State Profiles

The Population and Economy of Each U.S. State

First Edition, 1999

State Profiles
The Population and Economy of Each U.S. State

First Edition, 1999

EDITORS
Courtenay M. Slater and Martha G. Davis

ASSOCIATE EDITOR
Elizabeth Rogers

BERNAN PRESS
Lanham, MD

© 1999 Bernan Press, an imprint of Bernan Associates, a division of the Kraus Organization Limited.

ISBN: 0-89059-159-8

ISSN: 1524-3958

Printed by Automated Graphic Systems, Inc., White Plains, MD, on acid-free paper that meets the American National Standards Institute Z39-48 standard.

2000 1999   4 3 2 1

Bernan Press
4611-F Assembly Drive
Lanham, MD 20706-4391
email: info@bernan.com

CONTENTS

Preface vii
Using this Book ix

United States 1
Rankings 21

Alabama 31
Alaska 39
Arizona 47
Arkansas 55
California 63
Colorado 71
Connecticut 79
Delaware 87
District of Columbia 95
Florida 103
Georgia 111
Hawaii 119
Idaho 127
Illinois 135
Indiana 143
Iowa 151
Kansas 159
Kentucky 167
Louisiana 175
Maine 183
Maryland 191
Massachusetts 199
Michigan 207
Minnesota 215

Mississippi 223
Missouri 231
Montana 239
Nebraska 247
Nevada 255
New Hampshire 263
New Jersey 271
New Mexico 279
New York 287
North Carolina 295
North Dakota 303
Ohio 311
Oklahoma 319
Oregon 327
Pennsylvania 335
Rhode Island 343
South Carolina 351
South Dakota 359
Tennessee 367
Texas 375
Utah 383
Vermont 391
Virginia 399
Washington 407
West Virginia 415
Wisconsin 423
Wyoming 431

Notes and Definitions 439
Index 451

PREFACE

To TRACK U.S. ECONOMIC GROWTH, STANDARDS OF LIVING, THE effects on society of economic change, and the socio-economic progress of various demographic groups, it is necessary to go beyond the national picture. The answer to the question "How are Americans faring in the 1990s?" is very different for different groups of people, and the answer differs state by state. State economies and populations are growing at different rates and for different reasons, and this has major implications not only for government policies ranging from welfare reform to education to urban renewal, but for private investment strategies as well.

Analysis of states' economies reveals some surprises about how large or small certain factors really are and contradicts some common stereotypes:

Manufacturing of tobacco products provides less than 3 percent of all manufacturing employment in Virginia; Texas workers and proprietors derive only about 6 percent of their earnings from agriculture (including cattle) and oil combined; Wisconsin's dairy sector plus other farm industries constitute less than one percent of its economy.

States show a wide range of variation in their demographic and economic characteristics. For instance, in Wisconsin, 71 percent of the entire population age 16 and over was employed in 1997; in West Virginia, only 51 percent. Manufacturing output was 32 percent of Indiana's gross state product in 1996 and 28 percent in Kentucky, but only 5 percent in Nevada and 6 percent in Wyoming. All politics may be local, but adequate attention has not always been paid to critical differences in economic trends at the state and regional level. This book highlights the differing conditions in each state and region and is a valuable reference for those concerned with economic and social trends.

DATA SELECTION

SPACE CONSTRAINTS HAVE LIMITED THE AMOUNT OF DATA THAT could be provided for each state and placed a premium on the careful selection of the most meaningful data. In most cases, substantial additional detail is available from the source agencies, and these sources of additional information are listed in the notes.

Although the editors have taken care to select data that are accurate, meaningful, and useful, all statistical data are subject to error. Errors can arise from sampling variability, reporting errors, incomplete coverage, imputation, and other causes, and the range of error associated with state-level data typically is larger than that for national averages. Hence comparisons over time and among states should be interpreted with caution.

The data in this book meet the publication standards of the federal agencies from which they were obtained. The responsibilities of the editors and publisher of this volume are limited to reasonable care in the reproduction and presentation of data obtained from established sources.

ACKNOWLEDGEMENTS

THE ENORMOUS WORK LOAD OF PREPARING THE DATA FOR THIS volume, as well as much of the preparation of the text, was accomplished by the Associate Editor, Elizabeth Rogers. Katherine DeBrandt and Michael Ochs assisted with the data preparation and the writing of a number of chapters. James Rice, Kendall Golladay, and Steve Thomas spent many hours reviewing and fact-checking and editing the text, tables, and charts. The Bernan Press production group, under the direction of Sean Long, produced this book, with Benjamin Shupe taking the lead on art production and typesetting, Mary Reynolds setting up the tables, and with Dan Parham and Joyce Goodwine coordinating and assisting the many production elements of this book.

The editors are tremendously grateful to each of these colleagues for their assistance, and for the good humor and cooperative spirit in which this demanding project was carried out.

COURTENAY SLATER AND MARTHA DAVIS

USING THIS BOOK

The combination of text, data tables, and figures contained in *State Profiles* creates a concise analysis of trends in each U.S. state's population and economy, with detailed coverage of the 1990s supplemented by basic information for earlier years. In addition to the eight-page chapters for each state and the District of Columbia, which are the heart of this book, a U.S. overview, state rankings, notes and definitions, and an index also are included.

UNITED STATES. The chapter on the United States describes the overall national trends against which the data for each state can be compared, and gives examples of the range of variation among states. It also contains background information on data definitions in cases where understanding the definition is particularly important to correct interpretation of the data. Consulting each section of the U.S. chapter along with the corresponding section of a state chapter will assist in interpreting the state data.

RANKINGS. States are ranked on some 25 dimensions ranging from population growth through employment characteristics to state and local taxes. The District of Columbia has been ranked along with the states, but its special status as the nations capital and its typical characteristics of a central city, rather than a state, make it an outlier in many of the rankings. The federal government provides 30 percent of employment in the District and, associated with the high percentage of federal employment, 34 percent of the population age 25 and over hold college degrees—a higher percentage than any state. However, like many older central cities, the District has been experiencing a decline in population and has a high unemployment rate and an infant mortality rate above that for any state.

The eight-page chapters for each state and the District of Columbia follow the same standard design. Each page contains text highlighting elements shown in the tables and figures. Covered in each state chapter are the following topics:

OVERVIEW. Introductory paragraphs highlight key facets of the state's economic and demographic structure and summarize important recent trends. Charts compare the state's population growth to averages for the region and the nation and compare trends in the state's median household income and unemployment rate to the national trend.

POPULATION AND LABOR FORCE. Total population and households; age, race, and ethnic distribution of the population; percent living in metropolitan areas; birth and death rates; and labor force, employment, and unemployment. Figures illustrate the components of population change during the 1990s and compare household and population change during the 1980s to that in the 1990s.

HOUSEHOLD AND PERSONAL INCOME. Median household income and poverty rate compared to the national average; personal income by source and per capita income in current and constant dollars; and government transfer payments by type, with a comparison to U.S. trends.

ECONOMIC STRUCTURE. Employment and earnings for 1980 and each year from 1989 to 1997, with the distribution among major economic sectors and the average annual percent change during the 1990s; and a listing of the five leading private industries and the five fastest growing.

ECONOMIC STRUCTURE (CONTINUED). Average annual wages and salaries by sector compared to national averages; manufacturing as a percentage of gross state product and as value-added per worker; and trends in state exports of goods, including the top five export categories.

HOUSING. New home production rate compared to the national average; sales of existing homes; and home ownership rates.

AGRICULTURE. Number of farms, acreage, value of land and buildings, and farm income and expenses.

EDUCATION. Educational attainment; elementary and secondary school enrollment, per pupil expenditure, and teacher salaries; and higher education enrollment as a percent of the age 18 to 34 population, percent minority, and percent private.

HEALTH. Infant mortality; health insurance coverage; and death rates by leading causes.

GOVERNMENT. State and local taxes per capita and as a percent of personal income; state revenues by source, expenditures by function, debt, and cash and security holdings; and federal spending within the state by type and major program categories.

NOTES AND DEFINITIONS. Each chapter relies on the same standard set of federal data sources, sometimes supplemented to a limited degree by additional information from state-specific sources. Because the basic data sources are common to all chapters, the main body of the book includes very few footnotes. All the basic data sources are identified in the notes at the end of the book. The notes provide brief definitions, descriptions of methodology and data availability, descriptions of any calculations made by the editors, and references to sources of additional information. The notes on the basic data sources are organized by topic, following the structure of the state chapters. These notes by topic are followed by a listing of additional sources of information used for individual states.

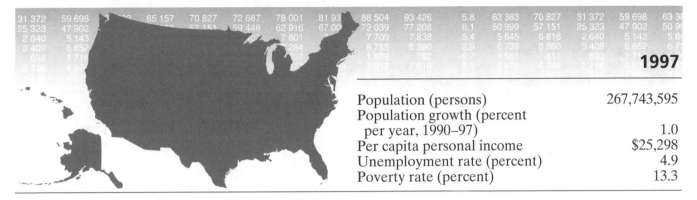

1997

Population (persons)	267,743,595
Population growth (percent per year, 1990–97)	1.0
Per capita personal income	$25,298
Unemployment rate (percent)	4.9
Poverty rate (percent)	13.3

THE MID-90S WERE A PERIOD OF INCREASING PROSPERITY FOR the United States, with real output growing more than 3 percent per year from 1994 to 1997, large gains in exports, strong growth of employment, and a declining unemployment rate. This impressive performance contrasted with the early 1990s, when a recession in 1990–91 was followed by an initially sluggish recovery, leading to widespread questioning of the vitality and international competitiveness of the U.S. economy.

Population growth in the 1990s has been a little more rapid than in the 1980s, and close to one-third of the growth has come from immigration, as individuals from other countries have been drawn to the economic opportunities and relatively open society found in the United States.

Almost all states followed (to some degree) the national pattern of recession in the early '90s and more vigorous economic growth as the decade progressed. The pace of growth and the degree of prosperity vary widely among states, however, as do patterns of population change. The individual state chapters in this book detail the year-to-year growth of output and employment in each state, identify each state's largest and most rapidly growing industries, and highlight the roles of manufacturing, agriculture, and exports. Population trends, changes in personal and household incomes, poverty rates, residential construction activity, education, health, and government finances also are covered.

This U.S. summary provides national totals or averages against which each state's data can be compared and summarizes the extent of variation among states for key indicators. It also provides supplementary information that may assist in interpreting national and state patterns of economic and demographic change.

The standard data tables in each state chapter contain annual data through 1997 (or the latest year available if 1997 data were not yet available). The year 1997 was chosen as the ending year in order to show as much data as possible for the same year, facilitating comparison. However, limited 1998 data by state are available, and a summary of key developments in 1998 is included in this introductory chapter.

POPULATION

Population and Labor Force

	1980	1990	1991	1992	1993	1994	1995	1996	1997	Change*
Population										
Total number of persons (thousands)	226 546	249 439	252 127	254 995	257 746	260 289	262 765	265 190	267 744	1.0
Percent Distribution:										
White, non-Hispanic	79.7	75.6	75.2	74.8	74.3	73.9	73.5	73.1	72.7	0.4
Black, non-Hispanic	11.5	11.8	11.8	11.9	11.9	12.0	12.0	12.0	12.1	1.4
Asian	1.6	3.0	3.1	3.3	3.4	3.5	3.6	3.7	3.7	4.1
Native American	0.7	0.8	0.8	0.8	0.8	0.9	0.9	0.9	0.9	1.6
Hispanic	6.4	9.1	9.3	9.6	9.8	10.1	10.4	10.7	11.0	3.8
In metropolitan areas	78.3	79.8	79.8	79.9	79.9	79.9	79.9	79.9	79.9	1.0
Total number of households (thousands)	80 390	91 946	93 179	94 654	95 358	95 988	97 386	98 751	NA	1.2
Labor Force (thousands)										
Population 16 and over	167 745	189 164	190 925	192 805	194 838	196 814	198 584	200 591	203 133	1.0
Civilian Labor Force	106 940	125 840	126 346	128 105	129 200	131 056	132 304	133 943	136 297	1.1
Employed	99 303	118 793	117 718	118 492	120 259	123 060	124 900	126 708	129 558	1.2
Percent of population	59.2	62.8	61.7	61.5	61.7	62.5	62.9	63.2	63.8	
Unemployment rate (percent)	7.1	5.6	6.8	7.5	6.9	6.1	5.6	5.4	4.9	

*Compound annual average percent change, 1990–1997.

THE U.S. POPULATION GREW AN AVERAGE OF 1 PERCENT PER year from 1990 to 1997. This was a little faster than the 0.9 percent per year growth during the 1980s and about equal to growth during the 1970s. States varied widely in their rate of population growth or decline. The most rapid growth occurred in a swath of states beginning in the Pacific Northwest and continuing through the Rocky Mountain states and into the Southwest. Georgia was the only state elsewhere in the nation to rival the population growth in those states.

COMPONENTS OF POPULATION CHANGE. A little over two-thirds of U.S. population growth from 1990 to 1997 was the result of natural increase (births minus deaths) and almost one-third the result of immigration from abroad. This level of immigration was higher than during the 1980s, when it accounted for about one-fourth of population growth. While immigration was a major factor in population growth in some states, it was of quite minor importance in others. For instance, immigration accounted for 97 percent of New Jersey's population growth and 76 percent of California's, it offset what would otherwise have been a population decline in New York, and it limited the extent of the population declines in Rhode Island, Connecticut, and the District of Columbia. In contrast, immigration accounted for less than 10 percent of population growth in each of the six most rapidly growing states—Nevada, Arizona, Idaho, Utah, Colorado, and Georgia.

Domestic migration—the movement of population already resident in the United States from one state to another—does not affect total U.S. population growth but was the major factor in population growth in some states and the cause of population decline in others. Net migration from other states, for instance, provided 74 percent of Nevada's population growth, and more than 50 percent of population growth in 11 other states. The population gains from domestic migration must be equaled by population losses in other states. Among states experiencing out-

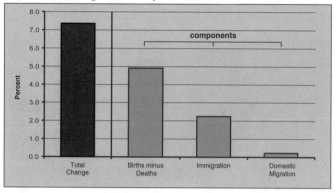

Population Change and Components: 1990–97

migration were New York and California, each of which had net out-migration of more than 5 percent of its population. (See rankings, page 21.)

RACE AND ETHNICITY. Among racial and ethnic groups, the non-Hispanic White population grew most slowly from 1990 to 1997, only 0.4 percent per year. The Black, non-Hispanic population grew more than three times as rapidly, 1.4 percent per year, and the Asian, Hispanic, and Native American populations more rapidly still. The Asian share of the U.S. population more than doubled from 1980 to 1997.

States vary widely in the racial and ethnic makeup of their populations and in the rates of growth of the different population groups. Non-Hispanic Whites were more than 96 percent of the 1997 populations of Maine, Vermont, and New Hampshire, but less than 30 percent of the populations of Hawaii and the District of Columbia. Neighboring states often present sharp contrasts in the racial and ethnic make up of their populations: Hispanics were 29 percent of the population of Texas in 1997, but less than 4 percent of the populations of the neighboring states of Oklahoma, Arkansas, and Louisiana. (See rankings, page 23.)

Ten Fastest-Growing States, Percent Population Change: 1990–1997

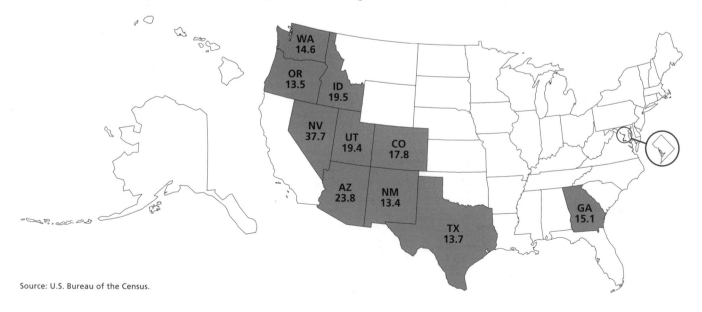

Source: U.S. Bureau of the Census.

METROPOLITAN AREAS. About 80 percent of the U.S. population lived in metropolitan areas in 1997, and this proportion has changed little since 1990. Among states, the proportion in metropolitan areas ranges from one-third or less in Montana, Vermont, and Wyoming to over 95 percent in California and Massachusetts and 100 percent in New Jersey and the District of Columbia. (See rankings, page 23.) Metropolitan areas, as officially defined by the federal government, consist of groups of counties that, although centered on a large concentration of urban population, may contain extensive rural areas.[1] Thus, although every county in New Jersey has been assigned to a metropolitan area, the state still has rural areas, and farming is an important economic activity. Metropolitan areas frequently, though not always, have lower unemployment and poverty rates and higher average incomes than non-metropolitan areas within the same state. This relationship does not necessarily extend to central cities within the metropolitan areas, however. Data for metropolitan areas sometimes are averages for a relatively impoverished central city and its more prosperous suburbs. This pattern is especially likely within older metropolitan areas in the Northeast and Midwest.

HOUSEHOLDS. There were about 100 million households in the United States in 1996. (Data by state for 1997 were not available at press time.) About 70 percent of U.S. households were family households, that is, households containing two or more related individuals—a married couple with or without children at home, a single parent with a child or children, or some other family group. The remaining 30 percent of households consisted of individuals living alone (55 percent of nonfamily households) or of two or more unrelated individuals sharing living quarters.

The state with the largest average household size was Utah, 3.08 persons per household in 1996. California and Texas also had well above average numbers of persons per household (2.96 and 2.71 respectively), reflecting their relatively large population shares under age 18 and their substantial recent immigrant populations. (Recent immigrants often must live in overcrowded quarters while establishing themselves economically.) As the two largest states, California and Texas heavily influence the national aver-

Average Annual Household and Population Growth

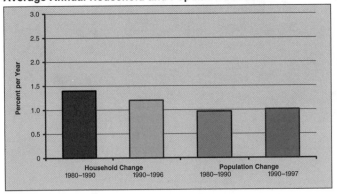

age household size. Thirty-seven states and the District of Columbia each had an average household size below the 2.63 national average in 1996, and the median states—those in the middle of a ranking of all states—were Arizona and Indiana, with an average of 2.57 persons per household. Average household size in Washington, D.C., at only 2.17 persons per household, was well below that of any state, and reflects a pattern, found in many cities, in which families with children tend to live in the surrounding suburbs while single individuals and childless couples are more likely to be city dwellers.

AGE. In 1997, 12.7 percent of the U.S. population was age 65 or older, only a slight increase from 12.5 percent in 1990. The small net change in population share is the result of two factors working in opposite directions. The share of the population age 65 to 74 actually fell from 1990 to 1997 (from 7.3 percent to 6.9), reflecting the low birth rates of the early 1930s. The share of the population age 75 and over rose (from 5.2 percent to 5.8), reflecting improved health status and longer lives. In future years, and especially after 2010, when the "baby boomers" born after 1944 begin reaching age 65, the percentage of the population aged 65 and over is expected to increase rapidly, reaching 18.5 percent by 2025.

Florida is the state with the largest population share age 65 and over, but it is an exception to the general pattern of heavy concentrations of older persons in states with slowly growing or declining populations and out-migration of younger people. Pennsylvania, Rhode Island, West Virginia, and Iowa—each with more than 15 percent of their populations in the aged 65 and over group—illustrate this more typical pattern. (See rankings, page 24)

Nationwide, the percentage of the population under age 18 rose slightly from 25.8 percent in 1990 to 26.0 percent in 1997. The share of the population under age 5 declined and that between ages 5 and 17 rose as the relatively large numbers of children born from 1989 through 1992 moved into the older age group. In about one-half the states, the share of the population under age 18 in 1997 was within one percentage point of the national average. Utah and Alaska led the list of states with larger shares under age 18, and others with large shares included the states along the southern border of the United States from Mississippi west to California, plus Wyoming and Idaho. States with smaller than average shares of children and youths all lay east of the Mississippi River and, not surprisingly, includ-

Population by Age; Births and Deaths

	1990	1997
Age distribution (percent)		
Under 5 years	7.6	7.2
5 to 17 years	18.2	18.8
18 to 64 years	61.8	61.3
65 years and over	12.5	12.7
Birth and death rates (per thousand population)		
Births	16.7	14.6
Deaths	8.6	8.6

ed states with declining populations and larger than average percentages of population over age 65.

BIRTHS AND DEATHS. The number of births in the United States reached its peak for recent decades in 1990, when there were 4.16 million babies born and the rate of births per 1,000 population reached 16.7. This was the highest rate since 1971, but far below the peak rates of the 1950s. By 1997, the birth rate had fallen again, down to 14.6, the lowest since the mid-70s. Utah is the only state in which the birth rate did not decline between 1990 and 1997, and Utah's 1997 birth rate of 21.3 was well above that of any other state. The lowest 1997 birth rates—12.5 or less— were found in the New England states of Maine, Vermont, New Hampshire, and Rhode Island and in West Virginia, Pennsylvania, and Montana.

The U.S. death rate has remained within the narrow range of 8.6 to 8.8 deaths per 1,000 population since at least 1980. This stability reflects an aging population, but one that is living longer. The median age of the population rose from 30 years in 1980 to 35 in 1997. Other things equal, an older population would have a higher death rate. But over the same period life expectancy at birth rose from 73.7 years in 1980 to 76.1 years in 1996, indicating improvements in the health status of the population that have helped keep the death rate from rising.

Alaska had the lowest death rate in both 1990 and 1997, but this was because of its relatively young population. When the rates for all states are adjusted to a standard age distribution, Alaska is within the mid-range of states. Hawaii is the state with the lowest age-adjusted rate. Utah had the second lowest rate, both before and after the age adjustment. In general, the highest age-adjusted death rates are found in the southern states, with Mississippi and Louisiana the highest, except for the District of Columbia.

Unemployment Rate: 1989–97

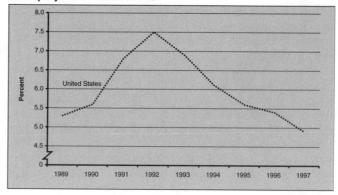

EMPLOYMENT AND UNEMPLOYMENT

THE RECESSION THAT BEGAN IN MID-1990 AND ENDED IN early 1991 caused the first year-to-year decline in total U.S. employment since 1982. Employment began to increase again in 1992, but not rapidly enough to match the increase in the number of people seeking work. Thus unemployment continued to rise during much of 1992. On an annual basis, the U.S. unemployment rate peaked at 7.5 percent in 1992 and then, as employment grew more rapidly, declined in each subsequent year, reaching 4.9 percent in 1997, the lowest rate in more than a quarter of a century.

As employment opportunities grew, more individuals were drawn into the labor force, and by 1997 the percentage of the civilian population age 16 and over holding jobs had reached a record 63.8 percent.

The early '90s recession and the subsequent period of growing prosperity were common to all regions of the

Average Annual Increase in Employment, 1990–1997

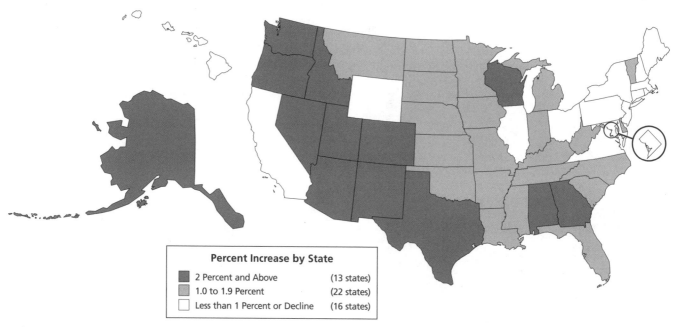

Percent Increase by State

- 2 Percent and Above (13 states)
- 1.0 to 1.9 Percent (22 states)
- Less than 1 Percent or Decline (16 states)

Source: Local area unemployment statistics, Bureau of Labor Statistics.

country. All but three states—Nebraska, South Dakota, and Wyoming—experienced some rise in unemployment in the early '90s, and all but one have seen unemployment decline after 1992. Some areas experienced sharper cyclical swings than others. Unemployment rates more than doubled from 1989 to 1992 in Massachusetts, Rhode Island, and New Jersey, but each of these states then saw large declines in unemployment after 1992. Massachusetts, where the unemployment rate peaked at 9.1 percent in 1992, had a 1997 unemployment rate of only 4.0 percent. Only Hawaii, where tourism has been hurt by the Japanese recession, had a higher unemployment rate in 1997 than in 1992. A few states, including Alaska, Montana, Oregon, and Arkansas, have seen unemployment come down after 1992, but rise again after 1994, while the U.S. rate continued to fall.

The rankings table on page 25 shows each state's average unemployment rate in 1997. The lowest unemployment rates are found in the Plains state of North Dakota and Nebraska, but at least one state in every region had a rate below the national average.

Additional perspective on labor market strength during the 1990s is gained by comparing rates of growth of employment. (See rankings, page 25.) States with higher unemployment may have had slow growth or a decline in employment, as in New York, or can have rapid growth of employment but even more rapid growth of population and labor force, as in Texas.

Vigorous employment growth was widespread throughout the West and South. California, however, is one notable exception, as the recession in the state was particularly severe and prolonged, with recovery beginning only in 1995. Wisconsin led the Midwest in employment growth, but ranked only 13th nationwide. In the Northeast, only Vermont and Delaware were close to the national average; all other northeastern states experienced either below-average employment growth or, in a few cases, actual declines.

Most states have seen a rise during the 1900s in the percentage of the population holding jobs. The actual percentage varies widely from state to state, however, reflecting the age distribution of the adult population, the degree of urbanization, the level of educational attainment, and other underlying factors, as well as the strength of the state's economy. (See rankings, page 25.)

INCOME

THE U.S. MEDIAN HOUSEHOLD INCOME, ADJUSTED FOR INFLATION, declined from 1989 to 1993. This decline resulted from a combination of slow growth of actual dollar incomes during and following the recession and a relatively high rate of inflation. Consumer prices increased 3.9 percent per year during this period. After 1993 employment and current-dollar incomes grew more rapidly and the rate of consumer price increase diminished, averaging

Per Capita Income, Selected Years
(percent of national average)

Region	1980	1989	1997
New England	106.4	121.8	120.3
Mid-Atlantic	108.2	116.6	115.6
Southeast	85.4	87.9	90.0
Great Lakes	101.6	98.2	99.8
Plains	94.6	92.9	95.3
Rocky Mountain	95.9	87.3	92.6
Southwest	96.3	86.8	89.9
Far West	114.7	108.3	103.0

2.7 percent per year from 1993 to 1997. Even so, inflation-adjusted median incomes in 1997 had not quite regained the 1989 level. The percentage of the population living in poverty followed a similar pattern. In 1989, the poverty rate of 12.8 percent was little different from 1980's 13.0 percent. It then rose to a peak of 15.1 percent in 1993, and, despite subsequent declines, remained higher in 1997 than it had been in 1989.

PER CAPITA INCOME. A more favorable picture is seen in the statistics on real per capita personal income, which fell less during the recession and then made a stronger recovery. By 1997, it was 10.2 percent higher than in 1989. Variation in average per capita incomes among the different regions of the country narrowed somewhat from 1989 to 1997, with those regions with below average incomes moving up and those with above average incomes moving down relative to the U.S. average. In both 1989 and 1997, the New England region had the highest per capita incomes and the Southwest the lowest. Changes during the 1980s were more dramatic than those from 1990 to 1997, with the Southwest, Rocky Mountain, Plains, and Great Lakes states all slipping relative to the national average, and New England and the Mid-Atlantic states surpassing the Far West to rank number 1 and number 2.

INCOME MEASUREMENT. The two income measures—household median income and per capita personal income—address somewhat different aspects of economic well-being. The household income data indicate the median, that is the midpoint in the range of all households' incomes, whereas per capita income is an average, or mean, derived by dividing aggregate personal income by the population. Faster growth of the average income rather than the median suggests that people in the upper income brackets have had larger increases in income than those with lower incomes, a trend that affects the average more than the median. Neither median household income nor per capita income directly measure income distribution, but other evidence indicates that inequality of household incomes continued to increase during the early and mid-90s.

Other differences in the definitions of the two measures and in the way they are computed also help account for their divergent patterns. The personal income measure

HOUSEHOLD INCOME AND PERSONS IN POVERTY	1989	1990	1991	1992	1993	1994	1995	1996	1997
Median household income (1997 dollars)	37 415	36 770	35 501	35 047	34 700	34 942	35 887	36 306	37 005
Persons in poverty (thousands)	31 528	33 585	35 708	38 014	39 265	38 059	36 425	36 529	35 574
Poverty rate (percent)	12.8	13.5	14.2	14.8	15.1	14.5	13.8	13.7	13.3

uses a more comprehensive definition of income, taking into account in-kind income from sources such as food stamps and medical benefits, whereas the standard measure of household income is limited to money income. This difference is significant when in-kind benefits are growing faster than money payments. Transfer payments have risen faster than any other source of income in the '90s, and their fastest growing component was medical benefits. Thus, it appears that rising government medical benefit payments have boosted personal income while not being counted in household incomes.

Changes in household income can be affected by changes in the average size of households. For example, when an employed young adult moves out of his or her parents' household and establishes separate living quarters, one household is replaced by two smaller ones; income per person does not change, but income per household declines. Nationwide, however, average household size has changed little during the 1990s, so the effect on household income has been relatively small.

In each state, these factors will play out differently in determining the relationship between median household and per capita income. Their trends may be similar or may diverge, depending on the weight of the high-income population in a state, the relative importance of in-kind benefits, and trends in the number of earners per household. In addition, the household income data, which are derived from the Current Population Survey, have sampling errors which are greater in an individual state than they are nationwide. For small states especially, these errors can lead to illusory changes in median household income from year to year, and it is wise to analyze broader multi-year trends.

COMPONENTS OF PERSONAL INCOME. Earnings are by far the largest source of personal income, accounting for 66 percent nationwide. Earnings include wages, salaries, most fringe benefits, and the net income of business proprietors. Information about earnings initially is collected based on the locations where people work. An "adjustment for residence" is then made to the data for each state to account for the earnings of those who work in one state and live in another (or in another country). A positive adjustment for residence indicates that, on balance, earnings are flowing into the state because residents cross state borders to work. A negative adjustment indicates that, on balance, workers are taking earnings out of the state to their residences elsewhere. The "adjustment for residence" in the U.S. totals is an estimate of the amount by which earnings within the United States by workers living in other countries exceed earnings of U.S. residents working abroad.

The other major components of personal income are dividends, interest and rent, at 17 percent of earnings nationwide, and transfer payments, at 16 percent of earnings nationwide. The great majority of transfer payments are government payments to individuals, and the largest of these are Social Security and medical payments. Also included are needs-based income maintenance payments, unemployment insurance benefits, and veterans benefits. Not surprisingly, states with larger concentrations of poverty tend to receive higher than average shares of transfer payments and smaller than average shares of dividends, interest, and rent, but the distributions also are affected by the percentage of elderly in the population and other factors.

TRANSFER PAYMENTS. Government transfer payments to individuals increased 63 percent from 1990 to 1997, but with large disparities among different categories of payments. Medical payments (largely Medicare and Medicaid) doubled during this period in part because of escalating medical prices and an aging population. By 1997, medical payments had surpassed Social Security to become the largest component of government payments to individuals. Excluding medical, all other transfers increased by only 46 percent, a quite moderate figure that reflects the effects of a strong economic recovery on income support and unemployment benefits.

Personal Income
(millions of dollars)

	1980	1989	1990	1991	1992	1993	1994	1995	1996	1997	Change*
Earnings by place of work	1 686 882	3 212 991	3 414 296	3 508 762	3 745 439	3 916 346	4 103 160	4 309 429	4 532 632	4 824 114	5.2
Wage and salary disbursements	1 370 268	2 586 070	2 743 797	2 812 349	2 974 792	3 081 486	3 234 155	3 422 404	3 624 975	3 885 389	5.2
Other labor income	139 687	272 996	300 431	322 518	351 116	384 864	404 718	401 412	386 723	392 712	4.7
Proprietor's income	176 927	353 925	370 068	373 895	419 531	449 996	464 287	485 613	520 934	546 013	5.6
Farm	12 556	32 803	31 491	26 704	32 854	31 576	29 582	19 968	32 165	30 252	-1.0
Nonfarm	164 371	321 122	338 577	347 191	386 677	418 420	434 705	465 645	488 769	515 761	6.1
(-) Personal contributions for social insurance	88 283	210 125	223 152	235 010	247 816	259 745	276 992	293 083	305 832	325 765	5.6
(+) Adjustment for residence	-488	-740	-790	-785	-778	-2 840	-3 219	-3 501	-3 530	-3 812	22.7
(=) Net earnings by place of residence	1 598 111	3 002 126	3 190 354	3 272 967	3 496 845	3 653 761	3 822 949	4 012 845	4 223 270	4 494 537	5.2
(+) Dividends, interest, and rent	366 045	852 535	900 214	904 818	884 375	903 830	963 501	1 031 489	1 117 844	1 165 828	4.0
(+) Transfer payments	322 202	625 963	687 738	769 806	858 144	911 894	954 600	1 015 804	1 067 876	1 110 344	7.4
(=) Total personal income	2 286 358	4 480 624	4 778 306	4 947 591	5 239 364	5 469 485	5 741 050	6 060 138	6 408 990	6 770 709	5.3
Farm Earnings	21 274	43 556	44 073	39 006	44 935	44 564	42 833	34 283	47 354	45 706	0.6
Nonfarm Earnings	2 265 084	4 437 068	4 734 233	4 908 585	5 194 429	5 424 921	5 698 217	6 025 855	6 361 636	6 725 003	5.3
Personal income per capita (dollars)											
Current dollars	10 062	18 153	19 156	19 624	20 546	21 220	22 056	23 063	24 169	25 298	4.2
1997 dollars	19 239	22 949	23 052	22 661	22 982	23 090	23 439	23 974	24 612	25 298	1.2

*Compound annual average percent change, 1989–1997

There were divergent trends among the various types of income maintenance payments. Unlike Social Security and Medicare, income maintenance payments are provided only to low-income persons or families who meet program eligibility requirements. The fastest growing program was Earned Income Tax Credits, which are payments to low-income families and individuals reporting earned income. The program has expanded during the 1990s as more low-wage earners found jobs, policy changes broadened eligibility, and the public became more familiar with the program. The average amount of credit per taxpayer in 1997 was $1,443, with 18.7 million families and individuals taking advantage of the credit. The total cost of $26.9 million comprised 92 percent of the transfer payment category "Other Income Maintenance," and it was the second largest income maintenance program next to Supplemental Security Income.

The category of transfers that did not increase was Family Assistance, which historically consisted of Aid to Families with Dependent Children. This program underwent radical reform when national legislation was enacted in 1996 to impose strong work requirements for beneficiaries, and give states broader discretion over other requirements for family assistance. (See sidebar, "The Impact of Welfare Reform.")

Supplemental Security Income (SSI) is a program which, unlike family assistance, is growing rapidly in virtually every state. There were 6.6 million SSI recipients in 1996, about one-half the number receiving Family Assistance, yet annual spending was larger. The program supports the needy aged, blind, and disabled, and during the past decade has come to be dominated by payments to the disabled, including children and adults under age 65. Between 1990 and 1996, the SSI rolls grew by 37 percent nationwide, with an actual decline in the number of recipients who were blind or over age 65 but a 56 percent increase in disabled recipients.

Unlike family welfare programs, the large majority of funds spent on SSI are federal rather than state funds, administered through the Social Security Administration. Some states pay a monthly supplement to the basic federal payment. In 1997 the basic federal payment was $484 for an individual living alone and $726 for a couple. Supplements were paid by 24 states and, for an aged individual, ranged from less than $10 in Hawaii, Nebraska, and Oregon to over $150 in California, Connecticut, and Alaska.

Government Transfer Payments
(millions of dollars)

	1996	1997	Change*
Total government payments to individuals	653 537	1 063 311	62.7
Retirement, disability, and health insurance ...	358 057	530 791	48.2
Social security	244 087	356 664	46.1
Government employee retirement	94 492	151 425	60.3
Medical payments	189 096	380 414	101.2
Income maintenance benefits	61 220	96 748	58.0
Supplemental Security Income	16 669	29 237	75.4
Family assistance	19 776	19 687	-0.5
Food stamps	14 741	18 741	27.1
Other income maintenance	10 034	29 083	189.8
Unemployment insurance benefits	18 330	20 271	10.6
Veterans benefits and other	26 834	35 087	30.8

THE IMPACT OF WELFARE REFORM

The U.S. federal/state family assistance program underwent radical restructuring when national legislation was enacted in 1996, both to impose strong work requirements for beneficiaries, and to give states broader discretion over other requirements for family assistance. The entitlement to aid was ended and the federal payment converted to a block grant.

Major criteria decided by each state include how much time recipients are given to find a job before benefits are reduced, and to what degree having young children affects the work requirement. Many states already had implemented reform prior to 1996 on a test basis. The results of these state initiatives and the new national legislation are apparent in declining welfare caseloads and spending totals, but the decline varies tremendously among the different states. States' rates of economic growth and levels of unemployment also have been critical factors in determining to what extent welfare recipients can get jobs and terminate their assistance.

The number of family aid recipients nationwide declined by 35 percent between January 1993 and January 1998, leaving 9.1 million recipients receiving aid. Trends in each state vary, ranging from declines of over 80 percent in Wisconsin and Wyoming to a 9 percent drop in Alaska. The caseload actually increased in Hawaii by 39 percent. Looking at the nine states with relatively small caseload declines (less than 20 percent) or an increase, seven had unemployment rates above the national average of 4.9 percent for 1997. They are the District of Columbia, Alaska, Hawaii, New York, California, Rhode Island, and Connecticut. For the other two states, Nevada's decline was modest because of the low number of recipients in the first place, and Washington's reduction in caseload appears to have been delayed until 1998.

In contrast, states with very large reductions (60 percent or more) in welfare caseload—Idaho, Mississippi, Wisconsin, and Wyoming—tend to have stronger economies. The largest of these states, Wisconsin, has experienced strong job growth and an unemployment rate below 4 percent, and it also was a pioneer in beginning welfare reform prior to the national legislation. Unemployment is higher in the other three states, which suggests that they may have reduced the number of aid recipients through sanctions and/or strong training and support programs. Notably, two of these states are very small and their changes reflect a reduction of only 15,000 to 17,000 people in each state.

The average level of monthly benefits per family varies greatly from state to state, which in turn affects the state's total family assistance costs and the dollar savings accruing to each state budget when caseloads decline. In January 1997, the maximum monthly payment for a family of three was over $700 in Suffolk County (New York), Hawaii, and Alaska, and over $600 in California and Connecticut, while it was less than $200 in Mississippi, Louisiana, Tennessee, and Alabama. Those states that historically have paid much higher benefits will now see larger dollar savings if they achieve reductions in welfare caseloads.

Government Payments to Individuals: 1997

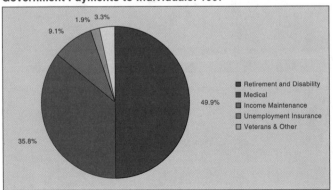

- 3.3%
- 1.9%
- 9.1%
- 35.8%
- 49.9%

- ■ Retirement and Disability
- ■ Medical
- ■ Income Maintenance
- ■ Unemployment Insurance
- □ Veterans & Other

Change in Welfare Caseloads, January 1993–January 1998
(Thousands of cases)

State	January 1993	January 1994	January 1995	January 1996	January 1997	January 1998	Change*
United States	14 115.0	14 275.9	13 930.0	12 876.7	11 423.0	9 131.7	-35.3
Alabama	141.7	135.1	121.8	108.3	91.7	61.8	-56.4
Alaska	35.0	37.5	37.3	35.4	36.2	31.7	-9.3
Arizona	194.1	202.4	195.1	171.6	151.5	113.2	-41.7
Arkansas	74.0	70.6	65.3	59.2	54.9	36.7	-50.4
California	2 415.1	2 621.4	2 692.2	2 648.8	2 476.6	2 144.5	-11.2
Colorado	123.3	118.1	110.7	99.7	87.4	55.4	-55.1
Connecticut	160.1	164.3	170.7	161.7	155.7	138.7	-13.4
Delaware	27.7	29.3	26.3	23.2	23.1	18.5	-33.1
District of Columbia	65.9	72.3	72.3	70.1	67.9	56.1	-14.8
Florida	701.8	689.1	657.3	575.6	478.3	320.9	-54.3
Georgia	402.2	396.7	388.9	367.7	306.6	220.1	-45.3
Hawaii	54.5	61.0	65.2	66.7	65.3	75.8	39.1
Idaho	21.1	23.3	24.1	23.5	19.8	4.4	-78.9
Illinois	685.5	710.0	710.0	663.2	601.9	526.9	-23.1
Indiana	209.9	218.1	197.2	147.1	122.0	95.7	-54.4
Iowa	100.9	110.6	103.1	91.7	78.3	69.5	-31.1
Kansas	87.5	87.4	81.5	70.8	57.5	38.5	-56.1
Kentucky	227.9	208.7	193.7	176.6	162.7	132.4	-41.9
Louisiana	263.3	252.9	258.2	239.2	206.6	118.4	-55.0
Maine	67.8	65.0	61.0	56.3	51.2	41.3	-39.2
Maryland	221.3	219.9	227.9	207.8	169.7	130.2	-41.2
Massachusetts	332.0	311.7	286.2	242.6	214.0	181.7	-45.3
Michigan	686.4	672.8	612.2	535.7	462.3	377.0	-45.1
Minnesota	191.5	189.6	180.5	171.9	160.2	141.1	-26.3
Mississippi	174.1	161.7	146.3	133.0	109.1	66.0	-62.1
Missouri	259.0	262.1	259.6	238.1	208.1	163.0	-37.1
Montana	34.8	35.4	34.3	32.6	28.1	20.1	-42.2
Nebraska	48.1	46.0	42.0	38.7	36.5	38.1	-20.7
Nevada	34.9	37.9	41.8	40.5	29.0	29.3	-16.3
New Hampshire	29.0	30.4	28.7	24.5	20.6	15.9	-45.0
New Jersey	349.9	334.8	321.2	293.8	256.1	217.3	-37.9
New Mexico	94.8	101.7	105.1	102.6	89.8	64.8	-31.7
New York	1 179.5	1 241.6	1 266.4	1 200.8	1 074.2	941.7	-20.2
North Carolina	331.6	334.5	317.8	282.1	253.3	192.2	-42.1
North Dakota	18.8	16.8	14.9	13.7	12.0	8.9	-52.7
Ohio	720.5	691.1	629.7	552.3	518.6	386.2	-46.4
Oklahoma	146.5	133.2	127.3	110.5	87.3	69.6	-52.5
Oregon	117.7	116.4	107.6	92.2	66.9	48.6	-58.7
Pennsylvania	604.7	615.6	611.2	553.1	484.3	395.1	-34.7
Rhode Island	61.1	62.7	62.4	60.7	54.8	54.5	-10.8
South Carolina	151.0	143.9	133.6	121.7	98.1	73.2	-51.5
South Dakota	20.3	19.4	17.7	16.8	14.1	10.5	-48.1
Tennessee	320.7	302.6	282.0	265.3	195.9	139.0	-56.7
Texas	785.3	796.3	765.5	714.5	626.6	439.8	-44.0
Utah	53.2	50.7	47.5	41.1	35.5	29.9	-43.8
Vermont	29.0	28.1	27.7	25.9	23.6	21.0	-27.4
Virginia	194.2	195.0	189.5	166.0	136.1	107.2	-44.8
Washington	286.3	292.6	290.9	276.0	263.8	228.7	-20.1
West Virginia	119.9	115.4	107.7	98.4	98.7	51.3	-57.2
Wisconsin	241.1	230.6	214.4	184.2	132.4	44.6	-81.5
Wyoming	18.3	16.7	15.4	13.5	10.3	2.9	-84.1

*Percent change, January 1993–January 1998.

ECONOMIC STRUCTURE

LEADING PRIVATE INDUSTRIES, 1997 (Worker and proprietor earnings, millions of dollars)		FASTEST EARNINGS GROWTH, 1990–97 (percent increase)	
Health services	$403 544	Securities brokers	146.6
Business services	301 024	Business services	110.2
Engineering and management services	176 914	Real estate	106.1
Construction specialties	176 463	Amusement and recreational services	103.4
Banks and other credit institutions	111 186	Social services	99.3

THE UNITED STATES, LIKE ALMOST ALL INDUSTRIALIZED countries, has predominantly a service-producing economy. The service-producing industries—also referred to as the trade and services sectors—accounted for 77 percent of gross domestic product (GDP) and 80 percent of employment in 1997. The service-producing industries are agricultural services (which includes landscaping and veterinary services as well as services to farmers); wholesale and retail trade; transportation and public utilities (including communications); finance, insurance, and real estate; government; and a wide spectrum of private services, ranging from business services, through health services, to personal services and community organizations.

EMPLOYMENT BY SECTOR. The service economy is not a new phenomenon. Service-producing industries provided over one-half of all U.S. employment in 1945. The share has been growing ever since. In recent decades, employment in trade and services as a share of all nonfarm employment has increased from 65 percent in 1969 to 80 percent in 1997. This growth was not evenly spread among the different service-producing industries, however. All of the increase in share occurred among private service-produc-

ing industries; government employment (federal, state, and local combined) declined as a percent of the total. Within the private service-producing sector, the shares of business services and health services have shown dramatic gains, the shares of wholesale and retail trade and of finance, insurance, and real estate have grown more modestly, and the share for transportation and utilities has fallen.

From 1989 to 1997, employment in private service-producing sectors grew 2.4 percent per year. Government employment grew only 0.6 percent per year, with declines in federal government employment offset by modest gains at the state and local level. Private, goods-producing employment was little changed, as declines in manufacturing, mining, and farming more than offset gains in construction.

WORKER AND PROPRIETOR EARNINGS. Economy-wide, worker and proprietor earnings grew a total of 50 percent from 1989 to 1997. Earnings reflect both employment growth and growth in current-dollar compensation per employee. They are among the best measures (available on a timely annual basis) of the economic importance of individual

Employment and Earnings by Sector

	1980	1989	1990	1991	1992	1993	1994	1995	1996	1997 Number	1997 Percent of total	Change*
Employment *(thousands of persons)*												
Total	114 231	137 318	139 185	138 786	139 411	142 006	145 650	149 363	152 657	156 400	100.0	1.6
Farm	3 798	3 196	3 147	3 092	3 043	3 008	2 948	2 979	2 945	2 954	1.9	-1.0
Nonfarm	110 433	134 122	136 038	135 694	136 368	138 998	142 702	146 384	149 712	153 446	98.1	1.7
Private nonfarm	91 675	113 374	114 806	114 453	114 933	117 487	121 099	124 745	128 056	131 665	84.2	1.9
Agriculture services, forestry, and fishing	909	1 374	1 452	1 509	1 494	1 631	1 734	1 786	1 890	1 971	1.3	4.6
Mining	1 278	1 047	1 043	1 023	935	934	936	885	824	833	0.5	-2.8
Construction	5 654	7 293	7 264	6 811	6 825	7 013	7 407	7 718	8 036	8 364	5.3	1.7
Manufacturing	20 781	19 998	19 635	19 025	18 711	18 745	19 053	19 201	19 198	19 414	12.4	-0.4
Transportation and public utilities	5 672	6 365	6 561	6 580	6 491	6 720	6 938	7 074	7 304	7 553	4.8	2.2
Wholesale trade	5 742	6 705	6 652	6 627	6 684	6 572	6 707	6 934	7 009	7 177	4.6	0.9
Retail trade	17 884	22 690	22 841	22 777	23 024	23 466	24 389	25 225	25 858	26 353	16.8	1.9
Finance, insurance, and real estate	8 756	10 667	10 696	10 524	10 293	10 502	10 813	11 018	11 353	11 777	7.5	1.2
Services	25 000	37 236	38 663	39 577	40 476	41 904	43 123	44 904	46 585	48 224	30.8	3.3
Government	18 758	20 748	21 232	21 241	21 435	21 511	21 603	21 639	21 656	21 781	13.9	0.6
Earnings *(millions of dollars)*												
Total	1 686 882	3 212 991	3 414 296	3 508 762	3 745 439	3 916 346	4 103 160	4 309 429	4 532 632	4 824 114	100.0	5.2
Farm	21 274	43 556	44 073	39 006	44 935	44 564	42 833	34 283	47 354	45 706	0.9	0.6
Nonfarm	1 665 608	3 169 435	3 370 223	3 469 756	3 700 504	3 871 782	4 060 327	4 275 146	4 485 278	4 778 408	99.1	5.3
Private nonfarm	1 400 762	2 664 511	2 823 160	2 892 132	3 093 919	3 242 564	3 409 193	3 603 515	3 794 790	4 063 372	84.2	5.4
Agriculture services, forestry, and fishing	7 693	19 264	22 053	22 939	24 099	25 183	26 651	27 511	28 133	30 243	0.6	5.8
Mining	36 419	32 261	34 697	37 123	36 566	36 762	36 397	37 936	39 409	42 608	0.9	3.5
Construction	106 587	201 007	204 482	191 943	194 757	205 471	225 623	238 439	256 378	274 769	5.7	4.0
Manufacturing	419 062	648 198	664 633	671 498	705 170	728 530	766 411	791 496	807 311	855 925	17.7	3.5
Transportation and public utilities	128 560	214 298	228 137	239 078	251 982	269 760	282 066	295 970	309 939	330 626	6.9	5.6
Wholesale trade	113 899	209 753	221 110	225 009	237 836	240 928	254 412	270 105	283 905	305 373	6.3	4.8
Retail trade	169 310	310 225	321 191	327 515	344 192	358 515	380 598	398 113	415 899	439 238	9.1	4.4
Finance, insurance, and real estate	102 253	222 638	238 463	248 912	288 960	316 142	321 030	346 692	378 561	411 417	8.5	8.0
Services	316 979	806 867	888 394	928 115	1 010 357	1 061 273	1 116 005	1 197 253	1 275 255	1 373 173	28.5	6.9
Government	264 846	504 924	547 063	577 624	606 585	629 218	651 134	671 631	690 488	715 036	14.8	4.4

*Compound annual average percent change, 1989–1997

industries within a state.

All but one of the industries with above average earnings growth were service-producing industries; chemicals and allied products was the only manufacturing industry to achieve above average growth. Leading the list in terms of growth was securities brokers, followed by the much larger business services industry. Leading the list in terms of size was the health services industry, followed by business services. These two industries rank among the five largest in virtually every state, and business services ranks among the five fastest growing in nearly every state.[2]

AVERAGE WAGES AND SALARIES. The data on average annual wages and salaries can be used to examine how earnings per worker vary among sectors of the economy and across states. The data have not been adjusted for inflation, so they do not directly measure changes over time in the purchasing power of these earnings. However, the Consumer Price Index can be used to calculate inflation-adjusted estimates. Real median household income and real per capita income also provide estimates of inflation-adjusted changes in income.

Wages and salaries include not only the wages of production and nonsupervisory workers, but also the salaries of managerial and professional employees; the compensation of corporate officers; and commissions, tips, and bonuses. Thus, the annual earnings of a manufacturing production worker or a retail sales clerk paid an hourly wage typically would be lower than the averages shown here. For example, retail trade workers in nonsupervisory jobs received an average hourly wage of $8.34 in 1997. The average work week was 28.9 hours, bringing the weekly wage to $241 and the annual wage for someone who worked a full 52 weeks to $12,532, or well below the $16,206 shown in the table—a figure which includes the salaries of managers and the commission, tips, and bonuses of retail workers who receive these forms of compensation.

By any measure, retail trade provides the lowest earnings of any nonfarm sector. (Earnings of farm proprietors make up an important—and highly variable—share of farm earnings. Hourly earnings of farm workers are below those in retail trade in many parts of the country.) The

Average Annual Wages and Salaries by Sector
(dollars)

	1989	1996	1997
All wage and salary workers	22 262	28 480	29 809
Farm	10 863	16 318	16 442
Nonfarm	22 354	28 563	29 900
Private nonfarm	22 323	28 441	29 867
Agriculture services, forestry, and fishing	14 193	17 103	17 941
Mining	35 865	47 412	49 800
Construction	25 340	30 374	31 765
Manufacturing	28 076	36 312	38 351
Transportation, communications, and public utilities	29 822	36 690	38 222
Wholesale trade	28 684	37 552	39 466
Retail trade	12 661	15 547	16 206
Finance, insurance, and real estate	28 807	41 931	44 993
Services	20 149	26 412	27 588
Government	22 495	29 153	30 062
Consumer Price Index, all urban consumers (1982-1984=100)	124.0	156.9	160.5

$8.34 per hour paid to retail trade workers in 1997 compares with an average of $12.28 for the private nonfarm economy as a whole, the average 28.9 hour retail trade work week compares with a private nonfarm average of 34.6, and the $16,206 for annual wages and salaries compares with a $29,900 nonfarm average. Retail trade provides 16.8 percent of all U.S. jobs. In comparison, mining, the sector with the highest wages and salaries, provides only 0.5 percent.

The only sector providing a larger share of employment than retail trade is services. Average wages and salaries in services were about 8 percent below the average for all private nonfarm workers, but the services average encompasses an extremely wide variation among different kinds of service jobs. Average hourly earnings for computer programming, for example, were $23.03 in 1997, while workers providing day care averaged $7.54, or less than one-third as much.

The manufacturing sector, which employs 12.4 percent of all workers, provides annual average wages and salaries 28 percent above the private nonfarm average, but earnings vary greatly among the different manufacturing industries. At the top of the pay scale in 1997, average hourly earnings of production workers in petroleum and coal products were $20.18; in tobacco products, $19.27; and in transportation equipment manufacturing, $17.56. At the bottom, apparel workers earned $8.25; leather workers, $8.98; and textile workers, $10.03.

Even within the same manufacturing industry, earnings can vary widely by state. Average hourly earnings in transportation equipment manufacturing were $22.08 in Michigan in 1997 but only $13.24 in Tennessee. Lower wage rates have been a major factor in attracting motor vehicle manufacture to Tennessee—where it was the fastest growing industry from 1989 to 1997—and to several other southern states.

Average annual wages and salaries of all workers in 1997 were highest in the New York, New Jersey, Connecticut, and Massachusetts complex, and in California. High earnings in these populous states brought the U.S. average substantially above the median. The median state, that is, the state that ranked at the mid-point of all the states, was Missouri, with average earnings of $27,098. Falling below this median were all of the plains states and all of the southeastern states except Georgia and Virginia.

MANUFACTURING. Employment in manufacturing in 1997 was about 3 percent lower than in 1989, and manufacturing provided only 12.4 percent of all jobs in 1997, compared to 14.6 percent in 1989. This decline in employment does not imply that the U.S. manufacturing sector is weak. Reorganization of production processes and investment in modern, computerized equipment have allowed more output to be produced with fewer workers. These changes have resulted in layoffs among manufacturing workers, including many managerial employees, but the changes also have cut costs and kept U.S. goods highly competitive in world trade.

Growth of manufacturing output was interrupted by the 1990–91 recession, but then was extremely vigorous from 1992 through 1997, with the gross domestic product

Gross Domestic Product and Manufacturing
(millions of dollars, except as noted)

	1989	1994	1995	1996
Gross domestic product, total	5 363 837	6 868 041	7 228 287	7 631 022
Manufacturing:				
Millions of dollars	1 013 500	1 216 094	1 285 428	1 332 093
Percent of total gross domestic product	18.9	17.7	17.8	17.5
Per worker (dollars)	50 681	63 826	66 945	69 387
New capital expenditures, manufacturing	98 738	112 784	128 473	139 323

(GDP) of the manufacturing sector rising more than 5 percent per year after adjustment for inflation. The decline of manufacturing output as a share of all current-dollar GDP results from a combination of rapid growth of some service-producing industries and the much lower rate of price increase in manufacturing than elsewhere in the economy. The GDP price index for manufacturing rose less than 1 percent from 1992 to 1997, compared with 12 percent rise in the price index for total GDP.

The mix of industries within manufacturing underwent rapid shifts from 1992 to 1997, with computers and other electronic products taking on greatly increased importance. Industrial machinery (which includes manufacture of computers) and electronic and other electrical equipment—two industries that together encompass much of "high-tech" manufacturing—doubled their inflation-adjusted output over the five years. In contrast, such traditional industries as apparel, textiles, paper, and lumber and wood products had only minimal growth of inflation-adjusted output.

States vary widely in their degree of dependence on manufacturing and in the specific manufacturing industries of greatest importance. Nationwide, the largest manufacturing industries, measured by worker and proprietor earnings, are industrial machinery, electronic and other electrical equipment, and chemicals. Others among the largest manufacturing industries are food and kindred products, motor vehicles, printing and publishing, and fabricated metal products.

The Great Lakes states of Indiana, Wisconsin, Michigan, Ohio, and Illinois still maintain their traditional lead as states with a large share of output attributable to manufacturing. The manufacturing share also is strikingly high in the South, with all the southern states except Florida and Virginia showing manufacturing as an above average share of GDP, and Kentucky, North and South Carolina, Arkansas, and Mississippi ranking among the top ten states. (See rankings, page 28.) In eastern states such as New York and New Jersey a declining manufacturing base and growth of service-producing industries have led manufacturing to become a fairly small part of their economies.

Some industries within manufacturing are heavily concentrated by region. Most striking are the 76 percent of all tobacco manufacturing and 66 percent of all textiles manufacturing located in the South Atlantic states (1996 data). The South Atlantic states also account for 25 percent of all furniture and fixtures production. Despite the southward shift of some production, 57 percent of all motor vehicle

manufacturing remains in the Great Lakes states, as does 38 percent of all primary metals manufacturing and 33 percent of fabricated metals. Printing and publishing is the one manufacturing industry in which the Mid-Atlantic states take the lead, with 20 percent of the total in 1996.

EXPORTS. In the mid-1990s, U.S. goods and services proved themselves highly competitive in world markets, with goods exports rising 34 percent from 1994 to 1997 and exports of services also growing strongly. Exports rose from 10.4 percent of GDP in 1994 to 11.9 percent in 1997. This growth was especially impressive because it was achieved during a period of strong domestic economic expansion. Typically, in such a period, export growth may slow, as a larger share of production is diverted to meet domestic demand, and imports may soar. From 1994 to 1997, however, imports grew a little less rapidly than exports. As a result, the trade deficit, while it remained a large absolute number, fell slightly relative to GDP, from 1.3 percent in 1994 to 1.2 percent in 1997.

Advanced technology products are a key to the strength of U.S. manufacturing exports. The five leading commodity groups—industrial machinery and computers, transportation equipment (which includes aircraft), electronic equipment, chemicals (which includes pharmaceuticals), and instruments—each include important high-tech components. Together these five groups accounted for more than 70 percent of U.S. manufactured exports in 1997.

Agricultural products have long been a strong factor in U.S. exports. With the more rapid growth of exports of manufactures, however, the agricultural share of total goods exports has diminished. Year-to-year fluctuations in foreign agricultural sales sometimes are large, reflecting changes in crop yields, world prices, and other highly variable factors. Comparing peak years, and including exports of manufactured food products, agricultural exports were 22.3 percent of total goods exports in 1974, 18.3 percent in 1981, and only 9.7 percent in 1996. However, trade in agricultural products consistently continues to produce large surpluses for the United States.

For trade in goods, Canada has long been the most important U.S trading partner, and, in 1997, Mexico surpassed Japan as the second largest market for U.S. exports. These two North American countries accounted for 32 percent of U.S. goods exports in 1997. Thirty-one percent went to Asian destinations, and 23 percent to Western Europe.

Exports of Goods
(millions of dollars)

	1994	1995	1996	1997
All goods	512 416	583 031	622 827	687 598
Manufactures	468 776	529 015	566 576	635 548
Agricultural and livestock products	23 896	31 122	34 132	29 440
Other commodities	19 744	22 894	22 119	22 610
Top goods exports, 1997:				
Industrial machinery and computers	88 528	103 239	111 983	127 707
Transportation equipment	88 159	85 752	96 568	112 259
Electronic and other electrical equipment	73 949	90 377	94 880	108 276
Chemicals and allied products	49 735	58 813	59 590	66 397
Scientific and professional instruments	28 162	31 392	34 804	39 397

Although exports are important to all states, states vary greatly in the relative value of their exports, in the destinations to which they export, and in the types of products exported. The data in this book give an indication of the importance of exports to a state, but, for several reasons, the data must be interpreted with caution. First, they pertain only to goods exports; comparable data about service exports are not available. Second, they identify the state where the seller of the export merchandise is located; often the seller also is the producer, and the production occurs in the same state as the sale, but this is not always the case. Third, even if the final product is produced in the state to which it is assigned, the product likely contains parts produced elsewhere.

In general, states in the South Atlantic, South Central, and Southwest regions experienced the most rapid export growth from 1994 to 1997, but there are exceptions to this general pattern. New Mexico, Arizona, Texas, Kentucky, North and South Carolina, Arkansas, and Alabama all had export growth above the national average, but so did Kansas, Colorado, Wisconsin, and Illinois. California, Texas, and New York—the three most populous states—each had even larger shares of exports. Together these states had 26 percent of the U.S. population in 1997 and 30 percent of exports. Florida, with the fourth largest population, had an export share below its population share, however, doubtless reflecting its large retired population and the relatively limited role of manufacturing in the Florida economy.

It is worth reiterating that these export data cover only goods exports; they do not measure the overall participation of a state in the international economy. Hawaii's goods exports may be small, but its earnings from spending by foreign visitors are a vital factor in its economy. Florida has seen rapid growth of its goods exports in the past 10 years, but more important may be Florida's popularity as an international tourist destination and its role as a transportation hub for movement of people and goods to Latin America.

HOUSING

NEW HOME CONSTRUCTION IS ONE OF THE MOST VOLATILE SECtors of the economy, exhibiting large swings in output depending upon the strength of the overall economy and the level of interest rates and also on the pace of new household formation and the amount of population migration among states and areas. A slump in housing production began prior to the overall recession of 1990–91 and hit bottom in 1991. Taking the 1989 to 1997 period,

New Home Production
(rate per 1,000 population)

Region	1989	1997
New England	4.5	3.4
Mid-Atlantic	4.2	3.1
Southeast	8.8	9.5
Great Lakes	5.1	5.5
Plains	4.5	5.8
Rocky Mountain	3.6	10.4
Southwest	3.5	8.7
Far West	9.4	5.3

which is the benchmark for this book, new housing output nationwide (including new mobile homes) gained about 13 percent over the entire period, but starting from the 1991 low, it had rebounded 55 percent by 1997.

There is tremendous state and regional variation in both the level of housing production and the rate of recovery since the recession. (See rankings, page 28.) The Rocky Mountain and Southwest regions stand out for their higher level of housing output per capita and their rate of increase since 1989, while the Southeast has had consistently strong output throughout the period. Dominated by gains in Texas, total housing production (including mobile home placements) increased 187 percent in the Southwest between 1989 and 1997, and, led by Colorado's recovery, production in the Rocky Mountain region grew 244 percent. These gains vastly outstripped even the rapid population growth in these regions. The resulting per capita levels of production were 50 to 60 percent higher than the U.S. average.

Weakness in new housing production was most marked throughout the decade in the Mid-Atlantic and New England regions, where population growth was minimal. A small offsetting factor is that the renovation market is more significant here than elsewhere, and it is not captured in building permit data. Output in the Far West has plummeted since 1989, brought down by the crash in California, from which the state has not recovered fully. California's weakness is reflected in the fact that its housing output represented 16 percent of the nation's total in 1989 but only 7 percent in 1997. The Great Lakes and Plains regions have experienced a moderately strong housing recovery since 1989, as population growth resumed in the 1990s after widespread out-migration during the 1980s.

A footnote to the housing production story is the steady uptrend in the share of total production consisting of manufactured housing (mobile homes). From a 13.2 per-

Housing Supply

	1989	1990	1991	1992	1993	1994	1995	1996	1997
Residential building permits (thousands)	1 338.4	1 110.8	948.8	1 094.9	1 199.1	1 371.6	1 332.5	1 425.6	1 441.1
New home production (including manufactured housing)									
Thousands of homes	1 541.2	1 306.2	1 123.1	1 306.9	1 441.6	1 657.7	1 643.2	1 745.3	1 737.6
Rate per 1,000 population	6.2	5.2	4.5	5.1	5.6	6.4	6.3	6.6	6.5
Existing home sales									
Thousands of homes	3 710	3 560	3 559	3 886	4 203	4 404	4 240	4 559	4 730
Change from previous year (percent)	-3.9	-4.0	0.0	9.2	8.2	4.8	-3.7	7.5	3.8
Home-ownership rate (percent of households)	63.9	63.9	64.1	64.1	64.0	64.0	64.7	65.4	65.7
Rental vacancy rate (percent of rental housing units)	7.4	7.2	7.4	7.4	7.3	7.4	7.6	7.8	7.7

cent share of total output in 1989, manufactured housing consistently represented over 17 percent of output from 1994 through 1997. It is a more affordable alternative to conventional housing, and, with the highest growth in population and housing concentrated in the Southwest and Southeast, where incomes are below national averages, the manufactured housing option has become a significant part of the U.S. housing market.

The record of the 1990s is more impressive for existing home re-sales (including single-family, apartment, condominium, and cooperatives) than for new production. Sales strength in the 1990s was unprecedented, exceeding the earlier sales peak of 1978–79. Sales volume was up 27 percent between 1989 and 1997. Median prices for sales of existing single-family homes advanced a strong 33 percent during this eight-year period. The price increases show large regional variations; the greatest rise came in the Midwest, up 49 percent from 1989 to 1997, with next highest price escalation in the South, at 29 percent. Price gains in the West were only 15 percent, and there was no price increase in the Northeast. The latter two regions had much higher prevailing prices in the 1989 base year, however, and prices had already escalated 47 and 63 percent, respectively, during the late '80s. The South and Midwest had only modest price gains during the late 1980s.[3]

The U.S. homeownership rate, that is, owner-occupied housing as a percentage of all occupied housing, changed little between 1989 and 1994 after declining during the 1980s. After 1994, strong household income gains and low mortgage interest rates fostered home purchase, and, by 1997, the homeownership rate slightly exceeded the previous record set in 1980. In recent years, there have been institutional changes in financing that allow greater numbers of moderate-income households to qualify for home purchase with low down payments. Increased homeownership is a public policy goal pursued in every region as a means of stabilizing neighborhoods and helping families accumulate wealth. The advance in homeownership rates has not come at an even pace across the states, however. Some states with rapid population growth and escalating home prices, such as Oregon, have seen declines in this rate, while in many Plains states, the stable, older-age population helps explain consistently high homeownership rates.

AGRICULTURE

FOR MANY YEARS, THE UNITED STATES HAS PRODUCED AN abundance of farm products both with progressively fewer

U.S. FARMS, 1997	
Number of farms (1997)	2 057 910
Total acres (thousands)	968 338
U.S. average acres per farm	471
Value of land and buildings (millions of dollars)	909 688
Average per farm	442 045

farms and farm workers, and with less acreage devoted to agriculture. In general, these trends continued in the 1990s, but at a slower pace than in the previous 10 years. According to the most recent Census of Agriculture (taken every five years), the number of farms in the United States declined by only 0.7 percent from 1992 to 1997. This compares with declines of 7.8 percent from 1987 to 1992 and 6.8 percent from 1982 to 1987. Land in farms declined 1.5 percent, compared to 2.0 and 2.3 percent, respectively, in the two previous five year periods.

Farm employment, which fell almost 16 percent from 1980 to 1989, fell a further 8 percent from 1989 to 1994, but remained virtually unchanged from 1994 to 1997, although wide year-to-year swings in farm activity make it difficult to say whether farm employment has stabilized or simply has paused in its declining trend. In any case, farm employment continues to diminish as a share of a growing employment total, dropping from 3.3 percent in 1980 to 2.3 percent in 1989 and 1.9 percent in 1997.

In no state did farm employment reach 10 percent of the employment total in 1997. The states with the largest farm share of employment—North and South Dakota, Iowa, and Nebraska—had percentages ranging from 8.5 to 5.9 percent. Kentucky led the southeastern states, with a 5.2 percent share. (See rankings, page 27.) In some states with notably important agricultural activity, including California and Florida, farm employment constituted a below average share of total employment. And in most northeastern states, farming generated less than 1 percent of total employment. The farm employment figures do not, however, measure the total importance of agriculture to any state's economy, as additional employment and income are generated by the provision of agricultural services, the processing of agricultural products, and the sale of farm equipment and supplies.

In federal statistics a farm is defined as any place with $1,000 of annual farm sales. Thus the total number of farms includes many for which farming generates only a minor fraction of total household income. In 1997, 50 percent of all farms had sales of less then $10,000, and 50 percent of all farm operators reported a principal occupation other than farming. By state, the percentage whose princi-

Farm Income
(millions of dollars)

	1980	1989	1990	1991	1992	1993	1994	1995	1996	1997
Gross income	156 566	198 078	202 968	200 613	202 600	217 569	210 864	223 619	231 482	241 446
Recipts from sales	146 884	173 058	180 136	178 677	179 765	189 560	187 956	200 363	207 395	216 097
Government payments	1 286	10 887	9 298	8 214	9 169	13 402	7 879	7 279	7 340	7 496
Imputed and miscellaneous income	8 397	14 133	13 534	13 721	13 666	14 607	15 029	15 976	16 747	17 852
(-) Production expenses	138 334	160 325	169 248	169 904	169 756	178 260	184 562	191 176	199 702	207 455
(=) Realized net income	18 232	37 752	33 719	30 709	32 844	39 309	26 302	32 443	31 781	33 990
(+) Inventory change	-6 109	-455	2 325	-1 042	5 044	-5 922	10 772	-9 301	7 674	2 375
(=) Net income	12 123	37 298	36 045	29 667	37 888	33 387	37 074	23 142	39 455	36 365
Corporate income	-433	4 495	4 554	2 963	5 034	1 811	7 492	3 173	7 290	6 113
Farm proprietors' income	12 556	32 803	31 491	26 704	32 854	31 576	29 582	19 968	32 165	30 252

pal occupation was farming varied from 36 percent in Tennessee to 74 percent in North Dakota. Nationwide, the 50 percent of farms with sales above $10,000 accounted for 98.5 percent of all farm sales, and the 18 percent of farms with sales above $100,000 for 87.4 percent of all sales.

The figures above refer to gross receipts from sales, before deduction of expenses. Gross cash receipts grew 25 percent from 1989 to 1997, but production expenses grew by a larger 29 percent, and inventory change varied widely from year to year. Net farm income in 1996 and 1997 averaged somewhat above 1989 and 1990, but the large year-to-year variations in net income make it difficult to say that this represents a trend.

Nationwide, farm sales in 1997 were just about evenly divided between crops and livestock and poultry. Individual states vary widely, however. Crops were 80 percent of total sales in Florida and 74 percent in California, while livestock and poultry and their products were 80 percent in Alabama, 71 percent in Wisconsin, and 69 percent in Texas.

EDUCATION

STATISTICS ON THE PERCENTAGE OF THE POPULATION AGE 25 and over who have completed high school or college provide summary indicators of the general educational level of the adult population. They measure past educational opportunity, not the current performance of the school system. Information on per pupil spending and teacher salaries provide indicators, albeit incomplete measures, of educational efforts currently being undertaken.

EDUCATIONAL ATTAINMENT. The percentages of the population that have completed high school and college refer to the entire population age 25 and over and hence include older generations who, on average, had less education than generally is received today. In 1997, 87.7 percent of persons age 25 to 44 had completed high school and 26.3 percent had completed four or more years of college; for those age 65 and over the corresponding figures were only 65.5 and 14.8 percent. Moreover, there was greater variation among the states with respect to high school completion for those age 65 and over than for younger generations. In Arizona, 82.5 percent of persons age 65 and over in 1997 had completed high school, in Kentucky, only 50.3 percent. For persons age 25 to 44, the percentage who had completed high school was uniformly higher and ranged from 94.3 percent in Wisconsin to 81.1 percent in

High School Completion: 1990–97

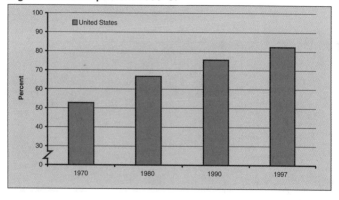

EDUCATIONAL ATTAINMENT	
Percent of population age 25 and over, 1997	
High school graduate or higher	82.1
College degree or higher	23.9

California.[4] The California figure undoubtedly is held down by the large number of immigrants in this age group coming from countries with less educational opportunity.

As recently as 1960, only 41.1 percent the U.S. population age 25 and over had completed high school and only 7.7 percent had completed college. In 1970, the percentages still were quite low: 52.3 percent for high school and 10.7 percent for college. Since then, all states have seen large gains in the percentages who have completed high school, and the states that had the lowest percentages have made the largest gains. In 1970, the percentage of the population age 25 and over who had completed high school ranged from a high of 67.3 percent in Utah to a low of 37.8 percent in South Carolina; by 1997, the percentages not only were higher, but the variation was less. Alaska had the highest percentage who had completed high school (92.1 percent) and Kentucky the lowest (75.4 percent). The District of Columbia and Massachusetts had the highest percentages who had completed college, Arkansas and West Virginia the lowest. (See rankings, page 29.)

ELEMENTARY AND SECONDARY EDUCATION. Of the nearly 50 million children enrolled in U.S. elementary and secondary schools in the 1995–96 school year, the great majority attended public schools. This was true in every state as well as nationwide. In no state did private school enrollment reach 20 percent of the total. The highest percentages enrolled in private school were in Delaware (19.1 percent), the District of Columbia (18 percent), Pennsylvania (16.2 percent), and Louisiana and Hawaii (both were 15.6 percent); the lowest were in Wyoming (2.2 percent), Utah (2.6 percent), Idaho (3.7 percent), and Oklahoma (3.8 percent).

Average teacher salaries in 1996–97 were highest in Alaska ($50,647) and Connecticut ($50,426). All of the Mid-Atlantic states paid salaries above the national average. The lowest salaries were found in the Plains, Southeast, and Southwest. South Dakota ranked last ($26,764). Second and third from the bottom were North Dakota ($27,711) and Mississippi ($27,720). Total expenditures per pupil to some extent paralleled the rankings for teacher salaries, but with notable exceptions. North and South Dakota and West Virginia, for example, rank substantially higher on per pupil expenditure than on teacher salaries. Part of the explanation lies in the high costs of maintaining small schools in rural areas and transporting students long distances to school.

HIGHER EDUCATION. The higher education enrollment figures include both 4-year and 2-year institutions and include professional and technical schools as well as colleges and universities. Enrollment in 2-year institutions was about 38 percent of the total in 1996, and this enrollment was overwhelmingly (96 percent) in public schools. Enrollment in 4-year institutions was about 66 percent public and 34 percent private. Although the majority of higher education students are between ages 18 and 24, the

Education Indicators

Elementary and secondary schools
Enrollment, 1995–1996
Total (thousands)	49 873
Percent in private schools	10.1
Expenditures per pupil (dollars), 1995–96	6 146
Average teacher salary (dollars), 1997–98	38 509

Higher education
Enrollment, 1996–1997
Total (thousands)	14 218
Percent of population 18–34	21.8
Percent minority	26.1
Percent in private schools	22.6

proportion age 25 and above has grown, rising from 34 percent in 1980 to 41 percent in 1996. The proportion attending part-time has grown slightly from 41 percent in 1980 to 43 percent in 1996.

Among the states, enrollees in higher education as a percent of the population ages 18 to 34 in 1996–97 ranged from a high of 30.9 percent in Nebraska to a low of 16.3 percent in Georgia. The percentage for the District of Columbia (47.9 percent) was well above that of any state. There was no clear geographic pattern to the states with the highest percentage enrolled, but seven of the eight states with the lowest percentages were southeastern states, and no southeastern state reached the national average.

HEALTH

SEVERAL HEALTH INDICATORS THAT ARE AVAILABLE FOR ALL states on a fairly current basis are presented in this book. Together they give a general picture of some of the health problems that may exist within a state and the degree of progress being made in providing the state's residents with adequate healthcare.

INFANT MORTALITY. The United States has made notable progress in recent years in reducing infant mortality. The infant mortality rate—the number of deaths of infants under one year per thousand live births—fell from 12.6 in 1980 to 9.2 in 1990 and then to an average of 7.2 for 1996–97. All states have seen reductions in infant mortality rates since 1980, and 1996–97 rates of 6.0 or less in 12 states ranging from Maine to Hawaii illustrate the possibilities for further reduction in the remaining states. A number of states with high infant mortality rates have established goals for reduction and programs to try to reach those goals.

Historically, infant mortality has been reduced through increased medical knowledge and the development of better medical equipment and facilities. Today, however, further progress in reducing infant mortality is dependent in large part on insuring that women understand the importance of early pre-natal care, obtain adequate nutrition, avoid smoking and drug use during pregnancy, and have access to available medical facilities. Among the states, higher rates of infant mortality tend to be found in states with high poverty rates, relatively large rural populations, and relatively low levels of educational attainment. (See rankings, page 29.) Apart from the District of Columbia, the highest 1996–97 rate was in Mississippi, but that state's

average rate of 10.3 for those years represented a major reduction from 17.0 in 1980 and 12.1 in 1990.

HEALTH INSURANCE. The percentage of the U.S. population lacking health insurance rose from 13.9 percent in 1990 to 16.1 percent in 1997. These numbers refer to persons who were without insurance coverage during the entire year. Persons covered by Medicare or Medicaid are counted as having health insurance.

Among the groups especially likely to lack insurance coverage are the working poor and the foreign-born population. About one-half of all full-time workers with incomes below the poverty level, and about 34 percent of all foreign-born, were without health insurance coverage during 1997. Among age groups, 30 percent of young adults between the ages of 18 and 24 lacked coverage. In contrast, thanks to Medicare, all but 1 percent of those aged 65 and over were covered by health insurance.

Among states, the proportion of the population lacking health insurance in 1997 ranged from only 8 percent in Hawaii and Wisconsin to over 24 percent in Arizona, Arkansas, and Texas. A number of factors, including specific state policies regarding Medicaid eligibility, age distribution of the population, and the prevalence of poverty influence the coverage rates of individual states. However, states with a high proportion of recent immigrants, including Texas, California, and Florida, stand out as being among those with the lowest rates of health insurance coverage. Some states with high poverty rates, including Arizona, Arkansas, and Mississippi, also fall into this category. Yet Tennessee, Louisiana, and Kentucky—also states with high poverty rates—had somewhat lower than average percentages of persons lacking health insurance in 1997.

DEATH RATES; CAUSES OF DEATH. Overall rates of death and the leading causes of death vary greatly by age. Children between ages 5 and 14 have the lowest death rate (21.7 per 100,000 in 1996), and, for these children, accidents are by far the leading cause of death. For young people ages 15 to 24, accidents remain the leading cause of death, but homicide and suicide also become important, and the overall death rate is four times as high (89.6 per 100,000 in 1996) as for the younger group. Death rates rise for each successively older age group, and diseases become more important as causes. For persons ages 45 to 64, cancer was the leading cause of death for women and heart disease for men. For those over age 65, heart disease was by far the leading cause, and the overall death rate was 5,061.1 per 100,000 in 1996.

Because of these great differences in death rates among age groups, comparing the death rate for a state with a

Health Indicators

	1990	1995	1996	1997
Infant mortality (rate per thousand live births)	9.2	7.6	7.3	7.1
Total deaths, age-adjusted (rate per thousand population)	5.2	5.0	4.9	4.8
Persons not covered by health insurance (percent of population)	13.9	15.4	15.6	16.1

Leading Causes of Death, 1996
(deaths per 100,000 population)

	Age-adjusted	Not age-adjusted
Deaths from all causes	491.6	872.5
Heart disease	134.5	276.4
Cancer	127.9	203.4
Cerebrovascular diseases	26.4	60.3
Chronic obstructive pulmonary disease	21.0	40.0
Diabetes mellitus	13.6	23.3
Pnemonia and influenza	12.8	31.6
HIV	11.1	11.7
Liver disease	7.5	9.4
Alzheimer's disease	2.7	8.1
Accidents and adverse effects	30.4	35.8
Motor vehicle accidents	16.2	16.5
Suicide	10.8	11.6
Homicide	8.5	7.9
Injury by firearm	12.9	12.8

large elderly population, such as Florida, to the rate for a state with a much more youthful population, such as Utah, does not provide good information about the relative health of each state's population. The overall death rate in Florida is higher simply because the population is older. A more useful approach is to compare the death rates for each age group. A shorthand way of making this more useful comparison is to look at "age-adjusted" death rates. These rates, computed by the U.S. Department of Health and Human Services, show what the death rates would have been in each state if all states had had identical percentages of their populations in each age group.

For the United States, the age-adjusted rate of death from all causes was 491.6 deaths per 100,000 population in 1996, which rounds to 4.9 per 1,000. (The total death rate from all causes often is expressed as the number of deaths per 1,000 population, but, because deaths from specific causes sometimes are relatively rare events, deaths by cause more often are expressed as the number of deaths per 100,000 population. State-level data on causes of death in 1997 were not available at press time.)

Based on age-adjusted data, heart disease and cancer are the leading causes of death in every state. Nationwide, they accounted for more than one-half of all deaths in 1996. Deaths from homicide showed perhaps the greatest variation by state, ranging from 1.8 per 100,000 in New Hampshire to 19.5 in Louisiana. (The rate in the District of Columbia was 72.9, but comparison of a large city to an entire state is particularly inappropriate in this case. Large cities almost invariably have violent crime rates higher than statewide averages.) The death rate from injury by firearm is a total of homicides, suicides, and accidents caused by firearms. Deaths caused by firearms were 10 per 100,000 or less in all of the New England states, New York, and New Jersey, as well as in Ohio, Wisconsin, Minnesota, Iowa, North Dakota, Nebraska, and Hawaii. In contrast, rates were 20 per 100,000 or above in Alabama, Mississippi, Louisiana, Nevada, and Alaska.

GOVERNMENT FINANCE

THE SERVICES PROVIDED BY STATE AND LOCAL GOVERNMENT also represent a major source of jobs and economic activity, employing about 11 percent of all workers in 1997.

AVERAGE STATE AND LOCAL TAXES, 1995–1996	
Per capita (dollars)	2 477
Percent of personal income	10.8

State and local budgets have been bolstered by the economy's expansion through the mid-90s. In the aggregate, states and localities increased direct spending by about 15 percent in the three years from fiscal 1993 to 1996. During the same period, revenues from their own sources—taxation and other charges—increased almost 18 percent, generating surpluses in most states. For all state governments, as of fiscal 1997, the aggregate of state assets in cash and securities was almost four times the amount of general debt outstanding. In addition to direct program expenditures, which totaled $503 billion in fiscal 1996, states spend significant amounts on transfers to localities, over $243 billion in the same year.

SPENDING BY FUNCTION: State and local spending for education, a topic which has received intense public discussion, increased 16 percent from fiscal 1993 to 1996, the same rate of increase as total direct general spending. Elementary and secondary education remains the largest function supported by local government, at $277 billion in fiscal 1996 (40 percent of all direct local spending). Hospital, health, and public welfare spending comprised 13.5 percent of local direct general spending. At the state level, public welfare alone represented about 32 percent of all direct spending, and, when hospitals and health are added on, the health and welfare category represented 42 percent of states' direct spending. However, education is the largest state spending area when state transfers to local education programs are included. In fact, of all the state-level education spending, 60 percent took the form

State Government Finances, 1996–1997

	Millions of dollars	Percent distribution	Dollars per capita
General revenue	814 382	100.0	3 049
Intergovernmental revenue	230 592	28.3	863
Taxes	443 335	54.4	1 660
General sales	147 069	18.1	551
Selective sales	68 668	8.4	257
License taxes	28 217	3.5	106
Individual income	144 668	17.8	542
Corporation net income	30 662	3.8	115
Other taxes	24 052	3.0	90
Other general revenue	72 303	8.9	526
General expenditure	788 176	100.0	2 951
Intergovernmental expenditure	264 207	33.5	989
Direct expenditure	523 969	66.5	1 962
General expenditure, by function			
Education	275 821	35.0	1 033
Public welfare	203 204	25.8	761
Hospitals and Health	63 193	8.0	237
Highways	60 204	7.6	225
Police protection and corrections	36 544	4.6	137
Natural resources, parks and recreation	16 809	2.1	63
Governmental administration	28 656	3.6	107
Interest on general debt	26 310	3.3	99
Other and unallocable	77 434	9.8	290
Debt at end of fiscal year	455 697	NA	1 706
Cash and security holdings	1 784 947	NA	6 683

of transfers to local government and 40 percent was direct spending, much of this going to higher education.

Other differences in spending between state and local government are the relatively larger amount spent on police and fire protection at the local level, though this is still only about 8 percent of direct general spending, and the proportionately larger local spending on administration. This reflects the decentralized office operations of multiple local governments, compared to the lower cost central structure of state government. At the state level, larger shares of budgets go to highways and corrections. Both levels spend 5 percent of their direct spending to pay interest on general debt.

States spent 34 percent of their general budgets on transfers of funds to localities in fiscal 1997, a significant revenue-sharing process that reinforces local government coffers. This state contribution is even larger in certain states, such as California, which uses 48 percent of its budget for local transfers. Arizona, Michigan, Minnesota, Nevada, and Wisconsin all shared more than 40 percent of state general spending through transfers. Seven states shared less than 20 percent of state general spending, most of them in New England (Alaska, Delaware, Hawaii, Maine, New Hampshire, Rhode Island, and Vermont). Hawaii shared less than 3 percent with localities.

SOURCES OF REVENUE: On the revenue side, states and localities have very different sources of funds. Local governments depend overwhelmingly on property taxes and current charges to users of services, which together made up 71.7 percent of all local general revenue (not including intergovernmental transfers) in fiscal 1996. Taxes other than property, including sales, income, and corporate taxes, contributed only about 16 percent of all local revenue. In contrast, these were 67 percent of each state's "own source" revenue, while current charges were a moderate 12 percent of the total and property taxes were an insignificant source. There is significant variation among states for certain categories. Seven states—Alaska, Florida, Nevada, South Dakota, Texas, Washington, and Wyoming—have no income tax and five states—Alaska, Delaware, Montana, New Hampshire and Oregon—have no general sales tax.

As the growing economy of the '90s has boosted incomes and consumer spending, the tax base of the states has grown accordingly, with an 18 percent increase in total tax collections between fiscal 1993 and 1996. General sales and individual income tax receipts increased 22 and 19 percent in the period, respectively.

In contrast, increases in the property tax base depend mostly upon a strong real estate market and the willingness of local governments to either raise assessments or rates, thus property tax collections by localities rose only 10 percent during this period. Local governments have raised current charges instead. Collections from these charges grew by over 27 percent during the three-year period. Charges comprise a wide range of service fees, with the largest being hospital service fees, which are 30.5 percent of the total. Next largest are sewer charges, at 18.3 percent of the total, education charges (including school lunch sales) at 10.6 percent, solid waste fees at 7.5 percent, and airport charges at 6.5 percent.

The state and local tax data in the state chapters of this book focus only on tax collections and do not include current charges. There is wide variation in the share of personal income represented by state and local taxes (excluding corporate income taxes) in each state, from over 13 percent in Alaska and New York, to less than 9 percent in New Hampshire and Tennessee. (See rankings, page 28.) Caution should be used in interpreting these shares as measures of the relative fiscal burdens on residents of different states. In some states, taxes are structured to fall heavily on out-of-state residents, such as tourists, or on businesses operating across state lines, such as oil companies. In addition, some state and local governments rely on user fees—not represented in these data—to finance activities that others pay for with general tax revenues.

Intergovernmental transfers play a critical role on the revenue side as well. Federal transfers are directed overwhelmingly to state governments, which receive 89 percent of federal inter-governmental transfers. Federal transfers to states in fiscal 1996 amounted to $208 billion, compared to the $549 billion states raised from their own general revenue base. However, states in turn passed on $230 billion in net transfers to the local level from either pass-through of federal funds or from states' own resources.

Remarkably, 16 states actually obtained less than half of their revenues from taxes in 1997, due to the significance of federal transfers, user fees, interest earnings, and miscellaneous revenue. These 16 mostly include states whose low incomes generate limited taxes, such as Tennessee, West Virginia, Louisiana, Montana and Alabama, as well as higher income states which have opted for relatively low taxes, such as Oregon. New York is also in this category because of its receipt of intergovernmental transfers totaling 40 percent of its general budget, the highest ratio of any state.

FEDERAL SPENDING IN STATES. The majority of federal spending is distributed to states and their residents in the form of payments to individuals, grants to state and local governments and nonprofit institutions, salaries and wages of federal workers, and defense and nondefense procurement contracts. Not included in the totals distributed to

Federal Spending

	Fiscal 1997, millions of dollars	Percent distribution
Total distributed to states and their residents	1 420 406	100.0
Payments to individuals	786 611	55.4
Retirement and disability	458 015	32.2
Medicare	206 049	14.5
Food Stamps	19 506	1.4
Supplemental Security Income	26 835	1.9
Grants	249 267	17.5
Medicaid and other health	113 918	8.0
Nutrition and family welfare	46 785	3.3
Education	17 134	1.2
Housing and community development	11 339	0.8
Salaries and wages	165 010	11.6
Defense procurement contracts	119 533	8.4
Non-defense procurement contracts	73 018	5.1

the states are federal monies not spent within the United States or that cannot reasonably be allocated, such as spending on the conduct of foreign affairs.

The majority of federal spending is distributed widely among the U.S. population, and as a result is distributed among states generally in proportion to their population. In 1997, 55.4 percent of federal spending within the states consisted of payments to individuals. About 85 percent of such payments were for Social Security, Medicare, and government retirement. These are distributed based on age and previous employment, not on income. The balance consists of veterans benefits, unemployment compensation, and miscellaneous individual payments, including Food Stamp and Supplemental Security Income (SSI) payments. The latter two are means-tested; that is, eligibility for these payments is conditional on low-income.

The second largest federal spending category is grants, primarily to state governments, which comprised 17.5 percent of federal funding in 1997. Nearly one-half of grant distributions is Medicaid support for poor people's medical care, which goes disproportionately to poorer states. Some of the remaining grants are distributed on needs-based formulas taking into account factors such as a state's number of poor children or amount of substandard housing.

One notable aspect of federal wage and salary payments is that federal employees are quite dispersed geographically because of regional and district offices, such as the many Social Security offices, and the varied locations of military bases. Thus, many states' economies benefit from federal employment and procurement of support goods and services. While Washington D.C. tends to be viewed as the center of federal employment, and indeed has the highest reliance on federal employment within its total employment base (30.1 percent), the city's federal employees earn only 6.8 percent of the total earned by federal employees nationwide (civilian and military). Neighboring Virginia and Maryland host a large share of federal wage earners, who represent 8.5 and 7.1 percent, respectively, of total employment in those two states. Hawaii and Alaska rely on federal employment for over 10 percent of their total jobs, and many South Atlantic states have over 4 percent of their employment in the federal sector. At the other end of the scale, many Midwestern states have a low share of federal employment, the lowest being in Michigan and Wisconsin at 1.5 percent of their total employment. (See rankings, page 27.)

Defense procurement, representing 8.4 percent of federal funds in fiscal 1997, is somewhat concentrated in states with aircraft, shipbuilding, and high-tech capacity. California is the leading state for such defense spending, receiving 15.5 percent of the 1997 national total, followed by Texas with 6.1 percent.

DEVELOPMENTS IN 1998

THE UNITED STATES CONTINUED ITS RECORD OF HEALTHY economic growth and low inflation in 1998, and all but a few states benefited, although in varying degrees. State-level data for 1998 was incomplete at press time, and the standard tables in the state chapters end with 1997 (or, in a few cases, 1996) so as to put as many different data items as possible on a common year. This section summarizes a few key indicators that recently have become available for 1998. These data are preliminary and may undergo considerable revision, but they provide general indications of each state's population change and economic performance in 1998.

POPULATION CHANGE, 1998. The U.S. population grew by 2.6 million in 1998, bringing the population total to 270.3 million. The 1.0 percent increase maintained the average rate of population growth from 1990 to 1997. Immigration accounted for more than one-third of the increase, a somewhat higher share than the average for 1990–97.

The most rapid population gains continued to be found in Nevada and Arizona. Four of the next five states, ranked by rate of population growth—Colorado, Texas, Utah, and Idaho—are in the Southwest or the Rocky Mountains. The Atlantic coast from North Carolina south to Florida formed an additional area of rapid population growth. Georgia moved into third place ranked on growth, Florida and North Carolina joined the top ten, and South Carolina ranked 11th.

California's 484,000 population increase was the largest absolute gain of any state, and, in contrast to the state's slow growth early in the 1990s, it ranked 9th in terms of percent population gain. Natural increase (births minus deaths) was the largest component of California's population growth, but immigration from abroad was almost as large. These growth factors were partly offset by net domestic out-migration equal to 0.3 percent of the state's 1997 population.

Connecticut and Rhode Island, both of which are states that lost population between 1990 and 1997, had small gains in 1998, but the District of Columbia continued to lose population, and North Dakota, Pennsylvania, and West Virginia also lost population. In general, these losses were due to domestic out-migration, although West Virginia, with its large proportion of elderly in the population, had not only net out-migration but also a small excess of deaths over births.

EMPLOYMENT AND UNEMPLOYMENT. Total U.S. civilian employment increased by 1.9 million workers, or 1.5 percent from 1997 to 1998, and the gain in payroll employment was even larger. The unemployment rate fell from 4.9 percent in 1997 to 4.5 percent in 1998, the lowest annual average since 1969. The employment to population ratio, which had reached a record 63.8 percent of the population age 16 and over in 1997, rose further to set a new record of 64.1 percent in 1998.

The states with the strongest percentage growth in employment—Arizona, Nevada, Colorado, and Utah—naturally enough were among the states with the most rapid population gains. Six states had civilian employment growth of more than 100,000—California (424,000 more people at work), Texas (311,000), Florida (137,000), Georgia (122,000), Virginia (108,000), and New York (103,000). These were not the states with the lowest unemployment rates (except for Virginia), but in each of these states the unemployment rate declined from 1997 to 1998. In California and New York the unemployment rate fell below 6 percent for the first time since 1990, the Texas rate

Population, Employment, Unemployment, and Exports, 1998

(Number of persons in thousands)

State	Population			Employed				Unemployed		Exports	
	Total	Change, 1997–1998		Total	Change, 1997–1998		Percent of population	Total	Rate	Millons of dollars	Percent change, 1997–1998
		Number	Percent		Number	Percent					
UNITED STATES	270 299	2 555	1.0	131 463	1 905	1.5	64.1	6 210	4.5	682 977	-0.7
Alabama	4 352	30	0.7	2 062	4	0.2	61.4	91	4.2	4 560	0.5
Alaska	614	4	0.7	299	9	3.1	70.0	18	5.8	760	-21.6
Arizona	4 669	115	2.5	2 178	95	4.6	61.8	94	4.1	10 753	-20.7
Arkansas	2 538	15	0.6	1 148	-2	-0.2	59.1	67	5.5	1 934	-12.5
California	32 667	484	1.5	15 361	424	2.8	62.5	969	5.9	98 809	-4.8
Colorado	3 971	79	2.0	2 159	78	3.7	71.6	86	3.8	10 733	-5.3
Connecticut	3 274	7	0.2	1 652	17	1.0	65.3	57	3.4	12 140	-5.9
Delaware	744	8	1.2	377	11	3.0	65.7	15	3.8	4 969	-2.7
District of Columbia	523	-7	-1.3	244	6	2.5	58.9	24	8.8	4 392	-10.0
Florida	14 916	239	1.6	6 918	137	2.0	59.6	310	4.3	23 173	1.2
Georgia	7 642	152	2.0	3 852	122	3.3	66.9	169	4.2	11 212	14.3
Hawaii	1 193	1	0.1	560	1	0.2	63.2	37	6.2	211	-30.3
Idaho	1 229	20	1.6	620	21	3.5	67.6	33	5.0	1 460	-14.9
Illinois	12 045	56	0.5	5 946	42	0.7	65.5	277	4.5	33 838	-1.1
Indiana	5 899	34	0.6	2 993	15	0.5	66.8	96	3.1	13 949	6.5
Iowa	2 862	8	0.3	1 526	-2	-0.1	70.0	43	2.8	3 412	9.5
Kansas	2 629	28	1.1	1 357	40	3.0	69.2	54	3.8	4 403	-14.2
Kentucky	3 936	26	0.7	1 835	21	1.2	60.8	89	4.6	7 440	7.8
Louisiana	4 369	15	0.4	1 945	54	2.9	59.4	118	5.7	4 392	0.4
Maine	1 244	2	0.2	622	-2	-0.3	63.5	29	4.4	1 664	4.7
Maryland	5 135	40	0.8	2 631	-11	-0.4	66.8	125	4.6	4 014	4.0
Massachusetts	6 147	33	0.5	3 164	35	1.1	66.6	109	3.3	16 467	-5.2
Michigan	9 817	37	0.4	4 835	82	1.7	64.8	194	3.9	39 269	3.6
Minnesota	4 725	38	0.8	2 613	74	2.9	73.5	68	2.5	13 499	-2.1
Mississippi	2 752	20	0.7	1 200	10	0.8	58.3	68	5.4	1 414	-0.5
Missouri	5 439	30	0.6	2 738	-32	-1.2	66.6	119	4.2	6 832	-3.0
Montana	880	2	0.2	442	11	2.6	64.8	26	5.6	390	-9.3
Nebraska	1 663	6	0.3	892	9	1.0	71.9	25	2.7	2 472	-0.9
Nevada	1 747	68	4.1	880	33	3.9	66.7	40	4.3	765	-5.2
New Hampshire	1 185	13	1.1	633	8	1.3	69.6	19	2.9	1 987	2.9
New Jersey	8 115	57	0.7	3 963	-19	-0.5	63.4	192	4.6	20 033	-3.8
New Mexico	1 737	13	0.8	780	16	2.1	60.2	51	6.2	1 896	6.5
New York	18 175	29	0.2	8 372	103	1.2	59.6	498	5.6	45 565	-6.8
North Carolina	7 546	116	1.6	3 663	-42	-1.1	64.5	131	3.5	12 920	-1.4
North Dakota	638	-3	-0.4	336	-3	-0.9	70.0	11	3.2	657	5.5
Ohio	11 209	17	0.1	5 437	-8	-0.1	63.5	242	4.3	24 815	-1.2
Oklahoma	3 347	25	0.8	1 554	19	1.2	61.6	74	4.5	2 623	-3.6
Oregon	3 282	39	1.2	1 664	37	2.3	65.3	98	5.6	8 144	-2.6
Pennsylvania	12 001	-10	-0.1	5 661	-7	-0.1	61.0	275	4.6	19 139	-0.8
Rhode Island	988	1	0.1	474	-2	-0.4	63.1	24	4.9	1 113	-1.2
South Carolina	3 836	48	1.3	1 884	41	2.2	64.0	75	3.8	5 857	3.2
South Dakota	738	0	0.1	386	8	2.1	70.6	11	2.9	374	-14.2
Tennessee	5 431	59	1.1	2 644	82	3.2	62.8	116	4.2	9 873	-0.4
Texas	19 760	374	1.9	9 631	311	3.3	65.9	487	4.8	59 029	4.9
Utah	2 100	35	1.7	1 023	15	1.5	69.3	40	3.8	3 099	-5.9
Vermont	591	2	0.4	319	5	1.6	69.2	11	3.4	2 758	6.4
Virginia	6 791	54	0.8	3 386	108	3.3	65.6	102	2.9	11 460	-0.5
Washington	5 689	75	1.3	2 895	48	1.7	66.9	145	4.8	37 960	19.6
West Virginia	1 811	-4	-0.2	747	-1	-0.1	51.4	53	6.6	1 178	-9.3
Wisconsin	5 224	22	0.4	2 853	12	0.4	71.9	99	3.4	9 221	-5.8
Wyoming	481	1	0.2	246	7	2.9	67.0	12	4.8	158	-10.0

fell below 5 percent, and the other three states each had a 1998 unemployment rate below the national average.

Only three states—Hawaii, New Mexico, and West Virginia—and the District of Columbia had unemployment rates still above 6 percent in 1998, and for West Virginia this was a major improvement from the recession induced 11.4 percent rate in 1992 and the lowest unemployment rate since 1978.

EXPORTS. In 1998, U.S. exports faced sharply reduced demand and increased competition in world markets because of severe recessions in Japan and other key Asian countries. Despite the adverse conditions, receipts from U.S. goods exports fell just 0.7 percent from 1997 to 1998. The drop was entirely due to lower prices in world markets; the volume of goods exported actually increased.

The impact of the "Asian crisis" varied greatly by state. California, with its Pacific Rim orientation and its concentration on high-tech goods, saw its exports drop by $5 billion (4.8 percent). Arizona had an even more severe swing: the state's exports had grown 37 percent in 1997, but fell back almost 21 percent in 1998. In contrast, export growth continued for the state of Washington, with a nearly 20 percent 1998 gain following a 24 percent increase in 1997.

Continued revival of the state's aircraft exports likely was a leading factor. Texas, the state that ranks second after California in export sales, had a gain of $2.7 billion in 1998, but New York, the third ranking state, saw its exports drop $3.3 billion.

---

1. In New England, metropolitan areas are defined in terms of cities and towns, but 1997 data on that basis were not available for use in this book. An alternative concept, New England County Metropolitan Areas (NECMAs), was used.

2. Business services encompasses a wide variety of services, ranging from sophisticated, well-paid computer programming services to more mundane services such as building cleaning and maintenance. The United States is in the process of moving to a new system of classifying industries, the North American Industry Classification System (NAICS). Among other changes, NAICS will divide business services among a number of more precisely defined industries. See the notes and definitions section in the back of this book for more information.

3. These price data are for the four U.S. regions as defined by the Bureau of the Census. The definitions differ from the eight economic regions as defined by the Bureau of Economic Analysis and used elsewhere in this book. See he notes and definitions section in the back of this book for regional definitions.

4. These comparisons are based on data for the 25 largest states; similar data by age are not readily available for smaller states.

Population, 1997 | | | Percent population change, 1990–1997, and components

State and rank	Population	State and rank	Population change (percent)	Natural increase (percent)	Domestic migration (percent)	International immigration (percent)
United States	267 743 595	**United States**	7.3	4.9	0.2	2.2
1. California	32 182 118	1. Nevada	37.7	7.1	28.0	2.9
2. Texas	19 385 699	2. Arizona	23.8	7.2	12.6	2.2
3. New York	18 146 200	3. Idaho	19.5	6.5	11.9	1.2
4. Florida	14 677 181	4. Utah	19.4	11.4	5.3	1.2
5. Pennsylvania	12 011 278	5. Colorado	17.8	6.5	10.2	1.4
6. Illinois	11 989 352	6. Georgia	15.1	6.0	8.2	1.1
7. Ohio	11 192 932	7. Washington	14.6	5.5	7.3	2.0
8. Michigan	9 779 984	8. Texas	13.7	7.8	3.0	3.2
9. New Jersey	8 058 384	9. Oregon	13.5	3.8	8.3	1.7
10. Georgia	7 489 982	10. New Mexico	13.4	7.2	4.5	1.9
11. North Carolina	7 430 675	11. Florida	12.7	2.5	6.9	3.5
12. Virginia	6 737 489	12. North Carolina	11.6	4.3	6.9	0.6
13. Massachusetts	6 114 440	13. Alaska	10.2	10.7	-1.6	1.2
14. Indiana	5 864 847	14. Delaware	9.9	4.6	4.0	1.0
15. Washington	5 614 151	14. Montana	9.9	3.4	6.5	0.3
16. Missouri	5 408 455	16. Tennessee	9.8	3.5	6.3	0.5
17. Tennessee	5 371 693	17. Virginia	8.4	4.9	2.1	1.7
18. Wisconsin	5 201 226	18. South Carolina	8.3	4.4	3.0	0.4
19. Maryland	5 094 924	19. California	7.5	8.3	-6.3	5.7
20. Minnesota	4 687 408	20. Arkansas	7.2	2.8	4.3	0.3
21. Arizona	4 553 249	21. Hawaii	7.1	7.5	-4.1	3.9
22. Louisiana	4 353 646	22. Alabama	6.8	3.5	2.7	0.3
23. Alabama	4 322 113	22. Minnesota	6.8	4.6	1.6	0.9
24. Kentucky	3 910 366	24. Maryland	6.2	5.1	-0.6	2.0
25. Colorado	3 892 029	25. Wisconsin	6.1	3.6	1.7	0.4
26. South Carolina	3 788 119	26. Mississippi	6.0	4.3	1.8	0.2
27. Oklahoma	3 321 611	27. Kentucky	5.9	3.2	2.5	0.3
28. Connecticut	3 267 240	27. South Dakota	5.9	3.9	1.6	0.5
29. Oregon	3 243 272	27. Wyoming	5.9	4.7	1.0	0.4
30. Iowa	2 854 330	30. Indiana	5.6	4.1	1.4	0.4
31. Mississippi	2 731 644	31. Missouri	5.5	3.1	1.9	0.5
32. Kansas	2 601 437	31. Oklahoma	5.5	3.3	1.8	0.7
33. Arkansas	2 523 186	33. New Hampshire	5.4	4.1	1.1	0.4
34. Utah	2 065 001	34. Michigan	5.0	4.4	-1.6	0.8
35. West Virginia	1 815 231	35. Kansas	4.9	4.0	-0.5	0.8
36. New Mexico	1 723 965	36. Nebraska	4.8	3.7	0.7	0.7
37. Nevada	1 678 691	37. Illinois	4.7	5.1	-3.7	2.5
38. Nebraska	1 657 009	38. Vermont	4.3	3.2	0.8	0.6
39. Maine	1 241 895	39. New Jersey	3.9	4.1	-3.8	3.8
40. Idaho	1 208 865	40. Louisiana	3.2	4.9	-2.0	0.5
41. Hawaii	1 192 057	41. Ohio	3.0	3.6	-0.9	0.4
42. New Hampshire	1 172 140	42. Iowa	2.7	2.6	-0.3	0.5
43. Rhode Island	987 263	43. Massachusetts	1.6	3.5	-3.5	1.9
44. Montana	878 730	44. West Virginia	1.3	0.6	0.8	0.2
45. South Dakota	737 755	45. Pennsylvania	1.0	1.9	-1.4	0.7
46. Delaware	735 143	46. Maine	0.9	2.0	-1.1	0.2
47. North Dakota	640 965	47. New York	0.8	4.4	-8.1	4.8
48. Alaska	609 655	48. North Dakota	0.6	3.1	-2.9	0.6
49. Vermont	588 632	49. Connecticut	-0.7	3.7	-5.8	1.7
50. District of Columbia	529 895	50. Rhode Island	-1.7	2.9	-5.6	1.3
51. Wyoming	480 043	51. District of Columbia	-12.2	3.8	-19.6	3.9

RANKINGS: RACE

Percent White, non-Hispanic, 1997		Percent Black, non-Hispanic, 1997		Percent Asian, 1997	
State and rank	Percent White, non-Hispanic	State and rank	Percent Black, non-Hispanic	State and rank	Percent Asian
United States	72.7	**United States**	12.1	**United States**	3.7
1. Maine	97.7	1. District of Columbia	61.9	1. Hawaii	63.1
2. Vermont	97.6	2. Mississippi	36.3	2. California	11.7
3. New Hampshire	96.7	3. Louisiana	31.8	3. Washington	5.5
4. West Virginia	95.7	4. South Carolina	29.9	4. New Jersey	5.3
5. Iowa	94.8	5. Georgia	28.2	4. New York	5.3
6. North Dakota	93.1	6. Maryland	27.0	6. Alaska	4.4
7. Minnesota	91.9	7. Alabama	25.8	6. Nevada	4.4
8. Montana	91.4	8. North Carolina	21.9	8. Maryland	3.8
9. Kentucky	91.3	9. Virginia	19.7	9. Virginia	3.5
10. Wyoming	90.7	10. Delaware	18.8	10. Massachusetts	3.4
11. Idaho	90.4	11. Tennessee	16.4	11. Illinois	3.2
12. Nebraska	90.1	12. Arkansas	16.0	12. Oregon	3.1
13. South Dakota	89.9	13. Illinois	14.9	13. District of Columbia	2.9
13. Wisconsin	89.9	14. Florida	14.6	14. Texas	2.7
15. Utah	89.3	14. New York	14.6	15. Minnesota	2.5
16. Indiana	88.5	16. Michigan	14.1	15. Utah	2.5
17. Oregon	88.4	17. New Jersey	13.2	17. Colorado	2.3
18. Rhode Island	87.5	18. Texas	11.6	17. Connecticut	2.3
19. Kansas	86.9	19. Ohio	11.3	19. Rhode Island	2.2
20. Pennsylvania	86.5	20. Missouri	11.1	20. Arizona	2.0
21. Missouri	86.0	21. Pennsylvania	9.4	20. Delaware	2.0
22. Ohio	85.9	22. Connecticut	8.4	22. Georgia	1.8
23. Massachusetts	85.4	23. Indiana	8.1	23. Kansas	1.7
24. Washington	83.8	24. Oklahoma	7.5	23. Florida	1.7
25. Tennessee	81.5	25. Kentucky	7.2	25. Pennsylvania	1.6
26. Michigan	81.3	26. Nevada	6.8	26. Michigan	1.5
27. Connecticut	81.2	27. California	6.6	26. Wisconsin	1.5
28. Arkansas	81.1	28. Kansas	5.6	28. New Mexico	1.4
29. Oklahoma	80.0	29. Wisconsin	5.4	29. Iowa	1.3
30. Colorado	79.0	30. Massachusetts	5.2	29. Nebraska	1.3
31. Delaware	75.7	31. Colorado	3.9	29. Oklahoma	1.3
32. North Carolina	73.6	32. Nebraska	3.8	32. Louisiana	1.2
33. Virginia	73.2	32. Rhode Island	3.8	32. North Carolina	1.2
34. Alaska	72.7	34. Alaska	3.7	34. Idaho	1.1
35. Nevada	72.6	35. Washington	3.3	34. Missouri	1.1
36. Alabama	72.3	36. West Virginia	3.1	34. New Hampshire	1.1
37. Illinois	72.0	37. Arizona	3.0	34. Ohio	1.1
38. New Jersey	69.7	38. Hawaii	2.7	38. Indiana	0.9
39. Florida	69.2	38. Minnesota	2.7	38. South Carolina	0.9
40. Arizona	68.3	40. Iowa	1.9	38. Tennessee	0.9
41. South Carolina	67.8	40. New Mexico	1.9	41. North Dakota	0.8
42. Georgia	67.1	42. Oregon	1.6	41. Vermont	0.8
43. New York	65.9	43. Utah	0.7	41. Wyoming	0.8
44. Maryland	65.5	43. Wyoming	0.7	44. Arkansas	0.7
45. Louisiana	64.0	45. New Hampshire	0.6	44. Kentucky	0.7
46. Mississippi	61.9	45. North Dakota	0.6	44. Maine	0.7
47. Texas	56.2	45. South Dakota	0.6	44. Mississippi	0.7
48. California	51.1	48. Maine	0.5	48. Alabama	0.6
49. New Mexico	48.6	48. Vermont	0.5	48. Montana	0.6
50. Hawaii	29.2	50. Idaho	0.4	48. South Dakota	0.6
51. District of Columbia	28.0	51. Montana	0.3	51. West Virginia	0.5

RANKINGS: RACE, ETHNICITY, AND METROPOLITAN POPULATION

Percent Native American, 1997		Percent Hispanic, 1997		Percent in metropolitan counties, 1997	
State and rank	Percent Native American	State and rank	Percent Hispanic	State and rank	Percent metropolitan
United States	0.9	**United States**	11.0	**United States**	79.9
1. Alaska	15.9	1. New Mexico	40.0	1. District of Columbia	100.0
2. New Mexico	9.1	2. California	30.8	1. New Jersey	100.0
3. South Dakota	7.9	3. Texas	29.4	3. Massachusetts	98.5
4. Oklahoma	7.8	4. Arizona	21.9	4. California	96.6
5. Montana	6.2	5. Nevada	15.1	5. Florida	92.8
6. Arizona	5.6	6. Florida	14.4	6. Maryland	92.7
7. North Dakota	4.6	7. Colorado	14.3	7. New York	91.8
8. Wyoming	2.2	8. New York	14.2	8. Rhode Island	91.6
9. Nevada	1.8	9. New Jersey	11.9	9. Connecticut	91.2
9. Washington	1.8	10. Illinois	9.9	10. Arizona	87.6
11. Oregon	1.4	11. Hawaii	8.0	11. Nevada	85.8
11. Utah	1.4	12. Connecticut	7.9	12. Pennsylvania	84.5
13. Idaho	1.3	13. District of Columbia	7.2	13. Texas	84.3
13. North Carolina	1.3	14. Idaho	7.1	14. Illinois	84.1
15. Minnesota	1.2	15. Utah	6.5	15. Colorado	84.0
16. California	1.0	16. Rhode Island	6.2	16. Washington	82.8
17. Colorado	0.9	17. Washington	6.1	17. Michigan	82.6
17. Kansas	0.9	18. Massachusetts	5.9	18. Delaware	81.7
17. Nebraska	0.9	18. Oregon	5.9	19. Ohio	81.0
17. Wisconsin	0.9	18. Wyoming	5.9	20. Virginia	78.0
21. Hawaii	0.6	21. Kansas	5.1	21. Utah	76.8
21. Michigan	0.6	22. Nebraska	4.1	22. Louisiana	75.2
23. Arkansas	0.5	23. Alaska	3.8	23. Hawaii	73.3
23. Maine	0.5	24. Oklahoma	3.7	24. Indiana	71.7
23. Rhode Island	0.5	25. Maryland	3.5	25. Oregon	70.3
23. Texas	0.5	25. Virginia	3.5	26. Minnesota	69.9
27. Alabama	0.4	27. Delaware	3.3	27. South Carolina	69.8
27. Florida	0.4	28. Georgia	2.8	28. Georgia	68.6
27. Louisiana	0.4	29. Louisiana	2.6	29. Missouri	67.9
27. Mississippi	0.4	29. Michigan	2.6	29. Tennessee	67.9
27. Missouri	0.4	31. Pennsylvania	2.5	31. Alabama	67.7
27. New York	0.4	31. Wisconsin	2.5	31. Wisconsin	67.7
33. Delaware	0.3	33. Indiana	2.3	33. North Carolina	66.9
33. District of Columbia	0.3	34. North Carolina	2.0	34. New Hampshire	62.5
33. Iowa	0.3	35. Iowa	1.9	35. Oklahoma	60.4
33. Maryland	0.3	36. Arkansas	1.8	36. New Mexico	56.9
33. New Jersey	0.3	37. Minnesota	1.7	37. Kansas	56.0
33. Vermont	0.3	37. Montana	1.7	38. Nebraska	51.5
33. Virginia	0.3	39. Missouri	1.5	39. Arkansas	48.5
40. Connecticut	0.2	39. Ohio	1.5	40. Kentucky	48.3
40. Georgia	0.2	41. New Hampshire	1.4	41. Iowa	44.5
40. Illinois	0.2	42. South Carolina	1.2	42. North Dakota	42.9
40. Indiana	0.2	43. North Carolina	1.1	43. West Virginia	41.8
40. Kentucky	0.2	43. South Dakota	1.1	44. Alaska	41.2
40. Massachusetts	0.2	43. Tennessee	1.1	45. Maine	39.9
40. New Hampshire	0.2	46. Alabama	0.9	46. Idaho	37.8
40. Ohio	0.2	46. Vermont	0.9	47. Mississippi	35.5
40. South Carolina	0.2	48. Kentucky	0.8	48. South Dakota	33.6
40. Tennessee	0.2	48. Mississippi	0.8	49. Montana	33.4
50. Pennsylvania	0.1	50. Maine	0.7	50. Vermont	32.4
50. West Virginia	0.1	51. West Virginia	0.6	51. Wyoming	29.6

RANKINGS: AGE AND BIRTH RATE

Percent age 65 years and over, 1997		Percent under 18 years, 1997		Birth rate, 1997	
State and rank	Percent age 65 and over	State and rank	Percent under 18 years	State and rank	Live births per 1,000 population
United States	12.7	**United States**	26.0	**United States**	14.6
1. Florida	18.5	1. Utah	33.4	1. Utah	21.3
2. Pennsylvania	15.8	2. Alaska	30.9	2. Texas	17.2
2. Rhode Island	15.8	3. Idaho	29.0	3. Arizona	16.6
4. West Virginia	15.1	4. New Mexico	28.9	4. California	16.3
5. Iowa	15.0	5. Texas	28.7	5. Nevada	16.1
6. Connecticut	14.4	6. Arizona	28.1	6. Alaska	15.9
6. North Dakota	14.4	7. California	27.7	7. Georgia	15.8
8. Arkansas	14.3	8. Mississippi	27.6	8. Mississippi	15.7
8. South Dakota	14.3	9. Wyoming	27.5	9. New Mexico	15.5
10. Massachusetts	14.1	10. Louisiana	27.4	10. Idaho	15.4
11. District of Columbia	13.9	11. Nebraska	26.8	11. Illinois	15.2
11. Maine	13.9	11. Illinois	26.7	11. Louisiana	15.2
13. Missouri	13.7	12. Minnesota	26.7	13. District of Columbia	14.9
13. Nebraska	13.7	12. South Dakota	26.7	14. Arkansas	14.6
13. New Jersey	13.7	15. Georgia	26.6	14. Hawaii	14.6
16. Kansas	13.5	16. Kansas	26.5	16. Colorado	14.5
17. New York	13.4	16. Oklahoma	26.5	16. New York	14.5
17. Ohio	13.4	18. Nevada	26.4	16. Oklahoma	14.5
17. Oklahoma	13.4	19. Arkansas	26.3	19. Kansas	14.4
20. Oregon	13.3	20. Colorado	26.1	19. North Carolina	14.4
21. Arizona	13.2	20. Montana	26.1	21. Indiana	14.2
21. Hawaii	13.2	22. Missouri	26.0	22. Alabama	14.1
21. Montana	13.2	22. Wisconsin	26.0	22. Nebraska	14.1
21. Wisconsin	13.2	24. Washington	25.9	22. Washington	14.1
25. Alabama	13.0	25. North Dakota	25.8	25. Delaware	14.0
26. Delaware	12.9	26. Michigan	25.6	25. New Jersey	14.0
27. Illinois	12.5	27. Hawaii	25.5	27. Tennessee	13.9
27. Indiana	12.5	27. Indiana	25.5	28. Maryland	13.8
27. Kentucky	12.5	29. Iowa	25.4	28. Minnesota	13.8
27. North Carolina	12.5	29. Ohio	25.4	28. Missouri	13.8
27. Tennessee	12.5	29. South Carolina	25.4	28. South Carolina	13.8
32. Michigan	12.4	32. New Hampshire	25.2	28. South Dakota	13.8
33. Minnesota	12.3	32. North Carolina	25.2	33. Michigan	13.7
33. Vermont	12.3	34. New York	25.1	33. Virginia	13.7
35. Mississippi	12.2	35. Oregon	25.0	35. Kentucky	13.6
36. New Hampshire	12.1	36. Maryland	24.9	35. Ohio	13.6
36. South Carolina	12.1	37. Alabama	24.8	37. Massachusetts	13.5
38. Maryland	11.5	38. New Jersey	24.7	37. Oregon	13.5
38. Nevada	11.5	38. Tennessee	24.7	39. Wyoming	13.4
38. Washington	11.5	38. Vermont	24.7	40. Connecticut	13.1
41. Louisiana	11.4	41. Kentucky	24.6	40. Florida	13.1
42. Idaho	11.3	42. Virginia	24.4	42. North Dakota	13.0
42. Wyoming	11.3	43. Delaware	24.3	43. Iowa	12.9
44. New Mexico	11.2	44. Connecticut	24.2	43. Wisconsin	12.9
44. Virginia	11.2	45. Maine	23.9	45. Rhode Island	12.5
46. California	11.1	46. Pennsylvania	23.8	46. Montana	12.3
47. Colorado	10.1	47. Florida	23.7	47. New Hampshire	12.3
47. Texas	10.1	47. Massachusetts	23.7	48. Pennsylvania	12.0
49. Georgia	9.9	47. Rhode Island	23.7	49. West Virginia	11.4
50. Utah	8.7	50. West Virginia	22.7	50. Vermont	11.3
51. Alaska	5.3	51. District of Columbia	20.3	51. Maine	11.0

RANKINGS: EMPLOYMENT

	Unemployment rank, 1997		Employment growth, 1990–1997		Employment to population ratio, 1997
State and rank	Percent unemployed	State and rank	Average annual increase in employment	State and rank	Employment to population ratio
United States	4.9	**United States**	1.2	**United States**	63.8
1. North Dakota	2.5	1. Nevada	4.3	1. Wisconsin	71.3
2. Nebraska	2.6	2. Idaho	3.7	2. Minnesota	70.9
3. New Hampshire	3.1	2. Utah	3.7	3. Utah	70.3
3. South Dakota	3.1	4. Colorado	3.2	4. New Hampshire	70.0
3. Utah	3.1	5. Arizona	2.9	5. Nebraska	69.7
6. Colorado	3.3	6. Georgia	2.6	6. Colorado	69.5
6. Iowa	3.3	7. Washington	2.4	7. Iowa	68.9
6. Minnesota	3.3	8. Alabama	2.3	8. Wyoming	68.7
9. Indiana	3.5	9. Alaska	2.1	9. North Dakota	68.2
10. North Carolina	3.6	9. New Mexico	2.1	9. Vermont	68.2
11. Wisconsin	3.7	9. Oregon	2.1	11. Maryland	66.7
12. Kansas	3.8	9. Texas	2.1	11. South Dakota	66.7
13. Delaware	4.0	13. Wisconsin	2.0	13. Missouri	66.6
13. Massachusetts	4.0	14. Montana	1.9	14. Idaho	66.3
13. Virginia	4.0	15. Missouri	1.8	14. Nevada	66.3
13. Vermont	4.0	15. South Dakota	1.8	16. Kansas	66.2
17. Nevada	4.1	15. Tennessee	1.8	17. Washington	65.9
17. Oklahoma	4.1	18. Indiana	1.7	18. Alaska	65.8
19. Michigan	4.2	19. Florida	1.6	19. Indiana	65.5
19. Missouri	4.2	19. Michigan	1.6	20. Georgia	65.2
21. Georgia	4.5	19. Minnesota	1.6	21. Illinois	65.1
21. South Carolina	4.5	19. North Carolina	1.6	22. Massachusetts	65.0
23. Arizona	4.6	23. Nebraska	1.5	23. North Carolina	64.4
23. Ohio	4.6	23. North Dakota	1.5	23. Texas	64.4
25. Illinois	4.7	23. South Carolina	1.5	25. Oregon	64.3
26. Florida	4.8	26. Iowa	1.4	26. Connecticut	63.9
26. Washington	4.8	26. Louisiana	1.4	27. Delaware	63.8
28. Alabama	5.1	28. Arkansas	1.3	28. Maine	63.6
28. Connecticut	5.1	28. Kentucky	1.3	29. Montana	63.5
28. Maryland	5.1	30. Mississippi	1.2	29. New Jersey	63.5
28. New Jersey	5.1	30. Vermont	1.2	31. South Carolina	63.2
28. Wyoming	5.1	32. Delaware	1.1	32. Michigan	62.9
33. Pennsylvania	5.2	32. Kansas	1.1	33. Ohio	62.7
34. Arkansas	5.3	34. Oklahoma	1.0	34. Virginia	62.2
34. Idaho	5.3	34. West Virginia	1.0	35. Arizona	61.1
34. Rhode Island	5.3	36. Illinois	0.9	35. Rhode Island	61.1
37. Kentucky	5.4	36. Maryland	0.9	37. California	61.7
37. Maine	5.4	36. Ohio	0.9	38. Hawaii	61.0
37. Montana	5.4	36. Wyoming	0.9	38. Tennessee	61.0
37. Tennessee	5.4	40. New Hampshire	0.8	40. Alabama	60.9
37. Texas	5.4	40. Virginia	0.8	41. Oklahoma	60.3
42. Mississippi	5.7	42. Hawaii	0.7	42. Pennsylvania	59.8
43. Oregon	5.8	43. California	0.6	43. Arkansas	59.3
44. Louisiana	6.1	44. Maine	0.5	43. New Mexico	59.3
45. New Mexico	6.2	44. Pennsylvania	0.5	45. Kentucky	59.2
46. California	6.3	46. Massachusetts	0.4	46. New York	58.9
47. Hawaii	6.4	46. New Jersey	0.4	47. Florida	58.7
48. New York	6.4	48. New York	-0.2	48. Louisiana	57.1
49. West Virginia	6.9	48. Rhode Island	-0.2	49. Mississippi	56.2
50. Alaska	7.9	50. Connecticut	-0.9	50. District of Columbia	55.1
50. District of Columbia	7.9	51. District of Columbia	-3.6	51. West Virginia	51.3

RANKINGS: INCOME AND POVERTY

Personal income per capita, 1997		Median household income, 1996–1997 average		Poverty rate, 1996–1997 average	
State and rank	Personal income per capita (dollars)	State and rank	Median household income (1997 dollars)	State and rank	Persons below the poverty level (percent)
United States	25 298	**United States**	36 656	**United States**	13.5
1. Connecticut	35 954	1. Alaska	50 992	1. New Hampshire	7.8
2. District of Columbia	35 290	2. New Jersey	48 289	2. Indiana	8.2
3. New Jersey	32 233	3. Maryland	45 844	3. Utah	8.3
4. Massachusetts	31 207	4. Connecticut	43 535	4. Alaska	8.5
5. New York	30 299	5. Colorado	42 562	4. Wisconsin	8.5
6. Maryland	28 671	6. Minnesota	42 248	6. Delaware	9.1
7. Delaware	28 443	7. Hawaii	41 832	7. New Jersey	9.3
8. Illinois	27 929	8. Delaware	41 622	8. Maryland	9.4
9. New Hampshire	27 806	9. Virginia	41 534	8. Colorado	9.4
10. Colorado	27 015	10. Massachusetts	41 212	10. Iowa	9.6
11. Nevada	26 553	11. Washington	41 040	10. Nevada	9.6
12. Washington	26 412	12. Illinois	40 873	12. Minnesota	9.7
13. Minnesota	26 295	13. New Hampshire	40 655	13. Nebraska	10.0
14. California	26 218	14. Utah	40 332	14. Connecticut	10.2
15. Virginia	26 172	15. Wisconsin	40 257	15. Kansas	10.5
16. Rhode Island	25 689	16. California	39 699	16. Washington	10.6
17. Hawaii	25 686	17. Michigan	39 434	17. Maine	10.7
18. Pennsylvania	25 678	18. Nevada	39 139	17. Missouri	10.7
19. Michigan	24 998	19. Indiana	37 421	19. Michigan	10.8
20. Alaska	24 945	20. Oregon	36 777	20. Vermont	11.0
21. Florida	24 795	21. Pennsylvania	36 609	21. Massachusetts	11.2
22. Ohio	24 203	22. Rhode Island	36 316	22. Pennsylvania	11.4
23. Wisconsin	24 199	23. North Carolina	36 129	23. Illinois	11.7
24. Kansas	24 014	24. New York	36 010	23. Oregon	11.7
25. Oregon	23 984	25. Missouri	35 802	25. North Carolina	11.8
26. Georgia	23 893	26. Ohio	35 493	26. Ohio	11.9
27. Missouri	23 723	27. Georgia	34 953	26. Rhode Island	11.9
28. Nebraska	23 656	28. Kansas	34 902	28. North Dakota	12.3
29. Texas	23 647	29. South Carolina	34 861	29. Virginia	12.5
30. Indiana	23 183	30. Nebraska	34 743	30. Wyoming	12.7
31. Iowa	23 177	31. Idaho	34 455	31. Hawaii	13.0
32. North Carolina	23 174	32. Texas	34 453	32. South Carolina	13.1
33. Vermont	23 018	33. Maine	34 132	33. Idaho	13.3
34. Tennessee	22 752	34. Vermont	34 077	34. South Dakota	14.2
35. Wyoming	22 611	35. Iowa	33 877	35. Florida	14.3
36. Arizona	21 994	36. Kentucky	33 305	36. Georgia	14.7
37. Maine	21 928	37. Arizona	32 552	37. Alabama	14.9
38. South Dakota	21 183	38. Wyoming	32 543	38. Tennessee	15.1
39. Alabama	20 699	39. D.C.	32 280	39. Oklahoma	15.2
40. South Carolina	20 651	40. Louisiana	32 108	40. Montana	16.3
41. Kentucky	20 599	41. North Dakota	31 927	41. Kentucky	16.5
42. Louisiana	20 473	42. Florida	31 900	42. New York	16.6
43. Idaho	20 393	43. Alabama	31 468	43. Texas	16.7
44. Utah	20 246	44. Tennessee	31 066	44. California	16.8
45. Oklahoma	20 214	45. South Dakota	29 949	45. West Virginia	17.5
46. North Dakota	20 213	46. Oklahoma	29 709	46. Louisiana	18.4
47. Montana	19 704	47. Montana	29 277	47. Arkansas	18.5
48. Arkansas	19 602	48. Mississippi	27 894	48. Mississippi	18.7
49. New Mexico	19 249	49. New Mexico	27 874	49. Arizona	18.9
50. West Virginia	18 734	50. Arkansas	26 954	50. D.C.	23.0
51. Mississippi	18 087	51. West Virginia	26 657	51. New Mexico	23.4

RANKINGS: EMPLOYMENT

State and rank	Percent of total employment	State and rank	Percent of total employment	State and rank	Percent of total employment
Federal government employment, civilian and military, 1997		**Farm employment, 1997**		**Manufacturing employment, 1997**	
United States	3.2	**United States**	1.9	**United States**	12.4
1. District of Columbia	30.0	1. North Dakota	8.5	1. Indiana	19.7
2. Hawaii	11.6	2. South Dakota	7.7	2. Wisconsin	19.2
3. Alaska	10.7	3. Iowa	6.4	3. North Carolina	18.5
4. Virginia	8.2	4. Nebraska	5.9	4. Michigan	18.4
5. Maryland	7.1	5. Kentucky	5.2	5. Arkansas	18.3
6. New Mexico	5.4	6. Montana	5.0	6. Mississippi	17.5
7. North Dakota	5.2	7. Idaho	4.8	7. South Carolina	17.3
8. Oklahoma	4.6	8. Kansas	4.7	8. Ohio	17.0
9. Mississippi	4.3	9. Oklahoma	4.4	9. Alabama	16.9
9. Washington	4.3	10. Arkansas	4.2	10. Tennessee	16.2
9. Wyoming	4.3	11. Mississippi	4.0	11. New Hampshire	15.5
12. Alabama	4.2	12. Wyoming	3.7	12. Kentucky	14.9
12. Georgia	4.2	13. Missouri	3.5	13. Rhode Island	14.8
14. North Carolina	4.0	14. Minnesota	3.4	14. Pennsylvania	14.5
14. South Carolina	4.0	15. Oregon	3.2	15. Minnesota	14.3
16. Kentucky	3.9	15. Wisconsin	3.2	16. Connecticut	14.0
16. Montana	3.9	17. Tennessee	2.9	16. Iowa	14.0
18. South Dakota	3.8	18. West Virginia	2.6	16. Illinois	14.0
19. Rhode Island	3.7	19. Alabama	2.4	19. Vermont	13.7
19. Utah	3.7	19. Washington	2.4	20. Georgia	13.5
21. Colorado	3.6	21. Texas	2.3	21. Oregon	13.1
22. West Virginia	3.5	22. Indiana	2.2	21. Maine	13.1
23. Louisiana	3.4	22. New Mexico	2.2	23. Missouri	12.9
24. Kansas	3.3	22. Vermont	2.2	24. Delaware	12.6
25. Idaho	3.2	25. North Carolina	1.9	24. Kansas	12.6
25. Maine	3.2	26. Louisiana	1.6	26. Massachusetts	11.9
27. Arizona	3.1	27. California	1.5	27. Washington	11.8
27. Delaware	3.1	27. Colorado	1.5	28. Idaho	11.4
27. Texas	3.1	27. Hawaii	1.5	29. California	11.2
30. Missouri	3.0	27. Maine	1.5	30. New Jersey	11.0
31. Florida	2.9	27. Utah	1.5	31. Utah	10.9
32. Arkansas	2.8	27. Virginia	1.5	32. Nebraska	10.4
32. California	2.8	33. Georgia	1.4	33. South Dakota	10.3
32. Nebraska	2.8	33. Illinois	1.4	34. Virginia	10.2
35. Vermont	2.6	33. Michigan	1.4	35. Texas	10.1
36. Pennsylvania	2.4	33. Ohio	1.4	36. Oklahoma	10.0
37. Nevada	2.3	33. South Carolina	1.4	37. West Virginia	9.9
37. Tennessee	2.3	38. Florida	1.1	38. New York	9.7
39. Illinois	2.2	38. Pennsylvania	1.1	39. Arizona	8.8
39. New Jersey	2.2	40. Delaware	0.9	40. Louisiana	8.7
39. Oregon	2.2	41. Arizona	0.8	41. Colorado	8.2
42. Connecticut	2.0	42. Maryland	0.7	42. Florida	6.4
42. Massachusetts	2.0	43. New York	0.6	42. Maryland	6.4
42. New York	2.0	44. New Hampshire	0.5	44. New Mexico	5.7
45. Ohio	1.9	45. Connecticut	0.4	44. North Dakota	5.7
46. Iowa	1.8	45. Nevada	0.4	46. Montana	5.6
47. Indiana	1.7	45. New Jersey	0.4	47. Alaska	4.8
47. Minnesota	1.7	48. Massachusetts	0.3	48. Nevada	4.1
47. New Hampshire	1.7	49. Alaska	0.2	48. Wyoming	4.1
50. Wisconsin	1.5	49. Rhode Island	0.2	50. Hawaii	2.7
51. Michigan	1.4	51. District of Columbia	0.0	51. District of Columbia	1.9

RANKINGS: MANUFACTURING, HOUSING, AND TAXES

Manufacturing output, 1996		Housing production, 1997		State and local taxes, 1997	
State and rank	Percent of gross state product	State and rank	Housing production per 1,000 population	State and rank	Percent of personal income
United States	17.5	**United States**	6.5	**United States**	10.8
1. Indiana	31.7	1. Nevada	22.4	1. New Hampshire	8.3
2. Kentucky	28.1	2. Arizona	14.2	2. Tennessee	8.6
3. Wisconsin	27.7	3. North Carolina	13.0	3. Alabama	9.1
4. Michigan	27.2	4. Georgia	12.7	4. Virginia	9.6
4. Ohio	27.2	5. Colorado	12.4	5. Indiana	9.7
6. North Carolina	27.0	5. South Carolina	12.4	5. Missouri	9.7
7. South Carolina	26.6	7. Florida	10.3	7. South Dakota	9.8
8. Arkansas	24.6	8. Idaho	10.2	8. Louisiana	9.9
9. Iowa	24.0	8. Utah	10.2	8. Michigan	9.9
10. Mississippi	23.4	10. Oregon	10.0	10. Delaware	10.0
11. Tennessee	22.9	11. Tennessee	9.4	10. Florida	10.0
12. Alabama	22.3	12. New Mexico	9.1	12. Colorado	10.1
13. New Hampshire	22.2	13. Washington	8.3	12. Pennsylvania	10.1
14. Missouri	21.4	14. Delaware	8.0	12. South Carolina	10.1
15. Delaware	21.2	15. Alabama	7.9	15. North Carolina	10.2
16. Pennsylvania	20.7	16. Texas	7.8	15. Oregon	10.2
17. Idaho	20.6	17. Virginia	7.5	17. Arkansas	10.3
18. Oregon	20.5	18. Indiana	7.3	17. Texas	10.3
19. Illinois	19.3	19. Mississippi	7.1	19. Illinois	10.4
20. Minnesota	19.2	20. Kentucky	7.0	19. Maryland	10.4
21. Louisiana	19.0	21. Arkansas	6.9	21. Oklahoma	10.5
22. Maine	18.5	22. Nebraska	6.8	21. Massachussets	10.5
23. Kansas	18.3	22. Wisconsin	6.8	21. West Virginia	10.5
24. Georgia	18.1	24. Kansas	6.4	24. California	10.6
24. Vermont	18.1	25. South Dakota	6.3	24. Georgia	10.6
24. West Virginia	18.1	26. Michigan	6.2	24. Montana	10.6
27. Oklahoma	17.3	27. North Dakota	6.1	27. Ohio	10.8
28. Connecticut	16.7	28. Minnesota	5.9	28. Idaho	10.9
28. Rhode Island	16.7	29. Missouri	5.8	28. Kansas	10.9
30. New Mexico	16.5	29. Wyoming	5.8	30. Mississippi	11.0
31. Texas	16.3	31. Oklahoma	5.6	31. New Jersey	11.1
32. Massachusetts	15.5	32. Louisiana	5.4	31. Rhode Island	11.1
33. Virginia	15.2	32. New Hampshire	5.4	33. Arizona	11.2
34. South Dakota	14.5	34. Maryland	5.3	33. Kentucky	11.2
35. Arizona	14.5	35. Maine	5.2	35. Connecticut	11.4
36. Nebraska	14.1	35. West Virginia	5.2	35. Iowa	11.4
37. Utah	14.0	37. Montana	5.1	35. Nevada	11.4
38. California	13.9	38. Ohio	4.7	35. North Dakota	11.4
39. New Jersey	13.7	39. Vermont	4.5	39. Nebraska	11.5
40. Washington	13.1	40. Illinois	4.3	40. Utah	11.6
41. Colorado	12.2	40. Iowa	4.3	41. Wyoming	11.7
42. New York	11.8	42. Alaska	4.2	42. Vermont	11.9
43. Maryland	8.6	43. Pennsylvania	3.7	43. Washington	12.0
44. Florida	8.1	44. California	3.5	44. New Mexico	12.1
45. Montana	7.7	44. New Jersey	3.5	45. District of Columbia	12.5
46. North Dakota	7.5	46. Hawaii	3.1	45. Minnesota	12.5
47. Wyoming	5.7	47. Connecticut	2.9	47. Maine	12.7
48. Alaska	4.8	48. Massachusetts	2.8	48. Wisconsin	12.8
48. Nevada	4.8	49. Rhode Island	2.7	49. Hawaii	12.9
50. Hawaii	3.1	50. New York	2.1	50. New York	13.4
51. District of Columbia	2.5	51. District Of Columbia	0.0	51. Alaska	13.6

RANKINGS: HEALTH AND EDUCATION

Infant mortality, 1996–1997 average		Percent without health insurance, 1997		College attainment rate, 1997	
State and rank	Deaths per 1,000 live births	State and rank	Percent of population	State and rank	Percent (over age 25) with college degree
United States	7.2	**United States**	16.1	**United States**	23.9
1. Maine	4.1	1. Hawaii	7.5	1. District of Columbia	33.7
2. Massachusetts	4.6	2. Wisconsin	8.0	2. Massachusetts	33.5
3. New Hampshire	5.1	3. Minnesota	9.2	3. Maryland	32.2
4. Washington	5.3	4. Vermont	9.5	4. Connecticut	30.0
5. Wyoming	5.6	5. Pennsylvania	10.1	5. Colorado	28.9
6. Iowa	5.7	6. Rhode Island	10.2	6. New Jersey	28.5
6. Oregon	5.7	7. Nebraska	10.8	7. Minnesota	28.3
8. Hawaii	5.9	8. Indiana	11.4	8. Virginia	28.0
8. North Dakota	5.9	8. Washington	11.4	9. Alaska	27.5
8. Rhode Island	5.9	10. Ohio	11.5	9. California	27.5
8. Utah	5.9	11. Michigan	11.6	9. Kansas	27.5
12. Nevada	6.0	12. Kansas	11.7	12. New Hampshire	27.0
13. California	6.1	13. New Hampshire	11.8	13. Delaware	26.8
14. Minnesota	6.2	13. South Dakota	11.8	14. Utah	26.7
14. New Mexico	6.2	15. Connecticut	12.0	15. Washington	26.1
14. Texas	6.2	15. Iowa	12.0	16. New York	25.8
17. New York	6.4	17. Illinois	12.4	17. Rhode Island	25.7
18. South Dakota	6.5	18. Massachusetts	12.6	18. Montana	25.2
19. Connecticut	6.6	18. Missouri	12.6	19. Illinois	25.0
19. Idaho	6.6	18. Virginia	12.6	20. Oregon	24.3
21. New Jersey	6.8	21. Delaware	13.1	21. Vermont	23.7
22. Alaska	6.9	22. Oregon	13.3	22. New Mexico	23.6
22. Wisconsin	6.9	23. Maryland	13.4	23. Missouri	22.9
24. Montana	7.1	23. Utah	13.4	23. Pennsylvania	22.9
25. Florida	7.4	25. Tennessee	13.6	25. North Carolina	22.6
25. Pennsylvania	7.4	26. Louisiana	14.9	26. Hawaii	22.5
27. Indiana	7.5	26. Maine	14.9	27. Texas	22.4
27. Ohio	7.5	28. Kentucky	15.0	27. Wisconsin	22.4
27. Vermont	7.5	29. Colorado	15.1	29. Georgia	22.3
27. Virginia	7.5	30. North Dakota	15.2	30. Wyoming	22.2
31. Colorado	7.6	31. Alabama	15.5	31. Iowa	21.7
32. Missouri	7.7	31. North Carolina	15.5	31. Florida	21.7
33. Kansas	7.9	31. Wyoming	15.5	33. Ohio	21.5
34. Delaware	8.0	34. District of Columbia	16.2	34. Nebraska	21.3
34. Kentucky	8.0	35. New Jersey	16.5	35. Michigan	21.0
34. Michigan	8.0	36. South Carolina	16.8	36. Mississippi	20.9
37. Illinois	8.1	37. West Virginia	17.2	37. North Dakota	20.5
38. Arkansas	8.2	38. Nevada	17.5	37. Oklahoma	20.5
38. West Virginia	8.2	38. New York	17.5	39. South Dakota	20.1
40. Oklahoma	8.3	40. Georgia	17.6	40. Maine	20.0
40. Nebraska	8.3	41. Idaho	17.7	41. Nevada	19.9
42. Georgia	8.4	42. Oklahoma	17.8	42. Arizona	19.5
42. South Carolina	8.4	43. Alaska	18.1	43. Idaho	19.4
42. Tennessee	8.4	44. Montana	19.5	44. Alabama	19.3
45. Maryland	8.7	45. Florida	19.6	45. South Carolina	19.2
46. Louisiana	8.8	46. Mississippi	20.1	46. Louisiana	18.1
47. North Carolina	9.4	47. California	21.5	47. Kentucky	17.6
48. Alabama	9.8	48. New Mexico	22.6	48. Tennessee	17.1
48. Arizona	9.8	49. Arkansas	24.4	49. Indiana	16.2
50. Mississippi	10.3	50. Arizona	24.5	50. West Virginia	14.7
51. District of Columbia	13.5	50. Texas	24.5	51. Arkansas	14.6

31 372	59 698		65 157	70 827	72 687	78 001	81 93	88 504	93 426	5.8	63 383	70 827	31 372	59 698	63 38
25 323	47 902		57 151	59 446	62 916	67 00		72 039	77 208	6.1	50 999	57 151	25 323	47 902	50 99
2 640	5 143				7 801			7 709	7 838	5.4	5 645	6 816	2 640	5 143	5 64
3 409	6 652			284				8 755	8 380	2.9	6 739	6 860	3 409	6 652	6 73
693	1 716			807				1 539	762	-9.7	1 561	811	693	1 716	
2 716	4 8							7 217	7 618	5.6	6 176	6 049	2 716	4 8	

1997

Population (persons)	4,322,113
Population rank	23rd
Population growth rank (1990–97)	22nd
Per capita personal income	$20,699
Unemployment rate (percent)	5.1
Poverty rate (percent)	15.7

WITH A 1997 POPULATION OF 4.3 MILLION, ALABAMA RANKED 23rd among the states in population size, and its population growth rate of 0.9 percent per year from 1990 to 1997 was just under the national average of 1.0 percent. The largest concentrations of population are in the Birmingham, Tuscaloosa, Anniston, and Gadsden metropolitan areas in the north-central part of the state, with a combined 1997 population of 1.2 million; the Huntsville, Decatur, and Florence metropolitan areas on the state's northern border, with 610,000; and the Mobile metropolitan area on the Gulf Coast, with 530,000. These areas also are centers of the state's manufacturing and are among the more prosperous areas of the state.

Alabama has achieved rates of employment and income growth somewhat higher than the national averages during the 1990s. Manufacturing is shifting from the traditional textiles and apparel toward motor vehicles, other transportation equipment, and electronics. The growth of the state's exports and the opening up of new export markets in Latin America have been particularly encouraging. Still, the state remains relatively poor, with median household income only some 86 percent of the national average. Educational attainment rates and per capita school spending are lower than national averages, and the infant mortality rate of 9.2 per 1,000 live births in 1997 was still well above the national average.

Average Annual Population Growth: 1990–97

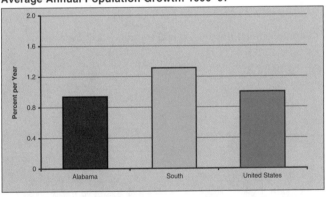

Median Household Income: 1989–97 (1997 dollars)

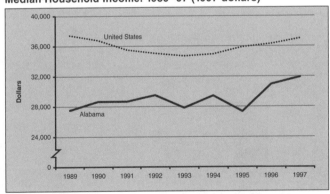

Unemployment Rate: 1989–97

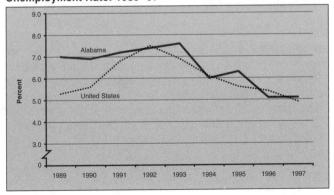

ALABAMA'S UNEMPLOYMENT RATE ROSE LESS THAN DID THE national rate during the early 1990s recession. The subsequent decline also was more gradual, but it was sufficient to bring the state's rate down to close to the national average by 1997, compared to being substantially above average in 1990. Labor force and employment in Alabama grew more rapidly than in the nation as a whole from 1990 to 1997 and more rapidly than did Alabama's adult population. The percentage of the population holding jobs rose from 56.4 percent in 1990 to 60.9 percent in 1997. Even so, the 1997 percentage was lower than the national average of 63.8 percent.

POPULATION AND LABOR FORCE

ALABAMA'S POPULATION GROWTH RATE FROM 1990 TO 1997 was very close to that for the nation as a whole. However, the 0.7 percent per year growth of the White non-Hispanic population was higher than the national average rate of 0.4 percent. Growth of the non-Hispanic Black population was about in line with national growth and was about twice as rapid as the growth of Alabama's non-Hispanic White population. Thus, at 25.8 percent, non-Hispanic Blacks were a larger share of the state's population total in 1997 than in 1990, and non-Hispanic Whites were a somewhat smaller share. Other groups made up only a tiny fraction of Alabama's population in 1990.

The metropolitan population grew almost twice as rapidly as the nonmetropolitan, and the metropolitan share reached 67.7 percent in 1995 through 1997. This rate still was lower than the national average of 79.9 percent, however.

Just over one-half of Alabama's 6.8 percent total population growth from 1990 to 1997 was due to natural increase (births minus deaths). In-migration from other states accounted for another 40 percent of the population gain and immigration from abroad for only 4 percent.

Population and Labor Force

	1980	1990	1991	1992	1993	1994	1995	1996	1997	Change* State	Change* U.S.
Population											
Total number of persons (thousands)	3 894	4 048	4 090	4 138	4 192	4 239	4 270	4 291	4 322	0.9	1.0
Percent distribution:											
White, Non-Hispanic	73.3	73.5	73.2	73.0	72.9	72.7	72.6	72.5	72.3	0.7	0.4
Black, Non-Hispanic	25.3	24.9	25.3	25.4	25.5	25.6	25.7	25.7	25.8	1.5	1.4
Asian	0.3	0.6	0.6	0.6	0.6	0.6	0.6	0.6	0.6	2.5	4.1
Native American	0.2	0.4	0.4	0.4	0.4	0.4	0.4	0.4	0.4	-1.5	1.6
Hispanic	0.9	0.7	0.6	0.6	0.7	0.7	0.8	0.8	0.9	4.6	3.8
In metropolitan areas	65.7	67.1	67.3	67.4	67.5	67.6	67.7	67.7	67.7	1.1	1.0
Total number of households (thousands)	1 342	1 507	1 532	1 558	1 574	1 582	1 603	1 624	NA	1.3	1.2
Labor Force (thousands)											
Population 16 and over	2 881	3 121	3 158	3 199	3 247	3 284	3 306	3 338	3 378	1.1	1.0
Civilian labor force	1 674	1 889	1 907	1 962	1 997	2 029	2 069	2 099	2 168	2.0	1.1
Employed	1 526	1 759	1 769	1 817	1 845	1 907	1 939	1 991	2 058	2.3	1.2
Percent of population	53.0	56.4	56.0	56.8	56.8	58.1	58.6	59.6	60.9		
Unemployment rate (percent)	8.8	6.9	7.2	7.4	7.6	6.0	6.3	5.1	5.1		

*Compound annual average percent change, 1990–1997; 1990–1996 for households.

Population Change and Components: 1990–97

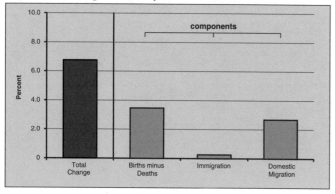

Average Annual Household and Population Growth

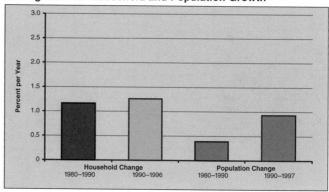

Population by Age; Births and Deaths

	1990 State	1990 U.S.	1997 State	1997 U.S.
Age distribution (percent)				
Under 5 years	7.1	7.6	6.8	7.2
5 to 17 years	18.8	18.2	18.0	18.8
18 to 64 years	61.2	61.8	62.2	61.3
65 years and over	12.9	12.5	13.0	12.7
Birth and death rates (per thousand population)				
Births	15.7	16.7	14.1	14.6
Deaths	9.7	8.6	9.9	8.6

BETWEEN 1990 AND 1997, ALABAMA SHOWED A 1 PERCENTage point gain in the share of its population in the 18 to 64 age group, compared to a decline of 0.5 percentage points nationally. The larger share for this working-age group was offset by a corresponding decline in the proportion of the population under age 18. The proportion of the population age 65 and over crept up slightly.

HOUSEHOLD AND PERSONAL INCOME

HOUSEHOLD INCOME AND PERSONS IN POVERTY	1990	1995	1996	1997 State	1997 U.S.
Median household income (1997 dollars)	28 682	27 372	30 997	31 939	37 005
Persons in poverty (thousands)	779	882	595	665	35 574
Poverty rate (percent)	19.2	20.1	14.0	15.7	13.3

ALABAMA EXPERIENCED GOOD GAINS IN HOUSEHOLD AND personal incomes and a sizable reduction in its poverty rate in 1996 and 1997. The poverty rate for those two years averaged 15 percent, compared to 20 percent in 1995 and 19 percent in 1990, and median household income (adjusted for inflation) moved strongly upward, with 1996–1997 averaging more than 10 percent above 1994–1995. The 1996–1997 income gain brought the state considerably closer to the national average. Alabama's median income was only 78 percent of the nation's average in 1990, but by 1996–1997 it had reached 86 percent.

Though the gain was less dramatic, real per capita personal income also moved closer to the U.S. average, rising from 79 percent of that average in 1990 to 82 percent in 1997. Earnings accounted for 65.5 percent of Alabama's 1997 personal income, just a little lower than the national average of 66.4 percent. Dividends, interest, and rent were only 14 percent, compared to 17.2 percent nationally, while transfer payments were 20.5 percent, compared to only 16.4 percent for the nation. Farming provided 1.2 percent of Alabama's personal income, almost double the nation's 0.7 percent share.

Government transfer payments to Alabama residents increased 67.9 percent from 1990 to 1997, well above the nation's 62.7 percent average rise. The difference was particularly large for income maintenance payments, which grew 88.6 percent in Alabama, compared to only 58 percent nationally. "Other income maintenance," a category consisting largely of the earned income tax credit, showed by far the largest percentage growth. The expansion of this credit during the 1990s has been of particular benefit to relatively low-wage states such as Alabama.

Personal Income
(millions of dollars)

	1980	1989	1990	1991	1992	1993	1994	1995	1996	1997	Change*
Earnings by place of work	22 321	41 295	43 908	46 235	49 518	51 976	54 761	57 263	59 315	62 392	5.3
Wages and salaries	18 374	33 308	35 477	37 039	39 593	41 263	43 492	45 975	47 955	50 614	5.4
Other labor income	1 835	3 653	4 028	4 344	4 820	5 267	5 576	5 546	5 323	5 354	4.9
Proprietors' income	2 112	4 335	4 403	4 852	5 104	5 446	5 693	5 743	6 037	6 423	5.0
Farm	138	814	703	1 006	864	911	899	685	778	920	1.5
Nonfarm	1 974	3 521	3 699	3 846	4 240	4 535	4 794	5 058	5 259	5 503	5.7
(–) Personal contributions for social insurance	1 299	2 851	3 029	3 234	3 434	3 638	3 908	4 185	4 322	4 563	6.1
(+) Adjustment for residence	343	502	513	516	546	547	594	641	662	715	NA
(=) **Net earnings by state of residence**	21 364	38 947	41 392	43 518	46 630	48 885	51 447	53 719	55 655	58 543	5.2
(+) Dividends, interest, and rent	3 663	8 780	9 241	9 442	9 474	9 591	10 345	11 152	12 053	12 503	4.5
(+) Transfer payments	5 151	9 770	10 957	12 048	13 479	14 454	15 206	16 475	17 452	18 356	8.2
(=) **Total personal income**	30 178	57 496	61 589	65 008	69 582	72 930	76 999	81 346	85 160	89 403	5.7
Farm	231	929	832	1 125	976	1 039	1 018	816	910	1 056	1.6
Nonfarm	29 947	56 568	60 757	63 883	68 606	71 891	75 981	80 529	84 251	88 347	5.7
Personal income per capita (dollars)											
Current dollars	7 737	14 266	15 214	15 894	16 814	17 395	18 193	19 086	19 864	20 699	4.8
1997 dollars	14 793	18 035	18 308	18 353	18 808	18 928	19 334	19 840	20 228	20 699	1.7

*Compound annual average percent change, 1989–1997

Government Transfer Payments

	Millions of dollars 1990	Millions of dollars 1997	Percent change* State	Percent change* U.S.
Total government payments to individuals	10 506	17 640	67.9	62.7
Retirement, disability, and insurance	6 018	9 037	50.2	48.2
Social Security	4 070	6 086	49.5	46.1
Government employee retirement	1 729	2 721	57.4	60.3
Medical payments	2 808	5 931	111.2	101.2
Income maintenance	914	1 723	88.6	58.0
Supplemental Security Income	359	635	77.2	75.4
Family assistance	66	69	5.3	-0.5
Food Stamps	339	381	12.4	27.1
Other income maintenance	151	638	323.2	189.8
Unemployment insurance benefits	203	220	8.1	10.6
Veterans benefits and other	563	730	29.7	30.8

*Percent change, 1990–1997

Government Payments to Individuals: 1997

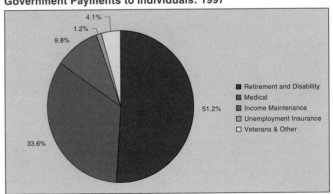

- Retirement and Disability
- Medical
- Income Maintenance
- Unemployment Insurance
- Veterans & Other

51.2%
33.6%
9.8%
1.2%
4.1%

ECONOMIC STRUCTURE

LEADING PRIVATE INDUSTRIES, 1997 (Worker and proprietor earnings, millions of dollars)		FASTEST EARNINGS GROWTH, 1989–97 (percent increase)	
Health services	$5 452	Real estate	256.5
Business services	2 434	Business services	121.1
Construction specialties	2 335	Construction specialties	93.2
Engineering and management services	1 872	Health services	86.0
Eating and drinking places	1 324	Eating and drinking places	76.1

LIKE MOST OF THE NATION, ALABAMA HAS SEEN MANUFACTURING decline as a share of overall economic activity during the 1990s. Manufacturing's role in the state's economy remains well above the national average, however, accounting for 17 percent of employment and 22 percent of worker and proprietor earnings in 1997, compared to 12 percent of employment and 18 of earnings nationally. The drop in manufacturing employment during the early-90s recession was considerably more moderate in Alabama than in the nation as a whole, and by 1995 the state's employment in manufacturing had risen well above 1989's prerecession peak. A fresh decline occurred in 1996 and 1997, however, so that the number of manufacturing jobs again fell slightly below the 1989 peak.

The 11,000 manufacturing jobs lost from 1995 to 1997 were far more than offset by gains in other sectors, so that 79,000 private nonfarm jobs were added to the Alabama economy over those two years. The sectors showing the largest gains were services (41,000 jobs), retail trade (20,000), and construction (12,000). As in many states, health services, business services, and construction specialties have been among the most rapidly growing industries during the 1990s, measured by worker and proprietor earnings; these also were Alabama's three largest industries in 1997, followed by engineering and management services, an industry consisting largely of additional types of business services.

Alabama's manufacturing activity is divided among a fairly large number of industries, with primary metals, paper and allied products, lumber and wood products, industrial machinery and equipment, and textiles—the largest five—being relatively similar in size. Among manufacturing industries, lumber and wood products and motor vehicles have shown the most rapid earnings growth during the 1990s, while growth of textiles and primary metals has lagged.

Farming has declined in relative importance during the 1990s, making up only 1.7 percent of earnings in 1997, compared to 2.2 percent in 1989. This share still was nearly double the national average of 0.9 percent, however.

Employment and Earnings by Sector

	1980	1989	1990	1991	1992	1993	1994	1995	1996	1997 Number	1997 Percent of total	Change*
Employment *(thousands of persons)*												
Total	1 736	2 020	2 058	2 075	2 113	2 174	2 189	2 249	2 279	2 325	100.0	1.8
Farm	83	63	63	61	60	59	58	58	54	56	2.4	-1.5
Nonfarm	1 653	1 956	1 995	2 014	2 053	2 115	2 131	2 190	2 225	2 269	97.6	1.9
Private nonfarm	1 304	1 586	1 617	1 634	1 667	1 727	1 746	1 808	1 844	1 887	81.2	2.2
Agricultural service, forestry, and fishing	11	17	18	19	19	22	23	24	25	26	1.1	5.6
Mining	18	13	15	14	13	12	12	13	12	12	0.5	-1.4
Construction	92	113	119	115	116	122	126	133	141	145	6.2	3.2
Manufacturing	376	397	395	391	394	398	400	404	396	393	16.9	-0.1
Transportation and public utilities	80	94	95	96	95	100	100	103	106	108	4.6	1.8
Wholesale trade	81	90	90	90	93	92	95	99	101	102	4.4	1.6
Retail trade	245	316	321	327	339	351	364	379	391	399	17.2	2.9
Finance, insurance, and real estate	98	109	111	109	107	113	105	107	110	115	4.9	0.7
Services	303	437	453	472	492	518	521	546	563	587	25.2	3.7
Government	348	371	377	380	386	388	386	383	380	382	16.4	0.4
Earnings *(millions of dollars)*												
Total	22 321	41 295	43 908	46 235	49 518	51 976	54 761	57 263	59 315	62 392	100.0	5.3
Farm	231	929	832	1 125	976	1 039	1 018	816	910	1 056	1.7	1.6
Nonfarm	22 090	40 366	43 076	45 110	48 542	50 937	53 743	56 447	58 406	61 336	98.3	5.4
Private nonfarm	17 626	32 393	34 501	35 930	38 884	40 953	43 263	45 642	47 518	50 134	80.4	5.6
Agricultural service, forestry, and fishing	92	199	238	272	294	309	341	347	335	345	0.6	7.1
Mining	558	504	586	586	559	556	572	615	623	630	1.0	2.8
Construction	1 378	2 353	2 649	2 615	2 692	2 845	3 109	3 337	3 707	3 903	6.3	6.5
Manufacturing	6 191	10 162	10 501	10 755	11 527	11 967	12 593	12 965	12 992	13 489	21.6	3.6
Transportation and public utilities	1 622	2 904	3 039	3 214	3 333	3 547	3 711	3 871	4 004	4 111	6.6	4.4
Wholesale trade	1 359	2 356	2 504	2 550	2 741	2 834	3 000	3 237	3 381	3 598	5.8	5.4
Retail trade	2 159	3 869	4 016	4 207	4 519	4 854	5 144	5 397	5 674	6 011	9.6	5.7
Finance, insurance, and real estate	983	1 880	2 027	2 092	2 397	2 637	2 822	3 062	3 322	3 576	5.7	8.4
Services	3 285	8 164	8 941	9 639	10 823	11 405	11 970	12 813	13 481	14 470	23.2	7.4
Government	4 463	7 974	8 575	9 180	9 658	9 984	10 480	10 805	10 888	11 202	18.0	4.3

*Compound annual average percent change, 1989–1997

ECONOMIC STRUCTURE (Continued)

THE AVERAGE ANNUAL EARNINGS OF ALABAMA WORKERS were 86 percent of the U.S. average in 1997, and this percentage was little changed from 1989. The Alabama average is about at the midpoint between Georgia to the east, with its higher wages, and Mississippi to the west, with its lower ones.

In transportation and public utilities, mining, and agricultural services, annual earnings in 1997 were about 95 percent of the national average, but these three sectors combined provided only 6 percent of total employment in the state. In manufacturing, Alabama wages and salaries were only 79 percent of the U.S. average, and, again, this percentage has shown little change since 1989. As is true nationally, retail trade provides by far the lowest earnings of any nonfarm sector; these low annual earnings result from a combination of low hourly wages, fewer hours worked per week on average, and many part-year workers.

Manufacturing contributed 22.3 percent of Alabama's gross state product in 1996, down from 24.2 percent in 1989, but well above the 1996 national average of 17.5 percent. Manufacturing activity is spread throughout the state, but concentrations are found in the Huntsville-Florence-Decatur area near the state's northern border and in Birmingham and the adjacent areas of Tuscaloosa, Anniston, and Gadsden in the north-central part of the state. An analysis by the Federal Reserve Bank of Atlanta indicates that the auto and aerospace industries in the north, as well as shipbuilding in the Gulf Coast area around Mobile, are expanding and creating relatively high-paying jobs, while loss of jobs in the apparel industry is impeding economic growth in the southern and central parts of the state.

The mid-1990s were years of strong export growth for the United States, and Alabama outpaced the nation, with total exports rising 46 percent from 1994 to 1997, compared to 34 percent nationally. Strongest growth came from exports of electric and electronic equipment, which substantially more than doubled over the four years. Although Canada and Japan are the largest export markets, Mexico and other Latin American countries have grown increasingly important in recent years and accounted for 27 percent of total exports in 1997.

Average Annual Wages and Salaries by Sector
(dollars)

	1989	1996	1997	
			State	U.S.
All wage and salary workers	19 213	24 646	25 517	29 809
Farm	7 272	14 024	11 530	16 442
Nonfarm	19 314	24 694	25 593	29 900
Private nonfarm	19 198	24 378	25 336	29 867
Agricultural service, forestry, and fishing	12 603	16 807	17 161	17 941
Mining	35 873	45 860	48 010	49 800
Construction	19 824	24 999	25 864	31 765
Manufacturing	22 372	28 903	30 370	38 351
Transportation and utilities	28 870	35 118	36 029	38 222
Wholesale trade	23 691	31 119	32 609	39 466
Retail trade	11 266	13 961	14 564	16 206
Finance, insurance, and real estate	22 461	31 618	33 355	44 993
Services	17 294	22 997	23 747	27 588
Government	19 736	25 989	26 667	30 062

Gross State Product and Manufacturing
(millions of dollars, except as noted)

	1989	1994	1995	1996
Gross state product, total	67 858	89 327	94 988	99 190
Manufacturing:				
Millions of dollars	16 419	19 816	21 858	22 131
Percent of total gross state product	24.2	22.2	23.0	22.3
Per worker (dollars)	41 407	49 576	54 049	55 956
New capital expenditures, manufacturing	NA	2 153	2 786	3 319

Exports of Goods
(millions of dollars)

	1994	1995	1996	1997
All goods	3 115	3 587	3 702	4 537
Manufactures	2 797	3 167	3 360	4 208
Agricultural and livestock products	69	125	65	70
Other commodities	249	295	278	260
Top goods exports, 1997:				
Electric and electronic equipment	488	610	820	1 140
Industrial machinery and computers	394	458	457	626
Paper products	333	501	440	443
Transportation equipment	592	419	401	358
Chemical products	220	293	335	357

HOUSING

THE RATE OF NEW HOME PRODUCTION IN ALABAMA WAS THE same as the national rate in 1990, and showed a similar recession-induced dip in 1991. The state's home production came back more strongly in 1992 and 1993, however, and remained moderately higher than the national pace through 1997. Sales of existing homes fell in 1994 and 1995 but then recovered, and, in 1997, were about one-third higher than in 1990. The 1997 median sales price of existing homes in the Birmingham metropolitan area was $118,900, compared to a national average of $124,000. Median prices in the Montgomery area ($94,100) and the Mobile area ($87,200) were much lower.

Throughout the 1990s, more than 40 percent of Alabama's new home production has consisted of manufactured housing (mobile homes), compared to less than 20 percent nationally.

Alabama's 1997 homeownership rate of 71.3 percent was up from 68.4 percent in 1990 and was higher than 1997's national average of 65.7 percent.

Homeownership Rates: 1989 and 1997

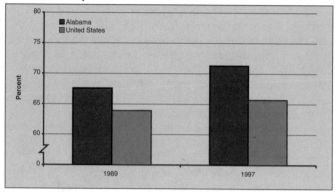

Housing Supply

	1989	1990	1991	1992	1993	1994	1995	1996	1997
Residential building permits (thousands)	12.0	12.5	11.3	13.9	16.1	19.1	20.1	19.9	17.7
New home production (including manufactured housing):									
Thousands of homes	20.6	21.0	19.2	23.6	27.2	33.5	34.5	35.4	34.1
Rate per 1,000 population									
Alabama	5.1	5.2	4.7	5.7	6.5	7.9	8.1	8.3	7.9
U.S.	6.2	5.2	4.5	5.1	5.6	6.4	6.3	6.6	6.5
Existing home sales:									
Thousands of homes	59.4	61.1	64.0	72.5	77.9	77.4	74.2	76.8	82.2
Change from previous year (percent)									
Alabama	-3.4	2.9	4.7	13.3	7.4	-0.6	-4.1	3.5	7.0
U.S.	-3.9	-4.0	0.0	9.2	8.2	4.8	-3.7	7.5	3.8
Home ownership rate (percent of households)	67.6	68.4	69.9	70.3	70.2	68.5	70.1	71.0	71.3
Rental vacancy rate (percent of rental housing units)	6.9	8.1	7.2	6.4	6.8	7.2	8.5	8.7	7.3

AGRICULTURE

POULTRY IS BIG BUSINESS IN ALABAMA, ACCOUNTING FOR 66 percent of the value of all farm sales in 1997. Yet less than 9 percent of Alabama's farmers reported poultry sales in that year. For these farms, poultry sales per farm averaged $586,000. This figure compared with an average value for all sales by all Alabama farms of only $75,000.

In Alabama, 62 percent of farm operators had a principal occupation other than farming in 1997, compared to 50 percent nationally, and 69 percent of farms had sales of less than $10,000. However, farms with sales more than

$10,000 accounted for 97 percent of the value of all sales.

From 1989 through 1997, net farm income in Alabama fluctuated within a range of $0.7 to $1.1 billion.

ALABAMA FARMS, 1997	
Number of farms	45 000
Total acres (thousands):	9 700
Average per farm	216
Value of land and buildings (millions of dollars)	14 356
Average per farm (dollars)	319 022

Farm Income
(millions of dollars)

	1980	1989	1990	1991	1992	1993	1994	1995	1996	1997
Gross income	2 200	3 390	3 404	3 488	3 417	3 603	3 681	3 605	3 860	4 052
Receipts from sales	1 943	2 843	2 915	2 982	2 841	2 978	3 050	2 967	3 215	3 319
Government payments	23	121	82	66	119	137	89	54	76	66
Imputed and miscellaneous income	233	426	406	440	457	488	541	584	569	667
(−) Production expenses	2 045	2 443	2 595	2 519	2 479	2 647	2 743	2 823	3 017	2 939
(=) Realized net income	154	948	809	969	939	957	938	782	843	1 113
(+) Inventory change	-17	-74	-51	96	0	-16	89	-37	42	-79
(=) Net income	138	873	757	1 065	939	940	1 027	745	884	1 035
Corporate income	0	60	54	60	74	30	128	60	107	115
Farm proprietors income	138	814	703	1 006	864	911	899	685	778	920

EDUCATION

EDUCATIONAL ATTAINMENT Percent of population age 25 and over, 1997	State	United States
High school graduate or higher	77.6	82.1
College graduate or higher	19.3	23.9

THE PERCENTAGE OF ALABAMA RESIDENTS AGE 25 AND OVER who had completed high school rose from 41.2 percent in 1970 to 66.9 percent in 1990 and 77.6 percent in 1997. The rapid gains in the 1990s have helped narrow the gap with the higher national average. Alabama's college completion rates were higher than the national average in 1970, but fell below when they showed no gain during the 1970s; gains since 1980 have been insufficient to catch up.

Elementary and secondary school expenditures per pupil were 77 percent of the national average in 1995–96.

This level was higher than those of Tennessee and Mississippi and about equal to that of Arkansas, but below those of other southern states.

Alabama has initiated comprehensive educational reforms in the 1990s, aimed not simply at increasing school completion rates, but at raising academic standards. The new standards increase the course requirements for high school graduation and introduce a more rigorous graduation exam. Another aspect of the reform aims to promote school readiness among at-risk preschoolers.

High School Completion: 1990–97

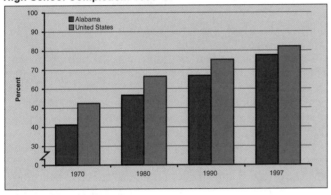

Education Indicators

	State	U.S.
Elementary and secondary schools		
Enrollment, 1995–96		
Total (thousands)	813	49 873
Percent in private schools	8.2	10.1
Expenditures per pupil (dollars), 1995–96	4 716	6 146
Average teacher salary (dollars), 1996–97	32 549	38 509
Higher education		
Enrollment, 1996–97		
Total (thousands)	220	14 218
Percent of population 18–34	20.5	21.8
Percent minority	26.9	26.1
Percent in private schools	10.5	22.6

HEALTH

AMONG THE GOALS OF HEALTHY ALABAMA 2000 IS REDUCtion of the state's infant mortality rate to 8 per 1,000 live births or fewer by the year 2000. In 1996 and 1997 the rate averaged 9.8 per 1,000, compared to 10.8 in 1990.

The state's overall death rate is higher than the national average. Adjusted for differences in the age distribution of the population, the rate of death from heart disease, the leading cause of death, was 20 percent high-

er than the national average in 1996, as was the rate for cerebrovascular diseases (strokes). However, deaths from accidents and adverse effects were half again as high as the national rate, as were deaths from injury by firearms.

The percent of the state's population not covered by health insurance has fallen since 1990, while the U.S. rate has risen. The two rates are now fairly close.

Health Indicators

	1990	1995	1996	1997
Infant mortality				
(rate per thousand live births)				
Alabama	10.8	9.8	10.3	9.2
U.S.	9.2	7.6	7.3	7.1
Total deaths, age-adjusted rate				
(rate per thousand population)				
Alabama	5.9	5.8	5.8	5.6
U.S.	5.2	5.0	4.9	4.8
Persons not covered by health insurance				
(percent of population)				
Alabama	17.4	13.5	12.9	15.5
U.S.	13.9	15.4	15.6	16.1

Leading Causes of Death, 1996
(deaths per 100,000 population)

	Age-adjusted		Not age-adjusted	
	State	U.S.	State	U.S.
Deaths from all causes	580.9	491.6	1002.3	872.5
Heart disease	161.3	134.5	315.9	276.4
Cancer	138.5	127.9	222.4	203.4
Cerebrovascular diseases	31.8	26.4	66.9	60.3
Chronic obstructive pulmonary disease	21.5	21.0	40.7	40.0
Diabetes mellitus	15.1	13.6	26.6	23.3
Pneumonia and influenza	12.9	12.8	31.1	31.6
HIV	8.1	11.1	8.3	11.7
Liver disease	7.3	7.5	9.5	9.4
Alzheimer's disease	3.6	2.7	10.2	8.1
Accidents and adverse effects	45.0	30.4	51.4	35.8
Motor vehicle accidents	27.2	16.2	27.5	16.5
Suicide	11.0	10.8	12.0	11.6
Homicide	13.0	8.5	12.4	7.9
Injury by firearm	20.0	12.9	20.4	12.8

GOVERNMENT

STATE AND LOCAL TAXES, 1995–96	State	U.S.
Per capita (dollars)	1 735	2 477
Percent of personal income	9.1	10.8

IN THE 1995–96 FISCAL YEAR, ALABAMA'S $1,735 PER CAPITA of state and local taxes (excluding corporate income taxes) were the lowest of any state and only 70 percent of the all-state average. Measured as a percent of personal income, Alabama taxes still were lower than the all-state average but were not quite the nation's lowest. Tennessee and New Hampshire collected somewhat more tax dollars per capita but also had higher per capita personal incomes, so their ratios of taxes to income were lower than those in Alabama. Local taxes were only 32 percent of Alabama's state and local total, compared to a 41 percent national average, indicating considerably above-average state-level responsibility for revenue collection.

General and selective sales taxes produced 52 percent of Alabama's total state-level tax revenue in fiscal year 1996–97, a little higher than the all-state average of 49 percent. Revenue from the individual income tax made up 31 percent of the state's total, compared to an all-state average of 33 percent, while corporate income taxes yielded just 4 percent, compared to an all-state average of 7 percent.

Total state-level general expenditure per capita in Alabama was 92 percent of the all-state average in 1996–97, but education spending was 16 percent more. These figures are for state government spending only; local spending on education would appear to be well below the national average, since total per-pupil expenditure in elementary and secondary schools was only 77 percent of the national average in 1995–96.

Interest on Alabama's general debt averaged $52 per capita in 1996–97, compared to a national average of $99. The state seemed in excellent financial shape at year-end, with debt equal to $875 per capita, compared to $1,706 nationally, and cash and security holdings more than five times the size of the debt.

Alabama's 1.7 percent share of federal funds distributed to states and their residents in fiscal 1997 was just about equal to the state's 1.6 percent share of the U.S. population. Reflecting Alabama's relatively low household incomes, the shares of food stamp and Supplementary Security Income payments coming to state residents exceeded the state's population share. Housing and community development grants were high relative to the state's population share, but grants for nutrition and family welfare were low. Shares of federal salaries and wages and defense procurement contracts were slightly higher than the state's population share.

State Government Finances, 1996–97

	Millions of dollars	Percent distribu-tion	Dollars per capita	
			State	U.S.
General revenue	11 487	100.0	2 660	3 049
Intergovernmental revenue	3 554	30.9	823	863
Taxes	5 484	47.7	1 270	1 660
General sales	1 506	13.1	349	551
Selective sales	1 361	11.8	315	257
License taxes	424	3.7	98	106
Individual income	1 688	14.7	391	542
Corporation net income	227	2.0	52	115
Other taxes	279	2.4	65	90
Other general revenue	2 449	21.3	567	526
General expenditure	11 669	100.0	2 702	2 951
Intergovernmental expenditure	3 292	28.2	762	989
Direct expenditure	8 376	71.8	1 939	1 962
General expenditure, by function:				
Education	5 175	44.4	1 198	1 033
Public welfare	2 538	21.7	588	761
Hospitals and health	1 449	12.4	336	237
Highways	837	7.2	194	225
Police protection and corrections	327	2.8	76	137
Natural resources, parks and recreation	192	1.6	45	63
Governmental administration	301	2.6	70	107
Interest on general debt	224	1.9	52	99
Other and unallocable	626	5.4	145	290
Debt at end of fiscal year	3 780	NA	875	1 706
Cash and security holdings	21 639	NA	5 010	6 683

Federal Spending within State

	Federal funds, fiscal 1997		
	Millions of dollars	Percent distribution	Percent of U.S. total*
Total within state	24 650	100.0	1.7
Payments to individuals	14 372	58.3	1.8
Retirement and disability	8 397	34.1	1.8
Medicare	3 705	15.0	1.8
Food stamps	394	1.6	2.0
Supplemental Security Income	651	2.6	2.4
Grants	3 858	15.7	1.5
Medicaid and other health	1 848	7.5	1.6
Nutrition and family welfare	576	2.3	1.2
Education	288	1.2	1.7
Housing and community development	229	0.9	2.0
Salaries and wages	2 902	11.8	1.8
Defense procurement contracts	2 159	8.8	1.8
Non-defense procurement contracts	1 072	4.3	1.5

*State population is 1.6 percent of the U.S. total.

31 372	59 698		65 157	70 827	72 687	78 001	81 93	88 504	93 426	5.8	63 383	70 827	31 372	59 698	63 3
25 323	47 902			57 151	59 446	62 916	67 00	72 039	77 208	6.1	50 999	57 151	25 323	47 902	50 9
2 640	5 143					7 801		7 709	7 838	5.4	5 645	6 816	2 640	5 143	5 6
3 409	6 652					7 284		8 755	8 380	2.9	6 739	6 860	3 409	6 652	6 7
693	1 716					007		1 539	762	-9.7	1 561	811	693	1 716	1 5
2 716	4 93							7 217	7 618	5.6	6 176	6 049	2 716	4 9	

1997

Population (persons)	609,655
Population rank	48th
Population growth rank (1990–97)	13th
Per capita personal income	$24,945
Unemployment rate (percent)	7.9
Poverty rate (percent)	8.8

WEAKENING MARKETS FOR OIL, ORES, LUMBER, AND FISH HURT the Alaska economy during the mid-1990s but did not cause a serious setback. Indeed, private sector employment grew faster in Alaska than in the United States from 1989 to 1997. The state's construction, retail trade, and services sectors outperformed the United States for the period. Tourism provided a growing source of income; healthcare is a large, stable industry; and business services and engineering are significant. A high level of federal, state, and local government employment also continued. Alaska did suffer job losses between 1993 and 1997 within its oil, fishing, lumber, and other manufacturing industries. The job loss associated with oil production declines in the mid-1990s was cushioned by steady oil exploration activity employing oil field services workers, though there has been a serious impact on state tax revenues.

A remarkable feature of living in Alaska is the state's annual payout of about $1,000 per resident, dividends from the "Permanent Fund" established using oil revenues. The fund is fulfilling its purpose in providing long-term benefits from the windfall revenues connected with North Slope oil production. After explosive population growth during the 1980s, population growth has continued at relatively high rates in the 1990s. This growth came despite out-migration linked to federal military cutbacks.

Average Annual Population Growth: 1990–97

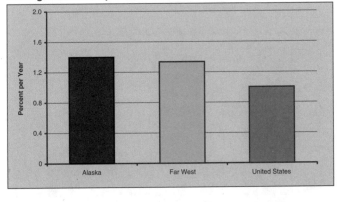

Median Household Income: 1989–97 (1997 dollars)

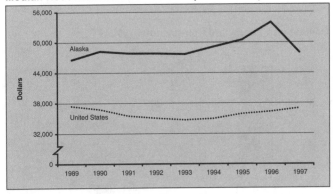

Unemployment Rate: 1989–97

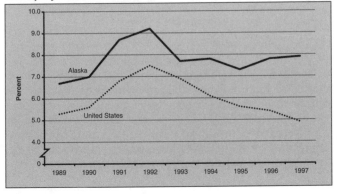

ALASKA'S UNEMPLOYMENT RATE HAS EXCEEDED U.S. averages throughout the entire decade and remained at a high 7.9 percent in 1997. Employment growth actually has been quite strong in Alaska in most years, even in 1992, but the labor force grew very fast (especially early in the decade) and outpaced the growth of jobs. Even with high unemployment, the state had an exceptionally high percentage of its adult population at work in 1997.

POPULATION AND LABOR FORCE

ALASKA'S POPULATION HAS GROWN STEADILY IN THE 1990S at an annual average of 1.4 percent, thanks to high birth rates and low death rates. This natural increase cushioned the blow of the out-migration that occurred in the 1990s, especially in 1993–94. Military personnel leaving four bases that were closed accounted for about 70 percent of the out-migration during 1993–97. This trend contrasted with the strong in-migration during the 1980s—when in-migration added 13 percent to the population, spurred by the early 1980s oil boom—and overall population grew at an exceptional 3.2 percent annual average. The state has strong Native American commu-nities, yet they comprise only 15.9 percent of all Alaskans. The state has the same white non-Hispanic population representation as the United States as a whole. The population continued to be spread among rural areas, with a proportion of metropolitan area population only half the U.S. average.

From 1995 to 1997, the labor force grew much faster than the adult population. Job growth also was strong, but did not quite keep up with the labor force, causing the unemployment rate to rise. Still, the ratio of employed to adult population has risen, reaching a high 65.8 percent in 1996 and 1997.

Population and Labor Force

	1980	1990	1991	1992	1993	1994	1995	1996	1997	Change* State	Change* U.S.
Population											
Total number of persons (thousands)	402	553	569	587	597	601	602	605	610	1.4	1.0
Percent distribution:											
White, Non-Hispanic	76.4	73.7	74.0	73.9	73.6	73.4	73.4	73.1	72.7	1.2	0.4
Black, Non-Hispanic	3.4	4.5	3.9	4.0	4.2	4.0	3.7	3.6	3.7	-1.4	1.4
Asian	2.1	3.5	3.8	3.8	3.9	4.0	4.1	4.3	4.4	4.6	4.1
Native American	16.0	15.4	15.6	15.5	15.4	15.5	15.6	15.9	15.9	1.9	1.6
Hispanic	2.3	3.4	3.3	3.3	3.4	3.5	3.6	3.7	3.8	3.1	3.8
In metropolitan areas	43.3	41.1	41.3	41.8	41.8	41.9	41.7	41.2	41.2	1.4	1.0
Total number of households (thousands)	131	189	194	202	206	207	210	214	NA	2.1	1.2
Labor Force (thousands)											
Population 16 and over	286	391	402	418	426	431	434	438	442	1.8	1.0
Civilian labor force	188	270	276	288	298	305	303	313	315	2.2	1.1
Employed	170	251	252	261	275	281	281	289	290	2.1	1.2
Percent of population	59.4	64.3	62.6	62.5	64.5	65.4	64.7	65.8	65.8		
Unemployment rate (percent)	9.7	7.0	8.7	9.2	7.7	7.8	7.3	7.8	7.9		

*Compound annual average percent change, 1990–1997; 1990–1996 for households.

Population Change and Components: 1990–97

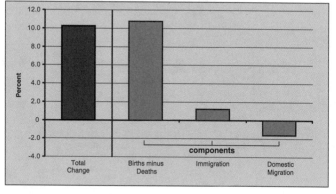

Average Annual Household and Population Growth

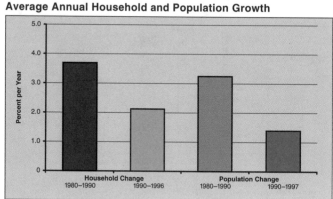

Population by Age; Births and Deaths

	1990 State	1990 U.S.	1997 State	1997 U.S.
Age distribution (percent)				
Under 5 years	10.3	7.6	8.1	7.2
5 to 17 years	21.8	18.2	22.8	18.8
18 to 64 years	63.9	61.8	63.8	61.3
65 years and over	4.1	12.5	5.3	12.7
Birth and death rates (per thousand population)				
Births	21.6	16.7	15.9	14.6
Deaths	4.0	8.6	4.1	8.6

ALASKA'S POPULATION IS YOUNGER THAN AVERAGE. A PARTIC-ularly large difference occurs in the number of school-age children, with a 4 percentage point higher concentration in Alaska than in other states, placing large demands on school resources. In contrast, the proportion of people age 65 and older in the state is only 42 percent as high as the average. With a lowered birth rate and lessened in-migration during the 1990s, however, the age profile of the state has moved closer to the average since 1990.

HOUSEHOLD AND PERSONAL INCOME

HOUSEHOLD INCOME AND PERSONS IN POVERTY	1990	1995	1996	1997 State	1997 U.S.
Median household income (1997 dollars)	48 258	50 503	53 990	47 994	37 005
Persons in poverty (thousands)	57	45	54	56	35 574
Poverty rate (percent)	11.4	7.1	8.2	8.8	13.3

PERSONAL INCOME PER CAPITA WAS 1.4 PERCENT LOWER IN Alaska than the United States in 1997, after it had been as much as 10 percent higher in the early 1990s. With most job gains coming in the low-wage service and retail sectors, personal income growth stagnated. Total wage and salary payments rose only three-fifths as fast as in the United States. Earnings of resident workers and proprietors stood at $16,942 per capita in 1997, virtually equal to earnings in the United States as a whole. (An unusually large net 6.6 percent of earnings went to out-of-state residents.) Per capita transfer payments to residents were 15.9 percent above average, and dividend and interest income was 27 percent lower than average for the United States.

Median household income in Alaska is considerably higher than for the United States as a whole, though the survey data have a high statistical error factor and may be less reliable than personal income data. Poverty rates have remained low despite the economic slowdown.

Transfer payments in Alaska differ markedly in their composition from the U.S. norm. Most remarkable, of course, is the roughly $1,000 per person state payment of dividends from the "Permanent Fund" (categorized as part of "veterans and other"). Retirement programs play a relatively minor role, given the small older population in the state. Because of the large federal and military presence here, government retirement payments overshadow Social Security in total size. Alaskans receive much less in transfers for medical care, retirement, and conventional income support than average. Still, there were larger than average increases in family assistance and food stamps during 1990–97 as the economy weakened.

Personal Income
(millions of dollars)

	1980	1989	1990	1991	1992	1993	1994	1995	1996	1997	Change*
Earnings by place of work	5 281	9 250	9 823	10 302	10 844	11 221	11 470	11 610	11 694	11 972	3.3
Wages and salaries	4 403	7 377	7 819	8 212	8 636	8 943	9 148	9 264	9 374	9 623	3.4
Other labor income	364	729	808	902	952	1 020	1 059	1 035	991	986	3.8
Proprietors' income	514	1 144	1 196	1 189	1 256	1 258	1 264	1 311	1 328	1 364	2.2
Farm	1	3	4	5	4	6	4	7	5	8	12.7
Nonfarm	513	1 141	1 192	1 184	1 252	1 252	1 260	1 305	1 323	1 356	2.2
(−) Personal contributions for social insurance	280	604	643	683	706	742	766	795	822	857	4.5
(+) Adjustment for residence	-332	-615	-653	-694	-724	-736	-752	-757	-770	-786	NA
(=) Net earnings by state of residence	4 669	8 030	8 527	8 926	9 415	9 743	9 953	10 059	10 102	10 329	3.2
(+) Dividends, interest, and rent	482	1 310	1 387	1 407	1 444	1 511	1 720	1 829	1 909	1 941	5.0
(+) Transfer payments	473	1 586	1 742	1 901	2 092	2 302	2 392	2 531	2 701	2 930	8.0
(=) Total personal income	5 624	10 927	11 656	12 233	12 951	13 556	14 065	14 419	14 711	15 199	4.2
Farm	4	6	8	8	8	10	8	10	9	11	7.5
Nonfarm	5 620	10 920	11 648	12 224	12 942	13 546	14 057	14 408	14 703	15 188	4.2
Personal income per capita (dollars)											
Current dollars	13 875	19 970	21 073	21 496	22 074	22 715	23 412	23 965	24 318	24 945	2.8
1997 dollars	26 530	25 247	25 359	24 822	24 691	24 717	24 880	24 912	24 764	24 945	-0.2

*Compound annual average percent change, 1989–1997

Government Transfer Payments

	Millions of dollars 1990	Millions of dollars 1997	Percent change* State	Percent change* U.S.
Total government payments to individuals	1 674	2 841	69.7	62.7
Retirement, disability, and insurance	607	1 051	73.1	48.2
Social Security	205	370	80.8	46.1
Government employee retirement	388	667	71.9	60.3
Medical payments	259	556	114.6	101.2
Income maintenance	133	235	77.2	58.0
Supplemental Security Income	27	43	62.5	75.4
Family assistance	65	99	52.5	-0.5
Food Stamps	27	52	94.3	27.1
Other income maintenance	14	41	185.1	189.8
Unemployment insurance benefits	79	100	26.9	10.6
Veterans benefits and other	596	899	50.7	30.8

*Percent change, 1990–1997

Government Payments to Individuals: 1997

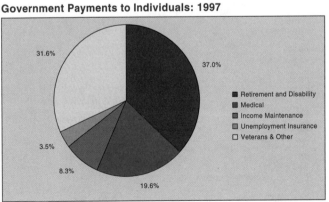

- Retirement and Disability 37.0%
- Medical 8.3%
- Income Maintenance 3.5%
- Unemployment Insurance 19.6%
- Veterans & Other 31.6%

ECONOMIC STRUCTURE

LEADING PRIVATE INDUSTRIES, 1997 (Worker and proprietor earnings, millions of dollars)		FASTEST EARNINGS GROWTH, 1989–97 (percent increase)	
Oil and gas extraction	$761	Membership organizations	101.0
Health services	686	General merchandise stores	90.5
Other transportation services	613	Health services	82.4
Construction specialties	446	Air transportation	79.0
Air transportation	401	Other transportation services	64.2

WHILE THE OIL INDUSTRY IS THE ONE MOST PEOPLE IDENTIFY with Alaska, and it remains the largest private-sector industry in the state, government is actually the largest sector. With a heavy federal civilian employment base, a substantial number of military installations, and very large state and local government workforce, government generated 30 percent of this economy's earnings in 1997 (60 percent of these earnings in the state/local sector). Cutbacks in state government and military base closings since 1993 have only slightly diminished its importance.

The main goods-producing sectors of the economy, oil, fishing, and manufacturing, have all experienced downturns since the early 1990s, from which there has been only partial recovery. However, job growth has been vigorous in other areas. Construction growth has been outstanding: offsetting flat demand in heavy construction, the light-construction sector has emerged to build residential and commercial projects. The services sector has provided much of the employment growth. Health services and air transportation are large and growing industries; Alaska's proximity to Asia means its airports see substantial air cargo landings, despite the state's small population size. Engineering is also an important industry showing moderate growth. Tourism is expanding, as reflected in the fast-growing yet relatively small recreation industry, and the state government rates it as the second largest private sector in Alaska.

Employment and Earnings by Sector

	1980	1989	1990	1991	1992	1993	1994	1995	1996	1997 Number	1997 Percent of total	Change*
Employment *(thousands of persons)*												
Total	244	331	341	350	354	361	367	368	373	380	100.0	1.7
Farm	1	1	1	1	1	1	1	1	1	1	0.2	-2.3
Nonfarm	243	330	340	349	353	361	367	368	373	379	99.8	1.7
Private nonfarm	163	235	242	250	253	260	269	273	279	286	75.4	2.5
Agricultural service, forestry, and fishing	9	15	14	14	14	15	15	13	14	15	3.9	0.1
Mining	8	11	13	13	12	12	12	11	11	11	3.0	-0.2
Construction	13	15	16	16	16	17	18	19	19	19	5.1	3.1
Manufacturing	15	18	19	20	20	19	19	20	19	18	4.8	0.3
Transportation and public utilities	19	25	25	26	26	27	28	28	28	29	7.7	2.2
Wholesale trade	6	8	9	9	9	9	9	10	10	10	2.6	1.9
Retail trade	28	46	47	49	51	52	57	58	59	61	16.1	3.8
Finance, insurance, and real estate	21	21	20	20	19	20	18	19	19	20	5.3	-0.5
Services	44	76	80	84	86	88	92	96	99	102	26.9	3.7
Government	80	95	99	99	100	101	98	95	94	93	24.4	-0.4
Earnings *(millions of dollars)*												
Total	5 281	9 250	9 823	10 302	10 844	11 221	11 470	11 610	11 694	11 972	100.0	3.3
Farm	4	6	8	8	8	10	8	10	9	11	0.1	7.5
Nonfarm	5 278	9 244	9 815	10 294	10 836	11 211	11 463	11 600	11 685	11 961	99.9	3.3
Private nonfarm	3 654	6 343	6 710	7 014	7 346	7 603	7 907	8 042	8 102	8 373	69.9	3.5
Agricultural service, forestry, and fishing	103	313	332	275	248	237	221	210	195	200	1.7	-5.4
Mining	359	736	845	932	908	868	908	883	887	880	7.3	2.2
Construction	613	676	702	697	700	807	891	903	902	907	7.6	3.7
Manufacturing	375	541	593	629	676	650	628	651	609	598	5.0	1.3
Transportation and public utilities	617	1 062	918	986	1 070	1 132	1 173	1 160	1 152	1 245	10.4	2.0
Wholesale trade	167	275	296	305	318	320	334	338	345	352	2.9	3.1
Retail trade	442	805	882	927	976	1 001	1 067	1 109	1 132	1 168	9.8	4.8
Finance, insurance, and real estate	200	296	313	333	367	417	436	443	455	473	3.9	6.0
Services	777	1 638	1 828	1 931	2 083	2 172	2 249	2 344	2 426	2 550	21.3	5.7
Government	1 624	2 901	3 105	3 280	3 490	3 608	3 556	3 558	3 583	3 588	30.0	2.7

*Compound annual average percent change, 1989–1997

ECONOMIC STRUCTURE (Continued)

AVERAGE ANNUAL WAGES FOR ALASKA WORKERS IN 1997 were 9 percent higher than those for the United States overall, because of a combination of the industry mix and level of wages in the state. The state's leading sector, government, paid wages about 20 percent above the average for the nation, and it is also disproportionately represented in the state economy. The relatively large mining sector, though it is small on an absolute basis, pays such high wages (60 percent above average) that it also raises the state average. Retail trade paid wages averaging 16 percent above national levels. In contrast, the services sector was more concentrated in low-wage industries, and wages averaged 7 percent below average; pay within the finance and wholesale trade sectors also fell below national levels in these fields.

Manufacturing has been a consistently small part of the Alaska economy, one of the smallest in the nation, because of the state's distance from materials sources and markets alike. Though manufacturing output value has grown modestly in recent years, employment in this sector has pretty steadily declined since 1992. The largest industries within the sector are food processing and lumber and wood products, and no other industry reaches the $100 million earnings level. With the decline in Alaska's fishing activity during the decade, fish processing output also has suffered.

Exports do not contribute greatly to supporting the Alaska economy and have not grown nearly as much as U.S. exports have during the 1994–97 period. Poor export performance for fish products and lumber, the state's leading exports as recently as 1993, account for the sluggish growth of total exports from Alaska in the mid-1990s. Exports of both products have declined significantly in the past four years. Crude oil and refined petroleum are now leading exports, but the largest export is metallic ores such as gold and zinc, the former a recently revived mining industry in the state.

Average Annual Wages and Salaries by Sector
(dollars)

	1989	1996	1997 State	1997 U.S.
All wage and salary workers	28 350	32 011	32 455	29 809
Farm	17 637	20 032	20 268	16 442
Nonfarm	28 357	32 017	32 461	29 900
Private nonfarm	28 133	30 338	30 820	29 867
Agricultural service, forestry, and fishing	25 031	26 847	28 062	17 941
Mining	62 472	79 729	79 701	49 800
Construction	41 960	45 415	45 717	31 765
Manufacturing	27 512	29 181	29 795	38 351
Transportation and utilities	40 612	39 487	40 618	38 222
Wholesale trade	31 038	33 737	34 570	39 466
Retail trade	16 509	18 690	18 774	16 206
Finance, insurance, and real estate	26 158	31 476	32 362	44 993
Services	21 763	24 914	25 595	27 588
Government	28 744	35 569	36 062	30 062

Gross State Product and Manufacturing
(millions of dollars, except as noted)

	1989	1994	1995	1996
Gross state product, total	23 065	21 853	23 674	24 161
Manufacturing:				
Millions of dollars	1 077	1 105	1 231	1 161
Percent of total gross state product	4.7	5.1	5.2	4.8
Per worker (dollars)	60 465	57 844	62 857	61 660
New capital expenditures, manufacturing	NA	107	119	81

Exports of Goods
(millions of dollars)

	1994	1995	1996	1997
All goods	888	892	850	969
Manufactures	486	406	345	332
Agricultural and livestock products	4	5	2	3
Other commodities	397	481	503	634
Top goods exports, 1997:				
Metallic ores and concentrates	98	195	216	363
Crude petroleum and natural gas	140	145	145	141
Fish and other marine products	122	95	101	69
Lumber and wood products	154	79	44	66
Industrial machinery and computers	16	24	29	50

HOUSING

NEW HOUSING PRODUCTION IN ALASKA HAS ADVANCED lethargically during most of the 1990s, with production rates per capita only about half of the national average because of the state's modest growth of incomes. However, the housing market picked up some momentum in 1996–97. Data on existing home sales are not available, but trends in this market typically parallel movements in the new home construction market. Overall, the housing market in Alaska is supported by strong underlying natural population growth and is not affected much by out-migration of military personnel or base closings, because these do not affect directly the demand for private housing units.

Home prices are not available from the National Association of Realtors, but a survey by the American Chamber of Commerce researchers found the average price of an existing home in Anchorage in 1997 was $176,485, or 30 percent above the mean for 321 U.S. cities surveyed. Rates of homeownership have jumped sharply

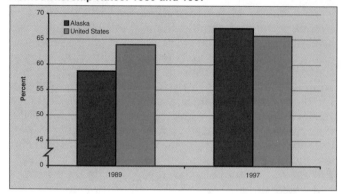

Homeownership Rates: 1989 and 1997

in the 1995–97 period, but this increase may be a statistical anomaly related to military personnel reductions changing the mix of renters and owners within the state.

Housing Supply

	1989	1990	1991	1992	1993	1994	1995	1996	1997
Residential building permits (thousands)	0.6	0.7	1.0	1.1	1.7	2.1	2.2	2.6	2.6
New home production (including manufactured housing):									
Thousands of homes	0.6	0.7	1.0	1.1	1.8	2.1	2.2	2.6	2.6
Rate per 1,000 population									
Alaska	1.1	1.3	1.8	1.9	3.0	3.5	3.7	4.3	4.3
U.S.	6.2	5.2	4.5	5.1	5.6	6.4	6.3	6.6	6.5
Existing home sales:									
Thousands of homes	6.6	NA	NA	NA	NA	NA	NA	NA	NA
Change from previous year (percent)									
Alaska	-27.5	NA	NA	NA	NA	NA	NA	NA	NA
U.S.	-3.9	-4.0	0.0	9.2	8.2	4.8	-3.7	7.5	3.8
Home ownership rate (percent of households)	58.7	58.4	57.1	55.5	55.4	58.8	60.9	62.9	67.2
Rental vacancy rate (percent of rental housing units)	11.0	6.8	5.7	5.8	4.9	4.5	6.0	5.9	7.4

Note: Manufactured housing data for 1989–97 suppressed because estimate was based on too few responses.

AGRICULTURE

THE STATE'S TINY FARMING SECTOR GENERATES LESS THAN one-tenth of one percent of Alaska personal income, because of the obvious climate constraints. There is some livestock production, whose revenues have been steady throughout the decade, but almost no crop production.

ALASKA FARMS, 1997	
Number of farms	510
Total acres (thousands):	920
Average per farm	1 804
Value of land and buildings (millions of dollars)	NA
Average per farm (dollars)	NA

Farm Income
(millions of dollars)

	1980	1989	1990	1991	1992	1993	1994	1995	1996	1997
Gross income	15	35	33	32	31	32	33	35	34	38
Receipts from sales	12	29	27	27	26	27	28	30	29	32
Government payments	0	1	1	1	2	2	1	2	1	1
Imputed and miscellaneous income	3	5	5	4	4	4	3	3	4	4
(−) Production expenses	15	31	28	27	26	26	28	27	28	28
(=) Realized net income	0	4	5	5	5	6	5	8	6	10
(+) Inventory change	1	-1	0	0	0	1	1	0	1	1
(=) Net income	1	4	5	5	5	7	5	8	7	10
Corporate income	0	1	1	1	1	1	2	2	2	3
Farm proprietors income	1	3	4	5	4	6	4	7	5	8

EDUCATION

EDUCATIONAL ATTAINMENT Percent of population age 25 and over, 1997	State	United States
High school graduate or higher	92.1	82.1
College graduate or higher	27.5	23.9

ALASKA RESIDENTS HAVE A HIGHER AVERAGE EDUCATIONAL attainment than the U.S. average in rates of earning both high school and college degrees. In both categories this state stands well above average, most likely because of the young age mix of the population and the strong relationship it has to amount of education. In addition, the disproportionate size of government in the state's job totals also translates to an educated workforce. The state spends the highest amount per pupil on public elementary and secondary schooling; at $9,012, this is a whopping 47 percent higher than the national average. This level of spending reflects a hefty premium in average salaries paid to attract teachers, and probably also reflects high transportation and overhead costs in the far-flung school districts of this large and highly rural state.

High School Completion: 1990–97

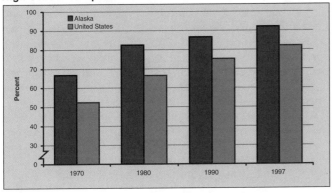

Education Indicators

	State	U.S.
Elementary and secondary schools		
Enrollment, 1995–96		
Total (thousands)	134	49 873
Percent in private schools	4.6	10.1
Expenditures per pupil (dollars), 1995–96	9 012	6 146
Average teacher salary (dollars), 1996–97	50 647	38 509
Higher education		
Enrollment, 1996–97		
Total (thousands)	29	14 218
Percent of population 18–34	19.2	21.8
Percent minority	19.4	26.1
Percent in private schools	3.5	22.6

HEALTH

HEALTH INDICATORS SHOW THAT ALASKANS ENJOY SLIGHTLY better than average health even after adjusting for the relatively young median age of the state. Infant mortality and overall death rates are a bit below average. Death from heart disease is particularly low in Alaska, while cancer and other major diseases cause death about as frequently here as in the United States overall. Deaths from accidents and adverse effects are particularly high in Alaska, possibly related to the number of mining and fishing jobs within the state. Suicide rates are double the national average, but deaths from HIV almost nonexistent in Alaska. In most recent years, a greater percentage of residents were covered by health insurance than the national average, but this ratio declined in 1997 to a level below the U.S. average.

Health Indicators

	1990	1995	1996	1997
Infant mortality				
(rate per thousand live births)				
Alaska	10.5	7.7	7.9	5.9
U.S.	9.2	7.6	7.3	7.1
Total deaths, age-adjusted rate				
(rate per thousand population)				
Alaska	5.3	4.9	4.7	4.5
U.S.	5.2	5.0	4.9	4.8
Persons not covered by health insurance				
(percent of population)				
Alaska	15.4	12.5	13.5	18.1
U.S.	13.9	15.4	15.6	16.1

Leading Causes of Death, 1996
(deaths per 100,000 population)

	Age-adjusted		Not age-adjusted	
	State	U.S.	State	U.S.
Deaths from all causes	473.5	491.6	425.4	872.5
Heart disease	96.8	134.5	85.0	276.4
Cancer	125.1	127.9	106.4	203.4
Cerebrovascular diseases	25.6	26.4	23.4	60.3
Chronic obstructive pulmonary disease	22.9	21.0	18.6	40.0
Diabetes mellitus	12.9	13.6	10.7	23.3
Pneumonia and influenza	6.2	12.8	5.9	31.6
HIV	NA	11.1	NA	11.7
Liver disease	8.8	7.5	8.9	9.4
Alzheimer's disease	4.8	2.7	4.1	8.1
Accidents and adverse effects	53.1	30.4	52.2	35.8
Motor vehicle accidents	16.5	16.2	16.1	16.5
Suicide	20.5	10.8	19.8	11.6
Homicide	7.0	8.5	6.9	7.9
Injury by firearm	21.0	12.9	20.3	12.8

GOVERNMENT

STATE AND LOCAL TAXES, 1995–96	State	U.S.
Per capita (dollars)	3 254	2 477
Percent of personal income	13.6	10.8

THE RELATIVE SIZE OF STATE AND LOCAL TAXES IN ALASKA IS heavily influenced by the taxation of oil production by the state. Including special taxes on the oil industry, included as "other taxes," the state and local tax bite in Alaska is $3254 per capita. This equals 13.6 percent of state personal income. However, adjusting for the disproportionate size of "other taxes" at the state level and instead using the U.S. average for this category, the state and local tax total drops to $1,642 per capita or about 34 percent less than the national average. This low total paid by ordinary Alaska residents reflects the absence of either a state sales tax or personal income tax, and this is the only state not to have at least one of these two general taxes. The need for general taxes is reduced by the receipt of ongoing interest earnings from the state's tremendously large "Permanent Fund," capitalized by North Slope oil taxes and now worth about $25 billion.

Spending levels per capita by state government in 1997 show the roughly $1,000 per person cash distributions to residents from the Permanent Fund under "other" expenditure, but also show spending higher than average in most other categories. The state makes relatively large transfers of funds to local governments, but also directly spends more than average on education, welfare and healthcare. Spending on highways and natural resources is extraordinarily large on a per capita basis, given the huge areas and small population in this state. With state tax coffers fairly flush in the early 1990s, these spending levels were easy to maintain, but with the onset of lower oil prices in 1997–98 and their negative effects on tax collections, the state is engaging in belt-tightening.

The relatively large numbers of federal civilian and military employees in Alaska bring in federal payroll at disproportionately large amounts, along with defense procurement from the private sector. A number of federal workers retire here as well, bringing retirement money into the state. These three factors account for a higher than average federal spending level within Alaska, even though the receipt of Social Security benefits and Medicare is very low in this young state. The state also wins federal grants at an above-average rate, partly due to the special needs of its minority and rural population.

State Government Finances, 1996–97

	Millions of dollars	Percent distribu-tion	Dollars per capita State	Dollars per capita U.S.
General revenue	7 425	100.0	12 192	3 049
Intergovernmental revenue	1 042	14.0	1 711	863
Taxes	1 619	21.8	2 659	1 660
General sales	0	0.0	0	551
Selective sales	96	1.3	158	257
License taxes	78	1.0	128	106
Individual income	0	0.0	0	542
Corporation net income	331	4.5	544	115
Other taxes	1 114	15.0	1 829	90
Other general revenue	4 764	64.2	7 822	526
General expenditure	5 160	100.0	8 472	2 951
Intergovernmental expenditure	1 015	19.7	1 667	989
Direct expenditure	4 145	80.3	6 806	1 962
General expenditure, by function:				
Education	1 199	23.2	1 969	1 033
Public welfare	742	14.4	1 219	761
Hospitals and health	188	3.6	308	237
Highways	590	11.4	968	225
Police protection and corrections	209	4.0	343	137
Natural resources, parks and recreation	304	5.9	500	63
Governmental administration	334	6.5	549	107
Interest on general debt	227	4.4	372	99
Other and unallocable	1 367	26.5	2 244	290
Debt at end of fiscal year	3 291	NA	5 403	1 706
Cash and security holdings	34 320	NA	56 355	6 683

Federal Spending within State

	Federal funds, fiscal 1997 Millions of dollars	Federal funds, fiscal 1997 Percent distribution	Federal funds, fiscal 1997 Percent of U.S. total*
Total within state	4 644	100.0	0.3
Payments to individuals	1 096	23.6	0.1
Retirement and disability	656	14.1	0.1
Medicare	163	3.5	0.1
Food stamps	48	1.0	0.2
Supplemental Security Income	26	0.6	0.1
Grants	1 374	29.6	0.6
Medicaid and other health	266	5.7	0.2
Nutrition and family welfare	183	3.9	0.4
Education	146	3.1	0.9
Housing and community development	100	2.2	0.9
Salaries and wages	1 284	27.6	0.8
Defense procurement contracts	645	13.9	0.5
Non-defense procurement contracts	211	4.5	0.3

*State population is 0.2 percent of the U.S. total.

31 372	59 698		65 157	70 827	72 687	78 001	81 93	88 504	93 426	5.8	63 383	70 827	31 372	59 698	63 3
25 323	47 902			57 151	59 446	62 916	67 00	72 039	77 208	6.1	50 999	57 151	25 323	47 902	50 9
2 640	5 143					7 801		7 709	7 838	5.4	5 645	6 816	2 640	5 143	5 6
3 409	6 652					284		8 755	8 360	2.9	6 739	6 860	3 409	6 652	6 7
693	1 716					07		1 539	762	9.7	1 561	811	693	1 716	1 5
716	4							7 217	7 618	5.6	5 178	6 049	716	4	

1997

Population (persons)	4,553,249
Population rank	21st
Population growth rank (1990–97)	2nd
Per capita personal income	$21,994
Unemployment rate (percent)	4.6
Poverty rate (percent)	17.2

ARIZONA HAS SEEN A BOOM IN POPULATION AND JOB GROWTH in the 1990s, with an economy diversifying through business services, electronics, and tourism. Yet it is not a prosperous state: the employment mix tilts toward lower wage service and retail trade industries, and its big retiree population typically has relatively low incomes. Thus, per capita income and median household income in the state stood at 87 to 90 percent of the U.S. levels in 1997.

The mining and farm sectors continued to shrink in importance during the 1990s, as did the historically large presence of U.S. military bases. In 1970, the government and military sector provided more jobs than any other major sector in the state, but in 1997 there were dispro-portionately fewer government jobs than average for the United States. In their place, Arizona has a respectable manufacturing base, booming business services industries, rapid expansion in homebuilding and related sectors to serve the flood of in-migrants, and a burgeoning tourist industry. By the late 1990s, there was political concern in the state about the social consequences of rapid growth.

Arizona is becoming more ethnically diverse because of the expansion of the Hispanic population. In 1997 its proportion of Hispanics (22 percent) was double the U.S. average, though still not as high as in California and Texas. Other minority groups are still small, and the state retains a large majority White non-Hispanic population.

Average Annual Population Growth: 1990–97

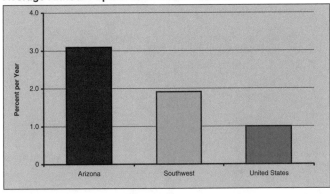

Median Household Income: 1989–97 (1997 dollars)

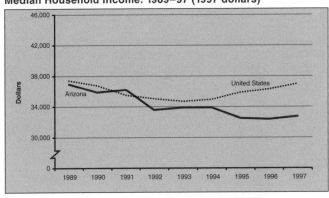

Unemployment Rate: 1989–97

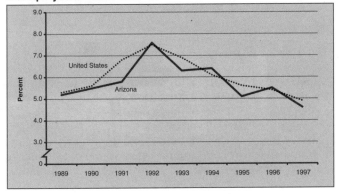

UNEMPLOYMENT HAS BEEN VERY LOW IN ARIZONA IN 1995–97, and rates have tracked the U.S. average fairly closely in the 1990s, with a bit less cyclical variation. Total employment increased at very strong rates, and Arizona's relatively small manufacturing sector decreases the volatility of employment trends.

POPULATION AND LABOR FORCE

RECENT POPULATION GROWTH IN ARIZONA HAS VASTLY OUT-stripped the U.S. averages, with a 23.8 percent increase during the 1990–97 period. The state has a younger population and higher birth rate than average, but the largest factor is a huge in-migration from other states, which by 1997 had added 12.6 percent to the 1990 population. Some of these migrants are retirees, but most appear to be working-age adults with children, judging by the age distribution. The 3.1 percent annual population growth rate in the 1990s duplicates that in the 1980s and has created an amazing 68 percent increase between 1980 and 1997. Arizona moved up to being the 21st largest state in the union, and its 1990–97 population increase (almost 900,000 people) was the fifth largest in absolute numbers (after Texas, California, Florida, and Georgia).

The Hispanic community in the state is the fastest growing major ethnic group, and it constituted 21.9 percent of the 1997 population, but the non-Hispanic White population was still more than 68 percent of total population. The significant Native American population (5.6 percent of the state) is decreasing as a proportion of the total, because in-migration does not add much to this group. Black and Asian populations remain a small percentage of the population.

Population and Labor Force

	1980	1990	1991	1992	1993	1994	1995	1996	1997	Change* State	Change* U.S.
Population											
Total number of persons (thousands)	2 718	3 679	3 762	3 867	3 994	4 148	4 307	4 432	4 553	3.1	1.0
Percent distribution:											
White, Non-Hispanic	74.6	71.5	71.1	70.5	70.1	69.7	69.3	68.8	68.3	2.4	0.4
Black, Non-Hispanic	2.7	3.2	2.9	2.9	2.9	2.9	3.0	3.0	3.0	2.2	1.4
Asian	0.9	1.6	1.7	1.7	1.8	1.9	1.9	2.0	2.0	6.5	4.1
Native American	5.7	5.8	5.9	5.9	5.8	5.7	5.7	5.6	5.6	2.7	1.6
Hispanic	16.3	18.7	19.3	19.8	20.3	20.6	21.0	21.5	21.9	5.5	3.8
In metropolitan areas	86.0	87.4	87.4	87.4	87.4	87.5	87.5	87.6	87.6	3.1	1.0
Total number of households (thousands)	957	1 369	1 392	1 432	1 466	1 518	1 624	1 687	NA	3.5	1.2
Labor Force (thousands)											
Population 16 and over	2 026	2 772	2 835	2 914	3 005	3 138	3 249	3 332	3 410	3.0	1.0
Civilian labor force	1 238	1 800	1 771	1 812	1 830	2 013	2 191	2 209	2 185	2.8	1.1
Employed	1 155	1 701	1 669	1 673	1 715	1 885	2 079	2 088	2 083	2.9	1.2
Percent of population	57.0	61.4	58.9	57.4	57.1	60.1	64.0	62.7	61.1		
Unemployment rate (percent)	6.7	5.5	5.8	7.6	6.3	6.4	5.1	5.5	4.6		

*Compound annual average percent change, 1990–1997; 1990–1996 for households.

Population Change and Components: 1990–97

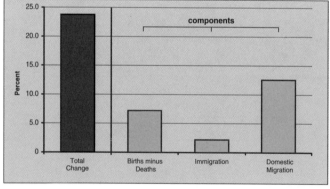

Average Annual Household and Population Growth

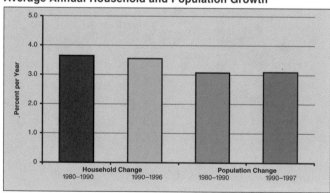

Population by Age; Births and Deaths

	1990 State	1990 U.S.	1997 State	1997 U.S.
Age distribution (percent)				
Under 5 years	8.3	7.6	8.2	7.2
5 to 17 years	19.0	18.2	19.9	18.8
18 to 64 years	59.6	61.8	58.7	61.3
65 years and over	13.1	12.5	13.2	12.7
Birth and death rates (per thousand population)				
Births	18.8	16.7	16.6	14.6
Deaths	7.8	8.6	8.2	8.6

ARIZONA'S IMAGE AS A RETIREE HAVEN IS SOMEWHAT ACCU-rate, reflected in a bit higher than average concentration of people over 65, but the higher proportion of children is the more remarkable feature. The 1997 birth rate was 16.6 per 100,000, 14 percent higher than the U.S. average, though it had declined from the 1990 level. The combination of large young and old populations gives the state a lower than average number of working-age adults to support the services needed by the dependent population.

HOUSEHOLD AND PERSONAL INCOME

HOUSEHOLD INCOME AND PERSONS IN POVERTY	1990	1995	1996	1997 State	1997 U.S.
Median household income (1997 dollars)	35 887	32 503	32 363	32 740	37 005
Persons in poverty (thousands)	484	700	980	797	35 574
Poverty rate (percent)	13.7	16.1	20.5	17.2	13.3

DESPITE SIGNIFICANT ECONOMIC GROWTH, ARIZONA INCOMES in the mid-1990s remain below U.S. averages and poverty remains high, partly because of the extremely high poverty rates among Native Americans. Median household income in 1997 was 88 percent of the national average, although household income was closer to the U.S. median in the early 1990s. Total personal income grew an impressive 74 percent from 1989 to 1997, but it reflected mostly the expansion of population. Real per capita income grew an average of 1.1 percent per year, about the same as nationally. Arizona's income per capita in 1997 was 87 percent of the U.S. average, a ratio that had remained remarkably constant through the 1990s. All major components of personal income are well below average: earnings per capita equaled 86 percent of the U.S. average in 1997,

dividends and interest were 88 percent of average, and transfers were 91 percent of average.

Transfer payments comprised 17 percent of Arizona's personal income in 1997 and rose somewhat faster than personal income overall during 1989–97. This was caused largely by spiraling medical payments and large increases in Supplemental Security Income (SSI) for the elderly and disabled. Social Security payments increased at about the same rate as income overall, though programs assisting the elderly comprise a high proportion of transfer payments. Family assistance grew at rates above the U.S. average in this period but more slowly than most other transfer programs. Other income maintenance exploded in size, because its main component is the fast-growing earned income tax credits program for low-income workers.

Personal Income
(millions of dollars)

	1980	1989	1990	1991	1992	1993	1994	1995	1996	1997	Change*
Earnings by place of work	18 560	39 548	41 681	43 511	46 523	50 150	54 857	60 071	64 996	70 419	7.5
Wages and salaries	15 104	32 550	34 194	35 406	37 652	40 032	43 974	48 326	52 856	57 713	7.4
Other labor income	1 468	3 174	3 478	3 813	4 235	4 706	5 246	5 407	5 457	5 608	7.4
Proprietors' income	1 988	3 824	4 009	4 293	4 637	5 412	5 637	6 338	6 682	7 097	8.0
Farm	332	512	453	555	486	647	283	510	415	371	-3.9
Nonfarm	1 656	3 312	3 556	3 738	4 151	4 765	5 354	5 828	6 267	6 726	9.3
(−) Personal contributions for social insurance	1 059	2 674	2 799	3 013	3 208	3 452	3 838	4 236	4 570	4 977	8.1
(+) Adjustment for residence	-79	168	233	224	242	218	214	216	248	264	NA
(=) Net earnings by state of residence	17 423	37 043	39 115	40 722	43 557	46 916	51 234	56 051	60 673	65 705	7.4
(+) Dividends, interest, and rent	4 573	11 803	12 129	12 119	11 908	12 508	13 583	14 842	16 333	17 353	4.9
(+) Transfer payments	3 628	8 817	9 860	11 007	12 535	13 537	14 519	15 562	16 366	17 124	8.7
(=) Total personal income	25 624	57 663	61 104	63 848	68 000	72 962	79 335	86 455	93 372	100 182	7.1
Farm	494	684	640	725	647	824	510	759	662	635	-0.9
Nonfarm	25 129	56 978	60 464	63 123	67 354	72 138	78 825	85 696	92 710	99 547	7.2
Personal income per capita (dollars)											
Current dollars	9 359	15 919	16 608	16 969	17 580	18 267	19 122	20 068	21 057	21 994	4.1
1997 dollars	17 895	20 125	19 986	19 595	19 664	19 877	20 321	20 861	21 443	21 994	1.1

*Compound annual average percent change, 1989–1997

Government Transfer Payments

	Millions of dollars 1990	Millions of dollars 1997	Percent change* State	Percent change* U.S.
Total government payments to individuals	9 428	16 397	73.9	62.7
Retirement, disability, and insurance	5 662	8 983	58.6	48.2
Social Security	3 657	6 099	66.8	46.1
Government employee retirement	1 633	2 505	53.4	60.3
Medical payments	2 402	5 241	118.2	101.2
Income maintenance	653	1 244	90.5	58.0
Supplemental Security Income	142	317	123.2	75.4
Family assistance	152	183	20.3	-0.5
Food Stamps	258	294	14.2	27.1
Other income maintenance	101	449	345.0	189.8
Unemployment insurance benefits	165	160	-3.0	10.6
Veterans benefits and other	546	769	40.9	30.8

*Percent change, 1990–1997

Government Payments to Individuals: 1997

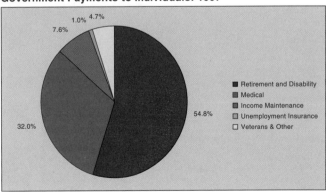

- Retirement and Disability — 54.8%
- Medical — 32.0%
- Income Maintenance — 7.6%
- Unemployment Insurance — 1.0%
- Veterans & Other — 4.7%

ECONOMIC STRUCTURE

LEADING PRIVATE INDUSTRIES, 1997 (Worker and proprietor earnings, millions of dollars)		FASTEST EARNINGS GROWTH, 1989–97 (percent increase)	
Health services	$5 788	Real estate	203.0
Business services	4 793	Business services	176.4
Construction specialties	3 483	Amusement and recreation services	170.4
Electronic and other electric equipment	2 872	Air transportation	142.8
Engineering and management services	2 609	Social services	127.5

SERVICES INDUSTRIES HAVE DOMINATED THE ARIZONA economy in the 1990s to an even greater extent than that of the United States, as business services (including computer services), engineering, and tourism-related industries flourish. Health services remains the leading industry, not surprising given the slightly disproportionate share of older residents. In addition, repair, educational, and social services all showed earnings growth of more than 100 percent from 1989 to 1997. Services jobs grew to comprise 32.5 percent of the state's employment base as of 1997. This trend has been complemented by fast growth in the construction industry and homebuilding-related sectors (such as building materials and real estate brokers), as production responded to the steady stream of in-migration.

Higher paid sectors of manufacturing and government represent a lower than average share of the Arizona economy. The federal military presence has shrunk during the 1990s, and the total federal payroll has declined as a percent of total earnings in the state (to 3.9 percent in 1997 from 6.1 percent in 1980). Manufacturing is where the state deviates most from national patterns, with a share of employment in this sector only 71 percent as great as the national average. However, manufacturing jobs did expand by 11 percent in 1989–97 and by 39 percent since 1980, a much better showing than the national manufacturing trend. Electronic equipment manufacturing is the largest and nearly the fastest growing of the manufacturing industries in the state, as high-tech industries expand. Aircraft manufacturing is the second largest industry in this sector.

Employment and Earnings by Sector

	1980	1989	1990	1991	1992	1993	1994	1995	1996	1997 Number	1997 Percent of total	Change*
Employment *(thousands of persons)*												
Total	1 285	1 883	1 907	1 921	1 945	2 030	2 167	2 291	2 407	2 502	100.0	3.6
Farm	21	19	19	20	21	19	19	19	20	19	0.8	0.1
Nonfarm	1 263	1 864	1 888	1 901	1 924	2 012	2 148	2 271	2 387	2 483	99.2	3.7
Private nonfarm	1 033	1 575	1 589	1 601	1 620	1 693	1 822	1 937	2 050	2 148	85.8	4.0
Agricultural service, forestry, and fishing	17	28	28	30	32	34	38	40	43	45	1.8	6.0
Mining	22	15	15	16	16	15	15	16	16	16	0.6	0.4
Construction	90	113	109	104	107	116	138	152	160	166	6.6	4.9
Manufacturing	158	197	194	185	182	186	199	205	211	219	8.8	1.4
Transportation and public utilities	55	79	85	86	85	90	96	101	107	113	4.5	4.6
Wholesale trade	53	82	82	83	87	87	95	103	111	116	4.6	4.4
Retail trade	226	340	344	350	354	367	400	419	437	453	18.1	3.7
Finance, insurance, and real estate	119	175	170	165	162	172	171	178	192	207	8.3	2.2
Services	293	546	562	581	596	626	670	724	772	813	32.5	5.1
Government	231	289	299	301	304	319	326	334	337	336	13.4	1.9
Earnings *(millions of dollars)*												
Total	18 560	39 548	41 681	43 511	46 523	50 150	54 857	60 071	64 996	70 419	100.0	7.5
Farm	494	684	640	725	647	824	510	759	662	635	0.9	-0.9
Nonfarm	18 066	38 864	41 041	42 786	45 877	49 327	54 347	59 313	64 333	69 784	99.1	7.6
Private nonfarm	14 826	31 805	33 476	34 795	37 533	40 588	45 091	49 631	54 215	59 186	84.0	8.1
Agricultural service, forestry, and fishing	136	312	350	392	423	456	503	549	595	644	0.9	9.5
Mining	719	474	508	563	617	596	585	668	803	744	1.1	5.8
Construction	1 798	2 714	2 659	2 613	2 750	3 077	3 865	4 440	4 771	5 127	7.3	8.3
Manufacturing	3 195	6 287	6 382	6 495	6 695	7 068	7 879	8 329	8 824	9 733	13.8	5.6
Transportation and public utilities	1 255	2 389	2 614	2 730	2 836	3 063	3 362	3 637	3 877	4 171	5.9	7.2
Wholesale trade	974	2 193	2 357	2 470	2 720	2 821	3 189	3 539	4 028	4 501	6.4	9.4
Retail trade	2 160	4 447	4 551	4 738	5 078	5 484	6 176	6 600	7 209	7 749	11.0	7.2
Finance, insurance, and real estate	1 126	2 771	2 867	2 925	3 553	4 149	4 463	5 022	5 638	6 131	8.7	10.4
Services	3 464	10 218	11 189	11 869	12 862	13 875	15 071	16 846	18 470	20 385	28.9	9.0
Government	3 240	7 059	7 565	7 991	8 343	8 738	9 256	9 681	10 119	10 598	15.0	5.2

*Compound annual average percent change, 1989–1997

ECONOMIC STRUCTURE (Continued)

AVERAGE WAGES IN ARIZONA WERE ABOUT 8 PERCENT BELOW the U.S. averages, reflecting both lower pay rates and the mix of sectors within the state. In the majority of sectors, wages were 5 to 8 percent below national norms, including services, government, and mining. There was a huge 24 percent gap between state and national wages within the finance, insurance, and real estate sector, because Arizona is not a center for investment banking and other high-end finance jobs. In contrast, retail trade wages were actually slightly above the national averages, and manufacturing wages were 4 percent above average in 1997 because of the predominance of high-productivity electronics and aircraft manufacturing.

The value of manufacturing output grew rapidly from 1992 to 1996, and, counter to the national trend, it actually increased faster than overall gross state product in Arizona. However, at 14.5 percent of gross state product, manufacturing still contributes less to the state economy than in an average state. Arizona's value of output per worker in manufacturing was higher than the U.S. average because of the industry mix: electronics and transportation equipment are by far the largest industries (and the only two with earnings over $1 billion). Also, because the sector's growth is relatively recent, the plant and equipment in the state are newer and afford higher productivity than the aging plant and equipment in traditional industrial states.

Exports are an increasingly important component of production demand in Arizona, especially in supporting the expansion of manufacturing. State exports have grown an impressive 95 percent during the 1994–97 period. Electronic equipment was the leading export good, and each of the top three exports more than doubled in value during the four year period from 1993 to 1997. Even agricultural commodities grew smartly; Arizona produces mainly vegetables, livestock, and dairy products.

Average Annual Wages and Salaries by Sector
(dollars)

	1989	1996	1997 State	1997 U.S.
All wage and salary workers	20 602	26 086	27 361	29 809
Farm	15 603	18 823	21 133	16 442
Nonfarm	20 636	26 130	27 396	29 900
Private nonfarm	20 179	25 888	27 115	29 867
Agricultural service, forestry, and fishing	11 012	14 417	15 179	17 941
Mining	33 552	48 399	45 387	49 800
Construction	21 595	26 719	27 922	31 765
Manufacturing	28 308	37 098	39 792	38 351
Transportation and utilities	27 532	33 658	34 676	38 222
Wholesale trade	25 566	34 037	36 626	39 466
Retail trade	12 496	16 391	17 041	16 206
Finance, insurance, and real estate	24 800	33 634	34 185	44 993
Services	18 551	23 837	24 981	27 588
Government	22 663	27 335	28 872	30 062

Gross State Product and Manufacturing
(millions of dollars, except as noted)

	1989	1994	1995	1996
Gross state product, total	65 667	95 360	103 951	111 520
Manufacturing:				
Millions of dollars	8 470	14 228	15 133	16 143
Percent of total gross state product	12.9	14.9	14.6	14.5
Per worker (dollars)	43 084	71 578	73 983	76 359
New capital expenditures, manufacturing	NA	1 385	2 250	2 914

Exports of Goods
(millions of dollars)

	1994	1995	1996	1997
All goods	6 971	8 403	9 938	13 557
Manufactures	6 633	7 910	9 561	13 139
Agricultural and livestock products	156	181	177	217
Other commodities	182	311	200	201
Top goods exports, 1997:				
Electric and electronic equipment	3 637	4 503	5 429	6 539
Industrial machinery and computers	827	884	1 098	3 238
Transportation equipment	655	718	943	1 229
Scientific and measuring instruments	432	522	559	622
Fabricated metal products	164	163	239	278

HOUSING

Housing construction has provided a major part of the impetus for economic growth in Arizona in the 1990s, as residential production per capita has been double the U.S. rates in most years of the decade. Housing production rebounded after a slight recession in 1991, so that by 1997 it had hit levels double those of 1990. The Phoenix-Mesa metropolitan area was second in the nation in its number of building permits in 1997, particularly attributable to single-family activity. Spin-off effects of the housing boom were earnings increases within both the real estate and building materials industries. Sales increases of existing homes generally exceeded U.S. rates but not by the same margins as for new production.

Homeownership rates increased in the early 1990s in Arizona, but the peak rate of 69.1 percent in 1993 has not been maintained in the face of continuing in-migration. The average sales price in the Phoenix area was $113,700 in 1997, an 8 percent increase over 1996. Prices are still below typical prices in California and the rest of the West

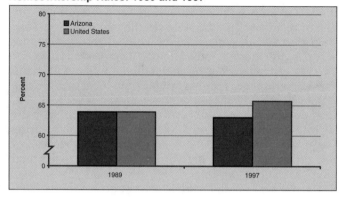

Homeownership Rates: 1989 and 1997

Coast, and represent one of the attractions of this state. Rises in rental vacancy rates in 1996–97 suggest a temporary oversupply of apartments, but one that can be expected to be absorbed by future population growth.

Housing Supply

	1989	1990	1991	1992	1993	1994	1995	1996	1997
Residential building permits (thousands)	23.8	23.0	23.5	31.8	38.7	51.8	52.7	53.7	57.8
New home production (including manufactured housing):									
Thousands of homes	27.0	26.2	26.1	35.3	43.0	57.5	59.2	60.7	64.7
Rate per 1,000 population									
Arizona	7.5	7.1	6.9	9.1	10.8	13.9	13.7	13.7	14.2
U.S.	6.2	5.2	4.5	5.1	5.6	6.4	6.3	6.6	6.5
Existing home sales:									
Thousands of homes	77.7	86.3	79.7	89.8	107.9	123.8	122.0	128.2	135.1
Change from previous year (percent)									
Arizona	-3.2	11.1	-7.6	12.7	20.2	14.7	-1.5	5.1	5.4
U.S.	-3.9	-4.0	0.0	9.2	8.2	4.8	-3.7	7.5	3.8
Home ownership rate (percent of households)	63.9	64.5	66.3	69.3	69.1	67.7	62.9	62.0	63.0
Rental vacancy rate (percent of rental housing units)	10.5	10.7	9.6	9.5	7.4	8.8	7.2	10.2	9.1

AGRICULTURE

The farming sector's net income has fluctuated in a moderate band during the 1990s, though 1997 was a particularly weak year. A rapidly growing vegetable industry, now the largest farm product area, and moderately growing dairy industry are the only positive elements in the sector. Livestock still is the second largest product but its revenues have been flat during the decade. Farm proprietors' income in 1997 was only about 5 percent of total proprietors' income in the state, compared with a 17 percent share in 1980. Corporate farming has a substantial

ARIZONA FARMS, 1997	
Number of farms	7 500
Total acres (thousands):	35 400
Average per farm	4 720
Value of land and buildings (millions of dollars)	14 868
Average per farm (dollars)	1 982 400

presence in the state, and the size of an average farm is a gigantic 4720 acres. The real estate value of an average farm is nearly $2 million.

Farm Income
(millions of dollars)

	1980	1989	1990	1991	1992	1993	1994	1995	1996	1997
Gross income	1 815	2 135	2 105	1 954	1 950	2 202	2 035	2 313	2 347	2 327
Receipts from sales	1 736	1 966	1 979	1 823	1 778	1 983	1 857	2 189	2 160	2 156
Government payments	5	85	43	40	76	114	72	9	57	47
Imputed and miscellaneous income	74	84	83	90	97	105	106	115	129	125
(–) Production expenses	1 606	1 430	1 480	1 401	1 368	1 455	1 591	1 706	1 733	1 882
(=) Realized net income	209	705	625	553	583	747	444	607	613	445
(+) Inventory change	122	-66	-65	93	12	-49	-46	21	-37	54
(=) Net income	332	638	560	646	594	698	398	628	576	499
Corporate income	0	127	107	90	109	51	115	118	161	128
Farm proprietors income	332	512	453	555	486	647	283	510	415	371

EDUCATION

EDUCATIONAL ATTAINMENT Percent of population age 25 and over, 1997	State	United States
High school graduate or higher	82.6	82.1
College graduate or higher	19.5	23.9

EDUCATIONAL ATTAINMENT IN ARIZONA IN 1997 WAS ABOUT average, considering the number of people with a high school degree, but significantly below average for college attainment.   Between 1990 and 1997, the proportion of adults who were college graduates actually declined (counter to the national trend), probably because in-migration of nongraduates. This decline placed the state in the lowest quartile among states for percent of population with college degrees.   However, Arizona has a relatively large share of young adults currently enrolled in higher education, which bodes well for future rates of attainment. With a fast-growing elementary and secondary school population, it is difficult to maintain the level of spending per pupil, and indeed Arizona's spending rate is about 20 percent below the U.S. average. Teacher salaries also are well below average. The state has a very low share of enrollment in private elementary and secondary schools.

High School Completion: 1990–97

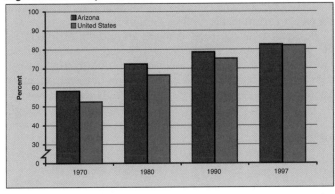

Education Indicators

	State	U.S.
Elementary and secondary schools		
Enrollment, 1995–96		
Total (thousands)	788	49 873
Percent in private schools	5.6	10.1
Expenditures per pupil (dollars), 1995–96	4 860	6 146
Average teacher salary (dollars), 1996–97	33 350	38 509
Higher education		
Enrollment, 1996–97		
Total (thousands)	277	14 218
Percent of population 18–34	25.8	21.8
Percent minority	25.5	26.1
Percent in private schools	8.4	22.6

HEALTH

HEALTH INDICATORS SHOW THE STATE WAS ABOUT AVERAGE for death rates but slightly worse than average for infant mortality. Infant mortality has not declined as much as in most states from 1990 to 1997. There is a lower incidence of death from major diseases among Arizonans than average (after adjustment for the state's higher number of older people), with an especially low rate of heart disease. In contrast, the state's death rates from accidents, firearms, homicide, and suicide are well above average. Health insurance coverage extends to a substantially lower percentage of the population in Arizona than nationally, with noncoverage at a startlingly high 24.5 percent. This rate is consistent with the lower prevalence of manufacturing jobs (which typically offer better employee benefits) and high incidence of poverty in the state.

Health Indicators

	1990	1995	1996	1997
Infant mortality				
(rate per thousand live births)				
Arizona	8.8	7.5	13.3	6.3
U.S.	9.2	7.6	7.3	7.1
Total deaths, age-adjusted rate				
(rate per thousand population)				
Arizona	4.8	5.0	4.8	4.7
U.S.	5.2	5.0	4.9	4.8
Persons not covered by health insurance				
(percent of population)				
Arizona	15.5	20.4	24.1	24.5
U.S.	13.9	15.4	15.6	16.1

Leading Causes of Death, 1996
(deaths per 100,000 population)

	Age-adjusted		Not age-adjusted	
	State	U.S.	State	U.S.
Deaths from all causes	475.2	491.6	826.4	872.5
Heart disease	114.5	134.5	231.3	276.4
Cancer	114.6	127.9	187.9	203.4
Cerebrovascular diseases	22.9	26.4	53.0	60.3
Chronic obstructive pulmonary disease	24.5	21.0	48.1	40.0
Diabetes mellitus	12.6	13.6	20.3	23.3
Pneumonia and influenza	12.6	12.8	28.7	31.6
HIV	7.3	11.1	7.5	11.7
Liver disease	10.0	7.5	12.3	9.4
Alzheimer's disease	3.2	2.7	10.1	8.1
Accidents and adverse effects	41.6	30.4	47.9	35.8
Motor vehicle accidents	22.1	16.2	22.5	16.5
Suicide	15.3	10.8	16.4	11.6
Homicide	10.9	8.5	10.1	7.9
Injury by firearm	18.7	12.9	18.8	12.8

GOVERNMENT

STATE AND LOCAL TAXES, 1995–96	State	U.S.
Per capita (dollars)	2 194	2 477
Percent of personal income	11.2	10.8

COMBINED STATE AND LOCAL TAXES ARE LIGHT IN ARIZONA on a per capita basis, with collections about 11 percent below the U.S. average in fiscal 1996. The division of revenues between state and local levels is a little heavier on the state part, compared with national averages, so local taxes are particularly low. However, considering the lower than average personal incomes in Arizona, the tax load is a bit heavier than for the United States overall, comprising 11.2 percent of total income.

The state of Arizona levies relatively low taxes per capita, with correspondingly *below-average spending on all the major services: education, welfare, and health. Low per capita state spending on education, combined with the disproportionately high school-age population, puts a double bind on education in the state. Conservative budget policies have limited state debt to very low levels and keep costs of administration down below U.S. averages. On the revenue side, the state receives less federal intergovernmental revenue than average and has lower than average individual income taxes (one factor in attracting retirees). In contrast, corporate income tax receipts and sales tax revenues are higher than average.

Federal spending in Arizona is about proportionate to its share of the national population; payments for Medicare and Medicaid are proportionately the lowest among all categories of benefits. Non-defense procurement has the greatest shortfall, with Arizona receiving only 0.9 percent of procurement nationally, though defense procurement spending is equal to the state's share of total population.

State Government Finances, 1996–97

	Millions of dollars	Percent distribution	Dollars per capita State	Dollars per capita U.S.
General revenue	11 499	100.0	2 524	3 049
Intergovernmental revenue	3 237	28.2	711	863
Taxes	6 834	59.4	1 500	1 660
General sales	2 855	24.8	627	551
Selective sales	948	8.2	208	257
License taxes	437	3.8	96	106
Individual income	1 668	14.5	366	542
Corporation net income	601	5.2	132	115
Other taxes	324	2.8	71	90
Other general revenue	1 428	12.4	313	526
General expenditure	11 266	100.0	2 473	2 951
Intergovernmental expenditure	4 528	40.2	994	989
Direct expenditure	6 738	59.8	1 479	1 962
General expenditure, by function:				
Education	4 033	35.8	885	1 033
Public welfare	2 688	23.9	590	761
Hospitals and health	614	5.4	135	237
Highways	1 167	10.4	256	225
Police protection and corrections	696	6.2	153	137
Natural resources, parks and recreation	211	1.9	46	63
Governmental administration	331	2.9	73	107
Interest on general debt	159	1.4	35	99
Other and unallocable	1 366	12.1	300	290
Debt at end of fiscal year	2 742	NA	602	1 706
Cash and security holdings	25 615	NA	5 623	6 683

Federal Spending within State

	Federal funds, fiscal 1997		
	Millions of dollars	Percent distribution	Percent of U.S. total*
Total within state	22 282	100.0	1.6
Payments to individuals	13 024	58.5	1.7
Retirement and disability	8 310	37.3	1.8
Medicare	3 120	14.0	1.5
Food stamps	312	1.4	1.6
Supplemental Security Income	332	1.5	1.2
Grants	3 836	17.2	1.5
Medicaid and other health	1 464	6.6	1.3
Nutrition and family welfare	782	3.5	1.7
Education	301	1.4	1.8
Housing and community development ..	204	0.9	1.8
Salaries and wages	2 574	11.6	1.6
Defense procurement contracts	1 970	8.8	1.6
Non-defense procurement contracts	665	3.0	0.9

*State population is 1.7 percent of the U.S. total.

31 372	59 698		65 157	70 827	72 687	78 001	81 93		88 504	93 426	5.8	63 383	70 827	31 372	59 698	63 38
25 323	47 902		57 151	59 446	62 916	67 00		72 039	77 208	6.1	50 999	57 151	25 323	47 902	50 99
2 640	5 143					7 801		7 709	7 838	5.4	5 645	6 816	2 640	5 143	5 64
3 409	6 652				284			8 755	8 380	2.9	6 739	6 860	3 409	6 652	6 73
693	1 716				07			1 539	762	-9.7	1 561	811	693	1 716	1 56
2 716	4 9			02				7 217	7 618	5.6	5 178	6 049	2 716	4 9	

1997

Population (persons)	2,523,186
Population rank	33rd
Population growth rank (1990–97)	20th
Per capita personal income	$19,602
Unemployment rate (percent)	5.3
Poverty rate (percent)	19.7

WITH A 1997 POPULATION OF 2.5 MILLION, ARKANSAS IS A relatively small state. Its population grew an average of 1.0 percent per year from 1990 to 1997, equal to the national rate of growth. Twenty-five percent of the state's population is in the Little Rock-North Little Rock and adjoining Pine Bluff metropolitan areas, roughly in the center of the state. Another concentration of population is found in the Fayetteville-Springdale-Rogers metropolitan area in the state's northwest corner. This relatively prosperous area contains only 10 percent of the state's population but accounted for fully one-third of the state's population growth from 1990 to 1997.

Agriculture and the manufacture of food products play major roles in the state's economy, with poultry being by far the leading agricultural product.

Arkansas' economy grew vigorously from 1992 through 1995, a period when much of the nation was still struggling to recover from recession. Employment growth was strong during these years, the unemployment rate fell, and home production enjoyed a modest boom. Then, in 1996 and 1997—while the nation was enjoying stronger economic growth—the state's economy seemed to stall: employment growth slowed, the unemployment rate rose, the number of persons in poverty increased, and the home production rate leveled off. Exports remained a bright spot, however, rising 11 percent each year in 1996 and 1997.

Average Annual Population Growth: 1990–97

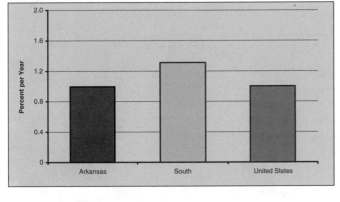

Median Household Income: 1989–97 (1997 dollars)

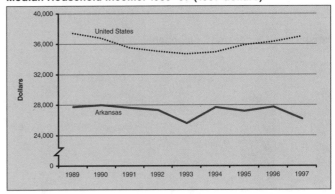

Unemployment Rate: 1989–97

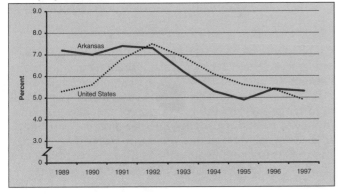

ARKANSAS' UNEMPLOYMENT RATE HIT A RECESSIONARY PEAK of 7.4 percent in 1991, then came down fairly rapidly through 1995. Since 1995 the rate has risen somewhat and appears stalled in a range somewhat higher than 5 percent. In general, unemployment rates are lower in metropolitan areas than elsewhere in the state: the 1997 rates were 3.9 percent in Little Rock-North Little Rock, 3.2 percent in Fayetteville-Springdale-Rogers, and 4.2 in Jonesboro. The Pine Bluff metropolitan area is an exception to this pattern; its unemployment rate rose above 11 percent during the early-1990s recession and, after falling from 1992–95, leveled off at 7.7 percent from 1995–97.

POPULATION AND LABOR FORCE

ARKANSAS' NON-HISPANIC WHITE POPULATION GREW 0.8 PER-cent per year from 1990 to 1997, compared to a national rate of 0.4 percent. The Black non-Hispanic population grew more rapidly than the White population but did not quite equal the national growth rate. Non-Hispanic Whites were 81 percent of the total population in 1997, and non-Hispanic Blacks were 16 percent. Other race and ethnic groups were only 3 percent of the total.

The metropolitan population grew more than twice as rapidly as the nonmetropolitan from 1990 to 1997 but still made up a little less than one-half of the 1997 total, com-pared to 80 percent nationally.

In-migration from other states accounted for 60 percent of Arkansas' 7.2 percent total population growth from 1990 to 1997 and natural increase (births minus deaths) for almost all of the remainder. Immigration from abroad accounted for only 4 percent. In-migration from other states has been concentrated in the Fayetteville-Springdale-Rogers metropolitan area, which has attracted working-age people drawn by expanding job opportuni-ties and retirees drawn by the lakes, recreational opportu-nities, and relatively low cost of living.

Population and Labor Force

	1980	1990	1991	1992	1993	1994	1995	1996	1997	Change* State	Change* U.S.
Population											
Total number of persons (thousands)	2 286	2 354	2 370	2 394	2 424	2 451	2 480	2 505	2 523	1.0	1.0
Percent distribution:											
White, Non-Hispanic	82.2	82.2	82.1	82.0	81.9	81.8	81.6	81.3	81.1	0.8	0.4
Black, Non-Hispanic	16.2	15.7	15.9	16.0	16.0	15.9	15.9	15.9	16.0	1.2	1.4
Asian	0.3	0.6	0.6	0.6	0.6	0.6	0.7	0.7	0.7	3.8	4.1
Native American	0.6	0.6	0.5	0.5	0.5	0.5	0.5	0.5	0.5	0.2	1.6
Hispanic	0.7	1.0	0.9	1.0	1.1	1.2	1.4	1.7	1.8	10.0	3.8
In metropolitan areas	44.9	47.2	47.4	47.6	47.9	48.0	48.2	48.3	48.5	1.4	1.0
Total number of households (thousands)	816	891	899	910	919	925	938	951	NA	1.1	1.2
Labor Force (thousands)											
Population 16 and over	1 703	1 804	1 818	1 833	1 862	1 883	1 903	1 926	1 940	1.0	1.0
Civilian labor force	1 000	1 126	1 116	1 154	1 165	1 207	1 220	1 230	1 214	1.1	1.1
Employed	924	1 048	1 033	1 069	1 093	1 143	1 160	1 164	1 150	1.3	1.2
Percent of population	54.3	58.1	56.8	58.3	58.7	60.7	61.0	60.4	59.3		
Unemployment rate (percent)	7.6	7.0	7.4	7.3	6.2	5.3	4.9	5.4	5.3		

*Compound annual average percent change, 1990–1997; 1990–1996 for households.

Population Change and Components: 1990–97

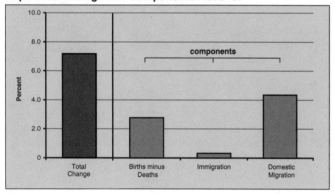

Average Annual Household and Population Growth

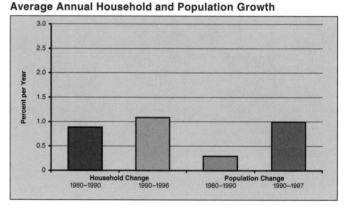

Population by Age; Births and Deaths

	1990 State	1990 U.S.	1997 State	1997 U.S.
Age distribution (percent)				
Under 5 years	7.1	7.6	7.0	7.2
5 to 17 years	19.2	18.2	19.3	18.8
18 to 64 years	58.8	61.8	59.5	61.3
65 years and over	14.8	12.5	14.3	12.7
Birth and death rates (per thousand population)				
Births	15.5	16.7	14.6	14.6
Deaths	10.5	8.6	11.0	8.6

CHANGES IN THE AGE DISTRIBUTION OF THE ARKANSAS POPU-lation aged 18 and over were in a direction opposite to the national trend from 1990 to 1997. The percentage of the Arkansas population age 18 to 64 rose, while the national percentage fell, and the proportion of the state's popula-tion aged 65 and over fell, while the national percentage rose. Even so, the state has a notably larger than average share of its population in the 65 and over age group and a smaller than average share in the working-age group.

HOUSEHOLD AND PERSONAL INCOME

HOUSEHOLD INCOME AND PERSONS IN POVERTY	1990	1995	1996	1997	
				State	U.S.
Median household income (1997 dollars)	27 981	27 186	27 745	26 162	37 005
Persons in poverty (thousands)	472	376	449	515	35 574
Poverty rate (percent)	19.6	14.9	17.2	19.7	13.3

ARKANSAS' POVERTY RATE IS SUBSTANTIALLY HIGHER THAN the U.S. average, and, although it seemed to be coming down from 1990 to 1995, the 1996–1997 average returned almost to the high 1989–1990 rate. Adjusted for inflation, median household income appears to have been declining throughout the 1990s; the 1996–1997 average was 3 percent lower than that for 1989–1990. This trend differs from that for the nation as a whole, which saw a faster decline in household incomes through mid-decade but rising incomes and a continuing decline in the poverty rate in 1996 and 1997. Arkansas' median household income was only 74 percent of the national average for 1996–1997.

Real per capita personal income has shown a somewhat more encouraging trend than median household income, increasing each year since 1991 and moving slightly closer to the U.S. average. It reached 77 percent of the national average in 1992, compared to 74 percent in 1989; from 1992 through 1997, it remained at 77 to 78 percent.

Farming provided 3.4 percent of Arkansas' personal income, far more than the nation's 0.7 percent share.

Government transfer payments to Arkansas residents increased 61.6 percent from 1990 to 1997, roughly equal to the national percentage increase. Income maintenance payments grew 95.7 percent in Arkansas, compared to only 58 percent nationally. "Other income maintenance," a category consisting largely of the earned income tax credit, showed by far the largest percent growth and grew at about double the national rate. The expansion of this credit during the 1990s has been of particular benefit to relatively low-wage states such as Arkansas. Unemployment insurance payments also grew considerably more rapidly in Arkansas than in the nation.

Personal Income
(millions of dollars)

	1980	1989	1990	1991	1992	1993	1994	1995	1996	1997	Change*
Earnings by place of work	11 962	21 723	22 823	24 284	26 625	27 974	29 751	31 355	32 987	34 586	6.0
Wages and salaries	9 336	16 454	17 697	18 620	20 175	21 042	22 446	23 891	25 104	26 606	6.2
Other labor income	960	1 873	2 086	2 287	2 566	2 814	3 019	2 996	2 881	2 894	5.6
Proprietors' income	1 665	3 395	3 040	3 377	3 885	4 118	4 286	4 468	5 002	5 086	5.2
Farm	210	965	646	747	1 023	1 004	1 134	1 214	1 614	1 465	5.4
Nonfarm	1 455	2 430	2 393	2 630	2 862	3 114	3 151	3 253	3 388	3 621	5.1
(−) Personal contributions for social insurance	638	1 430	1 516	1 622	1 761	1 866	2 022	2 161	2 239	2 370	6.5
(+) Adjustment for residence	-19	-167	-212	-232	-270	-322	-356	-324	-339	-336	NA
(=) Net earnings by state of residence	11 305	20 126	21 095	22 430	24 594	25 786	27 373	28 869	30 409	31 880	5.9
(+) Dividends, interest, and rent	2 580	5 256	5 488	5 500	5 394	5 487	5 734	6 197	6 769	7 154	3.9
(+) Transfer payments	3 225	5 949	6 438	7 073	7 856	8 431	8 773	9 427	9 944	10 419	7.3
(=) Total personal income	17 111	31 331	33 021	35 003	37 845	39 704	41 881	44 494	47 122	49 453	5.9
Farm	384	1 171	892	992	1 248	1 248	1 353	1 411	1 840	1 693	4.7
Nonfarm	16 726	30 160	32 128	34 011	36 596	38 457	40 527	43 083	45 283	47 760	5.9
Personal income per capita (dollars)											
Current dollars	7 476	13 353	14 026	14 766	15 807	16 380	17 086	17 935	18 802	19 602	4.9
1997 dollars	14 294	16 881	16 878	17 051	17 681	17 824	18 157	18 643	19 147	19 602	1.9

*Compound annual average percent change, 1989–1997

Government Transfer Payments

	Millions of dollars		Percent change*	
	1990	1997	State	U.S.
Total government payments to individuals	6 187	9 995	61.6	62.7
Retirement, disability, and insurance	3 466	5 073	46.4	48.2
Social Security	2 591	3 821	47.5	46.1
Government employee retirement	747	1 095	46.7	60.3
Medical payments	1 698	3 283	93.4	101.2
Income maintenance	484	948	95.7	58.0
Supplemental Security Income	187	337	79.7	75.4
Family assistance	60	57	-3.8	-0.5
Food Stamps	162	211	30.1	27.1
Other income maintenance	75	343	354.9	189.8
Unemployment insurance benefits	155	205	32.1	10.6
Veterans benefits and other	383	485	26.8	30.8

*Percent change, 1990–1997

Government Payments to Individuals: 1997

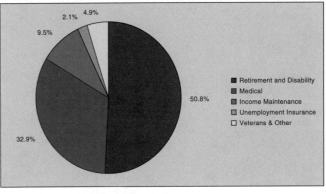

- Retirement and Disability — 50.8%
- Medical — 32.9%
- Income Maintenance — 9.5%
- Unemployment Insurance — 2.1%
- Veterans & Other — 4.9%

ECONOMIC STRUCTURE

LEADING PRIVATE INDUSTRIES, 1997 (Worker and proprietor earnings, millions of dollars)		FASTEST EARNINGS GROWTH, 1989–97 (percent increase)	
Health services	$3 229	Other transportation services	203.1
Farming	1 693	Real estate	143.6
Food and kindred products	1 419	General merchandise sales	124.2
Business services	1 279	Motor vehicles and equipment	119.8
Construction specialties	1 270	Business services	119.4

ARKANSAS IS ONE OF THE SMALL NUMBER OF STATES IN WHICH farming ranks among the top five industries, measured by worker and proprietor earnings. Together with the closely related food and kindred product manufacturing industry, also among the top five, food and farming accounted directly for 9 percent of earnings in 1997. Arkansas is the home of poultry giant Tyson Foods, many of whose contract growers and processing plants are located within the state.

Although farm earnings have grown during the 1990s, employment in farming fell a total of more than 12 percent, or 8,500 jobs, from 1989 to 1997. Farming still provided 4.2 percent of total employment in 1997, however, compared to only 1.9 percent nationally.

Arkansas' second largest manufacturing industry, fabricated metal products, is roughly one-half the size of food and kindred products. Ranking close in size after fabricated metals are lumber and wood products, paper, electron-ics, and industrial machinery. Motor vehicles was the most rapidly growing manufacturing industry but still accounted for less than 4 percent of manufacturing earnings in 1997. In total, manufacturing accounted for 18.3 percent of employment and 22.5 percent of earnings in 1997, compared to 12 percent of employment and 18 percent of earnings nationally. In contrast to the national pattern, manufacturing employment in Arkansas expanded during the first half of the 1990s. Growth was especially strong from 1992 to 1995, when nearly 23,000 new jobs were added, a 9 percent expansion. Expansion halted in 1995; in fact, employment in manufacturing in 1997 was 2 percent less than the level in 1995.

As befits the home state of Wal-Mart, general merchandise sales was among Arkansas' most rapidly growing industries from 1989 to 1997. Retail trade provided 17.5 percent of total employment in the state in 1997 but, with its relatively low wages, only 11 percent of earnings.

Employment and Earnings by Sector

	1980	1989	1990	1991	1992	1993	1994	1995	1996	1997 Number	1997 Percent of total	Change*
Employment *(thousands of persons)*												
Total	1 035	1 197	1 210	1 239	1 265	1 305	1 335	1 378	1 405	1 431	100.0	2.3
Farm	88	68	67	65	64	63	58	59	59	60	4.2	-1.6
Nonfarm	948	1 128	1 143	1 174	1 202	1 243	1 277	1 320	1 346	1 371	95.8	2.5
Private nonfarm	782	951	959	988	1 014	1 054	1 086	1 126	1 150	1 171	81.9	2.6
Agricultural service, forestry, and fishing	8	13	14	15	15	16	17	18	19	19	1.4	4.9
Mining	9	8	8	8	7	7	7	7	6	6	0.4	-3.5
Construction	57	60	62	63	66	70	73	79	82	83	5.8	4.3
Manufacturing	215	239	239	241	244	253	263	267	262	262	18.3	1.2
Transportation and public utilities	51	66	66	66	65	68	70	75	78	79	5.5	2.4
Wholesale trade	43	48	47	48	50	50	51	54	53	54	3.8	1.5
Retail trade	153	193	194	199	207	215	226	236	244	250	17.5	3.3
Finance, insurance, and real estate	56	63	62	62	63	65	62	64	66	68	4.8	1.0
Services	190	262	268	286	297	310	316	327	340	350	24.4	3.7
Government	165	178	184	186	188	189	191	193	196	199	13.9	1.5
Earnings *(millions of dollars)*												
Total	11 962	21 723	22 823	24 284	26 625	27 974	29 751	31 355	32 987	34 586	100.0	6.0
Farm	384	1 171	892	992	1 248	1 248	1 353	1 411	1 840	1 693	4.9	4.7
Nonfarm	11 577	20 552	21 930	23 292	25 377	26 726	28 397	29 944	31 147	32 893	95.1	6.1
Private nonfarm	9 714	17 143	18 222	19 286	21 128	22 337	23 817	25 165	26 158	27 677	80.0	6.2
Agricultural service, forestry, and fishing	65	140	157	183	209	218	234	237	233	253	0.7	7.7
Mining	151	139	144	149	145	152	148	160	163	176	0.5	3.0
Construction	922	1 136	1 247	1 253	1 371	1 497	1 625	1 789	1 945	2 014	5.8	7.4
Manufacturing	3 153	5 357	5 663	5 920	6 335	6 685	7 224	7 415	7 485	7 790	22.5	4.8
Transportation and public utilities	972	1 864	1 989	2 028	2 218	2 295	2 431	2 624	2 708	2 826	8.2	5.3
Wholesale trade	693	1 144	1 216	1 263	1 369	1 436	1 517	1 626	1 669	1 769	5.1	5.6
Retail trade	1 372	2 272	2 373	2 575	2 850	2 985	3 222	3 406	3 555	3 819	11.0	6.7
Finance, insurance, and real estate	508	961	999	1 050	1 184	1 324	1 364	1 458	1 547	1 675	4.8	7.2
Services	1 877	4 132	4 432	4 865	5 447	5 744	6 051	6 449	6 852	7 355	21.3	7.5
Government	1 864	3 409	3 709	4 006	4 249	4 390	4 581	4 779	4 989	5 216	15.1	5.5

*Compound annual average percent change, 1989–1997

ECONOMIC STRUCTURE (Continued)

THE AVERAGE ANNUAL EARNINGS OF ARKANSAS WORKERS were 80 percent of the U.S. average in 1980 but slipped to 76 percent by 1989 and still remained close to 76 percent in 1997. Arkansas' manufacturing workers earned only 68 percent of the national average in 1997. This level, too, was about the same as in 1989 but was down from 73 percent in 1980. Only in the retail trade sector did the state's wages and salaries exceed 90 percent of the national average, and this sector, both nationally and in the state, provided the lowest annual earnings of any nonfarm sector. The low worker earnings in retail trade stem from a combination of low hourly wages, fewer hours worked per week on average, and many part-year workers.

From 1989 through 1996, manufacturing's share of Arkansas' gross state product remained within the range of 23.9 to 25.9 percent; the 1996 figure was 24.6 percent, well above the national average of 17.5 percent. The 1996 manufacturing value per Arkansas worker of $53,000 was less than the national average of $69,000. This figure may reflect, in part, the large share of manufacturing represented by poultry processing, a relatively low value-added industry.

Food products, Arkansas' dominant manufacturing industry, also dominated its exports, accounting for one-third of all goods exports in 1997. No other industry came close in terms of value of exports, but, together, the next four, shown in the table, supplied another 37 percent of 1997 exports. Arkansas achieved strong growth of exports in the mid-1990s, with total goods exports growing 50 percent from 1994 to 1997, compared to a national average increase of 34 percent.

Average Annual Wages and Salaries by Sector
(dollars)

	1989	1996	1997 State	1997 U.S.
All wage and salary workers	16 955	21 741	22 640	29 809
Farm	10 375	13 400	12 501	16 442
Nonfarm	17 087	21 858	22 791	29 900
Private nonfarm	17 031	21 682	22 662	29 867
Agricultural service, forestry, and fishing	11 967	15 161	16 080	17 941
Mining	24 619	30 256	31 898	49 800
Construction	18 130	23 314	24 134	31 765
Manufacturing	19 400	24 799	25 984	38 351
Transportation and utilities	25 647	31 224	32 219	38 222
Wholesale trade	21 366	28 520	29 698	39 466
Retail trade	10 926	14 051	14 820	16 206
Finance, insurance, and real estate	21 230	27 861	29 863	44 993
Services	14 835	19 769	20 645	27 588
Government	17 330	22 703	23 411	30 062

Gross State Product and Manufacturing
(millions of dollars, except as noted)

	1989	1994	1995	1996
Gross state product, total	36 471	50 364	53 358	56 417
Manufacturing:				
Millions of dollars	9 432	12 782	13 689	13 898
Percent of total gross state product	25.9	25.4	25.7	24.6
Per worker (dollars)	39 540	48 591	51 242	52 996
New capital expenditures, manufacturing	NA	1 178	1 369	1 279

Exports of Goods
(millions of dollars)

	1994	1995	1996	1997
All goods	1 471	1 794	1 997	2 212
Manufactures	1 410	1 715	1 903	2 036
Agricultural and livestock products	42	39	42	46
Other commodities	19	40	52	129
Top goods exports, 1997:				
Food products	487	674	812	718
Chemical products	202	248	228	274
Electric and electronic equipment	137	155	168	200
Industrial machinery and computers	152	172	168	182
Transportation equipment	100	102	124	169

HOUSING

In contrast to the national pattern, Arkansas' rate of new home production increased rather than slumped in 1991. Consistent with the state's good employment gains and falling unemployment, the home production rate continued to rise through 1994, with a particularly strong gain in 1993. Since 1994, the state's home production rate has been relatively steady and has remained somewhat higher than the national rate. More than one-third of new home production from 1995 through 1997 consisted of manufactured housing (mobile homes), compared to less than 20 percent nationally.

Existing home sales were strong from 1992 through 1995, then showed little increase from 1995 to 1997. The 1997 median sales price of existing homes in the Little Rock-North Little Rock metropolitan area was $85,600 compared to a national average of $124,100.

Arkansas' 1997 homeownership rate of 66.7 percent was slightly higher than the U.S. rate of 65.7 percent. The state's rate rose during the early 1990s, peaking at 70.5 percent in 1993, then fell back approximately to the 1989 rate.

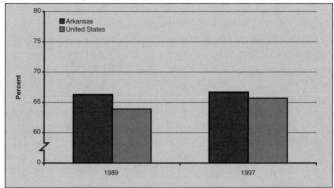

Homeownership Rates: 1989 and 1997

Housing Supply

	1989	1990	1991	1992	1993	1994	1995	1996	1997
Residential building permits (thousands)	6.3	5.9	6.9	7.9	10.0	12.4	11.7	11.1	11.0
New home production (including manufactured housing):									
Thousands of homes	9.5	8.6	10.2	11.4	15.1	17.7	18.0	17.9	17.3
Rate per 1,000 population									
Arkansas	4.0	3.7	4.3	4.8	6.2	7.2	7.3	7.1	6.9
U.S.	6.2	5.2	4.5	5.1	5.6	6.4	6.3	6.6	6.5
Existing home sales:									
Thousands of homes	47.5	44.8	43.4	47.8	52.8	52.3	57.5	59.7	58.7
Change from previous year (percent)									
Arkansas	0.0	-5.7	-3.1	10.1	10.5	-0.9	9.9	3.8	-1.7
U.S.	-3.9	-4.0	0.0	9.2	8.2	4.8	-3.7	7.5	3.8
Home ownership rate (percent of households)	66.3	67.8	68.6	70.3	70.5	68.1	67.2	66.6	66.7
Rental vacancy rate (percent of rental housing units)	8.0	7.9	8.6	6.9	7.2	6.8	7.4	7.2	8.1

AGRICULTURE

Poultry dominates Arkansas' Agriculture, accounting for 46 percent of the value of all farm sales in 1997. For the 12 percent of the state's farms that sold poultry, poultry sales per farm averaged $476,000.

In Arkansas, farming was the principal occupation for 51 percent of farm operators in 1997, about equal to the national average. Twenty-two percent of farms had sales of more than $100,000, a percentage considerably higher than that of other South Central states and higher than the national average of 18 percent. During 1992–97, net income from Arkansas farming topped $1 billion each year. The peak year was 1996, when income from farming reached 3.9 percent of total personal income.

ARKANSAS FARMS, 1997

Number of farms	42 500
Total acres (thousands):	14 800
Average per farm	348
Value of land and buildings (millions of dollars)	14 948
Average per farm (dollars)	351 718

Farm Income
(millions of dollars)

	1980	1989	1990	1991	1992	1993	1994	1995	1996	1997
Gross income	3 356	5 336	5 056	5 104	5 369	5 946	5 913	6 061	6 772	6 681
Receipts from sales	3 125	4 482	4 429	4 388	4 621	4 872	5 232	5 277	5 991	5 935
Government payments	35	440	313	353	410	705	303	384	362	275
Imputed and miscellaneous income	196	414	315	363	337	369	378	401	419	471
(−) Production expenses	2 928	4 137	4 390	4 554	4 364	4 678	4 876	4 615	5 100	5 047
(=) Realized net income	427	1 199	666	551	1 004	1 267	1 038	1 446	1 672	1 635
(+) Inventory change	-217	-157	31	240	101	-233	248	-132	149	1
(=) Net income	210	1 042	698	791	1 105	1 035	1 285	1 315	1 821	1 636
Corporate income	0	77	51	44	82	31	151	100	207	171
Farm proprietors income	210	965	646	747	1 023	1 004	1 134	1 214	1 614	1 465

EDUCATION

EDUCATIONAL ATTAINMENT Percent of population age 25 and over, 1997	State	United States
High school graduate or higher	76.9	82.1
College graduate or higher	14.6	23.9

THE PERCENTAGE OF ARKANSAS RESIDENTS AGE 25 AND OVER who had completed high school rose from 39.9 percent in 1970 to 66.3 percent in 1990 and 76.9 percent in 1997, thus narrowing the gap with the substantially higher national average. Although low by national standards, the state's high school completion rate is higher than that of four other South Central states. The state's college completion rate has more than doubled since 1970 but was still the lowest in the nation in 1997.

Elementary and secondary school per-pupil expendi-tures were 77 percent of the national average in 1995–96. This level exceeded those of Tennessee and Mississippi and was about equal to that of Alabama, but lower than those of other southern states.

Education in Arkansas is largely public education, with only 6 percent of elementary and secondary students and 11 percent of higher education students enrolled in private schools. The minority share of higher education enroll-ment is about equal to the minority share of Arkansas' total population.

High School Completion: 1990–97

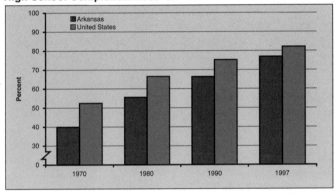

Education Indicators

	State	U.S.
Elementary and secondary schools		
Enrollment, 1995–96		
Total (thousands)	481	49 873
Percent in private schools	5.7	10.1
Expenditures per pupil (dollars), 1995–96	4 710	6 146
Average teacher salary (dollars), 1996–97	29 975	38 509
Higher education		
Enrollment, 1996–97		
Total (thousands)	101	14 218
Percent of population 18–34	17.1	21.8
Percent minority	18.5	26.1
Percent in private schools	11.2	22.6

HEALTH

ARKANSAS HAS MADE SOME PROGRESS IN REDUCING ITS infant mortality rate during the 1990s, but the gains have been less than those for the nation as a whole.

The state's overall death rate is somewhat higher than the national average. Adjusted for differences in the age distribution of the population, the rate of death from cere-brovascular diseases (strokes) was about one-third higher than the national rate in 1996. Rates for other diseases were closer to the national rate or, in some cases, below. However, deaths from motor vehicle accidents were near-ly 60 percent higher than the national average.

The percentage of the state's population not covered by health insurance has risen sharply since 1990 and in 1996 and 1997 averaged 45 percent higher than the national percentage.

Health Indicators

	1990	1995	1996	1997
Infant mortality				
(rate per thousand live births)				
Arkansas	9.2	8.8	8.0	8.4
U.S.	9.2	7.6	7.3	7.1
Total deaths, age-adjusted rate				
(rate per thousand population)				
Arkansas	5.6	5.6	5.5	5.7
U.S.	5.2	5.0	4.9	4.8
Persons not covered by health insurance				
(percent of population)				
Arkansas	17.4	17.9	21.7	24.4
U.S.	13.9	15.4	15.6	16.1

Leading Causes of Death, 1996
(deaths per 100,000 population)

	Age-adjusted		Not age-adjusted	
	State	U.S.	State	U.S.
Deaths from all causes	550.0	491.6	1057.2	872.5
Heart disease	147.8	134.5	331.6	276.4
Cancer	137.7	127.9	237.5	203.4
Cerebrovascular diseases	35.7	26.4	91.4	60.3
Chronic obstructive pulmonary disease	21.8	21.0	44.5	40.0
Diabetes mellitus	12.2	13.6	23.0	23.3
Pneumonia and influenza	13.8	12.8	37.7	31.6
HIV	5.2	11.1	5.0	11.7
Liver disease	5.8	7.5	7.8	9.4
Alzheimer's disease	2.4	2.7	7.5	8.1
Accidents and adverse effects	43.9	30.4	50.3	35.8
Motor vehicle accidents	25.7	16.2	25.3	16.5
Suicide	12.6	10.8	12.9	11.6
Homicide	9.9	8.5	9.5	7.9
Injury by firearm	17.2	12.9	17.1	12.8

GOVERNMENT

STATE AND LOCAL TAXES, 1995–96	State	U.S.
Per capita (dollars)	1 841	2 477
Percent of personal income	10.3	10.8

IN THE 1995–96 FISCAL YEAR, ARKANSAS' $1,841 PER CAPITA rate of state and local taxes (excluding corporate income taxes) was only 74 percent of the all-state average. Measured as a percentage of personal income, however, the gap was much narrower. Arkansas' state and local taxes equaled 10.3 percent of personal income, compared to 10.8 percent nationally, and the taxes-to-income ratio was higher than that of several other southern states with

State Government Finances, 1996–97

	Millions of dollars	Percent distribution	Dollars per capita	
			State	U.S.
General revenue	7 290	100.0	2 889	3 049
Intergovernmental revenue	2 264	31.1	898	863
Taxes	3 777	51.8	1 497	1 660
General sales	1 429	19.6	567	551
Selective sales	588	8.1	233	257
License taxes	222	3.0	88	106
Individual income	1 247	17.1	494	542
Corporation net income	230	3.2	91	115
Other taxes	61	0.8	24	90
Other general revenue	1 249	17.1	495	526
General expenditure	7 103	100.0	2 815	2 951
Intergovernmental expenditure	1 967	27.7	780	989
Direct expenditure	5 136	72.3	2 035	1 962
General expenditure, by function:				
Education	2 819	39.7	1 117	1 033
Public welfare	1 667	23.5	661	761
Hospitals and health	624	8.8	247	237
Highways	763	10.7	302	225
Police protection and corrections	266	3.7	106	137
Natural resources, parks and recreation	186	2.6	74	63
Governmental administration	246	3.5	98	107
Interest on general debt	122	1.7	48	99
Other and unallocable	409	5.8	162	290
Debt at end of fiscal year	2 248	NA	891	1 706
Cash and security holdings	11 899	NA	4 716	6 683

Federal Spending within State

	Federal funds, fiscal 1997		
	Millions of dollars	Percent distribution	Percent of U.S. total*
Total within state	12 593	100.0	0.9
Payments to individuals	8 439	67.0	1.1
Retirement and disability	5 076	40.3	1.1
Medicare	2 010	16.0	1.0
Food stamps	214	1.7	1.1
Supplemental Security Income	352	2.8	1.3
Grants	2 278	18.1	0.9
Medicaid and other health	1 085	8.6	1.0
Nutrition and family welfare	359	2.9	0.8
Education	177	1.4	1.0
Housing and community development	87	0.7	0.8
Salaries and wages	1 067	8.5	0.6
Defense procurement contracts	192	1.5	0.2
Non-defense procurement contracts	263	2.1	0.4

*State population is 0.9 percent of the U.S. total.

considerably higher incomes, including Florida, North Carolina, and Virginia. Local taxes were only 25 percent of Arkansas' state and local total, compared to a 41 percent national average, indicating considerably above-average state-level responsibility for revenue collection.

General and selective sales taxes produced 53 percent of Arkansas' total state-level tax revenue in fiscal year 1996–97, a little more than the all-state average of 49 percent. Revenue from the individual income tax made up 33 percent of the state's total, just equal to the all-state average, and corporate income taxes yielded 6 percent, compared to an all-state average of 7 percent.

Total state-level general expenditure per capita in Arkansas was 95 percent of the all-state average in 1996–97, and education spending was 8 percent higher than average. These figures are for state government spending only; local spending on education would appear to be well below the national average, because total per-pupil expenditure in elementary and secondary schools was only 77 percent of the national average in 1995–96.

Interest on Arkansas's general debt averaged $48 per capita in 1996–97, compared to a national average of $99. The state seemed in excellent financial shape at year-end, with debt equal to $891 per capita, compared to $1,706 nationally, and cash and security holdings more than five times the size of the debt.

Arkansas' 0.9 percent share of federal funds distributed to states and their residents in fiscal 1997 was just equal to the state's 0.9 percent share of the U.S. population. The state's share of defense and non-defense procurement contracts was much less than its population share, and its share of federal salaries and wages was a little below, while the share of payments to individuals was more.

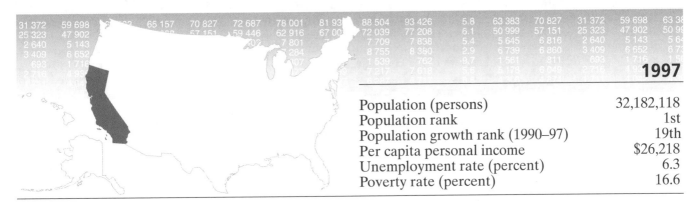

Population (persons)	32,182,118
Population rank	1st
Population growth rank (1990–97)	19th
Per capita personal income	$26,218
Unemployment rate (percent)	6.3
Poverty rate (percent)	16.6

CALIFORNIA'S ENORMOUS SIZE MAKES IT THE NATION'S LEADing economy and population center: 1 out of 8 Americans lives there and 1 out of 9 jobs is located there. The state continues to be a pace-setter as a multicultural society. With a large and rapidly growing Hispanic and Asian population, the proportion of non-Hispanic Whites had declined to 51 percent of the total population as of 1997. Yet the severity of the early 1990s recession in California put a dent in its economic dominance, as it lagged U.S. growth rates by almost every measure. High unemployment, low growth of jobs, and sub-par personal income growth in the 1989–95 period meant California's per capita and household median incomes grew very little in real dollars, falling to only a little above U.S. averages. After four years of no job growth, in 1995 a recovery began. However, employment growth in 1995–97 was about equal to national rates of increase, so the state did only slightly better than recoup the losses from its extended recession.

A flood of out-migration during the 1990–97 period equaled 6.3 percent of California's 1990 population, presenting a stark contrast to its rapid population growth in the 1980s. Thanks to continued strong foreign immigration, however, California's population did grow a moderate 7.5 percent overall in the 1990–97 period.

Average Annual Population Growth: 1990–97

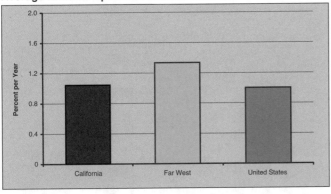

Median Household Income: 1989–97 (1997 dollars)

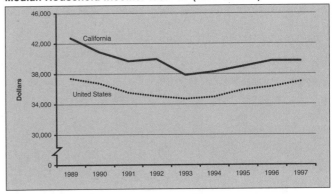

Unemployment Rate: 1989–97

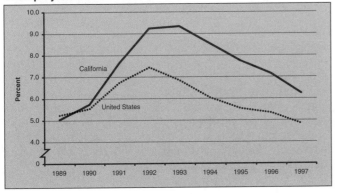

WITH SUBSTANTIAL JOB LOSSES STARTING IN 1991, UNEMployment spiraled upward above the 9 percent mark during the recession in 1991–93 and remained above the U.S. average all the way through 1997. Weakness was especially apparent in the manufacturing and construction sectors, whose decline was steeper and lasted longer than national averages prior to the sectors' respective comebacks in 1995–97. Defense cutbacks and a sharp decline in homebuilding contributed to the severity of the recession in California.

POPULATION AND LABOR FORCE

TOTAL POPULATION IN CALIFORNIA GREW AT ABOUT THE SAME rate as the U.S. overall from 1990 to 1997, but with marked differences in the components of growth. Out-migration offset most of the natural population increase, but foreign immigration was a major contributor to population growth. This was reflected in rapid growth in the Hispanic and Asian populations, which comprised over 42 percent of state population in 1997. The state is now home to over one-third of all Hispanics in the United States and 40 percent of the Asian-origin population. The 1990s experience of moderate population growth contrasts with California's 14.2 percent population increase from in-migration (foreign and domestic) in the 1980s and its 25 percent overall population increase in that decade.

The adult population has increased less than the overall population in the 1990s, limiting the size of the labor force. Indeed, the labor force hardly grew at all in 1990–95, as discouraged job seekers quit looking or even moved out of state. However, slow economic growth led to an increase in total employment from 1990 to 1997 that was even smaller than that of the labor force, and a fairly low percentage of the adult population held employment in 1997.

Population and Labor Force

	1980	1990	1991	1992	1993	1994	1995	1996	1997	Change* State	Change* U.S.
Population											
Total number of persons (thousands)	23 668	29 926	30 393	30 854	31 124	31 295	31 472	31 762	32 182	1.1	1.0
Percent distribution:											
White, Non-Hispanic	67.0	57.3	56.2	55.3	54.3	53.4	52.5	51.8	51.1	-0.6	0.4
Black, Non-Hispanic	7.5	7.2	7.0	7.0	6.9	6.8	6.8	6.7	6.6	-0.2	1.4
Asian	5.5	9.9	10.3	10.6	10.9	11.1	11.4	11.5	11.7	3.5	4.1
Native American	1.0	1.0	1.0	1.0	1.0	1.0	1.0	1.0	1.0	0.9	1.6
Hispanic	19.2	25.7	26.6	27.3	28.1	28.9	29.5	30.2	30.8	3.7	3.8
In metropolitan areas	96.8	96.8	96.7	96.7	96.7	96.7	96.6	96.6	96.6	1.1	1.0
Total number of households (thousands)	8 630	10 381	10 531	10 748	10 812	10 829	10 941	11 101	NA	1.1	1.2
Labor Force (thousands)											
Population 16 and over	18 127	22 740	22 982	23 288	23 444	23 511	23 615	23 821	24 201	0.9	1.0
Civilian labor force	11 584	15 193	15 177	15 404	15 360	15 450	15 412	15 512	15 941	0.7	1.1
Employed	10 794	14 319	14 004	13 973	13 918	14 122	14 203	14 391	14 937	0.6	1.2
Percent of population	59.5	63.0	60.9	60.0	59.4	60.1	60.1	60.4	61.7		
Unemployment rate (percent)	6.8	5.8	7.7	9.3	9.4	8.6	7.8	7.2	6.3		

*Compound annual average percent change, 1990–1997; 1990–1996 for households.

Population Change and Components: 1990–97

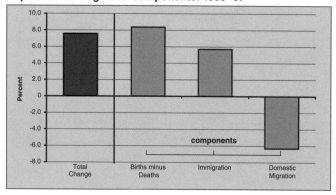

Average Annual Household and Population Growth

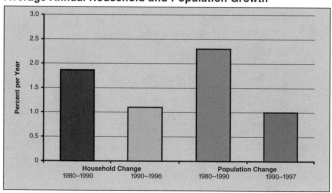

Population by Age; Births and Deaths

	1990 State	1990 U.S.	1997 State	1997 U.S.
Age distribution (percent)				
Under 5 years	8.5	7.6	8.2	7.2
5 to 17 years	18.2	18.2	19.5	18.8
18 to 64 years	62.9	61.8	61.2	61.3
65 years and over	10.5	12.5	11.1	12.7
Birth and death rates (per thousand population)				
Births	20.6	16.7	16.3	14.6
Deaths	7.2	8.6	NA	8.6

CALIFORNIA HAS A YOUNGER THAN AVERAGE POPULATION, with relatively more children under age 5 and a larger school-age population. With a relatively high birth rate, the young-age cohort will continue to swell, taxing the state's school resources. The working-age population declined between 1990 and 1997 as a share of the total, In contrast, those 65 years of age and older are an increasing part of the population, though still with a percentage share below the national average.

HOUSEHOLD AND PERSONAL INCOME

HOUSEHOLD INCOME AND PERSONS IN POVERTY	1990	1995	1996	1997 State	1997 U.S.
Median household income (1997 dollars)	40 880	38 976	39 703	39 694	37 005
Persons in poverty (thousands)	4 128	5 342	5 472	5 459	35 574
Poverty rate (percent)	13.9	16.7	16.9	16.6	13.3

CONSISTENT WITH THE STATE'S SLOW ECONOMIC GROWTH between 1989 and 1997, both major measures of income in California grew less than average. Median household income, while still at a level above the U.S. median, declined 7 percent from 1989 to 1997 (in real dollars) and reached a level closer to the U.S. average. Per capita personal income in real dollars grew only a total of 2.5 percent over 1989–97, compared with a national increase of 10.2 percent. Among components of personal income, nonfarm proprietors' income posted the strongest gain in earnings-related income.

Despite slow earnings growth in the 1990s, earnings per capita in 1997 remain about 4 percent higher in California than national averages. Dividends and interest per capita were 8 percent higher than for the United States, and transfer payments were 4 percent lower than nationally. Poverty rates increased between 1990 and 1997 to a level well above the U.S. average, reflecting the scarcity of new jobs and immigration of low-income families.

Transfer payments grew only moderately in California from 1990 to 1997. This stems primarily from the lower than average (compared to the United States) increases in medical payments and income maintenance programs. Retirement and disability payments grew at about an average rate. While Supplemental Security Income rose extremely rapidly in many states, it increased only 30 percent in California. Family assistance payments, however, increased somewhat during this period, when they were declining in many states under welfare reform regimes. Benefits under the earned income tax credit (part of "other" income maintenance) rose most rapidly of all.

Personal Income
(millions of dollars)

	1980	1989	1990	1991	1992	1993	1994	1995	1996	1997	Change*
Earnings by place of work	207 494	435 992	469 356	476 910	498 151	506 521	517 994	539 342	567 591	607 447	4.2
Wages and salaries	164 253	343 664	368 550	372 837	383 505	384 437	394 598	414 843	440 541	475 160	4.1
Other labor income	16 280	36 773	40 757	43 402	46 407	49 315	49 752	47 399	45 862	46 775	3.1
Proprietors' income	26 961	55 555	60 049	60 670	68 238	72 769	73 644	77 100	81 188	85 512	5.5
Farm	4 044	4 432	4 191	3 108	4 047	4 833	3 752	2 996	3 301	2 987	-4.8
Nonfarm	22 918	51 123	55 858	57 562	64 192	67 936	69 891	74 104	77 887	82 525	6.2
(−) Personal contributions for social insurance	10 411	28 998	31 082	32 610	33 823	34 561	36 011	37 241	38 553	40 819	4.4
(+) Adjustment for residence	14	-6	-44	-6	34	-391	-452	-732	-756	-855	NA
(=) **Net earnings by state of residence**	197 097	406 989	438 229	444 294	464 362	471 570	481 530	501 369	528 282	565 774	4.2
(+) Dividends, interest, and rent	47 655	109 523	118 405	117 574	115 589	116 424	122 721	133 351	145 127	152 201	4.2
(+) Transfer payments	36 837	74 450	82 663	91 304	104 723	110 137	114 070	119 549	124 610	128 041	7.0
(=) **Total personal income**	281 589	590 962	639 298	653 172	684 674	698 130	718 321	754 269	798 020	846 017	4.6
Farm	5 742	6 808	7 006	5 890	6 706	7 780	6 813	6 412	7 121	6 864	0.1
Nonfarm	275 847	584 154	632 292	647 282	677 969	690 350	711 509	747 857	790 898	839 153	4.6
Personal income per capita (dollars)											
Current dollars	11 831	20 226	21 360	21 476	22 163	22 388	22 899	23 901	25 050	26 218	3.3
1997 dollars	22 621	25 570	25 704	24 799	24 791	24 361	24 335	24 845	25 509	26 218	0.3

*Compound annual average percent change, 1989–1997

Government Transfer Payments

	Millions of dollars 1990	Millions of dollars 1997	Percent change* State	Percent change* U.S.
Total government payments to individuals	78 389	122 532	56.3	62.7
Retirement, disability, and insurance	39 594	57 433	45.1	48.2
Social Security	23 123	33 770	46.0	46.1
Government employee retirement	12 889	20 176	56.5	60.3
Medical payments	21 946	41 137	87.4	101.2
Income maintenance	11 775	17 760	50.8	58.0
Supplemental Security Income	4 309	5 601	30.0	75.4
Family assistance	5 320	6 198	16.5	-0.5
Food Stamps	1 027	2 301	124.1	27.1
Other income maintenance	1 120	3 661	227.0	189.8
Unemployment insurance benefits	2 213	2 707	22.3	10.6
Veterans benefits and other	2 861	3 495	22.2	30.8

*Percent change, 1990–1997

Government Payments to Individuals: 1997

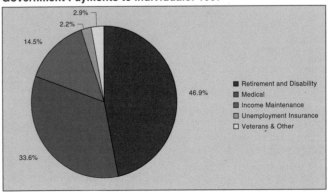

- Retirement and Disability — 46.9%
- Medical — 33.6%
- Income Maintenance — 14.5%
- Unemployment Insurance — 2.2%
- Veterans & Other — 2.9%

ECONOMIC STRUCTURE

LEADING PRIVATE INDUSTRIES, 1997 (Worker and proprietor earnings, millions of dollars)		FASTEST EARNINGS GROWTH, 1989–97 (percent increase)	
Business services	$49 436	Security brokers	129.6
Health services	43 759	Business services	105.6
Engineering and management services	27 905	Social services	91.0
Construction specialties	20 017	Amusement and recreation services	84.6
Electronic and other electric equipment	15 627	Motion pictures	82.4

WITH GENERAL WEAKNESS IN THE MANUFACTURING AND construction industries in the 1990s, service industries are increasingly predominant in California. Business services (which includes computer services in Silicon Valley and other technology centers) is the state's largest industry and also the second fastest growing. It contributes 8.1 percent of all earnings in the state, compared with a 6.2 percent share nationally. In manufacturing, the high-tech electronic equipment and industrial machinery industries (the two fastest growing industries in the manufacturing sector) both have rallied between 1995 and 1997, after a 15 percent decline in manufacturing employment occurred from 1989 to 1995. Yet there were still fewer manufacturing jobs in 1997 than there were in 1980, similar to the national decline in the sector. The state's construction employment through

1997 never recovered to the level of 1989. Construction is still a large sector, but construction specialties fell a notch from third to fourth largest earning industry in the state.

All of the fastest growing sectors during 1990–97 are in service industries, ranging from business services to amusement and social services. Educational services also grew rapidly. The real estate industry saw big earnings gains in 1995–97 related to continuing price increases in real estate and an active resale market, despite low new home output. However, federal government job cutbacks in California, from military base closings and civilian job reductions, weakened the state's economy starting in the mid-90s. Since a 1992 peak, federal government payroll reductions alone resulted in a $2.1 billion direct reduction in earnings in the state by 1997.

Employment and Earnings by Sector

	1980	1989	1990	1991	1992	1993	1994	1995	1996	1997 Number	1997 Percent of total	Change*
Employment *(thousands of persons)*												
Total	12 777	16 578	16 955	16 907	16 554	16 532	16 736	17 102	17 586	18 006	100.0	1.0
Farm	281	275	262	272	252	266	258	278	288	274	1.5	0.0
Nonfarm	12 495	16 303	16 692	16 634	16 302	16 267	16 477	16 824	17 299	17 732	98.5	1.1
Private nonfarm	10 397	13 916	14 246	14 190	13 869	13 871	14 090	14 442	14 919	15 340	85.2	1.2
Agricultural service, forestry, and fishing	206	282	295	298	301	324	349	361	389	400	2.2	4.5
Mining	54	58	57	58	53	50	50	45	42	42	0.2	-4.0
Construction	568	902	894	815	746	714	737	767	789	837	4.6	-0.9
Manufacturing	2 076	2 226	2 193	2 112	1 980	1 905	1 895	1 897	1 957	2 022	11.2	-1.2
Transportation and public utilities	593	685	715	723	700	723	738	747	773	806	4.5	2.0
Wholesale trade	629	839	851	826	822	784	792	825	832	856	4.8	0.3
Retail trade	2 007	2 625	2 676	2 654	2 625	2 623	2 682	2 754	2 816	2 867	15.9	1.1
Finance, insurance, and real estate	1 143	1 414	1 432	1 406	1 363	1 363	1 373	1 353	1 381	1 435	8.0	0.2
Services	3 122	4 885	5 132	5 298	5 280	5 384	5 476	5 691	5 940	6 077	33.8	2.8
Government	2 098	2 387	2 446	2 444	2 432	2 396	2 387	2 383	2 380	2 392	13.3	0.0
Earnings *(millions of dollars)*												
Total	207 494	435 992	469 356	476 910	498 151	506 521	517 994	539 342	567 591	607 447	100.0	4.2
Farm	5 742	6 808	7 006	5 890	6 706	7 780	6 813	6 412	7 121	6 864	1.1	0.1
Nonfarm	201 752	429 184	462 350	471 019	491 445	498 741	511 181	532 930	560 470	600 584	98.9	4.3
Private nonfarm	168 785	364 089	390 826	394 781	412 025	418 958	429 511	449 409	475 718	512 637	84.4	4.4
Agricultural service, forestry, and fishing	1 649	3 975	4 684	4 687	4 996	5 191	5 465	5 630	5 861	6 305	1.0	5.9
Mining	2 006	2 038	2 170	2 284	2 286	2 271	2 098	2 054	2 056	2 230	0.4	1.1
Construction	13 049	29 843	30 337	26 974	25 140	24 001	25 983	26 989	28 134	30 950	5.1	0.5
Manufacturing	43 722	78 529	80 851	81 367	81 638	80 613	81 727	83 683	87 956	96 313	15.9	2.6
Transportation and public utilities	14 428	25 295	27 173	28 607	29 735	31 578	32 625	34 132	35 694	38 447	6.3	5.4
Wholesale trade	13 319	27 770	29 864	29 669	30 995	30 100	31 579	33 356	35 054	37 606	6.2	3.9
Retail trade	21 863	42 934	44 961	45 238	46 377	46 823	48 542	49 943	51 460	54 489	9.0	3.0
Finance, insurance, and real estate	13 635	31 044	32 858	33 375	38 577	41 866	40 951	42 437	45 554	49 734	8.2	6.1
Services	45 116	122 661	137 929	142 581	152 280	156 514	160 540	171 185	183 949	196 565	32.4	6.1
Government	32 967	65 095	71 524	76 239	79 420	79 783	81 670	83 522	84 752	87 946	14.5	3.8

*Compound annual average percent change, 1989–1997

ECONOMIC STRUCTURE (Continued)

AVERAGE WAGES FOR THE ENTIRE STATE ECONOMY WERE 10.7 percent above national averages in 1997. The service sector displayed the highest wage relative to the U.S. figure, averaging 17 percent above national levels because of the large business and technology services components in California. Retail trade and government also paid relatively high average wages, at 13 to 14 percent above the U.S. average, and very high wages in the finance sector reflect major headquarters operations in the state. Manufacturing wages were 10.7 percent higher than the U.S. average, putting the state at some competitive disadvantage to the neighboring states of Arizona, Nevada, and Oregon. Only in agricultural services wages does California fall short of national averages, because of the lack of higher paying forestry and fishing industries.

The manufacturing sector, which is dominated by durable goods industries (70 percent of all manufacturing earnings), saw consistent job losses from 1989 through 1995, with a slight recovery in 1996–97. Transportation equipment other than motor vehicles (aircraft and ships) was the state's largest manufacturing industry in 1989 but since has been declining, with an earnings decline of 31 percent from 1989 to 1997 in current dollars. In 1997, the leading manufacturing industries were industrial machinery and electronic equipment, whose worker earnings grew 42 percent in three years (1994–97). The shrinkage in manufacturing overall shows up in its declining share of gross state product; by 1996 it was down to a proportion nearly 4 percentage points lower than nationally. Average value of manufacturing output per worker is about the same as the U.S. average.

Exports constituted an important element of demand for California's goods and its economic recovery in the mid-1990s, as exports have increased by one-third in the 1994–97 period. By far the leading exports are electronics and industrial machinery, and these are also the fastest growing major export sectors. About half the exports are to East Asia, with Japan the single largest overseas market. Overall, California is by far the largest exporter in the United States.

Average Annual Wages and Salaries by Sector
(dollars)

	1989	1996	1997 State	1997 U.S.
All wage and salary workers	24 836	31 291	33 003	29 809
Farm	11 778	17 268	18 968	16 442
Nonfarm	25 014	31 496	33 188	29 900
Private nonfarm	24 923	31 208	33 024	29 867
Agricultural service, forestry, and fishing	12 906	14 649	15 733	17 941
Mining	38 570	53 868	58 109	49 800
Construction	28 835	32 600	34 532	31 765
Manufacturing	30 833	39 744	42 479	38 351
Transportation and utilities	31 715	38 696	40 508	38 222
Wholesale trade	30 222	39 380	41 019	39 466
Retail trade	14 879	17 625	18 470	16 206
Finance, insurance, and real estate	31 887	43 440	47 106	44 993
Services	23 672	30 845	32 347	27 588
Government	25 439	32 888	34 000	30 062

Gross State Product and Manufacturing
(millions of dollars, except as noted)

	1989	1994	1995	1996
Gross state product, total	736 662	875 965	913 474	962 696
Manufacturing:				
Millions of dollars	112 188	119 276	125 531	134 179
Percent of total gross state product	15.2	13.6	13.7	13.9
Per worker (dollars)	50 399	62 938	66 179	68 567
New capital expenditures, manufacturing	NA	10 961	12 908	14 093

Exports of Goods
(millions of dollars)

	1994	1995	1996	1997
All goods	78 190	92 038	98 634	103 802
Manufactures	72 795	85 881	92 687	97 881
Agricultural and livestock products	3 216	3 321	3 243	3 458
Other commodities	2 180	2 836	2 704	2 463
Top goods exports, 1997:				
Electric and electronic equipment	19 801	25 932	27 199	27 715
Industrial machinery and computers	17 651	21 216	25 492	26 900
Transportation equipment	11 807	12 420	10 982	12 056
Scientific and measuring instruments	5 399	6 247	7 457	8 470
Food products	4 532	4 953	5 246	5 097

HOUSING

The loss of jobs and out-migration during 1990–97 took a toll on the homebuilding industry in California, where housing production remained well below its 1980s levels. Housing production per capita was substantially lower than the U.S. average throughout this period; the Riverside metro area was the only one in the state in the top 20 areas for building permits in 1997. Sales increases of existing homes lagged the national rates until a 1996–97 recovery. Home prices were flat for most of the decade in most areas, though prices remained very high in major metro areas. Price increases resumed after 1995 and are exploding in certain major markets such as the booming San Jose high-tech area. The state's median price for existing homes was $185,000 in May 1997, and in the San Francisco Bay area it reached $280,000.

Homeownership rates have remained exceptionally low in California, a full 10 points below the U.S. average, with a high percentage of immigrants, high unemployment in the 1990s, and higher than average cost of homes in most areas of the state. Vacancy rates for rental housing are at a healthy, below-average level attributable to continued immigration and a slow expansion of the rental housing stock.

Homeownership Rates: 1989 and 1997

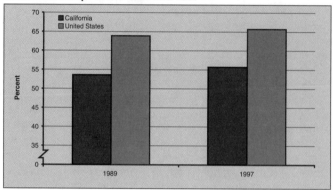

Housing Supply

	1989	1990	1991	1992	1993	1994	1995	1996	1997
Residential building permits (thousands)	237.7	163.2	106.0	97.8	84.3	97.0	83.9	92.1	109.6
New home production (including manufactured housing):									
Thousands of homes	249.0	173.6	112.2	103.4	88.1	100.7	87.1	95.8	114.5
Rate per 1,000 population									
California	8.5	5.8	3.7	3.3	2.8	3.2	2.8	3.0	3.5
U.S.	6.2	5.2	4.5	5.1	5.6	6.4	6.3	6.6	6.5
Existing home sales:									
Thousands of homes	539.3	453.0	425.4	427.3	435.0	482.5	425.6	505.4	555.4
Change from previous year (percent)									
California	-4.1	-16.0	-6.1	0.4	1.8	10.9	-11.8	18.8	9.9
U.S.	-3.9	-4.0	0.0	9.2	8.2	4.8	-3.7	7.5	3.8
Home ownership rate (percent of households)	53.6	53.8	54.5	55.3	56.0	55.5	55.4	55.0	55.7
Rental vacancy rate (percent of rental housing units)	5.9	6.0	6.2	7.5	8.2	7.9	8.5	7.2	6.5

AGRICULTURE

The farm sector of California is the country's biggest by far, with more than $25 billion in cash sales in 1997. There have been modest increases in revenue throughout the 1990s. Vegetable production grew the most; when added to the large fruits and nuts industry, the two generated 51 percent of all farm receipts in the state. However, subtracting the escalating costs of production, net income in 1995–97 averaged 10 percent less (in current dollars) than in the first three years of the decade. Income earned by corporate farms (24 percent of total) was a relatively high share compared to national averages in 1997. The average real estate value of a farm reached nearly $900,000 in California.

CALIFORNIA FARMS, 1997

Number of farms	84 000
Total acres (thousands):	30 000
Average per farm	357
Value of land and buildings (millions of dollars)	75 300
Average per farm (dollars)	896 429

Farm Income
(millions of dollars)

	1980	1989	1990	1991	1992	1993	1994	1995	1996	1997
Gross income	14 554	19 670	20 891	19 374	20 675	22 543	23 132	24 136	25 336	26 560
Receipts from sales	14 148	18 502	19 779	18 180	19 344	21 040	21 927	22 994	23 956	25 228
Government payments	14	372	252	261	430	522	273	240	301	221
Imputed and miscellaneous income	392	795	859	933	900	980	933	902	1 080	1 112
(−) Production expenses	10 809	14 313	15 584	16 121	15 860	17 255	18 080	20 247	21 049	22 700
(=) Realized net income	3 745	5 357	5 306	3 253	4 815	5 288	5 052	3 889	4 287	3 860
(+) Inventory change	298	-56	-285	301	69	-100	94	-254	184	74
(=) Net income	4 043	5 301	5 021	3 554	4 884	5 188	5 146	3 635	4 471	3 934
Corporate income	-1	869	830	446	837	355	1 393	639	1 170	946
Farm proprietors income	4 044	4 432	4 191	3 108	4 047	4 833	3 752	2 996	3 301	2 987

EDUCATION

EDUCATIONAL ATTAINMENT Percent of population age 25 and over, 1997	State	United States
High school graduate or higher	80.7	82.1
College graduate or higher	27.5	23.9

As one of the nation's most affluent areas, California displays high college education achievement levels, with 27.5 percent of its population college graduates. With a historically strong state university system and a dynamic high-tech industry, it ranks ninth in the United States for proportion of the adult population who are college graduates. Current enrollment as a percent of the young adult population is a bit above average. However, it has a smaller than average share of high school graduates, probably reflecting the limited schooling of its large immigrant community. Spending for public elementary and secondary schools has lagged and in 1996 stood at only 83 percent of the average spending nationally, ranking 37th in the nation. Much of the shortfall is attributable to the 1978 "Proposition 13" cap on local property taxes in California.

High School Completion: 1990–97

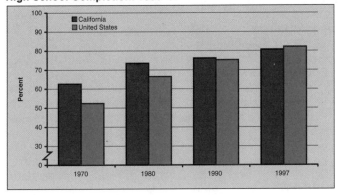

Education Indicators

	State	U.S.
Elementary and secondary schools		
Enrollment, 1995–96		
Total (thousands)	6 166	49 873
Percent in private schools	10.2	10.1
Expenditures per pupil (dollars), 1995–96	5 108	6 146
Average teacher salary (dollars), 1996–97	43 474	38 509
Higher education		
Enrollment, 1996–97		
Total (thousands)	1 883	14 218
Percent of population 18–34	22.5	21.8
Percent minority	48.7	26.1
Percent in private schools	13.7	22.6

HEALTH

Low death rates in the state indicate a fairly healthy population. Infant mortality rates in California are well below national averages, placing the state in the top quartile of states on this measure. This achievement is somewhat surprising given the state's high poverty rates in recent years. Total death rates, even adjusted for the relative youth of the state population, also are consistently lower than the nation's. There is an especially low incidence of death from heart disease and cancer. Apart from the state's well-known image for healthy lifestyle, the concentration of Asian and Hispanic population may reduce the incidence of these diseases. However, more than one-fifth of the population lacks health insurance coverage, a high rate caused by the large immigrant population and the high rate of poverty in the state.

Health Indicators

	1990	1995	1996	1997
Infant mortality				
(rate per thousand live births)				
California	7.9	6.3	6.1	6.0
U.S.	9.2	7.6	7.3	7.1
Total deaths, age-adjusted rate				
(rate per thousand population)				
California	5.0	4.6	4.5	NA
U.S.	5.2	5.0	4.9	4.8
Persons not covered by health insurance				
(percent of population)				
California	19.1	20.6	20.1	21.5
U.S.	13.9	15.4	15.6	16.1

Leading Causes of Death, 1996
(deaths per 100,000 population)

	Age-adjusted		Not age-adjusted	
	State	U.S.	State	U.S.
Deaths from all causes	447.4	491.6	700.9	872.5
Heart disease	117.1	134.5	214.0	276.4
Cancer	114.9	127.9	160.2	203.4
Cerebrovascular diseases	26.3	26.4	51.9	60.3
Chronic obstructive pulmonary disease	21.1	21.0	35.8	40.0
Diabetes mellitus	11.7	13.6	17.0	23.3
Pneumonia and influenza	15.9	12.8	35.0	31.6
HIV	12.4	11.1	13.2	11.7
Liver disease	9.9	7.5	11.1	9.4
Alzheimer's disease	2.4	2.7	6.2	8.1
Accidents and adverse effects	27.1	30.4	29.8	35.8
Motor vehicle accidents	13.0	16.2	13.3	16.5
Suicide	10.0	10.8	10.7	11.6
Homicide	10.3	8.5	9.6	7.9
Injury by firearm	13.2	12.9	12.8	12.8

GOVERNMENT

STATE AND LOCAL TAXES, 1995–96	State	U.S.
Per capita (dollars)	2 522	2 477
Percent of personal income	10.6	10.8

COMBINED STATE AND LOCAL TAX COLLECTIONS WERE 2 PERcent above the national average on a per capita basis in 1995–96, as state income and sales tax collections strengthened. This rate reflected California's above-average incomes; California taxes came to 10.6 percent of personal income that year, slightly below the 10.8 percent average tax rate nationally. The state government collected a higher proportion of the total taxes and the local level saw a lower share than in a typical state, partly because of caps on local property tax levies.

State-level sales and income taxes were somewhat higher than the national average, and California state government also receives a greater amount of federal assistance per capita than average. As a result, general spending at the state level per capita was 8 percent higher than the U.S. norm, but a huge portion of that (48.3 percent) is intergovernmental transfers to the local levels. With the constriction of local property tax revenues after Proposition 13, the state has stepped in to supplement local funds at a rate much higher than that undertaken in the average state. Overall state spending on education and welfare are substantially higher, per capita, than U.S. averages. Spending on administration and interest on general debt are relatively low, as is the accumulated level of debt at the end of fiscal 1997.

California received somewhat less than its proportionate share (by population) of total federal spending in 1997, primarily attributable to its lower share of retirees and federal workers. In the category of Social Security and government retirement, its residents received only 9.6 percent of retirement benefits paid in all states, while the state has 12.1 percent of the U.S. population. The state fared better for receipt of program grants, and bested most states for contract procurement, with 15.5 percent of defense contracting dollars going to state companies, by far the largest share of any state.

State Government Finances, 1996–97

	Millions of dollars	Percent distribution	Dollars per capita State	Dollars per capita U.S.
General revenue	103 929	100.0	3 221	3 049
Intergovernmental revenue	30 345	29.2	940	863
Taxes	61 667	59.3	1 911	1 660
General sales	19 974	19.2	619	551
Selective sales	5 248	5.1	163	257
License taxes	2 963	2.9	92	106
Individual income	23 273	22.4	721	542
Corporation net income	5 804	5.6	180	115
Other taxes	4 406	4.2	137	90
Other general revenue	11 917	11.5	369	526
General expenditure	102 853	100.0	3 187	2 951
Intergovernmental expenditure	49 636	48.3	1 538	989
Direct expenditure	53 217	51.7	1 649	1 962
General expenditure, by function:				
Education	35 546	34.6	1 102	1 033
Public welfare	30 205	29.4	936	761
Hospitals and health	9 001	8.8	279	237
Highways	4 581	4.5	142	225
Police protection and corrections	5 006	4.9	155	137
Natural resources, parks and recreation	2 260	2.2	70	63
Governmental administration	3 164	3.1	98	107
Interest on general debt	2 482	2.4	77	99
Other and unallocable	10 606	10.3	329	290
Debt at end of fiscal year	45 337	NA	1 405	1 706
Cash and security holdings	226 895	NA	7 032	6 683

Federal Spending within State

	Federal funds, fiscal 1997		
	Millions of dollars	Percent distribution	Percent of U.S. total*
Total within state	158 556	100.0	11.2
Payments to individuals	84 043	53.0	10.7
Retirement and disability	43 993	27.7	9.6
Medicare	23 663	14.9	11.5
Food stamps	2 245	1.4	11.5
Supplemental Security Income	3 797	2.4	14.1
Grants	28 885	18.2	11.6
Medicaid and other health	11 657	7.4	10.2
Nutrition and family welfare	5 862	3.7	12.5
Education	1 940	1.2	11.3
Housing and community development	1 060	0.7	9.3
Salaries and wages	17 587	11.1	10.7
Defense procurement contracts	18 508	11.7	15.5
Non-defense procurement contracts	7 737	4.9	10.6

*State population is 12.1 percent of the U.S. total.

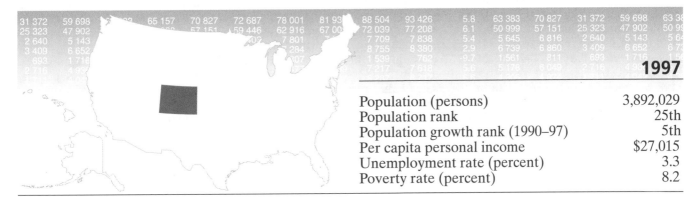

1997

Population (persons)	3,892,029
Population rank	25th
Population growth rank (1990–97)	5th
Per capita personal income	$27,015
Unemployment rate (percent)	3.3
Poverty rate (percent)	8.2

COLORADO INCREASED ITS POPULATION AND EMPLOYMENT base at a tremendous rate during the 1990s, as its appealing lifestyle and strong economy attracted new in-migrants from other states and abroad. Its nearly 18 percent population growth from 1990 to 1997 ranks as fifth fastest in the nation, and total earnings of workers and proprietors rose 80 percent, almost double the U.S. rate. The median household income in 1997 reached a level 17 percent above that of the nation. This is partly attributable to the high proportion of Colorado's population that was of working-age and partly to the high percentage of adults who were working in 1997, about 70 percent. In contrast, Coloradans received less in government transfer payments than average.

The state's profile as a mining and ranching center, complemented by skiing and other outdoor tourism, has evolved into an economy more similar to that of the nation and dominated by a services sector that includes computer services, health care, engineering, and management. The construction and real estate industries have boomed during the 1990s because of the strong influx of new households as well as the rising affluence of existing ones. The state's flavor also changed as minorities, mainly Hispanics, continued to grow as a proportion of total population, reaching 21 percent in 1997, compared to 13 percent in 1980.

Average Annual Population Growth: 1990–97

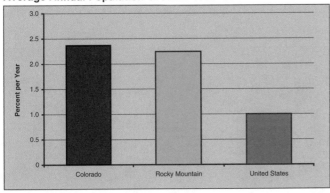

Median Household Income: 1989–97 (1997 dollars)

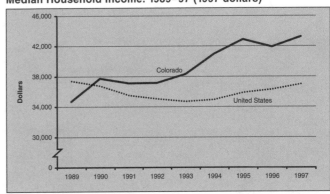

Unemployment Rate: 1989–97

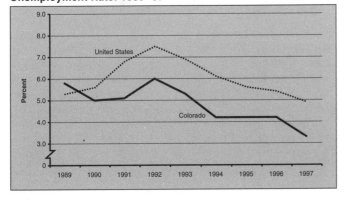

THOUGH ITS POPULATION AND LABOR FORCE HAVE GROWN substantially during the 1990s, Colorado's unemployment rate has declined fairly consistently from its decade high point of 6 percent in 1992. Reaching 3.3 percent in 1997, the state's unemployment was the eighth lowest in the nation, well below the U.S. average of 4.9 percent. The extraordinary expansion in the number of employed workers, which averaged 3.2 percent annual growth in 1990–97, boosted the ratio of employment to adult population up to nearly 70 percent in 1997, well above the national average.

POPULATION AND LABOR FORCE

DURING THE 1990S, COLORADO UNDERWENT TREMENDOUS population growth, led by strong domestic in-migration, which added 10 percent to the state's 1990 population. While Colorado's birth rate of 14.5 remained consistent with the U.S. birth rate of 14.6, the state's death rate of 6.6 was well below the national rate of 8.7, a condition that contributed to the state's rapid population growth. The state's popularity as a place with an excellent quality of life as well as plentiful jobs gave Colorado the eighth highest net domestic in-migration in the country from 1990 to 1997. The population growth of 2.4 percent annually from 1990 to 1997 was fifth highest in the nation and well above the national average of 1.0 percent. Colorado's ranking moved up from 26th to 25th largest state. These high rates of growth were most evident in the Asian and Hispanic communities. Both populations have significantly increased their proportions of Colorado's total population, starting in the 1980s. While the largest absolute growth was among the White non-Hispanic population, its proportion of the total population dropped to 79 percent.

Population and Labor Force

	1980	1990	1991	1992	1993	1994	1995	1996	1997	Change*	
										State	U.S.
Population											
Total number of persons (thousands)	2 890	3 304	3 368	3 461	3 562	3 654	3 738	3 814	3 892	2.4	1.0
Percent distribution:											
White, Non-Hispanic	82.9	80.6	80.5	80.3	80.0	79.8	79.6	79.3	79.0	2.1	0.4
Black, Non-Hispanic	3.5	4.1	3.9	4.0	4.0	4.0	4.0	3.9	3.9	1.6	1.4
Asian	1.2	1.9	1.9	2.0	2.1	2.1	2.2	2.3	2.3	5.3	4.1
Native American	0.7	0.9	0.9	0.9	0.9	0.9	0.9	0.9	0.9	2.3	1.6
Hispanic	11.8	12.9	13.1	13.2	13.4	13.6	13.8	14.0	14.3	3.9	3.8
In metropolitan areas	83.3	84.4	84.4	84.5	84.5	84.3	84.1	84.0	84.0	2.3	1.0
Total number of households (thousands)	1 061	1 282	1 306	1 348	1 388	1 424	1 466	1 502	NA	2.7	1.2
Labor Force (thousands)											
Population 16 and over	2 185	2 509	2 561	2 630	2 714	2 795	2 868	2 932	2 993	2.6	1.0
Civilian labor force	1 500	1 764	1 782	1 820	1 900	2 001	2 088	2 093	2 152	2.9	1.1
Employed	1 412	1 675	1 691	1 710	1 800	1 917	2 000	2 005	2 081	3.2	1.2
Percent of population	64.6	66.8	66.0	65.0	66.3	68.6	69.7	68.4	69.5		
Unemployment rate (percent)	5.9	5.0	5.1	6.0	5.3	4.2	4.2	4.2	3.3		

*Compound annual average percent change, 1990–1997; 1990–1996 for households.

Population Change and Components: 1990–97

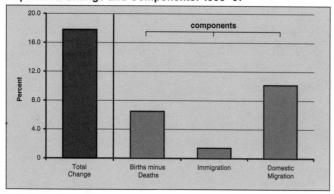

Average Annual Household and Population Growth

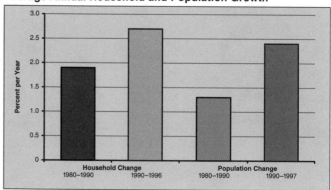

Population by Age; Births and Deaths

	1990		1997	
	State	U.S.	State	U.S.
Age distribution (percent)				
Under 5 years	7.9	7.6	7.0	7.2
5 to 17 years	18.8	18.2	19.1	18.8
18 to 64 years	63.3	61.8	63.8	61.3
65 years and over	10.0	12.5	10.1	12.7
Birth and death rates (per thousand population)				
Births	16.2	16.7	14.5	14.6
Deaths	6.5	8.6	6.6	8.6

THE PROPORTION OF PEOPLE IN COLORADO BETWEEN THE ages of 18 and 64 was 63.8 percent, significantly higher than the national percentage of 61.3, and apparently growing because of in-migration in this age segment. Though the percentage of the population over 65 increased slightly from 1990 to 1997, its proportion of 10.1 percent was well below the national 12.7 percent. The state had slightly more school-age children than average but a smaller than average proportion of children under age five.

HOUSEHOLD AND PERSONAL INCOME

HOUSEHOLD INCOME AND PERSONS IN POVERTY	1990	1995	1996	1997 State	1997 U.S.
Median household income (1997 dollars)	37 740	42 870	41 890	43 233	37 005
Persons in poverty (thousands)	461	335	412	320	35 574
Poverty rate (percent)	13.7	8.8	10.6	8.2	13.3

IN 1997, COLORADO'S MEDIAN HOUSEHOLD INCOME WAS $43,233, and the sixth highest in the nation. In contrast, the state's median income was 29th in the nation in 1989. Real income growth in Colorado averaged 2.8 percent per year, versus a decline nationwide. This growth is a reflection of Colorado's economic success during the 1990s, which has also contributed to a substantial decrease in the poverty rate. With Wisconsin, the state's 1997 poverty rate of 8.2 percent was the lowest poverty rate in the nation.

Growth in real personal income per capita in Colorado also was nearly 18 percent from 1989 to 1997, (compared to 10 percent nationwide). All components of income grew rapidly, except farm income. In 1997, the state's per capita income was nearly 7 percent higher than the national average, led by earnings that were 12 percent above average. In contrast, transfer payments were rela- tively small, 16 percent below average, while dividend and interest income was 9 percent above the national average per capita.

Transfer payments in Colorado grew nearly 73 percent from 1990 to 1997, not surprising given the rapid population growth. Even though the retiree population was relatively small, this group grew rapidly and increased the size of retirement payments in the state. Other income maintenance, consisting mostly of earned income tax credits, grew explosively and became much larger than the dwindling family assistance and food stamp programs. However, Supplemental Security Income nearly doubled during this period, paralleling a national increase. Unemployment insurance benefits increased much less than the national average, reflecting Colorado's low unemployment rate.

Personal Income
(millions of dollars)

	1980	1989	1990	1991	1992	1993	1994	1995	1996	1997	Change*
Earnings by place of work	23 975	43 387	46 757	49 560	53 844	58 784	62 238	67 091	72 062	78 151	7.6
Wages and salaries	19 450	34 681	37 148	39 574	42 733	45 801	48 969	52 883	57 178	62 484	7.6
Other labor income	1 735	3 448	3 862	4 351	4 818	5 332	5 665	5 744	5 795	5 980	7.1
Proprietors' income	2 790	5 258	5 747	5 635	6 293	7 651	7 604	8 465	9 088	9 687	7.9
Farm	138	454	723	465	446	768	231	263	361	375	-2.4
Nonfarm	2 652	4 804	5 024	5 170	5 848	6 883	7 373	8 202	8 727	9 312	8.6
(−) Personal contributions for social insurance	1 209	2 725	2 920	3 186	3 431	3 723	4 019	4 360	4 672	5 084	8.1
(+) Adjustment for residence	27	62	81	80	81	47	38	61	64	63	NA
(=) **Net earnings by state of residence**	22 793	40 723	43 918	46 453	50 494	55 109	58 257	62 793	67 454	73 129	7.6
(+) Dividends, interest, and rent	5 093	11 345	11 938	12 457	12 447	13 157	14 786	15 844	17 426	18 434	6.3
(+) Transfer payments	3 378	7 256	7 877	8 787	9 749	10 517	11 071	12 248	12 884	13 595	8.2
(=) **Total personal income**	31 264	59 325	63 733	67 698	72 690	78 783	84 115	90 884	97 764	105 158	7.4
Farm	288	616	910	643	624	964	481	535	633	667	1.0
Nonfarm	30 976	58 709	62 823	67 054	72 067	77 819	83 634	90 349	97 131	104 491	7.5
Personal income per capita (dollars)											
Current dollars	10 748	18 110	19 290	20 096	20 998	22 109	23 001	24 290	25 618	27 015	5.1
1997 dollars	20 551	22 895	23 213	23 206	23 488	24 058	24 443	25 249	26 088	27 015	2.1

*Compound annual average percent change, 1989–1997

Government Transfer Payments

	Millions of dollars 1990	Millions of dollars 1997	Percent change* State	Percent change* U.S.
Total government payments to individuals	7 448	12 852	72.6	62.7
Retirement, disability, and insurance	4 632	7 313	57.9	48.2
Social Security	2 547	4 104	61.1	46.1
Government employee retirement	1 676	2 712	61.8	60.3
Medical payments	1 713	3 903	127.8	101.2
Income maintenance	544	906	66.7	58.0
Supplemental Security Income	153	298	95.4	75.4
Family assistance	144	128	-10.8	-0.5
Food Stamps	163	175	7.4	27.1
Other income maintenance	84	304	262.7	189.8
Unemployment insurance benefits	164	167	1.5	10.6
Veterans benefits and other	395	563	42.5	30.8

*Percent change, 1990–1997

Government Payments to Individuals: 1997

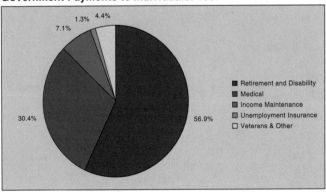

- ■ Retirement and Disability
- ■ Medical
- ■ Income Maintenance
- ▨ Unemployment Insurance
- ☐ Veterans & Other

56.9% 30.4% 7.1% 1.3% 4.4%

ECONOMIC STRUCTURE

LEADING PRIVATE INDUSTRIES, 1997 (Worker and proprietor earnings, millions of dollars)		FASTEST EARNINGS GROWTH, 1989–97 (percent increase)	
Business services	$6 501	Amusement and recreation services	189.4
Health services	5 384	Security brokers	179.1
Construction specialties	3 747	Real estate	176.0
Communications	3 643	Construction specialties	156.7
Engineering and management services	3 390	Business services	153.7

COLORADO'S LEADING INDUSTRIES WERE BUSINESS AND health services. The services sector played an even more central role than in a typical state, with three of the leading industries and 32.3 percent of all jobs in services. The fastest growing industry from 1989 to 1997 was amusement and recreational services, indicating vigorous growth in the state's tourism industry. However, the state saw rapid growth in better paying service sectors such as engineering and computer services. For example, IBM Corp. has a major presence in Denver, and Sun Microsystems is expanding into the state. Industrial machinery and equipment was the only manufacturing industry among Colorado's fifteen leading private industries, and manufacturing continued to be a small element in the state's economy, contributing a one-third smaller proportion of jobs (8.2 percent) than the U.S. average. Manufacturing's earnings and employment have both grown at a lower rate than the state's totals. Construction and agricultural services had the fastest growing employment of all the major sectors. Construction employed 83.9 percent more people in 1997 than it did in 1989, growing more than four times faster than in the nation and contributing to rapid earnings growth in real estate. The federal civilian and military work force was a bit larger than average in Colorado, but its proportion of total earnings in the state has declined from 6.3 percent in 1989 to 4.6 percent in 1997.

Employment and Earnings by Sector

	1980	1989	1990	1991	1992	1993	1994	1995	1996	1997 Number	1997 Percent of total	Change*
Employment *(thousands of persons)*												
Total	1 654	2 019	2 052	2 105	2 154	2 252	2 368	2 464	2 551	2 652	100.0	3.5
Farm	46	44	44	39	39	39	39	35	37	40	1.5	-1.3
Nonfarm	1 608	1 975	2 009	2 065	2 115	2 213	2 330	2 429	2 514	2 612	98.5	3.6
Private nonfarm	1 315	1 648	1 676	1 727	1 767	1 861	1 978	2 076	2 160	2 253	85.0	4.0
Agricultural service, forestry, and fishing	13	19	20	21	21	24	29	30	31	34	1.3	7.3
Mining	43	32	31	31	28	27	28	26	23	23	0.9	-4.3
Construction	102	94	97	103	115	127	145	154	164	173	6.5	7.9
Manufacturing	185	198	197	195	196	196	202	206	211	218	8.2	1.2
Transportation and public utilities	85	104	107	111	112	119	126	132	138	142	5.4	4.0
Wholesale trade	80	90	91	94	96	98	102	106	108	113	4.3	2.9
Retail trade	275	336	343	354	365	383	417	441	456	470	17.7	4.3
Finance, insurance, and real estate	160	185	180	177	177	187	184	195	208	224	8.4	2.4
Services	371	590	609	641	658	699	745	785	820	856	32.3	4.8
Government	294	327	333	338	348	353	352	353	355	359	13.5	1.2
Earnings *(millions of dollars)*												
Total	23 975	43 387	46 757	49 560	53 844	58 784	62 238	67 091	72 062	78 151	100.0	7.6
Farm	288	616	910	643	624	964	481	535	633	667	0.9	1.0
Nonfarm	23 687	42 771	45 847	48 917	53 220	57 820	61 757	66 556	71 429	77 484	99.1	7.7
Private nonfarm	19 510	34 973	37 495	39 945	43 672	47 827	51 463	55 807	60 332	65 892	84.3	8.2
Agricultural service, forestry, and fishing	102	232	257	272	312	352	396	422	452	502	0.6	10.1
Mining	1 334	1 090	1 095	1 148	1 143	1 240	1 208	1 308	1 351	1 457	1.9	3.7
Construction	1 946	2 368	2 510	2 792	2 792	3 863	4 456	4 749	5 279	5 736	7.3	11.7
Manufacturing	3 798	6 334	6 536	6 829	7 177	7 362	7 601	8 089	8 649	9 276	11.9	4.9
Transportation and public utilities	1 996	3 911	4 348	4 591	4 887	5 601	5 850	6 371	6 833	7 397	9.5	8.3
Wholesale trade	1 652	2 645	2 866	2 992	3 228	3 374	3 685	3 992	4 273	4 750	6.1	7.6
Retail trade	2 615	4 263	4 490	4 825	5 207	5 655	6 214	6 678	7 105	7 647	9.8	7.6
Finance, insurance, and real estate	1 535	2 845	3 013	3 193	3 828	4 493	4 630	5 116	5 637	6 255	8.0	10.3
Services	4 533	11 284	12 380	13 305	14 608	15 887	17 424	19 083	20 753	22 873	29.3	9.2
Government	4 177	7 797	8 352	8 971	9 548	9 993	10 294	10 749	11 097	11 592	14.8	5.1

*Compound annual average percent change, 1989–1997

ECONOMIC STRUCTURE (Continued)

THE AVERAGE WAGE IN COLORADO IN 1997, AT $29,506 ANNU-ally, was just below the national average of $29,809. In nearly every sector, wages were very close to the U.S. average; finance, insurance, and real estate was the only major sector with significantly lower average wages, which were less than 85 percent of the average. In the dominant services sector, wages averaged 2 percent above those of the nation, and in retail trade the wage advantage was 3 percent. Mining wages were 116 percent higher than the national average, and farm wages were nearly 109 percent of average. Farm wages showed the most dramatic change from 1989 to 1997, increasing by nearly 90 percent.

The value of output in manufacturing has been increasing more slowly than gross state product (GSP) since 1989. In 1996, it comprised just 12.2 percent of GSP, down from 12.9 percent in 1989. This is well below the U.S. average of 17.5 percent and places the state in the lowest quartile of states for percent of output within manufacturing. Colorado's manufacturing value added per worker remained slightly lower than the U.S. average. The state's leading manufacturing industry was industrial machinery and equipment, which was also its fastest growing major manufacturing industry. Next largest were printing and publishing and instruments manufacturing. New capital expenditures have remained fairly steady from 1994 to 1996.

Revenue generated from Colorado's exports grew by more than 45 percent from 1994 to 1997. The leading export in 1997 was industrial machinery and computers. Exports of electric and electronic equipment have more than doubled from 1994 to 1997 and were the fastest growing leading export during this period. Since 1994, food products have replaced scientific and measuring products as the third largest export.

Average Annual Wages and Salaries by Sector
(dollars)

	1989	1996	1997 State	1997 U.S.
All wage and salary workers	21 472	28 113	29 506	29 809
Farm	9 450	20 340	17 872	16 442
Nonfarm	21 593	28 161	29 590	29 900
Private nonfarm	21 470	28 064	29 598	29 867
Agricultural service, forestry, and fishing	13 132	17 834	18 527	17 941
Mining	41 962	55 624	57 780	49 800
Construction	23 632	29 868	31 099	31 765
Manufacturing	28 903	36 998	38 626	38 351
Transportation and utilities	30 467	39 817	42 519	38 222
Wholesale trade	27 745	37 768	40 248	39 466
Retail trade	12 175	15 889	16 709	16 206
Finance, insurance, and real estate	24 811	36 093	38 046	44 993
Services	19 537	26 594	28 077	27 588
Government	22 069	28 618	29 551	30 062

Gross State Product and Manufacturing
(millions of dollars, except as noted)

	1989	1994	1995	1996
Gross state product, total	69 588	100 712	107 903	116 227
Manufacturing:				
Millions of dollars	8 964	12 674	13 257	14 226
Percent of total gross state product	12.9	12.6	12.3	12.2
Per worker (dollars)	45 321	62 829	64 238	67 523
New capital expenditures, manufacturing	NA	1 590	1 502	1 528

Exports of Goods
(millions of dollars)

	1994	1995	1996	1997
All goods	7 802	9 689	10 065	11 329
Manufactures	7 641	9 423	9 824	11 057
Agricultural and livestock products	33	35	32	42
Other commodities	127	230	209	231
Top goods exports, 1997:				
Industrial machinery and computers	4 622	5 650	5 574	5 492
Electric and electronic equipment	1 293	1 743	2 031	2 965
Food products	450	540	612	830
Scientific and measuring instruments	574	623	691	760
Fabricated metal products	92	106	168	200

HOUSING

New home production in Colorado increased tremendously from 1990 to 1997 reflecting the rapid expansion of population and incomes. In 1990, the rate of home production per 1,000 residents was 3.9, well below the U.S. rate, but it accelerated sharply in 1992–93. It was almost double the national rate of production in 1994–97 and led to a boom in the construction industry. Sales of existing homes increased rapidly in 1992–93 but declined in 1994–95 when new construction surged. A moderate recovery in sales occurred in 1996–97. The median home price in 1997 in Denver was $140,600, well above the U.S. average but still lower than that for the western region. The state's homeownership rate also increased significantly during this period, reaching 64.1 percent. Apparently a number of in-migrants were able to afford to buy homes in the Colorado market, though the homeownership rate in 1997 was still the 13th lowest rate in the nation. Rental vacancy rates remained low after 1991; the 1997 rate of 3.7 percent was the lowest in the nation.

Homeownership Rates: 1989 and 1997

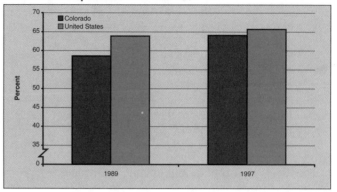

Housing Supply

	1989	1990	1991	1992	1993	1994	1995	1996	1997
Residential building permits (thousands)	11.1	11.9	14.1	23.5	29.9	37.2	38.6	41.1	43.1
New home production (including manufactured housing):									
Thousands of homes	11.8	12.8	15.2	25.0	32.6	41.0	42.5	45.6	48.3
Rate per 1,000 population									
Colorado	3.6	3.9	4.5	7.2	9.1	11.2	11.4	11.9	12.4
U.S.	6.2	5.2	4.5	5.1	5.6	6.4	6.3	6.6	6.5
Existing home sales:									
Thousands of homes	53.9	54.2	59.6	71.4	82.1	80.6	76.9	81.6	86.6
Change from previous year (percent)									
Colorado	-11.5	0.6	10.0	19.8	15.0	-1.8	-4.6	6.1	6.1
U.S.	-3.9	-4.0	0.0	9.2	8.2	4.8	-3.7	7.5	3.8
Home ownership rate (percent of households)	58.6	59.0	59.8	60.9	61.8	62.9	64.6	64.5	64.1
Rental vacancy rate (percent of rental housing units)	12.4	10.2	5.8	5.8	4.9	5.3	4.3	6.1	3.7

AGRICULTURE

Colorado ranked 30th in the nation for total number of farms. The average Colorado farm had 1,327 acres (well above the national average of 471), and the average farm was worth more than $780,000. This figure was well above the national average value. Colorado's gross farm income increased by only 14.3 percent from 1989 to 1997. During this same time period, production expenses increased by 23.2 percent. As a result, the net income has been somewhat lower in recent years than in the early 1990s. More than 70 percent of Colorado's farm revenue was derived from livestock and livestock products, with the balance in crops. Crop income has increased by nearly 20 percent since 1990, while livestock income has been flat.

COLORADO FARMS, 1997

Number of farms	24 500
Total acres (thousands):	32 500
Average per farm	1 327
Value of land and buildings (millions of dollars)	19 175
Average per farm (dollars)	782 653

Farm Income
(millions of dollars)

	1980	1989	1990	1991	1992	1993	1994	1995	1996	1997
Gross income	3 495	4 519	4 908	4 350	4 497	5 004	4 733	4 908	4 874	5 165
Receipts from sales	3 353	4 069	4 416	3 850	4 050	4 484	4 280	4 437	4 359	4 649
Government payments	18	183	237	217	203	250	177	168	176	176
Imputed and miscellaneous income	124	267	255	283	244	270	276	304	339	340
(−) Production expenses	3 407	3 795	4 046	3 880	3 935	4 183	4 340	4 552	4 510	4 675
(=) Realized net income	88	724	862	470	562	822	393	356	364	490
(+) Inventory change	50	-147	64	89	19	26	-27	-10	198	68
(=) Net income	138	577	926	559	582	847	366	346	562	558
Corporate income	0	123	203	94	136	79	135	83	200	183
Farm proprietors income	138	454	723	465	446	768	231	263	361	375

EDUCATION

EDUCATIONAL ATTAINMENT Percent of population age 25 and over, 1997	State	United States
High school graduate or higher	87.6	82.1
College graduate or higher	28.9	23.9

COLORADO HAD AMONG THE HIGHEST EDUCATION ATTAINMENT levels in the nation in 1997. More than 87 percent of the state's adults were high school graduates, which ranked Colorado eighth in the nation. Nearly 29 percent of the state's adults were college graduates, which placed Colorado fifth in the nation. While both percentages were increases from 1990, they both marked a drop in state's rankings among all states. Colorado's economic prosperity attracted well-educated in-migrants as well as generating resources for education. Both average teacher's salary and per pupil expenditures were below the U.S. average. Expenditures per pupil were depressed partly by the sheer growth in the student age population, up about 20 percent in 1990–97, and the slower growth for school budgets. The percentage of young adults age 18 to 34 enrolled in Colorado's postsecondary institutions was above the U.S. average, and Colorado had a significantly lower percentage of its postsecondary students in private schools than the national rate.

High School Completion: 1990–97

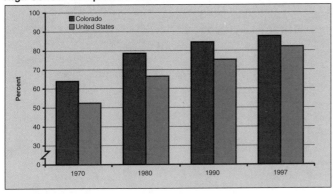

Education Indicators

	State	U.S.
Elementary and secondary schools		
Enrollment, 1995–96		
Total (thousands)	705	49 873
Percent in private schools	6.9	10.1
Expenditures per pupil (dollars), 1995–96	5 521	6 146
Average teacher salary (dollars), 1996–97	36 175	38 509
Higher education		
Enrollment, 1996–97		
Total (thousands)	243	14 218
Percent of population 18–34	26.6	21.8
Percent minority	18.2	26.1
Percent in private schools	13.9	22.6

HEALTH

GENERALLY, THE HEALTH OF COLORADO'S POPULATION seemed to be about equal to the national average. In 1997, Colorado's infant mortality rate remained steady at 7.6, just above the national average. The percentage of the state's population without health insurance remained fairly steady and was just below the national average of 16.1 percent. The total death rate remained well below the national rate. The age-adjusted death rates for major diseases were below average, with the exceptions of chronic obstructive pulmonary disease and Alzheimer's disease. The state's suicide death rate was well above the national average. Accidents and adverse effects, injuries by firearms, and motor vehicle death rates were all higher than the national rate.

Health Indicators

	1990	1995	1996	1997
Infant mortality *(rate per thousand live births)*				
Colorado	8.8	6.5	7.6	7.6
U.S.	9.2	7.6	7.3	7.1
Total deaths, age-adjusted rate *(rate per thousand population)*				
Colorado	4.5	4.4	4.3	4.2
U.S.	5.2	5.0	4.9	4.8
Persons not covered by health insurance *(percent of population)*				
Colorado	14.7	14.8	16.6	15.1
U.S.	13.9	15.4	15.6	16.1

Leading Causes of Death, 1996
(deaths per 100,000 population)

	Age-adjusted		Not age-adjusted	
	State	U.S.	State	U.S.
Deaths from all causes	432.0	491.6	672.9	872.5
Heart disease	98.2	134.5	172.6	276.4
Cancer	105.9	127.9	147.9	203.4
Cerebrovascular diseases	22.0	26.4	43.9	60.3
Chronic obstructive pulmonary disease	27.1	21.0	43.3	40.0
Diabetes mellitus	9.6	13.6	14.4	23.3
Pneumonia and influenza	12.5	12.8	25.7	31.6
HIV	5.7	11.1	6.4	11.7
Liver disease	7.3	7.5	8.9	9.4
Alzheimer's disease	3.2	2.7	7.7	8.1
Accidents and adverse effects	32.5	30.4	37.4	35.8
Motor vehicle accidents	17.6	16.2	17.5	16.5
Suicide	16.8	10.8	18.2	11.6
Homicide	5.9	8.5	5.6	7.9
Injury by firearm	13.6	12.9	14.0	12.8

GOVERNMENT

STATE AND LOCAL TAXES, 1995–96	State	U.S.
Per capita (dollars)	2 364	2 477
Percent of personal income	10.1	10.8

COLORADO'S TOTAL STATE AND LOCAL TAXES IN 1995–96 totaled $2,364 per capita, which represented 10.1 percent of personal income, below the national average. Nearly 49 percent of these taxes were local, indicating higher than average local-level taxes.

In 1997, total state government general revenue amounted to $2,555 per capita, lower than the national average because of lower intergovernmental revenue and lower taxes. Colorado's state taxes amounted to $1,359 per capita, as compared to $1,660 nationwide. Taxes on corporation net income of $58 per capita were significantly lower than the $115 nationally. General sales taxes also were relatively low. However, Colorado's individual income taxes per capita were 21 percent above average and accounted for more than 20 percent of the state's tax revenues, reflecting the high income levels in the state. Colorado's per capita state debt in 1997 was only half the national average, as a result of the state's history of fiscally conservative state government.

Federal spending in the state was above average in personnel and procurement areas and below average for other categories. Retirement and Medicare spending were low, because of the small retired population, and the state's affluence limited its receipt of needs-based grants-in-aid. The state's 2.1 percent share of salaries and wages was well above the state's 1.5 percent of the U.S. population.

State Government Finances, 1996–97

	Millions of dollars	Percent distribution	Dollars per capita State	Dollars per capita U.S.
General revenue	9 945	100.0	2 555	3 049
Intergovernmental revenue	2 596	26.1	667	863
Taxes	5 290	53.2	1 359	1 660
General sales	1 413	14.2	363	551
Selective sales	766	7.7	197	257
License taxes	261	2.6	67	106
Individual income	2 560	25.7	658	542
Corporation net income	224	2.3	58	115
Other taxes	65	0.7	17	90
Other general revenue	2 059	20.7	529	526
General expenditure	9 381	100.0	2 410	2 951
Intergovernmental expenditure	3 017	32.2	775	989
Direct expenditure	6 364	67.8	1 635	1 962
General expenditure, by function:				
Education	4 192	44.7	1 077	1 033
Public welfare	2 221	23.7	570	761
Hospitals and health	393	4.2	101	237
Highways	810	8.6	208	225
Police protection and corrections	511	5.4	131	137
Natural resources, parks and recreation	199	2.1	51	63
Governmental administration	334	3.6	86	107
Interest on general debt	236	2.5	61	99
Other and unallocable	487	5.2	125	290
Debt at end of fiscal year	3 402	NA	874	1 706
Cash and security holdings	23 591	NA	6 060	6 683

Federal Spending within State

	Federal funds, fiscal 1997		
	Millions of dollars	Percent distribution	Percent of U.S. total*
Total within state	19 629	100.0	1.4
Payments to individuals	9 467	48.2	1.2
Retirement and disability	6 092	31.0	1.3
Medicare	2 087	10.6	1.0
Food stamps	182	0.9	0.9
Supplemental Security Income	249	1.3	0.9
Grants	2 871	14.6	1.2
Medicaid and other health	1 128	5.7	1.0
Nutrition and family welfare	483	2.5	1.0
Education	197	1.0	1.1
Housing and community development	89	0.5	0.8
Salaries and wages	3 386	17.2	2.1
Defense procurement contracts	1 896	9.7	1.6
Non-defense procurement contracts	1 597	8.1	2.2

*State population is 1.5 percent of the U.S. total.

31 372	59 698		65 157	70 827	72 687	78 001	81 93	88 504	93 426	5.8	63 383	70 827	31 372	59 698	63 38
25 323	47 902			57 151	59 446	62 916	67 00	72 039	77 208	6.1	50 999	57 151	25 323	47 902	50 99
2 640	5 143				7 801		7 709	7 838	5.4	5 645	6 816	2 640	5 143	5 64
3 409	6 652				284		8 755	8 390	2.9	6 739	6 860	3 409	6 652	6 7
693	1 716				307		1 539	762	-9.7	1 561	811	693	1 716	1 5
2 716	4						7 217	7 618	5.6	9 178	6 049	2 716	4	

1997

Population (persons)	3,267,240
Population rank	28th
Population growth rank (1990–97)	49th
Per capita personal income	$35,954
Unemployment rate (percent)	5.1
Poverty rate (percent)	8.6

CONNECTICUT, LIKE SEVERAL OTHER NEW ENGLAND STATES, has experienced declines in manufacturing, an aging population, and a growing demand on social services. In addition, it was one of only two states to experience a decrease in population from 1990–1997; Rhode Island was the other. Population also declined in the District of Columbia. Connecticut's decline averaged 0.1 percent per year, and was caused by domestic out-migration. Median household income remained higher than the national median from 1989 to 1997, but declined thoughout the period, especially from 1989 to 1993. In 1997, as a result, the income of the family at the middle of the state's income distribution was down to 19 percent above the

U.S. average level. Transfer payments were the fastest growing component of aggregate personal incomes, with medical payments and food stamps growing at double-digit rates. Housing trends reflected demographics in the state, with new housing construction and sales of existing homes at lower rates than in the country as a whole.

Manufacturing became less important to the state over the 1990s, falling from almost 20 percent of gross state product in 1989 to 16.7 percent in 1996. Services and finance, insurance, and real estate grew quite quickly in the decade, with these two sectors dominating the top five fastest growing industries in the state from 1989 to 1997.

Average Annual Population Growth: 1990–97

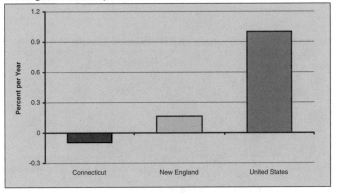

Median Household Income: 1989–97 (1997 dollars)

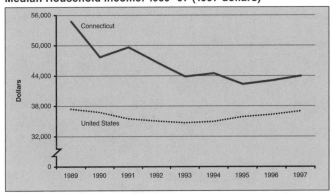

Unemployment Rate: 1989–97

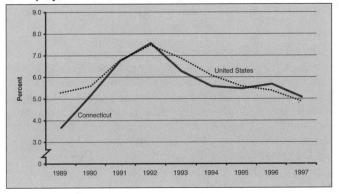

UNEMPLOYMENT RATES IN CONNECTICUT ROUGHLY PARALleled those in the United States as a whole throughout the 1990s. Reflecting the decrease in population in the state and an increasingly elderly population, the labor force contracted almost 1 percent per year from 1990 to 1997. As a result, the unemployment rate was virtually unchanged between those two years despite a similar percentage decline in employment.

POPULATION AND LABOR FORCE

THOUGH ALL OF THE NEW ENGLAND STATES HAD LOWER than average population growth, Connecticut's total population actually fell, at a rate of 0.1 percent per year. This decline, despite higher than average growth in the small Asian population, was caused by a drop in the White non-Hispanic population and slower than average growth in the Black non-Hispanic and Hispanic populations. Net domestic migration was the main factor in the decline of population in Connecticut, with an outflow accounting for a 5.8 percent population decline between 1990 and 1997.

Births less deaths and international immigration, accounting for increases of 3.7 and 1.7 percent respectively, failed to completely compensate for the loss.

Unemployment rose to a peak of 7.6 percent in 1992 and then declined, in line with national trends, to a 1997 level almost identical to that of 1990. Employment and the labor force declined faster than the working-age population, and thus the employment/population ratio, which had been well above the U.S. average in 1990, fell to 63.9 percent in 1997, about equal to national average.

Population and Labor Force

	1980	1990	1991	1992	1993	1994	1995	1996	1997	Change*	
										State	U.S.
Population											
Total number of persons (thousands)	3 108	3 289	3 287	3 272	3 270	3 265	3 262	3 264	3 267	-0.1	1.0
Percent distribution:											
White, Non-Hispanic	88.2	83.7	83.4	83.0	82.6	82.3	82.0	81.6	81.2	-0.5	0.4
Black, Non-Hispanic	6.8	8.1	8.1	8.2	8.2	8.3	8.3	8.4	8.4	0.4	1.4
Asian	0.7	1.6	1.7	1.8	1.9	2.0	2.1	2.2	2.3	5.5	4.1
Native American	0.2	0.2	0.2	0.2	0.2	0.2	0.2	0.2	0.2	1.1	1.6
Hispanic	4.0	6.5	6.7	6.9	7.1	7.3	7.5	7.7	7.9	2.9	3.8
In metropolitan areas	96.0	91.6	91.5	91.5	91.4	91.4	91.3	91.3	91.2	-0.1	1.0
Total number of households (thousands)	1 094	1 230	1 233	1 234	1 227	1 222	1 225	1 231	NA	0.0	1.2
Labor Force (thousands)											
Population 16 and over	2 402	2 616	2 604	2 584	2 571	2 562	2 556	2 559	2 559	-0.3	1.0
Civilian labor force	1 601	1 833	1 841	1 819	1 784	1 737	1 711	1 719	1 723	-0.9	1.1
Employed	1 507	1 739	1 716	1 681	1 673	1 641	1 617	1 620	1 635	-0.9	1.2
Percent of population	62.7	66.5	65.9	65.0	65.1	64.0	63.2	63.3	63.9		
Unemployment rate (percent)	5.9	5.2	6.8	7.6	6.3	5.6	5.5	5.7	5.1		

*Compound annual average percent change, 1990–1997; 1990–1996 for households.

Population Change and Components: 1990–97

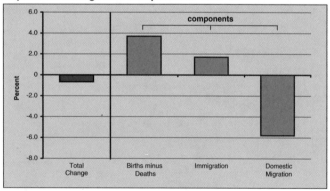

Average Annual Household and Population Growth

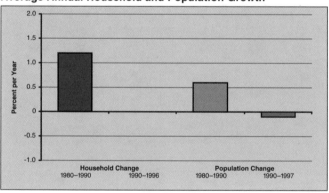

Population by Age; Births and Deaths

	1990		1997	
	State	U.S.	State	U.S.
Age distribution (percent)				
Under 5 years	7.1	7.6	6.6	7.2
5 to 17 years	15.8	18.2	17.6	18.8
18 to 64 years	63.6	61.8	61.4	61.3
65 years and over	13.5	12.5	14.4	12.7
Birth and death rates (per thousand population)				
Births	15.2	16.7	13.1	14.6
Deaths	8.4	8.6	8.9	8.6

CONNECTICUT'S POPULATION WAS OLDER THAN THE POPULATION of the United States as a whole in both 1990 and 1997, but the share of those over 65 in the state increased faster than in the nation. The share under age 18 rose faster than average but was still smaller than the national level, and the share age 18 to 64 fell to about the same as in the nation as a whole by 1997. The birth rate in 1997 of 13.1 per 1,000 was significantly lower than the U.S. rate.

HOUSEHOLD AND PERSONAL INCOME

HOUSEHOLD INCOME AND PERSONS IN POVERTY	1990	1995	1996	1997	
				State	U.S.
Median household income (1997 dollars)	47 732	42 382	43 085	43 985	37 005
Persons in poverty (thousands)	196	318	392	282	35 574
Poverty rate (percent)	6.0	9.7	11.7	8.6	13.3

MEDIAN HOUSEHOLD INCOME IN CONNECTICUT WAS 46 PER-cent above the U.S. average in 1989 but declined 20 percent in real terms from 1989 to 1993 and has changed little since then. In 1990, Connecticut's poverty rate, at 6.0 percent, was less than half the U.S. average of 13.5 percent. By 1995–97, the U.S. rate averaged 13.6 percent over the three years while Connecticut's rate, averaged 10 percent.

Aggregate nonfarm personal income increased at a 4.4 percent annual rate in Connecticut from 1989–1997, not as quickly as personal income in the United States. Adjustment for residence was positive—state residents earned more out of state than state firms paid to residents elsewhere—and rose 86 percent from 1989 to 1997. Per capita personal income was about 40 percent higher than the U.S. average in both 1989 and 1997 and did not show the relative deterioration evident in median income. This

may reflect a "hollowing out" of the state's income distribution—a loss of middle-class households (whose well-being is better reflected in the median income than in per capita income) while the proportion of low-income families rises and the incomes of high-income families (which do not affect median income) increase disproportionately.

Government payments to individuals grew by 7.5 percent per year on average from 1990 to 1997, a little faster than nationwide. Medical programs and Social Security were the largest programs, and medical programs and food stamps grew the fastest. Unemployment payments and family assistance (formerly known as Aid to Families with Dependent Children) declined over the eight-year period, contracting 2.6 percent and 1.4 percent per year, respectively.

Personal Income
(millions of dollars)

	1980	1989	1990	1991	1992	1993	1994	1995	1996	1997	Change*
Earnings by place of work	26 989	58 292	60 375	60 670	63 760	66 157	68 308	71 264	74 442	80 014	4.0
Wages and salaries	22 196	47 582	49 094	49 325	51 147	52 339	53 869	56 594	59 708	64 710	3.9
Other labor income	2 468	5 321	5 657	5 971	6 268	6 669	6 794	6 751	6 480	6 615	2.8
Proprietors' income	2 325	5 388	5 624	5 374	6 344	7 149	7 645	7 920	8 254	8 689	6.2
Farm	36	77	104	85	114	145	95	72	68	67	-1.7
Nonfarm	2 289	5 312	5 520	5 289	6 230	7 004	7 550	7 848	8 186	8 623	6.2
(–) Personal contributions for social insurance	1 375	3 589	3 726	3 897	4 023	4 128	4 333	4 569	4 756	5 120	4.5
(+) Adjustment for residence	1 534	2 647	2 913	2 958	3 751	3 635	3 611	4 348	4 657	4 922	NA
(=) Net earnings by state of residence	27 148	57 350	59 562	59 731	63 489	65 665	67 586	71 043	74 343	79 816	4.2
(+) Dividends, interest, and rent	7 070	17 651	17 918	17 445	16 836	16 997	17 966	19 350	21 406	22 300	3.0
(+) Transfer payments	4 144	8 419	9 521	10 661	12 425	12 926	13 413	14 385	14 801	15 449	7.9
(=) Total personal income	38 361	83 421	87 002	87 837	92 749	95 588	98 966	104 777	110 550	117 564	4.4
Farm	85	145	185	164	191	225	176	164	164	163	1.4
Nonfarm	38 276	83 275	86 817	87 673	92 559	95 362	98 790	104 613	110 386	117 402	4.4
Personal income per capita (dollars)											
Current dollars	12 322	25 407	26 453	26 712	28 305	29 201	30 269	32 073	33 835	35 954	4.4
1997 dollars	23 560	32 120	31 833	30 845	31 661	31 775	32 167	33 340	34 455	35 954	1.4

*Compound annual average percent change, 1989–1997

Government Transfer Payments

	Millions of dollars		Percent change*	
	1990	1997	State	U.S.
Total government payments to individuals	9 002	14 912	65.7	62.7
Retirement, disability, and insurance	4 649	6 965	49.8	48.2
Social Security	3 600	5 165	43.5	46.1
Government employee retirement	946	1 613	70.5	60.3
Medical payments	2 946	6 303	113.9	101.2
Income maintenance	747	998	33.6	58.0
Supplemental Security Income	185	291	57.8	75.4
Family assistance	322	292	-9.2	-0.5
Food Stamps	79	169	114.0	27.1
Other income maintenance	161	246	52.2	189.8
Unemployment insurance benefits	428	357	-16.5	10.6
Veterans benefits and other	232	289	24.8	30.8

*Percent change, 1990–1997

Government Payments to Individuals: 1997

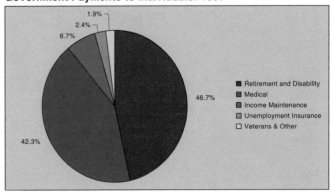

ECONOMIC STRUCTURE

LEADING PRIVATE INDUSTRIES, 1997 (Worker and proprietor earnings, millions of dollars)		FASTEST EARNINGS GROWTH, 1989–97 (percent increase)	
Health services	$7 333	Holding and investment companies	440.5
Business services	5 898	Security brokers	245.0
Insurance carriers	3 947	Amusement and recreation services	192.0
Engineering and management services	3 020	Business services	126.2
Transportation equip., excl. motor veh.	3 015	Social services	85.9

EMPLOYMENT DROPPED FROM 1989 THROUGH 1992, STAGNATed for two more years, and then rose from 1994 to 1997, yielding for the period as a whole a decline averaging 0.1 percent per year. Construction, manufacturing, and mining employment fell dramatically over the period, as did finance, real estate, and insurance. The only sectors to increase employment in any substantial way were services and transportation, communications, and public utilities. Agricultural services rose rapidly, but from a small base. Earnings in Connecticut rose over the decade, but at a slower rate than in the country as a whole. Only construc-tion sustained an earnings loss from 1989 to 1997, though all of the sectors in the state except for transportation, communications, and public utilities grew below the national average. Services, which grew only slightly slower than the national average, was also the biggest component of the economy, with 30.2 percent of all earnings. Most of the largest industries in the state were service industries, and the other two were nonmanufacturing. The fastest growing industries in the state were in either the services sector or the finance, insurance, and real estate sector.

Employment and Earnings by Sector

	1980	1989	1990	1991	1992	1993	1994	1995	1996	1997 Number	1997 Percent of total	Change*
Employment (thousands of persons)												
Total	1 709	2 050	2 017	1 940	1 921	1 942	1 927	1 952	1 987	2 029	100.0	-0.1
Farm	13	10	10	10	10	10	10	9	9	9	0.4	-1.5
Nonfarm	1 696	2 040	2 008	1 930	1 912	1 933	1 918	1 943	1 978	2 020	99.6	-0.1
Private nonfarm	1 483	1 804	1 767	1 693	1 684	1 706	1 688	1 714	1 749	1 792	88.3	-0.1
Agricultural service, forestry, and fishing	10	15	16	15	16	18	19	20	21	22	1.1	4.7
Mining	3	3	2	2	2	2	2	2	2	2	0.1	-5.4
Construction	67	112	97	84	85	85	87	89	92	97	4.8	-1.8
Manufacturing	448	368	349	330	314	303	295	289	285	285	14.0	-3.1
Transportation and public utilities	67	78	79	77	75	78	80	81	84	86	4.2	1.2
Wholesale trade	86	96	92	89	88	83	84	86	88	90	4.4	-0.8
Retail trade	261	328	317	301	301	301	306	312	317	322	15.8	-0.3
Finance, insurance, and real estate	155	235	232	225	215	215	186	187	189	193	9.5	-2.4
Services	387	568	581	569	588	621	630	649	672	696	34.3	2.6
Government	213	237	241	237	227	227	229	228	229	228	11.2	-0.5
Earnings (millions of dollars)												
Total	26 989	58 292	60 375	60 670	63 760	66 157	68 308	71 264	74 442	80 014	100.0	4.0
Farm	85	145	185	164	191	225	176	164	164	163	0.2	1.4
Nonfarm	26 904	58 146	60 190	60 506	63 569	65 932	68 133	71 100	74 279	79 851	99.8	4.0
Private nonfarm	23 963	51 441	53 037	53 032	55 922	57 900	59 805	62 678	65 638	71 051	88.8	4.1
Agricultural service, forestry, and fishing	80	270	292	284	305	337	358	374	387	414	0.5	5.5
Mining	220	81	61	61	70	93	84	92	95	101	0.1	2.8
Construction	1 297	4 006	3 328	2 901	2 920	3 058	3 193	3 275	3 441	3 749	4.7	-0.8
Manufacturing	9 636	14 142	14 370	14 464	14 620	14 517	14 764	14 938	15 344	16 448	20.6	1.9
Transportation and public utilities	1 442	2 851	2 976	3 033	3 089	3 352	3 499	3 802	3 927	4 142	5.2	4.8
Wholesale trade	1 780	4 118	4 142	4 101	4 315	4 165	4 219	4 523	4 776	5 323	6.7	3.3
Retail trade	2 428	5 539	5 456	5 291	5 402	5 554	5 724	5 844	5 988	6 253	7.8	1.5
Finance, insurance, and real estate	2 094	6 045	6 550	6 795	7 766	8 304	8 185	8 872	9 415	10 470	13.1	7.1
Services	4 985	14 388	15 862	16 102	17 435	18 521	19 779	20 959	22 264	24 150	30.2	6.7
Government	2 941	6 705	7 153	7 474	7 647	8 032	8 327	8 422	8 641	8 800	11.0	3.5

*Compound annual average percent change, 1989–1997

ECONOMIC STRUCTURE (Continued)

AVERAGE WAGES IN CONNECTICUT WERE HIGHER THAN U.S. average wages. Wages in every sector were higher, except for mining, which was only marginally lower. Finance, insurance, and real estate had the highest wages in 1997, followed by wholesale trade and manufacturing. Retail trade, agricultural services, and farm wages were the lowest-wage industries, as was the case in New England and the United States as a whole. Average wage growth in Connecticut was higher than in the United States, at 4.4 percent versus 3.5 percent per year.

Manufacturing comprised 16.7 percent of Connecticut's gross state product (GSP) in 1997, a little below the national average of 17.5 percent of gross domestic product. In 1989, manufacturing was a larger component of the Connecticut economy than it was in 1997, making up 19.6 percent of GSP and rendering manufacturing more important to Connecticut than to the United States as a whole at the time. Durable manufacturing was important to the state, with electronic goods, industrial machinery, and instruments the largest manufacturing subsectors. Though durable goods were very important, nondurable sectors such as chemicals, paper, printing, and publishing were also quite large. While industrial machinery was a large subsector, its growth was stagnant from 1989 to 1997.

The value of goods exports from Connecticut grew at a 7.9 percent annual rate from 1994 to 1997, led by chemicals, agricultural products, and three durable goods categories—transportation equipment, industrial machinery, and electric and electronic equipment. These were the five largest categories, and, except for electric and electronic equipment, they also had double-digit growth rates.

Average Annual Wages and Salaries by Sector
(dollars)

	1989	1996	1997 State	1997 U.S.
All wage and salary workers	26 978	35 838	38 115	29 809
Farm	10 464	16 462	17 344	16 442
Nonfarm	27 035	35 900	38 178	29 900
Private nonfarm	27 140	36 053	38 544	29 867
Agricultural service, forestry, and fishing	18 652	22 298	23 308	17 941
Mining	46 827	50 643	49 354	49 800
Construction	32 854	37 769	40 076	31 765
Manufacturing	33 276	46 977	50 759	38 351
Transportation and utilities	32 020	41 213	42 783	38 222
Wholesale trade	37 760	49 411	53 785	39 466
Retail trade	15 568	18 088	18 765	16 206
Finance, insurance, and real estate	35 076	57 844	65 076	44 993
Services	23 334	31 425	33 094	27 588
Government	26 362	34 946	35 823	30 062

Gross State Product and Manufacturing
(millions of dollars, except as noted)

	1989	1994	1995	1996
Gross state product, total	94 195	112 620	118 595	124 046
Manufacturing:				
Millions of dollars	18 449	19 056	19 888	20 712
Percent of total gross state product	19.6	16.9	16.8	16.7
Per worker (dollars)	50 167	64 665	68 887	72 741
New capital expenditures, manufacturing	NA	1 587	1 513	1 769

Exports of Goods
(millions of dollars)

	1994	1995	1996	1997
All goods	10 272	12 942	13 052	12 897
Manufactures	8 258	9 986	9 705	10 730
Agricultural and livestock products	1 045	1 728	2 331	1 501
Other commodities	970	1 228	1 017	666
Top goods exports, 1997:				
Chemical products	2 327	2 846	2 934	3 146
Transportation equipment	1 448	1 729	1 652	2 120
Agricultural products	1 019	1 703	2 318	1 483
Industrial machinery and computers	726	867	865	1 020
Electric and electronic equipment	664	721	770	802

HOUSING

CONNECTICUT'S HOUSING ACTIVITY STATISTICS ARE INCOMplete because the data for manufactured (mobile) homes have been suppressed for statistical reasons; however, manufactured home activity is generally low in New England. Building permits and home sales both declined sharply in 1990 but have recovered since. Existing home sales by 1996 had surpassed the levels of 1988–89, while building permits in 1997 were 25 percent above the 1991 low but 22 percent below 1989. Per capita building permits were less than half the national housing production rate, perhaps partly because of the lack of manufactured home data but also reflecting out-migration and the consequent population decline. Homeownership rates fluctuated throughout the decade, dipping to a low point in 1994 but then increasing to a high point only two years later and staying high the following year. The rental vacancy rate was likewise volatile, with the largest vacancy rate in 1995, which, at 15.2 percent of property to rent unoccupied, was almost three times the 1989 rate.

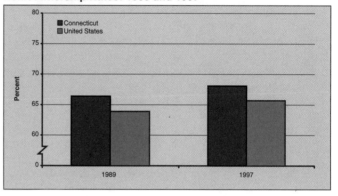

Homeownership Rates: 1989 and 1997

Housing Supply

	1989	1990	1991	1992	1993	1994	1995	1996	1997
Residential building permits (thousands)	12.0	7.6	7.5	8.0	9.2	9.5	8.6	8.5	9.3
New home production (including manufactured housing):									
Thousands of homes	12.0	7.6	7.5	8.0	9.2	9.5	8.6	8.5	9.4
Rate per 1,000 population									
Connecticut	3.7	2.3	2.3	2.4	2.8	2.9	2.6	2.6	2.9
U.S.	6.2	5.2	4.5	5.1	5.6	6.4	6.3	6.6	6.5
Existing home sales:									
Thousands of homes	41.0	34.3	37.6	40.0	45.9	49.8	51.4	49.2	55.0
Change from previous year (percent)									
Connecticut	-16.7	-16.3	9.6	6.4	14.8	8.5	3.2	-4.3	11.8
U.S.	-3.9	-4.0	0.0	9.2	8.2	4.8	-3.7	7.5	3.8
Home ownership rate (percent of households)	66.4	67.9	65.5	66.1	64.5	63.8	68.2	69.0	68.1
Rental vacancy rate (percent of rental housing units)	5.9	7.5	7.7	8.3	11.1	11.4	15.2	10.7	7.7

Note: Manufactured housing data for 1989–96 suppressed because estimate was based on too few responses.

AGRICULTURE

RECEIPTS FROM FARM SALES INCREASED OVER THE PERIOD from 1989 to 1997 and reached a peak in 1997. Production expenses also increased over the same time period. Net income fell generally after 1993, ending in 1997 only $1 million higher than in 1989. Total proprietors' income peaked in 1993 but by 1997 was less than half that amount. The average farm in Connecticut was far smaller than the average U.S. farm (470.5 acres) but was similar to those of its New England neighbors. Despite the small size of farms in the state, the average value was much higher than the

CONNECTICUT FARMS, 1997	
Number of farms	3 900
Total acres (thousands):	380
Average per farm	97
Value of land and buildings (millions of dollars)	2 850
Average per farm (dollars)	730 769

U.S. value ($442,045), probably because of high valuations of land for possible alternative uses in this highly urbanized state.

Farm Income
(millions of dollars)

	1980	1989	1990	1991	1992	1993	1994	1995	1996	1997
Gross income	325	440	488	472	514	532	525	504	532	543
Receipts from sales	299	396	447	432	469	486	481	461	492	498
Government payments	1	2	2	1	2	3	2	2	2	1
Imputed and miscellaneous income	26	41	39	39	42	43	41	41	38	43
(–) Production expenses	292	342	364	353	360	370	382	402	404	441
(=) Realized net income	33	98	124	119	153	162	142	101	128	102
(+) Inventory change	3	-1	8	-18	-6	-3	5	-8	-25	-5
(=) Net income	36	97	132	101	148	159	147	94	103	98
Corporate income	0	20	28	16	33	14	52	22	35	31
Farm proprietors income	36	77	104	85	114	145	95	72	68	67

EDUCATION

EDUCATIONAL ATTAINMENT Percent of population age 25 and over, 1997	State	United States
High school graduate or higher	84.0	82.1
College graduate or higher	30.0	23.9

CONNECTICUT RANKED 27TH AMONG STATES IN THE PERCENTage of the population over 25 with a high school diploma, yet was still above the national average of 82.1 percent. (The national average is pulled below the rate in the "middle" state by the large populations and relatively low educational attainment of several big states.) Among the New England states, Connecticut spent the most per elementary and secondary pupil, 43 percent more than the national average. Its teachers had the highest average salary in the region and were second only to Alaska in the nation as a whole. Higher education attainment was stronger in the state, which ranked fourth in the percentage of its population over 25 with a bachelor's degree in 1997. Of the population between the ages of 18 and 34, 20.3 percent were enrolled in higher education in 1996, similar to other states in the region. Minorities made up 17.5 percent of the student population in 1996, a rate far lower than in the nation as a whole, but second highest in the region after Massachusetts.

High School Completion: 1990–97

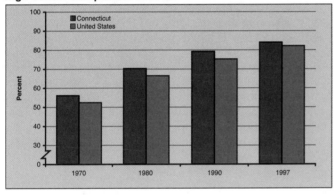

Education Indicators

	State	U.S.
Elementary and secondary schools		
Enrollment, 1995–96		
Total (thousands)	589	49 873
Percent in private schools	12.0	10.1
Expenditures per pupil (dollars), 1995–96	8 817	6 146
Average teacher salary (dollars), 1996–97	50 426	38 509
Higher education		
Enrollment, 1996–97		
Total (thousands)	155	14 218
Percent of population 18–34	20.3	21.8
Percent minority	17.5	26.1
Percent in private schools	37.2	22.6

HEALTH

IN MOST MEASURES OF HEALTH WITHIN A STATE, CONNECTICUT performed well. Infant mortality rates, death rates, and the percentage not covered by health insurance were lower than the national averages. Infant mortality and the death rate declined slightly through the 1990s, though the percentage without health insurance almost doubled from the regional low of 6.9 percent in 1990 to 12 percent in 1997. While the total crude death rate was higher, as were the crude death rates for HIV and cancer, when adjusted for age, these indicators fell below the national averages as well.

Health Indicators

	1990	1995	1996	1997
Infant mortality				
(rate per thousand live births)				
Connecticut	7.9	7.2	6.2	7.0
U.S.	9.2	7.6	7.3	7.1
Total deaths, age-adjusted rate				
(rate per thousand population)				
Connecticut	4.5	4.5	4.4	4.2
U.S.	5.2	5.0	4.9	4.8
Persons not covered by health insurance				
(percent of population)				
Connecticut	6.9	8.8	11.0	12.0
U.S.	13.9	15.4	15.6	16.1

Leading Causes of Death, 1996
(deaths per 100,000 population)

	Age-adjusted		Not age-adjusted	
	State	U.S.	State	U.S.
Deaths from all causes	443.2	491.6	902.8	872.5
Heart disease	126.0	134.5	303.2	276.4
Cancer	122.9	127.9	218.2	203.4
Cerebrovascular diseases	22.0	26.4	59.7	60.3
Chronic obstructive pulmonary disease	16.4	21.0	37.0	40.0
Diabetes mellitus	11.2	13.6	21.7	23.3
Pneumonia and influenza	11.7	12.8	34.9	31.6
HIV	10.9	11.1	12.0	11.7
Liver disease	6.7	7.5	9.3	9.4
Alzheimer's disease	2.1	2.7	7.3	8.1
Accidents and adverse effects	25.1	30.4	31.9	35.8
Motor vehicle accidents	10.1	16.2	10.0	16.5
Suicide	8.6	10.8	8.9	11.6
Homicide	6.0	8.5	5.3	7.9
Injury by firearm	8.2	12.9	7.5	12.8

GOVERNMENT

STATE AND LOCAL TAXES, 1995–96	State	U.S.
Per capita (dollars)	3 635	2 477
Percent of personal income	11.4	10.8

WITH COMBINED PER CAPITA STATE AND LOCAL TAXES OF $3,635, Connecticut's tax burden was significantly higher than that in the nation as a whole, which averaged $2,477 per capita, and was also high relative to the rest of New England. Calculated as a percent of total personal income in the state, state and local taxes equaled 11.4 percent of total income, while the national percentage was 10.8.

State taxes were one and one-half times the U.S. aver-age on a per capita basis. Individual income taxes, sales taxes (general and select), and corporate income taxes were all higher in the state. License taxes were the only major category lower than the national average, though only fractionally so. Expenditures by the state were also higher than in the country at large. State spending on education, natural resources, and parks and recreation were the only types below the national average. Government administration and the interest on general debt were far higher in the state, at one and one-half and three times the national average, respectively. Public welfare and law enforcement spending were also higher.

Connecticut received $18.1 billion in federal funds in 1997. This amount represented 1.3 percent of all federal funds spent in the 50 states and the District of Columbia, in contrast to Connecticut's 1.2 percent of total U.S. population. The Medicare and Medicaid programs commanded the highest relative levels of funding. Defense procurement was significant, both as a percentage of the total federal funds spent in Connecticut and as a percentage of the national total of defense procurement funds. Other procurement was quite small.

State Government Finances, 1996–97

	Millions of dollars	Percent distribu- tion	Dollars per capita State	Dollars per capita U.S.
General revenue	13 015	100.0	3 980	3 049
Intergovernmental revenue	2 944	22.6	900	863
Taxes	8 146	62.6	2 491	1 660
General sales	2 598	20.0	795	551
Selective sales	1 567	12.0	479	257
License taxes	341	2.6	104	106
Individual income	2 807	21.6	859	542
Corporation net income	530	4.1	162	115
Other taxes	302	2.3	92	90
Other general revenue	1 925	14.8	589	526
General expenditure	11 952	100.0	3 655	2 951
Intergovernmental expenditure	2 481	20.8	759	989
Direct expenditure	9 471	79.2	2 896	1 962
General expenditure, by function:				
Education	2 894	24.2	885	1 033
Public welfare	2 915	24.4	891	761
Hospitals and health	1 380	11.5	422	237
Highways	756	6.3	231	225
Police protection and corrections	603	5.0	185	137
Natural resources, parks and recreation	115	1.0	35	78
Governmental administration	584	4.9	179	107
Interest on general debt	948	7.9	290	99
Other and unallocable	1 757	14.7	537	290
Debt at end of fiscal year	17 051	NA	5 214	1 706
Cash and security holdings	22 887	NA	6 999	6 683

Federal Spending within State

	Federal funds, fiscal 1997		
	Millions of dollars	Percent distribution	Percent of U.S. total*
Total within state	18 124	100.0	1.3
Payments to individuals	10 285	56.7	1.3
Retirement and disability	5 831	32.2	1.3
Medicare	2 988	16.5	1.5
Food stamps	171	0.9	0.9
Supplemental Security Income	202	1.1	0.8
Grants	3 410	18.8	1.4
Medicaid and other health	1 691	9.3	1.5
Nutrition and family welfare	631	3.5	1.3
Education	173	1.0	1.0
Housing and community development ..	162	0.9	1.4
Salaries and wages	1 353	7.5	0.8
Defense procurement contracts	2 517	13.9	2.1
Non-defense procurement contracts	401	2.2	0.5

*State population is 1.2 percent of the U.S. total.

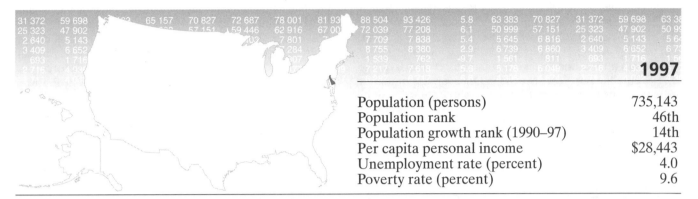

Population (persons)	735,143
Population rank	46th
Population growth rank (1990–97)	14th
Per capita personal income	$28,443
Unemployment rate (percent)	4.0
Poverty rate (percent)	9.6

DELAWARE WAS THE ONLY MID-ATLANTIC STATE TO EXPERIence positive net domestic migration as well as a population growth higher than the U.S. average. It also managed to maintain lower unemployment rates than the nation at large. Manufacturing employment actually fell by almost 16,000 from 1989 to 1997 but was compensated for by an increase in service employment of just over 27,000. Despite this, manufacturing remained important in the state, representing 21.2 percent of gross state product in 1996, higher than that of any other state in the region. Financial services grew in importance from 1989 to 1997, with employment and earnings growing far faster than regional and national rates. DuPont, the largest employer in the state, has been a major economic force for some time, contributing to the importance of the chemical industry and the manufacturing sector as a whole in the state. Favorable incorporation laws have also had an impact on the state's economy, with almost 292,000 companies incorporated in 1997, an increase of 4.4 percent over the previous year.

Median household income in Delaware was higher than the national level in 1997, though it was lower than incomes in both New Jersey and Maryland in the Mid-Atlantic. Incomes dropped slightly in the early part of the decade, but 1997 incomes were 3.7 percent higher than 1989 levels in inflation-adjusted terms.

Average Annual Population Growth: 1990–97

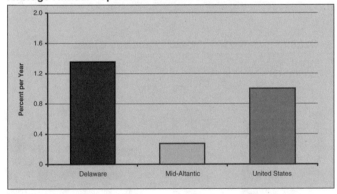

Median Household Income: 1989–97 (1997 dollars)

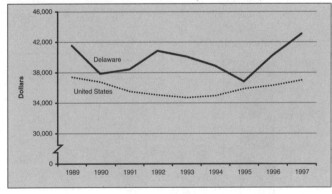

Unemployment Rate: 1989–97

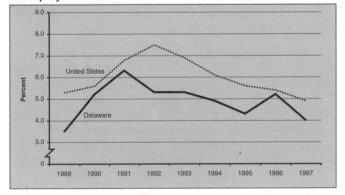

UNEMPLOYMENT IN DELAWARE WAS LOWER AND RECOVERED more quickly from recession than in the nation as a whole. Peaking at 6.3 percent in 1991, the unemployment rate fell to a regional low of 4 percent in 1997. Total employment dropped early in the 1990s but grew dramatically in subsequent years. Labor force growth was slow relative to the growth in the working-age population, which helped hold down unemployment.

POPULATION AND LABOR FORCE

DELAWARE, ALONE AMONG THE MID-ATLANTIC STATES, HAD an above-average population growth rate from 1990 to 1997. This growth was seen in every racial category, with the Black population growing 3.1 percent per year (as opposed to 1.5 percent per year in the country at large). The Asian population also grew much faster than average, at 5.8 percent per year. Much of Delaware's population growth stems from natural increases and domestic migration, the only Mid-Atlantic state to experience a gain in the latter. Net immigration also contributed to overall population growth. Of all Delaware's residents, 81.7 percent live in the metropolitan counties of New Castle and Kent (Wilmington and Dover metropolitan areas).

The labor force grew more slowly than the population age 16 and older in Delaware from 1990 to 1997, running counter to the national trend of increasing labor force participation and reflecting a population aging a little faster than the national average. This rate combined with employment growth to yield a low and declining unemployment rate after the recession's peak.

Population and Labor Force

	1980	1990	1991	1992	1993	1994	1995	1996	1997	Change* State	Change* U.S.
Population											
Total number of persons (thousands)	594	669	680	690	700	709	719	727	735	1.4	1.0
Percent distribution:											
White, Non-Hispanic	81.3	79.2	78.8	78.3	77.9	77.4	76.9	76.4	75.7	0.6	0.4
Black, Non-Hispanic	16.0	16.6	17.0	17.3	17.5	17.8	18.1	18.4	18.8	3.1	1.4
Asian	0.8	1.4	1.5	1.6	1.6	1.7	1.8	1.9	2.0	5.8	4.1
Native American	0.2	0.3	0.3	0.3	0.3	0.3	0.3	0.3	0.3	2.1	1.6
Hispanic	1.6	2.5	2.5	2.5	2.7	2.8	3.0	3.1	3.3	5.4	3.8
In metropolitan areas	83.5	83.0	82.9	82.7	82.5	82.3	82.1	81.8	81.7	1.1	1.0
Total number of households (thousands)	207	247	253	258	262	264	270	276	NA	1.8	1.2
Labor Force (thousands)											
Population 16 and over	451	520	528	534	542	548	558	566	574	1.4	1.0
Civilian labor force	284	359	359	366	374	382	382	383	382	0.9	1.1
Employed	262	340	337	346	354	364	365	363	366	1.1	1.2
Percent of population	58.1	65.4	63.8	64.8	65.4	66.4	65.5	64.2	63.8		
Unemployment rate (percent)	7.7	5.2	6.3	5.3	5.3	4.9	4.3	5.2	4.0		

*Compound annual average percent change, 1990–1997; 1990–1996 for households.

Population Change and Components: 1990–97

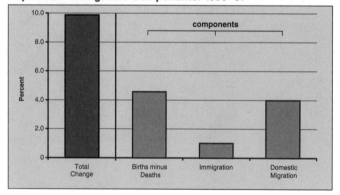

Average Annual Household and Population Growth

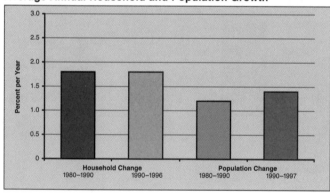

Population by Age; Births and Deaths

	1990 State	1990 U.S.	1997 State	1997 U.S.
Age distribution (percent)				
Under 5 years	7.5	7.6	6.7	7.2
5 to 17 years	17.2	18.2	17.5	18.8
18 to 64 years	63.2	61.8	62.9	61.3
65 years and over	12.1	12.5	12.9	12.7
Birth and death rates (per thousand population)				
Births	16.7	16.7	14.0	14.6
Deaths	8.6	8.6	8.9	8.6

IN 1997, DELAWARE HAD A SLIGHTLY OLDER POPULATION than did the United States. Though the number of people age 65 and older was just larger than the U.S. average, it had been below that average in 1990. Delaware had a higher than average proportion of people in the working-age group of 18 to 64. Delaware's birth rate of 14 per 1,000 is only slightly lower than the U.S. rate of 14.6, though the lower birth rate will help continue the trend of a smaller than average pre-school and school-age populations.

HOUSEHOLD AND PERSONAL INCOME

HOUSEHOLD INCOME AND PERSONS IN POVERTY	1990	1995	1996	1997 State	1997 U.S.
Median household income (1997 dollars)	37 827	36 784	40 211	43 033	37 005
Persons in poverty (thousands)	48	74	63	72	35 574
Poverty rate (percent)	6.9	10.3	8.6	9.6	13.3

REAL MEDIAN HOUSEHOLD INCOME IN DELAWARE GREW SUBstantially from 1989 to 1997, and was 16 percent above the national median in 1997. Declining in 1989, it stagnated through 1995, and resumed growth in 1996. Poverty in Delaware was 6.9 percent in 1990. By 1997, the rate had increased to 9.6 percent but remained far lower than the poverty rate in the United States, which stood at 13.3 percent.

Aggregate personal income in Delaware grew 5.5 percent per year from 1989 to 1997, slightly faster than in the United States. Wages and salaries grew at a similar pace, and proprietors' income grew 16.4 percent faster than the U.S. rate. Delawarians are likely to find jobs outside the state, which is reflected by the negative adjustment for place of residence (a way to account for the importance of in- and out-commuting). Delaware's per capita personal income grew a little slower than per capita income in the rest of the country but was above average in 1997 overall. When adjusted for inflation, personal per capita income grew 1.1 percent per year, the same as national growth.

Government transfer payments in Delaware increased more than 8 percent per year on average from 1990 to 1997, a growth rate higher that of than that of any other state in the region. The programs with the highest growth rates were medical payments, Supplemental Security Income, and "other income maintenance," which includes the earned income tax credit. None of Delaware's programs contracted from 1990 to 1997, though several grew at less than the total transfer payment rate, including family assistance and food stamps. Though Social Security was one of the slower growing programs, it was the largest, disbursing more than $1 billion in 1997.

Personal Income
(millions of dollars)

	1980	1989	1990	1991	1992	1993	1994	1995	1996	1997	Change*
Earnings by place of work	5 102	10 779	11 478	11 914	12 429	12 953	13 596	14 388	15 319	16 320	5.3
Wages and salaries	4 176	8 602	9 074	9 346	9 655	9 961	10 431	11 167	12 010	12 910	5.2
Other labor income	494	999	1 078	1 143	1 194	1 363	1 444	1 448	1 407	1 431	4.6
Proprietors' income	432	1 178	1 325	1 425	1 580	1 629	1 721	1 773	1 902	1 980	6.7
Farm	-6	172	114	106	90	91	85	53	74	60	-12.3
Nonfarm	438	1 005	1 212	1 319	1 490	1 538	1 636	1 721	1 828	1 919	8.4
(–) Personal contributions for social insurance	259	653	693	729	747	781	837	897	953	1 022	5.8
(+) Adjustment for residence	-259	-672	-735	-773	-800	-881	-961	-1 095	-1 198	-1 288	NA
(=) Net earnings by state of residence	4 584	9 454	10 050	10 412	10 882	11 291	11 798	12 396	13 169	14 010	5.0
(+) Dividends, interest, and rent	944	2 516	2 702	2 822	2 836	2 926	3 101	3 350	3 732	3 896	5.6
(+) Transfer payments	786	1 566	1 693	1 901	2 157	2 265	2 444	2 623	2 844	2 903	8.0
(=) Total personal income	6 314	13 536	14 445	15 134	15 875	16 482	17 344	18 369	19 744	20 808	5.5
Farm	14	194	138	130	112	114	109	79	102	89	-9.3
Nonfarm	6 301	13 342	14 306	15 005	15 762	16 368	17 235	18 290	19 642	20 720	5.7
Personal income per capita (dollars)											
Current dollars	10 614	20 563	21 590	22 261	23 041	23 605	24 549	25 666	27 291	28 443	4.1
1997 dollars	20 294	25 996	25 981	25 706	25 773	25 686	26 088	26 680	27 791	28 443	1.1

*Compound annual average percent change, 1989–1997

Government Transfer Payments

	Millions of dollars 1990	Millions of dollars 1997	Percent change* State	Percent change* U.S.
Total government payments to individuals	1 582	2 772	75.2	62.7
Retirement, disability, and insurance	955	1 527	59.8	48.2
Social Security	688	1 096	59.3	46.1
Government employee retirement	234	390	66.7	60.3
Medical payments	425	900	111.8	101.2
Income maintenance	102	197	93.6	58.0
Supplemental Security Income	22	46	102.5	75.4
Family assistance	31	41	33.8	-0.5
Food Stamps	26	39	47.8	27.1
Other income maintenance	22	71	223.4	189.8
Unemployment insurance benefits	41	64	54.5	10.6
Veterans benefits and other	59	84	43.5	30.8

*Percent change, 1990–1997

Government Payments to Individuals: 1997

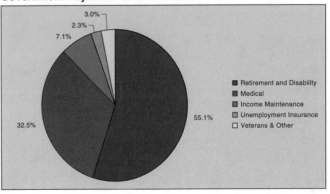

- Retirement and Disability
- Medical
- Income Maintenance
- Unemployment Insurance
- Veterans & Other

ECONOMIC STRUCTURE

LEADING PRIVATE INDUSTRIES, 1997 (Worker and proprietor earnings, millions of dollars)		FASTEST EARNINGS GROWTH, 1989–97 (percent increase)	
Chemicals and allied products	$2 724	Security brokers	258.8
Banks and other credit institutions	1 458	Banks and other credit institutions	196.1
Health services	1 273	Real estate	143.0
Construction specialties	798	Social services	104.2
Business services	755	Business services	101.5

TOTAL EMPLOYMENT INCREASED FROM 1989 TO 1997 AT A RATE of 1.3 percent per year, slightly less than the U.S. rate of 1.6 percent. As in many states in the region, employment growth in services and the small agricultural services sector was much higher than growth in total employment. Unlike in most other states, however, finance, insurance, and real estate employment grew rapidly in the same period and accounted for 12.8 percent of all employment in the state in 1997. The only major sector to experience a decline in employment was manufacturing, which decreased 2.9 percent per year on average. Construction employment growth was stagnant over the period.

Earnings in the state grew faster than did earnings nationwide. Finance, insurance, and real estate earnings rose faster than any other sector, at 12.8 percent per year on average. None of the nonfarm sectors experienced a decline in earnings from 1989 to 1997, but manufacturing earnings increased at a slower rate than the national average. Despite this, manufacturing still represented a larger percentage of Delaware earnings than of U.S. earnings (17.7 percent). Chemicals and allied products was the largest industry in the state, followed by banks and other credit institutions. The five fastest growing industries from 1989 to 1997 were in the finance, insurance, and real estate and services sectors.

Employment and Earnings by Sector

	1980	1989	1990	1991	1992	1993	1994	1995	1996	1997 Number	1997 Percent of total	Change*
Employment *(thousands of persons)*												
Total	312	418	422	418	417	424	428	441	452	464	100.0	1.3
Farm	6	5	5	5	4	4	4	4	4	4	0.9	-2.5
Nonfarm	306	413	417	413	412	420	424	437	448	460	99.1	1.4
Private nonfarm	252	355	358	354	353	359	362	374	385	398	85.6	1.4
Agricultural service, forestry, and fishing	2	3	3	3	3	4	4	4	4	5	1.0	4.5
Mining	0	0	0	0	0	0	0	0	0	0	0.0	0.0
Construction	18	27	27	24	24	24	23	25	28	28	6.1	0.4
Manufacturing	73	75	73	71	69	66	64	63	59	59	12.6	-2.9
Transportation and public utilities	14	17	17	17	16	17	17	17	17	18	3.8	0.5
Wholesale trade	11	14	14	14	13	13	14	15	15	15	3.2	1.1
Retail trade	51	70	70	69	71	72	74	77	79	81	17.4	1.9
Finance, insurance, and real estate	22	43	45	45	45	48	48	52	55	59	12.8	4.1
Services	63	106	109	110	111	115	117	121	127	133	28.6	2.9
Government	55	58	59	59	59	61	62	62	63	63	13.5	1.0
Earnings *(millions of dollars)*												
Total	5 102	10 779	11 478	11 914	12 429	12 953	13 596	14 388	15 319	16 320	100.0	5.3
Farm	14	194	138	130	112	114	109	79	102	89	0.5	-9.3
Nonfarm	5 089	10 585	11 339	11 784	12 316	12 839	13 487	14 309	15 217	16 231	99.5	5.5
Private nonfarm	4 370	9 243	9 897	10 251	10 741	11 179	11 751	12 474	13 297	14 261	87.4	5.6
Agricultural service, forestry, and fishing	14	39	43	46	45	48	52	57	61	67	0.4	7.2
Mining	26	8	9	14	11	6	6	7	8	9	0.1	0.9
Construction	395	811	850	892	920	879	822	917	1 097	1 148	7.0	4.4
Manufacturing	2 021	3 537	3 720	3 818	3 852	4 019	4 174	4 234	4 189	4 320	26.5	2.5
Transportation and public utilities	282	552	560	590	613	629	664	684	696	725	4.4	3.5
Wholesale trade	224	427	475	486	495	490	522	557	591	624	3.8	4.8
Retail trade	453	911	967	970	1 013	1 045	1 124	1 192	1 272	1 350	8.3	5.0
Finance, insurance, and real estate	210	857	945	1 013	1 165	1 321	1 489	1 709	1 951	2 249	13.8	12.8
Services	745	2 101	2 327	2 421	2 627	2 742	2 900	3 116	3 431	3 769	23.1	7.6
Government	719	1 342	1 442	1 533	1 575	1 660	1 736	1 835	1 920	1 971	12.1	4.9

*Compound annual average percent change, 1989–1997

ECONOMIC STRUCTURE (Continued)

AVERAGE WAGES IN DELAWARE IN 1997 WERE HIGHER THAN the national average but lower than the average for the Mid-Atlantic region. The only sector for which wages were higher than those for both the national and regional averages was manufacturing. Finance, insurance, and real estate wages were lower than average wages in the nation and the region. This relatively low wage rate may be due in part to the large presence of personal credit services and credit card issuers in the state, which tend to pay lower wages. Major sectors with faster growth than the state average in wages per hour were construction, manufacturing, finance, insurance, and real estate, and services.

Manufacturing contributed 21.2 percent of Delaware's gross state product in 1997. This was the highest ratio in the Mid-Atlantic. It was also higher than the national average, but has fallen faster, as Delaware's manufacturing employment declined while services and finance, insurance, and real estate were rising. The value of manufacturing output per worker in Delaware was lower than the national average.

Goods exports from Delaware rose 35.8 percent from 1994 to 1997. Chemical products was the top export, accounting for 71.5 percent of total goods exports, and increased 39.6 percent from 1994 to 1997. The only commodity group in the top five to lose export value was scientific and measuring instruments.

Average Annual Wages and Salaries by Sector
(dollars)

	1989	1996	1997 State	1997 U.S.
All wage and salary workers	23 247	30 043	31 419	29 809
Farm	10 885	18 678	16 330	16 442
Nonfarm	23 311	30 084	31 481	29 900
Private nonfarm	23 679	30 473	31 978	29 867
Agricultural service, forestry, and fishing	13 701	17 461	18 287	17 941
Mining	35 849	34 103	33 375	49 800
Construction	23 085	31 495	32 788	31 765
Manufacturing	37 716	51 357	53 371	38 351
Transportation and utilities	29 124	35 695	36 863	38 222
Wholesale trade	28 171	36 134	38 295	39 466
Retail trade	12 124	15 366	16 027	16 206
Finance, insurance, and real estate	23 973	36 114	39 326	44 993
Services	18 938	25 515	26 951	27 588
Government	21 340	28 002	28 739	30 062

Gross State Product and Manufacturing
(millions of dollars, except as noted)

	1989	1994	1995	1996
Gross state product, total	19 480	24 124	26 947	28 331
Manufacturing: Millions of dollars	5 110	5 750	6 146	5 993
Percent of total gross state product	26.2	23.8	22.8	21.2
Per worker (dollars)	68 576	89 604	97 986	101 821
New capital expenditures, manufacturing	NA	379	319	807

Exports of Goods
(millions of dollars)

	1994	1995	1996	1997
All goods	3 758	4 397	4 584	5 104
Manufactures	3 667	4 283	4 474	5 004
Agricultural and livestock products	58	68	59	50
Other commodities	34	46	52	50
Top goods exports, 1997:				
Chemical products	2 614	3 125	3 252	3 650
Rubber and plastic products	305	360	379	454
Scientific and measuring instruments	273	291	288	270
Textile mill products	126	134	129	175
Industrial machinery and computers	71	71	76	97

HOUSING

TOTAL NEW HOUSING SUPPLY IN DELAWARE WAS STEADY throughout the 1990s at somewhat less than the state's 1989 rate. On a per capita basis, however, Delaware exceeded the U.S. and regional averages for housing production. Likewise existing home sales were relatively steady but below their 1989 high. Homeownership is well above the national average. The rental vacancy rate started the decade lower than the national average, peaked at a high 10.6 percent in 1995, and has fallen back since.

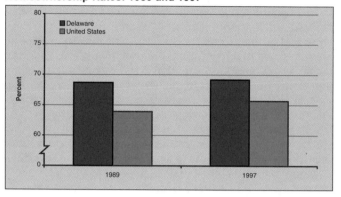

Homeownership Rates: 1989 and 1997

Housing Supply

	1989	1990	1991	1992	1993	1994	1995	1996	1997
Residential building permits (thousands)	5.8	5.1	4.3	4.6	4.9	5.0	4.6	4.4	4.7
New home production (including manufactured housing):									
Thousands of homes	7.5	6.4	5.4	6.2	6.5	6.1	6.1	5.9	5.8
Rate per 1,000 population									
Delaware	11.4	9.6	7.9	9.0	9.3	8.6	8.5	8.2	7.9
U.S.	6.2	5.2	4.5	5.1	5.6	6.4	6.3	6.6	6.5
Existing home sales:									
Thousands of homes	11.8	9.7	10.4	10.0	9.4	10.4	10.2	NA	NA
Change from previous year (percent)									
Delaware	-4.8	-17.8	7.2	-3.8	-6.0	10.6	-1.9	NA	NA
U.S.	-3.9	-4.0	0.0	9.2	8.2	4.8	-3.7	7.5	3.8
Home ownership rate (percent of households)	68.7	67.7	70.2	73.8	74.1	70.5	71.7	71.5	69.2
Rental vacancy rate (percent of rental housing units)	6.7	6.0	8.0	9.1	8.4	8.3	10.6	7.7	8.5

AGRICULTURE

FARM SALES IN DELAWARE DIPPED IN THE MIDDLE OF THE decade but grew in the latter half, surpassing the 1989 level again only in 1995. Production expenses increased throughout the time period, causing realized net income to decline. Government payments to the state were negligible, and corporate farms do not have a large presence in the state. The average farm in Delaware is larger than those in any of the other states in the region, and the value of the average farm in the state is the highest in the region.

DELAWARE FARMS, 1997	
Number of farms	2 400
Total acres (thousands):	565
Average per farm	235
Value of land and buildings (millions of dollars)	1 791
Average per farm (dollars)	746 250

Livestock and products, notably broilers (chicken), is Delaware's leading farm product.

Farm Income
(millions of dollars)

	1980	1989	1990	1991	1992	1993	1994	1995	1996	1997
Gross income	356	744	709	702	688	699	745	757	843	858
Receipts from sales	340	669	648	633	621	624	670	676	758	757
Government payments	1	5	3	3	3	6	6	3	5	6
Imputed and miscellaneous income	14	70	58	66	64	68	70	78	80	95
(−) Production expenses	364	553	582	594	586	591	650	688	761	776
(=) Realized net income	-8	191	128	108	102	107	95	69	81	82
(+) Inventory change	-4	4	1	9	1	-12	10	-9	9	-9
(=) Net income	-12	196	129	117	103	95	105	60	91	73
Corporate income	-6	23	15	10	12	5	20	7	17	12
Farm proprietors income	-6	172	114	106	90	91	85	53	74	60

EDUCATION

EDUCATIONAL ATTAINMENT Percent of population age 25 and over, 1997	State	United States
High school graduate or higher	84.4	82.1
College graduate or higher	26.8	23.9

DELAWARE RANKED 24TH IN THE NATION FOR THE PERCENTage of its residents over 25 holding high school diplomas, though both per-pupil spending and teacher salaries in elementary and secondary schools were higher than the U.S. average. A relatively large percentage of enrollment in elementary and secondary schools (19.1 percent) was private compared to the U.S. percentage (10.1 percent).

Higher educational attainment was stronger in Delaware, which ranked 13th in the nation overall for the percentage of the population over 25 holding a bachelor's degree. A relatively high percentage (24.1 percent) of the population ages 18 to 34 was enrolled in higher education in 1996, but the percentage of minorities enrolled was well under the national average.

High School Completion: 1990–97

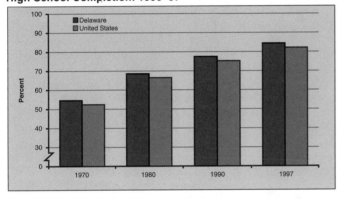

Education Indicators

	State	U.S.
Elementary and secondary schools		
Enrollment, 1995–96		
Total (thousands)	134	49 873
Percent in private schools	19.1	10.1
Expenditures per pupil (dollars), 1995–96	7 267	6 146
Average teacher salary (dollars), 1996–97	41 436	38 509
Higher education		
Enrollment, 1996–97		
Total (thousands)	45	14 218
Percent of population 18–34	24.1	21.8
Percent minority	19.4	26.1
Percent in private schools	18.4	22.6

HEALTH

DELAWARE HAD HIGHER THAN AVERAGE AGE-ADJUSTED DEATH rates for HIV, cancer, diabetes, heart disease, liver disease, and suicide in 1996. The total death rate was higher than the national average throughout the 1990s, and infant

mortality was higher in 1990 and 1996–97. Health insurance coverage rates have improved since 1995, and the rate of those not covered by insurance dropped to a decade low in 1997.

Health Indicators

	1990	1995	1996	1997
Infant mortality				
(rate per thousand live births)				
Delaware	10.1	7.5	7.7	8.2
U.S.	9.2	7.6	7.3	7.1
Total deaths, age-adjusted rate				
(rate per thousand population)				
Delaware	5.4	5.2	5.3	5.1
U.S.	5.2	5.0	4.9	4.8
Persons not covered by health insurance				
(percent of population)				
Delaware	13.9	15.7	13.4	13.1
U.S.	13.9	15.4	15.6	16.1

Leading Causes of Death, 1996
(deaths per 100,000 population)

	Age-adjusted		Not age-adjusted	
	State	U.S.	State	U.S.
Deaths from all causes	526.2	491.6	897.2	872.5
Heart disease	141.9	134.5	277.9	276.4
Cancer	147.4	127.9	232.9	203.4
Cerebrovascular diseases	23.9	26.4	47.7	60.3
Chronic obstructive pulmonary disease	20.9	21.0	38.5	40.0
Diabetes mellitus	15.8	13.6	26.5	23.3
Pneumonia and influenza	11.6	12.8	27.5	31.6
HIV	16.5	11.1	18.3	11.7
Liver disease	9.1	7.5	11.2	9.4
Alzheimer's disease	2.4	2.7	6.5	8.1
Accidents and adverse effects	28.5	30.4	33.2	35.8
Motor vehicle accidents	14.5	16.2	14.5	16.5
Suicide	11.9	10.8	13.4	11.6
Homicide	7.5	8.5	7.9	7.9
Injury by firearm	10.8	12.9	11.7	12.8

GOVERNMENT

STATE AND LOCAL TAXES, 1995–96	State	U.S.
Per capita (dollars)	2 593	2 477
Percent of personal income	10.0	10.8

STATE AND LOCAL TAXES (LESS CORPORATE TAX) TOOK A SIG-nificantly smaller share of personal income in Delaware (10.0 percent) than the national average (10.8 percent). But state per capita incomes were so high that this share yielded a greater than average per capita tax level. The percentage of taxes levied by local governments, at 19.3 percent, was the lowest in the country. State taxation was quite a bit higher than the national average on a per capi-ta calculation, however. Without a general sales tax, Delaware relies on higher than average personal income, corporate income, and selective sales taxes for revenue, and license taxes are 7.5 times higher than for the nation as a whole.

Expenditure in the state is likewise far higher than national levels. State education spending is almost one and one-half times that in the United States (per capita), and hospitals and healthcare are also better funded in the state. There is less spending on public welfare than in the nation as a whole. Police protection and corrections are very well funded in the state, at a level almost twice as high as for the country on average. Highway spending per capita was also quite high. Debt at the end of the financial year was almost three times the national level, but cash and security holdings were less than twice the U.S. average per capita.

Delaware received 0.2 percent of all federal funds dis-persed in 1997, which is slightly smaller than the 0.3 per-cent of the U.S. population it contains. The state receives about 0.2 percent to 0.3 percent of total funds for most programs. The largest programs in the state are retire-ment, Medicare and Medicaid, which get 39.3 percent, 15.2 percent, and 7.6 percent, respectively. Defense and non-defense procurement was low in the state, similar to that in other Mid-Atlantic states, and it represented only 3.0 percent and 1.5 percent, respectively, of all funds received.

State Government Finances, 1996–97

	Millions of dollars	Percent distribu-tion	Dollars per capita	
			State	U.S.
General revenue	3 469	100.0	4 740	3 049
Intergovernmental revenue	672	19.4	918	863
Taxes	1 743	50.2	2 381	1 660
General sales	0	0.0	0	551
Selective sales	253	7.3	346	257
License taxes	579	16.7	790	106
Individual income	663	19.1	906	542
Corporation net income	173	5.0	236	115
Other taxes	76	2.2	103	90
Other general revenue	1 054	30.4	1 440	526
General expenditure	3 098	100.0	4 233	2 951
Intergovernmental expenditure	576	18.6	787	989
Direct expenditure	2 522	81.4	3 446	1 962
General expenditure, by function:				
Education	1 070	34.5	1 462	1 033
Public welfare	501	16.2	684	761
Hospitals and health	227	7.3	311	237
Highways	262	8.5	359	225
Police protection and corrections	175	5.7	240	137
Natural resources, parks and recreation	81	2.6	111	63
Governmental administration	245	7.9	335	107
Interest on general debt	209	6.7	285	99
Other and unallocable	327	10.5	446	290
Debt at end of fiscal year	3 434	NA	4 692	1 706
Cash and security holdings	7 510	NA	10 260	6 683

Federal Spending within State

	Federal funds, fiscal 1997		
	Millions of dollars	Percent distribution	Percent of U.S. total*
Total within state	3 470	100.0	0.2
Payments to individuals	2 224	64.1	0.3
Retirement and disability	1 365	39.3	0.3
Medicare	528	15.2	0.3
Food stamps	41	1.2	0.2
Supplemental Security Income	47	1.4	0.2
Grants	678	19.5	0.3
Medicaid and other health	264	7.6	0.2
Nutrition and family welfare	131	3.8	0.3
Education	55	1.6	0.3
Housing and community development	28	0.8	0.2
Salaries and wages	383	11.0	0.2
Defense procurement contracts	105	3.0	0.1
Non-defense procurement contracts	51	1.5	0.1

*State population is 0.3 percent of the U.S. total.

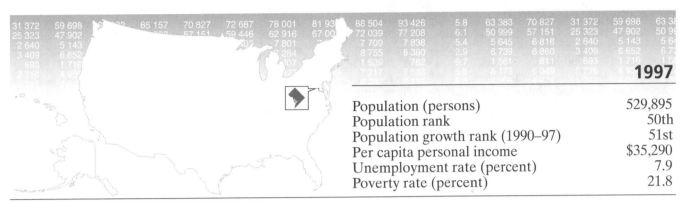

1997

Population (persons)	529,895
Population rank	50th
Population growth rank (1990–97)	51st
Per capita personal income	$35,290
Unemployment rate (percent)	7.9
Poverty rate (percent)	21.8

WASHINGTON, D.C., FACED A BLEAK PICTURE FOR ALL MAJOR indicators of economic health during the 1990s. Its unique political status as a federal district and controversial local leadership combined with the socioeconomic problems that typically plague older cities. The city also was affected by national trends toward shrinking government, while government-related high-tech contracting and spin-off companies concentrated in the surrounding suburbs.

The city's population fell by 12.4 percent from 1990 to 1997, as one in five residents moved out. This was only partially balanced by foreign immigration and natural population growth. The number of jobs located in the city declined by 8.7 percent from 1989 to 1997, a period when employment grew vigorously in the surrounding states as well as nationally. Total earnings for those working in the city grew about two-thirds as fast as nationally, and average wages continue to be extremely high. However, the share of these earnings taken home by commuters from outside the district in 1997 reached 60.4 percent.

The number of D.C. residents holding jobs actually declined by 23 percent from 1990 to 1997. Median household income for residents was 13.9 percent below the U.S. level, while incomes were above the U.S. average in most nearby suburbs. The city's record had been more hopeful in the 1980s, when population losses were moderate and employment increased by about 10 percent.

Average Annual Population Growth: 1990–97

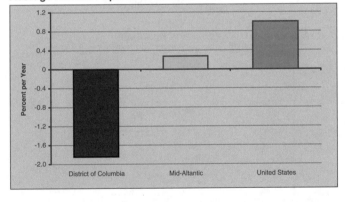

Median Household Income: 1989–97 (1997 dollars)

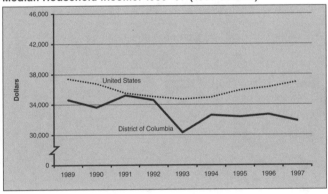

Unemployment Rate: 1989–97

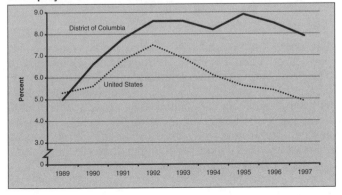

UNEMPLOYMENT RATES REMAINED CONSISTENTLY HIGH throughout the 1990s. The city lacked the manufacturing and construction jobs that typically are cyclical; thus, high unemployment in the District reflected the weakness of its economy. While the nation recovered from the early 1990s recession with strong increases in employment, total employment of D.C. residents declined every year and unemployment hardly dipped below 8 percent. Further, labor force participation declined by more than 5 points from 1990 to 1997, as job seekers became discouraged or young people never sought work at all. The employment to population ratio was a low 55.1 percent in 1997.

POPULATION AND LABOR FORCE

DECLINES IN POPULATION IN THE 1990S MARKED Washington, D.C., as one of the nation's most distressed cities. Out-migration consisted mostly of working- and middle-class families concerned about deteriorating schools and high crime rates, and it resulted in a 20.3 percent loss of total population from 1990 to 1997. Partly offsetting this loss, foreign immigration added 3.9 percent to the population and there was a 3.8 percent natural increase. Birth rates and death rates were both higher than the U.S. average during the 1990s, combining to create above-average natural growth (though birth rates declined markedly during the 1990s). These population declines accelerated the negative trend of the 1980s, when total migration (domestic and international) subtracted 9.5 percent from 1980 population levels.

The composition of the city's population became slightly more diverse in 1997 compared with 1990. The Black, non-Hispanic share fell slightly to 61.9 percent of the population, but the percentage of Hispanics rose two points to 7.2 percent and the Asian community grew to 2.9 percent. The non-Hispanic White population share edged up from 27.6 percent to 28.0 percent from 1996 to 1997. The size of an average household declined a bit, to 2.33 in 1996, as it appeared that out-migrants tended to be larger families.

Population and Labor Force

	1980	1990	1991	1992	1993	1994	1995	1996	1997	Change*	
										State	U.S.
Population											
Total number of persons (thousands)	638	604	594	585	577	566	552	540	530	-1.8	1.0
Percent distribution:											
White, Non-Hispanic	26.1	29.4	27.0	26.8	26.8	27.1	27.3	27.6	28.0	-2.6	0.4
Black, Non-Hispanic	69.7	62.9	65.1	64.8	64.3	63.6	63.1	62.5	61.9	-2.1	1.4
Asian	1.1	1.9	2.3	2.6	2.7	2.8	2.9	2.9	2.9	4.1	4.1
Native American	0.2	0.3	0.3	0.3	0.3	0.3	0.3	0.3	0.3	-0.6	1.6
Hispanic	2.8	5.7	5.6	5.8	6.2	6.5	6.8	7.0	7.2	1.5	3.8
In metropolitan areas	100.0	100.0	100.0	100.0	100.0	100.0	100.0	100.0	100.0	-1.9	1.0
Total number of households (thousands)	253	250	247	246	243	238	233	231	NA	-1.3	1.2
Labor Force (thousands)											
Population 16 and over	516	504	490	481	473	462	449	440	432	-2.2	1.0
Civilian labor force	323	329	315	310	307	300	284	271	258	-3.4	1.1
Employed	300	307	290	284	281	275	259	248	238	-3.6	1.2
Percent of population	58.2	61.0	59.2	59.0	59.4	59.5	57.6	56.3	55.1		
Unemployment rate (percent)	7.3	6.6	7.8	8.6	8.6	8.2	8.9	8.5	7.9		

*Compound annual average percent change, 1990–1997; 1990–1996 for households.

Population Change and Components: 1990–97

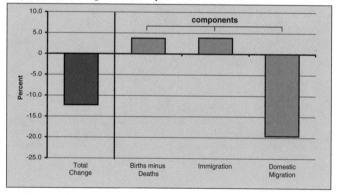

Average Annual Household and Population Growth

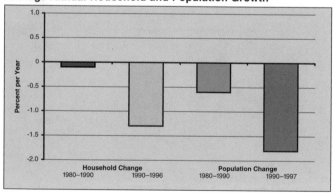

Population by Age; Births and Deaths

	1990		1997	
	State	U.S.	State	U.S.
Age distribution (percent)				
Under 5 years	6.1	7.6	6.3	7.2
5 to 17 years	12.5	18.2	14.0	18.8
18 to 64 years	68.7	61.8	65.9	61.3
65 years and over	12.8	12.5	13.9	12.7
Birth and death rates (per thousand population)				
Births	19.5	16.7	14.9	14.6
Deaths	12.0	8.6	11.7	8.6

THE CITY'S AGE DISTRIBUTION SHIFTED DURING THE 1990–97 period, reflecting the out-migration of working-age adults. The proportion of children and seniors in the population increased. Even so, the resulting age distribution in 1997 showed a much smaller than average proportion of children, due to the large number of singles, childless couples, and "empty nesters" who lived in the city. Those over 65 years of age also comprised a higher share of the population than the national average.

HOUSEHOLD AND PERSONAL INCOME

HOUSEHOLD INCOME AND PERSONS IN POVERTY	1990	1995	1996	1997	
				State	U.S.
Median household income (1997 dollars)	33 637	32 382	32 699	31 860	37 005
Persons in poverty (thousands)	120	122	130	113	35 574
Poverty rate (percent)	21.1	22.2	24.1	21.8	13.3

MEDIAN HOUSEHOLD INCOME IN THE DISTRICT IN 1997 WAS 86 percent as high as the national median, a gap in incomes that developed in the mid 1990s. With a declining proportion of adults at work, this trend was not surprising. Poverty rates have been well above average, as is typical for a large city, but they have not declined since 1990 despite the national downtrend.

Personal income figures appear to display an entirely different picture, showing an increase of 19 percent in real per capita income between 1989 and 1997. Further, the level of personal income per capita through the 1990s was generally about 40 percent above the national average. Transfer payments were 80 percent higher and dividends and interest 36 percent above average. These figures appear to reflect rapid income increases for higher income residents, while typical (median) households have not seen real income increases. Of the $35 billion earned by those working in the city in 1997, most was earned by residents of other jurisdictions. Netting in- and out-commuting, 39.6 percent of total earnings went to District residents, compared to 41.1 percent in 1980 and 48.6 percent in 1970.

Transfer payments were a large proportion of personal income in Washington (21.2 percent in 1997), mainly because of the high concentration of government retirees. Government retirement payments per capita were four times higher than nationally; this was the largest category of cash transfer payments in the city. Income maintenance payments per capita were double the U.S. average and grew rapidly, counter to the national trends. The poverty rate remained high and welfare reform was slow (though benefit levels were reduced), thus family assistance payments and food stamps increased from 1990 to 1997.

Personal Income
(millions of dollars)

	1980	1989	1990	1991	1992	1993	1994	1995	1996	1997	Change*
Earnings by place of work	14 028	26 487	28 410	29 648	31 252	32 556	33 395	33 741	34 039	34 952	3.5
Wages and salaries	12 464	23 171	24 631	25 629	26 913	27 790	28 513	28 811	29 181	30 063	3.3
Other labor income	796	1 950	2 162	2 363	2 566	2 734	2 813	2 749	2 633	2 614	3.7
Proprietors' income	768	1 367	1 617	1 657	1 773	2 033	2 069	2 181	2 226	2 275	6.6
Farm	0	0	0	0	0	0	0	0	0	0	0.0
Nonfarm	768	1 367	1 617	1 657	1 773	2 033	2 069	2 181	2 226	2 275	6.6
(−) Personal contributions for social insurance	736	1 678	1 802	1 907	1 995	2 081	2 140	2 167	2 185	2 259	3.8
(+) Adjustment for residence	-8 261	-15 416	-16 578	-17 460	-18 536	-19 360	-20 008	-20 255	-20 488	-21 120	NA
(=) Net earnings by state of residence	5 031	9 393	10 031	10 281	10 721	11 115	11 247	11 319	11 367	11 573	2.6
(+) Dividends, interest, and rent	1 107	2 614	2 645	2 643	2 612	2 596	2 804	2 869	3 115	3 135	2.3
(+) Transfer payments	1 784	2 622	2 809	3 126	3 392	3 553	3 608	3 594	3 762	3 959	5.3
(=) Total personal income	7 922	14 629	15 484	16 050	16 726	17 264	17 659	17 783	18 244	18 667	3.1
Farm	0	0	0	0	0	0	0	0	0	0	0.0
Nonfarm	7 922	14 629	15 484	16 050	16 726	17 264	17 659	17 783	18 244	18 667	3.1
Personal income per capita (dollars)											
Current dollars	12 412	23 438	25 646	27 040	28 607	29 921	31 205	32 197	33 830	35 290	5.2
1997 dollars	23 732	29 631	30 862	31 224	31 999	32 558	33 162	33 469	34 450	35 290	2.2

*Compound annual average percent change, 1989–1997

Government Transfer Payments

	Millions of dollars		Percent change*	
	1990	1997	State	U.S.
Total government payments to individuals	2 683	3 882	44.7	62.7
Retirement, disability, and insurance	1 416	1 864	31.6	48.2
Social Security	432	546	26.3	46.1
Government employee retirement	949	1 286	35.5	60.3
Medical payments	867	1 445	66.7	101.2
Income maintenance	222	385	73.3	58.0
Supplemental Security Income	55	86	57.0	75.4
Family assistance	91	141	55.1	-0.5
Food Stamps	45	90	99.7	27.1
Other income maintenance	32	69	116.1	189.8
Unemployment insurance benefits	90	79	-11.4	10.6
Veterans benefits and other	88	109	24.3	30.8

*Percent change, 1990–1997

Government Payments to Individuals: 1997

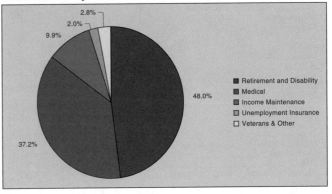

- Retirement and Disability
- Medical
- Income Maintenance
- Unemployment Insurance
- Veterans & Other

2.8%
2.0%
9.9%
48.0%
37.2%

ECONOMIC STRUCTURE

LEADING PRIVATE INDUSTRIES, 1997 (Worker and proprietor earnings, millions of dollars)		FASTEST EARNINGS GROWTH, 1989–97 (percent increase)	
Legal services	$3 666	Security brokers	127.3
Engineering and management services ..	2 819	Social services	73.0
Membership organizations	1 966	Business services	60.5
Health services	1 644	Real estate	53.3
Business services	1 544	Hotels and lodging	52.9

THE WASHINGTON, D.C., ECONOMY DERIVEED 60 PERCENT OF its earnings from the private sector (it was about 50 percent in 1980), but the leading private industries, legal services, accounting firms, and trade associations locate there because it is the nation's capital. The private services sector was the city's largest, contributing 43.5 percent of employment in 1997. This was the only sector that gained jobs from 1989 to 1997, up 2.3 percent, because those industries, as well as a pretty healthy tourism sector, are ancillary to the federal government. All other sectors, including government, showed substantial decreases in employment, reflecting the decline in population and retail, construction, manufacturing activity. Even finance-related employment declined as bank consolidation took hold, though one major employer in the city, the Federal National Mortgage Association (Fannie Mae), helped boost earnings in the fast-growing securities industry. Extensive layoffs in local government and a plateau in federal employment based in the city led to a slimmed-down government sector employing 17 percent fewer people in 1997 than in 1980. Total employment in 1997 had declined to a level just below that of 1980.

The retail sector suffered a broad-based decline during the 1990s as a number of major retail stores closed down and retail purchasing shifted to nearby suburban malls. As most of the earnings from city jobs went to suburban residents, personal income growth failed to translate commensurately into retail sales in the city, and worker earnings in the retail sector declined in current dollars. The construction sector declined even more, reflecting a slowdown in building activity but also the growing predominance of suburban firms undertaking work in the city.

Employment and Earnings by Sector

	1980	1989	1990	1991	1992	1993	1994	1995	1996	1997 Number	1997 Percent of total	Change*
Employment (thousands of persons)												
Total	706	778	787	775	768	768	748	733	716	710	100.0	-1.1
Farm	0	0	0	0	0	0	0	0	0	0	0.0	0.0
Nonfarm	706	778	787	775	768	768	748	733	716	710	100.0	-1.1
Private nonfarm	400	485	485	471	461	462	458	457	456	454	64.0	-0.8
Agricultural service, forestry, and fishing ..	4	6	7	8	8	9	9	9	10	10	1.4	5.6
Mining	0	1	1	1	0	0	0	0	0	0	0.0	NA
Construction	15	16	16	13	10	10	11	10	10	11	1.5	-5.0
Manufacturing	16	17	16	16	15	15	14	14	14	14	1.9	-2.6
Transportation and public utilities	28	25	25	24	23	23	22	22	22	21	3.0	-2.1
Wholesale trade	12	9	9	8	8	7	6	6	5	5	0.7	-6.0
Retail trade	55	60	58	53	52	51	51	51	49	47	6.6	-2.9
Finance, insurance, and real estate	50	50	47	45	41	41	37	36	36	37	5.2	-3.6
Services	220	302	306	304	303	306	307	308	309	309	43.5	0.3
Government	306	293	301	304	307	306	290	276	260	255	36.0	-1.7
Earnings (millions of dollars)												
Total	14 028	26 487	28 410	29 648	31 252	32 556	33 395	33 741	34 039	34 952	100.0	3.5
Farm	0	0	0	0	0	0	0	0	0	0	0.0	0.0
Nonfarm	14 028	26 487	28 410	29 648	31 252	32 556	33 395	33 741	34 039	34 952	100.0	3.5
Private nonfarm	7 128	15 504	16 720	16 959	17 783	18 500	19 088	19 632	20 314	20 811	59.5	3.7
Agricultural service, forestry, and fishing ..	100	222	250	267	276	314	319	328	336	348	1.0	5.8
Mining	30	6	8	11	10	12	11	15	15	17	0.0	12.7
Construction	280	499	525	439	371	352	368	367	380	416	1.2	-2.2
Manufacturing	402	798	820	822	835	853	876	905	931	965	2.8	2.4
Transportation and public utilities	736	1 171	1 170	1 187	1 230	1 253	1 250	1 296	1 324	1 347	3.9	1.8
Wholesale trade	290	352	384	390	404	353	310	309	298	311	0.9	-1.5
Retail trade	595	956	954	893	891	885	897	898	880	868	2.5	-1.2
Finance, insurance, and real estate	653	1 376	1 436	1 433	1 606	1 687	1 650	1 744	1 875	1 998	5.7	4.8
Services	4 042	10 125	11 172	11 517	12 160	12 791	13 407	13 768	14 275	14 541	41.6	4.6
Government	6 901	10 983	11 690	12 689	13 469	14 057	14 307	14 109	13 725	14 141	40.5	3.2

*Compound annual average percent change, 1989–1997

ECONOMIC STRUCTURE (Continued)

AVERAGE WAGES PAID TO THOSE WHO WORK IN WASHINGTON, D.C., generally were very high, fully 51 percent above those of the nation. Wages were much higher than the U.S. average in every sector except retail trade. Within services, the high averages reflected the high wages within law and accounting, as well as associations that dominate the sector. In government, which is 87 percent federal (by earnings), the workforce had a large proportion of high pay grades. The finance sector had the highest average pay of any major sector, partly because of specialized financial institutions such as Fannie Mae and the Student Loan Marketing Association (Sallie Mae). Wages in retail, construction, and low-skill jobs generally were modestly above U.S. averages because of the high cost of living in the area.

The city has no significant manufacturing sectors, because of its history as a government town, limited land and the high cost of land, and limited highway transportation access. The value of manufacturing output equaled only about 2.5 percent of gross state product in 1997, lower than that of any state. There is one leading industry, printing and publishing, whose $765 million in 1997 earnings comprised 79 percent of all manufacturing earnings. However, this amount decrease because *The Washington Post* recently moved its newspaper presses out of the District. Very small startup industries in electronics and transportation equipment began in 1996, and the city hopes to attract additional small high-tech companies.

With very little goods production in the District, few foreign exports are produced. The largest reported export, transportation equipment, and the small but equally puzzling amount of agricultural exports may reflect the export of goods produced elsewhere by a company with a District-based office.

Average Annual Wages and Salaries by Sector
(dollars)

	1989	1996	1997 State	1997 U.S.
All wage and salary workers	31 705	43 224	45 070	29 809
Farm	NA	NA	NA	16 442
Nonfarm	31 705	43 224	45 070	29 900
Private nonfarm	29 445	39 790	41 368	29 867
Agricultural service, forestry, and fishing	35 605	35 048	36 093	17 941
Mining	NA	NA	NA	49 800
Construction	28 739	34 840	36 973	31 765
Manufacturing	39 667	53 669	56 748	38 351
Transportation and utilities	42 578	55 824	59 978	38 222
Wholesale trade	37 914	51 467	55 842	39 466
Retail trade	15 047	16 998	17 681	16 206
Finance, insurance, and real estate	35 944	56 817	61 560	44 993
Services	29 572	40 243	41 262	27 588
Government	35 088	48 706	51 034	30 062

Gross State Product and Manufacturing
(millions of dollars, except as noted)

	1989	1994	1995	1996
Gross state product, total	38 006	48 142	49 686	51 197
Manufacturing:				
Millions of dollars	1 465	1 240	1 178	1 285
Percent of total gross state product	3.9	2.6	2.4	2.5
Per worker (dollars)	87 761	89 048	86 262	93 400
New capital expenditures, manufacturing	NA	44	67	44

Exports of Goods
(millions of dollars)

	1994	1995	1996	1997
All goods	5 151	5 324	5 085	4 881
Manufactures	5 004	5 127	4 897	4 766
Agricultural and livestock products	60	127	116	33
Other commodities	87	70	71	82
Top goods exports, 1997:				
Transportation equipment	2 766	2 520	3 284	2 549
Scientific and measuring instruments	162	180	81	420
Fabricated metal products	693	902	344	386
Industrial machinery and computers	276	283	245	372
Electric and electronic equipment	251	338	217	336

HOUSING

THE CITY'S HOUSING MARKET WAS EXTREMELY SOFT DURING most of the 1990s as the city experienced a population exodus. New home production was miniscule, because of the scarcity of vacant land in high-demand areas and market weakness elsewhere. Further, a lot of development was renovation and/or conversion into condominiums, which were not captured in the building permit statistics. Sales activity was better for existing homes, leaping upward in 1989 and continuing higher than previously in the 1980s. Another surge came in 1997, with renewed optimism about the city and a new federal tax benefit for homebuyers. Median home sales prices have been high since the early 1980s run-up, though prices declined during the 1990s and price levels equalized somewhat with those of the area suburbs. Median sales prices in the city in 1997 were about equal to the median price of $166,300 for the entire metro area.

Rates of homeownership were low in the District because of transience, the lack of affordability for many poor households, and the large stock of multifamily buildings. A city government loan program has assisted a num-

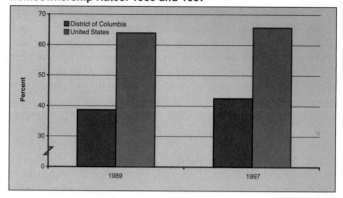

Homeownership Rates: 1989 and 1997

ber of working-class households to purchase, which, along with the federal tax credit, boosted the homeownership rate in 1995–97. Among rental units, the market deteriorated sharply after 1992, when the population outflow began to leave vacant large blocks of apartments in some neighborhoods.

Housing Supply

	1989	1990	1991	1992	1993	1994	1995	1996	1997
Residential building permits (thousands)	0.4	0.4	0.3	0.1	0.3	0.2	0.0	0.0	0.0
New home production (including manufactured housing):									
Thousands of homes	0.4	0.4	0.3	0.1	0.3	0.2	0.0	0.0	0.0
Rate per 1,000 population									
District of Columbia	0.6	0.7	0.5	0.2	0.5	0.4	0.0	0.0	0.0
U.S.	6.2	5.2	4.5	5.1	5.6	6.4	6.3	6.6	6.5
Existing home sales:									
Thousands of homes	15.5	13.1	12.5	12.4	12.3	12.3	11.6	10.8	14.2
Change from previous year (percent)									
District of Columbia	93.8	-15.5	-4.6	-0.8	-0.8	0.0	-5.7	-6.9	31.5
U.S.	-3.9	-4.0	0.0	9.2	8.2	4.8	-3.7	7.5	3.8
Home ownership rate (percent of households)	38.7	36.4	35.1	35.0	35.7	37.8	39.2	40.4	42.5
Rental vacancy rate (percent of rental housing units)	5.1	7.7	8.8	9.7	7.7	10.3	12.9	13.4	13.2

Note: Manufactured housing data for 1996 suppressed because estimate was based on too few responses.

AGRICULTURE

THERE ARE NO COMMERCIAL FARMS WITHIN THE DISTRICT OF Columbia and no official farm market activity.

EDUCATION

EDUCATIONAL ATTAINMENT Percent of population age 25 and over, 1997	State	United States
High school graduate or higher	80.3	82.1
College graduate or higher	33.7	23.9

EDUCATIONAL ATTAINMENT IN WASHINGTON, D.C., IS THE highest in the nation in the percentage of college graduates in the population, 33.7 percent, reflecting the highly skilled workers attracted to government, law, and related public policy professions in the city. Further, nearly half of current young adults are enrolled in higher education, a much higher rate than the average for the United States. This number partly reflects enrollment at four private universities serving primarily students originally from outside the District. In contrast, the disproportionate number of poor and older residents means the share of high school graduates, 80.3 percent, ranks the city among the lower half of states. Poor achievement levels in the public elementary and secondary schools have led to significant enrollment in private schools in the city, despite high average spending per pupil in the public schools. The high spending figure reflects high overhead spending on facilities and administration after enrollment dropped in the 1990s.

High School Completion: 1990–97

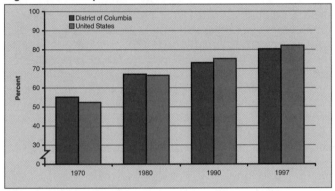

Education Indicators

	State	U.S.
Elementary and secondary schools		
Enrollment, 1995–96		
Total (thousands)	97	49 873
Percent in private schools	18.0	10.1
Expenditures per pupil (dollars), 1995–96	9 565	6 146
Average teacher salary (dollars), 1996–97	45 012	38 509
Higher education		
Enrollment, 1996–97		
Total (thousands)	74	14 218
Percent of population 18–34	47.9	21.8
Percent minority	45.7	26.1
Percent in private schools	90.0	22.6

HEALTH

CITY RESIDENTS ARE LESS HEALTHY THAN AVERAGE IN PART because of the high rate of poverty. Although rates of infant mortality have declined dramatically over the 1990–97 period, the 12.0 per thousand rate was still the highest in the nation. General death rates are also considerably higher than average, led by extremely high numbers of deaths from heart disease and cancer, including breast cancer (the District population has an especially high concentration of women). Death rates from homicide and HIV are also high, but the rate of death from motor vehicle accidents is low. The percent of the population covered by health insurance is about average, as the high rate of coverage among government workers is balanced by lower coverage among the many retail and service workers.

Health Indicators

	1990	1995	1996	1997
Infant mortality *(rate per thousand live births)*				
District of Columbia	20.7	16.2	14.9	12.0
U.S.	9.2	7.6	7.3	7.1
Total deaths, age-adjusted rate *(rate per thousand population)*				
District of Columbia	8.1	8.1	7.8	7.2
U.S.	5.2	5.0	4.9	4.8
Persons not covered by health insurance *(percent of population)*				
District of Columbia	19.2	17.3	14.8	16.2
U.S.	13.9	15.4	15.6	16.1

Leading Causes of Death, 1996
(deaths per 100,000 population)

	Age-adjusted		Not age-adjusted	
	State	U.S.	State	U.S.
Deaths from all causes	780.1	491.6	1219.4	872.5
Heart disease	154.2	134.5	298.0	276.4
Cancer	153.1	127.9	254.0	203.4
Cerebrovascular diseases	33.6	26.4	67.6	60.3
Chronic obstructive pulmonary disease	15.8	21.0	29.8	40.0
Diabetes mellitus	22.3	13.6	37.2	23.3
Pneumonia and influenza	17.0	12.8	37.4	31.6
HIV	87.6	11.1	99.6	11.7
Liver disease	14.3	7.5	17.7	9.4
Alzheimer's disease	2.1	2.7	7.4	8.1
Accidents and adverse effects	26.7	30.4	33.0	35.8
Motor vehicle accidents	10.5	16.2	10.9	16.5
Suicide	5.7	10.8	6.4	11.6
Homicide	72.9	8.5	59.8	7.9
Injury by firearm	60.7	12.9	49.2	12.8

GOVERNMENT

STATE AND LOCAL TAXES, 1995–96	State	U.S.
Per capita (dollars)	4 285	2 477
Percent of personal income	12.5	10.8

THE CITY OF WASHINGTON, D.C., CARRIES ON LOCAL GOVERN-ment functions as well as those of a state and supports itself primarily through taxes. Through most of the 1990s, a modest "federal payment" was made as compensation for local services provided to the federal sector. Still, the level of taxes per capita in Washington, D.C., is greater than average because of a large local government work-force and a shrinking population base to support it. Taxes

State Government Finances, 1996–97

	Millions of dollars	Percent distribu- tion	Dollars per capita	
			State	U.S.
General revenue	4 910	100.0	9 042	4 609
Intergovernmental revenue	1 871	38.1	3 446	885
Taxes	2 481	50.5	4 569	2 597
General sales	468	9.5	862	637
Selective sales	327	6.7	602	301
License taxes	17	0.3	31	52
Individual income	689	14.0	1 269	554
Corporation net income	154	3.1	284	121
Other taxes	826	16.8	1 521	933
Other general revenue	558	11.4	1 028	1 567
General expenditure	5 817	100.0	10 713	5 268
Intergovernmental expenditure	0	0.0	0	15
Direct expenditure	5 817	100.0	10 713	5 254
General expenditure, by function:				
Education	669	11.5	1 232	1 504
Public welfare	1 172	20.1	2 158	729
Hospitals and health	432	7.4	796	418
Highways	89	1.5	164	298
Police protection and corrections	540	9.3	994	310
Natural resources, parks and recreation	60	1.0	110	132
Governmental administration	308	5.3	567	234
Interest on general debt	313	5.4	576	222
Other and unallocable	2 234	38.4	4 114	1 422
Debt at end of fiscal year	4 137	NA	7 619	4 409
Cash and security holdings	4 727	NA	8 705	8 526

Federal Spending within State

	Federal funds, fiscal 1997		
	Millions of dollars	Percent distribution	Percent of U.S. total*
Total within state	23 125	100.0	1.6
Payments to individuals	2 978	12.9	0.4
Retirement and disability	1 521	6.6	0.3
Medicare	581	2.5	0.3
Food stamps	92	0.4	0.5
Supplemental Security Income	89	0.4	0.3
Grants	3 727	16.1	1.5
Medicaid and other health	826	3.6	0.7
Nutrition and family welfare	269	1.2	0.6
Education	428	1.9	2.5
Housing and community development	135	0.6	1.2
Salaries and wages	11 598	50.2	7.0
Defense procurement contracts	1 139	4.9	1.0
Non-defense procurement contracts	3 043	13.2	4.2

*State population is 0.2 percent of the U.S. total.

per capita of $4,285 in 1995–96 were 73 percent above the U.S. average, partly because of the high per capita person-al income in the city; taxes as a percent of income were 16 percent above the U.S. average.

Detailed revenue data from 1995–96 (the most recent available) show a very high level of income taxes per capi-ta compared to all state and local governments in the United States, and sales taxes are modestly above average. The high figure for "other taxes" in this case reflects most-ly local property taxes. The other major revenue compo-nent is intergovernmental transfers from the federal gov-ernment, which are high because of the "federal pay-ment"; combined with other federal grants-in-aid, the total comprised 38 percent of city revenue. Expenditure data show extraordinarily high expenses for public wel-fare, because of the large poor population and relatively generous benefits. Education spending per capita is not very high compared with a typical state and local govern-ment, because the total number of school-age children in the city is disproportionately low. Medical spending is very high because of the large Medicaid-eligible population and extensive use of the public hospital. Spending for administration and interest on the city's debt are also very high relative to the U.S. average, and the city had a very high level of debt for its size.

Not surprisingly, there is a high level of federal spend-ing in Washington, D.C., primarily through wages paid to federal workers. The wages paid in the city comprise 7 percent of all federal civilian and military wages paid throughout the United States. (Because much of this money is earned by residents commuting from Virginia and Maryland, the benefit to the city economy is diluted considerably.) The second largest federal expenditure is for non-defense procurement, much of which is spending to support basic building operations in the capital as well as policy research work. Grant funding is disproportion-ately large, especially in education, because of the city's high concentration of disadvantaged residents.

31 372	59 698		65 157	70 827	72 687	78 001	81 93	88 504	93 426	5.8	63 383	70 827	31 372	59 698	63 3
25 323	47 902		57 151	59 446	62 916	67 00		72 039	77 208	6.1	50 999	57 151	25 323	47 902	50 9
2 640	5 143			7 801				7 709	7 838	5.4	5 645	6 816	2 640	5 143	5 6
3 409	6 652		284					8 755	8 380	2.9	6 739	8 860	3 409	6 652	6 7
693	1 716		307					1 539	762	-9.7	1 561	811	693	1 716	1 6
2 716	4 93							7 217	7 618	-5.6	5 178	8 049	2 716		

1997

Population (persons)	14,677,181
Population rank	4th
Population growth rank (1990–97)	11th
Per capita personal income	$24,795
Unemployment rate (percent)	4.8
Poverty rate (percent)	14.3

FLORIDA IS PROJECTED TO SURPASS NEW YORK TO BECOME THE third most populous state, after California and Texas, by 2020. Its warm winter climate continues to make it a premier retirement location, a tourist mecca, and a world leader in production of fruits and vegetables.

Ninety-three percent of Florida's population lived in its 20 metropolitan areas. The two largest metropolitan areas, Tampa-St. Petersburg-Clearwater, with a population of 2.2 million in 1997, and Miami, with 2.0 million, contrasted in many respects. Miami, a city with a distinctly Latin flavor, was a major transportation hub and international financial center. In 1997, 56 percent of Miami's population was Hispanic, compared to only 9 percent for Tampa-St.

Petersburg-Clearwater. Persons aged 65 and older made up 14 percent of the metropolitan Miami population, somewhat more than the 13 percent U.S. average, but for Tampa-St. Petersburg-Clearwater the proportion was far higher at 22 percent.

Florida ranked second among the states in the value of its vegetable crop and led the nation in the production of tomatoes and sweet corn. Florida produces 75 percent of the nation's oranges. Yet only 3.5 percent of Florida's land area was used for vegetable fields and citrus crops, and Florida's 89,000 thousand farm jobs in 1997 were far outranked by 515,000 manufacturing jobs and 2.8 million jobs in the rapidly growing service sector.

Average Annual Population Growth: 1990–97

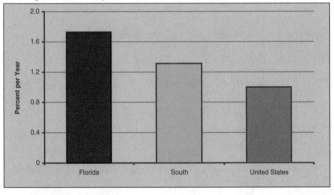

Median Household Income: 1989–97 (1997 dollars)

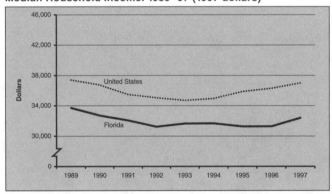

Unemployment Rate: 1989–97

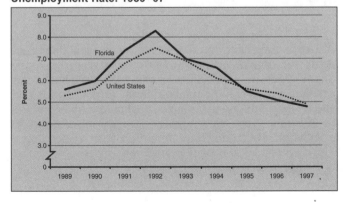

ALREADY ABOVE THE NATIONAL AVERAGE IN 1990, FLORIDA'S unemployment rate rose rapidly in the early-'90s recession, peaking at 8.3 percent in 1992. Since 1992, with employment growth above the national average, the state's unemployment rate has fallen steadily. It crept below the U.S. rate in 1995 and remained under the national average after that, falling to 4.8 percent in 1997.

POPULATION AND LABOR FORCE

FLORIDA WAS ONE OF THREE STATES—CALIFORNIA AND TEXAS were the others—with a population increase of more than one million from 1990 to 1997. Its 1.7 percent annual population growth was well above the national average but below the 2.0 percent rate of neighboring Georgia. Although rapid, 1990s population growth in Florida has been slower than in the 1980s, when it approached 3 percent annually.

More than one-half of Florida's population growth from 1990 to 1997 was due to net in-migration from other states and more than one-fourth to immigration from abroad. Only 20 percent was due to natural increase, that is, to the higher number of births than deaths.

Florida's already diverse population grew increasingly so during the 1990s. Hispanics were 14.4 percent of the population in 1997, compared to 12.2 percent in 1990. Blacks also increased their population share. Asians, although still less than 2 percent of the population, increased their numbers by 56 percent from 1990 to 1997.

Florida's labor force grew less rapidly than its population, suggesting that a high proportion of those moving into the state continue to be retirees. Even so, Florida's annual labor force growth of 1.4 percent from 1990 to 1997 was well above the 1.1 percent U.S. average.

Population and Labor Force

	1980	1990	1991	1992	1993	1994	1995	1996	1997	Change* State	Change* U.S.
Population											
Total number of persons (thousands)	9 746	13 019	13 290	13 502	13 712	13 954	14 180	14 425	14 677	1.7	1.0
Percent distribution:											
White, Non-Hispanic	76.7	73.1	72.6	72.1	71.6	71.0	70.3	69.7	69.2	0.9	0.4
Black, Non-Hispanic	13.5	13.2	13.4	13.6	13.8	14.1	14.2	14.4	14.6	3.1	1.4
Asian	0.6	1.2	1.3	1.4	1.4	1.5	1.6	1.7	1.7	6.5	4.1
Native American	0.3	0.3	0.3	0.3	0.3	0.3	0.3	0.4	0.4	5.0	1.6
Hispanic	8.8	12.2	12.5	12.7	13.0	13.3	13.7	14.1	14.4	4.1	3.8
In metropolitan areas	92.7	92.9	92.9	92.9	92.9	92.9	92.8	92.8	92.8	1.7	1.0
Total number of households (thousands)	3 744	5 135	5 237	5 340	5 379	5 451	5 551	5 648	NA	1.6	1.2
Labor Force (thousands)											
Population 16 and over	7 714	10 340	10 555	10 699	10 826	11 000	11 170	11 361	11 547	1.6	1.0
Civilian labor force	4 271	6 468	6 489	6 559	6 661	6 811	6 851	6 956	7 119	1.4	1.1
Employed	4 020	6 078	6 009	6 016	6 192	6 363	6 475	6 603	6 781	1.6	1.2
Percent of population	52.1	58.8	56.9	56.2	57.2	57.9	58.0	58.1	58.7		
Unemployment rate (percent)	5.9	6.0	7.4	8.3	7.0	6.6	5.5	5.1	4.8		

*Compound annual average percent change, 1990–1997; 1990–1996 for households.

Population Change and Components: 1990–97

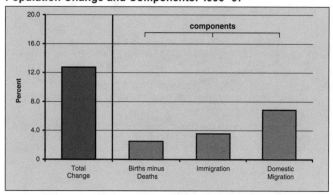

Average Annual Household and Population Growth

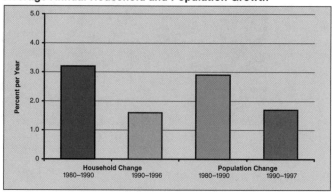

Population by Age; Births and Deaths

	1990 State	1990 U.S.	1997 State	1997 U.S.
Age distribution (percent)				
Under 5 years	6.9	7.6	6.5	7.2
5 to 17 years	16.0	18.2	17.2	18.8
18 to 64 years	58.8	61.8	57.8	61.3
65 years and over	18.2	12.5	18.5	12.7
Birth and death rates (per thousand population)				
Births	15.4	16.7	13.1	14.6
Deaths	10.4	8.6	10.6	8.6

ABOUT 2.7 MILLION, OR 18.5 PERCENT, OF FLORIDA'S residents were age 65 or over in 1997, the largest percentage of any state, although California and New York had larger absolute numbers of people in this age group. Florida's 65 and over population is projected to increase to 3.2 million by 2010 but to rise only slightly as a percent of the total population. Reflecting their longer life span, 57 percent of Florida's age 65 and over population, and 66 percent of those age 85 and over, were women.

HOUSEHOLD AND PERSONAL INCOME

HOUSEHOLD INCOME AND PERSONS IN POVERTY	1990	1995	1996	1997 State	1997 U.S.
Median household income (1997 dollars)	32 769	31 326	31 344	32 455	37 005
Persons in poverty (thousands)	1 896	2 321	2 037	2 056	35 574
Poverty rate (percent)	14.4	16.2	14.2	14.3	13.3

FLORIDA'S 1997 MEDIAN HOUSEHOLD INCOME OF $32,455 WAS about 12 percent below the national average and below that of any other South Atlantic state. Florida's large retired population helps account for the low household income; households made up of retirees have lower average incomes than do households with workers. However, household size also is smaller for retirees, so each household contains fewer people to support. Florida averaged 2.50 persons per household in 1996, compared to 2.65 nationally, and many of Florida's retirees lived alone. Florida's personal per capita income was within 2 percent of the national average in 1997 and above that of any other South Atlantic state except Virginia. Reflecting the large proportion of retirees, earnings made up only 57 percent of personal income, compared to 66 percent nationally. Twenty-four percent was from interest, dividends, and

rent, compared to 17.2 percent nationally, illustrating retirees' heavy reliance on these income sources.

Transfer payments were also a relatively high proportion of Florida's personal income—19.1 percent in 1997, compared to 16.4 percent nationally. Three-fourths of government transfers consisted of Social Security benefits and medical payments. Also significant were veterans benefits, retirement payments to former government employees, and Supplemental Security Income (SSI). Income maintenance other than SSI was less than 5 percent of all 1997 transfers. Family assistance payments rose only 10 percent from 1990 to 1997, implying a substantial decline once adjusted for inflation. "Other income maintenance," which consists largely of the earned income tax credit, grew "fivefold" to become the largest category within income maintenance.

Personal Income
(millions of dollars)

	1980	1989	1990	1991	1992	1993	1994	1995	1996	1997	Change*
Earnings by place of work	61 882	140 871	150 415	154 754	164 944	176 426	184 805	195 842	207 298	220 438	5.8
Wages and salaries	49 559	115 210	123 320	126 680	134 658	142 130	149 682	159 256	169 803	181 709	5.9
Other labor income	4 545	11 777	13 177	13 779	14 687	16 581	18 103	18 387	18 528	18 731	6.0
Proprietors' income	7 779	13 883	13 918	14 295	15 599	17 714	17 021	18 199	18 967	19 997	4.7
Farm	1 273	1 917	1 423	1 959	1 828	1 971	1 138	1 131	893	928	-8.7
Nonfarm	6 506	11 966	12 495	12 336	13 771	15 744	15 882	17 068	18 075	19 070	6.0
(−) Personal contributions for social insurance	3 152	9 263	9 822	10 347	11 021	11 746	12 614	13 447	14 043	14 970	6.2
(+) Adjustment for residence	10	458	558	612	653	524	532	459	490	522	NA
(=) **Net earnings by state of residence**	58 741	132 066	141 151	145 019	154 576	165 204	172 723	182 853	193 745	205 990	5.7
(+) Dividends, interest, and rent	23 306	64 500	67 907	68 628	63 710	69 465	73 055	76 374	84 081	88 023	4.0
(+) Transfer payments	15 933	36 035	39 946	44 848	50 542	54 383	57 870	62 188	65 827	69 334	8.5
(=) **Total personal income**	97 980	232 601	249 004	258 495	268 828	289 052	303 647	321 415	343 652	363 347	5.7
Farm	1 756	2 618	2 230	2 724	2 559	2 823	1 941	2 020	1 795	1 854	-4.2
Nonfarm	96 224	229 982	246 773	255 771	266 269	286 229	301 707	319 395	341 857	361 493	5.8
Personal income per capita (dollars)											
Current dollars	9 957	18 405	19 128	19 457	19 912	21 081	21 758	22 665	23 833	24 795	3.8
1997 dollars	19 038	23 268	23 018	22 468	22 273	22 939	23 122	23 560	24 270	24 795	0.8

*Compound annual average percent change, 1989–1997

Government Transfer Payments

	Millions of dollars 1990	Millions of dollars 1997	Percent change* State	Percent change* U.S.
Total government payments to individuals	38 421	66 991	74.4	62.7
Retirement, disability, and insurance	22 633	34 686	53.3	48.2
Social Security	16 438	25 471	54.9	46.1
Government employee retirement	5 640	8 381	48.6	60.3
Medical payments	11 538	24 814	115.1	101.2
Income maintenance	2 093	4 512	115.5	58.0
Supplemental Security Income	666	1 472	121.0	75.4
Family assistance	462	511	10.6	-0.5
Food Stamps	660	991	50.1	27.1
Other income maintenance	305	1 538	404.1	189.8
Unemployment insurance benefits	521	698	33.9	10.6
Veterans benefits and other	1 636	2 281	39.4	30.8

*Percent change, 1990–1997

Government Payments to Individuals: 1997

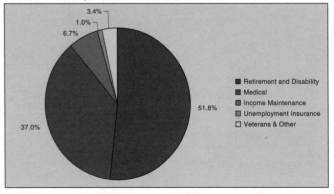

3.4%
1.0%
6.7%
51.8%
37.0%

- ■ Retirement and Disability
- ■ Medical
- ▨ Income Maintenance
- ▨ Unemployment Insurance
- ☐ Veterans & Other

ECONOMIC STRUCTURE

LEADING PRIVATE INDUSTRIES, 1997 (Worker and proprietor earnings, millions of dollars)		FASTEST EARNINGS GROWTH, 1989–97 (percent increase)	
Health services	$23 607	Business services	153.4
Business services	15 556	Security brokers	120.9
Construction specialties	8 585	Amusement and recreation services	110.3
Engineering and management services	8 368	Real estate	104.7
Eating and drinking places	6 492	Social services	104.1

THE NEEDS OF ITS LARGE ELDERLY POPULATION HELPED MAKE health care Florida's largest industry, providing 635,000 jobs in 1997 and generating $23.6 million in earnings. Health care needs, a booming tourist industry, and a large financial sector gave Florida a predominantly service-producing economy. Seventy-one percent of employment and 68 percent of earnings in 1997 were in private service-producing industries, compared to national averages of 65 percent and 59 percent, respectively.

Among Florida's top five industries—and, indeed, among its top ten or more, measured by earnings—all except construction specialties were part of the service-producing sector, as were each of the 10 industries with the most rapid earnings growth. The top five are shown above. Following them, with growth of 70 percent or more from 1989 to 1997, are air transportation, educational services, health services, engineering and management services, and agricultural services.

Not all of Florida's service industries grew so rapidly. Some major industries, including banking and eating and drinking places, grew only in line with the overall growth of Florida's economy, and, despite tourism's importance, the hotel industry grew a bit more slowly than the all-industry average.

Taking a broader look at employment, 1.4 million jobs were added to Florida's economy from 1989 to 1997, virtually all in service-producing industries. Employment in manufacturing, mining, and farming declined, and construction employment was flat. A long-range forecast by the Bureau of Economic and Business Research at the University of Florida projects that service-producing industries will continue to dominate job growth; ninety-five percent of job growth from 1995 to 2010 will be in these industries and the remainder in construction.

Employment and Earnings by Sector

	1980	1989	1990	1991	1992	1993	1994	1995	1996	1997 Number	1997 Percent of total	Change*
Employment *(thousands of persons)*												
Total	4 695	6 661	6 787	6 785	6 833	7 071	7 315	7 534	7 769	8 024	100.0	2.4
Farm	106	95	92	92	96	93	96	89	85	89	1.1	-0.8
Nonfarm	4 589	6 566	6 695	6 692	6 737	6 978	7 219	7 445	7 685	7 935	98.9	2.4
Private nonfarm	3 854	5 619	5 702	5 690	5 733	5 973	6 201	6 425	6 654	6 887	85.8	2.6
Agricultural service, forestry, and fishing	85	113	119	126	123	134	139	141	149	154	1.9	3.9
Mining	14	16	16	16	14	13	14	14	13	12	0.1	-3.8
Construction	325	455	436	386	381	403	413	425	449	460	5.7	0.1
Manufacturing	466	554	534	513	502	506	509	506	513	515	6.4	-0.9
Transportation and public utilities	245	303	315	319	317	334	347	356	373	388	4.8	3.1
Wholesale trade	235	315	316	316	325	324	335	349	363	376	4.7	2.3
Retail trade	850	1 276	1 291	1 275	1 287	1 325	1 374	1 409	1 466	1 487	18.5	1.9
Finance, insurance, and real estate	477	593	592	579	562	576	604	618	641	662	8.2	1.4
Services	1 155	1 993	2 083	2 160	2 222	2 357	2 466	2 607	2 687	2 833	35.3	4.5
Government	736	947	993	1 002	1 004	1 005	1 018	1 020	1 030	1 048	13.1	1.3
Earnings *(millions of dollars)*												
Total	61 882	140 871	150 415	154 754	164 944	176 426	184 805	195 842	207 298	220 438	100.0	5.8
Farm	1 756	2 618	2 230	2 724	2 559	2 823	1 941	2 020	1 795	1 854	0.8	-4.2
Nonfarm	60 126	138 252	148 185	152 030	162 385	173 603	182 864	193 822	205 503	218 584	99.2	5.9
Private nonfarm	50 283	115 670	123 003	125 325	134 823	144 756	153 037	162 835	173 263	184 757	83.8	6.0
Agricultural service, forestry, and fishing	590	1 386	1 570	1 682	1 753	1 867	1 983	2 016	2 130	2 267	1.0	6.3
Mining	680	351	345	339	340	328	316	356	398	357	0.2	0.2
Construction	5 152	10 382	10 373	9 212	9 255	10 321	10 966	11 528	12 620	13 275	6.0	3.1
Manufacturing	7 930	15 818	16 144	16 269	16 999	17 349	17 928	18 107	18 728	19 557	8.9	2.7
Transportation and public utilities	5 124	9 104	9 821	10 199	10 947	12 011	12 550	13 270	13 857	14 679	6.7	6.2
Wholesale trade	4 103	9 190	9 765	9 938	10 705	10 705	11 040	11 827	12 742	13 892	14 717	6.7	6.1
Retail trade	7 995	17 561	18 196	18 295	19 329	20 656	21 957	22 854	24 412	25 576	11.6	4.8
Finance, insurance, and real estate	4 855	11 056	11 499	11 823	13 746	15 296	15 698	17 138	18 687	20 258	9.2	7.9
Services	13 853	40 821	45 291	47 569	51 748	55 887	59 810	64 823	68 538	74 070	33.6	7.7
Government	9 844	22 582	25 182	26 705	27 563	28 847	29 827	30 987	32 240	33 827	15.3	5.2

*Compound annual average percent change, 1989–1997

ECONOMIC STRUCTURE (Continued)

FLORIDA'S $26,494 AVERAGE ANNUAL WAGE IN 1997 WAS about 11 percent below the national average. A gap was present in every sector except retail trade, the lowest paying nonfarm sector nationally. The largest gap was found in mining, but mining was a tiny share of Florida's economy and contained almost none of the oil and gas extraction that represents the high-wage component of mining elsewhere. More general factors that likely contributed to Florida's relatively low annual wages were the availability of immigrant labor and of retirees seeking to supplement pension income. Recent immigrants typically must settle for lower wages than comparably skilled long-time residents, and retirees already receiving pension income may choose desirable working conditions over higher wages. Also, they may often work part time, reducing the average annual wage relative to the hourly wage.

Florida's manufacturing sector was small relative to the total size of the Florida economy. Manufacturing makes up only about 8 percent of Florida's Gross State Product (GSP), less than one-half the national average of 17.5 percent, and far below other southern states, where manufacturing ranges from 15 to 28 percent of GSP. The relatively small role of manufacturing in the Florida economy reflected the dominance of tourism, financial services, and health care rather than any inherent weakness in the manufacturing sector. The slow growth of manufacturing earnings from 1989 to 1997 and the small decline in employment are in line with national trends. Manufacturing contributed $29.3 billion to Florida's GSP in 1996 and employed 515,000 workers in 1997.

Florida's manufacturing was diverse; no one industry dominated. The largest, electronic and other electrical products, accounted for 15 percent of Florida's $19.6 billion of manufacturing earnings in 1996. This industry will be an important contributor to any growth in manufacturing over the next 10 to 15 years. The University of Florida's Bureau of Business and Economic Research projects that, in combination, the electronics and instruments industries will add 23,000 Florida jobs between 1995 and 2010, substantially more than any other manufacturing industry.

Florida's exports, which reached almost $23 billion in 1997, were predominantly high-tech manufactured goods. The five leading export industries shown are all relatively high-tech; together they accounted for almost 70 percent of Florida's exports. Agricultural exports also were important to Florida. The $640 million of agricultural and livestock product exports in 1997 were supplemented by $961 million in exports of manufactured food products, bringing Florida's total agriculture-related exports to about $1.6 billion.

Average Annual Wages and Salaries by Sector
(dollars)

	1989	1996	1997 State	1997 U.S.
All wage and salary workers	20 225	25 592	26 494	29 809
Farm	11 617	16 983	15 751	16 442
Nonfarm	20 310	25 654	26 577	29 900
Private nonfarm	19 956	25 122	26 049	29 867
Agricultural service, forestry, and fishing	12 351	14 895	15 663	17 941
Mining	29 898	42 016	38 929	49 800
Construction	21 090	26 215	27 270	31 765
Manufacturing	25 219	32 245	33 751	38 351
Transportation and utilities	27 656	33 597	34 520	38 222
Wholesale trade	27 152	35 833	36 603	39 466
Retail trade	12 892	15 983	16 597	16 206
Finance, insurance, and real estate	25 055	35 102	37 771	44 993
Services	19 612	24 581	25 236	27 588
Government	22 062	28 526	29 476	30 062

Gross State Product and Manufacturing
(millions of dollars, except as noted)

	1989	1994	1995	1996
Gross state product, total	241 772	321 700	339 033	360 496
Manufacturing:				
Millions of dollars	23 700	26 723	28 210	29 286
Percent of total gross state product	9.8	8.3	8.3	8.1
Per worker (dollars)	42 748	52 548	55 772	57 091
New capital expenditures, manufacturing	NA	2 041	2 346	2 644

Exports of Goods
(millions of dollars)

	1994	1995	1996	1997
All goods	16 559	18 564	19 618	22 889
Manufactures	15 235	17 495	18 468	21 715
Agricultural and livestock products	911	580	652	640
Other commodities	413	489	499	533
Top goods exports, 1997:				
Industrial machinery and computers	3 409	4 097	4 744	5 770
Electric and electronic equipment	2 595	2 956	3 282	4 059
Transportation equipment	2 012	2 144	2 186	2 245
Chemical products	1 706	2 008	1 890	2 239
Scientific and measuring instruments	1 165	1 341	1 453	1 572

HOUSING

FLORIDA'S PACE OF NEW HOME PRODUCTION WAS EXTRAORDInarily high in 1989, more than double the U.S. rate of 6.2 homes per 1,000 population. The 1990–91 recessionary slump was correspondingly severe; the new home production rate fell 44 percent from 1989 to 1991, compared to a 27 percent drop nationwide, and was still well below the 1989 rate in 1997. Even so, reflecting the housing needs of a growing population, Florida's new home production rate remained above the U.S. average throughout the 1990s. Manufactured housing (mobile homes) made up 11 percent of Florida's new home production in 1997, well below the national average of 17 percent. Sales of existing homes fell only slightly in the 1990–91 recession, and, with lower interest rates and more favorable financing conditions, in 1994 through 1997 they averaged some 28 percent above 1989. Florida's homeownership rate was somewhat above the national average and has shown a modest, although irregular, upward trend during the 1990s.

Homeownership Rates: 1989 and 1997

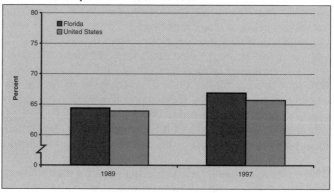

Housing Supply

	1989	1990	1991	1992	1993	1994	1995	1996	1997
Residential building permits (thousands)	165.0	126.3	95.3	102.0	115.1	128.6	122.9	125.0	134.0
New home production (including manufactured housing):									
Thousands of homes	188.4	144.9	109.9	121.9	132.8	145.3	138.2	140.1	150.5
Rate per 1,000 population									
Florida	14.9	11.1	8.3	9.0	9.7	10.4	9.7	9.7	10.3
U.S.	6.2	5.2	4.5	5.1	5.6	6.4	6.3	6.6	6.5
Existing home sales:									
Thousands of homes	177.6	183.3	176.0	179.2	208.9	229.7	220.3	225.5	234.4
Change from previous year (percent)									
Florida	-0.9	3.2	-4.0	1.8	16.6	10.0	-4.1	2.4	3.9
U.S.	-3.9	-4.0	0.0	9.2	8.2	4.8	-3.7	7.5	3.8
Home ownership rate (percent of households)	64.4	65.1	66.1	66.0	65.5	65.7	66.6	67.1	66.9
Rental vacancy rate (percent of rental housing units)	9.5	9.0	9.1	8.7	8.3	8.0	7.8	9.0	9.5

AGRICULTURE

TOTAL NET FARM INCOME AVERAGED $2.4 BILLION PER YEAR from 1989 to 1992 but has since trended downward. Two-thirds of Florida's $6 billion in 1997 agricultural sales came from fruits and nuts, vegetables, and nursery and greenhouse crops. Florida's annual production of oranges grew from 7.3 million metric tons in the late 1970s to 8.4 million in 1995–96, but its share of total world production fell from 20 percent to 15 percent, due primarily to an 80 percent increase in Brazilian production; Florida also was the leading southeastern milk producer. The state is noted

for its breeding of Thoroughbred horses, having produced 39 national champions, according to the Florida Agricultural Statistics Service.

FLORIDA FARMS, 1997	
Number of farms	40 000
Total acres (thousands):	10 300
Average per farm	258
Value of land and buildings (millions of dollars)	23 690
Average per farm (dollars)	592 250

Farm Income
(millions of dollars)

	1980	1989	1990	1991	1992	1993	1994	1995	1996	1997
Gross income	4 372	6 540	6 017	6 468	6 465	6 467	6 383	6 316	6 526	6 534
Receipts from sales	4 221	6 330	5 790	6 239	6 222	6 172	6 131	6 049	6 284	6 291
Government payments	7	38	37	41	53	111	59	56	23	19
Imputed and miscellaneous income	145	172	190	188	190	184	193	212	220	224
(–) Production expenses	3 156	3 897	4 052	4 036	3 934	4 270	4 364	4 703	4 963	4 959
(=) Realized net income	1 216	2 643	1 964	2 432	2 531	2 196	2 019	1 613	1 563	1 575
(+) Inventory change	57	-20	-12	36	11	24	29	-24	0	-43
(=) Net income	1 273	2 622	1 952	2 467	2 542	2 220	2 048	1 589	1 563	1 532
Corporate income	0	705	529	508	715	249	909	458	671	604
Farm proprietors income	1 273	1 917	1 423	1 959	1 828	1 971	1 138	1 131	893	928

EDUCATION

EDUCATIONAL ATTAINMENT Percent of population age 25 and over, 1997	State	United States
High school graduate or higher	81.4	82.1
College graduate or higher	21.7	23.9

THE EDUCATIONAL ATTAINMENT OF FLORIDA RESIDENTS AGE 25 and over was slightly below the U.S. average in 1997. However, the high school graduation percentage was the highest of any southern state, although Virginia was nearly tied at 81.3 percent. That Florida's educational attainment approaches the national average is due in part to the relatively high attainment of its older population. Much of Florida's older population consists of persons who could afford to migrate from other states—persons likely to have higher than average levels of income and education. Among Florida residents age 65 and over, 73.4 percent were high school graduates in 1997 and 17.3 percent had completed college, compared to national averages of 65.6 and 14.8 percent respectively.

Minority students made up almost one-third of 1996–97 enrollment in higher education in Florida; minorities made up 38 percent of Florida's population in the 18–34 age group in 1997, compared to 31 percent of Florida's total population.

High School Completion: 1990–97

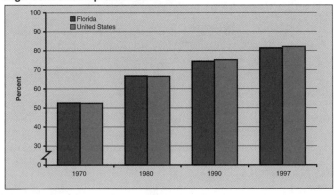

Education Indicators

	State	U.S.
Elementary and secondary schools Enrollment, 1995–96		
Total (thousands)	2 430	49 873
Percent in private schools	10.4	10.1
Expenditures per pupil (dollars), 1995–96	5 894	6 146
Average teacher salary (dollars), 1996–97	33 881	38 509
Higher education Enrollment, 1996–97		
Total (thousands)	641	14 218
Percent of population 18–34	20.2	21.8
Percent minority	32.7	26.1
Percent in private schools	17.2	22.6

HEALTH

BECAUSE OF THE HIGH PERCENTAGE OF OLDER PEOPLE IN Florida's population, the state's death rate was relatively high, but once adjusted to a standardized age distribution, it was about equal to the U.S. average, as was the infant mortality rate. The percentage of the Florida population not covered by health insurance was above the U.S. average. The health insurance estimates include Medicare and Medicaid as well as private health insurance, and national-ly almost 99 percent of the population age 65 and over is covered by health insurance. Assuming the same to be true in Florida, well over 20 percent of the population under age 65 may lack health insurance. Persons between ages 18 and 34 are the group most likely to lack health insurance, and it may be that Florida's substantial minority and immigrant population in this age group helps explain the high overall percentage lacking health insurance.

Health Indicators

	1990	1995	1996	1997
Infant mortality *(rate per thousand live births)*				
Florida	9.6	7.5	7.5	7.2
U.S.	9.2	7.6	7.3	7.1
Total deaths, age-adjusted rate *(rate per thousand population)*				
Florida	5.0	5.0	4.8	4.6
U.S.	5.2	5.0	4.9	4.8
Persons not covered by health insurance *(percent of population)*				
Florida	18.0	18.3	18.9	19.6
U.S.	13.9	15.4	15.6	16.1

Leading Causes of Death, 1996
(deaths per 100,000 population)

	Age-adjusted		Not age-adjusted	
	State	U.S.	State	U.S.
Deaths from all causes	478.4	491.6	1065.6	872.5
Heart disease	123.1	134.5	345.4	276.4
Cancer	127.5	127.9	261.8	203.4
Cerebrovascular diseases	22.8	26.4	68.6	60.3
Chronic obstructive pulmonary disease	20.1	21.0	53.5	40.0
Diabetes mellitus	12.1	13.6	26.4	23.3
Pneumonia and influenza	8.9	12.8	26.5	31.6
HIV	21.4	11.1	21.5	11.7
Liver disease	8.5	7.5	12.7	9.4
Alzheimer's disease	2.4	2.7	10.3	8.1
Accidents and adverse effects	31.5	30.4	37.5	35.8
Motor vehicle accidents	18.8	16.2	19.5	16.5
Suicide	13.1	10.8	15.0	11.6
Homicide	9.2	8.5	8.3	7.9
Injury by firearm	14.1	12.9	14.4	12.8

GOVERNMENT

STATE AND LOCAL TAXES, 1995–96	State	U.S.
Per capita (dollars)	2 260	2 477
Percent of personal income	10.0	10.8

FLORIDA HAS NO INDIVIDUAL INCOME TAX, AND TOTAL TAXES per capita in 1995–96 were below the national average both in dollar amount and as a percentage of personal income. Three-fourths of state tax receipts were from general and selective sales taxes, some significant portions of which were paid by visitors from out of state, so the amount of taxes actually paid by Florida residents was below the estimates shown here, which are derived by

dividing tax collections by the state's population.

Per capita state government spending for health, education, and public welfare was well below the national average, while spending on highways was near average and that on police protection was above. The 23 percent gap between Florida's spending on education and the national average was in part due to the lower than average percentage of the population that was of school age. However, even when per capita education spending was calculated on the population age 5 to 17 rather than on total population, Florida's spending still fell some 15 percent short of the national average. These figures were for state government spending only and do not reflect the extent to which localities may supplement the amount provided by the state. Per pupil spending data indicated a 4 percent gap below the U.S. level for elementary and secondary schools, suggesting that some of the gap in state spending was made up at the local level.

Interest on Florida's general debt averaged only $62 per capita in 1996–97, compared to a national average of $99. Florida appeared to be in sound financial shape at year end, with debt equal to $1,093 per capita, compared to $1,706 nationally, and cash and security holdings about four times the size of the debt.

Florida had 5.5 percent of the nation's population and received 5.8 percent of federal funds distributed to states and their residents in fiscal 1997. However, this larger than proportionate share was entirely due to Social Security and other retirement payments distributed to Florida's retirees, and to Medicare payments made on their behalf. In most other catagories Florida received a less than proportionate share.

State Government Finances, 1996–97

	Millions of dollars	Percent distribution	Dollars per capita State	Dollars per capita U.S.
General revenue	34 281	100.0	2 339	3 049
Intergovernmental revenue	8 297	24.2	566	863
Taxes	21 080	61.5	1 439	1 660
General sales	12 068	35.2	824	551
Selective sales	4 013	11.7	274	257
License taxes	1 370	4.0	94	106
Individual income	0	0.0	0	542
Corporation net income	1 233	3.6	84	115
Other taxes	2 396	7.0	164	90
Other general revenue	4 904	14.3	335	526
General expenditure	34 658	100.0	2 365	2 951
Intergovernmental expenditure	11 900	34.3	812	989
Direct expenditure	22 758	65.7	1 553	1 962
General expenditure, by function:				
Education	11 599	33.5	792	1 033
Public welfare	7 693	22.2	525	761
Hospitals and health	2 402	6.9	164	237
Highways	3 159	9.1	216	225
Police protection and corrections	2 169	6.3	148	137
Natural resources, parks and recreation	1 252	3.6	85	63
Governmental administration	1 536	4.4	105	107
Interest on general debt	905	2.6	62	99
Other and unallocable	3 944	11.4	269	290
Debt at end of fiscal year	16 022	NA	1 093	1 706
Cash and security holdings	65 401	NA	4 463	6 683

Federal Spending within State

	Federal funds, fiscal 1997 Millions of dollars	Federal funds, fiscal 1997 Percent distribution	Federal funds, fiscal 1997 Percent of U.S. total*
Total within state	82 645	100.0	5.8
Payments to individuals	56 691	68.6	7.2
Retirement and disability	33 689	40.8	7.4
Medicare	16 857	20.4	8.2
Food stamps	1 071	1.3	5.5
Supplemental Security Income	1 520	1.8	5.7
Grants	9 411	11.4	3.8
Medicaid and other health	4 053	4.9	3.6
Nutrition and family welfare	2 014	2.4	4.3
Education	775	0.9	4.5
Housing and community development	411	0.5	3.6
Salaries and wages	7 666	9.3	4.6
Defense procurement contracts	6 304	7.6	5.3
Non-defense procurement contracts	1 779	2.2	2.4

*State population is 5.5 percent of the U.S. total.

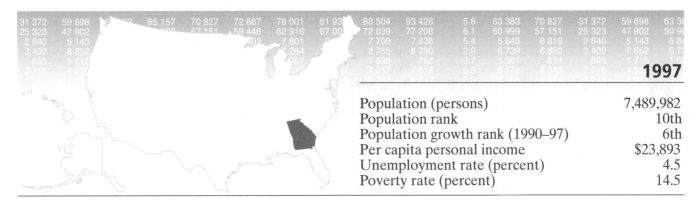

1997

Population (persons)	7,489,982
Population rank	10th
Population growth rank (1990–97)	6th
Per capita personal income	$23,893
Unemployment rate (percent)	4.5
Poverty rate (percent)	14.5

GEORGIA HAD THE MOST RAPID POPULATION GROWTH EAST OF the Rocky Mountain states during the 1990s, representing an increase from the state's already-rapid growth during the 1980s. Georgia's growth has been centered in the vibrant, prosperous Atlanta area. By 1997, almost 50 percent of Georgia's entire population lived in the 20-county Atlanta metropolitan area, which experienced a population increase of 726,000 from 1990 to 1997, bringing its total population to 3.6 million. When Georgia's smaller metropolitan areas—Albany, Athens, Macon, Savannah, and the Georgia parts of Chattanooga (TN-GA) and Columbus (GA-AL)—are added in, 69 percent of

Georgia's population lived in metropolitan areas in 1997, but this still was below the 80 percent U.S. average.

Long a hub of banking and commerce for the Southeast, Atlanta also is striving to become a major national center for high-tech industry. Private job growth in the Atlanta metropolitan area exceeded 5 percent per year in 1996 and 1997. Sparked by Atlanta, virtually every measure of Georgia's economy spelled growth and prosperity in the mid-1990s: household and personal incomes rose toward the national average, new home production rates were among the highest in the nation, and export growth was rapid.

Average Annual Population Growth: 1990–97

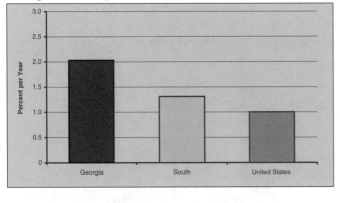

Median Household Income: 1989–97 (1997 dollars)

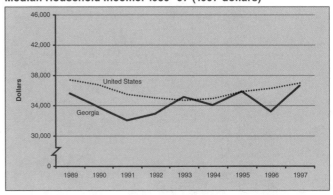

Unemployment Rate: 1989–97

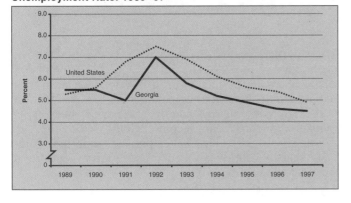

GEORGIA EXPERIENCED EXTRAORDINARY LABOR FORCE growth in 1996 and 1997, totaling 8.0 percent over the two years. Employment grew by an even more dramatic 8.4 percent. The percent of the population with jobs increased, and the unemployment rate fell to 4.5 percent. In the Atlanta metro area, the 1997 unemployment rate was an even lower 3.7 percent.

Earlier in the decade, Georgia experienced a sharp recession-induced increase in unemployment, which rose to 7.0 percent in 1992. This was below the national average for that year, however, and, since 1992, Georgia's unemployment rate has fallen as rapidly as the nation's.

POPULATION AND LABOR FORCE

GEORGIA'S POPULATION GREW 2 PERCENT PER YEAR FROM 1990 to 1997, compared to a national average of 1 percent. While all major groups in Georgia's population grew more rapidly than the national average, metropolitan growth was more rapid than nonmetropolitan, and minority groups grew more rapidly than the White non-Hispanic majority. Even so, while non-Hispanic Blacks constituted 28 percent of the Georgia population in 1997, other minority groups represented relatively small percentages. Hispanics made up not quite 3 percent, compared to almost 11 percent nationwide. Asians and Native Americans held even smaller percentages. In absolute numbers rather than percentages, the White non-Hispanic population grew by 448,000 from 1990 to 1997, the Black non-Hispanic population by 385,000 and the other groups combined by 150,000.

Well over one-half of Georgia's remarkable 15 percent total population growth from 1990 to 1997 was due to people moving into Georgia from elsewhere in the United States; total population gain from net domestic migration exceeded one-half million people. Natural increase (births minus deaths) accounted for another 40 percent of the population gain, and immigration from abroad for only 8 percent.

Population and Labor Force

	1980	1990	1991	1992	1993	1994	1995	1996	1997	Change* State	Change* U.S.
Population											
Total number of persons (thousands)	5 463	6 506	6 623	6 760	6 895	7 046	7 189	7 334	7 490	2.0	1.0
Percent distribution:											
White, Non-Hispanic	71.7	70.3	69.7	69.3	68.9	68.5	68.0	67.6	67.1	1.3	0.4
Black, Non-Hispanic	26.5	26.5	27.1	27.3	27.5	27.7	27.8	28.0	28.2	2.9	1.4
Asian	0.5	1.2	1.3	1.4	1.5	1.6	1.7	1.8	1.8	8.1	4.1
Native American	0.2	0.2	0.2	0.2	0.2	0.2	0.2	0.2	0.2	2.7	1.6
Hispanic	1.1	1.8	1.8	1.9	2.0	2.2	2.4	2.6	2.8	8.5	3.8
In metropolitan areas	64.2	67.2	67.4	67.7	67.8	68.1	68.3	68.5	68.6	2.3	1.0
Total number of households (thousands)	1 872	2 366	2 425	2 489	2 533	2 587	2 654	2 723	NA	2.4	1.2
Labor Force (thousands)											
Population 16 and over	4 027	4 950	5 043	5 144	5 241	5 368	5 481	5 596	5 721	2.1	1.0
Civilian labor force	2 543	3 300	3 264	3 354	3 467	3 578	3 617	3 739	3 907	2.4	1.1
Employed	2 380	3 118	3 099	3 119	3 265	3 392	3 441	3 567	3 730	2.6	1.2
Percent of population	59.1	63.0	61.4	60.6	62.3	63.2	62.8	63.7	65.2		
Unemployment rate (percent)	6.4	5.5	5.0	7.0	5.8	5.2	4.9	4.6	4.5		

*Compound annual average percent change, 1990–1997; 1990–1996 for households.

Population Change and Components: 1990–97

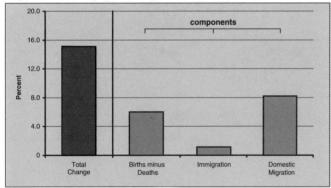

Average Annual Household and Population Growth

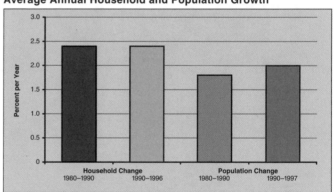

Population by Age; Births and Deaths

	1990 State	1990 U.S.	1997 State	1997 U.S.
Age distribution (percent)				
Under 5 years	7.8	7.6	7.5	7.2
5 to 17 years	19.0	18.2	19.1	18.8
18 to 64 years	63.1	61.8	63.6	61.3
65 years and over	10.1	12.5	9.9	12.7
Birth and death rates (per thousand population)				
Births	17.4	16.7	15.8	14.6
Deaths	8.0	8.6	7.9	8.6

THE AGE DISTRIBUTION OF GEORGIA'S POPULATION CHANGED LITTLE during the 1990s. The percentage of the population age 65 and over fell slightly from 1990 to 1997, in contrast to the national pattern of a small increase. The percentage under age 18 also dipped, and the share age 18 to 64 experienced a corresponding increase. Compared to the U.S. average, Georgia had a smaller percentage in the retirement years and larger percentages of children, youths, and working-age adults.

HOUSEHOLD AND PERSONAL INCOME

HOUSEHOLD INCOME AND PERSONS IN POVERTY	1990	1995	1996	1997 State	1997 U.S.
Median household income (1997 dollars)	33 845	35 911	33 242	36 663	37 005
Persons in poverty (thousands)	1 001	878	1 097	1 109	35 574
Poverty rate (percent)	15.8	12.1	14.8	14.5	13.3

GEORGIA'S INFLATION-ADJUSTED HOUSEHOLD INCOME FOL-lowed a somewhat irregular upward course after 1991 and, although it was still below the national average, the gap narrowed. Averaged over 1995 to 1997, Georgia's median household income was 97 percent of the U.S. level. This compares with only 92 percent in 1990.

Personal income per capita followed a similar pattern. The 94 percent of the U.S. average reached in 1995 through 1997 compares with 91 percent in 1990 and only 84 percent in 1980. Thanks to Georgia's growing population and strong economy, all major components of personal income grew more rapidly than the national average during the 1990s.

With persons in the working-age group, a somewhat higher than average percentage of its population and with a low unemployment rate, Georgia derived 70 percent of its personal income from worker and proprietor earnings in 1997, compared to 66 percent nationwide. The percentages coming from dividends, interest and rent, and transfer payments were correspondingly smaller.

Among transfer payments, "other income maintenance" showed extraordinary growth from 1990 to 1997. This category consists largely of the earned income tax credit, a benefit that goes to workers whose earnings fall below specified thresholds. It was the most rapidly growing type of transfer payment nationally, and its even more rapid growth in Georgia likely reflects the rapidly growing total number of workers, some portion of whom qualified for the credit.

Personal Income
(millions of dollars)

	1980	1989	1990	1991	1992	1993	1994	1995	1996	1997	Change*
Earnings by place of work	35 665	80 144	85 363	88 443	96 052	102 333	109 446	117 332	125 820	134 864	6.7
Wages and salaries	29 803	65 602	69 712	71 642	76 977	81 652	87 249	94 412	101 960	109 828	6.7
Other labor income	2 835	6 840	7 641	8 197	9 224	10 082	10 715	10 839	10 885	11 129	6.3
Proprietors' income	3 027	7 702	8 009	8 604	9 851	10 599	11 482	12 081	12 974	13 907	7.7
Farm	-102	1 143	973	1 306	1 363	1 308	1 624	1 544	1 767	1 944	6.9
Nonfarm	3 129	6 559	7 036	7 298	8 488	9 291	9 859	10 537	11 207	11 963	7.8
(−) Personal contributions for social insurance	1 932	5 137	5 483	5 763	6 151	6 597	7 139	7 704	8 228	8 844	7.0
(+) Adjustment for residence	8	-108	-92	-81	-96	-115	-141	-195	-238	-265	NA
(=) Net earnings by state of residence	33 741	74 899	79 788	82 598	89 805	95 621	102 166	109 434	117 354	125 756	6.7
(+) Dividends, interest, and rent	6 048	17 205	18 356	19 073	18 908	19 502	21 302	23 078	25 458	26 914	5.8
(+) Transfer payments	6 440	13 460	14 969	17 075	18 973	20 490	21 905	23 478	25 184	26 200	8.7
(=) Total personal income	46 228	105 564	113 112	118 746	127 686	135 613	145 373	155 990	167 996	178 870	6.8
Farm	58	1 337	1 192	1 511	1 557	1 531	1 831	1 773	1 997	2 180	6.3
Nonfarm	46 170	104 227	111 920	117 235	126 129	134 082	143 542	154 217	165 999	176 689	6.8
Personal income per capita (dollars)											
Current dollars	8 426	16 466	17 385	17 932	18 885	19 665	20 623	21 689	22 906	23 893	4.8
1997 dollars	16 111	20 817	20 921	20 707	21 124	21 398	21 916	22 546	23 326	23 893	1.7

*Compound annual average percent change, 1989–1997

Government Transfer Payments

	Millions of dollars 1990	Millions of dollars 1997	Percent change* State	Percent change* U.S.
Total government payments to individuals	14 193	24 610	73.4	62.7
Retirement, disability, and insurance	7 655	12 187	59.2	48.2
Social Security	5 089	8 133	59.8	46.1
Government employee retirement	2 349	3 781	61.0	60.3
Medical payments	4 129	8 524	106.5	101.2
Income maintenance	1 384	2 606	88.4	58.0
Supplemental Security Income	415	749	80.5	75.4
Family assistance	347	375	8.3	-0.5
Food Stamps	407	573	40.7	27.1
Other income maintenance	215	908	323.2	189.8
Unemployment insurance benefits	326	292	-10.5	10.6
Veterans benefits and other	699	1 001	43.1	30.8

*Percent change, 1990–1997

Government Payments to Individuals: 1997

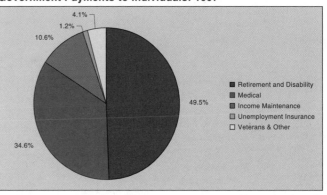

- Retirement and Disability
- Medical
- Income Maintenance
- Unemployment Insurance
- Veterans & Other

ECONOMIC STRUCTURE

LEADING PRIVATE INDUSTRIES, 1997 (Worker and proprietor earnings, millions of dollars)		FASTEST EARNINGS GROWTH, 1989–97 (percent increase)	
Health services	$9 918	Business services	178.5
Business services	9 384	Communications	161.1
Communications	5 034	Real estate	121.7
Construction specialties	4 911	Educational services	109.2
Engineering and management services	4 308	Engineering and management services	99.5

GEORGIA'S EXCEPTIONAL ECONOMIC GROWTH WAS SPREAD broadly among the major economic sectors, including manufacturing. While the nation was experiencing a decline in manufacturing employment during the 1980s, Georgia had an 8 percent increase. Manufacturing employment in Georgia then fell during the early-90s recession but began to climb again in 1992, a year ahead of the national employment comeback. By 1997, Georgia's manufacturing employment was 4 percent above the 1989 peak, whereas nationwide manufacturing jobs were still 3 percent below 1989. Manufacturing provided 13.5 percent of Georgia's jobs in 1997, compared to 12.4 percent nationally.

Even so, Georgia's economy was predominantly service producing. Private service-producing industries accounted for 63.3 percent of Georgia's employment in 1997, a little below the national average of 64.5 percent. Except for construction specialties, each of Georgia's five largest private industries were in the service producing sector, as were those that grew fastest from 1989 to 1997.

The government sector represented 14.9 percent of Georgia's 1997 job total, compared to 13.9 percent nationally, and farm employment was only 1.4 percent of the total, compared to 1.9 percent nationally.

Reflecting Georgia's importance as a transportation and distribution hub, the percentages of Georgia's workers employed in wholesale trade and in transportation, communications, and utilities were above the national averages. Each of these sectors employed 5.8 percent of Georgia's workers in 1997, compared to U.S. averages of 4.6 and 4.8 percent, respectively. Within the transportation sector, the air transport industry was particularly important, ranking sixth among all major industry groups in earnings growth, with worker and proprietor earnings up a total of 91.6 percent. Sparking the growth was the increased traffic at Atlanta's Hartsfield Airport, now in a race with Chicago's O'Hare to be the nation's busiest.

Employment and Earnings by Sector

	1980	1989	1990	1991	1992	1993	1994	1995	1996	1997 Number	1997 Percent of total	Change*
Employment *(thousands of persons)*												
Total	2 747	3 635	3 681	3 650	3 729	3 898	4 057	4 224	4 363	4 468	100.0	2.6
Farm	97	75	74	70	69	68	65	64	58	62	1.4	-2.3
Nonfarm	2 651	3 560	3 606	3 580	3 660	3 831	3 993	4 160	4 305	4 406	98.6	2.7
Private nonfarm	2 130	2 958	2 989	2 959	3 028	3 189	3 333	3 497	3 645	3 738	83.7	3.0
Agricultural service, forestry, and fishing	16	30	31	33	32	36	39	43	45	48	1.1	6.1
Mining	9	11	11	9	9	9	9	9	9	9	0.2	-2.1
Construction	139	213	212	191	191	201	217	235	249	255	5.7	2.3
Manufacturing	529	582	570	553	558	570	592	603	600	604	13.5	0.5
Transportation and public utilities	153	201	216	213	215	224	234	240	250	259	5.8	3.2
Wholesale trade	174	233	226	226	230	228	232	242	251	258	5.8	1.3
Retail trade	408	604	604	597	614	646	686	723	759	772	17.3	3.1
Finance, insurance, and real estate	200	244	244	244	240	253	266	277	287	298	6.7	2.5
Services	503	839	874	893	938	1 022	1 056	1 124	1 195	1 235	27.7	5.0
Government	520	603	617	620	632	642	659	663	660	667	14.9	1.3
Earnings *(millions of dollars)*												
Total	35 665	80 144	85 363	88 443	96 052	102 333	109 446	117 332	125 820	134 864	100.0	6.7
Farm	58	1 337	1 192	1 511	1 557	1 531	1 831	1 773	1 997	2 180	1.6	6.3
Nonfarm	35 607	78 807	84 170	86 932	94 496	100 801	107 616	115 560	123 823	132 684	98.4	6.7
Private nonfarm	28 999	65 408	69 611	71 498	78 451	84 021	90 019	97 184	104 764	112 739	83.6	7.0
Agricultural service, forestry, and fishing	136	372	411	447	470	514	576	641	675	740	0.5	9.0
Mining	237	313	317	284	302	311	323	344	350	369	0.3	2.1
Construction	2 074	4 829	5 058	4 521	4 704	5 190	5 838	6 517	7 247	7 644	5.7	5.9
Manufacturing	8 285	15 014	15 336	15 727	16 995	17 781	19 119	20 045	20 896	21 963	16.3	4.9
Transportation and public utilities	3 436	6 950	7 763	8 147	9 131	9 960	10 563	11 198	11 960	12 872	9.5	8.0
Wholesale trade	3 263	7 583	7 788	7 977	8 570	8 978	9 344	9 902	10 680	11 642	8.6	5.5
Retail trade	3 797	7 948	8 060	8 207	8 771	9 452	10 253	11 016	11 911	12 608	9.3	5.9
Finance, insurance, and real estate	2 023	5 301	5 591	5 872	6 621	7 202	7 448	8 154	8 919	9 834	7.3	8.0
Services	5 747	17 099	19 288	20 316	22 888	24 634	26 556	29 368	32 127	35 067	26.0	9.4
Government	6 608	13 399	14 560	15 434	16 044	16 781	17 597	18 376	19 058	19 944	14.8	5.1

*Compound annual average percent change, 1989–1997

ECONOMIC STRUCTURE (Continued)

THE ANNUAL EARNINGS OF GEORGIA WORKERS HAVE BEEN gaining on the national average. In 1997, average private nonfarm wages in Georgia were 97 percent of the U.S. average, up from 94 percent in 1990 and 90 percent in 1980. These gains likely are due in part to shifts in the composition of employment toward relatively high-wage industries such as business services, engineering and management services, and industrial machinery manufacture. The gains also reflect earnings above the national average in Georgia's important wholesale trade and transportation, communications, and utilities sectors.

Annual wages of Georgia's farm workers were less than one-half the nonfarm average and no more than 70 percent of the U.S. average for farm workers. The low annual wage reflects the part-year nature of farm work as well as the lower average hourly pay. Salaries of Georgia's government workers were 91 percent of the U.S. average in 1997, the same as in 1990.

Manufacturing contributed 18.1 percent to Georgia's 1996 gross state product (GSP), slightly more than the U.S. average of 17.5 percent. Reflecting the more rapid growth of service-producing industries, the manufacturing share of Georgia's GSP declined since 1989, as it did nationally.

Georgia's manufacturing was well diversified, with eight or more manufacturing industries each contributing 0.5 percent or more to 1996 GSP. The largest manufacturing industries, measured by worker and proprietor earnings in 1997, were textiles and food and kindred products. Among the most rapidly growing from 1989 to 1997 were lumber and wood products and industrial machinery. Those with below-average growth included printing and publishing, electronics, chemicals, paper, and textiles.

Growth of U.S. goods exports from 1994 to 1997 was quite rapid, totaling 34 percent over the four years. Georgia's goods exports grew an even larger 38 percent. The state's export base was well diversified; the five top industry categories account for only 56 percent of total exports. Important industries, in addition to the top five shown in the table, included textile mill products, apparel, food products, and scientific and measuring instruments.

Average Annual Wages and Salaries by Sector
(dollars)

	1989	1996	1997 State	1997 U.S.
All wage and salary workers	20 671	27 122	28 537	29 809
Farm	7 272	14 025	11 529	16 442
Nonfarm	20 779	27 177	28 623	29 900
Private nonfarm	20 849	27 362	28 909	29 867
Agricultural service, forestry, and fishing	13 773	18 011	18 701	17 941
Mining	29 130	38 361	40 523	49 800
Construction	21 251	27 756	29 007	31 765
Manufacturing	22 471	30 571	32 043	38 351
Transportation and utilities	30 491	40 266	42 156	38 222
Wholesale trade	29 951	39 596	42 065	39 466
Retail trade	12 255	15 176	15 871	16 206
Finance, insurance, and real estate	27 296	38 703	41 829	44 993
Services	19 118	25 878	27 446	27 588
Government	20 480	26 312	27 268	30 062

Gross State Product and Manufacturing
(millions of dollars, except as noted)

	1989	1994	1995	1996
Gross state product, total	133 542	185 982	200 751	216 033
Manufacturing:				
Millions of dollars	25 782	33 497	36 863	39 079
Percent of total gross state product	19.3	18.0	18.4	18.1
Per worker (dollars)	44 284	56 585	61 115	65 183
New capital expenditures, manufacturing	NA	3 486	3 642	3 847

Exports of Goods
(millions of dollars)

	1994	1995	1996	1997
All goods	7 108	8 627	8 618	9 810
Manufactures	6 568	8 064	8 062	9 215
Agricultural and livestock products	132	164	137	183
Other commodities	408	399	419	413
Top goods exports, 1997:				
Industrial machinery and computers	1 021	1 242	1 271	1 408
Chemical products	584	683	812	1 313
Electric and electronic equipment	746	789	852	1 079
Paper products	684	1 093	916	905
Transportation equipment	653	1 028	673	828

HOUSING

GEORGIA'S POPULATION WAS INCREASINGLY MADE UP OF homeowners. Almost 71 percent of Georgia households owned their homes in 1997, a rapid increase from less than 65 percent in 1989 and 1990. Nationwide, the homeownership rate was 65.7 percent in 1997.

The need to accommodate the rapidly growing population produced a residential construction boom in Georgia. The new home production rate was well above the U.S. average throughout the 1990s, but especially so from 1995 to 1997, when Georgia's new home production rate averaged 12.7 per thousand population, almost twice the national rate. Home construction activity was especially strong in the Atlanta area; two-thirds of the residential building permits issued in the state in 1997 were issued in the Atlanta metropolitan area.

Georgia's rapid growth produced its share of environmental problems and infrastructure needs. Crowded roads and airports, limits on water distribution and treatment, and an uphill struggle against air pollution in some areas

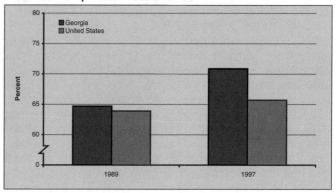

Homeownership Rates: 1989 and 1997

are factors that may constrain future growth. Some fast-growing communities have placed temporary moratoriums on new construction until the infrastructure can catch up and plans for future growth can be developed.

Housing Supply

	1989	1990	1991	1992	1993	1994	1995	1996	1997
Residential building permits (thousands)	50.5	41.3	37.6	44.6	53.9	64.9	72.2	74.9	75.1
New home production (including manufactured housing):									
Thousands of homes	61.2	52.2	47.1	55.2	66.8	82.1	91.3	94.3	94.9
Rate per 1,000 population									
Georgia	9.5	8.0	7.1	8.2	9.7	11.6	12.7	12.9	12.7
U.S.	6.2	5.2	4.5	5.1	5.6	6.4	6.3	6.6	6.5
Existing home sales:									
Thousands of homes	73.6	73.2	70.7	NA	NA	NA	NA	NA	NA
Change from previous year (percent)									
Georgia	-5.9	-0.5	-3.4	NA	NA	NA	NA	NA	NA
U.S.	-3.9	-4.0	0.0	9.2	8.2	4.8	-3.7	7.5	3.8
Home ownership rate (percent of households)	64.7	64.3	65.7	66.9	66.5	63.4	66.6	69.3	70.9
Rental vacancy rate (percent of rental housing units)	10.0	9.4	9.7	8.9	7.3	9.1	11.3	11.6	11.2

AGRICULTURE

IN THE YEARS 1994 THROUGH 1997 NET FARM INCOME AVERAGED just under $2 billion per year. Georgia is known for its peaches and pecans, but the principal commercial product group in 1997 was poultry and poultry products, accounting for 50 percent of the total value of agricultural sales. Next in importance was cotton and cottonseed, accounting for 12 percent of total sales value.

In Georgia farming was a part-time activity for many farmers. More than one-half of Georgia farm operators had a principal occupation other than farming in 1997, and

60 percent of farms had sales of less than $10,000. The 40 percent of farms with sales greater than $10,000 accounted for almost 99 percent of the value of sales.

GEORGIA FARMS, 1997	
Number of farms	43 000
Total acres (thousands):	11 800
Average per farm	274
Value of land and buildings (millions of dollars)	16 874
Average per farm (dollars)	392 419

Farm Income
(millions of dollars)

	1980	1989	1990	1991	1992	1993	1994	1995	1996	1997
Gross income	3 078	4 672	4 596	4 645	4 879	5 152	5 534	5 954	6 597	6 843
Receipts from sales	2 804	4 037	4 014	4 068	4 216	4 411	4 848	5 287	5 836	6 028
Government payments	29	173	131	98	182	225	140	67	115	109
Imputed and miscellaneous income	245	462	452	480	480	515	546	600	646	706
(−) Production expenses	3 115	3 409	3 457	3 413	3 404	3 719	3 888	4 182	4 610	4 603
(=) Realized net income	-37	1 263	1 139	1 233	1 475	1 433	1 646	1 773	1 987	2 240
(+) Inventory change	-101	-21	-79	162	22	-77	244	-73	59	-17
(=) Net income	-138	1 242	1 060	1 395	1 497	1 356	1 890	1 700	2 046	2 223
Corporate income	-35	99	87	89	134	48	267	156	279	279
Farm proprietors income	-102	1 143	973	1 306	1 363	1 308	1 624	1 544	1 767	1 944

EDUCATION

EDUCATIONAL ATTAINMENT Percent of population age 25 and over, 1997	State	United States
High school graduate or higher	78.8	82.1
College graduate or higher	22.3	23.9

THE PERCENTAGES OF GEORGIANS COMPLETING HIGH SCHOOL and college were somewhat below the national average, and per pupil school expenditure was only 87.5 percent of the national average in the 1994–95 school year. Georgia is using the proceeds of its state lottery to fund innovative educational efforts. By law, these lottery funds cannot be used to substitute for regular state and local spending on education but are to be used for statewide prekindergartens for 4-year-olds, technology for educational facilities, and HOPE scholarships.

HOPE—Helping Outstanding Pupils Educationally—scholarships are available to students graduating from high school with a B average. They provide tuition, fees, and a book allowance at state colleges, universities, or technical institutes or more limited scholarships at private colleges or universities within Georgia. Scholarships continue for four years, provided the student maintains a B average. In 1996, 97 percent of Georgia freshmen at the University of Georgia and 96 percent at the Georgia Institute of Technology held HOPE scholarships.

High School Completion: 1990–97

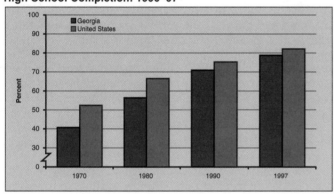

Education Indicators

	State	U.S.
Elementary and secondary schools		
Enrollment, 1995–96		
Total (thousands)	1 409	49 873
Percent in private schools	6.9	10.1
Expenditures per pupil (dollars), 1995–96	5 377	6 146
Average teacher salary (dollars), 1996–97	36 042	38 509
Higher education		
Enrollment, 1996–97		
Total (thousands)	318	14 218
Percent of population 18–34	16.3	21.8
Percent minority	30.8	26.1
Percent in private schools	21.6	22.6

HEALTH

THE HEALTH OF GEORGIA'S POPULATION APPEARS TO HAVE improved during the 1990s, but is still beneath national norms. Because of Georgia's relatively young population, the total death rate was below the national average, but, once adjusted to a standardized age distribution, it rose above. The age-adjusted rate was higher than that for most other South Atlantic states. Death rates from most of the major causes tended to be somewhat above the national

average, and that for injury by firearms was substantially higher. The infant mortality rate came down markedly during the 1990s but remained above the national average.

The percent of Georgia's population not covered by health insurance also was above the national average. Part of the explanation for this may lie in Georgia's relatively young population as young adults are the age group least likely to have health insurance coverage.

Health Indicators

	1990	1995	1996	1997
Infant mortality				
(rate per thousand live births)				
Georgia	12.4	9.4	9.0	7.7
U.S.	9.2	7.6	7.3	7.1
Total deaths, age-adjusted rate				
(rate per thousand population)				
Georgia	5.9	5.7	5.6	5.5
U.S.	5.2	5.0	4.9	4.8
Persons not covered by health insurance				
(percent of population)				
Georgia	16.2	17.9	17.8	17.6
U.S.	13.9	15.4	15.6	16.1

Leading Causes of Death, 1996
(deaths per 100,000 population)

	Age-adjusted		Not age-adjusted	
	State	U.S.	State	U.S.
Deaths from all causes	560.9	491.6	799.0	872.5
Heart disease	152.5	134.5	238.2	276.4
Cancer	129.7	127.9	169.1	203.4
Cerebrovascular diseases	34.8	26.4	57.9	60.3
Chronic obstructive pulmonary disease	23.8	21.0	34.4	40.0
Diabetes mellitus	12.7	13.6	17.6	23.3
Pneumonia and influenza	15.9	12.8	28.6	31.6
HIV	15.8	11.1	17.3	11.7
Liver disease	7.0	7.5	8.1	9.4
Alzheimer's disease	3.8	2.7	8.2	8.1
Accidents and adverse effects	37.1	30.4	40.7	35.8
Motor vehicle accidents	21.7	16.2	21.6	16.5
Suicide	11.2	10.8	11.8	11.6
Homicide	10.2	8.5	10.0	7.9
Injury by firearm	16.9	12.9	17.0	12.8

GOVERNMENT

STATE AND LOCAL TAXES, 1995–96	State	U.S.
Per capita (dollars)	2 256	2 477
Percent of personal income	10.6	10.8

GEORGIA'S STATE AND LOCAL TAXES PER CAPITA IN 1995–96 were below the national average, but, when measured as a percent of personal income, the difference was small. Local taxes were 42 percent of the state and local total, little different from the 41 percent national average.

Revenue from the individual income tax made up 43 percent of the state's total tax revenue in 1996–97, compared to an all-state average of 33 percent. Sales taxes produced 45 percent of the state's total tax revenue, below the all-state average of 49 percent. Corporate income taxes yielded just under 7 percent of the state's tax revenues, about an average share.

State general expenditure per capita in Georgia equaled about 93 percent of the average for all states in 1996–97. Per capita expenditures on education were 116 percent of the national average, while those on public welfare were only 94 percent, those on hospitals and health an even lower 76 percent, and those on highways a rock-bottom 64 percent. According to the Terry College of Business at the University of Georgia, Georgia's motor fuel tax is the lowest in the nation and inadequate to maintain and improve the surface transportation system. The figures in this paragraph are for state government spending only and do not reflect the extent to which localities may supplement the amounts provided by the state. Interest on Georgia's general debt averaged only $51 per capita in 1996–97, compared to a national average of $99. Georgia appeared to be in sound financial shape at year end, with debt equal to $826 per capita, compared to $1,706 nationally, and cash and security holdings approaching six times the size of the debt.

Georgia had 2.8 percent of the nation's population and received 2.5 percent of federal funds distributed to states and their residents in fiscal 1997. Georgia's somewhat lower than average population percentage in the 65 and over age group is reflected in the slightly less than proportionate share of retirement and disability payments and Medicare coming to Georgia. Since these payment categories accounted for 44 percent of all federal payments within Georgia, the state's share of the federal funds total is correspondingly reduced. Georgia received a somewhat larger than proportionate share of defense contracts and of federal salaries and wages. The latter probably reflects, in part, the Atlanta location of Southeast regional headquarters for a number of federal agencies.

State Government Finances, 1996–97

	Millions of dollars	Percent distribu- tion	Dollars per capita State	Dollars per capita U.S.
General revenue	19 714	100.0	2 633	3 049
Intergovernmental revenue	6 007	30.5	802	863
Taxes	10 898	55.3	1 456	1 660
General sales	3 916	19.9	523	551
Selective sales	990	5.0	132	257
License taxes	405	2.1	54	106
Individual income	4 741	24.1	633	542
Corporation net income	726	3.7	97	115
Other taxes	120	0.6	16	90
Other general revenue	2 809	14.3	375	526
General expenditure	20 448	100.0	2 731	2 951
Intergovernmental expenditure	6 141	30.0	820	989
Direct expenditure	14 307	70.0	1 911	1 962
General expenditure, by function:				
Education	8 938	43.7	1 194	1 033
Public welfare	5 335	26.1	713	761
Hospitals and health	1 344	6.6	180	237
Highways	1 084	5.3	145	225
Police protection and corrections	1 054	5.2	141	137
Natural resources, parks and recreation	543	2.7	72	63
Governmental administration	487	2.4	65	107
Interest on general debt	385	1.9	51	99
Other and unallocable	1 279	6.3	171	290
Debt at end of fiscal year	6 186	NA	826	1 706
Cash and security holdings	36 320	NA	4 852	6 683

Federal Spending within State

	Federal funds, fiscal 1997 Millions of dollars	Federal funds, fiscal 1997 Percent distribution	Federal funds, fiscal 1997 Percent of U.S. total*
Total within state	35 930	100.0	2.5
Payments to individuals	19 105	53.2	2.4
Retirement and disability	11 153	31.0	2.4
Medicare	4 728	13.2	2.3
Food stamps	604	1.7	3.1
Supplemental Security Income	782	2.2	2.9
Grants	5 896	16.4	2.4
Medicaid and other health	2 659	7.4	2.3
Nutrition and family welfare	1 172	3.3	2.5
Education	424	1.2	2.5
Housing and community development ..	295	0.8	2.6
Salaries and wages	5 707	15.9	3.5
Defense procurement contracts	3 902	10.9	3.3
Non-defense procurement contracts	871	2.4	1.2

*State population is 2.8 percent of the U.S. total.

1997

Population (persons)	1,192,057
Population rank	41st
Population growth rank (1990–97)	21st
Per capita personal income	$25,686
Unemployment rate (percent)	6.4
Poverty rate (percent)	13.9

HAWAII'S ECONOMIC GROWTH WAS HURT BY THE ASIAN ECOnomic weakness of the mid-1990s, as its leading sector, tourism, experienced some reduction in Asian and U.S. visitors. The travel and tourism industry, which was estimated by state analysts to comprise about 28 percent of gross state product in 1997, suffered a 9 percent constant-dollar drop in this activity from 1995 to 1997. At the same time, the state's economy was depressed by federal government cutbacks in personnel, procurement, and military forces. Further, population growth decelerated during the 1990s as residents began a net migration to other states.

These three negatives and the secondary effects filtering through the rest of the economy, such as a weak construc-

tion sector, led to employment declines in the state in three consecutive years, 1993–95, with a plateau in 1996–97. The federal government continued to play a large role in Hawaii: earnings from federal civilian employment contributed double the normal percentage of state earnings, and military personnel earnings were seven times those in a typical state. Real per capita income, after declining in several recent years, was essentially unchanged from 1996 to 1997. Per capita income was about equal to national averages in 1997, but, taking into account the high cost of living throughout the state, the purchasing power of its residents appears to have fallen below average.

Average Annual Population Growth: 1990–97

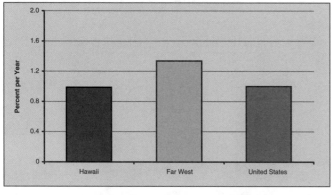

Median Household Income: 1989–97 (1997 dollars)

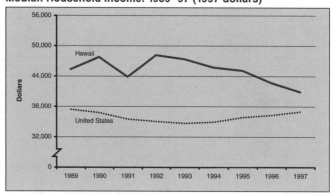

Unemployment Rate: 1989–97

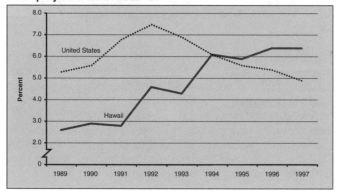

AFTER A COUNTERCYCLICAL ADVANCE IN JOB GROWTH DURING 1990–91, when Asia's strong economy and tourism boosted the state's fortunes, the ensuing weakness of Hawaii's economy has translated clearly into employment losses and higher unemployment. The weakening started in 1992 and worsened in 1994. Employment recovered slightly in 1996–97 but failed to keep pace with growth of the labor force. Only two states and the District of Columbia had higher unemployment in 1997.

POPULATION AND LABOR FORCE

TOTAL POPULATION GROWTH DURING THE 1990S WAS SLIGHTLY below the U.S. average and significantly below the Far West region's average. With quite a high rate of natural population increase, population was held down by net out-migration to other states of 4 percent (1990–97), an outflow that accelerated during the 1994–97 economic downturn in the state. A net inflow of military personnel in the early 1990s was a partial offset. A steady inflow of immigrants, consisting mostly of Asians, gave this state one of the highest immigration rates in the nation.

Hawaii's population remained the most heavily dominated by people of Asian and Pacific Islander descent,

comprising a steady 63 percent of the total. The non-Hispanic White population was down slightly during the decade, while the small Hispanic and Black communities grew slower than average from 1990 to 1997. Total population became a little less concentrated in metropolitan areas, unlike the steady proportion of metro population for the United States.

The labor force grew faster than the adult population during the 1990s. With a slower growth of actual employment, this trend left an increasing number of unemployed in Hawaii, as well as a decreasing proportion of the population at work.

Population and Labor Force

	1980	1990	1991	1992	1993	1994	1995	1996	1997	Change*	
										State	U.S.
Population											
Total number of persons (thousands)	965	1 113	1 132	1 151	1 164	1 176	1 183	1 187	1 192	0.9	1.0
Percent distribution:											
White, Non-Hispanic	32.2	31.8	31.0	30.9	30.6	30.3	30.0	29.6	29.2	-0.3	0.4
Black, Non-Hispanic	1.8	2.6	2.4	2.7	2.7	2.7	2.7	2.7	2.7	1.2	1.4
Asian	61.2	62.0	62.8	62.4	62.6	62.6	62.7	62.9	63.1	1.2	4.1
Native American	0.3	0.5	0.5	0.5	0.5	0.5	0.5	0.5	0.6	2.9	1.6
Hispanic	7.4	7.3	7.5	7.6	7.6	7.6	7.7	7.8	8.0	2.2	3.8
In metropolitan areas	79.1	75.3	74.8	74.5	74.2	74.0	73.7	73.5	73.3	0.5	1.0
Total number of households (thousands)	294	356	365	374	376	380	384	389	NA	1.5	1.2
Labor Force (thousands)											
Population 16 and over	723	861	873	886	892	900	905	910	916	0.9	1.0
Civilian labor force	440	550	574	584	586	580	576	594	597	1.2	1.1
Employed	418	534	558	557	561	545	543	556	559	0.7	1.2
Percent of population	57.8	62.0	63.9	62.9	62.9	60.6	60.0	61.1	61.0		
Unemployment rate (percent)	4.9	2.9	2.8	4.6	4.3	6.1	5.9	6.4	6.4		

*Compound annual average percent change, 1990–1997; 1990–1996 for households.

Population Change and Components: 1990–97

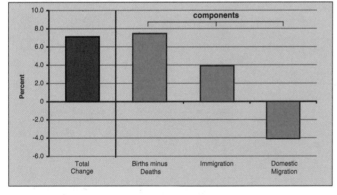

Average Annual Household and Population Growth

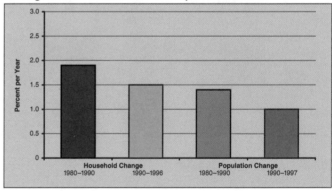

Population by Age; Births and Deaths

	1990		1997	
	State	U.S.	State	U.S.
Age distribution (percent)				
Under 5 years	7.6	7.6	7.5	7.2
5 to 17 years	17.5	18.2	18.0	18.8
18 to 64 years	63.6	61.8	61.3	61.3
65 years and over	11.2	12.5	13.2	12.7
Birth and death rates (per thousand population)				
Births	18.5	16.7	14.6	14.6
Deaths	6.1	8.6	6.7	8.6

THE AGE MIX IN THE STATE HAS MOVED CLOSER TO THAT OF THE nation since 1990, as the working-age segment of the population declined substantially and the share of those 65 and older increased commensurately. Though the share of school-age children increased from 1990 to 1997, Hawaii's birth rate has dropped sharply (to the national rate) since 1990, which portends a reversal of this trend. Relatively low death rates will continue to contribute to higher than average net natural population increase.

HOUSEHOLD AND PERSONAL INCOME

HOUSEHOLD INCOME AND PERSONS IN POVERTY	1990	1995	1996	1997	
				State	U.S.
Median household income (1997 dollars)	47 795	45 129	42 730	40 934	37 005
Persons in poverty (thousands)	121	122	142	164	35 574
Poverty rate (percent)	11.0	10.3	12.1	13.9	13.3

WHERE ONCE HAWAII BOASTED INCOMES WELL ABOVE THE U.S. average, the mid-1990s brought disappointing results. Income growth lagged behind the U.S. growth rate, starting with a decline in real income from 1993 to 1997. Both median household income and personal income per capita failed to keep up with inflation. Median household income in 1997 was 11 percent above that of the United States, compared with a 21 percent advantage in 1989. Hawaii's standard of living is affected by a cost of living significantly higher than average, about 20 percent higher by one survey.

Per capita personal income was 1.5 percent higher in the state than the nation in 1997; during the 1990s growth in real incomes was only half as fast in Hawaii as in the United States. Within components of per capita income, earnings of workers and proprietors were 1.2 percent

above the national level, and dividend and interest income was 2.2 percent below average. The state does not appear to have a large number of wealthy or retired people, despite its image.

Transfer payments were above typical U.S. levels in 1997 primarily because of the preponderance of former government employees (state and federal) receiving retirement benefits. In contrast, payments of Social Security were relatively low. Payment of family assistance and food stamp benefits was higher than average—and has increased more than average—because of both the weakness of the state economy and its slow movement toward welfare reform. Other income maintenance, primarily earned income tax credits, expanded sharply. Unemployment payments also grew much larger during the decade as the unemployment rate moved sharply higher.

Personal Income
(millions of dollars)

	1980	1989	1990	1991	1992	1993	1994	1995	1996	1997	Change*
Earnings by place of work	8 169	16 130	18 084	19 083	20 328	20 844	21 072	21 123	21 127	21 666	3.8
Wages and salaries	6 694	13 077	14 518	15 392	16 410	16 647	16 760	16 749	16 862	17 366	3.6
Other labor income	529	1 245	1 451	1 632	1 767	1 885	1 948	1 872	1 737	1 713	4.1
Proprietors' income	946	1 808	2 115	2 059	2 151	2 312	2 363	2 502	2 528	2 587	4.6
Farm	243	50	64	24	13	10	2	6	4	4	-27.1
Nonfarm	703	1 758	2 051	2 035	2 137	2 302	2 361	2 496	2 524	2 583	4.9
(−) Personal contributions for social insurance	452	1 031	1 143	1 228	1 297	1 320	1 354	1 372	1 375	1 412	4.0
(+) Adjustment for residence	0	0	0	0	0	0	0	0	0	0	NA
(=) Net earnings by state of residence	7 716	15 099	16 941	17 855	19 030	19 524	19 718	19 751	19 752	20 254	3.7
(+) Dividends, interest, and rent	1 543	3 498	3 881	4 012	3 700	4 028	4 363	4 806	5 010	5 078	4.8
(+) Transfer payments	1 304	2 633	3 134	3 231	3 642	3 959	4 251	4 777	4 937	5 146	8.7
(=) Total personal income	10 563	21 230	23 956	25 098	26 372	27 511	28 331	29 333	29 698	30 479	4.6
Farm	391	237	250	207	200	186	180	164	162	157	-5.0
Nonfarm	10 173	20 993	23 706	24 891	26 173	27 325	28 152	29 169	29 536	30 321	4.7
Personal income per capita (dollars)											
Current dollars	10 916	19 395	21 533	22 182	22 942	23 708	24 161	24 883	25 105	25 686	3.6
1997 dollars	20 872	24 520	25 912	25 614	25 662	25 798	25 676	25 866	25 565	25 686	0.6

*Compound annual average percent change, 1989–1997

Government Transfer Payments

	Millions of dollars		Percent change*	
	1990	1997	State	U.S.
Total government payments to individuals	3 002	4 982	65.9	62.7
Retirement, disability, and insurance	1 963	2 699	37.5	48.2
Social Security	1 112	1 386	24.7	46.1
Government employee retirement	830	1 289	55.3	60.3
Medical payments	613	1 313	114.0	101.2
Income maintenance	278	631	126.9	58.0
Supplemental Security Income	52	90	74.2	75.4
Family assistance	105	234	123.5	-0.5
Food Stamps	85	185	116.8	27.1
Other income maintenance	37	123	233.7	189.8
Unemployment insurance benefits	47	166	255.3	10.6
Veterans benefits and other	101	173	70.9	30.8

*Percent change, 1990–1997

Government Payments to Individuals: 1997

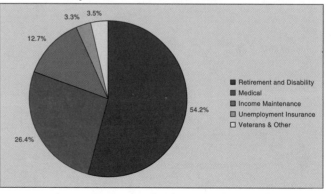

- ■ Retirement and Disability
- ■ Medical
- ■ Income Maintenance
- ☐ Unemployment Insurance
- ☐ Veterans & Other

ECONOMIC STRUCTURE

LEADING PRIVATE INDUSTRIES, 1997 (Worker and proprietor earnings, millions of dollars)		FASTEST EARNINGS GROWTH, 1989–97 (percent increase)	
Health services	$1 766	Educational services	121.7
Hotels and lodging	1 330	Social services	120.9
Other transportation	919	Amusement and recreation services	84.5
Business services	905	Real estate	75.2
Construction specialties	794	Electric, gas, and sanitary services	67.3

HAWAII'S ECONOMY IS OVERWHELMINGLY SERVICES ORIENTED because of its location and natural resources. The predominance of the tourism sector was reflected in the sizable hotel and restaurant businesses, with hotels as the second largest industry in the state in 1997, even though tourism had taken somewhat of a negative turn during the mid-1990s. Visitor arrivals in 1997 were down 1.4 percent from 1990 and total "visitor days" were flat during the same period as opposed to the 43 percent increase in visitor arrivals between 1985 and 1990. Remarkably, there was no relative drop-off of Asian tourists in recent years: from 1990 to 1997 the percentage of "eastbound" visitors actually increased from 32 percent to 40 percent, but spending per visitor may well have declined.

The significant size of the real estate industry derived from tourism-related development, as well as the high values involved in this state, where real estate is very costly. The number of government jobs was extraordinarily high—22.3 percent of total employment compared with

13.9 percent for the United States. There was a notable federal presence here (both military and civilian), even after cutbacks starting in 1993–94, and a large state government employment base. Employment in services, retail trade, and government, accounted for 72.3 percent of jobs, compared to 61.6 percent nationally.

Besides tourism, Hawaii also had sizable health care, business services, and education industries. Earnings in health care grew 67 percent from 1989 to 1997 as the proportion of older residents increased. The state estimates that education provided 8 percent of jobs and 5.4 percent of gross state product. Educational services for nonresidents provided a state income inflow, and there are plans to promote more "edu-tourism," educational trips for adults. Business services included a high-tech component that feeds off of federal research and development activity within marine research and surveying, aquaculture, and environmental management. Computer and telecommunication firms filled defense contracts as well as selling to businesses.

Employment and Earnings by Sector

	1980	1989	1990	1991	1992	1993	1994	1995	1996	1997 Number	1997 Percent of total	Change*
Employment *(thousands of persons)*												
Total	575	703	730	753	755	751	747	740	741	745	100.0	0.7
Farm	16	14	15	14	14	13	12	11	11	11	1.5	-3.2
Nonfarm	559	689	715	739	740	737	734	729	730	733	98.5	0.8
Private nonfarm	405	519	543	564	563	561	560	560	564	567	76.2	1.1
Agricultural service, forestry, and fishing	5	7	8	9	9	10	9	10	10	10	1.3	4.3
Mining	0	0	0	1	1	1	0	1	0	0	0.1	3.0
Construction	28	36	40	42	40	41	38	35	32	31	4.2	-2.0
Manufacturing	25	24	24	23	23	22	21	20	20	20	2.7	-2.6
Transportation and public utilities	33	42	45	47	46	45	45	46	46	47	6.3	1.2
Wholesale trade	20	25	26	27	27	26	26	25	25	25	3.3	-0.1
Retail trade	98	128	131	134	134	133	134	138	139	139	18.7	1.1
Finance, insurance, and real estate	63	59	61	61	62	62	62	61	62	63	8.4	0.8
Services	133	197	208	220	221	221	223	224	229	233	31.3	2.1
Government	155	170	172	174	178	176	175	169	166	166	22.3	-0.3
Earnings *(millions of dollars)*												
Total	8 169	16 130	18 084	19 083	20 328	20 844	21 072	21 123	21 127	21 666	100.0	3.8
Farm	391	237	250	207	200	186	180	164	162	157	0.7	-5.0
Nonfarm	7 778	15 893	17 834	18 876	20 128	20 658	20 892	20 959	20 964	21 509	99.3	3.9
Private nonfarm	5 419	11 723	13 328	14 071	14 962	15 380	15 541	15 649	15 723	15 998	73.8	4.0
Agricultural service, forestry, and fishing	36	94	117	141	146	150	144	150	143	141	0.6	5.2
Mining	21	5	7	13	17	17	16	21	19	16	0.1	15.1
Construction	610	1 397	1 681	1 834	1 826	1 897	1 712	1 588	1 461	1 378	6.4	-0.2
Manufacturing	493	774	779	793	817	792	820	783	772	799	3.7	0.4
Transportation and public utilities	715	1 312	1 436	1 540	1 674	1 671	1 665	1 697	1 741	1 824	8.4	4.2
Wholesale trade	327	644	740	765	786	795	794	791	788	798	3.7	2.7
Retail trade	906	2 060	2 287	2 296	2 425	2 487	2 570	2 636	2 635	2 655	12.3	3.2
Finance, insurance, and real estate	600	1 131	1 279	1 321	1 554	1 739	1 662	1 698	1 757	1 761	8.1	5.7
Services	1 711	4 307	5 002	5 368	5 716	5 831	6 157	6 285	6 406	6 627	30.6	5.5
Government	2 359	4 169	4 505	4 805	5 166	5 278	5 351	5 310	5 242	5 511	25.4	3.5

*Compound annual average percent change, 1989–1997

ECONOMIC STRUCTURE (Continued)

AVERAGE WAGES FOR ALL WORKERS IN HAWAII WERE 5 PER-cent below the national average in 1997, though the three dominant sectors met or exceeded the U.S. average. In services, by far the largest sector in the state, wages were at virtual parity with those in the nation, and retail trade and government wages were 8 percent and 3 percent above average, respectively. Thus, the lower overall average in the state derived from its industry mix: the heavier concentration of jobs within the low-wage services and retail sectors and the light weight of manufacturing in particular. The small manufacturing sector paid wages that were on average 19 percent below those of the United States, with wages also particularly low in finance and wholesale trade. Construction wages, in contrast, averaged 33 percent above those of the United States.

Manufacturing was a tiny part of the Hawaii economy, with the smallest contribution to total output of any state (although Washington, D.C., is lower). Representing only 3.1 percent of gross state product, its share of gross state product has even declined slightly since 1989, as the state lacks any of the high-growth industries propelling other states' manufacturing. The two leading manufacturing industries, printing and food products, displayed flat or declining earnings during 1989–97. Manufacturing output value per worker was relatively low because of this industry mix, and new capital investment decreased during the mid-1990s.

Hawaii's tourism was, of course, a major service export industry, but exports of goods were exceptionally small, only about 1 percent of gross state product. Food and raw agricultural products comprised two of the top five export goods, while refined petroleum products grew to become the leading export good.

Average Annual Wages and Salaries by Sector
(dollars)

	1989	1996	1997 State	1997 U.S.
All wage and salary workers	21 682	27 389	28 228	29 809
Farm	17 662	20 014	20 188	16 442
Nonfarm	21 749	27 476	28 318	29 900
Private nonfarm	21 178	26 768	27 350	29 867
Agricultural service, forestry, and fishing	16 710	20 453	21 168	17 941
Mining	42 243	50 143	51 604	49 800
Construction	34 072	42 431	42 397	31 765
Manufacturing	23 648	30 279	31 006	38 351
Transportation and utilities	27 514	34 549	35 951	38 222
Wholesale trade	24 787	31 352	32 616	39 466
Retail trade	14 037	17 360	17 562	16 206
Finance, insurance, and real estate	25 466	33 374	34 585	44 993
Services	20 521	26 812	27 423	27 588
Government	23 170	29 362	30 893	30 062

Gross State Product and Manufacturing
(millions of dollars, except as noted)

	1989	1994	1995	1996
Gross state product, total	28 756	35 249	36 034	36 317
Manufacturing:				
Millions of dollars	1 259	1 134	1 115	1 123
Percent of total gross state product	4.4	3.2	3.1	3.1
Per worker (dollars)	51 413	52 961	55 440	56 723
New capital expenditures, manufacturing	NA	203	113	79

Exports of Goods
(millions of dollars)

	1994	1995	1996	1997
All goods	237	256	295	303
Manufactures	183	211	247	256
Agricultural and livestock products	22	28	26	22
Other commodities	33	17	22	25
Top goods exports, 1997:				
Refined petroleum products	50	50	71	100
Transportation equipment	15	19	21	35
Food products	44	36	36	31
Scientific and measuring instruments	11	17	18	23
Agricultural products	18	24	24	21

HOUSING

HAWAII'S ECONOMIC STRENGTH IN THE EARLY 1990S TRANS-lated into stalwart housing construction numbers, with extremely high residential construction activity and employment in 1989–91. However, in 1996–97 construction permits fell by around 50 percent. The state's depressed economy and an acceleration of out-migration in those two years took a toll on housing production. A less extreme pattern appeared in the market for existing homes: the 1989–90 period supported very high sales rates, which dropped back toward more normal historical levels starting in 1991. There was a bit of further weakening in 1995–96 but not a large swing.

Home prices generally were high in Honolulu because of scarce land and high transportation costs for materials, even though homes usually forgo heating and air conditioning systems. Median sales price for existing homes in the Honolulu area in 1997 was $307,000, almost double the typical price in the Far West. This price accounts for the low rate of homeownership in the state, about 75 per-

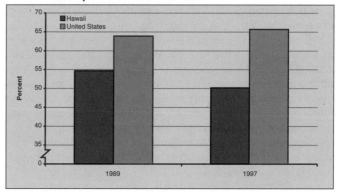

Homeownership Rates: 1989 and 1997

cent of the national average in 1997. The rate of rental vacancies remained in a fairly moderate range throughout the decade, because rental demand was sustained by the scarcity of affordable home-buying opportunities.

Housing Supply

	1989	1990	1991	1992	1993	1994	1995	1996	1997
Residential building permits (thousands)	9.6	8.7	9.2	7.8	6.6	7.3	6.6	3.9	3.7
New home production (including manufactured housing):									
Thousands of homes	9.6	8.7	9.2	7.8	6.6	7.3	6.6	3.9	3.7
Rate per 1,000 population									
Hawaii	8.8	7.8	8.1	6.8	5.7	6.2	5.6	3.3	3.1
U.S.	6.2	5.2	4.5	5.1	5.6	6.4	6.3	6.6	6.5
Existing home sales:									
Thousands of homes	21.2	19.2	12.2	11.6	12.5	13.1	10.0	9.8	11.1
Change from previous year (percent)									
Hawaii	3.9	-9.4	-36.5	-4.9	7.8	4.8	-23.7	-2.0	13.3
U.S.	-3.9	-4.0	0.0	9.2	8.2	4.8	-3.7	7.5	3.8
Home ownership rate (percent of households)	54.7	55.5	55.2	53.8	52.8	52.3	50.2	50.6	50.2
Rental vacancy rate (percent of rental housing units)	6.6	6.6	5.8	5.8	6.8	7.4	6.3	6.0	7.1

Note: Manufactured housing data for 1990–97 suppressed because estimate was based on too few responses.

AGRICULTURE

THE 1990S WAS A DISMAL PERIOD FOR HAWAIIAN AGRICUL-ture, as net income fell to nearly zero for the entire 1993–97 period. Total cash receipts in recent years have been lower in current dollars than they were in either 1980 or 1990, particularly attributable to declines in livestock sales. The better-known fruit and nut industry barely held steady, with an increase of 3 percent in revenues over the 1990–97 period before adjustment for inflation. Production expenses declined slightly over that time, yet net income has still fallen steadily since 1990. Net farm

income equaled only 0.5 percent of total personal income in 1997.

HAWAII FARMS, 1997	
Number of farms	4 600
Total acres (thousands):	1 590
Average per farm	346
Value of land and buildings (millions of dollars)	NA
Average per farm (dollars)	NA

Farm Income
(millions of dollars)

	1980	1989	1990	1991	1992	1993	1994	1995	1996	1997
Gross income	672	629	653	588	566	546	547	537	539	536
Receipts from sales	658	601	622	556	533	515	517	510	511	508
Government payments	1	0	1	1	2	3	3	1	1	1
Imputed and miscellaneous income	13	28	30	31	31	28	27	26	27	28
(−) Production expenses	432	549	558	549	535	528	547	526	527	527
(=) Realized net income	239	80	95	39	31	18	1	11	12	9
(+) Inventory change	4	-2	4	-7	-10	-7	5	-2	-3	-1
(=) Net income	243	77	99	32	21	11	5	9	9	8
Corporate income	0	27	35	9	7	2	3	3	5	4
Farm proprietors income	243	50	64	24	13	10	2	6	4	4

EDUCATION

EDUCATIONAL ATTAINMENT Percent of population age 25 and over, 1997	State	United States
High school graduate or higher	83.7	82.1
College graduate or higher	22.5	23.9

EDUCATIONAL STATISTICS FOR HAWAII SHOW THAT 83.7 PERcent of adults held high school degrees, which places the state in the middle of a ranking of all states. Spending on current public elementary and secondary schools was somewhat below average compared to the nation, as were average teacher salaries (in contrast to the salaries of other government workers in Hawaii). There was an above-average proportion of pupils attending private schools. The state's residents had less than average attainment of college degrees, because most tourism-related jobs do not require a college-educated workforce and there was not enough demand within high-tech, engineering, and other professional sectors to attract college-educated workers. However, the proportion of young adults who were enrolled in college in 1997 was equivalent to the national average.

High School Completion: 1990–97

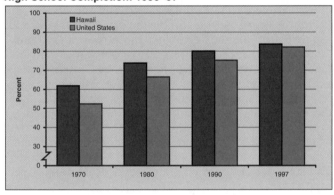

Education Indicators

	State	U.S.
Elementary and secondary schools		
Enrollment, 1995–96		
Total (thousands)	222	49 873
Percent in private schools	15.6	10.1
Expenditures per pupil (dollars), 1995–96	6 051	6 146
Average teacher salary (dollars), 1996–97	35 842	38 509
Higher education		
Enrollment, 1996–97		
Total (thousands)	61	14 218
Percent of population 18–34	21.6	21.8
Percent minority	70.6	26.1
Percent in private schools	22.8	22.6

HEALTH

THIS STATE BOASTS A HEALTHIER THAN AVERAGE POPULATION, based on basic mortality statistics. Infant mortality rates were somewhat better than average, and total death rates were very low. Death from heart disease and cancer ran about 20 percent lower than in the United States overall, probably reflecting the healthy eating habits of the majority-Asian population as well as the state's health-oriented environment. The state government also had unusually high spending on health care. Death from accidents, homicide, and HIV also ran well below average. A particularly high proportion of the state population was covered by health insurance, further supporting these favorable health results. This fact is unusual in an economy with large services and retail trade sectors, but the high rate of government employment raised the rate of insurance coverage.

Health Indicators

	1990	1995	1996	1997
Infant mortality				
(rate per thousand live births)				
Hawaii	6.7	5.8	5.8	6.0
U.S.	9.2	7.6	7.3	7.1
Total deaths, age-adjusted rate				
(rate per thousand population)				
Hawaii	4.1	3.9	3.9	3.8
U.S.	5.2	5.0	4.9	4.8
Persons not covered by health insurance				
(percent of population)				
Hawaii	7.3	8.9	8.6	7.5
U.S.	13.9	15.4	15.6	16.1

Leading Causes of Death, 1996
(deaths per 100,000 population)

	Age-adjusted		Not age-adjusted	
	State	U.S.	State	U.S.
Deaths from all causes	390.1	491.6	671.4	872.5
Heart disease	108.4	134.5	206.6	276.4
Cancer	100.5	127.9	157.2	203.4
Cerebrovascular diseases	24.4	26.4	52.1	60.3
Chronic obstructive pulmonary disease	10.6	21.0	20.2	40.0
Diabetes mellitus	10.8	13.6	18.1	23.3
Pneumonia and influenza	11.9	12.8	28.2	31.6
HIV	5.7	11.1	6.1	11.7
Liver disease	4.9	7.5	6.6	9.4
Alzheimer's disease	1.7	2.7	5.2	8.1
Accidents and adverse effects	25.6	30.4	31.1	35.8
Motor vehicle accidents	11.5	16.2	11.7	16.5
Suicide	10.4	10.8	10.7	11.6
Homicide	3.7	8.5	3.5	7.9
Injury by firearm	3.9	12.9	4.1	12.8

GOVERNMENT

STATE AND LOCAL TAXES, 1995—96	State	U.S.
Per capita (dollars)	3 189	2 477
Percent of personal income	12.9	10.8

STATE AND LOCAL TAXES IN HAWAII WERE UNUSUALLY HIGH, a full 28.7 percent above the U.S. average during 1995–96. The lion's share of taxing and spending was carried out at the state level (about 80 percent of the taxes), because local governments lack a substantial property tax base. Since the majority of land in Hawaii is owned by private trusts and leased under long-term lease by homeowners, the yield on property taxes is reduced below normal lev-

State Government Finances, 1996—97

	Millions of dollars	Percent distribution	Dollars per capita State	Dollars per capita U.S.
General revenue	5 527	100.0	4 656	3 049
Intergovernmental revenue	1 303	23.6	1 097	863
Taxes	3 088	55.9	2 601	1 660
General sales	1 457	26.4	1 228	551
Selective sales	469	8.5	395	257
License taxes	90	1.6	76	106
Individual income	977	17.7	823	542
Corporation net income	68	1.2	57	115
Other taxes	28	0.5	24	90
Other general revenue	1 136	20.6	957	526
General expenditure	5 421	100.0	4 567	2 951
Intergovernmental expenditure	156	2.9	131	989
Direct expenditure	5 265	97.1	4 435	1 962
General expenditure, by function:				
Education	1 557	28.7	1 312	1 033
Public welfare	983	18.1	828	761
Hospitals and health	515	9.5	434	237
Highways	322	5.9	271	225
Police protection and corrections	135	2.5	113	137
Natural resources, parks and recreation	215	4.0	181	63
Governmental administration	248	4.6	209	107
Interest on general debt	328	6.1	277	99
Other and unallocable	1 118	20.6	942	290
Debt at end of fiscal year	5 253	NA	4 425	1 706
Cash and security holdings	10 843	NA	9 135	6 683

Federal Spending within State

	Millions of dollars	Percent distribution	Percent of U.S. total*
Total within state	8 159	100.0	0.6
Payments to individuals	3 508	43.0	0.4
Retirement and disability	2 179	26.7	0.5
Medicare	650	8.0	0.3
Food stamps	194	2.4	1.0
Supplemental Security Income	83	1.0	0.3
Grants	1 137	13.9	0.5
Medicaid and other health	383	4.7	0.3
Nutrition and family welfare	250	3.1	0.5
Education	110	1.3	0.6
Housing and community development	69	0.8	0.6
Salaries and wages	2 330	28.6	1.4
Defense procurement contracts	926	11.3	0.8
Non-defense procurement contracts	151	1.9	0.2

*State population is 0.4 percent of the U.S. total.

els. State and local taxes comprised 12.9 percent of state personal income; this percentage rose recently because of the state's lack of income growth, and was substantially higher than the U.S. average. The full burden of state taxes did not fall on residents, however, because a significant portion of sales and accommodations taxes were paid by tourists.

State tax revenues per capita in 1997 were 57 percent higher than for an average state, which combined with relatively high federal transfers to yield total revenues 53 percent above average. It appears that about half of this discrepancy was related to the relative distribution of taxation between state and local government in Hawaii. Further, tourism had a favorable impact on state sales and use revenues (the state estimates this income at $420 million in 1998, which is more than 10 percent of all state taxes). However, individual income taxes borne by residents were also 50 percent above average on a per capita basis. State spending on education was much higher than the U.S. average, and much of this was direct spending rather than transfers to the local level. Other categories where spending was disproportionately high are health care, natural resources, administration, interest, and other. The state had an unusually high level of debt, on a per capita basis.

This state received a relatively high amount of federal money compared to its small population. This money was largely related to the military bases located in Hawaii, their employee salaries, pensions, and private procurement contracts in-state. In addition, the state had more federal civilian employees than average. Medicare and Medicaid expenditures were a bit below average, which relates to the better-than-normal health status of many Hawaiians. Non-defense procurement was below average.

31 372	59 698			65 157	70 827	72 687	78 001	81 93	88 504	93 426	5.8	63 383	70 827	31 372	59 698	63 38
25 323	47 902			57 151	59 446	62 916	67 00	72 039	77 208	6.1	50 999	57 151	25 323	47 902	50 99
2 640	5 143				7 801		7 709	7 838	5.4	5 645	6 816	2 640	5 143	5 64
3 409	6 652			7 284		8 755	8 380	2.9	6 739	6 860	3 409	6 652	6 7
693	1 716				1 539	762	9.7	1 561	811	693	1 716	9
2 716					7 217	7 618	5.6	5 178	6 049	2 716	9

1997

Population (persons)	1,208,865
Population rank	40th
Population growth rank (1990–97)	3rd
Per capita personal income	$20,393
Unemployment rate (percent)	5.3
Poverty rate (percent)	14.7

THE PRESENCE OF NUMEROUS THRIVING AND GROWING MANU-facturing and resource-based businesses testified to Idaho's fertile business climate. While traditional natural resource industries continued to be important, Idaho's economy developed vigorous manufacturing, retail trade, and service industries, which accounted for 55 percent of all the jobs in Idaho in 1997. Both employment and earnings grew by substantial rates from 1989 to 1997. However, both per capita and median household income remained significantly below the U.S. levels for 1997.

Population figures show a strong increase of 2.6 percent annually from 1990 to 1997 compared to a national aver-age 1.0 percent increase over the same period. The minority populations in Idaho showed significant increases from 1990 to 1997, specifically Asians and Hispanics, but minorities still account for less than 10 percent of the state's total population. Much of Idaho's tremendous growth from 1990 to 1997 came from domestic migration, which accounted for more than half of the state's growth. The state's expanding economy was able to accommodate the population growth, as is evident by the slightly lower unemployment rate and the steady poverty rate over the past several years, though both rates were higher than the national average.

Average Annual Population Growth: 1990–97

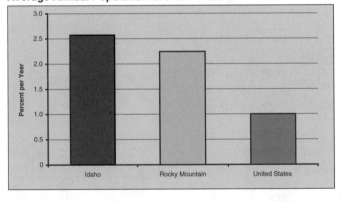

Median Household Income: 1989–97 (1997 dollars)

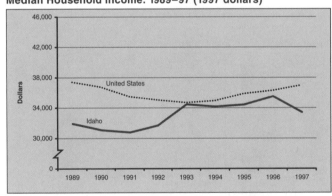

Unemployment Rate: 1989–97

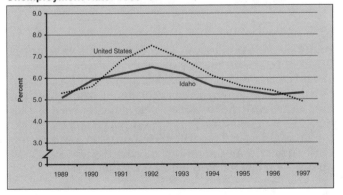

IDAHO'S UNEMPLOYMENT RATE REMAINED FAIRLY STEADY throughout the decade, despite substantial population growth in the working age group. During this period, Idaho's civilian labor force grew at a faster rate than the U.S. labor force. Except for 1997, the unemployment rate in Idaho has steadily declined since the recessionary high of 6.5 percent in 1992. 1997 also marked the first time since 1990 that Idaho's unemployment rate exceeded the national average. Idaho's 1997 unemployment rate of 5.3 was among the highest twenty in the nation, and the state was among only ten states whose unemployment rates had increased from the previous year.

POPULATION AND LABOR FORCE

IDAHO'S TOTAL POPULATION GREW 2.6 PERCENT ANNUALLY from 1990 to 1997, compared with the U.S. average of 1.0 percent. Idaho had the third highest percent change in population in the nation, as the state grew by nearly 20 percent from 1990 to 1997. Given the state's small size, this change represented an increase of only 200,000 people. The state has had a tremendously high rate of domestic in-migration and substantial immigration from abroad. Part of the population growth can be attributed to higher than average birth rates and lower than average death rates. The Hispanic and Asian populations had the highest rates of growth. From 1990 to 1997, the state's Hispanic population had an average annual growth rate of 7.0, well above the U.S. rate of 3.8. By 1997, Hispanics accounted for 7.1 percent of Idaho's population. The state had very small Black, Asian, and Native American populations. The Native American population showed the smallest increase in the state, as it grew by about 1,000, or an average annual rate of 1.5 percent. The population living within metropolitan areas remained very low, at 37.0 percent of total state population, indicating that many migrants are coming to small towns and rural areas.

Population and Labor Force

	1980	1990	1991	1992	1993	1994	1995	1996	1997	Change* State	Change* U.S.
Population											
Total number of persons (thousands)	944	1 012	1 039	1 066	1 100	1 134	1 164	1 186	1 209	2.6	1.0
Percent distribution:											
White, Non-Hispanic	94.0	91.9	92.0	91.7	91.4	91.2	90.9	90.7	90.4	2.4	0.4
Black, Non-Hispanic	0.3	0.7	0.3	0.3	0.4	0.4	0.4	0.4	0.4	-5.9	1.4
Asian	0.7	1.0	1.0	1.0	1.0	1.0	1.1	1.1	1.1	4.3	4.1
Native American	1.1	1.5	1.5	1.4	1.4	1.4	1.4	1.3	1.3	1.5	1.6
Hispanic	3.9	5.3	5.5	5.8	6.1	6.4	6.6	6.9	7.1	7.0	3.8
In metropolitan areas	34.1	36.0	36.3	36.5	36.7	37.0	37.3	37.6	37.8	3.3	1.0
Total number of households (thousands)	324	361	373	384	395	405	419	430	NA	3.0	1.2
Labor Force (thousands)											
Population 16 and over	672	731	757	779	808	836	863	884	903	3.1	1.0
Civilian labor force	429	493	509	532	548	591	600	617	633	3.6	1.1
Employed	395	463	477	497	514	559	568	585	599	3.7	1.2
Percent of population	58.8	63.4	63.0	63.8	63.6	66.9	65.9	66.2	66.3		
Unemployment rate (percent)	7.9	5.9	6.2	6.5	6.2	5.6	5.4	5.2	5.3		

*Compound annual average percent change, 1990–1997; 1990–1996 for households.

Population Change and Components: 1990–97

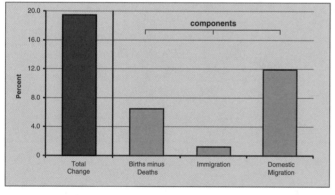

Average Annual Household and Population Growth

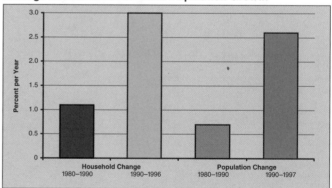

Population by Age; Births and Deaths

	1990 State	1990 U.S.	1997 State	1997 U.S.
Age distribution (percent)				
Under 5 years	8.1	7.6	7.6	7.2
5 to 17 years	22.8	18.2	21.5	18.8
18 to 64 years	57.0	61.8	59.7	61.3
65 years and over	12.0	12.5	11.3	12.7
Birth and death rates (per thousand population)				
Births	16.3	16.7	15.4	14.6
Deaths	7.4	8.6	7.4	8.6

IDAHO'S POPULATION BY AGE WAS QUITE DIFFERENT FROM THE U.S. profile. The proportion of people between the ages of 18 and 64 was well below average, while that for children remained well above. The proportion of school-age children decreased slightly since 1990 but remained higher than average, resulting in the need for greater resources for education spending. The birth rate of 15.4 was significantly higher than the national average, while the death rate of 7.4 remained well below the national rate.

HOUSEHOLD AND PERSONAL INCOME

HOUSEHOLD INCOME AND PERSONS IN POVERTY	1990	1995	1996	1997 State	1997 U.S.
Median household income (1997 dollars)	31 075	34 413	35 505	33 404	37 005
Persons in poverty (thousands)	157	167	140	183	35 574
Poverty rate (percent)	14.9	14.5	11.9	14.7	13.3

IDAHO'S MEDIAN HOUSEHOLD INCOME REMAINED LOWER THAN the national average during the 1990s, ranging from 4 to 10 percent below U.S. levels in most years. In 1997, it was at $33,404, only 90 percent of the national average. The state's poverty rate measured 14.7 percent in 1997, somewhat above the national average of 13.3 percent, and was one of the 15 highest rates in the nation.

Per capita personal income increased 42.8 percent in current dollars and nearly 13 percent in inflation-adjusted dollars from 1989 to 1997. Despite this growth, per capita personal income remained nearly 20 percent lower than the national average. Total earnings grew much faster than in the United States because of the higher population and job growth in Idaho; but again, earnings per capita remained only 81 percent as high as the national average. Income from transfer payments also was well below aver-

age. In 1997, adjustment for residence increased substantially from $130 million in 1989 to $246 million, indicating that 1.5 percent of net earnings of residents was earned in out-of-state jobs.

Transfer payments grew quite a lot faster than overall personal incomes. The fastest growth was in medical payments which grew by 119.7 percent from 1990 to 1997. Income maintenance grew by 107.8 percent, well above the national average of 58 percent. Much of this growth was centered on Supplemental Security Income (SSI), as well as on other income maintenance, which largely consists of earned income tax benefits. Unemployment insurance increased by 52.8 percent, significantly higher than the national increase of 10.6 percent; despite Idaho's decreased unemployment rate, the actual number of unemployed grew.

Personal Income
(millions of dollars)

	1980	1989	1990	1991	1992	1993	1994	1995	1996	1997	Change*
Earnings by place of work	5 985	10 144	11 140	11 576	12 778	14 197	14 959	15 902	16 648	17 535	7.1
Wages and salaries	4 488	7 247	7 969	8 531	9 309	9 994	10 926	11 742	12 335	13 117	7.7
Other labor income	417	755	867	964	1 088	1 218	1 361	1 365	1 322	1 329	7.3
Proprietors' income	1 080	2 142	2 304	2 081	2 382	2 985	2 672	2 796	2 991	3 089	4.7
Farm	259	685	774	604	606	914	365	387	471	385	-6.9
Nonfarm	821	1 457	1 530	1 477	1 775	2 071	2 307	2 408	2 519	2 704	8.0
(−) Personal contributions for social insurance	309	661	719	786	849	919	1 017	1 109	1 169	1 256	8.4
(+) Adjustment for residence	55	130	150	165	167	151	161	186	216	246	NA
(=) Net earnings by state of residence	5 731	9 613	10 570	10 955	12 096	13 429	14 103	14 979	15 696	16 525	7.0
(+) Dividends, interest, and rent	1 314	2 505	2 680	2 772	2 814	3 007	3 303	3 583	3 920	4 165	6.6
(+) Transfer payments	1 084	2 086	2 278	2 539	2 790	3 038	3 222	3 509	3 814	3 991	8.4
(=) Total personal income	8 129	14 203	15 528	16 267	17 700	19 474	20 628	22 071	23 430	24 681	7.2
Farm	407	859	977	802	808	1 136	649	700	782	725	-2.1
Nonfarm	7 722	13 344	14 551	15 465	16 892	18 338	19 978	21 371	22 647	23 956	7.6
Personal income per capita (dollars)											
Current dollars	8 575	14 283	15 346	15 658	16 597	17 686	18 168	18 947	19 729	20 393	4.6
1997 dollars	16 396	18 057	18 467	18 081	18 565	19 245	19 307	19 695	20 091	20 393	1.5

*Compound annual average percent change, 1989–1997

Government Transfer Payments

	Millions of dollars 1990	Millions of dollars 1997	Percent change* State	Percent change* U.S.
Total government payments to individuals	2 172	3 750	72.7	62.7
Retirement, disability, and insurance	1 395	2 184	56.5	48.2
Social Security	950	1 463	54.0	46.1
Government employee retirement	345	571	65.6	60.3
Medical payments	473	1 039	119.7	101.2
Income maintenance	122	253	107.8	58.0
Supplemental Security Income	33	80	141.1	75.4
Family assistance	21	20	-4.5	-0.5
Food Stamps	41	51	24.9	27.1
Other income maintenance	27	102	279.9	189.8
Unemployment insurance benefits	72	110	52.8	10.6
Veterans benefits and other	110	164	49.9	30.8

*Percent change, 1990–1997

Government Payments to Individuals: 1997

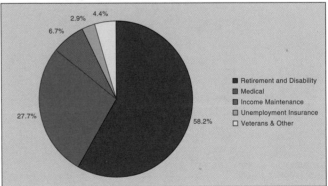

- Retirement and Disability
- Medical
- Income Maintenance
- Unemployment Insurance
- Veterans & Other

58.2% — 27.7% — 6.7% — 2.9% — 4.4%

ECONOMIC STRUCTURE

LEADING PRIVATE INDUSTRIES, 1997 (Worker and proprietor earnings, millions of dollars)		FASTEST EARNINGS GROWTH, 1989–97 (percent increase)	
Health services	$1 300	Real estate	363.4
Construction specialties	922	Electronic equipment manufacturing	228.4
Engineering and management services	764	Social services	202.0
Lumber and wood products	743	Electric, gas and sanitary services	180.5
Farming	725	Industrial machinery manufacturing	152.0

HEALTH SERVICES AND CONSTRUCTION SPECIALTIES WERE THE two leading private industries in Idaho, together accounting for more than $2 billion in worker earnings, equal to 16 percent of all private nonfarm earnings in the state. Services continued to be a major force in Idaho's economy, as two of the state's leading private industries were within the services sector. Services showed the largest increase of actual jobs, pushing the sector to just above 25 percent of total jobs. Real estate was the fastest growing industry, with growth of 363 percent from 1989 to 1997. Electronic and other electric equipment followed with an increase of 228 percent, and industrial machinery production was also among the fastest growing. Idaho was unusu-

al in having two manufacturing industries among its fastest growing, and this sector was expanding in the state while in the nation manufacturing employment had declined since 1989. Idaho's total employment increased by an average annual change of 3.8 percent from 1989 to 1997. During that period, construction showed the highest annual average increase in employment. Construction now comprises more than 7 percent of employment in Idaho. Construction earnings increased by more than 110 percent from 1989 to 1997, as did earnings in finance, insurance, and real estate. Total earnings increased by 72.9 percent. Only farm earnings showed a decrease from 1989 to 1997, falling more than 15 percent.

Employment and Earnings by Sector

	1980	1989	1990	1991	1992	1993	1994	1995	1996	1997 Number	1997 Percent of total	Change*
Employment *(thousands of persons)*												
Total	466	529	552	571	591	614	651	675	696	715	100.0	3.8
Farm	44	37	37	36	35	35	34	37	37	34	4.8	-0.9
Nonfarm	421	493	515	535	556	579	617	639	659	681	95.2	4.1
Private nonfarm	338	402	423	440	457	479	515	535	554	574	80.2	4.5
Agricultural service, forestry, and fishing	7	12	13	14	13	15	16	17	18	19	2.7	6.0
Mining	5	4	5	4	3	3	3	4	4	4	0.5	-1.4
Construction	27	28	31	33	37	40	46	48	49	51	7.1	8.0
Manufacturing	57	65	68	68	71	75	79	78	80	82	11.4	2.8
Transportation and public utilities	23	24	25	25	25	26	28	29	30	31	4.4	3.3
Wholesale trade	24	24	25	27	28	28	29	30	32	33	4.6	3.8
Retail trade	73	88	92	96	101	105	116	121	125	129	18.1	4.9
Finance, insurance, and real estate	32	34	35	35	35	37	36	37	37	38	5.4	1.7
Services	90	123	130	138	142	150	163	172	179	187	26.1	5.4
Government	83	90	93	95	99	101	101	103	105	107	15.0	2.2
Earnings *(millions of dollars)*												
Total	5 985	10 144	11 140	11 576	12 778	14 197	14 959	15 902	16 648	17 535	100.0	7.1
Farm	407	859	977	802	808	1 136	649	700	782	725	4.1	-2.1
Nonfarm	5 578	9 285	10 162	10 774	11 970	13 061	14 310	15 202	15 866	16 810	95.9	7.7
Private nonfarm	4 596	7 562	8 277	8 719	9 739	10 716	11 836	12 619	13 147	13 970	79.7	8.0
Agricultural service, forestry, and fishing	49	132	152	163	174	186	202	210	216	239	1.4	7.7
Mining	150	140	148	133	131	123	152	155	166	180	1.0	3.2
Construction	495	723	843	886	1 015	1 131	1 330	1 409	1 451	1 520	8.7	9.7
Manufacturing	1 076	1 818	1 930	1 956	2 237	2 503	2 847	2 939	2 956	3 111	17.7	6.9
Transportation and public utilities	459	660	698	766	821	935	985	1 050	1 112	1 186	6.8	7.6
Wholesale trade	369	542	602	638	694	724	793	837	906	966	5.5	7.5
Retail trade	671	1 063	1 163	1 226	1 343	1 457	1 585	1 668	1 771	1 881	10.7	7.4
Finance, insurance, and real estate	268	413	455	493	581	688	740	812	853	868	5.0	9.7
Services	1 060	2 070	2 287	2 459	2 743	2 969	3 201	3 538	3 716	4 019	22.9	8.6
Government	982	1 723	1 885	2 055	2 231	2 345	2 473	2 583	2 719	2 840	16.2	6.4

*Compound annual average percent change, 1989–1997

ECONOMIC STRUCTURE (Continued)

AVERAGE WAGES IN IDAHO REMAINED BELOW THE NATIONAL averages, with the exception of farming. The average wage for all workers was less than 80 percent of the national average. Finance, insurance, and real estate wages were only 63.8 percent of the national average of $44,993. Retail trade and manufacturing were closest to national averages but still remained less than 90 percent. Relatively moderate wage scales in manufacturing may help explain the expansion in jobs in Idaho. From 1989 to 1997, average wages in Idaho increased by 34.6 percent, slightly higher than the national average of 33.9 percent.

Manufacturing has increased from 19.3 percent of gross state product in 1989 to 20.6 percent in 1996, as manufacturing output more than kept up with the 69 percent growth in GSP over the eight years. Since 1989, manufacturing has grown by more than 80 percent. Idaho's output per worker remained higher than the national average. The state's leading manufacturing industries were lumber and wood products, food products, and industrial machinery. New capital expenditures more than doubled from 1994 to 1996.

Idaho's exports increased by just over 12 percent from 1994 to 1997, expanding at a lower rate than the state's overall state economy and much slower than U.S. exports during the same period. The largest export was industrial machinery and computers, which have grown by nearly 15 percent since 1994. The fastest growing major export was food products. Since 1994, the value of food exports has grown by more than 57 percent. A decline in exports of electronic equipment during 1996 and 1997 contributed to the relative weakness in the state's export picture.

Average Annual Wages and Salaries by Sector
(dollars)

	1989	1996	1997 State	1997 U.S.
All wage and salary workers	17 672	22 989	23 785	29 809
Farm	11 842	19 224	25 693	16 442
Nonfarm	17 880	23 102	23 741	29 900
Private nonfarm	18 027	23 043	23 712	29 867
Agricultural service, forestry, and fishing	11 365	14 548	15 155	17 941
Mining	29 274	35 528	37 088	49 800
Construction	22 164	25 907	26 572	31 765
Manufacturing	23 655	32 232	33 375	38 351
Transportation and utilities	25 295	30 295	30 805	38 222
Wholesale trade	19 784	26 051	26 930	39 466
Retail trade	11 045	14 024	14 500	16 206
Finance, insurance, and real estate	20 102	28 493	28 717	44 993
Services	16 710	21 494	22 178	27 588
Government	17 380	23 335	23 857	30 062

Gross State Product and Manufacturing
(millions of dollars, except as noted)

	1989	1994	1995	1996
Gross state product, total	16 544	24 505	26 885	27 898
Manufacturing:				
Millions of dollars	3 188	4 809	5 897	5 754
Percent of total gross state product	19.3	19.6	21.9	20.6
Per worker (dollars)	48 756	61 242	75 947	72 246
New capital expenditures, manufacturing	NA	1 637	6 284	6 424

Exports of Goods
(millions of dollars)

	1994	1995	1996	1997
All goods	1 531	1 893	1 610	1 716
Manufactures	1 469	1 831	1 539	1 634
Agricultural and livestock products	51	49	55	63
Other commodities	10	12	16	19
Top goods exports, 1997:				
Industrial machinery and computers	571	676	626	656
Electric and electronic equipment	518	649	438	484
Food products	154	213	225	243
Agricultural products	47	46	52	60
Chemical products	50	52	57	58

HOUSING

HOUSING PRODUCTION HAS INCREASED SUBSTANTIALLY SINCE the 1990–91 recession. Since 1989, home production rates in Idaho have remained well above the national average. Idaho's population growth, well above average, helped to stimulate increased housing production. High population growth in 1993 and 1994 is evident in the high numbers of home production, which peaked in 1994. Home production in Idaho from 1992 to 1994 was nearly double the U.S. rate. Homeownership rates have risen since 1989. After a slight decrease during the recession early this decade, homeownership rates increased to 72.3 percent in 1997. This was the twelfth highest homeownership rate in the nation. Rental vacancy rates increased steadily from an exceptionally low rate of 2.7 percent in 1992 to 6.8 percent in 1997.

Homeownership Rates: 1989 and 1997

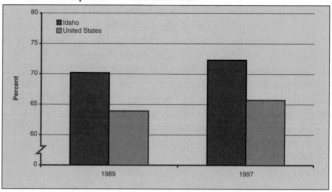

Housing Supply

	1989	1990	1991	1992	1993	1994	1995	1996	1997
Residential building permits (thousands)	4.8	5.7	6.6	9.6	11.6	12.6	10.7	10.8	10.3
New home production (including manufactured housing):									
Thousands of homes	5.5	6.8	7.8	11.2	13.7	15.8	13.3	13.0	12.3
Rate per 1,000 population									
Idaho	5.5	6.7	7.5	10.5	12.4	13.9	11.4	10.9	10.2
U.S.	6.2	5.2	4.5	5.1	5.6	6.4	6.3	6.6	6.5
Existing home sales:									
Thousands of homes	15.0	18.1	19.0	21.6	23.4	23.1	20.5	20.2	20.7
Change from previous year (percent)									
Idaho	14.5	20.7	5.0	13.7	8.3	-1.3	-11.3	-1.5	2.5
U.S.	-3.9	-4.0	0.0	9.2	8.2	4.8	-3.7	7.5	3.8
Home ownership rate (percent of households)	70.2	69.4	68.4	70.3	72.1	70.7	72.0	71.4	72.3
Rental vacancy rate (percent of rental housing units)	6.0	5.4	3.9	2.7	3.7	3.6	4.5	5.8	6.8

AGRICULTURE

WITH 22,000 FARMS IN 1997, IDAHO RANKED IN THE MIDDLE of the nation for the total number of farms. The state averaged 614 acres per farm, well above the national average of 471. The value of land and buildings in Idaho stood at about $13 billion in 1997, ranking thirtieth in the nation for total value of farmland and buildings. The gross income from farming increased by nearly 20 percent from 1989 to 1997, despite uneven growth during the 1990s. However, net income after expenses and inventory change declined pretty steadily after 1993 and was about 38 per-

cent lower in 1997 than in 1989. Idaho's farming income was earned nearly equally from livestock and related products, and crops.

IDAHO FARMS, 1997	
Number of farms	22 000
Total acres (thousands):	13 500
Average per farm	614
Value of land and buildings (millions of dollars)	12 960
Average per farm (dollars)	589 091

Farm Income
(millions of dollars)

	1980	1989	1990	1991	1992	1993	1994	1995	1996	1997
Gross income	2 473	3 353	3 532	3 340	3 414	3 613	3 671	3 800	4 005	3 992
Receipts from sales	2 365	3 098	3 239	3 024	3 115	3 279	3 365	3 518	3 688	3 675
Government payments	8	99	133	141	137	159	127	89	116	110
Imputed and miscellaneous income	100	156	160	175	162	174	179	193	201	207
(−) Production expenses	2 328	2 597	2 749	2 639	2 667	2 811	3 235	3 412	3 522	3 726
(=) Realized net income	145	756	783	701	748	802	436	389	483	266
(+) Inventory change	113	54	136	-15	-21	176	58	78	147	235
(=) Net income	259	810	919	686	726	978	494	467	630	501
Corporate income	0	126	144	83	120	65	129	79	159	116
Farm proprietors income	259	685	774	604	606	914	365	387	471	385

EDUCATION

EDUCATIONAL ATTAINMENT Percent of population age 25 and over, 1997	State	United States
High school graduate or higher	85.7	82.1
College graduate or higher	19.4	23.9

IDAHO RANKED IN THE TOP TWENTY STATES IN THE PROPORTION of its population with a high school degree. Nearly 86 percent of the state's population were high school graduates, well above the national percentage of just over 82 percent. Idaho had fewer elementary and secondary students enrolled in private school (3.7 percent) than the United States (10.1 percent). Idaho's teachers' salaries were among the lowest 15 states in the nation, which may suggest a lower cost of living, and per pupil expenditure of $4,465 was well below the U.S. average of $6,146. The high rate of educational attainment did not carry over to the post-secondary level. Idaho ranked among the bottom ten states in the nation for percent of state population holding college degrees. Less than 20 percent of Idaho residents graduated from college, compared with the national average of nearly 24 percent. The lower percentage of college graduates may reflect a lack of industries that require college degrees.

High School Completion: 1990–97

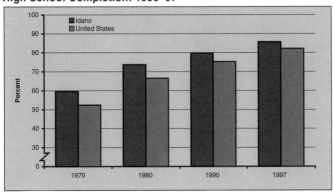

Education Indicators

	State	U.S.
Elementary and secondary schools		
Enrollment, 1995–96		
Total (thousands)	252	49 873
Percent in private schools	3.7	10.1
Expenditures per pupil (dollars), 1995–96	4 465	6 146
Average teacher salary (dollars), 1996–97	31 818	38 509
Higher education		
Enrollment, 1996–97		
Total (thousands)	60	14 218
Percent of population 18–34	21.3	21.8
Percent minority	6.5	26.1
Percent in private schools	17.5	22.6

HEALTH

OVERALL, THE HEALTH OF IDAHO RESIDENTS APPEARS TO HAVE been fairly close to the national average, according to major indicators. The percentage of Idaho's population without health insurance increased over the past several years. In 1996 it reached 16.5 percent, surpassing the national average. Idaho's 1997 infant mortality rate was 6.1, well below the U.S. average rate of 7.1. Idaho's death rate remained below the national average since 1990. With the exception of unintentional injuries, motor vehicle deaths, and suicide, Idaho's death rates for major causes were all below the national average. Idaho's heart disease and lung cancer death rates were both less than 75 percent of the national rates, and the state's cirrhosis death rate was less than 65 percent of average.

Health Indicators

	1990	1995	1996	1997
Infant mortality				
(rate per thousand live births)				
Idaho	8.7	6.1	7.1	6.1
U.S.	9.2	7.6	7.3	7.1
Total deaths, age-adjusted rate				
(rate per thousand population)				
Idaho	4.5	4.4	4.3	4.3
U.S.	5.2	5.0	4.9	4.8
Persons not covered by health insurance				
(percent of population)				
Idaho	15.2	14.0	16.5	17.7
U.S.	13.9	15.4	15.6	16.1

Leading Causes of Death, 1996
(deaths per 100,000 population)

	Age-adjusted		Not age-adjusted	
	State	U.S.	State	U.S.
Deaths from all causes	431.7	491.6	732.7	872.5
Heart disease	104.9	134.5	200.5	276.4
Cancer	109.4	127.9	167.1	203.4
Cerebrovascular diseases	25.5	26.4	57.8	60.3
Chronic obstructive pulmonary disease	22.7	21.0	40.1	40.0
Diabetes mellitus	12.5	13.6	20.4	23.3
Pneumonia and influenza	11.6	12.8	26.1	31.6
HIV	1.8	11.1	1.8	11.7
Liver disease	4.9	7.5	6.0	9.4
Alzheimer's disease	3.2	2.7	9.3	8.1
Accidents and adverse effects	41.5	30.4	47.3	35.8
Motor vehicle accidents	23.0	16.2	23.7	16.5
Suicide	13.8	10.8	14.9	11.6
Homicide	4.3	8.5	4.2	7.9
Injury by firearm	13.1	12.9	14.0	12.8

GOVERNMENT

STATE AND LOCAL TAXES, 1995–96	State	U.S.
Per capita (dollars)	2 009	2 477
Percent of personal income	10.9	10.8

In 1996, Idaho's state and local taxes amounted to $2,009 per capita. Though this was significantly lower than the national average, it was a slightly higher percentage of personal income. Only 28.8 percent of these taxes were local, as compared to 40.8 percent nationwide, indicating lower property taxes. Idaho's 1997 per capita state government revenue of $2,811 was less than the U.S. average of $3,049 though state taxes per capita were much closer to average. The state's per capita individual income taxes were slightly higher than nationally. While the state's general expenditures were lower than the national per capita expenditures, Idaho spent $1,112 for education per capita, while the national average was $1,033. Idaho's highway expenditures were also above the national average. The state's expenditures for public welfare amounted to $495 per capita, significantly lower than the $761 national per capita expenditure. Idaho's per capita debt was nearly $400 lower than the national per capita debt.

Idaho's proportion of the U.S. total federal grants and payments to individuals was lower than the state's proportion of the U.S. population. In 1997, Idaho comprised 0.5 percent of the nation's population, and only in nondefense procurement did the state receive a greater than 0.5 percent share. Defense procurements amounted to only 0.1 percent of the U.S. total. Total expenditures, total grants, and payments to individuals all amounted to 0.4 percent of the total, just under the state's share of the total population.

State Government Finances, 1996–97

	Millions of dollars	Percent distribution	Dollars per capita State	Dollars per capita U.S.
General revenue	3 402	100.0	2 811	3 049
Intergovernmental revenue	849	25.0	702	863
Taxes	1 961	57.6	1 620	1 660
General sales	622	18.3	514	551
Selective sales	302	8.9	249	257
License taxes	148	4.3	122	106
Individual income	712	20.9	588	542
Corporation net income	138	4.1	114	115
Other taxes	39	1.1	32	90
Other general revenue	592	17.4	489	526
General expenditure	3 251	100.0	2 686	2 951
Intergovernmental expenditure	1 067	32.8	882	989
Direct expenditure	2 183	67.2	1 804	1 962
General expenditure, by function:				
Education	1 346	41.4	1 112	1 033
Public welfare	599	18.4	495	761
Hospitals and health	130	4.0	108	237
Highways	397	12.2	328	225
Police protection and corrections	135	4.2	111	137
Natural resources, parks and recreation	136	4.2	113	63
Governmental administration	119	3.6	98	107
Interest on general debt	102	3.1	85	99
Other and unallocable	287	8.8	237	290
Debt at end of fiscal year	1 598	NA	1 321	1 706
Cash and security holdings	7 294	NA	6 028	6 683

Federal Spending within State

	Federal funds, fiscal 1997 Millions of dollars	Federal funds, fiscal 1997 Percent distribution	Federal funds, fiscal 1997 Percent of U.S. total*
Total within state	5 591	100.0	0.4
Payments to individuals	2 996	53.6	0.4
Retirement and disability	1 966	35.2	0.4
Medicare	597	10.7	0.3
Food stamps	52	0.9	0.3
Supplemental Security Income	71	1.3	0.3
Grants	932	16.7	0.4
Medicaid and other health	319	5.7	0.3
Nutrition and family welfare	159	2.8	0.3
Education	74	1.3	0.4
Housing and community development ..	21	0.4	0.2
Salaries and wages	627	11.2	0.4
Defense procurement contracts	143	2.6	0.1
Non-defense procurement contracts	744	13.3	1.0

*State population is 0.5 percent of the U.S. total.

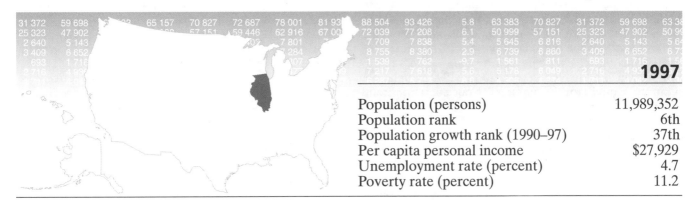

	1997
Population (persons)	11,989,352
Population rank	6th
Population growth rank (1990–97)	37th
Per capita personal income	$27,929
Unemployment rate (percent)	4.7
Poverty rate (percent)	11.2

THE OLD PICTURE OF ILLINOIS AS A STATE OF FARMING AND heavy industry is giving way to one of a diversified economy integrated into business services growth, as well as an increasing ethnic diversity in its population. One regional economics firm calculated that the Chicago area had the third highest concentration of high-tech workers (184,000), behind San Jose and Boston and was headquarters for 32 Fortune 500 companies. The state still had a strong base of high-paying jobs in manufacturing and wholesale trade, though neither sector was as dominant as it was 20 years ago. The number of manufacturing jobs in 1997 was 17 percent below the 1980 level. Agriculture comprised less than 1 percent of earnings in the state.

The state's strong economic growth yielded higher incomes per capita than the national average, but it had an anemic population growth rate caused by steady out-migration to other states. This trend resulted in total population growth only 60 percent as fast as the U.S. (though equal to the average growth for the Great Lakes region). A surprisingly large number of Hispanics lived in Illinois, reflecting moderately high ongoing immigration. The largest absolute growth in population from 1990 to 1997 came among the Hispanic population (up 231,000), and the non-Hispanic White population was down to 72 percent of the state's total.

Average Annual Population Growth: 1990–97

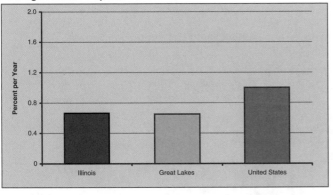

Median Household Income: 1989–97 (1997 dollars)

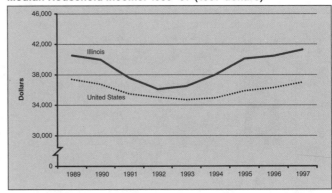

Unemployment Rate: 1989–97

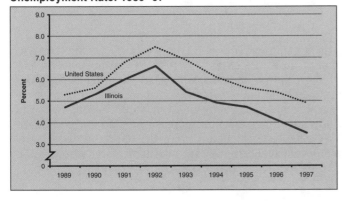

THE STATE UNEMPLOYMENT RATE WAS ABOVE THE U.S. AVERAGE and rose from 1989 to 1992, reflecting a marked decline in manufacturing employment in the state. In the mid-1990s jobs in the services and finance sectors grew strongly, while the labor force grew little or not at all, leading to lower unemployment rates. Out-migration continued to limit the growth of the labor force and hold down unemployment in 1996–97, so that unemployment reached a low 4.7 percent in 1997, compared to the 4.9 percent rate nationwide.

POPULATION AND LABOR FORCE

POPULATION GROWTH DURING THE 1990S PROCEEDED AT A rate only 60 percent as fast as that of the nation because of moderately severe out-migration. Though not as sharp as the 1980s out-migration of 7 percent of its population, the 1990–97 loss through out-migration was 3.7 percent. This decline was only partly balanced by international immigration, which added 2.5 percent to the 1990 population, about the same as for the nation. The out-migration trend appears not to be related primarily to unemployment, as the out-migration intensified in the mid-1990s even though economic conditions improved.

Hispanics and Asians displayed the fastest population growth, reflecting both immigration and natural increases. The non-Hispanic White population failed to grow during the 1990s, indicating that most out-migrants were White. Though Blacks still comprised the largest minority group in the state, 14.9 percent of total population, their growth was slower than that of other minority groups.

With modest population growth, the labor force followed suit and increased less than half as fast as it did nationwide during the 1990s. The number of employed adults grew faster, however, resulting in a significant increase in the ratio of employment to population and a decreased unemployment rate.

Population and Labor Force

	1980	1990	1991	1992	1993	1994	1995	1996	1997	Change* State	Change* U.S.
Population											
Total number of persons (thousands)	11 427	11 447	11 533	11 630	11 718	11 794	11 866	11 934	11 989	0.6	1.0
Percent distribution:											
White, Non-Hispanic	78.2	74.8	74.4	74.0	73.6	73.2	72.8	72.4	72.0	0.0	0.4
Black, Non-Hispanic	14.5	14.6	14.7	14.8	14.8	14.8	14.9	14.9	14.9	0.8	1.4
Asian	1.5	2.6	2.7	2.8	2.9	3.0	3.0	3.1	3.2	3.8	4.1
Native American	0.2	0.2	0.2	0.2	0.2	0.2	0.2	0.2	0.2	0.5	1.6
Hispanic	5.6	8.0	8.2	8.4	8.7	9.0	9.3	9.6	9.9	3.7	3.8
In metropolitan areas	82.8	83.8	83.8	83.9	83.9	84.0	84.0	84.1	84.1	0.6	1.0
Total number of households (thousands)	4 045	4 202	4 239	4 284	4 294	4 295	4 322	4 352	NA	0.6	1.2
Labor Force (thousands)											
Population 16 and over	8 609	8 818	8 845	8 891	8 942	8 974	9 001	9 031	9 068	0.4	1.0
Civilian labor force	5 551	5 917	5 922	6 022	6 022	6 034	6 111	6 166	6 196	0.7	1.1
Employed	5 093	5 548	5 493	5 561	5 570	5 692	5 796	5 840	5 904	0.9	1.2
Percent of population	59.2	62.9	62.1	62.6	62.3	63.4	64.4	64.7	65.1		
Unemployment rate (percent)	8.3	6.2	7.2	7.6	7.5	5.7	5.2	5.3	4.7		

*Compound annual average percent change, 1990–1997; 1990–1996 for households.

Population Change and Components: 1990–97

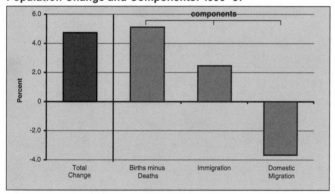

Average Annual Household and Population Growth

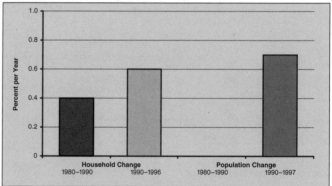

Population by Age; Births and Deaths

	1990 State	1990 U.S.	1997 State	1997 U.S.
Age distribution (percent)				
Under 5 years	7.5	7.6	7.6	7.2
5 to 17 years	18.1	18.2	19.1	18.8
18 to 64 years	61.8	61.8	60.9	61.3
65 years and over	12.5	12.5	12.5	12.7
Birth and death rates (per thousand population)				
Births	17.1	16.7	15.2	14.6
Deaths	9.0	8.6	8.7	8.6

THE AGE DISTRIBUTION IN ILLINOIS WAS NEARLY IDENTICAL TO that of the United States; in 1990, the proportions of very young children and people over 65 were the same in the state and the nation. However, there was an increase in the percentage of young children by 1997 (counter to the national trend), and the increase in school-age children was a bit faster in Illinois than the nation, reflecting the somewhat higher birth rate in Illinois. The working age population declined as a percent of the total.

HOUSEHOLD AND PERSONAL INCOME

HOUSEHOLD INCOME AND PERSONS IN POVERTY	1990	1995	1996	1997 State	1997 U.S.
Median household income (1997 dollars)	39 962	40 094	40 462	41 283	37 005
Persons in poverty (thousands)	1 606	1 459	1 429	1 349	35 574
Poverty rate (percent)	13.7	12.4	12.1	11.2	13.3

INCOMES WERE CONSISTENTLY HIGHER THAN AVERAGE IN Illinois during the 1990s, with median household income 12 percent higher and per capita income 10 percent higher than average for the nation in 1997. In fact, the state's relative prosperity has widened slightly since the early 1990s. The state's poverty rate declined accordingly and was at a level moderately below the U.S. rate in 1997.

Total personal income increased at the same rate in the state as the nation from 1989 to 1997, but the state's per capita income grew faster than the nation's as the Illinois population grew more slowly. The state's high per capita personal income was largely because of high wages and proprietors' earnings, which exceeded the national average by 13 percent in 1997. Dividends and interest income were above average by 16 percent, whereas transfer payments per capita were 6 percent below average.

Transfer payments in 1997 were below average in Illinois on a per capita basis because of lower than average medical and retirement payments, the largest two categories of transfers. In both cases the rate of growth of such payments during the 1990s was also relatively low. Income maintenance grew slowly during the decade because of significant reductions in welfare rolls, comparable to those in the nation, and a very small increase in the value of food stamps received. Other income maintenance, consisting primarily of earned income tax credits, grew rapidly but was still much below the national rate.

Personal Income
(millions of dollars)

	1980	1989	1990	1991	1992	1993	1994	1995	1996	1997	Change*
Earnings by place of work	93 515	160 120	169 224	174 022	187 670	196 180	206 635	216 565	227 538	241 880	5.3
Wages and salaries	76 470	130 712	138 519	142 347	150 551	156 296	164 083	173 716	183 041	195 961	5.2
Other labor income	8 234	14 152	15 690	16 707	17 964	19 821	21 047	20 924	19 998	20 263	4.6
Proprietors' income	8 811	15 256	15 016	14 968	19 156	20 064	21 504	21 924	24 498	25 656	6.7
Farm	77	1 561	1 066	248	1 046	792	1 292	-86	1 487	1 504	-0.5
Nonfarm	8 734	13 695	13 950	14 720	18 110	19 271	20 213	22 010	23 011	24 152	7.3
(–) Personal contributions for social insurance	4 873	10 393	11 010	11 606	12 170	12 847	13 719	14 372	14 734	15 633	5.2
(+) Adjustment for residence	386	-166	-264	-282	-329	-437	-493	-555	-538	-588	NA
(=) Net earnings by state of residence	89 027	149 561	157 950	162 134	175 171	182 896	192 423	201 638	212 265	225 659	5.3
(+) Dividends, interest, and rent	20 974	44 074	46 456	46 887	45 974	46 704	49 916	53 609	57 780	59 989	3.9
(+) Transfer payments	16 026	28 018	30 187	32 768	37 142	38 682	40 207	43 122	45 071	46 593	6.6
(=) Total personal income	126 028	221 653	234 593	241 788	258 288	268 281	282 546	298 369	315 117	332 241	5.2
Farm	324	1 832	1 383	556	1 373	1 137	1 619	244	1 814	1 834	0.0
Nonfarm	125 703	219 820	233 210	241 233	256 915	267 145	280 927	298 125	313 303	330 407	5.2
Personal income per capita (dollars)											
Current dollars	11 021	19 427	20 495	20 992	22 265	22 979	24 072	25 297	26 603	27 929	4.6
1997 dollars	21 073	24 560	24 663	24 240	24 905	25 004	25 581	26 296	27 091	27 929	1.6

*Compound annual average percent change, 1989–1997

Government Transfer Payments

	Millions of dollars 1990	Millions of dollars 1997	Percent change* State	Percent change* U.S.
Total government payments to individuals	28 409	44 450	56.5	62.7
Retirement, disability, and insurance	15 617	22 500	44.1	48.2
Social Security	11 773	15 971	35.7	46.1
Government employee retirement	3 256	5 887	80.8	60.3
Medical payments	8 060	15 670	94.4	101.2
Income maintenance	2 905	4 040	39.0	58.0
Supplemental Security Income	652	1 177	80.4	75.4
Family assistance	904	894	-1.1	-0.5
Food Stamps	865	914	5.7	27.1
Other income maintenance	484	1 054	118.0	189.8
Unemployment insurance benefits	964	1 197	24.2	10.6
Veterans benefits and other	863	1 043	20.8	30.8

*Percent change, 1990–1997

Government Payments to Individuals: 1997

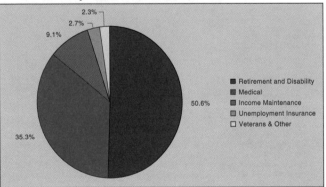

- Retirement and Disability — 50.6%
- Medical — 35.3%
- Income Maintenance — 9.1%
- Unemployment Insurance — 2.7%
- Veterans & Other — 2.3%

ECONOMIC STRUCTURE

LEADING PRIVATE INDUSTRIES, 1997 (Worker and proprietor earnings, millions of dollars)		FASTEST EARNINGS GROWTH, 1989–97 (percent increase)	
Health services	$17 543	Amusement and recreation services	145.4
Business services	16 958	Real estate	121.1
Engineering and management services	10 502	Social services	103.9
Construction specialties	9 185	Business services	101.5
Industrial machinery manufacturing	9 143	Security brokers	96.6

ILLINOIS'S ECONOMY MIRRORED THE STRUCTURE OF THE U.S. economy, and it experienced broad-based growth during the 1990s, led by the high-technology sector. The state hosted many high-tech companies such as Motorola and Ameritech, two of the top five private companies in the state. With the spin-off activity this sector engendered, business services was among the fastest growing industries and soon is expected to become the largest industry in the state. Engineering and management was the state's third largest industry and grew faster than average. Other large, rapidly growing service industries were social services and educational services. The finance sector employed a relatively large 9 percent of the workforce because Chicago is a regional banking headquarters (it is the nation's third largest metro area) and includes national institutions such as the Mercantile

Exchange and Board of Trade. Amusement and recreation was a small but fast-growing industry spurred by the vitality of Chicago's sports and convention business.

Burgeoning airline business for Chicago-based United Airlines and others made air transportation a rapidly growing industry, with earnings growth of 79 percent in 1989–97. Within manufacturing, only the industrial machinery industry remained in the top five private industries, and the fastest growing manufacturing segments were the most technology oriented: electronic equipment and chemicals (which includes pharmaceuticals such as Abbott Labs, which recently established a 1,500-job facility near Chicago). Construction, while it remained a large sector in the state, did not display earnings growth as rapid as did the overall state economy.

Employment and Earnings by Sector

	1980	1989	1990	1991	1992	1993	1994	1995	1996	1997 Number	1997 Percent of total	Change*
Employment *(thousands of persons)*												
Total	5 688	6 347	6 427	6 422	6 406	6 497	6 677	6 850	6 969	7 099	100.0	1.4
Farm	146	116	111	108	106	104	100	99	97	99	1.4	-2.0
Nonfarm	5 542	6 231	6 316	6 314	6 300	6 392	6 576	6 751	6 872	7 000	98.6	1.5
Private nonfarm	4 742	5 408	5 471	5 473	5 459	5 552	5 731	5 891	6 009	6 132	86.4	1.6
Agricultural service, forestry, and fishing	22	43	46	49	48	52	55	56	58	61	0.9	4.6
Mining	42	35	34	33	30	27	28	25	22	20	0.3	-6.7
Construction	234	294	304	289	287	291	305	315	324	333	4.7	1.6
Manufacturing	1 202	1 004	996	965	939	952	975	983	991	996	14.0	-0.1
Transportation and public utilities	298	335	341	344	336	349	361	366	377	387	5.5	1.8
Wholesale trade	348	393	378	378	376	363	367	367	374	367	5.2	-0.8
Retail trade	882	1 029	1 022	1 027	1 029	1 043	1 079	1 112	1 121	1 137	16.0	1.3
Finance, insurance, and real estate	474	554	564	559	552	559	589	597	611	636	9.0	1.7
Services	1 241	1 721	1 785	1 830	1 862	1 917	1 972	2 064	2 144	2 194	30.9	3.1
Government	799	823	845	841	841	840	845	859	863	868	12.2	0.7
Earnings *(millions of dollars)*												
Total	93 515	160 120	169 224	174 022	187 670	196 180	206 635	216 565	227 538	241 880	100.0	5.3
Farm	324	1 832	1 383	556	1 373	1 137	1 619	244	1 814	1 834	0.8	0.0
Nonfarm	93 190	158 288	167 841	173 466	186 298	195 044	205 015	216 320	225 724	240 046	99.2	5.3
Private nonfarm	81 623	138 055	146 088	150 299	161 923	169 547	178 663	189 013	197 286	210 517	87.0	5.4
Agricultural service, forestry, and fishing	250	662	786	822	873	904	954	983	1 027	1 127	0.5	6.9
Mining	1 263	923	952	968	927	809	838	804	790	735	0.3	-2.8
Construction	5 430	9 828	10 316	9 917	9 870	10 244	11 177	11 685	12 406	13 153	5.4	3.7
Manufacturing	26 488	34 409	35 649	35 783	37 579	39 505	42 227	43 701	44 662	47 783	19.8	4.2
Transportation and public utilities	7 349	11 701	12 374	12 977	13 709	14 778	15 370	16 055	16 626	17 767	7.3	5.4
Wholesale trade	7 650	13 365	13 860	14 139	14 761	14 727	15 370	16 227	16 293	17 337	7.2	3.3
Retail trade	8 872	14 465	14 743	15 032	15 728	16 330	17 218	18 101	18 564	19 562	8.1	3.8
Finance, insurance, and real estate	6 793	11 694	13 072	14 364	17 135	18 712	19 316	20 549	21 946	23 912	9.9	9.4
Services	17 529	41 007	44 336	46 297	51 341	53 538	56 194	60 907	64 973	69 141	28.6	6.7
Government	11 567	20 233	21 753	23 167	24 375	25 497	26 353	27 308	28 438	29 529	12.2	4.8

*Compound annual average percent change, 1989–1997

ECONOMIC STRUCTURE (Continued)

AVERAGE WAGES FOR ALL ILLINOIS WAGE AND SALARY WORKers were 9 percent above the U.S. average in 1997 and they grew slightly faster than nationwide wages during the 1990s. Wages were higher than average in every major sector, and the gap was largest in the highest paid sectors: in finance they were 8 percent above the already-high national average, reflecting the large regional banking and securities centers there. In wholesale trade and construction, wages were 10 percent and 25 percent above the U.S. levels, respectively. The diversified manufacturing sector had wages just 7 percent above those of the United States. Within the largest and lowest paid services and retail trade sectors, wages were closer to parity with (only 3 to 6 percent above) national averages.

Manufacturing was a slightly more important component of the Illinois economy than of an average state, but its share of the gross state product (19.3 percent in 1997) was the lowest of any of the Great Lakes states. Still, Illinois's value of manufacturing output was sixth highest in the nation, equivalent to that of Michigan. Though manufacturing output value did grow a healthy 4.7 percent annually from 1989 to 1996, the balance of the state economy grew slightly faster. The share of manufacturing earnings in nondurable goods industries was equal to the national average, reflecting the presence of large food processing, printing, and chemicals/pharmaceuticals companies that balanced the industrial and electronic equipment and metals production. Output value per worker was a bit higher than the U.S average in manufacturing.

Exports' strong growth over the past several years has helped sustain most of the state's large manufacturing industries. Total exports of goods grew about 13 percent annually over the 1994 to 1997 period, and the state ranked fifth in total exports in the nation. Manufacturing exports of $31.5 billion comprised a fairly large share of the state's manufacturing output. Industrial and electronic machinery alone represented 47 percent of total state exports. Export of agricultural goods grew very rapidly in the mid-1990s before dropping somewhat lower in 1997.

Average Annual Wages and Salaries by Sector
(dollars)

	1989	1996	1997 State	1997 U.S.
All wage and salary workers	23 879	30 805	32 434	29 809
Farm	10 829	16 446	14 993	16 442
Nonfarm	23 935	30 849	32 492	29 900
Private nonfarm	24 158	30 965	32 705	29 867
Agricultural service, forestry, and fishing	15 872	20 317	21 468	17 941
Mining	37 144	45 950	45 689	49 800
Construction	31 594	38 017	39 765	31 765
Manufacturing	29 434	38 311	41 142	38 351
Transportation and utilities	31 057	38 282	40 273	38 222
Wholesale trade	31 088	41 209	43 241	39 466
Retail trade	13 034	16 000	16 744	16 206
Finance, insurance, and real estate	31 152	45 566	48 767	44 993
Services	21 315	27 874	29 142	27 588
Government	22 683	30 172	31 227	30 062

Gross State Product and Manufacturing
(millions of dollars, except as noted)

	1989	1994	1995	1996
Gross state product, total	260 915	336 867	352 932	370 778
Manufacturing:				
Millions of dollars	51 656	66 680	68 723	71 444
Percent of total gross state product	19.8	19.8	19.5	19.3
Per worker (dollars)	51 458	68 385	69 940	72 092
New capital expenditures, manufacturing	NA	6 284	6 424	7 124

Exports of Goods
(millions of dollars)

	1994	1995	1996	1997
All goods	24 534	30 478	32 225	34 225
Manufactures	22 464	27 661	28 748	31 454
Agricultural and livestock products	2 870	3 954	4 593	4 234
Other commodities	464	522	483	414
Top goods exports, 1997:				
Industrial machinery and computers	6 642	7 663	8 153	9 066
Electric and electronic equipment	4 831	6 822	6 561	7 006
Chemical products	3 485	4 153	4 156	4 338
Transportation equipment	1 726	2 023	2 289	2 470
Agricultural products	1 589	2 276	2 964	2 314

HOUSING

ILLINOIS'S NEW HOMEBUILDING ACTIVITY DID NOT KEEP UP IN the 1990s with national trends, with new production only about two-thirds of that of the United States on a per capita basis in most years. While building permits in the Chicago area were fourth highest in the nation in 1997, growth was slow in the balance of the state. Overall, the figures reflect primarily the slow population growth in the state. Also, part of the demand inside Chicago was met through renovation of existing homes, which does not appear in these permit statistics. Sales of existing homes increased moderately in 1996–97 after slow activity during the mid-1990s. The median price of a home in the Chicago area was $158,900 in 1997, up about 4 percent from the previous year; prices remained higher than in cities in the adjacent states of Indiana and Wisconsin.

The state made progress in increasing the rate of home-ownership, which rose by five percentage points from 1990 to 1997. This reflects the growth in personal income in the state, moderate home price trends, and low interest rates.

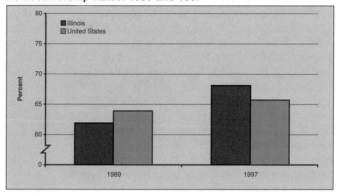

Homeownership Rates: 1989 and 1997

Rental vacancy rates, which remained in the moderate range during most of this decade, increased in 1996–97, possibly because of the uptick in out-migration and the larger number of homeowners.

Housing Supply

	1989	1990	1991	1992	1993	1994	1995	1996	1997
Residential building permits (thousands)	42.4	38.3	32.8	40.4	44.7	49.3	47.5	49.6	46.3
New home production (including manufactured housing):									
Thousands of homes	45.3	41.9	36.1	43.9	48.9	54.5	52.9	53.9	51.1
Rate per 1,000 population									
Illinois	4.0	3.7	3.1	3.8	4.2	4.6	4.5	4.6	4.3
U.S.	6.2	5.2	4.5	5.1	5.6	6.4	6.3	6.6	6.5
Existing home sales:									
Thousands of homes	162.7	160.9	168.1	186.2	193.9	188.4	183.5	191.6	199.7
Change from previous year (percent)									
Illinois	-3.2	-1.1	4.5	10.8	4.1	-2.8	-2.6	4.4	4.2
U.S.	-3.9	-4.0	0.0	9.2	8.2	4.8	-3.7	7.5	3.8
Home ownership rate (percent of households)	61.9	63.0	63.0	62.4	61.8	64.2	66.4	68.2	68.1
Rental vacancy rate (percent of rental housing units)	7.2	6.1	6.5	7.0	6.3	6.8	7.4	7.9	8.5

AGRICULTURE

NET FARM EARNINGS WERE RELATIVELY FLAT OVER THE PAST decade, although net income before inventory adjustment rose moderately. Farm product sales were up 2 percent during 1989–97 (using three-year averages), while production expenses increased 11 percent during the same period (quite a modest increase). There were strong increases in grain sales that offset declining income from livestock. Grain sales in 1997 were over three times as large as livestock receipts, and they were supported by solid growth in export demand for grain. Overall, however,

ILLINOIS FARMS, 1997	
Number of farms	76 000
Total acres (thousands):	28 000
Average per farm	368
Value of land and buildings (millions of dollars)	61 880
Average per farm (dollars)	814 211

farm income did not keep pace with the strong growth in Illinois's nonfarm sector. The average value of farms in the state was very high, more than $800,000.

Farm Income
(millions of dollars)

	1980	1989	1990	1991	1992	1993	1994	1995	1996	1997
Gross income	8 453	8 756	9 015	8 804	8 325	9 802	8 501	10 143	9 497	10 335
Receipts from sales	8 108	7 572	8 033	7 917	7 440	8 538	7 777	9 134	8 655	9 300
Government payments	36	726	507	441	481	851	303	544	387	552
Imputed and miscellaneous income	309	459	476	445	404	413	421	465	455	483
(–) Production expenses	7 346	7 934	8 028	7 978	8 240	8 302	8 377	8 295	9 108	8 776
(=) Realized net income	1 107	822	987	826	85	1 500	124	1 848	389	1 559
(+) Inventory change	-1 029	817	134	-568	1 020	-690	1 287	-1 953	1 231	67
(=) Net income	77	1 639	1 121	258	1 105	809	1 411	-105	1 619	1 626
Corporate income	0	78	55	10	59	17	119	-19	132	122
Farm proprietors income	77	1 561	1 066	248	1 046	792	1 292	-86	1 487	1 504

EDUCATION

EDUCATIONAL ATTAINMENT Percent of population age 25 and over, 1997	State	United States
High school graduate or higher	84.4	82.1
College graduate or higher	25.0	23.9

ILLINOIS HAD A BETTER EDUCATED POPULATION THAN AVERAGE, considering levels of attainment for both high school and college degrees. This was consistent with the relatively high household incomes in the state and its expanding and diversified economy. At the elementary and secondary level, government spending per pupil was virtually the same as the national average, though teacher salaries were high. A higher than average portion of students were enrolled in private schools. In higher education, the state ranked 19th among all states in the proportion of adults with college degrees and currently has a quite high percentage of young adults who are enrolled in school. Minority enrollment in college matched the share of minorities in the state's overall population.

High School Completion: 1990–97

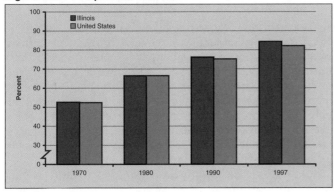

Education Indicators

	State	U.S.
Elementary and secondary schools		
Enrollment, 1995–96		
Total (thousands)	2 245	49 873
Percent in private schools	13.4	10.1
Expenditures per pupil (dollars), 1995–96	6 128	6 146
Average teacher salary (dollars), 1996–97	42 679	38 509
Higher education		
Enrollment, 1996–97		
Total (thousands)	721	14 218
Percent of population 18–34	24.8	21.8
Percent minority	28.3	26.1
Percent in private schools	26.1	22.6

HEALTH

DEATH RATES IN ILLINOIS WERE HIGHER THAN AVERAGE, surprising for a prosperous state with fairly low poverty. Its high infant mortality rate placed the state in the bottom quarter among all states, even though this rate has decreased markedly since 1990. The overall death rate was only slightly higher than the national average. Major diseases such as cancer and heart disease caused more fatalities in the state than average (as did homicide), while accidental death rates were relatively low. Health insurance coverage extended to a higher than average percentage of the Illinois population, reflecting the state's relatively high household incomes. The above-average coverage rate also related to its employment mix, which was heavier than average in manufacturing and finance (with high rates of coverage) and lighter in construction (with the least health insurance coverage of any sector).

Health Indicators

	1990	1995	1996	1997
Infant mortality				
(rate per thousand live births)				
Illinois	10.7	9.4	8.1	8.0
U.S.	9.2	7.6	7.3	7.1
Total deaths, age-adjusted rate				
(rate per thousand population)				
Illinois	5.4	5.3	5.1	4.9
U.S.	5.2	5.0	4.9	4.8
Persons not covered by health insurance				
(percent of population)				
Illinois	10.9	11.0	11.3	12.4
U.S.	13.9	15.4	15.6	16.1

Leading Causes of Death, 1996
(deaths per 100,000 population)

	Age-adjusted		Not age-adjusted	
	State	U.S.	State	U.S.
Deaths from all causes	508.2	491.6	895.6	872.5
Heart disease	142.7	134.5	289.8	276.4
Cancer	133.3	127.9	209.2	203.4
Cerebrovascular diseases	27.5	26.4	62.7	60.3
Chronic obstructive pulmonary disease	19.9	21.0	36.8	40.0
Diabetes mellitus	13.5	13.6	23.0	23.3
Pneumonia and influenza	13.8	12.8	33.3	31.6
HIV	9.0	11.1	9.5	11.7
Liver disease	7.6	7.5	9.5	9.4
Alzheimer's disease	2.9	2.7	8.8	8.1
Accidents and adverse effects	26.3	30.4	31.1	35.8
Motor vehicle accidents	13.5	16.2	13.5	16.5
Suicide	8.4	10.8	9.0	11.6
Homicide	12.0	8.5	10.7	7.9
Injury by firearm	12.9	12.9	12.0	12.8

GOVERNMENT

STATE AND LOCAL TAXES, 1995–96	State	U.S.
Per capita (dollars)	2 620	2 477
Percent of personal income	10.4	10.8

CONSIDERING TAXPAYERS' CAPACITY TO PAY, COMBINED STATE and local taxation in Illinois was below average: taxes equaled 10.4 percent of personal income, which was lower than the national rate of 10.8 percent. Total state and local taxes in Illinois were about 6 percent higher than the U.S. average on a per capita basis in 1995–96, because taxes at the local level were somewhat high, including property and sales taxes. There was roughly a fifty-fifty split in total

State Government Finances, 1996–97

	Millions of dollars	Percent distribution	Dollars per capita	
			State	U.S.
General revenue	32 068	100.0	2 696	3 049
Intergovernmental revenue	8 714	27.2	732	863
Taxes	18 545	57.8	1 559	1 660
General sales	5 296	16.5	445	551
Selective sales	3 500	10.9	294	257
License taxes	1 215	3.8	102	106
Individual income	6 287	19.6	528	542
Corporation net income	1 804	5.6	152	115
Other taxes	443	1.4	37	90
Other general revenue	4 810	15.0	404	526
General expenditure	31 266	100.0	2 628	2 951
Intergovernmental expenditure	9 148	29.3	769	989
Direct expenditure	22 118	70.7	1 859	1 962
General expenditure, by function:				
Education	9 160	29.3	770	1 033
Public welfare	9 164	29.3	770	761
Hospitals and health	2 549	8.2	214	237
Highways	2 597	8.3	218	225
Police protection and corrections	1 255	4.0	105	137
Natural resources, parks and recreation	463	1.5	39	63
Governmental administration	1 055	3.4	89	107
Interest on general debt	1 526	4.9	128	99
Other and unallocable	3 498	11.2	294	290
Debt at end of fiscal year	23 801	NA	2 001	1 706
Cash and security holdings	59 776	NA	5 025	6 683

Federal Spending within State

	Federal funds, fiscal 1997		
	Millions of dollars	Percent distribution	Percent of U.S. total*
Total within state	52 874	100.0	3.7
Payments to individuals	33 577	63.5	4.3
Retirement and disability	18 672	35.3	4.1
Medicare	9 145	17.3	4.4
Food stamps	927	1.8	4.8
Supplemental Security Income	1 254	2.4	4.7
Grants	9 678	18.3	3.9
Medicaid and other health	4 112	7.8	3.6
Nutrition and family welfare	2 041	3.9	4.4
Education	734	1.4	4.3
Housing and community development	739	1.4	6.5
Salaries and wages	5 404	10.2	3.3
Defense procurement contracts	1 250	2.4	1.0
Non-defense procurement contracts	1 939	3.7	2.7

*State population is 4.4 percent of the U.S. total.

collections between state and local levels, which placed Illinois among the lower half of states for the amount of state-level taxes.

The state budget in fiscal 1997 showed total tax collections per capita at a level 6 percent below the average for all states, primarily because of lower sales tax collections. Other tax categories were virtually the same as national averages. The state received less in intergovernmental transfers than the typical state and yielded a revenue total that was about 12 percent below average. On the expenditure side, therefore, the state was constrained to spend significantly less than average. It was in education that this shortfall was concentrated; Illinois spent only 75 percent as much (per capita) as the typical state on education. Much of this spending was reflected in the lower than average transfers from state to local government. For most other functions the state was close to the national averages. Its spending on interest on general debt was higher than average; however, the state has done some belt-tightening in recent years and now spends less than average on government administration. The state government workforce grew considerably less in the 1990s than private employment in Illinois.

Total federal expenditures in Illinois fell short of the state's proportionate share of U.S. population, mainly because of the modest federal workforce based here. Federal workers in the state comprised 3.4 percent of all civilian and 2.5 percent of all military earnings for the nation. Further, the state received a relatively low amount in Medicaid grants, though grants in other program areas, especially housing, were high. Procurement contracting was lower than average in Illinois, particularly defense contracting, because the state had few weapons and defense research firms and a limited military base presence.

31 372	59 698		65 157	70 827	72 687	78 001	81 93	88 504	93 426	5.8	63 383	70 827	31 372	59 698	63 3
25 323	47 902			57 151	59 446	62 916	67 00	72 039	77 208	6.1	50 999	57 151	25 323	47 902	50 9
2 640	5 143					7 801		7 709	7 838	5.4	5 645	6 816	2 640	5 143	5 6
3 409	6 652					264		8 755	8 380	2.9	6 739	6 860	3 409	6 652	6 7
693	1 716					07		1 539	762	-9.7	1 561	811	693	1 716	
2 716	4 9							7 217	7 618	5.	5 178	6 049	2 716		

1997

Population (persons)	5,864,847
Population rank	14th
Population growth rank (1990–97)	30th
Per capita personal income	$23,183
Unemployment rate (percent)	3.5
Poverty rate (percent)	8.8

INDIANA EXPERIENCED ONE OF THE MOST ACTIVE PERIODS OF growth in 1989–97 of any state, having successfully overcome the 1970s decline in its steel industry. With the state's relatively low production and housing costs, employment increased 13 percent faster than the strong U.S. rate from 1989 to 1997. Manufacturing still contributed an enormous portion of the jobs and output in the state—31.7 percent of its output in 1996, the most industrialized state in the nation. Manufacturing employment in 1997 was 3.7 percent higher than the 1980 level, countering the national downtrend. But major services and construction sectors also gained a more prominent role in the state's increasingly balanced economy. Housing produc-

tion per capita outstripped the U.S. rate throughout the 1990s. With this dynamic growth, per capita earnings advanced to a point only 4 percent below the national level, though average wages per worker were still relatively low.

Population growth was below the U.S. average in 1990–97, yet above average for the Great Lakes region. The reason was a moderate in-migration from other states in light of the strong job picture, though Indiana had very little foreign immigration. The 1990s growth stands in stark contrast to the 1980s, when Indiana had almost no net growth because of a 5 percent population loss from out-migration.

Average Annual Population Growth: 1990–97

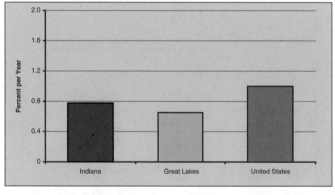

Median Household Income: 1989–97 (1997 dollars)

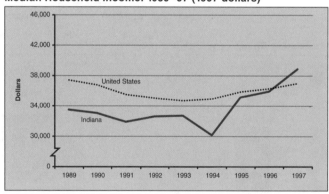

Unemployment Rate: 1989–97

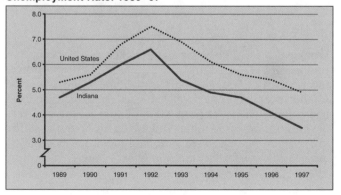

UNEMPLOYMENT RATES DURING THE 1989–97 PERIOD WERE consistently lower in Indiana than in the United States, and its 1997 rate of 3.5 percent was the lowest of any heavily industrialized state. Though it experienced the same cyclical downturn as the nation did in 1990–91, the state's job growth and reductions in unemployment have been stronger since then, and it had an above average proportion of adult population at work in 1997, 65.5 percent.

POPULATION AND LABOR FORCE

IN-MIGRATION FROM OTHER STATES COMBINED WITH NATURAL population growth to yield a 5.6 percent population increase for Indiana during 1990–97, compared with 7.3 percent for the United States. About half of the differential is accounted for by Indiana's lower in-migration, and half by its lower natural population increase. Still, the 1990s showed a significant improvement over the sluggish growth of the 1980s. The Indianapolis metropolitan area saw a population gain of 8.9 percent in the 1990s, as it grew faster than the northern region of the state.

The state had sparse Hispanic and Asian populations (only 2.3 and 0.9 percent of the total population, respec-

tively). It did not become a popular destination for immigrants. The largest minority population group was non-Hispanics Blacks, who comprised 8.1 percent in 1997. The state retained a remarkable predominance of non-Hispanic Whites, which comprised 88.5 percent of the population in 1997, virtually the same proportion as in 1990.

The state's labor force grew strongly during the 1990s, much faster than the population. With the increased labor force participation rate, and the success of these entrants in getting jobs, the state achieved an above average rate of employment to population.

Population and Labor Force

	1980	1990	1991	1992	1993	1994	1995	1996	1997	Change* State	Change* U.S.
Population											
Total number of persons (thousands)	5 490	5 555	5 601	5 648	5 701	5 741	5 787	5 827	5 865	0.8	1.0
Percent distribution:											
White, Non-Hispanic	90.3	89.3	89.5	89.3	89.2	89.0	88.8	88.7	88.5	0.6	0.4
Black, Non-Hispanic	7.5	7.9	7.8	7.9	7.9	8.0	8.0	8.0	8.1	1.2	1.4
Asian	0.4	0.7	0.7	0.7	0.8	0.8	0.8	0.9	0.9	4.0	4.1
Native American	0.2	0.2	0.2	0.2	0.2	0.2	0.2	0.2	0.2	0.5	1.6
Hispanic	1.6	1.9	1.8	1.9	1.9	2.0	2.1	2.2	2.3	3.7	3.8
In metropolitan areas	70.8	71.5	71.6	71.6	71.7	71.7	71.7	71.7	71.7	0.8	1.0
Total number of households (thousands)	1 927	2 065	2 101	2 133	2 149	2 156	2 182	2 209	NA	1.1	1.2
Labor Force (thousands)											
Population 16 and over	4 081	4 278	4 316	4 356	4 403	4 434	4 472	4 512	4 545	0.9	1.0
Civilian labor force	2 628	2 794	2 779	2 840	2 944	3 049	3 126	3 065	3 086	1.4	1.1
Employed	2 375	2 645	2 612	2 652	2 786	2 898	2 980	2 939	2 978	1.7	1.2
Percent of population	58.2	61.8	60.5	60.9	63.3	65.4	66.6	65.1	65.5		
Unemployment rate (percent)	9.6	5.3	6.0	6.6	5.4	4.9	4.7	4.1	3.5		

*Compound annual average percent change, 1990–1997; 1990–1996 for households.

Population Change and Components: 1990–97

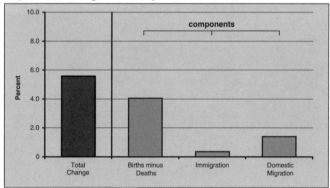

Average Annual Household and Population Growth

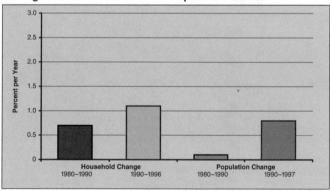

Population by Age; Births and Deaths

	1990 State	1990 U.S.	1997 State	1997 U.S.
Age distribution (percent)				
Under 5 years	7.2	7.6	6.9	7.2
5 to 17 years	18.7	18.2	18.6	18.8
18 to 64 years	61.6	61.8	61.9	61.3
65 years and over	12.5	12.5	12.5	12.7
Birth and death rates (per thousand population)				
Births	15.6	16.7	14.2	14.6
Deaths	8.9	8.6	8.3	8.6

WORKING AGE ADULTS WERE A RELATIVELY LARGE SEGMENT IN Indiana in 1997, and they were an increasing proportion of the population, countering the national trend toward a smaller proportion of people in this age group. Indiana had a slightly smaller proportion of very young and very old people compared to the United States. With the state's lower than average birth rate, its school-age population did not grow as fast as that of a typical state.

HOUSEHOLD AND PERSONAL INCOME

HOUSEHOLD INCOME AND PERSONS IN POVERTY	1990	1995	1996	1997 State	1997 U.S.
Median household income (1997 dollars)	33 068	35 159	35 953	38 889	37 005
Persons in poverty (thousands)	714	545	428	515	35 574
Poverty rate (percent)	13.0	9.6	7.5	8.8	13.3

HOUSEHOLD INCOMES IN INDIANA HAVE HISTORICALLY BEEN 7 to 10 percent below the U.S. median but gained ground in 1995–97 to reach approximate parity when considering the three–year average. The increased number of employed persons boosted incomes, despite the lower average wages per worker in Indiana. Poverty rates have remained below the U.S. average during the 1990s and decreased substantially after 1990 because of the strong economic growth.

The above-average growth of personal income in Indiana in 1989–97 narrowed the gap between the state and the United States (per capita) to 8 percent in 1997, and earnings per capita reached parity with the nation. The state's average income was pulled down by the low levels of dividend and interest income (18 percent below the United States per capita) and transfer payments (17 percent below the United States). Within earned income

categories, proprietors' income lagged behind the stronger growth of wages and salaries. Looking at earnings of those commuting into and out of Indiana, the net effect was a significant 2.5 percent of earnings of Indiana residents earned out of state.

Transfer payments grew at a distinctly slower pace in Indiana than in the United States during 1990–97. Retirement and medical payments growth was slower than average due to the stable number of older people. The advent of welfare reform reduced family assistance payments by 35 percent, though Supplemental Security Income (SSI) moved sharply higher. Rapid growth occurred in the earned income tax credit (the largest component of other income maintenance), which tripled in size to become the largest income maintenance program.

Personal Income
(millions of dollars)

	1980	1989	1990	1991	1992	1993	1994	1995	1996	1997	Change*
Earnings by place of work	38 233	65 411	68 727	70 847	76 562	81 398	86 712	90 487	93 892	98 960	5.3
Wages and salaries	31 251	52 845	55 717	57 709	61 489	64 593	68 967	72 688	76 077	80 534	5.4
Other labor income	3 571	6 037	6 531	7 064	7 899	9 179	9 860	9 831	8 837	8 912	5.0
Proprietors' income	3 411	6 528	6 480	6 074	7 174	7 626	7 885	7 968	8 978	9 514	4.8
Farm	218	654	512	-83	345	444	336	-4	697	859	3.5
Nonfarm	3 193	5 874	5 968	6 157	6 829	7 181	7 550	7 972	8 281	8 655	5.0
(−) Personal contributions for social insurance	1 964	4 215	4 451	4 722	5 019	5 363	5 805	6 142	6 360	6 713	6.0
(+) Adjustment for residence	574	1 343	1 488	1 517	1 669	1 752	1 899	2 103	2 243	2 418	NA
(=) Net earnings by state of residence	36 843	62 539	65 764	67 643	73 211	77 787	82 807	86 448	89 776	94 666	5.3
(+) Dividends, interest, and rent	7 794	15 413	16 406	16 435	16 237	16 655	17 976	19 061	20 322	21 046	4.0
(+) Transfer payments	6 572	12 061	13 193	14 632	16 520	17 574	18 246	18 595	19 584	20 234	6.7
(=) Total personal income	51 210	90 013	95 364	98 710	105 968	112 016	119 029	124 104	129 682	135 945	5.3
Farm	384	840	727	124	565	675	555	216	916	1 080	3.2
Nonfarm	50 826	89 172	94 637	98 586	105 403	111 341	118 474	123 888	128 766	134 866	5.3
Personal income per capita (dollars)											
Current dollars	9 327	16 296	17 167	17 624	18 763	19 651	20 731	21 442	22 251	23 183	4.5
1997 dollars	17 834	20 602	20 658	20 351	20 988	21 383	22 031	22 289	22 659	23 183	1.5

*Compound annual average percent change, 1989–1997

Government Transfer Payments

	Millions of dollars 1990	Millions of dollars 1997	Percent change* State	Percent change* U.S.
Total government payments to individuals	12 436	19 238	54.7	62.7
Retirement, disability, and insurance	7 276	10 368	42.5	48.2
Social Security	5 935	8 404	41.6	46.1
Government employee retirement	1 085	1 672	54.2	60.3
Medical payments	3 790	6 731	77.6	101.2
Income maintenance	763	1 301	70.5	58.0
Supplemental Security Income	177	374	110.8	75.4
Family assistance	182	119	-34.5	-0.5
Food Stamps	240	287	19.9	27.1
Other income maintenance	164	520	216.7	189.8
Unemployment insurance benefits	146	261	78.4	10.6
Veterans benefits and other	461	577	25.2	30.8

*Percent change, 1990–1997

Government Payments to Individuals: 1997

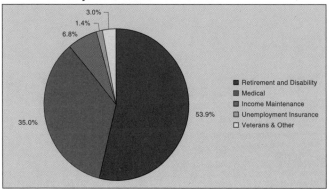

3.0%
1.4%
6.8%
53.9%
35.0%

■ Retirement and Disability
■ Medical
■ Income Maintenance
□ Unemployment Insurance
□ Veterans & Other

ECONOMIC STRUCTURE

LEADING PRIVATE INDUSTRIES, 1997 (Worker and proprietor earnings, millions of dollars)		FASTEST EARNINGS GROWTH, 1989–97 (percent increase)	
Health services	$8 545	Amusement and recreation services	196.6
Motor vehicles and equipment	4 832	Real estate	155.9
Construction specialties	4 046	Other transportation services	131.5
Primary metal industries	3 983	Social services	102.3
Business services	3 656	Business services	100.5

MANUFACTURING RETAINED MORE PROMINENCE IN THE Indiana economy than any other sector, and generated earnings 50 percent larger than the services sector. It employed one fifth of the state's workers, a share of jobs about 8 percentage points higher than U.S. averages. Motor vehicles and equipment became the state's second largest industry, particularly production of recreational vehicles, auto parts, and truck and bus bodies. There were nine other manufacturing industries with earnings above $1 billion, from steel (where it was the leading producer in the nation) to pharmaceuticals (Alka-Seltzer was invented here at Miles Laboratories).

However, other major sectors in the state grew faster in the 1990s than manufacturing: the state experienced a much higher job growth rate than the United States in the construction, wholesale trade, and finance sectors from 1989 to 1997. The services and finance sectors remained a smaller part of the economy than the national norm, yet four of the five fastest growing sectors of the 1990s were service- or finance-related industries. A boom in new home construction contributed to this trend. Thus, the composition of the state's employment base moved closer to the U.S. norm.

Employment and Earnings by Sector

	1980	1989	1990	1991	1992	1993	1994	1995	1996	1997 Number	1997 Percent of total	Change*
Employment *(thousands of persons)*												
Total	2 632	3 030	3 083	3 094	3 144	3 217	3 313	3 401	3 447	3 508	100.0	1.8
Farm	118	91	87	83	82	80	78	76	77	77	2.2	-2.1
Nonfarm	2 515	2 939	2 997	3 011	3 062	3 137	3 235	3 325	3 372	3 431	97.8	2.0
Private nonfarm	2 147	2 549	2 597	2 605	2 649	2 724	2 823	2 914	2 960	3 021	86.1	2.1
Agricultural service, forestry, and fishing	12	20	22	23	23	24	26	27	28	30	0.8	5.0
Mining	14	12	12	12	11	10	10	10	9	10	0.3	-2.9
Construction	125	160	165	164	167	172	183	189	194	202	5.8	3.0
Manufacturing	666	656	646	629	640	655	677	696	688	690	19.7	0.6
Transportation and public utilities	123	150	153	153	152	156	160	163	165	167	4.8	1.3
Wholesale trade	114	132	134	136	137	138	142	147	148	150	4.3	1.5
Retail trade	440	540	549	551	561	573	601	628	641	646	18.4	2.3
Finance, insurance, and real estate	169	178	183	185	186	189	193	197	202	209	6.0	2.0
Services	485	701	733	752	772	808	831	858	885	918	26.2	3.4
Government	367	390	400	406	413	413	413	411	413	410	11.7	0.6
Earnings *(millions of dollars)*												
Total	38 233	65 411	68 727	70 847	76 562	81 398	86 712	90 487	93 892	98 960	100.0	5.3
Farm	384	840	727	124	565	675	555	216	916	1 080	1.1	3.2
Nonfarm	37 849	64 570	68 001	70 724	75 997	80 723	86 157	90 271	92 976	97 881	98.9	5.3
Private nonfarm	33 273	56 156	58 864	60 989	65 735	70 072	75 167	79 009	81 368	86 119	87.0	5.5
Agricultural service, forestry, and fishing	95	243	277	298	327	344	363	382	397	429	0.4	7.4
Mining	467	349	395	371	358	344	360	350	357	403	0.4	1.8
Construction	2 353	4 079	4 242	4 373	4 470	4 797	5 426	5 722	6 056	6 506	6.6	6.0
Manufacturing	14 789	21 768	22 152	22 524	24 331	26 330	28 372	29 771	29 539	30 921	31.2	4.5
Transportation and public utilities	2 630	4 407	4 548	4 676	4 911	5 139	5 433	5 592	5 728	5 896	6.0	3.7
Wholesale trade	2 156	3 622	3 902	4 037	4 289	4 471	4 775	5 068	5 283	5 623	5.7	5.7
Retail trade	3 806	6 173	6 397	6 623	6 965	7 382	7 953	8 455	8 838	9 224	9.3	5.1
Finance, insurance, and real estate	1 660	3 121	3 385	3 560	4 159	4 494	4 844	4 931	5 323	5 760	5.8	8.0
Services	5 316	12 394	13 565	14 527	15 927	16 772	17 641	18 738	19 846	21 358	21.6	7.0
Government	4 576	8 414	9 137	9 734	10 262	10 651	10 990	11 262	11 608	11 761	11.9	4.3

*Compound annual average percent change, 1989–1997

ECONOMIC STRUCTURE (Continued)

AVERAGE WAGES PER WORKER IN INDIANA REMAINED WELL below national levels in 1997 despite the rapid job growth rates in the state. In every sector except manufacturing and construction, wages were below the national rates by percentages ranging from 12 percent to 28 percent (finance, insurance, real estate). Within the large manufacturing sector, wages were equivalent to national averages and the same held true in construction. The overall growth of average wages from 1989 to 1997, an average of 3.5 percent per year in current dollars, was the same in Indiana and the United States.

Manufacturing comprised 31.7 percent of the gross state product in 1997, the highest ratio in the nation (even though this share has declined since the 1980s). Manufacturing output was weighted toward durable goods industries, with a heavy concentration in steel, fabricated metals, and motor vehicles and equipment. (The value of production of electronic equipment, a dynamic industry nationally, was actually declining in Indiana.) This mix, plus sustained new capital expenditures, led to higher than average levels of manufacturing value per worker in Indiana, with increases from 1989 to 1996 slightly higher than was true nationwide.

Indiana experienced a boom in manufacturing exports during the 1994–97 period, though export demand still contributed a smaller than average share to the state economy. Particularly high growth rates occurred in exports of chemicals, including pharmaceuticals, and electronic equipment (despite the decline in output value of electronics in the state starting in 1995). Agricultural exports from this state were negligible.

Average Annual Wages and Salaries by Sector
(dollars)

	1989	1996	1997 State	1997 U.S.
All wage and salary workers	20 391	25 962	27 046	29 809
Farm	10 828	16 446	14 992	16 442
Nonfarm	20 452	26 004	27 103	29 900
Private nonfarm	20 601	26 127	27 309	29 867
Agricultural service, forestry, and fishing	12 491	16 560	17 227	17 941
Mining	36 092	41 881	44 012	49 800
Construction	24 151	29 992	31 425	31 765
Manufacturing	28 352	36 269	38 026	38 351
Transportation and utilities	26 930	32 678	33 679	38 222
Wholesale trade	25 209	32 922	34 777	39 466
Retail trade	10 760	13 673	14 257	16 206
Finance, insurance, and real estate	21 777	30 553	32 437	44 993
Services	16 369	21 908	22 815	27 588
Government	19 611	25 256	25 824	30 062

Gross State Product and Manufacturing
(millions of dollars, except as noted)

	1989	1994	1995	1996
Gross state product, total	105 830	141 358	148 801	155 797
Manufacturing:				
Millions of dollars	33 715	44 553	48 295	49 338
Percent of total gross state product	31.9	31.5	32.5	31.7
Per worker (dollars)	51 365	65 784	69 391	71 742
New capital expenditures, manufacturing	NA	4 411	4 746	4 739

Exports of Goods
(millions of dollars)

	1994	1995	1996	1997
All goods	9 534	11 052	12 119	13 097
Manufactures	9 384	10 898	11 951	12 931
Agricultural and livestock products	53	53	56	60
Other commodities	97	101	112	106
Top goods exports, 1997:				
Electric and electronic equipment	1 800	2 105	2 582	2 704
Transportation equipment	1 918	2 365	2 504	2 693
Chemical products	1 314	1 682	1 971	2 162
Industrial machinery and computers	1 510	1 700	1 867	2 082
Scientific and measuring instruments	1 131	993	805	813

HOUSING

HOMEBUILDING RECOVERED SMARTLY FROM THE 1991 RECESsion in Indiana, and housing production per capita remained above the U.S. average throughout the 1990–97 period, consistent with its strong economic growth. With the Indianapolis area leading the state in population growth, it ranked 21st in the nation in new building permits in 1997. Sales of existing homes also trended upward strongly in the 1990s, in accord with national increases, with an especially large jump in sales in Indiana in 1993. Home prices remained attractively low in the state: median home sales prices were $103,700 in 1997 in Indianapolis, substantially below those of other large Midwest metropolitan areas.

Rates of homeownership historically have been higher than average because of Indiana's nontransient population and low housing prices, and in 1996–97 they jumped to new highs, to rank fifth in the nation. Rental vacancy rates also stayed below the U.S. average, supported by the ongoing population in-migration to the state.

Homeownership Rates: 1989 and 1997

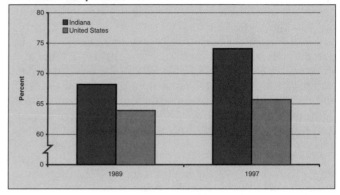

Housing Supply

	1989	1990	1991	1992	1993	1994	1995	1996	1997
Residential building permits (thousands)	26.5	25.0	23.9	28.7	30.8	34.4	35.7	37.2	35.2
New home production (including manufactured housing):									
Thousands of homes	32.6	31.4	29.8	34.5	36.8	41.8	43.7	45.2	42.6
Rate per 1,000 population									
Indiana	5.9	5.7	5.3	6.1	6.5	7.3	7.6	7.8	7.3
U.S.	6.2	5.2	4.5	5.1	5.6	6.4	6.3	6.6	6.5
Existing home sales:									
Thousands of homes	81.6	80.1	76.0	84.8	100.8	103.3	100.6	103.5	111.5
Change from previous year (percent)									
Indiana	0.0	-1.8	-5.1	11.6	18.9	2.5	-2.6	2.9	7.7
U.S.	-3.9	-4.0	0.0	9.2	8.2	4.8	-3.7	7.5	3.8
Home ownership rate (percent of households)	68.2	67.0	66.1	67.6	68.7	68.4	71.0	74.2	74.1
Rental vacancy rate (percent of rental housing units)	6.2	5.3	6.2	7.0	7.2	5.0	5.2	6.9	7.2

AGRICULTURE

INDIANA'S FARM SECTOR FARED WELL IN THE MID-1990S, AS total revenues climbed faster than production expenses since the early 1990s. Grain sales, the leading production segment in the state, increased 38 percent from the beginning of the decade through the 1995–97 period, while livestock production levels were flat. Realized net income tripled during the decade (looking at three-year averages), though when inventory changes are added the net income was not good in 1995. Overall, the farm sector performed better than in other Midwestern states, due to the dominance of the grain sector, which saw broad gains across the country.

INDIANA FARMS, 1997	
Number of farms	62 000
Total acres (thousands):	15 900
Average per farm	256
Value of land and buildings (millions of dollars)	31 323
Average per farm (dollars)	505 210

Farm Income
(millions of dollars)

	1980	1989	1990	1991	1992	1993	1994	1995	1996	1997
Gross income	5 115	5 162	5 672	5 222	5 059	6 229	5 131	6 134	6 240	6 238
Receipts from sales	4 839	4 495	5 093	4 693	4 538	5 541	4 678	5 553	5 690	5 611
Government payments	15	334	244	210	233	379	137	246	214	265
Imputed and miscellaneous income	262	333	335	319	288	309	316	335	336	362
(–) Production expenses	4 537	4 895	5 130	5 025	5 243	5 378	5 318	5 321	5 591	5 549
(=) Realized net income	578	268	541	197	-184	851	-187	813	648	689
(+) Inventory change	-360	448	19	-322	565	-390	581	-818	165	300
(=) Net income	218	716	561	-125	381	462	394	-6	813	989
Corporate income	0	61	49	-42	35	17	58	-2	116	129
Farm proprietors income	218	654	512	-83	345	444	336	-4	697	859

EDUCATION

EDUCATIONAL ATTAINMENT Percent of population age 25 and over, 1997	State	United States
High school graduate or higher	81.9	82.1
College graduate or higher	16.2	23.9

INDIANA'S PERCENTAGE OF HIGH SCHOOL GRADUATES APPROX-imated the U.S. norm, indicative of its healthy economy, stable base of population, low poverty rates, and small immigrant population. Its recent spending per pupil in public elementary and secondary schools was near the national average as well. Unlike most of the Midwest, Indiana had a lower percentage enrollment than aver-age in private elementary and secondary schools. In

higher education, the ratio of college graduates to pop-ulation was lower than average, consistent with the larg-er blue collar workforce and smaller high-tech and pro-fessional services sectors in Indiana. The percent of the current young adult population enrolled in higher edu-cation was also a bit below the U.S. average, and the low minority enrollment reflects the state's overall popula-tion mix.

High School Completion: 1990–97

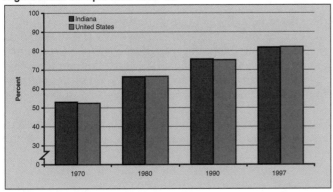

Education Indicators

	State	U.S.
Elementary and secondary schools		
Enrollment, 1995–96		
Total (thousands)	1 077	49 873
Percent in private schools	9.2	10.1
Expenditures per pupil (dollars), 1995–96	6 040	6 146
Average teacher salary (dollars), 1996–97	38 575	38 509
Higher education		
Enrollment, 1996–97		
Total (thousands)	286	14 218
Percent of population 18–34	19.9	21.8
Percent minority	11.1	26.1
Percent in private schools	22.8	22.6

HEALTH

MAJOR HEALTH INDICATORS SHOW A STATE WITH INFANT mortality rates that improved markedly from 1990 to a level near the national average in 1997, with total death rates approximately equal to national levels. Among major causes of death, heart disease, cancer, and stroke, the state had higher than average death rates, likely related to its level of industrialization and pollu-

tion, but it had lower rates for death from homicide and HIV infection. A higher than average proportion of Indiana residents had health insurance because of the high percentage of the population that was employed and its disproportionate concentration in the manufac-turing sector, that typically offers better benefits to employees.

Health Indicators

	1990	1995	1996	1997
Infant mortality *(rate per thousand live births)*				
Indiana	9.6	8.4	7.5	7.4
U.S.	9.2	7.6	7.3	7.1
Total deaths, age-adjusted rate *(rate per thousand population)*				
Indiana	5.2	5.2	5.1	4.6
U.S.	5.2	5.0	4.9	4.8
Persons not covered by health insurance *(percent of population)*				
Indiana	10.7	12.6	10.6	11.4
U.S.	13.9	15.4	15.6	16.1

Leading Causes of Death, 1996
(deaths per 100,000 population)

	Age-adjusted		Not age-adjusted	
	State	U.S.	State	U.S.
Deaths from all causes	506.8	491.6	906.9	872.5
Heart disease	142.7	134.5	287.9	276.4
Cancer	134.9	127.9	213.8	203.4
Cerebrovascular diseases	28.5	26.4	67.6	60.3
Chronic obstructive pulmonary disease	24.0	21.0	44.6	40.0
Diabetes mellitus	14.5	13.6	25.5	23.3
Pneumonia and influenza	12.0	12.8	29.2	31.6
HIV	3.8	11.1	4.0	11.7
Liver disease	5.9	7.5	7.5	9.4
Alzheimer's disease	3.5	2.7	10.1	8.1
Accidents and adverse effects	29.6	30.4	35.8	35.8
Motor vehicle accidents	16.4	16.2	16.6	16.5
Suicide	11.7	10.8	12.6	11.6
Homicide	7.4	8.5	6.8	7.9
Injury by firearm	13.6	12.9	13.8	12.8

GOVERNMENT

STATE AND LOCAL TAXES, 1995–96	State	U.S.
Per capita (dollars)	2 069	2 477
Percent of personal income	9.7	10.8

STATE AND LOCAL GOVERNMENT TAXES COMBINED EQUALED $2,069 per capita in Indiana in 1995–96, about 17 percent below the per capita average for the United States. Taxes at each level, state and local, were below average. Even though personal income in the state was also somewhat below average compared to the nation, the bite taken from personal income was significantly less in Indiana. State and local taxes combined comprised 9.7 percent of personal income, compared with an 10.8 percent share nationally.

State government spending per capita was about 12 percent below the U.S. norm in Indiana, with spending particularly lower for public welfare and health functions. Education spending per capita actually was higher than for the United States overall. The low levels of spending on administration and interest reflect the historical budget conservatism prevalent in the state. Overall state tax collections were 7 percent lower on a per capita basis in 1997 than for the United States, with sales taxes lower but individual income taxes higher than the U.S. average.

Federal spending within Indiana was somewhat lower than the state's share of population would indicate, due to the small number of federal employees in the state and its receipt of limited amounts of federal grants. In grant programs ranging from Medicaid to education and housing, the state received disproportionately small amounts of funding. Procurement spending was also below average in Indiana, though defense contracting ($1.7 billion) was the second highest in the Midwest. Only Social Security and government retirement spending were as high as those for an average state, on a per capita basis.

State Government Finances, 1996–97

	Millions of dollars	Percent distribu- tion	Dollars per capita	
			State	U.S.
General revenue	15 992	100.0	2 727	3 049
Intergovernmental revenue	3 859	24.1	658	863
Taxes	9 101	56.9	1 552	1 660
General sales	3 043	19.0	519	551
Selective sales	1 089	6.8	186	257
License taxes	194	1.2	33	106
Individual income	3 751	23.5	640	542
Corporation net income	904	5.7	154	115
Other taxes	120	0.8	20	90
Other general revenue	3 032	19.0	517	526
General expenditure	15 400	100.0	2 626	2 951
Intergovernmental expenditure	5 508	35.8	939	989
Direct expenditure	9 892	64.2	1 687	1 962
General expenditure, by function:				
Education	6 411	41.6	1 093	1 033
Public welfare	3 221	20.9	549	761
Hospitals and health	634	4.1	108	237
Highways	1 648	10.7	281	225
Police protection and corrections	572	3.7	97	137
Natural resources, parks and recreation	221	1.4	38	63
Governmental administration	372	2.4	63	107
Interest on general debt	288	1.9	49	99
Other and unallocable	2 034	13.2	347	290
Debt at end of fiscal year	6 140	NA	1 047	1 706
Cash and security holdings	23 269	NA	3 968	6 683

Federal Spending within State

	Federal funds, fiscal 1997		
	Millions of dollars	Percent distribution	Percent of U.S. total*
Total within state	25 398	100.0	1.8
Payments to individuals	15 918	62.7	2.0
Retirement and disability	9 915	39.0	2.2
Medicare	4 100	16.1	2.0
Food stamps	290	1.1	1.5
Supplemental Security Income	396	1.6	1.5
Grants	4 010	15.8	1.6
Medicaid and other health	1 883	7.4	1.7
Nutrition and family welfare	732	2.9	1.6
Education	289	1.1	1.7
Housing and community development	159	0.6	1.4
Salaries and wages	1 781	7.0	1.1
Defense procurement contracts	1 739	6.8	1.5
Non-defense procurement contracts	588	2.3	0.8

*State population is 2.2 percent of the U.S. total.

1997

Population (persons)	2,854,330
Population rank	30th
Population growth rank (1990–97)	42nd
Per capita personal income	$23,177
Unemployment rate (percent)	3.3
Poverty rate (percent)	9.6

DURING THE 1990S, IOWA EXPERIENCED A VERY HEALTHY 13 percent growth in jobs, which outpaced the U.S. economy, adding twice as many jobs in the state from 1990 to 1997 as were created from 1980 to 1990. The state had extremely low population growth from 1990 to 1997, with an increase of only 2.7 percent. The state's birth rate fell to 12.9 in 1997, not much higher than the death rate of 9.7, and there was steady domestic out-migration. However, the 1990s saw an improvement over the 1980s, when Iowa suffered a net loss of 4.3 percent of its population. In 1996,

manufacturing accounted for a higher than average 24 percent of the gross state product, with industrial machinery its leading industry. Agriculture remained a major force in Iowa's economy, accounting for nearly 7 percent of total earnings in 1997, while the services sector was somewhat smaller than average for the United States. Iowa's poverty rate was substantially lower than the national average, reflecting a fairly steady economy. The mortality rate and age-adjusted death rates from most major causes remained well below the national average.

Average Annual Population Growth: 1990–97

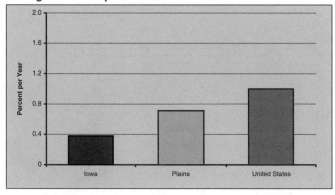

Median Household Income: 1989–97 (1997 dollars)

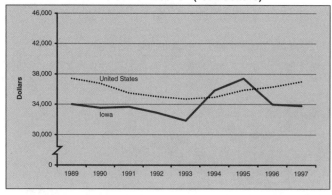

Unemployment Rate: 1989–97

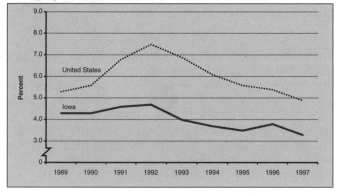

UNEMPLOYMENT HAS REMAINED CONSISTENTLY LOW IN IOWA during the 1990s, sharing very little in the national recession. In 1997, the unemployment rate dropped to a decade low of 3.3 percent. For both 1996 and 1997, Iowa held the sixth lowest unemployment rate in the nation. The labor force grew twice as fast as the working-age population, but employment grew even faster, holding the unemployment rate below 4 percent since 1994.

151

POPULATION AND LABOR FORCE

TOTAL POPULATION IN IOWA GREW 0.4 PERCENT ANNUALLY from 1990 to 1997, well below the U.S. average of 1.0 percent per year. As with many of its neighboring Plains states, Iowa's growth rate was among the lowest in the nation, though this was still an improvement over the state's 1980s population loss. Steady out-migration helped contribute to the state's low growth rate. A lower than average birth rate and higher than average death rate also contributed to a net increase of only 74,000 people from 1990 to 1997. For the first time in more than a decade, the non-Hispanic White population, which comprised nearly 95 percent of Iowa's total population, showed a decrease

in numbers from 1996 to 1997. With high rates of growth in other groups, Iowa had a slight net increase of only 5,000 people in 1997. The fastest growing groups were the Asian and Hispanic populations, which grew at annual rates of 4.2 and 5.5 percent, respectively from 1990 to 1997. The state's proportion of Black population has decreased since 1990, when it comprised 2.1 percent of the state's total population. The Hispanic population will soon become the state's largest minority. The proportion of people living in metro areas continued to be extremely low, at 45 percent, compared to the national average of 80 percent.

Population and Labor Force

	1980	1990	1991	1992	1993	1994	1995	1996	1997	Change* State	Change* U.S.
Population											
Total number of persons (thousands)	2 914	2 780	2 791	2 807	2 821	2 829	2 841	2 849	2 854	0.4	1.0
Percent distribution:											
White, Non-Hispanic	96.9	95.4	95.8	95.6	95.5	95.3	95.1	94.9	94.8	0.3	0.4
Black, Non-Hispanic	1.4	2.1	1.7	1.8	1.8	1.8	1.8	1.9	1.9	-1.1	1.4
Asian	0.5	1.0	1.0	1.0	1.1	1.2	1.2	1.2	1.3	4.2	4.1
Native American	0.2	0.3	0.3	0.3	0.3	0.3	0.3	0.3	0.3	1.1	1.6
Hispanic	0.9	1.3	1.3	1.3	1.4	1.5	1.6	1.8	1.9	5.5	3.8
In metropolitan areas	41.1	43.3	43.5	43.7	43.9	44.1	44.2	44.4	44.5	0.8	1.0
Total number of households (thousands)	1 053	1 064	1 069	1 083	1 084	1 084	1 093	1 103	NA	0.6	1.2
Labor Force (thousands)											
Population 16 and over	2 197	2 135	2 144	2 163	2 176	2 189	2 205	2 215	2 219	0.6	1.0
Civilian labor force	1 432	1 448	1 470	1 512	1 560	1 566	1 560	1 593	1 579	1.2	1.1
Employed	1 350	1 386	1 402	1 440	1 497	1 509	1 505	1 533	1 528	1.4	1.2
Percent of population	61.4	64.9	65.4	66.6	68.8	68.9	68.3	69.2	68.9		
Unemployment rate (percent)	5.8	4.3	4.6	4.7	4.0	3.7	3.5	3.8	3.3		

*Compound annual average percent change, 1990–1997; 1990–1996 for households.

Population Change and Components: 1990–97

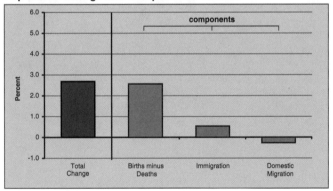

Average Annual Household and Population Growth

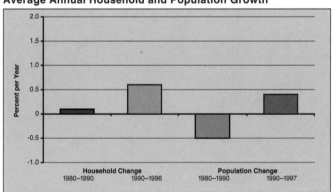

Population by Age; Births and Deaths

	1990 State	1990 U.S.	1997 State	1997 U.S.
Age distribution (percent)				
Under 5 years	7.0	7.6	6.4	7.2
5 to 17 years	18.9	18.2	19.0	18.8
18 to 64 years	58.8	61.8	59.5	61.3
65 years and over	15.3	12.5	15.0	12.7
Birth and death rates (per thousand population)				
Births	14.2	16.7	12.9	14.6
Deaths	9.7	8.6	9.7	8.6

IOWA'S POPULATION DISTRIBUTION WAS SLIGHTLY DIFFERENT from the national average. The state had a lower percentage of children under the age of 5 and a much greater share of people over the age of 65. A decreasing birth rate, well below the national average, may explain the shrinking proportion of Iowa's population that is under the age of 5. Since 1990, the percentage of the population between the ages of 18 and 64 has grown larger, but it is still clearly below the national average.

HOUSEHOLD AND PERSONAL INCOME

HOUSEHOLD INCOME AND PERSONS IN POVERTY	1990	1995	1996	1997 State	1997 U.S.
Median household income (1997 dollars)	33 510	37 407	33 971	33 783	37 005
Persons in poverty (thousands)	289	352	279	270	35 574
Poverty rate (percent)	10.4	12.2	9.6	9.6	13.3

IN 1997, IOWA'S $33,783 MEDIAN HOUSEHOLD INCOME remained 9 percent short of the national average, ranking 34th in the nation and reflecting the consistently low income position of the state during the 1990s. The poverty rate remained steady in 1997 at 9.6 percent, well below the national average of 13.3 percent. Iowa's low unemployment rate has helped contribute to the state's declining poverty rate.

From 1989 to 1997, Iowa's per capita personal income increased by 44.3 percent in current dollars, and 14 percent in inflation-adjusted dollars. Since 1989, the state's per capita income has been growing at a faster rate than average because of the combination of slow population growth and rapid earnings growth. The percentage of the working-age population holding jobs increased to 68.9 percent in 1997, far above the national average, and wages and

salaries grew by an average annual rate of 5.7 percent from 1989 to 1997. Still, total earnings per capita in 1997 were 8 percent short of the U.S. average. Transfer payments were 13 percent below average, and dividends and interest were 5 percent short of the national level.

Total government payments to individuals grew at a smaller rate compared to the national average. They were more heavily weighted toward retirement benefits than in the average state, and the rate of growth in medical payments was much less than for the United States overall. Income maintenance was also a smaller than average portion of total transfers, and within this category payments for family assistance decreased at a faster rate and food stamps increased at a much smaller rate than the national average. Other income maintenance (including the earned income credit) became the state's largest welfare program.

Personal Income
(millions of dollars)

	1980	1989	1990	1991	1992	1993	1994	1995	1996	1997	Change*
Earnings by place of work	19 547	30 940	32 467	33 275	36 073	36 077	40 178	41 085	44 680	47 091	5.4
Wages and salaries	15 195	23 032	24 539	25 569	27 245	28 417	30 265	32 000	33 703	35 815	5.7
Other labor income	1 571	2 580	2 853	3 090	3 409	3 721	4 002	3 976	3 823	3 858	5.2
Proprietors' income	2 781	5 328	5 074	4 616	5 419	3 938	5 911	5 109	7 155	7 418	4.2
Farm	332	1 848	1 712	1 177	1 852	185	2 012	1 049	2 905	2 850	5.6
Nonfarm	2 449	3 480	3 363	3 439	3 567	3 753	3 898	4 060	4 250	4 568	3.5
(−) Personal contributions for social insurance	1 101	2 123	2 258	2 378	2 496	2 630	2 836	3 017	3 142	3 340	5.8
(+) Adjustment for residence	52	240	261	288	308	247	236	273	268	296	NA
(=) **Net earnings by state of residence**	18 499	29 058	30 470	31 185	33 885	33 694	37 578	38 341	41 806	44 047	5.3
(+) Dividends, interest, and rent	5 495	8 917	9 460	9 487	9 470	9 618	9 847	10 261	11 132	11 813	3.6
(+) Transfer payments	3 674	6 516	7 003	7 622	8 201	8 762	9 059	9 521	9 942	10 250	5.8
(=) **Total personal income**	27 669	44 490	46 933	48 294	51 556	52 073	56 485	58 123	62 880	66 110	5.1
Farm	618	2 109	2 005	1 451	2 135	480	2 294	1 335	3 188	3 134	5.1
Nonfarm	27 051	42 382	44 928	46 843	49 422	51 593	54 190	56 788	59 692	62 975	5.1
Personal income per capita (dollars)											
Current dollars	9 495	16 058	16 885	17 305	18 369	18 465	19 965	20 462	22 078	23 177	4.7
1997 dollars	18 155	20 301	20 319	19 983	20 547	20 092	21 217	21 270	22 483	23 177	1.7

*Compound annual average percent change, 1989–1997

Government Transfer Payments

	Millions of dollars 1990	Millions of dollars 1997	Percent change* State	Percent change* U.S.
Total government payments to individuals	6 626	9 718	46.7	62.7
Retirement, disability, and insurance	4 014	5 528	37.7	48.2
Social Security	3 296	4 478	35.9	46.1
Government employee retirement	582	900	54.7	60.3
Medical payments	1 768	3 043	72.1	101.2
Income maintenance	412	632	53.3	58.0
Supplemental Security Income	87	155	78.1	75.4
Family assistance	160	144	-10.1	-0.5
Food Stamps	112	121	7.6	27.1
Other income maintenance	53	213	301.1	189.8
Unemployment insurance benefits	152	185	21.4	10.6
Veterans benefits and other	280	330	18.0	30.8

*Percent change, 1990–1997

Government Payments to Individuals: 1997

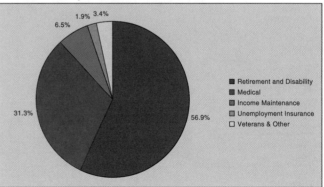

- Retirement and Disability
- Medical
- Income Maintenance
- Unemployment Insurance
- Veterans & Other

56.9% 31.3% 6.5% 1.9% 3.4%

ECONOMIC STRUCTURE

LEADING PRIVATE INDUSTRIES, 1997 (Worker and proprietor earnings, millions of dollars)		FASTEST EARNINGS GROWTH, 1989–97 (percent increase)	
Health services	$3 814	Amusement and recreation services	247.7
Farming	3 134	Social services	123.8
Industrial machinery manufacturing	2 220	Business services	107.3
Construction specialties	1 860	General building contractors	91.9
Business services	1 840	Construction specialties	91.8

IOWA'S MANUFACTURING SECTOR WAS SURPRISINGLY LARGE and generated a higher proportion of state employment and earnings than in the average state. Its 21.2 percent share of earnings in 1997 placed it in a virtual tie with the services sector for largest component of the Iowa economy, although the faster growth in services promises to make it the lead sector in the future. Total manufacturing earnings were among the slower growing sectors of the 1990s. The two leading manufacturing industries were industrial machinery and food products, accounting for about 40 percent of the sector's worker earnings. In 1997, Iowa's leading service industries were health services and business services, with the latter the fastest growing large industry. The other fastest growing sectors from 1989 to 1997 were amusement and recreational services and social services. The fastest rates of employment growth among the major sectors were in construction and agricultural services, though the construction job growth figure is a bit distorted by the very low level of jobs in 1989. Agriculture continued to be a strong part of the state's economy, as it contributed nearly 7 percent of total earnings and 6.4 percent of total employment in 1997. However, its size has declined (both in absolute and relative terms) since 1980, when farming represented 10.5 percent of all jobs in Iowa.

Employment and Earnings by Sector

	1980	1989	1990	1991	1992	1993	1994	1995	1996	1997 Number	1997 Percent of total	Change*
Employment *(thousands of persons)*												
Total	1 541	1 610	1 642	1 664	1 680	1 705	1 741	1 790	1 824	1 856	100.0	1.8
Farm	162	137	131	124	125	120	121	122	119	118	6.4	-1.8
Nonfarm	1 379	1 473	1 511	1 540	1 555	1 584	1 620	1 668	1 705	1 738	93.6	2.1
Private nonfarm	1 159	1 244	1 277	1 303	1 318	1 347	1 381	1 426	1 461	1 492	80.4	2.3
Agricultural service, forestry, and fishing	10	18	20	22	20	21	22	22	24	25	1.3	4.5
Mining	3	3	3	3	3	3	3	3	3	3	0.1	-0.5
Construction	74	66	71	73	77	79	85	89	93	95	5.1	4.7
Manufacturing	250	241	242	239	236	242	252	257	255	261	14.0	1.0
Transportation and public utilities	69	69	69	68	67	70	73	75	78	82	4.4	2.2
Wholesale trade	83	85	82	84	88	86	87	89	89	90	4.9	0.8
Retail trade	255	273	280	284	290	294	306	315	321	325	17.5	2.2
Finance, insurance, and real estate	109	105	109	111	110	115	107	110	112	115	6.2	1.2
Services	305	385	402	418	427	437	447	467	488	497	26.8	3.2
Government	221	229	234	237	237	238	239	242	244	246	13.2	0.9
Earnings *(millions of dollars)*												
Total	19 547	30 940	32 467	33 275	36 073	36 077	40 178	41 085	44 680	47 091	100.0	5.4
Farm	618	2 109	2 005	1 451	2 135	480	2 294	1 335	3 188	3 134	6.7	5.1
Nonfarm	18 929	28 831	30 462	31 824	33 938	35 597	37 884	39 750	41 492	43 957	93.3	5.4
Private nonfarm	16 185	24 056	25 351	26 413	28 282	29 723	31 765	33 400	34 878	37 120	78.8	5.6
Agricultural service, forestry, and fishing	115	250	302	317	351	345	325	329	332	351	0.7	4.4
Mining	104	65	69	79	82	78	77	77	79	86	0.2	3.6
Construction	1 298	1 500	1 718	1 795	1 941	2 050	2 336	2 514	2 730	2 846	6.0	8.3
Manufacturing	5 371	7 140	7 423	7 486	7 922	8 315	8 976	9 224	9 967	9 967	21.2	4.3
Transportation and public utilities	1 406	1 939	1 997	2 042	2 120	2 279	2 439	2 565	2 669	2 832	6.0	4.8
Wholesale trade	1 554	2 105	2 205	2 297	2 493	2 538	2 660	2 831	2 951	3 168	6.7	5.2
Retail trade	2 073	2 955	3 165	3 324	3 492	3 611	3 860	3 992	4 142	4 316	9.2	4.8
Finance, insurance, and real estate	1 054	1 892	2 019	2 177	2 387	2 601	2 753	2 926	3 106	3 372	7.2	7.5
Services	3 210	6 211	6 455	6 895	7 495	7 905	8 339	8 941	9 573	10 181	21.6	6.4
Government	2 744	4 775	5 111	5 412	5 656	5 874	6 118	6 350	6 614	6 837	14.5	4.6

*Compound annual average percent change, 1989–1997

ECONOMIC STRUCTURE (Continued)

IOWA'S AVERAGE WAGES AND SALARIES IN 1997 OF $24,134 were a full 19 percent below the national average of $29,809, contributing to Iowa's ability to attract new investment and jobs. Manufacturing wages were 12 percent below the national average. The construction sector's 1997 wages of $29,010 were the closest to the national average at 91.3 percent, a reflection of the high demand in the construction industry. The very low wages in services, only 73 percent as high as in services nationally, partly reflect the relative lack of high-end technology services in the state.

Manufacturing was a large part of Iowa's economy. In 1996, manufacturing accounted for 24 percent of the state's gross state product (GSP), placing Iowa among the top ten states ranked by this ratio. This percentage represented a slight decrease from the sector's share of GSP in earlier years. Value of manufacturing output per worker increased to $71,616 in 1996, up from $54,454 in 1989. While Iowa's manufacturing value per worker remained higher than the national average, it grew at a slower rate. New capital expenditures increased by more than 20 percent from 1995 to 1996, however, which may bode well for future productivity. One of the state's leading manufacturing industries was industrial machinery, whose earnings exceeded $2 billion in 1997.

Iowa increased its exports to foreign markets by nearly 34 percent from 1994 to 1997, led by industrial machinery and computer exports, which increased by 47 percent over the period. This rate slightly exceeded the growth of U.S. exports of this product group in the same period. The largest export sector in the state was industrial machinery, followed by electric and electronic equipment. Transportation equipment had the highest rate of growth for major sectors at 57.4 percent from 1994 to 1997, and exports of food products also grew substantially. Agricultural and livestock products exports increased significantly in 1996 and 1997, yet they account for a fairly small share of total exports.

Average Annual Wages and Salaries by Sector
(dollars)

	1989	1996	1997 State	1997 U.S.
All wage and salary workers	17 992	23 066	24 134	29 809
Farm	9 028	12 358	13 401	16 442
Nonfarm	18 183	23 223	24 277	29 900
Private nonfarm	18 060	23 019	24 146	29 867
Agricultural service, forestry, and fishing	12 341	14 962	15 085	17 941
Mining	25 767	29 752	32 498	49 800
Construction	21 667	28 340	29 010	31 765
Manufacturing	25 916	31 942	33 751	38 351
Transportation and utilities	25 453	30 936	31 707	38 222
Wholesale trade	21 591	29 180	30 792	39 466
Retail trade	9 952	12 672	13 103	16 206
Finance, insurance, and real estate	22 752	31 096	33 328	44 993
Services	14 251	19 337	20 184	27 588
Government	18 736	24 223	24 928	30 062

Gross State Product and Manufacturing
(millions of dollars, except as noted)

	1989	1994	1995	1996
Gross state product, total	52 196	68 728	71 362	76 315
Manufacturing:				
Millions of dollars	13 116	17 207	17 902	18 292
Percent of total gross state product	25.1	25.0	25.1	24.0
Per worker (dollars)	54 454	68 320	69 573	71 616
New capital expenditures, manufacturing	NA	1 785	1 726	2 100

Exports of Goods
(millions of dollars)

	1994	1995	1996	1997
All goods	2 331	2 578	2 695	3 117
Manufactures	2 137	2 388	2 485	2 892
Agricultural and livestock products	145	145	165	178
Other commodities	49	45	45	46
Top goods exports, 1997:				
Industrial machinery and computers	636	745	746	934
Electric and electronic equipment	320	311	297	375
Food products	235	296	296	338
Transportation equipment	144	190	187	227
Scientific and measuring instruments	154	163	209	193

HOUSING

New home production increased significantly from 1989 to 1997, but the rate of production per 1,000 residents remained about 40 percent below the national average. Existing home sales have remained relatively flat during the 1990s, with a substantial increase in both 1996 and 1997, when for the first time sales exceeded their 1989 level. The sluggish growth in both home construction and home sales can be attributed to the anemic population growth in the state throughout the 1990s, with almost no population growth in 1996 and 1997 when the U.S. housing market was at its strongest. Homeownership rates have fluctuated throughout the 1990s. The recession in the early 1990s caused a dramatic drop in homeownership rates, which fell to 66.3 percent in 1992. In 1997, the rate increased to 72.7 percent, giving the state the tenth highest rate in the nation. Iowa's stable population and moderate home prices generally contributed to high rates of homeownership. The rental vacancy rate increased in 1997 to 6.4 percent, from a low of 3.9 percent in 1992.

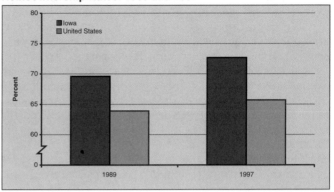

Homeownership Rates: 1989 and 1997

Housing Supply

	1989	1990	1991	1992	1993	1994	1995	1996	1997
Residential building permits (thousands)	7.4	7.6	8.0	10.5	10.6	12.5	11.3	12.0	10.7
New home production (including manufactured housing):									
Thousands of homes	9.2	9.3	9.5	13.3	12.6	14.5	13.6	14.5	12.3
Rate per 1,000 population									
Iowa	3.3	3.3	3.4	4.7	4.5	5.1	4.8	5.1	4.3
U.S.	6.2	5.2	4.5	5.1	5.6	6.4	6.3	6.6	6.5
Existing home sales:									
Thousands of homes	54.6	51.9	54.1	53.1	53.5	54.3	51.6	56.4	57.7
Change from previous year (percent)									
Iowa	-5.7	-4.9	4.2	-1.8	0.8	1.5	-5.0	9.3	2.3
U.S.	-3.9	-4.0	0.0	9.2	8.2	4.8	-3.7	7.5	3.8
Home ownership rate (percent of households)	69.6	70.7	68.4	66.3	68.2	70.1	71.4	72.8	72.7
Rental vacancy rate (percent of rental housing units)	8.5	7.8	7.0	3.9	4.3	4.9	5.3	5.5	6.4

AGRICULTURE

Iowa had the third highest number of farms in the nation in 1997. The size of Iowa's farms averaged 339 acres, well below the national average of 471. The value of land and buildings in Iowa increased from $40,360 million in 1994 to $52,124 in 1997. Gross income from farming increased nearly 25 percent from 1989 to 1997, and net farm income was up 50 percent from 1990 to 1997 (using three-year averages). Sales from crops was 53.6 percent of farm receipts, and the remainder was from livestock and their products. Crop revenue has increased by more than 60 percent since 1989, well above the 6.1 percent increase in revenue from livestock and their products.

IOWA FARMS, 1997

Number of farms	98 000
Total acres (thousands):	33 200
Average per farm	339
Value of land and buildings (millions of dollars)	52 124
Average per farm (dollars)	531 878

Farm Income
(millions of dollars)

	1980	1989	1990	1991	1992	1993	1994	1995	1996	1997
Gross income	11 212	11 629	12 234	12 212	12 254	12 890	11 072	13 896	13 629	14 449
Receipts from sales	10 756	10 095	10 916	11 023	11 098	11 143	9 820	12 532	12 551	13 120
Government payments	45	981	754	645	662	1 230	732	787	508	713
Imputed and miscellaneous income	412	553	563	544	494	518	520	578	569	616
(−) Production expenses	10 341	9 988	10 568	10 515	10 833	10 807	11 181	10 915	11 544	11 536
(=) Realized net income	872	1 642	1 665	1 697	1 421	2 083	-109	2 981	2 084	2 913
(+) Inventory change	-539	335	170	-455	574	-1 892	2 379	-1 848	1 179	257
(=) Net income	332	1 977	1 835	1 242	1 996	191	2 270	1 133	3 263	3 170
Corporate income	0	129	123	64	144	5	258	84	358	320
Farm proprietors income	332	1 848	1 712	1 177	1 852	185	2 012	1 049	2 905	2 850

EDUCATION

EDUCATIONAL ATTAINMENT Percent of population age 25 and over, 1997	State	United States
High school graduate or higher	86.7	82.1
College graduate or higher	21.7	23.9

IOWA RANKED TENTH IN THE NATION FOR THE PERCENTAGE OF its population with a high school degree. In 1997, nearly 87 percent of the state's population were high school graduates, compared to the national average of 82.1 percent. In contrast, 21.7 percent of the state's population held college degrees, which was below the national average of 23.9 percent, reflecting the state's relatively small number of technology, finance, and other white-collar professional jobs. Public spending on elementary and secondary schools was 6 percent lower than the national average, with per pupil expenditure amounting to $5,772. The average teacher's salary was $33,275, well below the national average. The lower salaries can be partially attributed to a lower cost of living in Iowa. Iowa's postsecondary enrollment had a greater proportion of minority students than the state's total population.

High School Completion: 1990–97

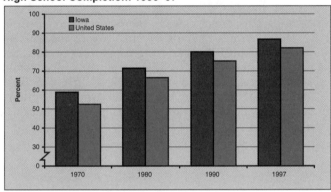

Education Indicators

	State	U.S.
Elementary and secondary schools		
Enrollment, 1995–96		
Total (thousands)	552	49 873
Percent in private schools	9.0	10.1
Expenditures per pupil (dollars), 1995–96	5 772	6 146
Average teacher salary (dollars), 1996–97	33 275	38 509
Higher education		
Enrollment, 1996–97		
Total (thousands)	177	14 218
Percent of population 18–34	27.0	21.8
Percent minority	7.7	26.1
Percent in private schools	28.9	22.6

HEALTH

THE PROPORTION OF IOWA RESIDENTS WITHOUT HEALTH INSURANCE slowly increased over the past several years, yet the 1997 rate of 12 percent remained well below the national average of 16.1 percent. This appears to be related to the low poverty rate and high ratio of employed adults in the state. Infant mortality dropped to a rate of 4.8 per 1,000 in 1997, giving Iowa the fourth lowest rate in the nation. The total death rate has dropped considerably since 1990, but at a slower rate than in the nation overall. Iowa's rates for major causes of death were all below the U.S. average (when adjusted for the age distribution of the state population), with the exceptions of Alzheimer's disease and motor vehicle death.

Health Indicators

	1990	1995	1996	1997
Infant mortality *(rate per thousand live births)*				
Iowa	8.1	8.2	6.5	4.8
U.S.	9.2	7.6	7.3	7.1
Total deaths, age-adjusted rate *(rate per thousand population)*				
Iowa	4.4	4.4	4.3	4.2
U.S.	5.2	5.0	4.9	4.8
Persons not covered by health insurance *(percent of population)*				
Iowa	8.1	11.3	11.6	12.0
U.S.	13.9	15.4	15.6	16.1

Leading Causes of Death, 1996
(deaths per 100,000 population)

	Age-adjusted		Not age-adjusted	
	State	U.S.	State	U.S.
Deaths from all causes	430.9	491.6	976.2	872.5
Heart disease	121.9	134.5	322.0	276.4
Cancer	120.2	127.9	227.7	203.4
Cerebrovascular diseases	25.2	26.4	79.7	60.3
Chronic obstructive pulmonary disease	21.0	21.0	47.2	40.0
Diabetes mellitus	9.9	13.6	21.2	23.3
Pneumonia and influenza	12.1	12.8	40.0	31.6
HIV	2.4	11.1	2.5	11.7
Liver disease	4.2	7.5	6.2	9.4
Alzheimer's disease	3.1	2.7	12.4	8.1
Accidents and adverse effects	29.1	30.4	38.3	35.8
Motor vehicle accidents	16.8	16.2	17.2	16.5
Suicide	10.6	10.8	11.3	11.6
Homicide	2.8	8.5	2.5	7.9
Injury by firearm	7.4	12.9	7.9	12.8

GOVERNMENT

STATE AND LOCAL TAXES, 1995–96	State	U.S.
Per capita (dollars)	2 377	2 477
Percent of personal income	11.4	10.8

TOTAL STATE AND LOCAL TAXES IN IOWA WERE 4 PERCENT lower, on a per capita basis, than the average in the nation in 1995–96. Given the relatively low average income in the state, however, these taxes consumed a greater portion of personal income than average. Iowa's per capita state-level general revenue of $2,931 was just below the national average of $3,049 in 1997, with taxes per capita equal to the U.S. average but with intergovernmental transfers from the federal government at a below-average level. Among various state taxes, the highest was the $603 per capita from individual income taxes. This amount was well above the $542 national average. The state's expenditures for education per capita amounted to $1,260, more than $200 higher than the national average. Iowa's per capita expenditures on interest for its general debt of $40 was only 40 percent of the national average, as the level of debt outstanding is very low. The state's other per capita general expenditures were relatively similar to the expenditures in a typical state.

With the exception of Social Security and government retirement, Iowa received a less than proportionate share of federal grants, procurements, and payments to individuals. Defense and other procurement were the lowest proportion, at only 0.4 percent and 0.5 percent of the U.S. total, as compared to Iowa's 1.1 percent of the U.S. total population, because there was relatively little defense-related production capacity in the state. Grants are often a reflection on the number of poor within a state, thus the lower proportion of grants for Iowa can be partially attributed to Iowa's low poverty rate.

State Government Finances, 1996–97

	Millions of dollars	Percent distribution	Dollars per capita State	Dollars per capita U.S.
General revenue	8 360	100.0	2 931	3 049
Intergovernmental revenue	2 008	24.0	704	863
Taxes	4 686	56.1	1 643	1 660
General sales	1 500	17.9	526	551
Selective sales	728	8.7	255	257
License taxes	421	5.0	148	106
Individual income	1 720	20.6	603	542
Corporation net income	221	2.6	78	115
Other taxes	96	1.1	34	90
Other general revenue	1 666	19.9	584	526
General expenditure	8 622	100.0	3 023	2 951
Intergovernmental expenditure	2 869	33.3	1 006	989
Direct expenditure	5 753	66.7	2 017	1 962
General expenditure, by function:				
Education	3 595	41.7	1 260	1 033
Public welfare	1 738	20.2	609	761
Hospitals and health	679	7.9	238	237
Highways	1 095	12.7	384	225
Police protection and corrections	259	3.0	91	137
Natural resources, parks and recreation	230	2.7	81	63
Governmental administration	312	3.6	109	107
Interest on general debt	114	1.3	40	99
Other and unallocable	601	7.0	211	290
Debt at end of fiscal year	2 014	NA	706	1 706
Cash and security holdings	18 888	NA	6 623	6 683

Federal Spending within State

	Federal funds, fiscal 1997		
	Millions of dollars	Percent distribution	Percent of U.S. total*
Total within state	13 542	100.0	1.0
Payments to individuals	8 096	59.8	1.0
Retirement and disability	5 256	38.8	1.1
Medicare	1 909	14.1	0.9
Food stamps	125	0.9	0.6
Supplemental Security Income	163	1.2	0.6
Grants	2 129	15.7	0.9
Medicaid and other health	1 005	7.4	0.9
Nutrition and family welfare	419	3.1	0.9
Education	150	1.1	0.9
Housing and community development	69	0.5	0.6
Salaries and wages	943	7.0	0.6
Defense procurement contracts	438	3.2	0.4
Non-defense procurement contracts	367	2.7	0.5

*State population is 1.1 percent of the U.S. total.

KANSAS

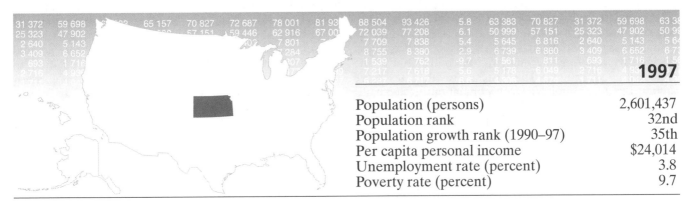

1997

Population (persons)	2,601,437
Population rank	32nd
Population growth rank (1990–97)	35th
Per capita personal income	$24,014
Unemployment rate (percent)	3.8
Poverty rate (percent)	9.7

KANSAS IS BECOMING LESS DEPENDENT ON AGRICULTURE AND meat packing, as its aircraft manufacturing, telecommunications industry, and services sector have seen vigorous growth in recent years. With education levels higher than the national average and wages below average, the state is attractive for companies seeking expansion. Overall, the state experienced worker earnings growth at a slightly above-average rate from 1989 to 1997, and a population growth a bit lower than average has resulted in faster growth of per capita income in the state. The state's $3 billion aircraft industry features plants of four major companies, Boeing, Raytheon, Cessna, and Learjet, and produces a majority of the nation's general aviation aircraft. Agriculture still carries a disproportionate weight in the state economy, and net income in farming has advanced more consistently than for the U.S. farm sector in the 1990s, yet farm employment in Kansas is declining just as in the nation.

Population growth in Kansas of 4.9 percent during the 1990 to 1997 period was similar to neighboring states, yet below the national average. Growth would have been lower in the state except for international immigration, which offset the domestic out-migration and has given Kansas an Hispanic community of significant size.

Average Annual Population Growth: 1990–97

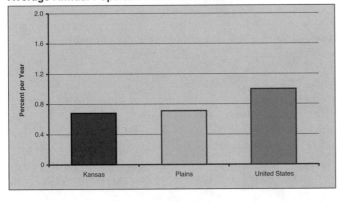

Median Household Income: 1989–97 (1997 dollars)

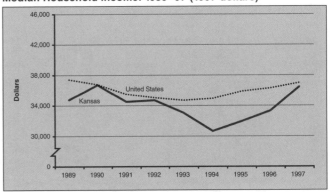

Unemployment Rate: 1989–97

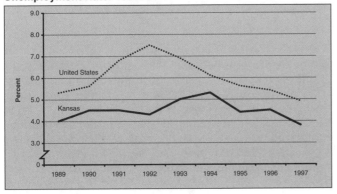

UNEMPLOYMENT HAS BEEN CONSISTENTLY LOW IN KANSAS throughout the 1990s, reaching a low point of 3.8 percent in 1997. This gave the state the 12th lowest unemployment rate in the nation. The increase in the number of employed adults, which averaged a strong 1.1 percent annually in the 1990s, exceeded the 1.0 percent growth of the labor force, which in turn exceeded the growth of the adult population. All these indicators of a strong labor market are consistent with the increase in the percentage of population employed, which exceeded 66 percent in 1997.

159

POPULATION AND LABOR FORCE

FROM 1990 TO 1997, KANSAS WAS ONE OF THE SLOWER GROW-ing states in the nation, ranking 35th among all states. The total population of Kansas grew by only 0.6 percent annually during this period, well below the U.S. rate of 1.0 percent. Kansas experienced some domestic out-migration during this period, while immigration contributed to the state's limited growth. The fastest growth rates were among the Asian and Hispanic populations, reflecting a national trend. Overall, both groups had significant increases in their proportions of the state's total popula-tion over the past two decades. The Black population did not grow appreciable from 1990-1997, reflecting some out-migration, thus Hispanics appear to be becoming the state's largest minority group. The state has become significantly more diverse than in 1980, with the White population declining from 90.5 percent of the population to about 87 percent in 1997. The population became increasingly concentrated in metropolitan areas, as the proportion grew to 56 percent in 1997, although it was still much below the national metro average of 80 percent.

Population and Labor Force

	1980	1990	1991	1992	1993	1994	1995	1996	1997	Change* State	Change* U.S.
Population											
Total number of persons (thousands)	2 364	2 481	2 494	2 518	2 538	2 558	2 575	2 585	2 601	0.6	1.0
Percent distribution:											
White, Non-Hispanic	90.5	88.2	88.3	87.9	87.8	87.5	87.3	87.1	86.9	0.4	0.4
Black, Non-Hispanic	5.3	5.8	5.7	5.8	5.8	5.8	5.7	5.7	5.6	0.2	1.4
Asian	0.7	1.3	1.4	1.4	1.5	1.5	1.6	1.6	1.7	4.1	4.1
Native American	0.8	0.9	0.9	0.9	0.9	0.9	0.9	0.9	0.9	0.3	1.6
Hispanic	2.7	3.9	3.9	4.1	4.3	4.5	4.7	4.9	5.1	4.6	3.8
In metropolitan areas	50.1	53.9	54.3	54.6	54.9	55.1	55.2	55.6	56.0	1.2	1.0
Total number of households (thousands)	872	945	948	959	962	965	975	982	NA	0.6	1.2
Labor Force (thousands)											
Population 16 and over	1 800	1 883	1 889	1 908	1 924	1 941	1 960	1 973	1 989	0.8	1.0
Civilian labor force	1 184	1 276	1 271	1 311	1 324	1 330	1 338	1 349	1 368	1.0	1.1
Employed	1 131	1 219	1 214	1 255	1 257	1 259	1 279	1 288	1 317	1.1	1.2
Percent of population	62.8	64.7	64.3	65.8	65.3	64.9	65.2	65.3	66.2		
Unemployment rate (percent)	4.5	4.5	4.5	4.3	5.0	5.3	4.4	4.5	3.8		

*Compound annual average percent change, 1990–1997; 1990–1996 for households.

Population Change and Components: 1990–97

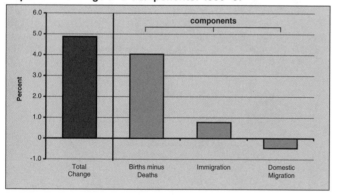

Average Annual Household and Population Growth

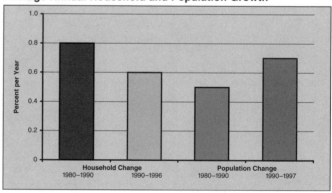

Population by Age; Births and Deaths

	1990 State	1990 U.S.	1997 State	1997 U.S.
Age distribution (percent)				
Under 5 years	7.7	7.6	6.9	7.2
5 to 17 years	19.0	18.2	19.6	18.8
18 to 64 years	59.5	61.8	59.9	61.3
65 years and over	13.8	12.5	13.5	12.7
Birth and death rates (per thousand population)				
Births	15.7	16.7	14.4	14.6
Deaths	9.0	8.6	9.2	8.6

KANSAS'S AGE DEMOGRAPHICS MOVED SLIGHTLY CLOSER TO the national norm between 1990 and 1997, but the state still has a relatively large senior population and a smaller working-age segment. The largest change came in a decrease in the percentage of the state's population under the age of 5, a legacy of the state's low birth rates over the past decade (though the state's birth rate has not declined as much as the U.S. birth rate has). The growth of the school-age population mirrors the national trend.

HOUSEHOLD AND PERSONAL INCOME

HOUSEHOLD INCOME AND PERSONS IN POVERTY	1990	1995	1996	1997	
				State	U.S.
Median household income (1997 dollars)	36 738	31 954	33 333	36 471	37 005
Persons in poverty (thousands)	259	273	287	250	35 574
Poverty rate (percent)	10.3	10.8	11.2	9.7	13.3

MEDIAN HOUSEHOLD INCOME (IN REAL TERMS) IN KANSAS rose to $36,471 in 1997, just below the national average. This was a recovery from median incomes in 1994–95 (which were only 88 to 89 percent of the national median), a period when earnings growth in Kansas had slowed significantly. The poverty rate remained below average in Kansas, with a downtick to 9.7 percent in 1997, the 15th lowest rate in the nation.

In Kansas, per capita personal income increased from 1989 to 1997 by 13.1 percent in inflation-adjusted dollars, compared with a 10.2 percent increase for the nation. At $24,014 in 1997, the state's per capita income is just under 95 percent of the national average. Earnings by place of work have increased faster than overall income, and earnings per capita are a quite high 93.7 percent of the U.S. average earnings. Transfer payment income is quite low in

Kansas, equaling 86 percent of the national average per capita, while dividend and interest income was at the same level as the U.S. average. Wages earned by Kansas residents commuting out of state in 1997 on net added 2.7 percent to earnings.

Total transfer payments have increased at a slower rate than the U.S. average. With the exception of Supplemental Security Income, the increases from 1990 to 1997 were all lower than the national average. Further, the weight of the faster growing medical payment category is smaller than average in Kansas, with a higher proportion of transfers consisting of retirement payments. Family assistance payments and unemployment insurance benefits both declined and food stamps showed only a slight increase. Other income maintenance grew quickly, reflecting rapidly expanding use of earned income tax credits.

Personal Income
(millions of dollars)

	1980	1989	1990	1991	1992	1993	1994	1995	1996	1997	Change*
Earnings by place of work	16 545	28 399	30 419	31 405	34 049	35 611	37 019	38 270	40 813	43 623	5.5
Wages and salaries	13 341	22 179	23 530	24 483	26 196	27 087	28 492	30 027	31 878	34 300	5.6
Other labor income	1 351	2 400	2 661	2 939	3 253	3 557	3 724	3 727	3 641	3 729	5.7
Proprietors' income	1 853	3 819	4 229	3 983	4 600	4 967	4 803	4 516	5 294	5 593	4.9
Farm	-66	553	1 134	772	1 148	1 166	925	411	987	993	7.6
Nonfarm	1 919	3 267	3 095	3 211	3 453	3 801	3 878	4 105	4 307	4 600	4.4
(−) Personal contributions for social insurance	940	1 953	2 067	2 194	2 309	2 436	2 610	2 763	2 904	3 122	6.0
(+) Adjustment for residence	704	924	965	932	972	1 003	979	1 062	1 138	1 176	NA
(=) Net earnings by state of residence	16 309	27 370	29 317	30 143	32 712	34 177	35 387	36 569	39 047	41 676	5.4
(+) Dividends, interest, and rent	4 188	8 373	8 898	9 067	8 703	8 787	8 988	10 050	10 745	11 341	3.9
(+) Transfer payments	3 074	5 806	6 288	6 903	7 551	7 919	8 418	8 748	9 002	9 295	6.1
(=) Total personal income	23 571	41 549	44 503	46 112	48 967	50 883	52 794	55 368	58 793	62 312	5.2
Farm	104	748	1 349	968	1 340	1 360	1 146	649	1 251	1 259	6.7
Nonfarm	23 468	40 801	43 154	45 144	47 626	49 522	51 647	54 719	57 542	61 053	5.2
Personal income per capita (dollars)											
Current dollars	9 950	16 802	17 940	18 500	19 464	20 075	20 672	21 547	22 796	24 014	4.6
1997 dollars	19 025	21 241	21 588	21 363	21 772	21 844	21 968	22 398	23 214	24 014	1.5

*Compound annual average percent change, 1989–1997

Government Transfer Payments

	Millions of dollars		Percent change*	
	1990	1997	State	U.S.
Total government payments to individuals	6 002	8 866	47.7	62.7
Retirement, disability, and insurance	3 581	5 099	42.4	48.2
Social Security	2 622	3 682	40.4	46.1
Government employee retirement	754	1 165	54.4	60.3
Medical payments	1 652	2 735	65.6	101.2
Income maintenance	347	538	55.1	58.0
Supplemental Security Income	66	147	122.6	75.4
Family assistance	107	93	-13.6	-0.5
Food Stamps	100	103	3.1	27.1
Other income maintenance	73	195	165.9	189.8
Unemployment insurance benefits	152	144	-5.2	10.6
Veterans benefits and other	270	349	29.4	30.8

*Percent change, 1990–1997

Government Payments to Individuals: 1997

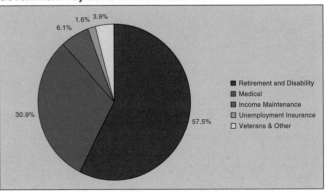

- Retirement and Disability — 57.5%
- Medical — 30.9%
- Income Maintenance — 6.1%
- Unemployment Insurance — 1.6%
- Veterans & Other — 3.9%

ECONOMIC STRUCTURE

LEADING PRIVATE INDUSTRIES, 1997 (Worker and proprietor earnings, millions of dollars)		FASTEST EARNINGS GROWTH, 1989–97 (percent increase)	
Health services	$3 612	Real estate	151.3
Transportation equip., excl. motor veh.	2 521	Social services	137.5
Business services	2 088	Communications	110.8
Construction specialties	1 652	Business services	80.7
Engineering and management services	1 262	Eating and drinking places	79.6

KANSAS' ECONOMIC STRUCTURE IS FAIRLY REFLECTIVE OF THE national economy, with a prominent aircraft manufacturing industry, automobile production, and significant telecommunications presence through a major Sprint telephone operation (employing 20,000 workers). Manufacturing job growth from 1989 to 1997 totaled about 12 percent, while the sector was cutting jobs nationwide. Communications industry earnings increased 110 percent between 1989 and 1997. The state's total employment distribution in 1997 showed its share of jobs in manufacturing, construction, and transportation and communications to be about equal to the national averages. The services sector is fast growing but remains a smaller than average part of the state economy. Three leading industries are in services—health services, business services, and engineering and management—though business services in Kansas is a smaller proportion of total earnings than it is nationwide. Construction earnings showed the highest rate of growth of any sector in Kansas, increasing 71 percent since 1989.

Employment growth in services, like telecommunications all have helped compensate for job losses or slow growth in more traditional sectors such as agriculture, and oil and gas production. Employment in farming and mining (oil) has decreased significantly during both the 1980s and 1990s, dropping from 7.7 and 2.7 percent of total employment in 1980 to 4.7 and 1.2 percent, respectively in 1997, though these sectors are still of above-average importance to the state economy.

Employment and Earnings by Sector

	1980	1989	1990	1991	1992	1993	1994	1995	1996	1997 Number	1997 Percent of total	Change*
Employment *(thousands of persons)*												
Total	1 314	1 466	1 484	1 502	1 516	1 538	1 567	1 601	1 637	1 685	100.0	1.8
Farm	101	86	85	84	82	80	77	78	80	79	4.7	-1.1
Nonfarm	1 213	1 380	1 399	1 418	1 434	1 458	1 490	1 523	1 557	1 606	95.3	1.9
Private nonfarm	986	1 127	1 142	1 159	1 166	1 187	1 213	1 250	1 289	1 336	79.3	2.1
Agricultural service, forestry, and fishing	8	14	15	16	15	17	17	18	19	20	1.2	4.5
Mining	35	30	29	28	24	28	25	23	20	20	1.2	-5.1
Construction	66	63	63	63	68	70	75	78	84	87	5.2	4.1
Manufacturing	195	190	191	190	188	188	194	197	202	212	12.6	1.4
Transportation and public utilities	74	75	75	75	74	76	78	78	80	83	4.9	1.2
Wholesale trade	69	74	75	75	77	74	74	79	80	82	4.9	1.2
Retail trade	199	237	238	243	248	252	263	274	284	291	17.3	2.6
Finance, insurance, and real estate	89	96	96	95	93	96	89	90	92	96	5.7	0.0
Services	252	348	360	373	379	387	398	413	427	446	26.5	3.1
Government	227	252	257	259	268	271	276	273	268	270	16.0	0.8
Earnings *(millions of dollars)*												
Total	16 545	28 399	30 419	31 405	34 049	35 611	37 019	38 270	40 813	43 623	100.0	5.5
Farm	104	748	1 349	968	1 340	1 360	1 146	649	1 251	1 259	2.9	6.7
Nonfarm	16 442	27 651	29 070	30 437	32 709	34 250	35 872	37 621	39 561	42 364	97.1	5.5
Private nonfarm	13 726	22 592	23 655	24 736	26 547	27 801	29 166	30 827	32 674	35 322	81.0	5.7
Agricultural service, forestry, and fishing	67	168	193	214	222	234	237	250	253	276	0.6	6.5
Mining	449	363	388	420	399	399	360	393	410	446	1.0	2.6
Construction	1 182	1 544	1 541	1 541	1 741	1 883	2 102	2 241	2 480	2 640	6.1	6.9
Manufacturing	3 752	5 519	5 733	5 944	6 289	6 458	6 858	7 128	7 598	8 263	18.9	5.2
Transportation and public utilities	1 555	2 408	2 493	2 619	2 761	2 893	3 044	3 057	3 189	3 446	7.9	4.6
Wholesale trade	1 313	2 057	2 224	2 278	2 443	2 447	2 564	2 830	3 011	3 243	7.4	5.9
Retail trade	1 751	2 797	2 907	3 056	3 263	3 453	3 641	3 827	4 020	4 308	9.9	5.5
Finance, insurance, and real estate	843	1 606	1 690	1 763	1 969	2 145	2 173	2 292	2 413	2 595	5.9	6.2
Services	2 813	6 130	6 486	6 901	7 461	7 889	8 188	8 808	9 300	10 106	23.2	6.4
Government	2 716	5 059	5 415	5 701	6 162	6 449	6 706	6 794	6 887	7 041	16.1	4.2

*Compound annual average percent change, 1989–1997

ECONOMIC STRUCTURE (Continued)

THE AVERAGE WAGE IN KANSAS AMOUNTED TO 84 PERCENT OF the national average in 1997. Two sectors with particularly low wages were mining, which is 63.6 percent of the national average, and finance, insurance, and real estate, whose wages are 71.5 percent of average. Average wages in manufacturing and transportation and utilities were relatively higher, at 88 percent and 95 percent of the U.S. averages, respectively. Only farm wages are higher than the national average, with the state's average wage more than $2,500 higher.

Manufacturing continues to play an important role in the state's economy. In 1996, manufacturing accounted for 18.3 percent of Kansas's gross state product (GSP), a slight increase from previous years and above the sector's share of U.S. output, which was 17.5 percent. Transportation equipment, excluding motor vehicles (primarily aircraft and parts) employed about 22 percent of all manufacturing workers in 1997, and according to the Kansas Department of Commerce and Housing, 1996 was a growth year for general aviation manufactures, with billings up 10 percent to a record $3.1 billion. The second largest manufacturing industry is food products, as Kansas is home to several large meat packers. The state's GSP grew at a rate equal to the national economy from 1989 to 1996, with an increase of 41.2 percent. Manufacturing output value per worker reached $61,538 1996, almost $8,000 less than the national average. New capital expenditures increased by nearly 25 percent from 1994 to 1996, however.

Kansas's export of products to foreign markets increased by 46.7 percent from 1994 to 1997, though exports were smaller proportion of Kansas' economy than of the U.S. The state's leading exports are transportation equipment, agricultural products, and food products; more than 30 percent of the state's aircraft output goes to export markets.

Transportation equipment exports grew 87 percent from 1994 to 1997, far outpacing other export growth. Chemical products increased significantly from 1994 to 1997, though they represented only 5 percent of state exports in 1997.

Average Annual Wages and Salaries by Sector
(dollars)

	1989	1996	1997	
			State	U.S.
All wage and salary workers	19 022	24 089	25 136	29 809
Farm	12 895	18 448	19 049	16 442
Nonfarm	19 099	24 148	25 197	29 900
Private nonfarm	19 315	24 429	25 620	29 867
Agricultural service, forestry, and fishing	12 160	15 389	16 207	17 941
Mining	23 894	30 208	31 668	49 800
Construction	22 130	26 758	27 898	31 765
Manufacturing	25 583	32 911	34 289	38 351
Transportation and utilities	28 640	34 154	36 342	38 222
Wholesale trade	24 677	33 180	35 219	39 466
Retail trade	10 903	13 662	14 362	16 206
Finance, insurance, and real estate	22 223	30 211	32 148	44 993
Services	16 332	21 528	22 382	27 588
Government	18 332	23 059	23 500	30 062

Gross State Product and Manufacturing
(millions of dollars, except as noted)

	1989	1994	1995	1996
Gross state product, total	48 175	61 929	64 146	68 014
Manufacturing:				
Millions of dollars	8 760	10 972	11 485	12 451
Percent of total gross state product	18.2	17.7	17.9	18.3
Per worker (dollars)	46 196	56 419	58 202	61 538
New capital expenditures, manufacturing	NA	1 213	1 326	1 515

Exports of Goods
(millions of dollars)

	1994	1995	1996	1997
All goods	3 498	4 461	4 971	5 133
Manufactures	2 450	2 804	3 193	3 846
Agricultural and livestock products	946	1 565	1 639	1 203
Other commodities	102	93	139	84
Top goods exports, 1997:				
Transportation equipment	688	736	884	1 288
Agricultural products	945	1 565	1 637	1 202
Food products	681	855	887	913
Industrial machinery and computers	309	349	399	458
Chemical products	142	166	253	270

HOUSING

New home production increased substantially from 1989 to 1997. After several years of slow growth, home production per 1,000 rates began to increase more strongly in 1992. Since 1993, they have been fairly consistent with the healthy national rates of home production. The number of existing home sales increased significantly from a decade low of just over 37,000 in 1991 to more than 61,000 in 1997. The growth of home sales in Kansas has been about 33 percent higher than the national growth of sales, following the state's much slower sales growth in the 1980s. The median sales price in Kansas' largest metro area, Wichita, was still only $83,200 in 1997. Despite this relative affordability, rates of homeownership declined from 1989 to 1997. They peaked at 69.8 percent in 1992 and fell to 66.5 percent in 1997, just above the national average rate. The 1997 rental vacancy rate of 9.4 percent was significantly higher than the national average of 7.7 percent, and gave the state the 12th highest rate in the nation.

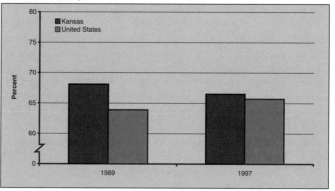

Homeownership Rates: 1989 and 1997

Housing Supply

	1989	1990	1991	1992	1993	1994	1995	1996	1997
Residential building permits (thousands)	8.6	8.5	7.8	9.8	11.0	13.0	12.7	14.7	13.6
New home production (including manufactured housing):									
Thousands of homes	10.2	9.9	9.3	11.1	13.1	16.2	15.9	18.1	16.5
Rate per 1,000 population									
Kansas	4.1	4.0	3.7	4.4	5.2	6.3	6.2	7.0	6.4
U.S.	6.2	5.2	4.5	5.1	5.6	6.4	6.3	6.6	6.5
Existing home sales:									
Thousands of homes	45.1	38.8	37.1	46.2	53.7	55.7	54.4	59.9	61.6
Change from previous year (percent)									
Kansas	-5.3	-14.0	-4.4	24.5	16.2	3.7	-2.3	10.1	2.8
U.S.	-3.9	-4.0	0.0	9.2	8.2	4.8	-3.7	7.5	3.8
Home ownership rate (percent of households)	68.1	69.0	69.7	69.8	68.9	69.0	67.5	67.5	66.5
Rental vacancy rate (percent of rental housing units)	9.3	7.8	6.9	5.9	6.2	9.0	6.2	9.9	9.4

AGRICULTURE

Agriculture has a substantial role in Kansas's economy and it has performed well during the 1990s, with earnings growth from 1989 to 1997 surpassing growth for nonfarm sectors in the same period. The state's gross farm income increased by 25.6 percent from 1989 to 1997, while production expenses grew at a lower rate. Net income increased 12.6 percent over the period (based on three-year averages). Since 1989, crop sales revenue has increased by 86.5 percent, as compared to an increase of 13.2 percent for livestock. As a result, crop revenue has grown from 33 percent of receipts from sales in 1989 to just under 44 percent in 1997, with the rest derived from the sales of livestock and their products.

KANSAS FARMS, 1997

Number of farms	64 000
Total acres (thousands):	47 800
Average per farm	747
Value of land and buildings (millions of dollars)	27 485
Average per farm (dollars)	429 453

Farm Income
(millions of dollars)

	1980	1989	1990	1991	1992	1993	1994	1995	1996	1997
Gross income	6 725	8 800	9 341	9 235	9 117	9 509	9 481	9 551	9 513	11 051
Receipts from sales	6 418	7 697	8 034	8 057	8 134	8 299	8 537	8 618	8 396	9 946
Government payments	93	588	835	698	592	784	468	422	555	530
Imputed and miscellaneous income	213	514	472	480	391	425	476	511	562	575
(−) Production expenses	6 570	7 836	8 283	7 980	8 084	8 165	8 477	8 533	8 936	9 620
(=) Realized net income	155	964	1 059	1 255	1 033	1 343	1 004	1 018	578	1 431
(+) Inventory change	-407	-275	360	-343	424	-70	387	-493	882	-17
(=) Net income	-252	688	1 419	912	1 457	1 274	1 391	525	1 460	1 414
Corporate income	-186	136	285	140	309	108	466	114	473	421
Farm proprietors income	-66	553	1 134	772	1 148	1 166	925	411	987	993

EDUCATION

EDUCATIONAL ATTAINMENT Percent of population age 25 and over, 1997	State	United States
High school graduate or higher	88.1	82.1
College graduate or higher	27.5	23.9

THE STATE'S EDUCATIONAL ATTAINMENT RATES ARE REMARK-ably high for a state with lower than average incomes and a somewhat large older population. More than 88 percent of its population has graduated from high school, placing Kansas as the sixth highest in the nation. Nearly 28 percent of the state's population holds college degrees, which ranks the state tenth in the nation. The percentages of both high school and college graduates have increased sig-

nificantly from 1990, when the state was ranked tenth and 19th, respectively. Kansas's per pupil expenditures are just below the national average, and the state's average teacher's salary is 93.1 percent of the national average. The proportion of young adults currently enrolled in post-secondary school is higher than average; the percentage of minority enrollment is slightly less than the minority representation in the state's population.

High School Completion: 1990–97

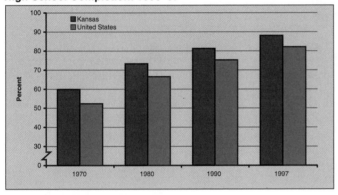

Education Indicators

	State	U.S.
Elementary and secondary schools		
Enrollment, 1995–96		
Total (thousands)	502	49 873
Percent in private schools	7.8	10.1
Expenditures per pupil (dollars), 1995–96	5 971	6 146
Average teacher salary (dollars), 1996–97	35 837	38 509
Higher education		
Enrollment, 1996–97		
Total (thousands)	172	14 218
Percent of population 18–34	28.1	21.8
Percent minority	12.6	26.1
Percent in private schools	9.8	22.6

HEALTH

HEALTH INDICATORS FOR KANSAS ARE ON THE FAVORABLE side. The 1997 infant mortality rate of 6.9 per 1,000 was just below the national rate of 7.1 per 1,000, and Kansas had the 33rd lowest infant mortality rate in the nation based on a two year average (1996–97). Generally, Kansas' 1996 age-adjusted death rates for leading causes were near average, with the exceptions of HIV, chronic liver disease and cirrhosis, and homicide, which were

all well below average. Motor vehicle accidents, accidents and adverse effects, and suicide death rates were significantly higher than the U.S. averages. The percentage of people without health insurance dropped from 12.4 in 1995 to 11.7 in 1997, ranking Kansas 12th lowest in the nation. This decrease marked a substantial improvement in rankings from 1995, when Kansas ranked 17th in the nation.

Health Indicators

	1990	1995	1996	1997
Infant mortality *(rate per thousand live births)*				
Kansas	8.4	7.0	8.9	6.9
U.S.	9.2	7.6	7.3	7.1
Total deaths, age-adjusted rate *(rate per thousand population)*				
Kansas	4.6	4.7	4.6	4.6
U.S.	5.2	5.0	4.9	4.8
Persons not covered by health insurance *(percent of population)*				
Kansas	10.8	12.4	11.4	11.7
U.S.	13.9	15.4	15.6	16.1

Leading Causes of Death, 1996
(deaths per 100,000 population)

	Age-adjusted		Not age-adjusted	
	State	U.S.	State	U.S.
Deaths from all causes	464.2	491.6	929.3	872.5
Heart disease	119.6	134.5	281.4	276.4
Cancer	121.9	127.9	207.8	203.4
Cerebrovascular diseases	26.0	26.4	73.0	60.3
Chronic obstructive pulmonary disease	22.0	21.0	44.0	40.0
Diabetes mellitus	12.6	13.6	23.4	23.3
Pneumonia and influenza	11.8	12.8	35.4	31.6
HIV	3.7	11.1	3.7	11.7
Liver disease	5.0	7.5	6.4	9.4
Alzheimer's disease	2.9	2.7	9.9	8.1
Accidents and adverse effects	33.9	30.4	41.8	35.8
Motor vehicle accidents	20.2	16.2	20.3	16.5
Suicide	12.1	10.8	13.0	11.6
Homicide	6.1	8.5	5.6	7.9
Injury by firearm	12.5	12.9	12.7	12.8

GOVERNMENT

STATE AND LOCAL TAXES, 1995–96	State	U.S.
Per capita (dollars)	2 379	2 477
Percent of personal income	10.9	10.8

LOOKING AT TAXES (EXCEPT CORPORATE) AT BOTH THE STATE and local levels in Kansas, combined taxes on a per capita basis amounted to $2,379 in 1995–96, just below the national average and representing an average percentage of personal income. In 1997, Kansas's per capita state government revenue was well below the national average. The state received nearly the same amount of per capita revenue from taxes but has lower than average intergovernmental income. The per capita individual income taxes were $583, higher than the nation's $542, and other taxes were around national average levels. The state's general expenditures were about $300 lower per capita than nationally. However, per capita state spending on education was $1,170 as compared to the all-state average of $1,033. The average state spent more per capita on public welfare and police protection and corrections expenditures than Kansas, while Kansas spent a significantly higher amount on highways. Kansas's debt at the end of the fiscal year was $467 per capita, much lower than the national average of $1,706.

Kansas' share of total federal expenditures in 1997 was a little less than its 1.0 percent proportion of the nation's population, led by retirement and Medicare spending of approximately average levels. Total salaries paid to federal workers in Kansas were also of average size. The state fell short in procurement, as Kansas received 0.6 percent of the nation's defense procurements and 0.4 percent of non-defense procurement. Medicaid grants totaled 0.7 percent of the U.S. total. Housing and community development grants amounted to only 0.5 percent of the U.S. total.

State Government Finances, 1996–97

	Millions of dollars	Percent distribution	Dollars per capita State	Dollars per capita U.S.
General revenue	7 264	100.0	2 799	3 049
Intergovernmental revenue	1 840	25.3	709	863
Taxes	4 230	58.2	1 630	1 660
General sales	1 476	20.3	569	551
Selective sales	531	7.3	205	257
License taxes	212	2.9	82	106
Individual income	1 513	20.8	583	542
Corporation net income	291	4.0	112	115
Other taxes	207	2.8	80	90
Other general revenue	1 195	16.4	460	526
General expenditure	6 875	100.0	2 649	2 951
Intergovernmental expenditure	2 326	33.8	896	989
Direct expenditure	4 549	66.2	1 753	1 962
General expenditure, by function:				
Education	3 037	44.2	1 170	1 033
Public welfare	1 124	16.4	433	761
Hospitals and health	605	8.8	233	237
Highways	1 013	14.7	390	225
Police protection and corrections	247	3.6	95	137
Natural resources, parks and recreation	171	2.5	66	63
Governmental administration	254	3.7	98	107
Interest on general debt	71	1.0	28	99
Other and unallocable	352	5.1	136	290
Debt at end of fiscal year	1 211	NA	467	1 706
Cash and security holdings	8 826	NA	3 401	6 683

Federal Spending within State

	Federal funds, fiscal 1997		
	Millions of dollars	Percent distribution	Percent of U.S. total*
Total within state	12 647	100.0	0.9
Payments to individuals	7 360	58.2	0.9
Retirement and disability	4 725	37.4	1.0
Medicare	1 859	14.7	0.9
Food stamps	112	0.9	0.6
Supplemental Security Income	159	1.3	0.6
Grants	1 893	15.0	0.8
Medicaid and other health	762	6.0	0.7
Nutrition and family welfare	404	3.2	0.9
Education	170	1.3	1.0
Housing and community development	62	0.5	0.5
Salaries and wages	1 589	12.6	1.0
Defense procurement contracts	681	5.4	0.6
Non-defense procurement contracts	308	2.4	0.4

*State population is 1.0 percent of the U.S. total.

31 372	59 698		65 157	70 827	72 687	78 001	81 93	88 504	93 426	5.8	63 383	70 827	31 372	59 698	63 3
25 323	47 902			57 151	59 446	62 916	67 00	72 039	77 208	6.1	50 999	57 151	25 323	47 902	50 9
2 640	5 143					7 801		7 709	7 838	5.4	5 645	6 816	2 640	5 143	5 6
3 409	6 652					284		8 755	8 380	2.9	6 739	6 860	3 409	6 652	6 7
693	1 716					007		1 539	762	-9.7	1 581	811	693	1 716	1 5
2 716	4 93							7 217	7 618	5.6	5 178	6 049	2 716	4 9	

1997

Population (persons)	3,910,366
Population rank	24th
Population growth rank (1990–97)	27th
Per capita personal income	$20,599
Unemployment rate (percent)	5.4
Poverty rate (percent)	15.9

KENTUCKY MAY BE BEST KNOWN FOR RAISING THOROUGHBRED horses and distilling bourbon whiskey, or, more prosaically, for mining coal and growing tobacco. But Toyota manufacturing and UPS parcel shipping have been the forces behind the state's economic growth during the 1990s. The state recovered more quickly from the early-90s recession than did the nation as a whole, and employment growth from 1989 to 1997 was above the national average. Led by the production of motor vehicles and equipment, employment in the manufacturing sector grew in Kentucky while it shrank nationwide. Despite strong manufacturing and transportation sectors, wages and salaries were below the national average, and the state's poverty rate was high.

Studies conducted at the University of Kentucky emphasize that a higher ratio of employment to population and a better-educated, better-paid work force will be needed in order to bring the incomes of the state's residents up to national averages.

Spurred by a 1989 Kentucky Supreme Court ruling, the state has instituted sweeping educational reforms. Between the 1988–89 and 1995-96 school years, per pupil expenditure rose more rapidly than in any other state, although it still had reached only 90 percent of the national average by the latter year. Kentucky also has achieved greater equality of spending among richer and poorer school districts within the state.

Average Annual Population Growth: 1990–97

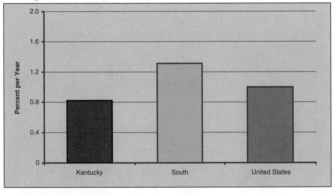

Median Household Income: 1989–97 (1997 dollars)

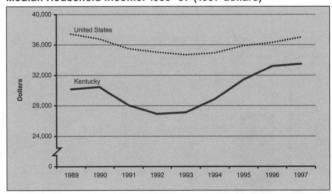

Unemployment Rate: 1989–97

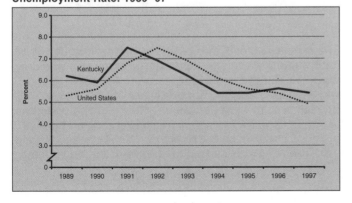

KENTUCKY'S UNEMPLOYMENT RATE ROSE SHARPLY AS RECESSION took hold in 1991. Then from 1991 to 1994 it came down rapidly, so that it was below the national rate from 1992 through 1994. After 1994, the state's rate stalled in the neighborhood of 5.5 percent, while the national rate continued to drop. However, with strong employment growth in 1997, the unemployment rate began to creep down again. Unemployment rates in the state's larger metropolitan areas were below the state average in 1997; the Lexington rate was only 2.7 percent, the Kentucky portion of the Louisville area was, 4.3 percent, and the Kentucky portion of the Cincinnati area was, 4.0 percent.

167

POPULATION AND LABOR FORCE

KENTUCKY'S POPULATION GREW A TOTAL OF 5.9 PERCENT FROM 1990 to 1997, somewhat more slowly than the national average. The Black and White non-Hispanic populations grew in line with the total. The Asian and Hispanic populations grew more rapidly but remained a tiny percentage of the state's total. Over one-half of the state's population growth came from natural increase (births minus deaths), and almost all the rest from migration from other states. Immigration from abroad accounted for about 5 percent.

The largest concentrations of the population are in the north-central triangle formed by Lexington, Louisville, and the Kentucky portion of the Cincinnati metropolitan area. Thirty-nine percent of the state's population lived in these three metropolitan areas in 1997. All or part of four additional metropolitan areas are within the state, but, even so, only 48 percent of the population lived in metropolitan areas in 1997, compared to 80 percent nationwide.

Labor force and employment growth from 1990 to 1997 exceeded growth of the working-age population, and the percentage of the population holding jobs rose, but, at 59.2 percent in 1997, remained below the national average (63.8 percent in 1997).

Population and Labor Force

	1980	1990	1991	1992	1993	1994	1995	1996	1997	Change* State	Change* U.S.
Population											
Total number of persons (thousands)	3 661	3 693	3 716	3 758	3 794	3 824	3 856	3 883	3 910	0.8	1.0
Percent distribution:											
White, Non-Hispanic	91.8	91.4	91.6	91.6	91.5	91.5	91.4	91.3	91.3	0.8	0.4
Black, Non-Hispanic	7.0	7.2	7.1	7.2	7.1	7.2	7.2	7.2	7.2	0.8	1.4
Asian	0.3	0.5	0.5	0.5	0.6	0.6	0.6	0.6	0.7	3.9	4.1
Native American	0.1	0.2	0.2	0.2	0.2	0.2	0.2	0.2	0.2	-0.8	1.6
Hispanic	0.7	0.7	0.6	0.6	0.7	0.7	0.7	0.7	0.8	2.3	3.8
In metropolitan areas	47.4	48.3	48.4	48.5	48.4	48.4	48.3	48.3	48.3	0.8	1.0
Total number of households (thousands)	1 263	1 380	1 397	1 418	1 430	1 437	1 457	1 478	NA	1.1	1.2
Labor Force (thousands)											
Population 16 and over	2 717	2 855	2 875	2 904	2 942	2 970	3 004	3 035	3 066	1.0	1.0
Civilian labor force	1 662	1 767	1 755	1 767	1 802	1 824	1 861	1 865	1 917	1.2	1.1
Employed	1 529	1 662	1 624	1 645	1 690	1 726	1 761	1 760	1 814	1.3	1.2
Percent of population	56.3	58.2	56.5	56.6	57.4	58.1	58.6	58.0	59.2		
Unemployment rate (percent)	8.0	5.9	7.5	6.9	6.2	5.4	5.4	5.6	5.4		

*Compound annual average percent change, 1990–1997; 1990–1996 for households.

Population Change and Components: 1990–97

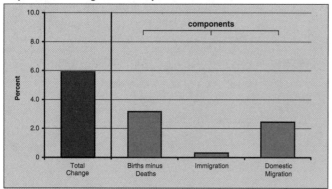

Average Annual Household and Population Growth

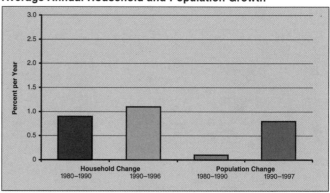

Population by Age; Births and Deaths

	1990 State	1990 U.S.	1997 State	1997 U.S.
Age distribution (percent)				
Under 5 years	6.8	7.6	6.6	7.2
5 to 17 years	18.8	18.2	18.0	18.8
18 to 64 years	61.8	61.8	62.9	61.3
65 years and over	12.6	12.5	12.5	12.7
Birth and death rates (per thousand population)				
Births	14.8	16.7	13.6	14.6
Deaths	9.5	8.6	9.8	8.6

THE PROPORTION OF KENTUCKY'S POPULATION UNDER AGE 18 fell by a full percentage point from 1990 to 1997, while the proportion of the population age 18 to 64 rose by a corresponding amount. The proportion age 65 and over was little changed. In 1997, the share of the state's population age 18 to 64 was above the national average, and the share of those under age 18 was below. The share age 65 and over also was below the national average, but only slightly.

HOUSEHOLD AND PERSONAL INCOME

HOUSEHOLD INCOME AND PERSONS IN POVERTY	1990	1995	1996	1997	
				State	U.S.
Median household income (1997 dollars)	30 430	31 394	33 157	33 452	37 005
Persons in poverty (thousands)	628	572	658	623	35 574
Poverty rate (percent)	17.3	14.7	17.0	15.9	13.3

KENTUCKY'S 1996–97 MEDIAN HOUSEHOLD INCOME, ADJUSTed for inflation, was 9 percent higher than in 1990. Thus, Kentucky gained on the national average, which showed no increase over this period. Kentucky's poverty rate has fluctuated from year-to-year, but, averaged over three-year spans, rose faster than the U.S. average in the early 1990s and came down faster in more recent years, narrowing the gap with the national average.

Maintaining the trend established during the 1980s, Kentucky's inflation-adjusted personal income per capita increased during the 1990s, but, unlike median household income, has not gained on the national average. An analysis conducted at the University of Kentucky concludes that catching up to the national average will require a better-educated, better-paid work force and/or an increase in the ratio of employment to population. At best, the catch-up process may take 20 years or more.

Earnings provided 65 percent of Kentucky's personal income in 1997, compared to 66 percent nationally. Dividends, interest, and rent were 15 percent, compared to 17 percent nationally. Transfer payments, however, were 20 percent, compared to only 16 percent nationally. This relatively high reliance on transfers reflects Kentucky's low average wages and relatively high poverty rate.

Government transfers rose 69 percent from 1990 to 1997. The largest increase was in "other income maintenance," a category consisting largely of the earned income tax credit, a benefit going to lower-wage workers and their families. Program expansion and employment growth in this relatively low-wage state help explain the increase. In contrast, family assistance payments actually declined slightly and food stamp payments grew very little.

Personal Income
(millions of dollars)

	1980	1989	1990	1991	1992	1993	1994	1995	1996	1997	Change*
Earnings by place of work	21 911	36 951	39 090	40 500	44 161	46 322	48 733	50 566	52 910	56 570	5.5
Wages and salaries	16 998	28 897	30 989	32 177	34 858	36 279	38 365	40 556	42 794	45 715	5.9
Other labor income	1 992	3 232	3 624	3 894	4 370	5 008	5 282	5 205	4 879	4 985	5.6
Proprietors' income	2 921	4 823	4 478	4 428	4 932	5 035	5 086	4 804	5 237	5 870	2.5
Farm	423	883	776	805	998	823	828	451	690	1 071	2.4
Nonfarm	2 498	3 940	3 702	3 623	3 934	4 212	4 259	4 354	4 547	4 799	2.5
(−) Personal contributions for social insurance	1 126	2 482	2 637	2 810	3 017	3 181	3 416	3 653	3 832	4 078	6.4
(+) Adjustment for residence	80	45	60	44	-130	-199	-291	-354	-441	-480	NA
(=) Net earnings by state of residence	20 864	34 515	36 514	37 733	41 014	42 942	45 026	46 559	48 637	52 012	5.3
(+) Dividends, interest, and rent	3 987	8 831	9 403	9 520	9 382	9 344	9 834	10 627	11 490	12 004	3.9
(+) Transfer payments	4 858	8 886	9 785	11 164	12 282	12 993	13 483	14 575	15 456	16 486	8.0
(=) Total personal income	29 709	52 231	55 702	58 417	62 678	65 279	68 343	71 761	75 584	80 503	5.6
Farm	570	1 042	960	983	1 169	1 011	1 008	637	883	1 264	2.4
Nonfarm	29 139	51 190	54 742	57 434	61 509	64 267	67 334	71 124	74 701	79 239	5.6
Personal income per capita (dollars)											
Current dollars	8 108	14 204	15 085	15 726	16 706	17 212	17 872	18 609	19 470	20 599	4.8
1997 dollars	15 503	17 957	18 153	18 159	18 687	18 729	18 993	19 344	19 827	20 599	1.7

*Compound annual average percent change, 1989–1997

Government Transfer Payments

	Millions of dollars		Percent change*	
	1990	1997	State	U.S.
Total government payments to individuals	9 358	15 833	69.2	62.7
Retirement, disability, and insurance	5 167	7 740	49.8	48.2
Social Security	3 701	5 501	48.7	46.1
Government employee retirement	1 004	1 697	69.0	60.3
Medical payments	2 547	5 658	122.2	101.2
Income maintenance	987	1 621	64.2	58.0
Supplemental Security Income	350	694	98.3	75.4
Family assistance	193	186	-3.6	-0.5
Food Stamps	345	362	4.9	27.1
Other income maintenance	99	379	281.3	189.8
Unemployment insurance benefits	214	249	16.4	10.6
Veterans benefits and other	443	564	27.4	30.8

*Percent change, 1990–1997

Government Payments to Individuals: 1997

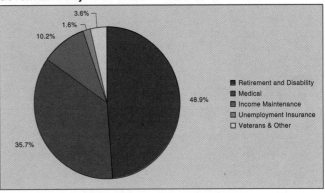

- Retirement and Disability
- Medical
- Income Maintenance
- Unemployment Insurance
- Veterans & Other

48.9%
35.7%
10.2%
1.6%
3.6%

ECONOMIC STRUCTURE

LEADING PRIVATE INDUSTRIES, 1997 (Worker and proprietor earnings, millions of dollars)		FASTEST EARNINGS GROWTH, 1989–97 (percent increase)	
Health services	$5 564	Air transportation	335.8
Construction specialties	2 161	Other transportation services	275.0
Business services	2 050	Motor vehicles and equipment	142.7
Motor vehicles and equipment	1 848	Business services	112.3
Eating and drinking places	1 433	General merchandise stores	85.7

AS IS THE CASE THROUGHOUT THE NATION, KENTUCKY NOW has a predominantly service-producing economy, with the service-producing sectors providing 72 percent of all jobs in 1997. Kentucky stands out among the states, however, for the strong growth of its manufacturing sector during the 1990s . Other notable aspects of the Kentucky economy are the relatively large share of its work force employed in farming, as well as the continuing decline of the traditionally important mining sector.

Kentucky's most rapidly growing industry from 1989 to 1997 was transportation by air, with worker and proprietor earnings increasing more than 300 percent. Important elements in its growth include expansion of United Parcel Service operations in Louisville, and expansion of air cargo operations at the Greater Cincinnati/Northern Kentucky airport.

The second-most rapidly growing industry was motor vehicle and equipment manufacturing, with the Toyota plant in Georgetown, and the facilities across the state that supply this plant, accounting for much of the growth. Sparked by motor vehicle and equipment manufacturing, Kentucky saw manufacturing employment grow by 1.4 percent per year from 1989 to 1997, a period during which U.S. manufacturing employment declined at an 0.4 percent rate. Virtually all of Kentucky's manufacturing job growth occurred between 1992 and 1997.

While manufacturing has been growing, mining has continued to decline. Although Kentucky still is one of the top three coal-producing states, employment in mining has declined from 3.5 percent of all jobs in 1980 to 2.1 percent in 1989 and only 1.2 percent in 1997. In absolute terms, the number of mining jobs fell by 32,000, or 55 percent, from 1980 to 1997.

Employment in farming also has declined during the 1990s, but still accounted for 5.2 percent of all employment in 1997, compared to a national average of only 1.9 percent.

Employment and Earnings by Sector

	1980	1989	1990	1991	1992	1993	1994	1995	1996	1997 Number	1997 Percent of total	Change*
Employment *(thousands of persons)*												
Total	1 646	1 877	1 915	1 916	1 964	2 005	2 049	2 103	2 136	2 189	100.0	1.9
Farm	137	127	125	119	122	119	112	114	110	114	5.2	-1.4
Nonfarm	1 509	1 750	1 789	1 797	1 842	1 886	1 937	1 989	2 026	2 075	94.8	2.2
Private nonfarm	1 232	1 453	1 489	1 493	1 527	1 569	1 618	1 666	1 703	1 748	79.9	2.3
Agricultural service, forestry, and fishing	9	18	19	20	20	21	22	23	24	25	1.2	4.5
Mining	58	39	40	36	34	32	32	29	26	26	1.2	-4.8
Construction	84	100	101	98	105	109	114	116	120	126	5.8	3.0
Manufacturing	283	291	293	288	293	302	314	323	321	326	14.9	1.4
Transportation and public utilities	82	91	95	95	94	97	104	106	110	114	5.2	2.9
Wholesale trade	66	76	76	77	80	78	80	85	87	88	4.0	1.9
Retail trade	248	321	325	325	334	344	358	371	380	388	17.7	2.4
Finance, insurance, and real estate	98	95	97	97	96	99	91	92	95	98	4.5	0.4
Services	303	423	443	456	472	488	503	521	540	556	25.4	3.5
Government	276	296	300	304	315	317	319	323	323	327	14.9	1.2
Earnings *(millions of dollars)*												
Total	21 911	36 951	39 090	40 500	44 161	46 322	48 733	50 566	52 910	56 570	100.0	5.5
Farm	570	1 042	960	983	1 169	1 011	1 008	637	883	1 264	2.2	2.4
Nonfarm	21 341	35 910	38 130	39 517	42 992	45 311	47 725	49 929	52 026	55 307	97.8	5.5
Private nonfarm	17 887	29 741	31 485	32 310	35 121	37 317	39 482	41 332	43 151	46 142	81.6	5.6
Agricultural service, forestry, and fishing	74	229	252	282	297	311	321	339	348	378	0.7	6.5
Mining	1 952	1 540	1 672	1 516	1 509	1 470	1 479	1 356	1 303	1 326	2.3	-1.9
Construction	1 383	2 182	2 204	2 165	2 426	2 646	2 844	2 888	3 119	3 391	6.0	5.7
Manufacturing	5 383	8 479	8 983	8 941	9 716	10 347	11 086	11 500	11 661	12 444	22.0	4.9
Transportation and public utilities	1 670	2 653	2 812	2 985	3 188	3 341	3 567	3 702	3 911	4 198	7.4	5.9
Wholesale trade	1 168	1 900	2 019	2 108	2 252	2 311	2 478	2 703	2 829	3 054	5.4	6.1
Retail trade	2 242	3 730	3 863	4 034	4 337	4 616	4 917	5 166	5 418	5 762	10.2	5.6
Finance, insurance, and real estate	866	1 634	1 742	1 810	2 050	2 326	2 320	2 465	2 645	2 845	5.0	7.2
Services	3 149	7 394	7 938	8 469	9 345	9 951	10 470	11 212	11 916	12 745	22.5	7.0
Government	3 454	6 169	6 645	7 207	7 870	7 993	8 243	8 596	8 875	9 164	16.2	5.1

*Compound annual average percent change, 1989–1997

ECONOMIC STRUCTURE (Continued)

THE $25,028 AVERAGE ANNUAL WAGE OR SALARY EARNED BY Kentucky workers in 1997 was 84 percent of the national average, and this percentage was unchanged from 1989. The Kentucky average also was low relative to the adjacent states of Tennessee, Virginia, Ohio, Illinois, and Indiana, although higher than that of West Virginia. The highest average earnings were in mining, but this sector employed only 1.2 percent of all workers in 1997. Among sectors employing larger numbers of workers, manufacturing and transportation and utilities provided the highest earnings. These earnings also were among those closest to the national average, reaching 88 and 91 percent, respectively. It is in the services sector, where Kentucky wages and salaries were only 80 percent of the national average, that Kentucky lags most seriously behind. This is the sector providing the largest number of jobs and the most rapid job growth, and thus the sector in which much of the transition to a better-paying job mix must be found if Kentucky is to reach its goal of approaching national average incomes.

Manufacturing contributed 28.1 percent of Kentucky gross state product (GSP) in 1996, far above the national average and second in the nation after Indiana. Manufacturing's share of Kentucky GSP dipped during the early-90s recession, but by 1996 had climbed back to the 1989 level. This contrasted with the national pattern of decline from an 18.9 percent share in 1989 to 17.5 percent in 1996. The value of manufacturing output per Kentucky worker was 20 percent above the U.S. average in 1996.

Kentucky's exports continued to boom in the mid-90s, with exports of goods growing 65 percent from 1994 to 1997, compared to 34 percent nationwide. This rapid growth continued a trend established in the late 1980s. The two leading export industries, transportation equipment (which includes motor vehicles and parts) and industrial machinery (which includes computers) accounted for 39 percent of all goods exports in 1997. Tobacco products rank third in leading exports, but have shown much less growth. Canada is the most important market for Kentucky exports, taking over one-third of all exports in 1997 and a far higher share of exports of motor vehicles. Asian countries purchased over one-quarter of Kentucky's total goods exports and about three-quarters of the state's exports of tobacco products.

Average Annual Wages and Salaries by Sector
(dollars)

	1989	1996	1997 State	1997 U.S.
All wage and salary workers	18 746	24 026	25 028	29 809
Farm	6 966	11 803	9 423	16 442
Nonfarm	18 912	24 133	25 194	29 900
Private nonfarm	18 875	23 959	25 144	29 867
Agricultural service, forestry, and fishing	13 469	16 074	16 981	17 941
Mining	33 020	40 186	41 130	49 800
Construction	20 278	25 492	26 854	31 765
Manufacturing	25 347	31 901	33 733	38 351
Transportation and utilities	26 966	33 315	34 669	38 222
Wholesale trade	22 938	30 127	32 039	39 466
Retail trade	10 467	13 507	14 118	16 206
Finance, insurance, and real estate	22 457	30 229	32 075	44 993
Services	15 453	21 059	21 982	27 588
Government	19 067	24 912	25 419	30 062

Gross State Product and Manufacturing
(millions of dollars, except as noted)

	1989	1994	1995	1996
Gross state product, total	64 785	86 059	90 617	95 410
Manufacturing:				
Millions of dollars	18 147	23 819	25 926	26 833
Percent of total gross state product	28.0	27.7	28.6	28.1
Per worker (dollars)	62 402	75 814	80 317	83 604
New capital expenditures, manufacturing	NA	2 410	2 489	3 076

Exports of Goods
(millions of dollars)

	1994	1995	1996	1997
All goods	4 188	5 030	5 824	6 904
Manufactures	4 052	4 811	5 582	6 664
Agricultural and livestock products	51	74	46	68
Other commodities	86	145	197	172
Top goods exports, 1997:				
Transportation equipment	879	959	1 134	1 544
Industrial machinery and computers	609	690	951	1 182
Tobacco products	809	968	862	869
Electric and electronic equipment	429	479	546	620
Apparel	61	170	312	496

HOUSING

Kentucky entered the 1990s with a new home production rate below the U.S. average, but home construction activity in the state suffered less than in the United States as a whole during the 1990–91 recession, so that, by 1991 the U.S. home production rate had fallen below that of Kentucky. From 1991 to 1997 both rates were generally on a rising trend, and the Kentucky rate remained above the national average. Manufactured housing (mobile homes) has accounted for about one-third of all new homes produced during the 1990s, compared to less than 20 percent nationwide.

Sales of existing homes also held up better in Kentucky than in the nation during the recession, but then leveled off during the mid-90s, although fluctuating year-to-year from 1992 to 1997. The median sales price of existing homes was $100,600 in the Lexington metropolitan area in 1997 and $96,800 in the Louisville area, compared to $124,100 nationally. With relatively favorable financing conditions and rising incomes and employment, the per-

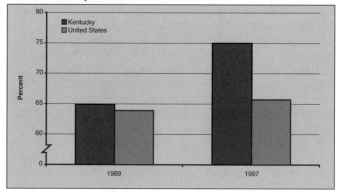

Homeownership Rates: 1989 and 1997

centage of Kentucky households owning their own homes rose from 65 percent in 1989 to 75 percent in 1997; nationwide, the corresponding figures were 64 percent in 1989 and 66 percent in 1997.

Housing Supply

	1989	1990	1991	1992	1993	1994	1995	1996	1997
Residential building permits (thousands)	12.7	11.8	12.0	14.7	15.9	18.6	17.6	18.8	18.1
New home production (including manufactured housing):									
Thousands of homes	19.1	17.6	18.2	22.7	23.7	27.9	29.0	29.2	27.3
Rate per 1,000 population									
Kentucky	5.2	4.8	4.9	6.1	6.2	7.3	7.5	7.5	7.0
U.S.	6.2	5.2	4.5	5.1	5.6	6.4	6.3	6.6	6.5
Existing home sales:									
Thousands of homes	62.2	66.4	67.8	78.7	83.3	81.1	78.2	78.8	81.1
Change from previous year (percent)									
Kentucky	2.1	6.8	2.1	16.1	5.8	-2.6	-3.6	0.8	2.9
U.S.	-3.9	-4.0	0.0	9.2	8.2	4.8	-3.7	7.5	3.8
Home ownership rate (percent of households)	64.9	65.8	67.2	69.0	68.8	70.6	71.2	73.2	75.0
Rental vacancy rate (percent of rental housing units)	7.2	5.8	7.6	8.7	8.5	7.6	5.1	5.8	9.4

AGRICULTURE

Kentucky agriculture is characterized by a large number of small farms; average farm size is only one-third the national average. Average sales per farm were also about one-third the national average in 1997. Only 7 percent of farms had sales above $100,000, accounting for 65 percent of sales. Farming was the principal occupation for only 41 percent of Kentucky's farm operators in 1997, compared to a national average of 50 percent.

Kentucky ranks second after North Carolina in the growing of tobacco, a crop requiring relatively small

acreage. Fifty-five percent of Kentucky farms sold tobacco in 1997, and the crop accounted for 27 percent of the value of all agricultural sales.

KENTUCKY FARMS, 1997	
Number of farms	88 000
Total acres (thousands):	13 900
Average per farm	158
Value of land and buildings (millions of dollars)	20 155
Average per farm (dollars)	229 034

Farm Income
(millions of dollars)

	1980	1989	1990	1991	1992	1993	1994	1995	1996	1997
Gross income	3 121	3 445	3 587	3 661	3 696	3 959	3 696	3 657	4 155	4 202
Receipts from sales	2 894	3 035	3 183	3 253	3 189	3 432	3 205	3 134	3 576	3 637
Government payments	10	118	82	73	72	97	55	67	75	83
Imputed and miscellaneous income	217	292	323	335	434	431	436	456	504	482
(–) Production expenses	2 437	2 661	2 813	2 854	2 874	2 978	2 939	3 047	3 232	3 313
(=) Realized net income	684	784	774	807	822	982	757	610	923	889
(+) Inventory change	-261	136	33	21	214	-147	122	-142	-192	240
(=) Net income	423	919	807	828	1 036	835	879	468	731	1 130
Corporate income	0	37	31	23	38	12	51	18	41	59
Farm proprietors income	423	883	776	805	998	823	828	451	690	1 071

EDUCATION

EDUCATIONAL ATTAINMENT Percent of population age 25 and over, 1997	State	United States
High school graduate or higher	75.4	82.1
College graduate or higher	17.6	23.9

RESPONDING TO THE KENTUCKY SUPREME COURT'S SWEEPING 1989 ruling that the state's entire school system was unconstitutional in its failure to provide adequate school funding and equal educational opportunity for all children, Kentucky has initiated comprehensive educational reform. The state's plan includes increased funding, correction of funding disparities between richer and poorer areas, and removal of political influence from the system. By 1995–96, Kentucky's per pupil expenditure for elementary and secondary schooling had reached 90 percent of the national average and, among southern states, was exceeded only by Florida and West Virginia. Kentucky's high school completion rate reached 75.4 percent in 1997, compared to 64.6 percent as recently as 1990. Yet, despite this marked improvement, it remains the lowest in the nation. The college completion rate of 17.6 percent is above that of several other South Central states, but is low by national standards.

High School Completion: 1990–97

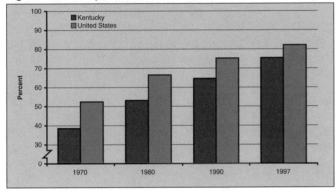

Education Indicators

	State	U.S.
Elementary and secondary schools		
Enrollment, 1995–96		
Total (thousands)	727	49 873
Percent in private schools	9.2	10.1
Expenditures per pupil (dollars), 1995–96	5 545	6 146
Average teacher salary (dollars), 1996–97	33 950	38 509
Higher education		
Enrollment, 1996–97		
Total (thousands)	178	14 218
Percent of population 18–34	18.4	21.8
Percent minority	9.5	26.1
Percent in private schools	17.1	22.6

HEALTH

KENTUCKY'S INFANT MORTALITY RATE APPEARS TO HAVE FALLEN slightly during the 1990s, but the improvement has not matched that of the nation as a whole. Thus, Kentucky's rate, which in 1990 was below the national average, was higher than the nation's in 1996 and 1997.

The state's overall death rate is above the national average. Adjusted for differences in the age distribution of the population, the rate of death from heart disease, the leading cause of death, was 16 percent above the national average in 1996, as was the rate for cancer. The rate for chronic obstructive pulmonary diseases (lung diseases) was 33 percent above the nation's. The death rate from injury by firearm, however, was about equal to the national average and was below that of any other southern state.

The percent of the state's population without health insurance has increased since 1990.

Health Indicators

	1990	1995	1996	1997
Infant mortality				
(rate per thousand live births)				
Kentucky	8.5	7.6	7.6	8.3
U.S.	9.2	7.6	7.3	7.1
Total deaths, age-adjusted rate				
(rate per thousand population)				
Kentucky	5.7	5.5	5.5	5.5
U.S.	5.2	5.0	4.9	4.8
Persons not covered by health insurance				
(percent of population)				
Kentucky	13.2	14.6	15.4	15.0
U.S.	13.9	15.4	15.6	16.1

Leading Causes of Death, 1996
(deaths per 100,000 population)

	Age-adjusted		Not age-adjusted	
	State	U.S.	State	U.S.
Deaths from all causes	547.0	491.6	959.7	872.5
Heart disease	155.7	134.5	306.7	276.4
Cancer	149.0	127.9	232.4	203.4
Cerebrovascular diseases	29.5	26.4	66.5	60.3
Chronic obstructive pulmonary disease	27.9	21.0	50.1	40.0
Diabetes mellitus	14.6	13.6	25.2	23.3
Pneumonia and influenza	13.4	12.8	33.9	31.6
HIV	3.5	11.1	3.6	11.7
Liver disease	6.9	7.5	8.9	9.4
Alzheimer's disease	3.3	2.7	9.8	8.1
Accidents and adverse effects	38.2	30.4	44.7	35.8
Motor vehicle accidents	20.5	16.2	20.8	16.5
Suicide	11.4	10.8	12.6	11.6
Homicide	6.0	8.5	6.0	7.9
Injury by firearm	13.1	12.9	14.0	12.8

GOVERNMENT

STATE AND LOCAL TAXES, 1995–96	State	U.S.
Per capita (dollars)	2 093	2 477
Percent of personal income	11.2	10.8

IN THE 1995–96 FISCAL YEAR, KENTUCKY'S PER CAPITA STATE and local taxes (excluding corporate income taxes) were 16 percent below the all-state average. However, because Kentucky incomes also are below the national average, taxes were a higher than average share of personal income, 11.2 percent in the state compared to the 10.8 percent national average.

Local taxes were only 24 percent of the state and local

State Government Finances, 1996–97

	Millions of dollars	Percent distribu- tion	Dollars per capita	
			State	U.S.
General revenue	12 431	100.0	3 181	3 049
Intergovernmental revenue	3 464	27.9	886	863
Taxes	6 819	54.9	1 745	1 660
General sales	1 883	15.1	482	551
Selective sales	1 311	10.5	336	257
License taxes	427	3.4	109	106
Individual income	2 205	17.7	564	542
Corporation net income	293	2.4	75	115
Other taxes	700	5.6	179	90
Other general revenue	2 148	17.3	550	526
General expenditure	11 634	100.0	2 977	2 951
Intergovernmental expenditure	2 918	25.1	747	989
Direct expenditure	8 716	74.9	2 230	1 962
General expenditure, by function:				
Education	4 398	37.8	1 125	1 033
Public welfare	3 207	27.6	821	761
Hospitals and health	751	6.5	192	237
Highways	1 091	9.4	279	225
Police protection and corrections	382	3.3	98	137
Natural resources, parks and recreation	321	2.8	82	63
Governmental administration	468	4.0	120	107
Interest on general debt	384	3.3	98	99
Other and unallocable	633	5.4	162	290
Debt at end of fiscal year	7 120	NA	1 822	1 706
Cash and security holdings	24 059	NA	6 156	6 683

Federal Spending within State

	Federal funds, fiscal 1997		
	Millions of dollars	Percent distribution	Percent of U.S. total*
Total within state	21 245	100.0	1.5
Payments to individuals	11 901	56.0	1.5
Retirement and disability	6 939	32.7	1.5
Medicare	2 895	13.6	1.4
Food stamps	375	1.8	1.9
Supplemental Security Income	693	3.3	2.6
Grants	3 829	18.0	1.5
Medicaid and other health	1 880	8.8	1.7
Nutrition and family welfare	670	3.2	1.4
Education	274	1.3	1.6
Housing and community development	149	0.7	1.3
Salaries and wages	2 273	10.7	1.4
Defense procurement contracts	1 139	5.4	1.0
Non-defense procurement contracts	1 615	7.6	2.2

*State population is 1.5 percent of the U.S. total.

total in 1995–96, compared to a 41 percent national average. With this relatively heavy reliance on state-level tax collection, state taxes per capita were $1,745 in 1996–97, or 5 percent above the all-state average. Sales taxes produced 47 percent of all state tax revenue in fiscal year 1996-97, individual income tax 32 percent, and corporate income taxes just 4 percent tax revenue. Each of these sources produced a somewhat lower percentage of total tax revenue than was the case for the all-state average. A higher than average proportion from "other" taxes made up the difference.

Total state-level general expenditure per capita in Kentucky was slightly above the all-state average in 1996-97. State spending on education was by far the largest functional category, and it was 9 percent higher than the all-state average. Total state and local expenditure per elementary and secondary school pupil increased 30 percent between the 1988–89 and 1995–96 school years, the most rapid increase of any state, and, ranked on per pupil expenditure, Kentucky moved from 45th in the nation in 1988–89 to 31st in 1995–96. Prompted by the 1989 Kentucky Supreme Court ruling, Kentucky also has moved toward substantially greater equality of per pupil expenditure among richer and poorer areas of the state.

Kentucky's 1.5 percent share of federal funds distributed to states and their residents in fiscal 1997 was just equal to the state's 1.5 percent share of the U.S. population. The totals for payments to individuals and for grants also were in line with the state's population. As is the case nationally, these two categories make up almost three-quarters of all federal payments within the state. Reflecting the state's relatively low household incomes, the shares of food stamp and Supplementary Security Income payments coming to state residents exceeded the state's population share. Defense procurement contracts were low relative to population but non-defense contract payments were high.

31 372	59 698		65 157	70 827	72 687	78 001	81 93	88 504	93 426	5.8	63 383	70 827	31 372	59 698	63 3
25 323	47 902		57 151	59 446	62 916	67 00	72 039	77 208	6.1	50 999	57 151	25 323	47 902	50 9	
2 640	5 143			7 801		7 709	7 838	5.4	5 645	6 816	2 640	5 143	5 6		
3 409	6 652			284		8 755	8 380	2.9	6 739	6 860	3 409	6 652	6 7		
693	1 716			07		1 539	762	-9.7	1 561	811	693	1 716	1 5		
2 716	4 9					7 217	7 618	5.6	5 178	6 049	2 716	4 9			

1997

Population (persons)	4,353,646
Population rank	22nd
Population growth rank (1990–97)	40th
Per capita personal income	$20,473
Unemployment rate (percent)	6.1
Poverty rate (percent)	16.3

LOUISIANA, AND PARTICULARLY NEW ORLEANS, WITH ITS HIS-toric attractions, jazz performances, and Mardi Gras festi-val, long has drawn tourists from around the world. The introduction of river boat casinos and the expansion of New Orleans' convention and tourist facilities have helped tourism become even bigger business for Louisiana in the last few years. Tourism, shipbuilding, and a halt to the decline in petroleum-related activity have brought growth of population and employment to Louisiana in the mid-90s, following stagnation in the 1980s.

Recent growth has been centered in the southern part of the state, particularly in the Baton Rouge, Lake Charles, and Lafayette metropolitan areas, while the Shreveport-Bossier City area in the northwest and the mid-state Alexandria area have had higher unemployment rates and slowly growing or declining populations. Coastal areas of Louisiana are expected to continue to benefit from tourism, from the introduction of new extraction technol-ogy for off-shore oil, and from a shipbuilding industry operating at essentially full capacity.

The more prosperous economy of the mid-90s brought gains in real median household incomes and a reduction in the state's poverty rate. The poverty rate remained far above the national average, however, and the high inci-dence of poverty is reflected in a high infant mortality rate and educational attainment rates below the U.S. average.

Average Annual Population Growth: 1990–97

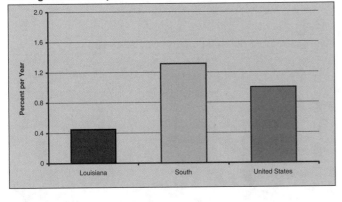

Median Household Income: 1989–97 (1997 dollars)

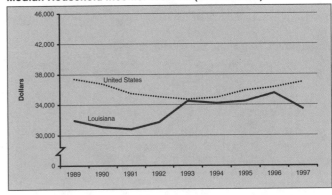

Unemployment Rate: 1989–97

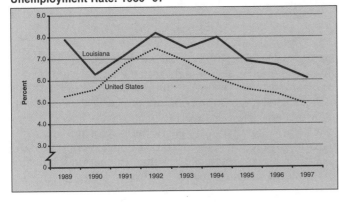

THE LOUISIANA UNEMPLOYMENT RATE REACHED A RECESSION-related peak of 8.2 percent in 1992, but good employment growth then brought the rate down to 6.1 percent by 1997. This rate was still well above the U.S. average of 4.9 per-cent, however.

At 5.5 percent, the 1997 unemployment rate in the New Orleans metropolitan area was below the state average, as was the 5.3 percent rate in the Baton Rouge area and the 3.5 percent rate in the nearby Houma area, but the rate in the Shreveport-Bossier area in the northwest corner of the state was a substantially higher 6.9 percent.

POPULATION AND LABOR FORCE

LOUISIANA'S POPULATION GREW 3.2 PERCENT FROM 1990 TO 1997. While this was a distinct increase relative to the 1980s, when the state's population grew scarcely at all, this level of growth remained pale relative to the 1970s, when the population grew 15.4 percent. Louisiana's population growth in the 1980s and 1990s has lagged behind that of the neighboring states of Arkansas, Mississippi, and Texas, as well as behind the national average.

Most of Louisiana's population growth during the 1990s has been in the southern part of the state, with the most rapid growth in the Baton Rouge, Lake Charles, and Lafayette metropolitan areas. The Shreveport-Bossier City area in the north has grown very little, and the population of the mid-state Alexandria area has declined.

Louisiana's White, non-Hispanic population declined slightly from 1990 to 1997. Each of the other population groups showed some growth, but none reached their national average rate of growth.

Natural increase (births minus deaths) added almost 5 percent to Louisiana's population from 1990 to 1997, and foreign immigration another 0.5 percent, but there was partly offsetting out-migration to other states equal to 2 percent of the 1990 population.

Population and Labor Force

	1980	1990	1991	1992	1993	1994	1995	1996	1997	Change* State	Change* U.S.
Population											
Total number of persons (thousands)	4 206	4 219	4 241	4 272	4 286	4 307	4 328	4 340	4 354	0.4	1.0
Percent distribution:											
White, Non-Hispanic	67.6	66.2	65.5	65.2	64.9	64.7	64.4	64.2	64.0	0.0	0.4
Black, Non-Hispanic	29.1	30.1	30.8	31.0	31.2	31.4	31.6	31.7	31.8	1.2	1.4
Asian	0.6	1.0	1.0	1.1	1.1	1.1	1.2	1.2	1.2	3.2	4.1
Native American	0.3	0.5	0.4	0.4	0.4	0.4	0.4	0.4	0.4	0.2	1.6
Hispanic	2.4	2.3	2.3	2.4	2.4	2.4	2.5	2.6	2.6	2.2	3.8
In metropolitan areas	74.3	74.9	74.9	75.0	75.1	75.1	75.1	75.1	75.2	0.5	1.0
Total number of households (thousands)	1 412	1 499	1 514	1 534	1 539	1 543	1 559	1 572	NA	0.8	1.2
Labor Force (thousands)											
Population 16 and over	3 044	3 136	3 148	3 174	3 194	3 216	3 238	3 276	3 309	0.8	1.0
Civilian labor force	1 788	1 837	1 915	1 935	1 888	1 941	1 953	1 998	2 014	1.3	1.1
Employed	1 667	1 721	1 777	1 777	1 746	1 785	1 818	1 863	1 891	1.4	1.2
Percent of population	54.8	54.9	56.5	56.0	54.7	55.5	56.2	56.9	57.1		
Unemployment rate (percent)	6.7	6.3	7.2	8.2	7.5	8.0	6.9	6.7	6.1		

*Compound annual average percent change, 1990–1997; 1990–1996 for households.

Population Change and Components: 1990–97

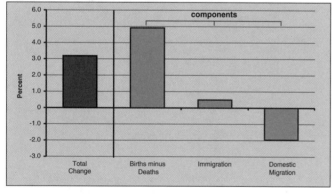

Average Annual Household and Population Growth

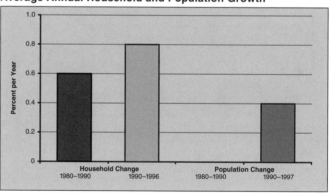

Population by Age; Births and Deaths

	1990 State	1990 U.S.	1997 State	1997 U.S.
Age distribution (percent)				
Under 5 years	7.9	7.6	7.2	7.2
5 to 17 years	20.7	18.2	20.2	18.8
18 to 64 years	60.2	61.8	61.2	61.3
65 years and over	11.1	12.5	11.4	12.7
Birth and death rates (per thousand population)				
Births	17.1	16.7	15.2	14.6
Deaths	8.9	8.6	9.2	8.6

LOUISIANA'S POPULATION IS RELATIVELY YOUNG, WITH THE proportion under age 18 higher than average and the proportion over age 64 lower than average. From 1990 to 1997, however, the proportion under age 18 declined, with a particularly large drop in the proportion under 5. There was a corresponding increase in the proportion age 18 to 64, bringing the state close to the national average in 1997. Louisiana's birth rate is higher than the nation's, but, like the national rate, declined from 1990 to 1997.

HOUSEHOLD AND PERSONAL INCOME

HOUSEHOLD INCOME AND PERSONS IN POVERTY	1990	1995	1996	1997 State	1997 U.S.
Median household income (1997 dollars)	27 513	29 434	30 956	33 260	37 005
Persons in poverty (thousands)	952	849	873	691	35 574
Poverty rate (percent)	23.6	19.7	20.5	16.3	13.3

LOUISIANA HAD EXTREMELY SLOW GROWTH OF EMPLOYMENT and earnings during the 1980s. The effects of this slump can be seen in the data on income and poverty. In 1980, real per capita personal income in Louisiana had been at 87 percent of the U.S. average; by 1989 it had fallen to only 75 percent. Similarly, the state's median household income averaged only 77 percent of the nation's in 1989–90, and the poverty rate was 23.6 percent in 1990.

During the early 1990s, it was U.S. average incomes (adjusted for inflation) that failed to grow, while Louisiana recovered some lost ground. By 1996–97, the state's median household income had risen to 88 percent of the national average, and the poverty rate, although still high, had come down to a 1996–97 average of 18.4 percent. Since 1994, real per capita personal income in Louisiana, growing at about the same rate as the national average, has hovered near 81 percent of the U.S. average.

Earnings provided 64 percent of Louisiana's personal income in 1997, compared to 66 percent nationwide. Dividends, interest, and rent were 15 percent, compared to 17 percent nationwide. Transfer payments, however, were 21 percent, compared to only 16 percent nationwide. This relatively high reliance on transfers reflects the state's low average wages and relatively high poverty rate.

Government transfers rose 67 percent from 1990 to 1997. The largest increase was in "other income maintenance," a category consisting largely of the earned income tax credit. Supplemental Security Income payments also showed a large rise, but, in contrast, family assistance payments actually declined by more than one-third and food stamp payments by 12 percent.

Personal Income
(millions of dollars)

	1980	1989	1990	1991	1992	1993	1994	1995	1996	1997	Change*
Earnings by place of work	28 998	40 351	43 563	46 039	48 528	50 372	53 022	55 870	58 167	61 552	5.4
Wages and salaries	23 662	31 918	34 502	36 419	38 171	39 333	41 654	44 124	46 181	49 383	5.6
Other labor income	2 532	3 545	4 028	4 414	4 683	5 100	5 221	5 346	5 262	5 331	5.2
Proprietors' income	2 805	4 889	5 033	5 206	5 674	5 940	6 147	6 400	6 724	6 838	4.3
Farm	60	264	184	254	297	281	367	407	535	346	3.4
Nonfarm	2 744	4 625	4 850	4 952	5 376	5 659	5 780	5 993	6 189	6 492	4.3
(−) Personal contributions for social insurance	1 459	2 518	2 714	2 914	3 012	3 147	3 406	3 647	3 811	4 066	6.2
(+) Adjustment for residence	-332	-137	-124	-132	-117	-136	-138	-144	-158	-176	NA
(=) Net earnings by state of residence	27 207	37 697	40 725	42 994	45 398	47 089	49 479	52 079	54 198	57 309	5.4
(+) Dividends, interest, and rent	4 943	9 897	10 299	10 259	9 962	10 216	10 811	11 506	12 466	12 952	3.4
(+) Transfer payments	4 932	10 331	11 309	12 882	14 611	16 119	17 602	17 913	18 452	18 833	7.8
(=) Total personal income	37 082	57 925	62 332	66 135	69 971	73 424	77 892	81 498	85 117	89 094	5.5
Farm	181	399	348	420	452	449	514	541	688	502	2.9
Nonfarm	36 901	57 526	61 984	65 715	69 519	72 975	77 378	80 957	84 428	88 593	5.5
Personal income per capita (dollars)											
Current dollars	8 781	13 620	14 774	15 594	16 381	17 135	18 085	18 828	19 608	20 473	5.2
1997 dollars	16 790	17 219	17 779	18 007	18 323	18 645	19 219	19 572	19 967	20 473	2.2

*Compound annual average percent change, 1989–1997

Government Transfer Payments

	Millions of dollars 1990	Millions of dollars 1997	Percent change* State	Percent change* U.S.
Total government payments to individuals	10 850	18 133	67.1	62.7
Retirement, disability, and insurance	5 436	7 892	45.2	48.2
Social Security	3 777	5 333	41.2	46.1
Government employee retirement	1 521	2 386	56.8	60.3
Medical payments	3 462	7 432	114.7	101.2
Income maintenance	1 302	2 048	57.3	58.0
Supplemental Security Income	377	725	92.2	75.4
Family assistance	196	126	-35.7	-0.5
Food Stamps	562	496	-11.7	27.1
Other income maintenance	166	700	321.2	189.8
Unemployment insurance benefits	135	134	-0.8	10.6
Veterans benefits and other	515	628	21.8	30.8

*Percent change, 1990–1997

Government Payments to Individuals: 1997

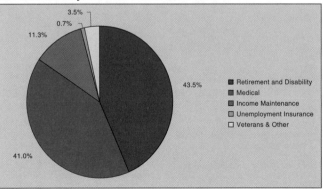

- ■ Retirement and Disability
- ■ Medical
- ■ Income Maintenance
- ☐ Unemployment Insurance
- ☐ Veterans & Other

ECONOMIC STRUCTURE

LEADING PRIVATE INDUSTRIES, 1997 (Worker and proprietor earnings, millions of dollars)		FASTEST EARNINGS GROWTH, 1989–97 (percent increase)	
Health services	$5 898	Amusement and recreation services	402.8
Oil and gas extraction	3 055	Industrial machinery manufacturing	126.5
Business services	2 497	Engineering and management services	77.5
Chemicals and allied products	2 288	Construction specialties	76.9
Construction specialties	2 229	Heavy construction contractors	76.6

AS IS THE CASE THROUGHOUT THE NATION, LOUISIANA NOW has a predominantly service-producing economy, with the service-producing sectors providing 79 percent of all jobs in 1997. The manufacturing sector, though highly productive, accounted for only 8.7 percent of 1997 employment, compared to 12.4 percent nationally. Distinctive features of the Louisiana economy include the dramatic expansion of amusement and recreation services during the 1990s, the importance of the shipbuilding industry, and the continued, although diminished, importance of oil and gas related industries.

The mining sector, which includes oil and gas extraction, accounted for 2.7 percent of employment in 1997, but this does not measure the total contribution of oil and gas to the economy. When petroleum-related employment in oil refining, pipelines, and chemicals is added to that in oil and gas production, jobs in this group of activities totaled some 87,000 in 1995. This total was far below a short-lived peak of 145,000 in 1982, however. Employment in these industries declined rapidly in the 1980s, then more slowly in the early 1990s, and seems to have leveled-out or begun to grow again in the mid-90s.

Shipbuilding has been among the important manufacturing industries in coastal Louisiana, and growth in this industry has created what a recent analysis refers to as "a critical shortage" of skilled workers. One New Orleans shipyard has addressed this problem by building a worker training center.

New Orleans long has been a major tourist destination, but the introduction of riverboat casinos in the 1990s has produced explosive growth in the amusement and recreation services industry, which was by far the most rapidly growing Louisiana industry from 1989 to 1997. Cruise ship tourism to New Orleans also is growing, thanks to expansion of the cruise ship terminal, and the expansion of the city's convention center has sparked a hotel building boom in the city. Concern now is being expressed, however, that tourism will suffer if improvements are not made to New Orleans' airport to keep pace with the expanding hotel and convention facilities.

Employment and Earnings by Sector

	1980	1989	1990	1991	1992	1993	1994	1995	1996	1997 Number	1997 Percent of total	Change*
Employment *(thousands of persons)*												
Total	1 968	1 967	2 018	2 047	2 058	2 105	2 148	2 204	2 248	2 296	100.0	2.0
Farm	58	47	44	42	41	40	37	37	37	37	1.6	-2.7
Nonfarm	1 910	1 921	1 973	2 005	2 017	2 065	2 111	2 167	2 211	2 259	98.4	2.0
Private nonfarm	1 561	1 551	1 594	1 621	1 626	1 675	1 715	1 766	1 811	1 859	81.0	2.3
Agricultural service, forestry, and fishing	14	21	21	22	21	24	24	24	26	27	1.2	3.3
Mining	101	67	68	68	58	57	59	57	58	62	2.7	-1.0
Construction	163	111	121	127	130	133	139	143	151	156	6.8	4.3
Manufacturing	218	183	189	193	192	193	195	195	196	199	8.7	1.1
Transportation and public utilities	134	119	123	122	117	121	124	122	125	128	5.6	1.0
Wholesale trade	106	91	90	93	94	92	94	98	98	101	4.4	1.4
Retail trade	301	328	329	332	339	351	363	377	387	394	17.2	2.3
Finance, insurance, and real estate	124	121	119	117	113	119	111	114	117	122	5.3	0.1
Services	401	511	533	546	562	585	606	637	654	670	29.2	3.5
Government	349	370	379	385	391	390	396	400	400	400	17.4	1.0
Earnings *(millions of dollars)*												
Total	28 998	40 351	43 563	46 039	48 528	50 372	53 022	55 870	58 167	61 552	100.0	5.4
Farm	181	399	348	420	452	449	514	541	688	502	0.8	2.9
Nonfarm	28 817	39 952	43 215	45 619	48 076	49 924	52 508	55 329	57 479	61 050	99.2	5.4
Private nonfarm	24 516	32 866	35 466	37 276	39 225	40 814	43 089	45 477	47 495	50 645	82.3	5.6
Agricultural service, forestry, and fishing	131	219	254	269	271	286	291	289	290	308	0.5	4.3
Mining	2 407	2 223	2 414	2 586	2 344	2 403	2 373	2 528	2 782	3 202	5.2	4.7
Construction	3 168	2 642	2 956	3 143	3 315	3 400	3 660	3 838	4 244	4 523	7.3	7.0
Manufacturing	4 803	5 853	6 334	6 704	7 044	7 243	7 713	7 927	8 113	8 564	13.9	4.9
Transportation and public utilities	2 788	3 482	3 693	3 893	3 984	4 156	4 319	4 417	4 526	4 832	7.8	4.2
Wholesale trade	2 029	2 360	2 486	2 627	2 738	2 777	2 928	3 119	3 231	3 472	5.6	4.9
Retail trade	2 928	3 958	4 111	4 280	4 503	4 714	4 997	5 328	5 503	5 764	9.4	4.8
Finance, insurance, and real estate	1 280	2 043	2 128	2 204	2 404	2 628	2 716	2 913	3 049	3 257	5.3	6.0
Services	4 981	10 085	11 090	11 570	12 621	13 207	14 092	15 119	15 757	16 724	27.2	6.5
Government	4 301	7 087	7 749	8 343	8 851	9 109	9 419	9 852	9 984	10 405	16.9	4.9

*Compound annual average percent change, 1989–1997

ECONOMIC STRUCTURE (Continued)

IN 1980, THE AVERAGE ANNUAL WAGE OR SALARY EARNED BY Louisiana workers was 98 percent of the U.S. average. By 1997, this ratio had fallen to 84 percent. This widened gap with the U.S. average is explained in part by the diminished share of petroleum-related employment in the state's overall jobs picture and the increased share of employment in services. The petroleum-related industries of oil and gas extraction, petroleum refining, and chemicals manufacturing each are relatively well-paid, a fact reflected in 1997 Louisiana wages and salaries in mining and manufacturing that were 96 percent of the U.S. average. In contrast, the state's average wages and salaries in services were only 81 percent of the nation's, with one factor in this gap being the state's relatively large concentration of workers in low-wage tourist-related service industries.

Although employment in manufacturing was only 8.7 percent of all Louisiana employment in 1996, manufacturing accounted for 19 percent of that year's gross state product (GSP). The 1996 GSP share was about equal to 1989, but represented a recovery from a lower share in 1992 through 1994. Manufacturing value per worker in the state was about two-thirds higher than the national average, reflecting the high value-added per worker that typifies petroleum refining and chemicals manufacturing, two of Louisiana's more important manufacturing industries. New capital expenditures in manufacturing were strong in the mid-90s, particularly in 1992 and 1996. Further expansion of facilities for producing chemicals and plastics is planned or underway by Exxon, Shell Chemical, and Marathon Oil, indicating good future growth prospects for these high-value industries.

Agricultural products show up as Louisiana's top goods exports, but, in fact, many of these agricultural exports actually are produced in the Midwest, with sales and shipping handled in Louisiana's port cities. Among export goods actually produced in Louisiana, chemicals are the most important. Louisiana's goods exports grew considerably more slowly than the national average from 1994 through 1997. In contrast, shipping activity at Louisiana's ports was strong. The state is a major gateway for U.S. exports of grains, food, petrochemicals, and forest products, and imports are also big business. Inbound cargoes of its leading import commodities—steel, copper, and coffee—showed double-digit increases in 1997.

Average Annual Wages and Salaries by Sector
(dollars)

	1989	1996	1997 State	1997 U.S.
All wage and salary workers	19 060	23 881	25 013	29 809
Farm	10 374	13 400	12 502	16 442
Nonfarm	19 123	23 938	25 085	29 900
Private nonfarm	19 607	24 336	25 498	29 867
Agricultural service, forestry, and fishing	13 267	16 546	17 079	17 941
Mining	33 832	44 435	47 694	49 800
Construction	21 783	26 741	27 966	31 765
Manufacturing	27 459	35 012	36 703	38 351
Transportation and utilities	26 687	33 088	34 584	38 222
Wholesale trade	24 021	30 563	31 855	39 466
Retail trade	10 947	13 447	13 918	16 206
Finance, insurance, and real estate	21 500	29 517	30 928	44 993
Services	16 927	21 547	22 468	27 588
Government	17 434	22 426	23 472	30 062

Gross State Product and Manufacturing
(millions of dollars, except as noted)

	1989	1994	1995	1996
Gross state product, total	83 679	103 880	112 944	121 143
Manufacturing:				
Millions of dollars	16 156	17 322	22 733	22 989
Percent of total gross state product	19.3	16.7	20.1	19.0
Per worker (dollars)	88 526	88 826	116 364	117 538
New capital expenditures, manufacturing	NA	2 646	3 008	3 267

Exports of Goods
(millions of dollars)

	1994	1995	1996	1997
All goods	3 577	4 581	4 731	4 373
Manufactures	2 465	2 953	2 614	2 731
Agricultural and livestock products	1 028	1 509	2 003	1 511
Other commodities	85	119	115	132
Top goods exports, 1997:				
Agricultural products	1 023	1 501	1 993	1 497
Chemical products	643	827	813	839
Industrial machinery and computers	499	467	480	520
Food products	459	559	345	361
Primary metals	73	181	88	152

HOUSING

IN 1989 AND 1990, A PERIOD OF ECONOMIC DIFFICULTY IN Louisiana, the state's new home production rate was quite low, scarcely one-third of the U.S. per capita average, and, in another indicator of hard times, the rental vacancy rate was over 13 percent. As economic conditions began to improve after 1991, the home production rate rose fairly steadily through 1996, although it did not quite catch up to the U.S. average, and the rental vacancy rate dropped to more normal levels. Sales of existing homes also have risen during the 1990s, albeit at an irregular pace. The median sales price of existing homes was $93,300 in the New Orleans metropolitan area in 1997, $92,300 in the Baton Rouge area, and only $78,200 in the Shreveport area, compared with a national average of $124,000.

Manufactured housing (mobile homes) has accounted for 30 percent or more of all new homes each year from 1993 to 1997, compared to less than 20 percent nationwide.

Homeownership Rates: 1989 and 1997

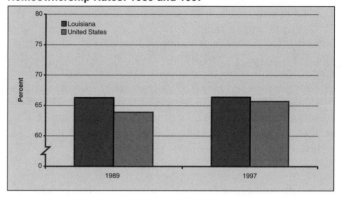

The percent of Louisiana households who own their own homes has not changed much during the 1990s and was slightly above the national average in 1997.

Housing Supply

	1989	1990	1991	1992	1993	1994	1995	1996	1997
Residential building permits (thousands)	6.1	6.5	7.2	9.8	11.2	14.8	14.7	18.0	15.1
New home production (including manufactured housing):									
Thousands of homes	7.4	8.1	8.8	13.0	15.9	21.2	23.8	26.2	23.6
Rate per 1,000 population									
Louisiana	1.7	1.9	2.1	3.0	3.7	4.9	5.5	6.0	5.4
U.S.	6.2	5.2	4.5	5.1	5.6	6.4	6.3	6.6	6.5
Existing home sales:									
Thousands of homes	40.8	41.6	47.1	47.0	49.3	51.4	50.4	50.9	52.9
Change from previous year (percent)									
Louisiana	2.5	2.0	13.2	-0.2	4.9	4.3	-1.9	1.0	3.9
U.S.	-3.9	-4.0	0.0	9.2	8.2	4.8	-3.7	7.5	3.8
Home ownership rate (percent of households)	66.3	67.8	68.9	66.7	65.4	65.8	65.3	64.9	66.4
Rental vacancy rate (percent of rental housing units)	13.2	13.1	9.5	7.8	7.2	9.4	9.6	7.8	8.4

AGRICULTURE

COTTON AND COTTONSEED ARE LOUISIANA'S MOST IMPORTANT agricultural products, accounting for 16 percent of all 1997 sales. However, this was down from 22 percent in 1992, and the number of farms marketing cotton fell by 39 percent over the five years. Other major farm products are soybeans (12 percent of 1997 sales) and poultry and poultry products (14 percent).

Farming was the principal occupation for 47 percent of Louisiana's farm operators in 1997, not far from the national average of 50 percent. Forty percent of farms had

sales above $10,000; these farms accounted for 98 percent of all sales.

LOUISIANA FARMS, 1997

Number of farms	26 500
Total acres (thousands):	8 500
Average per farm	321
Value of land and buildings (millions of dollars)	10 455
Average per farm (dollars)	394 528

Farm Income
(millions of dollars)

	1980	1989	1990	1991	1992	1993	1994	1995	1996	1997
Gross income	1 792	2 298	2 259	1 962	2 341	2 427	2 411	2 397	2 675	2 526
Receipts from sales	1 642	1 874	1 948	1 620	1 930	1 908	2 079	2 066	2 316	2 189
Government payments	20	250	155	175	271	367	181	164	199	157
Imputed and miscellaneous income	130	174	157	168	140	152	151	166	160	180
(−) Production expenses	1 668	1 866	1 989	2 000	1 944	2 025	2 069	1 964	2 147	2 101
(=) Realized net income	124	432	271	-38	397	402	342	433	528	425
(+) Inventory change	-64	-148	-72	308	-74	-112	77	10	80	-36
(=) Net income	60	284	198	269	323	291	419	443	608	389
Corporate income	0	20	14	15	26	9	52	36	74	43
Farm proprietors income	60	264	184	254	297	281	367	407	535	346

EDUCATION

EDUCATIONAL ATTAINMENT Percent of population age 25 and over, 1997	State	United States
High school graduate or higher	75.7	82.1
College graduate or higher	18.1	23.9

THE PERCENT OF LOUISIANA RESIDENTS AGE 25 AND OVER who had completed high school rose from 42.3 percent in 1970 to 68.3 percent in 1990 and 75.7 percent in 1997. Despite these gains, the state's 1997 high school completion rate still was the second lowest of any state. The state's college completion rate doubled from 1970 to 1997. Like a number of other states, Louisiana is attempting to improve educational quality by introducing rigorous statewide testing requirements and standards for holding schools accountable for student achievement.

In contrast to other southern states, a fairly high percentage of Louisiana's elementary and secondary students, 15.6 percent compared to 10.1 percent nationwide, attended private schools in 1995–96. The percentage of higher education students attending private schools was substantially below the national average, however. The minority share of higher education enrollment was higher than the national average, but somewhat below the 36 percent minority share of Louisiana's total population.

High School Completion: 1990–97

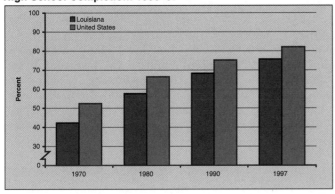

Education Indicators

	State	U.S.
Elementary and secondary schools		
Enrollment, 1995–96		
Total (thousands)	945	49 873
Percent in private schools	15.6	10.1
Expenditures per pupil (dollars), 1995–96	4 988	6 146
Average teacher salary (dollars), 1996–97	28 347	38 509
Higher education		
Enrollment, 1996–97		
Total (thousands)	204	14 218
Percent of population 18–34	18.8	21.8
Percent minority	32.6	26.1
Percent in private schools	14.2	22.6

HEALTH

AN ANALYSIS BY THE LOUISIANA OFFICE OF PUBLIC HEALTH ranked the state 48th in the nation on a set of health indicators, and placed much of the blame on a lack of access to routine and preventive healthcare, which, in turn, is a result of the state's high poverty rate and inadequate number of health care providers.

Louisiana had an unusually high percentage of the population who are not covered by health insurance and an infant mortality rate that, remained well above the national average in 1997.

Adjusted for differences in the age distribution of the population, death rates from heart disease and cancer were high by national standards. The 1996 rate for diabetes was 75 percent above the national average and that from injury by firearm almost twice the national average.

Health Indicators

	1990	1995	1996	1997
Infant mortality				
(rate per thousand live births)				
Louisiana	11.1	9.8	8.4	9.1
U.S.	9.2	7.6	7.3	7.1
Total deaths, age-adjusted rate				
(rate per thousand population)				
Louisiana	6.2	6.0	5.9	5.8
U.S.	5.2	5.0	4.9	4.8
Persons not covered by health insurance				
(percent of population)				
Louisiana	19.7	20.5	20.9	19.5
U.S.	13.9	15.4	15.6	16.1

Leading Causes of Death, 1996
(deaths per 100,000 population)

	Age-adjusted		Not age-adjusted	
	State	U.S.	State	U.S.
Deaths from all causes	587.8	491.6	909.9	872.5
Heart disease	154.6	134.5	270.4	276.4
Cancer	148.5	127.9	214.1	203.4
Cerebrovascular diseases	31.7	26.4	59.2	60.3
Chronic obstructive pulmonary disease	19.9	21.0	33.1	40.0
Diabetes mellitus	23.8	13.6	37.3	23.3
Pneumonia and influenza	11.4	12.8	24.0	31.6
HIV	13.7	11.1	13.8	11.7
Liver disease	7.1	7.5	8.5	9.4
Alzheimer's disease	3.7	2.7	9.4	8.1
Accidents and adverse effects	37.7	30.4	41.7	35.8
Motor vehicle accidents	20.9	16.2	20.9	16.5
Suicide	11.9	10.8	12.2	11.6
Homicide	19.5	8.5	18.3	7.9
Injury by firearm	25.2	12.9	24.2	12.8

GOVERNMENT

STATE AND LOCAL TAXES, 1995–96	State	U.S.
Per capita (dollars)	1 870	2 477
Percent of personal income	9.9	10.8

IN THE 1995–96 FISCAL YEAR, LOUISIANA'S STATE AND LOCAL taxes (excluding corporate income taxes) were $1,870 per capita, or only 75 percent of the all-state average. Louisiana personal incomes also were below the average, so that, measured as a percent of personal income, taxes came closer to the all-state average. Even so, state and local taxes were only 9.9 percent of personal income, compared to a 10.8 percent national average. In

Louisiana, 44 percent of state and local taxes were collected at the local level, a little higher share than the 41 percent national average.

At the state level, Louisiana total general revenue per capita in 1997 was 2 percent higher than the all-state average; taxes, however, were 22 percent lower. Much of the difference is explained by Louisiana's large per capita receipts of "other general revenue," a category that includes royalties paid for oil and gas rights. It is this royalty income that helps Louisiana keep its taxes relatively low. Individual income taxes per capita were one-third below the all state average in 1997, and general and selective sales taxes were about 22 percent lower.

Total state-level general expenditure per capita was within 1 percent of the all-state average in 1996–97. Education was the largest functional spending category, and the state's per capita spending was 1 percent above the average for all states. These figures are for state government spending only; local spending on education would appear to be well below the national average, since total per-pupil expenditure in elementary and secondary schools was only 81 percent of the national average in 1995–96.

Louisiana's general debt averaged $1,615 per capita in 1996-97, or 95 percent as high as the national average of $1,706. Interest on this debt, however, was $125 per capita, or 26 percent higher than the national average of $99. Cash and security holdings at year end were almost 4 times as large as the general debt, a ratio roughly equal to the all-state average.

Louisiana's 1.7 percent share of federal funds distributed to states and their residents in fiscal 1997 was slightly above the state's 1.6 percent share of the U.S. population. Reflecting the state's relatively low household incomes and high poverty rate, several individual categories of payments, including food stamps, Supplemental Security Income, and Medicaid and other health-related grants, were particularly high relative to the state's population share. Medicare spending also was high despite a lower-than-average population age 65 and over. Shares of federal salaries and wages and defense and non-defense procurement contracts were somewhat low relative to the state's population share.

State Government Finances, 1996–97

	Millions of dollars	Percent distribu-tion	Dollars per capita State	Dollars per capita U.S.
General revenue	13 529	100.0	3 109	3 049
Intergovernmental revenue	4 329	32.0	995	863
Taxes	5 646	41.7	1 297	1 660
General sales	1 828	13.5	420	551
Selective sales	931	6.9	214	257
License taxes	436	3.2	100	106
Individual income	1 560	11.5	358	542
Corporation net income	380	2.8	87	115
Other taxes	511	3.8	118	90
Other general revenue	3 554	26.3	817	526
General expenditure	12 790	100.0	2 939	2 951
Intergovernmental expenditure	3 171	24.8	729	989
Direct expenditure	9 619	75.2	2 210	1 962
General expenditure, by function:				
Education	4 558	35.6	1 047	1 033
Public welfare	2 960	23.1	680	761
Hospitals and health	1 459	11.4	335	237
Highways	850	6.6	195	225
Police protection and corrections	609	4.8	140	137
Natural resources, parks and recreation	503	3.9	116	63
Governmental administration	483	3.8	111	107
Interest on general debt	544	4.3	125	99
Other and unallocable	824	6.4	189	290
Debt at end of fiscal year	7 030	NA	1 615	1 706
Cash and security holdings	26 722	NA	6 140	6 683

Federal Spending within State

	Federal funds, fiscal 1997 Millions of dollars	Federal funds, fiscal 1997 Percent distribution	Federal funds, fiscal 1997 Percent of U.S. total*
Total within state	23 451	100.0	1.7
Payments to individuals	13 354	56.9	1.7
Retirement and disability	6 686	28.5	1.5
Medicare	4 069	17.4	2.0
Food stamps	512	2.2	2.6
Supplemental Security Income	760	3.2	2.8
Grants	4 911	20.9	2.0
Medicaid and other health	2 795	11.9	2.5
Nutrition and family welfare	819	3.5	1.8
Education	357	1.5	2.1
Housing and community development	211	0.9	1.9
Salaries and wages	2 066	8.8	1.3
Defense procurement contracts	1 743	7.4	1.5
Non-defense procurement contracts	1 034	4.4	1.4

*State population is 1.6 percent of the U.S. total.

31 372	59 698		65 157	70 827	72 687	78 001	81 93	88 504	93 426	5.8	63 383	70 827	31 372	59 698	63 38
25 323	47 902		57 151	59 446	62 916	67 00		72 039	77 208	6.1	50 999	57 151	25 323	47 902	50 9
2 640	5 143			7 801				7 709	7 838	5.4	5 645	6 816	2 640	5 143	5 6
3 409	6 652		284					8 755	8 380	2.9	6 739	6 860	3 409	6 652	6 7
693	1 718		07					1 539	762	-9.7	1 561	811	693	1 716	1 5
716	4							7 217	7 618	5.6	5 178	6 049			

1997

Population (persons)	1,241,895
Population rank	39th
Population growth rank (1990–97)	46th
Per capita personal income	$21,928
Unemployment rate (percent)	5.4
Poverty rate (percent)	10.1

THE RECESSION OF THE EARLY 1990S LINGERED LONGER IN Maine than in the rest of the country, and as of 1997 its unemployment rate, which had been well below the U.S. average in 1989, was still somewhat above the U.S. rate. Median household incomes in real terms, already below the U.S. average in 1989, dropped 10 percent from 1989 to 1991. Household income recovery has been erratic, and as of 1997 the income of the median household was only 89 percent of the national average. Manufacturing employment fell faster than in any other sector from 1989 to 1997, but services and retail trade employment rose.

Manufacturing earnings grew over the period, though not as fast as service earnings did.

Population growth was almost stagnant throughout the decade, with domestic out-migration almost canceling out gains from births less deaths. A rural state (only around 40 percent of the population lived in a metropolitan county), Maine also had a relatively large percentage of people 65 and older. As in other states with large older populations, the fastest growing (and largest) transfer payment category was medical payments. The 1997 poverty rate was high for the region but has remained lower than the U.S. average.

Average Annual Population Growth: 1990–97

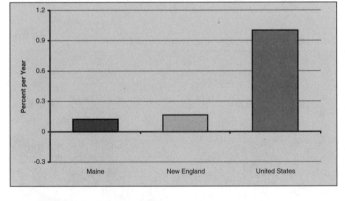

Median Household Income: 1989–97 (1997 dollars)

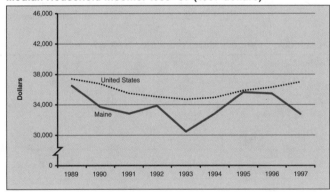

Unemployment Rate: 1989–97

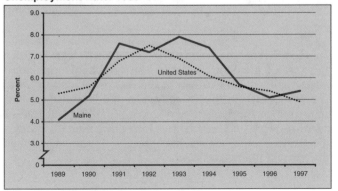

UNEMPLOYMENT IN MAINE ENDED THE 1980S AT A LOW 4.1 percent but in the years 1991–94 was above the national average. In 1995–97, the rate fell back to near the U.S. average. The labor force decreased as employment fell in 1993 and hit a decade low point in 1994. Employment also fell in 1997, but a corresponding labor force drop prevented the unemployment rate from rising more than a few tenths of a point.

POPULATION AND LABOR FORCE

MAINE'S POPULATION GREW FAR SLOWER, AT 0.1 PERCENT PER year during the period 1990 to 1997, than the population of New England or the United States as a whole. With a predominately White population (97.7 percent in 1997), the faster growth in the small Asian populations did not appreciably alter total population growth. The Black population in the state fell sharply, but from a very small base. Only 39.9 percent of Mainers live in metropolitan coun-

ties, which makes Maine the least metropolitan state in New England, except for Vermont, and the seventh least metropolitan state in the United States. The population 16 and over grew steadily between 1990 and 1997, but the civilian labor force was more irregular, hitting peaks in 1992 and 1996, years of strong employment growth. The unemployment rate rose in the early 1990s, reaching a high point in 1993 of 7.9 percent.

Population and Labor Force

| | 1980 | 1990 | 1991 | 1992 | 1993 | 1994 | 1995 | 1996 | 1997 | Change* | |
										State	U.S.
Population											
Total number of persons (thousands)	1 125	1 231	1 235	1 234	1 236	1 235	1 233	1 238	1 242	0.1	1.0
Percent distribution:											
White, Non-Hispanic	98.6	97.5	98.0	97.9	97.9	97.9	97.9	97.8	97.7	0.2	0.4
Black, Non-Hispanic	0.3	0.8	0.4	0.4	0.4	0.4	0.4	0.4	0.5	-7.2	1.4
Asian	0.3	0.6	0.6	0.6	0.6	0.6	0.6	0.7	0.7	2.1	4.1
Native American	0.4	0.5	0.5	0.5	0.5	0.5	0.5	0.4	0.5	-0.9	1.6
Hispanic	0.5	0.7	0.6	0.6	0.6	0.6	0.6	0.7	0.7	0.0	3.8
In metropolitan areas	36.0	40.3	40.1	40.0	40.0	40.2	40.1	40.0	39.9	0.0	1.0
Total number of households (thousands)	395	465	470	474	474	473	477	483	NA	0.6	1.2
Labor Force (thousands)											
Population 16 and over	846	957	960	961	964	965	967	975	981	0.3	1.0
Civilian labor force	507	635	642	650	632	614	640	666	659	0.5	1.1
Employed	468	602	593	604	582	569	603	632	624	0.5	1.2
Percent of population	55.3	62.9	61.8	62.8	60.4	59.0	62.4	64.8	63.6		
Unemployment rate (percent)	7.8	5.2	7.6	7.2	7.9	7.4	5.7	5.1	5.4		

*Compound annual average percent change, 1990–1997; 1990–1996 for households.

Population Change and Components: 1990–97

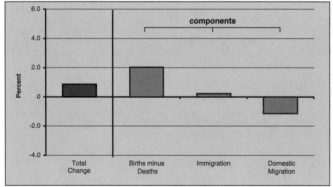

Average Annual Household and Population Growth

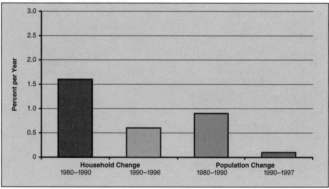

Population by Age; Births and Deaths

| | 1990 | | 1997 | |
	State	U.S.	State	U.S.
Age distribution (percent)				
Under 5 years	7.0	7.6	5.6	7.2
5 to 17 years	18.0	18.2	18.3	18.8
18 to 64 years	61.7	61.8	62.1	61.3
65 years and over	13.3	12.5	13.9	12.7
Birth and death rates (per thousand population)				
Births	14.1	16.7	11.0	14.6
Deaths	9.0	8.6	9.6	8.6

IN 1997, MAINE HAD A SLIGHTLY OLDER POPULATION THAN the rest of the United States. The preschool population was smaller in Maine than in the rest of the country, and the percentage in the school-age group was also smaller than that of the United States. With a 1997 birth rate of 11.0 for every 1,000 residents, a lower rate than the national average of 14.6, smaller preschool and school-age groups will likely continue.

HOUSEHOLD AND PERSONAL INCOME

HOUSEHOLD INCOME AND PERSONS IN POVERTY	1990	1995	1996	1997	
				State	U.S.
Median household income (1997 dollars)	33 726	35 658	35 492	32 772	37 005
Persons in poverty (thousands)	162	138	135	124	35 574
Poverty rate (percent)	13.1	11.2	11.2	10.1	13.3

MEDIAN HOUSEHOLD INCOME IN MAINE FELL OVERALL FROM 1989 to 1997, when adjusted for inflation. The majority of this decline occurred in three stages in 1990–91, 1993, and 1997, with declines in each period of 10.1, 10.0, and 7.7 percent, respectively. The two main periods of growth in household income, 1992 and 1993–95, were not enough to keep incomes above the 1989 mark. Poverty rates in Maine were fairly high compared to other states in New England but were below U.S. rates in the 1990s. The poverty rate in Maine is also different from the rest of the region because it was fairly stable, while the rest of the region experienced fluctuating rates during the 1990s.

Aggregate personal income in Maine grew 3 percent per year from 1989 to 1997, which was considerably lower than the U.S. growth rate. Growth in wages and salaries also lagged behind the U.S. average, increasing only 3.4 percent annually while U.S. wages and salaries increased 5.2 percent. The only component of personal income not to trail the U.S. average was transfer payments. On a per capita basis (i.e., aggregate income divided by the population), personal income was below the U.S. average in 1989 and had fallen further behind by 1997, to 86.7 percent of the national average.

Government payments to individuals in Maine grew 7.4 percent per year from 1990 to 1997. Medical payments were the fastest-growing component; next in size was Social Security. Other fast-growing programs were Supplemental Security Income and other income maintenance. Family assistance, which is what is commonly thought of as welfare, and unemployment insurance benefits were the only two programs to decrease over the period.

Personal Income
(millions of dollars)

	1980	1989	1990	1991	1992	1993	1994	1995	1996	1997	Change*
Earnings by place of work	6 598	14 124	14 620	14 446	15 038	15 435	15 871	16 384	17 028	17 942	3.0
Wages and salaries	5 271	10 994	11 396	11 281	11 705	11 978	12 419	12 919	13 467	14 329	3.4
Other labor income	543	1 317	1 417	1 452	1 518	1 619	1 529	1 505	1 503	1 518	1.8
Proprietors' income	784	1 813	1 806	1 713	1 815	1 839	1 923	1 959	2 059	2 094	1.8
Farm	0	74	93	41	108	87	59	14	38	-13	0.0
Nonfarm	784	1 739	1 714	1 672	1 707	1 752	1 863	1 945	2 021	2 107	2.4
(−) Personal contributions for social insurance	348	885	912	936	983	1 032	1 099	1 168	1 209	1 281	4.7
(+) Adjustment for residence	-2	93	94	89	105	128	162	198	218	244	NA
(=) Net earnings by state of residence	6 248	13 331	13 801	13 598	14 160	14 531	14 935	15 414	16 037	16 906	3.0
(+) Dividends, interest, and rent	1 412	3 847	3 892	3 822	3 738	3 720	4 001	4 197	4 563	4 717	2.6
(+) Transfer payments	1 695	3 096	3 433	3 941	4 332	4 573	4 763	5 034	5 336	5 613	7.7
(=) Total personal income	9 356	20 274	21 127	21 361	22 230	22 823	23 698	24 646	25 936	27 236	3.8
Farm	46	129	157	104	169	151	122	86	113	63	-8.6
Nonfarm	9 310	20 145	20 970	21 257	22 061	22 672	23 576	24 560	25 823	27 173	3.8
Personal income per capita (dollars)											
Current dollars	8 302	16 618	17 159	17 298	18 001	18 456	19 177	19 970	20 941	21 928	3.5
1997 dollars	15 874	21 009	20 649	19 975	20 135	20 083	20 379	20 759	21 325	21 928	0.5

*Compound annual average percent change, 1989–1997

Government Transfer Payments

	Millions of dollars		Percent change*	
	1990	1997	State	U.S.
Total government payments to individuals	3 276	5 414	65.2	62.7
Retirement, disability, and insurance	1 767	2 639	49.4	48.2
Social Security	1 241	1 849	49.0	46.1
Government employee retirement	475	731	53.9	60.3
Medical payments	937	2 019	115.6	101.2
Income maintenance	293	410	39.9	58.0
Supplemental Security Income	57	110	93.7	75.4
Family assistance	109	83	-23.6	-0.5
Food Stamps	67	100	49.0	27.1
Other income maintenance	60	116	93.3	189.8
Unemployment insurance benefits	124	110	-11.1	10.6
Veterans benefits and other	156	235	50.9	30.8

*Percent change, 1990–1997

Government Payments to Individuals: 1997

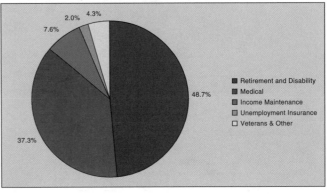

- Retirement and Disability — 48.7%
- Medical — 37.3%
- Income Maintenance — 7.6%
- Unemployment Insurance — 2.0%
- Veterans & Other — 4.3%

ECONOMIC STRUCTURE

LEADING PRIVATE INDUSTRIES, 1997 (Worker and proprietor earnings, millions of dollars)		FASTEST EARNINGS GROWTH, 1989–97 (percent increase)	
Health services	$1 941	Social services	156.0
Paper and allied products	813	Business services	78.1
Construction specialties	772	Real estate	77.9
Business services	628	Electric, gas and sanitary services	74.3
Miscellaneous retail stores	517	Educational services	69.9

TOTAL EMPLOYMENT IN MAINE INCREASED FROM 1989 TO 1997 at a rate of 0.7 percent per year. Manufacturing employment declined by 1.8 percent per year, with most of the decline taking place between 1989 and 1992. Services had the largest percentage of total employment and increased at an impressive 3 percent per year over the period. Finance, insurance, and real estate; services; and transportation, communications, and utilities earnings grew at paces of 6.1 percent, 5.7 percent, and 4.6 percent per year,

respectively. Health services was the largest industry in Maine in 1997, earning $1.9 billion. The top manufacturing industry, paper and allied products, was ranked second overall, earning $813 million. The two industries ranking next, special trade construction and business services, routinely rank in the top five in New England. Miscellaneous retail stores was the fifth largest industry in Maine, highlighting the importance to the state of retail outlet stores such as L.L. Bean.

Employment and Earnings by Sector

	1980	1989	1990	1991	1992	1993	1994	1995	1996	1997 Number	1997 Percent of total	Change*
Employment *(thousands of persons)*												
Total	555	708	706	684	687	699	711	720	731	747	100.0	0.7
Farm	16	12	12	12	12	12	12	12	11	11	1.5	-1.1
Nonfarm	539	696	695	672	675	687	699	708	720	736	98.5	0.7
Private nonfarm	441	586	582	561	566	579	596	607	618	634	84.9	1.0
Agricultural service, forestry, and fishing	12	12	12	12	12	15	15	14	15	16	2.2	4.0
Mining	0	0	0	0	0	0	0	0	0	0	0.0	0.0
Construction	29	53	48	41	42	42	43	45	47	47	6.3	-1.4
Manufacturing	119	114	110	104	101	100	101	101	98	98	13.1	-1.8
Transportation and public utilities	24	27	28	27	27	28	29	29	30	31	4.1	1.6
Wholesale trade	22	28	27	26	26	26	27	28	29	29	3.9	0.5
Retail trade	87	132	130	125	128	131	136	139	140	143	19.1	1.0
Finance, insurance, and real estate	27	42	41	40	39	40	40	41	42	44	5.9	0.7
Services	120	179	185	185	191	197	205	211	217	226	30.2	3.0
Government	98	111	113	111	109	108	103	101	102	102	13.7	-1.0
Earnings *(millions of dollars)*												
Total	6 598	14 124	14 620	14 446	15 038	15 435	15 871	16 384	17 028	17 942	100.0	3.0
Farm	46	129	157	104	169	151	122	86	113	63	0.4	-8.6
Nonfarm	6 552	13 995	14 462	14 342	14 869	15 284	15 749	16 298	16 915	17 880	99.6	3.1
Private nonfarm	5 349	11 562	11 834	11 596	12 072	12 511	12 996	13 507	14 059	14 947	83.3	3.3
Agricultural service, forestry, and fishing	82	173	185	196	187	176	176	173	169	178	1.0	0.3
Mining	34	8	7	5	6	7	7	6	5	5	0.0	-4.9
Construction	436	1 260	1 137	906	925	947	964	1 015	1 129	1 158	6.5	-1.0
Manufacturing	1 889	3 059	3 086	2 993	3 044	3 087	3 152	3 200	3 202	3 364	18.7	1.2
Transportation and public utilities	430	748	786	799	831	895	939	972	1 005	1 068	6.0	4.6
Wholesale trade	335	746	759	726	743	763	802	851	916	968	5.4	3.3
Retail trade	722	1 702	1 703	1 677	1 767	1 861	1 932	1 991	2 036	2 149	12.0	3.0
Finance, insurance, and real estate	268	724	763	800	867	944	956	987	1 058	1 163	6.5	6.1
Services	1 153	3 141	3 407	3 494	3 703	3 830	4 068	4 313	4 539	4 894	27.3	5.7
Government	1 203	2 433	2 629	2 745	2 797	2 773	2 753	2 791	2 857	2 932	16.3	2.4

*Compound annual average percent change, 1989–1997

ECONOMIC STRUCTURE (Continued)

AVERAGE 1997 WAGES IN MAINE WERE LOWER THAN AVERAGE wages in the United States and New England. Average wages were highest in finance, insurance, and real estate, manufacturing, and wholesale trade, much as they were for the country and the region. However, the average wages in these categories were 23.6 percent, 19.6 percent and 15.9 percent below the U.S. average, respectively. The sectors with the lowest average wages in 1997 were retail trade, farm, and agricultural services, again similar to the U.S. ranking. However, farm and agricultural services wages in 1997 were higher than the U.S. wages, at 5.5 percent and 1.4 percent, respectively. Retail wages in Maine were only 7.5 percent lower. The overall growth of average wages in Maine from 1989 to 1997 was 3.3 percent, slightly slower than the U.S. rate of 3.5 percent.

Manufacturing comprised 18.5 percent of gross state product (GSP) in Maine in 1997, slightly higher than the national average of 17.5 percent. Manufacturing's share of GSP fell from 1989 to 1997 by about the same rate as in the United States as a whole. Manufacturing production was almost evenly split between durable and nondurable goods.

Exports from Maine increased rapidly from 1994 to 1997. There was a slight dip in total goods exports in 1996 but overall growth of 39.6 percent between 1994 and 1997. The dominant export category was electric and electronic equipment, which more than doubled during the period and accounted for one-third of all Maine goods exports in 1997. All of the top five goods exported increased, though electric and electronic equipment and lumber and wood products experienced significant declines in 1996 and relatively large gains in 1997.

Average Annual Wages and Salaries by Sector
(dollars)

	1989	1996	1997 State	1997 U.S.
All wage and salary workers	18 829	23 458	24 455	29 809
Farm	10 462	16 461	17 347	16 442
Nonfarm	18 898	23 510	24 503	29 900
Private nonfarm	18 621	23 132	24 198	29 867
Agricultural service, forestry, and fishing	14 034	17 608	18 199	17 941
Mining	29 704	21 062	22 462	49 800
Construction	21 756	26 000	27 068	31 765
Manufacturing	23 639	30 470	32 268	38 351
Transportation and utilities	24 864	29 598	30 787	38 222
Wholesale trade	24 663	30 511	31 738	39 466
Retail trade	11 731	14 388	14 986	16 206
Finance, insurance, and real estate	23 813	32 158	34 358	44 993
Services	16 616	21 396	22 278	27 588
Government	20 068	25 241	25 940	30 062

Gross State Product and Manufacturing
(millions of dollars, except as noted)

	1989	1994	1995	1996
Gross state product, total	22 830	26 238	27 748	28 894
Manufacturing:				
Millions of dollars	4 537	4 717	5 355	5 333
Percent of total gross state product	19.9	18.0	19.3	18.5
Per worker (dollars)	39 969	46 641	53 231	54 461
New capital expenditures, manufacturing	NA	563	653	740

Exports of Goods
(millions of dollars)

	1994	1995	1996	1997
All goods	1 139	1 318	1 249	1 590
Manufactures	984	1 138	1 052	1 361
Agricultural and livestock products	45	51	56	70
Other commodities	110	129	141	159
Top goods exports, 1997:				
Electric and electronic equipment	241	317	260	523
Paper products	179	246	258	239
Lumber and wood products	114	121	113	127
Fish and other marine products	89	96	107	125
Industrial machinery and computers	58	68	78	86

HOUSING

NEW HOUSING PRODUCTION IN MAINE WAS HIGH IN 1989 BUT had fallen by 1991 to a lower level and has remained near there since then. Measured as a combination of building permits issued and manufactured housing put in place, new housing production per capita did not share in the national housing recovery, though it was higher than in many other states in the region. Existing home sales grew over the decade, ending the period at a high point, though still below the 1988 level. The homeownership rate remained far above the national rate, 74.9 percent in Maine in 1997 versus 65.7 percent in the United States as a whole. The rental vacancy rate, a measure of the percentage of unoccupied rental units, was relatively high over the early 1990s but declined starting in 1995, and by 1997 was below the national average.

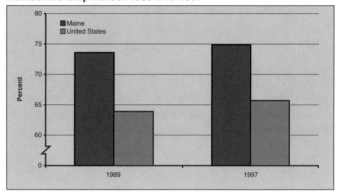

Homeownership Rates: 1989 and 1997

Housing Supply

	1989	1990	1991	1992	1993	1994	1995	1996	1997
Residential building permits (thousands)	6.4	4.8	3.7	4.3	3.8	4.6	4.4	4.7	4.7
New home production (including manufactured housing):									
Thousands of homes	9.2	7.4	5.6	6.1	5.1	6.1	5.8	6.7	6.5
Rate per 1,000 population									
Maine	7.5	6.0	4.5	4.9	4.1	4.9	4.7	5.4	5.2
U.S.	6.2	5.2	4.5	5.1	5.6	6.4	6.3	6.6	6.5
Existing home sales:									
Thousands of homes	9.0	NA	NA	10.3	11.6	13.1	13.1	14.2	14.7
Change from previous year (percent)									
Maine	-51.1	NA	NA	NA	12.6	12.9	0.0	8.4	3.5
U.S.	-3.9	-4.0	0.0	9.2	8.2	4.8	-3.7	7.5	3.8
Home ownership rate (percent of households)	73.6	74.2	72.0	72.0	71.9	72.6	76.7	76.5	74.9
Rental vacancy rate (percent of rental housing units)	6.0	9.7	10.8	10.7	10.4	11.0	8.6	7.2	6.1

AGRICULTURE

CASH RECEIPTS FROM FARMING CHANGED LITTLE OVER THE 1989–97 period, but production expenses rose, and net income was negative in 1997. Both corporate and noncorporate farms suffered losses.

The average farm in Maine was smaller than the average U.S. farm, though it was larger than the average in many of the other states in the region. Despite the relatively large size of Maine's farms compared to other New England states, the value of an average farm was lower than in the other New England states and in the nation as a whole.

MAINE FARMS, 1997	
Number of farms	7 300
Total acres (thousands):	1 340
Average per farm	184
Value of land and buildings (millions of dollars)	1 742
Average per farm (dollars)	238 630

Farm Income
(millions of dollars)

	1980	1989	1990	1991	1992	1993	1994	1995	1996	1997
Gross income	473	506	551	502	524	529	526	517	530	541
Receipts from sales	441	451	504	456	475	470	474	464	489	495
Government payments	3	7	7	6	10	20	14	14	5	4
Imputed and miscellaneous income	28	48	40	40	39	39	38	39	36	42
(−) Production expenses	481	436	455	449	444	454	483	515	506	553
(=) Realized net income	-8	71	96	53	80	75	43	2	24	-12
(+) Inventory change	8	15	10	-8	44	16	31	14	23	-9
(=) Net income	0	85	107	46	124	91	75	17	47	-21
Corporate income	0	11	14	4	16	5	15	2	9	-8
Farm proprietors income	0	74	93	41	108	87	59	14	38	-13

EDUCATION

EDUCATIONAL ATTAINMENT Percent of population age 25 and over, 1997	State	United States
High school graduate or higher	85.8	82.1
College graduate or higher	20.0	23.9

MAINE RANKED 15TH IN THE COUNTRY IN THE PERCENTAGE OF its population over the age of 25 holding a high school diploma. This percentage ranked the state second in New England. Per pupil spending in elementary and secondary schools was slightly higher than the national average, though the average teacher salary was the lowest in the region and almost $5,000 less than the average teacher salary in the United States. Unlike other states in the region, Maine's rank in the percentage of the population over 25 with a bachelor's degree was very low, in 40th place. In 1997, 20.0 percent of the population between the ages of 18 and 34 was enrolled in higher education, which was lower than the U.S. percentage (21.8). Further, minorities made up only 4 percent of those enrolled, the lowest in the nation.

High School Completion: 1990–97

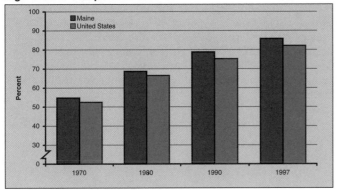

Education Indicators

	State	U.S.
Elementary and secondary schools		
Enrollment, 1995–96		
Total (thousands)	230	49 873
Percent in private schools	7.3	10.1
Expenditures per pupil (dollars), 1995–96	6 546	6 146
Average teacher salary (dollars), 1996–97	33 800	38 509
Higher education		
Enrollment, 1996–97		
Total (thousands)	56	14 218
Percent of population 18–34	19.4	21.8
Percent minority	4.0	26.1
Percent in private schools	31.9	22.6

HEALTH

MAINE'S MAJOR HEALTH INDICATORS SHOWED A STATE WITH above-average crude death rates in cancer, diabetes, Alzheimer's disease, heart disease, pneumonia and influenza, chronic obstructive pulmonary diseases (including emphysema), liver disease, and suicide. When adjusted for changes in the age composition in the state, several causes of death, including diabetes, heart disease, pneumonia and influenza, and liver disease, fell below the national age-adjusted rate. The age-adjusted total death rate fell slightly in the 1990s and remained lower than the national rate in each year. Infant mortality rates in 1997, at 3.7 per 1,000 live births, were the lowest in the nation. Maine had below average rates of health insurance noncoverage, though the 1997 rate of 14.9 percent not covered by health insurance was the highest in the region.

Health Indicators

	1990	1995	1996	1997
Infant mortality				
(rate per thousand live births)				
Maine	6.2	6.5	4.4	3.7
U.S.	9.2	7.6	7.3	7.1
Total deaths, age-adjusted rate				
(rate per thousand population)				
Maine	4.9	4.8	4.6	4.6
U.S.	5.2	5.0	4.9	4.8
Persons not covered by health insurance				
(percent of population)				
Maine	11.2	13.5	12.1	14.9
U.S.	13.9	15.4	15.6	16.1

Leading Causes of Death, 1996
(deaths per 100,000 population)

	Age-adjusted		Not age-adjusted	
	State	U.S.	State	U.S.
Deaths from all causes	463.0	491.6	944.3	872.5
Heart disease	123.3	134.5	284.8	276.4
Cancer	135.5	127.9	237.4	203.4
Cerebrovascular diseases	22.7	26.4	58.8	60.3
Chronic obstructive pulmonary disease	24.6	21.0	53.0	40.0
Diabetes mellitus	12.6	13.6	24.4	23.3
Pneumonia and influenza	10.5	12.8	32.3	31.6
HIV	3.2	11.1	3.4	11.7
Liver disease	7.0	7.5	9.9	9.4
Alzheimer's disease	4.0	2.7	14.3	8.1
Accidents and adverse effects	24.7	30.4	31.8	35.8
Motor vehicle accidents	14.0	16.2	14.2	16.5
Suicide	11.8	10.8	13.8	11.6
Homicide	2.3	8.5	2.3	7.9
Injury by firearm	8.4	12.9	9.9	12.8

GOVERNMENT

STATE AND LOCAL TAXES, 1995–96	State	U.S.
Per capita (dollars)	2 542	2 477
Percent of personal income	12.7	10.8

STATE AND LOCAL TAXES PER CAPITA IN MAINE WERE 2.6 percent over the national average at $2,542 per capita in the fiscal year 1995–96. But Maine's low incomes meant that a quite high ratio of taxes to personal income was required; at 12.7 percent it was the highest tax ratio in the region. Around 60 percent of taxation was at the state level, with the remaining local taxation primarily property tax, which was very similar to national trends. State taxes were lower in Maine than they were in the rest of the country on a per capita basis. Corporate income taxes were also substantially lower, at 68.1 percent of the national average. This advantage was offset by a higher than average individual income tax of $621.43 per capita, 114.7 percent higher than in the United States as a whole. Per capita state expenditures were higher than the national average, mainly reflecting above-average spending on public welfare, highways, natural resources, and interest on debt.

Federal spending within Maine totaled $7.3 billion dollars in 1997, about 0.5 percent of total U.S. federal funds distributed to the 50 states and the District of Columbia. Maine also had about 0.5 percent of the total U.S. population. Maine had a 1997 share of Medicare spending below that population proportion, but the Medicaid share was noticeably higher. Defense procurement was important to the state, contributing 12.7 percent of total funds and representing 0.8 percent of all defense funds released to the states.

State Government Finances, 1996–97

	Millions of dollars	Percent distribu- tion	Dollars per capita State	Dollars per capita U.S.
General revenue	4 059	100.0	3 268	3 049
Intergovernmental revenue	1 299	32.0	1 046	863
Taxes	2 019	49.8	1 626	1 660
General sales	683	16.8	550	551
Selective sales	282	6.9	227	257
License taxes	117	2.9	94	106
Individual income	772	19.0	621	542
Corporation net income	97	2.4	78	115
Other taxes	69	1.7	55	90
Other general revenue	741	18.2	596	526
General expenditure	3 961	100.0	3 189	2 951
Intergovernmental expenditure	773	19.5	622	989
Direct expenditure	3 188	80.5	2 567	1 962
General expenditure, by function:				
Education	1 122	28.3	903	1 033
Public welfare	1 337	33.7	1 076	761
Hospitals and health	262	6.6	211	237
Highways	362	9.1	292	225
Police protection and corrections	105	2.7	85	137
Natural resources, parks and recreation	125	3.2	101	63
Governmental administration	159	4.0	128	107
Interest on general debt	173	4.4	139	99
Other and unallocable	316	8.0	254	290
Debt at end of fiscal year	3 203	NA	2 579	1 706
Cash and security holdings	6 400	NA	5 153	6 683

Federal Spending within State

	Federal funds, fiscal 1997		
	Millions of dollars	Percent distribution	Percent of U.S. total*
Total within state	7 250	100.0	0.5
Payments to individuals	3 915	54.0	0.5
Retirement and disability	2 436	33.6	0.5
Medicare	847	11.7	0.4
Food stamps	104	1.4	0.5
Supplemental Security Income	103	1.4	0.4
Grants	1 501	20.7	0.6
Medicaid and other health	767	10.6	0.7
Nutrition and family welfare	253	3.5	0.5
Education	85	1.2	0.5
Housing and community development	49	0.7	0.4
Salaries and wages	755	10.4	0.5
Defense procurement contracts	918	12.7	0.8
Non-defense procurement contracts	100	1.4	0.1

*State population is 0.5 percent of the U.S. total.

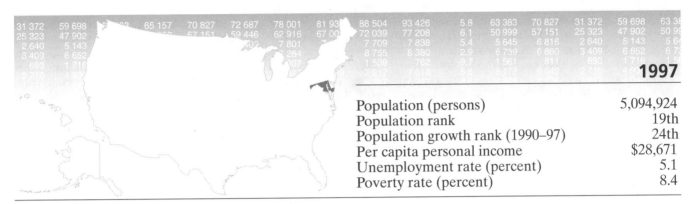

1997

Population (persons)	5,094,924
Population rank	19th
Population growth rank (1990–97)	24th
Per capita personal income	$28,671
Unemployment rate (percent)	5.1
Poverty rate (percent)	8.4

LIKE MANY OTHER STATES IN THE MID-ATLANTIC REGION, Maryland has had net domestic out-migration during the 1990s and, as a result, slower population growth than the U.S. average. But there are proportionately more people in the working-age group than in the nation or other states in the region, and fewer seniors. The unemployment rate was lower than the nation's from 1989 to 1997.

Median household income in the state rose slightly from 1989 to 1997 and remained significantly higher than the U.S. median throughout. The state also had lower than average poverty rates. Local and state taxation appears high when expressed in per capita dollar terms but was lower as a percentage of personal income than the U.S. average.

Services employment and earnings grew rapidly in Maryland, as did finance, insurance, and real estate earnings. All private nonfarm sectors experienced earnings growth from 1989 to 1997. Manufacturing, not a large component of the economy in terms of gross state product (8.6 percent), lost employment over the time period.

Average Annual Population Growth: 1990–97

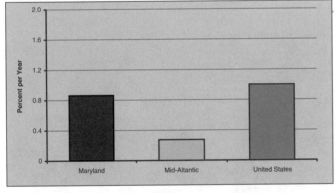

Median Household Income: 1989–97 (1997 dollars)

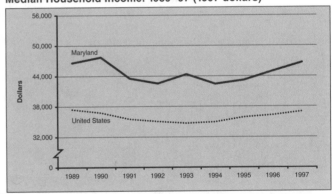

Unemployment Rate: 1989–97

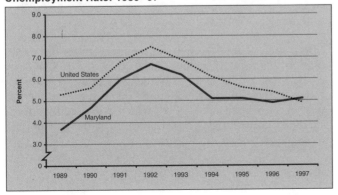

THE UNEMPLOYMENT RATE IN MARYLAND GENERALLY FOL-lowed the cyclical path of the national rate, but at a lower level. Its 1992 peak was associated with a large increase in the labor force from the year before (2.2 percent) rather than a fall in employment (which actually gained 1.4 percent from the year before). In 1994 through 1997, the Maryland rate was about unchanged, in contrast to the continued downward trend in the United States.

POPULATION AND LABOR FORCE

POPULATION GROWTH WAS SLIGHTLY SLOWER IN MARYLAND than it was in the rest of the country. The White non-Hispanic population declined slightly, while the Black, Hispanic, and Asian populations grew faster than nation-wide. The natural rate of increase (births less deaths) was the main factor behind growth in the state, though international immigration accounted for about one-third of the increase. Offsetting these sources of growth was a significant domestic out-migration from 1990 to 1997, as in many states in the region. Metropolitan counties, primarily in the Baltimore and Washington, D.C. metropolitan areas, are home to 92.7 percent of Marylanders.

The labor force grew faster than the population from 1990 to 1997. The employment growth rate was intermediate between the two, leading to small increases in both the employment/population ratio and the unemployment rate. Maryland's employment/population ratio was well above the national average, and its unemployment rate was below the U.S. rate in most years.

Population and Labor Force

	1980	1990	1991	1992	1993	1994	1995	1996	1997	Change* State	Change* U.S.
Population											
Total number of persons (thousands)	4 217	4 797	4 856	4 903	4 943	4 985	5 023	5 058	5 095	0.9	1.0
Percent distribution:											
White, Non-Hispanic	74.1	69.7	69.0	68.5	67.9	67.3	66.7	66.1	65.5	0.0	0.4
Black, Non-Hispanic	22.5	24.4	25.0	25.3	25.6	25.9	26.3	26.7	27.0	2.3	1.4
Asian	1.6	3.0	3.1	3.2	3.4	3.5	3.6	3.7	3.8	4.4	4.1
Native American	0.2	0.3	0.3	0.3	0.3	0.3	0.3	0.3	0.3	1.6	1.6
Hispanic	1.5	2.8	2.8	2.9	3.0	3.1	3.3	3.4	3.5	4.5	3.8
In metropolitan areas	93.0	92.8	92.8	92.8	92.8	92.8	92.8	92.7	92.7	0.8	1.0
Total number of households (thousands)	1 461	1 749	1 778	1 806	1 816	1 830	1 853	1 871	NA	1.1	1.2
Labor Force (thousands)											
Population 16 and over	3 215	3 737	3 772	3 799	3 821	3 855	3 883	3 923	3 959	0.8	1.0
Civilian labor force	2 158	2 609	2 620	2 677	2 672	2 696	2 715	2 788	2 784	0.9	1.1
Employed	2 018	2 487	2 463	2 498	2 505	2 558	2 577	2 652	2 642	0.9	1.2
Percent of population	62.8	66.6	65.3	65.7	65.6	66.4	66.4	67.6	66.7		
Unemployment rate (percent)	6.5	4.7	6.0	6.7	6.2	5.1	5.1	4.9	5.1		

*Compound annual average percent change, 1990–1997; 1990–1996 for households.

Population Change and Components: 1990–97

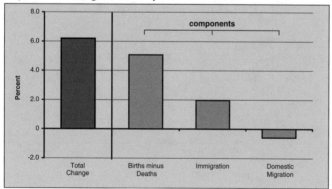

Average Annual Household and Population Growth

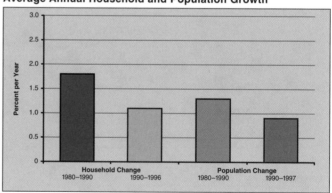

Population by Age; Births and Deaths

	1990 State	1990 U.S.	1997 State	1997 U.S.
Age distribution (percent)				
Under 5 years	7.7	7.6	6.8	7.2
5 to 17 years	16.9	18.2	18.1	18.8
18 to 64 years	64.6	61.8	63.6	61.3
65 years and over	10.8	12.5	11.5	12.7
Birth and death rates (per thousand population)				
Births	16.8	16.7	13.8	14.6
Deaths	8.0	8.6	8.2	8.6

MARYLAND, IN 1997, HAD A LARGER PERCENTAGE OF ITS POPulation in the working-age group than the U.S. average and a smaller than average percentage in every other age group. The birth rate of 13.8 per 1,000 is less than the U.S. rate of 14.6 births per 1,000, which could contribute to smaller than average pre-school and school-age populations in the state in the future.

HOUSEHOLD AND PERSONAL INCOME

HOUSEHOLD INCOME AND PERSONS IN POVERTY	1990	1995	1996	1997 State	1997 U.S.
Median household income (1997 dollars)	47 717	43 222	45 002	46 685	37 005
Persons in poverty (thousands)	468	520	522	422	35 574
Poverty rate (percent)	9.9	10.1	10.3	8.4	13.3

THE MEDIAN HOUSEHOLD INCOME IN MARYLAND, IN INFLA-tion-adjusted terms, fell in 1991 and, despite subsequent recovery had not quite regained the 1990 level by 1997. In 1997 median income in Maryland was 26 percent higher than the U.S. average. The poverty rate rose in the middle of the decade, but by 1997 had fallen below its 1989 level. In each year it was far below the poverty rate for the United States as a whole.

Aggregate personal income in Maryland grew at a slower pace than personal income in the nation. Wages and salaries paid in the state grew at a fairly steady pace each year (4.4 percent per year) and proprietors' income grew 4.1 percent per year. In 1997, nearly $14 billion, net, was brought into Maryland by residents who worked elsewhere, many in Washington, D.C. Per capita personal income grew slightly, when adjusted for inflation, and was 13.3 percent higher than the national average in 1997.

Government total transfer payments grew at an annual rate of 7.3 percent in Maryland from 1990 to 1997. Medical payments, Supplemental Security Income, and "other income maintenance" (mainly the earned income tax credit) grew faster than other transfer payment categories. Family assistance payments fell over the seven-year period. Old Age, Survivors and Disability Insurance (Social Security), while growing more slowly than the average annual rate for total transfer payments, paid out the largest amount of money in 1997, at $5.8 billion.

Personal Income
(millions of dollars)

	1980	1989	1990	1991	1992	1993	1994	1995	1996	1997	Change*
Earnings by place of work	30 126	65 171	69 162	70 104	72 895	75 748	79 042	82 356	85 990	91 626	4.4
Wages and salaries	25 463	54 112	57 386	58 116	60 063	61 940	64 797	67 725	71 141	76 368	4.4
Other labor income	2 284	5 115	5 656	5 918	6 354	6 815	7 216	7 158	6 936	7 065	4.1
Proprietors' income	2 378	5 944	6 121	6 070	6 478	6 994	7 029	7 473	7 913	8 193	4.1
Farm	-13	273	242	197	232	205	158	67	193	116	-10.1
Nonfarm	2 392	5 672	5 878	5 873	6 247	6 789	6 871	7 405	7 720	8 076	4.5
(−) Personal contributions for social insurance	1 706	4 323	4 601	4 771	4 917	5 105	5 410	5 653	5 859	6 250	4.7
(+) Adjustment for residence	4 949	10 404	10 924	11 420	12 127	12 482	12 831	13 000	13 447	13 918	NA
(=) Net earnings by state of residence	33 368	71 251	75 485	76 752	80 105	83 125	86 463	89 702	93 578	99 294	4.2
(+) Dividends, interest, and rent	6 827	18 139	19 139	19 407	19 071	19 710	21 102	22 596	24 417	25 325	4.3
(+) Transfer payments	5 996	12 100	13 234	14 929	16 270	17 197	18 712	18 992	20 178	21 441	7.4
(=) Total personal income	46 191	101 490	107 858	111 089	115 446	120 033	126 277	131 290	138 173	146 060	4.7
Farm	·64	354	338	289	321	299	253	175	306	231	-5.2
Nonfarm	46 128	101 136	107 520	110 799	115 125	119 734	126 024	131 115	137 867	145 829	4.7
Personal income per capita (dollars)											
Current dollars	10 926	21 469	22 482	22 872	23 541	24 275	25 313	26 115	27 305	28 671	3.7
1997 dollars	20 891	27 142	27 054	26 411	26 332	26 415	26 900	27 147	27 805	28 671	0.7

*Compound annual average percent change, 1989–1997

Government Transfer Payments

	Millions of dollars 1990	Millions of dollars 1997	Percent change* State	Percent change* U.S.
Total government payments to individuals	12 573	20 585	63.7	62.7
Retirement, disability, and insurance	7 706	11 595	50.5	48.2
Social Security	3 887	5 816	49.6	46.1
Government employee retirement	3 415	5 314	55.6	60.3
Medical payments	3 301	6 652	101.5	101.2
Income maintenance	889	1 398	57.2	58.0
Supplemental Security Income	191	374	95.9	75.4
Family assistance	316	272	-14.2	-0.5
Food Stamps	214	310	44.7	27.1
Other income maintenance	168	443	163.8	189.8
Unemployment insurance benefits	279	353	26.7	10.6
Veterans benefits and other	399	587	47.3	30.8

*Percent change, 1990–1997

Government Payments to Individuals: 1997

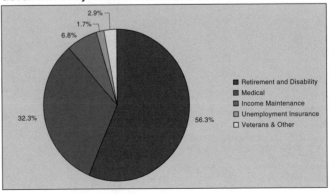

- ■ Retirement and Disability
- ■ Medical
- ■ Income Maintenance
- ▨ Unemployment Insurance
- ☐ Veterans & Other

2.9%
1.7%
6.8%
56.3%
32.3%

ECONOMIC STRUCTURE

LEADING PRIVATE INDUSTRIES, 1997 (Worker and proprietor earnings, millions of dollars)		FASTEST EARNINGS GROWTH, 1989–97 (percent increase)	
Health services	$8 264	Securities brokers	267.8
Business services	7 017	Hotels and lodging	146.6
Engineering and management services ..	5 318	Social services	119.2
Construction specialties	4 172	Real estate	86.9
Eating and drinking places	1 983	Amusement and recreation services	79.4

TOTAL EMPLOYMENT IN MARYLAND INCREASED BY 177,000—an annual rate of 0.8 percent per year—from 1989 to 1997. This was entirely accounted for by growth in services; changes in other sectors were small and offsetting. Services provided 34 percent of the state's jobs in 1997. Total earnings grew from 1989 to 1997 at an average annual rate of 4.4 percent. All private nonfarm sectors experienced growth in the period, with services and finance, insurance, and real estate growing faster than the rest. Manufacturing grew at 2.2 percent per year despite falling employment. As in other states in the Mid-Atlantic, service industries held several of the top earning spots. The top four industries were health services, business services, engineering and management, and special trade construction. Eating and drinking places was fifth in the state, underlining the importance of tourism to the state surrounding the Chesapeake Bay. In addition, two of the five fastest growing industries (hotels and amusement and recreation services) also depend heavily on tourism in the state.

Employment and Earnings by Sector

	1980	1989	1990	1991	1992	1993	1994	1995	1996	1997 Number	1997 Percent of total	Change*
Employment *(thousands of persons)*												
Total	2 074	2 729	2 757	2 687	2 661	2 686	2 737	2 790	2 834	2 907	100.0	0.8
Farm	30	23	22	22	22	22	21	20	19	19	0.7	-2.2
Nonfarm	2 045	2 706	2 734	2 665	2 639	2 665	2 717	2 770	2 815	2 887	99.3	0.8
Private nonfarm	1 572	2 215	2 229	2 166	2 140	2 166	2 218	2 269	2 315	2 385	82.0	0.9
Agricultural service, forestry, and fishing ..	15	25	26	26	25	28	29	29	31	32	1.1	3.1
Mining	3	4	4	4	3	3	3	3	2	3	0.1	-5.5
Construction	124	205	198	171	162	162	168	170	175	183	6.3	-1.4
Manufacturing	241	215	213	200	191	188	187	184	183	186	6.4	-1.8
Transportation and public utilities	96	117	118	119	116	118	123	124	126	129	4.4	1.2
Wholesale trade	92	121	116	114	113	109	111	114	116	118	4.1	-0.3
Retail trade	356	483	475	462	459	458	471	483	487	495	17.0	0.3
Finance, insurance, and real estate	149	230	232	225	212	218	226	228	233	241	8.3	0.6
Services	496	815	847	846	859	883	900	933	962	1 000	34.4	2.6
Government	473	491	505	499	498	499	499	501	500	503	17.3	0.3
Earnings *(millions of dollars)*												
Total	30 126	65 171	69 162	70 104	72 895	75 748	79 042	82 356	85 990	91 626	100.0	4.4
Farm	64	354	338	289	321	299	253	175	306	231	0.3	-5.2
Nonfarm	30 062	64 817	68 825	69 814	72 574	75 450	78 789	82 180	85 684	91 395	99.7	4.4
Private nonfarm	22 723	51 080	53 916	54 003	56 518	58 782	61 456	64 133	67 068	72 143	78.7	4.4
Agricultural service, forestry, and fishing ..	113	381	415	401	410	432	467	469	487	515	0.6	3.8
Mining	186	79	83	101	83	71	73	71	71	81	0.1	0.3
Construction	2 143	5 761	5 790	5 045	4 763	4 795	5 247	5 428	5 748	6 241	6.8	1.0
Manufacturing	4 924	7 083	7 339	7 246	7 347	7 391	7 722	7 818	7 903	8 428	9.2	2.2
Transportation and public utilities	2 048	3 893	4 051	4 216	4 304	4 507	4 766	4 894	5 073	5 297	5.8	3.9
Wholesale trade	1 820	3 871	3 970	3 995	4 119	4 175	4 367	4 590	4 837	5 177	5.7	3.7
Retail trade	3 450	7 232	7 274	7 214	7 454	7 454	7 820	8 055	8 252	8 675	9.5	2.3
Finance, insurance, and real estate	1 619	4 325	4 628	4 692	5 495	6 052	6 125	6 350	6 787	7 449	8.1	7.0
Services	6 421	18 454	20 365	21 092	22 543	23 914	24 869	26 460	27 910	30 280	33.0	6.4
Government	7 339	13 737	14 908	15 811	16 055	16 668	17 333	18 047	18 616	19 252	21.0	4.3

*Compound annual average percent change, 1989–1997

ECONOMIC STRUCTURE (Continued)

MARYLAND'S AVERAGE WAGE WAS SLIGHTLY HIGHER THAN THE national average, though lower than that of the Mid-Atlantic region, which, with average wages of $35,323 per worker, was the region with the highest pay. Several sectors in Maryland had average wages higher than the national average yet lower than the regional one. Included in this category were agricultural services, construction, manufacturing, services, and wholesale trade. Wages were lower compared to both the U.S. average and the mid-Atlantic average in mining and finance, insurance, and real estate. Average wages rose at a 3.9 percent annual rate from 1989 to 1997, slightly faster than the U.S. rate.

The value of manufacturing output, as a percentage of gross state product, was lower in Maryland (at 8.6 percent in 1996) than in any other Mid-Atlantic state and only half the national average. Value of manufacturing output per worker was also lower than nationally.

Goods exports from Maryland grew 35.5 percent from 1994 to 1997. Electrical, electronic, and industrial machinery were the top export categories. Of the top five goods exports, only one group, transportation equipment did not see export gains.

Average Annual Wages and Salaries by Sector
(dollars)

	1989	1996	1997 State	1997 U.S.
All wage and salary workers	23 058	29 808	31 211	29 809
Farm	10 884	18 677	16 321	16 442
Nonfarm	23 094	29 834	31 251	29 900
Private nonfarm	22 326	28 679	30 235	29 867
Agricultural service, forestry, and fishing	16 570	20 148	20 897	17 941
Mining	28 742	36 556	37 277	49 800
Construction	25 273	31 073	32 744	31 765
Manufacturing	28 986	38 043	40 141	38 351
Transportation and utilities	29 700	37 185	38 547	38 222
Wholesale trade	29 910	39 353	41 347	39 466
Retail trade	14 020	16 678	17 356	16 206
Finance, insurance, and real estate	27 586	38 992	42 916	44 993
Services	21 611	28 619	30 065	27 588
Government	25 987	34 181	35 165	30 062

Gross State Product and Manufacturing
(millions of dollars, except as noted)

	1989	1994	1995	1996
Gross state product, total	108 351	132 942	137 353	143 190
Manufacturing:				
Millions of dollars	10 977	11 307	11 996	12 317
Percent of total gross state product	10.1	8.5	8.7	8.6
Per worker (dollars)	51 002	60 321	65 219	67 484
New capital expenditures, manufacturing	NA	785	996	1 182

Exports of Goods
(millions of dollars)

	1994	1995	1996	1997
All goods	2 848	3 439	3 510	3 861
Manufactures	2 576	2 977	3 055	3 412
Agricultural and livestock products	76	150	152	119
Other commodities	196	312	303	329
Top goods exports, 1997:				
Electric and electronic equipment	346	499	486	663
Industrial machinery and computers	455	568	618	620
Chemical products	316	380	394	384
Transportation equipment	361	312	268	311
Scientific and measuring instruments	255	311	255	310

HOUSING

THE NEW HOUSING SUPPLY IN MARYLAND WAS SUBSTANTIALly higher per 1,000 residents than in other states in the region, with the exception of Delaware. New housing production, the combination of building permits issued and new manufactured housing put into place, declined generally from 1989 to 1997, though there were increases in 1992 and 1997. Housing production per capita was higher than the national average early in the decade but fell below it in 1994 through 1997. Existing home sales declined from 1989 to 1991 and again in 1994 and 1995, with fewer homes sold in 1997 than in six of the previous eight years. Homeownership rates were fairly average throughout the decade and then shot up in the last three years of the period, particularly in 1997. The rental vacancy rate fluctuated to a greater extent, experiencing a high point in 1993 and rising again in 1997.

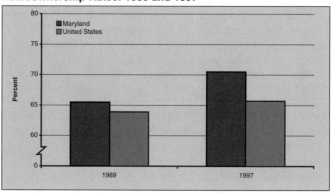

Homeownership Rates: 1989 and 1997

Housing Supply

	1989	1990	1991	1992	1993	1994	1995	1996	1997
Residential building permits (thousands)	40.6	32.0	25.2	32.4	30.0	29.0	26.6	25.1	26.0
New home production (including manufactured housing):									
Thousands of homes	42.1	33.1	26.7	33.0	31.2	29.8	28.0	25.9	27.1
Rate per 1,000 population									
Maryland	8.9	6.9	5.5	6.7	6.3	6.0	5.6	5.1	5.3
U.S.	6.2	5.2	4.5	5.1	5.6	6.4	6.3	6.6	6.5
Existing home sales:									
Thousands of homes	76.8	67.1	66.8	69.0	73.4	69.5	58.7	60.3	66.4
Change from previous year (percent)									
Maryland	-5.9	-12.6	-0.4	3.3	6.4	-5.3	-15.5	2.7	10.1
U.S.	-3.9	-4.0	0.0	9.2	8.2	4.8	-3.7	7.5	3.8
Home ownership rate (percent of households)	65.5	64.9	63.8	64.8	65.5	64.1	65.8	66.9	70.5
Rental vacancy rate (percent of rental housing units)	5.5	5.2	6.7	7.2	8.7	8.1	5.7	6.7	8.0

AGRICULTURE

FARM SALES INCREASED FROM 1989 TO 1997 IN GENERAL, though the mid-decade was fairly stagnant for cash receipts. Production expenses also rose sporadically, causing realized net income to fall in most of the years in the period. As production expenses increased, government payments remained virtually flat and at very low levels. Corporate farms did not have a very large presence in the state. The average farm in Maryland was smaller than its U.S. counterpart and was smaller even than the average farm in most Mid-Atlantic states. The average farm's value, however, was greater than that of the typical U.S. farm, suggesting a high demand for farmland for development.

MARYLAND FARMS, 1997	
Number of farms	13 000
Total acres (thousands):	2 100
Average per farm	162
Value of land and buildings (millions of dollars)	8 400
Average per farm (dollars)	646 154

Farm Income
(millions of dollars)

	1980	1989	1990	1991	1992	1993	1994	1995	1996	1997
Gross income	1 040	1 567	1 591	1 575	1 571	1 627	1 600	1 660	1 780	1 841
Receipts from sales	936	1 377	1 419	1 391	1 379	1 414	1 390	1 440	1 562	1 585
Government payments	4	24	17	15	16	26	16	15	18	19
Imputed and miscellaneous income	100	166	155	169	176	187	194	204	200	236
(−) Production expenses	1 050	1 268	1 331	1 347	1 348	1 364	1 447	1 513	1 582	1 671
(=) Realized net income	-9	299	260	228	223	263	153	146	198	170
(+) Inventory change	-11	3	10	-15	37	-49	39	-71	33	-32
(=) Net income	-21	302	270	213	260	214	191	76	232	138
Corporate income	-7	29	27	17	28	9	33	9	39	21
Farm proprietors income	-13	273	242	197	232	205	158	67	193	116

EDUCATION

EDUCATIONAL ATTAINMENT Percent of population age 25 and over, 1997	State	United States
High school graduate or higher	84.7	82.1
College graduate or higher	32.2	23.9

MARYLAND RANKED 22ND IN THE COUNTRY IN THE PERCENT-age of population over 25 that held a high school diploma in 1997. Per pupil spending in elementary and secondary schools was 20 percent above the U.S. level, and teacher salaries were 7 percent higher. Private schools accounted for about 13.4 percent of all elementary and secondary students, a higher percentage than in the United States (10.1 percent). Maryland ranked third, however, in the percent-age of its population over 25—nearly one-third—that holds a bachelor's degree; only the District of Columbia and Massachusetts were higher. Of the population between the ages of 18 and 34, 20.6 percent were enrolled in higher education in 1996, slightly less than the national rate. Maryland had the highest percentage of minority students in the mid-Atlantic region, but it was somewhat below the minority percentage in its population.

High School Completion: 1990–97

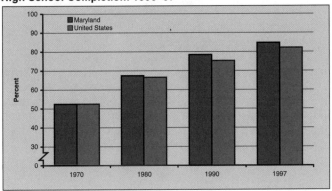

Education Indicators

	State	U.S.
Elementary and secondary schools Enrollment, 1995–96		
Total (thousands)	931	49 873
Percent in private schools	13.4	10.1
Expenditures per pupil (dollars), 1995–96	7 382	6 146
Average teacher salary (dollars), 1996–97	41 148	38 509
Higher education Enrollment, 1996–97		
Total (thousands)	261	14 218
Percent of population 18–34	20.6	21.8
Percent minority	32.2	26.1
Percent in private schools	16.7	22.6

HEALTH

MARYLAND HAD A HIGHER THAN AVERAGE AGE-ADJUSTED death rate throughout the 1990s, though it fell slightly from 1990 to 1997. Infant mortality was also higher than the national average, with the 1997 rate the fifth highest in the country. Health insurance coverage was stronger in Maryland than the U.S. percentage. The crude death rates for HIV, diabetes, and homicide were higher than the national death rates. However, when adjusted for changes in the age composition over time within the state, rates for several other causes of death were also higher than the national age-adjusted rates, including cancer, pneumonia and influenza, and injury by firearm.

Health Indicators

	1990	1995	1996	1997
Infant mortality *(rate per thousand live births)*				
Maryland	9.5	8.9	8.4	9.0
U.S.	9.2	7.6	7.3	7.1
Total deaths, age-adjusted rate *(rate per thousand population)*				
Maryland	5.4	5.3	5.2	5.0
U.S.	5.2	5.0	4.9	4.8
Persons not covered by health insurance *(percent of population)*				
Maryland	12.7	15.3	11.4	13.4
U.S.	13.9	15.4	15.6	16.1

Leading Causes of Death, 1996
(deaths per 100,000 population)

	Age-adjusted		Not age-adjusted	
	State	U.S.	State	U.S.
Deaths from all causes	520.1	491.6	827.3	872.5
Heart disease	131.6	134.5	235.5	276.4
Cancer	136.3	127.9	200.4	203.4
Cerebrovascular diseases	26.2	26.4	52.2	60.3
Chronic obstructive pulmonary disease	20.1	21.0	34.7	40.0
Diabetes mellitus	17.5	13.6	27.9	23.3
Pneumonia and influenza	13.5	12.8	28.4	31.6
HIV	18.4	11.1	20.9	11.7
Liver disease	6.9	7.5	8.4	9.4
Alzheimer's disease	2.7	2.7	7.2	8.1
Accidents and adverse effects	23.4	30.4	28.0	35.8
Motor vehicle accidents	12.8	16.2	12.9	16.5
Suicide	9.2	10.8	9.9	11.6
Homicide	13.4	8.5	11.9	7.9
Injury by firearm	16.0	12.9	15.1	12.8

GOVERNMENT

STATE AND LOCAL TAXES, 1995–96	State	U.S.
Per capita (dollars)	2 721	2 477
Percent of personal income	10.4	10.8

IN LOCAL AND STATE TAXES COMBINED (EXCLUDING CORPO-rate income taxes), Maryland taxes were a smaller percentage of personal income than the national average. But Maryland's high per capita income meant that the dollar amount of these taxes per capita exceeded the national average by 10 percent. A slightly larger percentage of local and state tax was collected by local authorities (43.2 percent in Maryland and 40.8 percent nationally), of which most was property tax. State taxes alone were only slightly higher than the national average, on a per capita basis. General sales and license taxes were lower in the state, but individual income taxes were higher. Corporate taxation per capita in the state was half the national level. Direct expenditure per capita was also higher in Maryland, though state expenditures on education, public welfare, and hospitals were lower than average. The categories with higher per capita spending were highways and especially police protection and corrections, with a level substantially higher than that of the United States. There was a slightly higher than average per capita debt at the end of the 1996–97 fiscal year, but a larger amount of cash and security holdings as well.

Maryland received 2.7 percent of all federal expenditures in 1997, which was significantly higher than its 1.9 percent share of total U.S. population. Reflecting the state's proximity to Washington, D.C., and its large federal establishments, salaries, wages, and procurement spending far exceeded the state's population share. Retirement payments were the largest category and were higher than population share, reflecting the many federal retirees.

State Government Finances, 1996–97

	Millions of dollars	Percent distribu-tion	Dollars per capita State	Dollars per capita U.S.
General revenue	14 800	100.0	2 905	3 049
Intergovernmental revenue	3 411	23.1	670	863
Taxes	8 604	58.1	1 689	1 660
General sales	2 095	14.2	411	551
Selective sales	1 600	10.8	314	257
License taxes	350	2.4	69	106
Individual income	3 769	25.5	740	542
Corporation net income	343	2.3	67	115
Other taxes	448	3.0	88	90
Other general revenue	2 784	18.8	547	526
General expenditure	14 002	100.0	2 749	2 951
Intergovernmental expenditure	3 536	25.3	694	989
Direct expenditure	10 466	74.7	2 055	1 962
General expenditure, by function:				
Education	4 401	31.4	864	1 033
Public welfare	3 023	21.6	593	761
Hospitals and health	1 099	7.9	216	237
Highways	1 245	8.9	244	225
Police protection and corrections	992	7.1	195	137
Natural resources, parks and recreation	474	3.4	93	63
Governmental administration	668	4.8	131	107
Interest on general debt	602	4.3	118	99
Other and unallocable	1 498	10.7	294	290
Debt at end of fiscal year	9 873	NA	1 938	1 706
Cash and security holdings	40 443	NA	7 939	6 683

Federal Spending within State

	Federal funds, fiscal 1997		
	Millions of dollars	Percent distribution	Percent of U.S. total*
Total within state	38 869	100.0	2.7
Payments to individuals	16 013	41.2	2.0
Retirement and disability	10 165	26.2	2.2
Medicare	3 806	9.8	1.8
Food stamps	323	0.8	1.7
Supplemental Security Income	374	1.0	1.4
Grants	4 664	12.0	1.9
Medicaid and other health	2 423	6.2	2.1
Nutrition and family welfare	743	1.9	1.6
Education	275	0.7	1.6
Housing and community development	212	0.5	1.9
Salaries and wages	7 556	19.4	4.6
Defense procurement contracts	3 869	10.0	3.2
Non-defense procurement contracts	4 574	11.8	6.3

*State population is 1.9 percent of the U.S. total.

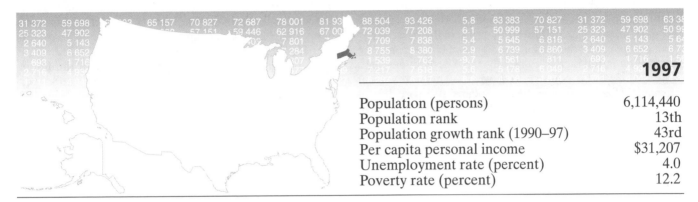

1997

Population (persons)	6,114,440
Population rank	13th
Population growth rank (1990–97)	43rd
Per capita personal income	$31,207
Unemployment rate (percent)	4.0
Poverty rate (percent)	12.2

MASSACHUSETTS HAD MODEST POPULATION GROWTH IN THE 1990s, and what growth the state had was confined to the school-age and over-65 age groups. Out-migration to other states largely negated the effect of natural increase (births minus deaths). However, a larger proportion of the stable working-age population entered the labor force over the decade, and an even larger proportion found employment. Job growth was strongest in services but also occurred in transportation, communications, and utilities and the small agricultural services sector. Average wages per worker grew faster than the national average, and overall per capita income stayed about 25 percent above the national average. Transfer payments grew faster than aggregate personal income.

The income of the median household fell in real terms, though it was still above the national average as of 1997. This decrease suggests that there was some erosion of the middle class in the state despite overall growth. Though Massachusetts was a state heavily dependent on manufacturing in the past, the service sector was already larger than manufacturing in 1989, measured by aggregate worker earnings, and more than twice as large by 1997. The share of gross state product accounted for by manufacturing fell from 19.2 percent in 1989 to 15.5 percent in 1996. Massachusetts is a highly urbanized state, with the vast majority of people living in metropolitan counties.

Average Annual Population Growth: 1990–97

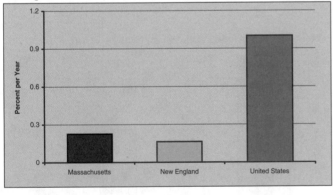

Median Household Income: 1989–97 (1997 dollars)

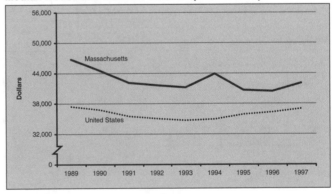

Unemployment Rate: 1989–97

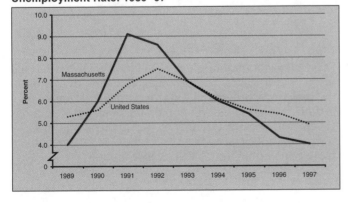

THE MASSACHUSETTS UNEMPLOYMENT RATE ROSE HIGHER, but then fell faster and further, than the U.S. rate over the years 1989 to 1997. The 1991 unemployment rate of 9.1 percent was the highest in the region. By 1997, Massachusetts at 4.0 percent unemployment had lower unemployment than most states, even while many of the states in New England had still lower unemployment.

POPULATION AND LABOR FORCE

MASSACHUSETTS'S POPULATION GREW A TOTAL OF 1.6 PERCENT from 1990 to 1997, in the bottom 20 percent of all U.S. states but third highest in New England. The White population declined over the period, at a rate of 0.2 percent per year, compared to the national increase of 0.4 percent. The Asian population increased rapidly at 5.4 percent per year, faster than in the country as a whole. The numbers of Hispanic, Blacks, and Native Americans also rose, but at rates lower than the national average. Population growth was confined to the 5–17 and 65 and over age groups. The working-age portion of the population (16 and older) declined from 1990 to 1993 and then started to rise again, ending up in 1997 at just above the 1990 level. The civilian labor force rose somewhat faster, and after 1992, employment growth outstripped both, bringing down the unemployment rate. A high concentration of people (98.5 percent) in Massachusetts lived in metropolitan areas in 1997, a level relatively unchanged throughout the decade.

Population and Labor Force

	1980	1990	1991	1992	1993	1994	1995	1996	1997	Change* State	Change* U.S.
Population											
Total number of persons (thousands)	5 737	6 018	5 997	5 992	6 008	6 027	6 058	6 083	6 114	0.2	1.0
Percent distribution:											
White, Non-Hispanic	92.5	87.8	87.6	87.2	86.8	86.4	86.1	85.8	85.4	-0.2	0.4
Black, Non-Hispanic	3.7	4.8	4.8	4.9	5.0	5.0	5.1	5.1	5.2	1.3	1.4
Asian	0.9	2.4	2.6	2.8	2.9	3.0	3.2	3.3	3.4	5.4	4.1
Native American	0.2	0.2	0.2	0.2	0.2	0.2	0.2	0.2	0.2	0.7	1.6
Hispanic	2.5	4.9	5.0	5.1	5.3	5.4	5.5	5.7	5.9	2.9	3.8
In metropolitan areas	96.4	98.5	98.5	98.5	98.5	98.5	98.5	98.5	98.5	0.2	1.0
Total number of households (thousands)	2 033	2 247	2 249	2 264	2 264	2 269	2 297	2 322	NA	0.5	1.2
Labor Force (thousands)											
Population 16 and over	4 460	4 810	4 767	4 749	4 744	4 752	4 775	4 794	4 816	0.0	1.0
Civilian labor force	2 867	3 228	3 162	3 145	3 164	3 173	3 164	3 172	3 260	0.1	1.1
Employed	2 706	3 033	2 876	2 876	2 945	2 982	2 994	3 035	3 129	0.4	1.2
Percent of population	60.7	63.1	60.3	60.6	62.1	62.8	62.7	63.3	65.0		
Unemployment rate (percent)	5.6	6.0	9.1	8.6	6.9	6.0	5.4	4.3	4.0		

*Compound annual average percent change, 1990–1997; 1990–1996 for households.

Population Change and Components: 1990–97

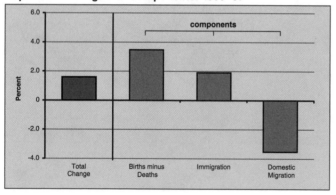

Average Annual Household and Population Growth

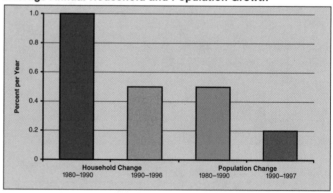

Population by Age; Births and Deaths

	1990 State	1990 U.S.	1997 State	1997 U.S.
Age distribution (percent)				
Under 5 years	7.0	7.6	6.5	7.2
5 to 17 years	15.5	18.2	17.2	18.8
18 to 64 years	64.0	61.8	62.2	61.3
65 years and over	13.6	12.5	14.1	12.7
Birth and death rates (per thousand population)				
Births	15.4	16.7	13.5	14.6
Deaths	8.8	8.6	8.9	8.6

LIKE MANY OTHER STATES IN NEW ENGLAND, Massachusetts had an older population than the United States had a whole. The percentage of the population in the preschool and school range was smaller than average in 1997, while the elderly population constituted a larger group. With a birth rate of 13.5 per 1,000 people in 1997, which was lower than the U.S. average of 14.6, trends in these population groups will likely continue.

HOUSEHOLD AND PERSONAL INCOME

HOUSEHOLD INCOME AND PERSONS IN POVERTY	1990	1995	1996	1997	
				State	U.S.
Median household income (1997 dollars)	44 511	40 624	40 400	42 023	37 005
Persons in poverty (thousands)	626	665	622	732	35 574
Poverty rate (percent)	10.7	11.0	10.1	12.2	13.3

THE INCOME OF THE MEDIAN HOUSEHOLD IN MASSACHUSETTS, when adjusted for inflation, fell from 1989 to 1993 and has improved little since. The state's median household income was above the U.S. median by 13.6 percent in 1997 but had been 25 percent higher in 1989. Poverty in the state was below the U.S. average in the 1990s, though it was closer to that average in 1997 than it had been in 1990.

Per capita personal income, however, was 25 percent above the U.S. average in 1989 and grew about as fast as in the nation. Personal income averages the cash and in-kind incomes of everyone in the state, while median household income represents the cash income of the household at the middle; the differences in trend between the two are suggestive of growth in the proportion of lower income people along with income gains for the high-income people not represented by the median.

Transfer payments were the fastest growing component of aggregate income but did not rise as quickly as in the rest of the country. Adjustment for residence was negative, indicating net commuting into the state to earn income, and increased 6.9 percent per year.

Transfer payments have grown about twice as fast as personal income in Massachusetts, with the fastest average yearly growth from 1990 to 1997 occurring in the Supplemental Security Income program (9.5 percent) and medical payments (9 percent). Other payments that are given primarily to the elderly, such as Social Security, grew about as fast as total transfer payments. Income maintenance payments, on the whole, grew at a much slower rate, and the family assistance program, actually declined by 5 percent per year on average.

Personal Income
(millions of dollars)

	1980	1989	1990	1991	1992	1993	1994	1995	1996	1997	Change*
Earnings by place of work	45 168	100 012	101 547	101 024	107 119	111 609	116 493	123 373	130 377	139 499	4.2
Wages and salaries	37 576	81 888	83 188	82 388	86 111	89 270	93 436	99 454	106 000	114 239	4.2
Other labor income	3 722	8 681	9 122	9 573	10 280	10 979	11 482	11 270	11 084	11 244	3.3
Proprietors' income	3 871	9 443	9 237	9 063	10 728	11 361	11 575	12 650	13 292	14 016	5.1
Farm	55	97	71	95	101	101	66	50	70	87	-1.4
Nonfarm	3 816	9 346	9 166	8 968	10 627	11 259	11 509	12 600	13 222	13 929	5.1
(–) Personal contributions for social insurance	2 264	6 117	6 253	6 390	6 628	6 933	7 391	7 804	8 102	8 690	4.5
(+) Adjustment for residence	-482	-1 991	-2 103	-2 180	-2 300	-2 502	-2 711	-2 856	-3 178	-3 388	NA
(=) **Net earnings by state of residence**	42 423	91 904	93 191	92 454	98 191	102 174	106 392	112 713	119 097	127 422	4.2
(+) Dividends, interest, and rent	10 109	26 442	26 746	26 415	25 213	25 664	27 332	30 265	32 943	34 296	3.3
(+) Transfer payments	9 413	17 806	19 750	22 597	23 635	24 366	25 593	27 163	27 836	29 190	6.4
(=) **Total personal income**	61 945	136 152	139 687	141 466	147 039	152 204	159 317	170 141	179 876	190 908	4.3
Farm	109	166	152	173	176	181	147	141	165	183	1.2
Nonfarm	61 835	135 986	139 535	141 293	146 862	152 023	159 170	170 000	179 711	190 725	4.3
Personal income per capita (dollars)											
Current dollars	10 780	22 634	23 211	23 593	24 541	25 335	26 426	28 073	29 559	31 207	4.1
1997 dollars	20 612	28 614	27 931	27 244	27 451	27 568	28 083	29 182	30 101	31 207	1.1

*Compound annual average percent change, 1989–1997

Government Transfer Payments

	Millions of dollars		Percent change*	
	1990	1997	State	U.S.
Total government payments to individuals	18 728	28 062	49.8	62.7
Retirement, disability, and insurance	8 609	12 283	42.7	48.2
Social Security	6 178	8 826	42.8	46.1
Government employee retirement	2 298	3 310	44.0	60.3
Medical payments	6 741	12 304	82.5	101.2
Income maintenance	1 625	1 936	19.1	58.0
Supplemental Security Income	400	755	88.7	75.4
Family assistance	674	463	-31.3	-0.5
Food Stamps	222	252	13.7	27.1
Other income maintenance	329	466	41.5	189.8
Unemployment insurance benefits	1 075	724	-32.6	10.6
Veterans benefits and other	678	815	20.2	30.8

*Percent change, 1990–1997

Government Payments to Individuals: 1997

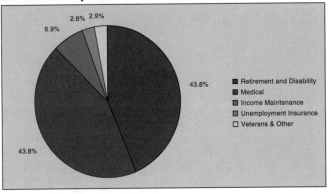

- Retirement and Disability
- Medical
- Income Maintenance
- Unemployment Insurance
- Veterans & Other

ECONOMIC STRUCTURE

LEADING PRIVATE INDUSTRIES, 1997 (Worker and proprietor earnings, millions of dollars)		FASTEST EARNINGS GROWTH, 1989–97 (percent increase)	
Health services	$13 820	Securities brokers	202.9
Business services	11 028	Electric, gas and sanitary services	108.5
Engineering and management services	8 389	Business services	98.6
Educational services	4 373	Real estate	79.2
Securities brokers	4 330	Engineering and management services	66.0

TOTAL EMPLOYMENT IN MASSACHUSETTS DECLINED IN 1990 and 1991 but grew steadily each year afterward, for an average annual gain of 0.6 percent. The fastest growing nonfarm sectors are services and agricultural services, forestry, fisheries, and other, though the latter grew from a small base in 1989. Manufacturing employment fell at a rate of 2.6 percent per year overall, despite managing slight gains in 1996 and 1997. Total earnings grew in the same period, as did earnings in every nonfarm sector. The fastest growing sectors in Massachusetts were finance, insurance, and real estate, services, and transportation, communications, and public utilities. Manufacturing earnings grew 1.7 percent per year. The largest industries in Massachusetts, as in other states within the region, are mostly service oriented. Educational services earned $4.3 billion in 1997, underlining the importance of private schools and universities to the economy. The top-placed manufacturing industry, industrial machinery, was number six.

Employment and Earnings by Sector

	1980	1989	1990	1991	1992	1993	1994	1995	1996	1997 Number	1997 Percent of total	Change*
Employment (thousands of persons)												
Total	3 142	3 751	3 646	3 486	3 517	3 587	3 660	3 748	3 825	3 922	100.0	0.6
Farm	16	13	13	13	12	12	12	11	11	11	0.3	-2.0
Nonfarm	3 126	3 738	3 633	3 473	3 505	3 575	3 649	3 737	3 815	3 911	99.7	0.6
Private nonfarm	2 685	3 285	3 183	3 037	3 077	3 143	3 220	3 303	3 381	3 473	88.5	0.7
Agricultural service, forestry, and fishing	20	31	29	29	29	33	34	34	36	38	1.0	2.8
Mining	2	3	3	2	2	2	3	3	2	2	0.1	-2.5
Construction	109	189	162	139	142	151	161	167	173	181	4.6	-0.5
Manufacturing	688	574	533	497	480	469	466	462	462	466	11.9	-2.6
Transportation and public utilities	132	142	145	140	138	145	150	150	154	160	4.1	1.5
Wholesale trade	156	191	180	171	171	167	172	178	180	183	4.7	-0.5
Retail trade	500	624	593	556	562	569	589	603	613	625	15.9	0.0
Finance, insurance, and real estate	239	306	299	286	279	284	300	304	311	321	8.2	0.6
Services	837	1 226	1 238	1 217	1 273	1 324	1 345	1 402	1 448	1 496	38.2	2.5
Government	442	453	451	436	428	432	429	433	434	439	11.2	-0.4
Earnings (millions of dollars)												
Total	45 168	100 012	101 547	101 024	107 119	111 609	116 493	123 373	130 377	139 499	100.0	4.2
Farm	109	166	152	173	176	181	147	141	165	183	0.1	1.2
Nonfarm	45 059	99 846	101 396	100 851	106 942	111 428	116 346	123 232	130 212	139 317	99.9	4.3
Private nonfarm	38 673	87 866	88 827	88 251	94 152	97 911	102 212	108 650	115 099	123 663	88.6	4.4
Agricultural service, forestry, and fishing	194	574	581	574	571	567	587	603	639	690	0.5	2.3
Mining	201	76	79	66	74	67	72	73	67	76	0.1	0.0
Construction	1 918	6 058	5 091	4 307	4 391	4 787	5 263	5 516	5 929	6 409	4.6	0.7
Manufacturing	12 841	20 841	20 489	20 309	20 809	20 709	21 143	21 866	22 573	23 910	17.1	1.7
Transportation and public utilities	2 887	4 960	5 180	5 429	5 794	6 251	6 486	6 836	7 127	7 579	5.4	5.4
Wholesale trade	2 891	6 924	6 969	6 805	7 155	7 165	7 622	8 189	8 712	9 340	6.7	3.8
Retail trade	4 335	9 827	9 523	9 129	9 478	9 843	10 343	10 716	11 271	11 850	8.5	2.4
Finance, insurance, and real estate	2 938	8 053	8 452	8 399	9 509	10 487	11 048	12 138	13 252	14 340	10.3	7.5
Services	10 468	30 551	32 462	33 232	36 370	38 035	39 648	42 713	45 528	49 469	35.5	6.2
Government	6 386	11 980	12 568	12 600	12 791	13 516	14 134	14 583	15 114	15 654	11.2	3.4

*Compound annual average percent change, 1989–1997

ECONOMIC STRUCTURE (Continued)

MASSACHUSETTS HAD AN AVERAGE WAGE IN 1997 THAT WAS higher than both the U.S. and the New England averages. There was only one sector that was lower than the U.S. average, mining, and though it was 22.9 percent lower than the U.S. average, it was 1.1 percent higher than the average in New England. Finance, insurance, and real estate was the sector with the fastest growing average wage. Construction and agricultural wages in Massachusetts in 1997 were highest when compared against both the U.S. and New England average wages, followed by finance, insurance, and real estate; wholesale trade; and services. Average wages grew 4.3 percent from 1989 to 1997, faster than the U.S. rate of 3.5 percent.

Manufacturing in Massachusetts dropped significantly as a percentage of gross state product between 1989 and 1996. Most of this decline occurred between 1989 and 1994. From 1994 through 1996, the manufacturing share was between 1.8 and 2.1 percentage points below the U.S. share. Manufacturing production was tilted heavily to durable goods production, which was twice as large as nondurable goods production.

Goods exports in Massachusetts grew quickly from 1994 to 1997, increasing 38 percent over the period. Of the export commodities in the top five, one, chemical products, was a nondurable good.

Average Annual Wages and Salaries by Sector
(dollars)

	1989	1996	1997	
			State	U.S.
All wage and salary workers	24 936	33 167	34 878	29 809
Farm	10 464	16 461	17 344	16 442
Nonfarm	24 963	33 194	34 905	29 900
Private nonfarm	25 036	33 384	35 228	29 867
Agricultural service, forestry, and fishing	19 859	23 322	24 200	17 941
Mining	33 365	34 423	38 414	49 800
Construction	29 784	37 678	39 618	31 765
Manufacturing	31 843	43 036	45 634	38 351
Transportation and utilities	30 958	37 777	38 877	38 222
Wholesale trade	33 122	45 704	48 164	39 466
Retail trade	14 250	17 256	17 909	16 206
Finance, insurance, and real estate	32 332	51 668	55 261	44 993
Services	23 020	31 353	33 186	27 588
Government	24 505	31 988	32 815	30 062

Gross State Product and Manufacturing
(millions of dollars, except as noted)

	1989	1994	1995	1996
Gross state product, total	158 232	185 988	195 874	208 591
Manufacturing:				
Millions of dollars	30 347	29 587	30 700	32 265
Percent of total gross state product	19.2	15.9	15.7	15.5
Per worker (dollars)	52 885	63 492	66 424	69 798
New capital expenditures, manufacturing	NA	2 344	2 756	2 860

Exports of Goods
(millions of dollars)

	1994	1995	1996	1997
All goods	12 586	14 396	15 368	17 368
Manufactures	12 133	13 931	14 865	16 919
Agricultural and livestock products	50	46	42	38
Other commodities	403	419	462	411
Top goods exports, 1997:				
Industrial machinery and computers	3 908	4 319	4 599	5 018
Electric and electronic equipment	2 688	3 263	3 214	3 780
Scientific and measuring instruments	1 910	2 159	2 471	2 809
Chemical products	717	896	1 024	1 225
Fabricated metal products	449	476	550	706

HOUSING

HOUSING PRODUCTION IN MASSACHUSETTS ROUGHLY FOL-lowed the performance of other states in the region, which was the only region not to thrive in the housing expansion of 1991–97. The amount of new construction (building permits plus manufactured housing put in place) per 1,000 people, a way of comparing activity between states of varying size, was significantly lower than the U.S. rate of 6.5 per 1,000 in 1997. On the other hand, existing home sales regained all their recession losses and by 1994 were back at prerecession levels; they increased 40 percent from 1989 to 1997, faster than U.S. sales, which increased 27.5 percent. Homeownership rates were consistently lower than U.S. rates. Rental vacancy rates reached a decade high point of 8.8 percent in 1992 but have declined since to well below the national average.

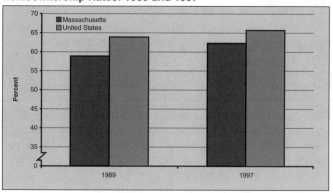

Homeownership Rates: 1989 and 1997

Housing Supply

	1989	1990	1991	1992	1993	1994	1995	1996	1997
Residential building permits (thousands)	21.3	14.3	12.7	16.4	17.5	18.1	16.4	17.3	17.2
New home production (including manufactured housing):									
Thousands of homes	22.0	14.5	12.7	16.5	17.8	18.5	16.7	17.3	17.4
Rate per 1,000 population									
Massachusetts	3.7	2.4	2.1	2.8	3.0	3.1	2.8	2.8	2.8
U.S.	6.2	5.2	4.5	5.1	5.6	6.4	6.3	6.6	6.5
Existing home sales:									
Thousands of homes	67.4	44.0	49.6	57.6	66.0	68.7	68.1	81.9	94.3
Change from previous year (percent)									
Massachusetts	-11.9	-34.7	12.7	16.1	14.6	4.1	-0.9	20.3	15.1
U.S.	-3.9	-4.0	0.0	9.2	8.2	4.8	-3.7	7.5	3.8
Home ownership rate (percent of households)	58.9	58.6	60.2	61.8	60.7	60.6	60.2	61.7	62.3
Rental vacancy rate (percent of rental housing units)	5.0	6.9	8.3	8.8	7.8	7.1	6.2	5.8	5.2

Note: Manufactured housing data for 1991 and 1996 suppressed because estimate was based on too few responses.

AGRICULTURE

FARM RECEIPTS ROSE FROM 1989 TO 1997, THOUGH GROWTH was fairly flat through 1995. Production expenses were quite high and increased throughout the decade. Expenses were never high enough to render realized net income negligible or negative, but net income in 1997 was about the same as in 1989. Corporate farming grew over the period; about one-third of net income went to corporate farms in 1996 and 1997. Total net farm proprietors' income reached its peak in 1992 and 1993. Farms tended to be smaller in terms of acreage, but were nevertheless worth slightly more than those in the United States, on average.

MASSACHUSETTS FARMS, 1997	
Number of farms	6 200
Total acres (thousands):	570
Average per farm	92
Value of land and buildings (millions of dollars)	3 534
Average per farm (dollars)	570 000

Farm Income
(millions of dollars)

	1980	1989	1990	1991	1992	1993	1994	1995	1996	1997
Gross income	351	484	474	509	508	501	506	488	550	587
Receipts from sales	317	420	421	457	455	449	455	441	505	535
Government payments	1	4	3	1	5	4	5	2	2	1
Imputed and miscellaneous income	34	60	51	51	49	48	46	44	43	51
(−) Production expenses	299	356	384	385	377	382	403	420	429	456
(=) Realized net income	52	128	90	124	132	119	102	67	121	131
(+) Inventory change	3	-5	1	-10	0	-7	2	-2	-12	-1
(=) Net income	55	123	91	114	131	112	105	66	109	129
Corporate income	0	26	20	19	31	10	39	16	39	42
Farm proprietors income	55	97	71	95	101	101	66	50	70	87

EDUCATION

EDUCATIONAL ATTAINMENT Percent of population age 25 and over, 1997	State	United States
High school graduate or higher	85.9	82.1
College graduate or higher	33.5	23.9

MASSACHUSETTS RANKED 14TH IN THE UNITED STATES AND first in the region in the proportion of its population 25 and over with a high school diploma. Per pupil spending in elementary and secondary schools was higher than in the rest of the country, as were teacher salaries, though salaries were substantially lower than those in neighboring Connecticut. Massachusetts was second in the nation in the percentage of the population over 25 with a bachelor's degree and was the highest ranking New England state. In 1996, 26.5 percent of people aged 18 to 34 were enrolled in higher education, higher than the national average. The number of minorities enrolled in 1996 was lower than the U.S. average, yet Massachusetts had the highest percentage in all of New England.

High School Completion: 1990–97

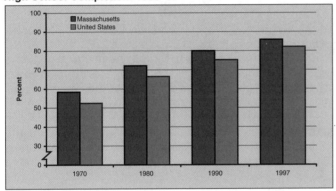

Education Indicators

	State	U.S.
Elementary and secondary schools		
Enrollment, 1995–96		
Total (thousands)	1 041	49 873
Percent in private schools	12.1	10.1
Expenditures per pupil (dollars), 1995–96	7 613	6 146
Average teacher salary (dollars), 1996–97	43 806	38 509
Higher education		
Enrollment, 1996–97		
Total (thousands)	410	14 218
Percent of population 18–34	26.5	21.8
Percent minority	17.7	26.1
Percent in private schools	57.7	22.6

HEALTH

THE AGE-ADJUSTED DEATH RATE (THE RATE IN WHICH changes in the age composition of the population are taken into account) in Massachusetts was consistently lower than the national average in the 1990s, falling steadily from 1990 to 1997. Infant mortality was likewise lower than the national average, reaching near the nationwide low point in 1997 with a rate of 4.3 percent. Health insurance was relatively accessible to the resident population in Massachusetts, which had a lower rate of those in need of health insurance than the country at large. Crude death rates for cancer, Alzheimer's disease, heart disease, and chronic obstructive pulmonary diseases (including emphysema) were above average, but when adjusted for age, rates for heart disease and chronic obstructive pulmonary diseases fell below the national rate.

Health Indicators

	1990	1995	1996	1997
Infant mortality *(rate per thousand live births)*				
Massachusetts	7.0	5.2	4.9	4.3
U.S.	9.2	7.6	7.3	7.1
Total deaths, age-adjusted rate *(rate per thousand population)*				
Massachusetts	4.7	4.5	4.4	4.2
U.S.	5.2	5.0	4.9	4.8
Persons not covered by health insurance *(percent of population)*				
Massachusetts	9.1	11.1	12.4	12.6
U.S.	13.9	15.4	15.6	16.1

Leading Causes of Death, 1996
(deaths per 100,000 population)

	Age-adjusted		Not age-adjusted	
	State	U.S.	State	U.S.
Deaths from all causes	440.5	491.6	908.2	872.5
Heart disease	116.4	134.5	276.5	276.4
Cancer	130.9	127.9	229.0	203.4
Cerebrovascular diseases	19.9	26.4	55.1	60.3
Chronic obstructive pulmonary disease	18.1	21.0	40.1	40.0
Diabetes mellitus	11.4	13.6	22.2	23.3
Pneumonia and influenza	14.5	12.8	45.9	31.6
HIV	8.9	11.1	10.0	11.7
Liver disease	7.0	7.5	9.4	9.4
Alzheimer's disease	2.9	2.7	10.4	8.1
Accidents and adverse effects	14.7	30.4	21.0	35.8
Motor vehicle accidents	7.2	16.2	7.5	16.5
Suicide	7.5	10.8	8.0	11.6
Homicide	3.6	8.5	3.1	7.9
Injury by firearm	4.0	12.9	3.8	12.8

GOVERNMENT

STATE AND LOCAL TAXES, 1995–96	State	U.S.
Per capita (dollars)	2 937	2 477
Percent of personal income	10.5	10.8

DESPITE ITS REPUTATION FOR BEING A HIGH-TAX STATE, Massachusetts's state and local taxes (other than corporate) actually consumed a smaller share of the state's personal income (10.5 percent) than the national average (10.8 percent). But given the state's high income levels, per capita taxes were substantially higher than the U.S. average. A smaller percentage of taxation was levied by local governments, while at the state level, general taxes were 131 percent higher than taxes in the rest of the country, calculated on a per capita basis. Sales taxes (general and selected), license taxes, and other taxes were lower, but individual income and corporation net income taxes were 216.7 percent and 172.8 percent larger, respectively, than the U.S. average. State per capita expenditures were higher by 126 percent, but state spending for education was only 78 percent of the per capita outlay of the average state government. Public welfare spending was higher per capita, as was spending on health and hospitals, highways, and police protection and corrections.

Federal funds disbursed in Massachusetts totaled $37.1 billion in 1997, which was about 2.6 percent of all funds disbursed in the 50 states and the District of Columbia. The population of the state equaled 2.3 percent of the total U.S. population. Direct payments to individuals roughly paralleled total funds distributed, but with lower than average payments for food stamps and Supplemental Security Income, the category that drove up the group was Medicare. Likewise, in grants given to the state, Medicaid raised spending levels. Salaries and wages were significantly less than 2.6 percent, but housing and community affairs grants to Massachusetts were well above the state's share of population and aggregate federal spending. Defense procurement was quite important to the state and accounted for 13.2 percent of all federal funds spent there.

State Government Finances, 1996–97

	Millions of dollars	Percent distribution	Dollars per capita State	Dollars per capita U.S.
General revenue	23 811	100.0	3 892	3 049
Intergovernmental revenue	5 809	24.4	949	863
Taxes	13 305	55.9	2 175	1 660
General sales	2 876	12.1	470	551
Selective sales	1 341	5.6	219	257
License taxes	431	1.8	70	106
Individual income	7 182	30.2	1 174	542
Corporation net income	1 213	5.1	198	115
Other taxes	262	1.1	43	90
Other general revenue	4 697	19.7	768	526
General expenditure	23 589	100.0	3 856	2 951
Intergovernmental expenditure	5 637	23.9	921	989
Direct expenditure	17 952	76.1	2 934	1 962
General expenditure, by function:				
Education	4 956	21.0	810	1 033
Public welfare	5 881	24.9	961	761
Hospitals and health	2 212	9.4	362	237
Highways	2 144	9.1	350	225
Police protection and corrections	1 078	4.6	176	137
Natural resources, parks and recreation	345	1.5	56	63
Governmental administration	982	4.2	161	107
Interest on general debt	1 771	7.5	289	99
Other and unallocable	4 219	17.9	690	290
Debt at end of fiscal year	29 386	NA	4 803	1 706
Cash and security holdings	35 435	NA	5 792	6 683

Federal Spending within State

	Federal funds, fiscal 1997		
	Millions of dollars	Percent distribution	Percent of U.S. total*
Total within state	37 086	100.0	2.6
Payments to individuals	20 283	54.7	2.6
Retirement and disability	10 528	28.4	2.3
Medicare	6 283	16.9	3.0
Food stamps	260	0.7	1.3
Supplemental Security Income	614	1.7	2.3
Grants	7 490	20.2	3.0
Medicaid and other health	3 871	10.4	3.4
Nutrition and family welfare	1 134	3.1	2.4
Education	379	1.0	2.2
Housing and community development	358	1.0	3.2
Salaries and wages	2 824	7.6	1.7
Defense procurement contracts	4 885	13.2	4.1
Non-defense procurement contracts	1 233	3.3	1.7

*State population is 2.3 percent of the U.S. total.

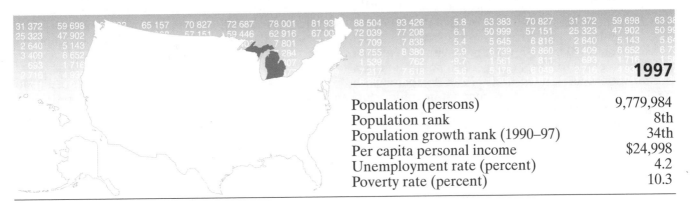

1997

Population (persons)	9,779,984
Population rank	8th
Population growth rank (1990–97)	34th
Per capita personal income	$24,998
Unemployment rate (percent)	4.2
Poverty rate (percent)	10.3

MANUFACTURING STILL REIGNED AS THE PREEMINENT SECTOR in the Michigan economy in 1997. The state's healthy manufacturing growth in the 1993–97 period brought the state out of a deep 1991–92 recession, and it maintained the state's traditional position of higher than national average incomes and low poverty rates. A number of service industries were also growing in the state, such as business services and Detroit-based Northwest Airlines. The construction industry expanded more rapidly from 1993 to 1997 than did construction nationally. Yet the predominance of automobile manufacturing and related metals and rubber-plastics industries (17 percent of all earnings in 1997 came from these three) still leaves the state vulnerable in the future to large cyclical swings.

Population in the 1990–97 period grew only two-thirds as fast as the U.S. average because of continued out-migration to other states, though the rates of departure dropped off substantially from the pace during the 1980s. Out-migration occurred mostly in the early 1990s, when unemployment was very high, which suggests that future migration may depend on the health of manufacturing and other sectors in the state economy. Michigan saw very little foreign immigration and has only small Hispanic and Asian communities (4 percent of the population). Yet with its large Black population, it had the second largest proportion of minorities in the Midwest, after Illinois.

Average Annual Population Growth: 1990–97

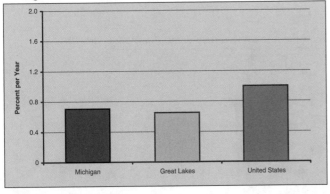

Median Household Income: 1989–97 (1997 dollars)

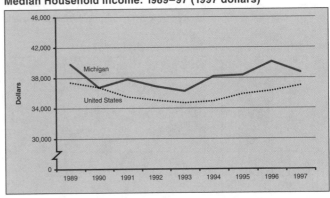

Unemployment Rate: 1989–97

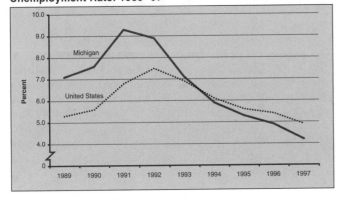

MICHIGAN'S ECONOMY IS MARKED BY LARGE SWINGS IN ITS unemployment rate, influenced heavily by the fortunes of the automobile and other manufacturing industries. Once this sector began recovering in 1993, the state unemployment rate stayed lower than the U.S. average in 1994–97 and was a remarkably low 4.2 percent in 1997. The unemployment declines since 1991 came while the labor force was expanding faster than overall population, giving Michigan a healthy increase throughout the 1990s in the percent of the population at work.

POPULATION AND LABOR FORCE

Michigan's population growth from 1990 to 1997 was not as strong as the U.S. average but represented an improvement from the no-growth trend of the 1980s. The state's population growth was largely due to natural increase from 1990 to 1997, while net migration (foreign and domestic) led to a slight 1.0 percent population loss. Out-migration decelerated in the 1990s compared with the 6.3 percent population loss from out-migration during the 1980s. There was a small amount of foreign immigration in the 1990s, which resulted in the state's high growth rates among Hispanics and Asians, both of which are small communities in absolute size. Blacks are the state's largest minority population, representing 14.1 percent of the total. Non-Hispanic Whites comprised more than 81 percent of Michigan's total population in 1997.

Labor force and employment growth between 1990 and 1997 were above the U.S. average, reflecting Michigan's high unemployment in 1990 and its subsequent rebound from recession after 1990.

Population and Labor Force

	1980	1990	1991	1992	1993	1994	1995	1996	1997	Change* State	Change* U.S.
Population											
Total number of persons (thousands)	9 262	9 311	9 390	9 465	9 523	9 586	9 663	9 734	9 780	0.7	1.0
Percent distribution:											
White, Non-Hispanic	84.3	82.2	82.1	82.0	81.9	81.7	81.6	81.4	81.3	0.5	0.4
Black, Non-Hispanic	12.8	13.8	13.9	13.9	14.0	14.1	14.1	14.1	14.1	1.0	1.4
Asian	0.7	1.2	1.2	1.2	1.3	1.3	1.4	1.5	1.5	4.7	4.1
Native American	0.5	0.6	0.6	0.6	0.6	0.6	0.6	0.6	0.6	0.3	1.6
Hispanic	1.7	2.3	2.2	2.3	2.3	2.4	2.4	2.5	2.6	2.3	3.8
In metropolitan areas	83.3	82.8	82.8	82.7	82.7	82.7	82.7	82.7	82.6	0.7	1.0
Total number of households (thousands)	3 195	3 419	3 452	3 493	3 494	3 500	3 534	3 576	NA	0.7	1.2
Labor Force (thousands)											
Population 16 and over	6 873	7 119	7 177	7 240	7 286	7 340	7 407	7 505	7 562	0.9	1.0
Civilian labor force	4 293	4 598	4 592	4 690	4 753	4 823	4 814	4 897	4 962	1.1	1.1
Employed	3 759	4 248	4 165	4 274	4 418	4 539	4 556	4 659	4 753	1.6	1.2
Percent of population	54.7	59.7	58.0	59.0	60.6	61.8	61.5	62.1	62.9		
Unemployment rate (percent)	12.4	7.6	9.3	8.9	7.1	5.9	5.3	4.9	4.2		

*Compound annual average percent change, 1990–1997; 1990–1996 for households.

Population Change and Components: 1990–97

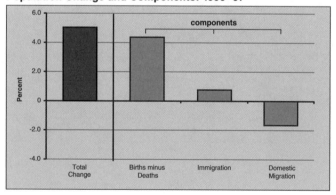

Average Annual Household and Population Growth

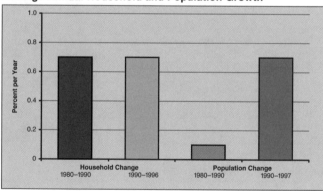

Population by Age; Births and Deaths

	1990 State	1990 U.S.	1997 State	1997 U.S.
Age distribution (percent)				
Under 5 years	7.6	7.6	6.7	7.2
5 to 17 years	18.7	18.2	18.9	18.8
18 to 64 years	61.7	61.8	62.0	61.3
65 years and over	11.9	12.5	12.4	12.7
Birth and death rates (per thousand population)				
Births	16.5	16.7	13.7	14.6
Deaths	8.5	8.6	8.6	8.6

The birth rate in Michigan has declined more steeply than in the United States from 1990 to 1997. Low birth rates yielded a smaller than average proportion of young children in Michigan as of 1997 and a smaller increase in school-age population compared to national trends. The state retained a larger than average cohort of working-age adults, and the proportion of people 65 years and older is about the same as for the United States overall.

HOUSEHOLD AND PERSONAL INCOME

HOUSEHOLD INCOME AND PERSONS IN POVERTY	1990	1995	1996	1997 State	1997 U.S.
Median household income (1997 dollars)	36 763	38 362	40 125	38 742	37 005
Persons in poverty (thousands)	1 315	1 174	1 068	1 006	35 574
Poverty rate (percent)	14.3	12.2	11.2	10.3	13.3

MEDIAN HOUSEHOLD INCOME IN MICHIGAN INCREASED slightly in inflation-adjusted dollars over the 1990–97 period, up to a level of $38,742, or about 5 percent above the national average. This appeared to stem from the state's significantly higher concentration of high-wage manufacturing workers than in most states. Poverty rates fell during the 1990s, as residents benefited from an economic recovery and the state conducted one of the nation's most aggressive programs to move families off welfare (some welfare recipients found jobs and others may have migrated to other states).

Personal income per capita was virtually equivalent in Michigan and the United States in much of the 1990s, standing at $24,998 for the state in 1997. Total wages per capita in Michigan were 5 percent higher than in the United States, but the values of transfer payments and dividends and interest were 6 percent and 3 percent lower, respectively. Nonfarm proprietors' income in Michigan is significantly lower in the aggregate than nationally (40 percent smaller), and it grew only two-thirds as fast as did wages during the 1990s.

Michigan's welfare reform and slow population growth shaped a trend toward moderate increases in transfer payments between 1990 and 1997. Welfare reform cut total payments for family assistance by a dramatic 55 percent, though medical payments on behalf of public assistance recipients still grew to more than double the 1990 level. Medicare payments grew less quickly than they did nationally, and reductions in unemployment triggered reduced unemployment benefits payments. Supplemental Security Income payments were up 94 percent from 1990 to 1997, outpacing the national average growth.

Personal Income
(millions of dollars)

	1980	1989	1990	1991	1992	1993	1994	1995	1996	1997	Change*
Earnings by place of work	70 372	119 814	124 183	125 226	133 918	143 425	154 750	163 428	167 130	176 027	4.9
Wages and salaries	57 819	98 907	102 778	103 708	110 169	115 408	125 010	133 112	140 192	148 486	5.2
Other labor income	7 796	11 912	12 523	12 929	14 928	18 269	19 746	19 659	16 090	16 275	4.0
Proprietors' income	4 757	8 995	8 882	8 588	8 821	9 748	9 994	10 656	10 849	11 266	2.9
Farm	363	617	309	170	127	183	41	237	31	66	-24.4
Nonfarm	4 394	8 378	8 573	8 418	8 694	9 565	9 953	10 419	10 818	11 200	3.7
(−) Personal contributions for social insurance	3 364	7 579	7 869	8 166	8 624	9 168	10 095	10 778	11 169	11 821	5.7
(+) Adjustment for residence	343	477	457	476	534	519	593	649	692	735	NA
(=) Net earnings by state of residence	67 351	112 712	116 771	117 535	125 829	134 777	145 248	153 299	156 653	164 941	4.9
(+) Dividends, interest, and rent	13 301	29 766	31 341	31 776	31 239	31 644	35 448	37 783	40 405	41 103	4.1
(+) Transfer payments	14 660	23 963	25 991	29 300	30 911	32 991	33 438	35 179	36 570	38 284	6.0
(=) Total personal income	95 312	166 441	174 102	178 612	187 979	199 411	214 135	226 261	233 628	244 329	4.9
Farm	552	903	672	554	555	596	471	663	501	545	-6.1
Nonfarm	94 760	165 539	173 430	178 058	187 424	198 815	213 664	225 598	233 127	243 784	5.0
Personal income per capita (dollars)											
Current dollars	10 298	17 987	18 700	19 021	19 858	20 937	22 353	23 434	24 009	24 998	4.2
1997 dollars	19 690	22 740	22 503	21 964	22 213	22 782	23 755	24 360	24 449	24 998	1.2

*Compound annual average percent change, 1989–1997

Government Transfer Payments

	Millions of dollars 1990	Millions of dollars 1997	Percent change* State	Percent change* U.S.
Total government payments to individuals	24 657	36 550	48.2	62.7
Retirement, disability, and insurance	12 744	18 530	45.4	48.2
Social Security	10 038	14 238	41.8	46.1
Government employee retirement	2 370	3 986	68.2	60.3
Medical payments	6 947	13 197	90.0	101.2
Income maintenance	2 995	2 975	-0.7	58.0
Supplemental Security Income	486	945	94.3	75.4
Family assistance	1 284	577	-55.0	-0.5
Food Stamps	696	645	-7.4	27.1
Other income maintenance	530	809	52.7	189.8
Unemployment insurance benefits	1 188	942	-20.7	10.6
Veterans benefits and other	782	905	15.7	30.8

*Percent change, 1990–1997

Government Payments to Individuals: 1997

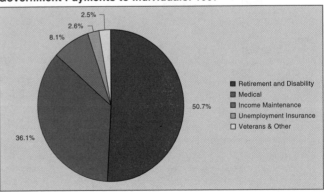

- Retirement and Disability — 50.7%
- Medical — 36.1%
- Income Maintenance — 8.1%
- Unemployment Insurance — 2.6%
- Veterans & Other — 2.5%

ECONOMIC STRUCTURE

LEADING PRIVATE INDUSTRIES, 1997 (Worker and proprietor earnings, millions of dollars)		FASTEST EARNINGS GROWTH, 1989–97 (percent increase)	
Motor vehicles and equipment	$21 206	Real estate	136.4
Health services	14 375	Air transportation	125.9
Business services	9 629	Other transportation services	104.2
Industrial machinery manufacturing	7 116	Business services	85.1
Construction specialties	6 463	Social services	77.1

THE COMPOSITION OF MICHIGAN'S ECONOMY TILTS STRONGLY toward manufacturing, which in 1997 contributed 31.2 percent of total worker earnings in the state, a share that was about 50 percent higher than that of manufacturing nationally. Of the entire national motor vehicle and equipment industry, 37 percent of total worker earnings in the industry were located in Michigan. However, even with strong auto sales in the mid-1990s, this sector's growth was not keeping up with the overall state economy: its share of jobs declined more than two percentage points, from 20.7 in 1989 to 18.4 percent in 1997. There were 12 manufacturing industries in the state with earnings of more than $1 billion but the only major one with rapid growth in the 1989–97

period was rubber and plastics.

Michigan in 1997 had a smaller proportion of service and government jobs than in the United States overall, though business services is the state's fastest growing large industry. Other large private service industries whose earnings grew at an above-average pace in the 1990s were social services, engineering, education, and health services. Air transportation was a small yet expanding industry, linked to Northwest Airlines and the greater emphasis on its hub in Detroit. Because the majority of this state's fast-growing industries of the 1990s were in the and finance service categories, Michigan's economic mix was moving slowly in the direction of the United States norm.

Employment and Earnings by Sector

	1980	1989	1990	1991	1992	1993	1994	1995	1996	1997 Number	1997 Percent of total	Change*
Employment (thousands of persons)												
Total	4 039	4 745	4 810	4 757	4 789	4 849	5 030	5 182	5 295	5 397	100.0	1.6
Farm	97	81	82	83	80	76	77	80	75	74	1.4	-1.1
Nonfarm	3 942	4 664	4 728	4 675	4 709	4 773	4 953	5 103	5 219	5 323	98.6	1.7
Private nonfarm	3 319	4 021	4 073	4 021	4 056	4 122	4 306	4 456	4 569	4 669	86.5	1.9
Agricultural service, forestry, and fishing	18	32	35	36	36	39	43	44	46	49	0.9	5.3
Mining	16	17	16	16	15	15	16	15	13	13	0.2	-3.3
Construction	156	207	212	199	203	206	221	235	252	266	4.9	3.2
Manufacturing	993	984	954	916	919	926	975	1 003	993	993	18.4	0.1
Transportation and public utilities	166	176	180	178	174	178	187	190	197	202	3.8	1.8
Wholesale trade	169	213	215	216	220	217	223	229	235	242	4.5	1.6
Retail trade	677	833	853	845	850	858	888	917	940	955	17.7	1.7
Finance, insurance, and real estate	258	323	323	322	314	320	335	346	360	370	6.9	1.7
Services	866	1 236	1 284	1 292	1 324	1 363	1 418	1 478	1 534	1 578	29.2	3.1
Government	623	643	655	654	653	651	647	646	650	654	12.1	0.2
Earnings (millions of dollars)												
Total	70 372	119 814	124 183	125 226	133 918	143 425	154 750	163 428	167 130	176 027	100.0	4.9
Farm	552	903	672	554	555	596	471	663	501	545	0.3	-6.1
Nonfarm	69 821	118 911	123 511	124 672	133 363	142 829	154 279	162 764	166 629	175 482	99.7	5.0
Private nonfarm	60 182	102 895	106 186	106 475	114 208	122 995	133 953	142 076	145 091	152 797	86.8	5.1
Agricultural service, forestry, and fishing	165	424	479	501	534	559	639	677	723	789	0.4	8.1
Mining	541	399	382	409	408	429	413	434	405	430	0.2	1.0
Construction	3 273	6 091	6 306	5 875	5 899	6 255	7 048	7 732	8 572	9 287	5.3	5.4
Manufacturing	27 536	40 982	40 442	39 590	42 750	47 379	53 137	55 383	52 931	54 899	31.2	3.7
Transportation and public utilities	4 073	6 102	6 373	6 479	6 758	7 208	7 727	8 007	8 309	8 848	5.0	4.8
Wholesale trade	3 722	7 126	7 501	7 708	8 223	8 611	9 254	9 910	10 470	11 305	6.4	5.9
Retail trade	6 569	10 672	11 024	11 180	11 709	12 065	12 887	13 582	14 245	14 993	8.5	4.3
Finance, insurance, and real estate	2 871	5 477	5 881	6 150	7 012	7 611	7 846	8 445	9 132	9 611	5.5	7.3
Services	11 432	25 624	27 798	28 582	30 915	32 878	35 002	37 907	40 304	42 636	24.2	6.6
Government	9 639	16 016	17 325	18 196	19 155	19 834	20 326	20 689	21 538	22 685	12.9	4.4

*Compound annual average percent change, 1989–1997

ECONOMIC STRUCTURE (Continued)

AVERAGING ALL SECTORS TOGETHER, ANNUAL PAY FOR WAGE and salaried workers in Michigan in 1997 was 8 percent above the national average, a differential that persisted throughout the 1990s. Wages were especially high in manufacturing, both in absolute terms and relative to the U.S. average in that sector: $48,521 per year, compared to only $38,351 in the nation. Wages in wholesale trade and construction were also substantially above the U.S. averages. The pattern did not carry over to the large services sector, where wages were 2 percent below average in Michigan, or retail trade, with 4 percent lower wages than the U.S. average. The state's finance sector also had wages much below average (a 19 percent gap) because it was not a financial center with many high-end jobs.

Despite the prominence of manufacturing in the Michigan economy, it contributed a declining share of gross state product over time, reaching a 27.2 percent share in 1996. The motor vehicle industry represented about 39 percent of total manufacturing earnings in 1997, and earnings in that industry grew only about 60 percent as fast as did total state earnings. Value added per worker grew a bit slower in Michigan manufacturing than for the whole United States from 1989 to 1996, though it was still higher than average because of the preponderance of durable goods industries (80 percent of all manufacturing).

Exports played a critical role in supporting the state's economy, because of the relatively high levels of exports of automobiles and parts and industrial machinery. Michigan had the fifth highest level of exports of all states in 1997. Exports of industrial machinery advanced steadily through the mid-1990s, and those of transportation equipment jumped 75 percent from 1993 and 1994 and then plateaued. The state's fastest growth among major exports between 1994 and 1997 came in chemical products, and the poorest performance was the decline in fabricated metal exports.

Average Annual Wages and Salaries by Sector
(dollars)

	1989	1996	1997 State	1997 U.S.
All wage and salary workers	24 135	30 906	32 156	29 809
Farm	11 424	19 999	20 691	16 442
Nonfarm	24 208	30 958	32 210	29 900
Private nonfarm	24 463	31 097	32 299	29 867
Agricultural service, forestry, and fishing	15 001	19 222	20 323	17 941
Mining	30 624	40 190	42 219	49 800
Construction	28 284	33 574	34 851	31 765
Manufacturing	35 668	46 640	48 521	38 351
Transportation and utilities	31 543	37 876	39 756	38 222
Wholesale trade	31 468	41 575	43 659	39 466
Retail trade	11 904	14 839	15 480	16 206
Finance, insurance, and real estate	24 617	34 669	36 402	44 993
Services	19 983	26 215	27 112	27 588
Government	22 851	30 138	31 674	30 062

Gross State Product and Manufacturing
(millions of dollars, except as noted)

	1989	1994	1995	1996
Gross state product, total	184 552	240 645	251 794	263 336
Manufacturing:				
Millions of dollars	53 353	70 690	71 463	71 683
Percent of total gross state product	28.9	29.4	28.4	27.2
Per worker (dollars)	54 197	72 492	71 240	72 179
New capital expenditures, manufacturing	NA	6 158	7 835	7 728

Exports of Goods
(millions of dollars)

	1994	1995	1996	1997
All goods	36 812	37 102	38 128	37 920
Manufactures	36 196	36 393	37 498	37 241
Agricultural and livestock products	171	181	174	198
Other commodities	445	528	456	482
Top goods exports, 1997:				
Transportation equipment	23 547	23 241	23 689	21 588
Industrial machinery and computers	3 991	4 169	4 281	5 333
Electric and electronic equipment	1 870	1 778	1 805	1 962
Chemical products	1 157	1 315	1 669	1 930
Fabricated metal products	1 367	1 158	1 300	1 252

HOUSING

HOUSING PRODUCTION IN MICHIGAN WAS SURPRISINGLY active during 1991 to 1997, given the moderate growth in population. Total production per capita was about equal to national rates throughout this time, prompting a growth rate of construction jobs from 1990 to 1997 that surpassed the growth of any other major sector in the state. The Detroit-Ann Arbor metropolitan area ranked 12th in the nation in new housing building permits in 1997. Housing activity included an increase in placement of mobile homes, which represent a surprisingly high 19 percent of all housing supplied in 1997. Significant increases in sales of existing homes in Michigan paralleled U.S. trends in the 1992–94 period, but sales were weaker in the state during 1996 and 1997. Nonetheless, prices of existing homes in the Detroit area advanced 7 percent in 1997, rising to a median price of $119,600.

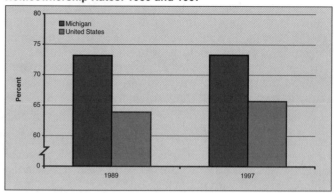

Homeownership Rates: 1989 and 1997

Rates of homeownership historically have been high, because of the nontransient population, above-average incomes, and moderate home prices. Rental vacancy rates have tended to be at or below national averages but in 1994–97 took a turn upward that could deter major apartment construction activity until the market improves.

Housing Supply

	1989	1990	1991	1992	1993	1994	1995	1996	1997
Residential building permits (thousands)	45.7	38.9	33.8	37.0	39.8	46.5	47.2	52.4	49.2
New home production (including manufactured housing):									
Thousands of homes	56.6	48.9	42.4	46.9	49.0	56.9	58.4	64.5	61.0
Rate per 1,000 population									
Michigan	6.1	5.3	4.5	5.0	5.1	5.9	6.0	6.6	6.2
U.S.	6.2	5.2	4.5	5.1	5.6	6.4	6.3	6.6	6.5
Existing home sales:									
Thousands of homes	151.6	145.0	145.0	157.3	170.6	184.2	176.3	179.8	180.3
Change from previous year (percent)									
Michigan	2.7	-4.4	0.0	8.5	8.5	8.0	-4.3	2.0	0.3
U.S.	-3.9	-4.0	0.0	9.2	8.2	4.8	-3.7	7.5	3.8
Home ownership rate (percent of households)	73.2	72.3	70.6	70.6	72.3	72.0	72.2	73.3	73.3
Rental vacancy rate (percent of rental housing units)	7.5	7.3	7.2	7.7	7.9	8.9	8.8	10.2	8.9

AGRICULTURE

THE FARMING SECTOR IN MICHIGAN, WHICH IS MUCH SMALLER than in other Midwest states, suffered through a series of difficult years in the mid-1990s. Average revenues for the 1995–97 period were only 13 percent above those of 1989–91, while production expenses rose much more rapidly. Among the three major farm products in the state, grain sales increased modestly during the 1990s, but dairy product revenues advanced only slightly and meat-animal sales declined. Total net income of farm proprietors and corporate farms was down 70 percent between the 1995–97 period and the start of the decade, as 1994, 1996, and 1997 were particularly bad years.

MICHIGAN FARMS, 1997	
Number of farms	51 000
Total acres (thousands):	10 500
Average per farm	206
Value of land and buildings (millions of dollars)	16 800
Average per farm (dollars)	329 412

Farm Income
(millions of dollars)

	1980	1989	1990	1991	1992	1993	1994	1995	1996	1997
Gross income	3 104	3 733	3 757	3 813	3 749	3 965	3 861	4 181	4 126	4 087
Receipts from sales	2 829	3 130	3 329	3 416	3 368	3 477	3 500	3 762	3 731	3 656
Government payments	11	262	169	124	143	241	102	151	110	121
Imputed and miscellaneous income	264	341	259	274	238	246	259	268	285	310
(–) Production expenses	2 742	3 228	3 477	3 610	3 596	3 826	3 875	3 842	3 925	4 193
(=) Realized net income	362	505	279	204	153	139	-14	340	201	-105
(+) Inventory change	1	168	58	-21	-13	51	62	-77	-165	181
(=) Net income	363	672	338	182	140	190	48	262	36	76
Corporate income	0	56	29	12	13	7	7	25	5	10
Farm proprietors income	363	617	309	170	127	183	41	237	31	66

EDUCATION

EDUCATIONAL ATTAINMENT Percent of population age 25 and over, 1997	State	United States
High school graduate or higher	86.0	82.1
College graduate or higher	21.0	23.9

THE EDUCATIONAL ATTAINMENT OF MICHIGAN RESIDENTS HIStorically has matched U.S. levels for the proportion with high school diplomas, but it lags the nation when it comes to percent of college graduates in the population. The relatively large proportion of blue-collar jobs and lack of major high-tech centers probably account for this trend. The percentage of the state's adult population with college degrees in 1997, 21 percent, ranked Michigan in the lower half of all states, though a higher than average proportion of current young adults were in college in 1996. For public elementary and secondary schools, per pupil spending is dramatically higher in Michigan than in the United States overall, as are average teacher salaries, reflecting the state government's emphasis on education programs and the relatively small growth in student population.

High School Completion: 1990—97

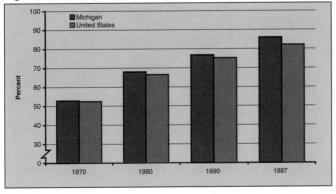

Education Indicators

	State	U.S.
Elementary and secondary schools		
Enrollment, 1995—96		
Total (thousands)	1 831	49 873
Percent in private schools	10.3	10.1
Expenditures per pupil (dollars), 1995—96...............	7 166	6 146
Average teacher salary (dollars), 1996—97...............	44 251	38 509
Higher education		
Enrollment, 1996—97		
Total (thousands)	547	14 218
Percent of population 18—34................................	23.0	21.8
Percent minority	17.5	26.1
Percent in private schools	16.1	22.6

HEALTH

ONE MAJOR HEALTH INDICATOR, INFANT MORTALITY, SHOWS A worse than average situation in Michigan, placing it in the bottom quartile of states for this key health indicator. This is a surprising result for a prosperous state with a relatively low poverty rate. Total death rates were about the same as in the United States in 1997, though Michigan had a higher incidence of death from heart disease and cancer (based on 1996 data). Deaths from accidental causes were a little below the national average. The percentage of Michigan's population covered by health insurance has been consistently high in the 1990s, reflecting the high percentage of workers in unionized and manufacturing jobs, which are more likely to offer employee benefits. Michigan in 1997 had 11.6 percent of the population not covered by insurance, compared with 16.1 percent nationally.

Health Indicators

	1990	1995	1996	1997
Infant mortality *(rate per thousand live births)*				
Michigan	10.7	8.3	7.9	8.1
U.S.	9.2	7.6	7.3	7.1
Total deaths, age-adjusted rate *(rate per thousand population)*				
Michigan	5.3	5.1	5.0	4.9
U.S.	5.2	5.0	4.9	4.8
Persons not covered by health insurance *(percent of population)*				
Michigan	9.4	9.7	8.9	11.6
U.S.	13.9	15.4	15.6	16.1

Leading Causes of Death, 1996
(deaths per 100,000 population)

	Age-adjusted		Not age-adjusted	
	State	U.S.	State	U.S.
Deaths from all causes	502.4	491.6	871.6	872.5
Heart disease	147.0	134.5	292.0	276.4
Cancer	131.7	127.9	204.1	203.4
Cerebrovascular diseases	27.2	26.4	60.0	60.3
Chronic obstructive pulmonary disease	21.1	21.0	38.4	40.0
Diabetes mellitus	14.3	13.6	24.5	23.3
Pneumonia and influenza	13.8	12.8	31.4	31.6
HIV	5.0	11.1	5.3	11.7
Liver disease	8.0	7.5	10.1	9.4
Alzheimer s disease	2.3	2.7	6.2	8.1
Accidents and adverse effects	27.1	30.4	32.1	35.8
Motor vehicle accidents	16.1	16.2	16.5	16.5
Suicide	10.8	10.8	11.6	11.6
Homicide	9.0	8.5	8.4	7.9
Injury by firearm	13.1	12.9	12.9	12.8

GOVERNMENT

STATE AND LOCAL TAXES, 1995–96	State	U.S.
Per capita (dollars)	2 360	2 477
Percent of personal income	9.9	10.8

THE COMBINED LEVELS OF STATE PLUS LOCAL GOVERNMENT taxes within Michigan were about 5 percent below the national average, on a per capita calculation, in 1995–96. While state-level taxation was higher than average, the very low tax bite at the local government level in Michigan brought the total down. Since Michigan was a relatively prosperous state with high income per capita, the tax burden as a percent of personal income, 9.9 per-cent, was nearly a full percentage point lower than the comparable U.S. figure for 1995–96.

States taxes in 1997 overall were substantially above the U.S. average on a per capita basis, especially sales tax collections, which are one-third above the national average. Individual income taxes and corporate income taxes were also high, with selective sales taxes the only major category that was below average. Almost all the extra revenue collection was reflected in the state's much higher than average education spending, much of which appears to have been transferred to local governments for their school programs, thus helping hold down the pressure on local government taxes. Spending on hospitals and health was also above average, but public welfare spending was below the national average per capita.

Michigan received a distinctly below-average share of federal dollars during 1997, compared to the large size of the state's population, because of the low level of federal civilian and military employment in-state. Procurement contracts were also particularly small, especially in defense contracting, with less than 1 percent of such spending in Michigan. Income support and medical payments were received in rough proportion to the state's population, as were most categories of grants-in-aid. Nutrition and family welfare grants was the only category where the state received higher than average amounts.

State Government Finances, 1996–97

	Millions of dollars	Percent distribution	Dollars per capita State	Dollars per capita U.S.
General revenue	33 857	100.0	3 464	3 049
Intergovernmental revenue	8 267	24.4	846	863
Taxes	19 856	58.6	2 032	1 660
General sales	7 132	21.1	730	551
Selective sales	1 740	5.1	178	257
License taxes	1 016	3.0	104	106
Individual income	5 930	17.5	607	542
Corporation net income	2 229	6.6	228	115
Other taxes	1 809	5.3	185	90
Other general revenue	5 734	16.9	587	526
General expenditure	32 546	100.0	3 330	2 951
Intergovernmental expenditure	14 145	43.5	1 447	989
Direct expenditure	18 401	56.5	1 883	1 962
General expenditure, by function:				
Education	14 309	44.0	1 464	1 033
Public welfare	6 723	20.7	688	761
Hospitals and health	3 467	10.7	355	237
Highways	2 059	6.3	211	225
Police protection and corrections	1 544	4.8	158	137
Natural resources, parks and recreation	380	1.2	39	63
Governmental administration	718	2.2	73	107
Interest on general debt	787	2.4	81	99
Other and unallocable	2 559	7.9	262	290
Debt at end of fiscal year	14 431	NA	1 477	1 706
Cash and security holdings	60 166	NA	6 156	6 683

Federal Spending within State

	Federal funds, fiscal 1997		
	Millions of dollars	Percent distribution	Percent of U.S. total*
Total within state	41 236	100.0	2.9
Payments to individuals	27 687	67.1	3.5
Retirement and disability	15 938	38.7	3.5
Medicare	7 638	18.5	3.7
Food stamps	715	1.7	3.7
Supplemental Security Income	964	2.3	3.6
Grants	8 401	20.4	3.4
Medicaid and other health	3 732	9.1	3.3
Nutrition and family welfare	1 941	4.7	4.1
Education	619	1.5	3.6
Housing and community development	339	0.8	3.0
Salaries and wages	2 741	6.6	1.7
Defense procurement contracts	1 098	2.7	0.9
Non-defense procurement contracts	912	2.2	1.2

*State population is 3.7 percent of the U.S. total.

31 372	59 698		65 157	70 827	72 687	78 001	81 93	88 504	93 426	5.8	63 383	70 827	31 372	59 698	63 3
25 323	47 902			57 151	59 446	62 916	67 00	72 039	77 208	6.1	50 999	57 151	25 323	47 902	50 9
2 640	5 143				7 801			7 709	7 838	5.4	5 645	6 816	2 640	5 143	5 6
3 409	6 652				284			8 755	8 380	2.9	6 739	6 860	3 409	6 652	6 7
693	1 716				07			1 539	762	-9.7	1 561	811	693	1 716	4
2 716								7 217	7 818	5.6	5 178	8 049	2 716		

1997

Population (persons)	4,687,408
Population rank	20th
Population growth rank (1990–97)	22nd
Per capita personal income	$26,295
Unemployment rate (percent)	3.3
Poverty rate (percent)	9.6

DURING THE 1990S, MINNESOTA EXPERIENCED VIGOROUS growth in employment and earnings, exceeding even the strong U.S. averages and making a standout performance within the Northern region. Its 1990s population growth was slightly below the U.S. average but above average for its region. In-migration has helped boost its population and employment figures. As the state's economy prospered, the per capita income has exceeded the national average. Minnesota has a strong record on education and has among the highest education attainment levels in the nation. The state's poverty, unemployment, and infant mortality rates have remained well below the national rates. While agriculture's impact on the state's economy continues to decline, the services sector has grown substantially and now dominates the state's leading industries, which include healthcare, business services, and engineering and management services. Though not growing as rapidly as the service sector, the high paying manufacturing sector is also expanding and provides a disproportionately large share of jobs in the state.

Average Annual Population Growth: 1990—97

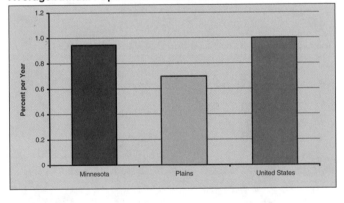

Median Household Income: 1989—97 (1997 dollars)

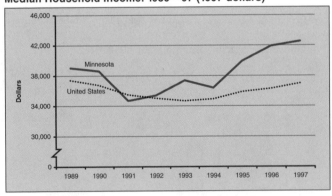

Unemployment Rate: 1989—97

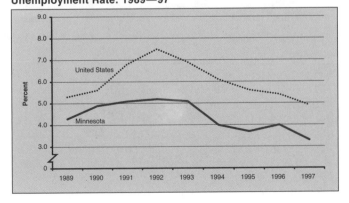

MINNESOTA'S UNEMPLOYMENT RATE HAS DECLINED SUBSTANtially over the past decade, though it never climbed very high even during the recession of the early 1990s. During the early half of the 1990s, the unemployment rate hovered around 5.0 percent; since 1994, the rate has been at 4.0 percent or below. In 1997, the rate dropped to 3.3 percent, the seventh lowest unemployment rate in the nation. Nearly 71 percent of Minnesota's population is employed, an exceptionally high employment ratio that has increased a bit since the early 1990s. The number of jobs is growing significantly faster than the population, allowing the state to maintain its low unemployment rate.

POPULATION AND LABOR FORCE

MINNESOTA'S POPULATION GREW BY 0.9 PERCENT ANNUALLY from 1990 to 1997, just below the national average of 1.0 percent. In 1997, Minnesota ranked as the 20th largest state in terms of population, the same position it held in 1990. Domestic and international in-migration of more than 100,000 has helped add to the state's population growth, which otherwise has been slowed by a below-average birth rate. The composition of Minnesota's population has shifted somewhat from 1990 to 1997. The White non-

Hispanic population maintained its high proportion of the state's population, at just below 92 percent of the total, but this level represented a 1.5 percentage point drop from 1990. Both the Asian and Hispanic populations had average annual rates of significantly higher than the national averages for both populations. The Asian population's high growth rate is bringing its size closer to the Black population, which holds the position as the largest minority in Minnesota.

Population and Labor Force

	1980	1990	1991	1992	1993	1994	1995	1996	1997	Change* State	Change* U.S.
Population											
Total number of persons (thousands)	4 076	4 387	4 428	4 472	4 524	4 566	4 605	4 648	4 687	0.9	1.0
Percent distribution:											
White, Non-Hispanic	96.2	93.4	93.6	93.3	93.0	92.7	92.5	92.2	91.9	0.7	0.4
Black, Non-Hispanic	1.3	2.4	2.2	2.3	2.4	2.5	2.6	2.7	2.7	2.8	1.4
Asian	0.8	1.8	1.9	2.0	2.1	2.2	2.3	2.4	2.5	5.6	4.1
Native American	0.9	1.1	1.2	1.2	1.2	1.2	1.2	1.2	1.2	2.0	1.6
Hispanic	0.8	1.3	1.3	1.3	1.4	1.5	1.5	1.6	1.7	4.6	3.8
In metropolitan areas	65.6	68.9	69.1	69.2	69.4	69.5	69.6	69.7	69.9	1.1	1.0
Total number of households (thousands)	1 445	1 648	1 667	1 689	1 702	1 716	1 740	1 763	NA	1.1	1.2
Labor Force (thousands)											
Population 16 and over	3 062	3 325	3 355	3 383	3 426	3 465	3 505	3 550	3 582	1.1	1.0
Civilian labor force	2 111	2 386	2 414	2 415	2 476	2 577	2 595	2 603	2 625	1.4	1.1
Employed	1 985	2 269	2 290	2 289	2 349	2 474	2 499	2 500	2 539	1.6	1.2
Percent of population	64.8	68.2	68.3	67.7	68.6	71.4	71.3	70.4	70.9		
Unemployment rate (percent)	5.9	4.9	5.1	5.2	5.1	4.0	3.7	4.0	3.3		

*Compound annual average percent change, 1990–1997; 1990–1996 for households.

Population Change and Components: 1990–97

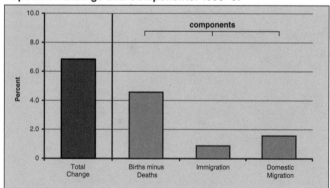

Average Annual Household and Population Growth

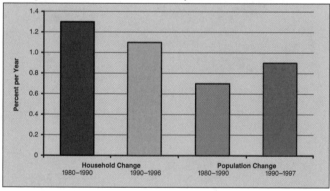

Population by Age; Births and Deaths

	1990 State	1990 U.S.	1997 State	1997 U.S.
Age distribution (percent)				
Under 5 years	7.8	7.6	6.7	7.2
5 to 17 years	19.0	18.2	20.0	18.8
18 to 64 years	60.7	61.8	61.0	61.3
65 years and over	12.5	12.5	12.3	12.7
Birth and death rates (per thousand population)				
Births	15.5	16.7	13.8	14.6
Deaths	8.0	8.6	7.9	8.6

THE AGE DISTRIBUTION OF MINNESOTA'S POPULATION SHOWS proportionately fewer children under the age of five in 1997 compared with 1990, significantly lower than the national average. The birth rate of 13.8 per 1,000 has dropped some since 1990, remaining just below the national average. The proportion of the population age 18 to 64 has grown from 1990 to 1997, counter to the national trend, contributing to the rapid growth of the labor force in the state.

HOUSEHOLD AND PERSONAL INCOME

HOUSEHOLD INCOME AND PERSONS IN POVERTY	1990	1995	1996	1997 State	1997 U.S.
Median household income (1997 dollars)	38 639	39 949	41 932	42 564	37 005
Persons in poverty (thousands)	524	427	458	457	35 574
Poverty rate (percent)	12.0	9.2	9.8	9.6	13.3

IN 1997, MINNESOTA'S MEDIAN HOUSEHOLD INCOME, AT $42,564, was the tenth highest in the nation. The state's median income was 115 percent of the national average of $37,005, a gap that has widened since 1990 as Minnesota's economy has thrived. Since 1990, Minnesota's poverty rate has dropped from 12.0 percent to 9.6 percent, well below the national average. This drop placed the state among the 15 lowest poverty rates in the nation. The increasing number of jobs and Minnesota's general prosperity have helped to lower the state's poverty rate.

Minnesota's 1997 per capita personal income of $26,295 was about 4 percent above the national average and has been growing at a slightly faster rate than U.S. averages. Nearly 71 percent of the state's population held jobs in 1997, marking the fourth consecutive year with more than 70 percent of the population employed. With the state's flourishing job market, worker and proprietors' earnings per capita reached a level 9 percent above the national average. In contrast, transfer payments per capita were 13 percent below that of the United States, while dividend and interest income per capita was at an average level in 1997.

From 1990 to 1997, transfer payments have been growing at a slower rate than nationwide, primarily because of slower growth of medical payments in Minnesota. The fastest growth was in "other income maintenance," dominated by the earned income tax credit, and Supplemental Security Income. Minnesota's payments for food stamps and family assistance have both decreased in real dollars.

Personal Income
(millions of dollars)

	1980	1989	1990	1991	1992	1993	1994	1995	1996	1997	Change*
Earnings by place of work	31 372	59 698	63 383	65 157	70 827	72 687	78 001	81 932	88 504	93 426	5.8
Wages and salaries	25 323	47 902	50 999	53 038	57 151	59 446	62 916	67 008	72 039	77 208	6.1
Other labor income	2 640	5 143	5 645	6 129	6 816	7 403	7 801	7 858	7 709	7 838	5.4
Proprietors' income	3 409	6 652	6 739	5 989	6 860	5 838	7 284	7 067	8 755	8 380	2.9
Farm	693	1 716	1 561	760	811	-316	807	268	1 539	762	-9.7
Nonfarm	2 716	4 936	5 178	5 230	6 049	6 154	6 477	6 799	7 217	7 618	5.6
(−) Personal contributions for social insurance	1 711	4 042	4 306	4 559	4 874	5 133	5 541	5 927	6 287	6 717	6.6
(+) Adjustment for residence	-100	-457	-457	-484	-497	-535	-595	-649	-672	-772	-833	NA
(=) **Net earnings by state of residence**	29 561	55 199	58 593	60 101	65 418	66 959	71 811	75 334	81 444	85 876	5.7
(+) Dividends, interest, and rent	6 628	14 255	15 003	15 520	15 730	16 063	17 343	18 292	19 496	20 362	4.6
(+) Transfer payments	5 299	10 384	11 290	12 244	13 324	14 180	14 956	15 825	16 481	16 969	6.3
(=) **Total personal income**	41 489	79 838	84 886	87 866	94 472	97 202	104 110	109 451	117 421	123 207	5.6
Farm	919	1 982	1 887	1 089	1 163	24	1 160	616	1 922	1 153	-6.6
Nonfarm	40 570	77 856	82 999	86 776	93 309	97 178	102 949	108 834	115 499	122 054	5.8
Personal income per capita (dollars)											
Current dollars	10 156	18 404	19 349	19 844	21 124	21 486	22 794	23 759	25 260	26 295	4.6
1997 dollars	19 419	23 267	23 284	22 915	23 629	23 380	24 223	24 698	25 723	26 295	1.5

*Compound annual average percent change, 1989–1997

Government Transfer Payments

	Millions of dollars 1990	Millions of dollars 1997	Percent change* State	Percent change* U.S.
Total government payments to individuals	10 640	16 119	51.5	62.7
Retirement, disability, and insurance	5 627	8 255	46.7	48.2
Social Security	4 101	5 889	43.6	46.1
Government employee retirement	1 187	2 004	68.8	60.3
Medical payments	3 315	5 669	71.0	101.2
Income maintenance	897	1 287	43.5	58.0
Supplemental Security Income	156	309	98.2	75.4
Family assistance	370	379	2.3	-0.5
Food Stamps	174	183	5.0	27.1
Other income maintenance	197	416	111.5	189.8
Unemployment insurance benefits	344	368	7.1	10.6
Veterans benefits and other	457	539	17.9	30.8

*Percent change, 1990–1997

Government Payments to Individuals: 1997

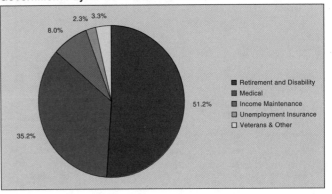

- Retirement and Disability — 51.2%
- Medical — 35.2%
- Income Maintenance — 8.0%
- Unemployment Insurance — 2.3%
- Veterans & Other — 3.3%

ECONOMIC STRUCTURE

LEADING PRIVATE INDUSTRIES, 1997 (Worker and proprietor earnings, millions of dollars)		FASTEST EARNINGS GROWTH, 1989–97 (percent increase)	
Health services	$7 751	Securities brokers	170.0
Business services	5 920	Business services	165.5
Industrial machinery manufacturing	3 818	Amusement and recreation services	137.3
Construction specialties	3 674	Real estate	126.9
Engineering and management services	2 324	Rubber and plastics manufacturing	95.0

HEALTH SERVICES AND BUSINESS SERVICES WERE Minnesota's two leading private industries in 1997, joined by engineering and management services in the top five ranking. Security industries brokers was the fastest growing industry from 1989 to 1997, but more impressive was the 165.5 percent earnings growth in the huge business services industry, representing a $3.7 billion increase over the eight years. The important role of the services sector is similar to the structure of the U.S. economy, as services provides about 30 percent of all jobs in both the state and the nation. The number of services jobs grew substantially faster than any other sector in Minnesota from 1989 to 1997. The two other industries in the state's top five, industrial machinery and construction specialties, indicate the importance of manufacturing and construction in the state's economy. Each sector provides a larger than average share of jobs; manufacturing jobs represented 14.3 percent of the 1997 total, compared to a 12.4 percent share of U.S. jobs. In contrast, the proportion of workers employed by all levels of government is nearly 2 percentage points lower than the national average. Mining and farm employment were the only two industries with decreases in jobs from 1989 to 1997. During this period, farm earnings have decreased by more than 40 percent, reducing almost by half the farm industry's contribution to Minnesota's total earnings. The total number of jobs in Minnesota has been increasing fairly steadily throughout the 1990s, but the growth accelerated from 1994 to 1997.

Employment and Earnings by Sector

	1980	1989	1990	1991	1992	1993	1994	1995	1996	1997 Number	1997 Percent of total	Change*
Employment *(thousands of persons)*												
Total	2 254	2 654	2 707	2 739	2 785	2 842	2 933	3 029	3 096	3 166	100.0	2.2
Farm	138	117	116	115	112	109	107	109	106	106	3.4	-1.2
Nonfarm	2 116	2 537	2 590	2 624	2 673	2 733	2 825	2 919	2 990	3 060	96.6	2.4
Private nonfarm	1 808	2 193	2 233	2 264	2 309	2 366	2 454	2 542	2 612	2 680	84.6	2.5
Agricultural service, forestry, and fishing	14	19	20	21	21	23	24	25	26	27	0.8	4.1
Mining	16	10	10	9	9	9	9	9	9	9	0.3	-0.7
Construction	105	119	120	117	124	125	129	134	140	146	4.6	2.6
Manufacturing	383	413	412	410	411	421	432	442	446	453	14.3	1.2
Transportation and public utilities	113	122	127	130	128	130	135	139	144	150	4.7	2.6
Wholesale trade	124	136	136	139	143	142	148	153	160	161	5.1	2.1
Retail trade	384	449	454	456	464	476	498	517	527	534	16.9	2.2
Finance, insurance, and real estate	170	196	200	202	201	210	221	227	234	241	7.6	2.7
Services	499	730	754	779	808	830	858	896	927	960	30.3	3.5
Government	308	344	357	360	364	367	372	377	378	380	12.0	1.3
Earnings *(millions of dollars)*												
Total	31 372	59 698	63 383	65 157	70 827	72 687	78 001	81 932	88 504	93 426	100.0	5.8
Farm	919	1 982	1 887	1 089	1 163	24	1 160	616	1 922	1 153	1.2	-6.6
Nonfarm	30 453	57 715	61 496	64 068	69 664	72 663	76 840	81 316	86 582	92 273	98.8	6.0
Private nonfarm	26 190	49 571	52 601	54 695	59 816	62 472	66 143	70 233	75 037	80 400	86.1	6.2
Agricultural service, forestry, and fishing	125	267	307	316	344	356	362	372	383	406	0.4	5.4
Mining	557	338	374	384	381	374	399	432	451	462	0.5	4.0
Construction	2 088	3 498	3 630	3 495	3 839	3 997	4 315	4 600	5 025	5 397	5.8	5.6
Manufacturing	7 687	13 845	14 323	14 780	15 891	16 446	17 330	17 945	18 792	19 961	21.4	4.7
Transportation and public utilities	2 543	4 157	4 351	4 578	4 786	4 859	5 014	5 296	5 532	6 056	6.5	4.8
Wholesale trade	2 611	4 367	4 599	4 831	5 245	5 422	5 904	6 326	7 014	7 344	7.9	6.7
Retail trade	3 313	5 667	5 857	5 967	6 366	6 765	7 210	7 595	7 959	8 409	9.0	5.1
Finance, insurance, and real estate	1 780	3 931	4 318	4 666	5 396	5 990	6 218	6 617	7 233	7 782	8.3	8.9
Services	5 486	13 503	14 842	15 678	17 569	18 262	19 392	21 049	22 648	24 582	26.3	7.8
Government	4 264	8 144	8 895	9 373	9 848	10 192	10 697	11 083	11 545	11 874	12.7	4.8

*Compound annual average percent change, 1989–1997

ECONOMIC STRUCTURE (Continued)

WHILE MINNESOTA'S AVERAGE WAGES ARE JUST BELOW THE national average, several of Minnesota's major sectors have wages that are above the U.S. average. In 1997, manufacturing wages were 3 percent above the national average in the sector, construction wages were more than 16 percent above the national average, and farm wages were more than 20 percent higher than average. Service sector wages averaged 6 percent below the United States, however. Overall, Minnesota's average wages are fairly consistent with the national averages, with more than half of the major sectors' average wages falling within 95 percent to 105 percent of the national wages.

Manufacturing is playing a decreasingly significant role in Minnesota's economy over time. Manufacturing as a percent of the gross state product has been decreasing, from 22.4 percent in 1989 to 19.2 percent in 1996. While the value of manufacturing output has continued to grow by nearly 27 percent during this period, it has been growing at slower rates than the state's overall output, which has grown by nearly 50 percent since 1989. Industrial machinery is the state's leading manufacturing industry. Manufacturing output value per worker in Minnesota amounted to $60,837 in 1996, only 87.7 percent of the national average. Minnesota's manufacturing value per worker has grown at a significantly slower rate than average since 1989. New capital expenditures have increased significantly from 1994 to 1996, however.

Exports of Minnesota products have increased by nearly 38 percent from 1994 to 1997. Agricultural and livestock product exports dropped in 1997, though agricultural product exports are the leading export and remain about 50 percent higher than they were in 1994. Among the top exports, food products have increased most slowly in the past three years, while industrial machinery and computers and scientific and measuring equipment increased by greater than average amounts. Export demand has helped boost output of instruments, which was Minnesota's fastest growing manufacturing industry in the 1989–97 period.

Average Annual Wages and Salaries by Sector
(dollars)

	1989	1996	1997 State	1997 U.S.
All wage and salary workers	21 797	28 265	29 639	29 809
Farm	11 424	19 999	20 691	16 442
Nonfarm	21 901	28 323	29 700	29 900
Private nonfarm	21 922	28 414	29 907	29 867
Agricultural service, forestry, and fishing	14 128	17 789	18 614	17 941
Mining	35 543	45 899	46 569	49 800
Construction	28 334	35 217	37 038	31 765
Manufacturing	29 772	37 536	39 497	38 351
Transportation and utilities	30 876	35 956	38 164	38 222
Wholesale trade	29 473	39 971	41 610	39 466
Retail trade	11 680	14 806	15 559	16 206
Finance, insurance, and real estate	27 493	40 709	43 184	44 993
Services	18 027	24 583	25 876	27 588
Government	21 788	27 807	28 496	30 062

Gross State Product and Manufacturing
(millions of dollars, except as noted)

	1989	1994	1995	1996
Gross state product, total	95 452	124 617	131 358	141 573
Manufacturing:				
Millions of dollars	21 398	24 609	25 823	27 115
Percent of total gross state product	22.4	19.7	19.7	19.2
Per worker (dollars)	51 835	56 990	58 403	60 837
New capital expenditures, manufacturing	NA	2 194	2 766	2 847

Exports of Goods
(millions of dollars)

	1994	1995	1996	1997
All goods	10 011	12 404	13 884	13 793
Manufactures	7 201	8 115	8 812	9 590
Agricultural and livestock products	2 673	4 178	4 950	3 982
Other commodities	137	111	123	222
Top goods exports, 1997:				
Agricultural products	2 663	4 171	4 943	3 974
Industrial machinery and computers	1 563	1 787	1 975	2 182
Food products	1 508	1 718	1 715	1 801
Scientific and measuring instruments	1 021	1 167	1 354	1 416
Electric and electronic equipment	892	988	1 008	1 090

HOUSING

WHILE MINNESOTA'S HOUSING PRODUCTION HAS INCREASED from its level in 1990, it was stronger than the U.S. construction rate during the early 1990s but a bit weaker than average during 1994–97. The number of building permits declined in 1997, reflecting a lower population growth from 1996 to 1997 than in previous years. Home sales have increased quite rapidly in most years of the 1990s, and despite a weak performance in 1994–95 there has been a general strengthening of existing .home sales since the early 1990s recession. The rate of homeownership has increased from 68.0 percent in 1990 to 75.4 percent in 1997, the highest rate of homeownership in the nation. In 1997, the rental vacancy rate dropped for the second consecutive year, giving Minnesota the fourth lowest rental vacancy rate in the nation.

Homeownership Rates: 1989 and 1997

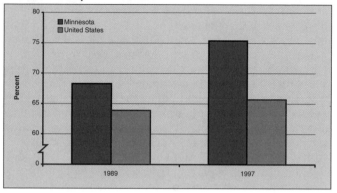

Housing Supply

	1989	1990	1991	1992	1993	1994	1995	1996	1997
Residential building permits (thousands)	25.1	23.5	21.1	26.4	27.3	25.6	25.5	27.0	24.9
New home production (including manufactured housing):									
Thousands of homes	26.9	25.1	22.2	28.3	29.4	27.5	28.5	30.1	27.8
Rate per 1,000 population									
Minnesota	6.2	5.7	5.0	6.3	6.5	6.0	6.2	6.5	5.9
U.S.	6.2	5.2	4.5	5.1	5.6	6.4	6.3	6.6	6.5
Existing home sales:									
Thousands of homes	62.7	64.8	66.3	75.7	81.8	82.1	76.7	85.8	88.0
Change from previous year (percent)									
Minnesota	-11.4	3.3	2.3	14.2	8.1	0.4	-6.6	11.9	2.6
U.S.	-3.9	-4.0	0.0	9.2	8.2	4.8	-3.7	7.5	3.8
Home ownership rate (percent of households)	68.3	68.0	68.9	66.7	65.8	68.9	73.3	75.4	75.4
Rental vacancy rate (percent of rental housing units)	5.8	6.5	6.6	5.4	4.9	5.2	6.7	5.5	4.7

AGRICULTURE

IN 1997, MINNESOTA HAS THE FIFTH HIGHEST NUMBER OF farms in the nation. Minnesota's farms average 343 acres, well below the national average of 471 acres. The value of farmland and buildings in Minnesota has not increased significantly since 1993, so its rank has dropped from fifth to eighth in the nation. Minnesota's net farm income has decreased by 54 percent from 1989 to 1997, which can be attributed to growing production costs, with particularly weak performance in 1993 through 1995. The state's revenue from sales is fairly evenly divided between livestock and crops, with the former accounting for 53.3 percent and the latter, 46.7 percent. Total crop revenue has increased at a slightly higher rate than has livestock income.

MINNESOTA FARMS, 1997

Number of farms	87 000
Total acres (thousands):	29 800
Average per farm	343
Value of land and buildings (millions of dollars)	30 992
Average per farm (dollars)	356 230

Farm Income
(millions of dollars)

	1980	1989	1990	1991	1992	1993	1994	1995	1996	1997
Gross income	7 211	8 217	8 244	8 610	7 903	7 980	7 340	8 742	9 862	9 176
Receipts from sales	6 852	7 132	7 217	7 680	6 986	6 656	6 209	7 755	8 973	8 093
Government payments	70	600	512	436	422	823	622	468	349	417
Imputed and miscellaneous income	290	485	515	494	495	501	509	519	539	666
(–) Production expenses	6 166	6 572	7 043	7 230	7 142	7 523	7 954	7 908	8 369	8 856
(=) Realized net income	1 045	1 646	1 201	1 380	761	458	-614	834	1 492	320
(+) Inventory change	-352	176	460	-583	107	-885	1 514	-547	217	519
(=) Net income	693	1 822	1 661	797	868	-427	900	287	1 709	839
Corporate income	0	106	100	37	57	-111	93	19	171	77
Farm proprietors income	693	1 716	1 561	760	811	-316	807	268	1 539	762

EDUCATION

EDUCATIONAL ATTAINMENT Percent of population age 25 and over, 1997	State	United States
High school graduate or higher	87.9	82.1
College graduate or higher	28.3	23.9

MINNESOTA HAS ONE OF THE STRONGEST EDUCATION RECORDS in the nation. The state ranks seventh in the nation in both the percentage of adults with high school diplomas and the percentage holding college degrees. Nearly 88 percent of Minnesota's population are high school graduates, and more than 28 percent have earned bachelor's degrees. The state has the fifth highest increase of percentage of population with college degrees in the nation from 1990, when the state's percentage with college degrees was 21.8 percent. The well-educated population is both a reflection of and a cause of the state's general prosperity. Average teacher salaries are just below the national average and per pupil expenditures are just about equal to the average. A slightly greater percentage of minorities are enrolled in postsecondary institutions than make up Minnesota's total population, and a relatively large percentage of all young adults is currently enrolled.

High School Completion: 1990–97

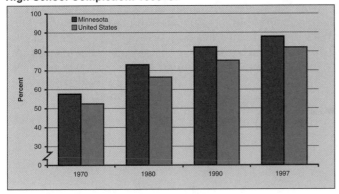

Education Indicators

	State	U.S.
Elementary and secondary schools		
Enrollment, 1995–96		
Total (thousands)	922	49 873
Percent in private schools	9.4	10.1
Expenditures per pupil (dollars), 1995–96	6 162	6 146
Average teacher salary (dollars), 1996–97	37 975	38 509
Higher education		
Enrollment, 1996–97		
Total (thousands)	275	14 218
Percent of population 18–34	24.7	21.8
Percent minority	8.9	26.1
Percent in private schools	24.2	22.6

HEALTH

THE HEALTH OF MINNESOTA'S POPULATION APPEARS TO BE well above average in the nation. Minnesota's infant mortality rate has been steadily declining over the past few years. In 1997, the rate fell to 5.9 per 1,000. Minnesota has the third lowest overall death rate in the nation. Death rates for all major causes are below the U.S. average, particularly for heart disease. The number of people without health insurance, at 9.2 percent, is less than two-thirds of the national average and the third lowest in the United States.

Health Indicators

	1990	1995	1996	1997
Infant mortality *(rate per thousand live births)*				
Minnesota	7.3	6.7	6.4	5.9
U.S.	9.2	7.6	7.3	7.1
Total deaths, age-adjusted rate *(rate per thousand population)*				
Minnesota	4.3	4.3	4.1	4.0
U.S.	5.2	5.0	4.9	4.8
Persons not covered by health insurance *(percent of population)*				
Minnesota	8.9	8.0	10.2	9.2
U.S.	13.9	15.4	15.6	16.1

Leading Causes of Death, 1996
(deaths per 100,000 population)

	Age-adjusted		Not age-adjusted	
	State	U.S.	State	U.S.
Deaths from all causes	413.2	491.6	798.3	872.5
Heart disease	98.4	134.5	215.4	276.4
Cancer	118.3	127.9	189.9	203.4
Cerebrovascular diseases	24.6	26.4	65.0	60.3
Chronic obstructive pulmonary disease	18.3	21.0	36.1	40.0
Diabetes mellitus	12.9	13.6	23.8	23.3
Pneumonia and influenza	8.9	12.8	26.7	31.6
HIV	3.5	11.1	3.8	11.7
Liver disease	5.0	7.5	6.3	9.4
Alzheimer's disease	3.0	2.7	9.9	8.1
Accidents and adverse effects	26.3	30.4	35.3	35.8
Motor vehicle accidents	13.5	16.2	13.6	16.5
Suicide	10.1	10.8	10.5	11.6
Homicide	4.0	8.5	3.8	7.9
Injury by firearm	8.1	12.9	8.1	12.8

GOVERNMENT

STATE AND LOCAL TAXES, 1995–96	State	U.S.
Per capita (dollars)	2 977	2 477
Percent of personal income	12.5	10.8

STATE AND LOCAL TAXES IN MINNESOTA IN 1995–96 ADDED up to $2,977 per capita, 20 percent higher than the $2,477 nationwide. This rate is only partly accounted for by the relatively high incomes in the state; these taxes represent 12.5 percent of personal income, compared with the national rate of 10.8 percent. Only 31.2 percent of these taxes are local taxes, as compared to 40.8 percent nationwide, indicating relatively low property taxation at the local level. At the state level, revenue was 20 percent above average, with taxes 44 percent higher than the U.S. level per capita. Individual income taxes amounted to $1,020 per capita, well above the $542 average and accounting for most of the tax differential. Minnesota's education expenditures by the state amounted to $1,318 per capita. This amount was significantly higher than the U.S. average. Public welfare expenditures were also higher per capita in Minnesota than in the nation. The state's per capita debt was nearly $700 lower than the national average, however.

Minnesota's receipts of federal grants, procurements, and payments to individuals are either at or below the state's proportion of the U.S. population. Defense and other procurement were both less than 1.0 percent of the U.S. total, significantly lower than Minnesota's 1.8 percent of the U.S. population. Payments to individuals amounted to 1.4 percent, while total grants were 1.7 percent of the U.S. total. Both education grants and Medicaid payments were also below 1.8 percent.

State Government Finances, 1996–97

	Millions of dollars	Percent distribution	Dollars per capita State	Dollars per capita U.S.
General revenue	17 207	100.0	3 672	3 049
Intergovernmental revenue	3 626	21.1	774	863
Taxes	11 223	65.2	2 395	1 660
General sales	3 115	18.1	665	551
Selective sales	1 661	9.7	354	257
License taxes	821	4.8	175	106
Individual income	4 779	27.8	1 020	542
Corporation net income	699	4.1	149	115
Other taxes	148	0.9	32	90
Other general revenue	2 358	13.7	503	526
General expenditure	16 796	100.0	3 584	2 951
Intergovernmental expenditure	6 942	41.3	1 481	989
Direct expenditure	9 854	58.7	2 103	1 962
General expenditure, by function:				
Education	6 176	36.8	1 318	1 033
Public welfare	4 459	26.5	951	761
Hospitals and health	930	5.5	198	237
Highways	1 255	7.5	268	225
Police protection and corrections	415	2.5	88	137
Natural resources, parks and recreation	459	2.7	98	63
Governmental administration	493	2.9	105	107
Interest on general debt	309	1.8	66	99
Other and unallocable	2 300	13.7	491	290
Debt at end of fiscal year	4 862	NA	1 038	1 706
Cash and security holdings	36 925	NA	7 880	6 683

Federal Spending within State

	Federal funds, fiscal 1997		
	Millions of dollars	Percent distribution	Percent of U.S. total*
Total within state	20 006	100.0	1.4
Payments to individuals	11 323	56.6	1.4
Retirement and disability	7 062	35.3	1.5
Medicare	2 684	13.4	1.3
Food stamps	199	1.0	1.0
Supplemental Security Income	266	1.3	1.0
Grants	4 321	21.6	1.7
Medicaid and other health	1 990	9.9	1.7
Nutrition and family welfare	850	4.2	1.8
Education	242	1.2	1.4
Housing and community development ..	180	0.9	1.6
Salaries and wages	1 638	8.2	1.0
Defense procurement contracts	1 090	5.4	0.9
Non-defense procurement contracts	594	3.0	0.8

*State population is 1.8 percent of the U.S. total.

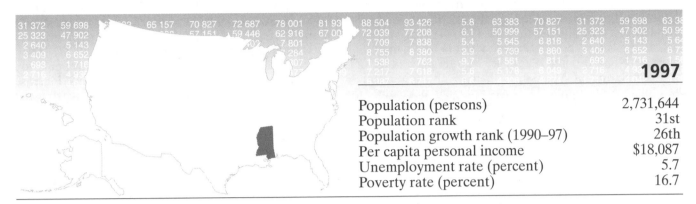

31 372	59 698		65 157	70 827	72 687	78 001	81 93	88 504	93 426	5.8	63 383	70 827	31 372	59 698	63 38
25 323	47 902		57 151	59 446	62 916	67 00	72 039	77 208	6.1	50 999	57 151	25 323	47 902	50 9

1997

Population (persons)	2,731,644
Population rank	31st
Population growth rank (1990–97)	26th
Per capita personal income	$18,087
Unemployment rate (percent)	5.7
Poverty rate (percent)	16.7

COTTON NO LONGER IS KING IN MISSISSIPPI, IF EVER IT WAS. Poultry now is the leader in agricultural sales, and agriculture's share of the economy has diminished in the 1990s. The introduction of gambling casinos has given a strong boost to tourist-related industries in the 1990s, especially from 1992 through 1994. Amusement and recreation services and hotels were the most rapidly-growing industries from 1989 to 1997, and the demand for new hotels and new housing brought boom times for construction.

Economic growth continued from 1995 through 1997, although at a less rapid pace than during the previous three years. Unemployment and poverty have been reduced during the 1990s, and gains in median household incomes and real personal incomes per capita have brought Mississippi closer to the national averages. Even so, Mississippi remained among the poorest states in the nation, with the fourth highest poverty rate, the highest 1996-97 infant mortality rate except for the District of Columbia, and median and per capita incomes at or near the bottom of the state rankings.

Population growth in Mississippi from 1990 to 1997 was a little slower than in the United States as a whole, largely because of the very limited amount of foreign immigration. Non-Hispanic Blacks were 36 percent of the state's population in 1997 and non-Hispanic Whites were 62 percent; other groups were only 2 percent.

Average Annual Population Growth: 1990–97

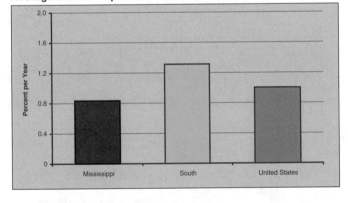

Median Household Income: 1989–97 (1997 dollars)

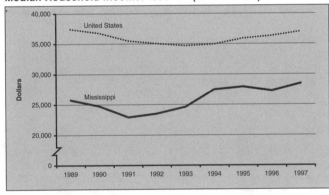

Unemployment Rate: 1989–97

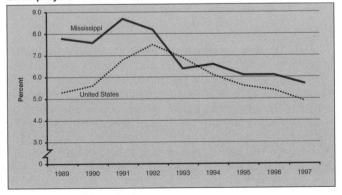

MISSISSIPPI'S UNEMPLOYMENT RATE WAS WELL ABOVE THE U.S. average in 1990, and recession pushed the rate higher in 1991. Employment growth resumed in 1992, however, and the unemployment rate came down rapidly in 1992 and 1993. There was a further, but smaller, decline from 1993 to 1997. The 1997 rate still was above the U.S. average, but the gap was less than at the beginning of the decade. The percentage of Mississippi adults holding jobs in 1997 was higher than in 1990, but considerably lower than the U.S. average of 63.8 percent.

POPULATION AND LABOR FORCE

MISSISSIPPI'S WHITE AND BLACK NON-HISPANIC POPULA-tions grew in line with U.S. averages from 1990 to 1997. However, the percent gains in the Asian and Hispanic populations were smaller than the U.S. averages, keeping Mississippi's total population growth rate below the U.S. average. Non-Hispanic Blacks are a larger percentage of the population of Mississippi than of any other state (although Washington, D.C. has a higher percentage). Other minority groups, although growing, remained a very small share of the total population.

Only 35.5 percent of the state's population lived in metropolitan areas in 1997. The percentage has increased during the 1990s, but still is less than one-half of the U.S. average of 80 percent. The state's largest metropolitan areas are Jackson, with a 1997 population of 425,000, and Biloxi-Gulfport-Pascagoula with 343,000.

Over 70 percent of the state's 6.0 percent population growth from 1990 to 1997 came from natural increase (births minus deaths) and almost all the rest from net movement into Mississippi from other states. Less than 4 percent of the total came from immigration from abroad.

Population and Labor Force

	1980	1990	1991	1992	1993	1994	1995	1996	1997	Change* State	Change* U.S.
Population											
Total number of persons (thousands)	2 521	2 577	2 591	2 610	2 636	2 663	2 690	2 710	2 732	0.8	1.0
Percent distribution:											
White, Non-Hispanic	63.6	63.7	62.9	62.7	62.5	62.4	62.3	62.1	61.9	0.4	0.4
Black, Non-Hispanic	34.8	34.7	35.6	35.8	35.9	36.0	36.1	36.2	36.3	1.4	1.4
Asian	0.3	0.6	0.5	0.5	0.6	0.6	0.6	0.7	0.7	3.7	4.1
Native American	0.3	0.3	0.3	0.3	0.4	0.3	0.4	0.4	0.4	1.9	1.6
Hispanic	1.0	0.7	0.6	0.7	0.7	0.7	0.7	0.8	0.8	2.1	3.8
In metropolitan areas	32.0	34.0	34.1	34.4	34.7	35.0	35.2	35.4	35.5	1.5	1.0
Total number of households (thousands)	827	911	924	934	941	948	964	979	NA	1.2	1.2
Labor Force (thousands)											
Population 16 and over	1 809	1 969	1 979	1 992	2 015	2 041	2 070	2 092	2 116	1.0	1.0
Civilian labor force	1 061	1 184	1 190	1 191	1 216	1 253	1 257	1 257	1 262	0.9	1.1
Employed	982	1 094	1 086	1 094	1 138	1 170	1 180	1 180	1 190	1.2	1.2
Percent of population	54.3	55.5	54.9	54.9	56.5	57.3	57.0	56.4	56.2		
Unemployment rate (percent)	7.5	7.6	8.7	8.2	6.4	6.6	6.1	6.1	5.7		

*Compound annual average percent change, 1990–1997; 1990–1996 for households.

Population Change and Components: 1990–97

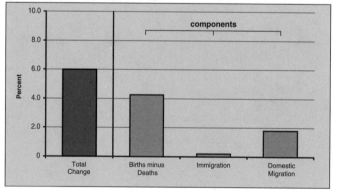

Average Annual Household and Population Growth

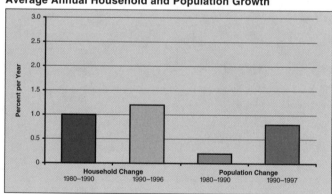

Population by Age; Births and Deaths

	1990 State	1990 U.S.	1997 State	1997 U.S.
Age distribution (percent)				
Under 5 years	7.6	7.6	7.4	7.2
5 to 17 years	20.9	18.2	20.2	18.8
18 to 64 years	59.2	61.8	60.2	61.3
65 years and over	12.4	12.5	12.2	12.7
Birth and death rates (per thousand population)				
Births	16.9	16.7	15.7	14.6
Deaths	9.8	8.6	10.1	8.6

MISSISSIPPI HAS A RELATIVELY HIGH BIRTH RATE, AND ONE that declined less than the U.S. average from 1990 to 1997. Reflecting the high birth rate, children under age 18 are a larger share of the state's total population than is the case nationwide. The percentage of the population between ages 18 and 64 increased between 1990 to 1997, while the national average percentage declined. Even so, in 1997 Mississippi still had a smaller percentage in this working-age group than did the nation.

HOUSEHOLD AND PERSONAL INCOME

HOUSEHOLD INCOME AND PERSONS IN POVERTY	1990	1995	1996	1997 State	1997 U.S.
Median household income (1997 dollars)	24 779	27 948	27 289	28 499	37 005
Persons in poverty (thousands)	684	630	575	455	35 574
Poverty rate (percent)	25.7	23.5	20.6	16.7	13.3

FROM 1990 TO 1996–97, MISSISSIPPI HAD A GAIN IN INFLA-tion-adjusted median household income of more than 12 percent. With no gain in the U.S. average over these years, Mississippi incomes rose from 67 percent of the national average in 1990 to 76 percent in 1996–97. The state's poverty rate, which was 20 percent or higher from 1990 through 1995, declined to an average of 18.7 percent in 1996–97—a figure still well above the U.S. average. The state's real personal income per capita increased almost twice as fast as the U.S. average from 1989 to 1997, rising from 66 percent of the U.S. average in 1989 to 71 percent in 1997. Even so, Mississippi had the lowest per capita income of any state in 1997 and was near the bottom of the rankings for median household income.

Earnings provided 64 percent of Mississippi's personal income in 1997, compared to 66 percent nationwide.

The "adjustment for residence," which measures the net amount earned by Mississippi residents from work in other states, was 2 percent of personal income. Dividends, interest, and rent were only 12 percent, compared to 17 percent nationwide. However, in part because of the state's low average wages and high poverty rate, transfer payments were 23 percent, compared to only 16 percent nationwide.

The largest transfer payment increase from 1990 to 1997 was in "other income maintenance," a category consisting largely of the earned income tax credit. Medical payments also showed a large rise, but, in contrast, Supplemental Security Income payments rose less than the U.S. average, and family assistance payments actually declined by 44 percent and food stamp payments by 18 percent.

Personal Income
(millions of dollars)

	1980	1989	1990	1991	1992	1993	1994	1995	1996	1997	Change*
Earnings by place of work	12 470	20 946	22 033	23 154	24 937	26 726	29 128	30 323	31 815	33 366	6.0
Wages and salaries	10 017	16 598	17 557	18 283	19 475	20 882	22 764	24 018	25 151	26 650	6.1
Other labor income	941	1 852	2 037	2 218	2 476	2 729	2 940	2 940	2 857	2 875	5.7
Proprietors' income	1 511	2 497	2 439	2 653	2 986	3 114	3 424	3 365	3 807	3 842	5.5
Farm	68	354	152	277	355	234	477	361	676	538	5.4
Nonfarm	1 443	2 143	2 287	2 376	2 631	2 880	2 947	3 004	3 131	3 304	5.6
(–) Personal contributions for social insurance	688	1 504	1 588	1 680	1 793	1 940	2 140	2 306	2 419	2 581	7.0
(+) Adjustment for residence	410	707	752	786	806	816	828	922	947	1 037	NA
(=) **Net earnings by state of residence**	12 192	20 148	21 197	22 261	23 950	25 602	27 816	28 939	30 343	31 822	5.9
(+) Dividends, interest, and rent	2 125	4 590	4 814	4 953	4 782	4 809	5 123	5 487	5 909	6 173	3.8
(+) Transfer payments	3 190	6 144	6 737	7 444	8 235	8 861	9 369	10 198	10 921	11 392	8.0
(=) **Total personal income**	17 507	30 882	32 748	34 657	36 967	39 272	42 308	44 623	47 173	49 386	6.0
Farm	208	505	334	460	525	418	643	510	846	709	4.3
Nonfarm	17 299	30 377	32 414	34 198	36 442	38 854	41 665	44 113	46 327	48 677	6.1
Personal income per capita (dollars)											
Current dollars	6 932	11 996	12 707	13 377	14 164	14 903	15 887	16 585	17 402	18 087	5.3
1997 dollars	13 254	15 166	15 291	15 447	15 843	16 217	16 883	17 240	17 721	18 087	2.2

*Compound annual average percent change, 1989–1997

Government Transfer Payments

	Millions of dollars 1990	Millions of dollars 1997	Percent change* State	Percent change* U.S.
Total government payments to individuals	6 447	10 946	69.8	62.7
Retirement, disability, and insurance	3 321	5 010	50.8	48.2
Social Security	2 393	3 585	49.8	46.1
Government employee retirement	839	1 321	57.4	60.3
Medical payments	1 718	3 964	130.7	101.2
Income maintenance	903	1 380	52.8	58.0
Supplemental Security Income	298	515	72.4	75.4
Family assistance	90	51	-43.8	-0.5
Food Stamps	360	296	-17.8	27.1
Other income maintenance	155	519	235.2	189.8
Unemployment insurance benefits	117	128	9.4	10.6
Veterans benefits and other	388	464	19.8	30.8

*Percent change, 1990–1997

Government Payments to Individuals: 1997

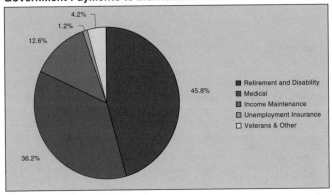

- Retirement and Disability — 45.8%
- Medical — 36.2%
- Income Maintenance — 12.6%
- Unemployment Insurance — 1.2%
- Veterans & Other — 4.2%

ECONOMIC STRUCTURE

LEADING PRIVATE INDUSTRIES, 1997 (Worker and proprietor earnings, millions of dollars)		FASTEST EARNINGS GROWTH, 1989–97 (percent increase)	
Health services	$2 945	Amusement and recreation services	1 053.8
Construction specialties	1 143	Hotels and lodging	514.4
Business services	927	Business services	130.9
Lumber and wood products	864	Construction specialties	111.0
Trucking and warehousing	768	Health services	108.7

THE INTRODUCTION OF GAMBLING CASINOS HAS BEEN THE TOP 1990s economic story for Mississippi. Amusement and recreation services and hotels were the state's two most rapidly growing industries from 1989 to 1997, and these and other tourist-related industries have provided a major boost to employment and incomes. Employment in the services sector grew at a 5.3 percent annual rate from 1989 to 1997, with gains of some 9 percent per year in 1993 and 1994—the start-up years for the casino business. The demand for new hotels also brought a boom in the construction industry. The resultant pick-up in economic activity can be seen in the strong real income gains registered from 1992 to 1994 and in the drop in the unemployment rate from 8.7 percent in 1991 to 6.4 percent in 1993.

The 1991 to 1994 rate of economic expansion was too rapid to be maintained, but economic growth in Mississippi has continued, albeit at a more moderate pace. And casinos can claim much of the credit. The 29 casinos regulated by the state are reported to have employed over 33,800 workers in 1998 and to have generated about $2 billion in annual revenue.

While services boomed, manufacturing employment declined slightly from 1989 to 1997. The pattern within this time period was one of growing employment from 1989 to 1994 and a fairly sharp decline (more than 7 percent) from 1994 to 1997. Much of the job loss was in the apparel industry.

The mining sector, which includes oil and gas extraction, is a small but important part of the Mississippi economy. Employment in this sector declined during the 1980s and the early 1990s, but appears to have stabilized after 1992. Earnings in this sector grew somewhat more rapidly than the economy-wide average. Related construction and repair work on offshore drilling rigs helps support the Mississippi shipbuilding industry.

Farm employment was 8 percent of the employment total in 1980, but had fallen to 5 percent by 1990. Although the number of farm jobs stabilized after 1990, the share of total employment fell slightly further, to 4 percent, by 1997.

Employment and Earnings by Sector

	1980	1989	1990	1991	1992	1993	1994	1995	1996	1997 Number	1997 Percent of total	Change*
Employment *(thousands of persons)*												
Total	1 114	1 196	1 208	1 217	1 242	1 297	1 347	1 378	1 400	1 425	100.0	2.2
Farm	87	57	55	52	52	53	50	54	56	57	4.0	0.0
Nonfarm	1 028	1 140	1 153	1 165	1 190	1 244	1 297	1 323	1 344	1 369	96.0	2.3
Private nonfarm	801	905	916	929	950	1 000	1 049	1 073	1 093	1 115	78.2	2.6
Agricultural service, forestry, and fishing	8	12	12	13	13	14	15	15	15	16	1.2	4.0
Mining	15	10	10	10	9	9	9	9	8	9	0.6	-1.9
Construction	58	56	57	55	58	64	68	72	76	78	5.5	4.3
Manufacturing	230	251	253	255	259	263	269	265	254	249	17.5	-0.1
Transportation and public utilities	47	54	53	54	53	56	58	61	63	64	4.5	2.3
Wholesale trade	46	44	44	44	46	46	47	48	48	49	3.4	1.3
Retail trade	155	188	189	190	195	203	211	221	228	233	16.3	2.7
Finance, insurance, and real estate	54	60	60	60	59	61	62	63	65	67	4.7	1.3
Services	187	231	238	249	259	284	310	320	336	350	24.5	5.3
Government	227	235	237	236	240	244	248	250	251	254	17.8	1.0
Earnings *(millions of dollars)*												
Total	12 470	20 946	22 033	23 154	24 937	26 726	29 128	30 323	31 815	33 366	100.0	6.0
Farm	208	505	334	460	525	418	643	510	846	709	2.1	4.3
Nonfarm	12 262	20 441	21 700	22 695	24 412	26 308	28 485	29 813	30 969	32 656	97.9	6.0
Private nonfarm	9 797	16 073	17 097	17 913	19 430	21 042	22 892	23 883	24 857	26 314	78.9	6.4
Agricultural service, forestry, and fishing	64	139	162	175	189	186	207	206	192	217	0.6	5.7
Mining	255	182	192	199	196	210	210	222	251	298	0.9	6.4
Construction	850	1 058	1 146	1 121	1 232	1 467	1 651	1 722	1 902	2 024	6.1	8.5
Manufacturing	3 229	5 405	5 674	5 896	6 372	6 692	7 119	7 172	7 062	7 256	21.7	3.8
Transportation and public utilities	864	1 448	1 515	1 587	1 687	1 817	1 941	2 060	2 142	2 257	6.8	5.7
Wholesale trade	734	1 042	1 108	1 146	1 223	1 282	1 378	1 430	1 482	1 583	4.7	5.4
Retail trade	1 358	2 187	2 259	2 362	2 532	2 704	2 873	3 042	3 222	3 422	10.3	5.8
Finance, insurance, and real estate	536	966	1 010	1 042	1 142	1 237	1 302	1 374	1 429	1 515	4.5	5.8
Services	1 908	3 646	4 031	4 385	4 855	5 446	6 211	6 656	7 176	7 741	23.2	9.9
Government	2 465	4 368	4 603	4 782	4 982	5 266	5 594	5 930	6 112	6 342	19.0	4.8

*Compound annual average percent change, 1989–1997

ECONOMIC STRUCTURE (Continued)

THE $22,157 ANNUAL WAGE OR SALARY EARNED BY THE AVERage Mississippi worker in 1997 was only 74 percent of the U.S. average, little changed from 1989. It also was the lowest of any southern state, although wages in the plains states of South and North Dakota and Montana were lower. Employment growth in Mississippi has been heavily centered in relatively low-paying tourist-related industries. This job growth has reduced unemployment and helped lower the poverty rate but has not worked to raise average wages and salaries. In manufacturing, there has been some expansion of the better-paying chemicals and industrial machinery industries, but the largest manufacturing industries continue to be lumber and furniture and fixtures—industries toward the lower end of the manufacturing pay scale.

Except for a recessionary dip in 1991, manufacturing accounted for slightly over 25 percent of Mississippi's gross state product (GSP) from 1989 through 1994. The share diminished noticeably in 1995 and 1996, although the 1996 share of 23.4 percent still was well above the 17.5 percent national average. Manufacturing's declining share of the state's GSP stemmed from a marked slowing in the rate of growth of manufacturing output value. Employment in manufacturing declined after 1994. Within manufacturing, however, there was some shift toward higher-technology industries with better future growth prospects. The chemicals, industrial machinery (including computers), and plastics industries grew fairly rapidly while apparel manufacturing underwent a major decline. Mississippi's largest manufacturing industries, measured by worker and proprietor earnings, are lumber and wood products and the closely related furniture and fixtures industry. These two industries had only moderate growth from 1989 to 1997.

Growth of Mississippi goods exports from 1994 to 1997 was led by a 165 percent increase in exports of manufactured food products. Exports of agricultural and livestock products also more than doubled. In total, the state's goods exports grew 29 percent from 1994 to 1997, a strong performance but somewhat below the 34 percent increase for the United States as a whole. Well over one-half of Mississippi's exports are shipped to markets in the Americas—Canada, Mexico, or South and Central America. Exports to Mexico nearly doubled from 1994 to 1997 with apparel and agricultural and livestock products accounting for much of the gain.

Average Annual Wages and Salaries by Sector
(dollars)

	1989	1996	1997 State	1997 U.S.
All wage and salary workers	16 478	21 285	22 157	29 809
Farm	10 374	13 401	12 502	16 442
Nonfarm	16 563	21 366	22 263	29 900
Private nonfarm	16 446	21 230	22 201	29 867
Agricultural service, forestry, and fishing	11 871	15 921	16 817	17 941
Mining	24 081	31 493	34 446	49 800
Construction	17 985	23 224	24 395	31 765
Manufacturing	18 610	24 293	25 553	38 351
Transportation and utilities	24 957	31 337	33 015	38 222
Wholesale trade	21 263	28 280	29 622	39 466
Retail trade	10 348	12 967	13 548	16 206
Finance, insurance, and real estate	20 354	26 917	28 225	44 993
Services	14 289	19 937	20 762	27 588
Government	16 942	21 865	22 491	30 062

Gross State Product and Manufacturing
(millions of dollars, except as noted)

	1989	1994	1995	1996
Gross state product, total	37 217	50 751	53 647	56 406
Manufacturing:				
Millions of dollars	9 488	12 859	13 197	13 208
Percent of total gross state product	25.5	25.3	24.6	23.4
Per worker (dollars)	37 840	47 871	49 765	52 081
New capital expenditures, manufacturing	NA	1 254	1 384	1 660

Exports of Goods
(millions of dollars)

	1994	1995	1996	1997
All goods	1 100	1 369	1 222	1 421
Manufactures	1 055	1 261	1 145	1 307
Agricultural and livestock products	29	81	52	65
Other commodities	16	27	24	49
Top goods exports, 1997:				
Food products	77	139	160	204
Industrial machinery and computers	105	107	132	190
Electric and electronic equipment	160	179	163	139
Apparel	28	55	90	111
Paper products	122	169	119	91

HOUSING

MISSISSIPPI'S NEW HOME PRODUCTION RATE WAS LOW RELAtive to the U.S. average in 1989, but its further decline in the 1990–91 recession was less marked. A rapid increase in home production beginning in 1992 brought the Mississippi rate above that of the United States by 1994, and there was a further increase in 1995. A strong pick-up in existing home sales from 1991 to 1993 is additional evidence of the state's rapid economic expansion in those years. With slower economic growth from 1995 to 1997, new home production and sales of existing homes leveled off, and a higher rental vacancy rate suggested that housing supply had caught up with demand.

The increase in production of manufactured housing (mobile homes) from 1991 to 1996 was more rapid than that of conventional housing, and, by 1996, manufactured housing accounted for 50 percent of all housing production, compared to 18 percent nationally.

The homeownership rate in Mississippi is higher than

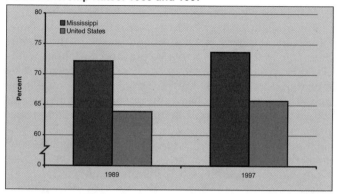

Homeownership Rates: 1989 and 1997

the U.S. average and rose more rapidly from 1990 to 1997, reaching 73.7 percent of all households in the latter year, compared to 65.7 percent nationwide.

Housing Supply

	1989	1990	1991	1992	1993	1994	1995	1996	1997
Residential building permits (thousands)	6.6	5.9	5.2	6.3	8.1	10.9	10.8	10.4	10.1
New home production (including manufactured housing):									
Thousands of homes	11.1	9.8	8.8	11.2	14.1	18.6	21.1	20.8	19.5
Rate per 1,000 population									
Mississippi	4.3	3.8	3.4	4.3	5.4	7.0	7.8	7.7	7.1
U.S.	6.2	5.2	4.5	5.1	5.6	6.4	6.3	6.6	6.5
Existing home sales:									
Thousands of homes	36.5	34.7	35.2	39.2	43.6	43.5	46.1	46.7	47.7
Change from previous year (percent)									
Mississippi	-0.3	-4.9	1.4	11.4	11.2	-0.2	6.0	1.3	2.1
U.S.	-3.9	-4.0	0.0	9.2	8.2	4.8	-3.7	7.5	3.8
Home ownership rate (percent of households)	72.2	69.4	71.8	70.4	69.7	69.2	71.1	73.0	73.7
Rental vacancy rate (percent of rental housing units)	10.5	8.7	7.8	7.4	8.0	7.9	13.2	13.2	11.5

AGRICULTURE

POULTRY RATHER THAN COTTON NOW DOMINATES MISSISSIPPI agriculture. Poultry and poultry products were marketed by only 6 percent of the state's farms in 1997 but accounted for 38 percent of all agricultural sales, bringing each poultry farmer an impressive $618,000 on average.

Cotton and cottonseed provided 18 percent of sales receipts in 1997, down from 26 percent in 1992, and the number of farms marketing cotton fell by almost 50 percent over the five years. Farmers selling cotton and cottonseed received an average of $324,000 from these sales

MISSISSIPPI FARMS, 1997	
Number of farms	43 000
Total acres (thousands):	12 500
Average per farm	291
Value of land and buildings (millions of dollars)	11 875
Average per farm (dollars)	276 163

in 1997, little more than one-half the average received from poultry sales, but well above the $100,000 average received by all farms from all sales.

Farm Income
(millions of dollars)

	1980	1989	1990	1991	1992	1993	1994	1995	1996	1997
Gross income	2 416	3 046	2 999	2 825	3 301	3 569	3 477	3 717	4 045	4 015
Receipts from sales	2 225	2 423	2 542	2 355	2 751	2 871	2 931	3 231	3 488	3 438
Government payments	19	325	186	176	280	384	226	134	198	170
Imputed and miscellaneous income	172	298	271	293	270	315	321	353	359	407
(–) Production expenses	2 114	2 565	2 754	2 858	2 814	3 078	3 210	3 145	3 392	3 465
(=) Realized net income	302	482	245	-33	487	492	267	573	652	550
(+) Inventory change	-234	-103	-83	325	-105	-251	269	-184	104	46
(=) Net income	68	379	163	292	382	241	536	389	756	596
Corporate income	0	25	11	15	27	7	59	28	80	58
Farm proprietors income	68	354	152	277	355	234	477	361	676	538

EDUCATION

EDUCATIONAL ATTAINMENT Percent of population age 25 and over, 1997	State	United States
High school graduate or higher	77.5	82.1
College graduate or higher	20.9	23.9

AMONG MISSISSIPPI RESIDENTS AGE 25 AND OVER IN 1997, 77.5 percent had completed high school; the comparable 1990 figure was only 64.3 percent. The percentage who had completed college more than doubled between 1970 and 1997, with much of the gain occurring since 1990. Like a number of other states, Mississippi currently is attempting to improve educational quality by introducing more rigorous testing requirements and holding individual schools accountable for their students' achievement.

Elementary and secondary school expenditures per pupil in 1995–96 were 69 percent of the national average, noticeably below other southern states. Teachers salaries, at 72 percent of the national average, were similarly low.

Only 9 percent of Mississippi's higher education students attended private schools in 1997, compared to 23 percent nationwide. The minority share of higher education enrollment was higher than the national average, but below the 38 percent minority share of Mississippi's total population.

High School Completion: 1990–97

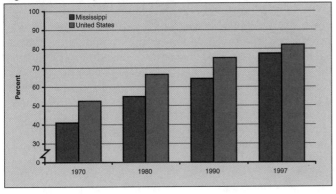

Education Indicators

	State	U.S.
Elementary and secondary schools Enrollment, 1995–96		
Total (thousands)	556	49 873
Percent in private schools	9.0	10.1
Expenditures per pupil (dollars), 1995–96	4 250	6 146
Average teacher salary (dollars), 1996–97	27 720	38 509
Higher education Enrollment, 1996–97		
Total (thousands)	126	14 218
Percent of population 18–34	18.5	21.8
Percent minority	32.7	26.1
Percent in private schools	9.0	22.6

HEALTH

MISSISSIPPI'S INFANT MORTALITY RATE AVERAGED 10.4 PER thousand live births from 1995 through 1997, an improvement from 1990 but still well above the national average. The State Department of Health has set a goal of reducing the rate to 7.5 by 2003. Emphasis on early prenatal care, reduction of smoking and drug abuse by pregnant women, teen pregnancy prevention, and social support services are elements of the effort to achieve this goal.

Adjusted for differences in the age distribution of the population, the state's overall death rate is well above the national average, and the highest of any southern state. There has been no apparent reduction in the rate during the 1990s. The 1996 death rate from heart disease, the leading cause of death, was 39 percent above the national average. The death rate from motor vehicle accidents was almost twice the national average.

Health Indicators

	1990	1995	1996	1997
Infant mortality *(rate per thousand live births)*				
Mississippi	12.1	10.5	9.7	10.9
U.S.	9.2	7.6	7.3	7.1
Total deaths, age-adjusted rate *(rate per thousand population)*				
Mississippi	6.1	6.2	6.0	6.1
U.S.	5.2	5.0	4.9	4.8
Persons not covered by health insurance *(percent of population)*				
Mississippi	19.9	19.7	18.5	20.1
U.S.	13.9	15.4	15.6	16.1

Leading Causes of Death, 1996
(deaths per 100,000 population)

	Age-adjusted		Not age-adjusted	
	State	U.S.	State	U.S.
Deaths from all causes	603.5	491.6	982.4	872.5
Heart disease	187.4	134.5	351.2	276.4
Cancer	141.4	127.9	212.0	203.4
Cerebrovascular diseases	32.1	26.4	62.9	60.3
Chronic obstructive pulmonary disease	21.9	21.0	37.1	40.0
Diabetes mellitus	12.6	13.6	19.8	23.3
Pneumonia and influenza	14.8	12.8	32.7	31.6
HIV	8.8	11.1	8.5	11.7
Liver disease	8.0	7.5	9.4	9.4
Alzheimer's disease	2.2	2.7	6.0	8.1
Accidents and adverse effects	50.2	30.4	55.6	35.8
Motor vehicle accidents	31.6	16.2	31.9	16.5
Suicide	11.2	10.8	11.4	11.6
Homicide	14.1	8.5	13.8	7.9
Injury by firearm	20.8	12.9	20.7	12.8

GOVERNMENT

STATE AND LOCAL TAXES, 1995–96	State	U.S.
Per capita (dollars)	1 819	2 477
Percent of personal income	11.0	10.8

AS A PERCENTAGE OF PERSONAL INCOME, MISSISSIPPI'S PER capita state and local taxes (excluding corporate income taxes) in the 1995–96 fiscal year were slightly higher than the national average rate. This relatively high ratio stems from Mississippi's low per capita incomes; the actual per capita dollar amount of state and local taxes was the third lowest in the nation and just 73 percent of the all-state average. Local taxes were only 26 percent of the state and local total, compared to a 41 percent national average, indicating considerably above average state-level responsibility for revenue collection.

With the explosive growth of tourism during the 1990s, general and selective sales taxes have been a lucrative revenue source for the state, which, despite the low incomes of residents, raised more dollars per capita than the national average. Revenue from the individual income tax, on the other hand, was far below the all-state per capita average.

Total state-level general expenditure per capita in Mississippi was within 1 percent of the all-state average in 1996–97. Education was by far the largest functional category of spending and was at 98 percent of the all-state average per capita. These figures are for state government spending only; local spending on education appeared to be well below the national average, since total per-pupil expenditure in elementary and secondary schools was only 69 percent of the national average in 1995–96.

Interest on Mississippi's general debt averaged $55 per capita in 1996–97, compared to a national average of $99. The state seemed in excellent financial shape at year end, with debt equal to $899 per capita, compared to $1,706 nationwide, and cash and security holdings almost 6 times the size of the debt.

Mississippi's 1.1 percent share of federal funds distributed to states and their residents in fiscal 1997 was a little higher than the state's 1.0 percent share of the U.S. population. Reflecting relatively low household incomes, the shares of food stamp and Supplementary Security Income payments coming to state residents were especially high relative to the state's population share. Shares for Medicaid and other health related grants, and for education grants, also were somewhat high. The share of federal non-defense procurement contracts was noticeably low relative to the state's share of the U.S. population.

State Government Finances, 1996–97

	Millions of dollars	Percent distribution	Dollars per capita	
			State	U.S.
General revenue	7 895	100.0	2 891	3 049
Intergovernmental revenue	2 904	36.8	1 063	863
Taxes	4 017	50.9	1 471	1 660
General sales	1 916	24.3	702	551
Selective sales	749	9.5	274	257
License taxes	266	3.4	97	106
Individual income	791	10.0	290	542
Corporation net income	226	2.9	83	115
Other taxes	68	0.9	25	90
Other general revenue	974	12.3	357	526
General expenditure	8 014	100.0	2 934	2 951
Intergovernmental expenditure	2 686	33.5	983	989
Direct expenditure	5 328	66.5	1 951	1 962
General expenditure, by function:				
Education	2 752	34.3	1 008	1 033
Public welfare	1 891	23.6	693	761
Hospitals and health	670	8.4	245	237
Highways	776	9.7	284	225
Police protection and corrections	268	3.4	98	137
Natural resources, parks and recreation	278	3.5	102	63
Governmental administration	265	3.3	97	107
Interest on general debt	152	1.9	55	99
Other and unallocable	962	12.0	352	290
Debt at end of fiscal year	2 455	NA	899	1 706
Cash and security holdings	14 574	NA	5 337	6 683

Federal Spending within State

	Federal funds, fiscal 1997		
	Millions of dollars	Percent distribution	Percent of U.S. total*
Total within state	15 091	100.0	1.1
Payments to individuals	8 701	57.7	1.1
Retirement and disability	4 699	31.1	1.0
Medicare	2 158	14.3	1.0
Food stamps	315	2.1	1.6
Supplemental Security Income	546	3.6	2.0
Grants	2 856	18.9	1.1
Medicaid and other health	1 453	9.6	1.3
Nutrition and family welfare	517	3.4	1.1
Education	237	1.6	1.4
Housing and community development	98	0.6	0.9
Salaries and wages	1 542	10.2	0.9
Defense procurement contracts	1 362	9.0	1.1
Non-defense procurement contracts	366	2.4	0.5

*State population is 1.0 percent of the U.S. total.

31 372	59 698		65 157	70 827	72 687	78 001	81 93	88 504	93 426	5.8	63 383	70 827	31 372	59 698	63 3
25 323	47 902			57 151	59 446	62 916	67 00	72 039	77 208	6.1	50 999	57 151	25 323	47 902	50 9
2 640	5 143				02	7 801		7 709	7 838	5.4	5 645	6 816	2 640	5 143	5 6
3 409	6 652				284			8 755	8 380	2.9	6 739	6 860	3 409	6 652	6 7
693	1 716				762		07	1 539	762	-9.7	1 561	811	693	1 716	1 5
2 716	1 93							7 217	7 618	5.6	5 178	6 04	2 716		

1997

Population (persons)	5,408,455
Population rank	16th
Population growth rank (1990–97)	32nd
Per capita personal income	$23,723
Unemployment rate (percent)	4.2
Poverty rate (percent)	11.8

DURING THE 1990S, MISSOURI'S ECONOMY HAS BEEN RELA-tively strong, growing at about the same pace as the U.S. economy. Vigorous employment growth has helped the state's unemployment rate to drop considerably over recent years. Services, especially with the large healthcare and business services industries, has continued to be the state's largest sector, though manufacturing is a larger than average source of earnings and employment. Over the past decade, the construction industry has seen tremendous growth in employment and earnings with the increase in demand for housing. While agricultural products continue to be among the state's leading exports, agriculture contributes only about 1 percent of all worker earnings in the state's economy. The state's median household income was just below the national average in 1997, though the gap in per capita income is greater. During the 1990s, Missouri has enjoyed moderate population growth, just below the national average. Minorities make up more than 14 percent of the total population, though the minority groups are growing at a rate lower than the U.S. rate.

Average Annual Population Growth: 1990–97

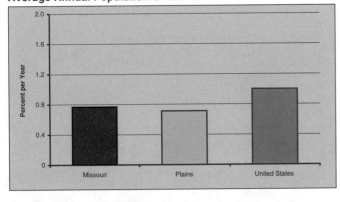

Median Household Income: 1989–97 (1997 dollars)

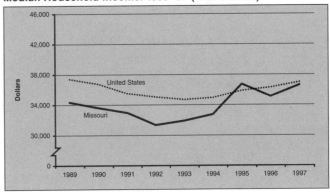

Unemployment Rate: 1989–97

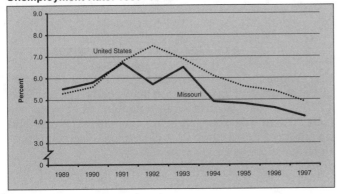

IN 1997, MISSOURI'S UNEMPLOYMENT RATE DROPPED TO 4.2 percent, below the national average. The 1997 rate marked a substantial decrease from rates during the early 1990s recession and gave the state the 19th lowest unemployment rate in the nation in 1997. During the 1990s, the state's labor force grew at nearly double the rate of the population, and employment increased more rapidly. Both the services and construction industries even had substantial increases in employment during this period. From 1989 to 1997, they accounted for nearly 250,000 additional jobs, 63 percent of the state's new jobs during this period.

POPULATION AND LABOR FORCE

MISSOURI'S TOTAL POPULATION GREW 0.8 PERCENT ANNUALLY from 1990 to 1997, just below the national rate of 1.0 percent. From 1990 to 1997, there was little change in the racial breakdown of the state's population, though the White non-Hispanic population decreased by almost a full percent. In 1997, the White non-Hispanic population accounted for 86 percent of the population, and the only minority group of significant size was Blacks, with just over 11 percent of the population. About one-third of Missouri's population growth can be attributed to domes-

tic in-migration, so in this respect Missouri resembles its Southern neighbors. International migration to Missouri has also contributed to the state's growth. The in-migration has helped offset the state's declining birth rate. Missouri's birth rate fell to 13.8 per 1,000 live births in 1997, while the state's 1997 death rate of 10.1 per 1,000 population was one of the highest in the nation.

The proportion of residents in metropolitan areas, about 68 percent, is substantially below the national rate of 80 percent.

Population and Labor Force

	1980	1990	1991	1992	1993	1994	1995	1996	1997	Change*	
										State	U.S.
Population											
Total number of persons (thousands)	4 917	5 126	5 158	5 194	5 238	5 291	5 337	5 369	5 408	0.8	1.0
Percent distribution:											
White, Non-Hispanic	87.7	86.7	86.8	86.7	86.5	86.4	86.3	86.1	86.0	0.6	0.4
Black, Non-Hispanic	10.4	10.7	10.8	10.8	10.9	11.0	11.0	11.1	11.1	1.3	1.4
Asian	0.5	0.9	0.9	0.9	0.9	1.0	1.0	1.0	1.1	4.1	4.1
Native American	0.3	0.4	0.4	0.4	0.4	0.4	0.4	0.4	0.4	-0.2	1.6
Hispanic	1.1	1.4	1.2	1.3	1.3	1.4	1.4	1.5	1.5	2.3	3.8
In metropolitan areas	67.4	68.2	68.3	68.2	68.2	68.1	68.0	67.9	67.9	0.7	1.0
Total number of households (thousands)	1 793	1 961	1 976	1 994	2 001	2 009	2 031	2 052	NA	0.8	1.2
Labor Force (thousands)											
Population 16 and over	3 737	3 948	3 967	3 990	4 024	4 062	4 098	4 131	4 161	0.8	1.0
Civilian labor force	2 307	2 594	2 656	2 668	2 661	2 698	2 833	2 905	2 893	1.6	1.1
Employed	2 140	2 443	2 479	2 515	2 489	2 567	2 698	2 772	2 770	1.8	1.2
Percent of population	57.3	61.9	62.5	63.0	61.9	63.2	65.8	67.1	66.6		
Unemployment rate (percent)	7.2	5.8	6.7	5.7	6.5	4.9	4.8	4.6	4.2		

*Compound annual average percent change, 1990–1997; 1990–1996 for households.

Population Change and Components: 1990–97

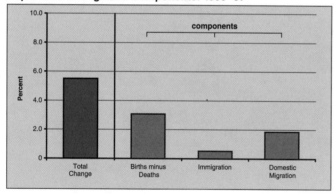

Average Annual Household and Population Growth

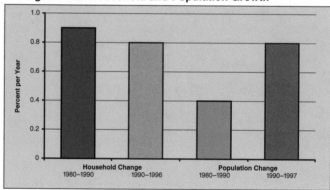

Population by Age; Births and Deaths

	1990		1997	
	State	U.S.	State	U.S.
Age distribution (percent)				
Under 5 years	7.3	7.6	6.8	7.2
5 to 17 years	18.4	18.2	19.2	18.8
18 to 64 years	60.3	61.8	60.3	61.3
65 years and over	14.0	12.5	13.7	12.7
Birth and death rates (per thousand population)				
Births	15.5	16.7	13.8	14.6
Deaths	9.8	8.6	10.1	8.6

FROM 1990 TO 1997, MISSOURI'S POPULATION AGE BREAKDOWN changed slightly. The pre-school age group proportion dropped. However, the state had a larger than average percentage of its population between the ages of 5 and 17. The percentage of the state's population between the ages of 18 and 64 was well below the national figure, and it continued to maintain its greater than average proportion of its population over the age of 65.

HOUSEHOLD AND PERSONAL INCOME

HOUSEHOLD INCOME AND PERSONS IN POVERTY	1990	1995	1996	1997	
				State	U.S.
Median household income (1997 dollars)	33 564	36 676	35 051	36 553	37 005
Persons in poverty (thousands)	700	484	500	627	35 574
Poverty rate (percent)	13.4	9.4	9.5	11.8	13.3

MISSOURI'S 1997 MEDIAN HOUSEHOLD INCOME OF $36,553 was just under the national average. This was the 25th highest in the nation, up from 1994, when the state was ranked 34th in the nation. The state's poverty rate was 11.8 percent, significantly lower than the national rate of 13.3. In 1997, Missouri had the 25th lowest poverty rate in the nation, well below its rank of 8th in 1995.

Per capita personal income increased 10.6 percent in inflation-adjusted dollars from 1989 to 1997. In 1997, Missouri's per capita income was just under 94 percent of the national average, though it has been growing at a slightly faster rate than nationwide. Net earnings per capita were only 91 percent as high as the U.S. average, while transfer payments and dividend and interest income were close to the national average. Growth of proprietors' income was significantly slower than that of wage earners.

Adjustment for residence has been a substantial factor throughout the 1990s, as a net $3.4 billion, or 3.7 percent of total earnings left the state via out-of-state residents working in Missouri.

Total government payments to individuals grew by a slightly higher rate than the national average, mainly because Missouri's medical payments grew by nearly 120 percent from 1990 to 1997, well above the U.S. growth. Total income maintenance grew at a faster rate than nationwide; the differential was due entirely to the much faster than average growth of "other" income maintenance, which is primarily earned income tax credits. Supplemental Security Income grew faster and food stamps slower than the U.S. average. Family assistance, now the smallest program, did not increase at all, following the national welfare trend.

Personal Income
(millions of dollars)

	1980	1989	1990	1991	1992	1993	1994	1995	1996	1997	Change*
Earnings by place of work	34 550	62 651	65 049	66 717	71 113	73 981	78 708	82 727	87 043	92 547	5.0
Wages and salaries	28 135	50 147	52 626	53 854	56 755	58 980	62 647	66 739	70 419	75 217	5.2
Other labor income	2 829	5 438	5 918	6 372	7 175	7 859	8 425	8 452	8 003	8 121	5.1
Proprietors' income	3 586	7 066	6 504	6 491	7 183	7 143	7 635	7 536	8 622	9 209	3.4
Farm	67	682	410	295	455	104	364	-71	683	893	3.4
Nonfarm	3 519	6 384	6 094	6 196	6 728	7 039	7 271	7 607	7 939	8 316	3.4
(−) Personal contributions for social insurance	1 809	4 094	4 281	4 483	4 696	4 930	5 328	5 702	5 939	6 333	5.6
(+) Adjustment for residence	-1 555	-2 451	-2 563	-2 556	-2 666	-2 791	-2 862	-3 042	-3 228	-3 398	NA
(=) Net earnings by state of residence	31 186	56 106	58 205	59 677	63 751	66 260	70 518	73 983	77 876	82 816	5.0
(+) Dividends, interest, and rent	8 154	17 798	18 816	19 058	18 956	18 618	19 760	21 173	22 505	23 373	3.5
(+) Transfer payments	6 753	12 524	13 403	15 675	16 594	17 948	18 595	19 911	20 918	21 962	7.3
(=) Total personal income	46 093	86 429	90 424	94 410	99 301	102 826	108 872	115 067	121 299	128 151	5.0
Farm	237	844	600	480	655	312	564	131	884	1 094	3.3
Nonfarm	45 856	85 585	89 823	93 930	98 646	102 514	108 309	114 936	120 415	127 057	5.1
Personal income per capita (dollars)											
Current dollars	9 365	16 961	17 640	18 305	19 119	19 631	20 615	21 610	22 615	23 723	4.3
1997 dollars	17 906	21 442	21 227	21 137	21 386	21 361	21 908	22 464	23 030	23 723	1.3

*Compound annual average percent change, 1989–1997

Government Transfer Payments

	Millions of dollars		Percent change*	
	1990	1997	State	U.S.
Total government payments to individuals	12 766	21 101	65.3	62.7
Retirement, disability, and insurance	7 390	10 642	44.0	48.2
Social Security	5 586	7 937	42.1	46.1
Government employee retirement	1 510	2 378	57.5	60.3
Medical payments	3 578	7 867	119.9	101.2
Income maintenance	944	1 629	72.5	58.0
Supplemental Security Income	239	479	100.2	75.4
Family assistance	246	245	-0.8	-0.5
Food Stamps	327	379	15.8	27.1
Other income maintenance	131	526	301.1	189.8
Unemployment insurance benefits	308	266	-13.6	10.6
Veterans benefits and other	546	697	27.5	30.8

*Percent change, 1990–1997

Government Payments to Individuals: 1997

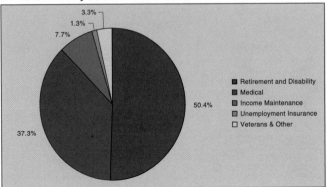

- Retirement and Disability
- Medical
- Income Maintenance
- Unemployment Insurance
- Veterans & Other

ECONOMIC STRUCTURE

LEADING PRIVATE INDUSTRIES, 1997 (Worker and proprietor earnings, millions of dollars)		FASTEST EARNINGS GROWTH, 1989–97 (percent increase)	
Health services	$8 382	Amusement and recreation services	197.8
Business services	4 283	Security brokers	147.8
Construction specialties	3 932	Real estate	117.1
Communications	2 394	Social services	109.1
Engineering and management services	2 331	Educational services	76.7

IN 1997, SERVICES WAS MISSOURI'S LEADING SECTOR AND included three of the state's leading industries: health, business, and engineering and management services. The services industry's employment has increased by 210,000 jobs, or 27.2 percent, from 1989 to 1997, while Missouri's total employment increased by 13.2 percent. Service sector earnings have grown by more than 65 percent during the same period. Amusement and recreational services was the state's fastest growing industry from 1989 to 1997, increasing by nearly 200 percent, and all the other fastest growing industries are in services or finance. Fast-growing employment sectors during this period also included agricultural services and construction; construction employment increased at double the rate of overall employment in the state. The mining, farming, and manufacturing industries all had fewer employees in 1997 than in 1989. Manufacturing had the largest actual decrease, by eliminating more than 20,000 jobs. Still, manufacturing is the state's second leading sector by earnings, comprising nearly 20 percent of the state's total earnings in 1997, slightly higher than its proportion in the U.S. economy.

Employment and Earnings by Sector

	1980	1989	1990	1991	1992	1993	1994	1995	1996	1997 Number	1997 Percent of total	Change*
Employment *(thousands of persons)*												
Total	2 554	2 959	2 987	2 964	2 981	3 062	3 138	3 210	3 277	3 351	100.0	1.6
Farm	148	131	128	125	126	121	121	122	121	118	3.5	-1.4
Nonfarm	2 406	2 828	2 858	2 839	2 855	2 940	3 017	3 088	3 156	3 234	96.5	1.7
Private nonfarm	2 036	2 432	2 452	2 433	2 446	2 527	2 599	2 662	2 719	2 789	83.2	1.7
Agricultural service, forestry, and fishing	14	22	˙24	25	25	27	29	29	30	32	1.0	4.8
Mining	9	8	8	8	8	7	7	7	7	6	0.2	-3.4
Construction	116	147	146	138	145	153	170	173	178	185	5.5	2.9
Manufacturing	449	452	448	429	423	423	428	435	432	431	12.9	-0.6
Transportation and public utilities	156	175	178	176	172	179	180	181	188	196	5.8	1.4
Wholesale trade	145	153	150	151	152	147	150	155	157	160	4.8	0.5
Retail trade	394	494	492	489	492	511	532	547	561	570	17.0	1.8
Finance, insurance, and real estate	189	209	214	209	204	211	213	215	221	228	6.8	1.1
Services	562	771	794	809	826	869	890	919	947	981	29.3	3.1
Government	370	397	406	407	409	413	418	426	438	445	13.3	1.4
Earnings *(millions of dollars)*												
Total	34 550	62 651	65 049	66 717	71 113	73 981	78 708	82 727	87 043	92 547	100.0	5.0
Farm	237	844	600	480	655	312	564	131	884	1 094	1.2	3.3
Nonfarm	34 313	61 807	64 448	66 237	70 458	73 669	78 144	82 596	86 159	91 453	98.8	5.0
Private nonfarm	29 510	53 191	55 169	56 439	60 334	63 183	67 164	71 129	74 067	78 816	85.2	5.0
Agricultural service, forestry, and fishing	112	308	351	343	371	387	400	408	420	454	0.5	5.0
Mining	332	211	203	251	225	229	211	245	232	239	0.3	1.6
Construction	2 095	3 783	3 657	3 498	3 768	4 122	5 025	5 316	5 625	6 001	6.5	5.9
Manufacturing	8 649	13 771	14 030	14 019	14 823	15 303	16 148	17 015	17 049	18 068	19.5	3.5
Transportation and public utilities	3 496	5 577	5 877	6 018	6 197	6 474	6 689	6 938	7 284	7 750	8.4	4.2
Wholesale trade	2 922	4 659	4 852	4 906	5 199	5 104	5 370	5 743	6 009	6 334	6.9	4.0
Retail trade	3 599	6 056	6 151	6 389	6 822	7 181	7 623	7 965	8 289	8 646	9.3	4.6
Finance, insurance, and real estate	1 931	3 978	4 294	4 423	4 914	5 316	5 532	5 857	6 264	6 750	7.3	6.8
Services	6 374	14 849	15 754	16 592	18 014	19 066	20 165	21 643	22 895	24 556	26.5	6.5
Government	4 803	8 616	9 280	9 798	10 124	10 486	10 980	11 467	12 092	12 637	13.7	4.9

*Compound annual average percent change, 1989–1997

ECONOMIC STRUCTURE (Continued)

IN 1997, MISSOURI'S AVERAGE WAGES EQUALED ONLY 90.9 percent of the national average. With the exception of construction, every sector's wages were substantially below average. The gap was smaller in manufacturing sector, where wages were 5 percent below the U.S. average. From 1989 to 1997, Missouri's average farm wages showed the greatest increase by growing more than 48 percent. The state's average wage grew by 33 percent during the same period, about the same as wage growth nationwide.

Missouri's gross state product (GSP) increased by 42.2 percent from 1989 to 1997. During this period, manufacturing's share of the state's GSP has remained high. In 1989, manufacturing accounted for 23.1 percent of Missouri's GSP; by 1997 it had fallen slightly to 21.4 percent. Despite this decrease, manufacturing output continues to contribute an above-average share of GSP. Though not among the state's five largest industries, chemicals and allied products and transportation equipment excluding motor vehicles are the biggest manufacturing industries, with worker earnings of $2.3 billion and $2.0 billion in 1997. Missouri's manufacturing value of output per worker has increased substantially since 1994, and in 1996 was well above the national average of $69,387. However, new capital expenditures fell sharply in 1996 after a major increase in 1995.

Missouri's largest goods exports in 1997 were chemical products and agricultural products. The value of the state's overall exports has increased by nearly 35 percent since 1994, slightly less than the increase in U.S. exports in the same period. The state's agricultural product exports increased more than 60 percent. Manufactured goods exports have increased 30.0 percent during the same period, though industrial machinery and computers showed a large increase from 1994 to 1997. Both chemical products and transportation equipment showed small increases from 1994 to 1997, with almost no increase after 1995.

Average Annual Wages and Salaries by Sector
(dollars)

	1989	1996	1997 State	1997 U.S.
All wage and salary workers	20 375	25 961	27 098	29 809
Farm	9 028	12 358	13 402	16 442
Nonfarm	20 454	26 039	27 169	29 900
Private nonfarm	20 565	26 255	27 459	29 867
Agricultural service, forestry, and fishing	12 924	16 429	16 948	17 941
Mining	32 306	36 764	38 122	49 800
Construction	24 429	31 172	32 540	31 765
Manufacturing	26 731	34 256	36 552	38 351
Transportation and utilities	29 118	34 907	36 166	38 222
Wholesale trade	26 670	34 873	36 228	39 466
Retail trade	11 455	14 530	14 983	16 206
Finance, insurance, and real estate	24 207	33 643	35 633	44 993
Services	17 550	23 603	24 539	27 588
Government	19 880	24 922	25 660	30 062

Gross State Product and Manufacturing
(millions of dollars, except as noted)

	1989	1994	1995	1996
Gross state product, total	102 025	129 110	137 483	145 123
Manufacturing:				
Millions of dollars	23 539	27 465	30 415	31 122
Percent of total gross state product	23.1	21.3	22.1	21.4
Per worker (dollars)	52 073	64 148	69 879	72 125
New capital expenditures, manufacturing	NA	2 608	3 039	2 415

Exports of Goods
(millions of dollars)

	1994	1995	1996	1997
All goods	5 235	5 690	6 590	7 043
Manufactures	4 393	4 858	5 122	5 712
Agricultural and livestock products	738	697	1 355	1 182
Other commodities	104	135	113	149
Top goods exports, 1997:				
Chemical products	1 389	1 525	1 594	1 530
Agricultural products	735	694	1 351	1 179
Industrial machinery and computers	543	616	666	825
Electric and electronic equipment	523	490	584	618
Transportation equipment	470	569	564	570

HOUSING

WITH THE EXCEPTION OF 1994, MISSOURI'S HOUSING PRODUCTION rates per capita have remained lower than the U.S. rate in the 1990s. Still, housing production has increased 44.4 percent from 18,400 units in 1990 to 31,200 units in 1997. Sales of existing homes have also increased significantly during this period. From 1990 to 1997, Missouri's home sales increased 43.1 percent. In 1996, Missouri's homeownership rates climbed up above 70 percent for the first time during the decade, well above the national average, spurred on by healthy income growth and low interest rates. In 1997, Missouri had the 16th highest homeownership rate in the nation. This was quite a change from 1989, when the state had the 13th lowest homeownership rate in the nation. Rental vacancy rates have remained consistently above the national average, ranking 16th highest in the nation in 1997.

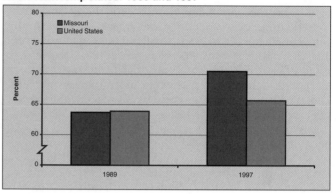

Homeownership Rates: 1989 and 1997

Housing Supply

	1989	1990	1991	1992	1993	1994	1995	1996	1997
Residential building permits (thousands)	18.0	15.3	16.1	20.1	21.7	26.4	24.3	26.3	25.2
New home production (including manufactured housing):									
Thousands of homes	21.6	18.4	19.6	24.9	27.4	34.4	32.4	33.9	31.2
Rate per 1,000 population									
Missouri	4.2	3.6	3.8	4.8	5.2	6.5	6.1	6.3	5.8
U.S.	6.2	5.2	4.5	5.1	5.6	6.4	6.3	6.6	6.5
Existing home sales:									
Thousands of homes	81.0	84.1	82.7	98.8	106.4	110.2	108.3	113.7	115.9
Change from previous year (percent)									
Missouri	11.0	3.8	-1.7	19.5	7.7	3.6	-1.7	5.0	1.9
U.S.	-3.9	-4.0	0.0	9.2	8.2	4.8	-3.7	7.5	3.8
Home ownership rate (percent of households)	63.7	64.0	64.2	65.2	66.4	68.4	69.4	70.2	70.5
Rental vacancy rate (percent of rental housing units)	8.3	9.6	11.1	9.9	9.4	10.1	10.0	8.6	8.9

AGRICULTURE

IN 1997, MISSOURI HAD THE THIRD HIGHEST NUMBER OF farms in the nation and, the ninth highest total value of farmland and buildings. The average number of acres per farm was 293, well below the national average of 471. Receipts from sales grew by nearly 40 percent from 1989 to 1997. Production expenses have been increasing steadily throughout the decade but at a slower rate than gross income. While income from crops remains lower than income from livestock and livestock products, it has grown by 50 percent from 1989 to 1997, significantly higher than the 29.5 percent growth of livestock revenue. Overall, the state's farm economy has remained fairly strong in the past decade except for weak years in 1993 and 1995.

MISSOURI FARMS, 1997	
Number of farms	102 000
Total acres (thousands):	29 900
Average per farm	293
Value of land and buildings (millions of dollars)	30 199
Average per farm (dollars)	296 069

Farm Income
(millions of dollars)

	1980	1989	1990	1991	1992	1993	1994	1995	1996	1997
Gross income	4 927	5 086	5 048	4 960	5 193	5 431	5 555	5 525	5 899	6 705
Receipts from sales	4 491	4 304	4 346	4 301	4 524	4 582	4 883	4 828	5 165	5 948
Government payments	79	356	299	269	294	455	267	257	291	278
Imputed and miscellaneous income	357	426	403	390	375	393	404	440	443	480
(−) Production expenses	4 327	4 444	4 657	4 780	4 995	5 133	5 289	5 290	5 663	5 684
(=) Realized net income	601	642	391	180	198	298	266	235	236	1 022
(+) Inventory change	-533	79	44	129	287	-191	137	-324	517	-44
(=) Net income	67	721	435	308	485	107	404	-89	754	978
Corporate income	0	39	25	14	30	3	39	-18	71	85
Farm proprietors income	67	682	410	295	455	104	364	-71	683	893

EDUCATION

EDUCATIONAL ATTAINMENT Percent of population age 25 and over, 1997	State	United States
High school graduate or higher	80.1	82.1
College graduate or higher	22.9	23.9

MISSOURI RANKS NEAR THE MIDDLE OF THE NATION IN ITS education attainment levels. More than 80 percent of the state's population are high school graduates, and nearly 23 percent have earned college degrees. These numbers are just below the U.S. averages. The education attainment levels have increased significantly from 1990, when only 73.9 percent of the state's population had graduated from high school, and 17.8 percent were college graduates.

Missouri's average teacher salary was only 89 percent of the national average teacher salary, and per pupil expenditures were about 10 percent below the national average. Within higher education, in contrast to the state's lower than average attainment level, a higher than average proportion of young adults is currently enrolled. Nearly 35 percent of the state's postsecondary students attend private schools, well above the 22.6 percent nationally.

High School Completion: 1990–97

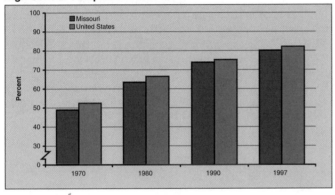

Education Indicators

	State	U.S.
Elementary and secondary schools		
Enrollment, 1995–96		
Total (thousands)	1 017	49 873
Percent in private schools	12.5	10.1
Expenditures per pupil (dollars), 1995–96	5 626	6 146
Average teacher salary (dollars), 1996–97	34 342	38 509
Higher education		
Enrollment, 1996–97		
Total (thousands)	290	14 218
Percent of population 18–34	22.9	21.8
Percent minority	13.8	26.1
Percent in private schools	34.9	22.6

HEALTH

INFANT MORTALITY IN MISSOURI IN 1997 WAS JUST ABOVE THE national average, the 23rd highest infant mortality rate in the nation. The state has one of the 14th highest death rates in the nation, well above the U.S. rate, even after adjustment for age differences. For most major causes of death, Missouri's death rate is higher than average. The state's motor vehicle death rate is 30 percent higher than

the national rate. The percentage of Missouri's population that is without health insurance has declined since 1995. During this same period, the national percentage has been increasing. Missouri's percentage without health insurance (12.6 percent) is well below the national average of 16.1 and ranks the state the 16th in the nation in the percent of population with health insurance.

Health Indicators

	1990	1995	1996	1997
Infant mortality				
(rate per thousand live births)				
Missouri	9.4	7.4	8.1	7.3
U.S.	9.2	7.6	7.3	7.1
Total deaths, age-adjusted rate				
(rate per thousand population)				
Missouri	5.3	5.3	5.2	5.2
U.S.	5.2	5.0	4.9	4.8
Persons not covered by health insurance				
(percent of population)				
Missouri	12.7	14.6	13.2	12.6
U.S.	13.9	15.4	15.6	16.1

Leading Causes of Death, 1996
(deaths per 100,000 population)

	Age-adjusted		Not age-adjusted	
	State	U.S.	State	U.S.
Deaths from all causes	517.9	491.6	1006.0	872.5
Heart disease	149.0	134.5	340.1	276.4
Cancer	132.6	127.9	223.2	203.4
Cerebrovascular diseases	27.4	26.4	70.5	60.3
Chronic obstructive pulmonary disease	22.8	21.0	46.7	40.0
Diabetes mellitus	12.9	13.6	23.8	23.3
Pneumonia and influenza	14.0	12.8	40.4	31.6
HIV	5.8	11.1	6.0	11.7
Liver disease	5.8	7.5	7.8	9.4
Alzheimer's disease	2.5	2.7	8.3	8.1
Accidents and adverse effects	36.7	30.4	44.6	35.8
Motor vehicle accidents	20.9	16.2	21.0	16.5
Suicide	13.2	10.8	14.2	11.6
Homicide	9.3	8.5	8.7	7.9
Injury by firearm	15.7	12.9	16.0	12.8

GOVERNMENT

STATE AND LOCAL TAXES, 1995–96	State	U.S.
Per capita (dollars)	2 101	2 477
Percent of personal income	9.7	10.8

IN 1996, THE COMBINATION OF STATE AND LOCAL TAXES IN Missouri amounted to $2,101 per capita, below the national average of $2,477. These taxes represented just 9.7 percent of personal income, among the lowest percentages in the nation. In 1997, Missouri's per capita state government revenue amounted to $2,550, well below the national average of $3,049. Per capita individual income taxes totaling $562 were slightly higher in Missouri than nationwide, but the state's per capita general sales taxes, license taxes, and corporation net income taxes were all lower than the U.S. per capita amounts for all other states. Missouri's general expenditures are lower per capita than nationwide. State expenditures for education amounted to $935, about 10 percent below U.S. levels. With few exceptions, the state's per capita expenditures were much lower than the national per capita amounts. The U.S. per capita debt amounted to $1,706 in 1997, well above Missouri's $1,403.

Missouri received a greater than proportional share of total federal government expenditures, including payments to individuals and procurement. Defense procurement spending in the state amounted to 4.0 percent of the U.S. total because of aircraft purchases, well above Missouri's 2.0 percent of the U.S. population. With the exception of Medicaid grants, Missouri received a slightly lower proportion of federal grants. Missouri received just 1.7 percent of the total U.S education grants. The state's residents received only 1.8 percent of the total federal salaries and wages.

State Government Finances, 1996–97

	Millions of dollars	Percent distribution	Dollars per capita State	Dollars per capita U.S.
General revenue	13 774	100.0	2 550	3 049
Intergovernmental revenue	3 720	27.0	689	863
Taxes	7 816	56.7	1 447	1 660
General sales	2 592	18.8	480	551
Selective sales	1 110	8.1	205	257
License taxes	562	4.1	104	106
Individual income	3 038	22.1	562	542
Corporation net income	411	3.0	76	115
Other taxes	102	0.7	19	90
Other general revenue	2 238	16.2	414	526
General expenditure	13 082	100.0	2 422	2 951
Intergovernmental expenditure	3 944	30.1	730	989
Direct expenditure	9 138	69.9	1 692	1 962
General expenditure, by function:				
Education	5 051	38.6	935	1 033
Public welfare	3 066	23.4	568	761
Hospitals and health	1 010	7.7	187	237
Highways	1 265	9.7	234	225
Police protection and corrections	524	4.0	97	137
Natural resources, parks and recreation	301	2.3	56	63
Governmental administration	637	4.9	118	107
Interest on general debt	443	3.4	82	99
Other and unallocable	785	6.0	145	290
Debt at end of fiscal year	7 579	NA	1 403	1 706
Cash and security holdings	32 267	NA	5 973	6 683

Federal Spending within State

	Federal funds, fiscal 1997 Millions of dollars	Percent distribution	Percent of U.S. total*
Total within state	31 833	100.0	2.2
Payments to individuals	16 625	52.2	2.1
Retirement and disability	9 993	31.4	2.2
Medicare	4 447	14.0	2.2
Food stamps	403	1.3	2.1
Supplemental Security Income	481	1.5	1.8
Grants	4 652	14.6	1.9
Medicaid and other health	2 277	7.2	2.0
Nutrition and family welfare	827	2.6	1.8
Education	298	0.9	1.7
Housing and community development	221	0.7	1.9
Salaries and wages	3 033	9.5	1.8
Defense procurement contracts	4 749	14.9	4.0
Non-defense procurement contracts	1 576	5.0	2.2

*State population is 2.0 percent of the U.S. total.

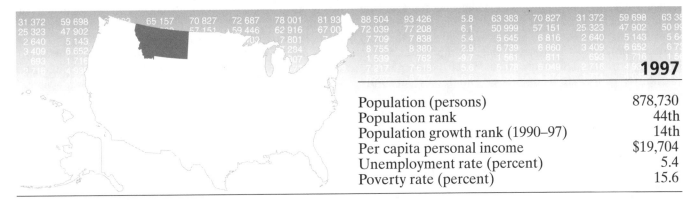

31 372	59 698		65 157	70 827	72 687	78 001	81 93	88 504	93 426	5.8	63 383	70 827	31 372	59 698	63 38
25 323	47 902			57 151	59 446	62 916	67 00	72 039	77 208	6.1	50 999	57 151	25 323	47 902	50 99
2 640	5 143					7 801		7 709	7 838	5.4	5 645	6 816	2 640	5 143	5 64
3 409	6 652				284			8 755	8 380	2.9	6 739	6 860	3 409	6 652	6 73
693	1 716				762			1 539	762	-9.7	1 561	811	693	1 716	1 5
2 716								7 217	7 618	5.6	6 178	6 049	2 716		

1997

Population (persons)	878,730
Population rank	44th
Population growth rank (1990–97)	14th
Per capita personal income	$19,704
Unemployment rate (percent)	5.4
Poverty rate (percent)	15.6

WITH EXPANDING SERVICES AND RETAIL TRADE SECTORS Montana's economy grew slightly faster than that of the United States in the 1990s. A growing tourist trade and a quality of life that attracts in-migrants from other states appear to be the touchstones of the state's success. Over 50,000 Americans migrated into Montana in 1990–97, adding more than 6 percent to the population. Many of them appear to be working-age adults who contribute to the state's labor force. Though there is a vital business services sector, the state largely has missed out on high-technology manufacturing and services growth that is driving much of the nation's growth in the 1990s; the manufacturing sector is relatively small and is still dominated by the lumber industry. However, the traditional natural resources-based industries—mining, agriculture, and lumber, and wood manufacturing—contributed only 8.1 percent of total earnings in 1997, compared to 12.5 percent in 1989.

Because of the substantial migration, population growth in Montana during the 1990s continued at an above-average pace. However, the state had one of the nation's smallest populations, the third lowest density of population, and the lowest proportion living in a metropolitan area. Though the rural flavor of the state is attractive to many in-migrants, it also may limit the development of industries dependent upon proximity to large market.

Average Annual Population Growth: 1990–97

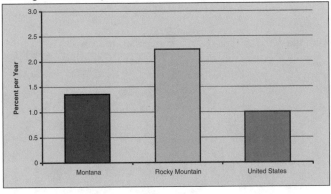

Median Household Income: 1989–97 (1997 dollars)

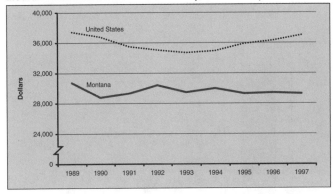

Unemployment Rate: 1989–97

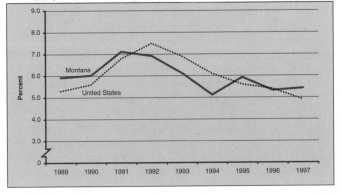

MONTANA'S UNEMPLOYMENT RATE INCREASED SUBSTANTIALLY during the early 1990s recession, though not to the heights reached by the U.S. unemployment rate because the state has a relatively smaller number of manufacturing and construction jobs. Since then, unemployment declined fairly steadily with the rapid growth of jobs in Montana. There was a pause in job growth in 1995 according to the household survey data, but growth resumed the following year. For the entire 1989 to 1997 period, employment increased much faster in Montana than in the United States, slightly faster than the increase in the state labor force as well.

POPULATION AND LABOR FORCE

TOTAL POPULATION IN MONTANA GREW 1.4 PERCENT ANNUALLY from 1990 to 1997, tying with Delaware for the 14th highest percent increase in the nation during this period. Contributing to the state's high growth rate was the substantial domestic and international net migration, which together amounted to more than 50,000 people; almost two-thirds of the total increase. The largest absolute growth was among the White non-Hispanic population, which increased by 61,000 and still represents 91.4 percent of the state's total population. The relatively large Native American and the smaller Hispanic populations had the highest rates of growth during this period, while the Asian population grew by only 1,000. The breakdown of Montana's population by race has stayed much the same from 1990 to 1997. The number of people living in non-metropolitan areas has increased slightly since 1990, and in 1997 amounted to two-thirds of Montana's population.

The in-migration of working-age adults caused a significant growth in Montana's labor force, averaging 1.8 percent per year in the 1990s. The strong economy has accommodated this increase through vigorous employment growth, which has exceeded the growth of the labor force.

Population and Labor Force

	1980	1990	1991	1992	1993	1994	1995	1996	1997	Change* State	Change* U.S.
Population											
Total number of persons (thousands)	787	800	808	822	840	855	868	877	879	1.4	1.0
Percent distribution:											
White, Non-Hispanic	93.4	91.4	91.7	91.7	91.7	91.6	91.5	91.5	91.4	1.4	0.4
Black, Non-Hispanic	0.2	0.7	0.3	0.3	0.3	0.3	0.3	0.3	0.3	-9.9	1.4
Asian	0.4	0.6	0.6	0.6	0.6	0.6	0.6	0.6	0.6	1.4	4.1
Native American	4.8	5.9	6.1	6.1	6.0	6.1	6.1	6.1	6.2	2.2	1.6
Hispanic	1.3	1.7	1.6	1.6	1.6	1.7	1.7	1.7	1.7	1.7	3.8
In metropolitan areas	24.0	33.8	33.9	34.0	34.0	33.8	33.7	33.6	33.4	1.2	1.0
Total number of households (thousands)	284	306	309	315	321	326	335	341	NA	1.8	1.2
Labor Force (thousands)											
Population 16 and over	585	599	607	618	633	648	664	675	679	1.8	1.0
Civilian labor force	370	401	407	422	426	440	437	446	455	1.8	1.1
Employed	348	377	378	393	400	417	411	422	431	1.9	1.2
Percent of population	59.4	62.9	62.2	63.5	63.2	64.4	61.9	62.5	63.5		
Unemployment rate (percent)	6.1	6.0	7.1	6.9	6.1	5.1	5.9	5.3	5.4		

*Compound annual average percent change, 1990–1997; 1990–1996 for households.

Population Change and Components: 1990–97

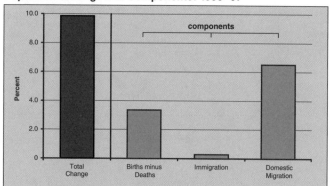

Average Annual Household and Population Growth

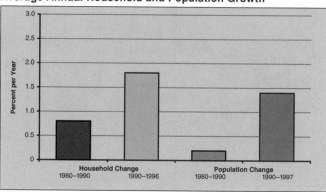

Population by Age; Births and Deaths

	1990 State	1990 U.S.	1997 State	1997 U.S.
Age distribution (percent)				
Under 5 years	7.5	7.6	6.2	7.2
5 to 17 years	20.4	18.2	19.9	18.8
18 to 64 years	58.7	61.8	60.7	61.3
65 years and over	13.3	12.5	13.2	12.7
Birth and death rates (per thousand population)				
Births	14.5	16.7	12.3	14.6
Deaths	8.6	8.6	8.9	8.6

SINCE 1990, MONTANA'S POPULATION HAS GRADUALLY GOTten older. The percent of the state's population under 18 dropped from 27.9 percent in 1990 to 26.1 percent in 1997. The percentage under age 5 showed the largest decrease by falling from 7.5 percent in 1990 to 6.2 percent in 1997. The state's population over age 64 remained high compared to U.S. norms, while the percent of the population between the ages of 18 and 64 rose from 58.7 percent in 1990 to 60.7 percent in 1997 in part due to in-migration.

HOUSEHOLD AND PERSONAL INCOME

HOUSEHOLD INCOME AND PERSONS IN POVERTY	1990	1995	1996	1997	
				State	U.S.
Median household income (1997 dollars)	28 705	29 232	29 342	29 212	37 005
Persons in poverty (thousands)	134	133	155	139	35 574
Poverty rate (percent)	16.3	15.3	17.0	15.6	13.3

IN 1997, MONTANA'S MEDIAN HOUSEHOLD INCOME RANKED fourth lowest in the nation. At $29,212 it was less than 80 percent of the U.S. median. Since 1990, the state's median income has increased by 1.8 percent, in constant dollars, and has remained in the range of 78 to 86 percent of the U.S. median. The state's poverty rate of 15.6 percent in 1997 was higher than the U.S. rate and was among the highest 15 state's in the nation, partly because of the high poverty rates among the Native American population.

Montana's per capita income increased by 9.8 percent in inflation-adjusted dollars from 1989 to 1997, which is slightly less than the national average increase. The state's 1997 per capita income of $19,704 amounted to less than 78 percent of the national average, primarily reflecting the very low earnings of workers and proprietors. Low wage levels in the state led to per capita earnings only 71 per-

cent as high as the U.S. average in 1997. Transfer payments are much closer to the national average per capita (only 4 percent lower), while dividend and interest income was 88 percent as high as in the nation.

From 1990 to 1997, government payments to individuals grew by 49.8 percent, below the national increase of 62.7 percent. The slow growth of retirement income, as well as the disproportionate weight of this category of transfers in Montana, accounted for the moderate overall increase. Medical payments also increased more slowly in the state and comprised a smaller share of the total compared to U.S. norms. In contrast, all forms of income maintenance increased well above the national average. Other income maintenance, which is primarily earned income tax credits, more than tripled in Montana and now overshadows other welfare programs.

Personal Income
(millions of dollars)

	1980	1989	1990	1991	1992	1993	1994	1995	1996	1997	Change*
Earnings by place of work	4 896	7 266	7 654	8 394	8 911	9 863	9 906	10 374	10 808	11 355	5.7
Wages and salaries	3 869	5 355	5 705	6 070	6 517	6 944	7 337	7 695	8 139	8 530	6.0
Other labor income	343	551	603	665	753	829	892	912	900	901	6.3
Proprietors' income	684	1 360	1 346	1 659	1 641	2 091	1 677	1 767	1 769	1 924	4.4
Farm	-7	312	263	438	321	676	175	175	107	187	-6.2
Nonfarm	691	1 047	1 083	1 221	1 319	1 415	1 502	1 591	1 662	1 737	6.5
(−) Personal contributions for social insurance	297	548	584	634	690	740	788	838	882	926	6.8
(+) Adjustment for residence	13	-4	-6	-16	-8	-18	-19	-12	-10	-10	NA
(=) Net earnings by state of residence	4 612	6 714	7 064	7 744	8 213	9 105	9 099	9 524	9 916	10 419	5.6
(+) Dividends, interest, and rent	1 331	2 545	2 653	2 684	2 725	2 776	2 936	3 137	3 267	3 384	3.6
(+) Transfer payments	1 032	2 090	2 310	2 455	2 667	2 879	3 002	3 245	3 373	3 513	6.7
(=) Total personal income	6 975	11 349	12 028	12 883	13 605	14 761	15 038	15 906	16 557	17 316	5.4
Farm	116	403	364	532	412	776	304	318	249	338	-2.2
Nonfarm	6 859	10 946	11 664	12 351	13 193	13 985	14 734	15 588	16 308	16 977	5.6
Personal income per capita (dollars)											
Current dollars	8 842	14 193	15 038	15 947	16 540	17 572	17 589	18 310	18 886	19 704	4.2
1997 dollars	16 906	17 943	18 096	18 415	18 501	19 121	18 692	19 033	19 232	19 704	1.2

*Compound annual average percent change, 1989–1997

Government Transfer Payments

	Millions of dollars		Percent change*	
	1990	1997	State	U.S.
Total government payments to individuals	2 223	3 331	49.8	62.7
Retirement, disability, and insurance	1 431	1 958	36.8	48.2
Social Security	844	1 233	46.1	46.1
Government employee retirement	339	521	53.6	60.3
Medical payments	497	912	83.3	101.2
Income maintenance	138	240	74.4	58.0
Supplemental Security Income	29	54	88.3	75.4
Family assistance	42	48	14.3	-0.5
Food Stamps	42	55	31.0	27.1
Other income maintenance	25	84	228.6	189.8
Unemployment insurance benefits	48	67	39.2	10.6
Veterans benefits and other	109	153	41.1	30.8

*Percent change, 1990–1997

Government Payments to Individuals: 1997

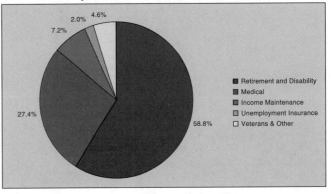

- Retirement and Disability — 58.8%
- Medical — 27.4%
- Income Maintenance — 7.2%
- Unemployment Insurance — 2.0%
- Veterans & Other — 4.6%

ECONOMIC STRUCTURE

LEADING PRIVATE INDUSTRIES, 1997 (Worker and proprietor earnings, millions of dollars)		FASTEST EARNINGS GROWTH, 1989–97 (percent increase)	
Health services	$1 166	Real estate	275.9
Construction specialties	491	Amusement and recreation services	156.8
Business services	383	General building contractors	148.0
Eating and drinking places	360	Construction specialties	132.3
Farming	338	Business services	132.2

MONTANA'S ECONOMY IS MARKED BY A HIGHER THAN AVERAGE reliance on jobs in farming and retail trade, with a much lower than average proportion of jobs in manufacturing. Farms and ranches employ 5 percent of the state workforce, compared to 1.9 percent in the nation overall, and retail trade jobs also comprise a share 3 percentage points above average (19.7 compared to 16.8 percent of total jobs). Retail trade jobs are growing faster than average, buoyed by tourism. The amusement and recreation industry also reflects the growing tourist trade, although Montana's outdoor-oriented tourism has not spurred much growth in the hotel industry.

The construction sector, though not particularly large in its share of jobs, grew at the fastest rate of any major sector in the state in the 1990s. Services jobs also grew faster than average, and was as in most states the dominant sector, in Montana. The healthcare industry is particularly dominant here, with worker and proprietor earnings comprising 10.3 percent of all earnings, a share 2 percentage points greater than in the U.S. economy.

Only the mining and farming industries showed a decrease in employment from 1989 to 1997. Farming lost nearly 4,200 jobs during this period, and its share of total employment declined from 8.1 percent in 1980 to 5 percent in 1997.

Employment and Earnings by Sector

	1980	1989	1990	1991	1992	1993	1994	1995	1996	1997 Number	1997 Percent of total	Change*
Employment *(thousands of persons)*												
Total	394	427	436	447	460	473	497	513	527	534	100.0	2.8
Farm	32	31	31	30	29	29	27	27	27	27	5.0	-1.8
Nonfarm	362	396	406	418	431	445	470	485	500	507	95.0	3.1
Private nonfarm	288	318	325	337	348	362	386	403	417	425	79.5	3.7
Agricultural service, forestry, and fishing ..	4	6	6	7	6	7	8	8	9	9	1.7	6.2
Mining	10	8	8	7	7	7	7	7	7	7	1.3	-1.9
Construction	22	18	19	21	24	25	28	30	32	32	6.1	7.4
Manufacturing	26	26	26	26	27	28	28	29	29	30	5.6	1.5
Transportation and public utilities	26	23	24	24	24	24	25	26	26	27	5.0	1.7
Wholesale trade	19	17	17	18	19	19	19	20	20	20	3.7	2.0
Retail trade	69	77	78	82	86	88	96	100	104	105	19.7	4.0
Finance, insurance, and real estate	25	28	28	28	27	29	29	30	32	32	6.1	1.9
Services	86	114	119	124	127	136	144	152	159	162	30.4	4.5
Government	75	78	80	81	83	83	83	83	83	83	15.5	0.7
Earnings *(millions of dollars)*												
Total	4 896	7 266	7 654	8 394	8 911	9 863	9 906	10 374	10 808	11 355	100.0	5.7
Farm	116	403	364	532	412	776	304	318	249	338	3.0	-2.2
Nonfarm	4 780	6 863	7 290	7 862	8 499	9 087	9 602	10 055	10 559	11 017	97.0	6.1
Private nonfarm	3 822	5 317	5 642	6 107	6 627	7 128	7 564	7 978	8 396	8 813	77.6	6.5
Agricultural service, forestry, and fishing ..	23	62	73	81	91	98	94	94	91	96	0.8	5.7
Mining	252	244	234	281	270	258	259	288	276	297	2.6	2.5
Construction	413	391	421	485	555	616	708	769	826	876	7.7	10.6
Manufacturing	515	640	662	677	724	769	782	783	822	863	7.6	3.8
Transportation and public utilities	555	681	717	767	790	849	883	899	910	941	8.3	4.1
Wholesale trade	335	391	420	441	475	503	532	554	575	596	5.3	5.4
Retail trade	624	879	937	1 020	1 106	1 175	1 248	1 300	1 365	1 425	12.6	6.2
Finance, insurance, and real estate	221	326	340	369	430	494	512	554	601	626	5.5	8.5
Services	882	1 705	1 838	1 985	2 186	2 367	2 547	2 736	2 931	3 092	27.2	7.7
Government	957	1 546	1 648	1 756	1 872	1 959	2 038	2 077	2 162	2 204	19.4	4.5

*Compound annual average percent change, 1989–1997

ECONOMIC STRUCTURE (Continued)

IN 1997, MONTANA'S AVERAGE WAGE AMOUNTED TO ONLY 72.9 percent of the U.S. average, the third lowest average wage in the nation. Wages in the services sector were an even lower 70 percent of the U.S average, while retail trade wages were 81 percent of average. Farming is the only sector in which Montana's average wages higher than the U.S. average. The average Montana farm wage $25,695 was, well above the U.S. average of $16,442, and farm wages have shown the highest growth, increasing 117 percent from 1989 to 1997. The state's finance, insurance, and real estate wages were the lowest when compared to the national average, only 60 percent as high.

Employment and earnings in Montana's manufacturing sector grew at a much slower rate than in the state's overall economy, thus weakening the manufacturing sector's position in Montana's economy. In 1996, manufacturing comprised 7.7 percent of the state's gross state product (GSP), a drop from 8.8 percent in 1989. Montana's GSP grew by 45.7 percent from 1989 to 1996, while manufacturing grew by 27.2 percent. Manufacturing of lumber and wood products, an industry with shrinking employment, remained Montana's leading manufacturing component, representing one-third of the sector's total earnings and holding down the growth of manufacturing in the state. The small industrial machinery industry was one of the fastest growing in the state, however. Montana's manufacturing output value per worker amounted to $48,856 in 1996, just over 70 percent of the national average. In 1996, the state's new capital expenditures increased slightly from the previous year but were still well below 1994 levels.

Montana's exports to foreign markets have grown by more than 65 percent since 1994, without adjustment for inflation, though they represent a very small component of the state's economy. Primary metals were the state's largest export and the third fastest growing major export from 1994 to 1997, though the jump in metals exports in 1997 does not necessarily reflect a long-term trend. Chemical products, ranked third overall, showed the largest rate of growth over the past four years, increasing 218.7 percent. Neither chemicals nor primary metals had become a growth industry in the state, however.

Average Annual Wages and Salaries by Sector
(dollars)

	1989	1996	1997 State	1997 U.S.
All wage and salary workers	16 762	20 902	21 734	29 809
Farm	11 842	19 223	25 695	16 442
Nonfarm	16 875	20 932	21 678	29 900
Private nonfarm	16 514	20 241	21 068	29 867
Agricultural service, forestry, and fishing	10 639	12 366	13 240	17 941
Mining	32 591	41 212	43 954	49 800
Construction	21 517	25 434	27 054	31 765
Manufacturing	22 541	26 780	27 994	38 351
Transportation and utilities	26 010	32 478	33 138	38 222
Wholesale trade	21 027	26 601	27 340	39 466
Retail trade	10 487	12 650	13 198	16 206
Finance, insurance, and real estate	19 644	26 016	27 089	44 993
Services	14 146	18 628	19 335	27 588
Government	17 952	23 433	23 924	30 062

Gross State Product and Manufacturing
(millions of dollars, except as noted)

	1989	1994	1995	1996
Gross state product, total	12 702	16 867	17 722	18 509
Manufacturing:				
Millions of dollars	1 124	1 296	1 362	1 430
Percent of total gross state product	8.8	7.7	7.7	7.7
Per worker (dollars)	42 670	45 549	47 508	48 856
New capital expenditures, manufacturing	NA	154	134	137

Exports of Goods
(millions of dollars)

	1994	1995	1996	1997
All goods	260	279	341	430
Manufactures	192	206	264	340
Agricultural and livestock products	22	28	33	29
Other commodities	46	45	44	61
Top goods exports, 1997:				
Primary metals	54	50	97	146
Industrial machinery and computers	41	70	72	71
Chemical products	13	17	16	41
Metallic ores and concentrates	14	12	8	23
Agricultural products	7	13	24	19

HOUSING

Housing production in Montana has more than tripled since 1989, propelled by both population growth and in-migration rates higher than the nation's as a whole, and by healthy growth in employment in the state. However, Montana's home production rates remained somewhat below the national average. A significant portion of this production has consisted of manufactured (mobile) homes, representing 30 percent to 40 percent of total production. In 1997 the share of mobile homes rose to a high of 45 percent of new home production, as such homes offer an affordable option for the relatively low-income household typical in Montana. Existing home sales declined during 1993–95, after a sales spurt in 1992, and they have yet to regain the levels attained in 1992. Rates of homeownership have remained fairly steady since 1989. They peaked at 69.9 percent in 1992 and have edged down since, reaching 67.5 percent in 1997, which is still above the national average. After dipping down to 3.4 percent,

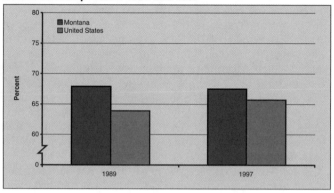

Homeownership Rates: 1989 and 1997

the state's rental vacancy rates have been increasing. Still, in 1997 Montana had the sixth lowest rental vacancy rate in the nation.

Housing Supply

	1989	1990	1991	1992	1993	1994	1995	1996	1997
Residential building permits (thousands)	0.7	1.2	1.5	2.1	2.9	3.0	3.1	2.7	2.5
New home production (including manufactured housing):									
Thousands of homes	1.2	1.7	2.1	3.2	4.6	4.7	4.5	4.3	4.5
Rate per 1,000 population									
Montana	1.5	2.1	2.6	3.9	5.5	5.5	5.2	4.9	5.1
U.S.	6.2	5.2	4.5	5.1	5.6	6.4	6.3	6.6	6.5
Existing home sales:									
Thousands of homes	13.0	12.7	13.9	16.6	16.2	15.6	13.8	14.2	14.9
Change from previous year (percent)									
Montana	4.0	-2.3	9.4	19.4	-2.4	-3.7	-11.5	2.9	4.9
U.S.	-3.9	-4.0	0.0	9.2	8.2	4.8	-3.7	7.5	3.8
Home ownership rate (percent of households)	67.9	69.1	69.6	69.9	69.7	68.8	68.7	68.6	67.5
Rental vacancy rate (percent of rental housing units)	9.7	8.1	6.6	4.2	3.4	3.5	3.6	5.1	5.0

AGRICULTURE

The state's average farm is 2,483 acres, far above the national average of 471. This number gave the state the fifth highest average number of acres per farm. However, the state's gross farm income has increased by only 16.3 percent from 1989 to 1997. Production expenses increased by 30 percent during the same period. As a result of weakness in sales, net farm income including inventory change has declined by 50 percent from 1990 to 1997 (looking at three-year averages). Montana derives slightly more of its receipts from sales of live-

stock and livestock products than from crops. Receipts from crops grew significantly faster from 1989 to 1997 than receipts from livestock.

MONTANA FARMS, 1997	
Number of farms	24 000
Total acres (thousands):	59 600
Average per farm	2 483
Value of land and buildings (millions of dollars)	18 178
Average per farm (dollars)	757 417

Farm Income
(millions of dollars)

	1980	1989	1990	1991	1992	1993	1994	1995	1996	1997
Gross income	1 640	2 160	2 241	2 167	2 366	2 431	2 483	2 395	2 538	2 513
Receipts from sales	1 497	1 722	1 787	1 689	1 908	1 918	2 047	2 015	2 091	2 087
Government payments	58	289	300	320	299	338	256	190	241	231
Imputed and miscellaneous income	84	148	154	158	160	175	180	190	206	195
(–) Production expenses	1 655	1 919	1 942	1 906	1 868	1 964	2 190	2 261	2 344	2 495
(=) Realized net income	-15	241	299	261	498	467	293	134	194	18
(+) Inventory change	-1	122	8	230	-121	251	-65	72	-56	218
(=) Net income	-16	363	307	491	377	718	228	207	138	236
Corporate income	-9	51	43	53	56	42	53	31	31	49
Farm proprietors income	-7	312	263	438	321	676	175	175	107	187

EDUCATION

EDUCATIONAL ATTAINMENT Percent of population age 25 and over, 1997	State	United States
High school graduate or higher	88.6	82.1
College graduate or higher	25.2	23.9

MONTANA'S EDUCATIONAL ATTAINMENT IS WELL ABOVE THE national average. More than 88 percent of the population over age 25 are high school graduates, which gives Montana the fifth highest percentage in the nation. More than 25 percent of the state's residents have earned their college degrees. This is the 18th highest rate in the nation. Montana's percent of college graduates has grown tremendously from 1990, when it was the 25th highest in the nation, suggesting that many of the in-migrants may be college educated. The state has one of the lowest average teacher salaries in the nation, reflecting the limitations on public service spending in a state where incomes are so low. Per pupil expenditures were also lower than the national average. While minorities represent only 8.8 percent of the state's total population, they comprise 11.2 percent of postsecondary enrollment.

High School Completion: 1990–97

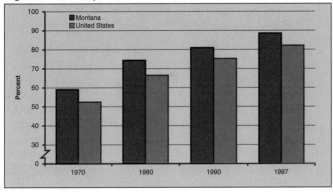

Education Indicators

	State	U.S.
Elementary and secondary schools		
Enrollment, 1995–96		
Total (thousands)	174	49 873
Percent in private schools	4.9	10.1
Expenditures per pupil (dollars), 1995–96	5 847	6 146
Average teacher salary (dollars), 1996–97	29 950	38 509
Higher education		
Enrollment, 1996–97		
Total (thousands)	43	14 218
Percent of population 18–34	23.0	21.8
Percent minority	11.2	26.1
Percent in private schools	11.9	22.6

HEALTH

MONTANA'S INFANT MORTALITY RATE DROPPED SLIGHTLY FROM 7.3 per 1,000 in 1996 to 6.9 in 1997, moving the state's rate below the national average. Montana's overall death rate remains below average. For major diseases, Montana's death rates are all lower than the national rates; rate from heart disease, adjusted to a standard age distribution, is 83 percent of the national average. However, Montana's death rates for suicide, motor vehicles deaths, unintentional injuries, and firearm deaths were all well above the U.S. average. The homicide death rates were low in comparison to the national average. In 1997, Montana residents without health insurance came close to 20 percent. The state has the eighth highest percentage of uninsured residents in the nation. The state's relatively high number of jobs in the farm and retail trade sectors tends to yield higher number of uninsured workers.

Health Indicators

	1990	1995	1996	1997
Infant mortality				
(rate per thousand live births)				
Montana	9.0	7.0	7.3	6.9
U.S.	9.2	7.6	7.3	7.1
Total deaths, age-adjusted rate				
(rate per thousand population)				
Montana	4.8	4.7	4.6	4.6
U.S.	5.2	5.0	4.9	4.8
Persons not covered by health insurance				
(percent of population)				
Montana	14.0	12.7	13.6	19.5
U.S.	13.9	15.4	15.6	16.1

Leading Causes of Death, 1996
(deaths per 100,000 population)

	Age-adjusted		Not age-adjusted	
	State	U.S.	State	U.S.
Deaths from all causes	458.1	491.6	876.4	872.5
Heart disease	111.7	134.5	243.7	276.4
Cancer	116.0	127.9	201.1	203.4
Cerebrovascular diseases	24.0	26.4	62.5	60.3
Chronic obstructive pulmonary disease	30.5	21.0	61.9	40.0
Diabetes mellitus	11.3	13.6	21.4	23.3
Pneumonia and influenza	9.9	12.8	28.2	31.6
HIV	NA	11.1	NA	11.7
Liver disease	7.1	7.5	9.6	9.4
Alzheimer's disease	3.2	2.7	10.7	8.1
Accidents and adverse effects	38.2	30.4	45.3	35.8
Motor vehicle accidents	21.5	16.2	21.7	16.5
Suicide	18.6	10.8	19.8	11.6
Homicide	4.4	8.5	4.2	7.9
Injury by firearm	16.8	12.9	17.7	12.8

GOVERNMENT

STATE AND LOCAL TAXES, 1995–96	State	U.S.
Per capita (dollars)	1 941	2 477
Percent of personal income	10.6	10.8

STATE AND LOCAL TAXES IN MONTANA (EXCLUDING CORPO-rate) were 78.4 percent of the national average per capita in 1995–96. This rate mainly was a reflection of the state's low per capita income, but these taxes were also slightly below average as a percent of personal income. Local taxes represented only 33.5 percent of these taxes, lower than the 40.8 percent nationwide, indicating lower property taxes. Montana's state government per capita general

State Government Finances, 1996–97

	Millions of dollars	Percent distribu-tion	Dollars per capita State	Dollars per capita U.S.
General revenue	2 879	100.0	3 275	3 049
Intergovernmental revenue	959	33.3	1 091	863
Taxes	1 309	45.5	1 489	1 660
General sales	0	0.0	0	551
Selective sales	274	9.5	312	257
License taxes	151	5.3	172	106
Individual income	406	14.1	462	542
Corporation net income	82	2.8	93	115
Other taxes	395	13.7	449	90
Other general revenue	611	21.2	695	526
General expenditure	2 826	100.0	3 215	2 951
Intergovernmental expenditure	715	25.3	813	989
Direct expenditure	2 111	74.7	2 401	1 962
General expenditure, by function:				
Education	1 020	36.1	1 160	1 033
Public welfare	501	17.7	570	761
Hospitals and health	192	6.8	218	237
Highways	344	12.2	391	225
Police protection and corrections	106	3.8	120	137
Natural resources, parks and recreation	151	5.4	172	63
Governmental administration	143	5.1	162	107
Interest on general debt	131	4.6	149	99
Other and unallocable	239	8.5	272	290
Debt at end of fiscal year	2 056	NA	2 339	1 706
Cash and security holdings	6 727	NA	7 653	6 683

Federal Spending within State

	Federal funds, fiscal 1997		
	Millions of dollars	Percent distribution	Percent of U.S. total*
Total within state	5 236	100.0	0.4
Payments to individuals	2 572	49.1	0.3
Retirement and disability	1 685	32.2	0.4
Medicare	526	10.0	0.3
Food stamps	55	1.1	0.3
Supplemental Security Income	57	1.1	0.2
Grants	1 180	22.5	0.5
Medicaid and other health	415	7.9	0.4
Nutrition and family welfare	167	3.2	0.4
Education	101	1.9	0.6
Housing and community development	43	0.8	0.4
Salaries and wages	595	11.4	0.4
Defense procurement contracts	80	1.5	0.1
Non-defense procurement contracts	180	3.4	0.2

*State population is 0.3 percent of the U.S. total.

revenue of $3,275 in 1997 was higher than the national average of $3,050. Montana's per capita individual income taxes totaled $462, well below the national average of $542, and there is no general sales tax in Montana. Selective sales taxes, license taxes, and other taxes are all higher than average, however. The state also receives 26 percent more in intergovernmental transfers than the typical state. The state's per capita general expenditure amounted to $3,215, well above the average of $2,951, as the state ran a much smaller operating surplus than the average state. Montana spends a slightly larger proportion on education, highways, and interest on general debt. The state's per capita debt at the end of the fiscal year amounted to $2,339, somewhat higher than the national average of $1,706.

Montana received a greater than proportional share of federal spending, particularly in the category of grants. The percentage of education grants was nearly double Montana's proportion of the nation's population, which is 0.3 percent. Montana's shares of Medicaid grants, nutrition and family welfare grants, and housing and community development grants were all greater than 0.3 percent, reflecting higher poverty rates among the state's residents. Defense procurement amounted to 0.1 percent of the U.S. total, well below the state's proportion of the U.S. population, because the state has very little manufacturing or research capacity.

31 372	59 698		65 157	70 827	72 687	78 001	81 93	88 504	93 426	5.8	63 383	70 827	31 372	59 698	63 38
25 323	47 902		57 151	59 446	62 916	67 00	72 039	77 208	6.1	50 999	57 151	25 323	47 902	50 99
2 640	5 143		7 801					7 709	7 838	5.4	5 645	6 816	2 640	5 143	5 64
3 409	6 652		284					8 755	8 380	2.9	6 739	6 860	3 409	6 652	6 7
693	1 716		07					1 539	762	-9.7	1 561	811	693	1 716	1 5
2 716								7 217	7 618		5 178	6 049	2 716		

1997

Population (persons)	1,657,009
Population rank	38th
Population growth rank (1990–97)	36th
Per capita personal income	$23,656
Unemployment rate (percent)	2.6
Poverty rate (percent)	9.8

NEBRASKA TODAY IS NO LONGER DOMINATED BY THE FARMING sector, but trends in farm output and prices still have a powerful effect on the state economy. This is the fourth largest farm producing state, second in the region only to Iowa, with cattle still its leading farm product. Farming and food product manufacturing, together generated $2.8 billion in worker earnings, or 9.6 percent of the state total, in 1997. Add to this the indirect effects on farm implement dealers, grain handlers, and small-town retailers, and the farm sector still wields mighty influence here.

A newer factor in Nebraska's economy is the influx of business services that exploit telecommunications to conduct "teleservicing" operations in remote locations. Jobs ranging from telemarketing and taking orders to managing computer network servers for data transmitted over phone lines helped boost Nebraska's business services industry to an energetic growth of 164 percent over the 1989 to 1997 period. The large number of high school graduates here, coupled with generally low wages, are an effective magnet for investment from out-of-state companies.

Total employment growth in the state averaged 2.1 percent annually during the 1989–97 period, much higher than the U.S. growth rate, even while population growth was modest. Per capita income has risen a bit faster than in an average state during the 1990s, although it remained only 94 percent as high in 1997.

Average Annual Population Growth: 1990–97

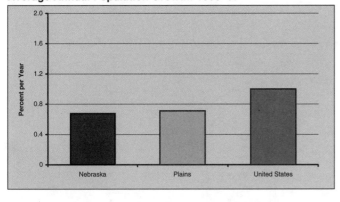

Median Household Income: 1989–97 (1997 dollars)

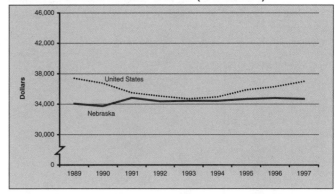

Unemployment Rate: 1989–97

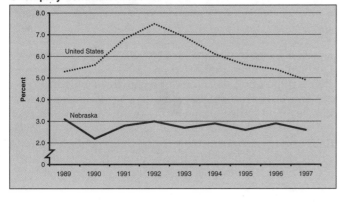

NEBRASKA'S ASTOUNDINGLY LOW UNEMPLOYMENT RATE OF 2.6 percent in 1997 was the nation's second lowest, behind North Dakota, and the rate has remained low during all phases of the business cycle in the 1990s. The tight labor market has drawn workers into the labor force in such numbers that labor force growth is nearly double that of the adult population, while employment also grew rapidly. The state has one of the nation's highest ratios of employment to population, at 70 percent.

POPULATION AND LABOR FORCE

NEBRASKA'S POPULATION HAS BEEN GROWING AT A SOMEWHAT lower rate than the national average; at 0.7 percent annually from 1990 to 1997, the increase was typical of growth in the Plains states. The 1990s growth was significantly faster than the minimal 1.5 percent total increase for the entire decade of the 1980s. The state's below-average birth rate has contributed to the low population growth, though international immigration and domestic in-migration helped offset this factor. The highest rates of growth during this period were in the Asian and Hispanic populations. Nebraska's Hispanic population grew by an

average annual rate of 8.3 percent, and the Asian population grew annually by 6.8 percent. The Hispanic population now accounts for 4.1 percent of Nebraska's total population, which has led the Hispanic population to surpass the Black population to become the largest minority in Nebraska. The state's population remains pretty evenly split between metropolitan and nonmetropolitan areas, leaving the metro population share much lower than the national average of 80 percent. Nebraska's largest metro area, Omaha, had a population of 687,000 in 1996.

Population and Labor Force

	1980	1990	1991	1992	1993	1994	1995	1996	1997	Change* State	Change* U.S.
Population											
Total number of persons (thousands)	1 570	1 581	1 591	1 602	1 612	1 622	1 635	1 648	1 657	0.7	1.0
Percent distribution:											
White, Non-Hispanic	94.1	92.2	92.3	91.9	91.6	91.2	90.8	90.4	90.1	0.3	0.4
Black, Non-Hispanic	3.0	3.8	3.6	3.7	3.7	3.7	3.7	3.8	3.8	0.6	1.4
Asian	0.5	0.8	0.9	0.9	1.0	1.1	1.2	1.2	1.3	6.8	4.1
Native American	0.6	0.8	0.8	0.8	0.9	0.9	0.9	0.9	0.9	2.4	1.6
Hispanic	1.8	2.5	2.5	2.8	3.0	3.3	3.6	3.9	4.1	8.3	3.8
In metropolitan areas	46.4	50.0	50.2	50.4	50.5	50.7	50.9	51.3	51.5	1.1	1.0
Total number of households (thousands)	571	602	606	614	615	616	624	631	NA	0.8	1.2
Labor Force (thousands)											
Population 16 and over	1 180	1 194	1 202	1 214	1 223	1 232	1 246	1 259	1 266	0.8	1.0
Civilian labor force	763	814	835	838	858	880	898	910	906	1.5	1.1
Employed	732	796	812	813	836	855	874	883	883	1.5	1.2
Percent of population	62.0	66.7	67.5	67.0	68.3	69.4	70.2	70.1	69.7		
Unemployment rate (percent)	4.1	2.2	2.8	3.0	2.7	2.9	2.6	2.9	2.6		

*Compound annual average percent change, 1990–1997; 1990–1996 for households.

Population Change and Components: 1990–97

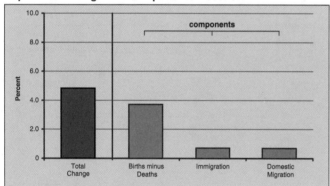

Average Annual Household and Population Growth

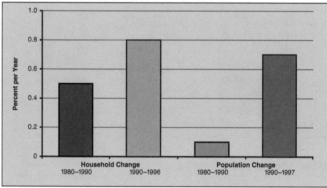

Population by Age; Births and Deaths

	1990 State	1990 U.S.	1997 State	1997 U.S.
Age distribution (percent)				
Under 5 years	7.6	7.6	6.9	7.2
5 to 17 years	19.6	18.2	19.9	18.8
18 to 64 years	58.7	61.8	59.4	61.3
65 years and over	14.1	12.5	13.7	12.7
Birth and death rates (per thousand population)				
Births	15.4	16.7	14.1	14.6
Deaths	9.4	8.6	9.2	8.6

NEBRASKA'S AGE DEMOGRAPHICS WERE SLIGHTLY CLOSER TO national averages in 1997 than 1990. The proportion of state's population 65 and older came down a bit, though it remains larger than average, and the working-age population segment is rising, suggesting the in-migration of people between 18 and 64 years of age. The state has a lower than average proportion of its population under 5, due to a low and dropping birth rate. From 1990 to 1997, the state's birth rate dropped from 15.4 to 14.1 per 1,000.

HOUSEHOLD AND PERSONAL INCOME

HOUSEHOLD INCOME AND PERSONS IN POVERTY	1990	1995	1996	1997	
				State	U.S.
Median household income (1997 dollars)	33 748	34 679	34 794	34 692	37 005
Persons in poverty (thousands)	167	159	169	163	35 574
Poverty rate (percent)	10.3	9.6	10.2	9.8	13.3

NEBRASKA'S 1997 MEDIAN HOUSEHOLD INCOME OF $34,692, was less than 94 percent of the national median. Since the state's median income did not increase (in real dollars) between 1995 and 1997, its relative position worsened from near-parity with the U.S. median in 1993 and 1994. Still, with the state's high percentage of its population working, the poverty rate remained low through the 1995–97 period. The 1997 poverty rate of 9.8 percent was significantly lower than the national average of 13.3 percent, and Nebraska had the 16th lowest 1996–97 average poverty rate in the nation.

In 1997, Nebraska's per capita income was 94 percent of the national average, though it had been growing faster than the nation's since 1989. Earnings by place of work have increased quite substantially, 5.5 percent annually, but proprietors' income has grown at a considerably slow-er average annual rate of 2.6 percent. Total earnings per capita were about 95 percent as high as in the nation in 1997, while dividend and interest income was slightly closer to the U.S. average at 98 percent. Transfer payments were substantially below average at only 85 percent of the U.S. level per capita.

Total government transfer payments increased by 56.7 percent from 1990 to 1997, slightly less than the national average increase of 62.7 percent. Total income maintenance payments increased by 69.1 percent, with Supplemental Security Income increasing by 84 percent, and other income maintenance increasing by 273 percent because of the huge expansion in use of earned income tax credits by the working poor. Family assistance payments decreased by 5.8 percent during this period, reflecting the effects of welfare reform and job availability.

Personal Income
(millions of dollars)

	1980	1989	1990	1991	1992	1993	1994	1995	1996	1997	Change*
Earnings by place of work	10 494	18 874	20 401	21 100	22 450	23 242	24 568	25 548	28 063	28 930	5.5
Wages and salaries	8 483	13 938	14 985	15 692	16 617	17 294	18 384	19 640	20 885	22 319	6.1
Other labor income	780	1 446	1 627	1 787	2 002	2 193	2 320	2 330	2 295	2 331	6.1
Proprietors' income	1 232	3 490	3 789	3 620	3 831	3 755	3 864	3 578	4 884	4 280	2.6
Farm	-100	1 563	1 911	1 758	1 820	1 511	1 359	971	2 133	1 281	-2.5
Nonfarm	1 332	1 927	1 877	1 862	2 011	2 244	2 505	2 607	2 751	2 999	5.7
(−) Personal contributions for social insurance	588	1 282	1 367	1 446	1 516	1 609	1 739	1 857	1 936	2 070	6.2
(+) Adjustment for residence	-204	-355	-371	-389	-423	-453	-465	-480	-493	-537	NA
(=) Net earnings by state of residence	9 703	17 237	18 663	19 264	20 510	21 180	22 364	23 211	25 635	26 324	5.4
(+) Dividends, interest, and rent	2 800	5 116	5 335	5 365	5 804	5 887	5 762	6 069	6 559	7 061	4.1
(+) Transfer payments	1 866	3 429	3 720	4 022	4 383	4 719	4 902	5 210	5 547	5 809	6.8
(=) Total personal income	14 369	25 782	27 717	28 652	30 697	31 785	33 029	34 489	37 741	39 195	5.4
Farm	95	1 781	2 148	1 970	2 024	1 718	1 594	1 224	2 413	1 563	-1.6
Nonfarm	14 273	24 001	25 570	26 681	28 673	30 068	31 434	33 265	35 328	37 632	5.8
Personal income per capita (dollars)											
Current dollars	9 139	16 371	17 536	18 010	19 153	19 710	20 356	21 078	22 891	23 656	4.7
1997 dollars	17 474	20 697	21 102	20 797	21 424	21 447	21 632	21 911	23 311	23 656	1.7

*Compound annual average percent change, 1989–1997

Government Transfer Payments

	Millions of dollars		Percent change*	
	1990	1997	State	U.S.
Total government payments to individuals	3 537	5 543	56.7	62.7
Retirement, disability, and insurance	2 191	3 091	41.1	48.2
Social Security	1 669	2 306	38.2	46.1
Government employee retirement	400	631	58.0	60.3
Medical payments	922	1 815	96.8	101.2
Income maintenance	205	347	69.1	58.0
Supplemental Security Income	48	88	84.0	75.4
Family assistance	62	59	-5.8	-0.5
Food Stamps	61	71	17.3	27.1
Other income maintenance	35	129	273.0	189.8
Unemployment insurance benefits	35	45	31.3	10.6
Veterans benefits and other	185	245	32.7	30.8

*Percent change, 1990–1997

Government Payments to Individuals: 1997

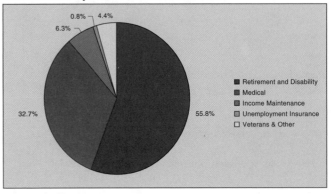

0.8% 4.4%
6.3%
32.7%
55.8%

- ■ Retirement and Disability
- ■ Medical
- ■ Income Maintenance
- ▨ Unemployment Insurance
- ☐ Veterans & Other

ECONOMIC STRUCTURE

LEADING PRIVATE INDUSTRIES, 1997 (Worker and proprietor earnings, millions of dollars)		FASTEST EARNINGS GROWTH, 1989–97 (percent increase)	
Health services	$2 277	Electric, gas and sanitary services	276.8
Business services	1 931	Business services	164.1
Farming	1 563	Other transportation	130.4
Food and kindred products	1 226	Heavy construction contractors	130.0
Construction specialties	1 065	Agricultural services	94.6

HEALTH AND BUSINESS SERVICES ARE NEBRASKA'S LEADING private industries, as over the past decade the services sector has been the fastest growing of the state's large sectors, in terms of earnings. Business services, which includes companies that handle telemarketing, service calls, and computerized databases over telephone lines, grew quickly from 1989-97, second only to electric, gas, and sanitary services. Still, the service sector as a whole has a relatively smaller share of employment and earnings than in the U.S. economy. Similarly, manufacturing employment and earnings grew more rapidly in the state than in the nation, yet manufacturing remains smaller than average, providing 10 percent of all jobs.

The finance, insurance, and real estate sector is relatively large for a small state, because of the long-time base of some large banks and insurance companies in Omaha and Lincoln. The sector's share of total employment in the state is similar to the national average. Nebraska's farm sector provides a larger than average base of jobs, with nearly 6 percent of all 1997 jobs in farming compared with 1.9 percent nationally. The number of farming jobs has declined steadily, however, and is a much smaller proportion of the total compared to 1980, when it comprised more than 10 percent of state jobs. A recovery in the construction sector in the 1990s led to rapid job growth, but part of this growth was recouping job losses in construction during the 1980s.

Employment and Earnings by Sector

	1980	1989	1990	1991	1992	1993	1994	1995	1996	1997 Number	1997 Percent of total	Change*
Employment *(thousands of persons)*												
Total	879	970	992	999	1 006	1 028	1 070	1 098	1 126	1 146	100.0	2.1
Farm	90	74	72	70	69	69	66	67	69	68	5.9	-1.1
Nonfarm	789	896	920	929	937	959	1 004	1 031	1 057	1 078	94.1	2.3
Private nonfarm	638	737	757	767	774	797	841	869	895	916	79.9	2.8
Agricultural service, forestry, and fishing	7	10	11	12	11	13	15	15	16	17	1.4	5.9
Mining	3	3	3	3	3	2	3	3	2	2	0.2	-2.7
Construction	43	39	41	42	43	48	51	53	55	57	5.0	4.9
Manufacturing	98	100	103	102	104	106	112	115	117	119	10.4	2.2
Transportation and public utilities	55	53	53	54	53	55	57	59	60	63	5.5	2.1
Wholesale trade	52	55	56	55	57	56	55	56	56	57	5.0	0.4
Retail trade	144	160	163	166	168	171	183	189	195	197	17.2	2.6
Finance, insurance, and real estate	66	72	74	74	73	75	76	79	80	82	7.2	1.6
Services	171	244	253	261	263	272	290	300	313	322	28.1	3.6
Government	151	159	163	161	163	162	163	162	162	162	14.1	0.2
Earnings *(millions of dollars)*												
Total	10 494	18 874	20 401	21 100	22 450	23 242	24 568	25 548	28 063	28 930	100.0	5.5
Farm	95	1 781	2 148	1 970	2 024	1 718	1 594	1 224	2 413	1 563	5.4	-1.6
Nonfarm	10 399	17 093	18 253	19 129	20 426	21 524	22 974	24 324	25 650	27 367	94.6	6.1
Private nonfarm	8 521	13 756	14 600	15 248	16 429	17 429	18 768	19 942	21 140	22 722	78.5	6.5
Agricultural service, forestry, and fishing	59	148	172	190	209	249	266	278	265	286	1.0	8.6
Mining	79	53	62	63	64	61	59	60	59	64	0.2	2.4
Construction	726	896	936	962	1 025	1 153	1 388	1 472	1 636	1 674	5.8	8.1
Manufacturing	1 765	2 603	2 725	2 830	3 060	3 223	3 574	3 727	3 882	4 135	14.3	6.0
Transportation and public utilities	1 215	1 721	1 751	1 848	1 967	2 089	2 196	2 340	2 441	2 804	9.7	6.3
Wholesale trade	943	1 342	1 472	1 478	1 595	1 618	1 611	1 694	1 771	1 890	6.5	4.4
Retail trade	1 233	1 743	1 817	1 905	1 979	2 089	2 254	2 376	2 523	2 641	9.1	5.3
Finance, insurance, and real estate	705	1 294	1 374	1 430	1 588	1 699	1 765	1 895	1 967	2 063	7.1	6.0
Services	1 796	3 955	4 291	4 541	4 944	5 248	5 655	6 100	6 594	7 166	24.8	7.7
Government	1 878	3 337	3 654	3 881	3 997	4 095	4 206	4 382	4 510	4 645	16.1	4.2

*Compound annual average percent change, 1989–1997

ECONOMIC STRUCTURE (Continued)

NEBRASKA'S 1997 AVERAGE WAGE REMAINED SUBSTANTIALLY below the national average, at 82.6 percent of the national level. For all major sectors, except farming and transportation, communications, and public utilities, the state's wages were lower than average. Wages were particularly low in manufacturing and services, at 80 percent and 81 percent of the U.S. averages, respectively. The leading manufacturing industry, food products, is one of the lower paying manufacturing industries, and the Nebraska service sector has fewer high-paying engineering and law jobs than the average for the nation. The state's average wages increased by 37 percent from 1989 to 1997. The biggest increase during this period came in services wages, which increased by 48 percent.

Manufacturing production grew faster in the state than in the nation in 1989–97. But at 14.1 percent of gross state product, manufacturing output is a smaller proportion of the Nebraska economy than in an average state. The state's leading manufacturing industry is food and kindred products, capitalizing in the proximity of farm products from the state's large agricultural sector. The second largest industry is industrial machinery, growing at a healthy pace. The state's 1996 manufacturing value per worker amounted to $56,892, less than 82 percent of the national average, influenced by the relatively lower productivity than marks the food products industry. Nebraska's manufacturing value per worker is growing at a significantly slower rate than the U.S. average. New capital expenditures dropped from their peak in 1995, but they remained higher than the level of 1994.

Nebraska's exports have increased by 27.4 percent from 1994 to 1997, a much smaller increase than for the nation overall. From 1996 to 1997, exports increased by only 1.7 percent. The state's leading exports in 1997 were food products, industrial machinery and computers, and agricultural products, the latter two of which displayed strong growth since 1994. Electric and electronic equipment exports were flat in this period. Agricultural products showed the highest rate of growth among the state's leading exports, increasing more than 170 percent from 1994 to 1997.

Average Annual Wages and Salaries by Sector
(dollars)

	1989	1996	1997	
			State	U.S.
All wage and salary workers	17 912	23 428	24 610	29 809
Farm	12 895	18 448	19 048	16 442
Nonfarm	18 019	23 511	24 699	29 900
Private nonfarm	17 732	23 142	24 427	29 867
Agricultural service, forestry, and fishing	11 129	13 380	14 788	17 941
Mining	22 579	27 517	29 389	49 800
Construction	20 445	28 095	27 693	31 765
Manufacturing	22 800	29 084	30 522	38 351
Transportation and utilities	29 173	35 669	39 683	38 222
Wholesale trade	21 655	27 496	29 171	39 466
Retail trade	10 005	12 905	13 452	16 206
Finance, insurance, and real estate	22 711	30 533	31 680	44 993
Services	15 185	21 310	22 475	27 588
Government	19 104	25 142	25 927	30 062

Gross State Product and Manufacturing
(millions of dollars, except as noted)

	1989	1994	1995	1996
Gross state product, total	31 044	42 109	43 673	47 187
Manufacturing:				
Millions of dollars	4 520	6 257	6 347	6 662
Percent of total gross state product	14.6	14.9	14.5	14.1
Per worker (dollars)	45 079	55 786	54 992	56 892
New capital expenditures, manufacturing	NA	555	803	693

Exports of Goods
(millions of dollars)

	1994	1995	1996	1997
All goods	1 958	2 255	2 453	2 494
Manufactures	1 860	2 149	2 201	2 247
Agricultural and livestock products	85	94	229	223
Other commodities	12	12	23	24
Top goods exports, 1997:				
Food products	1 210	1 477	1 427	1 325
Industrial machinery and computers	137	140	193	246
Agricultural products	81	93	227	220
Electric and electronic equipment	117	123	131	138
Transportation equipment	122	110	119	122

HOUSING

NEBRASKA'S HOUSING PRODUCTION HAS INCREASED FROM 6,900 units in 1991 to 11,300 units in 1997, making a substantial recovery from the 1990–91 recession. Nonetheless, Nebraska's home production rate per 1,000 people remained lower than the national rate until 1996, when the state rate finally exceeded the national rate. In 1997, Nebraska's rate was 6.8 per 1,000, compared with the national rate of 6.5 per 1,000. This lower home production rate through most of the 1990s can be attributed to Nebraska's slower growing population. Sales of existing homes were flat through 1996, a year in which sales were only at about the same level as they had been in 1989. In 1997 sales rebounded a bit, but overall in the 1990s they increased only half as much as nationally. Prices remain low in the state; 1997's median sales price in Omaha was only $93,600. The state's homeownership rate has fluctuated between 66 percent and 69 percent during the 1990s and, in 1997, was slightly higher than the national average of 65.7 percent. Nebraska has the 16th lowest

Homeownership Rates: 1989 and 1997

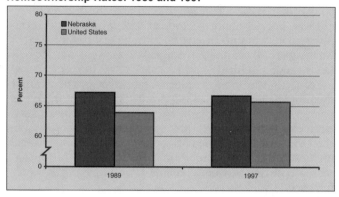

homeownership rate in the nation. The state's rental vacancy rate has remained quite moderate in recent years, coming down from the 1991 high of 8.1 percent.

Housing Supply

	1989	1990	1991	1992	1993	1994	1995	1996	1997
Residential building permits (thousands)	6.0	6.8	6.2	6.7	7.8	7.9	8.2	10.1	9.9
New home production (including manufactured housing):									
Thousands of homes	6.4	7.3	6.9	7.3	8.3	8.4	9.2	11.5	11.3
Rate per 1,000 population									
Nebraska	4.1	4.6	4.3	4.6	5.1	5.2	5.6	7.0	6.8
U.S.	6.2	5.2	4.5	5.1	5.6	6.4	6.3	6.6	6.5
Existing home sales:									
Thousands of homes	20.9	19.3	19.9	22.4	23.2	23.3	21.1	20.3	23.4
Change from previous year (percent)									
Nebraska	4.5	-7.7	3.1	12.6	3.6	0.4	-9.4	-3.8	15.3
U.S.	-3.9	-4.0	0.0	9.2	8.2	4.8	-3.7	7.5	3.8
Home ownership rate (percent of households)	67.2	67.3	67.5	68.4	67.7	68.0	67.1	66.8	66.7
Rental vacancy rate (percent of rental housing units)	6.6	6.5	8.1	7.5	5.9	5.5	5.5	6.6	6.3

AGRICULTURE

NEBRASKA HAS 55,000 FARMS, WHICH RANKS THE STATE 15TH highest in the nation. The state averages 855 acres per farm, well above the national average of 471. Nebraska ranks fifth in the nation for value of farmland and buildings. The state's gross farm income has increased by only 3.5 percent from 1989-1991 to 1995-1997, and net farm income decreased 6.5 percent during the period. Crop revenue accounted for 38.6 percent of revenue from cash receipts in 1997, but the majority of revenue is still derived from cattle and hogs.

NEBRASKA FARMS, 1997	
Number of farms	55 000
Total acres (thousands):	47 000
Average per farm	855
Value of land and buildings (millions of dollars)	31 960
Average per farm (dollars)	581 091

Farm Income
(millions of dollars)

	1980	1989	1990	1991	1992	1993	1994	1995	1996	1997
Gross income	7 501	10 589	10 040	10 478	9 762	10 405	9 275	10 651	10 291	11 243
Receipts from sales	7 233	9 523	8 935	9 492	8 898	9 172	8 472	9 660	9 345	10 213
Government payments	83	542	625	491	479	806	348	507	389	455
Imputed and miscellaneous income	185	524	481	495	386	427	455	484	557	575
(−) Production expenses	7 094	7 923	8 294	8 037	7 926	8 357	8 214	8 449	8 755	9 480
(=) Realized net income	407	2 666	1 747	2 441	1 836	2 048	1 061	2 202	1 537	1 763
(+) Inventory change	-636	-844	496	-453	337	-432	767	-1 037	1 298	-105
(=) Net income	-229	1 822	2 243	1 988	2 172	1 616	1 828	1 165	2 835	1 658
Corporate income	-129	259	331	230	352	105	468	194	702	378
Farm proprietors income	-100	1 563	1 911	1 758	1 820	1 511	1 359	971	2 133	1 281

EDUCATION

EDUCATIONAL ATTAINMENT Percent of population age 25 and over, 1997	State	United States
High school graduate or higher	86.0	82.1
College graduate or higher	21.3	23.9

WITH 86 PERCENT OF THE STATE'S ADULT POPULATION HAVING graduated from high school, Nebraska ranks among the top 15 states in the nation. However, the percentage of college graduates, at 21.3 percent, is lower than the national percentage of 23.9 percent, which places Nebraska among the 20 lowest states in the nation. Both of these rates mark substantial increases from the education attainment levels of 1990, when 81.8 percent had graduated from high school and 18.9 percent from college. Nebraska has a higher than average percentage of young adults currently

enrolled in higher education, which signals further increases in college attainment rates in the future. Minorities comprise only 7.8 percent of the state's post-secondary enrollment, substantially less than the nearly 10 percent of Nebraska's total population consisting of minorities.

Per pupil expenditures in elementary and secondary schools were nearly identical to the national average, but the average teacher's salary of $31,768 was well below the U.S. average of $38,507, reflecting generally lower average wages in the state.

High School Completion: 1990–97

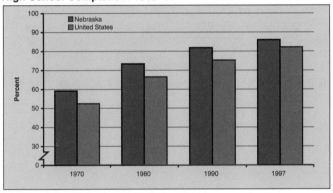

Education Indicators

	State	U.S.
Elementary and secondary schools		
Enrollment, 1995–96		
Total (thousands)	331	49 873
Percent in private schools	12.5	10.1
Expenditures per pupil (dollars), 1995–96	6 083	6 146
Average teacher salary (dollars), 1996–97	31 768	38 509
Higher education		
Enrollment, 1996–97		
Total (thousands)	119	14 218
Percent of population 18–34	30.9	21.8
Percent minority	7.9	26.1
Percent in private schools	16.4	22.6

HEALTH

OVERALL, THE HEALTH OF NEBRASKA'S POPULATION APPEARS to be better than the national average. The state's age-adjusted death rate for all causes fell slightly in the 1990s and was lower than the U.S. death rate in 1997. The infant mortality rate, while lower in the first half of the 1990s, rose in 1996 and 1997, surpassing the U.S. rate. With the exceptions of the age-adjusted death rates for Alzheimer's disease, chronic obstructive pulmonary diseases, motor

vehicle accidents, and suicide, Nebraska's death rates for major causes are lower than the U.S. rates. The state's age-adjusted death rates for HIV, homicide, and liver disease are all well below the national rates. Following a national trend, Nebraska's population without health insurance rose substantially from 8.5 percent in 1990 to 10.8 percent in 1997. This rate remained well below the national rate of 16.1 percent.

Health Indicators

	1990	1995	1996	1997
Infant mortality *(rate per thousand live births)*				
Nebraska	8.3	7.4	8.7	7.9
U.S.	9.2	7.6	7.3	7.1
Total deaths, age-adjusted rate *(rate per thousand population)*				
Nebraska	4.7	4.5	4.5	4.4
U.S.	5.2	5.0	4.9	4.8
Persons not covered by health insurance *(percent of population)*				
Nebraska	8.5	9.0	11.4	10.8
U.S.	13.9	15.4	15.6	16.1

Leading Causes of Death, 1996
(deaths per 100,000 population)

	Age-adjusted		Not age-adjusted	
	State	U.S.	State	U.S.
Deaths from all causes	445.7	491.6	937.2	872.5
Heart disease	122.7	134.5	302.8	276.4
Cancer	115.8	127.9	201.3	203.4
Cerebrovascular diseases	24.1	26.4	69.0	60.3
Chronic obstructive pulmonary disease	22.4	21.0	47.4	40.0
Diabetes mellitus	9.7	13.6	20.2	23.3
Pneumonia and influenza	10.8	12.8	34.6	31.6
HIV	3.8	11.1	3.7	11.7
Liver disease	3.7	7.5	4.9	9.4
Alzheimer's disease	3.4	2.7	12.7	8.1
Accidents and adverse effects	29.5	30.4	39.2	35.8
Motor vehicle accidents	17.5	16.2	18.2	16.5
Suicide	11.1	10.8	11.4	11.6
Homicide	3.4	8.5	3.0	7.9
Injury by firearm	9.8	12.9	9.7	12.8

GOVERNMENT

STATE AND LOCAL TAXES, 1995–96	State	U.S.
Per capita (dollars)	2 454	2 477
Percent of personal income	11.5	10.8

IN 1995–96, NEBRASKANS PAID 11.5 PERCENT OF PERSONAL incomes in state and local taxes (except corporate) combined, well above the national rate of 10.8 percent. Yet Nebraska's per capita taxes were slightly less than the national average, reflecting the state's lower average incomes. At the state level, Nebraska's general revenues amounted to $2,860 per capita in 1997. This amount was significantly lower than the national average. With the exception of individual income taxes, state taxes per capita were lower in Nebraska than the national average. The state's per capita individual income taxes amounted to $566, just above the national per capita individual income tax of $551. Nebraska's per capita general expenditures were 7 percent lower than the U.S. average. The state's per capita expenditures for public welfare were significantly lower than national expenditures. Nebraska's per capita debt at the end of the fiscal year was $902, amounting to only 53 percent of the per capita debt for all state government.

Federal grants and payments to individuals in Nebraska were all fairly proportional to the state's 0.6 percent of the U.S. population. Nebraska received a greater share of Social Security and government retirement payments but a smaller share of Medicare payments. The state also received a lower share of defense and other procurement: defense procurement amounted to only 0.2 percent of the U.S. total.

State Government Finances, 1996–97

	Millions of dollars	Percent distribution	Dollars per capita State	Dollars per capita U.S.
General revenue	4 740	100.0	2 861	3 049
Intergovernmental revenue	1 164	24.6	703	863
Taxes	2 548	53.8	1 538	1 660
General sales	866	18.3	522	551
Selective sales	416	8.8	251	257
License taxes	165	3.5	100	106
Individual income	937	19.8	566	542
Corporation net income	137	2.9	83	115
Other taxes	27	0.6	16	90
Other general revenue	1 028	21.7	620	526
General expenditure	4 548	100.0	2 744	2 951
Intergovernmental expenditure	1 210	26.6	730	989
Direct expenditure	3 337	73.4	2 014	1 962
General expenditure, by function:				
Education	1 588	34.9	958	1 033
Public welfare	1 030	22.7	622	761
Hospitals and health	544	12.0	328	237
Highways	596	13.1	360	225
Police protection and corrections	151	3.3	91	137
Natural resources, parks and recreation	154	3.4	93	63
Governmental administration	128	2.8	77	107
Interest on general debt	90	2.0	54	99
Other and unallocable	266	5.9	161	290
Debt at end of fiscal year	1 494	NA	902	1 706
Cash and security holdings	6 895	NA	4 161	6 683

Federal Spending within State

	Federal funds, fiscal 1997 Millions of dollars	Percent distribution	Percent of U.S. total*
Total within state	7 838	100.0	0.6
Payments to individuals	4 479	57.1	0.6
Retirement and disability	3 010	38.4	0.7
Medicare	973	12.4	0.5
Food stamps	72	0.9	0.4
Supplemental Security Income	87	1.1	0.3
Grants	1 341	17.1	0.5
Medicaid and other health	543	6.9	0.5
Nutrition and family welfare	277	3.5	0.6
Education	106	1.4	0.6
Housing and community development	63	0.8	0.6
Salaries and wages	974	12.4	0.6
Defense procurement contracts	262	3.3	0.2
Non-defense procurement contracts	259	3.3	0.4

*State population is 0.6 percent of the U.S. total.

31 372	59 698		65 157	70 827	72 687	78 001	81 93	88 504	93 426	5.8	63 383	70 827	31 372	59 698	63 3
25 323	47 902		57 151	59 446		62 916	67 00	72 039	77 208	6.1	50 999	57 151	25 323	47 902	50 9
2 640	5 143				7 801			7 709	7 838	5.4	5 645	6 816	2 640	5 143	5 6
3 409	6 652				284		07	8 755	8 380	2.9	6 739	6 860	3 409	6 652	6 7
693	1 716				762			1 539	762	-9.7	1 561	811	693	1 716	
716	4 9							217	618	5	178	6 049	716		

1997

Population (persons)	1,678,691
Population rank	37th
Population growth rank (1990–97)	1st
Per capita personal income	$26,553
Unemployment rate (percent)	4.1
Poverty rate (percent)	11.0

NEVADA ACHIEVED DISTINCTION AS THE GAMBLING CENTER OF the nation and, more recently, as the state with the fastest rate of population growth. People are pouring in to take advantage of plentiful jobs paying increasingly competitive wages and perhaps hoping to escape the problems of large urban areas in California and elsewhere. As a result, the state's population jumped 37.8 percent from 1990 to 1997, on top of a 50 percent increase logged in the 1980s. The Las Vegas metropolitan area grew 48 percent from 1990 to 1997, the fastest in the nation. Still, the state ranks 37th in total size, just ahead of Nebraska, and the 1990s increase in absolute terms was about one-fifth of the increase in California's population. With its large popula-

tion shifts, Nevada is changing toward mirroring the racial diversity of the country, with minority population representing about 28 percent of the state total in 1997.

The state's economy grew rapidly, with an increase of more than 51 percent in total employment, and it managed to sustain above-average per capita incomes. While a number of basic retail and construction industries have grown at extraordinary rates, the state's basic dependence on gambling-related businesses remains strong. Hotel and entertainment jobs associated with the gambling industry contributed 19.8 percent of all earnings in the state in 1997, down slightly from the 23.9 percent share in 1980. A small manufacturing sector is growing but remains tiny.

Average Annual Population Growth: 1990–97

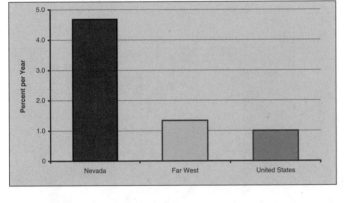

Median Household Income: 1989–97 (1997 dollars)

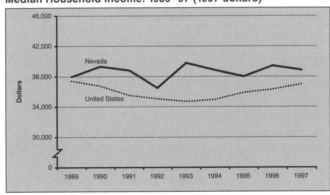

Unemployment Rate: 1989–97

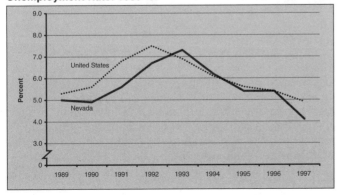

UNEMPLOYMENT RATES IN NEVADA HAVE FLUCTUATED IN approximate accord with the cyclical changes in the U.S. unemployment rate during the 1990s. Because of exceptional increases in employment in the mid 1990s, the state's unemployment rate declined to 4.1 percent in 1997, lower than the national average. However, the higher unemployment rates of the 1992–93 period in Nevada were not caused by any cyclical downturn of manufacturing or construction. Instead, they appear to reflect the economy's difficulty in consistently keeping pace with rapid expansion in the labor force, which grew 30 percent between 1989 and 1994.

POPULATION AND LABOR FORCE

NEVADA'S RECENT POPULATION GROWTH RATES HAVE BEEN OFF the charts, with a 37.6 percent rise from 1990 to 1997 and a 50 percent increase in the previous decade, resulting in a population doubling over those 17 years. However, Nevada still remains a small state, and 11 other states displayed larger absolute gains in population during 1990–97.

Three-quarters of the increase for Nevada came from in-migration from other states, with a relatively smaller amount of international immigration. Immigration brought a 2.7 percent population increase, around the same proportion as for the United States overall. Natural population increase fueled a 7 percent rise, which is unusu-

ally high. The state's birth rate declined from 1990 to 1997, but it still exceeds the national average.

With a doubling in the number of Hispanics between 1990 and 1997, Nevada reached a new level of ethnic diversity. As of 1997, Hispanics constituted 15.1 percent of total population, a higher share than their national representation; non-Hispanic Blacks were 6.8 percent of the state's population. Considering the fast-growing Asian population and the state's higher than average proportion of Native Americans, the state's total minority population percentage reached a level similar to the national population profile.

Population and Labor Force

	1980	1990	1991	1992	1993	1994	1995	1996	1997	Change*	
										State	U.S.
Population											
Total number of persons (thousands)	800	1 219	1 285	1 333	1 382	1 458	1 528	1 600	1 679	4.7	1.0
Percent distribution:											
White, Non-Hispanic	83.3	78.3	78.0	77.3	76.5	75.6	74.6	73.7	72.6	3.6	0.4
Black, Non-Hispanic	6.3	6.8	6.5	6.6	6.6	6.7	6.8	6.8	6.8	4.8	1.4
Asian	1.9	3.3	3.5	3.6	3.8	3.9	4.1	4.2	4.4	9.0	4.1
Native American	1.8	1.7	1.8	1.8	1.8	1.8	1.8	1.7	1.8	5.0	1.6
Hispanic	6.8	10.5	10.9	11.4	11.9	12.6	13.5	14.2	15.1	10.2	3.8
In metropolitan areas	83.2	84.4	84.7	84.8	85.0	85.4	85.5	85.6	85.8	4.9	1.0
Total number of households (thousands)	304	466	496	517	535	562	591	619	NA	4.8	1.2
Labor Force (thousands)											
Population 16 and over	614	932	990	1 026	1 060	1 117	1 171	1 223	1 278	4.6	1.0
Civilian labor force	431	665	692	714	743	782	802	840	883	4.1	1.1
Employed	404	632	653	666	689	733	759	794	847	4.3	1.2
Percent of population	65.8	67.9	66.0	64.9	65.1	65.7	64.8	64.9	66.3		
Unemployment rate (percent)	6.2	4.9	5.6	6.7	7.3	6.2	5.4	5.4	4.1		

*Compound annual average percent change, 1990–1997; 1990–1996 for households.

Population Change and Components: 1990–97

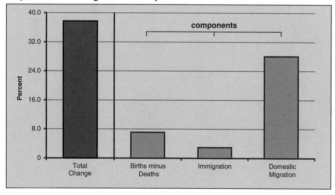

Average Annual Household and Population Growth

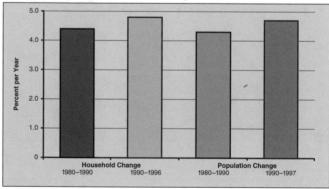

Population by Age; Births and Deaths

	1990		1997	
	State	U.S.	State	U.S.
Age distribution (percent)				
Under 5 years	8.2	7.6	7.7	7.2
5 to 17 years	17.8	18.2	18.7	18.8
18 to 64 years	63.4	61.8	62.1	61.3
65 years and over	10.6	12.5	11.5	12.7
Birth and death rates (per thousand population)				
Births	18.0	16.7	16.1	14.6
Deaths	7.7	8.6	8.0	8.6

NEVADA HAS SEEN IN-MIGRATION IN ALL AGE GROUPS DURING the 1990s. The proportion of school-age children is effectively equal to the national average, but is growing rapidly. The state has a slightly higher than average percentage of working-age adults. It also has a lower than average concentration of people over 65 years of age, although this segment of the population grew at a faster rate than the state's overall population in the 1990s.

HOUSEHOLD AND PERSONAL INCOME

HOUSEHOLD INCOME AND PERSONS IN POVERTY	1990	1995	1996	1997	
				State	U.S.
Median household income (1997 dollars)	39 324	38 002	39 424	38 854	37 005
Persons in poverty (thousands)	119	173	133	190	35 574
Poverty rate (percent)	9.8	11.1	8.1	11.0	13.3

MEDIAN HOUSEHOLD INCOME IN NEVADA WAS $38,854 IN 1997, 5 percent higher than the national median, continuing its consistent 1990s record of income above the national norm. This fits with the state's profile of relatively fewer retirees and a high ratio of employees to population. The state poverty rate stood at 11.0 percent in 1997, below the national average.

The level of personal income per capita was 5 percent above the national average in 1997; however, the earnings component was 8.7 percent higher per capita than in the nation. Dividends and interest were 6.5 percent higher, and transfer payments per capita were 12 percent lower than the U.S. average and grew 10.1 percent from 1989 to 1997, after adjustment for inflation—growth roughly equal to the national average. Among the components, business proprietors' income grew the fastest, up 139 percent over the eight years. One damper for the state tax base was the money earned by Nevada workers living out of state, which had a net effect of exporting 1.9 percent of the total in-state earnings in 1997.

Transfer payments were a relatively small 13.8 percent of personal income in 1997. Transfers in Nevada consist disproportionately of retirement and disability benefits, with a smaller than average percentage in medical and income maintenance benefits, reflecting the large proportion of the population that is employed. Indeed, there was a huge jump in receipt of the earned income tax credit from 1990 to 1997 (now the largest income maintenance program in the state). There were also large increases in Supplemental Security Income (SSI). Family assistance is the smallest welfare program, and it grew very modestly considering the state's population increases.

Personal Income
(millions of dollars)

	1980	1989	1990	1991	1992	1993	1994	1995	1996	1997	Change*
Earnings by place of work	7 417	16 161	18 307	19 273	21 198	22 959	25 450	27 859	30 756	33 250	9.4
Wages and salaries	6 302	13 514	15 099	15 778	17 143	18 497	20 508	22 545	25 095	27 298	9.2
Other labor income	468	1 116	1 319	1 464	1 668	1 865	2 083	2 167	2 226	2 292	9.4
Proprietors' income	647	1 531	1 888	2 031	2 387	2 597	2 859	3 147	3 435	3 659	11.5
Farm	35	49	50	46	35	69	29	14	13	8	-20.6
Nonfarm	612	1 482	1 838	1 985	2 352	2 528	2 830	3 132	3 423	3 652	11.9
(−) Personal contributions for social insurance	345	951	1 062	1 136	1 222	1 326	1 494	1 652	1 824	1 989	9.7
(+) Adjustment for residence	-168	-336	-370	-373	-386	-447	-496	-533	-592	-646	NA
(=) Net earnings by state of residence	6 904	14 874	16 874	17 765	19 589	21 186	23 459	25 674	28 340	30 615	9.4
(+) Dividends, interest, and rent	1 440	4 041	4 573	4 821	4 974	5 104	5 737	6 463	7 353	7 779	8.5
(+) Transfer payments	1 075	2 791	3 180	3 882	4 393	4 655	4 908	5 376	5 730	6 130	10.3
(=) Total personal income	9 420	21 706	24 628	26 468	28 956	30 945	34 105	37 512	41 423	44 524	9.4
Farm	60	78	80	74	61	98	65	54	53	51	-5.2
Nonfarm	9 360	21 628	24 548	26 394	28 895	30 847	34 039	37 458	41 371	44 474	9.4
Personal income per capita (dollars)											
Current dollars	11 626	19 084	20 209	20 598	21 727	22 384	23 377	24 525	25 876	26 553	4.2
1997 dollars	22 229	24 126	24 319	23 785	24 303	24 357	24 843	25 494	26 350	26 553	1.2

*Compound annual average percent change, 1989–1997

Government Transfer Payments

	Millions of dollars		Percent change*	
	1990	1997	State	U.S.
Total government payments to individuals	3 024	5 882	94.5	62.7
Retirement, disability, and insurance	1 967	3 466	76.2	48.2
Social Security	1 034	2 107	103.8	46.1
Government employee retirement	566	1 057	86.9	60.3
Medical payments	703	1 708	142.9	101.2
Income maintenance	141	343	143.5	58.0
Supplemental Security Income	33	90	171.8	75.4
Family assistance	29	45	57.0	-0.5
Food Stamps	44	70	60.5	27.1
Other income maintenance	35	138	290.3	189.8
Unemployment insurance benefits	88	160	82.1	10.6
Veterans benefits and other	125	205	63.8	30.8

*Percent change, 1990–1997

Government Payments to Individuals: 1997

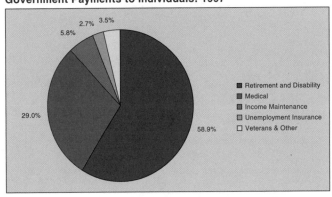

- Retirement and Disability — 58.9%
- Medical — 29.0%
- Income Maintenance — 5.8%
- Unemployment Insurance — 2.7%
- Veterans & Other — 3.5%

ECONOMIC STRUCTURE

LEADING PRIVATE INDUSTRIES, 1997 (Worker and proprietor earnings, millions of dollars)		FASTEST EARNINGS GROWTH, 1989–97 (percent increase)	
Hotels and lodging	$5 622	Real estate	394.0
Construction specialties	2 554	Business services	176.9
Health services	2 150	Construction specialties	150.4
Business services	1 620	Air transportation	149.9
Engineering and management services	1 184	Heavy construction contractors	125.6

SERVICES PLAY A DOMINANT ROLE IN THE NEVADA ECONOMY, as much of it has been built up around the casinos, the tourists who visit, and the ancillary services to those tourists and the businesses they frequent. Fifty-eight percent of all employment in the state is within the services and retail trade sectors (compared with a 48 percent share nationally). Except for construction specialties, the four largest industries in the state are services. Within the services sector itself, the state has substantial earnings in only five industries: the four in the top five plus amusement and recreation, with earnings of $952 million in 1997. Even the growing air transportation industry is likely fueled primarily by the gambling industry. There is a continued narrowness to the economic base in Nevada.

Nonetheless, there was substantial growth (in percentage terms) in employment in all other sectors across the board. Fastest growth in percentage terms came in construction, as the state entered a fantastic boom in homebuilding and also expansion of its infrastructure to accommodate rapid population growth. Both heavy construction and the specialty contractor industries grew rapidly. The manufacturing sector experienced a high rate of growth, though it still contributed only 4 percent of all jobs in 1997. Earnings of the finance, insurance, and real estate sector more than tripled in the 1989–97 period. It contained two of the fastest growing earnings industries—real estate and insurance (the latter is too small to appear on the list of fastest growing industries).

Employment and Earnings by Sector

	1980	1989	1990	1991	1992	1993	1994	1995	1996	1997 Number	1997 Percent of total	Change*
Employment *(thousands of persons)*												
Total	490	720	763	781	789	831	914	969	1 036	1 090	100.0	5.3
Farm	5	5	5	4	4	4	4	4	4	5	0.4	-1.5
Nonfarm	484	715	758	776	784	827	909	965	1 031	1 085	99.6	5.4
Private nonfarm	413	629	668	681	686	726	805	858	919	969	88.9	5.5
Agricultural service, forestry, and fishing	3	5	6	7	6	7	8	9	11	12	1.1	10.4
Mining	7	15	16	15	15	14	14	15	16	16	1.5	0.9
Construction	31	56	58	51	50	58	69	76	90	97	8.9	7.2
Manufacturing	20	27	28	28	28	32	37	40	42	44	4.1	6.2
Transportation and public utilities	26	33	35	36	36	39	42	45	48	51	4.7	5.6
Wholesale trade	14	24	26	27	28	28	30	33	36	38	3.5	5.7
Retail trade	77	112	117	122	124	128	142	152	164	174	16.0	5.7
Finance, insurance, and real estate	37	49	52	53	52	57	60	66	71	76	7.0	5.6
Services	200	307	329	343	346	363	402	421	441	460	42.2	5.2
Government	71	86	90	95	99	101	105	108	112	117	10.7	3.9
Earnings *(millions of dollars)*												
Total	7 417	16 161	18 307	19 273	21 198	22 959	25 450	27 859	30 756	33 250	100.0	9.4
Farm	60	78	80	74	61	98	65	54	53	51	0.2	-5.2
Nonfarm	7 357	16 084	18 226	19 199	21 137	22 861	25 384	27 805	30 704	33 200	99.8	9.5
Private nonfarm	6 275	13 843	15 722	16 400	18 082	19 635	21 957	24 120	26 734	28 970	87.1	9.7
Agricultural service, forestry, and fishing	28	76	90	92	99	111	127	146	177	196	0.6	12.5
Mining	174	538	595	606	634	643	654	719	823	845	2.5	5.8
Construction	751	1 644	1 813	1 623	1 676	2 075	2 462	2 740	3 517	3 864	11.6	11.3
Manufacturing	372	725	790	816	956	1 022	1 192	1 317	1 458	1 577	4.7	10.2
Transportation and public utilities	564	1 004	1 117	1 200	1 259	1 377	1 517	1 627	1 763	1 916	5.8	8.4
Wholesale trade	262	697	800	844	932	952	1 038	1 150	1 299	1 442	4.3	9.5
Retail trade	831	1 647	1 806	1 915	2 067	2 189	2 460	2 673	2 984	3 272	9.8	9.0
Finance, insurance, and real estate	343	742	839	875	1 125	1 422	1 602	1 929	2 194	2 329	7.0	15.4
Services	2 949	6 770	7 872	8 429	9 334	9 844	10 907	11 818	12 519	13 529	40.7	9.0
Government	1 083	2 241	2 505	2 800	3 055	3 226	3 427	3 684	3 970	4 230	12.7	8.3

*Compound annual average percent change, 1989–1997

ECONOMIC STRUCTURE (Continued)

AVERAGE WAGES PER WORKER IN NEVADA WERE 2.7 PERCENT below the national average, but showed large deviations among sectors. Wages in the dominant services sector are at parity with national wage levels, reflecting relatively high wages within the big hotel casinos. Wages are much higher than the U.S. averages for the construction, retail trade, and government sectors, in order to attract workers to these fast-growing areas. Wages in the state lag the nation most sharply within the finance sector, where they are 24 percent less than the U.S. average, but also in the small manufacturing sector.

Manufacturing is a small but fast-growing sector within Nevada, and its growth could ultimately help diversify the state's economy. In 1996, value of manufacturing output represented 4.8 percent of gross state product, a ratio that had grown slightly since the 1980s as the sector kept pace with the rapidly growing economy in Nevada. The largest manufacturing industry in 1997 was printing, with $208 million in earnings, and next came miscellaneous manufacturing at $206 million. Manufacturing output value per worker in 1996, $58,622, was 15 percent below the national average reflecting the state's mix of industries.

Export production is not a significant component in the Nevada economy, because of the small manufacturing and farm sectors. Exports in 1996 were sixth lowest of all states, even though the rate of growth in percentage terms was quite high between 1993 and 1997. Exports include several types of commercial and electronic equipment, as well as miscellaneous manufacturing goods.

Average Annual Wages and Salaries by Sector
(dollars)

	1989	1996	1997 State	1997 U.S.
All wage and salary workers	21 632	28 117	28 999	29 809
Farm	9 447	20 340	17 873	16 442
Nonfarm	21 687	28 134	29 026	29 900
Private nonfarm	21 253	27 459	28 377	29 867
Agricultural service, forestry, and fishing	16 542	19 205	19 816	17 941
Mining	35 081	48 292	49 635	49 800
Construction	26 997	34 500	35 499	31 765
Manufacturing	24 175	31 896	33 057	38 351
Transportation and utilities	27 029	34 101	34 754	38 222
Wholesale trade	27 230	34 777	36 382	39 466
Retail trade	14 029	17 931	18 540	16 206
Finance, insurance, and real estate	23 387	33 282	34 051	44 993
Services	20 595	26 421	27 405	27 588
Government	24 408	32 829	33 609	30 062

Gross State Product and Manufacturing
(millions of dollars, except as noted)

	1989	1994	1995	1996
Gross state product, total	28 099	44 502	48 670	53 687
Manufacturing:				
Millions of dollars	1 151	2 003	2 293	2 589
Percent of total gross state product	4.1	4.5	4.7	4.8
Per worker (dollars)	42 103	54 269	57 456	61 453
New capital expenditures, manufacturing	NA	216	260	206

Exports of Goods
(millions of dollars)

	1994	1995	1996	1997
All goods	458	711	692	807
Manufactures	420	659	632	732
Agricultural and livestock products	7	5	6	5
Other commodities	31	47	54	70
Top goods exports, 1997:				
Miscellaneous manufactures	70	94	158	154
Industrial machinery and computers	69	131	95	119
Electric and electronic equipment	55	93	102	117
Scientific and measuring instruments	67	81	71	88
Transportation equipment	15	50	55	73

HOUSING

RATES OF HOUSING PRODUCTION PER CAPITA IN NEVADA WERE extraordinarily high during the 1990s because of the continuous in-migration. Total production, including multi-family units and mobile homes, proceeded at rates three to four times the national average for most of the decade. In 1997, building permits for the Las Vegas area (the country's 34th largest metro area) totaled 30,876, about the same as for Chicago (the third largest area), and it ranked fifth in the nation. This growth led to a large boost in the construction sector over the 1989–97 period. Sales of existing homes did not increase as vigorously.

Nevada historically has had a lower proportion of homeowners than has the United States overall, with a 6 to 10 percent gap below the U.S. rate. With rapid increases in population and households, the supply of available, affordable homes has come under pressure, keeping ownership rates low. In 1996–97, however, the rates of ownership moved up noticeably in Nevada. Within the rental housing market, vacancy rates have fluctuated but are sur

Homeownership Rates: 1989 and 1997

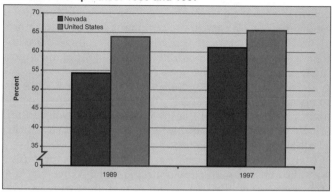

prisingly high for a growing state. High vacancies in 1989–93 indicated some overbuilding of new units, but vacancies have moderated in the mid–1990s.

Housing Supply

	1989	1990	1991	1992	1993	1994	1995	1996	1997
Residential building permits (thousands)	29.3	25.1	21.0	17.3	23.3	31.1	32.8	37.2	34.8
New home production (including manufactured housing):									
Thousands of homes	31.5	27.3	23.1	19.2	25.0	33.3	35.0	39.9	37.6
Rate per 1,000 population									
Nevada	27.7	22.4	18.0	14.4	18.1	22.8	22.9	24.9	22.4
U.S.	6.2	5.2	4.5	5.1	5.6	6.4	6.3	6.6	6.5
Existing home sales:									
Thousands of homes	21.4	26.2	25.6	25.6	30.5	32.9	29.6	31.8	29.7
Change from previous year (percent)									
Nevada	2.4	22.4	-2.3	0.0	19.1	7.9	-10.0	7.4	-6.6
U.S.	-3.9	-4.0	0.0	9.2	8.2	4.8	-3.7	7.5	3.8
Home ownership rate (percent of households)	54.3	55.8	55.8	55.1	55.8	55.8	58.6	61.1	61.2
Rental vacancy rate (percent of rental housing units)	10.9	8.4	8.5	9.0	9.1	6.1	6.8	7.1	7.5

AGRICULTURE

THE FARM SECTOR IS NOT A MAJOR FACTOR IN THE STATE ECONomy. Livestock and hay are the leading products but their sales have been flat through the 1990s. There were 2,500 farms in the state in 1997 of huge average size (3,520 acres) and value ($1.2 million per farm), yet net farm income represented only 0.1 percent of the state's personal income. This situation placed Nevada among the five lowest states for net farm earnings.

NEVADA FARMS, 1997

Number of farms	2 500
Total acres (thousands):	8 800
Average per farm	3 520
Value of land and buildings (millions of dollars)	3 080
Average per farm (dollars)	1232000

Farm Income
(millions of dollars)

	1980	1989	1990	1991	1992	1993	1994	1995	1996	1997
Gross income	293	314	360	333	332	358	368	343	344	370
Receipts from sales	274	280	327	298	288	316	328	301	301	327
Government payments	1	6	5	6	11	7	5	4	3	2
Imputed and miscellaneous income	17	27	28	29	33	35	35	38	41	41
(−) Production expenses	279	270	288	276	273	289	337	332	343	353
(=) Realized net income	14	44	72	56	60	69	31	12	1	17
(+) Inventory change	21	16	-11	-3	-17	6	8	5	16	-6
(=) Net income	35	60	60	53	42	75	40	17	17	10
Corporate income	0	11	11	7	7	5	11	3	5	3
Farm proprietors income	35	49	50	46	35	69	29	14	13	8

EDUCATION

EDUCATIONAL ATTAINMENT Percent of population age 25 and over, 1997	State	United States
High school graduate or higher	85.4	82.1
College graduate or higher	19.9	23.9

A RELATIVELY HIGH PROPORTION OF ADULTS IN NEVADA, 85.4 percent, have earned high school degrees, consistent with the high rates of employment in the state and the smaller than average cohort of older people. In contrast, with the small number of conventional professional jobs in Nevada, the proportion of the population holding college degrees is lower than national averages. Spending per pupil for public elementary and secondary schools is 13 percent below U.S. averages, which is typical for states experiencing rapid growth where educational resources cannot keep pace with the population. Still, public schools overwhelmingly predominate for both elementary/secondary and higher education, with only a tiny proportion of private school enrollment in the state.

High School Completion: 1990–97

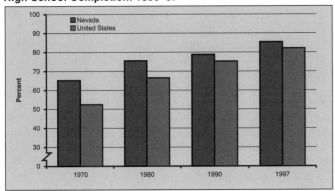

Education Indicators

	State	U.S.
Elementary and secondary schools Enrollment, 1995–96		
Total (thousands)	277	49 873
Percent in private schools	4.4	10.1
Expenditures per pupil (dollars), 1995–96	5 320	6 146
Average teacher salary (dollars), 1996–97	37 340	38 509
Higher education Enrollment, 1996–97		
Total (thousands)	74	14 218
Percent of population 18–34	19.0	21.8
Percent minority	23.0	26.1
Percent in private schools	2.1	22.6

HEALTH

MAJOR HEALTH INDICATORS FOR NEVADA TRACK THE NATIONAL trends fairly closely. Infant mortality has declined during the 1990s, as for most states, and is slightly below national averages. Overall death rates, however, are a little above national totals (after adjustment for age differentials). Death from heart disease is below average in the state, but deaths from suicide occur at double the national rate per capita. The proportion of the population lacking health insurance, 17.5 percent in 1997, is around the national average.

Health Indicators

	1990	1995	1996	1997
Infant mortality *(rate per thousand live births)*				
Nevada	8.4	5.7	6.2	5.7
U.S.	9.2	7.6	7.3	7.1
Total deaths, age-adjusted rate *(rate per thousand population)*				
Nevada	5.7	5.6	5.5	5.3
U.S.	5.2	5.0	4.9	4.8
Persons not covered by health insurance *(percent of population)*				
Nevada	16.5	18.7	15.6	17.5
U.S.	13.9	15.4	15.6	16.1

Leading Causes of Death, 1996
(deaths per 100,000 population)

	Age-adjusted		Not age-adjusted	
	State	U.S.	State	U.S.
Deaths from all causes	550.5	491.6	822.4	872.5
Heart disease	146.9	134.5	241.0	276.4
Cancer	136.7	127.9	199.1	203.4
Cerebrovascular diseases	27.9	26.4	49.7	60.3
Chronic obstructive pulmonary disease	33.7	21.0	55.5	40.0
Diabetes mellitus	10.8	13.6	16.4	23.3
Pneumonia and influenza	13.7	12.8	23.3	31.6
HIV	7.9	11.1	8.8	11.7
Liver disease	11.0	7.5	13.2	9.4
Alzheimer's disease	2.9	2.7	6.0	8.1
Accidents and adverse effects	34.9	30.4	37.7	35.8
Motor vehicle accidents	19.9	16.2	20.5	16.5
Suicide	19.8	10.8	20.9	11.6
Homicide	13.5	8.5	12.8	7.9
Injury by firearm	22.3	12.9	22.4	12.8

GOVERNMENT

STATE AND LOCAL TAXES, 1995–96	State	U.S.
Per capita (dollars)	2 661	2 477
Percent of personal income	11.4	10.8

TOTAL STATE AND LOCAL TAX RECEIPTS WERE 7 PERCENT HIGHer in Nevada than national averages, on a per capita basis, in 1995–96. Both state and local levels of government benefited from strong sales tax collections (65 percent of total tax revenue), which included selective sales taxes that transferred much of the tax burden to out-of-state visitors. Local property taxes were a smaller proportion of local taxes than typical in the nation. Calculated as a percent of personal income, total state and local taxes were 11.4 percent of income, which is higher than the national average. However, the actual impact on local residents is lessened substantially by the large contributions of visitors to the sales tax revenues.

Revenues and spending at the state level in 1997 were both moderately lower than the U.S. averages on a per capita basis. Total tax collections are actually a bit higher than national averages, based on the powerful engine of sales tax collections in a tourist mecca attracting out-of-state visitors. Selective sales tax receipts are also well above national norms allowing the state to function without any income taxes at the individual or corporate level. The state's revenue totals were eroded, however, by the low levels of intergovernmental receipts from the federal government. This level of federal aid is linked to the low poverty and other conditions of distress in the state.

State spending on education is comparable to typical national levels, on a per capita basis, with intergovernmental transfers to the local level actually a bit higher than average. However, spending on public welfare and health are significantly lower than U.S. norms, reflecting the relatively low numbers of poor and older people.

Federal spending for payments to individuals in Nevada is proportionate to its 0.6 percent share of U.S. population, but receipt of federal grants and procurement is lower than that share. Grants for Medicaid and other health programs were relatively lowest in the state, but education and family welfare grants were also lower than average. Procurement spending was minimal, especially for defense contracts, given the small manufacturing and high-tech industries in Nevada. Salaries paid to federal civilian and military personnel were nearly equal to the state's share of population.

State Government Finances, 1996–97

	Millions of dollars	Percent distribution	Dollars per capita State	Dollars per capita U.S.
General revenue	4 386	100.0	2 616	3 049
Intergovernmental revenue	830	18.9	495	863
Taxes	3 034	69.2	1 809	1 660
General sales	1 699	38.7	1 013	551
Selective sales	903	20.6	538	257
License taxes	303	6.9	180	106
Individual income	0	0.0	0	542
Corporation net income	0	0.0	0	115
Other taxes	130	3.0	78	90
Other general revenue	523	11.9	312	526
General expenditure	4 328	100.0	2 581	2 951
Intergovernmental expenditure	1 772	40.9	1 056	989
Direct expenditure	2 556	59.1	1 524	1 962
General expenditure, by function:				
Education	1 677	38.7	1 000	1 033
Public welfare	654	15.1	390	761
Hospitals and health	156	3.6	93	237
Highways	370	8.5	221	225
Police protection and corrections	220	5.1	131	137
Natural resources, parks and recreation	81	1.9	48	63
Governmental administration	201	4.6	120	107
Interest on general debt	156	3.6	93	99
Other and unallocable	814	18.8	485	290
Debt at end of fiscal year	2 769	NA	1 651	1 706
Cash and security holdings	12 360	NA	7 370	6 683

Federal Spending within State

	Federal funds, fiscal 1997		
	Millions of dollars	Percent distribution	Percent of U.S. total*
Total within state	7 115	100.0	0.5
Payments to individuals	4 576	64.3	0.6
Retirement and disability	2 949	41.4	0.6
Medicare	1 012	14.2	0.5
Food stamps	75	1.1	0.4
Supplemental Security Income	93	1.3	0.3
Grants	1 100	15.5	0.4
Medicaid and other health	310	4.4	0.3
Nutrition and family welfare	172	2.4	0.4
Education	69	1.0	0.4
Housing and community development	69	1.0	0.6
Salaries and wages	824	11.6	0.5
Defense procurement contracts	256	3.6	0.2
Non-defense procurement contracts	294	4.1	0.4

*State population is 0.6 percent of the U.S. total.

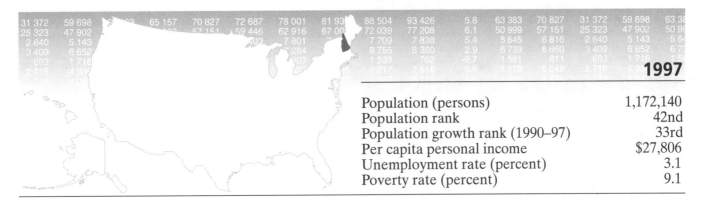

31 372	59 698		65 157	70 827	72 687	78 001	81 93	88 504	93 426	5.8	63 383	70 827	31 372	59 698	63 3
25 323	47 902			57 151	59 446	62 916	67 00	72 039	77 208	6.1	50 999	57 151	25 323	47 902	50 9
2 640	5 143			02	7 801		7 709	7 838	5.4	5 645	6 816	2 640	5 143	5 6
3 409	6 652				284	8 755	8 380	2.9	6 739	6 860	3 409	6 652	6 7
693	1 716			07	1 539	762	-9.7	1 561	811	693	1 716	1 5
2 716	4 93				217	7 618	5.6	178	6 049	2 716	

1997

Population (persons)	1,172,140
Population rank	42nd
Population growth rank (1990–97)	33rd
Per capita personal income	$27,806
Unemployment rate (percent)	3.1
Poverty rate (percent)	9.1

NEW HAMPSHIRE EXPERIENCED GROWTH IN POPULATION AND employment in the 1990s, and by 1997 its unemployment rate was one of the lowest in the nation. Wages in the state grew above the national rate. Growth in per capita personal and median household income was somewhat below the national growth rates, though both measures of income level remained above the national average. Manufacturing, which declined as a proportion of the economy in other states in the region, remained high in New Hampshire. This strength in manufacturing, combined with limited employment growth in retail trade, resulted in full-time jobs accounting for more than 80 percent of all employment, according to the Economic and Labor Market Information Bureau of New Hampshire.

New Hampshire's state and local taxes (other than corporate) were the lowest percentage of personal income in the nation, and the state's relative reliance on local property taxation was the greatest of any state. State corporate taxes per capita were higher than the U.S. average, but the state government spent less per capita than the average state. New Hampshire's spending on education was just half the national per capita average, while spending on interest on debt was triple the national average.

Average Annual Population Growth: 1990–97

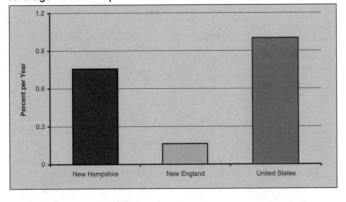

Median Household Income: 1989–97 (1997 dollars)

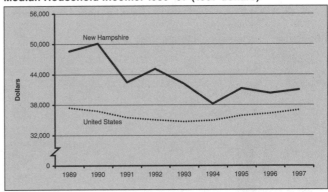

Unemployment Rate: 1989–97

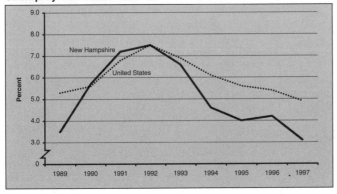

THE UNEMPLOYMENT RATE IN NEW HAMPSHIRE WAS SIMILAR to that in the country at large through 1992. Thereafter, however, unemployment fell faster than it did nationwide. By 1997, the rate was 3.1 percent, among the lowest in the nation.

POPULATION AND LABOR FORCE

TOTAL POPULATION IN NEW HAMPSHIRE GREW FASTER THAN in any other New England state, even though somewhat more slowly than the U.S. average between 1990 and 1997. There was higher growth in New Hampshire in the White, non-Hispanic, and Asian populations. Births less deaths accounted for most of the population gain, though domestic migration was a small but significant component of growth. New Hampshire has a fairly urban population, with almost two-thirds living in metropolitan counties.

The total population and its working-age (16 and older) component declined in 1991, as the recession reduced employment. By 1993, however, growth in both population and jobs had resumed. Over the entire 1990–97 period, employment growth outstripped labor force growth to bring the unemployment rate down.

Population and Labor Force

	1980	1990	1991	1992	1993	1994	1995	1996	1997	Change* State	Change* U.S.
Population											
Total number of persons (thousands)	921	1 112	1 107	1 114	1 122	1 133	1 146	1 160	1 172	0.8	1.0
Percent distribution:											
White, Non-Hispanic	98.4	96.9	97.4	97.3	97.1	97.0	96.9	96.8	96.7	0.7	0.4
Black, Non-Hispanic	0.5	0.9	0.5	0.6	0.6	0.6	0.6	0.6	0.6	-5.1	1.4
Asian	0.4	0.9	0.9	0.9	1.0	1.0	1.0	1.1	1.1	4.3	4.1
Native American	0.2	0.2	0.2	0.2	0.2	0.2	0.2	0.2	0.2	0.4	1.6
Hispanic	0.6	1.1	1.0	1.1	1.2	1.3	1.3	1.4	1.4	4.6	3.8
In metropolitan areas	58.1	61.8	61.7	61.9	62.1	62.2	62.2	62.3	62.5	0.9	1.0
Total number of households (thousands)	323	411	413	417	419	423	431	439	NA	1.1	1.2
Labor Force (thousands)											
Population 16 and over	696	849	841	842	847	857	868	882	893	0.7	1.0
Civilian labor force	469	628	621	610	616	624	633	623	646	0.4	1.1
Employed	447	592	576	565	575	595	608	597	625	0.8	1.2
Percent of population	64.2	69.7	68.5	67.0	67.9	69.5	70.1	67.7	70.0		
Unemployment rate (percent)	4.7	5.7	7.2	7.5	6.6	4.6	4.0	4.2	3.1		

*Compound annual average percent change, 1990–1997; 1990–1996 for households.

Population Change and Components: 1990–97

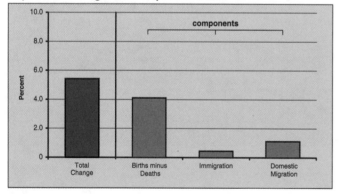

Average Annual Household and Population Growth

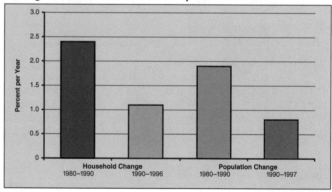

Population by Age; Births and Deaths

	1990 State	1990 U.S.	1997 State	1997 U.S.
Age distribution (percent)				
Under 5 years	7.6	7.6	6.3	7.2
5 to 17 years	17.3	18.2	19.0	18.8
18 to 64 years	63.8	61.8	62.7	61.3
65 years and over	11.3	12.5	12.1	12.7
Birth and death rates (per thousand population)				
Births	15.8	16.7	12.3	14.6
Deaths	7.7	8.6	8.1	8.6

NEW HAMPSHIRE IN 1997 HAD A POPULATION WITH MORE school- and working-age people than average and a lower percentage of those who are pre-school-age and age 65 and over. The birth rate of 12.3 births per 1,000 is lower than the U.S. rate of 14.6 per 1,000.

HOUSEHOLD AND PERSONAL INCOME

HOUSEHOLD INCOME AND PERSONS IN POVERTY	1990	1995	1996	1997	
				State	U.S.
Median household income (1997 dollars)	50 109	41 253	40 311	40 998	37 005
Persons in poverty (thousands)	68	60	73	109	35 574
Poverty rate (percent)	6.3	5.3	6.4	9.1	13.3

NEW HAMPSHIRE'S BETTER-THAN-AVERAGE PERFORMANCE ON the unemployment front did not extend to its income measures. While both median household income and per capita personal income remained above the national averages in 1997, neither had matched the U.S. growth rate. The income of the median household, in real terms, had not recovered from recession lows, declining 0.7 percent per year on average from 1989 to 1997. Poverty rates in the state were far below the national rates, but indicated a possible uptrend as of 1997. (This must be considered tentative, as the sampling errors for a small state are large.)

Per capita personal income rose more slowly than the national average. Increases in aggregate earnings and wages and salaries also lagged behind those of the country, but transfer payments increased at a faster rate. The adjustment for residence was not only positive, indicating that commuting New Hampshire residents on net brought in earnings from other states, but also increased 4.8 percent per year from 1989 to 1997.

Transfer payments to individuals grew by 7.9 percent per year on average between 1990 and 1997. Medical programs, Supplemental Security Income, and other income maintenance programs grew faster than other programs between 1990 and 1997. Social Security was the largest single program, with 1997 disbursements of $1.6 billion. Unemployment payments was the only program to decline, falling by nearly one-half from 1990 to 1997. Family assistance, formerly called Aid to Families with Dependent Children, did not decline but grew only 0.7 percent per year.

Personal Income
(millions of dollars)

	1980	1989	1990	1991	1992	1993	1994	1995	1996	1997	Change*
Earnings by place of work	6 059	15 033	14 921	14 770	15 793	16 484	17 483	18 666	19 727	21 239	4.4
Wages and salaries	4 890	11 737	11 786	11 635	12 356	12 744	13 588	14 630	15 617	16 980	4.7
Other labor income	522	1 321	1 364	1 405	1 532	1 672	1 778	1 789	1 756	1 798	3.9
Proprietors' income	646	1 974	1 772	1 729	1 906	2 068	2 118	2 246	2 354	2 462	2.8
Farm	-1	29	20	20	35	31	23	22	23	17	-6.5
Nonfarm	647	1 945	1 752	1 709	1 871	2 037	2 094	2 224	2 331	2 444	2.9
(−) Personal contributions for social insurance	315	962	978	998	1 062	1 115	1 208	1 308	1 381	1 493	5.6
(+) Adjustment for residence	800	1 868	1 967	2 034	2 108	2 200	2 296	2 341	2 582	2 728	NA
(=) Net earnings by state of residence	6 543	15 939	15 910	15 806	16 839	17 568	18 570	19 699	20 928	22 474	4.4
(+) Dividends, interest, and rent	1 494	4 555	4 649	4 641	4 479	4 563	4 951	5 243	5 740	5 970	3.4
(+) Transfer payments	1 129	2 214	2 488	3 231	3 440	3 353	3 816	4 109	4 066	4 164	8.2
(=) Total personal income	9 166	22 708	23 047	23 678	24 758	25 484	27 337	29 051	30 734	32 608	4.6
Farm	14	48	42	42	56	54	46	48	50	44	-1.2
Nonfarm	9 151	22 660	23 005	23 636	24 702	25 430	27 291	29 004	30 684	32 564	4.6
Personal income per capita (dollars)											
Current dollars	9 917	20 559	20 729	21 383	22 237	22 719	24 110	25 341	26 490	27 806	3.8
1997 dollars	18 962	25 991	24 945	24 692	24 874	24 721	25 622	26 342	26 976	27 806	0.8

*Compound annual average percent change, 1989–1997

Government Transfer Payments

	Millions of dollars		Percent change*	
	1990	1997	State	U.S.
Total government payments to individuals	2 335	3 969	70.0	62.7
Retirement, disability, and insurance	1 439	2 182	51.6	48.2
Social Security	1 020	1 601	57.0	46.1
Government employee retirement	348	516	48.3	60.3
Medical payments	604	1 391	130.3	101.2
Income maintenance	115	196	71.4	58.0
Supplemental Security Income	26	55	113.1	75.4
Family assistance	36	38	4.9	-0.5
Food Stamps	23	34	43.4	27.1
Other income maintenance	29	70	140.7	189.8
Unemployment insurance benefits	64	34	-46.9	10.6
Veterans benefits and other	113	165	46.0	30.8

*Percent change, 1990–1997

Government Payments to Individuals: 1997

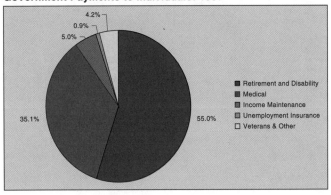

- 4.2%
- 0.9%
- 5.0%
- 35.1%
- 55.0%

■ Retirement and Disability
■ Medical
■ Income Maintenance
▨ Unemployment Insurance
□ Veterans & Other

ECONOMIC STRUCTURE

LEADING PRIVATE INDUSTRIES, 1997 (Worker and proprietor earnings, millions of dollars)		FASTEST EARNINGS GROWTH, 1989–97 (percent increase)	
Health services	$1 920	Electric, gas and sanitary services	133.9
Business services	1 301	Electronic equipment manufacturing	109.7
Industrial machinery manufacturing	989	Real estate	96.1
Electronic and other electric equipment	907	Social services	86.5
Construction specialties	847	Business services	79.4

TOTAL EMPLOYMENT IN NEW HAMPSHIRE GREW AT A MODER-ate annual rate between 1989 and 1997, with declines in 1990 and 1991. The fastest growing sectors were agricultural services, forestry, fishery, and other; services; and wholesale trade. The mining sector suffered losses in employment over the eight-year span, as did manufacturing and construction, despite recoveries in the latter two industries that started in 1992. Total earnings in mining grew 4.4 percent per year. Construction was the only private nonfarm sector to experience a decline in earnings,

falling on average 1.1 percent per year. Services and manufacturing were the sectors with the highest earnings in 1997, but services earnings had increased far faster than manufacturing earnings. Health services ranked as the highest earning industry in the state, followed by business services, both of which are typical for states in the region. Unlike other states in the region, two manufacturing industries, industrial machinery and equipment and electronic and other electrical equipment, placed in the top five industries.

Employment and Earnings by Sector

	1980	1989	1990	1991	1992	1993	1994	1995	1996	1997 Number	1997 Percent of total	Change*
Employment *(thousands of persons)*												
Total	483	666	648	622	635	648	673	696	716	736	100.0	1.3
Farm	6	5	5	4	4	4	4	4	4	4	0.5	-3.0
Nonfarm	477	661	643	618	630	644	669	692	712	732	99.5	1.3
Private nonfarm	409	583	564	541	554	568	592	614	633	652	88.6	1.4
Agricultural service, forestry, and fishing	3	6	6	6	6	7	7	7	8	8	1.1	5.0
Mining	1	1	1	1	1	1	1	1	1	1	0.1	-3.0
Construction	28	50	42	36	37	37	39	42	43	44	6.0	-1.7
Manufacturing	122	118	110	104	103	103	107	109	111	114	15.5	-0.5
Transportation and public utilities	17	22	22	21	22	23	24	24	25	26	3.5	1.9
Wholesale trade	20	26	25	25	26	27	27	29	30	32	4.4	2.6
Retail trade	83	131	126	118	123	127	133	138	140	144	19.6	1.2
Finance, insurance, and real estate	32	51	50	48	46	46	47	48	49	51	6.9	-0.1
Services	104	177	182	183	191	198	207	216	226	232	31.5	3.4
Government	68	78	79	77	76	76	77	78	80	80	10.9	0.3
Earnings *(millions of dollars)*												
Total	6 059	15 033	14 921	14 770	15 793	16 484	17 483	18 666	19 727	21 239	100.0	4.4
Farm	14	48	42	42	56	54	46	48	50	44	0.2	-1.2
Nonfarm	6 044	14 984	14 879	14 728	15 737	16 430	17 437	18 618	19 677	21 195	99.8	4.4
Private nonfarm	5 245	13 249	13 016	12 826	13 750	14 381	15 291	16 419	17 392	18 810	88.6	4.5
Agricultural service, forestry, and fishing	19	79	84	84	89	93	96	102	105	115	0.5	4.8
Mining	34	18	14	14	15	16	18	19	20	20	0.1	1.3
Construction	446	1 352	1 036	860	881	964	1 076	1 159	1 237	1 237	5.8	-1.1
Manufacturing	1 989	3 703	3 676	3 576	3 838	3 850	4 109	4 244	4 505	4 895	23.0	3.6
Transportation and public utilities	323	726	776	799	862	945	1 064	1 132	1 193	1 261	5.9	7.1
Wholesale trade	336	861	851	841	928	992	1 067	1 281	1 319	1 496	7.0	7.1
Retail trade	698	1 862	1 791	1 712	1 836	1 968	2 117	2 220	2 296	2 474	11.6	3.6
Finance, insurance, and real estate	298	953	958	994	1 077	1 113	1 133	1 223	1 287	1 447	6.8	5.4
Services	1 101	3 695	3 829	3 946	4 224	4 442	4 700	5 123	5 507	5 866	27.6	5.9
Government	799	1 735	1 864	1 902	1 987	2 049	2 146	2 199	2 285	2 385	11.2	4.1

*Compound annual average percent change, 1989–1997

ECONOMIC STRUCTURE (Continued)

NEW HAMPSHIRE'S AVERAGE WAGES IN 1997 WERE SLIGHTLY lower than average wages in the United States and moderately lower than the regional average for New England. Mining wages in New Hampshire were substantially lower than the national average, but mining earnings represented slightly more than one-tenth of one percent of total private earnings in the state. Finance, insurance, and real estate average wages were 13.7 percent below U.S. average wages and 28.4 percent below the regional average. Wholesale trade remained the sector with the highest average wages, a position it held from 1989 through 1997. The overall growth of average wages in New Hampshire was 3.9 percent per year, slightly higher than the U.S. rate.

Manufacturing, as a percentage of gross state product (GSP), remained high in New Hampshire. With manufacturing at 22.2 percent of GSP in 1997, the state's manufacturing to GSP ratio was almost five percentage points higher than in the nation. The ratio of manufacturing to GSP decreased from 1989 to 1996, but did not as much as that of U.S. manufacturing. New Hampshire factories are not among the nation's most productive; the value of manufacturing output per worker was 31 percent below the U.S. average.

Total exports rose steadily in New Hampshire from 1994 to 1997, increasing by 55 percent over the period. Of the top five exported goods, four were manufactured durable goods. Leather, the sole nondurable good in the top five, was the fastest growing, increasing by 30.7 percent per year between 1994 and 1997—an unusual strong performance for an industry that is in decline throughout most of the nation.

Average Annual Wages and Salaries by Sector
(dollars)

	1989	1996	1997 State	1997 U.S.
All wage and salary workers	21 149	27 168	28 725	29 809
Farm	10 470	16 465	17 345	16 442
Nonfarm	21 181	27 196	28 753	29 900
Private nonfarm	21 337	27 419	29 071	29 867
Agricultural service, forestry, and fishing	15 812	18 888	19 797	17 941
Mining	27 602	33 330	34 094	49 800
Construction	24 647	30 080	32 504	31 765
Manufacturing	27 594	36 367	38 812	38 351
Transportation and utilities	27 475	34 581	35 764	38 222
Wholesale trade	30 148	42 405	44 595	39 466
Retail trade	12 909	15 816	16 737	16 206
Finance, insurance, and real estate	25 281	35 463	38 817	44 993
Services	19 238	25 297	26 420	27 588
Government	20 236	25 814	26 737	30 062

Gross State Product and Manufacturing
(millions of dollars, except as noted)

	1989	1994	1995	1996
Gross state product, total	23 989	29 288	31 802	34 108
Manufacturing:				
Millions of dollars	5 430	5 998	6 887	7 557
Percent of total gross state product	22.6	20.5	21.7	22.2
Per worker (dollars)	45 846	56 052	63 415	68 118
New capital expenditures, manufacturing	NA	400	442	529

Exports of Goods
(millions of dollars)

	1994	1995	1996	1997
All goods	1 248	1 479	1 745	1 931
Manufactures	1 198	1 420	1 674	1 859
Agricultural and livestock products	17	20	21	23
Other commodities	33	39	49	49
Top goods exports, 1997:				
Industrial machinery and computers	424	493	550	583
Electric and electronic equipment	161	232	265	333
Leather products	64	70	145	144
Transportation equipment	71	110	156	142
Scientific and measuring instruments	94	100	132	118

HOUSING

HOUSING ACTIVITY IN NEW HAMPSHIRE EXCEEDED THE U.S. per capita rate in 1989, but it fell sharply in 1990 and has recovered only modestly since. The rate of new housing production (building permits plus manufactured housing put in place) per 1,000 people was lower than the U.S. rate for the rest of the period. Existing home sales in New Hampshire fell in 1989 and 1990 but have since surpassed their earlier highs. Homeownership in New Hampshire generally exceeds the U.S. average rate and has been stable. In contrast, the rental vacancy rate fluctuated a great deal, reaching a high point in 1991 but falling below the U.S. average in 1995–97.

Homeownership Rates: 1989 and 1997

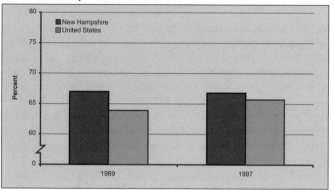

Housing Supply

	1989	1990	1991	1992	1993	1994	1995	1996	1997
Residential building permits (thousands)	7.3	4.1	3.5	4.0	4.2	4.7	4.4	4.9	5.4
New home production (including manufactured housing):									
Thousands of homes	8.4	4.9	3.8	4.3	4.5	5.3	5.0	5.6	6.3
Rate per 1,000 population									
New Hampshire	7.6	4.4	3.4	3.9	4.0	4.7	4.4	4.8	5.4
U.S.	6.2	5.2	4.5	5.1	5.6	6.4	6.3	6.6	6.5
Existing home sales:									
Thousands of homes	9.7	7.9	9.3	12.0	13.6	16.2	NA	NA	NA
Change from previous year (percent)									
New Hampshire	-29.7	-18.6	17.7	29.0	13.3	19.1	NA	NA	NA
U.S.	-3.9	-4.0	0.0	9.2	8.2	4.8	-3.7	7.5	3.8
Home ownership rate (percent of households)	67.0	65.0	66.8	66.6	65.4	65.1	66.0	65.0	66.8
Rental vacancy rate (percent of rental housing units)	7.7	9.7	11.0	9.5	6.7	7.7	5.4	5.6	6.2

AGRICULTURE

FARM RECEIPTS IN NEW HAMPSHIRE REMAINED MOSTLY FLAT from 1989 through 1995, showing a modest advance in 1996–97. Production expenses were high and rose faster than income, so net income was lower in 1997 despite higher receipts. Corporate farms had virtually no presence in the state. Total net farm proprietor's income reached its high point in 1992. The average size of New Hampshire farms was less than half the U.S. average, yet the value per farm was slightly higher than nationwide.

NEW HAMPSHIRE FARMS, 1997	
Number of farms	2 400
Total acres (thousands):	430
Average per farm	179
Value of land and buildings (millions of dollars)	1 118
Average per farm (dollars)	465 833

Farm Income
(millions of dollars)

	1980	1989	1990	1991	1992	1993	1994	1995	1996	1997
Gross income	112	178	162	161	173	174	173	180	189	188
Receipts from sales	96	137	138	138	150	151	151	159	170	167
Government payments	1	2	2	1	2	2	1	1	1	1
Imputed and miscellaneous income	15	39	22	21	21	21	20	20	18	20
(–) Production expenses	111	132	137	136	136	137	142	150	153	162
(=) Realized net income	1	46	25	25	37	37	31	30	36	27
(+) Inventory change	-3	-11	-1	-2	5	-3	1	-4	-5	-4
(=) Net income	-2	35	24	23	42	34	32	27	31	22
Corporate income	-1	6	4	3	7	2	8	5	8	5
Farm proprietors income	-1	29	20	20	35	31	23	22	23	17

EDUCATION

EDUCATIONAL ATTAINMENT Percent of population age 25 and over, 1997	State	United States
High school graduate or higher	85.1	82.1
College graduate or higher	27.0	23.9

NEW HAMPSHIRE RANKED 20TH IN THE NATION IN THE POPU-lation over age 25 holding high school diplomas, and ranked third in New England. Both per pupil spending and teacher salaries were slightly below the U.S. average. Private school enrollment accounted for 10.4 percent of total enrollment, which was just about the same proportion as in the United States (10.1 percent). New Hampshire ranked 12th in the percent of population age 25 and over holding bachelor's degrees, again ranking the state third in the region. In 1996, 22.8 percent of the population age 18 to 34 were enrolled in higher education, a percentage somewhat above the national level (21.8 percent). Like many New England states, New Hampshire had a small minority presence in higher education, but it was slightly higher than that of neighboring states Vermont and Maine.

High School Completion: 1990–97

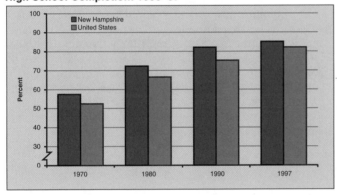

Education Indicators

	State	U.S.
Elementary and secondary schools		
Enrollment, 1995–96		
Total (thousands)	217	49 873
Percent in private schools	10.4	10.1
Expenditures per pupil (dollars), 1995–96	5 958	6 146
Average teacher salary (dollars), 1996–97	36 867	38 509
Higher education		
Enrollment, 1996–97		
Total (thousands)	64	14 218
Percent of population 18–34	22.8	21.8
Percent minority	5.0	26.1
Percent in private schools	43.6	22.6

HEALTH

NEW HAMPSHIRE HAD LOWER THAN AVERAGE AGE-ADJUSTED death rates throughout the 1990s, dropping slightly from 1990 to 1997. Infant mortality was also very low when compared to the U.S. rate, and the 1997 rate was the sixth lowest in the nation. The percentage of people in New Hampshire without health insurance was relatively low, 11.8 percent compared with a national average of 16.1 per-cent. The rates for the following causes of death were higher in New Hampshire than in the country, both in the raw data and on an age-adjusted basis: malignant neo-plasms (cancer), diabetes, Alzheimer's disease, chronic obstructive pulmonary disease (including emphysema), and suicide. Cancer had the highest death rate of all caus-es in the state in 1996.

Health Indicators

	1990	1995	1996	1997
Infant mortality				
(rate per thousand live births)				
New Hampshire	7.1	5.5	5.7	4.4
U.S.	9.2	7.6	7.3	7.1
Total deaths, age-adjusted rate				
(rate per thousand population)				
New Hampshire	4.7	4.6	4.5	4.4
U.S.	5.2	5.0	4.9	4.8
Persons not covered by health insurance				
(percent of population)				
New Hampshire	9.9	10.0	9.5	11.8
U.S.	13.9	15.4	15.6	16.1

Leading Causes of Death, 1996
(deaths per 100,000 population)

	Age-adjusted		Not age-adjusted	
	State	U.S.	State	U.S.
Deaths from all causes	449.4	491.6	808.2	872.5
Heart disease	122.3	134.5	251.0	276.4
Cancer	136.1	127.9	205.3	203.4
Cerebrovascular diseases	24.5	26.4	59.0	60.3
Chronic obstructive pulmonary disease	21.8	21.0	42.4	40.0
Diabetes mellitus	14.8	13.6	24.6	23.3
Pneumonia and influenza	6.4	12.8	17.5	31.6
HIV	3.1	11.1	3.6	11.7
Liver disease	7.2	7.5	9.2	9.4
Alzheimer's disease	4.1	2.7	11.6	8.1
Accidents and adverse effects	20.0	30.4	24.5	35.8
Motor vehicle accidents	11.5	16.2	11.5	16.5
Suicide	11.1	10.8	11.8	11.6
Homicide	1.8	8.5	1.9	7.9
Injury by firearm	8.0	12.9	8.3	12.8

GOVERNMENT

STATE AND LOCAL TAXES, 1995–96	State	U.S.
Per capita (dollars)	2 099	2 477
Percent of personal income	8.3	10.8

NEW HAMPSHIRE HAD THE LOWEST RATE OF STATE AND LOCAL taxation, relative to personal income, in the nation—its taxes, other than corporate, were 8.3 percent of personal income in 1995–96. Only one other state (Tennessee) had a rate less than 9 percent. Furthermore, 73 percent of New Hampshire's taxes are levied at the local level—by far the highest percentage of any state; only two other states levy more than 50 percent. At the state level, very low individ-

ual taxation rates and no sales tax kept the overall rate low, although selective sales taxes and corporation net income taxes are higher than the national per capita rate. Likewise expenditure at the state level was lower in New Hampshire, with total expenditure 84.7 percent of the national average. State education spending per capita was half that in the typical state. State per capita spending exceeded the average modestly in public welfare, highways, and government administration, and state spending on interest and debt were triple the national average. In all other categories, New Hampshire spent less than the average state.

New Hampshire received $5.1 billion dollars in federal funds in 1997. This amount was 0.4 percent of all federal funds distributed to the nation, about the same as New Hampshire's share of the total population. Retirement programs were the largest category, and the only category where the New Hampshire share exceeded (by a small amount) its population share; in all other categories of federal disbursements, New Hampshire received less than its population share.

State Government Finances, 1996–97

	Millions of dollars	Percent distribu-tion	Dollars per capita State	Dollars per capita U.S.
General revenue	2 796	100.0	2 383	3 049
Intergovernmental revenue	988	35.3	842	863
Taxes	915	32.7	780	1 660
General sales	0	0.0	0	551
Selective sales	459	16.4	391	257
License taxes	121	4.3	103	106
Individual income	53	1.9	45	542
Corporation net income	208	7.5	178	115
Other taxes	74	2.7	63	90
Other general revenue	893	31.9	761	526
General expenditure	2 891	100.0	2 465	2 951
Intergovernmental expenditure	414	14.3	353	989
Direct expenditure	2 478	85.7	2 112	1 962
General expenditure, by function:				
Education	624	21.6	532	1 033
Public welfare	905	31.3	771	761
Hospitals and health	180	6.2	153	237
Highways	306	10.6	261	225
Police protection and corrections	89	3.1	76	137
Natural resources, parks and recreation	42	1.4	36	63
Governmental administration	151	5.2	129	107
Interest on general debt	380	13.1	324	99
Other and unallocable	215	7.4	184	290
Debt at end of fiscal year	5 848	NA	4 986	1 706
Cash and security holdings	9 090	NA	7 749	6 683

Federal Spending within State

	Federal funds, fiscal 1997 Millions of dollars	Federal funds, fiscal 1997 Percent distribution	Federal funds, fiscal 1997 Percent of U.S. total*
Total within state	5 057	100.0	0.4
Payments to individuals	3 074	60.8	0.4
Retirement and disability	2 069	40.9	0.5
Medicare	686	13.6	0.3
Food stamps	35	0.7	0.2
Supplemental Security Income	46	0.9	0.2
Grants	949	18.8	0.4
Medicaid and other health	441	8.7	0.4
Nutrition and family welfare	145	2.9	0.3
Education	60	1.2	0.4
Housing and community development	30	0.6	0.3
Salaries and wages	480	9.5	0.3
Defense procurement contracts	388	7.7	0.3
Non-defense procurement contracts	99	2.0	0.1

*State population is 0.4 percent of the U.S. total.

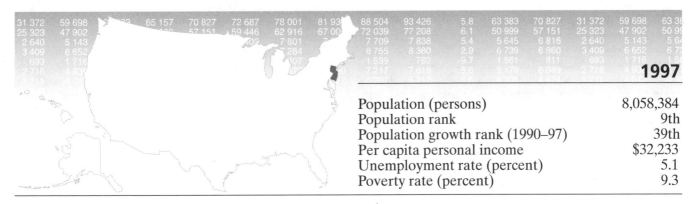

31 372	59 698		65 157	70 827	72 687	78 001	81 93	88 504	93 426	5.8	63 383	70 827	31 372	59 698	63 3
25 323	47 902		57 151	59 446	62 916	67 00	72 039	77 208	6.1	50 999	57 151	25 323	47 902	50 9
2 640	5 143			7 801			7 709	7 838	5.4	5 645	6 816	2 640	5 143	5 6
3 409	6 652			7 284			8 755	8 360	2.9	6 739	6 860	3 409	6 652	6 7
693	1 716						1 539	762	-9.7	1 561	811	693	1 716	1
2 716	4 93						7 217	7 618	5.6	5 178	6 049	2 716		

1997

Population (persons)	8,058,384
Population rank	9th
Population growth rank (1990–97)	39th
Per capita personal income	$32,233
Unemployment rate (percent)	5.1
Poverty rate (percent)	9.3

WITH ITS PROXIMITY TO NEW YORK CITY AND PHILADELPHIA, New Jersey's economy is more dependent on services than other states in the region or than in the nation as a whole. The importance of manufacturing to the state has been diminishing, while strong increases in employment in services have offset job losses in manufacturing and brought unemployment down from a 1992 high point to near the U.S. level. Median household income was far higher than in the country at large but fell by almost 1 percent per year (when adjusted for inflation) from 1990 to 1997.

New Jersey's population increased from 1990 to 1997, though more slowly than the U.S. rate. While the natural rate of increase and international immigration both contributed to growth, a relatively large level of net domestic out-migration hampered it. The fastest growing transfer payment component was medical payments, and with an older than average population, this component will probably continue to grow. Per capita state and local taxation remains high, though it represents only a slightly larger share of state personal income than in the rest of the country.

Average Annual Population Growth: 1990—97

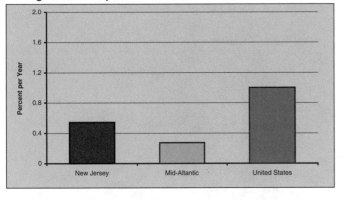

Median Household Income: 1989—97 (1997 dollars)

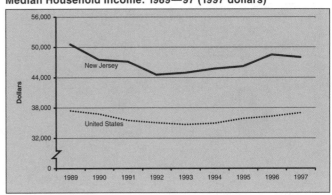

Unemployment Rate: 1989—97

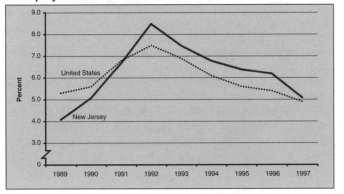

THE UNEMPLOYMENT RATE IN NEW JERSEY WAS LOWER THAN the U.S. average in 1989–90, but rose to a higher peak (8.5 percent) in 1992 and remained well above the national average until 1997. Employment decreased each year from 1991 to 1993, which was the driving force behind increasing unemployment despite a fall in the labor force in the same years. Since then employment growth has resumed, bringing the unemployment rate back down to its 1990 level.

POPULATION AND LABOR FORCE

NEW JERSEY'S POPULATION GREW MORE SLOWLY THAN THE population of the United States during the period 1990–97, and the state's White non-Hispanic population actually declined by 0.3 percent per year in the same period. Growth levels in the Black and Hispanic populations almost reached U.S. levels, but the Asian population growth rate was considerably higher in New Jersey. Natural increase and international immigration contributed about equally to population growth in the state. The increase in population from international immigra-

tion was completely offset, however, by the large domestic out-migration from New Jersey to other states. The entire state of New Jersey is composed of metropolitan counties.

The population over age 16 grew less than the total from 1990 to 1997, as did the labor force. With employment and labor force both increasing 0.4 percent per year from 1990 to 1997, the unemployment rate was the same in 1990 and 1997, though there were raised unemployment levels in the early 1990s.

Population and Labor Force

	1980	1990	1991	1992	1993	1994	1995	1996	1997	Change* State	Change* U.S.
Population											
Total number of persons (thousands)	7 365	7 758	7 784	7 826	7 873	7 916	7 962	8 008	8 058	0.5	1.0
Percent distribution:											
White, Non-Hispanic	79.3	74.1	73.3	72.7	72.1	71.5	70.9	70.3	69.7	-0.3	0.4
Black, Non-Hispanic	12.3	12.7	12.9	13.0	13.1	13.1	13.1	13.2	13.2	1.0	1.4
Asian	1.5	3.6	3.8	4.1	4.3	4.5	4.7	5.0	5.3	6.1	4.1
Native American	0.1	0.2	0.2	0.2	0.2	0.2	0.3	0.3	0.3	3.8	1.6
Hispanic	6.7	9.6	9.9	10.3	10.6	10.9	11.2	11.6	11.9	3.7	3.8
In metropolitan areas	100.0	100.0	100.0	100.0	100.0	100.0	100.0	100.0	100.0	0.5	1.0
Total number of households (thousands)	2 549	2 795	2 813	2 838	2 839	2 841	2 866	2 889	NA	0.6	1.2
Labor Force (thousands)											
Population 16 and over	5 652	6 138	6 135	6 141	6 154	6 167	6 192	6 230	6 273	0.3	1.0
Civilian labor force	3 594	4 067	4 041	4 031	3 989	4 016	4 064	4 135	4 198	0.5	1.1
Employed	3 334	3 861	3 770	3 690	3 691	3 743	3 804	3 878	3 982	0.4	1.2
Percent of population	59.0	62.9	61.5	60.1	60.0	60.7	61.4	62.2	63.5		
Unemployment rate (percent)	7.2	5.1	6.7	8.5	7.5	6.8	6.4	6.2	5.1		

*Compound annual average percent change, 1990–1997; 1990–1996 for households.

Population Change and Components: 1990–97

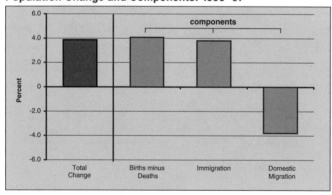

Average Annual Household and Population Growth

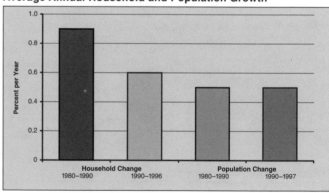

Population by Age; Births and Deaths

	1990 State	1990 U.S.	1997 State	1997 U.S.
Age distribution (percent)				
Under 5 years	7.1	7.6	6.9	7.2
5 to 17 years	16.3	18.2	17.8	18.8
18 to 64 years	63.3	61.8	61.6	61.3
65 years and over	13.3	12.5	13.7	12.7
Birth and death rates (per thousand population)				
Births	15.8	16.7	14.0	14.6
Deaths	9.1	8.6	8.9	8.6

NEW JERSEY'S POPULATION WAS, ON AVERAGE, OLDER THAN that of the United States. The smaller pre-school and school-age groups may persist because the state has a lower than U.S. average birth rate of 14 births for every 1,000 persons (1997). The state's share of working-age population share is slightly higher than that of the U.S., and its share of population over age 65 is significantly higher than nationwide, which is typical of other states in the region.

HOUSEHOLD AND PERSONAL INCOME

HOUSEHOLD INCOME AND PERSONS IN POVERTY	1990	1995	1996	1997	
				State	U.S.
Median household income (1997 dollars)	47 565	46 259	48 557	48 021	37 005
Persons in poverty (thousands)	711	617	726	737	35 574
Poverty rate (percent)	9.2	7.8	9.2	9.3	13.3

MEDIAN HOUSEHOLD INCOME IN NEW JERSEY FELL SLIGHTLY from 1989 to 1997, at a rate of 0.7 percent per year, when adjusted for inflation, but was still far higher than median household income in the country at large. Income began to fall in 1990, declining by 11.9 percent by 1992. The subsequent rise from 1992 to 1996 was not enough to return income in the state to its 1989 level, and it fell again in 1997. The poverty rate in New Jersey was well below the national average and was also considerably lower than neighboring New York state (which had a poverty rate of 16.5 percent in 1997, 7.2 percentage points higher than New Jersey).

Aggregate personal income rose in New Jersey from 1989 to 1997, but at a slower rate than in the United States as a whole (which rose 5.3 percent per year), as did wages and salaries and proprietors' income. The adjustment by place of residence was positive, indicating net payments from out of state to New Jersey, and increased by more than 5 percent per year. Per capita personal income rose by almost 4 percent, slightly below the U.S. average.

Transfer payments rose quickly in New Jersey, though not as quickly as in the country at large. The fastest growing component from 1990 to 1997 was other income maintenance (which includes the earned income tax credit), followed closely by medical payments. Medical payments and old age, survivors, and disability insurance (Social Security) were the largest programs, representing about 73 percent of government payments to individuals. Family aid was the only program to decline in the seven-year period.

Personal Income
(millions of dollars)

	1980	1989	1990	1991	1992	1993	1994	1995	1996	1997	Change*
Earnings by place of work	58 047	122 816	128 786	130 235	138 824	144 366	149 965	156 190	162 702	171 767	4.3
Wages and salaries	47 903	101 054	105 799	106 700	112 861	116 657	121 158	126 555	132 779	141 175	4.3
Other labor income	5 073	10 282	10 993	11 625	12 692	13 762	14 371	14 159	13 766	13 825	3.8
Proprietors' income	5 071	11 479	11 994	11 910	13 271	13 946	14 436	15 476	16 157	16 767	4.8
Farm	51	157	115	105	104	134	129	113	120	62	-11.1
Nonfarm	5 019	11 322	11 880	11 805	13 167	13 813	14 308	15 363	16 036	16 705	5.0
(−) Personal contributions for social insurance	3 156	8 383	8 805	9 178	9 669	9 866	10 455	10 961	11 407	11 977	4.6
(+) Adjustment for residence	6 606	10 114	10 511	10 393	11 746	11 698	11 586	12 435	14 022	15 104	NA
(=) Net earnings by state of residence	61 497	124 547	130 493	131 450	140 901	146 197	151 097	157 663	165 317	174 894	4.3
(+) Dividends, interest, and rent	14 581	38 959	40 518	40 738	39 881	40 228	42 559	45 070	48 110	49 708	3.1
(+) Transfer payments	10 794	19 999	22 024	24 965	28 561	29 757	30 634	32 604	33 840	34 965	7.2
(=) Total personal income	86 872	183 505	193 035	197 153	209 344	216 183	224 290	235 337	247 267	259 567	4.4
Farm	124	251	226	217	215	250	246	247	261	203	-2.6
Nonfarm	86 747	183 254	192 809	196 936	209 129	215 932	224 043	235 090	247 006	259 363	4.4
Personal income per capita (dollars)											
Current dollars	11 777	23 751	24 885	25 334	26 758	27 474	28 351	29 581	30 901	32 233	3.9
1997 dollars	22 518	30 027	29 946	29 254	29 931	29 896	30 129	30 749	31 467	32 233	0.9

*Compound annual average percent change, 1989–1997

Government Transfer Payments

	Millions of dollars		Percent change*	
	1990	1997	State	U.S.
Total government payments to individuals	20 798	33 458	60.9	62.7
Retirement, disability, and insurance	11 498	16 903	47.0	48.2
Social Security	8 393	12 072	43.8	46.1
Government employee retirement	2 511	4 108	63.6	60.3
Medical payments	6 229	12 440	99.7	101.2
Income maintenance	1 472	2 239	52.1	58.0
Supplemental Security Income	347	640	84.5	75.4
Family assistance	478	378	-20.9	-0.5
Food Stamps	308	431	40.1	27.1
Other income maintenance	339	790	132.8	189.8
Unemployment insurance benefits	1 035	1 154	11.5	10.6
Veterans benefits and other	564	722	27.9	30.8

*Percent change, 1990–1997

Government Payments to Individuals: 1997

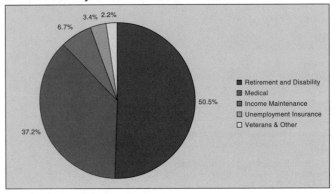

- Retirement and Disability
- Medical
- Income Maintenance
- Unemployment Insurance
- Veterans & Other

ECONOMIC STRUCTURE

LEADING PRIVATE INDUSTRIES, 1997 (Worker and proprietor earnings, millions of dollars)		FASTEST EARNINGS GROWTH, 1989–97 (percent increase)	
Health services	$14 877	Securities brokers	209.5
Business services	13 255	Air transportation	205.0
Engineering and management services	8 716	Communications	100.6
Chemicals and allied products	8 159	Other transportation	89.9
Communications	6 081	Business services	87.1

TOTAL EMPLOYMENT IN NEW JERSEY ROSE MODESTLY FROM 1989 to 1997, adding 107,000 jobs at a rate of 0.3 percent per year. Agricultural services, forestry, and fisheries grew faster than any other private nonfarm sector, but did so from a very small base. Services employment added 245,000 jobs, offsetting losses elsewhere and accounting for all the net job growth. Construction and manufacturing declined 1.8 percent and 3.4 percent per year, respectively. Total earnings rose 4.3 percent per year, with losses only for construction and the tiny farm sector. Finance, insurance, and real estate had small employment gains but large increases in earnings. Services had the largest percentage of total earnings by far (30.1 percent), followed by government (14 percent). Manufacturing, which in 1980 had 28.6 percent of total earnings, had only 15.6 percent in 1997. Three of the top five industries in New Jersey were services (health, business, and engineering and management), making the state more dependent on services than many of the other states in the region. Chemicals and allied products, the only manufacturing industry in the top five, and communications rounded out the list. The top five fastest growing industries included two in the transportation sector and also highlighted the importance of the financial and business services in the state.

Employment and Earnings by Sector

	1980	1989	1990	1991	1992	1993	1994	1995	1996	1997 Number	1997 Percent of total	Change*
Employment *(thousands of persons)*												
Total	3 608	4 391	4 338	4 209	4 208	4 238	4 279	4 344	4 399	4 498	100.0	0.3
Farm	20	16	16	16	16	15	15	16	16	17	0.4	0.5
Nonfarm	3 588	4 375	4 322	4 193	4 191	4 223	4 264	4 328	4 383	4 481	99.6	0.3
Private nonfarm	3 023	3 785	3 723	3 603	3 605	3 636	3 677	3 743	3 802	3 897	86.6	0.4
Agricultural service, forestry, and fishing	20	29	29	28	29	31	32	34	35	37	0.8	2.9
Mining	5	5	5	4	4	4	4	3	3	3	0.1	-5.0
Construction	144	226	204	175	172	176	180	184	187	195	4.3	-1.8
Manufacturing	799	654	602	569	540	529	521	511	495	495	11.0	-3.4
Transportation and public utilities	214	254	256	253	253	263	271	274	280	286	6.3	1.5
Wholesale trade	235	297	290	278	279	276	278	281	285	289	6.4	-0.3
Retail trade	549	671	656	637	638	639	649	666	672	685	15.2	0.3
Finance, insurance, and real estate	250	421	412	391	385	386	403	410	421	434	9.7	0.4
Services	806	1 228	1 269	1 269	1 304	1 332	1 337	1 380	1 424	1 473	32.8	2.3
Government	565	590	599	589	586	587	586	585	581	584	13.0	-0.1
Earnings *(millions of dollars)*												
Total	58 047	122 816	128 786	130 235	138 824	144 366	149 965	156 190	162 702	171 767	100.0	4.3
Farm	124	251	226	217	215	250	246	247	261	203	0.1	-2.6
Nonfarm	57 923	122 565	128 560	130 018	138 609	144 115	149 719	155 943	162 441	171 563	99.9	4.3
Private nonfarm	49 579	105 995	110 507	110 885	118 294	122 748	127 409	133 043	139 081	147 434	85.8	4.2
Agricultural service, forestry, and fishing	167	505	532	525	549	594	645	668	702	740	0.4	4.9
Mining	304	181	191	164	189	215	247	211	201	234	0.1	3.3
Construction	2 909	7 976	7 280	6 248	6 143	6 484	6 887	7 018	7 279	7 774	4.5	-0.3
Manufacturing	16 581	24 193	23 968	23 939	24 734	24 842	25 373	25 577	25 612	26 798	15.6	1.3
Transportation and public utilities	5 068	9 430	9 941	10 508	11 106	12 188	13 152	13 704	14 395	15 050	8.8	6.0
Wholesale trade	4 679	10 954	11 417	11 265	12 307	12 450	13 050	13 473	14 149	15 150	8.8	4.1
Retail trade	5 432	11 208	11 342	11 213	11 550	11 907	12 396	12 739	13 108	13 669	8.0	2.5
Finance, insurance, and real estate	3 055	8 826	9 355	9 531	11 035	12 119	11 999	12 868	14 239	15 275	8.9	7.1
Services	11 385	32 723	36 480	37 492	40 681	41 949	43 660	46 784	49 396	52 743	30.7	6.1
Government	8 344	16 569	18 053	19 133	20 315	21 367	22 310	22 900	23 360	24 129	14.0	4.8

*Compound annual average percent change, 1989–1997

ECONOMIC STRUCTURE (Continued)

AVERAGE WAGES IN NEW JERSEY WERE SIGNIFICANTLY HIGHer than wages in the United States as a whole and moderately higher than wages in the mid-Atlantic region. Finance, insurance and real estate wages in New Jersey were higher than in the country on average (but were lower than such incomes in the region, which includes New York) and grew 7.0 percent per year from 1989 to 1997, almost twice the growth rate for average wages in the state. Almost all private nonfarm sectors had wages higher than regional and national levels. Average wages in the state grew 4.2 percent per year in the nine-year period, slightly faster than the U.S. wage growth rate.

Manufacturing in New Jersey, expressed as a percentage of gross state product, fell from 17.6 percent in 1989 to 13.7 percent in 1996. Exactly the same as the 1996 mid-Atlantic ratio, it was far below the ratio of neighboring state Pennsylvania and highlights the large and growing importance of the service industries in the state. Manufacturing production leaned heavily toward non-durable goods manufacturing, which was 64.1 percent of all manufacturing output in 1996. The value of manufacturing output per worker was below the U.S. average.

Goods exports from New Jersey increased 24.2 percent from 1994 to 1997. Chemical products, the top exported goods group, increased exports by 55.0 percent in the same time period. Of the top five exported goods groups, all increased the amount exported by at least 10 percent.

Average Annual Wages and Salaries by Sector
(dollars)

	1989	1996	1997 State	1997 U.S.
All wage and salary workers	26 400	35 304	36 750	29 809
Farm	10 884	18 679	16 321	16 442
Nonfarm	26 433	35 335	36 793	29 900
Private nonfarm	26 491	34 985	36 516	29 867
Agricultural service, forestry, and fishing	18 222	22 225	22 946	17 941
Mining	36 677	45 465	49 296	49 800
Construction	32 294	38 507	39 976	31 765
Manufacturing	32 042	44 097	46 462	38 351
Transportation and utilities	32 267	43 315	44 731	38 222
Wholesale trade	33 640	45 377	48 007	39 466
Retail trade	15 472	18 698	19 228	16 206
Finance, insurance, and real estate	31 301	50 481	53 684	44 993
Services	24 206	32 153	33 433	27 588
Government	26 112	37 247	38 333	30 062

Gross State Product and Manufacturing
(millions of dollars, except as noted)

	1989	1994	1995	1996
Gross state product, total	206 121	255 777	266 134	276 377
Manufacturing:				
Millions of dollars	36 287	37 485	37 919	37 985
Percent of total gross state product	17.6	14.7	14.2	13.7
Per worker (dollars)	55 477	71 904	74 259	76 705
New capital expenditures, manufacturing	NA	2 596	2 639	2 570

Exports of Goods
(millions of dollars)

	1994	1995	1996	1997
All goods	16 761	18 369	18 458	20 815
Manufactures	15 646	17 119	17 283	19 689
Agricultural and livestock products	269	308	395	344
Other commodities	845	941	780	783
Top goods exports, 1997:				
Chemical products	3 975	4 643	4 859	6 161
Electric and electronic equipment	2 693	2 679	2 623	2 992
Industrial machinery and computers	1 901	2 002	1 824	2 101
Transportation equipment	1 260	1 312	1 510	1 551
Scientific and measuring instruments	1 229	1 249	1 349	1 463

HOUSING

THE LEVEL OF NEW HOUSING SUPPLY IN NEW JERSEY WAS strong in 1989 but fell in 1990 and remained weak until 1993. Construction building in the state, rather than mobile home placement, provided the majority of new housing in the state, which is typical for the region. The rate of new housing units per 1,000 residents was far below the U.S. average. Existing home sales also faltered in 1990 but then started growing in 1992 and by 1996–97 were far above their previous highs. Homeownership rates hovered around 65 percent for most of the decade but then dropped 1.8 percentage points in 1996 and 1997, falling below the U.S. average. The rental vacancy rate fluctuated throughout the period from 1989 to 1997, remaining below the U.S. average, and fell to a low point in 1997.

Homeownership Rates: 1989 and 1997

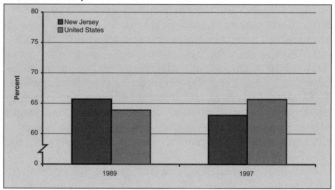

Housing Supply

	1989	1990	1991	1992	1993	1994	1995	1996	1997
Residential building permits (thousands)	30.3	17.5	14.9	19.1	25.2	25.4	21.5	24.2	28.0
New home production (including manufactured housing):									
Thousands of homes	30.9	18.0	14.9	19.4	25.4	25.8	21.9	24.2	28.3
Rate per 1,000 population									
New Jersey	4.0	2.3	1.9	2.5	3.2	3.3	2.8	3.0	3.5
U.S.	6.2	5.2	4.5	5.1	5.6	6.4	6.3	6.6	6.5
Existing home sales:									
Thousands of homes	126.6	114.8	118.8	132.1	139.0	145.4	138.3	147.8	157.3
Change from previous year (percent)									
New Jersey	-5.2	-9.3	3.5	11.2	5.2	4.6	-4.9	6.9	6.4
U.S.	-3.9	-4.0	0.0	9.2	8.2	4.8	-3.7	7.5	3.8
Home ownership rate (percent of households)	65.7	65.0	64.8	64.6	64.5	64.1	64.9	64.6	63.1
Rental vacancy rate (percent of rental housing units)	4.6	5.9	7.7	6.9	8.2	7.1	6.6	7.7	5.5

Note: Manufactured housing data for 1991 and 1996 suppressed because estimate was based on too few responses.

AGRICULTURE

BASED ON THREE-YEAR AVERAGES, FARM CASH RECEIPTS ROSE 18 percent between 1989–91 and 1995–97, while production expenses rose 25 percent, leading to some decline in realized net income. Corporate farms were not a significant presence in the state, but they did seem to become more important in 1994–96. Total net farm proprietors' incomes were at their highest in 1989 and did not again reach that level. The average farm size was the smallest in the region but average farm value was the highest, which could reflect both the high value of the state's fruit and vegetable crops and land values for alternative uses in this urbanized state.

NEW JERSEY FARMS, 1997	
Number of farms	9 400
Total acres (thousands):	830
Average per farm	88
Value of land and buildings (millions of dollars)	6 881
Average per farm (dollars)	732 021

Farm Income
(millions of dollars)

	1980	1989	1990	1991	1992	1993	1994	1995	1996	1997
Gross income	512	756	744	740	744	803	874	877	900	871
Receipts from sales	443	674	655	658	650	705	772	770	804	777
Government payments	1	21	16	4	11	7	8	5	3	4
Imputed and miscellaneous income	68	61	73	78	84	91	95	101	93	91
(−) Production expenses	456	562	607	618	620	644	693	731	735	785
(=) Realized net income	56	194	137	121	124	158	181	146	165	87
(+) Inventory change	-4	-2	4	2	6	-13	7	-4	8	-1
(=) Net income	51	193	141	123	130	145	188	142	173	85
Corporate income	0	36	27	18	26	11	59	29	52	24
Farm proprietors income	51	157	115	105	104	134	129	113	120	62

EDUCATION

EDUCATIONAL ATTAINMENT Percent of population age 25 and over, 1997	State	United States
High school graduate or higher	84.8	82.1
College graduate or higher	28.5	23.9

NEW JERSEY WAS RANKED 21ST IN THE PERCENT OF ITS POPU-lation age 25 and over holding a high school diploma, despite spending the most per pupil in the nation. Teacher salaries were also high, earning New Jersey a place in the top four highest paying states, along with Alaska, Connecticut, and New York. New Jersey ranked 6th in the percent of its population holding a bachelor's degree. Only 17.6 percent of the population between the ages of 18 and 34 were enrolled in higher education in 1996. Minorities made up 29.5 percent of those enrolled in higher educa-tion, slightly higher than the average for the United States (26.1 percent).

High School Completion: 1990–97

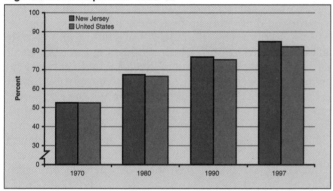

Education Indicators

	State	U.S.
Elementary and secondary schools		
Enrollment, 1995–96		
Total (thousands)	1 405	49 873
Percent in private schools	14.8	10.1
Expenditures per pupil (dollars), 1995–96	9 955	6 146
Average teacher salary (dollars), 1996–97	49 349	38 509
Higher education		
Enrollment, 1996–97		
Total (thousands)	328	14 218
Percent of population 18–34	17.6	21.8
Percent minority	29.5	26.1
Percent in private schools	19.4	22.6

HEALTH

NEW JERSEY HAD AN AGE-ADJUSTED TOTAL DEATH RATE about the same as the country's, after taking into account the state's older population. The infant mortality rate was a bit lower than the U.S. rate. The percentage of people without health insurance was lower in New Jersey at the beginning of the decade but passed the U.S. level in 1996. The main causes of death in New Jersey were cancer and heart dis-ease. Both of these rates were also above the national aver-age when unadjusted for changes in age composition over time. However, when adjusted for age, heart disease fell below the national rate. Two other causes with above-aver-age age-adjusted death rates were HIV and diabetes.

Health Indicators

	1990	1995	1996	1997
Infant mortality *(rate per thousand live births)*				
New Jersey	9.0	6.6	7.3	6.3
U.S.	9.2	7.6	7.3	7.1
Total deaths, age-adjusted rate *(rate per thousand population)*				
New Jersey	5.2	5.0	4.8	4.6
U.S.	5.2	5.0	4.9	4.8
Persons not covered by health insurance *(percent of population)*				
New Jersey	10.0	14.2	16.7	16.5
U.S.	13.9	15.4	15.6	16.1

Leading Causes of Death, 1996
(deaths per 100,000 population)

	Age-adjusted		Not age-adjusted	
	State	U.S.	State	U.S.
Deaths from all causes	482.2	491.6	916.4	872.5
Heart disease	131.0	134.5	298.8	276.4
Cancer	133.7	127.9	229.3	203.4
Cerebrovascular diseases	23.0	26.4	53.8	60.3
Chronic obstructive pulmonary disease	16.8	21.0	35.2	40.0
Diabetes mellitus	16.3	13.6	29.6	23.3
Pneumonia and influenza	12.1	12.8	30.5	31.6
HIV	20.0	11.1	22.0	11.7
Liver disease	7.4	7.5	9.9	9.4
Alzheimer's disease	2.4	2.7	7.5	8.1
Accidents and adverse effects	23.0	30.4	28.7	35.8
Motor vehicle accidents	9.8	16.2	10.4	16.5
Suicide	6.7	10.8	7.3	11.6
Homicide	5.5	8.5	4.9	7.9
Injury by firearm	5.4	12.9	4.9	12.8

GOVERNMENT

STATE AND LOCAL TAXES, 1995–96	State	U.S.
Per capita (dollars)	3 292	2 477
Percent of personal income	11.1	10.8

NEW JERSEY'S STATE AND LOCAL TAXES, OTHER THAN CORPOrate, took up only a little higher percentage of personal income than the national average (11.1 versus 10.8). Combined with the state's above-average incomes, this situation yielded a level of taxes per capita that was one-third higher than that of the average state. Local taxation was almost half of total local and state receipts; nationwide, it was only about 40 percent. State taxes were only slightly higher than the average state's, with lower sales and license taxes. Individual income and corporate taxes were higher per capita.

Direct expenditure in the state was also slightly higher than for the nation on a per capita calculation. State spending per capita on education, health, and public welfare was lower than in the country. Highway spending in the state was also lower than in the country at large. The state exceeded the national average rate of spending on police and corrections, natural parks and recreation, governmental administration, and interest. Debt at the end of the fiscal year was twice as high as the national level, but there was a correspondingly larger amount of cash and security holdings per capita in the state.

New Jersey received about 2.8 percent of all federally allocated funds in 1997, which was less than its 3.0 percent of the U.S. population. Social Security and other retirement and especially Medicare disbursements were higher as a percentage of funds allocated, though the retirement programs were the larger by far, with 35.4 percent of all funds disbursed to the state (Medicare had 17.6 percent). Salaries and wages were below New Jersey's population share, as were defense and non-defense procurement. Defense procurement was about 7.5 percent and non-defense procurement was 2.8 percent of federal funds spent in New Jersey.

State Government Finances, 1996–97

	Millions of dollars	Percent distribution	Dollars per capita State	Dollars per capita U.S.
General revenue	26 963	100.0	3 348	3 049
Intergovernmental revenue	6 363	23.6	790	863
Taxes	14 415	53.5	1 790	1 660
General sales	4 415	16.4	548	551
Selective sales	2 777	10.3	345	257
License taxes	742	2.8	92	106
Individual income	4 825	17.9	599	542
Corporation net income	1 264	4.7	157	115
Other taxes	391	1.4	49	90
Other general revenue	6 185	22.9	768	526
General expenditure	23 053	100.0	2 863	2 951
Intergovernmental expenditure	6 383	27.7	793	989
Direct expenditure	16 671	72.3	2 070	1 962
General expenditure, by function:				
Education	7 282	31.6	904	1 033
Public welfare	4 826	20.9	599	761
Hospitals and health	1 729	7.5	215	237
Highways	1 593	6.9	198	225
Police protection and corrections	1 239	5.4	154	137
Natural resources, parks and recreation	617	2.7	77	63
Governmental administration	965	4.2	120	107
Interest on general debt	1 377	6.0	171	99
Other and unallocable	3 427	14.9	426	290
Debt at end of fiscal year	26 591	NA	3 302	1 706
Cash and security holdings	63 138	NA	7 840	6 683

Federal Spending within State

	Federal funds, fiscal 1997 Millions of dollars	Federal funds, fiscal 1997 Percent distribution	Federal funds, fiscal 1997 Percent of U.S. total*
Total within state	39 862	100.0	2.8
Payments to individuals	25 071	62.9	3.2
Retirement and disability	14 094	35.4	3.1
Medicare	7 020	17.6	3.4
Food stamps	454	1.1	2.3
Supplemental Security Income	585	1.5	2.2
Grants	6 915	17.3	2.8
Medicaid and other health	3 217	8.1	2.8
Nutrition and family welfare	1 210	3.0	2.6
Education	441	1.1	2.6
Housing and community development	432	1.1	3.8
Salaries and wages	3 476	8.7	2.1
Defense procurement contracts	2 971	7.5	2.5
Non-defense procurement contracts	1 127	2.8	1.5

*State population is 3.0 percent of the U.S. total.

1997

Population (persons)	1,723,965
Population rank	36th
Population growth rank (1990–97)	10th
Per capita personal income	$19,249
Unemployment rate (percent)	6.2
Poverty rate (percent)	21.2

NEW MEXICO'S GROWTH OF BOTH POPULATION AND EMPLOYMENT exceeded national averages in the 1990s. The state's economy contains disparate elements, however: one a prospering cluster of high-technology research and industry, and the other a services economy offering relatively low wages. Throughout the decade, residents, on average, continued to have incomes well below national averages, with fairly high unemployment and a low proportion of adults at work. Hispanics and Native Americans, both groups whose members, on average, earn less than Whites, comprise 49 percent of the state's population.

The state markets itself as a center for emerging high-technology industries that can feed off the state's large scientific brain trust. Two giant federal research laboratories, Los Alamos and Sandia, both offer their technical know-how and procurement needs to foster start-up high-tech companies, creating jobs making things as diverse as nuclear isotopes used in medical diagnostics and precision mirrors used in U.S. weapons systems. Still, research and manufacturing supported a very small proportion of employment in the state,(although Intel located its largest computer chip factory here) so there is a narrow base of good-paying private sector jobs. Reliance on federal government (including military) jobs remained high, making the state vulnerable to cutbacks such as the layoffs at Los Alamos in the mid-1990s.

Average Annual Population Growth: 1990–97

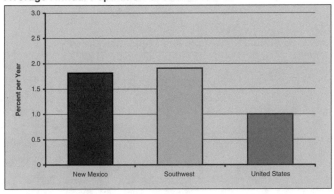

Median Household Income: 1989–97 (1997 dollars)

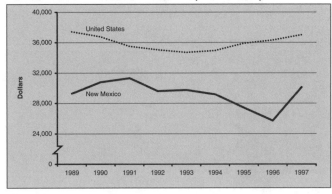

Unemployment Rate: 1989–97

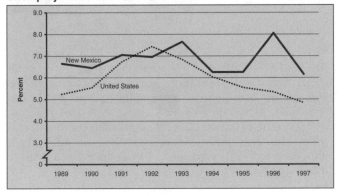

UNEMPLOYMENT WAS RELATIVELY HIGH IN NEW MEXICO throughout the 1990s, and the state has suffered its own peculiar business cycle from layoffs in its federal labs and military cutbacks. Unemployment has remained above U.S. averages throughout the 1989–97 period except 1992 and remained somewhat high in 1997. The ratio of employment to adult population hovered between 59 and 60 percent through the 1990s, at a time when this ratio was higher and rising in the rest of the nation.

POPULATION AND LABOR FORCE

POPULATION GROWTH IN NEW MEXICO proceeded at 1.9 percent annually, nearly double the U.S. rate during the 1990–1997 period, because of high birth rates and strong in-migration from other states. The in-migration of 68,000 people during the 1990s, though much smaller than the migration into neighboring Arizona and Nevada, translated to a 4.5 percent population gain given the state's small population. There has been surprisingly little international immigration during the 1990s, despite the large Hispanic community, perhaps because of the relatively low wages in the state. An unusually large percentage of state population remains in nonmetropolitan areas.

New Mexico is by far the most Hispanic state in the United States in percentage terms, but only the 8th largest in actual numbers. California has 14 times as many Hispanic residents. Combined with the large Native American community and a small percentage of both Blacks and Asians, the minority population outnumbers the non-Hispanic White community (48.6 percent). The labor force grew 2.1 percent a year from 1990 to 1997, almost double the national rate. The number of jobs increased a little faster, leaving unemployment at about the same level in 1997 as in 1990. A downturn in employment in 1996 was corrected by gains in 1997.

Population and Labor Force

	1980	1990	1991	1992	1993	1994	1995	1996	1997	Change* State	Change* U.S.
Population											
Total number of persons (thousands)	1 303	1 520	1 547	1 581	1 615	1 654	1 684	1 708	1 724	1.9	1.0
Percent distribution:											
White, Non-Hispanic	53.0	50.7	50.2	49.8	49.7	49.6	49.5	49.0	48.6	1.2	0.4
Black, Non-Hispanic	1.7	2.2	1.8	1.9	1.9	1.9	1.9	1.9	1.9	-0.3	1.4
Asian	0.6	1.0	1.1	1.1	1.2	1.2	1.3	1.3	1.4	6.3	4.1
Native American	8.2	8.9	9.2	9.2	9.2	9.1	9.1	9.1	9.1	2.2	1.6
Hispanic	36.6	38.0	38.6	38.8	38.9	39.0	39.2	39.6	40.0	2.6	3.8
In metropolitan areas	51.8	55.6	55.8	56.0	56.3	56.4	56.6	56.7	56.9	2.2	1.0
Total number of households (thousands)	441	543	554	569	578	592	607	619	NA	2.2	1.2
Labor Force (thousands)											
Population 16 and over	939	1 113	1 135	1 160	1 184	1 217	1 244	1 270	1 288	2.1	1.0
Civilian labor force	562	708	726	741	756	778	791	798	815	2.0	1.1
Employed	520	662	674	689	698	729	741	734	764	2.1	1.2
Percent of population	55.4	59.5	59.4	59.4	58.9	59.9	59.6	57.8	59.3		
Unemployment rate (percent)	7.5	6.5	7.1	7.0	7.7	6.3	6.3	8.1	6.2		

*Compound annual average percent change, 1990–1997; 1990–1996 for households.

Population Change and Components: 1990–97

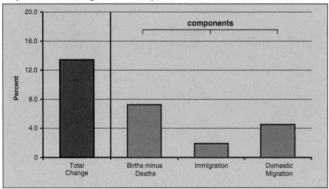

Average Annual Household and Population Growth

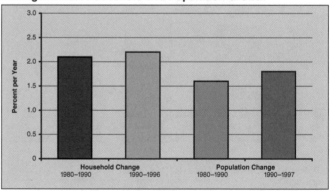

Population by Age; Births and Deaths

	1990 State	1990 U.S.	1997 State	1997 U.S.
Age distribution (percent)				
Under 5 years	8.6	7.6	7.7	7.2
5 to 17 years	21.2	18.2	21.1	18.8
18 to 64 years	59.5	61.8	60.0	61.3
65 years and over	10.7	12.5	11.2	12.7
Birth and death rates (per thousand population)				
Births	18.1	16.7	15.5	14.6
Deaths	7.0	8.6	7.4	8.6

THE STATE POPULATION HAS A YOUNGER THAN AVERAGE PROfile, with a particularly high percentage of school-age children. The adult population, both working-age and over age 65, is proportionately smaller. The birth rate remained higher than average, suggesting that the state will continue to have a larger than average number of children. However, since 1990 the state has moved closer to national averages: its birth rate has declined, and it has an increasing proportion of senior citizens.

HOUSEHOLD AND PERSONAL INCOME

HOUSEHOLD INCOME AND PERSONS IN POVERTY	1990	1995	1996	1997	
				State	U.S.
Median household income (1997 dollars)	30 748	27 372	25 662	30 086	37 005
Persons in poverty (thousands)	319	457	472	387	35 574
Poverty rate (percent)	20.9	25.3	25.5	21.2	13.3

INCOME REMAINS VERY LOW IN NEW MEXICO, THE LOWEST IN the Southwest region, as much of its population lives in rural areas without access to good jobs and those who have jobs tend to earn low wages. The level of median household income during the 1990s has ranged from 75 to 85 percent of the national median; in 1997 it was 81 percent of the U.S. median. The rate of poverty is extremely high, above 25 percent in recent years, although it declined to 21.2 percent in 1997.

Per capita personal income was a steady 76 to 78 percent of the U.S. averages throughout the 1990s, depicting some loss of relative standing compared to 1980 when the state average was 82 percent of the national. The largest factor in the state's low income was the depressed level of earnings by workers and proprietors, averaging 27 percent below the U.S. level in 1997. Dividend and interest income

also was low, 30 percent below national levels, while transfer payments were closer to average (only 7 percent below the U.S. average).

Transfer payments comprise a high share of the state's personal income partly because of the state's high percentage of federal retirees and veterans, though total transfers are a bit below average in absolute amount. Total transfers increased at a faster rate than nationwide from 1990 to 1997, but this increase was entirely due to the faster population growth. Rapid growth in medical payments outpaced the U.S. growth, as did payments of Supplemental Security Income. Poverty remains high so family assistance payments increased; however, they were outpaced by payments of "other" income maintenance, primarily consisting of earned income tax credits, now the largest income maintenance program in New Mexico.

Personal Income
(millions of dollars)

	1980	1989	1990	1991	1992	1993	1994	1995	1996	1997	Change*
Earnings by place of work	8 068	14 298	15 329	16 370	17 553	18 980	19 981	21 263	21 906	23 017	6.1
Wages and salaries	6 600	11 465	12 296	13 018	13 843	14 802	15 887	17 070	17 697	18 656	6.3
Other labor income	615	1 218	1 366	1 490	1 644	1 809	1 881	1 939	1 873	1 886	5.6
Proprietors' income	854	1 616	1 666	1 862	2 066	2 369	2 213	2 254	2 336	2 475	5.5
Farm	121	290	313	318	377	433	260	202	204	231	-2.8
Nonfarm	733	1 325	1 353	1 544	1 689	1 935	1 953	2 052	2 133	2 244	6.8
(−) Personal contributions for social insurance	445	1 004	1 073	1 167	1 233	1 329	1 448	1 576	1 652	1 758	7.3
(+) Adjustment for residence	-3	51	56	59	63	52	57	63	76	92	NA
(=) Net earnings by state of residence	7 621	13 345	14 311	15 262	16 384	17 704	18 590	19 750	20 329	21 350	6.0
(+) Dividends, interest, and rent	1 558	3 698	3 939	3 842	3 871	3 984	4 333	4 585	5 025	5 243	4.5
(+) Transfer payments	1 623	3 438	3 758	4 210	4 662	5 061	5 439	6 023	6 473	6 704	8.7
(=) Total personal income	10 802	20 481	22 008	23 314	24 917	26 749	28 362	30 358	31 827	33 297	6.3
Farm	190	379	413	413	473	538	394	349	350	387	0.3
Nonfarm	10 612	20 103	21 595	22 901	24 444	26 211	27 968	30 009	31 477	32 910	6.4
Personal income per capita (dollars)											
Current dollars	8 250	13 619	14 479	15 064	15 752	16 545	17 127	18 003	18 599	19 249	4.4
1997 dollars	15 774	17 217	17 424	17 395	17 620	18 003	18 201	18 714	18 940	19 249	1.4

*Compound annual average percent change, 1989–1997

Government Transfer Payments

	Millions of dollars		Percent change*	
	1990	1997	State	U.S.
Total government payments to individuals	3 591	6 424	78.9	62.7
Retirement, disability, and insurance	2 149	3 380	57.3	48.2
Social Security	1 247	1 990	59.5	46.1
Government employee retirement	815	1 293	58.7	60.3
Medical payments	770	1 866	142.4	101.2
Income maintenance	353	721	104.2	58.0
Supplemental Security Income	90	178	97.3	75.4
Family assistance	68	154	125.1	-0.5
Food Stamps	123	158	28.8	27.1
Other income maintenance	72	231	222.2	189.8
Unemployment insurance benefits	61	80	32.6	10.6
Veterans benefits and other	259	377	45.8	30.8

*Percent change, 1990–1997

Government Payments to Individuals: 1997

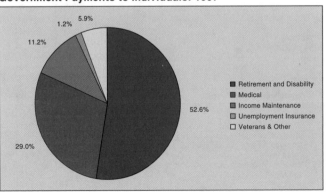

- Retirement and Disability
- Medical
- Income Maintenance
- Unemployment Insurance
- Veterans & Other

52.6% · 29.0% · 11.2% · 1.2% · 5.9%

ECONOMIC STRUCTURE

LEADING PRIVATE INDUSTRIES, 1997 (Worker and proprietor earnings, millions of dollars)		FASTEST EARNINGS GROWTH, 1989–97 (percent increase)	
Health services	$1 843	Electronic equipment manufacturing	232.2
Engineering and management services ..	1 479	Real estate	212.0
Business services	952	Social services	162.7
Construction specialties	890	Other transportation services	120.2
Eating and drinking places	676	General building contractors	109.0

NEW MEXICO HAS SUCCESSFULLY PROMOTED PRIVATE SECTOR growth that capitalizes on its wealth of government science and technology laboratories, such as biotechology and environmental services, resulting in the engineering and management industry that is now the second largest in the state. With continued operation of the Los Alamos and Sandia National Laboratories, the state has one of the nation's highest ratios of scientists and engineers in its workforce. A diverse array of technology-based business services also has grown in the state, such as Citigroup's 700-person credit card center and MCI telephone operations, fueled by the relatively low prevailing wages in New Mexico. With its above-average population growth, the state also has seen a large increase in jobs in construction, real estate, and retail trade during the 1990s.

Manufacturing employment grew more modestly than these other sectors but much faster than the national trend. The growth in production of computer chips and other electronic components, led by Intel's 5,000-worker production facility here (its largest in the United States), has come to dominate the state's manufacturing sector, which has no other major industry. Manufacturing remained underrepresented as a component of the New Mexico economy, compared with national averages, and government remained a much larger than average component of the state's. With about 15,000 research jobs at the national laboratories, and significant military installations, the federal civilian and military presence still loomed large. Combined with state and local government workforces, total government comprised 25 percent of all earnings in the state in 1997, down only slightly from its 26.7 percent share in 1989.

Employment and Earnings by Sector

	1980	1989	1990	1991	1992	1993	1994	1995	1996	1997 Number	1997 Percent of total	Change*
Employment *(thousands of persons)*												
Total	598	755	766	791	804	832	866	899	908	923	100.0	2.5
Farm	22	20	20	20	21	20	20	20	21	20	2.2	0.4
Nonfarm	576	736	746	771	783	812	845	878	888	903	97.8	2.6
Private nonfarm	431	566	571	593	602	629	660	691	701	714	77.4	2.9
Agricultural service, forestry, and fishing ..	4	8	8	10	10	11	11	12	12	13	1.4	5.8
Mining	31	20	20	22	19	20	20	20	19	19	2.1	-0.6
Construction	39	43	41	40	44	49	56	61	59	59	6.4	4.1
Manufacturing	36	48	48	47	46	48	51	51	52	53	5.7	1.3
Transportation and public utilities	31	33	34	34	34	34	35	36	38	39	4.2	1.9
Wholesale trade	23	27	28	28	30	30	31	32	32	32	3.5	2.1
Retail trade	98	133	134	138	142	147	156	164	167	170	18.4	3.2
Finance, insurance, and real estate	38	49	47	47	47	48	50	52	55	55	6.0	1.6
Services	131	206	210	226	232	240	249	263	268	274	29.7	3.6
Government	145	169	176	178	180	183	185	187	187	189	20.4	1.4
Earnings *(millions of dollars)*												
Total	8 068	14 298	15 329	16 370	17 553	18 980	19 981	21 263	21 906	23 017	100.0	6.1
Farm	190	379	413	413	473	538	394	349	350	387	1.7	0.3
Nonfarm	7 878	13 919	14 915	15 957	17 081	18 443	19 588	20 914	21 556	22 630	98.3	6.3
Private nonfarm	5 826	10 101	10 773	11 528	12 395	13 531	14 457	15 477	16 018	16 896	73.4	6.6
Agricultural service, forestry, and fishing ..	29	78	87	101	112	123	130	142	146	161	0.7	9.4
Mining	801	537	612	670	658	702	702	742	764	820	3.6	5.4
Construction	655	873	863	871	1 001	1 203	1 454	1 597	1 578	1 619	7.0	8.0
Manufacturing	558	1 166	1 228	1 285	1 303	1 404	1 563	1 601	1 684	1 857	8.1	6.0
Transportation and public utilities	669	1 012	1 070	1 123	1 154	1 211	1 230	1 260	1 300	1 366	5.9	3.8
Wholesale trade	385	616	660	688	750	783	841	894	911	972	4.2	5.9
Retail trade	889	1 537	1 641	1 757	1 926	2 068	2 201	2 359	2 457	2 590	11.3	6.7
Finance, insurance, and real estate	330	612	638	664	780	910	960	1 048	1 113	1 165	5.1	8.4
Services	1 511	3 669	3 975	4 369	4 711	5 126	5 377	5 835	6 066	6 346	27.6	7.1
Government	2 052	3 818	4 142	4 429	4 686	4 911	5 130	5 436	5 538	5 734	24.9	5.2

*Compound annual average percent change, 1989–1997

ECONOMIC STRUCTURE (Continued)

OVERALL, WAGES PAID IN 1997 WERE 18 PERCENT LOWER IN New Mexico than the U.S. average. This pattern was true in every sector except for farm wages, where wages jumped higher in 1997 because of strong farm performance. Among major sectors, average wages in services and retail trade were 14 percent and 9 percent below average, respectively. In government, wages were closer to parity, at 8 percent below the U.S. average. Manufacturing wages advanced faster than average in New Mexico, to reach a point 16 percent below the national average, but in construction, wages were a distant 24 percent below the U.S average.

The predominance of electronic equipment manufacturing within this state, and its rapid growth, are reflected in the total output figures for the sector. That output includes computer chips and other components manufactured by Intel and Phillips (two of the three largest manufacturing employers). With a huge increase in this production starting in 1994, the total manufacturing value of output jumped upward in that year and has continued at almost that level in 1995–96. (Earnings and employment data show a more moderate increase.) With manufacturing comprising 16.5 percent of gross state product in 1997, New Mexico nearly reaches the U.S. average for share of output from manufacturing. Manufacturing carries a much smaller share of employment, however; 5.7 percent of all jobs are in this sector, only about half of the sector's weight in U.S. employment.

The value of output per worker in New Mexico manufacturing has skyrocketed, reflecting the high productivity in electronics, biotechnology, communications, precision optics, and weapons systems production. The state claims the highest manufacturing output per worker of any state. Capital expenditures are advancing strongly.

Exports of electronic equipment led the way to large increases in total exports from New Mexico between 1994 and 1997. Taking into account a gigantic increase in electronics exports in 1997, exports in this industry increased sixfold from 1994 to 1997. Even with no other exports of significant size, the state's total exports almost tripled. Primary markets for the state's exports are Asia and Mexico, which may portend some slowdown in further growth in the short run. Exports remained a small percentage of total gross state product compared with the leading export states.

Average Annual Wages and Salaries by Sector
(dollars)

	1989	1996	1997 State	1997 U.S.
All wage and salary workers	18 633	23 663	24 584	29 809
Farm	15 602	18 823	21 134	16 442
Nonfarm	18 661	23 712	24 616	29 900
Private nonfarm	17 879	22 625	23 599	29 867
Agricultural service, forestry, and fishing	10 446	12 875	13 845	17 941
Mining	30 385	38 991	41 282	49 800
Construction	17 954	23 398	24 308	31 765
Manufacturing	22 014	29 612	32 307	38 351
Transportation and utilities	27 709	31 879	33 043	38 222
Wholesale trade	21 605	28 061	29 590	39 466
Retail trade	10 935	14 188	14 729	16 206
Finance, insurance, and real estate	19 700	26 330	28 282	44 993
Services	18 134	23 105	23 694	27 588
Government	20 695	26 934	27 654	30 062

Gross State Product and Manufacturing
(millions of dollars, except as noted)

	1989	1994	1995	1996
Gross state product, total	24 985	40 885	40 759	42 698
Manufacturing:				
Millions of dollars	1 565	8 356	6 492	7 027
Percent of total gross state product	6.3	20.4	15.9	16.5
Per worker (dollars)	32 702	163 446	127 142	135 544
New capital expenditures, manufacturing	NA	393	228	488

Exports of Goods
(millions of dollars)

	1994	1995	1996	1997
All goods	488	427	917	1 780
Manufactures	451	385	893	1 739
Agricultural and livestock products	16	21	12	10
Other commodities	22	20	13	30
Top goods exports, 1997:				
Electric and electronic equipment	203	215	686	1 450
Refined petroleum products	50	38	54	68
Industrial machinery and computers	69	38	40	55
Transportation equipment	26	13	29	55
Scientific and measuring instruments	17	21	27	33

HOUSING

Housing production grew at a rapid pace during the mid-1990s, as measured by building permits, with even greater increases (in percentage terms) in the placement of mobile homes. With rapid population growth in some areas and household incomes still below average, mobile homes provide a more affordable market niche in the state. About 60 percent of all building permits in 1997 were issued for the Albuquerque metro area, with about 25 percent of these for multifamily units, a strong showing in the apartment sector.

The housing market for existing homes in New Mexico has been fairly strong, as expected with its population growth rate, but it weakened during 1994–97 compared with the 1992–93 period. Migration patterns show the highest in-migration during the earlier period, which is when existing home sales were advancing strongly, and the decline of in-migration in 1996–97 shows up in home sales declines in those years. The

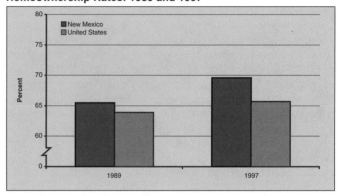

Homeownership Rates: 1989 and 1997

median home price in 1997 in Albuquerque was $126,700, only 79 percent as high as the median for the Western region.

Housing Supply

	1989	1990	1991	1992	1993	1994	1995	1996	1997
Residential building permits (thousands)	6.7	6.0	6.1	7.2	8.9	11.5	11.0	10.2	10.3
New home production (including manufactured housing):									
Thousands of homes	9.1	7.7	8.0	10.4	14.0	16.0	17.4	16.5	15.8
Rate per 1,000 population									
New Mexico	6.1	5.1	5.2	6.6	8.7	9.7	10.3	9.6	9.1
U.S.	6.2	5.2	4.5	5.1	5.6	6.4	6.3	6.6	6.5
Existing home sales:									
Thousands of homes	21.9	23.6	24.4	29.2	31.0	30.4	28.9	26.7	25.5
Change from previous year (percent)									
New Mexico	6.8	7.8	3.4	19.7	6.2	-1.9	-4.9	-7.6	-4.5
U.S.	-3.9	-4.0	0.0	9.2	8.2	4.8	-3.7	7.5	3.8
Home ownership rate (percent of households)	65.5	68.6	69.5	70.5	69.1	66.8	67.0	67.1	69.6
Rental vacancy rate (percent of rental housing units)	12.7	13.7	13.2	7.8	3.5	5.1	4.8	7.1	9.5

AGRICULTURE

Farming has fared relatively well in New Mexico during the 1990s compared with some of the major farm states, though earnings have not grown as much as the rest of the state economy. The sector's total performance is depressed by the poor showing of its largest segment, meat animals, but an outstanding growth in the up-and-coming dairy industry yielded its 146 percent revenue gain over the decade. The state claims to have the fastest growing dairy industry in the country, and the world's largest mozzarella cheese factory. Dairy products accounted for

NEW MEXICO FARMS, 1997	
Number of farms	13 500
Total acres (thousands):	43 500
Average per farm	3 222
Value of land and buildings (millions of dollars)	12 180
Average per farm (dollars)	902 222

29 percent of agricultural sales in 1997. However, net income of the total farm sector declined 27 percent between the 1989–91 period and the 1995–97 period.

Farm Income
(millions of dollars)

	1980	1989	1990	1991	1992	1993	1994	1995	1996	1997
Gross income	1 279	1 630	1 648	1 601	1 649	1 752	1 731	1 614	1 857	2 052
Receipts from sales	1 195	1 482	1 501	1 456	1 506	1 590	1 584	1 464	1 698	1 913
Government payments	21	65	64	58	60	76	61	55	59	39
Imputed and miscellaneous income	63	84	83	87	83	86	87	95	100	99
(−) Production expenses	1 041	1 244	1 261	1 277	1 204	1 290	1 463	1 388	1 599	1 746
(=) Realized net income	237	386	387	324	445	462	269	225	258	306
(+) Inventory change	-117	-44	-20	31	-7	-3	63	10	0	-20
(=) Net income	121	342	367	355	438	459	332	236	258	286
Corporate income	0	52	53	38	60	25	72	33	54	55
Farm proprietors income	121	290	313	318	377	433	260	202	204	231

EDUCATION

EDUCATIONAL ATTAINMENT Percent of population age 25 and over, 1997	State	United States
High school graduate or higher	78.0	82.1
College graduate or higher	23.6	23.9

EDUCATION LEVELS IN THE GENERAL POPULATION SHOWED below-average attainment of high school diplomas in New Mexico, consistent with the low incomes of its population. On this score, it ranks 10th lowest in the nation and lowest in the Southwest region. As a poor state, it spends only three-quarters as much per pupil on elementary and sec- ondary education as U.S. averages. In contrast, because of its role as a center for scientific research, the state has an average proportion of college graduates, ranking 21st in the country as a percent of adult population. It also has a large share of current population enrolled in college, many of whom are minorities.

High School Completion: 1990–97

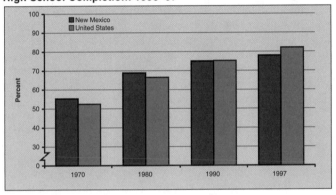

Education Indicators

	State	U.S.
Elementary and secondary schools		
Enrollment, 1995–96		
Total (thousands)	353	49 873
Percent in private schools	6.5	10.1
Expenditures per pupil (dollars), 1995–96	4 587	6 146
Average teacher salary (dollars), 1996–97	29 715	38 509
Higher education		
Enrollment, 1996–97		
Total (thousands)	104	14 218
Percent of population 18–34	25.8	21.8
Percent minority	43.7	26.1
Percent in private schools	5.7	22.6

HEALTH

HEALTH INDICATORS SHOW AN UNUSUALLY HEALTHY POPULA- tion, given the low incomes and high poverty in this state. Infant mortality has ranked consistently below U.S. averages, as have total death rates. Deaths from heart disease and cancer are markedly below average, probably attributable to the state's "clean" industry and generally high environmental quality, as well as the lower incidence of these diseases within the Hispanic community. However, deaths from accidents are very high, including motor vehicle accidents, as is true in much of the South. Both suicide and homicide rates are also substantially above average. A large percentage of the state population lacks health insurance, not surpris- ing in light of the low proportion of the state that is employed, the high rate of poverty, and the prevalence of low-wage jobs.

Health Indicators

	1990	1995	1996	1997
Infant mortality *(rate per thousand live births)*				
New Mexico	9.0	6.2	5.9	6.4
U.S.	9.2	7.6	7.3	7.1
Total deaths, age-adjusted rate *(rate per thousand population)*				
New Mexico	4.9	4.9	4.7	4.7
U.S.	5.2	5.0	4.9	4.8
Persons not covered by health insurance *(percent of population)*				
New Mexico	22.2	25.6	22.3	22.6
U.S.	13.9	15.4	15.6	16.1

Leading Causes of Death, 1996
(deaths per 100,000 population)

	Age-adjusted		Not age-adjusted	
	State	U.S.	State	U.S.
Deaths from all causes	470.7	491.6	728.4	872.5
Heart disease	103.6	134.5	186.5	276.4
Cancer	108.8	127.9	159.9	203.4
Cerebrovascular diseases	22.7	26.4	46.2	60.3
Chronic obstructive pulmonary disease	22.5	21.0	38.1	40.0
Diabetes mellitus	16.7	13.6	25.2	23.3
Pneumonia and influenza	11.7	12.8	24.5	31.6
HIV	4.9	11.1	5.0	11.7
Liver disease	12.8	7.5	14.5	9.4
Alzheimer's disease	2.4	2.7	5.9	8.1
Accidents and adverse effects	51.2	30.4	55.9	35.8
Motor vehicle accidents	26.3	16.2	25.9	16.5
Suicide	17.9	10.8	18.6	11.6
Homicide	11.6	8.5	10.9	7.9
Injury by firearm	18.9	12.9	18.9	12.8

GOVERNMENT

STATE AND LOCAL TAXES, 1995–96	State	U.S.
Per capita (dollars)	2 168	2 477
Percent of personal income	12.1	10.8

TOTAL STATE AND LOCAL TAXES ARE WELL BELOW AVERAGE IN New Mexico; at $2,168 per capita they are only 87.5 percent as high as the national average. Within the total, state taxes comprised a major share (actually higher than the average for all states), with extremely low taxes at the local level. Local governments typically rely heavily on property taxes, and New Mexico's abundance of federally owned property and Native American reservations placed

limits on this tax base. The two levels of government combined consume a higher proportion of personal income (12.1 percent) than average for the United States, because of the low per capita incomes in New Mexico.

State government in 1997 both collected taxes and received federal transfers at above-average rates per capita. Sales tax collections per capita are well above average, but income taxes are below average because of the small tax base in this low-income state. Receipt of other general revenue is particularly high in the state, partly reflecting interest earnings on the state's hefty cash holdings (which are significantly bigger than average). Overall, revenue collected by the state was one-third higher than by the typical state in 1997. Expenditures also were high, particularly on education and health, which were 41 percent and 44 percent higher than average for all states on a per capita basis. This rate included generous transfers to support local government programs, because local governments have a fairly small tax base.

New Mexico derived some net benefit financially from transactions with the federal government, as its residents and businesses received payments well in excess of their share of the national population. Grants in all major social welfare programs are above average, not surprising given the high poverty rates and large concentration of Native Americans here. Federal salaries for civilian and military workers are also relatively large in the aggregate. The largest factor of all is non-defense procurement, the purchase of goods and services from the private sector for the major federal research laboratories and military bases, much of it probably technical equipment.

State Government Finances, 1996–97

	Millions of dollars	Percent distribution	Dollars per capita State	Dollars per capita U.S.
General revenue	6 963	100.0	4 025	3 049
Intergovernmental revenue	1 973	28.3	1 141	863
Taxes	3 322	47.7	1 920	1 660
General sales	1 346	19.3	778	551
Selective sales	461	6.6	266	257
License taxes	134	1.9	77	106
Individual income	748	10.7	432	542
Corporation net income	173	2.5	100	115
Other taxes	461	6.6	267	90
Other general revenue	1 668	23.9	964	526
General expenditure	6 486	100.0	3 749	2 951
Intergovernmental expenditure	2 075	32.0	1 199	989
Direct expenditure	4 411	68.0	2 550	1 962
General expenditure, by function:				
Education	2 516	38.8	1 454	1 033
Public welfare	1 253	19.3	724	761
Hospitals and health	591	9.1	341	237
Highways	644	9.9	372	225
Police protection and corrections	244	3.8	141	137
Natural resources, parks and recreation	128	2.0	74	63
Governmental administration	257	4.0	149	107
Interest on general debt	124	1.9	72	99
Other and unallocable	730	11.3	422	290
Debt at end of fiscal year	2 458	NA	1 421	1 706
Cash and security holdings	18 665	NA	10 789	6 683

Federal Spending within State

	Federal funds, fiscal 1997		
	Millions of dollars	Percent distribution	Percent of U.S. total*
Total within state	12 454	100.0	0.9
Payments to individuals	4 763	38.2	0.6
Retirement and disability	3 045	24.4	0.7
Medicare	891	7.2	0.4
Food stamps	171	1.4	0.9
Supplemental Security Income	186	1.5	0.7
Grants	2 425	19.5	1.0
Medicaid and other health	897	7.2	0.8
Nutrition and family welfare	416	3.3	0.9
Education	205	1.6	1.2
Housing and community development	74	0.6	0.7
Salaries and wages	1 595	12.8	1.0
Defense procurement contracts	494	4.0	0.4
Non-defense procurement contracts	3 039	24.4	4.2

*State population is 0.6 percent of the U.S. total.

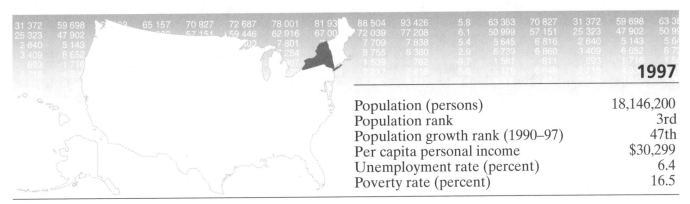

1997

Population (persons)	18,146,200
Population rank	3rd
Population growth rank (1990–97)	47th
Per capita personal income	$30,299
Unemployment rate (percent)	6.4
Poverty rate (percent)	16.5

A LOWER MEDIAN HOUSEHOLD INCOME AND A MUCH LARGER than average personal income per capita point to an increasing disparity in New York between upper income groups and the rest of the population. Average wages in the finance, insurance, and real estate sector in New York, at over $83,000 per year, were the highest of any industry in any state, but median household income fell from 1990 to 1997 when adjusted for inflation and was lower than the U.S. level. Employment was stagnant overall as a large increase in services was largely offset by contractions elsewhere. The largest industries in the state were in services or finance, insurance, and real estate.

The population of New York showed almost no growth from 1990 to 1997. Natural increase and international in-migration were substantial, yet a very large domestic out-migration from the state canceled these factors out. With a population older than that of the United States as a whole, New York's spending on retirement payments and medical payments increased over the time period as well. Metropolitan counties, which are centered around and include the metropolitan areas of New York-Northern New Jersey-Long Island, Albany-Schenectady-Troy, Syracuse, Utica-Rome, Binghamton, Elmira, Rochester, and Jamestown, hold 91.8 percent of the state's population.

Average Annual Population Growth: 1990–97

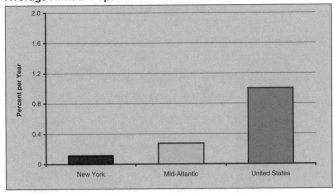

Median Household Income: 1989–97 (1997 dollars)

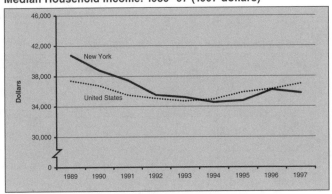

Unemployment Rate: 1989–97

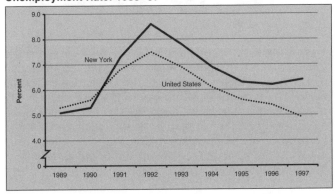

UNEMPLOYMENT IN NEW YORK WAS LOWER THAN THE national average in 1989–90 but has been higher ever since, peaking at 8.6 percent in 1992 and recovering only to 6.4 percent in 1997. This was the fourth highest rate in the nation in that year. A declining working-age population and flat labor force were not enough to offset the effects on unemployment of employment declines.

POPULATION AND LABOR FORCE

New York's population was nearly stagnant in the years from 1990 to 1997. The White non-Hispanic population declined in this time period and the Black and the Hispanic populations grew at significantly slower rates than in the country. The Asian population was the fastest growing, at 4.2 percent per year, similar to the national average rate. Natural increase (births less deaths) contributed to growth in the state between 1990 and 1997, along with international in-migration, but a very high level of domestic out-migration from New York virtually canceled out any growth. New York is a predominantly metropolitan state, with only 8.2 percent of the population living in nonmetropolitan counties.

The population over 16 and the labor force declined slightly between 1990 and 1997. Employment was stagnant as well. The employment to population ratio was flat and fell further below the U.S. average, while the unemployment rate rose.

Population and Labor Force

	1980	1990	1991	1992	1993	1994	1995	1996	1997	Change* State	Change* U.S.
Population											
Total number of persons (thousands)	17 558	18 002	18 028	18 079	18 139	18 152	18 145	18 142	18 146	0.1	1.0
Percent distribution:											
White, Non-Hispanic	75.2	69.4	68.7	68.3	67.8	67.3	66.8	66.4	65.9	-0.6	0.4
Black, Non-Hispanic	13.1	14.2	14.4	14.4	14.5	14.5	14.5	14.6	14.6	0.5	1.4
Asian	1.9	4.0	4.2	4.4	4.6	4.7	4.9	5.1	5.3	4.2	4.1
Native American	0.3	0.4	0.4	0.4	0.4	0.4	0.4	0.4	0.4	0.8	1.6
Hispanic	9.5	12.3	12.6	12.8	13.1	13.4	13.7	13.9	14.2	2.2	3.8
In metropolitan areas	91.9	91.8	91.7	91.7	91.7	91.7	91.7	91.7	91.8	0.1	1.0
Total number of households (thousands)	6 340	6 639	6 661	6 706	6 702	6 684	6 709	6 737	NA	0.2	1.2
Labor Force (thousands)											
Population 16 and over	13 519	14 185	14 139	14 123	14 135	14 113	14 084	14 057	14 049	-0.1	1.0
Civilian labor force	7 978	8 843	8 732	8 659	8 651	8 605	8 509	8 614	8 835	0.0	1.1
Employed	7 381	8 375	8 096	7 911	7 973	8 010	7 970	8 076	8 269	-0.2	1.2
Percent of population	54.6	59.0	57.3	56.0	56.4	56.8	56.6	57.5	58.9		
Unemployment rate (percent)	7.5	5.3	7.3	8.6	7.8	6.9	6.3	6.2	6.4		

*Compound annual average percent change, 1990–1997; 1990–1996 for households.

Population Change and Components: 1990–97

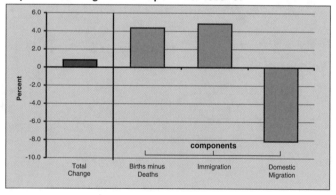

Average Annual Household and Population Growth

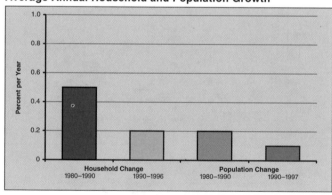

Population by Age; Births and Deaths

	1990 State	1990 U.S.	1997 State	1997 U.S.
Age distribution (percent)				
Under 5 years	7.2	7.6	7.2	7.2
5 to 17 years	16.6	18.2	17.9	18.8
18 to 64 years	63.2	61.8	61.5	61.3
65 years and over	13.0	12.5	13.4	12.7
Birth and death rates (per thousand population)				
Births	16.5	16.7	14.5	14.6
Deaths	9.4	8.6	8.9	8.6

New York has a population older than that of the United States as a whole. The porportion of its population 65 and over is higher than the national average and rising faster. The proportion in the working-age population (18 to 64) declined markedly from 1990 to 1997. The school-age group grew, though it still was a smaller than average percentage of the population. The pre-school age group made up the same percentage of the population in New York as it does in the United States.

HOUSEHOLD AND PERSONAL INCOME

HOUSEHOLD INCOME AND PERSONS IN POVERTY	1990	1995	1996	1997	
				State	U.S.
Median household income (1997 dollars)	38 794	34 783	36 222	35 798	37 005
Persons in poverty (thousands)	2 571	3 020	3 058	2 979	35 574
Poverty rate (percent)	14.3	16.5	16.7	16.5	13.3

MEDIAN HOUSEHOLD INCOME IN NEW YORK FELL I2.I PERcent in real terms between 1989 and 1997 and ended the period lower than median household income in the country, the only mid-Atlantic state to do so. The poverty rate was also higher in New York, and it rose from 14.3 percent in 1990 to an average of 16.6 in 1995–97, while the national poverty rate stood at 13.5 in 1990 and 13.6 in 1995–97.

Aggregate personal income in New York grew 4.3 percent per year from 1989 to 1997, lower than the nation's 5.3 percent rate. Wages and salaries in the state grew far slower than in the nation, though nonfarm proprietors' income rose faster. New York had a growing negative adjustment for residence, indicating a large and increasing number of in-commuters from neighboring states. New York's personal income per capita was almost 20 percent higher than the national per capita income and grew at the U.S. rate. Total and per capita personal income reflect the above-average income gains for upper-income groups, which do not raise median income.

Transfer payments (government payments to individuals) in New York increased slightly faster in the state than nationally. The two largest programs in the state were medical payments, which were a significantly larger share than nationally, and Social Security. The fastest growing programs were "other income maintenance," which includes the earned income tax credit, medical payments, and Supplemental Security Income. The only program to contract between 1990 and 1997 was unemployment benefits; Aid to Families with Dependent Children, a program whose spending was unchanged nationwide, grew 3.3 percent per year in New York.

Personal Income
(millions of dollars)

	1980	1989	1990	1991	1992	1993	1994	1995	1996	1997	Change*
Earnings by place of work	143 996	286 975	303 541	305 905	326 925	335 073	342 640	358 813	376 658	396 965	4.1
Wages and salaries	117 219	235 935	248 148	247 693	261 924	266 573	272 564	285 170	301 981	320 424	3.9
Other labor income	11 402	22 220	24 396	26 018	28 146	30 038	31 174	30 970	29 784	29 856	3.8
Proprietors' income	15 376	28 821	30 997	32 194	36 855	38 462	38 902	42 673	44 893	46 685	6.2
Farm	289	430	374	263	308	311	177	20	160	-56	0.0
Nonfarm	15 087	28 391	30 623	31 931	36 547	38 152	38 725	42 652	44 734	46 741	6.4
(–) Personal contributions for social insurance	7 460	18 486	19 632	20 219	21 273	21 744	22 523	23 306	24 281	25 578	4.1
(+) Adjustment for residence	-7 376	-13 343	-14 145	-14 025	-16 249	-16 203	-16 138	-17 901	-19 753	-21 177	NA
(=) **Net earnings by state of residence**	129 160	255 146	269 764	271 660	289 402	297 126	303 979	317 606	332 624	350 210	4.0
(+) Dividends, interest, and rent	33 548	79 189	82 587	81 710	77 739	77 514	82 291	86 604	92 480	95 426	2.4
(+) Transfer payments	31 277	58 063	63 619	72 089	81 230	85 610	90 061	96 223	101 778	103 896	7.5
(=) **Total personal income**	193 986	392 398	415 971	425 460	448 371	460 249	476 331	500 433	526 883	549 531	4.3
Farm	533	716	711	594	631	652	522	413	569	356	-8.4
Nonfarm	193 453	391 682	415 260	424 865	447 740	459 597	475 809	500 020	526 314	549 176	4.3
Personal income per capita (dollars)											
Current dollars	11 043	21 820	23 107	23 600	24 799	25 373	26 239	27 578	29 055	30 299	4.2
1997 dollars	21 115	27 585	27 806	27 252	27 739	27 609	27 884	28 667	29 588	30 299	1.2

*Compound annual average percent change, 1989–1997

Government Transfer Payments

	Millions of dollars		Percent change*	
	1990	1997	State	U.S.
Total government payments to individuals	60 174	99 774	65.8	62.7
Retirement, disability, and insurance	26 947	40 734	51.2	48.2
Social Security	18 903	26 091	38.0	46.1
Government employee retirement	6 907	12 581	82.1	60.3
Medical payments	23 030	44 003	91.1	101.2
Income maintenance	6 679	11 095	66.1	58.0
Supplemental Security Income	1 582	2 947	86.3	75.4
Family assistance	2 423	3 033	25.2	-0.5
Food Stamps	1 123	1 711	52.3	27.1
Other income maintenance	1 551	3 404	119.4	189.8
Unemployment insurance benefits	1 803	1 758	-2.5	10.6
Veterans benefits and other	1 715	2 183	27.3	30.8

*Percent change, 1990–1997

Government Payments to Individuals: 1997

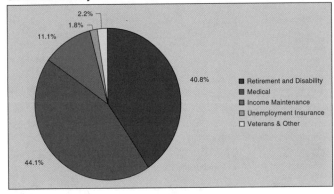

- Retirement and Disability
- Medical
- Income Maintenance
- Unemployment Insurance
- Veterans & Other

ECONOMIC STRUCTURE

LEADING PRIVATE INDUSTRIES, 1997 (Worker and proprietor earnings, millions of dollars)		FASTEST EARNINGS GROWTH, 1989–97 (percent increase)	
Securities brokers	$39 391	Securities brokers	141.6
Health services	33 924	Social services	71.3
Business services	24 389	Motion pictures	68.6
Banks and other credit institutions	16 217	Communications	57.0
Legal services	14 141	Health services	56.7

TOTAL EMPLOYMENT IN NEW YORK WAS STAGNANT FROM 1989 to 1997, growing only 0.1 percent per year on average over the time period. Services added nearly 450,000 jobs, offsetting substantial declines in manufacturing and government. The government decline is unusual—in the country at large, gains made at state and local governments outweigh federal job cutbacks. Earnings in New York, like employment, grew more slowly than nationally. The earnings gain in finance, insurance, and real estate was the most impressive, with an annual average growth rate of 9.3 percent, despite a very modest increase in employment. This sector accounts for one-fifth of all New York earnings, compared with 8.5 percent nationwide. The five largest industries in New York as measured by earnings were all either services (business, legal, and health) or financial services (security and commodities brokers and services and depository and nondepository credit institutions), with securities and commodities brokers leading them all. The largest manufacturing industry in New York was publishing and printing, which ranked ninth overall.

Employment and Earnings by Sector

	1980	1989	1990	1991	1992	1993	1994	1995	1996	1997 Number	1997 Percent of total	Change*
Employment (thousands of persons)												
Total	8 622	9 852	9 802	9 579	9 511	9 538	9 585	9 653	9 755	9 909	100.0	0.1
Farm	84	66	66	65	65	64	63	61	59	58	0.6	-1.6
Nonfarm	8 538	9 786	9 736	9 514	9 446	9 474	9 522	9 592	9 695	9 851	99.4	0.1
Private nonfarm	7 200	8 280	8 204	8 016	7 973	8 002	8 065	8 173	8 293	8 451	85.3	0.3
Agricultural service, forestry, and fishing	39	52	55	56	57	62	63	64	68	70	0.7	3.8
Mining	14	12	12	11	10	10	10	9	8	8	0.1	-4.8
Construction	271	444	427	382	364	359	364	368	373	386	3.9	-1.7
Manufacturing	1 492	1 220	1 152	1 091	1 047	1 017	993	977	960	959	9.7	-3.0
Transportation and public utilities	480	454	477	476	460	466	468	471	476	484	4.9	0.8
Wholesale trade	528	506	492	469	457	453	453	458	456	460	4.6	-1.2
Retail trade	1 181	1 395	1 366	1 344	1 325	1 334	1 351	1 381	1 401	1 424	14.4	0.3
Finance, insurance, and real estate	897	1 088	1 069	1 038	1 015	1 013	1 054	1 066	1 083	1 103	11.1	0.2
Services	2 298	3 109	3 154	3 148	3 237	3 287	3 310	3 378	3 468	3 557	35.9	1.7
Government	1 338	1 506	1 532	1 499	1 474	1 471	1 457	1 419	1 403	1 400	14.1	-0.9
Earnings (millions of dollars)												
Total	143 996	286 975	303 541	305 905	326 925	335 073	342 640	358 813	376 658	396 965	100.0	4.1
Farm	533	716	711	594	631	652	522	413	569	356	0.1	-8.4
Nonfarm	143 463	286 260	302 830	305 311	326 294	334 421	342 118	358 400	376 089	396 610	99.9	4.2
Private nonfarm	122 663	242 557	255 440	257 221	276 872	283 056	289 059	304 543	321 387	340 782	85.8	4.3
Agricultural service, forestry, and fishing	367	939	1 041	1 075	1 091	1 150	1 186	1 218	1 236	1 296	0.3	4.1
Mining	841	356	348	290	283	302	324	320	321	336	0.1	-0.7
Construction	5 239	14 543	14 166	12 678	11 769	11 794	12 627	12 885	13 325	14 022	3.5	-0.5
Manufacturing	30 937	44 468	44 857	44 658	45 807	45 445	45 571	45 899	46 467	48 272	12.2	1.0
Transportation and public utilities	12 087	17 472	18 968	19 490	20 067	20 794	21 095	21 942	22 796	23 436	5.9	3.7
Wholesale trade	11 137	19 175	19 742	19 120	19 825	19 844	20 331	20 930	21 571	22 792	5.7	2.2
Retail trade	11 307	21 686	21 966	21 772	22 468	22 639	23 906	24 508	25 177	26 528	6.7	2.6
Finance, insurance, and real estate	17 091	39 023	42 193	44 788	54 493	57 583	56 665	64 051	72 719	79 283	20.0	9.3
Services	33 656	84 894	92 158	93 349	101 069	103 504	107 355	112 790	117 774	124 818	31.4	4.9
Government	20 800	43 703	47 390	48 089	49 422	51 365	53 058	53 857	54 702	55 828	14.1	3.1

*Compound annual average percent change, 1989–1997

ECONOMIC STRUCTURE (Continued)

AVERAGE WAGES IN NEW YORK WERE CONSIDERABLY HIGHER in 1997 than the national and regional levels. Every sector had higher wages, except for the tiny mining sector. New York's finance, insurance, and real estate sector had the highest wage in the nation—$83,557 per worker; this wage was 85.7 percent higher than the national average. Other sectors with notably higher wages include manufacturing (14.8 percent above the U.S. average), construction (19.6 percent), wholesale trade (17.6 percent), and services (15.2 percent). Average wages in New York grew 4.3 percent annually from 1989 to 1997, faster than the U.S. rate of 3.7 percent annually, led by growth in the finance, insurance, and real estate sector.

Manufacturing importance, that is the sector's percentage of gross state product (GSP), was lower in New York than it was in the United States or in the region. Manufacturing value was 11.8 percent of GSP in 1997, down from 14 percent in 1989. Manufacturing output value per worker was lower than the national average.

Goods exports from New York rose 31.2 percent from 1994 to 1997. The top 5 export commodities were all durable goods, and all increased their exports from 1994 to 1997. Primary metals grew the fastest, increasing 21.2 percent per year on average.

Average Annual Wages and Salaries by Sector
(dollars)

	1989	1996	1997 State	1997 U.S.
All wage and salary workers	27 246	36 312	38 023	29 809
Farm	10 463	16 460	17 344	16 442
Nonfarm	27 296	36 368	38 077	29 900
Private nonfarm	27 334	36 420	38 302	29 867
Agricultural service, forestry, and fishing	20 472	23 872	24 482	17 941
Mining	44 770	46 915	49 098	49 800
Construction	30 900	36 866	38 002	31 765
Manufacturing	31 843	42 127	44 022	38 351
Transportation and utilities	34 122	42 256	42 948	38 222
Wholesale trade	34 429	44 173	46 426	39 466
Retail trade	14 637	17 254	18 008	16 206
Finance, insurance, and real estate	43 121	75 523	83 557	44 993
Services	23 612	30 570	31 787	27 588
Government	27 117	36 110	36 952	30 062

Gross State Product and Manufacturing
(millions of dollars, except as noted)

	1989	1994	1995	1996
Gross state product, total	474 860	565 161	587 714	613 287
Manufacturing:				
Millions of dollars	66 550	69 546	69 970	72 154
Percent of total gross state product	14.0	12.3	11.9	11.8
Per worker (dollars)	54 552	70 036	71 648	75 197
New capital expenditures, manufacturing	NA	3 912	4 732	5 331

Exports of Goods
(millions of dollars)

	1994	1995	1996	1997
All goods	37 260	44 080	44 965	48 885
Manufactures	32 146	38 095	38 795	42 577
Agricultural and livestock products	1 784	2 520	2 921	2 477
Other commodities	3 330	3 465	3 249	3 831
Top goods exports, 1997:				
Industrial machinery and computers	5 235	6 256	5 778	7 218
Primary metals	3 048	4 671	6 014	5 426
Scientific and measuring instruments	3 312	3 706	4 203	4 536
Electric and electronic equipment	3 568	4 058	3 587	4 387
Transportation equipment	2 970	3 887	3 808	4 346

HOUSING

THE SUPPLY OF NEW HOUSING IN NEW YORK, WHEN MEASured as building permits plus manufactured housing (mobile homes), showed declines in 1990 and 1991, stagnation through 1995, and some increase in 1996–97. On a per capita basis, home production was less than one-third of the U.S. rate. Existing home sales fell in 1989 and 1990 but have recovered and now surpass pre-recession levels. Homeownership was low in the state—only Hawaii and the District of Columbia have lower rates. Rental vacancy rates were relatively stable, except for a very tight period in 1989 and a relatively loose period in 1996, and were well below the national average.

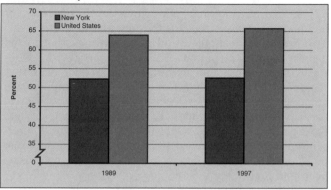

Homeownership Rates: 1989 and 1997

Housing Supply

	1989	1990	1991	1992	1993	1994	1995	1996	1997
Residential building permits (thousands)	48.7	35.0	28.6	29.9	28.6	31.1	28.1	34.9	32.9
New home production (including manufactured housing):									
Thousands of homes	55.9	41.9	33.4	35.0	34.2	36.4	32.7	40.3	38.1
Rate per 1,000 population									
New York	3.1	2.3	1.9	1.9	1.9	2.0	1.8	2.2	2.1
U.S.	6.2	5.2	4.5	5.1	5.6	6.4	6.3	6.6	6.5
Existing home sales:									
Thousands of homes	140.2	125.5	127.2	136.3	143.0	156.3	150.4	165.8	171.0
Change from previous year (percent)									
New York	-12.6	-10.5	1.4	7.2	4.9	9.3	-3.8	10.2	3.1
U.S.	-3.9	-4.0	0.0	9.2	8.2	4.8	-3.7	7.5	3.8
Home ownership rate (percent of households)	52.3	53.3	52.6	53.3	52.8	52.5	52.7	52.7	52.6
Rental vacancy rate (percent of rental housing units)	3.7	4.9	5.5	5.8	5.5	5.9	6.3	6.9	6.2

AGRICULTURE

FARM SALES FLUCTUATED FROM 1989 TO 1997 BUT ULTIMATEly ended slightly lower than 1989 levels. Production expenses also fluctuated but increased at a faster pace, eventually outstripping sales, resulting in net losses in 1997. Government payments were small and did not increase as production expenses grew. Corporate farm earnings were also negligible. Total net farm proprietors' income was fairly high until 1994 but began to slip in that year, with net losses in 1997. The average farm in New York was smaller than the average U.S. farm, but it was larger than those in other mid-Atlantic states. The average value per farm was lower than both the regional and the national average.

NEW YORK FARMS, 1997	
Number of farms	36 000
Total acres (thousands):	7 700
Average per farm	214
Value of land and buildings (millions of dollars)	10 703
Average per farm (dollars)	297 306

Farm Income
(millions of dollars)

	1980	1989	1990	1991	1992	1993	1994	1995	1996	1997
Gross income	2 754	3 198	3 257	3 144	3 188	3 236	3 193	3 190	3 309	3 186
Receipts from sales	2 590	2 953	3 024	2 925	2 950	2 966	2 952	2 954	3 093	2 936
Government payments	6	76	59	41	48	72	42	44	43	40
Imputed and miscellaneous income	158	169	173	177	190	198	199	193	173	210
(−) Production expenses	2 527	2 715	2 867	2 846	2 815	2 867	3 007	3 149	3 157	3 295
(=) Realized net income	227	482	389	297	373	369	186	41	152	-110
(+) Inventory change	62	-9	24	-14	-31	-45	24	-19	37	30
(=) Net income	289	473	413	283	343	324	210	23	188	-80
Corporate income	0	43	39	20	34	13	33	2	29	-24
Farm proprietors income	289	430	374	263	308	311	177	20	160	-56

EDUCATION

EDUCATIONAL ATTAINMENT Percent of population age 25 and over, 1997	State	United States
High school graduate or higher	80.0	82.1
College graduate or higher	25.8	23.9

NEW YORK WAS RANKED 38TH IN THE COUNTRY IN THE PER-cent of the population age 25 and over holding a high school diploma. This ranking was despite high levels of spending in elementary and secondary schools. Per pupil expenditures were the third highest in the nation, following New Jersey and Washington, D.C. Teacher salaries were also third highest, following Alaska and Connecticut. New York's place in the percentage of population holding

a bachelor's degree was slightly higher, at 16th. Of the population between the ages of 16 and 34, 23.1 percent were enrolled in higher education in 1996, slightly higher than the U.S. level. Minority enrollment was also higher than the U.S. level, at 31.7 percent, close to the minority share in the state's population. In higher education, 44.3 percent of enrollment was at private institutions, almost twice the rate in the United States (22.6 percent).

High School Completion: 1990–97

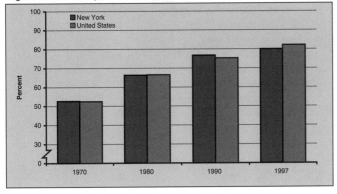

Education Indicators

	State	U.S.
Elementary and secondary schools		
Enrollment, 1995–96		
Total (thousands)	3 279	49 873
Percent in private schools	14.2	10.1
Expenditures per pupil (dollars), 1995–96	9 549	6 146
Average teacher salary (dollars), 1996–97	49 560	38 509
Higher education		
Enrollment, 1996–97		
Total (thousands)	1 028	14 218
Percent of population 18–34	23.1	21.8
Percent minority	31.7	26.1
Percent in private schools	44.3	22.6

HEALTH

NEW YORK HAD AN AGE-ADJUSTED DEATH RATE THAT STARTED the 1990s higher than the national average but then started to decline toward the end of the decade. Infant mortality was about the same as the national rate in 1995, though the 1996 rate declined a bit further than the U.S. rate and was well below the it by 1997. The rate of those without health insurance was fairly low in New

York in 1990, but after 1996 it exceeded the national average. The largest causes of death were cancer and heart disease, both of which were near or above the national average in terms of crude and age-adjusted death rates. The only other causes of death above the national average (age-adjusted) were HIV and pneumonia and influenza.

Health Indicators

	1990	1995	1996	1997
Infant mortality *(rate per thousand live births)*				
New York	9.6	7.7	6.7	6.1
U.S.	9.2	7.6	7.3	7.1
Total deaths, age-adjusted rate *(rate per thousand population)*				
New York	5.5	5.1	4.9	4.7
U.S.	5.2	5.0	4.9	4.8
Persons not covered by health insurance *(percent of population)*				
New York	12.1	15.2	17.0	17.5
U.S.	13.9	15.4	15.6	16.1

Leading Causes of Death, 1996
(deaths per 100,000 population)

	Age-adjusted		Not age-adjusted	
	State	U.S.	State	U.S.
Deaths from all causes	488.4	491.6	904.0	872.5
Heart disease	151.0	134.5	345.0	276.4
Cancer	126.6	127.9	209.8	203.4
Cerebrovascular diseases	19.7	26.4	45.4	60.3
Chronic obstructive pulmonary disease	16.6	21.0	33.6	40.0
Diabetes mellitus	10.9	13.6	19.4	23.3
Pneumonia and influenza	14.1	12.8	36.0	31.6
HIV	29.0	11.1	31.3	11.7
Liver disease	7.3	7.5	9.4	9.4
Alzheimer's disease	1.0	2.7	3.2	8.1
Accidents and adverse effects	21.4	30.4	26.1	35.8
Motor vehicle accidents	9.3	16.2	9.7	16.5
Suicide	6.7	10.8	7.3	11.6
Homicide	8.3	8.5	7.5	7.9
Injury by firearm	8.5	12.9	7.9	12.8

GOVERNMENT

STATE AND LOCAL TAXES, 1995–96	State	U.S.
Per capita (dollars)	3 697	2 477
Percent of personal income	13.4	10.8

STATE AND LOCAL TAXES PER CAPITA (LESS CORPORATE TAXES) in New York were the highest of any state and surpassed only by the District of Columbia. As a percentage of total personal income, they were exceeded only by Alaska. Local taxes (mostly property) were more than half of total taxation, which far exceeds the U.S. percentage of 40.8 percent. The state taxation rate per capita was also higher, mostly because of a significantly higher individual income tax, as sales and license taxes were lower and selective sales taxes were only moderately higher.

Total expenditure by the state (also in a per capita calculation) was higher by about a quarter than the national level. Though state education and highway spending were proportionately lower in the state, other categories such as hospitals and health and public welfare were well funded in comparison. Corrections spending was slightly higher on a per capita basis, but police protection was far lower than in the country at large. The debt at the end of the fiscal year was more than twice the national level, as were per capita interest payments.

New York received 6.9 percent of all federally dispersed funds in 1997, a level slightly higher than its 6.8 percent of the population. The state received significantly more than this population share of Medicare, food stamps, Supplemental Security Income, Medicaid, family assistance, and housing and community development grants, but much less in salaries, wages, and procurement.

State Government Finances, 1996–97

	Millions of dollars	Percent distribution	Dollars per capita	
			State	U.S.
General revenue	75 383	100.0	4 156	3 049
Intergovernmental revenue	30 470	40.4	1 680	863
Taxes	34 865	46.3	1 922	1 660
General sales	7 353	9.8	405	551
Selective sales	4 787	6.3	264	257
License taxes	945	1.3	52	106
Individual income	17 554	23.3	968	542
Corporation net income	3 042	4.0	168	115
Other taxes	1 183	1.6	65	90
Other general revenue	10 048	13.3	554	526
General expenditure	70 017	100.0	3 860	2 951
Intergovernmental expenditure	25 638	36.6	1 414	989
Direct expenditure	44 379	63.4	2 447	1 962
General expenditure, by function:				
Education	16 243	23.2	896	1 033
Public welfare	27 594	39.4	1 521	761
Hospitals and health	5 459	7.8	301	237
Highways	2 764	3.9	152	225
Police protection and corrections	2 632	3.8	145	137
Natural resources, parks and recreation	627	0.9	35	63
Governmental administration	3 467	5.0	191	107
Interest on general debt	3 767	5.4	208	99
Other and unallocable	7 464	10.7	412	290
Debt at end of fiscal year	74 078	NA	4 084	1 706
Cash and security holdings	153 766	NA	8 478	6 683

Federal Spending within State

	Federal funds, fiscal 1997		
	Millions of dollars	Percent distribution	Percent of U.S. total*
Total within state	98 138	100.0	6.9
Payments to individuals	56 988	58.1	7.2
Retirement and disability	29 751	30.3	6.5
Medicare	16 586	16.9	8.0
Food stamps	1 788	1.8	9.2
Supplemental Security Income	2 541	2.6	9.5
Grants	27 484	28.0	11.0
Medicaid and other health	15 299	15.6	13.4
Nutrition and family welfare	5 460	5.6	11.7
Education	1 340	1.4	7.8
Housing and community development	1 509	1.5	13.3
Salaries and wages	7 039	7.2	4.3
Defense procurement contracts	3 157	3.2	2.6
Non-defense procurement contracts	2 621	2.7	3.6

*State population is 6.8 percent of the U.S. total.

31 372	59 698		65 157	70 827	72 687	78 001	81 93	88 504	93 426	5.8	63 383	70 827	31 372	59 698	63 38
25 323	47 902		57 151	59 446	62 916	67 00		72 039	77 208	6.1	50 999	57 151	25 323	47 902	50 99
2 640	5 143			7 801				7 709	7 838	5.4	5 645	6 816	2 640	5 143	5 64
3 409	6 652		284					8 755	8 380	2.9	6 739	6 860	3 409	6 652	6 7
693	1 716		07					1 539	762	-9.7	1 561	811	693	1 716	1 5
716	1 93							7 217	7 618	5	5 178	6 049	716	9	

1997

Population (persons)	7,430,675
Population rank	11th
Population growth rank (1990–97)	12th
Per capita personal income	$23,174
Unemployment rate (percent)	3.6
Poverty rate (percent)	11.4

NORTH CAROLINA, STRETCHING OVER 500 MILES FROM ITS Atlantic Coast barrier islands in the East to the Appalachian mountains in the west, is the nation's 11th most populous state and among the top 25 percent of all states in rate of population growth during the 1990s. Located in the central third of the state is a complex of seven adjacent metropolitan areas, the largest of which are Raleigh-Durham-Chapel Hill toward the east, Greensboro-Winston Salem-High Point in the center, and Charlotte-Gastonia-Rock Hill (NC-SC) to the southwest. Five additional metropolitan areas lie wholly or partly within the state. Even so, the share of the population living in metropolitan areas in 1997 was only 67 percent, compared to 80 percent nationwide.

Despite declines or sluggish growth in such traditional manufacturing sectors as textiles, furniture, and tobacco, North Carolina has achieved measurable gains in economic well-being during the 1990s. Employment has grown rapidly, per capita income has increased, and the unemployment rate is well below the national average. Home construction has boomed, especially in the prosperous, rapidly-growing Charlotte and Raleigh-Durham areas. Agriculture has had a succession of good years, with net farm income rising above $3 billion in 1996 and 1997.

Average Annual Population Growth: 1990–97

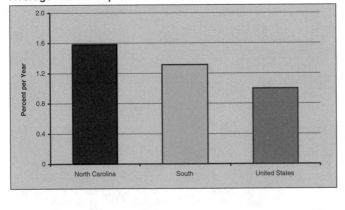

Median Household Income: 1989–97 (1997 dollars)

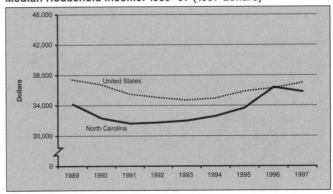

Unemployment Rate: 1989–97

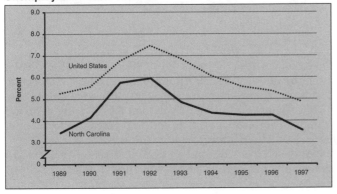

NORTH CAROLINA'S 1997 UNEMPLOYMENT RATE OF 3.6 PERcent was among the lowest in the nation. The rate has remained well below the national average throughout the 1990s, having peaked at 6 percent during the early 1990s recession, when the national rate was 7.5 percent, and having continued to average 1.5 percentage points below the national rate over the next five years.

Employment growth was especially strong in 1996, when the number at work rose by 4.2 percent; this was followed by a sturdy 2.3 percent further gain in 1997, when the proportion of the population age 16 and over holding jobs reached 64.4 percent.

POPULATION AND LABOR FORCE

NORTH CAROLINA'S POPULATION GREW 1.6 PERCENT PER YEAR from 1990 to 1997, compared with a national average of 1.0 percent. Metropolitan growth was more rapid than non-metropolitan, and minority groups grew more rapidly than the White, non-Hispanic majority.

Non-Hispanic Blacks constituted 22 percent of the North Carolina population in 1997—a share that has remained roughly constant since 1980. Despite rapid growth, other minority groups remained quite small percentages of the total. Hispanics doubled their population share from 1980 to 1997 but were still only 2 percent of the

state's population, compared to almost 11 percent nationwide. Asians and Native Americans were even smaller percentages. In absolute numbers rather than percentages, the White non-Hispanic population grew by 469,000 from 1990 to 1997, the Black non-Hispanic population by 190,000 and other groups combined by about 110,000.

Almost 60 percent of North Carolina's 11.5 percent total population growth from 1990 to 1997 was due to in-migration from other states. Natural increase (births minus deaths) accounted for almost 37 percent of the population gain and immigration from abroad for only 5 percent.

Population and Labor Force

	1980	1990	1991	1992	1993	1994	1995	1996	1997	Change*	
										State	U.S.
Population											
Total number of persons (thousands)	5 882	6 657	6 748	6 833	6 949	7 061	7 186	7 309	7 431	1.6	1.0
Percent distribution:											
White, Non-Hispanic	75.3	75.1	74.8	74.6	74.4	74.2	74.0	73.8	73.6	1.3	0.4
Black, Non-Hispanic	22.2	21.6	22.0	22.0	22.1	22.0	22.0	22.0	21.9	1.8	1.4
Asian	0.4	0.9	0.8	0.9	1.0	1.0	1.1	1.2	1.2	6.9	4.1
Native American	1.1	1.2	1.2	1.2	1.2	1.3	1.3	1.3	1.3	2.4	1.6
Hispanic	1.0	1.3	1.2	1.3	1.4	1.5	1.7	1.9	2.0	8.1	3.8
In metropolitan areas	63.7	66.1	66.2	66.3	66.4	66.5	66.7	66.8	66.9	1.8	1.0
Total number of households (thousands)	2 043	2 517	2 568	2 609	2 646	2 680	2 738	2 796	NA	1.8	1.2
Labor Force (thousands)											
Population 16 and over	4 443	5 214	5 287	5 335	5 415	5 493	5 585	5 674	5 754	1.4	1.0
Civilian labor force	2 855	3 468	3 512	3 548	3 557	3 597	3 631	3 783	3 844	1.5	1.1
Employed	2 668	3 324	3 308	3 335	3 381	3 440	3 473	3 618	3 705	1.6	1.2
Percent of population	60.1	63.8	62.6	62.5	62.4	62.6	62.2	63.8	64.4		
Unemployment rate (percent)	6.6	4.2	5.8	6.0	4.9	4.4	4.3	4.3	3.6		

*Compound annual average percent change, 1990–1997; 1990–1996 for households.

Population Change and Components: 1990–97

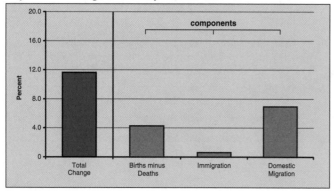

Average Annual Household and Population Growth

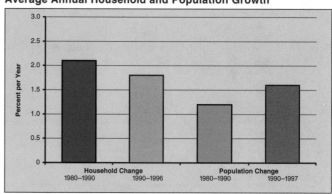

Population by Age; Births and Deaths

	1990		1997	
	State	U.S.	State	U.S.
Age distribution (percent)				
Under 5 years	7.1	7.6	7.0	7.2
5 to 17 years	17.3	18.2	18.2	18.8
18 to 64 years	63.5	61.8	62.3	61.3
65 years and over	12.1	12.5	12.5	12.7
Birth and death rates (per thousand population)				
Births	15.8	16.7	14.4	14.6
Deaths	8.6	8.6	8.9	8.6

THE AGE DISTRIBUTION OF NORTH CAROLINA'S POPULATION has changed little during the 1990s, and it differs little from the national distribution. Retirees as well as workers and their families have migrated into the state during the 1990s. The percent of the population age 65 and over rose slightly from 1990 to 1997, and the percent age 17 and under somewhat more, so that the percent age 18 to 64 experienced a corresponding decline. Each of these moderate shifts has been in line with national trends.

HOUSEHOLD AND PERSONAL INCOME

HOUSEHOLD INCOME AND PERSONS IN POVERTY	1990	1995	1996	1997	
				State	U.S.
Median household income (1997 dollars)	32 332	33 679	36 418	35 840	37 005
Persons in poverty (thousands)	829	877	885	839	35 574
Poverty rate (percent)	13.0	12.6	12.2	11.4	13.3

NORTH CAROLINA'S INFLATION-ADJUSTED MEDIAN HOUSE-hold income followed a strong, if somewhat irregular, upward course from 1992 to 1997, bringing it closer to the national average. During 1995–97, the state's median household income averaged 97 percent of the U.S. level, compared to only 91 percent as recently as 1992–93. North Carolina's 1997 poverty rate was well below the national average and the lowest of any southern state.

Personal income per capita also has moved toward the national average. North Carolina stood at only 80 percent of the U.S. average in 1980 and 87 percent in 1990, but was above 91 percent each year from 1995 through 1997.

North Carolina derived 68 percent of its personal income from worker and proprietor earnings in 1997, slightly above the 66 percent national average. The 15 percent from dividends, interest and rent was a little below the national average, while the share coming from transfer payments was just at the average. The relatively large, and growing, negative adjustment for residence indicates that on balance workers were commuting into North Carolina from other states.

The 1.8 percent farm share of 1997 personal income, although small, was close to three times the national average and has remained relatively constant in recent years. Among transfer payments, "other income maintenance," showed by far the largest percent growth from 1990 to 1997. This category consists largely of the earned income tax credit, a benefit that goes to workers whose earnings fall below specified thresholds. It was the most rapidly growing type of transfer payment nationwide, and its even more rapid growth in North Carolina likely reflects the relatively rapid growth of the total work force.

Personal Income
(millions of dollars)

	1980	1989	1990	1991	1992	1993	1994	1995	1996	1997	Change*
Earnings by place of work	36 948	79 100	83 717	86 264	94 126	100 298	106 370	112 630	119 066	127 682	6.2
Wages and salaries	30 571	64 007	67 713	69 552	75 412	79 538	84 512	90 310	96 030	103 494	6.2
Other labor income	2 785	6 590	7 238	7 816	8 871	9 850	10 496	10 453	10 260	10 485	6.0
Proprietors' income	3 592	8 504	8 766	8 896	9 843	10 911	11 363	11 866	12 776	13 703	6.1
Farm	403	1 366	1 776	2 061	1 969	2 339	2 348	2 191	2 550	2 720	9.0
Nonfarm	3 189	7 138	6 990	6 835	7 875	8 572	9 015	9 675	10 227	10 984	5.5
(−) Personal contributions for social insurance	2 046	5 337	5 668	5 968	6 435	6 891	7 443	8 008	8 457	9 090	6.9
(+) Adjustment for residence	-3	-432	-480	-485	-533	-617	-688	-776	-845	-923	NA
(=) **Net earnings by state of residence**	34 899	73 332	77 569	79 811	87 157	92 790	98 239	103 846	109 764	117 669	6.1
(+) Dividends, interest, and rent	6 120	16 666	17 728	17 947	17 810	18 438	19 869	21 820	24 267	25 794	5.6
(+) Transfer payments	6 704	13 913	15 532	17 735	19 598	21 753	22 558	25 214	27 164	28 611	9.4
(=) **Total personal income**	47 722	103 910	110 829	115 494	124 565	132 981	140 667	150 880	161 194	172 073	6.5
Farm	658	1 654	2 116	2 397	2 294	2 698	2 695	2 549	2 919	3 085	8.1
Nonfarm	47 064	102 257	108 714	113 097	122 272	130 283	137 972	148 331	158 275	168 988	6.5
Personal income per capita (dollars)											
Current dollars	8 090	15 827	16 649	17 115	18 230	19 140	19 919	20 994	22 054	23 174	4.9
1997 dollars	15 468	20 009	20 035	19 763	20 391	20 827	21 168	21 823	22 458	23 174	1.9

*Compound annual average percent change, 1989–1997

Government Transfer Payments

	Millions of dollars		Percent change*	
	1990	1997	State	U.S.
Total government payments to individuals	14 737	27 443	86.2	62.7
Retirement, disability, and insurance	8 515	13 721	61.1	48.2
Social Security	6 236	10 000	60.4	46.1
Government employee retirement	2 123	3 522	65.9	60.3
Medical payments	3 963	9 827	148.0	101.2
Income maintenance	1 212	2 451	102.3	58.0
Supplemental Security Income	468	795	70.1	75.4
Family assistance	268	324	20.9	-0.5
Food Stamps	301	459	52.4	27.1
Other income maintenance	175	873	398.6	189.8
Unemployment insurance benefits	325	381	17.2	10.6
Veterans benefits and other	722	1 062	47.0	30.8

*Percent change, 1990–1997

Government Payments to Individuals: 1997

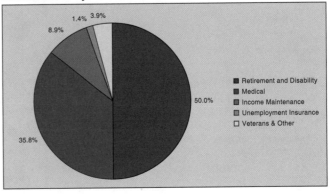

- Retirement and Disability — 50.0%
- Medical — 35.8%
- Income Maintenance — 8.9%
- Unemployment Insurance — 1.4%
- Veterans & Other — 3.9%

ECONOMIC STRUCTURE

LEADING PRIVATE INDUSTRIES, 1997 (Worker and proprietor earnings, millions of dollars)		FASTEST EARNINGS GROWTH, 1989–97 (percent increase)	
Health services	$9 469	Real estate	154.5
Business services	6 268	Business services	154.0
Construction specialties	5 313	Social services	149.2
Textile mill products	4 991	Health services	112.8
Industrial machinery manufacturing	3 624	Banks and other credit institutions	111.7

MANUFACTURING EMPLOYMENT IN NORTH CAROLINA HAS declined in the 1990s, with much of the drop occurring between 1995 and 1997, when 30,000 manufacturing jobs were lost, a 3.4 percent decline over the two years. This decline was more than offset by strong job growth in other industry sectors, however, so that total private nonfarm employment rose nearly 6 percent from 1995 to 1997, with the service sector alone contributing 113,000 jobs.

Although North Carolina, like the nation as a whole, is increasingly a service-producing economy, manufacturing is still important, accounting for 18.5 percent of total employment and 23.8 percent of worker and proprietor earnings, compared to national averages of 12.4 and 17.7 percent, respectively. Two of North Carolina's five largest industries—textile mill products and industrial machinery—are within the manufacturing sector. However, faced by stiff competition from abroad, earnings in textile mill products have shown little growth in the 1990s, and earnings in the closely related apparel industry, as well as in

tobacco manufacturing have declined. Industrial machinery manufacturing had slightly below average earnings growth, while the chemical industry, although smaller, has had above average growth.

Of special importance to the state is the banking industry, having ranked sixth in size (measured by worker and proprietor earnings) in 1997 and fifth in rate of growth from 1989 to 1997. Charlotte, the state's largest city, long has been recognized as one of the nation's leading banking centers.

Each of the state's most rapidly growing industries from 1989 to 1997 was within the service-producing sector, and each more than doubled in size. Real estate was the fastest growing industry, with business services second.

Farm employment was 1.9 percent of total employment in both 1996 and 1997, just equal to the national average. Earnings of farm workers and proprietors, however, accounted for almost 2.5 percent of total earnings in both years, compared to only about 1 percent nationwide.

Employment and Earnings by Sector

	1980	1989	1990	1991	1992	1993	1994	1995	1996	1997 Number	1997 Percent of total	Change*
Employment *(thousands of persons)*												
Total	3 060	3 865	3 918	3 893	3 995	4 121	4 241	4 382	4 485	4 612	100.0	2.2
Farm	151	95	96	98	97	91	88	93	87	88	1.9	-1.0
Nonfarm	2 909	3 769	3 823	3 794	3 898	4 029	4 153	4 289	4 398	4 524	98.1	2.3
Private nonfarm	2 383	3 157	3 208	3 182	3 246	3 368	3 480	3 610	3 709	3 821	82.8	2.4
Agricultural service, forestry, and fishing	21	35	38	39	38	44	45	48	52	55	1.2	6.0
Mining	6	6	7	7	5	5	5	5	5	5	0.1	-2.3
Construction	160	239	242	223	227	239	252	267	284	302	6.6	3.0
Manufacturing	840	888	872	845	854	868	882	884	866	854	18.5	-0.5
Transportation and public utilities	130	166	170	172	172	178	183	187	193	198	4.3	2.2
Wholesale trade	130	181	179	178	181	179	187	194	193	201	4.4	1.3
Retail trade	431	636	643	639	653	673	699	732	753	775	16.8	2.5
Finance, insurance, and real estate	172	218	224	222	216	226	236	246	258	272	5.9	2.8
Services	493	788	834	856	900	956	990	1 045	1 106	1 158	25.1	4.9
Government	526	612	615	612	653	662	673	680	689	703	15.2	1.8
Earnings *(millions of dollars)*												
Total	36 948	79 100	83 717	86 264	94 126	100 298	106 370	112 630	119 066	127 682	100.0	6.2
Farm	658	1 654	2 116	2 397	2 294	2 698	2 695	2 549	2 919	3 085	2.4	8.1
Nonfarm	36 289	77 446	81 601	83 867	91 833	97 601	103 675	110 081	116 147	124 597	97.6	6.1
Private nonfarm	29 957	64 520	67 590	69 138	75 569	80 630	86 079	91 639	96 969	104 383	81.8	6.2
Agricultural service, forestry, and fishing	152	411	464	482	503	540	577	618	660	742	0.6	7.7
Mining	210	175	186	188	127	136	160	170	177	198	0.2	1.6
Construction	2 112	5 152	5 244	4 883	5 202	5 805	6 954	7 704	8 561	8 561	6.7	6.6
Manufacturing	12 183	22 308	22 758	23 143	25 260	26 455	27 847	28 750	29 064	30 426	23.8	4.0
Transportation and public utilities	2 496	5 187	5 457	5 677	6 015	6 416	6 873	7 189	7 562	7 950	6.2	5.5
Wholesale trade	2 242	4 996	5 241	5 367	5 743	5 966	6 468	6 918	7 106	7 761	6.1	5.7
Retail trade	3 747	8 026	8 222	8 397	8 970	9 465	10 163	10 866	11 415	12 267	9.6	5.4
Finance, insurance, and real estate	1 574	3 840	4 141	4 250	4 878	5 513	5 840	6 505	7 335	8 146	6.4	9.9
Services	5 242	14 424	15 877	16 753	18 870	20 334	21 778	23 669	25 946	28 332	22.2	8.8
Government	6 332	12 926	14 011	14 729	16 263	16 971	17 596	18 442	19 178	20 215	15.8	5.7

*Compound annual average percent change, 1989–1997

ECONOMIC STRUCTURE (Continued)

THE ANNUAL EARNINGS OF NORTH CAROLINA WORKERS HAVE been moving closer to the national average, but still were relatively low. In 1980, private nonfarm workers had annual earnings equal to only 83 percent of the national average, but by 1989 this had risen to 86 percent, and by 1997 to 88 percent.

The 1997 figure of $26,271 for all wage and salary workers also was 88 percent of the national average. Wages and salaries in each major sector were below the national average, and the gap was particularly large in manufacturing, which was only 82 percent of the national average. In part, this gap reflects the dominance of the textile industry—a relatively low wage industry—in the state's manufacturing.

Manufacturing constituted 27 percent of North Carolina's gross state product (GSP) in 1996, substantially above the national average of 17.5 percent. This was the largest share of any South Atlantic state, although neighboring South Carolina was a close second. Growth of manufacturing has not kept pace with overall growth of North Carolina's GSP, however, so that the manufacturing share has declined from 32.1 percent in 1989 to 27.0 percent in 1996. Much of the decline occurred from 1994 to 1996. Among important manufacturing industries failing to keep pace with total GSP growth during these two years were electronic equipment, textiles, apparel, tobacco, and chemicals.

The United States experienced strong export growth from 1994 to 1997, and North Carolina's goods exports grew even more rapidly than the national average; a total of 46 percent, compared to 34 percent nationwide. The state's exports are fairly heavily concentrated in the top five industries, which accounted for 62 percent of all goods exports in 1997. Exports of chemical products almost doubled between 1993 and 1997, and exports of industrial machinery and computers rose 80 percent. Exports of apparel almost tripled, bringing this industry to fourth place in the export rankings. In contrast, exports of tobacco products, at $350 million in 1997, were less than half what they were in 1993.

Average Annual Wages and Salaries by Sector
(dollars)

	1989	1996	1997 State	1997 U.S.
All wage and salary workers	19 195	25 088	26 271	29 809
Farm	10 083	12 494	11 494	16 442
Nonfarm	19 270	25 182	26 385	29 900
Private nonfarm	19 206	25 114	26 389	29 867
Agricultural service, forestry, and fishing	12 802	16 624	17 417	17 941
Mining	30 505	37 043	39 392	49 800
Construction	19 121	25 239	26 682	31 765
Manufacturing	21 998	29 315	31 277	38 351
Transportation and utilities	28 152	35 422	36 649	38 222
Wholesale trade	25 809	34 374	36 038	39 466
Retail trade	11 614	14 684	15 362	16 206
Finance, insurance, and real estate	24 123	36 157	38 286	44 993
Services	17 171	23 090	24 087	27 588
Government	19 550	25 486	26 367	30 062

Gross State Product and Manufacturing
(millions of dollars, except as noted)

	1989	1994	1995	1996
Gross state product, total	136 904	182 268	192 219	204 229
Manufacturing:				
Millions of dollars	43 955	53 053	53 804	55 075
Percent of total gross state product	32.1	29.1	28.0	27.0
Per worker (dollars)	49 491	60 159	60 854	63 612
New capital expenditures, manufacturing	NA	5 011	5 049	4 880

Exports of Goods
(millions of dollars)

	1994	1995	1996	1997
All goods	8 969	10 567	11 587	13 102
Manufactures	8 225	9 773	10 744	12 170
Agricultural and livestock products	635	688	715	764
Other commodities	110	106	128	168
Top goods exports, 1997:				
Industrial machinery and computers	1 451	1 796	2 016	2 090
Chemical products	1 135	1 419	1 610	1 953
Electric and electronic equipment	1 084	1 182	1 386	1 553
Apparel	698	1 098	1 233	1 449
Textile mill products	743	910	997	1 075

HOUSING

PROSPERITY AND A GROWING POPULATION HAVE PRODUCED A residential construction boom in North Carolina. The new home production rate has been well above the U.S. average throughout the 1990s, and especially so from 1994 to 1997, when the state's new home production rate averaged 13.1 per thousand population, fully twice the national rate. Home construction in 1997 was especially strong in the Charlotte and Raleigh-Durham metropolitan areas; together these two areas contain about one-third of the state's population, but accounted for almost one-half of all building permits issued in 1997. Sales of existing homes also were strong in North Carolina during the mid-1990s. However, a marked increase in the rental vacancy rate suggests that supply may have caught up with demand and that the housing production rate may fall.

Over 70 percent of North Carolina's households owned their homes in 1997. Nationwide, the 1997 rate was 65.7.

Despite the residential building boom, North Carolina has substantial pockets of substandard housing, especially

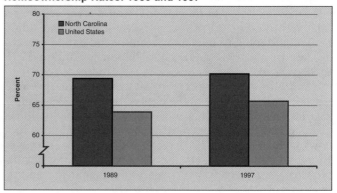

Homeownership Rates: 1989 and 1997

in rural areas, and the state recently began a new initiative to assist owners of substandard housing in the installation of adequate plumbing facilities.

Housing Supply

	1989	1990	1991	1992	1993	1994	1995	1996	1997
Residential building permits (thousands)	48.4	40.8	39.0	48.2	53.3	62.9	60.9	67.0	73.0
New home production (including manufactured housing):									
Thousands of homes	66.5	59.8	55.9	68.7	77.6	93.3	90.2	100.2	96.5
Rate per 1,000 population									
North Carolina	10.1	9.0	8.3	10.1	11.2	13.2	12.6	13.7	13.0
U.S.	6.2	5.2	4.5	5.1	5.6	6.4	6.3	6.6	6.5
Existing home sales:									
Thousands of homes	127.5	135.9	139.9	160.2	185.0	204.1	201.0	212.5	228.0
Change from previous year (percent)									
North Carolina	-5.3	6.6	2.9	14.5	15.5	10.3	-1.5	5.7	7.3
U.S.	-3.9	-4.0	0.0	9.2	8.2	4.8	-3.7	7.5	3.8
Home ownership rate (percent of households)	69.4	69.0	69.3	68.6	68.8	68.7	70.1	70.4	70.2
Rental vacancy rate (percent of rental housing units)	7.4	7.2	7.7	7.0	5.6	6.1	8.2	8.0	9.7

AGRICULTURE

NORTH CAROLINA IS THE NATION'S LEADING GROWER OF tobacco, and tobacco accounted for 15 percent of 1997 agricultural sales. Even more important than tobacco were hogs and pigs (34 percent of sales) and poultry and poultry products (28 percent). North Carolina is among the leading producers of blueberries, strawberries, peanuts, and Christmas trees, and is exceeded only by Idaho in the quantity of trout sold. However, these items account for relatively minor percentages of total sales.

Farm income has grown fairly steadily during the 1990s.

NORTH CAROLINA FARMS, 1997	
Number of farms	57 000
Total acres (thousands):	9 000
Average per farm	158
Value of land and buildings (millions of dollars)	18 450
Average per farm (dollars)	323 684

Net income exceeded $3 billion in 1997, up nearly two-thirds from 1990. The number of farms in North Carolina decreased about 5 percent from 1992 to 1997.

Farm Income
(millions of dollars)

	1980	1989	1990	1991	1992	1993	1994	1995	1996	1997
Gross income	3 933	5 643	6 244	6 266	6 660	7 297	7 761	8 467	9 579	10 094
Receipts from sales	3 529	4 782	5 410	5 448	5 761	6 293	6 702	7 233	8 307	8 762
Government payments	13	94	73	53	75	132	78	41	78	88
Imputed and miscellaneous income	390	767	761	764	824	872	982	1 192	1 193	1 245
(−) Production expenses	3 542	4 119	4 281	4 277	4 509	4 859	5 238	5 967	6 624	6 895
(=) Realized net income	390	1 524	1 963	1 988	2 151	2 438	2 523	2 500	2 954	3 199
(+) Inventory change	13	-14	10	247	60	8	316	-32	107	15
(=) Net income	403	1 510	1 972	2 235	2 211	2 446	2 840	2 468	3 062	3 214
Corporate income	0	144	196	174	242	107	492	277	512	494
Farm proprietors income	403	1 366	1 776	2 061	1 969	2 339	2 348	2 191	2 550	2 720

EDUCATION

EDUCATIONAL ATTAINMENT Percent of population age 25 and over, 1997	State	United States
High school graduate or higher	78.4	82.1
College graduate or higher	22.6	23.9

NORTH CAROLINA HAS MADE GREAT STRIDES IN EDUCATIONAL attainment over the past quarter-century. In 1970, only 38.5 percent of North Carolinians over age 25 had completed high school, compared to 52.4 percent nationwide. By 1997, that percentage in North Carolina had risen to 78.4 percent, much closer to the national average of 82.1 percent. Only 8.4 percent of the state's residents held a bachelor's degree in 1970, compared to 22.6 percent in 1997.

Although per pupil expenditures and average teachers salaries remain well below the national average, North Carolina has received national recognition for its educational progress. The National Educational Goals Panel has identified North Carolina as the state showing the most significant improvement during the 1990s. Fourth and eighth grade reading scores and fourth grade math scores on the National Assessment of Education Progress (NAEP) now exceed national averages, and the state led the nation in point gains on SAT scores from 1988 to 1998.

High School Completion: 1990–97

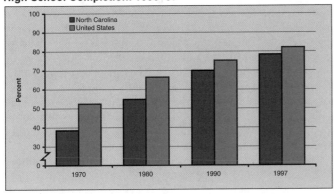

Education Indicators

	State	U.S.
Elementary and secondary schools		
Enrollment, 1995–96		
Total (thousands)	1 265	49 873
Percent in private schools	6.4	10.1
Expenditures per pupil (dollars), 1995–96	5 090	6 146
Average teacher salary (dollars), 1996–97	31 225	38 509
Higher education		
Enrollment, 1996–97		
Total (thousands)	373	14 218
Percent of population 18–34	20.1	21.8
Percent minority	24.8	26.1
Percent in private schools	18.8	22.6

HEALTH

NORTH CAROLINA'S AGE-ADJUSTED DEATH RATE WAS ABOVE the national average, and this excess is spread fairly evenly across most of the leading causes of death. A critical health need is to reduce the state's high infant mortality rate. While the national infant mortality rate has come down from 9.2 deaths per thousand live births in 1990 to an average of 7.3 in 1995–97, the North Carolina rate has dropped only from 10.6 to 9.3, a rate above that of any other South Atlantic state. The State has addressed this problem through its Baby Love program, a set of initiatives to improve health care for low-income women and their babies. Included in this effort are expanded Medicaid eligibility, emphasis on early prenatal care, childbirth and parenting classes, and screening of all newborns for certain health problems.

Health Indicators

	1990	1995	1996	1997
Infant mortality				
(rate per thousand live births)				
North Carolina	10.6	9.2	9.2	9.6
U.S.	9.2	7.6	7.3	7.1
Total deaths, age-adjusted rate				
(rate per thousand population)				
North Carolina	5.5	5.4	5.4	5.2
U.S.	5.2	5.0	4.9	4.8
Persons not covered by health insurance				
(percent of population)				
North Carolina	13.8	14.3	16.0	15.5
U.S.	13.9	15.4	15.6	16.1

Leading Causes of Death, 1996
(deaths per 100,000 population)

	Age-adjusted		Not age-adjusted	
	State	U.S.	State	U.S.
Deaths from all causes	537.4	491.6	905.3	872.5
Heart disease	144.9	134.5	271.3	276.4
Cancer	133.8	127.9	207.5	203.4
Cerebrovascular diseases	34.1	26.4	72.8	60.3
Chronic obstructive pulmonary disease	22.9	21.0	41.1	40.0
Diabetes mellitus	15.3	13.6	24.8	23.3
Pneumonia and influenza	14.9	12.8	34.5	31.6
HIV	10.6	11.1	11.3	11.7
Liver disease	7.4	7.5	9.4	9.4
Alzheimer's disease	3.4	2.7	9.3	8.1
Accidents and adverse effects	36.3	30.4	42.8	35.8
Motor vehicle accidents	20.4	16.2	20.6	16.5
Suicide	11.5	10.8	12.4	11.6
Homicide	9.7	8.5	9.2	7.9
Injury by firearm	15.9	12.9	16.1	12.8

GOVERNMENT

STATE AND LOCAL TAXES, 1995–96	State	U.S.
Per capita (dollars)	2 123	2 477
Percent of personal income	10.2	10.8

NORTH CAROLINA'S STATE AND LOCAL TAXES PER CAPITA IN 1995–96 were somewhat below the national average, both in dollars and as a percent of personal income. Local taxes were only 30 percent of the state and local total, compared to a 41 percent national average, indicating considerably above average state-level responsibility for revenue collection.

At the state level, total taxes per capita actually exceed-

State Government Finances, 1996–97

	Millions of dollars	Percent distribu- tion	Dollars per capita	
			State	U.S.
General revenue	21 696	100.0	2 922	3 049
Intergovernmental revenue	6 318	29.1	851	863
Taxes	12 678	58.4	1 708	1 660
General sales	3 057	14.1	412	551
Selective sales	2 259	10.4	304	257
License taxes	775	3.6	104	106
Individual income	5 459	25.2	735	542
Corporation net income	981	4.5	132	115
Other taxes	147	0.7	20	90
Other general revenue	2 699	12.4	364	526
General expenditure	20 955	100.0	2 822	2 951
Intergovernmental expenditure	7 315	34.9	985	989
Direct expenditure	13 640	65.1	1 837	1 962
General expenditure, by function:				
Education	8 561	40.9	1 153	1 033
Public welfare	4 733	22.6	637	761
Hospitals and health	1 682	8.0	226	237
Highways	1 888	9.0	254	225
Police protection and corrections	1 155	5.5	156	137
Natural resources, parks and recreation	499	2.4	67	63
Governmental administration	592	2.8	80	107
Interest on general debt	297	1.4	40	99
Other and unallocable	1 548	7.4	208	290
Debt at end of fiscal year	5 677	NA	765	1 706
Cash and security holdings	42 723	NA	5 754	6 683

Federal Spending within State

	Federal funds, fiscal 1997		
	Millions of dollars	Percent distribution	Percent of U.S. total*
Total within state	34 592	100.0	2.4
Payments to individuals	20 491	59.2	2.6
Retirement and disability	12 691	36.7	2.8
Medicare	4 750	13.7	2.3
Food stamps	482	1.4	2.5
Supplemental Security Income	743	2.1	2.8
Grants	6 798	19.7	2.7
Medicaid and other health	3 542	10.2	3.1
Nutrition and family welfare	1 122	3.2	2.4
Education	417	1.2	2.4
Housing and community development	224	0.6	2.0
Salaries and wages	4 887	14.1	3.0
Defense procurement contracts	1 083	3.1	0.9
Non-defense procurement contracts	878	2.5	1.2

*State population is 2.8 percent of the U.S. total.

ed the all-state average. Revenue from the individual income tax made up 43 percent of the state's total tax revenue in 1996-97, compared to an all-state average of 33 percent, while general and selective sales taxes produced 42 percent of the North Carolina's total tax revenue, compared to an all-state average of 49 percent. Corporate income taxes yielded just under 8 percent of the state's tax revenues, a little above the all-state average of 7 percent.

State general expenditure per capita in North Carolina equaled about 96 percent of the average for all states in 1996–97. Per capita expenditures on education were 112 percent of the all-state average. This figures is for state government spending only; local spending appeared to be well below the national average, since total per-pupil expenditure in elementary and secondary schools was only 83 percent of the national average in 1995–96.

Interest on North Carolina's general debt averaged only $40 per capita in 1996-97, compared to a national average of $99. The state appeared to be in excellent financial shape at year end, with debt equal to $765 per capita, compared to $1,706 nationwide, and cash and security holdings about 7.5 times the size of the debt.

North Carolina had 2.8 percent of the nation's population and received 2.4 percent of federal funds distributed to states and their residents in fiscal 1997. The difference is in part due to federal defense and nondefense contract payments that were disproportionately low relative to the state's population. The share of total wages and salaries paid to federal workers slightly exceeded the state's population share, however. The distribution of federal funds among categories other than contracts and wages and salaries was roughly in line with the state's population.

31 372	59 698		65 157	70 827	72 687	78 001	81 93	88 504	93 426	5.8	63 383	70 827	31 372	59 698	63 38
25 323	47 902			57 151	59 446	62 916	67 00	72 039	77 208	6.1	50 999	57 151	25 323	47 902	50 99
2 640	5 143					7 801		7 709	7 838	5.4	5 645	6 816	2 640	5 143	5 64
3 409	6 652						284	8 755	8 380	2.9	6 739	6 660	3 409	6 652	6 73
693	1 716							1 539	762	-9.7	1 561	811	693	1 716	1 56
2 716								7 217	7 618	5.6	3 178	6 049	2 716		

1997

Population (persons)	640,965
Population rank	47th
Population growth rank (1990–97)	48th
Per capita personal income	$20,213
Unemployment rate (percent)	2.5
Poverty rate (percent)	13.6

NORTH DAKOTA'S POPULATION GROWTH RATE OF 0.1 PERCENT per year during the 1990s was the fourth slowest of any state. Nontheless, the state's economy grew rapidly with employment and earnings growth that substantially exceeded national trends. Low prevailing wages probably were one factor attracting new jobs in services and manufacturing, sectors that grew faster than average. The healthcare industry was particularly large here, partly reflecting the concentration of older residents. The state's traditional economic base of farming has not grown as fast as the nonfarm sector; though the state is a leader in wheat production, it is following the national trend of declining farm employment. The historically large federal government presence also has ebbed. Employment in the farm and government sectors combined has declined as a percent of total employment, from 33 percent in 1980 to 25 percent in 1997, though the latter figure is still large compared to most states. Recent growth was concentrated in mainstream industries, as the state slowly shifted closer to the national average of jobs by sector.

Median household income in North Dakota fell short of the national average by about 15 percent, though the discrepancy is partly compensated for by the low cost of housing in the state. Per capita income has increased during the 1989 to 1997 period at a rate that exceeded the national average.

Average Annual Population Growth: 1990–97

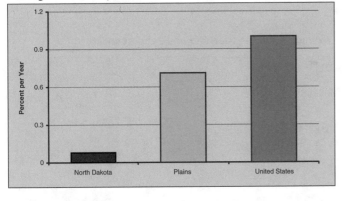

Median Household Income: 1989–97 (1997 dollars)

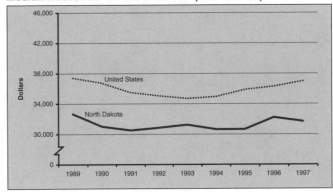

Unemployment Rate: 1989–97

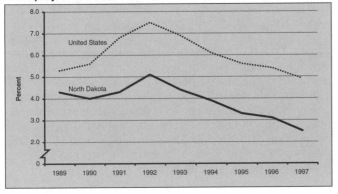

NORTH DAKOTA'S UNEMPLOYMENT RATE HAS DECLINED QUITE dramatically since its recession high point, moving from a moderate 5.1 percent in 1992 down to an astonishing 2.5 percent in 1997. It beat out Nebraska for the honor of lowest unemployment rate in the nation. Remarkably, despite the state's very low population growth, there was moderate growth in the labor force and even stronger growth in employment, beating out the job growth rate in the nation. The tight labor market apparently is drawing in nontraditional workers, as the ratio of employment to population moved up steadily.

303

POPULATION AND LABOR FORCE

OVER THE 1990–97 PERIOD, THE STATE HAS HAD A TOTAL POPulation growth of only 0.6 percent, well below the national average. The state has grown by only less than 4,000 people since 1990, representing the fourth lowest percent increase in the nation. The 1997 population level remained lower than in 1980, as the minimal growth in the 1990s could not compensate for losses during the 1980s. This low rate growth can be attributed to substantial out-migration and an above-average death rate because of the high proportion of older residents. The Native American population is the state's largest minority group and grew to 4.6 percent of the population, up from 3.1 percent in 1980. The White non-Hispanic and Black populations have both declined in absolute numbers since 1990. North Dakota's White, non-Hispanic population was still an overwhelming majority, at over 93 percent of the total population. The percent of state population living in metropolitan areas, about 43 percent, was the tenth lowest among all states, although this ratio creeped higher in the state during the 1990s. The largest city, Fargo, had a population of about 80,000 in 1997.

Population and Labor Force

	1980	1990	1991	1992	1993	1994	1995	1996	1997	Change* State	Change* U.S.
Population											
Total number of persons (thousands)	653	637	634	635	637	640	641	643	641	0.1	1.0
Percent distribution:											
White, Non-Hispanic	95.7	93.8	94.0	93.8	93.7	93.6	93.4	93.2	93.1	0.0	0.4
Black, Non-Hispanic	0.4	0.9	0.6	0.6	0.6	0.6	0.6	0.6	0.6	-6.7	1.4
Asian	0.4	0.6	0.6	0.7	0.7	0.7	0.8	0.8	0.8	3.9	4.1
Native American	3.1	3.9	4.2	4.2	4.3	4.4	4.4	4.5	4.6	2.4	1.6
Hispanic	0.5	0.8	0.8	0.8	0.8	0.8	0.9	1.0	1.1	3.3	3.8
In metropolitan areas	35.9	40.4	40.9	41.4	41.8	42.2	42.5	42.7	42.9	0.9	1.0
Total number of households (thousands)	228	241	240	242	242	242	244	247	NA	0.4	1.2
Labor Force (thousands)											
Population 16 and over	486	484	481	483	485	489	492	497	497	0.4	1.0
Civilian labor force	303	318	313	314	320	337	336	344	348	1.3	1.1
Employed	288	305	300	298	306	324	325	334	339	1.5	1.2
Percent of population	59.3	63.1	62.4	61.8	63.1	66.2	66.0	67.2	68.2		
Unemployment rate (percent)	5.0	4.0	4.3	5.1	4.4	3.9	3.3	3.1	2.5		

*Compound annual average percent change, 1990–1997; 1990–1996 for households.

Population Change and Components: 1990–97

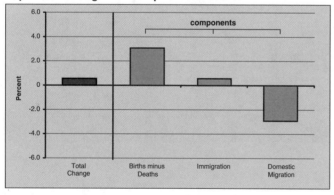

Average Annual Household and Population Growth

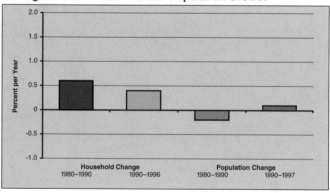

Population by Age; Births and Deaths

	1990 State	1990 U.S.	1997 State	1997 U.S.
Age distribution (percent)				
Under 5 years	7.4	7.6	6.4	7.2
5 to 17 years	19.5	18.2	19.4	18.8
18 to 64 years	58.9	61.8	59.8	61.3
65 years and over	14.3	12.5	14.4	12.7
Birth and death rates (per thousand population)				
Births	14.5	16.7	13.0	14.6
Deaths	8.9	8.6	9.5	8.6

NORTH DAKOTA'S POPULATION HAS BEEN GRADUALLY GROWing older. The proportion of population that was children under 18 declined by 1 percentage point since 1990, while the share of working age adults grew by 1 percentage point. However, this segment is smaller than average compared to the nation. The state had a significantly greater proportion of its population over age 64 than the United States as a whole. Birth rates have fallen between 1990 and 1997, while death rates increased.

HOUSEHOLD AND PERSONAL INCOME

HOUSEHOLD INCOME AND PERSONS IN POVERTY	1990	1995	1996	1997 State	1997 U.S.
Median household income (1997 dollars)	31 024	30 635	32 192	31 661	37 005
Persons in poverty (thousands)	87	76	69	87	35 574
Poverty rate (percent)	13.7	12.0	11.0	13.6	13.3

NORTH DAKOTA'S 1997 MEDIAN HOUSEHOLD INCOME OF $31,661 amounted to only 86 percent of the national average. Throughout the 1990s, the state's median income has ranged from 84 to 90 percent of the U.S. median income. The state's poverty rate of 13.6 percent in 1997 was higher than in 1995–96 and similar to the U.S. average of 13.3 percent.

The state's total personal income per capita increased by nearly 17 percent in inflation-adjusted dollars from 1989 to 1997, a much greater increase than that nationwide and a contrast with the stagnation in median household income. At $20,213, North Dakota's per capita income remains about 80 percent of the national average, however. With the state's low average wages and its relatively small working age population, earnings per capita were only 76 percent as high as the U.S. average in 1997.

Transfers per capita were closer to average at 93 percent, and income from dividends and interest was 83 percent of average. The adjustment for residence indicates that in 1997 workers commuting into North Dakota earned a total of $242 million more than North Dakota residents working elsewhere.

Growth of government transfer payments in the state from 1990 to 1997 was well below the national average, increasing only 44.3 percent. This is a modest increase even considering the state's minimal population growth. Both of the two major categories of transfers, retirement and medical payments, grew much more slowly than nationwide. Family assistance decreased by nearly 12 percent, and food stamps grew at a much slower rate than the national average. Earned income tax credits, the major component of other income maintenance, grew rapidly.

Personal Income
(millions of dollars)

	1980	1989	1990	1991	1992	1993	1994	1995	1996	1997	Change*
Earnings by place of work	3 552	6 032	6 627	6 767	7 565	7 591	8 333	8 278	9 394	9 166	5.4
Wages and salaries	3 195	4 669	4 957	5 195	5 537	5 819	6 139	6 534	6 927	7 306	5.8
Other labor income	255	427	476	525	578	638	682	687	676	680	6.0
Proprietors' income	101	936	1 193	1 047	1 449	1 134	1 512	1 057	1 791	1 179	2.9
Farm	-426	244	503	320	679	263	565	89	772	122	-8.3
Nonfarm	527	692	690	727	770	871	947	968	1 019	1 057	5.4
(−) Personal contributions for social insurance	242	463	498	532	552	585	620	663	692	727	5.8
(+) Adjustment for residence	-141	-173	-180	-189	-208	-237	-251	-264	-278	-292	NA
(=) Net earnings by state of residence	3 169	5 395	5 948	6 047	6 806	6 768	7 461	7 351	8 424	8 147	5.3
(+) Dividends, interest, and rent	1 164	1 851	2 060	1 973	1 957	1 986	1 993	2 139	2 267	2 325	2.9
(+) Transfer payments	773	1 589	1 720	1 797	1 955	2 106	2 159	2 238	2 360	2 482	5.7
(=) Total personal income	5 106	8 835	9 729	9 817	10 718	10 860	11 612	11 728	13 051	12 954	4.9
Farm	-348	325	592	402	759	344	657	188	882	233	-4.1
Nonfarm	5 454	8 510	9 136	9 415	9 958	10 516	10 955	11 540	12 169	12 721	5.2
Personal income per capita (dollars)											
Current dollars	7 803	13 669	15 264	15 480	16 867	17 043	18 157	18 287	20 308	20 213	5.0
1997 dollars	14 920	17 281	18 368	17 875	18 867	18 545	19 295	19 009	20 680	20 213	2.0

*Compound annual average percent change, 1989–1997

Government Transfer Payments

	Millions of dollars 1990	Millions of dollars 1997	Percent change* State	Percent change* U.S.
Total government payments to individuals	1 649	2 380	44.3	62.7
Retirement, disability, and insurance	953	1 268	33.0	48.2
Social Security	658	893	35.6	46.1
Government employee retirement	142	228	60.6	60.3
Medical payments	490	821	67.4	101.2
Income maintenance	89	141	57.8	58.0
Supplemental Security Income	18	32	72.8	75.4
Family assistance	25	22	-11.7	-0.5
Food Stamps	26	28	9.8	27.1
Other income maintenance	20	59	193.1	189.8
Unemployment insurance benefits	25	32	24.2	10.6
Veterans benefits and other	91	119	31.0	30.8

*Percent change, 1990–1997

Government Payments to Individuals: 1997

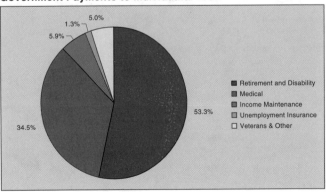

- Retirement and Disability — 53.3%
- Medical — 34.5%
- Income Maintenance — 5.9%
- Unemployment Insurance — 1.3%
- Veterans & Other — 5.0%

ECONOMIC STRUCTURE

LEADING PRIVATE INDUSTRIES, 1997 (Worker and proprietor earnings, millions of dollars)		FASTEST EARNINGS GROWTH, 1989–97 (percent increase)	
Health services	$1 104	Business services	193.5
Construction specialties	364	Industrial machinery manufacturing	146.9
Business services	327	Other transportation services	145.6
Electric, gas and sanitary services	255	Social services	113.9
Auto dealers and service stations	229	Construction specialties	97.9

NORTH DAKOTA'S LEADING INDUSTRY WAS HEALTH SERVICES, and it was more than three times larger than any other industry in the state in 1997. Representing 12 percent of all earnings, healthcare carries a weight in the state economy about 50 percent greater than in the U.S. economy. From 1989 to 1997, the fastest growing industry was business services, which increased by nearly 194 percent to become the third largest private industry in the state. The services sector grew faster than most sectors in the state, yet remained a smaller than average part of the state economy. Manufacturing jobs were a much smaller proportion of total employment than in an average state, though this sector too showed rapid growth in the 1990s.

Construction earnings showed the highest rate of growth during this period by nearly doubling. Government and farming were the only major sectors that showed decreases in employment from 1989 to 1997. However, both of these sectors remained more important to the state's economy than in typical states. The share of employment in the farm sector in North Dakota in 1997 was about 6.5 percentage points above average, and government jobs' percentage was 2.5 points higher than in the nation. Earnings of federal military personnel comprised 3.5 percent of state earnings, more than triple their average share, and federal civilian earnings were above average as well.

Employment and Earnings by Sector

	1980	1989	1990	1991	1992	1993	1994	1995	1996	1997 Number	1997 Percent of total	Change*
Employment *(thousands of persons)*												
Total	356	373	376	385	390	399	414	425	434	441	100.0	2.1
Farm	52	42	42	41	41	40	39	39	38	38	8.5	-1.4
Nonfarm	304	330	334	344	349	359	375	386	396	404	91.5	2.5
Private nonfarm	237	257	261	271	276	285	303	313	323	331	75.1	3.2
Agricultural service, forestry, and fishing	2	3	4	4	4	4	5	5	5	5	1.2	5.8
Mining	8	5	5	5	5	4	4	5	5	5	1.1	0.2
Construction	22	16	16	16	17	18	20	21	23	23	5.2	4.7
Manufacturing	17	17	18	19	19	21	23	23	23	25	5.7	4.7
Transportation and public utilities	19	20	20	21	21	22	23	23	23	24	5.3	2.0
Wholesale trade	22	21	20	21	21	21	21	22	22	23	5.2	1.3
Retail trade	58	61	62	64	66	68	72	74	76	76	17.3	2.8
Finance, insurance, and real estate	18	22	22	22	22	23	23	23	24	25	5.6	1.6
Services	71	92	94	100	102	105	112	117	122	126	28.5	3.9
Government	67	73	73	72	74	73	73	73	73	72	16.4	-0.1
Earnings *(millions of dollars)*												
Total	3 552	6 032	6 627	6 767	7 565	7 591	8 333	8 278	9 394	9 166	100.0	5.4
Farm	-348	325	592	402	759	344	657	188	882	233	2.5	-4.1
Nonfarm	3 900	5 706	6 034	6 365	6 806	7 246	7 675	8 090	8 512	8 933	97.5	5.8
Private nonfarm	3 105	4 332	4 593	4 858	5 220	5 616	6 027	6 364	6 750	7 134	77.8	6.4
Agricultural service, forestry, and fishing	19	49	55	48	57	66	66	66	65	66	0.7	3.8
Mining	201	140	157	170	168	173	163	175	188	200	2.2	4.5
Construction	404	328	346	356	394	440	492	545	620	632	6.9	8.5
Manufacturing	265	401	426	460	499	549	630	665	686	756	8.2	8.2
Transportation and public utilities	402	581	600	645	678	732	769	786	804	826	9.0	4.5
Wholesale trade	413	519	548	555	600	630	675	695	742	782	8.5	5.3
Retail trade	493	630	665	700	745	792	844	878	920	961	10.5	5.4
Finance, insurance, and real estate	191	297	315	334	373	407	430	455	481	512	5.6	7.0
Services	715	1 386	1 481	1 592	1 707	1 827	1 959	2 098	2 246	2 399	26.2	7.1
Government	795	1 374	1 441	1 507	1 586	1 630	1 648	1 726	1 762	1 799	19.6	3.4

*Compound annual average percent change, 1989–1997

ECONOMIC STRUCTURE (Continued)

NORTH DAKOTA'S AVERAGE WAGES WERE BELOW THE NATION-al average in every sector, with the exception of farm wages (16 percent above average). The greatest disparity was in finance, insurance, and real estate; the national average of $44,933 was 68 percent higher than the state average of $26,815. Wages in construction and retail trade were closer to the U.S. rate, 86 percent and 78 percent of average, respectively, while in services and manufacturing wages averaged only 71 percent of the U.S. levels. Overall, the state's average wages were about 27 percent less than the U.S. average.

With its gross state product (GSP) growing by nearly 50 percent from 1989 to 1996, North Dakota was among the top 20 in the nation for the GSP growth rate. Since manufacturing has gained the largest percentage increase in employment and second largest percentage increase in earnings of any major sector in the state, its output represented an increasing share of GSP during the 1990s. It reached 7.8 percent of GSP in 1995 and retreated slightly in 1996, though these ratios are still among the lowest in the nation. Industrial machinery and equipment is the state's leading private manufacturing industry. The state's manufacturing value of output per worker amounted to $50,722, nearly $19,000 less than the national average. New capital expenditures have increased by more than 45 percent from 1994 to 1996.

North Dakota's total exports to foreign markets grew by 60.2 percent from 1994 to 1997, without adjustment for inflation. However, exports remain a relatively small component of demand for the state's output, since manufacturing is so limited. In 1997, the largest export by far from the state was industrial machinery and equipment, having accounted for more than $278 million. It was followed by food products, which have shown a remarkable increase of 270 percent since 1994. Chemical products have also shown rapid growth from 1994 to 1997, with an increase of more than 250 percent. Agricultural and livestock products have had uneven growth since 1994, evident in the significant drop from $72.5 million in 1996 to $65.3 million in 1997.

Average Annual Wages and Salaries by Sector
(dollars)

	1989	1996	1997 State	1997 U.S.
All wage and salary workers	16 555	20 952	21 723	29 809
Farm	12 895	18 448	19 050	16 442
Nonfarm	16 635	20 996	21 769	29 900
Private nonfarm	16 434	20 745	21 573	29 867
Agricultural service, forestry, and fishing	11 529	13 456	13 984	17 941
Mining	30 626	36 978	38 757	49 800
Construction	20 366	26 582	27 296	31 765
Manufacturing	20 629	26 521	27 370	38 351
Transportation and utilities	26 349	32 322	33 654	38 222
Wholesale trade	21 351	27 318	28 314	39 466
Retail trade	9 525	12 087	12 652	16 206
Finance, insurance, and real estate	19 855	25 689	26 815	44 993
Services	14 812	18 868	19 585	27 588
Government	17 193	21 869	22 466	30 062

Gross State Product and Manufacturing
(millions of dollars, except as noted)

	1989	1994	1995	1996
Gross state product, total	10 482	13 680	14 477	15 701
Manufacturing:				
Millions of dollars	719	970	1 128	1 184
Percent of total gross state product	6.9	7.1	7.8	7.5
Per worker (dollars)	41 455	42 932	48 696	50 722
New capital expenditures, manufacturing	NA	114	147	165

Exports of Goods
(millions of dollars)

	1994	1995	1996	1997
All goods	389	489	576	623
Manufactures	319	402	470	526
Agricultural and livestock products	37	51	72	65
Other commodities	33	36	34	32
Top goods exports, 1997:				
Industrial machinery and computers	195	227	259	278
Food products	25	32	74	94
Transportation equipment	48	91	84	86
Agricultural products	32	45	67	58
Chemical products	6	14	16	21

HOUSING

NORTH DAKOTA'S HOUSING PRODUCTION HAS INCREASED SUB-stantially from the 1990–91 recession. New home production has increased by more than 62 percent since 1991. Since 1992, home production has managed to remain rather high, about the same as the U.S. rate per 1,000 population, despite the state's low population growth. Sales of existing homes have reflected weaker demand; since 1990, home sales have increased by 14.4 percent, well below the national increase of 32.9 percent. The median sales price in the state's largest metro area, Fargo, was $86,000 in 1997, one of the lowest prices among all metropolitan areas and 19 percent below average for the Midwest. Homeownership rates have fluctuated during the 1990s; in some years homeowners moved out of state and the ownership rate declined. However, the 68.1 percent ownership rate in 1997 is well above the national rate of 65.7 percent. Rental vacancy rates have increased to 8.3 percent in 1997, from a decade low of 4.8 percent in 1993.

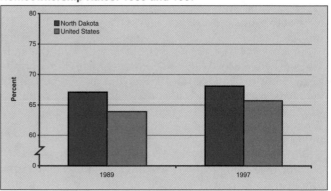

Homeownership Rates: 1989 and 1997

Housing Supply

	1989	1990	1991	1992	1993	1994	1995	1996	1997
Residential building permits (thousands)	2.2	1.5	2.1	2.6	2.9	3.4	3.2	2.3	3.2
New home production (including manufactured housing):									
Thousands of homes	2.4	1.5	2.4	3.1	3.3	4.1	3.8	3.0	3.9
Rate per 1,000 population									
North Dakota	3.7	2.4	3.8	4.9	5.2	6.4	5.9	4.7	6.1
U.S.	6.2	5.2	4.5	5.1	5.6	6.4	6.3	6.6	6.5
Existing home sales:									
Thousands of homes	10.3	10.4	10.3	11.9	11.8	10.9	10.6	12.0	11.9
Change from previous year (percent)									
North Dakota	1.0	1.0	-1.0	15.5	-0.8	-7.6	-2.8	13.2	-0.8
U.S.	-3.9	-4.0	0.0	9.2	8.2	4.8	-3.7	7.5	3.8
Home ownership rate (percent of households)	67.1	67.2	65.4	63.7	62.7	63.3	67.3	68.2	68.1
Rental vacancy rate (percent of rental housing units)	7.9	8.0	6.2	5.1	4.8	5.1	6.7	8.5	8.3

Note: Manufactured housing data for 1990 suppressed because estimate was based on too few responses.

AGRICULTURE

THOUGH AGRICULTURE IS AN IMPORTANT SECTOR IN THE North Dakota economy, the state ranks near the middle in a ranking of states by value of farm sales number of farms and for total value of farmland and buildings. It was the country's second leading wheat producer, however. The state averaged 1,318 acres per farm, well above the national average of 471. Net income fluctuated dramatically from year to year in the 1990s, but there has been a downtrend from the early 1990s until 1997, looking at three-year averages. North Dakota derived nearly 80 percent of

receipts from sales from crops. Revenue from crop sales grew by more than 54 percent from 1989 to 1997, while livestock revenue grew by only 0.5 percent.

NORTH DAKOTA FARMS, 1997	
Number of farms	30 500
Total acres (thousands):	40 200
Average per farm	1 318
Value of land and buildings (millions of dollars)	16 482
Average per farm (dollars)	540 393

Farm Income
(millions of dollars)

	1980	1989	1990	1991	1992	1993	1994	1995	1996	1997
Gross income	2 811	3 035	3 214	3 328	3 590	3 876	3 716	3 800	3 989	3 888
Receipts from sales	2 581	2 369	2 470	2 626	2 977	3 117	3 062	3 290	3 388	3 293
Government payments	117	475	545	534	443	565	457	296	353	362
Imputed and miscellaneous income	113	191	199	168	170	195	197	214	247	233
(–) Production expenses	2 525	2 863	3 022	3 052	3 108	3 232	3 412	3 467	3 744	3 735
(=) Realized net income	286	172	192	276	482	644	304	333	245	153
(+) Inventory change	-729	77	320	49	209	-379	277	-243	549	-27
(=) Net income	-443	249	512	325	691	265	581	90	794	126
Corporate income	-17	4	9	4	12	2	16	2	22	3
Farm proprietors income	-426	244	503	320	679	263	565	89	772	122

EDUCATION

EDUCATIONAL ATTAINMENT Percent of population age 25 and over, 1997	State	United States
High school graduate or higher	82.6	82.1
College graduate or higher	20.5	23.9

NORTH DAKOTA HAD A PERCENTAGE OF HIGH SCHOOL GRADUATES similar to the national average, but a lower rate of college graduates. The state ranked 29th in the nation with 82.6 percent of its residents having high school diplomas. The state drops to 37th when ranked by percent of population having college degrees, though it had a higher than average current enrollment of young adults. North Dakota's average teacher's salary was the second lowest in the nation, lower than South Dakota's average teacher's salary by $947. A relatively high proportion of school budgets must be devoted to facilities and transportation of students who are spread out in such a large state area. The state's expenditures per pupil were significantly below the national average and ranked among the 15 lowest in the nation, reflecting the state's limited tax base to support education budgets.

High School Completion: 1990–97

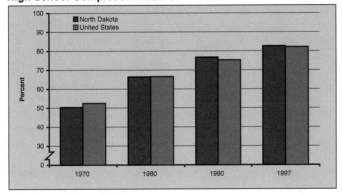

Education Indicators

	State	U.S.
Elementary and secondary schools		
Enrollment, 1995–96		
Total (thousands)	126	49 873
Percent in private schools	5.8	10.1
Expenditures per pupil (dollars), 1995–96	4 979	6 146
Average teacher salary (dollars), 1996–97	27 711	38 509
Higher education		
Enrollment, 1996–97		
Total (thousands)	41	14 218
Percent of population 18–34	26.3	21.8
Percent minority	8.2	26.1
Percent in private schools	9.3	22.6

HEALTH

NORTH DAKOTA'S INFANT MORTALITY JUMPED TO 7.4 PER 1,000 live births in 1997, up from 4.3 in 1996, costing the state its ranking of the lowest infant mortality rate in the nation. Throughout the 1990s, the state's overall death rate has remained fairly steady, and well below the national average. Generally, the state's age-adjusted death rates for major causes were near or below the national average. North Dakota's injury by firearm, liver disease, and Alzheimer's age-adjusted death rates were below the U.S. rates. The percentage of people without health insurance jumped from the lowest in the nation in 1994 to number thirty in 1997, at 15.2 percent, just below the national rate of 16.1. While this rate may reflect some sampling error, it does suggest that the new jobs added in 1997 are less likely to offer health insurance.

Health Indicators

	1990	1995	1996	1997
Infant mortality				
(rate per thousand live births)				
North Dakota	8.0	7.2	4.3	7.4
U.S.	9.2	7.6	7.3	7.1
Total deaths, age-adjusted rate				
(rate per thousand population)				
North Dakota	4.4	4.3	4.2	4.3
U.S.	5.2	5.0	4.9	4.8
Persons not covered by health insurance				
(percent of population)				
North Dakota	6.3	8.3	9.8	15.2
U.S.	13.9	15.4	15.6	16.1

Leading Causes of Death, 1996
(deaths per 100,000 population)

	Age-adjusted		Not age-adjusted	
	State	U.S.	State	U.S.
Deaths from all causes	421.4	491.6	934.1	872.5
Heart disease	114.4	134.5	291.7	276.4
Cancer	118.8	127.9	216.3	203.4
Cerebrovascular diseases	26.8	26.4	78.9	60.3
Chronic obstructive pulmonary disease	18.8	21.0	43.4	40.0
Diabetes mellitus	10.9	13.6	25.5	23.3
Pneumonia and influenza	10.8	12.8	37.6	31.6
HIV	NA	11.1	NA	11.7
Liver disease	5.7	7.5	8.1	9.4
Alzheimer's disease	1.6	2.7	7.3	8.1
Accidents and adverse effects	29.9	30.4	37.8	35.8
Motor vehicle accidents	16.5	16.2	16.8	16.5
Suicide	11.8	10.8	12.0	11.6
Homicide	NA	8.5	NA	7.9
Injury by firearm	8.4	12.9	8.5	12.8

GOVERNMENT

STATE AND LOCAL TAXES, 1995–96	State	U.S.
Per capita (dollars)	2 122	2 477
Percent of personal income	11.4	10.8

IN 1995–96, NORTH DAKOTA'S PER CAPITA STATE AND LOCAL taxes, at $2,122, were only 85.7 percent of the national average, but because of the low level of income, this figure represented a greater-than-average percentage of personal income. The local tax share was low and state level taxes alone were equal to the U.S. average per capita, according to 1997 data. North Dakota's state general revenue per capita was more than $700 greater than the national aver-age, because of very high intergovernmental income. North Dakota's per capita individual income taxes were significantly lower than the national average, but selective sales tax and "other" tax collections were much higher than average. The state's per capita general expenditures were also well above the national average. State per capita education and highway expenditures were significantly higher than the U.S. average, reflecting the fact that the costs of operating highways and school facilities over a large area are spread among a relatively small number of residents in this sparsely populated state. High education expenditures at the state level apparently have failed to compensate fully for low local education budgets, result-ing in the low total of spending per pupil. The state's per capita debt in 1997 was $300 less than the national aver-age.

While North Dakota comprised 0.2 percent of the U.S. population, the state's share of federal grants was general-ly higher than 0.2 percent of the U.S. total. For example, North Dakota received 0.4 percent of U.S. total grants and education grants. Payments to individuals were in propor-tion to the state's population, but salaries paid to federal workers in the state were relatively large. Only in defense and Supplemental Security Income did North Dakota receive a less than proportional share of the U.S. total. Overall, the state's share of U.S. total expenditures was 0.3 percent.

State Government Finances, 1996–97

	Millions of dollars	Percent distribu-tion	Dollars per capita	
			State	U.S.
General revenue	2 427	100.0	3 786	3 049
Intergovernmental revenue	812	33.5	1 267	863
Taxes	1 064	43.8	1 660	1 660
General sales	311	12.8	486	551
Selective sales	295	12.1	460	257
License taxes	77	3.2	120	106
Individual income	163	6.7	255	542
Corporation net income	75	3.1	117	115
Other taxes	143	5.9	222	90
Other general revenue	551	22.7	860	526
General expenditure	2 222	100.0	3 466	2 951
Intergovernmental expenditure	540	24.3	843	989
Direct expenditure	1 682	75.7	2 624	1 962
General expenditure, by function:				
Education	773	34.8	1 206	1 033
Public welfare	452	20.4	706	761
Hospitals and health	102	4.6	159	237
Highways	230	10.4	359	225
Police protection and corrections	30	1.4	47	137
Natural resources, parks and recreation	112	5.1	175	63
Governmental administration	81	3.7	127	107
Interest on general debt	57	2.6	90	99
Other and unallocable	383	17.2	598	290
Debt at end of fiscal year	900	NA	1 404	1 706
Cash and security holdings	4 562	NA	7 117	6 683

Federal Spending within State

	Federal funds, fiscal 1997		
	Millions of dollars	Percent distribution	Percent of U.S. total*
Total within state	4 204	100.0	0.3
Payments to individuals	1 762	41.9	0.2
Retirement and disability	1 107	26.3	0.2
Medicare	421	10.0	0.2
Food stamps	30	0.7	0.2
Supplemental Security Income	32	0.8	0.1
Grants	1 115	26.5	0.4
Medicaid and other health	264	6.3	0.2
Nutrition and family welfare	136	3.2	0.3
Education	71	1.7	0.4
Housing and community development	39	0.9	0.3
Salaries and wages	575	13.7	0.3
Defense procurement contracts	120	2.9	0.1
Non-defense procurement contracts	109	2.6	0.1

*State population is 0.2 percent of the U.S. total.

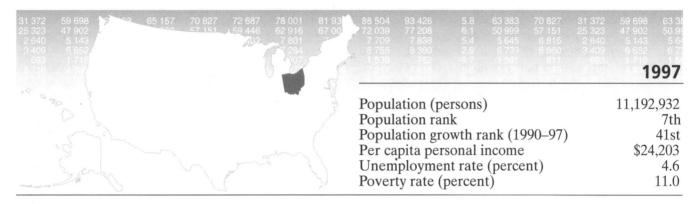

1997

Population (persons)	11,192,932
Population rank	7th
Population growth rank (1990–97)	41st
Per capita personal income	$24,203
Unemployment rate (percent)	4.6
Poverty rate (percent)	11.0

OHIO CONTINUED TO EXPERIENCE RELATIVELY SLOW GROWTH associated with the "Rustbelt" region of the Midwest, albeit to a less severe degree than in the 1980s. The state's growth of population and employment in the 1990s lagged somewhat behind both the nation and its Great Lakes neighbors. Median income stayed near national medians until 1996, when it dipped below. Ohio remained home to a wide array of major manufacturing industries, especially motor vehicles and related production, but manufacturing employment decreased (just as it did nationally). The state's strongest growth sectors in 1989–97 were construction and finance. There were broad signs of vibrant growth in the Columbus and Cincinnati areas, to counterbalance the sluggish economy surrounding Cleveland and Youngstown to the north.

The state's modest growth record throughout the 1990s is a recovery from its 1980s doldrums, when there was a more significant lag in growth of total employment and population. Cumulative population growth during the 1990–97 period was 3.0 percent, compared with only 0.6 percent between 1980 and 1990. The difference is the result of a major slowdown in out-migration. But unlike most other large states, Ohio had little international immigration to boost its population and economic growth. Ethnically, the state remains unchanged since 1990, with a large, stable Black population and few other minorities.

Average Annual Population Growth: 1990–97

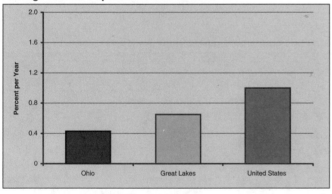

Median Household Income: 1989–97 (1997 dollars)

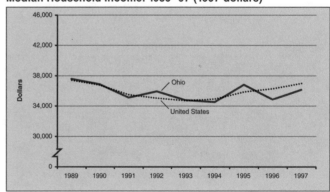

Unemployment Rate: 1989–97

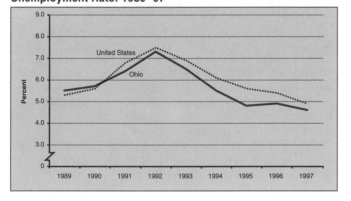

UNEMPLOYMENT IN OHIO HAS BEEN LOWER THAN NATIONAL rates during the entire 1991–97 period, with a 1997 rate of only 4.6 percent. Even with slower growth of employment compared to the United States, unemployment rates have stayed below average as the labor force also grew more slowly. Though the state had a disproportionate concentration of manufacturing jobs, which tend to move with volatility in the business cycle, its unemployment rate stayed below the U.S. average during the recession of the early 1990s.

POPULATION AND LABOR FORCE

THE POPULATION IN OHIO GREW A TOTAL OF 3.0 PERCENT from 1990 to 1997, less than half the growth rate of the nation (7.3 percent). Natural population growth is slowed by the lower than average birth rate. In addition, there was little foreign immigration, a net plus of only 0.4 percent over the seven years, compared to the U.S. rate of 2.2 percent. A trickle of out-migration to other states continued to reduce the state's population in the 1990s, though not nearly to the same extent as in the previous decade.

Population growth in the Columbus and Cincinnati metro areas was at least five times greater than that in the Cleveland area, which grew only 1.1 percent in 1990–97. Ohio's population is not as diverse as the nation's, with Blacks comprising the only significant minority group. Blacks represented 11.4 percent of the 1997 population, almost the same ratio as in the United States. Hispanics and Asians combined constituted only 2.6 of Ohio's population, with the remaining 86 percent non-Hispanic Whites.

The labor force grew faster than the adult population during the 1990s, and employment grew faster yet. This growth brought an increase in the employment to population ratio, though it was still below the U.S. average.

Population and Labor Force

	1980	1990	1991	1992	1993	1994	1995	1996	1997	Change* State	Change* U.S.
Population											
Total number of persons (thousands)	10 798	10 862	10 931	11 003	11 063	11 100	11 138	11 170	11 193	0.4	1.0
Percent distribution:											
White, Non-Hispanic	88.3	86.9	86.9	86.7	86.5	86.4	86.2	86.1	85.9	0.3	0.4
Black, Non-Hispanic	9.9	10.6	10.7	10.8	10.9	11.0	11.1	11.2	11.3	1.3	1.4
Asian	0.5	0.9	0.9	0.9	1.0	1.0	1.0	1.1	1.1	3.7	4.1
Native American	0.1	0.2	0.2	0.2	0.2	0.2	0.2	0.2	0.2	0.1	1.6
Hispanic	1.1	1.4	1.3	1.4	1.4	1.4	1.5	1.5	1.5	1.7	3.8
In metropolitan areas	81.4	81.4	81.4	81.3	81.3	81.2	81.1	81.0	81.0	0.4	1.0
Total number of households (thousands)	3 834	4 088	4 134	4 178	4 187	4 187	4 223	4 260	NA	0.7	1.2
Labor Force (thousands)											
Population 16 and over	8 108	8 386	8 433	8 480	8 531	8 563	8 608	8 652	8 682	0.5	1.0
Civilian labor force	5 089	5 409	5 438	5 496	5 491	5 542	5 585	5 643	5 707	0.8	1.1
Employed	4 663	5 099	5 089	5 095	5 131	5 235	5 319	5 365	5 445	0.9	1.2
Percent of population	57.5	60.8	60.3	60.1	60.1	61.1	61.8	62.0	62.7		
Unemployment rate (percent)	8.4	5.7	6.4	7.3	6.5	5.5	4.8	4.9	4.6		

*Compound annual average percent change, 1990–1997; 1990–1996 for households.

Population Change and Components: 1990–97

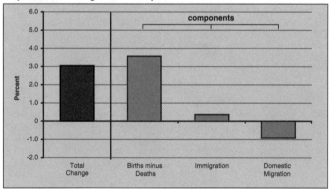

Average Annual Household and Population Growth

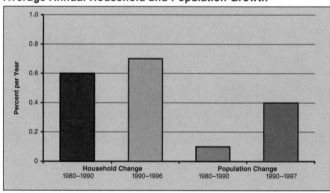

Population by Age; Births and Deaths

	1990 State	1990 U.S.	1997 State	1997 U.S.
Age distribution (percent)				
Under 5 years	7.2	7.6	6.7	7.2
5 to 17 years	18.3	18.2	18.7	18.8
18 to 64 years	61.5	61.8	61.3	61.3
65 years and over	13.0	12.5	13.4	12.7
Birth and death rates (per thousand population)				
Births	15.4	16.7	13.6	14.6
Deaths	9.1	8.6	9.4	8.6

OHIO'S POPULATION WAS OLDER THAN THE U.S. AVERAGE, showing a smaller than average cohort of young children under age 5 years and a higher proportion of seniors over age 65 years in 1997. The percentage of the population in between, both school-age children and working-age adults, tracked the national averages nearly exactly. Thus, the available pool of workers (absent out-migration) should remain about average, as children currently in school eventually enter the workforce.

HOUSEHOLD AND PERSONAL INCOME

HOUSEHOLD INCOME AND PERSONS IN POVERTY	1990	1995	1996	1997 State	1997 U.S.
Median household income (1997 dollars)	36 856	36 798	34 852	36 134	37 005
Persons in poverty (thousands)	1 256	1 285	1 424	1 231	35 574
Poverty rate (percent)	11.5	11.5	12.7	11.0	13.3

MEDIAN INCOME FOR OHIO HOUSEHOLDS IN 1997 WAS $36,134, about two percent below the national median. This gap appeared in 1996, when median incomes in the state fell below national levels for the first time in the 1990s. From 1990 through 1995, median incomes were virtually equal in the state and the nation. Poverty remained consistently below national averages during the mid-1990s.

Personal income per capita in Ohio remained about 4 percent below national averages in the 1990s. Ohio incomes have fallen a bit relative to U.S. income levels since 1980. Most components of personal income grew in Ohio at rates similar to national rates in the 1990s, except for the slow growth of nonfarm proprietors' income. (In the United States overall, rapid growth in this component reflects expansion in contractors and small businesses.)

The level of proprietors' income per capita in 1997 was only 78 percent of the national average, while dividend and interest income were also low, at 89 percent of U.S. norms. Wage income per capita was about equal to the national average, however, apparently reflecting the higher proportion of earners who are employees.

With the disproportionate number of persons over age 65 boosting retirement payments, transfer payments in Ohio comprise a higher than average share of personal income. Yet they grew during the 1990s at rates well below the national pace. Ohio's slower growth came especially in medical payments and income maintenance payments. A huge jump in Supplemental Security Income was offset by a 30 percent decline in family assistance and a 21 percent decline in food stamps. Other income maintenance, primarily earned income tax credits, surged 85 percent.

Personal Income
(millions of dollars)

	1980	1989	1990	1991	1992	1993	1994	1995	1996	1997	Change*
Earnings by place of work	80 235	133 723	140 657	143 650	153 163	160 551	169 875	177 717	183 775	194 651	4.8
Wages and salaries	66 579	110 240	115 755	117 878	124 766	129 358	137 207	144 650	151 392	160 873	4.8
Other labor income	7 172	11 618	12 456	13 165	14 724	16 736	17 750	17 421	15 909	16 049	4.1
Proprietors' income	6 483	11 865	12 446	12 607	13 673	14 457	14 918	15 647	16 473	17 730	5.1
Farm	417	835	807	292	663	449	663	503	749	1 303	5.7
Nonfarm	6 066	11 030	11 639	12 315	13 011	14 008	14 256	15 143	15 724	16 427	5.1
(−) Personal contributions for social insurance	4 198	8 705	9 171	9 620	10 049	10 628	11 490	12 281	12 832	13 618	5.8
(+) Adjustment for residence	-311	-1 010	-1 077	-1 113	-1 180	-1 257	-1 334	-1 358	-1 348	-1 450	NA
(=) Net earnings by state of residence	75 726	124 007	130 409	132 917	141 934	148 666	157 051	164 078	169 596	179 583	4.7
(+) Dividends, interest, and rent	15 747	32 610	34 328	34 881	33 583	34 534	36 342	38 959	41 826	43 271	3.6
(+) Transfer payments	15 388	29 680	32 040	35 396	38 838	40 592	42 331	44 480	46 188	47 886	6.2
(=) Total personal income	106 861	186 297	196 777	203 194	214 356	223 792	235 724	247 517	257 610	270 741	4.8
Farm	590	1 052	1 062	543	935	734	935	776	1 021	1 576	5.2
Nonfarm	106 271	185 246	195 714	202 651	213 421	223 058	234 790	246 740	256 589	269 165	4.8
Personal income per capita (dollars)											
Current dollars	9 894	17 203	18 117	18 592	19 487	20 237	21 246	22 233	23 078	24 203	4.4
1997 dollars	18 918	21 748	21 801	21 469	21 798	22 021	22 578	23 111	23 501	24 203	1.3

*Compound annual average percent change, 1989–1997

Government Transfer Payments

	Millions of dollars 1990	Millions of dollars 1997	Percent change* State	Percent change* U.S.
Total government payments to individuals	30 705	45 836	49.3	62.7
Retirement, disability, and insurance	17 763	25 275	42.3	48.2
Social Security	11 720	16 213	38.3	46.1
Government employee retirement	4 076	6 655	63.3	60.3
Medical payments	8 353	15 280	82.9	101.2
Income maintenance	2 797	3 368	20.4	58.0
Supplemental Security Income	482	1 103	128.7	75.4
Family assistance	933	650	-30.3	-0.5
Food Stamps	888	704	-20.7	27.1
Other income maintenance	494	911	84.5	189.8
Unemployment insurance benefits	758	712	-6.1	10.6
Veterans benefits and other	1 034	1 201	16.1	30.8

*Percent change, 1990–1997

Government Payments to Individuals: 1997

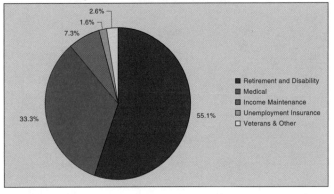

- ■ Retirement and Disability
- ■ Medical
- ■ Income Maintenance
- □ Unemployment Insurance
- □ Veterans & Other

55.1% 33.3% 7.3% 1.6% 2.6%

ECONOMIC STRUCTURE

LEADING PRIVATE INDUSTRIES, 1997 (Worker and proprietor earnings, millions of dollars)		FASTEST EARNINGS GROWTH, 1989–97 (percent increase)	
Health services	$17 765	Other transportation services	153.5
Business services	9 261	Real estate	133.9
Industrial machinery manufacturing	7 843	Business services	107.7
Construction specialties	7 231	Social services	100.1
Motor vehicles and equipment	6 732	Banks and other credit institutions	67.8

OHIO REMAINED A PROMINENT MEMBER OF THE BAND OF industrialized Great Lakes states, where manufacturing still dominates the economy. Over one-quarter of the gross state product derived from manufacturing, and its share of total employment in the state was 17 percent (compared to 12.5 percent in the United States). Two of its top five industries (industrial machinery and motor vehicles) were in manufacturing, and five other manufacturing industries had earnings above $3 billion in 1997. However, employment in manufacturing fell by 12 percent since 1980, a greater decline than the long-term downtrend in manufacturing nationwide.

Ohio is not keeping up with the nation in services sector growth, even though this is the state's fastest growing major sector. Healthcare is the largest industry and service-type industries made up all of the five fastest growth industries of the 1990s. Major metropolitan areas in Ohio remained centers of commerce supporting business services and finance sector jobs. The expanding social services industry responded to the decline in welfare caseloads, and air transportation was a small but booming industry. The construction sector also saw large employment gains in the 1990s, which brought it up to about the same proportion of the economy as the national average.

Employment and Earnings by Sector

	1980	1989	1990	1991	1992	1993	1994	1995	1996	1997 Number	1997 Percent of total	Change*
Employment *(thousands of persons)*												
Total	5 215	5 848	5 898	5 892	5 907	6 010	6 197	6 370	6 474	6 599	100.0	1.5
Farm	130	111	108	103	100	98	95	93	90	93	1.4	-2.2
Nonfarm	5 086	5 737	5 790	5 789	5 807	5 912	6 102	6 277	6 384	6 506	98.6	1.6
Private nonfarm	4 374	4 981	5 018	5 012	5 019	5 123	5 311	5 481	5 588	5 708	86.5	1.7
Agricultural service, forestry, and fishing	22	40	42	44	44	47	51	52	54	57	0.9	4.6
Mining	39	31	30	28	25	26	25	24	22	21	0.3	-4.7
Construction	229	278	282	269	273	286	305	313	324	335	5.1	2.3
Manufacturing	1 275	1 142	1 126	1 090	1 074	1 075	1 098	1 127	1 122	1 119	17.0	-0.3
Transportation and public utilities	247	253	255	252	248	255	266	270	278	285	4.3	1.5
Wholesale trade	237	280	278	283	282	280	289	298	305	311	4.7	1.3
Retail trade	866	1 028	1 032	1 032	1 039	1 064	1 113	1 155	1 182	1 194	18.1	1.9
Finance, insurance, and real estate	350	391	394	399	390	401	430	442	455	473	7.2	2.4
Services	1 109	1 537	1 578	1 615	1 643	1 688	1 734	1 799	1 847	1 913	29.0	2.8
Government	711	756	772	777	788	789	791	796	797	798	12.1	0.7
Earnings *(millions of dollars)*												
Total	80 235	133 723	140 657	143 650	153 163	160 551	169 875	177 717	183 775	194 651	100.0	4.8
Farm	590	1 052	1 062	543	935	734	935	776	1 021	1 576	0.8	5.2
Nonfarm	79 644	132 671	139 595	143 107	152 229	159 816	168 941	176 941	182 754	193 075	99.2	4.8
Private nonfarm	70 080	115 287	120 923	123 417	131 410	138 125	146 394	153 477	158 478	167 956	86.3	4.8
Agricultural service, forestry, and fishing	205	514	583	627	679	700	748	781	801	863	0.4	6.7
Mining	1 182	745	684	819	750	667	695	812	737	818	0.4	1.2
Construction	4 530	7 253	7 714	7 383	7 589	8 303	9 150	9 542	10 141	10 822	5.6	5.1
Manufacturing	29 121	41 025	41 677	41 578	44 220	46 469	48 927	50 362	50 362	52 317	26.9	3.1
Transportation and public utilities	5 686	7 876	8 196	8 403	8 776	9 261	9 790	10 050	10 371	10 933	5.6	4.2
Wholesale trade	4 908	8 420	8 936	9 265	9 622	9 968	10 728	11 410	12 003	12 938	6.6	5.5
Retail trade	7 715	12 303	12 931	13 282	14 157	14 691	15 809	16 652	17 405	18 210	9.4	5.0
Finance, insurance, and real estate	3 572	7 158	7 582	8 021	8 949	9 759	10 089	10 688	11 467	12 545	6.4	7.3
Services	13 162	29 992	32 619	34 040	36 668	38 308	40 459	43 183	45 191	48 511	24.9	6.2
Government	9 564	17 384	18 672	19 690	20 819	21 691	22 547	23 464	24 276	25 120	12.9	4.7

*Compound annual average percent change, 1989–1997

ECONOMIC STRUCTURE (Continued)

AVERAGE WAGE LEVELS IN OHIO WERE BROADLY LOWER THAN for the nation in 1997, a 4.1 percent gap overall, which had grown larger during the 1990s as the national economy recovered more strongly than that of the state. Only two major sectors, manufacturing and construction, countered this general trend. Wages in manufacturing averaged 6 percent higher in Ohio than in the United States, given the disproportionate weight of unionized jobs in heavy manufacturing. Construction wages were a slight 1.4 percent above national averages in the sector. In contrast, wages within the finance and services sectors were 21 percent and 11 percent below U.S. levels for these categories, respectively, and in trade and government the wage gaps were 3 percent and 7 percent.

Output value in Ohio manufacturing grew by 31 percent between 1989 and 1996, a rate equal to the increase nationwide. Among the state's large manufacturing industries, growth was fastest in chemicals, as total worker earnings increased 51 percent during 1989–97, and worker earnings increased a moderate 32 to 36 percent in the big industrial machinery and motor vehicles industries. With the predominance of older plants, overall value of output per worker has grown more slowly in Ohio than the U.S. average. However, it still remained a bit higher than the U.S. level as of 1996 because of the disproportionate weight of durable goods within Ohio manufacturing

Ohio ranked seventh among U.S. states in its value of merchandise exports in 1997, based on its extensive capacity in the core export category of heavy manufacturing. It had healthy increases from 1994 to 1997 in its two largest export goods: transportation equipment and industrial machinery. Agricultural and commodity exports were a tiny fraction of the total. The state's overall increase in exports during the period, 29 percent, was slightly lower than the 35 percent increase in U.S. exports and goods.

Average Annual Wages and Salaries by Sector
(dollars)

	1989	1996	1997 State	1997 U.S.
All wage and salary workers	21 841	27 366	28 573	29 809
Farm	10 828	16 446	14 993	16 442
Nonfarm	21 883	27 397	28 616	29 900
Private nonfarm	22 010	27 327	28 584	29 867
Agricultural service, forestry, and fishing	14 727	18 228	19 140	17 941
Mining	31 964	38 262	40 391	49 800
Construction	25 083	30 749	32 213	31 765
Manufacturing	31 129	38 682	40 647	38 351
Transportation and utilities	29 104	34 190	35 582	38 222
Wholesale trade	28 026	36 470	38 465	39 466
Retail trade	11 321	14 444	15 028	16 206
Finance, insurance, and real estate	24 444	33 391	35 626	44 993
Services	18 193	23 611	24 568	27 588
Government	21 161	27 816	28 804	30 062

Gross State Product and Manufacturing
(millions of dollars, except as noted)

	1989	1994	1995	1996
Gross state product, total	216 820	276 742	292 103	304 353
Manufacturing:				
Millions of dollars	63 125	75 770	81 535	82 669
Percent of total gross state product	29.1	27.4	27.9	27.2
Per worker (dollars)	55 288	69 016	72 336	73 709
New capital expenditures, manufacturing	NA	6 245	7 952	NA

Exports of Goods
(millions of dollars)

	1994	1995	1996	1997
All goods	19 478	20 926	22 555	25 106
Manufactures	18 837	20 241	21 523	24 039
Agricultural and livestock products	181	138	125	97
Other commodities	461	548	907	970
Top goods exports, 1997:				
Transportation equipment	4 753	4 721	5 090	6 047
Industrial machinery and computers	4 208	4 576	4 933	5 460
Chemical products	2 421	2 861	2 957	3 119
Electric and electronic equipment	1 938	1 861	1 880	1 978
Rubber and plastic products	1 102	1 251	1 228	1 336

HOUSING

THE HOUSING MARKET IN OHIO GREW AT A MODERATE RATE during the 1990–97 period, with total new housing production (including mobile homes and apartments) of 4.5 to 5 per 1,000 population during most of that time. With Ohio's population growth and in-migration rates lagging those of the United States, housing production was slower than the national rate of production per capita. New home and apartment construction in 1997 was much stronger in the Columbus and Cincinnati areas than in Cleveland. Sales of existing single-family homes in Ohio grew more slowly than in the country for most of the 1990s.

Rates of homeownership in Ohio stayed consistently high during the 1990s, exceeding the rates prevailing in the United States overall, because of the less transient, typically older population in the state and generally moderate home prices. Vacancy rates in the Ohio rental housing market, which were below average during the late 1980s and early 1990s, climbed higher in 1996–97,

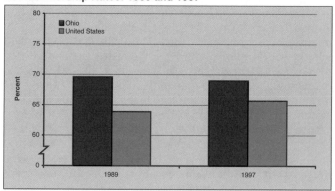

Homeownership Rates: 1989 and 1997

which will dampen further apartment building in the short term.

Housing Supply

	1989	1990	1991	1992	1993	1994	1995	1996	1997
Residential building permits (thousands)	41.2	38.5	35.8	42.6	44.2	47.2	44.8	49.3	46.5
New home production (including manufactured housing):									
Thousands of homes	47.4	44.1	41.7	49.9	51.4	54.9	53.2	57.5	53.1
Rate per 1,000 population									
Ohio	4.4	4.1	3.8	4.5	4.6	4.9	4.8	5.2	4.7
U.S.	6.2	5.2	4.5	5.1	5.6	6.4	6.3	6.6	6.5
Existing home sales:									
Thousands of homes	163.4	151.6	149.8	167.4	179.1	186.4	182.8	192.7	187.3
Change from previous year (percent)									
Ohio	1.7	-7.2	-1.2	11.7	7.0	4.1	-1.9	5.4	-2.8
U.S.	-3.9	-4.0	0.0	9.2	8.2	4.8	-3.7	7.5	3.8
Home ownership rate (percent of households)	69.6	68.7	68.7	69.1	68.5	67.4	67.9	69.2	69.0
Rental vacancy rate (percent of rental housing units)	5.9	5.5	5.4	6.2	7.1	6.8	7.4	8.1	8.9

AGRICULTURE

THE FARM ECONOMY IN OHIO DURING THE 1990s FARED MUCH better than did farming for the United States because of its strong grain sector, and farm earnings grew almost as fast as did nonfarm earnings. Net farm income grew 37 percent during the 1990s (using three-year averages), despite decreases in government subsidies. (Comparisons using 1997 alone are misleading because of the very strong farm performance that year.) Grain sales increased 38 percent during the decade and were especially high in 1997, while sales were flat or declining for meat animals

and dairy products. Still, the number of farm jobs declined 17 percent from 1989 to 1997.

OHIO FARMS, 1997	
Number of farms	73 000
Total acres (thousands):	15 100
Average per farm	207
Value of land and buildings (millions of dollars)	31 861
Average per farm (dollars)	436 452

Farm Income
(millions of dollars)

	1980	1989	1990	1991	1992	1993	1994	1995	1996	1997
Gross income	4 621	5 024	5 331	5 049	4 988	5 567	5 237	5 786	5 806	6 352
Receipts from sales	4 321	4 250	4 630	4 394	4 317	4 779	4 562	5 027	5 051	5 561
Government payments	9	274	197	157	166	265	117	167	163	186
Imputed and miscellaneous income	291	501	504	499	505	523	557	592	592	605
(−) Production expenses	3 839	4 281	4 541	4 533	4 593	4 776	4 789	4 872	5 070	5 160
(=) Realized net income	782	744	790	516	396	791	447	913	736	1 192
(+) Inventory change	-365	156	80	-207	322	-328	307	-367	113	268
(=) Net income	417	899	870	309	718	463	755	546	849	1 460
Corporate income	0	65	63	17	55	14	92	43	100	158
Farm proprietors income	417	835	807	292	663	449	663	503	749	1 303

EDUCATION

EDUCATIONAL ATTAINMENT Percent of population age 25 and over, 1997	State	United States
High school graduate or higher	86.2	82.1
College graduate or higher	21.5	23.9

THE EDUCATIONAL ATTAINMENT OF OHIO RESIDENTS WAS higher than average in percentage of high school graduates in 1997, yet the state ranked in the lower half of the nation in its proportion of college degree holders. The high rate of high school graduates is consistent with its urbanized, industrial base; in contrast, the somewhat large population over age 65 and the relative lack of growth in high-technology service sectors may account for its lower proportion of college graduates. The state lags the nation slightly in the proportion of the current young adult population enrolled in higher education. At the elementary and secondary level, Ohio spent 2 percent more per public school pupil than the U.S. average, and it had a slightly above-average share of students attending private schools.

High School Completion: 1990–97

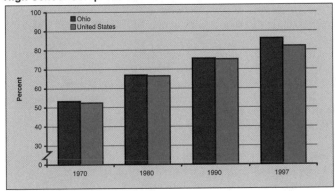

Education Indicators

	State	U.S.
Elementary and secondary schools		
Enrollment, 1995–96		
Total (thousands)	2 091	49 873
Percent in private schools	12.2	10.1
Expenditures per pupil (dollars), 1995–96	6 266	6 146
Average teacher salary (dollars), 1996–97	38 831	38 509
Higher education		
Enrollment, 1996–97		
Total (thousands)	538	14 218
Percent of population 18–34	20.0	21.8
Percent minority	14.0	26.1
Percent in private schools	24.6	22.6

HEALTH

OHIO HAD A SIGNIFICANTLY LARGER THAN AVERAGE PERCENTage of its population covered by health insurance in 1997 compared to the United States, probably because of the disproportionate size of the manufacturing sector and the low rate of poverty. The total death rate, however, was above average even when adjusted for the state's older than average age distribution. Death from heart disease and cancer was relatively high on an age-adjusted basis. However, deaths related to accidents, suicide, and HIV were below national norms in 1996. The homicide rate was particularly low. Infant mortality rates, although they declined impressively between 1990 and 1997, were somewhat above the national average in 1997.

Health Indicators

	1990	1995	1996	1997
Infant mortality *(rate per thousand live births)*				
Ohio	9.8	8.7	7.7	7.2
U.S.	9.2	7.6	7.3	7.1
Total deaths, age-adjusted rate *(rate per thousand population)*				
Ohio	5.3	5.2	5.0	5.0
U.S.	5.2	5.0	4.9	4.8
Persons not covered by health insurance *(percent of population)*				
Ohio	10.3	11.9	11.5	11.5
U.S.	13.9	15.4	15.6	16.1

Leading Causes of Death, 1996
(deaths per 100,000 population)

	Age-adjusted		Not age-adjusted	
	State	U.S.	State	U.S.
Deaths from all causes	503.9	491.6	941.6	872.5
Heart disease	144.5	134.5	306.2	276.4
Cancer	136.4	127.9	226.7	203.4
Cerebrovascular diseases	25.6	26.4	60.6	60.3
Chronic obstructive pulmonary disease	23.1	21.0	45.9	40.0
Diabetes mellitus	17.8	13.6	32.3	23.3
Pneumonia and influenza	11.9	12.8	29.8	31.6
HIV	5.7	11.1	5.9	11.7
Liver disease	6.1	7.5	8.3	9.4
Alzheimer's disease	2.8	2.7	8.8	8.1
Accidents and adverse effects	24.7	30.4	30.5	35.8
Motor vehicle accidents	12.6	16.2	12.8	16.5
Suicide	8.6	10.8	9.4	11.6
Homicide	4.8	8.5	4.5	7.9
Injury by firearm	8.8	12.9	9.0	12.8

GOVERNMENT

STATE AND LOCAL TAXES, 1995–96	State	U.S.
Per capita (dollars)	2 430	2 477
Percent of personal income	10.8	10.8

TOTAL STATE AND LOCAL TAXES IN OHIO WERE ABOUT 2 PERcent below the U.S. average on a per capita basis in 1995–96. As a share of income, these taxes consumed 10.8 percent of personal income, down from 11.3 percent the previous year but exactly the same as the national average, given the lower per capita income in Ohio. State taxes alone were below average, while higher per capita local taxes made up some of the difference.

State Government Finances, 1996–97

	Millions of dollars	Percent distribution	Dollars per capita	
			State	U.S.
General revenue	30 792	100.0	2 753	3 049
Intergovernmental revenue	8 993	29.2	804	863
Taxes	16 418	53.3	1 468	1 660
General sales	5 234	17.0	468	551
Selective sales	2 821	9.2	252	257
License taxes	1 355	4.4	121	106
Individual income	6 141	19.9	549	542
Corporation net income	737	2.4	66	115
Other taxes	129	0.4	12	90
Other general revenue	5 382	17.5	481	526
General expenditure	30 705	100.0	2 745	2 951
Intergovernmental expenditure	10 442	34.0	933	989
Direct expenditure	20 263	66.0	1 811	1 962
General expenditure, by function:				
Education	11 233	36.6	1 004	1 033
Public welfare	7 961	25.9	712	761
Hospitals and health	2 228	7.3	199	237
Highways	2 468	8.0	221	225
Police protection and corrections	1 467	4.8	131	137
Natural resources, parks and recreation	409	1.3	37	63
Governmental administration	1 121	3.7	100	107
Interest on general debt	865	2.8	77	99
Other and unallocable	2 953	9.6	264	290
Debt at end of fiscal year	13 437	NA	1 201	1 706
Cash and security holdings	113 511	NA	10 148	6 683

Federal Spending within State

	Federal funds, fiscal 1997		
	Millions of dollars	Percent distribution	Percent of U.S. total [*]
Total within state	50 998	100.0	3.6
Payments to individuals	32 691	64.1	4.2
Retirement and disability	19 423	38.1	4.2
Medicare	8 620	16.9	4.2
Food stamps	749	1.5	3.8
Supplemental Security Income	1 174	2.3	4.4
Grants	8 906	17.5	3.6
Medicaid and other health	4 238	8.3	3.7
Nutrition and family welfare	2 043	4.0	4.4
Education	604	1.2	3.5
Housing and community development	490	1.0	4.3
Salaries and wages	4 298	8.4	2.6
Defense procurement contracts	2 712	5.3	2.3
Non-defense procurement contracts	1 892	3.7	2.6

[*]State population is 4.2 percent of the U.S. total.

At the state level, Ohio taxes and spends less than average for states around the country, which is somewhat unusual for an older, urban state. Total state taxes per capita in 1997 were 12 percent below the average for all states. Sales tax collections per capita were somewhat below average, and corporate income tax revenue was only 57 percent as high as nationally. Individual income tax receipts were about equal to the average. On the spending side, Ohio is a bit below average in all program categories, from education to administration. It follows the national pattern of transferring substantial sums (though less than an average state) to local education and other programs. The state's cash and securities holdings are particularly strong, with assets of over $10,000 per person.

The state's 3.6 percent share of total federal spending is less than the its 4.2 percent share of the U.S. population. Payments under the largest programs, Social Security and Medicare, are in line with the state population. Medicaid spending is lower, in light of the state's low poverty rate, while spending is a bit higher on nutrition and family welfare programs. However, Ohio has a less than proportional share of total federal employee salaries (because of the smaller than average federal presence in the state) and federal procurement. Total contracts with Ohio establishments in both the defense and non-defense areas are less than commensurate with the state's population.

31 372	59 698			65 157	70 827	72 687	78 001	81 93		88 504	93 426	5.8	63 383	70 827	31 372	59 698	63 38
25 323	47 902			57 151	59 446		62 916	67 00		72 039	77 208	6.1	50 999	57 151	25 323	47 902	50 99
2 640	5 143					702	7 801			7 709	7 838	5.4	5 645	6 816	2 640	5 143	5 64
3 409	6 652						284			8 755	8 380	2.9	6 739	6 860	3 409	6 652	6 7
693	1 716						307			1 539	762	-9.7	1 561	811	693	1 716	1 5
2 716	4 93									2 217	7 618	5	178	049	2 716		

1997

Population (persons)	3,321,611
Population rank	27th
Population growth rank (1990–97)	31st
Per capita personal income	$20,214
Unemployment rate (percent)	4.1
Poverty rate (percent)	13.7

OKLAHOMA IS A SOUTHWESTERN STATE BUT IN MANY respects it more resembles its Plains states neighbors to the north. Its economy strived to regain ground lost in the 1980s oil-related recession, and it has not succeeded as well as Texas has in attracting new jobs and in-migrants to rebuild. The oil industry has contracted in real terms since the early 1980s; in four of eight years during 1989–97 its earnings declined. Other industries have partially filled the void, but there is no high-tech boom here, and the state's largest manufacturing industry, industrial machinery, languished throughout 1990s. The economy relied somewhat heavily on government: transfer payments were relatively large, as was government employment (Oklahoma City is a federal

regional headquarters). Incomes and average wages in Oklahoma have remained 15 to 20 percent below U.S. average levels.

The state's population grew slower in the 1990s than that of any other Southwestern state. (Paradoxically it moved up in population rank from 28th to 27th since 1990.) Though its 1990s growth record was stronger than that of the 1980s, the state still experienced a slow natural population increase and low in-migration. Without the foreign immigration that is reshaping the rest of the region, the state is missing a growth catalyst. The Hispanic population was 3.7 percent, low for the region, while Native Americans remained the largest minority group.

Average Annual Population Growth: 1990–97

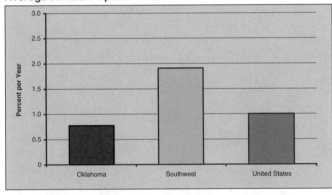

Median Household Income: 1989–97 (1997 dollars)

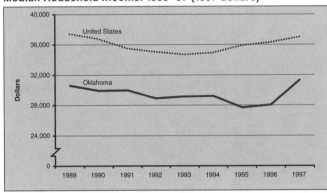

Unemployment Rate: 1989–97

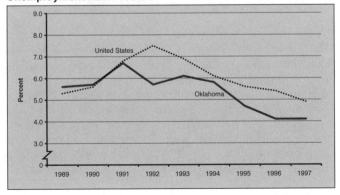

UNEMPLOYMENT RATES IN THE STATE GENERALLY FOLLOWED the national cyclical pattern of the 1990s, though rates in Oklahoma were lower than U.S. rates from 1992 through 1997. However, this reflects lower than average growth of the labor force rather than faster employment growth. State job growth lagged behind the U.S. performance of the 1990s, and Oklahoma continued to have one of the lower percentages of its adult population at work (60.3 percent in 1997).

POPULATION AND LABOR FORCE

OKLAHOMA'S POPULATION INCREASED ONLY 5.6 PERCENT from 1990 to 1997, lagging behind nationwide growth. But the bigger story is the turnaround from the dismal figures of the 1980s, when the economy sagged and the state lost 3.6 percent of its population to net out-migration (though overall population increased). In contrast, there was a plus 2.4 percent from in-migration (domestic and international) during 1990–97. This was largely domestic migration, with only modest foreign immigration. The state had slow natural population increase during the 1990s: its slightly low birth rate paired with an above-average death rate.

The state's largely White, non-Hispanic population is unique in the Southwest region. The Hispanic community, while growing rapidly comprises less than 4 percent of the population, in contrast to neighboring Texas's 29 percent. Native Americans, the largest minority group, comprised 7.8 of the population in 1997. Oklahoma had the second highest proportion of Native Americans among states, after New Mexico, and the second highest absolute number, after California. The Black population, representing 7.5 percent of Oklahomans, is growing faster than average and is projected to become the largest minority group by the year 2000.

Population and Labor Force

	1980	1990	1991	1992	1993	1994	1995	1996	1997	Change* State	Change* U.S.
Population											
Total number of persons (thousands)	3 025	3 147	3 166	3 204	3 229	3 248	3 271	3 296	3 322	0.8	1.0
Percent distribution:											
White, Non-Hispanic	85.1	81.0	80.9	80.7	80.6	80.5	80.4	80.2	80.0	0.6	0.4
Black, Non-Hispanic	6.7	7.4	7.4	7.5	7.5	7.5	7.5	7.5	7.5	1.0	1.4
Asian	0.7	1.1	1.1	1.1	1.2	1.2	1.2	1.3	1.3	2.5	4.1
Native American	5.7	8.1	8.1	8.1	8.0	8.0	7.9	7.9	7.8	0.3	1.6
Hispanic	1.9	2.9	2.8	3.0	3.1	3.2	3.4	3.5	3.7	4.5	3.8
In metropolitan areas	57.0	59.5	59.7	60.0	60.1	60.2	60.1	60.2	60.4	1.0	1.0
Total number of households (thousands)	1 119	1 206	1 211	1 230	1 235	1 238	1 250	1 265	NA	0.8	1.2
Labor Force (thousands)											
Population 16 and over	2 281	2 395	2 410	2 439	2 459	2 475	2 496	2 523	2 544	0.9	1.0
Civilian labor force	1 368	1 514	1 500	1 521	1 529	1 544	1 546	1 576	1 601	0.8	1.1
Employed	1 302	1 428	1 399	1 433	1 436	1 454	1 474	1 512	1 535	1.0	1.2
Percent of population	57.1	59.6	58.1	58.8	58.4	58.8	59.0	59.9	60.3		
Unemployment rate (percent)	4.8	5.7	6.7	5.7	6.1	5.8	4.7	4.1	4.1		

*Compound annual average percent change, 1990–1997; 1990–1996 for households.

Population Change and Components: 1990–97

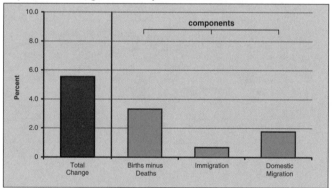

Average Annual Household and Population Growth

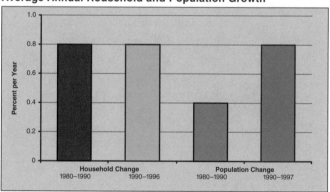

Population by Age; Births and Deaths

	1990 State	1990 U.S.	1997 State	1997 U.S.
Age distribution (percent)				
Under 5 years	7.3	7.6	6.8	7.2
5 to 17 years	19.4	18.2	19.7	18.8
18 to 64 years	59.8	61.8	60.1	61.3
65 years and over	13.5	12.5	13.4	12.7
Birth and death rates (per thousand population)				
Births	15.1	16.7	14.5	14.6
Deaths	9.7	8.6	10.1	8.6

OKLAHOMA HAD A SLIGHTLY HIGHER THAN AVERAGE PROPORTION of children under age 18 in 1997, though the difference had diminished since 1990 and promises to diminish further because of the state's low birth rates. The actual growth in the number of children was a moderate 4.4 percent from 1990 to 1997, limiting the strain on school resources. The population age 65 years and older was also disproportionately high in Oklahoma in 1997, leaving a substantially smaller proportion of working-age adults.

HOUSEHOLD AND PERSONAL INCOME

HOUSEHOLD INCOME AND PERSONS IN POVERTY	1990	1995	1996	1997	
				State	U.S.
Median household income (1997 dollars)	29 944	27 709	28 067	31 351	37 005
Persons in poverty (thousands)	481	548	556	456	35 574
Poverty rate (percent)	15.6	17.1	16.6	13.7	13.3

HOUSEHOLD INCOMES IN OKLAHOMA IN THE 1990S GENERAL-ly were 80 to 82 percent of national levels. Median household income in 1997 was 85 percent of that of the United States, after four years of vigorous job growth in the state. Poverty rates have responded favorably to the economic growth by declining since 1995. However, the 1997 poverty rate of 13.7 percent was only a return to the rate that prevailed in 1980 and remained slightly above average.

Per capita income in 1997 was 80 percent of the U.S. average, a slight slippage from the state's relative position in the early 1990s. In contrast, in 1980 per capita income was 94 percent as high as the U.S. average. Total earnings per capita were 22 percent below U.S. levels, because of low wage rates plus a low percentage of adults at work. Per capita dividend and interest income also was behind U.S. averages, reflecting the relatively small number of affluent residents. Farm income showed no increase over the 1989–97 period. Residents working in other states brought a net earnings inflow of 1.7 percent of total resident earnings in 1997.

Transfer payments in 1997 represented an above-average 20.1 percent share of personal income in Oklahoma. A large proportion of it comes in Social Security and other retirement benefits, because of the state's proportion of residents age 65 and older. Medical payments comprised a smaller than average share of transfer payments, though they did increase faster than any other component from 1990 to 1997. Reductions in welfare rolls cut family assistance spending a dramatic 38 percent in current dollars, but there were huge increases in "other" income maintenance (mostly earned income tax credits) and Supplemental Security Income.

Personal Income
(millions of dollars)

	1980	1989	1990	1991	1992	1993	1994	1995	1996	1997	Change*
Earnings by place of work	21 342	31 883	33 818	35 141	37 174	39 089	40 169	41 230	43 258	45 655	4.6
Wages and salaries	16 667	24 489	26 047	27 144	28 483	29 383	30 326	31 615	33 403	35 051	4.6
Other labor income	1 731	2 647	2 916	3 194	3 500	3 788	3 993	3 903	3 890	3 898	5.0
Proprietors' income	2 943	4 747	4 855	4 802	5 191	5 919	5 850	5 712	5 965	6 706	4.4
Farm	210	708	680	504	656	884	684	229	234	683	-0.4
Nonfarm	2 734	4 039	4 175	4 298	4 536	5 035	5 167	5 483	5 732	6 023	5.1
(−) Personal contributions for social insurance	1 108	2 154	2 289	2 444	2 574	2 672	2 808	2 957	3 089	3 235	5.2
(+) Adjustment for residence	171	493	546	576	609	614	664	704	730	782	NA
(=) Net earnings by state of residence	20 405	30 222	32 075	33 273	35 210	37 031	38 026	38 976	40 899	43 203	4.6
(+) Dividends, interest, and rent	4 357	8 200	8 595	8 438	8 471	8 380	8 975	9 340	9 946	10 351	3.0
(+) Transfer payments	4 014	7 858	8 465	9 269	10 255	10 841	11 416	12 402	12 964	13 498	7.0
(=) Total personal income	28 776	46 280	49 135	50 981	53 937	56 253	58 416	60 718	63 809	67 052	4.7
Farm	311	830	822	642	783	1 020	812	385	383	835	0.1
Nonfarm	28 465	45 450	48 314	50 338	53 154	55 232	57 605	60 333	63 425	66 218	4.8
Personal income per capita (dollars)											
Current dollars	9 463	14 691	15 613	16 101	16 833	17 422	17 984	18 560	19 363	20 214	4.1
1997 dollars	18 094	18 573	18 788	18 592	18 829	18 958	19 112	19 293	19 718	20 214	1.1

*Compound annual average percent change, 1989–1997

Government Transfer Payments

	Millions of dollars		Percent change*	
	1990	1997	State	U.S.
Total government payments to individuals	8 116	12 975	59.9	62.7
Retirement, disability, and insurance	4 846	7 155	47.6	48.2
Social Security	3 188	4 604	44.4	46.1
Government employee retirement	1 489	2 152	44.5	60.3
Medical payments	1 988	3 984	100.5	101.2
Income maintenance	637	1 015	59.3	58.0
Supplemental Security Income	192	322	67.6	75.4
Family assistance	141	87	-38.0	-0.5
Food Stamps	195	247	26.3	27.1
Other income maintenance	109	359	229.4	189.8
Unemployment insurance benefits	121	104	-14.2	10.6
Veterans benefits and other	523	717	37.0	30.8

*Percent change, 1990–1997

Government Payments to Individuals: 1997

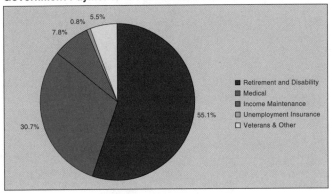

- Retirement and Disability — 55.1%
- Medical — 30.7%
- Income Maintenance — 7.8%
- Unemployment Insurance — 0.8%
- Veterans & Other — 5.5%

ECONOMIC STRUCTURE

LEADING PRIVATE INDUSTRIES, 1997 (Worker and proprietor earnings, millions of dollars)		FASTEST EARNINGS GROWTH, 1989–97 (percent increase)	
Health services	$3 889	Chemicals and allied products	171.9
Business services	2 350	Social services	113.1
Oil and gas extraction	2 116	Real estate	96.5
Construction specialties	1 452	Business services	83.0
Industrial machinery manufacturing	1 326	Trucking and warehousing	80.3

OKLAHOMA'S ECONOMY HAS NECESSARILY BECOME MORE diversified over the past 20 years as the oil and gas industry has shrunk in real terms. While oil and gas earnings were by far the largest of any industry in the state in 1980, by 1997 they ranked only third, behind health and business services. Despite this decline, the mining sector in 1997 still contributed a much higher proportion of all jobs (3.0 percent) and earnings (4.8 percent) than in a typical state. Farming is another traditional sector that continued as a larger than average force in the Oklahoma economy. Government is the third sector that is unusually large in Oklahoma, comprising 16.6 percent of all jobs in 1997 compared with 14.4 percent nationwide. Federal civilian and military earnings were about 70 percent higher than the national average, as a proportion of total earnings, while state government also contributed a somewhat high-er proportion of total jobs and earnings.

Conversely, manufacturing had a smaller than average weight in the state's job picture, about 2 percentage points lower than in the United States in 1997, with industrial machinery the sector's only large industry with earnings over $1 billion. There were somewhat less than average shares of employment in services and finance sectors also, even though three of the fastest growing industries are social services, real estate, and business services. Trucking and warehousing grew at triple the U.S. rate. However, a variety of service industries that grew nationwide are stagnant in Oklahoma, ranging from hotels to personal services to legal services. Declines in real earnings in several retail industries, such as food and apparel, suggest that residents are shopping more in neighboring states.

Employment and Earnings by Sector

	1980	1989	1990	1991	1992	1993	1994	1995	1996	1997 Number	1997 Percent of total	Change*
Employment *(thousands of persons)*												
Total	1 551	1 632	1 663	1 679	1 692	1 719	1 753	1 796	1 843	1 883	100.0	1.8
Farm	89	82	83	82	84	83	81	82	83	84	4.4	0.2
Nonfarm	1 461	1 550	1 580	1 596	1 608	1 636	1 672	1 714	1 760	1 800	95.6	1.9
Private nonfarm	1 184	1 248	1 273	1 289	1 292	1 323	1 362	1 402	1 449	1 488	79.0	2.2
Agricultural service, forestry, and fishing	9	15	16	18	17	19	20	21	21	22	1.2	4.7
Mining	106	84	81	79	71	67	69	63	56	56	3.0	-4.9
Construction	85	67	70	69	72	78	83	87	90	90	4.8	3.6
Manufacturing	195	171	175	176	170	175	180	179	183	189	10.0	1.3
Transportation and public utilities	79	77	80	81	81	84	86	86	92	95	5.1	2.8
Wholesale trade	74	67	66	68	70	66	67	71	71	72	3.8	0.9
Retail trade	238	263	266	273	279	285	298	308	319	322	17.1	2.6
Finance, insurance, and real estate	107	98	99	98	96	98	98	100	104	108	5.8	1.2
Services	291	405	418	427	436	450	461	488	514	533	28.3	3.5
Government	277	303	308	308	316	313	310	312	311	312	16.6	0.4
Earnings *(millions of dollars)*												
Total	21 342	31 883	33 818	35 141	37 174	39 089	40 169	41 230	43 258	45 655	100.0	4.6
Farm	311	830	822	642	783	1 020	812	385	383	835	1.8	0.1
Nonfarm	21 031	31 053	32 996	34 499	36 391	38 069	39 358	40 845	42 874	44 821	98.2	4.7
Private nonfarm	17 513	24 693	26 230	27 325	28 784	30 260	31 441	32 636	34 449	36 228	79.4	4.9
Agricultural service, forestry, and fishing	69	148	171	194	209	218	229	232	230	239	0.5	6.1
Mining	2 162	1 953	2 079	2 226	2 164	2 225	2 037	2 030	2 108	2 207	4.8	1.5
Construction	1 502	1 520	1 598	1 496	1 583	1 697	1 939	2 029	2 167	2 180	4.8	4.6
Manufacturing	3 858	5 204	5 503	5 749	5 983	6 278	6 694	6 634	6 912	7 322	16.0	4.4
Transportation and public utilities	1 710	2 491	2 719	2 910	3 099	3 360	3 333	3 408	3 623	3 782	8.3	5.4
Wholesale trade	1 507	1 778	1 846	1 951	2 065	1 924	1 997	2 134	2 208	2 325	5.1	3.4
Retail trade	2 278	3 208	3 292	3 462	3 643	3 808	4 012	4 175	4 401	4 545	10.0	4.5
Finance, insurance, and real estate	1 054	1 489	1 615	1 722	1 878	2 020	2 079	2 138	2 273	2 385	5.2	6.1
Services	3 373	6 902	7 408	7 615	8 159	8 729	9 121	9 855	10 527	11 244	24.6	6.3
Government	3 518	6 360	6 766	7 174	7 608	7 809	7 917	8 209	8 425	8 593	18.8	3.8

*Compound annual average percent change, 1989–1997

ECONOMIC STRUCTURE (Continued)

AVERAGE WAGES IN OKLAHOMA WERE ABOUT 20 PERCENT lower than U.S. averages in 1997, and they increased more slowly during the 1989–97 period. State wages came closest to average within the oil-dominated mining sector and are within 80 to 85 percent of national levels in retail trade, manufacturing (which is dominated in the state by fairly high productivity industries), and government. Within services and construction, average wages were only 76 percent as high as the U.S. levels in those sectors. The higher wage components of the business services industry, such as computer services, have a smaller than average presence in Oklahoma, and construction activity has shifted away from higher wage heavy construction over the past decade.

Manufacturing contributed a surprisingly large 17.3 percent to gross state product in 1997 in Oklahoma, a share that has risen since 1987 as manufacturing output grew by more than double the rate in the sector nationwide. Chemicals and allied products was the fastest growing, in percentage terms, but there were also significant earnings increases in fabricated metals, transportation equipment (excluding motor vehicles), and food products. Industrial machinery output has languished because of cutbacks in the oil industry it serves. Manufacturing output value per worker for the sector is nearly as high as the national average.

Exports were not a significantly large sector within Oklahoma and they have not grown nearly as fast as have exports for the entire country between 1994 and 1997, helping account for the sub-par growth rates within the state. Industrial machinery was by far the largest export good from Oklahoma, but these exports have grown less than 25 percent as fast as have U.S. exports of machinery during the same period. Chemical products displayed the fastest growth of exports for the state, but the value is still relatively small in absolute terms. Agricultural exports plummeted from 1994 to 1996, and only partially recovered in 1997.

Average Annual Wages and Salaries by Sector
(dollars)

	1989	1996	1997 State	1997 U.S.
All wage and salary workers	19 387	23 044	23 666	29 809
Farm	12 067	13 534	13 954	16 442
Nonfarm	19 444	23 114	23 735	29 900
Private nonfarm	19 535	22 754	23 442	29 867
Agricultural service, forestry, and fishing	11 638	13 623	14 155	17 941
Mining	34 799	43 081	43 647	49 800
Construction	20 699	23 444	24 074	31 765
Manufacturing	25 929	30 154	31 119	38 351
Transportation and utilities	29 659	33 553	34 083	38 222
Wholesale trade	23 523	28 962	29 790	39 466
Retail trade	11 241	13 317	13 698	16 206
Finance, insurance, and real estate	21 560	27 649	28 343	44 993
Services	16 385	20 185	20 863	27 588
Government	19 158	24 421	24 824	30 062

Gross State Product and Manufacturing
(millions of dollars, except as noted)

	1989	1994	1995	1996
Gross state product, total	53 791	65 957	68 611	72 767
Manufacturing:				
Millions of dollars	9 343	11 026	11 941	12 587
Percent of total gross state product	17.4	16.7	17.4	17.3
Per worker (dollars)	54 574	61 420	66 867	68 754
New capital expenditures, manufacturing	NA	753	733	1 015

Exports of Goods
(millions of dollars)

	1994	1995	1996	1997
All goods	2 172	2 467	2 538	2 722
Manufactures	1 990	2 178	2 285	2 489
Agricultural and livestock products	37	31	20	27
Other commodities	144	259	233	205
Top goods exports, 1997:				
Industrial machinery and computers	689	817	821	870
Chemical products	239	280	309	310
Electric and electronic equipment	259	217	214	272
Fabricated metal products	151	149	165	213
Transportation equipment	153	158	235	190

HOUSING

THE HOUSING SECTOR IN OKLAHOMA HAS REFLECTED THE modest growth of the state's overall economy and population, lagging national growth trends throughout the 1990–97 period. Total production of new housing per capita was significantly lower than in the nation, until an upturn in 1997 brought production rates closer to average. Mobile homes, a more affordable alternative to conventional houses, contributed substantially to the new home production figures in the mid-1990s, representing 40 percent of total production in 1997, compared to 20 percent in 1990. Existing home sales also have been a bit weaker than the national total sales figures. The median home price in the Oklahoma City area was $77,000 in 1997, one of the lowest of all large metropolitan areas.

By 1997, homeownership had become slightly less prevalent than in the early 1990s, but the rate stayed higher than the national average. Oklahoma's nontransient population, low home prices, and large contingent of older residents all contribute to a relatively high rate of owner-

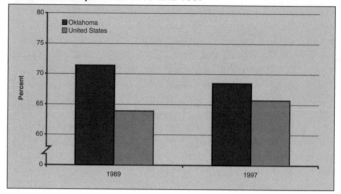

Homeownership Rates: 1989 and 1997

ship. Rental vacancy rates remained high throughout the 1990s, suggesting a continuing overhang of excess capacity from apartments built before the 1980s oil bust.

Housing Supply

	1989	1990	1991	1992	1993	1994	1995	1996	1997
Residential building permits (thousands)	5.6	5.3	5.9	7.7	8.7	9.5	10.1	10.6	11.2
New home production (including manufactured housing):									
Thousands of homes	6.6	6.6	6.9	9.2	11.7	12.7	15.0	16.1	18.7
Rate per 1,000 population									
Oklahoma	2.1	2.1	2.2	2.9	3.6	3.9	4.6	4.9	5.6
U.S.	6.2	5.2	4.5	5.1	5.6	6.4	6.3	6.6	6.5
Existing home sales:									
Thousands of homes	49.1	53.4	52.5	57.6	61.5	59.7	57.7	60.6	64.2
Change from previous year (percent)									
Oklahoma	4.9	8.8	-1.7	9.7	6.8	-2.9	-3.4	5.0	5.9
U.S.	-3.9	-4.0	0.0	9.2	8.2	4.8	-3.7	7.5	3.8
Home ownership rate (percent of households)	71.4	70.3	69.2	68.9	70.3	68.5	69.8	68.4	68.5
Rental vacancy rate (percent of rental housing units)	14.7	14.6	9.5	9.7	11.5	8.9	10.3	11.0	11.4

AGRICULTURE

THE FARM ECONOMY IN THE STATE IS DOMINATED BY THE CATtle industry, which brought in 74 percent of cash receipts in 1997. Grain production took a distant second place, and even those sales have not risen significantly. The state's farm earnings situation in the 1990s was lackluster. Net farm income fluctuated between $600 million and $900 million during most of the 1990s, but with much worse performance in 1995–96. The average farm size in the state is unusually low for the region and falls below the U.S. average, as does the average value of land and buildings on farms in the state.

OKLAHOMA FARMS, 1997

Number of farms	73 000
Total acres (thousands):	34 000
Average per farm	466
Value of land and buildings (millions of dollars)	19 380
Average per farm (dollars)	265 479

Farm Income
(millions of dollars)

	1980	1989	1990	1991	1992	1993	1994	1995	1996	1997
Gross income	3 803	4 615	4 634	4 908	4 639	5 101	4 999	4 641	4 518	5 570
Receipts from sales	3 565	3 949	4 011	4 302	4 084	4 458	4 461	4 130	3 928	4 931
Government payments	35	235	319	291	248	324	207	165	237	206
Imputed and miscellaneous income	204	431	304	315	307	318	331	347	353	434
(−) Production expenses	3 404	3 861	3 982	4 165	3 884	4 084	4 425	4 309	4 338	4 827
(=) Realized net income	399	754	651	743	755	1 017	574	332	180	743
(+) Inventory change	-190	44	119	-188	-3	-86	282	-68	111	89
(=) Net income	210	798	770	555	752	931	857	264	291	832
Corporate income	0	91	90	51	96	48	173	35	57	149
Farm proprietors income	210	708	680	504	656	884	684	229	234	683

EDUCATION

EDUCATIONAL ATTAINMENT Percent of population age 25 and over, 1997	State	United States
High school graduate or higher	85.2	82.1
College graduate or higher	20.5	23.9

FOR A RELATIVELY POOR STATE, THE HIGH SCHOOL ATTAINMENT of Oklahoma residents is outstanding. At 85.2 percent, Oklahoma is in the top third of states for proportion of high school graduates. Spending per elementary and secondary pupil is much lower than the U.S. average, however, and teacher salaries were about 24 percent below national levels in 1997, reflecting the state's low general wage scales and the limited local tax revenues

available. Attainment of college degrees is less prevalent than average for the nation; college graduates comprise 20.5 percent of the state, for which Oklahoma ranks 37th in the nation. Current enrollment shows that the proportion of young adults enrolled in higher education is a bit above average. The percent enrolled in private colleges is much more limited than is typical in the United States.

High School Completion: 1990–97

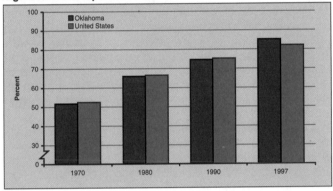

Education Indicators

	State	U.S.
Elementary and secondary schools		
Enrollment, 1995–96		
Total (thousands)	641	49 873
Percent in private schools	3.8	10.1
Expenditures per pupil (dollars), 1995–96	4 881	6 146
Average teacher salary (dollars), 1996–97	29 270	38 509
Higher education		
Enrollment, 1996–97		
Total (thousands)	177	14 218
Percent of population 18–34	22.9	21.8
Percent minority	21.0	26.1
Percent in private schools	12.9	22.6

HEALTH

HEALTH INDICATORS SHOW A MIXED RECORD FOR THE STATE. Infant mortality rates were above the average for the nation in 1997, but the rate has declined in the past three years and tends to indicate good availability of healthcare in a somewhat rural state. However, overall death rates, even adjusted for the age mix of the state, were noticeably higher than U.S. averages. Death rates were particularly high from

heart disease, stroke, and motor vehicle and other accidents. The suicide rate was well above average, and death from HIV infection is substantially below average. Relative to the nation, a larger percentage of the state's population is not covered by health insurance, though this percentage decreased in 1996–97 as the economy recovered more fully from recession and the poverty rate declined.

Health Indicators

	1990	1995	1996	1997
Infant mortality *(rate per thousand live births)*				
Oklahoma	9.2	8.3	8.9	7.6
U.S.	9.2	7.6	7.3	7.1
Total deaths, age-adjusted rate *(rate per thousand population)*				
Oklahoma	5.4	5.4	5.4	5.4
U.S.	5.2	5.0	4.9	4.8
Persons not covered by health insurance *(percent of population)*				
Oklahoma	18.6	19.2	17.0	17.8
U.S.	13.9	15.4	15.6	16.1

Leading Causes of Death, 1996
(deaths per 100,000 population)

	Age-adjusted		Not age-adjusted	
	State	U.S.	State	U.S.
Deaths from all causes	536.2	491.6	1003.3	872.5
Heart disease	158.9	134.5	342.8	276.4
Cancer	129.6	127.9	215.9	203.4
Cerebrovascular diseases	30.0	26.4	73.3	60.3
Chronic obstructive pulmonary disease	24.7	21.0	47.4	40.0
Diabetes mellitus	12.5	13.6	21.9	23.3
Pneumonia and influenza	15.5	12.8	41.1	31.6
HIV	5.6	11.1	5.5	11.7
Liver disease	6.8	7.5	8.8	9.4
Alzheimer's disease	2.3	2.7	7.6	8.1
Accidents and adverse effects	41.1	30.4	47.9	35.8
Motor vehicle accidents	24.0	16.2	24.5	16.5
Suicide	13.6	10.8	14.1	11.6
Homicide	8.6	8.5	8.1	7.9
Injury by firearm	15.6	12.9	15.8	12.8

GOVERNMENT

STATE AND LOCAL TAXES, 1995–96	State	U.S.
Per capita (dollars)	1 937	2 477
Percent of personal income	10.5	10.8

STATE PLUS LOCAL TAXES IN OKLAHOMA OF $1,937 PER PERson in 1995–96 were well below normal—about 22 percent below the U.S. average levels. The state-level taxes comprised a high percentage of the total because of the broadbased income and sales taxes in the state. Local taxes (primarily property tax) contributed a fairly low proportion (30 percent) of total taxes. With low total tax receipts, the tax burden as a percentage of personal income was below average for all states, despite the low incomes prevalent in Oklahoma.

Total state government revenue in 1997 was substantially below average because of the low level of state-generated revenue plus a below-average receipt of transfers from the federal level (covering Medicaid and other programs). State tax receipts per capita were about 8 percent below the U.S. average for states, with particularly low sales tax revenues, partly due to the sluggish retail economy. Individual income tax revenues were around the average, but corporate income tax collections were less than in a typical state. Total spending by the state was below average, but spending for education was surprisingly strong in 1997, exceeding the U.S. averages. In contrast, spending on public welfare and health were both much below the average. Reflecting past conservative spending patterns in the state, the expense for interest on general debt is only half of the national average, on a per capita basis, and the level of debt outstanding is two-thirds that of an average state.

The state's receipt of federal funds overall was proportionate to its share of U.S. population in 1997. Social Security and Medicare benefits paid in the state were a bit higher, though federal Medicaid spending per capita was below average in Oklahoma. Salaries paid to federal employees brought the state one-third more than its proportionate share of such salaries. In contrast, procurement (both defense and non-defense contracting) was particularly low here.

State Government Finances, 1996–97

	Millions of dollars	Percent distribution	Dollars per capita State	Dollars per capita U.S.
General revenue	8 704	100.0	2 624	3 049
Intergovernmental revenue	2 170	24.9	654	863
Taxes	5 061	58.1	1 526	1 660
General sales	1 273	14.6	384	551
Selective sales	668	7.7	201	257
License taxes	701	8.0	211	106
Individual income	1 698	19.5	512	542
Corporation net income	221	2.5	67	115
Other taxes	501	5.8	151	90
Other general revenue	1 474	16.9	444	526
General expenditure	8 286	100.0	2 498	2 951
Intergovernmental expenditure	2 625	31.7	791	989
Direct expenditure	5 661	68.3	1 707	1 962
General expenditure, by function:				
Education	3 691	44.5	1 113	1 033
Public welfare	1 723	20.8	520	761
Hospitals and health	616	7.4	186	237
Highways	806	9.7	243	225
Police protection and corrections	405	4.9	122	137
Natural resources, parks and recreation	207	2.5	62	63
Governmental administration	354	4.3	107	107
Interest on general debt	165	2.0	50	99
Other and unallocable	320	3.9	96	290
Debt at end of fiscal year	3 795	NA	1 144	1 706
Cash and security holdings	16 869	NA	5 086	6 683

Federal Spending within State

	Federal funds, fiscal 1997		
	Millions of dollars	Percent distribution	Percent of U.S. total*
Total within state	17 396	100.0	1.2
Payments to individuals	10 383	59.7	1.3
Retirement and disability	6 427	36.9	1.4
Medicare	2 596	14.9	1.3
Food stamps	255	1.5	1.3
Supplemental Security Income	296	1.7	1.1
Grants	2 770	15.9	1.1
Medicaid and other health	1 160	6.7	1.0
Nutrition and family welfare	588	3.4	1.3
Education	242	1.4	1.4
Housing and community development	151	0.9	1.3
Salaries and wages	2 629	15.1	1.6
Defense procurement contracts	738	4.2	0.6
Non-defense procurement contracts	450	2.6	0.6

*State population is 1.2 percent of the U.S. total.

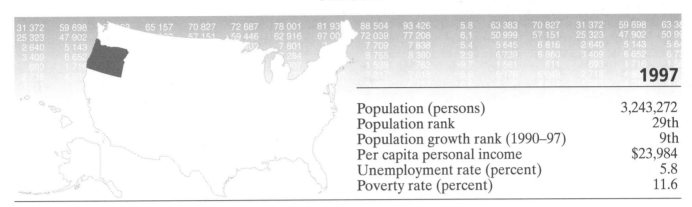

1997

Population (persons)	3,243,272
Population rank	29th
Population growth rank (1990–97)	9th
Per capita personal income	$23,984
Unemployment rate (percent)	5.8
Poverty rate (percent)	11.6

OREGON HAS EXPERIENCED A GROWTH SURGE DURING THE 1990s that is enlarging its population and strengthening its economic base toward the high-tech end, but only slightly boosted its per capita income toward parity with U.S. averages. Job growth has been far in excess of the national average, and population growth was almost double the rate in the nation from 1990 to 1997. Expansions in high-tech manufacturing and construction industries have led its economy: earnings in electronic equipment manufacturing grew by 298 percent from 1989 to 1997 to become the second largest industry in the sector. Manufacturing production overall grew as fast as the rest of the state economy, so that the value of manufacturing production represented 20.5 percent of the economy in 1997, higher than the U.S. average.

Population growth in Oregon of 13.4 percent in the 1990s overtook the state's traditional slow-growth policies, as the population was boosted by a strong in-migration from California and other states. The flood of migration was such that total in-migration in the 1990s has added seven times more new residents than the 1980s rate (counting domestic and international immigration). The population remains much more predominantly White non-Hispanic than average and has a higher proportion of working-age and higher proportion of elderly people than the United States as a whole.

Average Annual Population Growth: 1990–97

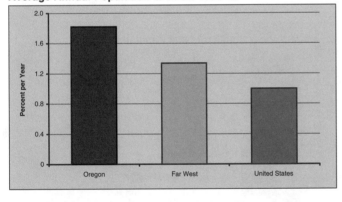

Median Household Income: 1989–97 (1997 dollars)

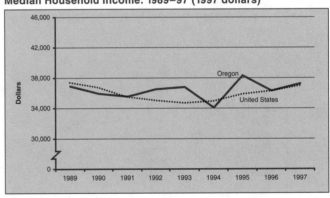

Unemployment Rate: 1989–97

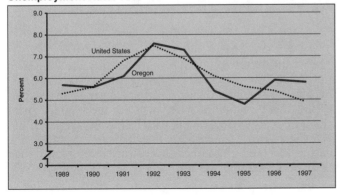

UNEMPLOYMENT FLUCTUATES ON A CYCLICAL BASIS SIMILAR to that in the nation, especially since manufacturing and construction employment have a slightly higher share of Oregon jobs than the average in the United States. Unemployment rates have been somewhat above the U.S. rates for 1996 and 1997, as even a 3.4 percent increase in employment in those two years could not keep pace with a striking 4.5 percent increase in Oregon's labor force.

POPULATION AND LABOR FORCE

POPULATION IN OREGON GREW BY 13.4 PERCENT BETWEEN 1990 and 1997, with a growth rate of 18 percent in the Portland metro area. The state had the 9th highest growth rate in the country, about the same rate as neighboring Washington and almost double that of California. Migrants from other states contributed most to the expansion, adding 8.3 percent to the 1990 population by 1997, with a 1.7 percent increase from immigrants (less than the U.S. average rate of immigration). With a low birth rate, Oregon has a slower than average natural increase in population. A goodly share of the in-migrants are moving to small towns and rural areas in the state, thus the non-metropolitan areas are maintaining their substantial share (around 30 percent) of the state's population.

Despite large percentage increases in the small minority population in the 1990s, the state retains a remarkably high predominance of White non-Hispanic population, at 88 percent, in contrast to the multicultural society of neighboring California. The Hispanic population is the largest minority group, with 5.9 percent of the 1997 population, and if its 7.5 percent annual growth rate continues, this community will soon become a major influence.

Population and Labor Force

	1980	1990	1991	1992	1993	1994	1995	1996	1997	Change* State	Change* U.S.
Population											
Total number of persons (thousands)	2 633	2 859	2 919	2 974	3 035	3 087	3 141	3 195	3 243	1.8	1.0
Percent distribution:											
White, Non-Hispanic	93.4	90.5	90.5	90.1	89.8	89.5	89.0	88.7	88.4	1.5	0.4
Black, Non-Hispanic	1.4	1.9	1.6	1.6	1.6	1.6	1.6	1.6	1.6	-0.7	1.4
Asian	1.6	2.5	2.6	2.7	2.8	2.8	2.9	3.0	3.1	5.3	4.1
Native American	1.2	1.4	1.4	1.4	1.4	1.4	1.4	1.4	1.4	1.5	1.6
Hispanic	2.5	4.0	4.2	4.4	4.7	5.0	5.3	5.6	5.9	7.5	3.8
In metropolitan areas	68.3	69.9	70.0	70.1	70.1	70.1	70.1	70.2	70.3	1.9	1.0
Total number of households (thousands)	992	1 103	1 131	1 157	1 180	1 197	1 223	1 249	NA	2.1	1.2
Labor Force (thousands)											
Population 16 and over	2 001	2 192	2 247	2 290	2 346	2 390	2 437	2 488	2 529	2.1	1.0
Civilian labor force	1 297	1 490	1 514	1 547	1 596	1 646	1 653	1 718	1 728	2.1	1.1
Employed	1 189	1 407	1 422	1 429	1 480	1 557	1 573	1 616	1 627	2.1	1.2
Percent of population	59.4	64.2	63.3	62.4	63.1	65.1	64.5	65.0	64.3		
Unemployment rate (percent)	8.3	5.6	6.1	7.6	7.3	5.4	4.8	5.9	5.8		

*Compound annual average percent change, 1990–1997; 1990–1996 for households.

Population Change and Components: 1990–97

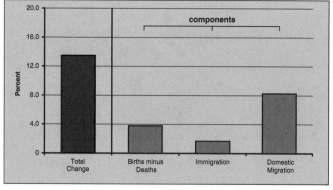

Average Annual Household and Population Growth

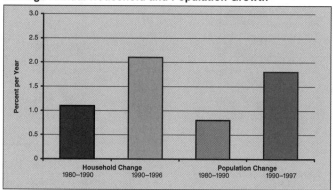

Population by Age; Births and Deaths

	1990 State	1990 U.S.	1997 State	1997 U.S.
Age distribution (percent)				
Under 5 years	7.3	7.6	6.6	7.2
5 to 17 years	18.6	18.2	18.4	18.8
18 to 64 years	60.3	61.8	61.7	61.3
65 years and over	13.7	12.5	13.3	12.7
Birth and death rates (per thousand population)				
Births	15.1	16.7	13.5	14.6
Deaths	8.8	8.6	8.9	8.6

THE AGE DISTRIBUTION HERE IS TILTED SLIGHTLY TO WORKING-age adults, which actually comprised an increasing proportion of the population during the 1990–97 period because of in-migration, while it was a decreasing segment of the U.S. population. Oregon has a moderately lower share of children, in keeping with its low birth rate. It has a higher share of elderly people than is typical for the nation, although this cohort is growing more slowly than the overall state population.

HOUSEHOLD AND PERSONAL INCOME

HOUSEHOLD INCOME AND PERSONS IN POVERTY	1990	1995	1996	1997 State	1997 U.S.
Median household income (1997 dollars)	35 957	38 307	36 306	37 247	37 005
Persons in poverty (thousands)	267	360	382	382	35 574
Poverty rate (percent)	9.2	11.2	11.8	11.6	13.3

THE MEDIAN INCOME OF OREGON HOUSEHOLDS HAS GENERally tracked the national median since the late 1980s, and it was nearly unchanged from 1989 to 1997 after adjustment for inflation. Decreases in average household size have been one factor holding down median household income. Poverty rates in Oregon have remained relatively low during the 1990s, because of the state's economic expansion, and reflected its low concentration of minority groups, who typically face higher poverty rates.

Per capita personal income was 5 to 10 percent lower than the U.S. average in the same period. However, the gap in per capita personal income between Oregon and the national average narrowed during the 1995–97 period, as per capita incomes increased 50 percent faster than the U.S. average. Oregon's lower relative position for per capita income may reflect its lower noncash transfer payments,

which are not included in the household income data. Personal income data show a 2.7 percent negative adjustment to total earnings of Oregon residents, reflecting incommuting by workers who live in other states, primarily Washington state.

Overall transfer payments rose faster than overall personal income during the 1990–97 period (as was true nationwide), but there was modest growth in Social Security payments and a precipitous drop in family assistance from welfare reform and job availability. In contrast, big increases came in medical payments, government retirement programs, and Supplemental Security Income, which increased 92 percent. The fastest increase came in other income maintenance, consisting primarily of earned income tax credits, now the largest income maintenance program here.

Personal Income
(millions of dollars)

	1980	1989	1990	1991	1992	1993	1994	1995	1996	1997	Change*
Earnings by place of work	19 403	32 458	35 487	37 082	39 664	42 433	45 468	48 581	52 342	56 344	7.1
Wages and salaries	15 404	25 479	27 706	28 975	30 967	32 775	35 226	38 147	41 465	44 967	7.4
Other labor income	1 518	2 803	3 163	3 396	3 670	4 012	4 288	4 409	4 406	4 533	6.2
Proprietors' income	2 481	4 175	4 619	4 711	5 027	5 645	5 953	6 026	6 472	6 845	6.4
Farm	293	344	324	323	338	468	257	103	175	110	-13.3
Nonfarm	2 188	3 831	4 295	4 388	4 689	5 177	5 696	5 923	6 296	6 736	7.3
(−) Personal contributions for social insurance	1 060	2 258	2 433	2 636	2 816	3 011	3 258	3 531	3 783	4 079	7.7
(+) Adjustment for residence	-278	-535	-629	-674	-745	-882	-983	-1 189	-1 435	-1 542	NA
(=) **Net earnings by state of residence**	18 064	29 665	32 426	33 772	36 102	38 540	41 227	43 862	47 124	50 723	6.9
(+) Dividends, interest, and rent	4 565	9 130	9 688	9 901	9 977	10 490	11 419	12 336	13 465	14 257	5.7
(+) Transfer payments	3 698	6 934	7 691	8 557	9 470	10 204	10 663	11 624	12 454	12 811	8.0
(=) **Total personal income**	26 327	45 729	49 805	52 230	55 549	59 234	63 309	67 822	73 044	77 791	6.9
Farm	480	616	657	658	662	824	630	525	650	591	-0.5
Nonfarm	25 847	45 114	49 148	51 572	54 887	58 410	62 678	67 297	72 393	77 200	6.9
Personal income per capita (dollars)											
Current dollars	9 968	16 387	17 422	17 890	18 671	19 512	20 497	21 579	22 852	23 984	4.9
1997 dollars	19 059	20 717	20 965	20 658	20 885	21 232	21 782	22 431	23 271	23 984	1.8

*Compound annual average percent change, 1989–1997

Government Transfer Payments

	Millions of dollars 1990	Millions of dollars 1997	Percent change* State	Percent change* U.S.
Total government payments to individuals	7 336	12 289	67.5	62.7
Retirement, disability, and insurance	4 482	7 176	60.1	48.2
Social Security	3 136	4 639	47.9	46.1
Government employee retirement	1 143	2 274	99.0	60.3
Medical payments	1 710	3 466	102.7	101.2
Income maintenance	514	801	55.7	58.0
Supplemental Security Income	114	219	91.6	75.4
Family assistance	157	104	-33.6	-0.5
Food Stamps	173	210	21.0	27.1
Other income maintenance	70	268	282.4	189.8
Unemployment insurance benefits	282	400	41.9	10.6
Veterans benefits and other	348	446	28.3	30.8

*Percent change, 1990–1997

Government Payments to Individuals: 1997

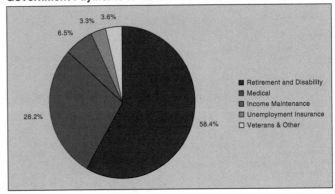

- Retirement and Disability — 58.4%
- Medical — 28.2%
- Income Maintenance — 6.5%
- Unemployment Insurance — 3.3%
- Veterans & Other — 3.6%

ECONOMIC STRUCTURE

LEADING PRIVATE INDUSTRIES, 1997 (Worker and proprietor earnings, millions of dollars)		FASTEST EARNINGS GROWTH, 1989–97 (percent increase)	
Health services	$4 557	Electronic equipment manufacturing	297.9
Business services	3 249	Real estate	225.6
Construction specialties	2 822	Amusement and recreation services	157.9
Lumber and wood products	2 334	Business services	157.0
Electronic and equipment manufacturing	2 073	Construction specialties	137.7

JOB GROWTH IN OREGON OUTPACED THE U.S. PERFORMANCE IN every sector, except agricultural services, in 1989–97, with the greatest spark provided by the phenomenal growth in business services and electronic equipment manufacturing. The growth of high-tech computer-related manufacturing is stimulated by both domestic and export demand for high-tech products. The state government now classifies 28 percent of manufacturing jobs in the state as "high technology," and increases in electronic equipment earnings accounted for 39 percent of the total increase in manufacturing earnings during 1989–97. Intel is now the state's second largest private employer, with 11,000 jobs in computer chip manufacturing. Lumber production is still the leading manufacturing industry, but limited demand has reduced its growth. Lumber's share of manufacturing earnings has dropped from 31 percent to 21 percent of the sector between 1989 and 1997. The three leading industries, lumber, electronics, and industrial machinery, comprised 50 percent of all the state's manufacturing earnings in 1997.

Within the large services sector, business services growth produced 29 percent of all earnings growth, and two other service type industries, real estate, and amusement and recreation services, are also among the five fastest growing industries of the 1990s. Rapid earnings growth of more than 90 percent also occurred in engineering, social services, and educational services. The construction sector boomed during the 1990s, as construction employment grew by a remarkable 65 percent during 1989–97 (compared with 15 percent growth nationwide). Expanded construction activity has included both small-scale building and heavy construction of new infrastructure needed for the growing population.

Employment and Earnings by Sector

	1980	1989	1990	1991	1992	1993	1994	1995	1996	1997 Number	1997 Percent of total	Change*
Employment *(thousands of persons)*												
Total	1 353	1 587	1 638	1 649	1 668	1 713	1 798	1 870	1 942	2 000	100.0	2.9
Farm	61	62	64	63	58	60	62	64	66	64	3.2	0.4
Nonfarm	1 293	1 525	1 574	1 586	1 610	1 653	1 736	1 806	1 876	1 936	96.8	3.0
Private nonfarm	1 084	1 296	1 337	1 347	1 366	1 409	1 491	1 559	1 626	1 683	84.1	3.3
Agricultural service, forestry, and fishing	19	28	29	29	28	31	34	34	36	38	1.9	4.1
Mining	3	2	3	3	3	3	3	3	3	3	0.2	2.9
Construction	68	70	77	78	79	82	92	101	110	115	5.7	6.5
Manufacturing	226	235	236	228	225	229	241	246	253	263	13.1	1.4
Transportation and public utilities	68	74	75	76	75	78	81	83	87	90	4.5	2.5
Wholesale trade	71	84	85	87	90	88	93	98	96	101	5.1	2.4
Retail trade	228	274	280	283	290	299	320	332	344	354	17.7	3.2
Finance, insurance, and real estate	117	109	112	112	113	117	115	120	125	132	6.6	2.4
Services	283	420	440	450	463	482	514	542	570	587	29.4	4.3
Government	209	229	237	239	243	245	245	247	250	253	12.6	1.2
Earnings *(millions of dollars)*												
Total	19 403	32 458	35 487	37 082	39 664	42 433	45 468	48 581	52 342	56 344	100.0	7.1
Farm	480	616	657	658	662	824	630	525	650	591	1.0	-0.5
Nonfarm	18 922	31 842	34 830	36 424	39 002	41 609	44 837	48 056	51 692	55 753	99.0	7.3
Private nonfarm	15 944	26 651	29 168	30 355	32 492	34 768	37 744	40 718	44 015	47 735	84.7	7.6
Agricultural service, forestry, and fishing	152	377	447	452	472	463	537	497	447	481	0.9	3.1
Mining	109	49	57	67	70	79	70	77	80	84	0.1	7.0
Construction	1 372	1 887	2 267	2 318	2 323	2 549	2 957	3 423	3 993	4 332	7.7	11.0
Manufacturing	4 743	6 928	7 180	7 289	7 609	8 063	8 825	9 381	9 949	10 899	19.3	5.8
Transportation and public utilities	1 540	2 319	2 401	2 542	2 652	2 804	2 978	3 170	3 357	3 574	6.3	5.6
Wholesale trade	1 436	2 352	2 596	2 686	2 910	2 999	3 259	3 618	3 808	4 205	7.5	7.5
Retail trade	2 240	3 574	3 908	4 160	4 408	4 714	5 064	5 313	5 699	6 076	10.8	6.9
Finance, insurance, and real estate	1 018	1 732	1 892	2 035	2 346	2 689	2 881	3 067	3 399	3 784	6.7	10.3
Services	3 333	7 432	8 418	8 806	9 702	10 409	11 175	12 173	13 283	14 299	25.4	8.5
Government	2 978	5 191	5 662	6 069	6 510	6 841	7 093	7 338	7 677	8 018	14.2	5.6

*Compound annual average percent change, 1989–1997

ECONOMIC STRUCTURE (Continued)

AVERAGE WAGES IN OREGON REMAINED SLIGHTLY BELOW national averages. Only in construction, retail trade, and agricultural services were wages above the national average. (The latter reflects higher wages in the timber industry.) Wages in manufacturing were closer to parity but still average 3.5 percent less than those in the United States, probably reflecting the weight of the lumber industry in the state. Services sector wages were unusually low, with a 12 percent shortfall below the national average.

Manufacturing has been a healthy sector in Oregon, maintaining its 20.5 percent share of state output through the 1990s (as of 1996). Though manufacturing employment rose less than other sectors, it still represents an above-average share of Oregon jobs (13.1 percent compared to 12.4 percent in the United States). Output per worker was slightly above average in Oregon in 1997, whereas it was below average in 1989, reflecting the shift toward electronics production. New capital investment in this sector has grown by impressive margins. From less than $1 billion per year during the 1980s, it has mushroomed to $3.3 billion in 1996, with significant investment in the computer chip industry, which portends well for future earnings growth.

Exports have played a vital role in supporting the economic expansion of this state, with more than half of all exports going to Asia. Oregon's exports in 1996 consisted 48 percent of high-technology products, 25 percent agricultural products, and 13 percent wood products, according to a state analysis. The importance of agricultural products within this mix is exceptionally high. Wood products were once more significant in size, but exports softened markedly in the 1996–97 period. Oregon is not a leading export state in total value, but its exports represent a higher than average share of the state economy.

Average Annual Wages and Salaries by Sector
(dollars)

	1989	1996	1997 State	1997 U.S.
All wage and salary workers	19 814	26 576	27 948	29 809
Farm	10 066	15 290	16 058	16 442
Nonfarm	20 008	26 789	28 158	29 900
Private nonfarm	19 844	26 570	28 007	29 867
Agricultural service, forestry, and fishing	14 243	18 874	19 486	17 941
Mining	27 594	33 879	34 694	49 800
Construction	23 999	33 017	34 932	31 765
Manufacturing	25 868	34 813	37 020	38 351
Transportation and utilities	27 871	34 263	35 546	38 222
Wholesale trade	26 032	36 941	38 857	39 466
Retail trade	12 087	16 175	16 841	16 206
Finance, insurance, and real estate	23 059	32 466	34 946	44 993
Services	17 089	23 280	24 330	27 588
Government	20 743	27 914	28 947	30 062

Gross State Product and Manufacturing
(millions of dollars, except as noted)

	1989	1994	1995	1996
Gross state product, total	52 932	74 724	80 805	86 967
Manufacturing:				
Millions of dollars	11 516	14 496	16 522	17 868
Percent of total gross state product	21.8	19.4	20.4	20.5
Per worker (dollars)	48 982	60 224	67 160	70 509
New capital expenditures, manufacturing	NA	1 352	2 070	3 345

Exports of Goods
(millions of dollars)

	1994	1995	1996	1997
All goods	6 987	9 902	8 481	8 359
Manufactures	4 552	6 410	5 005	5 420
Agricultural and livestock products	2 265	3 253	3 309	2 769
Other commodities	170	239	167	170
Top goods exports, 1997:				
Agricultural products	2 264	3 252	3 307	2 766
Industrial machinery and computers	1 162	2 001	1 336	1 543
Electric and electronic equipment	859	1 507	1 628	1 540
Lumber and wood products	762	735	506	535
Transportation equipment	412	438	357	454

HOUSING

HOUSING PRODUCTION HAS BEEN STRONG IN OREGON, AS would be expected in an area with such a powerful population uptrend, beating U.S. average housing production rates handily. After a cyclical downturn in 1991–92, there has been high production each year. The Portland metro area has grown particularly rapidly, and building permits for new residential construction there ranked 9th in the nation in 1997. Sales of existing homes have not gained as strongly.

Home prices in the Portland area, while they increased a dramatic 55 percent from 1992 to 1997, remained much lower than in Seattle or San Francisco, one of the elements attracting the state's large numbers of in-migrants. The median home price in Portland in 1997 was $152,400, up from $97,000 in 1992. Some analysts cite the restrictive land use policies of the area as a cause for the jump in housing prices, but certainly the strength of demand is a factor. Statewide, homeownership rates had been about equal to national rates until in 1995 a decline began in

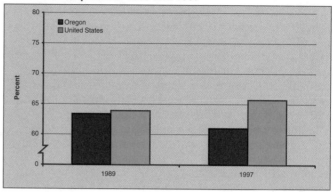

Homeownership Rates: 1989 and 1997

Oregon, attributable to the continuing influx of new residents and spiraling home prices. The same factors have kept rental vacancy rates extremely low.

Housing Supply

	1989	1990	1991	1992	1993	1994	1995	1996	1997
Residential building permits (thousands)	23.1	22.9	16.4	17.0	20.5	24.1	26.2	27.8	27.0
New home production (including manufactured housing):									
Thousands of homes	26.9	27.1	20.8	22.2	26.9	32.1	32.5	34.1	32.4
Rate per 1,000 population									
Oregon	9.6	9.5	7.1	7.5	8.9	10.4	10.3	10.7	10.0
U.S.	6.2	5.2	4.5	5.1	5.6	6.4	6.3	6.6	6.5
Existing home sales:									
Thousands of homes	53.2	56.6	48.1	52.5	58.8	58.1	59.0	58.9	60.1
Change from previous year (percent)									
Oregon	8.8	6.4	-15.0	9.1	12.0	-1.2	1.5	-0.2	2.0
U.S.	-3.9	-4.0	0.0	9.2	8.2	4.8	-3.7	7.5	3.8
Home ownership rate (percent of households)	63.4	64.4	65.2	64.3	63.8	63.9	63.2	63.1	61.0
Rental vacancy rate (percent of rental housing units)	4.2	3.3	5.1	4.9	5.6	3.9	4.0	5.9	5.4

AGRICULTURE

FARM INCOME SHOWED A SUBSTANTIAL WEAKENING DURING 1995–97, with average net earnings during that period of only $170 million, a 60 percent decline from the previous five years' average. Sales of livestock declined a bit over the decade, while production of hay and fruits increased, yet overall production cost increases swamped the revenue increases. Net income including inventory change was equal to only 3.7 percent of total farm revenue in 1997. Farm income represented approximately 1 percent of total personal income in the state.

OREGON FARMS, 1997	
Number of farms	37 500
Total acres (thousands):	17 500
Average per farm	467
Value of land and buildings (millions of dollars)	17 500
Average per farm (dollars)	466 667

Farm Income
(millions of dollars)

	1980	1989	1990	1991	1992	1993	1994	1995	1996	1997
Gross income	1 986	2 962	3 097	3 229	3 271	3 564	3 580	3 592	3 770	3 968
Receipts from sales	1 768	2 453	2 574	2 731	2 604	2 711	2 799	2 852	3 000	3 211
Government payments	6	60	89	89	87	93	74	52	73	63
Imputed and miscellaneous income	212	448	434	408	579	760	707	688	697	694
(−) Production expenses	1 795	2 561	2 696	2 765	2 851	3 156	3 256	3 478	3 594	3 785
(=) Realized net income	191	400	401	464	420	408	325	114	177	183
(+) Inventory change	102	9	-13	-94	-11	95	30	11	62	-38
(=) Net income	293	410	388	370	410	503	355	126	239	145
Corporate income	0	66	64	47	71	35	98	22	64	36
Farm proprietors income	293	344	324	323	338	468	257	103	175	110

EDUCATION

EDUCATIONAL ATTAINMENT Percent of population age 25 and over, 1997	State	United States
High school graduate or higher	84.7	82.1
College graduate or higher	24.3	23.9

OREGON'S PROSPERITY PARTLY REFLECTS ITS STABLE SOCIAL conditions, and rapid population growth presents possibly its biggest social challenge. Educational attainment has increased steadily over the last three decades, as it has in the United States overall. The 24.3 percent of Oregon's adult population holding college degrees is slightly above average (it ranks 20th in the nation), and the share of young adults currently enrolled in higher education is above average. The population holding high school degrees is also relatively high, ranking 22nd in the nation. Expenditures per pupil in elementary and secondary schools were about 7 percent above the national level, which is more remarkable given the surge in the numbers of students in this decade. Teachers' salaries were higher than average as well. The proportion of elementary and secondary students enrolled in private schools (7.6 percent) is particularly low in Oregon.

High School Completion: 1990–97

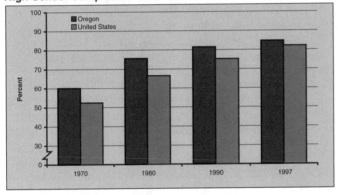

Education Indicators

	State	U.S.
Elementary and secondary schools		
Enrollment, 1995–96		
Total (thousands)	571	49 873
Percent in private schools	7.6	10.1
Expenditures per pupil (dollars), 1995–96	6 615	6 146
Average teacher salary (dollars), 1996–97	40 900	38 509
Higher education		
Enrollment, 1996–97		
Total (thousands)	165	14 218
Percent of population 18–34	22.7	21.8
Percent minority	13.0	26.1
Percent in private schools	14.4	22.6

HEALTH

OREGON BOASTS LOWER DEATH RATES THAN THE U.S. AVERage, indicating a better than average level of health in the state. This situation may be attributable in part to the lifestyle and health of the large number of in-migrants. Overall death rates are below the average, after adjustment for the state's age distribution. Infant mortality is among the ten lowest states in the country, and the state has relatively low rates of death from cancer and particularly heart disease. Deaths from accidents are somewhat high, however, except for motor vehicle accidents. A greater share of the state population is covered by health insurance than is typical for the nation. This fact is related to the state's low poverty rates and low numbers of immigrants.

Health Indicators

	1990	1995	1996	1997
Infant mortality *(rate per thousand live births)*				
Oregon	8.3	6.1	5.6	5.8
U.S.	9.2	7.6	7.3	7.1
Total deaths, age-adjusted rate *(rate per thousand population)*				
Oregon	4.8	4.7	4.6	4.5
U.S.	5.2	5.0	4.9	4.8
Persons not covered by health insurance *(percent of population)*				
Oregon	12.4	12.5	15.3	13.3
U.S.	13.9	15.4	15.6	16.1

Leading Causes of Death, 1996
(deaths per 100,000 population)

	Age-adjusted		Not age-adjusted	
	State	U.S.	State	U.S.
Deaths from all causes	464.9	491.6	902.5	872.5
Heart disease	105.3	134.5	239.4	276.4
Cancer	123.5	127.9	209.5	203.4
Cerebrovascular diseases	30.5	26.4	81.8	60.3
Chronic obstructive pulmonary disease	25.5	21.0	51.2	40.0
Diabetes mellitus	11.8	13.6	22.3	23.3
Pneumonia and influenza	10.7	12.8	30.1	31.6
HIV	6.1	11.1	6.4	11.7
Liver disease	7.6	7.5	9.8	9.4
Alzheimer's disease	4.0	2.7	13.1	8.1
Accidents and adverse effects	35.5	30.4	42.2	35.8
Motor vehicle accidents	16.7	16.2	16.6	16.5
Suicide	14.7	10.8	16.2	11.6
Homicide	5.0	8.5	4.7	7.9
Injury by firearm	12.5	12.9	13.3	12.8

GOVERNMENT

STATE AND LOCAL TAXES, 1995–96	State	U.S.
Per capita (dollars)	2 165	2 477
Percent of personal income	10.2	10.8

COMBINED STATE AND LOCAL TAXES IN OREGON WERE $2,165 per capita in 1995–96, compared with the higher average nationwide of $2,477, with taxes at both the state and local level being relatively low. Property tax rate cuts were instituted in some localities in the early 1990s, holding local tax collections below the national average, and in fact local property tax collections declined slightly between 1995 and 1996. As a percent of personal income,

state and local taxes comprised 10.2 percent of income, a substantial decrease from the previous year's 11 percent and lower than the average for the United States.

Despite relatively low tax collections, the state budget was greater than that of an average state in 1997 on a per capita basis. Supporting that budget is a relatively high state income tax but no general sales tax, so that total tax collections per capita actually were lower than the national average. However, other nontax revenues were high, and intergovernmental revenue from the federal government was 25 percent higher than average, yielding total revenues 14 percent above the United States average. Education spending in particular was about 8 percent higher (per capita) than in the United States overall. Spending also was higher on highways and state government administration but comparable in most other categories.

Federal spending in Oregon of $14.7 billion in 1997 was less than the state's proportionate share of total federal spending, based on population, attributable mainly to relatively low Medicare costs and the small number of federal jobs in the state. Procurement contracts were also an extremely small factor in the state economy, and community development and housing contracts and grants were lower than average. Retirement spending, the largest category, was at average levels.

State Government Finances, 1996–97

	Millions of dollars	Percent distribution	Dollars per capita	
			State	U.S.
General revenue	11 286	100.0	3 480	3 049
Intergovernmental revenue	3 518	31.2	1 085	863
Taxes	4 946	43.8	1 525	1 660
General sales	0	0.0	0	551
Selective sales	674	6.0	208	257
License taxes	512	4.5	158	106
Individual income	3 273	29.0	1 009	542
Corporation net income	384	3.4	118	115
Other taxes	103	0.9	32	90
Other general revenue	2 822	25.0	870	526
General expenditure	10 367	100.0	3 197	2 951
Intergovernmental expenditure	3 208	30.9	989	989
Direct expenditure	7 159	69.1	2 208	1 962
General expenditure, by function:				
Education	3 603	34.8	1 111	1 033
Public welfare	2 390	23.1	737	761
Hospitals and health	805	7.8	248	237
Highways	1 024	9.9	316	225
Police protection and corrections	576	5.6	178	137
Natural resources, parks and recreation	295	2.8	91	63
Governmental administration	661	6.4	204	107
Interest on general debt	361	3.5	111	99
Other and unallocable	653	6.3	201	290
Debt at end of fiscal year	5 841	NA	1 801	1 706
Cash and security holdings	24 103	NA	7 432	6 683

Federal Spending within State

	Federal funds, fiscal 1997		
	Millions of dollars	Percent distribution	Percent of U.S. total*
Total within state	14 665	100.0	1.0
Payments to individuals	9 253	63.1	1.2
Retirement and disability	5 904	40.3	1.3
Medicare	1 950	13.3	0.9
Food stamps	219	1.5	1.1
Supplemental Security Income	206	1.4	0.8
Grants	3 182	21.7	1.3
Medicaid and other health	1 264	8.6	1.1
Nutrition and family welfare	524	3.6	1.1
Education	200	1.4	1.2
Housing and community development	94	0.6	0.8
Salaries and wages	1 422	9.7	0.9
Defense procurement contracts	164	1.1	0.1
Non-defense procurement contracts	415	2.8	0.6

*State population is 1.2 percent of the U.S. total.

PENNSYLVANIA

31 372	59 698		65 157	70 827	72 687	78 001	81 93	88 504	93 426	5.8	63 383	70 827	31 372	59 698	63 38
25 323	47 902		57 151	59 446	62 916	67 00		72 039	77 208	6.1	50 999	57 151	25 323	47 902	50 99
2 640	5 143			7 801				7 709	7 838	5.4	5 645	6 816	2 640	5 143	5 64
3 409	6 652			284				8 755	8 380	2.9	6 739	6 860	3 409	6 652	6 7
693	1 716			07				1 539	762	-9.7	1 561	811	693	1 716	
2 716	4 9							7 217	7 616	5.6	5 178	6 048	2 716	4 9	

1997

Population (persons)	12,011,278
Population rank	5th
Population growth rank (1990–97)	45th
Per capita personal income	$25,678
Unemployment rate (percent)	5.2
Poverty rate (percent)	11.2

LIKE OTHER MID-ATLANTIC STATES, PENNSYLVANIA HAS HAD negligible population growth, domestic out-migration, and an aging population in the 1990s. However, both its labor force and employment rate grew faster than the working-age population, and its unemployment rate remained near the national level. Growth in services employment was strong, more than offsetting losses in manufacturing. Both median household income and per capita personal income rose faster than national level, and by 1997 were above the national levels even while transfer payments were growing more slowly.

The poverty rate was lower than the national average.

Most of Pennsylvania's population—84.5 percent—lived in the 11 metropolitan areas of Allentown-Bethlehem-Easton, Altoona, Harrisburg-Lebanon-Carlisle, Johnstown, Lancaster, Philadelphia, Pittsburgh, Reading, Scranton-Wilkes-Barre-Hazleton, Sharon, and State College. This represents a small decline from the 1990 proportion of 84.9 percent. The new housing production rate was stagnant in the state, but the resale market was strong and homeownership was high.

Average Annual Population Growth: 1990–97

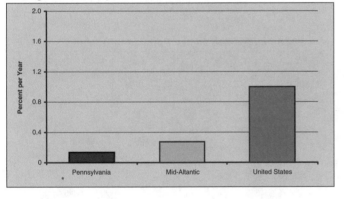

Median Household Income: 1989–97 (1997 dollars)

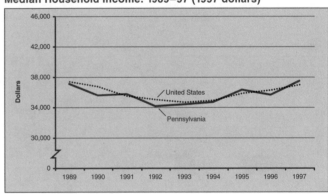

Unemployment Rate: 1989–97

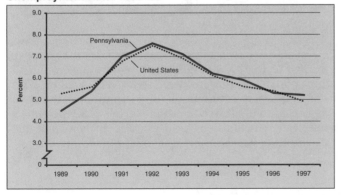

PENNSYLVANIA'S UNEMPLOYMENT RATE STARTED THE DECADE below the national average but was slightly above it in 1997. During the years of recession in the early 1990s the unemployment rate was very close to the national rate, peaking at essentially the same level in 1992, as employment fell while labor force growth continued. Since then, job growth has outstripped labor force growth, bringing unemployment down each year.

335

POPULATION AND LABOR FORCE

POPULATION GROWTH IN PENNSYLVANIA WAS ALMOST STAGNANT from 1990 to 1997 at 0.1 percent per year, which was a significantly slower rate than for the nation as a whole (1.0 percent per year). The White population did not grow at all, and every other racial category grew less rapidly than the national average, though Asian population growth was only marginally lower. Net domestic out-migration was relatively high and was the main cause of slow growth in the state, nearly canceling out the natural increase in population. Most of the state's population (84.5 percent) lived in metropolitan counties.

While the state's population over age 16 grew at the same rate as total population, both employment and the labor force in the state grew much faster from 1990 to 1997. The employment/population ratio rose from 58.2 percent to nearly 60 percent, but still remained below the national ratio, reflecting the state's older population. The unemployment rate in 1997 was back down to its 1990 level.

Population and Labor Force

	1980	1990	1991	1992	1993	1994	1995	1996	1997	Change*	
										State	U.S.
Population											
Total number of persons (thousands)	11 864	11 896	11 943	11 981	12 022	12 040	12 040	12 034	12 011	0.1	1.0
Percent distribution:											
White, Non-Hispanic	89.3	87.5	87.6	87.3	87.2	87.0	86.8	86.6	86.5	0.0	0.4
Black, Non-Hispanic	8.7	9.1	9.1	9.2	9.2	9.3	9.3	9.3	9.4	0.5	1.4
Asian	0.6	1.2	1.2	1.3	1.4	1.4	1.5	1.5	1.6	4.0	4.1
Native American	0.1	0.1	0.1	0.1	0.1	0.1	0.1	0.1	0.1	0.1	1.6
Hispanic	1.3	2.1	2.0	2.1	2.2	2.3	2.3	2.4	2.5	3.1	3.8
In metropolitan areas	84.9	84.9	84.8	84.8	84.7	84.7	84.6	84.5	84.5	0.1	1.0
Total number of households (thousands)	4 220	4 496	4 528	4 562	4 559	4 552	4 575	4 594	NA	0.4	1.2
Labor Force (thousands)											
Population 16 and over	9 170	9 402	9 426	9 433	9 457	9 466	9 476	9 493	9 485	0.1	1.0
Civilian labor force	5 435	5 791	5 826	5 886	5 889	5 829	5 837	5 900	5 979	0.5	1.1
Employed	5 010	5 476	5 419	5 440	5 470	5 469	5 495	5 587	5 668	0.5	1.2
Percent of population	54.6	58.2	57.5	57.7	57.8	57.8	58.0	58.9	59.8		
Unemployment rate (percent)	7.8	5.4	7.0	7.6	7.1	6.2	5.9	5.3	5.2		

*Compound annual average percent change, 1990–1997; 1990–1996 for households.

Population Change and Components: 1990–97

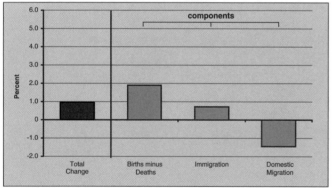

Average Annual Household and Population Growth

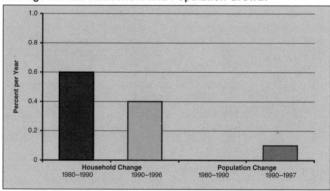

Population by Age; Births and Deaths

	1990		1997	
	State	U.S.	State	U.S.
Age distribution (percent)				
Under 5 years	6.8	7.6	6.1	7.2
5 to 17 years	16.7	18.2	17.7	18.8
18 to 64 years	61.1	61.8	60.3	61.3
65 years and over	15.4	12.5	15.8	12.7
Birth and death rates (per thousand population)				
Births	14.5	16.7	12.0	14.6
Deaths	10.3	8.6	10.6	8.6

PENNSYLVANIA HAD A MUCH LARGER PERCENTAGE OF PEOPLE over age 65 in 1997 than did the United States, while all other population groups were relatively smaller. This trend is likely to continue, as the birth rate for the state was considerably lower than that of the U.S. The state's death rate (unadjusted for age) was higher than the national level which reflects the older population.

HOUSEHOLD AND PERSONAL INCOME

HOUSEHOLD INCOME AND PERSONS IN POVERTY	1990	1995	1996	1997	
				State	U.S.
Median household income (1997 dollars)	35 618	36 359	35 700	37 517	37 005
Persons in poverty (thousands)	1 328	1 464	1 374	1 337	35 574
Poverty rate (percent)	11.0	12.2	11.6	11.2	13.3

REAL MEDIAN HOUSEHOLD INCOME IN PENNSYLVANIA FELL after 1989, but by 1997 had recovered to a level one percent higher than 1989. The U.S. national median declined in real terms over the period, and as a result Pennsylvania, having started the decade a little below the national average, was above it in 1997. The poverty rate in the state was lower than the national rate throughout the decade, though it was higher than in neighboring Delaware, Maryland, and New Jersey.

Aggregate personal income grew 4.4 percent per year from 1989 to 1997, at a slower pace than the national rate (5.3 percent per year). Wages and salaries also grew slower in the state than in the country, while nonfarm proprietors' income growth lagged far behind. The adjustment for residence was positive and grew rapidly, as more Pennsylvanians commuted out of state and

brought income in. Personal income in the state in 1997 was 1.5 percent higher than nationwide. On a per capita basis, personal income grew 1.3 percent from 1989 to 1997 when adjusted for inflation.

Government transfer payments increased 55.5 percent from 1990 to 1997, or 6.5 percent per year. This was slower than the national average rate of 7.2 percent. The largest programs in the state were Social Security and medical payments, while the fastest growing programs were "other income maintenance programs" (which includes the earned income tax credit), Supplemental Security Income, and medical payments. The only program in the decline was family assistance (formerly known as "Aid to Families with Dependent Children"), which, similar to the national rate, declined 0.1 percent per year.

Personal Income
(millions of dollars)

	1980	1989	1990	1991	1992	1993	1994	1995	1996	1997	Change*
Earnings by place of work	86 665	148 650	157 505	161 172	171 425	177 936	184 002	190 718	198 601	208 722	4.3
Wages and salaries	69 942	117 792	124 524	127 422	134 430	138 157	143 525	150 057	157 238	166 742	4.4
Other labor income	8 129	13 496	14 687	15 977	17 311	18 713	19 402	18 963	18 373	18 455	4.0
Proprietors' income	8 594	17 363	18 294	17 774	19 684	21 066	21 075	21 698	22 990	23 525	3.9
Farm	233	636	547	249	680	571	378	117	494	155	-16.2
Nonfarm	8 361	16 726	17 747	17 524	19 004	20 494	20 697	21 581	22 496	23 370	4.3
(−) Personal contributions for social insurance	4 557	9 868	10 434	10 935	11 570	12 212	12 890	13 447	13 749	14 447	4.9
(+) Adjustment for residence	-413	841	981	973	1 085	1 127	1 286	1 583	1 632	1 774	NA
(=) Net earnings by state of residence	81 694	139 623	148 052	151 210	160 941	166 850	172 398	178 854	186 484	196 048	4.3
(+) Dividends, interest, and rent	17 692	41 787	44 257	44 393	42 891	43 333	45 521	48 422	52 641	54 162	3.3
(+) Transfer payments ... ̈	19 653	35 306	38 118	42 954	47 172	49 926	51 082	53 029	56 224	58 430	6.5
(=) Total personal income	119 039	216 716	230 427	238 557	251 004	260 109	269 002	280 305	295 349	308 640	4.5
Farm	464	942	907	606	1 027	936	744	533	930	596	-5.6
Nonfarm	118 576	215 774	229 520	237 951	249 977	259 173	268 257	279 772	294 419	308 044	4.6
Personal income per capita (dollars)											
Current dollars	10 030	18 264	19 371	19 977	20 951	21 635	22 336	23 270	24 530	25 678	4.4
1997 dollars	19 178	23 090	23 310	23 068	23 435	23 542	23 736	24 189	24 980	25 678	1.3

*Compound annual average percent change, 1989–1997

Government Transfer Payments

	Millions of dollars		Percent change*	
	1990	1997	State	U.S.
Total government payments to individuals	36 130	56 199	55.5	62.7
Retirement, disability, and insurance	19 913	27 457	37.9	48.2
Social Security	14 726	20 123	36.7	46.1
Government employee retirement	3 960	5 975	50.9	60.3
Medical payments	11 006	21 647	96.7	101.2
Income maintenance	2 824	4 218	49.4	58.0
Supplemental Security Income	637	1 246	95.7	75.4
Family assistance	862	855	-0.8	-0.5
Food Stamps	692	837	20.9	27.1
Other income maintenance	633	1 280	102.2	189.8
Unemployment insurance benefits	1 259	1 510	19.9	10.6
Veterans benefits and other	1 128	1 367	21.2	30.8

*Percent change, 1990–1997

Government Payments to Individuals: 1997

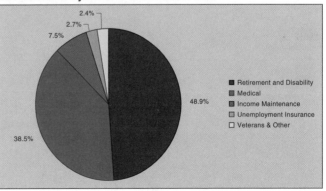

- 48.9% Retirement and Disability
- 38.5% Medical
- 7.5% Income Maintenance
- 2.7% Unemployment Insurance
- 2.4% Veterans & Other

ECONOMIC STRUCTURE

LEADING PRIVATE INDUSTRIES, 1997 (Worker and proprietor earnings, millions of dollars)		FASTEST EARNINGS GROWTH, 1989–97 (percent increase)	
Health services	$22 445	Air transportation	239.6
Business services	10 343	Real estate	131.3
Construction specialties	7 878	Securities brokers	129.2
Engineering and management services	7 003	Other transportation	125.5
Chemicals and allied products	5 751	Social services	97.9

EMPLOYMENT IN PENNSYLVANIA GREW AT RATE OF 0.8 PER year from 1989 to 1997, just one-half of the national rate. As in other states in the region, mining, construction, and manufacturing industries lost jobs, though the fall in construction was less severe in Pennsylvania than it was in other states. More than offsetting the loss of 123,000 jobs in these industries were the 375,000 (net) new jobs in services and another 136,000 in retail trade and finance, insurance, and real estate. Likewise, earnings growth lagged behind the national average by about a percentage point per year in total and in most industries. None of the private nonfarm sectors ended the nine year period with lower earnings, and unlike many states, there were no periods of dramatic drops in earnings. The fastest earnings growth was in finance, insurance, and real estate. Of the five largest industries in Pennsylvania, three are services (health, business, and engineering). Chemicals and allied products, the highest ranking manufacturing industry, and special trade construction were also in the top 5.

Employment and Earnings by Sector

	1980	1989	1990	1991	1992	1993	1994	1995	1996	1997 Number	1997 Percent of total	Change*
Employment *(thousands of persons)*												
Total	5 638	6 270	6 343	6 275	6 280	6 315	6 392	6 472	6 559	6 693	100.0	0.8
Farm	98	83	80	81	80	74	74	73	72	76	1.1	-1.1
Nonfarm	5 540	6 187	6 262	6 193	6 200	6 241	6 318	6 399	6 486	6 618	98.9	0.8
Private nonfarm	4 787	5 430	5 490	5 427	5 433	5 470	5 544	5 626	5 718	5 857	87.5	1.0
Agricultural service, forestry, and fishing	26	43	46	47	46	49	52	53	55	57	0.9	3.8
Mining	55	37	37	33	31	29	28	27	26	26	0.4	-4.2
Construction	254	339	336	312	311	310	319	320	325	337	5.0	-0.1
Manufacturing	1 349	1 080	1 048	1 008	980	973	977	972	964	971	14.5	-1.3
Transportation and public utilities	292	291	300	298	296	309	313	313	318	326	4.9	1.4
Wholesale trade	261	300	296	292	293	285	283	288	283	287	4.3	-0.6
Retail trade	904	1 062	1 064	1 054	1 058	1 060	1 080	1 111	1 132	1 149	17.2	1.0
Finance, insurance, and real estate	374	462	469	468	469	464	480	485	499	513	7.7	1.3
Services	1 273	1 816	1 895	1 915	1 948	1 992	2 011	2 057	2 116	2 191	32.7	2.4
Government	753	757	773	766	767	770	774	773	768	761	11.4	0.1
Earnings *(millions of dollars)*												
Total	86 665	148 650	157 505	161 172	171 425	177 936	184 002	190 718	198 601	208 722	100.0	4.3
Farm	464	942	907	606	1 027	936	744	533	930	596	0.3	-5.6
Nonfarm	86 201	147 708	156 598	160 566	170 398	177 000	183 257	190 185	197 671	208 126	99.7	4.4
Private nonfarm	75 404	129 031	136 288	139 126	147 886	153 582	159 064	165 314	171 971	182 109	87.2	4.4
Agricultural service, forestry, and fishing	228	640	749	791	836	866	902	920	928	973	0.5	5.4
Mining	1 982	1 422	1 541	1 445	1 448	1 407	1 395	1 413	1 447	1 519	0.7	0.8
Construction	4 836	9 939	10 117	9 448	9 693	9 909	10 575	10 681	11 125	11 878	5.7	2.3
Manufacturing	27 974	34 450	35 103	35 373	36 876	37 909	39 433	40 391	41 434	43 457	20.8	2.9
Transportation and public utilities	6 704	9 924	10 684	11 067	11 742	12 437	12 856	13 157	13 571	14 272	6.8	4.6
Wholesale trade	5 122	9 198	9 608	9 801	10 323	10 274	10 705	11 164	11 269	12 005	5.8	3.4
Retail trade	8 223	14 524	14 954	15 262	15 944	16 456	17 137	17 823	18 436	19 363	9.3	3.7
Finance, insurance, and real estate	4 334	9 282	10 019	10 495	11 958	12 878	13 124	13 951	15 187	15 977	7.7	7.0
Services	16 001	39 651	43 509	45 446	49 065	51 446	52 937	55 816	58 574	62 665	30.0	5.9
Government	10 797	18 677	20 310	21 439	22 512	23 418	24 194	24 871	25 701	26 016	12.5	4.2

*Compound annual average percent change, 1989–1997

ECONOMIC STRUCTURE (Continued)

PENNSYLVANIA'S AVERAGE WAGE IN 1997 WAS JUST A BIT BELOW the national average. However, average wage growth in Pennsylvania was 3.8 percent from 1989 to 1997, slightly higher than the national rate of 3.5 percent. Pennsylvania wages were above the national average only in construction, government, and the small agricultural services sector; the average manufacturing wage was slightly below the national average, as were the remaining sectors.

Pennsylvania is traditionally thought of as a strong manufacturing state, but 15 states had higher ratios of manufacturing to gross state product than Pennsylvania's 20.7 percent in 1996. However, this ratio was still above the national average and, unlike the declining national average, was little changed between 1989 and 1996.

Goods exports from Pennsylvania grew 31.3 percent from 1994 to 1997. The top 5 exports were all among manufacturing products, chemicals, and four major durable goods categories. Primary metals, transportation equipment, and industrial machinery were the fastest-growing major exports.

Average Annual Wages and Salaries by Sector
(dollars)

	1989	1996	1997 State	1997 U.S.
All wage and salary workers	21 856	28 320	29 467	29 809
Farm	10 885	18 676	16 320	16 442
Nonfarm	21 909	28 357	29 524	29 900
Private nonfarm	21 794	28 031	29 278	29 867
Agricultural service, forestry, and fishing	15 597	19 445	20 024	17 941
Mining	33 160	41 476	42 043	49 800
Construction	26 331	31 706	33 413	31 765
Manufacturing	27 233	36 264	38 171	38 351
Transportation and utilities	29 700	36 586	37 913	38 222
Wholesale trade	27 939	36 237	38 134	39 466
Retail trade	11 886	14 775	15 415	16 206
Finance, insurance, and real estate	26 317	38 270	40 147	44 993
Services	19 792	26 060	27 070	27 588
Government	22 606	30 383	31 101	30 062

Gross State Product and Manufacturing
(millions of dollars, except as noted)

	1989	1994	1995	1996
Gross state product, total	234 534	296 781	313 293	328 540
Manufacturing:				
Millions of dollars	49 050	60 181	65 989	68 074
Percent of total gross state product	20.9	20.3	21.1	20.7
Per worker (dollars)	45 403	61 618	67 902	70 650
New capital expenditures, manufacturing	NA	4 788	5 441	5 151

Exports of Goods
(millions of dollars)

	1994	1995	1996	1997
All goods	14 699	17 680	17 446	19 298
Manufactures	13 756	16 551	16 400	18 172
Agricultural and livestock products	86	79	93	120
Other commodities	857	1 051	952	1 006
Top goods exports, 1997:				
Chemical products	2 731	3 571	3 336	3 537
Industrial machinery and computers	2 520	2 942	3 080	3 444
Electric and electronic equipment	2 338	2 455	2 424	2 841
Primary metals	921	1 741	1 460	1 501
Transportation equipment	1 030	1 201	1 132	1 480

HOUSING

New housing production in Pennsylvania declined in 1990 and 1991 and has not shown a sustained recovery. Looking at the production rate per 1,000 population, which enables comparisons between states of different sizes, it never fell beneath 3.4 new homes produced per 1,000, a rate higher than the strongest year in neighboring New York state. The lack of recovery in subsequent years kept Pennsylvania's production rate below the U.S. average, however, and this gap is growing. Existing home sales also declined from 1989 to 1991 but rebounded to the 1988 level in 1997. Homeownership rates were high for the nation and the region, and fluctuated between 71.5 and 74 percent. Rental vacancy rates were also quite high, and hit a peak of 10.1 percent in 1997.

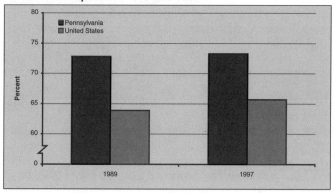

Homeownership Rates: 1989 and 1997

Housing Supply

	1989	1990	1991	1992	1993	1994	1995	1996	1997
Residential building permits (thousands)	45.5	37.2	34.6	38.3	40.1	40.2	36.3	37.9	39.9
New home production (including manufactured housing):									
Thousands of homes	52.3	44.1	41.0	45.0	47.1	47.5	42.9	44.2	44.3
Rate per 1,000 population									
Pennsylvania	4.4	3.7	3.4	3.8	3.9	3.9	3.6	3.7	3.7
U.S.	6.2	5.2	4.5	5.1	5.6	6.4	6.3	6.6	6.5
Existing home sales:									
Thousands of homes	193.8	182.7	179.2	204.4	216.1	216.4	217.2	224.3	233.3
Change from previous year (percent)									
Pennsylvania	-13.9	-5.7	-1.9	14.1	5.7	0.1	0.4	3.3	4.0
U.S.	-3.9	-4.0	0.0	9.2	8.2	4.8	-3.7	7.5	3.8
Home ownership rate (percent of households)	72.8	73.8	74.0	73.1	72.0	71.8	71.5	71.7	73.3
Rental vacancy rate (percent of rental housing units)	6.0	7.2	7.1	7.0	7.5	8.0	8.0	8.7	10.1

AGRICULTURE

Farm sales fluctuated between 1989 and 1997, but ended the period higher. Production expenses also grew, but grew at a faster pace, causing realized net value to shrink starting primarily in 1994. Corporate farms were a very small part of farming in Pennsylvania. Total net farm proprietors' earnings, like net income, fell over the decade, but unlike in other Mid-Atlantic states, were never negative. The average farm was much smaller than, yet was worth roughly the same as, an average U.S. farm.

PENNSYLVANIA FARMS, 1997	
Number of farms	50 000
Total acres (thousands):	7 700
Average per farm	154
Value of land and buildings (millions of dollars)	20 251
Average per farm (dollars)	405 020

Farm Income
(millions of dollars)

	1980	1989	1990	1991	1992	1993	1994	1995	1996	1997
Gross income	3 094	4 129	4 258	4 044	4 222	4 392	4 322	4 324	4 675	4 724
Receipts from sales	2 834	3 764	3 929	3 709	3 864	4 030	3 964	3 951	4 318	4 308
Government payments	8	68	41	34	49	45	33	41	37	35
Imputed and miscellaneous income	252	297	288	301	310	317	325	332	320	381
(−) Production expenses	2 858	3 513	3 680	3 675	3 627	3 705	3 918	4 097	4 193	4 467
(=) Realized net income	236	616	578	369	595	687	404	227	483	258
(+) Inventory change	-3	68	12	-105	146	-97	29	0	81	-83
(=) Net income	233	684	590	265	740	590	433	127	564	175
Corporate income	0	48	43	15	60	19	55	11	70	20
Farm proprietors income	233	636	547	249	680	571	378	117	494	155

EDUCATION

EDUCATIONAL ATTAINMENT Percent of population age 25 and over, 1997	State	United States
High school graduate or higher	82.4	82.1
College graduate or higher	22.9	23.9

PENNSYLVANIA WAS RANKED 31ST IN THE PERCENT OF THE population age 25 and over with a high school diploma, and was fourth in the Mid-Atlantic region. Per pupil spending was higher than the U.S. level by 18.0 percent and teacher's salaries were 18.9 percent greater. There was a greater percentage of elementary and secondary students enrolled in private schools (16.2 percent) than in the rest of the Mid-Atlantic and the country (10.1). Pennsylvania ranked 24th in the percentage of the population age 25 and over with a bachelor's degree in 1997, also placing it at the bottom of the Mid-Atlantic region. Of the population age 18 to 34, 22.6 percent were enrolled in higher education in 1996, very similar to the national level of 21.8 percent. Only 14.2 percent of enrolled students in 1996 were minorities, much lower than in the United States and also the neighboring states of New York and New Jersey, but similar to the proportion of minorities in Pennsylvania's population.

High School Completion: 1990–97

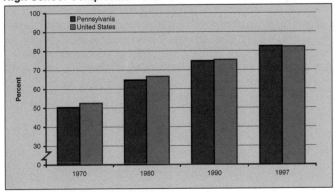

Education Indicators

	State	U.S.
Elementary and secondary schools		
Enrollment, 1995–96		
Total (thousands)	2 134	49 873
Percent in private schools	16.2	10.1
Expenditures per pupil (dollars), 1995–96	7 492	6 146
Average teacher salary (dollars), 1996–97	47 429	38 509
Higher education		
Enrollment, 1996–97		
Total (thousands)	622	14 218
Percent of population 18–34	22.6	21.8
Percent minority	14.2	26.1
Percent in private schools	46.1	22.6

HEALTH

PENNSYLVANIA HAD SLIGHTLY HIGHER AGE-ADJUSTED (WHERE changes in the age composition over time are taken into account) death rates over the 1990s, though they fell slightly over the period. Infant mortality was about the same in Pennsylvania and the country. Health insurance coverage was quite good in the state, which had a much lower percentage of those without insurance all through the 1990s. Several causes of death were above the national average using the crude death rate, including cancer, diabetes, heart disease, cerebrovascular diseases (stroke), pneumonia and influenza, chronic obstructive pulmonary diseases (including emphysema), and accidents and adverse effects. However, when these rates are adjusted for age, the latter four are less than the national average.

Health Indicators

	1990	1995	1996	1997
Infant mortality *(rate per thousand live births)*				
Pennsylvania	9.6	7.8	7.4	7.4
U.S.	9.2	7.6	7.3	7.1
Total deaths, age-adjusted rate *(rate per thousand population)*				
Pennsylvania	5.2	5.0	5.0	4.9
U.S.	5.2	5.0	4.9	4.8
Persons not covered by health insurance *(percent of population)*				
Pennsylvania	10.1	9.9	9.5	10.1
U.S.	13.9	15.4	15.6	16.1

Leading Causes of Death, 1996
(deaths per 100,000 population)

	Age-adjusted		Not age-adjusted	
	State	U.S.	State	U.S.
Deaths from all causes	502.6	491.6	1072.3	872.5
Heart disease	145.7	134.5	362.2	276.4
Cancer	133.3	127.9	253.1	203.4
Cerebrovascular diseases	25.7	26.4	71.8	60.3
Chronic obstructive pulmonary disease	19.0	21.0	44.9	40.0
Diabetes mellitus	14.5	13.6	29.6	23.3
Pneumonia and influenza	12.1	12.8	36.6	31.6
HIV	8.5	11.1	8.8	11.7
Liver disease	6.2	7.5	9.1	9.4
Alzheimer's disease	2.1	2.7	7.8	8.1
Accidents and adverse effects	28.8	30.4	36.8	35.8
Motor vehicle accidents	12.7	16.2	13.2	16.5
Suicide	11.0	10.8	11.8	11.6
Homicide	6.8	8.5	5.9	7.9
Injury by firearm	11.3	12.9	11.0	12.8

GOVERNMENT

STATE AND LOCAL TAXES, 1995–96	State	U.S.
Per capita (dollars)	2 387	2 477
Percent of personal income	10.1	10.8

PENNSYLVANIA'S STATE AND LOCAL TAXES (EXCEPT CORPO-rate) came to 10.1 percent of personal income, below the all-state average of 10.8, in 1995–1996. On a per capita basis, these taxes came to 3.6 percent less than the national average. In 1996-97, total state-level taxation also was slightly lower on a per capita basis, and state sales and personal income taxes, which have the most direct impact on individuals, both were below their national averages. Per capita corporate taxes, license taxes and selective sales taxes (gas tax, for example) were all higher in the state.

State-level spending was lower in Pennsylvania than in the nation. State expenditures on welfare, hospitals, and health was higher, while those for education and police protection and corrections were lower than nationwide levels. Debt at the end of the fiscal year was considerably lower than the U.S. average, while cash and security holdings were only slightly below the average.

Federal funds disbursed in Pennsylvania in 1997 were 4.6 percent of all funds allocated in the United States, which was slightly higher than the percentage of people living in the state. Retirement and Medicare were the two largest categories and both had a larger than proportionate share, as did the smaller Medicaid program. Salaries and wages as well as defense and non-defense procurement received far less federal funds that the population might otherwise suggest, but housing and community development grants received more.

State Government Finances, 1996–97

	Millions of dollars	Percent distribu-tion	Dollars per capita State	Dollars per capita U.S.
General revenue	35 212	100.0	2 929	3 049
Intergovernmental revenue	9 420	26.8	784	863
Taxes	19 377	55.0	1 612	1 660
General sales	6 055	17.2	504	551
Selective sales	3 166	9.0	263	257
License taxes	1 920	5.5	160	106
Individual income	5 575	15.8	464	542
Corporation net income	1 576	4.5	131	115
Other taxes	1 086	3.1	90	90
Other general revenue	6 415	18.2	534	526
General expenditure	33 709	100.0	2 804	2 951
Intergovernmental expenditure	9 844	29.2	819	989
Direct expenditure	23 864	70.8	1 985	1 962
General expenditure, by function:				
Education	10 513	31.2	875	1 033
Public welfare	10 019	29.7	834	761
Hospitals and health	3 076	9.1	256	237
Highways	2 493	7.4	207	225
Police protection and corrections	1 725	5.1	144	137
Natural resources, parks and recreation	544	1.6	45	63
Governmental administration	1 086	3.2	90	107
Interest on general debt	1 181	3.5	98	99
Other and unallocable	3 073	9.1	256	290
Debt at end of fiscal year	15 368	NA	1 279	1 706
Cash and security holdings	77 929	NA	6 483	6 683

Federal Spending within State

	Federal funds, fiscal 1997 Millions of dollars	Percent distribution	Percent of U.S. total*
Total within state	65 980	100.0	4.6
Payments to individuals	42 962	65.1	5.5
Retirement and disability	24 541	37.2	5.4
Medicare	12 765	19.3	6.2
Food stamps	867	1.3	4.4
Supplemental Security Income	1 159	1.8	4.3
Grants	11 715	17.8	4.7
Medicaid and other health	5 749	8.7	5.0
Nutrition and family welfare	2 247	3.4	4.8
Education	666	1.0	3.9
Housing and community development	698	1.1	6.2
Salaries and wages	5 267	8.0	3.2
Defense procurement contracts	3 036	4.6	2.5
Non-defense procurement contracts	2 090	3.2	2.9

*State population is 4.5 percent of the U.S. total.

31 372	59 698			65 157	70 827	72 687	78 001	81 93	88 504	93 426	5.8	63 383	70 827	31 372	59 698	63 38
25 323	47 902			57 151	59 446		62 916	67 00	72 039	77 208	6.1	50 999	57 151	25 323	47 902	50 99
2 640	5 143						7 801		7 709	7 838	5.4	5 645	6 816	2 640	5 143	5 64
3 409	6 652						284		8 755	8 380	2.9	6 739	6 860	3 409	6 652	6 7
693	1 718						07		1 539	782	-9.7	1 561	811	893	1 716	1 6
2 716	93								7 217	7 618	-5.6	5 178	6 049			

1997

Population (persons)	987,263
Population rank	43rd
Population growth rank (1990–97)	50th
Per capita personal income	$25,689
Unemployment rate (percent)	5.3
Poverty rate (percent)	12.7

RHODE ISLAND WAS ONE OF ONLY TWO STATES TO EXPERIENCE a population loss from 1990 to 1997 (Connecticut was the other. The District of Columbia also lost population). This loss was driven primarily by domestic out-migration that was almost twice the natural increase in the time period. The White and Black populations both fell, and the Asian population grew far slower in the state than nationwide.

The early 1990s recession hit the state particularly hard, with unemployment significantly higher than national levels for much of the period. Private nonfarm employment declined 6.6 percent between 1989 and 1991; it has recovered since, but not quite to the 1989 level. Manufacturing and construction employment were hardest hit, but service employment experienced almost no losses in the mid-1990s and gained 2.3 percent on average per year from 1989 to 1997. Manufacturing declined in importance in the state from 1989 to 1996, falling from more than 20 percent of the economy to 16.7 percent, well below the national ratio.

Real median household incomes in Rhode Island fell by more than 11 percent from 1990 to 1997. In 1989 household income in the state was 4.2 percent above the national average; in recent years it has averaged only about half a percent higher. Likewise, the poverty rates for the state, once well below the national average, are now closer, less than 1 percentage point lower in 1997.

Average Annual Population Growth: 1990–97

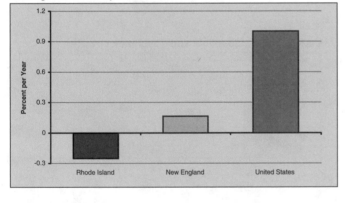

Median Household Income: 1989–97 (1997 dollars)

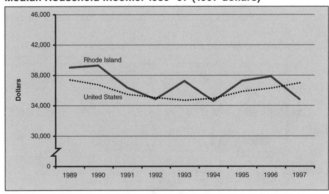

Unemployment Rate: 1989–97

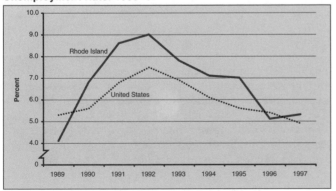

UNEMPLOYMENT IN RHODE ISLAND WAS HIGHER THAN THE national average for most years between 1990 and 1997. In particular, in the years surrounding the 1991 recession, unemployment rates in the state were up to 1.5 percentage points higher and stayed high until 1995. From 1990 to 1997, however, the labor force declined in line with the decline in working-age population and more than the downtrend in employment over the period. As a result, by 1996–97 the Rhode Island unemployment rate was closer to the national average.

POPULATION AND LABOR FORCE

RHODE ISLAND EXPERIENCED A DECLINE IN POPULATION from 1990 to 1997, one of the two states in New England to do so. Only Hispanics and the small Native American population grew faster than the U.S. average. The White non-Hispanic population decreased by just under 4 percent from 1990 to 1997, the Black non-Hispanic population fell 0.2 percent per year, and the Asian population growth rate in Rhode Island was half of the U.S. average. Rhode Island has a large concentration of people in metropolitan coun-

ties (91.6 percent of the population). Though the rate of births less deaths from 1990 to 1997 was similar to that of other states in the region, domestic out-migration was substantial, leading to the fall in population.

The employment to population ratio hovered around 60 percent throughout the period. The unemployment rate rose from 6.8 percent at the beginning of the period to the high point of 9 percent in 1992, then declined to just over 5 percent in 1996 and 1997, the lowest rates since 1989.

Population and Labor Force

	1980	1990	1991	1992	1993	1994	1995	1996	1997	Change* State	Change* U.S.
Population											
Total number of persons (thousands)	947	1 005	1 004	1 000	998	993	989	988	987	-0.2	1.0
Percent distribution:											
White, Non-Hispanic	93.8	89.4	89.4	89.2	88.9	88.5	88.2	87.9	87.5	-0.6	0.4
Black, Non-Hispanic	2.8	3.8	3.6	3.6	3.6	3.6	3.7	3.7	3.8	-0.2	1.4
Asian	0.7	1.9	2.0	2.0	2.0	2.1	2.1	2.2	2.2	1.9	4.1
Native American	0.3	0.4	0.4	0.4	0.4	0.4	0.5	0.5	0.5	1.7	1.6
Hispanic	2.0	4.7	4.8	5.0	5.3	5.5	5.8	6.0	6.2	4.0	3.8
In metropolitan areas	93.5	91.3	91.2	91.3	91.5	91.6	91.7	91.7	91.6	-0.2	1.0
Total number of households (thousands)	339	378	380	381	378	376	376	378	NA	0.0	1.2
Labor Force (thousands)											
Population 16 and over	738	803	799	794	788	783	779	779	779	-0.4	1.0
Civilian labor force	471	519	512	521	512	501	487	494	502	-0.5	1.1
Employed	437	484	468	474	472	465	454	468	476	-0.2	1.2
Percent of population	59.2	60.2	58.6	59.7	59.8	59.4	58.2	60.1	61.1		
Unemployment rate (percent)	7.2	6.8	8.6	9.0	7.8	7.1	7.0	5.1	5.3		

*Compound annual average percent change, 1990–1997; 1990–1996 for households.

Population Change and Components: 1990–97

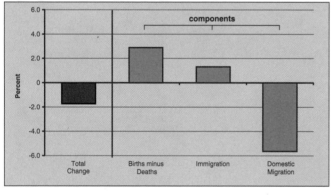

Average Annual Household and Population Growth

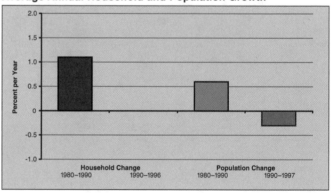

Population by Age; Births and Deaths

	1990 State	1990 U.S.	1997 State	1997 U.S.
Age distribution (percent)				
Under 5 years	6.8	7.6	6.3	7.2
5 to 17 years	15.7	18.2	17.4	18.8
18 to 64 years	62.6	61.8	60.5	61.3
65 years and over	15.0	12.5	15.8	12.7
Birth and death rates (per thousand population)				
Births	15.1	16.7	12.5	14.6
Deaths	9.5	8.6	9.9	8.6

RHODE ISLAND HAD AN OLDER THAN AVERAGE POPULATION in 1997; the number of elderly persons rose and was above the national proportion, while both the working-age and preschool-age populations declined from the 1990 level. The group ages 5 through 17 was the only other age group to increase. With lower than average birth rates, trends seen in the preschool age will continue, and will eventually start affecting school-age numbers.

HOUSEHOLD AND PERSONAL INCOME

HOUSEHOLD INCOME AND PERSONS IN POVERTY	1990	1995	1996	1997 State	1997 U.S.
Median household income (1997 dollars)	39 257	37 238	37 835	34 797	37 005
Persons in poverty (thousands)	71	102	104	120	35 574
Poverty rate (percent)	7.5	10.6	11.0	12.7	13.3

REAL MEDIAN HOUSEHOLD INCOMES FELL 11.3 PERCENT IN the two years from 1990 to 1992 and have fluctuated since then with little, if any, perceivable uptrend. Poverty in Rhode Island was below U.S. rates but by 1997, at 12.7 percent, was edging closer to the national rate of 13.3 percent.

Aggregate personal income is the sum of all incomes earned in the state from business and government sources. Personal income grew in the state, but more slowly than the national growth rate of 5.2 percent per year. Earnings and wages, as well as proprietors' income, also increased less rapidly. Transfer payments was the only category to increase at a faster pace than in the country as a whole. Adjustment for residence, a calculation of the importance of commuting (both in and out of a state), was positive and increased 6.4 percent per year, indicating that more people are leaving the state for work. Per capita personal income is derived by dividing aggregate income by the population and is different from the income of the median or typical household. Per capita personal income was a little below the U.S. average and rose less from 1989 to 1997.

Transfer payments grew 59.7 percent from 1990 to 1997, or 6.9 percent per year on average. The fastest growth occurred in Supplemental Security Income, followed by medical payments and other income maintenance. Retirement and health insurance programs were the largest categories in the state in 1997. Family assistance, formerly known as Aid to Families with Dependent Children, and veterans benefits grew the least.

Personal Income
(millions of dollars)

	1980	1989	1990	1991	1992	1993	1994	1995	1996	1997	Change*
Earnings by place of work	6 344	12 705	12 985	12 656	13 415	13 897	14 189	14 824	15 244	16 114	3.0
Wages and salaries	5 272	10 336	10 633	10 353	10 871	11 230	11 532	12 120	12 545	13 362	3.3
Other labor income	528	1 146	1 210	1 201	1 337	1 402	1 315	1 297	1 256	1 258	1.2
Proprietors' income	543	1 224	1 142	1 101	1 207	1 265	1 341	1 406	1 444	1 495	2.5
Farm	2	26	23	26	30	37	24	25	23	22	-2.0
Nonfarm	541	1 198	1 120	1 076	1 177	1 229	1 318	1 381	1 421	1 473	2.6
(−) Personal contributions for social insurance	380	899	942	975	1 034	1 083	1 140	1 189	1 216	1 269	4.4
(+) Adjustment for residence	119	621	662	693	721	766	852	890	949	1 019	NA
(=) Net earnings by state of residence	6 083	12 427	12 705	12 374	13 102	13 580	13 901	14 525	14 977	15 863	3.1
(+) Dividends, interest, and rent	1 497	3 806	3 810	3 702	3 581	3 643	3 762	3 955	4 219	4 329	1.6
(+) Transfer payments	1 609	2 964	3 273	3 981	4 145	4 465	4 507	4 762	4 863	5 174	7.2
(=) Total personal income	9 189	19 197	19 789	20 057	20 828	21 688	22 170	23 242	24 059	25 366	3.5
Farm	8	35	33	35	38	46	33	35	34	33	-0.7
Nonfarm	9 181	19 162	19 756	20 022	20 789	21 642	22 138	23 207	24 025	25 333	3.6
Personal income per capita (dollars)											
Current dollars	9 685	19 184	19 698	19 977	20 811	21 725	22 304	23 480	24 344	25 689	3.7
1997 dollars	18 518	24 253	23 704	23 068	23 279	23 640	23 702	24 407	24 790	25 689	0.7

*Compound annual average percent change, 1989–1997

Government Transfer Payments

	Millions of dollars 1990	Millions of dollars 1997	Percent change* State	Percent change* U.S.
Total government payments to individuals	3 135	5 007	59.7	62.7
Retirement, disability, and insurance	1 602	2 335	45.8	48.2
Social Security	1 133	1 582	39.6	46.1
Government employee retirement	387	636	64.4	60.3
Medical payments	990	1 957	97.7	101.2
Income maintenance	246	401	62.9	58.0
Supplemental Security Income	53	110	108.6	75.4
Family assistance	108	146	34.8	-0.5
Food Stamps	46	66	45.0	27.1
Other income maintenance	40	79	99.1	189.8
Unemployment insurance benefits	180	160	-10.7	10.6
Veterans benefits and other	118	154	30.8	30.8

*Percent change, 1990–1997

Government Payments to Individuals: 1997

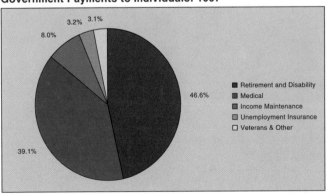

- Retirement and Disability 46.6%
- Medical 39.1%
- Income Maintenance 8.0%
- Unemployment Insurance 3.2%
- Veterans & Other 3.1%

ECONOMIC STRUCTURE

LEADING PRIVATE INDUSTRIES, 1997 (Worker and proprietor earnings, millions of dollars)		FASTEST EARNINGS GROWTH, 1989–97 (percent increase)	
Health services	$2 002	Electric, gas and sanitary services	118.9
Business services	916	Real estate	94.2
Miscellaneous manufacturing	575	Business services	81.3
Construction specialties	501	Health services	62.5
Educational services	478	Primary metal industries	58.5

EMPLOYMENT IN RHODE ISLAND SLIPPED SLIGHTLY FROM 1989 to 1997. In private nonfarm employment (which also fell at 0.1 percent per year), employment in services and agricultural services, forestry, fisheries, and other grew, but fell in construction and manufacturing. Mining employment, which fell in many states, actually rose slightly from 1989 to 1997, even with a fallback from the high point of 1993. Earnings grew in Rhode Island, but not as fast as earnings growth in other states in the region. Earnings grew fastest in the services sector, in the transportation, communications, and utilities sector; and in the finance, insurance, and real estate sector. Mining earnings also grew rapidly, but from a very small base. Manufacturing earnings remained nearly level and construction earnings fell; the only component to do so. Three of the top five industries were service industries (health, business, and education), with miscellaneous manufacturing and special trade construction rounding out the list.

Employment and Earnings by Sector

	1980	1989	1990	1991	1992	1993	1994	1995	1996	1997 Number	1997 Percent of total	Change*
Employment *(thousands of persons)*												
Total	486	566	555	529	534	539	539	547	552	561	100.0	-0.1
Farm	2	2	1	1	1	1	1	1	1	1	0.2	-2.6
Nonfarm	484	564	553	527	533	537	538	546	550	560	99.8	-0.1
Private nonfarm	411	489	476	451	457	461	464	472	476	484	86.4	-0.1
Agricultural service, forestry, and fishing	4	5	5	5	5	6	6	6	6	6	1.1	2.3
Mining	0	0	0	0	0	0	0	0	0	0	0.1	0.5
Construction	18	29	27	22	22	22	22	23	24	24	4.4	-2.3
Manufacturing	133	112	102	95	93	92	91	88	85	83	14.8	-3.6
Transportation and public utilities	15	17	18	17	16	17	18	18	18	19	3.4	1.1
Wholesale trade	21	25	21	20	20	20	20	21	20	20	3.6	-2.3
Retail trade	74	95	90	84	87	88	89	91	92	94	16.7	-0.1
Finance, insurance, and real estate	31	43	43	41	40	40	40	40	41	43	7.6	-0.1
Services	115	162	168	168	174	177	179	185	190	195	34.7	2.3
Government	72	76	77	76	76	76	73	74	74	75	13.4	-0.1
Earnings *(millions of dollars)*												
Total	6 344	12 705	12 985	12 656	13 415	13 897	14 189	14 824	15 244	16 114	100.0	3.0
Farm	8	35	33	35	38	46	33	35	34	33	0.2	-0.7
Nonfarm	6 336	12 670	12 953	12 621	13 377	13 852	14 156	14 789	15 210	16 081	99.8	3.0
Private nonfarm	5 317	10 726	10 861	10 531	11 157	11 549	11 860	12 366	12 711	13 453	83.5	2.9
Agricultural service, forestry, and fishing	37	101	104	105	103	98	97	101	103	105	0.7	0.5
Mining	26	5	5	4	7	8	9	8	8	9	0.1	7.8
Construction	283	852	818	620	603	603	665	679	711	764	4.7	-1.4
Manufacturing	2 055	2 967	2 891	2 811	2 934	2 976	2 963	2 969	2 962	3 069	19.0	0.4
Transportation and public utilities	289	511	552	544	598	702	713	750	778	827	5.1	6.2
Wholesale trade	367	728	675	622	664	678	703	771	776	818	5.1	1.5
Retail trade	631	1 313	1 283	1 213	1 301	1 334	1 349	1 381	1 409	1 501	9.3	1.7
Finance, insurance, and real estate	361	854	899	880	939	994	1 002	1 033	1 075	1 195	7.4	4.3
Services	1 269	3 395	3 634	3 731	4 007	4 156	4 360	4 673	4 889	5 165	32.1	5.4
Government	1 019	1 944	2 092	2 090	2 220	2 303	2 297	2 422	2 499	2 628	16.3	3.8

*Compound annual average percent change, 1989–1997

ECONOMIC STRUCTURE (Continued)

AVERAGE WAGES IN RHODE ISLAND WERE LOWER THAN THE national and New England regional averages in 1997, but wages in agricultural services were far higher in Rhode Island than for the United States as a whole. Government wages were higher than the national and regional averages. Construction wages were between the national and regional averages, but finance, insurance, and real estate wages were substantially below both, as were manufacturing and mining wages. Average wages grew 3.8 percent per year from 1989 to 1997, slightly faster than the U.S. rate of 3.5 percent.

Manufacturing, as a percent of gross state product (GSP) in Rhode Island in 1997, measured 16.7 percent, or almost one percentage point below the U.S. average. In 1989, manufacturing was a larger part of the economy at 20.5 percent of GSP. Two-thirds of manufacturing was durable goods manufacturing.

Total goods exports from Rhode Island grew 11.3 percent from 1994 to 1997, but there was a decline in 1995–96. Of the top five exported goods, two decreased the amount exported between 1994 and 1997. Industrial machinery and computers fell nearly 38 percent from 1994 to 1995, then increased 30 percent from 1995 to 1997, for a net lost of over 19 percent throughout the period. Scrap and waste exports fell almost 12 percent from 1994 to 1997.

Average Annual Wages and Salaries by Sector
(dollars)

	1989	1996	1997 State	1997 U.S.
All wage and salary workers	20 777	26 725	28 058	29 809
Farm	10 472	16 459	17 346	16 442
Nonfarm	20 794	26 738	28 071	29 900
Private nonfarm	20 259	25 931	27 262	29 867
Agricultural service, forestry, and fishing	19 874	22 627	22 958	17 941
Mining	27 497	30 951	31 311	49 800
Construction	26 669	31 079	33 028	31 765
Manufacturing	22 924	31 209	33 346	38 351
Transportation and utilities	25 404	32 484	33 873	38 222
Wholesale trade	26 668	36 327	37 819	39 466
Retail trade	12 672	14 975	15 766	16 206
Finance, insurance, and real estate	27 251	35 168	38 011	44 993
Services	18 787	25 021	25 973	27 588
Government	23 759	31 035	32 389	30 062

Gross State Product and Manufacturing
(millions of dollars, except as noted)

	1989	1994	1995	1996
Gross state product, total	20 836	23 875	25 046	25 629
Manufacturing:				
Millions of dollars	4 272	4 134	4 249	4 282
Percent of total gross state product	20.5	17.3	17.0	16.7
Per worker (dollars)	38 226	45 511	48 252	50 391
New capital expenditures, manufacturing	NA	259	284	401

Exports of Goods
(millions of dollars)

	1994	1995	1996	1997
All goods	1 012	957	955	1 126
Manufactures	885	794	812	1 006
Agricultural and livestock products	1	1	1	1
Other commodities	126	162	142	119
Top goods exports, 1997:				
Electric and electronic equipment	154	147	157	201
Industrial machinery and computers	230	143	169	186
Miscellaneous manufactures	142	131	116	153
Chemical products	52	51	39	89
Scrap and waste	93	117	96	82

HOUSING

New housing activity in Rhode Island, as measured by building permits, fell 38 percent from 1989 to 1991 and since then has recovered little of the ground lost. For Rhode Island, the housing production rate per 1,000 persons shown is not directly comparable with the U.S. rate, since the state's manufactured housing data have been suppressed for statistical reasons and are unavoidably counted as zero. However, mobile home placement in the Northeast and in urban areas tends to be low. The Rhode Island production rate calculated here is less than one-half of the U.S. per capita rate of housing production. Existing home sales fell less sharply than new home building from 1989 to 1991 and have since recovered to levels higher than in 1988–89, significantly exceeding U.S. growth rates. Homeownership was far lower in Rhode Island than nationwide throughout the decade and there was no real change in the rates after an abrupt decline in 1990.

Homeownership Rates: 1989 and 1997

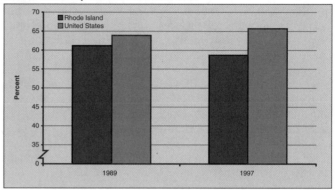

Housing Supply

	1989	1990	1991	1992	1993	1994	1995	1996	1997
Residential building permits (thousands)	3.9	3.0	2.4	2.6	2.6	2.5	2.3	2.5	2.7
New home production (including manufactured housing):									
Thousands of homes	3.9	3.0	2.4	2.6	2.6	2.5	2.3	2.5	2.7
Rate per 1,000 population									
Rhode Island	3.9	3.0	2.4	2.6	2.6	2.5	2.3	2.5	2.7
U.S.	6.2	5.2	4.5	5.1	5.6	6.4	6.3	6.6	6.5
Existing home sales:									
Thousands of homes	9.5	7.8	7.8	10.0	11.0	11.6	11.5	12.9	14.3
Change from previous year (percent)									
Rhode Island	-13.6	-17.9	0.0	28.2	10.0	5.5	-0.9	12.2	10.9
U.S.	-3.9	-4.0	0.0	9.2	8.2	4.8	-3.7	7.5	3.8
Home ownership rate (percent of households)	61.2	58.5	58.2	56.8	57.6	56.5	57.9	56.6	58.7
Rental vacancy rate (percent of rental housing units)	7.4	9.6	9.6	8.7	8.6	8.0	7.1	7.2	6.0

Note: Manufactured housing data for 1989–97 suppressed because estimate was based on too few responses.

AGRICULTURE

Farm income in Rhode Island was small and increased slightly over the decade, and production expenses grew at a faster rate than income but by an equivalent dollar amount. Corporate farms had a presence in the state, though they did not dominate. Total net farm proprietors' income hit its peak in 1993 but has fallen since then because of increasing production expenses. There were no appreciable government payments to the state in the decade. The number of acres per farm was quite low when compared to both the U.S. average and regional levels, yet

farms were also, on average, worth more than one and one-half times the average U.S. farm. This level may reflect high property values in densely populated areas.

RHODE ISLAND FARMS, 1997

Number of farms	700
Total acres (thousands):	63
Average per farm	90
Value of land and buildings (millions of dollars)	498
Average per farm (dollars)	711 429

Farm Income
(millions of dollars)

	1980	1989	1990	1991	1992	1993	1994	1995	1996	1997
Gross income	37	80	77	77	83	88	89	88	92	92
Receipts from sales	33	73	71	71	76	80	81	80	85	84
Government payments	0	0	0	0	0	0	0	0	0	0
Imputed and miscellaneous income	3	6	7	6	7	8	7	7	7	8
(–) Production expenses	35	45	47	46	44	47	50	53	54	57
(=) Realized net income	2	35	30	32	39	41	39	34	38	35
(+) Inventory change	0	0	0	0	1	0	0	0	0	-1
(=) Net income	2	34	30	32	40	41	39	34	38	34
Corporate income	0	8	7	6	10	4	16	9	15	12
Farm proprietors income	2	26	23	26	30	37	24	25	23	22

EDUCATION

EDUCATIONAL ATTAINMENT Percent of population age 25 and over, 1997	State	United States
High school graduate or higher	77.5	82.1
College graduate or higher	25.7	23.9

RHODE ISLAND WAS RANKED 45TH IN HIGH SCHOOL COMPLETION in the country, falling behind every other state in the region and coming behind states such as Alabama and Mississippi, which have historically low secondary education completion levels. Unlike these states, however, Rhode Island had above average per pupil spending (ranked second in the region) and teacher salaries. A higher than average percentage (13.6) of secondary and elementary stu-

dents were enrolled in private schools. Rhode Island ranked 14th in the percentage of the population holding bachelor's degrees or higher. A very substantial 29.5 percent of the population age 18 to 34 was enrolled in higher education in 1996, a level much higher than the 21.8 percent found in the United States as a whole. Minority enrollment was about half of what it was in the country in 1996, and almost half of all students enrolled were enrolled at private institutions.

High School Completion: 1990–97

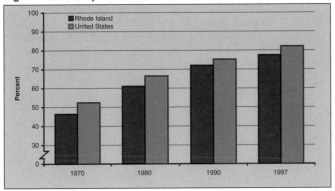

Education Indicators

	State	U.S.
Elementary and secondary schools		
Enrollment, 1995–96		
Total (thousands)	173	49 873
Percent in private schools	13.6	10.1
Expenditures per pupil (dollars), 1995–96	7 936	6 146
Average teacher salary (dollars), 1996–97	43 019	38 509
Higher education		
Enrollment, 1996–97		
Total (thousands)	72	14 218
Percent of population 18–34	29.5	21.8
Percent minority	13.0	26.1
Percent in private schools	48.3	22.6

HEALTH

RHODE ISLAND'S AGE-ADJUSTED DEATH RATE (IN WHICH changes over time in the age composition of the population are taken into consideration) was lower than the national rate, but there was a slight increase in 1997. Infant mortality was about the same in Rhode Island as in the rest of the country, though there was a dip in the rate in

1996. The number of people without health insurance was fairly low compared to the United States and similar to other states in the region. Cancer and heart diseases were the leading causes of death in the state, but only cancer and liver disease had age-adjusted death rates higher than the national average.

Health Indicators

	1990	1995	1996	1997
Infant mortality				
(rate per thousand live births)				
Rhode Island	8.1	7.2	5.2	6.6
U.S.	9.2	7.6	7.3	7.1
Total deaths, age-adjusted rate				
(rate per thousand population)				
Rhode Island	4.9	4.6	4.4	4.5
U.S.	5.2	5.0	4.9	4.8
Persons not covered by health insurance				
(percent of population)				
Rhode Island	11.1	12.9	9.9	10.2
U.S.	13.9	15.4	15.6	16.1

Leading Causes of Death, 1996
(deaths per 100,000 population)

	Age-adjusted		Not age-adjusted	
	State	U.S.	State	U.S.
Deaths from all causes	437.5	491.6	964.0	872.5
Heart disease	125.5	134.5	329.7	276.4
Cancer	137.4	127.9	254.1	203.4
Cerebrovascular diseases	19.4	26.4	59.1	60.3
Chronic obstructive pulmonary disease	16.1	21.0	41.4	40.0
Diabetes mellitus	12.8	13.6	26.9	23.3
Pneumonia and influenza	10.3	12.8	32.6	31.6
HIV	6.4	11.1	6.8	11.7
Liver disease	7.7	7.5	10.3	9.4
Alzheimer's disease	2.6	2.7	10.1	8.1
Accidents and adverse effects	14.3	30.4	21.0	35.8
Motor vehicle accidents	7.5	16.2	7.9	16.5
Suicide	7.8	10.8	8.4	11.6
Homicide	3.1	8.5	2.8	7.9
Injury by firearm	5.0	12.9	5.3	12.8

GOVERNMENT

STATE AND LOCAL TAXES, 1995–96	State	U.S.
Per capita (dollars)	2 650	2 477
Percent of personal income	11.1	10.8

RHODE ISLAND'S STATE AND LOCAL TAXES (LESS CORPORATE tax) per capita were slightly higher than the national level. These taxes also represented a relatively higher percentage of personal income. A larger than average percentage of state and local taxes was collected at the local level, almost entirely from property taxes. Rhode Island's per capita state tax was almost identical to the national average in 1997. Sales taxes and the corporate net tax were lower per capita, but the individual income tax was 19.7 percent higher than the national average. Per capita general expenditures were a little higher in the state than in the rest of the United States. Education, however, did not benefit from this higher level of spending, receiving only 89.7 percent of the level of national spending per capita. Spending on general administration in Rhode Island was 116.8 percent higher than the national average, and interest paid on the debt was 103 percent higher.

Federal funds in Rhode Island totaled $5.9 billion in 1997, or about 0.4 percent of funds disbursed from the federal government to the 50 states and the District of Columbia. Grants and the subcomponents of grants were able to draw in a larger share of federal funds than the population of the state might suggest. Medicaid and nutrition and family welfare were the driving factors behind the increase, though grants for education roughly followed the results for total grants. Defense procurement funds were proportionately small, and non-defense procurement was smaller still. Though defense funding was low comparatively, it still represented 4.4 percent of total funds given to the state.

State Government Finances, 1996–97

	Millions of dollars	Percent distribution	Dollars per capita State	Dollars per capita U.S.
General revenue	3 501	100.0	3 547	3 049
Intergovernmental revenue	1 109	31.7	1 123	863
Taxes	1 644	47.0	1 666	1 660
General sales	490	14.0	496	551
Selective sales	324	9.2	328	257
License taxes	80	2.3	81	106
Individual income	640	18.3	648	542
Corporation net income	89	2.5	90	115
Other taxes	22	0.6	22	90
Other general revenue	748	21.4	758	526
General expenditure	3 373	100.0	3 417	2 951
Intergovernmental expenditure	506	15.0	513	989
Direct expenditure	2 866	85.0	2 904	1 962
General expenditure, by function:				
Education	914	27.1	926	1 033
Public welfare	869	25.8	881	761
Hospitals and health	328	9.7	332	237
Highways	192	5.7	194	225
Police protection and corrections	153	4.5	155	137
Natural resources, parks and recreation	56	1.7	57	63
Governmental administration	215	6.4	218	107
Interest on general debt	300	8.9	304	99
Other and unallocable	346	10.3	351	290
Debt at end of fiscal year	5 302	NA	5 372	1 706
Cash and security holdings	9 587	NA	9 713	6 683

Federal Spending within State

	Federal funds, fiscal 1997 Millions of dollars	Percent distribution	Percent of U.S. total*
Total within state	5 892	100.0	0.4
Payments to individuals	3 562	60.5	0.5
Retirement and disability	1 957	33.2	0.4
Medicare	905	15.4	0.4
Food stamps	71	1.2	0.4
Supplemental Security Income	93	1.6	0.3
Grants	1 198	20.3	0.5
Medicaid and other health	542	9.2	0.5
Nutrition and family welfare	224	3.8	0.5
Education	73	1.2	0.4
Housing and community development	61	1.0	0.5
Salaries and wages	709	12.0	0.4
Defense procurement contracts	257	4.4	0.2
Non-defense procurement contracts	98	1.7	0.1

*State population is 0.4 percent of the U.S. total.

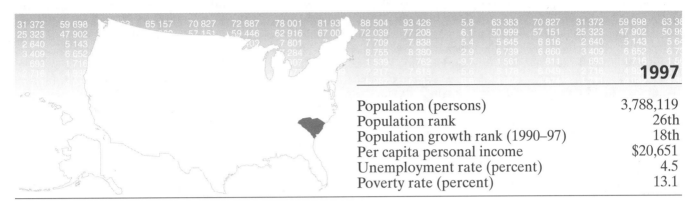

1997

Population (persons)	3,788,119
Population rank	26th
Population growth rank (1990–97)	18th
Per capita personal income	$20,651
Unemployment rate (percent)	4.5
Poverty rate (percent)	13.1

WITH A 1997 POPULATION OF 3.8 MILLION, SOUTH CAROLINA stands at the midpoint of the states in terms of population size, and its population growth rate of 1.0 percent per year from 1990 to 1997 was just equal to the national average. Although famous for the gracious, historic coastal city of Charleston and the nearby barrier islands, the largest concentration of population and economic activity is inland. The largest metropolitan area, Greenville-Spartanburg-Anderson, with a 1997 population of 905,000, is located along the state's northern border with North Carolina. Adjacent York County, part of the Charlotte-Gastonia-Rock Hill (NC-SC) metropolitan area, adds another 151,000 to the population total for this part of the state.

The period from 1990 to 1993 was a difficult one economically for much of South Carolina: employment grew little, real per capita incomes stagnated, and the unemployment rate rose to 7.6 percent by 1993, well above the national average. The years since 1993 have seen considerable improvement. Despite loss of jobs in traditional manufacturing industries such as textiles and apparel, overall employment growth accelerated, the unemployment rate fell to 4.5 percent by 1997, real per capita income showed strong gains, exports grew briskly, and residential construction boomed. Looking ahead, the state has undertaken initiatives to build a skilled work force and research and development base.

Average Annual Population Growth: 1990–97

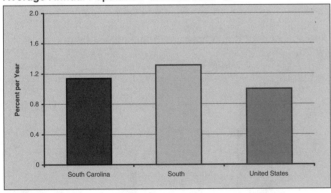

Median Household Income: 1989–97 (1997 dollars)

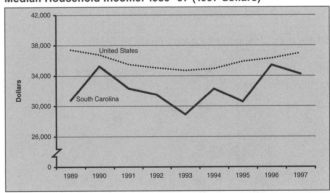

Unemployment Rate: 1989–97

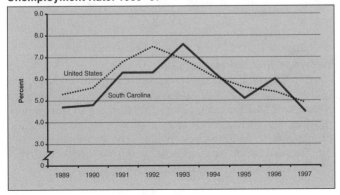

AFTER PEAKING AT 7.6 PERCENT IN 1993, SOUTH CAROLINA'S unemployment rate fell markedly over the next four years and, at 4.5 percent by 1997, was a little below that year's national average of 4.9 percent. The lower unemployment rate reflects stronger growth of employment after 1994. Employment grew at an average rate of 2.6 percent per year from 1994 to1997, compared to only 0.8 percent from 1990 to 1994. The proportion of the age 16 and over population holding jobs averaged 61.8 percent in 1995–97, compared to 60.9 percent from 1990 to 1994. However, the 1995–97 average still was well below the national average of 63.3 percent during the same period.

POPULATION AND LABOR FORCE

SOUTH CAROLINA'S POPULATION GREW IN LINE WITH THE national average rate of 1.0 percent per year from 1990 to 1997. The 0.8 percent per year growth of the White non-Hispanic population was above the national average rate of 0.4 percent. Growth of each of the other race and ethnic groups, although faster than that for non-Hispanic Whites, was a little below the national average. Non-Hispanic Whites were 68.7 percent of the population in 1990, and this proportion had fallen only slightly, to 67.8 percent by 1997.

Non-Hispanic Blacks constituted about 30 percent of the South Carolina population in 1997—a share that has remained roughly constant since 1980. Other minority groups are quite small percentages of the total. In absolute numbers rather than percentages, the White non-Hispanic population grew by 146,000 from 1990 to 1997, the Black non-Hispanic population by 98,000, and other groups combined by about 17,000.

Over one-half of South Carolina's 8.3 percent total population growth from 1990 to 1997 was the result of natural increase (births minus deaths). In-migration from other states accounted for more than one-third of the growth, and immigration from abroad for only 4 percent.

Population and Labor Force

	1980	1990	1991	1992	1993	1994	1995	1996	1997	Change* State	Change* U.S.
Population											
Total number of persons (thousands)	3 122	3 499	3 559	3 599	3 635	3 667	3 699	3 737	3 788	1.0	1.0
Percent distribution:											
White, Non-Hispanic	68.3	68.7	68.4	68.3	68.1	68.1	67.9	67.9	67.8	0.8	0.4
Black, Non-Hispanic	30.0	29.3	29.8	29.9	30.0	30.0	30.0	30.0	29.9	1.3	1.4
Asian	0.4	0.7	0.7	0.7	0.7	0.7	0.8	0.8	0.9	3.8	4.1
Native American	0.2	0.3	0.2	0.2	0.2	0.2	0.2	0.2	0.2	0.5	1.6
Hispanic	1.1	1.1	0.9	1.0	1.0	1.0	1.1	1.1	1.2	3.3	3.8
In metropolitan areas	67.7	69.5	69.7	69.7	69.7	69.7	69.6	69.6	69.8	1.1	1.0
Total number of households (thousands)	1 030	1 258	1 291	1 315	1 328	1 331	1 352	1 376	NA	1.5	1.2
Labor Force (thousands)											
Population 16 and over	2 303	2 683	2 730	2 761	2 791	2 816	2 847	2 876	2 916	1.2	1.0
Civilian labor force	1 388	1 739	1 769	1 796	1 827	1 824	1 865	1 865	1 931	1.5	1.1
Employed	1 293	1 656	1 657	1 683	1 687	1 709	1 771	1 753	1 843	1.5	1.2
Percent of population	56.1	61.7	60.7	61.0	60.5	60.7	62.2	61.0	63.2		
Unemployment rate (percent)	6.9	4.8	6.3	6.3	7.6	6.3	5.1	6.0	4.5		

*Compound annual average percent change, 1990–1997; 1990–1996 for households.

Population Change and Components: 1990–97

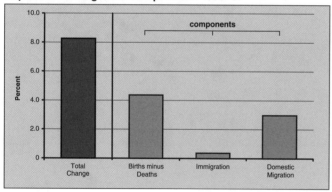

Average Annual Household and Population Growth

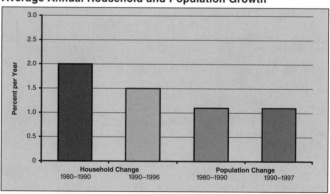

Population by Age; Births and Deaths

	1990 State	1990 U.S.	1997 State	1997 U.S.
Age distribution (percent)				
Under 5 years	7.5	7.6	6.8	7.2
5 to 17 years	18.8	18.2	18.7	18.8
18 to 64 years	62.4	61.8	62.5	61.3
65 years and over	11.3	12.5	12.1	12.7
Birth and death rates (per thousand population)				
Births	16.8	16.7	13.8	14.6
Deaths	8.5	8.6	8.8	8.6

THE PERCENT OF SOUTH CAROLINA'S POPULATION AGE 65 AND over was well below the national average in 1990. Since then it has increased more rapidly than that average, but at 12.1 percent in 1997 still had not reached the nation's average of 12.7 percent. The proportion of the state's population age 18 to 64 has remained relatively constant, in contrast to a decline nationwide. The proportion under age 18 has fallen, with almost all of the drop occurring among those under age five.

HOUSEHOLD AND PERSONAL INCOME

HOUSEHOLD INCOME AND PERSONS IN POVERTY	1990	1995	1996	1997	
				State	U.S.
Median household income (1997 dollars)	35 287	30 616	35 460	34 262	37 005
Persons in poverty (thousands)	548	744	482	500	35 574
Poverty rate (percent)	16.2	19.9	13.0	13.1	13.3

AFTER FLUCTUATING WITHIN A FAIRLY NARROW RANGE OF $29,000 to $32,000 from 1991 to 1995, South Carolina's inflation-adjusted median household income showed gains in 1996–97, when it averaged $34,861 per year, or 95 percent of the national average. South Carolina's poverty rate, which was substantially above the national average in 1980 and 1990, fell to 13.1 percent in 1997, roughly equal to the national average of 13.3 percent.

Personal income per capita has moved gradually toward the national average, with much of the gain occurring in the 1980s. South Carolina was at only 76 percent of that average in 1980, but was at 80.5 percent in 1990 and above 81 percent each year from 1994 through 1997.

South Carolina derived 66 percent of its personal income from worker and proprietor earnings in 1997, just equal to the national average. The 15 percent from dividends, interest, and rent was a little below the average, while the 19 percent from transfer payments was a little above. The relatively large positive adjustment for residence indicates that earnings of South Carolina residents who commute to jobs in other states substantially exceed earnings of workers who commute into South Carolina. The 0.6 percent farm share of 1997 personal income was nearly equal to the 0.7 percent national average and has remained relatively constant in recent years.

Among transfer payments, Social Security and medical payments grew somewhat faster than the U.S. average from 1990 to 1997, and income maintenance payments grew considerably faster. "Other income maintenance," largely the earned income tax credit, showed by far the largest percent growth, substantially exceeding even its rapid national average growth.

Personal Income
(millions of dollars)

	1980	1989	1990	1991	1992	1993	1994	1995	1996	1997	Change*
Earnings by place of work	18 165	36 596	39 420	40 357	42 673	44 878	47 089	49 420	51 488	54 738	5.2
Wages and salaries	15 393	30 551	32 795	33 508	35 208	36 734	38 482	40 722	42 695	45 626	5.1
Other labor income	1 367	3 157	3 527	3 725	4 119	4 523	4 785	4 792	4 652	4 720	5.2
Proprietors' income	1 406	2 887	3 098	3 124	3 346	3 621	3 821	3 906	4 142	4 392	5.4
Farm	-45	259	171	275	255	227	355	256	329	389	5.2
Nonfarm	1 451	2 628	2 927	2 849	3 092	3 394	3 466	3 650	3 813	4 002	5.4
(−) Personal contributions for social insurance	971	2 532	2 717	2 843	2 986	3 168	3 384	3 624	3 796	4 055	6.1
(+) Adjustment for residence	284	520	501	489	514	513	592	693	771	840	NA
(=) **Net earnings by state of residence**	17 478	34 584	37 205	38 003	40 202	42 222	44 296	46 489	48 463	51 522	5.1
(+) Dividends, interest, and rent	2 823	6 841	8 240	8 291	8 188	8 443	9 105	9 836	10 851	11 314	6.5
(+) Transfer payments	3 673	7 592	8 535	9 613	10 675	11 458	12 286	13 183	14 092	14 814	8.7
(=) **Total personal income**	23 974	49 016	53 979	55 907	59 065	62 123	65 688	69 508	73 407	77 650	5.9
Farm	43	345	269	366	340	326	447	357	431	494	4.6
Nonfarm	23 931	48 672	53 711	55 541	58 725	61 796	65 241	69 151	72 975	77 156	5.9
Personal income per capita (dollars)											
Current dollars	7 648	14 180	15 427	15 725	16 441	17 139	17 979	18 871	19 751	20 651	4.8
1997 dollars	14 623	17 927	18 564	18 158	18 390	18 650	19 106	19 616	20 113	20 651	1.8

*Compound annual average percent change, 1989–1997

Government Transfer Payments

	Millions of dollars		Percent change*	
	1990	1997	State	U.S.
Total government payments to individuals	8 133	14 199	74.6	62.7
Retirement, disability, and insurance	4 689	7 520	60.4	48.2
Social Security	3 109	5 058	62.7	46.1
Government employee retirement	1 439	2 257	56.8	60.3
Medical payments	2 171	4 650	114.2	101.2
Income maintenance	655	1 301	98.6	58.0
Supplemental Security Income	245	425	73.4	75.4
Family assistance	101	78	-22.2	-0.5
Food Stamps	195	275	40.9	27.1
Other income maintenance	114	523	357.2	189.8
Unemployment insurance benefits	146	181	23.5	10.6
Veterans benefits and other	472	547	15.9	30.8

*Percent change, 1990–1997

Government Payments to Individuals: 1997

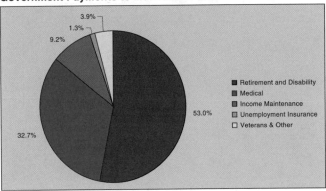

- ■ Retirement and Disability
- ■ Medical
- ■ Income Maintenance
- □ Unemployment Insurance
- □ Veterans & Other

53.0% 32.7% 9.2% 3.9% 1.3%

ECONOMIC STRUCTURE

LEADING PRIVATE INDUSTRIES, 1997 (Worker and proprietor earnings, millions of dollars)		FASTEST EARNINGS GROWTH, 1989–97 (percent increase)	
Health services	$3 558	Motor vehicles and equipment	270.2
Textile mill products	2 422	Business services	134.1
Business services	2 310	Real estate	122.2
Construction specialties	2 250	Health services	98.4
Chemicals and allied products	2 068	Other transportation services	92.6

THE STRUCTURE OF THE SOUTH CAROLINA ECONOMY HAS undergone changes in the 1990s, and further changes lie ahead as the state strives to continue moving toward a high-tech economy and improved standards of living. The South Carolina Technology Advisory Council—created to recommend steps to attract high-tech industry—has reported that, while the state has attracted high-tech manufacturing activity, it lags in developing research facilities; high-tech business services; and small, innovative high-tech companies. Development of these entities and of a more technologically sophisticated workforce are required if jobs being lost in traditional manufacturing industries are to be replaced with well-paying high-tech jobs.

Manufacturing's share of total South Carolina employment fell from 21 percent in 1989 to 17 percent in 1997, but this percentage still was well above the national average of 12.4 percent. Two of South Carolina's five largest industries—textile mill products and chemicals—are within the manufacturing sector, and industrial machinery manufac-

turing ranked sixth in 1997. However, faced by stiff competition from abroad, worker and proprietor earnings in textile mill products have shown almost no growth in the 1990s, and chemicals and industrial machinery had below-average earnings growth from 1989 to 1997. Employment in manufacturing fell by 24,000 jobs from 1989 to 1997, with 14,000 of the loss occurring in 1996 and 1997. Much of the loss was due to declining employment in textiles and apparel. In contrast, motor vehicle manufacturing has been South Carolina's most rapidly growing industry in the 1990s, and this growth is forecast to continue.

Retail trade stands out as a sector in which employment and earnings growth in South Carolina has exceeded the national average. This industry typically offers relatively low-paying, low-skill jobs, however; in 1997, it provided 19 percent of the state's total employment, but only 11 percent of worker and proprietor earnings. Wholesale trade, a sector with above-average worker earnings, also grew rapidly but accounted for less than 4 percent of total employment.

Employment and Earnings by Sector

	1980	1989	1990	1991	1992	1993	1994	1995	1996	1997 Number	1997 Percent of total	Change*
Employment *(thousands of persons)*												
Total	1 527	1 871	1 921	1 900	1 913	1 948	1 997	2 045	2 085	2 148	100.0	1.7
Farm	60	38	37	36	35	34	32	31	28	30	1.4	-2.7
Nonfarm	1 467	1 833	1 884	1 864	1 878	1 914	1 965	2 014	2 056	2 118	98.6	1.8
Private nonfarm	1 153	1 479	1 522	1 499	1 509	1 549	1 604	1 662	1 704	1 759	81.9	2.2
Agricultural service, forestry, and fishing	10	14	16	16	16	18	19	20	21	22	1.0	5.6
Mining	2	3	3	2	2	2	2	2	2	2	0.1	-1.2
Construction	92	122	134	120	113	116	119	123	131	138	6.4	1.5
Manufacturing	398	395	388	376	378	382	386	385	375	371	17.3	-0.8
Transportation and public utilities	58	71	74	73	72	74	78	81	84	87	4.1	2.6
Wholesale trade	56	65	66	64	63	63	65	70	73	77	3.6	2.1
Retail trade	216	320	331	328	335	342	358	375	389	403	18.8	2.9
Finance, insurance, and real estate	79	108	109	107	104	106	112	117	123	127	5.9	2.0
Services	242	381	403	412	425	446	465	489	507	530	24.7	4.2
Government	313	354	362	365	368	365	361	353	352	359	16.7	0.2
Earnings *(millions of dollars)*												
Total	18 165	36 596	39 420	40 357	42 673	44 878	47 089	49 420	51 488	54 738	100.0	5.2
Farm	43	345	269	366	340	326	447	357	431	494	0.9	4.6
Nonfarm	18 123	36 251	39 152	39 991	42 333	44 552	46 642	49 063	51 057	54 244	99.1	5.2
Private nonfarm	14 397	28 810	31 174	31 525	33 584	35 602	37 667	39 996	41 723	44 443	81.2	5.6
Agricultural service, forestry, and fishing	80	197	228	231	241	253	265	296	306	330	0.6	6.7
Mining	72	66	70	73	66	70	69	75	77	81	0.1	2.6
Construction	1 245	2 624	3 186	2 810	2 661	2 848	3 010	3 215	3 622	3 860	7.1	4.9
Manufacturing	5 987	10 205	10 545	10 763	11 607	12 117	12 632	12 959	12 872	13 415	24.5	3.5
Transportation and public utilities	1 129	2 171	2 294	2 345	2 424	2 544	2 713	2 814	2 903	3 031	5.5	4.3
Wholesale trade	911	1 663	1 792	1 786	1 859	1 945	2 095	2 327	2 511	2 761	5.0	6.5
Retail trade	1 780	3 790	4 060	4 134	4 422	4 749	5 006	5 376	5 665	6 043	11.0	6.0
Finance, insurance, and real estate	756	1 692	1 771	1 836	2 019	2 226	2 312	2 522	2 732	2 958	5.4	7.2
Services	2 437	6 402	7 229	7 548	8 284	8 850	9 564	10 414	11 037	11 964	21.9	8.1
Government	3 725	7 441	7 978	8 466	8 750	8 950	8 975	9 066	9 334	9 801	17.9	3.5

*Compound annual average percent change, 1989–1997

ECONOMIC STRUCTURE (Continued)

THE AVERAGE ANNUAL EARNINGS OF SOUTH CAROLINA workers were 82 percent of the U.S. average in 1997, and this percentage changed little during the 1980s and 1990s. The 1997 figure of $24,464 also was well below the averages for the neighboring states of Georgia and North Carolina. Among sectors with relatively important shares of South Carolina's employment total, wholesale trade, transportation and public utilities, and manufacturing provided the highest annual earnings. Retail trade had by far the lowest annual earnings, the result of a combination of low hourly wages, fewer hours worked per week on average, and many part-year workers.

Manufacturing has contributed about 27 percent of South Carolina's gross state product (GSP) in recent years, placing the state among the highest in the south and well above the 1997 national average of 17 percent. Although the manufacturing share of GSP has shown little change since 1989, employment in manufacturing has fallen 7 percent. This relationship indicates good productivity gains; that is, considerable restructuring of manufacturing to provide increased output with fewer employees. A large increase in capital investment in 1995 and 1996 suggests that this restructuring is continuing. Still, manufacturing output per worker in the state was below the national average, reflecting, in part, the dominance of the textile industry, an industry in which output per worker was well below the all-manufacturing average.

South Carolina has had some success in increasing its exports of higher technology manufactures in the last few years. Exports of electric and electronic equipment rose 48 percent from 1994 to 1997, and exports of transportation equipment—which includes motor vehicles—more than quadrupled. Exports of industrial machinery, chemicals, and textiles grew more slowly, but total exports of all manufactured goods were up 63 percent, compared to 37 percent nationwide. Manufactured goods made up 98 percent of South Carolina's total goods exports in 1997, compared to 87 percent nationwide, and the top five industry groups made up about two-thirds of all goods exports.

Average Annual Wages and Salaries by Sector
(dollars)

	1989	1996	1997 State	1997 U.S.
All wage and salary workers	18 552	23 598	24 464	29 809
Farm	7 273	14 026	11 529	16 442
Nonfarm	18 629	23 635	24 523	29 900
Private nonfarm	18 393	23 509	24 426	29 867
Agricultural service, forestry, and fishing	14 420	17 431	17 801	17 941
Mining	26 292	34 077	36 039	49 800
Construction	20 089	26 074	26 659	31 765
Manufacturing	22 753	30 303	32 074	38 351
Transportation and utilities	27 703	31 930	32 543	38 222
Wholesale trade	23 639	31 760	32 895	39 466
Retail trade	11 071	14 054	14 514	16 206
Finance, insurance, and real estate	21 305	28 779	30 598	44 993
Services	15 481	20 978	21 785	27 588
Government	19 481	24 152	24 930	30 062

Gross State Product and Manufacturing
(millions of dollars, except as noted)

	1989	1994	1995	1996
Gross state product, total	61 736	80 684	85 270	89 476
Manufacturing:				
Millions of dollars	16 715	22 123	23 520	23 768
Percent of total gross state product	27.1	27.4	27.6	26.6
Per worker (dollars)	42 277	57 383	61 105	63 450
New capital expenditures, manufacturing	NA	2 156	2 826	2 782

Exports of Goods
(millions of dollars)

	1994	1995	1996	1997
All goods	3 510	4 498	4 925	5 674
Manufactures	3 398	4 353	4 799	5 541
Agricultural and livestock products	55	70	64	77
Other commodities	57	74	62	56
Top goods exports, 1997:				
Electric and electronic equipment	755	955	904	1 120
Transportation equipment	227	314	829	1 006
Industrial machinery and computers	597	756	711	695
Chemical products	443	608	583	607
Textile mill products	308	377	374	403

HOUSING

EVEN THOUGH ITS POPULATION HAS GROWN ONLY IN LINE with the national average, South Carolina's new home production rate has been well above the nation's throughout the 1990s, and was roughly double the national rate in 1996 and 1997. This suggests that, as the state prospers, more vacation homes are being built and more substandard housing is being replaced. A high rental vacancy rate in 1996 and 1997 also suggests that housing supply may have outpaced demand and that the building boom may taper off. Well over one-third of South Carolina's new home production in recent years has consisted of manufactured housing (also called "mobile homes"), compared to less than 20 percent nationwide.

South Carolina's homeownership rate is well above the national average and increased during the 1990s. Over 74 percent of households owned their homes in 1997, up from 71 percent in 1989. Nationwide, the homeownership rate was 65.7 percent in 1997.

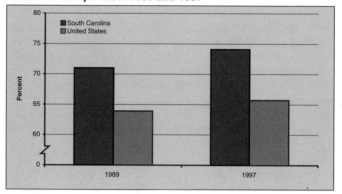

Homeownership Rates: 1989 and 1997

Housing Supply

	1989	1990	1991	1992	1993	1994	1995	1996	1997
Residential building permits (thousands)	21.2	21.3	18.7	20.2	21.1	24.6	24.0	29.4	30.1
New home production (including manufactured housing):									
Thousands of homes	33.5	33.6	27.4	31.6	34.9	38.7	40.7	49.2	46.5
Rate per 1,000 population									
South Carolina	9.7	9.6	7.7	8.8	9.6	10.6	11.1	13.2	12.4
U.S.	6.2	5.2	4.5	5.1	5.6	6.4	6.3	6.6	6.5
Existing home sales:									
Thousands of homes	52.2	57.8	53.9	58.9	62.2	67.3	68.9	74.2	81.5
Change from previous year (percent)									
South Carolina	-5.1	10.7	-6.7	9.3	5.6	8.2	2.4	7.7	9.8
U.S.	-3.9	-4.0	0.0	9.2	8.2	4.8	-3.7	7.5	3.8
Home ownership rate (percent of households)	71.0	71.4	73.1	71.0	71.1	72.0	71.3	72.9	74.1
Rental vacancy rate (percent of rental housing units)	9.1	8.4	11.1	10.0	10.6	12.3	9.3	14.1	15.1

AGRICULTURE

THE MID-1990S WERE A GOOD PERIOD FOR SOUTH CAROLINA agriculture, with net farm income averaging $389 million per year from 1994 through 1997. The state's agricultural sales in 1997 were evenly divided between crops and livestock. Within livestock, poultry and poultry products was by far the most important sales category, accounting for 37 percent of all agricultural sales. Among crops, tobacco was the most important, accounting for 13 percent of all agricultural sales.

In South Carolina, as elsewhere in the nation, farming is only a part-time activity for many farmers. Sixty percent of South Carolina farm operators had a principal occupation other than farming in 1997.

SOUTH CAROLINA FARMS, 1997	
Number of farms	21 500
Total acres (thousands):	5 000
Average per farm	233
Value of land and buildings (millions of dollars)	7 000
Average per farm (dollars)	325 581

Farm Income
(millions of dollars)

	1980	1989	1990	1991	1992	1993	1994	1995	1996	1997
Gross income	1 218	1 459	1 404	1 398	1 418	1 511	1 606	1 638	1 827	1 914
Receipts from sales	1 104	1 286	1 233	1 233	1 234	1 291	1 420	1 467	1 639	1 716
Government payments	13	73	63	49	73	103	60	35	43	43
Imputed and miscellaneous income	101	101	108	115	112	117	126	136	145	155
(–) Production expenses	1 145	1 151	1 154	1 156	1 126	1 224	1 251	1 333	1 468	1 475
(=) Realized net income	74	309	250	241	293	287	354	305	359	439
(+) Inventory change	-135	-22	-60	56	-9	-50	69	-18	31	16
(=) Net income	-61	286	190	297	284	237	424	286	390	455
Corporate income	-16	27	18	22	29	10	69	30	61	65
Farm proprietors income	-45	259	171	275	255	227	355	256	329	389

EDUCATION

EDUCATIONAL ATTAINMENT Percent of population age 25 and over, 1997	State	United States
High school graduate or higher	77.3	82.1
College graduate or higher	19.2	23.9

SOUTH CAROLINA HAS MADE NOTABLE PROGRESS IN EDUCA-tional attainment over the past quarter century. In 1970, only 37.8 percent of South Carolinians over age 25 had complet-ed high school, compared to 52.4 percent nationwide. By 1997, South Carolina's percentage had increased to 77.3 per-cent, much closer to that year's national average of 82.1 per-cent. Only 8.9 percent of the state's residents had completed four years of college in 1970, compared to 10.7 percent nationwide; in 1997 the comparable rates were 19.2 percent

for the state and 23.9 percent nationwide. In the 1996–97 school year, 18.4 percent of South Carolinians age 18 to 34 were enrolled in higher education, compared to 21.8 percent nationwide.

Per pupil expenditures in 1995–96 were 83 percent of the national average, and the average teacher salary was 85 per-cent. Only 7 percent of elementary and secondary school stu-dents and 15 percent of those in higher education attend pri-vate schools, about one-third below the national percentages.

High School Completion: 1990–97

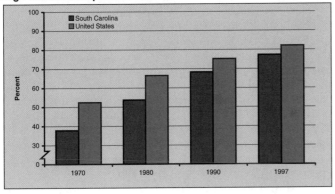

Education Indicators

	State	U.S.
Elementary and secondary schools		
Enrollment, 1995–96		
Total (thousands)	696	49 873
Percent in private schools	7.2	10.1
Expenditures per pupil (dollars), 1995–96	5 096	6 146
Average teacher salary (dollars), 1996–97	32 659	38 509
Higher education		
Enrollment, 1996–97		
Total (thousands)	174	14 218
Percent of population 18–34	18.4	21.8
Percent minority	26.1	26.1
Percent in private schools	14.9	22.6

HEALTH

SOUTH CAROLINA'S INFANT MORTALITY RATE HAS FALLEN DUR-ing the 1990s, from 11.7 deaths per 1,000 live births in 1990 to an average of 8.4 per 1,000 in 1996 and 1997, and the gap between the state rate and the national rate has been reduced by more than one-half. The state's overall death rate remained high, however. Adjusted for differences in the age distribution of the population, the rate of death from heart disease, the leading cause of death, was 16 per-

cent above the national average in 1996, and the rate for cerebrovascular diseases (strokes) was 50 percent higher than the national rate. Deaths from motor vehicle acci-dents also occurred at a rate one-half again as high as the national rate.

The percent of the South Carolina population lacking health insurance has remained fairly constant in the 1990s, while the national rate has increased.

Health Indicators

	1990	1995	1996	1997
Infant mortality *(rate per thousand live births)*				
South Carolina	11.7	9.6	7.9	8.8
U.S.	9.2	7.6	7.3	7.1
Total deaths, age-adjusted rate *(rate per thousand population)*				
South Carolina	5.9	5.8	5.8	5.5
U.S.	5.2	5.0	4.9	4.8
Persons not covered by health insurance *(percent of population)*				
South Carolina	16.2	14.6	17.1	16.8
U.S.	13.9	15.4	15.6	16.1

Leading Causes of Death, 1996
(deaths per 100,000 population)

	Age-adjusted		Not age-adjusted	
	State	U.S.	State	U.S.
Deaths from all causes	580.6	491.6	920.7	872.5
Heart disease	156.0	134.5	273.0	276.4
Cancer	137.8	127.9	206.0	203.4
Cerebrovascular diseases	39.4	26.4	77.1	60.3
Chronic obstructive pulmonary disease	23.3	21.0	39.4	40.0
Diabetes mellitus	16.5	13.6	25.3	23.3
Pneumonia and influenza	14.5	12.8	29.8	31.6
HIV	13.7	11.1	14.4	11.7
Liver disease	7.6	7.5	9.4	9.4
Alzheimer's disease	3.8	2.7	9.3	8.1
Accidents and adverse effects	41.6	30.4	46.4	35.8
Motor vehicle accidents	24.1	16.2	24.4	16.5
Suicide	12.6	10.8	13.4	11.6
Homicide	10.4	8.5	10.2	7.9
Injury by firearm	16.7	12.9	17.0	12.8

GOVERNMENT

STATE AND LOCAL TAXES, 1995–96	State	U.S.
Per capita (dollars)	1 913	2 477
Percent of personal income	10.1	10.8

IN THE 1995–96 FISCAL YEAR, SOUTH CAROLINA'S $1,913 OF state and local taxes per capita was only 77 percent of the all-state average and tied with South Dakota for the seventh lowest in the nation. Measured as a percent of personal income, these taxes still were below the all-state average, but the gap was considerably more narrow. Local taxes were only 31 percent of the state and local total, compared to a 41 percent national average, indicating considerably above-average state-level responsibility for revenue collection.

General and selective sales taxes produced more than 50 percent of South Carolina's total state-level tax revenue, close to the all-state average of 49 percent. Revenue from the individual income tax made up 36 percent of the state's total tax revenue in 1996–97, compared to an all-state average of 33 percent, while corporate income taxes yielded between 4 and 5 percent of the state's tax revenues, compared to an all-state average of 7 percent.

State general expenditure per capita in South Carolina was just about equal to the average for all states in 1996–97, as were per capita expenditures on education. These figures are for state government spending only. Local spending on education appeared to be well below the national average, because total per-pupil expenditure in elementary and secondary schools was only 83 percent of the national average in 1995–96.

Interest on South Carolina's general debt averaged $55 per capita in 1996–97, compared to a national average of $99. The state appeared to be in sound financial shape at year end, with debt equal to $1,423 per capita, compared to $1,706 nationwide, and cash and security holdings approaching four times the size of the debt.

South Carolina's 1.3 percent share of federal funds distributed to states and their residents in fiscal 1997 was just about equal to the state's 1.4 percent share of the U.S. population. Payments under nondefense procurement contracts were above the state's population share. Other federal funds categories were roughly in line with the state's population, with Supplemental Security Income payments being a little higher and grants for nutrition and family welfare and housing and community development a little lower.

State Government Finances, 1996–97

	Millions of dollars	Percent distribu-tion	Dollars per capita	
			State	U.S.
General revenue	10 750	100.0	2 859	3 049
Intergovernmental revenue	3 162	29.4	841	863
Taxes	5 381	50.1	1 431	1 660
General sales	2 032	18.9	540	551
Selective sales	703	6.5	187	257
License taxes	411	3.8	109	106
Individual income	1 933	18.0	514	542
Corporation net income	239	2.2	64	115
Other taxes	63	0.6	17	90
Other general revenue	2 207	20.5	587	526
General expenditure	11 127	100.0	2 959	2 951
Intergovernmental expenditure	2 929	26.3	779	989
Direct expenditure	8 198	73.7	2 180	1 962
General expenditure, by function:				
Education	3 903	35.1	1 038	1 033
Public welfare	2 622	23.6	697	761
Hospitals and health	1 314	11.8	350	237
Highways	665	6.0	177	225
Police protection and corrections	589	5.3	157	137
Natural resources, parks and recreation	223	2.0	59	63
Governmental administration	316	2.8	84	107
Interest on general debt	209	1.9	55	99
Other and unallocable	1 287	11.6	342	290
Debt at end of fiscal year	5 350	NA	1 423	1 706
Cash and security holdings	20 140	NA	5 356	6 683

Federal Spending within State

	Federal funds, fiscal 1997		
	Millions of dollars	Percent distribution	Percent of U.S. total*
Total within state	18 962	100.0	1.3
Payments to individuals	11 017	58.1	1.4
Retirement and disability	6 899	36.4	1.5
Medicare	2 368	12.5	1.1
Food stamps	280	1.5	1.4
Supplemental Security Income	433	2.3	1.6
Grants	3 302	17.4	1.3
Medicaid and other health	1 686	8.9	1.5
Nutrition and family welfare	483	2.5	1.0
Education	235	1.2	1.4
Housing and community development ..	115	0.6	1.0
Salaries and wages	2 077	11.0	1.3
Defense procurement contracts	901	4.8	0.8
Non-defense procurement contracts	1 503	7.9	2.1

*State population is 1.4 percent of the U.S. total.

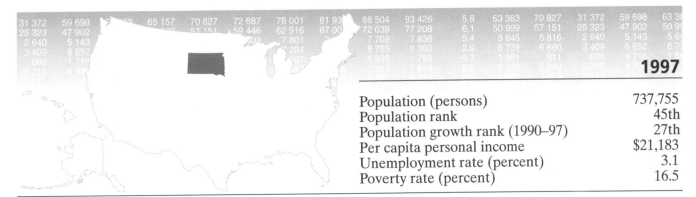

1997

Population (persons)	737,755
Population rank	45th
Population growth rank (1990–97)	27th
Per capita personal income	$21,183
Unemployment rate (percent)	3.1
Poverty rate (percent)	16.5

SOUTH DAKOTA HAS BEEN DIVERSIFYING ITS ECONOMY BY attracting a variety of services and light manufacturing industries with its low wages and pro-business tax climate. Within the services sector, employment has grown faster than in the United States during the 1990s, as firms exploit telephone technology to establish satellite offices for such various services as warranty administration (General Electric appliances), loan servicing, insurance claims, and credit cards. As one state official said, firms are realizing they do not need to be located in major metropolitan areas to be successful.

Manufacturing also is growing faster than average, because the industrial machinery industry is compensating for the lower growth in the food products industry. Farming is still a major part of the state economy, and the sector consistently has performed fairly well during the 1990s, although farm employment is on a path of slow long-term decline. Per capita income is growing faster in the state than nationwide, but it remained 16 percent below the U.S. average in 1997.

Population growth in the state has been less vigorous than job growth during the 1990s, yet the 5.9 percent population growth from 1990 to 1997 was a change from no growth during the 1980s. The 1990s rate of growth is below the national average because of a low natural rate of increase and little of foreign immigration.

Average Annual Population Growth: 1990–97

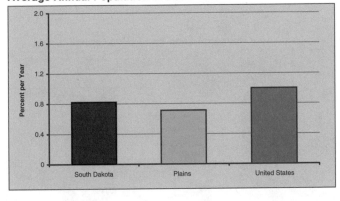

Median Household Income: 1989–97 (1997 dollars)

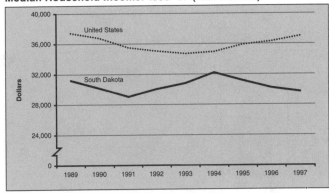

Unemployment Rate: 1989–97

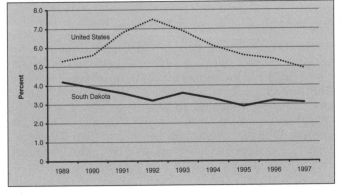

DURING THE 1990S, THE UNEMPLOYMENT RATE IN SOUTH Dakota has remained consistently below 4 percent, displaying no negative effects from the national recession early in the decade. The 1997 rate of 3.1 percent was third lowest in the nation. The state's labor force grew at an average annual rate of 1.8 percent, which is remarkable for a state with modest population growth, and household employment grew 1.9 percent annually. The state attained a ratio of employment to population that was well above average, though there was a flattening of employment and labor force growth in 1997.

POPULATION AND LABOR FORCE

THE TOTAL POPULATION OF SOUTH DAKOTA INCREASED BY 0.8 percent annually from 1990 to 1997, which is just below the national average of 1.0 percent but stronger growth than neighboring Nebraska or North Dakota. The record of the 1990s has been a substantial improvement over that of the 1980s, when the state's population hardly grew because of out-migration. The trend shifted to slight in-migration during the 1990s, combined with modest natural population growth. The state's White population is an overwhelming majority, about 90 percent, but in 1997 the White non-Hispanic population decreased for the second consecutive year, though it was still more than 30,000 higher than in 1990. The Asian and Hispanic populations showed the highest rates of growth, yet together represented less than 2 percent of the state's total population. Native Americans remained the state's leading minority with nearly 8 percent of the total population. Most of the population lives in nonmetropolitan areas, and the largest metro area, Sioux Falls, had a population of 160,000. South Dakota has the fourth lowest metro area population, as a percent of total population.

Population and Labor Force

	1980	1990	1991	1992	1993	1994	1995	1996	1997	Change*	
										State	U.S.
Population											
Total number of persons (thousands)	691	697	708	715	723	729	735	737	738	0.8	1.0
Percent distribution:											
White, Non-Hispanic	92.3	90.7	91.1	90.8	90.7	90.7	90.6	90.2	89.9	0.7	0.4
Black, Non-Hispanic	0.3	1.0	0.5	0.6	0.6	0.6	0.5	0.6	0.6	-5.3	1.4
Asian	0.3	0.5	0.5	* 0.5	0.5	0.6	0.6	0.6	0.6	3.4	4.1
Native American	6.6	7.0	7.4	* 7.5	7.5	7.5	7.5	7.7	7.9	2.5	1.6
Hispanic	0.6	0.9	0.8	0.8	0.9	0.9	1.0	1.0	1.1	2.7	3.8
In metropolitan areas	28.1	31.8	32.3	32.6	32.8	33.0	33.2	33.4	33.6	1.6	1.0
Total number of households (thousands)	243	259	260	263	265	267	270	273	NA	0.9	1.2
Labor Force (thousands)											
Population 16 and over	512	517	527	531	539	547	554	562	566	1.3	1.0
Civilian labor force	335	347	351	353	361	378	387	393	390	1.7	1.1
Employed	318	334	338	342	348	365	375	380	378	1.8	1.2
Percent of population	62.1	64.6	64.1	64.3	64.7	66.8	67.8	67.6	66.7		
Unemployment rate (percent)	4.9	3.9	3.6	3.2	3.6	3.3	2.9	3.2	3.1		

*Compound annual average percent change, 1990–1997; 1990–1996 for households.

Population Change and Components: 1990–97

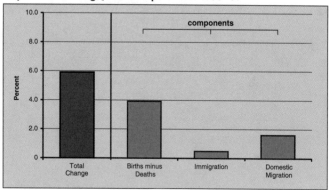

Average Annual Household and Population Growth

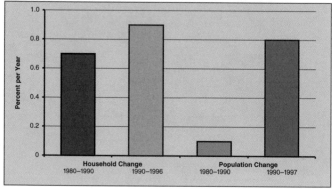

Population by Age; Births and Deaths

	1990		1997	
	State	U.S.	State	U.S.
Age distribution (percent)				
Under 5 years	7.9	7.6	6.7	7.2
5 to 17 years	20.7	18.2	20.0	18.8
18 to 64 years	56.7	61.8	59.0	61.3
65 years and over	14.7	12.5	14.3	12.7
Birth and death rates (per thousand population)				
Births	15.8	16.7	13.8	14.6
Deaths	9.1	8.6	9.5	8.6

SOUTH DAKOTA'S AGE DISTRIBUTION MOVED TOWARD THE national average between 1990 and 1997, except for the sharp decline in the proportion of children under age five. The share for school-age children also declined, but the working-age population increased as a percent of the total. The 1997 proportion of senior citizens, was high, but exceeded the U.S. average by less than in 1990. The state's birth rate dropped to 13.8 percent in 1997, while the death rate increased from 1990 to 1997.

HOUSEHOLD AND PERSONAL INCOME

HOUSEHOLD INCOME AND PERSONS IN POVERTY	1990	1995	1996	1997	
				State	U.S.
Median household income (1997 dollars)	30 173	31 150	30 203	29 694	37 005
Persons in poverty (thousands)	93	103	82	117	35 574
Poverty rate (percent)	13.3	14.5	11.8	16.5	13.3

SOUTH DAKOTA'S MEDIAN HOUSEHOLD INCOME REMAINED significantly lower than the national median throughout the 1990s, ranging from 80 to 92 percent. In 1997, the state's median income dropped for the third year in row, falling to the lowest median income since 1992. This decrease gave South Dakota the fifth lowest household income in the nation. The rate of poverty climbed quite dramatically from 11.8 in 1996 to 16.5 in 1997 giving South Dakota the eighth highest poverty rate in the nation.

With robust earnings growth and modest population growth, per capita income has moved up smartly, amounting to $21,183 in 1997, about 84 percent of the national average, a slight gain in its relative position since the early 1990s. All major components of income (earnings, transfer payments, and dividends and interest) were 13 percent to 16 percent below average on a per capita basis in 1997. A negative adjustment for residence has rapidly increased since 1989, indicating an increase in the earnings going to out-of-state residents.

From 1990 to 1997, transfer payments grew faster than personal incomes overall, but not as fast as transfer payments nationwide. The slower growth in state's transfer payments was primarily because of the slower growth in medical payments, despite South Dakota's somewhat larger older population eligible for Medicare. The highest percentages of growth have been in income maintenance. Supplemental Security Income and other income maintenance primarily earned income tax credits had the largest percent increases. Family assistance dropped considerably more than the national average, despite a substantial increase in the poverty rate from 1990 to 1997.

Personal Income
(millions of dollars)

	1980	1989	1990	1991	1992	1993	1994	1995	1996	1997	Change*
Earnings by place of work	3 696	6 704	7 524	7 911	8 590	9 027	9 782	9 775	10 889	11 175	6.6
Wages and salaries	2 819	4 646	5 052	5 403	5 853	6 229	6 667	7 113	7 489	7 932	6.9
Other labor income	244	493	565	635	716	801	868	874	858	866	7.3
Proprietors' income	633	1 564	1 906	1 873	2 022	1 997	2 247	1 788	2 542	2 377	5.4
Farm	37	596	881	775	856	765	921	408	1 095	793	3.6
Nonfarm	596	968	1 026	1 098	1 165	1 232	1 326	1 380	1 447	1 584	6.3
(−) Personal contributions for social insurance	220	479	513	552	589	624	677	727	756	804	6.7
(+) Adjustment for residence	18	-34	-50	-61	-76	-100	-127	-147	-162	-174	NA
(=) **Net earnings by state of residence**	3 494	6 191	6 961	7 299	7 926	8 303	8 978	8 901	9 972	10 197	6.4
(+) Dividends, interest, and rent	1 101	2 002	2 114	2 187	2 240	2 244	2 284	2 451	2 554	2 761	4.1
(+) Transfer payments	829	1 587	1 715	1 849	2 029	2 170	2 279	2 451	2 596	2 674	6.7
(=) **Total personal income**	5 424	9 780	10 789	11 335	12 195	12 717	13 541	13 803	15 122	15 632	6.0
Farm	115	677	968	855	934	843	1 010	503	1 201	900	3.6
Nonfarm	5 310	9 103	9 821	10 480	11 261	11 874	12 531	13 300	13 922	14 733	6.2
Personal income per capita (dollars)											
Current dollars	7 852	14 038	15 488	16 011	17 051	17 598	18 558	18 782	20 503	21 183	5.3
1997 dollars	15 013	17 747	18 638	18 488	19 073	19 149	19 722	19 524	20 879	21 183	2.2

*Compound annual average percent change, 1989–1997

Government Transfer Payments

	Millions of dollars		Percent change*	
	1990	1997	State	U.S.
Total government payments to individuals	1 644	2 564	56.0	62.7
Retirement, disability, and insurance	966	1 383	43.2	48.2
Social Security	744	1 026	38.0	46.1
Government employee retirement	202	331	64.1	60.3
Medical payments	447	823	84.1	101.2
Income maintenance	99	179	81.4	58.0
Supplemental Security Income	27	51	92.0	75.4
Family assistance	23	22	-5.5	-0.5
Food Stamps	36	38	6.4	27.1
Other income maintenance	14	69	402.8	189.8
Unemployment insurance benefits	12	17	34.6	10.6
Veterans benefits and other	119	162	35.8	30.8

*Percent change, 1990–1997

Government Payments to Individuals: 1997

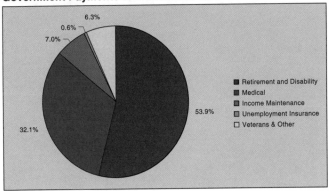

- Retirement and Disability — 53.9%
- Medical — 32.1%
- Income Maintenance — 7.0%
- Unemployment Insurance — 0.6%
- Veterans & Other — 6.3%

ECONOMIC STRUCTURE

LEADING PRIVATE INDUSTRIES, 1997 (Worker and proprietor earnings, millions of dollars)		FASTEST EARNINGS GROWTH, 1989–97 (percent increase)	
Health services	$1 193	Industrial machinery manufacturing	373.6
Farming	900	Amusement and recreation services	214.1
Industrial machinery manufacturing	508	Business services	146.5
Construction specialties	407	Social services	129.4
Banks and other credit institutions	370	Hotels and lodging	104.4

HEALTH SERVICES IS A DOMINANT INDUSTRY IN SOUTH Dakota, representing more than 10 percent of all worker earnings in the state in 1997. Tourism-related service businesses are two of the five fastest growing industries in the state, along with rapidly growing business services and social services. Clearly, services is growing strongly as a sector, yet it remains a smaller than average sector compared to the U.S. norm. Business services in particular is a relatively small industry in the state: typically, earnings in this industry are more than 6 percent of the total, while in South Dakota they equal 3 percent. Similarly, manufacturing is undergoing strong growth in the state, concentrated in industrial machinery, but this sector's contribution to state earnings is still 4 percentage points below average.

The construction sector was the second fastest growing in the state, after manufacturing, with growth in both general building and heavy construction projects. This increase followed a decade of zero net growth in construction employment from 1980 to 1989. Farming remained part of the backbone of South Dakota, with its 1997 earnings placing it as the second ranking industry. It provides 7.7 percent of the state's jobs as compared to 1.9 percent nationwide, even though there has been an absolute decline in farm employment through the past decades (over 13 percent of 1980s jobs in the state were in farming).

South Dakota has a surprisingly large number of jobs in the finance sector for a nonurban state. The credit institutions industry is growing faster than average, because of expansion of such operations as bank credit cards and loan servicing. One Minneapolis-based consumer finance company has located 1,100 jobs in Rapid City during a recent three-year period, servicing its national portfolio of mobile-home loans.

Employment and Earnings by Sector

	1980	1989	1990	1991	1992	1993	1994	1995	1996	1997 Number	1997 Percent of total	Change*
Employment (thousands of persons)												
Total	354	398	411	423	434	445	468	481	490	499	100.0	2.9
Farm	47	43	42	42	41	41	39	38	38	38	7.7	-1.4
Nonfarm	306	356	369	381	392	404	429	443	452	461	92.3	3.3
Private nonfarm	241	287	299	310	320	332	357	372	383	393	78.6	4.0
Agricultural service, forestry, and fishing	3	4	4	5	5	5	6	6	6	7	1.4	6.7
Mining	3	3	3	3	3	3	3	3	3	3	0.5	-2.2
Construction	17	17	19	19	20	21	23	23	24	25	5.0	4.7
Manufacturing	27	34	36	37	39	41	46	48	50	52	10.3	5.4
Transportation and public utilities	17	18	18	18	18	19	20	21	22	22	4.5	2.8
Wholesale trade	19	20	20	21	21	20	21	21	21	21	4.3	1.1
Retail trade	61	68	71	74	76	78	84	87	89	90	18.0	3.5
Finance, insurance, and real estate	21	26	27	27	27	28	30	32	34	36	7.2	4.2
Services	73	97	101	107	110	116	124	129	134	137	27.5	4.5
Government	65	69	70	71	72	72	72	71	69	68	13.7	-0.1
Earnings (millions of dollars)												
Total	3 696	6 704	7 524	7 911	8 590	9 027	9 782	9 775	10 889	11 175	100.0	6.6
Farm	115	677	968	855	934	843	1 010	503	1 201	900	8.0	3.6
Nonfarm	3 582	6 027	6 555	7 056	7 657	8 184	8 772	9 271	9 689	10 276	92.0	6.9
Private nonfarm	2 825	4 740	5 179	5 579	6 095	6 557	7 104	7 569	8 002	8 562	76.6	7.7
Agricultural service, forestry, and fishing	25	76	92	105	114	113	124	124	119	130	1.2	6.9
Mining	83	101	95	111	120	103	106	117	110	114	1.0	1.5
Construction	260	353	405	419	465	502	571	594	636	684	6.1	8.6
Manufacturing	435	725	796	849	955	1 048	1 205	1 308	1 403	1 536	13.7	9.8
Transportation and public utilities	331	497	508	544	574	618	648	669	696	738	6.6	5.0
Wholesale trade	322	440	465	499	532	546	581	622	655	683	6.1	5.6
Retail trade	497	729	812	869	915	990	1 047	1 094	1 137	1 203	10.8	6.5
Finance, insurance, and real estate	192	380	411	448	491	536	560	612	665	727	6.5	8.5
Services	681	1 438	1 594	1 735	1 930	2 102	2 262	2 428	2 581	2 748	24.6	8.4
Government	757	1 287	1 377	1 477	1 562	1 627	1 668	1 702	1 686	1 713	15.3	3.6

*Compound annual average percent change, 1989–1997

ECONOMIC STRUCTURE (Continued)

SOUTH DAKOTA'S AVERAGE WAGES IN EVERY SECTOR WERE below the national average, with the exception of farm wages, which were 16 percent above the U.S. average in 1997. The greatest disparity in 1997 average wages was in finance, insurance, and real estate, where the national average was $18,576 higher. Wages in the fast-growing manufacturing and services sectors remain only 69 to 70 percent of their respective U.S. averages. Overall, the state's average salary was 71.1 percent of the national average. This figure gave South Dakota the lowest average salary in the nation. The largest percent increase was in farming, which increased by nearly 50 percent between 1989 and 1997. South Dakota's average wages overall grew by a slightly greater rate than the national average.

Manufacturing has been playing an increasing role in the state's economy, thanks to phenomenal growth in industrial machinery and equipment production. New facilities have been attracted to the state from neighboring states, such as Iowa and Minnesota, by its low wage and low tax environment. South Dakota levies neither corporate income taxes nor business inventory taxes. From 1989 to1996, the state's gross state product (GSP) increased by 70.4 percent, while the value of output in manufacturing has increased 146.7 percent. In 1996, manufacturing accounted for 14.5 percent of the state's GSP, up from 10.0 percent in 1990, but a percentage still in the lowest one-half of states. The value of output per worker amounted to $59,231 in 1996, well below the national average. New capital expenditures trended slightly downward in 1996 for the second consecutive year.

South Dakota's exports to foreign markets grew by nearly 65 percent from 1994 to 1997, without adjustment for inflation, although exports remain a very limited portion of the total state economy. The state's largest exports were industrial machinery and computers. Since 1994, food products have increased by more than 400 percent, becoming South Dakota's fifth highest export, though exports of raw agricultural products are minimal. Electric and electronic equipment has also shown rapid growth from 1994 to 1997, moving from the fourth to the second leading export.

Average Annual Wages and Salaries by Sector
(dollars)

	1989	1996	1997 State	1997 U.S.
All wage and salary workers	15 617	20 345	21 185	29 809
Farm	12 896	18 449	19 051	16 442
Nonfarm	15 673	20 373	21 216	29 900
Private nonfarm	15 267	20 033	20 961	29 867
Agricultural service, forestry, and fishing	10 755	13 529	13 726	17 941
Mining	33 251	38 713	40 057	49 800
Construction	18 509	23 540	24 866	31 765
Manufacturing	18 821	25 037	26 615	38 351
Transportation and utilities	22 653	27 659	29 076	38 222
Wholesale trade	19 026	26 072	26 801	39 466
Retail trade	9 573	12 200	12 771	16 206
Finance, insurance, and real estate	19 416	25 216	26 417	44 993
Services	13 681	18 766	19 391	27 588
Government	16 985	21 824	22 338	30 062

Gross State Product and Manufacturing
(millions of dollars, except as noted)

	1989	1994	1995	1996
Gross state product, total	11 907	17 466	18 662	20 289
Manufacturing:				
Millions of dollars	1 196	1 987	2 686	2 951
Percent of total gross state product	10.0	11.4	14.4	14.5
Per worker (dollars)	35 329	43 439	55 394	59 231
New capital expenditures, manufacturing	NA	255	219	214

Exports of Goods
(millions of dollars)

	1994	1995	1996	1997
All goods	264	349	397	435
Manufactures	252	334	383	418
Agricultural and livestock products	4	7	10	8
Other commodities	7	7	5	9
Top goods exports, 1997:				
Industrial machinery and computers	96	162	145	160
Electric and electronic equipment	25	31	42	65
Scientific and measuring instruments	43	44	53	51
Primary metals	43	36	56	37
Food products	6	9	15	31

HOUSING

SINCE 1989, SOUTH DAKOTA'S HOUSING MARKETS HAVE strengthened with the positive trend in population growth, and production has increased significantly. This recovery in production hit its peak in 1994, when it reached 8.8 per 1,000 people, as compared to the national average of 6.4 per 1,000. While housing production has decreased since 1994, it remains about even with the national rate. A slowdown in the state's population growth in 1996 and 1997 has contributed to a decrease in housing production from 1996 to 1997. Sales of existing homes have also been generally strong in the 1990s; starting in 1992 they moved upward every year except 1994. In-migrants to South Dakota found housing prices low, another attraction for business relocation; the median 1997 sales price in the state's largest metro area, Sioux Falls, was $90,200, well below the Midwest average. Rates of homeownership remained slightly above the U.S. average, despite a slight drop from 1996 to 1997. The rental

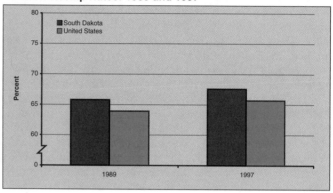

Homeownership Rates: 1989 and 1997

vacancy rate has increased substantially in 1996–97, as the population growth slowed, leading to the fourth highest rental vacancy rate in the nation in 1997.

Housing Supply

	1989	1990	1991	1992	1993	1994	1995	1996	1997
Residential building permits (thousands)	2.1	2.8	2.5	3.2	3.7	4.6	3.8	3.6	3.2
New home production (including manufactured housing):									
Thousands of homes	2.8	3.4	3.3	4.1	5.0	6.4	5.1	5.1	4.7
Rate per 1,000 population									
South Dakota	4.0	4.9	4.7	5.7	6.9	8.8	6.9	6.9	6.4
U.S.	6.2	5.2	4.5	5.1	5.6	6.4	6.3	6.6	6.5
Existing home sales:									
Thousands of homes	10.8	11.6	11.3	12.7	13.7	13.2	13.3	13.9	15.2
Change from previous year (percent)									
South Dakota	-5.3	7.4	-2.6	12.4	7.9	-3.6	0.8	4.5	9.4
U.S.	-3.9	-4.0	0.0	9.2	8.2	4.8	-3.7	7.5	3.8
Home ownership rate (percent of households)	65.8	66.2	66.1	66.5	65.6	66.4	67.5	67.8	67.6
Rental vacancy rate (percent of rental housing units)	7.1	5.3	4.5	3.1	4.3	5.3	5.9	9.9	12.6

AGRICULTURE

SOUTH DAKOTA RANKED IN THE MIDDLE OF THE NATION FOR total number of farms and averages 1,354 acres per farm, compared to the national average of 471. Though farming is an unusually large part of the state economy, the absolute size of farm marketing sales places the state 19th in the nation. Production expenses have grown at a slower rate than gross income, allowing for an increase during the 1990s in net income. In 1997, South Dakota derived roughly equal shares of its receipts from sales of crops and of livestock and livestock products. This

situation marked a considerable change from 1989, when crops accounted for only 33 percent of receipts from sales.

SOUTH DAKOTA FARMS, 1997	
Number of farms	32 500
Total acres (thousands):	44 000
Average per farm	1 354
Value of land and buildings (millions of dollars)	14 300
Average per farm (dollars)	440 000

Farm Income
(millions of dollars)

	1980	1989	1990	1991	1992	1993	1994	1995	1996	1997
Gross income	3 119	3 796	3 943	4 076	3 982	4 289	4 125	4 402	4 278	5 036
Receipts from sales	2 940	3 249	3 406	3 600	3 511	3 635	3 610	3 913	3 775	4 504
Government payments	65	340	333	286	272	432	289	245	230	268
Imputed and miscellaneous income	114	207	204	190	199	222	226	245	273	264
(–) Production expenses	2 713	3 051	3 282	3 272	3 273	3 415	3 516	3 523	3 743	3 934
(=) Realized net income	407	745	661	805	708	874	609	880	534	1 102
(+) Inventory change	-369	-110	277	8	204	-90	411	-444	673	-234
(=) Net income	37	635	937	812	912	784	1 020	435	1 208	867
Corporate income	0	39	57	37	56	19	98	27	113	74
Farm proprietors income	37	596	881	775	856	765	921	408	1 095	793

EDUCATION

EDUCATIONAL ATTAINMENT Percent of population age 25 and over, 1997	State	United States
High school graduate or higher	85.6	82.1
College graduate or higher	20.1	23.9

THE PROPORTION OF SOUTH DAKOTA RESIDENTS WITH A HIGH school diploma is higher than the national average. The state ranks 17th in the nation, with the percentage of high school graduates reaching 85.6 percent in 1997. However, the state ranks only 39th in the nation by percentage of college graduates, at just over 20 percent, because of the state's relatively small professional and technical workforce and larger than average population over age 65. South Dakota has the lowest average teacher salary in the nation. In 1997, South Dakota's teachers' salaries amounted to 70 percent of the national average. Expenditures per pupil are also significantly lower than the national average. Spending is constrained by the state's limited tax base and its conservative tax policies, thus reducing the amount of state aid to local school districts.

High School Completion: 1990–97

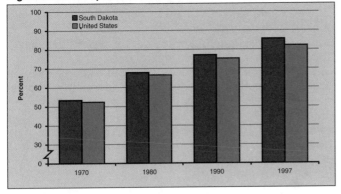

Education Indicators

	State	U.S.
Elementary and secondary schools Enrollment, 1995–96		
Total (thousands)	155	49 873
Percent in private schools	6.5	10.1
Expenditures per pupil (dollars), 1995–96	4 780	6 146
Average teacher salary (dollars), 1996–97	26 764	38 509
Higher education Enrollment, 1996–97		
Total (thousands)	35	14 218
Percent of population 18–34	20.7	21.8
Percent minority	8.8	26.1
Percent in private schools	19.2	22.6

HEALTH

GENERALLY SPEAKING, SOUTH DAKOTA RESIDENTS HAVE about average health, based on death rates, and better than average rates of coverage by health insurance. Infant mortality rates have improved over the 1990s, and, the 1997 rate of 7.6 per 1,000 live births was just above the national average and well below the state's 1995 rate of 9.5. The state's total death rate has been fairly steady since 1990 and remains somewhat below the national average. For the most part, age-adjusted death rates for major causes were below the national average. Suicide, motor vehicle, and accident death rates were significantly higher than the average U.S. rates. The percentage of people without health insurance showed as an uptick in 1997, following the national trend toward less health insurance coverage, but the state has remained in a better than average position for insurance coverage throughout the 1990s.

Health Indicators

	1990	1995	1996	1997
Infant mortality *(rate per thousand live births)*				
South Dakota	10.1	9.5	5.4	7.6
U.S.	9.2	7.6	7.3	7.1
Total deaths, age-adjusted rate *(rate per thousand population)*				
South Dakota	4.5	4.6	4.5	4.5
U.S.	5.2	5.0	4.9	4.8
Persons not covered by health insurance *(percent of population)*				
South Dakota	11.6	9.4	9.5	11.8
U.S.	13.9	15.4	15.6	16.1

Leading Causes of Death, 1996
(deaths per 100,000 population)

	Age-adjusted		Not age-adjusted	
	State	U.S.	State	U.S.
Deaths from all causes	449.8	491.6	928.0	872.5
Heart disease	123.8	134.5	300.0	276.4
Cancer	119.5	127.9	210.4	203.4
Cerebrovascular diseases	22.6	26.4	65.9	60.3
Chronic obstructive pulmonary disease	17.4	21.0	40.1	40.0
Diabetes mellitus	12.4	13.6	24.4	23.3
Pneumonia and influenza	12.5	12.8	38.9	31.6
HIV	NA	11.1	NA	11.7
Liver disease	7.2	7.5	8.7	9.4
Alzheimer's disease	2.7	2.7	10.6	8.1
Accidents and adverse effects	38.2	30.4	46.7	35.8
Motor vehicle accidents	22.1	16.2	23.5	16.5
Suicide	16.4	10.8	16.9	11.6
Homicide	NA	8.5	NA	7.9
Injury by firearm	10.9	12.9	11.3	12.8

GOVERNMENT

STATE AND LOCAL TAXES, 1995–96	State	U.S.
Per capita (dollars)	1 913	2 477
Percent of personal income	9.8	10.8

IN 1995–96, TOTAL PER CAPITA STATE AND LOCAL TAXES (except corporate) in South Dakota amounted to $1,913, significantly lower than the national average. These taxes represented just 9.8 percent of personal income, also well below the national rate of 10.8 percent. Local taxes account for more than 50 percent of these taxes, well above the 40.8 percent nationwide.

South Dakota's 1997 state government per capita gen-eral revenue was 15 percent less than the average state's per capita revenue, and tax revenues alone were even further below average, at 63 percent of the national norm. The state derives about an average amount of revenue from general sales taxes, selective sales taxes, and license taxes. It has no individual income tax and limited corporate income taxes. The state's per capita expenditures are also lower than average. Education spending at the state level is especially low, 76 percent as high as average states, as are state transfers of funds to local government school and other programs. The two main exceptions were highway and natural resources and parks and recreation expenditures, which are higher. South Dakota's 1997 debt was $800 higher per capita than the U.S. fiscal year debt, which has resulted in a significantly higher per capita expenditure on interest on general debt.

Total federal expenditures in South Dakota were in proportion to the state's 0.3 percent of the U.S. population. The state receives a greater share of education grants, housing and community development grants, and total grants. Both Medicaid grants and Medicare payments are 0.2 percent of the U.S. total. In defense and other procurement, South Dakota received a less than proportional share of the U.S. total.

State Government Finances, 1996–97

	Millions of dollars	Percent distribu-tion	Dollars per capita	
			State	U.S.
General revenue	1 920	100.0	2 602	3 049
Intergovernmental revenue	673	35.1	912	863
Taxes	768	40.0	1 041	1 660
General sales	411	21.4	557	551
Selective sales	198	10.3	269	257
License taxes	94	4.9	127	106
Individual income	0	0.0	0	542
Corporation net income	37	1.9	50	115
Other taxes	29	1.5	39	90
Other general revenue	479	24.9	649	526
General expenditure	1 947	100.0	2 639	2 951
Intergovernmental expenditure	435	22.4	590	989
Direct expenditure	1 512	77.6	2 049	1 962
General expenditure, by function:				
Education	581	29.9	788	1 033
Public welfare	389	20.0	527	761
Hospitals and health	99	5.1	134	237
Highways	282	14.5	382	225
Police protection and corrections	76	3.9	103	137
Natural resources, parks and recreation	102	5.2	138	63
Governmental administration	82	4.2	111	107
Interest on general debt	117	6.0	158	99
Other and unallocable	219	11.2	297	290
Debt at end of fiscal year	1 841	NA	2 494	1 706
Cash and security holdings	5 697	NA	7 719	6 683

Federal Spending within State

	Federal funds, fiscal 1997		
	Millions of dollars	Percent distribution	Percent of U.S. total*
Total within state	4 216	100.0	0.3
Payments to individuals	2 083	49.4	0.3
Retirement and disability	1 308	31.0	0.3
Medicare	457	10.8	0.2
Food stamps	39	0.9	0.2
Supplemental Security Income	52	1.2	0.2
Grants	1 097	26.0	0.4
Medicaid and other health	267	6.3	0.2
Nutrition and family welfare	130	3.1	0.3
Education	87	2.1	0.5
Housing and community development ..	50	1.2	0.4
Salaries and wages	511	12.1	0.3
Defense procurement contracts	87	2.1	0.1
Non-defense procurement contracts	166	3.9	0.2

*State population is 0.3 percent of the U.S. total.

31 372	59 698		65 157	70 827	72 687	78 001	81 93	88 504	93 426	5.8	63 383	70 827	31 372	59 698	63 38
25 323	47 902		57 151	59 446	62 916	67 00		72 039	77 208	6.1	50 999	57 151	25 323	47 902	50 99
2 640	5 143			7 801			7 709	7 838	5.4	5 645	6 816	2 640	5 143	5 6
3 409	6 652			284			8 755	8 380	2.9	6 739	6 860	3 409	6 652	6 7
693	1 716			07			1 539	762	-9.7	1 561	811	693	1 716	1 5
							7 217	7 616	5.6	5 178	6 049	2 716		

1997

Population (persons)	5,371,693
Population rank	17th
Population growth rank (1990–97)	16th
Per capita personal income	$22,752
Unemployment rate (percent)	5.4
Poverty rate (percent)	14.3

THE YEARS 1992 THROUGH 1994 WERE BOOM TIMES FOR Tennessee. Employment rose more than 10 percent from 1991 to 1994, and the unemployment rate fell almost two percentage points. Household and personal incomes gained on the national averages, and workers were drawn to Tennessee from other states. Population growth generated rapid increases in home construction.

Economic growth continued from 1995 through 1997, but at a more moderate pace. Motor vehicle and equipment manufacturing emerged during the 1990s as Tennessee's largest manufacturing industry. Tennessee's manufacturing is diverse, however, with at least a dozen important manufacturing industries. Over 16 percent of

workers were employed in manufacturing in 1997, compared to 12.4 percent nationwide. Even so, Tennessee's economy, like the nation's, is predominately a service economy, with health services, business services, and amusement and recreation services among the large and rapidly growing industries of the 1990s.

Despite the gains of the 1990s, Tennessee is not yet a wealthy state. Per capita incomes were 90 percent of the national average, and the 1997 poverty rate still was above the U.S. average. Achievements in health and education have been impressive, but the percentage of adults who had completed high school still was the third lowest in the nation in 1997, and the infant mortality rate still was high.

Average Annual Population Growth: 1990–97

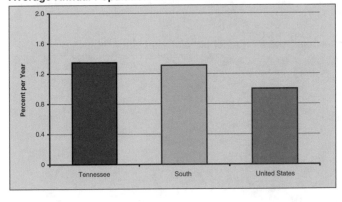

Median Household Income: 1989–97 (1997 dollars)

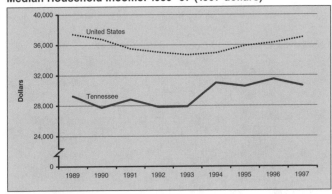

Unemployment Rate: 1989–97

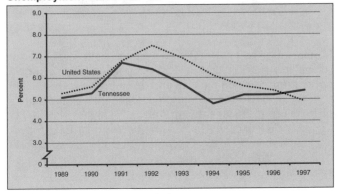

TENNESSEE'S UNEMPLOYMENT RATE WAS SLIGHTLY BELOW THE national average in 1990 and rose less than the nation's through 1992. Strong job growth from 1992 to 1994 then brought the state's unemployment rate down sooner and more rapidly than the nation's. From 1995 to 1997, however, Tennessee's expansion slowed, and the state's unemployment rate crept up while the national rate continued to decline. Similarly, the percentage of the adult population holding jobs rose rapidly from 1992 to 1994, then fell back somewhat in 1995 through 1997.

POPULATION AND LABOR FORCE

THE NEARLY 10 PERCENT GROWTH OF TENNESSEE'S POPULA-
tion from 1990 to 1997 exceeded the U.S. average and was
a considerable pick-up from the 1980s. The White, non-
Hispanic population grew almost three times as rapidly as
the national average, and, although other population
groups grew even faster, non-Hispanic Whites still were
more than 80 percent of the population in 1997. Non-
Hispanic Blacks were 16 percent, and other minority
groups were quite small percentages.

Slightly over one-half of Tennessee's 1997 population
lived in the three major metropolitan areas of Nashville,
Memphis, and Knoxville. Nashville has continued its rapid

population growth during the 1990s, reaching a population
of 1.1 million in 1997. Knoxville also has grown rapidly, but
growth in the Tennessee portion of the Memphis metropolitan area has been below the average for the state.
Altogether, 68 percent of the population lived in metropolitan areas in 1997, compared to 80 percent nationwide.

Tennessee's strong economy has encouraged migration
from other states, and this domestic in-migration accounted for almost two-thirds of population growth from 1990
to 1997. Natural increase (births minus deaths) provided
about one-third of population growth and immigration
from abroad only a small amount.

Population and Labor Force

	1980	1990	1991	1992	1993	1994	1995	1996	1997	Change* State	Change* U.S.
Population											
Total number of persons (thousands)	4 591	4 891	4 946	5 012	5 082	5 158	5 235	5 307	5 372	1.3	1.0
Percent distribution:											
White, Non-Hispanic	83.1	82.6	82.4	82.3	82.1	81.9	81.8	81.6	81.5	1.1	0.4
Black, Non-Hispanic	15.6	15.7	16.0	16.1	16.2	16.3	16.3	16.3	16.4	1.9	1.4
Asian	0.3	0.7	0.7	0.7	0.8	0.8	0.9	0.9	0.9	5.4	4.1
Native American	0.2	0.2	0.2	0.2	0.2	0.2	0.2	0.2	0.2	1.6	1.6
Hispanic	0.7	0.8	0.7	0.7	0.8	0.8	0.9	1.0	1.1	5.0	3.8
In metropolitan areas	66.6	67.9	67.9	68.0	68.0	68.0	68.0	68.0	67.9	1.3	1.0
Total number of households (thousands)	1 619	1 854	1 887	1 921	1 941	1 965	2 002	2 041	NA	1.6	1.2
Labor Force (thousands)											
Population 16 and over	3 462	3 810	3 856	3 901	3 952	4 011	4 076	4 143	4 198	1.4	1.0
Civilian labor force	2 080	2 387	2 421	2 455	2 500	2 665	2 701	2 744	2 708	1.8	1.1
Employed	1 928	2 261	2 258	2 298	2 357	2 537	2 561	2 603	2 562	1.8	1.2
Percent of population	55.7	59.4	58.6	58.9	59.6	63.3	62.8	62.8	61.0		
Unemployment rate (percent)	7.3	5.3	6.7	6.4	5.7	4.8	5.2	5.2	5.4		

*Compound annual average percent change, 1990–1997; 1990–1996 for households.

Population Change and Components: 1990–97

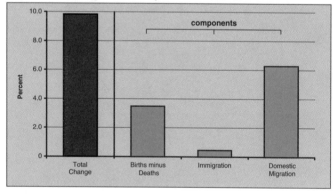

Average Annual Household and Population Growth

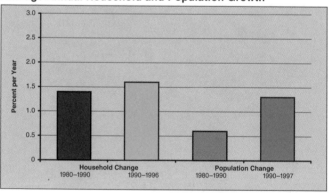

Population by Age; Births and Deaths

	1990 State	1990 U.S.	1997 State	1997 U.S.
Age distribution (percent)				
Under 5 years	6.9	7.6	6.7	7.2
5 to 17 years	18.0	18.2	17.9	18.8
18 to 64 years	62.4	61.8	62.8	61.3
65 years and over	12.7	12.5	12.5	12.7
Birth and death rates (per thousand population)				
Births	15.4	16.7	13.9	14.6
Deaths	9.5	8.6	9.8	8.6

MIGRATION INTO TENNESSEE OF WORKERS ATTRACTED BY THE
strong job market caused the proportion of the state's
population between ages 18 and 64 to increase from 1990
to 1997, in contrast to a national decline. Thus, the state's
proportion in this age group—already higher than average in 1990—exceeded the national average by 1.5 percentage points by 1997. The proportion under age 18 was
well below the national average, and the proportion over
age 64 was a little below.

HOUSEHOLD AND PERSONAL INCOME

HOUSEHOLD INCOME AND PERSONS IN POVERTY	1990	1995	1996	1997	
				State	U.S.
Median household income (1997 dollars)	27 743	30 557	31 496	30 636	37 005
Persons in poverty (thousands)	833	846	878	791	35 574
Poverty rate (percent)	16.9	15.5	15.9	14.3	13.3

FROM 1989 TO 1996–97, TENNESSEE HAD A GAIN IN INFLA-tion-adjusted median household income of more than 6 percent. With no gain in the U.S. average over these years, Tennessee incomes rose from 78 percent of the national average in 1989 to 85 percent in 1996–97, with most of the gain achieved during the state's 1992–94 economic expansion. Real personal income per capita also benefited from the 1992–94 growth spurt, rising from 87 percent of the national average in 1991 to 91 percent in 1994 and remaining between 90 or 92 percent during the next three years. The state's poverty rate has declined during the 1990s, bringing it closer to the U.S. average.

Earnings provided 68 percent of Tennessee resident's personal income in 1997, compared to only 66 percent nationwide. The negative "adjustment for residence," which measures the net amount earned by residents of other states from working in Tennessee, was 1 percent of all earnings by place of work. Dividends, interest, and rent were 14 percent of personal income, compared to 17 percent nationwide, and transfer payments were 18 percent, compared to 16 percent nationwide.

Government transfer payments rose 73 percent from 1990 to 1997, compared to a U.S. average of 63 percent. "Other income maintenance," a category consisting largely of the earned income tax credit, was the most rapidly growing transfer program both in Tennessee and in the nation. Medical payments also showed a large rise, but, in contrast, food stamp payments rose only 18 percent in the state, and family assistance payments, which were about level for the nation as a whole, declined by 30 percent in Tennessee.

Personal Income
(millions of dollars)

	1980	1989	1990	1991	1992	1993	1994	1995	1996	1997	Change*
Earnings by place of work	28 823	56 055	59 238	61 895	67 959	72 770	77 870	82 291	85 163	90 447	6.2
Wages and salaries	23 261	44 791	47 303	49 187	53 291	56 446	60 549	64 635	67 652	72 266	6.2
Other labor income	2 271	4 872	5 384	5 869	6 613	7 405	7 932	7 973	7 541	7 661	5.8
Proprietors' income	3 292	6 392	6 552	6 840	8 054	8 919	9 388	9 682	9 970	10 520	6.4
Farm	135	246	215	280	389	321	387	186	99	173	-4.3
Nonfarm	3 157	6 146	6 337	6 560	7 665	8 598	9 001	9 497	9 871	10 347	6.7
(–) Personal contributions for social insurance	1 504	3 559	3 770	4 011	4 289	4 607	5 019	5 363	5 542	5 896	6.5
(+) Adjustment for residence	-469	-697	-731	-723	-643	-775	-858	-924	-894	-989	NA
(=) Net earnings by state of residence	26 851	51 799	54 737	57 162	63 027	67 388	71 993	76 004	78 728	83 562	6.2
(+) Dividends, interest, and rent	4 883	11 746	12 289	12 357	12 255	12 405	13 384	14 675	16 035	16 663	4.5
(+) Transfer payments	5 733	11 400	12 736	14 442	16 223	17 480	18 237	19 883	20 981	21 911	8.5
(=) Total personal income	37 467	74 944	79 761	83 960	91 505	97 273	103 614	110 562	115 744	122 136	6.3
Farm	239	360	345	403	506	450	511	313	231	305	-2.1
Nonfarm	37 228	74 584	79 416	83 557	90 999	96 824	103 103	110 249	115 513	121 831	6.3
Personal income per capita (dollars)											
Current dollars	8 145	15 438	16 309	16 976	18 255	19 139	20 088	21 118	21 808	22 752	5.0
1997 dollars	15 574	19 517	19 626	19 603	20 419	20 826	21 348	21 952	22 208	22 752	1.9

*Compound annual average percent change, 1989–1997

Government Transfer Payments

	Millions of dollars		Percent change*	
	1990	1997	State	U.S.
Total government payments to individuals	12 167	21 087	73.3	62.7
Retirement, disability, and insurance	6 383	9 792	53.4	48.2
Social Security	4 788	7 383	54.2	46.1
Government employee retirement	1 352	2 144	58.6	60.3
Medical payments	3 836	8 364	118.0	101.2
Income maintenance	1 121	1 853	65.3	58.0
Supplemental Security Income	385	659	71.4	75.4
Family assistance	183	127	-30.3	-0.5
Food Stamps	390	459	17.8	27.1
Other income maintenance	164	607	270.6	189.8
Unemployment insurance benefits	277	339	22.2	10.6
Veterans benefits and other	550	740	34.6	30.8

*Percent change, 1990–1997

Government Payments to Individuals: 1997

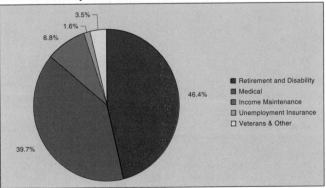

- Retirement and Disability
- Medical
- Income Maintenance
- Unemployment Insurance
- Veterans & Other

ECONOMIC STRUCTURE

LEADING PRIVATE INDUSTRIES, 1997 (Worker and proprietor earnings, millions of dollars)		FASTEST EARNINGS GROWTH, 1989–97 (percent increase)	
Health services	$9 097	Motor vehicles and equipment	166.9
Business services	4 427	Real estate	161.4
Construction specialties	3 582	Amusement and recreation services	134.7
Engineering and management services	3 206	Business services	124.7
Trucking and warehousing	2 440	Engineering and management services	106.3

TENNESSEE'S DIVERSIFIED MANUFACTURING SECTOR PROVIDED jobs for 16.2 percent of the state's workers in 1997, compared with a 12.4 percent U.S. average. Even so, Tennessee's economy, like the nation's, is a predominantly service economy. Service-producing sectors provided three-quarters of all nonfarm jobs in 1997. Four of the five largest industries, as measured by worker and proprietor earnings, were service-producing industries, as were four of the five fastest growing.

Although motor vehicle and equipment manufacturing was the state's most rapidly growing industry from 1989 to 1997, housing demands created by population and employment growth helped make real estate a close second. Attractions such as Nashville's Opryland U.S.A. contributed to the growth of amusement and recreation services, making it the third most rapidly growing industry. Ranking fourth and fifth in growth were business services

and engineering and management services (another group of services provided primarily to businesses). These already were large industries in 1989, but together they provided about $4 billion more in worker and proprietor earnings in 1997 than in the earlier year. Largest of all in 1997 was the health services industry. It, too, has grown much faster than the all-industry average, generating about $4 billion more in earnings in 1997 than it did in 1989.

Farm employment declined 11 percent from 1980 to 1990 and a further 14 percent from 1990 to 1997, providing only 2.9 percent of all jobs in the latter year. But this still was higher than the 1.9 percent farm share of total U.S. employment. Farm earnings fluctuate from year to year, but even in 1994—the peak year for the 1990s—they made up only 0.7 percent of total earnings of Tennessee workers and proprietors, and, in 1997, the share was only 0.3 percent.

Employment and Earnings by Sector

	1980	1989	1990	1991	1992	1993	1994	1995	1996	1997 Number	1997 Percent of total	Change*
Employment (thousands of persons)												
Total	2 264	2 754	2 790	2 797	2 862	2 957	3 080	3 176	3 221	3 288	100.0	2.2
Farm	125	113	111	106	109	102	97	97	94	96	2.9	-1.9
Nonfarm	2 139	2 642	2 679	2 691	2 753	2 855	2 982	3 079	3 127	3 192	97.1	2.4
Private nonfarm	1 772	2 265	2 293	2 302	2 364	2 462	2 582	2 679	2 723	2 793	84.9	2.7
Agricultural service, forestry, and fishing	11	18	20	22	21	24	26	28	29	30	0.9	6.5
Mining	11	9	9	8	7	7	7	7	7	7	0.2	-4.3
Construction	112	153	148	143	149	159	168	181	187	193	5.9	3.0
Manufacturing	513	535	530	516	527	542	554	553	534	531	16.2	-0.1
Transportation and public utilities	100	134	136	138	139	147	156	160	168	177	5.4	3.6
Wholesale trade	116	138	138	139	142	141	146	151	152	156	4.7	1.6
Retail trade	334	453	461	460	473	491	514	537	549	563	17.1	2.8
Finance, insurance, and real estate	154	167	165	162	160	163	196	204	213	221	6.7	3.6
Services	420	658	685	715	746	786	816	858	884	914	27.8	4.2
Government	368	377	387	388	389	393	400	400	405	399	12.1	0.7
Earnings (millions of dollars)												
Total	28 823	56 055	59 238	61 895	67 959	72 770	77 870	82 291	85 163	90 447	100.0	6.2
Farm	239	360	345	403	506	450	511	313	231	305	0.3	-2.1
Nonfarm	28 585	55 695	58 893	61 492	67 453	72 320	77 359	81 977	84 932	90 143	99.7	6.2
Private nonfarm	23 784	47 482	50 007	52 284	57 973	62 257	66 541	70 804	73 435	78 489	86.8	6.5
Agricultural service, forestry, and fishing	86	224	259	275	298	316	355	384	395	423	0.5	8.3
Mining	388	280	289	273	262	270	245	252	263	290	0.3	0.5
Construction	1 687	3 447	3 393	3 306	3 666	4 093	4 553	5 010	5 321	5 731	6.3	6.6
Manufacturing	8 248	14 076	14 562	14 995	16 555	17 668	18 685	18 959	18 849	19 567	21.6	4.2
Transportation and public utilities	2 005	4 019	4 283	4 558	4 879	5 260	5 613	5 969	6 225	6 809	7.5	6.8
Wholesale trade	2 074	3 746	3 971	4 160	4 454	4 631	4 948	5 272	5 480	5 888	6.5	5.8
Retail trade	3 044	5 830	6 045	6 330	6 987	7 444	8 078	8 621	9 063	9 633	10.6	6.5
Finance, insurance, and real estate	1 390	2 880	2 992	3 176	3 619	4 034	4 231	4 621	5 112	5 604	6.2	8.7
Services	4 862	12 981	14 211	15 212	17 252	18 540	19 834	21 715	22 725	24 543	27.1	8.3
Government	4 800	8 212	8 887	9 208	9 480	10 064	10 818	11 174	11 497	11 654	12.9	4.5

*Compound annual average percent change, 1989–1997

ECONOMIC STRUCTURE (Continued)

THE $26,758 AVERAGE ANNUAL WAGE OR SALARY EARNED BY Tennessee workers in 1997 was 90 percent of the U.S. average, and, among the 12 states in the Southeast, was topped only in Virginia and Georgia. In manufacturing, however, despite the importance of the relatively high-paying motor vehicle industry, workers' earnings were only 85 percent of the U.S. average, helping to explain the state's success in attracting manufacturing jobs. Wages and salaries in Tennessee's retail trade sector were 99 percent of the national average; retail trade, however, paid the lowest wages and salaries of any nonfarm sector, both in the state and nationwide. The state's farm wages were by far the lowest of any sector and were the farthest below national norms, at only 57 percent of the U.S. average.

Manufacturing held at 24 to 25 percent of Tennessee's Gross State Product from 1989 through 1994, but the share declined somewhat in 1995 and 1996. Employment in manufacturing also declined from 1994 to 1996. Within Tennessee's well-diversified manufacturing sector, there has been some shift toward higher-value, better-paying industries during the 1990s. Measured by worker and proprietor earnings, motor vehicle and equipment manufacture was the state's most rapidly growing industry from 1989 to 1997, and had become its largest manufacturing industry by 1997. Chemical products was close behind in size, though more slowly growing. In contrast, the poorly-paying apparel industry declined sharply during the 1990s and, by 1997, ranked behind at least 9 other manufacturing industries.

Chemical products and transportation equipment (largely motor vehicles and parts) are Tennessee's leading goods exports, virtually tied for first place in 1997. Agricultural exports also are important, but have fluctuated widely from year to year. Industrial machinery and computers, electronic and electrical equipment, and paper products also are major export categories, and the first two exhibited above average growth from 1994 to 1997. Overall, Tennessee's exports of manufactured goods grew 37 percent from 1994 to 1997, fully equal to the strong national average of 36 percent.

Exports to the Americas—Canada, Mexico, and South and Central America—made up 45 percent of Tennessee's 1997 export total. Exports to Mexico grew 58 percent from 1994 to 1997, with transportation equipment and electronic and electrical equipment accounting for most of the increase. Exports to South and Central American grew 82 percent.

Average Annual Wages and Salaries by Sector
(dollars)

	1989	1996	1997 State	1997 U.S.
All wage and salary workers	19 547	25 563	26 758	29 809
Farm	6 966	11 803	9 423	16 442
Nonfarm	19 632	25 619	26 843	29 900
Private nonfarm	19 583	25 622	26 935	29 867
Agricultural service, forestry, and fishing	11 982	15 788	16 616	17 941
Mining	28 281	37 387	43 690	49 800
Construction	21 256	27 267	29 256	31 765
Manufacturing	22 991	31 015	32 533	38 351
Transportation and utilities	26 908	33 002	34 710	38 222
Wholesale trade	25 036	33 464	34 999	39 466
Retail trade	11 612	15 369	16 036	16 206
Finance, insurance, and real estate	23 904	34 165	36 390	44 993
Services	17 984	23 774	25 015	27 588
Government	19 879	25 600	26 315	30 062

Gross State Product and Manufacturing
(millions of dollars, except as noted)

	1989	1994	1995	1996
Gross state product, total	91 646	127 852	134 873	140 750
Manufacturing:				
Millions of dollars	23 245	31 124	31 720	32 244
Percent of total gross state product	25.4	24.3	23.5	22.9
Per worker (dollars)	43 481	56 175	57 341	60 400
New capital expenditures, manufacturing	NA	3 010	2 986	3 353

Exports of Goods
(millions of dollars)

	1994	1995	1996	1997
All goods	7 506	9 461	9 328	9 917
Manufactures	6 104	6 974	7 298	8 358
Agricultural and livestock products	1 227	2 314	1 852	1 294
Other commodities	176	172	178	265
Top goods exports, 1997:				
Chemical products	1 318	1 453	1 363	1 503
Transportation equipment	1 110	1 175	1 296	1 494
Agricultural products	1 225	2 314	1 850	1 293
Industrial machinery and computers	724	879	992	1 095
Paper products	760	971	898	995

HOUSING

Tennessee's rate of new home production followed the national pattern of recessionary slowdown in 1990 and 1991 and recovery beginning in 1992. Tennessee's recovery was particularly strong from 1991 to 1994, reflecting the state's strong overall economic growth. From 1994 to 1997, new home production leveled off, but at a rate nearly half again as high as the national average. Sales of existing homes followed a similar pattern of strong increase from 1991 to 1994 and more moderate gains thereafter; for the entire 1989–1997 period, sales rose twice as fast in the state as they did nationwide.

The homeownership rate dipped in 1993 and 1994 and the rental vacancy rate was very low, a combination of factors consistent with a high rate of population in-migration during those years. As these new residents found homes of their own, the rental vacancy rate and the homeownership rate both rose from 1995 through 1997.

The median sales price of existing homes in the rapidly-growing Nashville metropolitan area was $115,200 in

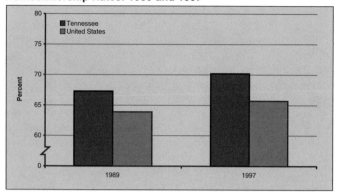

Homeownership Rates: 1989 and 1997

1997, not far below the national average of $124,100. Prices in the state's other large metropolitan areas were lower, $103,700 in Memphis, $99,000 in Knoxville and $92,200 in Chattanooga.

Housing Supply

	1989	1990	1991	1992	1993	1994	1995	1996	1997
Residential building permits (thousands)	24.2	20.2	19.3	23.3	27.0	31.9	35.1	40.5	34.1
New home production (including manufactured housing):									
Thousands of homes	31.9	27.7	26.9	34.1	39.0	46.2	49.9	55.9	50.5
Rate per 1,000 population									
Tennessee	6.6	5.7	5.4	6.8	7.7	9.0	9.5	10.5	9.4
U.S.	6.2	5.2	4.5	5.1	5.6	6.4	6.3	6.6	6.5
Existing home sales:									
Thousands of homes	95.2	92.7	92.0	102.2	120.5	129.8	133.6	142.9	149.9
Change from previous year (percent)									
Tennessee	1.4	-2.6	-0.8	11.1	17.9	7.7	2.9	7.0	4.9
U.S.	-3.9	-4.0	0.0	9.2	8.2	4.8	-3.7	7.5	3.8
Home ownership rate (percent of households)	67.3	68.3	68.0	67.4	64.1	65.2	67.0	68.8	70.2
Rental vacancy rate (percent of rental housing units)	9.1	9.5	8.5	6.0	4.6	4.6	5.4	5.4	7.2

AGRICULTURE

Tennessee, has many small farms; average farm size is only one-third the national average. Farming was the principal occupation for only 36 percent of Tennessee's farmers in 1997, compared to 50 percent nationwide.

Tennessee agriculture is relatively evenly divided between crops and livestock. Leading products, in 1997 included cattle and calves (20 percent of sales), poultry and poultry products (14 percent), soybeans (11 percent), and cotton (10 percent). The number of farms selling cotton fell 46 percent from 1992 to 1997, a pattern similar to

TENNESSEE FARMS, 1997	
Number of farms	80 000
Total acres (thousands):	11 800
Average per farm	148
Value of land and buildings (millions of dollars)	19 470
Average per farm (dollars)	243 375

that of other southern cotton-growing states.

Net farm income during 1995–1997 was less than one-half the average of the previous three years.

Farm Income
(millions of dollars)

	1980	1989	1990	1991	1992	1993	1994	1995	1996	1997
Gross income	2 233	2 513	2 441	2 266	2 525	2 625	2 628	2 571	2 845	2 718
Receipts from sales	1 923	2 000	2 058	1 897	2 106	2 151	2 223	2 201	2 414	2 293
Government payments	19	141	91	70	116	161	96	47	80	76
Imputed and miscellaneous income	292	372	292	299	303	313	309	323	350	349
(–) Production expenses	1 996	2 191	2 165	2 168	2 238	2 297	2 313	2 435	2 559	2 583
(=) Realized net income	236	322	276	97	288	328	315	136	285	135
(+) Inventory change	-102	-67	-53	191	117	-2	98	57	-180	48
(=) Net income	135	255	223	288	405	326	413	193	105	183
Corporate income	0	9	8	8	16	5	26	8	6	10
Farm proprietors income	135	246	215	280	389	321	387	186	99	173

EDUCATION

EDUCATIONAL ATTAINMENT Percent of population age 25 and over, 1997	State	United States
High school graduate or higher	76.1	82.1
College graduate or higher	17.1	23.9

THE PERCENT OF TENNESSEE RESIDENTS AGE 25 AND OVER who had completed high school rose from 41.8 percent in 1970 to 67.1 percent in 1990 and 76.1 percent in 1997. Despite these gains, the state's 1997 high school attainment rate was the third lowest of any state. The state's college completion rate doubled from 1970 to 1990, but has risen only slightly since.

Elementary and secondary school expenditures per pupil in 1995–96 were 74 percent of the national average; among southern states, only Mississippi was lower. Teachers' salaries, at 88 percent of the national average, compared favorably with a number of southern states, however.

The percent of the population age 18 to 34 enrolled in higher education was a little below the national average in 1997, and the percent attending private schools was close to the national figure. The minority share of higher education enrollment was roughly equal to the minority share of Tennessee's total population.

High School Completion: 1990–97

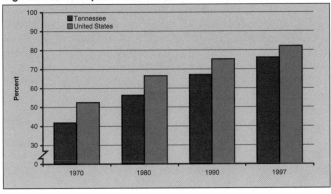

Education Indicators

	State	U.S.
Elementary and secondary schools		
Enrollment, 1995–96		
Total (thousands)	974	49 873
Percent in private schools	8.3	10.1
Expenditures per pupil (dollars), 1995–96	4 548	6 146
Average teacher salary (dollars), 1996–97	33 789	38 509
Higher education		
Enrollment, 1996–97		
Total (thousands)	247	14 218
Percent of population 18–34	18.8	21.8
Percent minority	18.2	26.1
Percent in private schools	21.4	22.6

HEALTH

TENNESSEE'S INNOVATIVE TENNCARE PROGRAM, INTRODUCED in 1994, places its Medicaid-eligible population in managed care programs, and extends health benefit coverage to large numbers of additional individuals who have been denied private health insurance because of chronic health conditions or who are unable to afford private health insurance. The program now covers about 1.2 million people, or more than 20 percent of Tennessee's population.

The program can cite many positive achievements, but has proved more costly than expected, and cost-saving modifications are presently under discussion.

Tennessee has reduced its infant mortality rate from 10.3 per thousand live births in 1990 to 8.4 in 1996 and 1997. As might be expected, given the Tenncare program, the percent of the population lacking health insurance is below the national average.

Health Indicators

	1990	1995	1996	1997
Infant mortality				
(rate per thousand live births)				
Tennessee	10.3	9.3	8.4	8.4
U.S.	9.2	7.6	7.3	7.1
Total deaths, age-adjusted rate				
(rate per thousand population)				
Tennessee	5.7	5.7	5.6	5.6
U.S.	5.2	5.0	4.9	4.8
Persons not covered by health insurance				
(percent of population)				
Tennessee	13.7	14.8	15.2	13.6
U.S.	13.9	15.4	15.6	16.1

Leading Causes of Death, 1996
(deaths per 100,000 population)

	Age-adjusted		Not age-adjusted	
	State	U.S.	State	U.S.
Deaths from all causes	559.4	491.6	966.6	872.5
Heart disease	155.6	134.5	305.3	276.4
Cancer	139.3	127.9	218.4	203.4
Cerebrovascular diseases	34.4	26.4	75.4	60.3
Chronic obstructive pulmonary disease	24.3	21.0	43.2	40.0
Diabetes mellitus	13.9	13.6	23.5	23.3
Pneumonia and influenza	14.7	12.8	34.6	31.6
HIV	7.0	11.1	7.3	11.7
Liver disease	7.6	7.5	9.7	9.4
Alzheimer's disease	3.0	2.7	8.5	8.1
Accidents and adverse effects	42.9	30.4	49.6	35.8
Motor vehicle accidents	24.2	16.2	24.6	16.5
Suicide	12.0	10.8	13.0	11.6
Homicide	10.5	8.5	10.1	7.9
Injury by firearm	17.9	12.9	18.1	12.8

GOVERNMENT

STATE AND LOCAL TAXES, 1995–96	State	U.S.
Per capita (dollars)	1 778	2 477
Percent of personal income	8.6	10.8

IN THE 1995–96 FISCAL YEAR, TENNESSEE'S $1,778 PER CAPI-ta state and local taxes (excluding corporate income taxes) were the second lowest in the nation and only 72 percent of the all-state average. Measured as a percent of personal income, taxes still were below the all-state average, measuring only 8.6 percent of the state's personal income, compared to 10.8 percent nationwide. Local taxes were 40 percent of the state and local total, about equal to the 41 percent national average.

Tennessee relies heavily on sales taxes. General and selective sales taxes produced over three-quarters of all state-level tax revenue in fiscal year 1996–97, and their per capita dollar yield was 17 percent above the U.S. average, despite the state's below average incomes. License taxes provided an unusually high 11 percent. Corporate income taxes yielded 7 percent of the total, just equal to the national average, but the individual income tax produced only $24 per capita, compared with a national average of $542.

Total state-level general expenditure per capita in was 84 percent of the all-state average in 1996–97, as was spending on education. Local spending on education also would appear to be well below the national average, since total per-pupil expenditure in elementary and secondary schools was only 74 percent of the national average in 1995–96. State-level spending on public welfare was 30 percent of all general expenditure, an unusually high proportion, but, even so, the $743 per capita spent on this category was a little below the national average.

Interest on Tennessee's general debt averaged $38 per capita in 1996–97, compared to a national average of $99, and the debt itself equaled only $618 per capita, compared to $1,706 nationwide. Cash and security holdings were almost 7 times the size of the general debt.

Tennessee's 2.0 percent share of federal funds distributed to states and their residents in fiscal 1997 was equal to the state's 2.0 percent share of the U.S. population. As is the case nationwide, payments to individuals and grants made up about three-quarters of all federal funds distributed within the state. Reflecting the state's relatively low household incomes, the shares of food stamp and Supplementary Security Income payments coming to state residents as well as the state's share of Medicaid and other health related grants exceeded the state's population share. The 4.4 percent share of non-defense procurement contracts coming to businesses within the state was notably high, while the share of defense procurement contracts was low.

State Government Finances, 1996–97

	Millions of dollars	Percent distribution	Dollars per capita	
			State	U.S.
General revenue	13 366	100.0	2 490	3 049
Intergovernmental revenue	5 065	37.9	944	863
Taxes	6 616	49.5	1 233	1 660
General sales	3 840	28.7	715	551
Selective sales	1 247	9.3	232	257
License taxes	738	5.5	137	106
Individual income	128	1.0	24	542
Corporation net income	480	3.6	89	115
Other taxes	184	1.4	34	90
Other general revenue	1 684	12.6	314	526
General expenditure	13 304	100.0	2 478	2 951
Intergovernmental expenditure	3 645	27.4	679	989
Direct expenditure	9 659	72.6	1 799	1 962
General expenditure, by function:				
Education	4 670	35.1	870	1 033
Public welfare	3 987	30.0	743	761
Hospitals and health	1 118	8.4	208	237
Highways	1 299	9.8	242	225
Police protection and corrections	565	4.3	105	137
Natural resources, parks and recreation	266	2.0	50	63
Governmental administration	331	2.5	62	107
Interest on general debt	203	1.5	38	99
Other and unallocable	866	6.5	161	290
Debt at end of fiscal year	3 315	NA	618	1 706
Cash and security holdings	22 632	NA	4 216	6 683

Federal Spending within State

	Federal funds, fiscal 1997		
	Millions of dollars	Percent distribution	Percent of U.S. total*
Total within state	28 855	100.0	2.0
Payments to individuals	16 415	56.9	2.1
Retirement and disability	9 422	32.7	2.1
Medicare	4 393	15.2	2.1
Food stamps	477	1.7	2.4
Supplemental Security Income	696	2.4	2.6
Grants	5 111	17.7	2.1
Medicaid and other health	2 649	9.2	2.3
Nutrition and family welfare	785	2.7	1.7
Education	318	1.1	1.9
Housing and community development	219	0.8	1.9
Salaries and wages	2 624	9.1	1.6
Defense procurement contracts	1 164	4.0	1.0
Non-defense procurement contracts	3 220	11.2	4.4

*State population is 2.0 percent of the U.S. total.

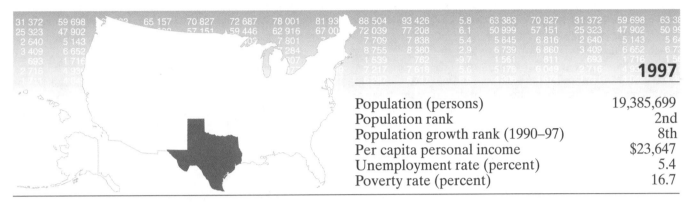

1997

Population (persons)	19,385,699
Population rank	2nd
Population growth rank (1990–97)	8th
Per capita personal income	$23,647
Unemployment rate (percent)	5.4
Poverty rate (percent)	16.7

THE TEXAS ECONOMY OF THE 1990S HAS BEEN RAPIDLY becoming a microcosm of the United States. The nation's third largest economy, it experienced strong growth in personal and business services, new manufacturing jobs, a resurgent construction industry, and an expanding state and local government sector to serve the growing population. High-tech industries proliferated, exemplified by the founding of Dell Computers in Austin. The state's traditional oil- and cattle-based economy was superseded by a modern diversifying economy. Oil and the rest of the mining sector directly contributed only 4.4 percent of total state earnings in 1997; the farm sector, including agricultural services, represented 1.3 percent of earnings.

Incomes advanced strongly during 1989–97, as employment grew an impressive 24 percent. By the early 1990s, Texas had recovered from its oil-related downturn of the 1980s. Further, the state has enjoyed steady growth each year during the 1990s. Per capita income, which averaged less than 90 percent of that of the United States in the late 1980s, came up to 93 percent of the U.S. average by 1997. Population growth was very strong—a 14 percent increase during 1990–97—which pushed the state up to second place, topping New York. The rise of the Hispanic population in Texas also reshaped the state's culture. One in five U.S. Hispanics lived in Texas as of 1997, and they represented about 30 percent of the state's population.

Average Annual Population Growth: 1990–97

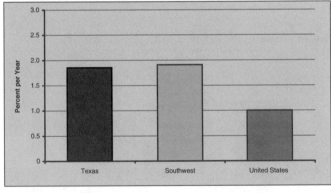

Median Household Income: 1989–97 (1997 dollars)

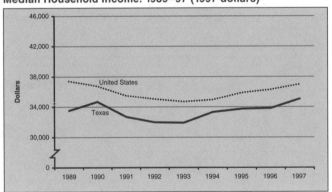

Unemployment Rate: 1989–97

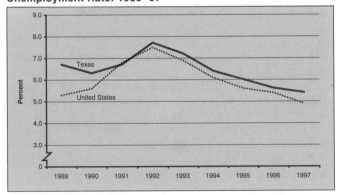

TEXAS'S UNEMPLOYMENT RATE GENERALLY HAS STAYED HIGHer than the U.S. rate in the 1990s, though unemployment moderated considerably compared to the oil-bust years of the 1980s. With vigorous job growth throughout the 1990s, by the mid-1990s Texas reached quite low unemployment rates, 5.4 percent by 1997. Given its growing and younger than average adult population, the state's labor force grew nearly 15 percent during 1990–97, with the percentage of its adult population at work higher than the U.S. average.

POPULATION AND LABOR FORCE

RAPID POPULATION GROWTH IN TEXAS IN THE 1990S HAS added 2.34 million people, about the same absolute increase as in California. Texas had rapid in-migration from home and abroad (its domestic in-migration contrasted with California's out-migration in the 1990s) and higher than average natural increase. The birth rate of 17.2 per 1,000 population was higher than the U.S. rate, and it also fell less than the national rate from 1990 to 1997. Texas's population increase reflected a continuation of its 1980s rates of natural increase and an acceleration of migration over the 1980s record.

The state had the third highest concentration of Hispanic population in the nation in percentage terms (29.4 percent in 1997) and the second highest number of Hispanics, after California. The Hispanic population grew from both natural increase and in-migration. With a Black non-Hispanic population comprising 12.2 percent of Texas's population, the overall minority representation was 43.8 percent in 1997, which make Texas one of the most diverse multicultural centers of the nation. The White non-Hispanic share of the population, now 56.2 percent, is expected soon to comprise less than 50 percent. More than 84 percent of the state's population lived within metropolitan areas, higher than the national average.

Population and Labor Force

	1980	1990	1991	1992	1993	1994	1995	1996	1997	Change*	
										State	U.S.
Population											
Total number of persons (thousands)	14 229	17 045	17 349	17 662	18 009	18 348	18 694	19 033	19 386	1.9	1.0
Percent distribution:											
White, Non-Hispanic	65.9	60.6	60.0	59.3	58.7	58.1	57.5	56.9	56.2	0.8	0.4
Black, Non-Hispanic	11.9	11.7	11.7	11.6	11.6	11.6	11.6	11.6	11.6	1.7	1.4
Asian	0.9	2.0	2.1	2.2	2.3	2.4	2.5	2.6	2.7	6.4	4.1
Native American	0.4	0.4	0.4	0.4	0.5	0.5	0.5	0.5	0.5	3.3	1.6
Hispanic	21.0	25.5	26.2	26.7	27.3	27.8	28.3	28.9	29.4	4.0	3.8
In metropolitan areas	81.1	83.5	83.7	83.9	84.0	84.1	84.0	84.2	84.3	2.0	1.0
Total number of households (thousands)	4 929	6 071	6 196	6 341	6 458	6 570	6 741	6 894	NA	2.1	1.2
Labor Force (thousands)											
Population 16 and over	10 456	12 650	12 885	13 117	13 385	13 650	13 939	14 208	14 479	1.9	1.0
Civilian labor force	6 737	8 616	8 755	8 999	9 161	9 409	9 588	9 674	9 850	1.9	1.1
Employed	6 386	8 071	8 165	8 308	8 504	8 803	9 011	9 130	9 320	2.1	1.2
Percent of population	61.1	63.8	63.4	63.3	63.5	64.5	64.6	64.3	64.4		
Unemployment rate (percent)	5.2	6.3	6.7	7.7	7.2	6.4	6.0	5.6	5.4		

*Compound annual average percent change, 1990–1997; 1990–1996 for households.

Population Change and Components: 1990–97

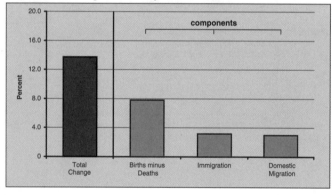

Average Annual Household and Population Growth

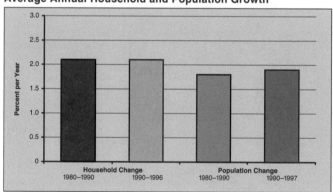

Population by Age; Births and Deaths

	1990		1997	
	State	U.S.	State	U.S.
Age distribution (percent)				
Under 5 years	8.4	7.6	8.3	7.2
5 to 17 years	20.4	18.2	20.4	18.8
18 to 64 years	61.2	61.8	61.2	61.3
65 years and over	10.1	12.5	10.1	12.7
Birth and death rates (per thousand population)				
Births	18.6	16.7	17.2	14.6
Deaths	7.4	8.6	7.3	8.6

TEXAS'S 1997 POPULATION MIX WAS SUBSTANTIALLY WEIGHTED toward youth, with 28.7 percent of its population under 18 years of age. This differential represents an extra 485,000 children in Texas. The large number of children in the state, which grew at the same 14 percent rate in 1990–97 as the overall population, was straining school resources in the state. There was about the same proportion of working-age adults as nationwide, while the share age 65 and older was lower than average.

HOUSEHOLD AND PERSONAL INCOME

HOUSEHOLD INCOME AND PERSONS IN POVERTY	1990	1995	1996	1997 State	1997 U.S.
Median household income (1997 dollars)	34 664	33 742	33 831	35 075	37 005
Persons in poverty (thousands)	2 684	3 270	3 180	3 297	35 574
Poverty rate (percent)	15.9	17.4	16.6	16.7	13.3

INCOMES REMAINED BELOW NATIONAL AVERAGES IN TEXAS, AS measured either by median household income or per capita personal income. Median income had exceeded the national average in 1984–85 but by 1991 had fallen to 91 percent of the U.S. average, then it recovered by 1997 to a level about 5 percent below the U.S. median. Poverty rates in the state have consistently been high during the 1990s, with only a small decline during its 1996–97 acceleration of economic growth.

Personal income per capita increased more than 16 percent in real terms from 1989 to 1997 and advanced at a faster rate than the U.S. average. This rate is more remarkable given the rapid growth in population. The below-average level of income in Texas was because of to a lower average receipt of transfer payments and dividends and interest, while earnings per capita were virtually the same as for the United States. Proprietors' income rose a dramatic 104 percent between 1989 and 1997, and even farm proprietors did well, in contrast to the farm sector nationwide.

Transfer payments per capita are relatively low in Texas because of its small older population and low benefits levels, but they have risen more rapidly than average. The largest increase came in medical payments, which grew more than 150 percent in 1990–97. Income maintenance programs also grew faster than average. Despite the continued high poverty rate in the state, traditional welfare program rolls were trimmed and food stamp spending grew little. But there was an explosion of "other" income maintenance, largely earned income tax credits, which now overshadow the standard assistance programs. Supplemental Security Income spending also shot up 98 percent.

Personal Income
(millions of dollars)

	1980	1989	1990	1991	1992	1993	1994	1995	1996	1997	Change*
Earnings by place of work	112 556	202 672	221 449	236 061	252 467	268 344	282 248	302 083	321 095	350 423	7.1
Wages and salaries	89 982	156 854	169 389	179 069	191 107	200 152	210 852	225 923	242 354	266 271	6.8
Other labor income	9 316	17 447	19 891	22 195	22 425	23 939	25 086	25 237	25 200	26 160	5.2
Proprietors' income	13 258	28 371	32 169	34 797	38 934	44 253	46 310	50 923	53 540	57 992	9.3
Farm	188	1 285	2 026	1 996	2 415	3 222	2 306	1 620	1 334	2 059	6.1
Nonfarm	13 071	27 085	30 144	32 801	36 519	41 031	44 005	49 303	52 206	55 933	9.5
(−) Personal contributions for social insurance	5 719	12 476	13 504	14 542	15 470	16 330	17 546	19 009	20 169	22 037	7.4
(+) Adjustment for residence	-548	-463	-500	-573	-582	-720	-783	-815	-848	-966	NA
(=) **Net earnings by state of residence**	106 289	189 733	207 446	220 945	236 414	251 293	263 919	282 259	300 078	327 420	7.1
(+) Dividends, interest, and rent	20 889	47 486	49 753	49 173	48 541	49 446	53 171	56 170	61 140	64 775	4.0
(+) Transfer payments	15 326	33 530	37 497	41 901	48 614	52 352	55 584	60 290	64 226	67 492	9.1
(=) **Total personal income**	142 504	270 749	294 697	312 020	333 569	353 092	372 673	398 718	425 443	459 688	6.8
Farm	680	1 902	2 740	2 691	3 057	3 912	2 950	2 406	2 088	2 823	5.1
Nonfarm	141 824	268 846	291 957	309 329	330 513	349 180	369 723	396 313	423 355	456 865	6.9
Personal income per capita (dollars)											
Current dollars	9 939	16 110	17 288	17 976	18 867	19 578	20 271	21 279	22 285	23 647	4.9
1997 dollars	19 004	20 367	20 804	20 758	21 104	21 304	21 542	22 120	22 693	23 647	1.9

*Compound annual average percent change, 1989–1997

Government Transfer Payments

	Millions of dollars 1990	Millions of dollars 1997	Percent change* State	Percent change* U.S.
Total government payments to individuals	35 438	64 496	82.0	62.7
Retirement, disability, and insurance	19 848	30 401	53.2	48.2
Social Security	13 209	20 030	51.6	46.1
Government employee retirement	6 128	9 744	59.0	60.3
Medical payments	9 603	24 352	153.6	101.2
Income maintenance	3 299	6 140	86.1	58.0
Supplemental Security Income	756	1 494	97.7	75.4
Family assistance	449	431	-4.1	-0.5
Food Stamps	1 514	1 673	10.5	27.1
Other income maintenance	581	2 542	337.9	189.8
Unemployment insurance benefits	830	1 018	22.6	10.6
Veterans benefits and other	1 858	2 585	39.1	30.8

*Percent change, 1990–1997

Government Payments to Individuals: 1997

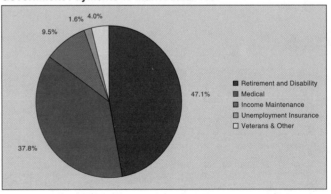

- Retirement and Disability
- Medical
- Income Maintenance
- Unemployment Insurance
- Veterans & Other

47.1% 37.8% 9.5% 1.6% 4.0%

ECONOMIC STRUCTURE

LEADING PRIVATE INDUSTRIES, 1997 (Worker and proprietor earnings, millions of dollars)		FASTEST EARNINGS GROWTH, 1989–97 (percent increase)	
Health services	$26 522	Transportation services	165.1
Business services	23 045	Business services	140.2
Oil and gas extraction	14 866	Communications	129.2
Engineering and management services	12 866	Real estate	113.9
Construction specialties	12 545	Industrial machinery manufacturing	112.4

TEXAS'S ECONOMIC STRUCTURE HAS COME TO RESEMBLE THAT of the United States, judging by the sectoral distribution of employment, and high technology has become an important force in the state's services and manufacturing. Health and business services were the largest industries, as they were nationwide. The oil and gas industry did play a larger than average role but not a dominant one, and comprised 4.4 percent of 1997 earnings compared to 0.9 percent nationwide. Employment in the mining sector (which includes oil) declined substantially during the 1989–97.

Four of the fastest growing industries were service-producing ones. Business services, which includes computer services, was the fastest growing very large industry, as annual earnings increased by $13.5 billion comparing 1997 with 1989. The "Telecom Corridor" in Richardson had the nation's highest concentration of telecommunications firms (350 firms); space-related research and spin-offs in applied technology were focused in Houston. Health services, the state's largest industry, grew a robust 88 percent over the period. Smaller service industries such as invest-

ment and securities companies, transportation services, and social services grew at dramatic rates. The Dallas-Fort Worth airport ranked third in the United States for passenger traffic. Construction has been the fastest growing overall sector during the 1990s, with job growth of 40 percent. Construction earnings expansion was led by general contractors and specialties companies, while heavy construction showed little growth.

Manufacturing played a bit smaller role than in an average state, but manufacturing jobs increased and were more numerous in 1997 than in 1980 (contrary to the national downtrend). Texas added more new manufacturing jobs than any other state from 1990 to 1997. Nearly every major computer maker had a plant here, as did aerospace equipment manufacturers and microelectronics makers from Sony to Motorola to Lucent Technologies. Growth of jobs in the government sector was significantly faster than the national average for that sector because of substantial growth in both the state and local government-workforce in Texas.

Employment and Earnings by Sector

	1980	1989	1990	1991	1992	1993	1994	1995	1996	1997 Number	1997 Percent of total	Change*
Employment *(thousands of persons)*												
Total	7 511	9 065	9 287	9 467	9 550	9 854	10 192	10 531	10 815	11 237	100.0	2.7
Farm	276	243	245	243	244	261	255	256	260	259	2.3	0.8
Nonfarm	7 234	8 822	9 042	9 224	9 306	9 593	9 937	10 274	10 555	10 978	97.7	2.8
Private nonfarm	6 077	7 417	7 603	7 775	7 813	8 064	8 365	8 667	8 945	9 346	83.2	2.9
Agricultural service, forestry, and fishing	59	93	100	108	104	113	119	125	130	137	1.2	5.0
Mining	313	292	291	294	268	288	282	262	241	248	2.2	-2.0
Construction	529	487	498	505	520	539	578	618	650	680	6.1	4.3
Manufacturing	1 068	1 011	1 022	1 021	1 008	1 031	1 058	1 079	1 105	1 134	10.1	1.4
Transportation and public utilities	399	456	478	485	487	506	527	547	571	604	5.4	3.6
Wholesale trade	437	462	467	483	485	489	494	510	518	539	4.8	1.9
Retail trade	1 198	1 495	1 525	1 566	1 604	1 652	1 725	1 787	1 837	1 890	16.8	3.0
Finance, insurance, and real estate	582	732	720	704	680	698	749	773	804	848	7.5	1.8
Services	1 493	2 387	2 503	2 610	2 656	2 747	2 832	2 966	3 089	3 266	29.1	4.0
Government	1 157	1 405	1 439	1 450	1 493	1 529	1 572	1 608	1 610	1 631	14.5	1.9
Earnings *(millions of dollars)*												
Total	112 556	202 672	221 449	236 061	252 467	268 344	282 248	302 083	321 095	350 423	100.0	7.1
Farm	680	1 902	2 740	2 691	3 057	3 912	2 950	2 406	2 088	2 823	0.8	5.1
Nonfarm	111 876	200 770	218 710	233 370	249 410	264 432	279 298	299 677	319 006	347 600	99.2	7.1
Private nonfarm	96 426	168 755	184 242	197 102	210 483	223 396	236 478	254 865	272 664	299 124	85.4	7.4
Agricultural service, forestry, and fishing	538	1 066	1 229	1 387	1 474	1 594	1 659	1 761	1 769	1 937	0.6	7.7
Mining	7 232	9 091	10 024	11 732	11 701	12 149	11 895	12 731	13 658	15 398	4.4	6.8
Construction	10 244	12 249	12 910	13 278	14 221	15 116	16 815	18 315	20 110	21 506	6.1	7.3
Manufacturing	22 251	34 859	37 412	39 570	41 593	43 274	46 363	50 283	52 476	56 712	16.2	6.3
Transportation and public utilities	9 407	16 412	17 904	19 651	21 094	23 451	24 588	26 820	28 881	31 903	9.1	8.7
Wholesale trade	9 214	14 194	15 372	16 537	17 153	17 601	18 684	19 927	21 176	23 578	6.7	6.5
Retail trade	11 969	19 914	21 196	22 405	23 508	24 749	26 747	28 240	29 676	31 689	9.0	6.0
Finance, insurance, and real estate	6 507	12 644	13 668	14 454	16 272	18 443	18 995	20 355	22 170	24 406	7.0	8.6
Services	19 064	48 325	54 528	58 088	63 467	67 019	70 732	76 434	82 747	91 996	26.3	8.4
Government	15 449	32 015	34 468	36 269	38 927	41 037	42 819	44 812	46 343	48 475	13.8	5.3

*Compound annual average percent change, 1989–1997

ECONOMIC STRUCTURE (Continued)

AVERAGE WAGES IN TEXAS GREW TO WITHIN 98 PERCENT OF the national averages, as they increased an average of 0.2 percent per year faster than U.S. trends. Wages remained high in the very productive mining (oil and gas) sector, and manufacturing wages were on a par with national averages for the sector. However, wages in construction were 6 percent below U.S. levels, and in government they were 10 percent below average. In the finance sector they were 13 percent lower, as Texas had a lower concentration of the high-end investment and insurance jobs. In other major sectors, wages in Texas were similar to those of the United States.

Manufacturing contributed 16.3 percent of gross state product in 1996 in Texas, a slightly smaller proportion than the national average but a share that more than kept pace with the growth of the state economy over the prior ten years. Production of chemicals was the leading manufacturing industry in the state, with $12.2 billion in earnings in 1997; this was the nation's largest chemical industry and produced 40 percent of U.S. industrial organic chemicals and 20 percent of U.S. plastics resins. Electronics and industrial machinery were next largest, with earnings in electronics that more than doubled over the 1989–97 period. Texas ranked second in the nation in microelectronics output, with the highest new capital investment in the industry. In contrast, the aircraft industry here has lost 30,680 jobs during the 1990s as defense cutbacks took effect. Value of manufacturing output per worker in the three leading industries averaged more than $150,000, which gave this sector an above-average productivity compared to U.S. manufacturing.

Exports were an important element in the state's economic growth, and Texas in 1997 was the second largest exporting state in the country, with $56.3 billion in goods exported. Export demand was a major factor bolstering the growth of the electronics and industrial machinery industries in the state, as these were the fastest growing of the major export products. Growth of exports of refined petroleum was among the smallest of any product in the state. The state's location adjacent to Mexico appears to have been a major advantage for its manufacturing base, as Mexico was the leading market for its exports of electronics and computers and other industrial machinery.

Average Annual Wages and Salaries by Sector
(dollars)

	1989	1996	1997 State	1997 U.S.
All wage and salary workers	21 416	27 609	29 110	29 809
Farm	12 066	13 534	13 954	16 442
Nonfarm	21 480	27 694	29 197	29 900
Private nonfarm	21 608	28 027	29 651	29 867
Agricultural service, forestry, and fishing	12 950	16 248	17 043	17 941
Mining	39 422	56 278	60 265	49 800
Construction	22 792	28 908	29 886	31 765
Manufacturing	27 315	36 077	38 445	38 351
Transportation and utilities	29 190	37 258	39 390	38 222
Wholesale trade	28 297	37 890	40 593	39 466
Retail trade	12 533	15 665	16 330	16 206
Finance, insurance, and real estate	25 601	36 559	38 977	44 993
Services	19 016	25 349	26 730	27 588
Government	20 943	26 226	27 122	30 062

Gross State Product and Manufacturing
(millions of dollars, except as noted)

	1989	1994	1995	1996
Gross state product, total	356 588	484 099	514 206	551 830
Manufacturing:				
Millions of dollars	61 045	77 313	84 350	89 725
Percent of total gross state product	17.1	16.0	16.4	16.3
Per worker (dollars)	60 354	73 053	78 156	81 234
New capital expenditures, manufacturing	NA	10 082	11 584	13 218

Exports of Goods
(millions of dollars)

	1994	1995	1996	1997
All goods	40 489	45 193	48 252	56 293
Manufactures	38 295	42 779	45 988	53 806
Agricultural and livestock products	1 015	1 143	1 026	1 123
Other commodities	1 179	1 270	1 238	1 364
Top goods exports, 1997:				
Electric and electronic equipment	7 889	10 036	10 661	13 566
Industrial machinery and computers	8 632	9 288	10 194	11 883
Chemical products	7 105	8 994	7 916	8 390
Transportation equipment	3 187	2 510	3 040	3 918
Refined petroleum products	1 677	2 052	2 365	2 684

HOUSING

HOUSING MARKETS IN THE STATE WERE WEAK DURING THE early 1990s but activity picked up considerably starting in 1994 when economic growth accelerated. New production exceeded the national average rate during 1994–97, supporting a significant growth in construction jobs. In 1997, three of the state's metropolitan areas ranked in the top 25 for building permits, led by Dallas, which ranked third. In the mid-1990s, 20 to 25 percent of total production consisted of new mobile home placements as a lower cost alternative to conventional houses. Sales of existing homes exhibited an uptrend through the decade, except for a temporary decline in sales in 1995. The median home price in the Dallas area was $112,000 in 1997, up 8 percent over the previous year but still very modest compared to most large cities. Prices in Houston were lower.

Rates of homeownership in Texas were lower than average and declined in the weak economy of early 1990s. High rates of in-migration from other states and countries, also have limited the rate of homeownership. Rental

Homeownership Rates: 1989 and 1997

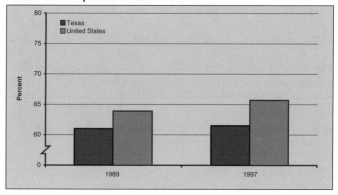

vacancy rates, which were sky-high during the mid-1980s as a result of previous overbuilding, have steadily declined in the 1990s as new households moved into the state. By 1997, the vacancy rate was about average.

Housing Supply

	1989	1990	1991	1992	1993	1994	1995	1996	1997
Residential building permits (thousands)	41.3	47.1	51.9	64.2	77.8	102.6	105.1	118.8	126.0
New home production (including manufactured housing):									
Thousands of homes	45.0	51.3	57.1	73.2	92.6	124.4	136.7	151.0	152.5
Rate per 1,000 population									
Texas	2.7	3.0	3.3	4.1	5.1	6.8	7.3	7.9	7.8
U.S.	6.2	5.2	4.5	5.1	5.6	6.4	6.3	6.6	6.5
Existing home sales:									
Thousands of homes	213.1	240.0	242.0	242.7	258.8	266.9	256.8	275.0	293.1
Change from previous year (percent)									
Texas	-5.4	12.6	0.8	0.3	6.6	3.1	-3.8	7.1	6.6
U.S.	-3.9	-4.0	0.0	9.2	8.2	4.8	-3.7	7.5	3.8
Home ownership rate (percent of households)	61.0	59.7	59.0	58.3	58.7	59.7	61.4	61.8	61.5
Rental vacancy rate (percent of rental housing units)	12.5	9.7	9.6	8.9	8.9	7.9	8.2	8.0	8.4

AGRICULTURE

THE FARM ECONOMY IN TEXAS HAS NOT KEPT PACE WITH THE expansion in other sectors in the 1990s, but Texas claims the second highest farm sales in the nation, after California. Net farm income expanded steadily in the early 1990s and then declined in 1994 through 1996, rebounding in 1997. Revenues from the leading product, cattle and livestock, have stayed on a plateau in the 1990s (declining in real terms), but poultry and grain production have increased through the decade. The role of corporate farming appears have to been increasing, as

TEXAS FARMS, 1997

Number of farms	205 000
Total acres (thousands):	129 000
Average per farm	629
Value of land and buildings (millions of dollars)	77 400
Average per farm (dollars)	377 561

this sector's share of net farm income has increased, up to 21 percent in 1997.

Farm Income
(millions of dollars)

	1980	1989	1990	1991	1992	1993	1994	1995	1996	1997
Gross income	10 875	15 381	16 031	16 106	15 727	17 571	16 965	17 166	16 814	17 653
Receipts from sales	10 163	12 910	13 945	14 187	13 405	14 967	14 894	15 214	14 624	15 385
Government payments	232	1 249	975	778	1 162	1 421	863	643	765	649
Imputed and miscellaneous income	481	1 223	1 111	1 141	1 160	1 183	1 208	1 309	1 426	1 619
(–) Production expenses	10 046	12 652	13 725	13 839	13 407	14 276	14 081	15 444	14 775	15 544
(=) Realized net income	829	2 730	2 306	2 267	2 320	3 294	2 884	1 722	2 039	2 109
(+) Inventory change	-641	-1 220	71	-23	517	131	129	189	-314	492
(=) Net income	188	1 510	2 377	2 245	2 837	3 426	3 013	1 911	1 725	2 601
Corporate income	0	225	351	248	422	203	707	291	391	542
Farm proprietors income	188	1 285	2 026	1 996	2 415	3 222	2 306	1 620	1 334	2 059

EDUCATION

EDUCATIONAL ATTAINMENT Percent of population age 25 and over, 1997	State	United States
High school graduate or higher	78.5	82.1
College graduate or higher	22.4	23.9

FOR ALL THE GROWTH AND PROMINENCE OF THE STATE OF Texas, it faces significant challenges in education. The educational attainment level of its population in 1997 was below average for achievement of college degrees (ranking 25th in the nation), and the state ranked a dismal 38th for high school degree attainment. These figures reflect the significant stream of relatively poorly educated adult immigrants who entering Texas. But the present educa-

tional system has also been strained by a burgeoning school-age population swelled by in-migration and high birth rates. Low per pupil spending (85 percent of the U.S. average) reflected the high numbers of children, as well as the low tax levels in the state. Enrollment of young adults in higher education in 1997 was a lower percentage of the 18–34 age group than the national average rate of enrollment.

High School Completion: 1990–97

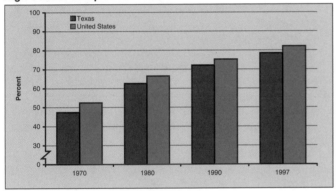

Education Indicators

	State	U.S.
Elementary and secondary schools		
Enrollment, 1995–96		
Total (thousands)	3 978	49 873
Percent in private schools	5.8	10.1
Expenditures per pupil (dollars), 1995–96	5 473	6 146
Average teacher salary (dollars), 1996–97	32 644	38 509
Higher education		
Enrollment, 1996–97		
Total (thousands)	955	14 218
Percent of population 18–34	19.6	21.8
Percent minority	37.3	26.1
Percent in private schools	12.3	22.6

HEALTH

HEALTH INDICATORS SHOWED SURPRISINGLY LOW INFANT mortality rates for a state that had high poverty and immigration rates. Infant mortality of 6.2 per 1,000 births in 1997 was below the average for all states. Overall death rates from most major causes were very similar to U.S. averages. Death from cancer was a bit below average and deaths from diabetes and accidents, including

motor vehicle accidents, were a little above average. A very high proportion of state residents, nearly one-quarter, lacked health insurance in 1997. This rate was considerably higher than national averages because of the state's high rate of poverty and the large number of immigrants and recent interstate migrants with little job tenure.

Health Indicators

	1990	1995	1996	1997
Infant mortality				
(rate per thousand live births)				
Texas	8.1	6.5	6.1	6.3
U.S.	9.2	7.6	7.3	7.1
Total deaths, age-adjusted rate				
(rate per thousand population)				
Texas	5.3	5.0	4.9	4.9
U.S.	5.2	5.0	4.9	4.8
Persons not covered by health insurance				
(percent of population)				
Texas	21.1	24.5	24.3	24.5
U.S.	13.9	15.4	15.6	16.1

Leading Causes of Death, 1996
(deaths per 100,000 population)

	Age-adjusted		Not age-adjusted	
	State	U.S.	State	U.S.
Deaths from all causes	492.5	491.6	731.7	872.5
Heart disease	134.0	134.5	221.8	276.4
Cancer	124.7	127.9	167.3	203.4
Cerebrovascular diseases	27.7	26.4	51.5	60.3
Chronic obstructive pulmonary disease	21.5	21.0	33.3	40.0
Diabetes mellitus	16.9	13.6	24.0	23.3
Pneumonia and influenza	10.8	12.8	21.2	31.6
HIV	10.4	11.1	10.8	11.7
Liver disease	8.9	7.5	10.2	9.4
Alzheimer's disease	3.4	2.7	7.9	8.1
Accidents and adverse effects	34.3	30.4	38.0	35.8
Motor vehicle accidents	20.5	16.2	20.7	16.5
Suicide	11.1	10.8	11.6	11.6
Homicide	8.5	8.5	8.3	7.9
Injury by firearm	13.6	12.9	13.7	12.8

GOVERNMENT

STATE AND LOCAL TAXES, 1995–96	State	U.S.
Per capita (dollars)	2 128	2 477
Percent of personal income	10.3	10.8

THE TOTAL STATE AND LOCAL TAX BURDEN WAS BELOW AVERage in Texas, primarily because of the state level policies. State taxes were a lower than average share of the state and local total (53 percent) than in an average state. Total taxes per capita, $2,128 in 1995–96, were 14 percent below the average state and local taxation rates in the nation. Similarly, these taxes comprised a smaller share of personal income for Texas taxpayers than comparable taxes

in the rest of the country.

Texas's conservative, small-government philosophy remained intact, according to its state government tax and spending record of 1997. State spending in Texas was well below the average for all states, and Texas levied low taxes and received lower than average transfers from the federal government. Total tax receipts in 1997 were $1,184 per capita at the state level, reflecting a significant gap of 29 percent below the national norm. The absence of income taxes levied on either individuals or corporations accounts for the differential, as sales and license tax receipts were about average.

Spending for education from the state level was about 10 percent lower than the average state, despite the larger than average proportion of school-age population in Texas. The state paid much smaller than average intergovernmental transfers from state to local governments, usually the main vehicle for state aid to education. Three other major program areas, public welfare, health, and highways, were between 22 percent and 28 percent smaller on a per capita basis in Texas than nationwide. Direct administrative costs and interest on state debt were both substantially smaller (per capita) than in typical states. State debt per capita at year-end was only 38 percent as high as that of the average state.

Federal spending in Texas was disproportionately small for the large size of its population, with only 6.3 percent of federal spending occurring in the state. The population's young age mix held down receipt of Social Security and Medicare, which were by far the largest dollar categories of spending. Grants were also lower than average, while federal employee salaries paid in-state were closer to the state's proportion of total population. Cutbacks in spending on military hardware reduced defense procurement here, though other procurement was still disproportionately high.

State Government Finances, 1996–97

	Millions of dollars	Percent distribution	Dollars per capita State	U.S.
General revenue	45 546	100.0	2 343	3 049
Intergovernmental revenue	13 800	30.3	710	863
Taxes	23 025	50.6	1 184	1 660
General sales	11 362	24.9	584	551
Selective sales	7 042	15.5	362	257
License taxes	3 265	7.2	168	106
Individual income	0	0.0	0	542
Corporation net income	0	0.0	0	115
Other taxes	1 355	3.0	70	90
Other general revenue	8 721	19.1	449	526
General expenditure	44 124	100.0	2 270	2 951
Intergovernmental expenditure	12 806	29.0	659	989
Direct expenditure	31 318	71.0	1 611	1 962
General expenditure, by function:				
Education	18 303	41.5	942	1 033
Public welfare	11 525	26.1	593	761
Hospitals and health	3 293	7.5	169	237
Highways	3 291	7.5	169	225
Police protection and corrections	2 546	5.8	131	137
Natural resources, parks and recreation	639	1.5	33	63
Governmental administration	1 239	2.8	64	107
Interest on general debt	843	1.9	43	99
Other and unallocable	2 445	5.5	126	290
Debt at end of fiscal year	12 462	NA	641	1 706
Cash and security holdings	121 587	NA	6 255	6 683

Federal Spending within State

	Federal funds, fiscal 1997		
	Millions of dollars	Percent distribution	Percent of U.S. total*
Total within state	88 898	100.0	6.3
Payments to individuals	48 379	54.4	6.2
Retirement and disability	27 312	30.7	6.0
Medicare	12 474	14.0	6.1
Food stamps	1 783	2.0	9.1
Supplemental Security Income	1 569	1.8	5.8
Grants	14 644	16.5	5.9
Medicaid and other health	7 034	7.9	6.2
Nutrition and family welfare	2 702	3.0	5.8
Education	1 347	1.5	7.9
Housing and community development	583	0.7	5.1
Salaries and wages	10 897	12.3	6.6
Defense procurement contracts	7 347	8.3	6.1
Non-defense procurement contracts	5 935	6.7	8.1

*State population is 7.3 percent of the U.S. total.

31 372	59 698		65 157	70 827	72 687	78 001	81 93	88 504	93 426	5.8	63 383	70 827	31 372	59 698	63 3
25 323	47 902		57 151	59 446	62 916	67 00	72 039	77 208	6.1	50 999	57 151	25 323	47 902	50 9
2 640	5 143		7 801		7 709	7 838	5.4	5 645	6 816	2 640	5 143	5 6
3 409	6 652		5 284		8 755	8 380	2.9	6 739	6 860	3 409	6 652	6 7
693	1 716				1 839	762	9.7	1 561	811	693	1 716	1 5
2 716					7 217	7 618	5.0	6 178	6 049	2 716		

1997

Population (persons)	2,065,001
Population rank	34th
Population growth rank (1990–97)	4th
Per capita personal income	$20,246
Unemployment rate (percent)	3.1
Poverty rate (percent)	8.9

UTAH'S ECONOMY HAS GROWN AT A REMARKABLY FAST RATE during the 1990s. The state experienced a 42 percent increase in employment from 1989 to 1997, nearly triple the U.S. rate. A population boom, led predominantly by the high rate of natural increase flowing from the high birth rate, precipitated rapid growth in the state's construction, services, and retail trade sectors. Further, the manufacturing sector grew smartly, as output of motor vehicles and equipment and instruments. Per capita income grew at double the national rate from 1989 to 1997, though it remained much lower than the U.S. average level. However, the median Utah household had income above the national median, and median household income grew 0.9 percent per year in real terms in contrast to the national decline. This difference and the low poverty rate may reflect a greater proportion of two-income households in Utah and also suggest that Utah's income and population gains, unlike in many parts of the country, have been concentrated in the middle class.

The state's population grew more than 19 percent from 1990 to 1997, the fourth largest gain in the nation in percentage terms. Unlike neighboring Nevada and Arizona, whose population growth spurts derive from monumental in-migration from other states, 60 percent of Utah's growth was due to natural increase (births minus deaths).

Average Annual Population Growth: 1990–97

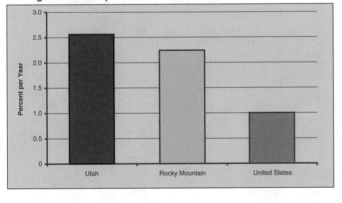

Median Household Income: 1989–97 (1997 dollars)

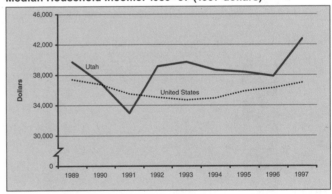

Unemployment Rate: 1989–97

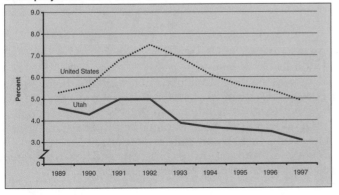

UTAH'S UNEMPLOYMENT RATE HAS NEVER BEEN HIGH DURING the 1990s, remaining consistently lower than its level of 1980. The rate declined steadily since its high point of 5.0 percent in 1992, down to 3.1 percent in 1997, one of the lowest rates in the nation. The stupendous increase in adult population led to a 27 percent increase in the labor force during the 1990–97 period, but employment growth outstripped even this labor force growth, with an increasing ratio of employment to adult population.

POPULATION AND LABOR FORCE

TOTAL POPULATION IN UTAH GREW 2.6 PERCENT ANNUALLY from 1990 to 1997, compared to the U.S. average of 1.0 percent per year. In 1997, Utah had the fourth highest population percent change in the nation. Even when the state was experiencing slower economic times in the 1980s, the rate of growth of the population for the decade still exceeded that of the nation. This rapid growth over two decades amounted to a 41 percent increase in population from 1980 to 1997. This rise moved Utah up to the 34th largest state in the nation. Utah's rapid rate of population growth was primarily attributable to natural increase rather than net in-migration, though in-migration added 5 percent to the population in this decade. The White non-Hispanic population decreased in proportion to the state total, yet it had the largest absolute growth and still made up nearly 90 percent of Utah's population. Only the Asian and Hispanic populations showed an increase in proportion of the total state population. In 1997, Hispanics accounted for 6.5 percent of the state's population, making them Utah's largest minority group. Despite a national trend toward urbanization, the proportion of Utah's population living in nonmetropolitan areas increased.

Population and Labor Force

	1980	1990	1991	1992	1993	1994	1995	1996	1997	Change*	
										State	U.S.
Population											
Total number of persons (thousands)	1 461	1 730	1 771	1 819	1 872	1 942	1 991	2 022	2 065	2.6	1.0
Percent distribution:											
White, Non-Hispanic	92.5	91.0	91.0	90.8	90.6	90.3	90.0	89.7	89.3	2.2	0.4
Black, Non-Hispanic	0.6	0.9	0.6	0.7	0.7	0.7	0.7	0.7	0.7	-2.0	1.4
Asian	1.4	2.0	2.1	2.1	2.2	2.3	2.3	2.4	2.5	5.8	4.1
Native American	1.4	1.4	1.5	1.5	1.4	1.5	1.4	1.4	1.4	2.2	1.6
Hispanic	4.1	4.9	5.1	5.2	5.3	5.6	5.8	6.1	6.5	6.6	3.8
In metropolitan areas	77.5	77.8	77.8	77.8	77.6	77.4	77.1	76.9	76.8	2.3	1.0
Total number of households (thousands)	449	537	553	571	586	600	621	639	NA	2.9	1.2
Labor Force (thousands)											
Population 16 and over	974	1 162	1 198	1 241	1 288	1 337	1 380	1 420	1 456	3.3	1.0
Civilian labor force	816	843	865	916	975	987	1 012	1 040	1 063	3.5	1.1
Employed	781	801	821	880	938	951	977	1 008	1 023	3.7	1.2
Percent of population	80.2	68.9	68.5	70.9	72.8	71.2	70.8	71.0	70.3		
Unemployment rate (percent)	6.3	4.3	5.0	5.0	3.9	3.7	3.6	3.5	3.1		

*Compound annual average percent change, 1990–1997; 1990–1996 for households.

Population Change and Components: 1990–97

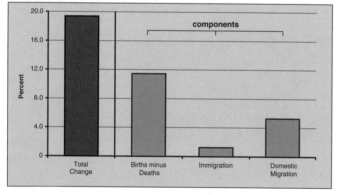

Average Annual Household and Population Growth

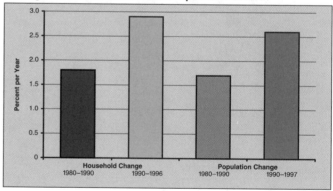

Population by Age; Births and Deaths

	1990		1997	
	State	U.S.	State	U.S.
Age distribution (percent)				
Under 5 years	9.9	7.6	9.5	7.2
5 to 17 years	26.3	18.2	23.9	18.8
18 to 64 years	55.0	61.8	57.8	61.3
65 years and over	8.7	12.5	8.7	12.7
Birth and death rates (per thousand population)				
Births	21.1	16.7	21.3	14.6
Deaths	5.3	8.6	5.5	8.6

THE BREAKDOWN OF UTAH'S POPULATION BY AGE MOVED IN the direction of national averages from 1990 to 1997. There was an increased percentage of the population between the ages of 18 and 64 in 1997 (boosting the size of the labor force tremendously in the 1990s). Utah's population under age 18 was still remarkably high, though the state had a significantly smaller proportion of its population over 64. The state's high birth rate and low death rate reflected Utah's overall young population.

HOUSEHOLD AND PERSONAL INCOME

HOUSEHOLD INCOME AND PERSONS IN POVERTY	1990	1995	1996	1997 State	1997 U.S.
Median household income (1997 dollars)	37 014	38 419	37 888	42 775	37 005
Persons in poverty (thousands)	143	168	153	185	35 574
Poverty rate (percent)	8.2	8.4	7.7	8.9	13.3

SINCE 1992, UTAH HAS MAINTAINED A RELATIVELY HIGH MEDI-an household income, ranging from 4 percent to 16 percent above the national median. In 1997, Utah had the ninth highest median household income in the country, 15 percent greater than the national median. Household income in Utah likely was boosted by a large average household size—the largest number of persons per household of any state—and an above-average prevalence of two-earner households. The poverty rate of 8.9 percent was the seventh lowest rate in the nation in 1997, a slight drop from the third best position in 1996.

Earnings of workers and proprietors increased tremendously during the 1990s, because Utah has enjoyed an economic boom. Total earnings per capita stood at 88 percent of the national level in 1997, however, since wage rates were low in Utah and the adult population was a relative-ly small proportion of the total. Overall, the state's per capita income stood at just 80 percent of the national average. The average was brought down by extremely low receipt of transfer payments and dividends and interest income, which were only 62 to 67 percent of the national averages on a per capita basis.

Government transfers generally grew more slowly than the national average, after adjustment for the state's large population increase. Its transfers consisted of a higher proportion of retirement payments and a lesser share of medical payments, though the latter did grow more rapidly in Utah than nationally. Family assistance has declined substantially and food stamp spending has not grown at all in the 1990s, reflecting job growth and low poverty rates. Other income maintenance, which was primarily earned income tax credits, grew explosively.

Personal Income
(millions of dollars)

	1980	1989	1990	1991	1992	1993	1994	1995	1996	1997	Change*
Earnings by place of work	9 311	17 124	18 750	20 105	21 819	23 608	25 665	27 896	30 134	32 613	8.4
Wages and salaries	7 650	14 087	15 277	16 396	17 712	18 860	20 523	22 417	24 461	26 650	8.3
Other labor income	722	1 435	1 639	1 847	2 089	2 358	2 556	2 655	2 641	2 717	8.3
Proprietors' income	940	1 602	1 835	1 863	2 018	2 390	2 586	2 824	3 032	3 245	9.2
Farm	18	152	186	164	210	235	116	79	80	90	-6.3
Nonfarm	922	1 450	1 649	1 699	1 808	2 156	2 471	2 746	2 952	3 155	10.2
(−) Personal contributions for social insurance	546	1 140	1 228	1 333	1 432	1 544	1 695	1 848	1 989	2 160	8.3
(+) Adjustment for residence	50	22	15	9	5	-3	-7	-5	5	7	NA
(=) **Net earnings by state of residence**	8 815	16 006	17 538	18 782	20 392	22 061	23 963	26 043	28 151	30 460	8.4
(+) Dividends, interest, and rent	1 535	3 437	3 569	3 651	3 683	3 954	4 300	4 708	5 228	5 525	6.1
(+) Transfer payments	1 462	3 138	3 479	3 870	4 228	4 608	4 757	5 146	5 446	5 705	7.8
(=) **Total personal income**	11 812	22 581	24 586	26 302	28 303	30 624	33 021	35 897	38 825	41 689	8.0
Farm	64	203	246	222	271	301	201	172	173	190	-0.8
Nonfarm	11 749	22 379	24 340	26 080	28 033	30 322	32 820	35 726	38 652	41 499	8.0
Personal income per capita (dollars)											
Current dollars	8 021	13 238	14 213	14 847	15 546	16 336	17 122	18 182	19 244	20 246	5.5
1997 dollars	15 337	16 736	17 103	17 144	17 389	17 776	18 196	18 900	19 597	20 246	2.4

*Compound annual average percent change, 1989–1997

Government Transfer Payments

	Millions of dollars 1990	Millions of dollars 1997	Percent change* State	Percent change* U.S.
Total government payments to individuals	3 286	5 380	63.7	62.7
Retirement, disability, and insurance	2 103	3 155	50.0	48.2
Social Security	1 170	1 879	60.6	46.1
Government employee retirement	709	1 077	51.9	60.3
Medical payments	709	1 545	117.9	101.2
Income maintenance	220	362	64.4	58.0
Supplemental Security Income	38	86	126.1	75.4
Family assistance	68	51	-24.4	-0.5
Food Stamps	74	77	3.8	27.1
Other income maintenance	40	148	266.5	189.8
Unemployment insurance benefits	66	82	24.7	10.6
Veterans benefits and other	188	236	25.6	30.8

*Percent change, 1990–1997

Government Payments to Individuals: 1997

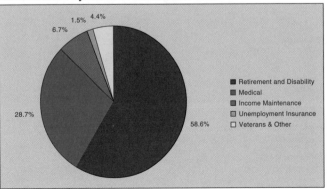

- 58.6% Retirement and Disability
- 28.7% Medical
- 6.7% Income Maintenance
- 1.5% Unemployment Insurance
- 4.4% Veterans & Other

ECONOMIC STRUCTURE

LEADING PRIVATE INDUSTRIES, 1997 (Worker and proprietor earnings, millions of dollars)		FASTEST EARNINGS GROWTH, 1989–97 (percent increase)	
Health services	$2 368	Real estate	365.0
Business services	2 126	Motor vehicles and equipment	364.2
Construction specialties	1 716	Business services	206.7
Engineering and management services	937	Construction specialties	193.0
Banks and other credit institutions	884	Instruments and related products	176.5

UTAH'S LEADING PRIVATE INDUSTRIES IN 1997 WERE HEALTH services and business services. Including the fourth-ranked engineering and management services, service industries occupied three of the top five leading industry earners spots, providing nearly 30 percent of Utah's employment in 1997. The services industry has added more than 130,000 jobs since 1989. The construction sector was the fastest growing employment component in the state economy as construction jobs have more than doubled in this decade, buoyed by building of housing and infrastructure for the growing population. This increase also led to explosive growth of earnings in the real estate industry, up 365 percent from 1989 to 1997. Manufacturing played a smaller than average role in the state economy, contributing about 15 percent of total earnings, or about 3 percentage points less than the national average. However, the manufacturing sector has displayed steady job growth here during the 1990s, while the U.S. manufacturing sector has been shrinking, and two of the five fastest growing industries have been in manufacturing. Finance, insurance, and real estate had the highest rate of growth in earnings of any sector from 1989 to 1997, increasing 190 percent, with banks and similar institutions comprising the fifth largest industry in the state. As a result, the sector accounted for 7.4 percent of the state's earnings in 1997, up from 4.9 percent in 1989.

Employment and Earnings by Sector

	1980	1989	1990	1991	1992	1993	1994	1995	1996	1997 Number	1997 Percent of total	Change*
Employment *(thousands of persons)*												
Total	689	903	943	968	986	1 033	1 112	1 174	1 234	1 283	100.0	4.5
Farm	20	19	19	18	18	18	18	17	18	19	1.5	0.1
Nonfarm	669	885	924	950	968	1 016	1 094	1 157	1 216	1 264	98.5	4.6
Private nonfarm	531	720	754	777	792	838	918	978	1 034	1 077	84.0	5.2
Agricultural service, forestry, and fishing	3	6	6	7	7	8	9	10	11	12	0.9	9.9
Mining	19	9	10	10	10	10	10	9	9	9	0.7	0.5
Construction	42	41	43	47	52	57	70	79	85	90	7.0	10.4
Manufacturing	90	108	112	111	112	116	124	130	136	140	10.9	3.3
Transportation and public utilities	36	45	47	47	47	51	54	57	60	62	4.9	4.2
Wholesale trade	36	42	43	45	45	45	47	51	53	54	4.2	3.1
Retail trade	111	150	157	162	170	177	196	209	220	228	17.8	5.4
Finance, insurance, and real estate	51	70	69	69	65	75	82	88	95	100	7.8	4.6
Services	141	250	268	280	285	300	327	344	365	381	29.7	5.4
Government	138	164	170	173	176	177	176	179	182	187	14.6	1.6
Earnings *(millions of dollars)*												
Total	9 311	17 124	18 750	20 105	21 819	23 608	25 665	27 896	30 134	32 613	100.0	8.4
Farm	64	203	246	222	271	301	201	172	173	190	0.6	-0.8
Nonfarm	9 247	16 921	18 504	19 883	21 549	23 307	25 464	27 725	29 961	32 423	99.4	8.5
Private nonfarm	7 384	13 452	14 757	15 870	17 292	18 914	20 892	22 945	24 942	27 069	83.0	9.1
Agricultural service, forestry, and fishing	22	49	55	64	73	81	89	102	117	129	0.4	13.0
Mining	530	328	360	368	396	398	401	418	419	453	1.4	4.1
Construction	764	955	1 054	1 184	1 296	1 468	1 826	2 149	2 379	2 606	8.0	13.4
Manufacturing	1 623	2 880	3 074	3 202	3 378	3 572	3 882	4 214	4 526	4 837	14.8	6.7
Transportation and public utilities	823	1 447	1 549	1 640	1 746	1 913	2 039	2 125	2 254	2 424	7.4	6.7
Wholesale trade	660	1 086	1 152	1 251	1 257	1 317	1 438	1 581	1 747	1 872	5.7	7.0
Retail trade	956	1 655	1 799	1 921	2 160	2 354	2 694	2 986	3 235	3 549	10.9	10.0
Finance, insurance, and real estate	457	833	906	1 003	1 216	1 544	1 704	1 961	2 203	2 414	7.4	14.2
Services	1 549	4 220	4 809	5 237	5 768	6 267	6 819	7 409	8 062	8 786	26.9	9.6
Government	1 864	3 469	3 748	4 013	4 257	4 393	4 572	4 780	5 019	5 353	16.4	5.6

*Compound annual average percent change, 1989–1997

ECONOMIC STRUCTURE (Continued)

DESPITE RECENT RAPID JOB GROWTH, UTAH'S AVERAGE WAGES remained below the national average, in 1997 only 85 percent of the U.S. average. With the exception of farm wages, Utah's wages for all major sectors were below average. The largest difference was in finance, insurance, and real estate wages, which amounted to only 70.5 percent of the national average. Manufacturing and construction wages also were particularly low, 82 percent and 83 percent of the U.S. average, respectively. The services and retail trade sectors showed a relatively higher average wage, 88 percent and 95 percent of the national levels. Since 1989, wages in agricultural services and finance, insurance, and real estate have increased by nearly 50 percent, the most rapid of the major sectors.

The value of Utah's gross state product (GSP) grew by 19.9 percent from 1994 to 1996. This was the second highest increase in the nation, after that of Nevada. Manufacturing continued to play a lower than average but significant role in the state's economy, its output equaled 14 percent of the GSP. Though factory output has been growing during the 1990s, it has not kept pace with the dramatic growth in the rest of the economy, thus its reduced role since 1989. The state's leading manufacturing industry in 1997 was industrial machinery and equipment, which was among the state's 15 leading private industry earners. In 1996, manufacturing output per worker amounted to $51,913, just 74.8 percent of the national average, and new capital expenditures decreased substantially from 1994 to 1996.

Utah's exports increased by more than 47 percent from 1994 to 1997, without adjustment for inflation, growing faster than the state's overall economy. The largest export in 1997 was primary metals, which fluctuated greatly over the past four years and held down the growth rate for total exports. In contrast, the three equipment industry export categories all grew to at least double their 1994 levels. The fastest growing of the three was transportation equipment, which grew 133 percent from 1994 to 1997. Agricultural and livestock products exports increased tremendously from just under $5 million in 1995 to more than $23 million in 1997.

Average Annual Wages and Salaries by Sector
(dollars)

	1989	1996	1997 State	1997 U.S.
All wage and salary workers	18 953	24 240	25 358	29 809
Farm	9 449	20 339	17 872	16 442
Nonfarm	19 018	24 257	25 395	29 900
Private nonfarm	18 985	24 161	25 324	29 867
Agricultural service, forestry, and fishing	10 690	15 391	15 892	17 941
Mining	34 672	43 609	45 334	49 800
Construction	21 593	25 091	26 406	31 765
Manufacturing	24 049	30 093	31 447	38 351
Transportation and utilities	28 677	33 444	34 801	38 222
Wholesale trade	24 170	31 521	33 311	39 466
Retail trade	10 651	14 478	15 354	16 206
Finance, insurance, and real estate	21 172	29 595	31 736	44 993
Services	17 453	23 147	24 130	27 588
Government	19 136	24 691	25 721	30 062

Gross State Product and Manufacturing
(millions of dollars, except as noted)

	1989	1994	1995	1996
Gross state product, total	28 365	42 007	45 554	50 352
Manufacturing:				
Millions of dollars	4 187	5 877	6 468	7 051
Percent of total gross state product	14.8	14.0	14.2	14.0
Per worker (dollars)	38 916	47 551	49 652	51 913
New capital expenditures, manufacturing	NA	1 249	913	930

Exports of Goods
(millions of dollars)

	1994	1995	1996	1997
All goods	2 233	2 313	2 768	3 293
Manufactures	1 852	1 793	2 379	2 968
Agricultural and livestock products	5	5	24	23
Other commodities	376	515	365	302
Top goods exports, 1997:				
Primary metals	752	364	439	784
Transportation equipment	213	231	419	497
Electric and electronic equipment	222	319	362	463
Industrial machinery and computers	194	317	448	399
Chemical products	141	125	202	222

HOUSING

Housing production has increased dramatically in Utah since the 1990–91 recession. In 1990, production was just over 7,000 units, and by 1996 it was up to more than 25,000. The rate of home production per 1,000 people increased significantly from 4.5 in 1989 to 10.2 in 1997. Though this figure represents a slight decrease from 12.5 in 1996, Utah's home production rate consistently has been well above the national average since 1991. The state's high population growth helped propel Utah's housing production by increasing the demand for housing. Rates of homeownership also increased from 70.1 percent in 1990 to 72.5 percent in 1997, for the 11th highest homeownership rate in the nation. Perhaps because of the burst of new building, existing home sales have been fairly flat after a spike in sales during 1990–92. Rental vacancy rates have generally been extremely high in Utah during this decade, surprising for a rapidly growing state. The 1997 rate of 14.4 percent gave Utah the second highest rental vacancy rate in the nation.

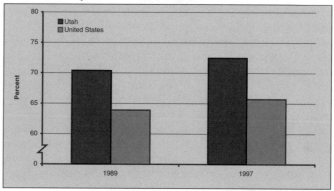

Homeownership Rates: 1989 and 1997

Housing Supply

	1989	1990	1991	1992	1993	1994	1995	1996	1997
Residential building permits (thousands)	6.0	7.3	8.9	12.8	17.3	18.6	20.9	23.5	19.3
New home production (including manufactured housing):									
Thousands of homes	6.4	7.7	9.0	13.5	18.1	19.9	22.5	25.2	21.0
Rate per 1,000 population									
Utah	3.8	4.5	5.1	7.4	9.7	10.3	11.4	12.5	10.2
U.S.	6.2	5.2	4.5	5.1	5.6	6.4	6.3	6.6	6.5
Existing home sales:									
Thousands of homes	20.3	22.1	26.3	31.5	31.2	32.4	31.6	33.8	30.0
Change from previous year (percent)									
Utah	-1.9	8.9	19.0	19.8	-1.0	3.8	-2.5	7.0	-11.2
U.S.	-3.9	-4.0	0.0	9.2	8.2	4.8	-3.7	7.5	3.8
Home ownership rate (percent of households)	70.4	70.1	70.7	70.0	68.9	69.3	71.5	72.7	72.5
Rental vacancy rate (percent of rental housing units)	10.6	12.6	14.9	14.6	15.7	7.1	12.3	13.4	14.4

AGRICULTURE

Utah, as an area dominated by desert and mountains had among the 15 lowest number of farms in the nation. The state averaged 821 acres per farm, well above the national average size. While the total value for farmland and buildings was rather low compared to those in other states, Utah had the second highest increase in value in the nation from 1993 to 1997, with a gain of 50.0 percent. Since 1989, Utah's farm production expenses have grown by nearly 45 percent, well above the 25.4 percent growth of gross income, resulting in a decrease in net farm income of more than 35 percent. Livestock and their products accounted for 76.5 percent of Utah's receipts from sales.

UTAH FARMS, 1997

Number of farms	13 400
Total acres (thousands):	11 000
Average per farm	821
Value of land and buildings (millions of dollars)	8 250
Average per farm (dollars)	615 672

Farm Income
(millions of dollars)

	1980	1989	1990	1991	1992	1993	1994	1995	1996	1997
Gross income	643	905	904	881	935	1 008	1 002	985	1 052	1 135
Receipts from sales	575	802	794	770	814	879	875	856	915	1 004
Government payments	5	35	35	33	36	37	32	25	21	20
Imputed and miscellaneous income	63	68	74	77	85	92	94	104	115	111
(–) Production expenses	649	705	722	699	726	767	874	909	967	1 020
(=) Realized net income	-7	200	181	181	209	240	128	76	85	114
(+) Inventory change	24	-28	30	0	34	8	19	15	16	-3
(=) Net income	18	172	211	181	243	248	147	91	101	111
Corporate income	0	20	26	17	33	13	32	13	21	21
Farm proprietors income	18	152	186	164	210	235	116	79	80	90

EDUCATION

EDUCATIONAL ATTAINMENT Percent of population age 25 and over, 1997	State	United States
High school graduate or higher	89.5	82.1
College graduate or higher	26.7	23.9

UTAH WAS ONE OF THE BEST EDUCATED STATES IN THE NATION, with nearly 90 percent of the state's adult population having earned a high school diploma. Utah had the nation's third highest percentage of high school graduates. More than 26 percent of the state's residents had college degrees, which placed Utah among the 15 states with the highest percentage of college graduates. In both per pupil expenditures in elementary and secondary schools and average teacher salaries, Utah ranked well below the U.S. average, however. In 1997, Utah had the 11th lowest average teacher salary in the nation. The low per pupil expenditures can be partly attributed to the high number of school-aged children. The percentage of children attending private schools was extremely low in Utah. In higher education, a relatively large proportion of young adults were currently enrolled in colleges, but minorities appeared to be underrepresented in Utah's postsecondary education. Only 6.8 percent of the state's college enrollment were minorities, as compared to 11.0 percent of the state's total population.

High School Completion: 1990–97

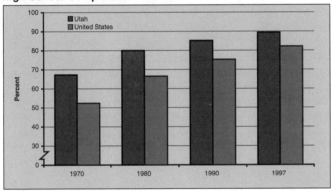

Education Indicators

	State	U.S.
Elementary and secondary schools Enrollment, 1995–96		
Total (thousands)	490	49 873
Percent in private schools	2.6	10.1
Expenditures per pupil (dollars), 1995–96	3 867	6 146
Average teacher salary (dollars), 1996–97	31 750	38 509
Higher education Enrollment, 1996–97		
Total (thousands)	152	14 218
Percent of population 18–34	27.2	21.8
Percent minority	6.8	26.1
Percent in private schools	24.7	22.6

HEALTH

UTAH'S HEALTH STATISTICS WERE A FAVORABLE INDICATION OF the state's high living standards. The state's infant mortality rate decreased slightly to 5.8 per 1,000 in 1997, which was well below the national average of 7.1 per 1,000. The 1997 rate was the ninth lowest in the nation. Utah's overall death rate was significantly lower than the national average. The death rates for major causes were generally below the average. Both suicides and drug-related death rates were considerably higher in Utah than in the United States; however, homicides, HIV, cirrhosis, and lung cancer death rates were all well below the national rates. Utah ranked 24th in the nation for percentage of population without health insurance, with a rate of uninsured considerably less than the national average. The high rates of insurance were supported by Utah's growing economy and low poverty rate.

Health Indicators

	1990	1995	1996	1997
Infant mortality *(rate per thousand live births)*				
Utah	7.5	5.4	5.9	5.8
U.S.	9.2	7.6	7.3	7.1
Total deaths, age-adjusted rate *(rate per thousand population)*				
Utah	4.2	4.2	4.1	4.0
U.S.	5.2	5.0	4.9	4.8
Persons not covered by health insurance *(percent of population)*				
Utah	9.0	11.7	12.0	13.4
U.S.	13.9	15.4	15.6	16.1

Leading Causes of Death, 1996
(deaths per 100,000 population)

	Age-adjusted		Not age-adjusted	
	State	U.S.	State	U.S.
Deaths from all causes	406.5	491.6	555.5	872.5
Heart disease	95.3	134.5	144.3	276.4
Cancer	89.8	127.9	105.2	203.4
Cerebrovascular diseases	23.8	26.4	42.2	60.3
Chronic obstructive pulmonary disease	17.0	21.0	23.0	40.0
Diabetes mellitus	16.1	13.6	20.9	23.3
Pneumonia and influenza	12.8	12.8	23.6	31.6
HIV	3.5	11.1	3.2	11.7
Liver disease	4.3	7.5	4.4	9.4
Alzheimer's disease	2.8	2.7	5.9	8.1
Accidents and adverse effects	29.6	30.4	32.2	35.8
Motor vehicle accidents	16.9	16.2	17.1	16.5
Suicide	14.7	10.8	14.3	11.6
Homicide	3.3	8.5	3.3	7.9
Injury by firearm	10.8	12.9	10.6	12.8

GOVERNMENT

STATE AND LOCAL TAXES, 1995–96	State	U.S.
Per capita (dollars)	2 058	2 477
Percent of personal income	11.6	10.8

REFLECTING UTAH'S RELATIVELY LOW PER CAPITA INCOME, ITS state and local taxes combined (excluding corporate) absorbed more personal income than the national average—11.6 percent versus 10.8—yet yielded tax revenues per capita that were 17 percent below the national average. Of these taxes, only 33.7 percent were local, as compared to 40.8 percent nationwide, indicating lower local property taxes in Utah. Utah's state government per capi-

ta general revenue was 6 percent less than the national per capita revenue in 1997. Per capita individual income taxes were equal to the national average, while corporation taxes were just under the national average. The state's per capita general sales tax was more than the national average, while both selective sales taxes and license taxes were lower. Utah's state government spent $1,469 per capita on education, significantly more than the national average of $1,033, necessitated by the very high numbers of school-age children and low local taxation in the state. However, spending on public welfare was substantially below average. Utah's overall per capita state expenditures of $3,053 were just above the national per capita expenditures of $2,951.

In general in 1997, Utah's shares of federal grants, procurement, and payments to individuals were lower than Utah's 0.8 percent of the U.S. population. The two exceptions were salaries and wages and non-defense procurement. Medicare payments, housing and community development grants, and defense procurement were all well below 0.8 percent of the U.S. total because of the state's low numbers of elderly and poor residents and its lack of defense-related industry.

State Government Finances, 1996–97

	Millions of dollars	Percent distribu-tion	Dollars per capita	
			State	U.S.
General revenue	5 903	100.0	2 867	3 049
Intergovernmental revenue	1 592	27.0	773	863
Taxes	3 011	51.0	1 462	1 660
General sales	1 265	21.4	614	551
Selective sales	315	5.3	153	257
License taxes	90	1.5	44	106
Individual income	1 128	19.1	548	542
Corporation net income	177	3.0	86	115
Other taxes	35	0.6	17	90
Other general revenue	1 300	22.0	631	526
General expenditure	6 285	100.0	3 053	2 951
Intergovernmental expenditure	1 673	26.6	813	989
Direct expenditure	4 612	73.4	2 240	1 962
General expenditure, by function:				
Education	3 025	48.1	1 469	1 033
Public welfare	990	15.7	481	761
Hospitals and health	492	7.8	239	237
Highways	584	9.3	283	225
Police protection and corrections	233	3.7	113	137
Natural resources, parks and recreation	198	3.2	96	63
Governmental administration	296	4.7	144	107
Interest on general debt	130	2.1	63	99
Other and unallocable	338	5.4	164	290
Debt at end of fiscal year	2 451	NA	1 190	1 706
Cash and security holdings	12 538	NA	6 089	6 683

Federal Spending within State

	Federal funds, fiscal 1997		
	Millions of dollars	Percent distribution	Percent of U.S. total*
Total within state	8 478	100.0	0.6
Payments to individuals	4 165	49.1	0.5
Retirement and disability	2 808	33.1	0.6
Medicare	793	9.4	0.4
Food stamps	79	0.9	0.4
Supplemental Security Income	91	1.1	0.3
Grants	1 602	18.9	0.6
Medicaid and other health	610	7.2	0.5
Nutrition and family welfare	311	3.7	0.7
Education	124	1.5	0.7
Housing and community development	38	0.4	0.3
Salaries and wages	1 388	16.4	0.8
Defense procurement contracts	433	5.1	0.4
Non-defense procurement contracts	773	9.1	1.1

*State population is 0.8 percent of the U.S. total.

		1997
Population (persons)		588,632
Population rank		49th
Population growth rank (1990–97)		38th
Per capita personal income		$23,018
Unemployment rate (percent)		4.0
Poverty rate (percent)		9.3

THOUGH THE RECESSION OF THE EARLY 1990S IMPACTED THE Vermont economy, it was less detrimental in the state than it was in other states in the region. The unemployment rate was substantially lower than the national rate even during the height of the recession. The poverty rate was also lower than the national level. However, Vermont started the decade in 1989 with median household income well above the U.S. average but it was 5 percent below by 1997. Average per capita income and wages remained lower as well throughout the decade.

Employment in the state grew overall from 1989 to 1997 but declined in manufacturing and construction, while services increased rapidly. Sector earnings for manufacturing and services were roughly similar in 1989, but by 1997, manufacturing earnings had dropped to 72 percent of service earnings. Despite this loss, manufacturing remained relatively important to the economy, representing about 18 percent of total gross state product in 1996.

The population of Vermont was largely White non-Hispanic and rural. It had the largest percentage of people living in nonmetropolitan counties in New England and was only behind Wyoming in the country at large. The state actually gained people through domestic migration, helping the state grow faster than most other New England states, though the average annual population growth rate was still lower than the national rate.

Average Annual Population Growth: 1990–97

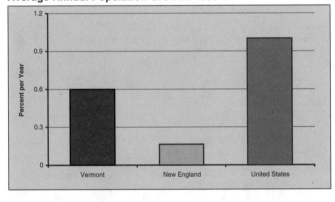

Median Household Income: 1989–97 (1997 dollars)

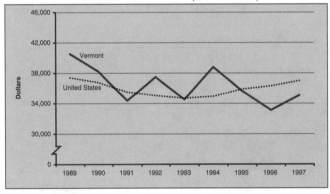

Unemployment Rate: 1989–97

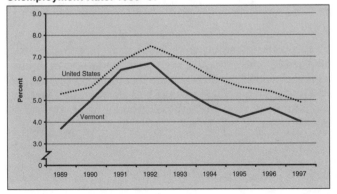

VERMONT HAD LOWER THAN AVERAGE UNEMPLOYMENT RATES throughout the decade; even at its high point in 1992, the unemployment rate was more than one percentage point lower than the national average. With rates below 5 percent since 1995, Vermont's employment has steadily grown since 1991. The unemployment high point in 1992 was associated with an increase in the labor force of just over 6,500 people, which exceeded the increase in employment of around 5,330.

POPULATION AND LABOR FORCE

VERMONT WAS OVERWHELMINGLY WHITE NON-HISPANIC—97.6 percent of the population in 1997. The Black non-Hispanic, Asian, and Hispanic populations all grew rapidly, but each from extremely small bases, and the Native American population declined. The state was very rural, with only 32.4 percent of the population living in metropolitan counties, though the percentage of the population living in metropolitan areas grew 1 percent per year between 1990 and 1997, far faster than in other states in the region except for New Hampshire.

Unemployment rates were lower in Vermont over the eight-year period than in other states in the region, with a low of 4 percent in 1997 and a high of 6.7 percent in 1992.

Population and Labor Force

	1980	1990	1991	1992	1993	1994	1995	1996	1997	Change* State	Change* U.S.
Population											
Total number of persons (thousands)	511	564	567	570	574	579	582	586	589	0.6	1.0
Percent distribution:											
White, Non-Hispanic	98.6	97.5	98.1	98.0	97.9	97.8	97.8	97.7	97.6	0.6	0.4
Black, Non-Hispanic	0.2	0.8	0.3	0.4	0.5	0.4	0.5	0.5	0.5	-5.8	1.4
Asian	0.3	0.6	0.6	0.7	0.7	0.7	0.8	0.8	0.8	4.3	4.1
Native American	0.2	0.3	0.3	0.3	0.3	0.3	0.3	0.3	0.3	-1.8	1.6
Hispanic	0.7	0.8	0.7	0.7	0.7	0.8	0.8	0.8	0.9	2.5	3.8
In metropolitan areas	26.0	31.5	31.6	31.7	31.9	32.2	32.2	32.3	32.4	1.0	1.0
Total number of households (thousands)	178	211	214	216	218	220	223	227	NA	1.2	1.2
Labor Force (thousands)											
Population 16 and over	385	436	438	440	443	448	453	458	461	0.8	1.0
Civilian labor force	250	304	304	310	316	315	319	324	327	1.0	1.1
Employed	235	289	284	290	299	300	305	309	314	1.2	1.2
Percent of population	61.0	66.3	64.9	65.8	67.4	67.0	67.5	67.5	68.2		
Unemployment rate (percent)	6.4	5.0	6.4	6.7	5.5	4.7	4.2	4.6	4.0		

*Compound annual average percent change, 1990–1997; 1990–1996 for households.

Population Change and Components: 1990–97

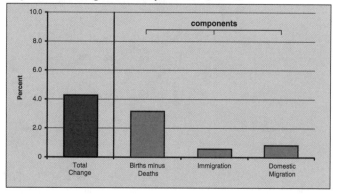

Average Annual Household and Population Growth

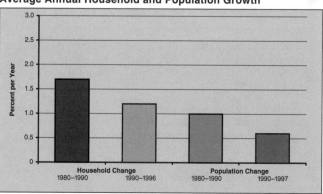

Population by Age; Births and Deaths

	1990 State	1990 U.S.	1997 State	1997 U.S.
Age distribution (percent)				
Under 5 years	7.4	7.6	5.9	7.2
5 to 17 years	18.0	18.2	18.8	18.8
18 to 64 years	62.9	61.8	63.0	61.3
65 years and over	11.7	12.5	12.3	12.7
Birth and death rates (per thousand population)				
Births	14.7	16.7	11.3	14.6
Deaths	8.2	8.6	8.9	8.6

VERMONT HAD A HIGHER THAN AVERAGE PERCENTAGE OF PEOPLE between the ages of 18 and 64 and had lower or equivalent percentages in all other age categories. The birth rate of 11.3 births per 1,000 in 1997 was the second lowest in the nation (next to Maine), contributing to a very small preschool-age group.

HOUSEHOLD AND PERSONAL INCOME

HOUSEHOLD INCOME AND PERSONS IN POVERTY	1990	1995	1996	1997	
				State	U.S.
Median household income (1997 dollars)	38 188	35 622	33 100	35 053	37 005
Persons in poverty (thousands)	61	61	74	54	35 574
Poverty rate (percent)	10.9	10.3	12.6	9.3	13.3

MEDIAN HOUSEHOLD INCOME IN VERMONT DECLINED over the decade, as real incomes in 1997 stood at only 86.5 percent of their 1989 levels. Poverty rates fluctuated from 1995 to 1997, reaching levels near the national level in 1996 but dropping to a decade low in 1997.

Personal income is based on aggregate data from business and government sources. Per capita personal income represents aggregate data divided by population rather than the income of the median household. Personal income per capita was below the national average and expanded at a slower rate. Wages and salaries also grew more slowly, as did proprietors' income, which grew very slowly when compared with either the national increase in proprietor's income or with earnings and wages within the state. The adjustment for residence increased by 6.3 percent, indicat-

ing that an increasing number of Vermonters are leaving the state for employment, though the amount of the adjustment is quite small compared to personal income.

Total transfer payments grew in Vermont by 7.3 percent per year on average. The programs that saw the largest growth were medical payments, Supplemental Security Income, and food stamps, growing at an average annual rate (of 10.6 percent, 7.5 percent, and 7.4 percent), respectively. While Social Security payments only grew 6 percent per year in Vermont, it was by far still the largest program, with disbursements of more than $813 million in 1997. Unemployment payments and family assistance (formerly Aid to Families with Dependent Children) payments declined, contracting by 2.6 percent and 0.9 percent per year, respectively.

Personal Income
(millions of dollars)

	1980	1989	1990	1991	1992	1993	1994	1995	1996	1997	Change*
Earnings by place of work	3 136	6 769	6 978	6 998	7 504	7 815	8 130	8 468	8 872	9 272	4.0
Wages and salaries	2 435	5 246	5 434	5 465	5 783	6 024	6 269	6 593	6 943	7 325	4.3
Other labor income	245	579	625	663	710	780	820	822	798	795	4.1
Proprietors' income	456	944	919	870	1 011	1 011	1 040	1 053	1 131	1 152	2.5
Farm	79	95	65	54	124	82	75	51	88	65	-4.6
Nonfarm	377	849	854	816	887	929	965	1 001	1 043	1 087	3.1
(−) Personal contributions for social insurance	164	427	446	465	491	516	547	580	604	636	5.1
(+) Adjustment for residence	13	52	53	54	55	53	59	66	71	86	NA
(=) Net earnings by state of residence	2 984	6 395	6 585	6 587	7 068	7 352	7 642	7 954	8 339	8 721	4.0
(+) Dividends, interest, and rent	754	1 984	2 030	2 041	2 013	2 014	2 184	2 411	2 606	2 693	3.9
(+) Transfer payments	684	1 222	1 364	1 520	1 681	1 762	1 861	2 013	2 065	2 143	7.3
(=) Total personal income	4 423	9 601	9 979	10 147	10 762	11 128	11 688	12 378	13 010	13 557	4.4
Farm	111	128	104	92	161	121	115	97	135	113	-1.5
Nonfarm	4 312	9 473	9 875	10 055	10 601	11 006	11 572	12 281	12 875	13 444	4.5
Personal income per capita (dollars)											
Current dollars	8 629	17 215	17 678	17 896	18 879	19 388	20 185	21 237	22 184	23 018	3.7
1997 dollars	16 499	21 764	21 273	20 665	21 117	21 097	21 451	22 076	22 591	23 018	0.7

*Compound annual average percent change, 1989–1997

Government Transfer Payments

	Millions of dollars		Percent change*	
	1990	1997	State	U.S.
Total government payments to individuals	1 272	2 029	59.4	62.7
Retirement, disability, and insurance	680	1 014	49.1	48.2
Social Security	541	814	50.3	46.1
Government employee retirement	121	181	49.4	60.3
Medical payments	344	698	102.8	101.2
Income maintenance	137	189	38.0	58.0
Supplemental Security Income	31	52	65.7	75.4
Family assistance	53	44	-16.6	-0.5
Food Stamps	24	39	64.8	27.1
Other income maintenance	29	54	85.9	189.8
Unemployment insurance benefits	53	50	-6.1	10.6
Veterans benefits and other	58	78	33.7	30.8

*Percent change, 1990–1997

Government Payments to Individuals: 1997

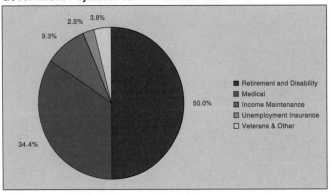

- Retirement and Disability 50.0%
- Medical 34.4%
- Income Maintenance 9.3%
- Unemployment Insurance 2.5%
- Veterans & Other 3.8%

ECONOMIC STRUCTURE

LEADING PRIVATE INDUSTRIES, 1997 (Worker and proprietor earnings, millions of dollars)		FASTEST EARNINGS GROWTH, 1989–97 (percent increase)	
Health services	$899	Social services	100.1
Electronic and other electric equipment ...	521	Business services	97.1
Construction specialties	407	Other transportation services	95.0
Business services	373	Educational services	74.7
Educational services	244	Food and kindred products	69.7

TOTAL EMPLOYMENT IN VERMONT GREW AT A MODERATE 1.3 percent per year on average from 1989 to 1997. Mining employment, which fell in every other state in the region, rose slightly in Vermont, though this increase was from a small base and also included a fall in employment that was not arrested until 1994. Construction was the only sector to suffer significant employment loss from 1989 to 1997, though manufacturing experienced a very slight drop. Employment in agricultural services, forestry, and fisheries; services; and transportation, communication, and utilities grew rapidly. Services and transportation, communications, and utilities had the fastest earnings growth. Finance, insurance, and real estate, which was stagnant in terms of employment growth over the period, reached earnings growth of 4.8 percent per year. Construction was the only sector to experience earnings loss, though the loss was very small. Three of the top five industries in Vermont were services (health, business, and education).

Employment and Earnings by Sector

	1980	1989	1990	1991	1992	1993	1994	1995	1996	1997 Number	1997 Percent of total	Change*
Employment *(thousands of persons)*												
Total	266	345	344	338	345	353	363	370	377	383	100.0	1.3
Farm	14	10	10	10	10	9	9	9	9	8	2.2	-2.2
Nonfarm	252	335	334	328	335	343	353	362	368	374	97.8	1.4
Private nonfarm	213	290	287	281	288	295	305	313	320	325	85.0	1.5
Agricultural service, forestry, and fishing	2	4	4	4	4	5	5	5	5	6	1.5	4.7
Mining	1	1	1	1	1	1	1	1	1	1	0.2	0.6
Construction	15	28	25	22	22	23	23	24	24	25	6.5	-1.6
Manufacturing	55	53	51	49	48	49	50	51	52	52	13.7	-0.1
Transportation and public utilities	10	12	13	13	13	13	14	14	15	15	4.0	2.6
Wholesale trade	10	13	13	13	14	14	14	15	14	14	3.6	0.7
Retail trade	40	59	58	57	58	60	62	64	66	67	17.4	1.4
Finance, insurance, and real estate	15	22	22	21	21	21	21	21	22	22	5.7	0.1
Services	64	97	101	102	106	111	115	118	121	124	32.4	3.1
Government	39	45	47	47	48	48	48	49	49	49	12.8	1.1
Earnings *(millions of dollars)*												
Total	3 136	6 769	6 978	6 998	7 504	7 815	8 130	8 468	8 872	9 272	100.0	4.0
Farm	111	128	104	92	161	121	115	97	135	113	1.2	-1.5
Nonfarm	3 025	6 641	6 874	6 906	7 343	7 694	8 015	8 371	8 737	9 159	98.8	4.1
Private nonfarm	2 583	5 678	5 821	5 793	6 160	6 472	6 753	7 065	7 394	7 752	83.6	4.0
Agricultural service, forestry, and fishing	15	46	53	54	56	57	58	57	57	60	0.6	3.3
Mining	28	16	17	18	18	19	21	20	21	23	0.2	4.9
Construction	209	643	575	487	499	524	545	582	608	631	6.8	-0.2
Manufacturing	925	1 525	1 552	1 564	1 610	1 639	1 660	1 725	1 813	1 897	20.5	2.8
Transportation and public utilities	197	356	377	383	408	441	460	488	508	531	5.7	5.1
Wholesale trade	146	362	362	370	412	420	449	466	458	472	5.1	3.4
Retail trade	338	761	765	750	793	838	882	915	946	992	10.7	3.4
Finance, insurance, and real estate	133	356	381	373	413	442	445	472	495	518	5.6	4.8
Services	592	1 613	1 740	1 795	1 951	2 091	2 233	2 339	2 487	2 628	28.3	6.3
Government	442	963	1 053	1 113	1 183	1 222	1 261	1 305	1 343	1 407	15.2	4.9

*Compound annual average percent change, 1989–1997

ECONOMIC STRUCTURE (Continued)

AVERAGE WAGES IN VERMONT WERE LOWER THAN WAGES IN the United States or New England on average in 1997. In every sector, wages were lower, but finance, real estate, and insurance; mining; and wholesale trade wages were lowest in comparison. Retail trade wages, the lowest within Vermont, had the most similarity to wages in the rest of the country. Manufacturing wages were also 10.2 percent lower in Vermont. Average wages in the state grew slightly slower than they did in the rest of the country.

Manufacturing, as a percentage of gross state product, was higher in Vermont in 1997 than it was in the United States as a whole, though less important in the state than in 1989. Manufacturing output value fell slightly in 1995 but grew overall from 1989 to 1997. Durable goods represented 72.6 percent of all manufacturing in the state.

Goods exports from Vermont increased 12.5 percent between 1994 and 1997, though the increase occurred entirely in 1995. Industrial machinery was the only exported good in the top five that did not increase its value of exports between 1994 and 1997. Other commodities exports, which includes re-exported goods, fell dramatically from 1994 to 1997, losing 44.6 percent of its value.

Average Annual Wages and Salaries by Sector
(dollars)

	1989	1996	1997 State	1997 U.S.
All wage and salary workers	18 994	23 832	24 833	29 809
Farm	10 464	16 460	17 340	16 442
Nonfarm	19 086	23 900	24 898	29 900
Private nonfarm	19 011	23 745	24 702	29 867
Agricultural service, forestry, and fishing	15 045	17 627	17 879	17 941
Mining	24 342	28 296	30 031	49 800
Construction	20 988	25 466	26 369	31 765
Manufacturing	26 315	32 958	34 457	38 351
Transportation and utilities	26 345	30 714	31 769	38 222
Wholesale trade	23 689	30 320	31 614	39 466
Retail trade	11 962	14 274	14 802	16 206
Finance, insurance, and real estate	23 693	32 278	33 907	44 993
Services	15 887	21 439	22 321	27 588
Government	19 464	24 657	25 871	30 062

Gross State Product and Manufacturing
(millions of dollars, except as noted)

	1989	1994	1995	1996
Gross state product, total	11 175	13 555	13 867	14 611
Manufacturing:				
Millions of dollars	2 391	2 510	2 478	2 645
Percent of total gross state product	21.4	18.5	17.9	18.1
Per worker (dollars)	45 169	50 442	48 917	51 102
New capital expenditures, manufacturing	NA	365	795	706

Exports of Goods
(millions of dollars)

	1994	1995	1996	1997
All goods	2 304	2 684	2 611	2 592
Manufactures	2 211	2 626	2 535	2 538
Agricultural and livestock products	13	11	12	9
Other commodities	81	47	64	45
Top goods exports, 1997:				
Electric and electronic equipment	1 775	2 202	2 056	1 983
Industrial machinery and computers	145	136	121	138
Transportation equipment	29	28	38	54
Fabricated metal products	51	26	59	51
Lumber and wood products	30	35	36	44

HOUSING

Housing production per capita was lower in Vermont than in the United States as a whole. Building permits never recovered from a precipitous drop in 1990, and manufactured housing production was down as well. Manufactured housing (mobile homes) put in place per 1,000 people was higher in Vermont than in the country at large from 1989–93 and then again in 1997. This is quite unusual, for New England states generally do not heavily use manufactured housing, which is primarily concentrated in the South. Sales of existing homes boomed in 1991–93 after a big drop in 1989, but have declined since then. Homeownership rates were higher than national rates, often by 5 or more percentage points. Rental vacancy rates started low but hit an anomalous high in 1994, twice as high as in 1993 or 1995, and ended the period only slightly higher than 1989 rates.

Homeownership Rates: 1989 and 1997

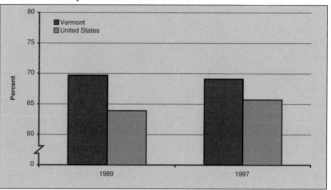

Housing Supply

	1989	1990	1991	1992	1993	1994	1995	1996	1997
Residential building permits (thousands)	3.6	2.4	2.0	2.3	2.3	2.4	2.3	2.1	1.8
New home production (including manufactured housing):									
Thousands of homes	4.4	3.0	2.5	2.9	2.9	2.9	2.8	2.6	2.6
Rate per 1,000 population									
Vermont	7.9	5.3	4.4	5.1	5.1	5.0	4.8	4.4	4.4
U.S.	6.2	5.2	4.5	5.1	5.6	6.4	6.3	6.6	6.5
Existing home sales:									
Thousands of homes	6.2	6.1	8.1	9.5	11.0	10.9	8.8	8.4	8.1
Change from previous year (percent)									
Vermont	-34.7	-1.6	32.8	17.3	15.8	-0.9	-19.3	-4.5	-3.6
U.S.	-3.9	-4.0	0.0	9.2	8.2	4.8	-3.7	7.5	3.8
Home ownership rate (percent of households)	69.7	72.6	70.8	70.8	68.5	69.4	70.4	70.3	69.1
Rental vacancy rate (percent of rental housing units)	2.9	6.2	6.5	5.3	5.2	10.3	5.3	4.2	3.7

AGRICULTURE

Farm receipts in Vermont fluctuated over the decade but ended up higher in 1997 than in 1989. Government payments to farmers in Vermont were quite low but still higher than in other states in the region, directly related to the predominance of dairy farms in the state. Production expenses increased over the decade as well but did not show the constant growth seen in other states in the region. Total net farm proprietors' income reached a high point in 1991–92. The average farm was smaller than the average U.S. farm but was larger than average farms in

any other New England state, again because of the large number of dairy farms in the state. The value per farm was lower, however.

VERMONT FARMS, 1997	
Number of farms	6 000
Total acres (thousands):	1 350
Average per farm	225
Value of land and buildings (millions of dollars)	2 093
Average per farm (dollars)	348 833

Farm Income
(millions of dollars)

	1980	1989	1990	1991	1992	1993	1994	1995	1996	1997
Gross income	413	508	522	493	538	542	533	526	580	569
Receipts from sales	384	453	477	450	493	499	489	482	540	522
Government payments	1	7	6	3	6	3	4	4	4	3
Imputed and miscellaneous income	27	48	39	40	39	40	40	39	36	43
(–) Production expenses	351	409	433	432	434	437	458	476	479	504
(=) Realized net income	62	99	88	61	105	105	75	50	101	65
(+) Inventory change	17	1	-20	-6	26	-21	7	4	-6	5
(=) Net income	79	100	68	56	130	83	82	54	95	70
Corporate income	0	4	3	2	7	2	6	3	7	5
Farm proprietors income	79	95	65	54	124	82	75	51	88	65

EDUCATION

EDUCATIONAL ATTAINMENT Percent of population age 25 and over, 1997	State	United States
High school graduate or higher	84.4	82.1
College graduate or higher	23.7	23.9

VERMONT RANKED 26TH IN THE NATION IN THE PERCENTAGE of the population holding a high school diploma in 1997. Spending per pupil was slightly higher in Vermont than in the country on average, and teacher's salaries were just under the national average. Private school enrollment was relatively small at 8.4 percent of total enrollment, compared to 10.1 percent nationwide. Vermont ranked 21st nationally in the percentage of the population holding a bachelor's degree. In 1996, 25.1 percent of the population aged 18 to 34 were enrolled in institutions of higher learning. Minority enrollment was very low in Vermont, as in many other New England states—only 4.5 percent of students in 1996. Of higher education students, 42.6 percent in Vermont attended a private school in 1996, a figure almost double the national average.

High School Completion: 1990–97

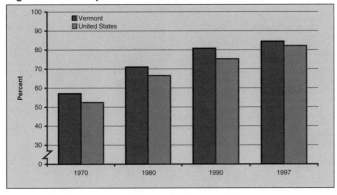

Education Indicators

	State	U.S.
Elementary and secondary schools		
Enrollment, 1995–96		
Total (thousands)	115	49 873
Percent in private schools	8.4	10.1
Expenditures per pupil (dollars), 1995–96	6 837	6 146
Average teacher salary (dollars), 1996–97	37 200	38 509
Higher education		
Enrollment, 1996–97		
Total (thousands)	35	14 218
Percent of population 18–34	25.1	21.8
Percent minority	4.5	26.1
Percent in private schools	42.6	22.6

HEALTH

VERMONT'S AGE-ADJUSTED DEATH RATE (WHERE CHANGES IN the age composition within a state over time are taken into account) was consistently lower than the national average, with a slight increase in Vermont and a decrease in the U.S. in 1997 bringing the two closer together. Infant mortality was lower than nationwide, though the 1996 rate in Vermont was higher. The number of people without health insurance was quite low in Vermont as compared to the U.S. average. The main causes of death in Vermont were cancer and heart disease (as they are in the country as a whole). However, the causes of death that were higher in Vermont than elsewhere in the country were malignant neoplasms, diabetes, Alzheimer's disease, and chronic obstructive pulmonary diseases (including emphysema).

Health Indicators

	1990	1995	1996	1997
Infant mortality				
(rate per thousand live births)				
Vermont	6.4	6.0	8.9	6.1
U.S.	9.2	7.6	7.3	7.1
Total deaths, age-adjusted rate				
(rate per thousand population)				
Vermont	4.8	4.7	4.5	4.7
U.S.	5.2	5.0	4.9	4.8
Persons not covered by health insurance				
(percent of population)				
Vermont	9.5	13.2	11.1	9.5
U.S.	13.9	15.4	15.6	16.1

Leading Causes of Death, 1996
(deaths per 100,000 population)

	Age-adjusted		Not age-adjusted	
	State	U.S.	State	U.S.
Deaths from all causes	450.0	491.6	827.3	872.5
Heart disease	120.4	134.5	252.6	276.4
Cancer	128.3	127.9	205.0	203.4
Cerebrovascular diseases	22.2	26.4	54.5	60.3
Chronic obstructive pulmonary disease	22.2	21.0	41.3	40.0
Diabetes mellitus	15.6	13.6	26.2	23.3
Pneumonia and influenza	10.7	12.8	28.7	31.6
HIV	NA	11.1	NA	11.7
Liver disease	4.2	7.5	5.3	9.4
Alzheimer's disease	4.3	2.7	12.9	8.1
Accidents and adverse effects	26.2	30.4	33.0	35.8
Motor vehicle accidents	13.9	16.2	14.3	16.5
Suicide	10.3	10.8	11.2	11.6
Homicide	NA	8.5	NA	7.9
Injury by firearm	9.1	12.9	9.5	12.8

GOVERNMENT

STATE AND LOCAL TAXES, 1995–96	State	U.S.
Per capita (dollars)	2 501	2 477
Percent of personal income	11.9	10.8

STATE AND LOCAL TAXES PER CAPITA (LESS CORPORATE TAX) were slightly higher than the U.S. average, but because of Vermont's below-average incomes, the average tax rate required to yield this level of taxes, 11.9 percent of personal income, was substantially higher than the national average rate of 10.8 percent. Vermont's state government, however, had lower taxes per capita than the average state. Sales taxes and corporate net income taxes were

State Government Finances, 1996–97

	Millions of dollars	Percent distribu-tion	Dollars per capita State	Dollars per capita U.S.
General revenue	2 053	100.0	3 485	3 049
Intergovernmental revenue	667	32.5	1 132	863
Taxes	899	43.8	1 527	1 660
General sales	184	9.0	312	551
Selective sales	225	11.0	383	257
License taxes	68	3.3	115	106
Individual income	323	15.7	549	542
Corporation net income	45	2.2	77	115
Other taxes	54	2.6	91	90
Other general revenue	486	23.7	826	526
General expenditure	1 971	100.0	3 346	2 951
Intergovernmental expenditure	312	15.8	530	989
Direct expenditure	1 658	84.2	2 816	1 962
General expenditure, by function:				
Education	645	32.7	1 095	1 033
Public welfare	523	26.5	888	761
Hospitals and health	59	3.0	99	237
Highways	191	9.7	324	225
Police protection and corrections	74	3.7	125	137
Natural resources, parks and recreation	74	3.8	126	63
Governmental administration	116	5.9	196	107
Interest on general debt	112	5.7	190	99
Other and unallocable	178	9.0	303	290
Debt at end of fiscal year	2 037	NA	3 459	1 706
Cash and security holdings	3 672	NA	6 234	6 683

Federal Spending within State

	Federal funds, fiscal 1997 Millions of dollars	Percent distribution	Percent of U.S. total*
Total within state	2 757	100.0	0.2
Payments to individuals	1 612	58.5	0.2
Retirement and disability	988	35.8	0.2
Medicare	353	12.8	0.2
Food stamps	41	1.5	0.2
Supplemental Security Income	43	1.6	0.2
Grants	704	25.5	0.3
Medicaid and other health	293	10.6	0.3
Nutrition and family welfare	132	4.8	0.3
Education	52	1.9	0.3
Housing and community development	17	0.6	0.1
Salaries and wages	267	9.7	0.2
Defense procurement contracts	98	3.6	0.1
Non-defense procurement contracts	52	1.9	0.1

*State population is 0.2 percent of the U.S. total.

significantly lower than the national levels. Individual income tax was almost identical in Vermont and the country, but selective sales taxes (such as gas taxes) were 48.9 percent higher. Total and general expenditures were slightly higher. Education spending was just over the national level per capita, unusual for a New England state, and public welfare spending was 16.7 percent higher. Spending for hospitals and health was far lower, but highways and police protection and correction were higher.

Vermont received 0.2 percent of all federally allocated funds in 1997, which is commensurate with its 0.2 percent of the U.S. population. Direct payments to individuals were higher than the population figures would suggest, while grants were lower. Procurement funds, both defense and non-defense, were also low compared to the state population, though they did represent 3.6 percent and 1.9 percent of total federal funds allocated to Vermont, respectively.

31 372	59 698		65 157	70 827	72 687	78 001	81 93	88 504	93 426	5.8	63 383	70 827	31 372	59 698	63 3
25 323	47 902		57 151	59 446	62 916	67 00	72 039	77 208	6.1	50 999	57 151	25 323	47 902	50 9
2 640	5 143			7 801		7 709	7 838	5.4	5 645	6 816	2 640	5 143	5 6
3 409	6 652			284		8 755	8 380	2.9	6 739	6 860	3 409	6 652	6 7
693	1 716			07		1 539	762	-9.7	1 581	811	693	1 716	1 5
716						817	618	5.8	5 178	6 049	716	4 9	

1997

Population (persons)	6,737,489
Population rank	12th
Population growth rank (1990–97)	17th
Per capita personal income	$26,172
Unemployment rate (percent)	4.0
Poverty rate (percent)	12.7

VIRGINIA IS THE NATION'S 12TH MOST POPULOUS STATE AND among those whose population has grown more rapidly than the national average during the 1990s. The state's 1990s population and employment growth have not matched the breakneck expansion of the 1980s, however, and cutbacks in defense spending have hit parts of Virginia hard. Even so, the state largely has shared in the nation's mid-1990s prosperity. Rapid growth of private service-producing industries, including business services, real estate, engineering and management services, banking, and communications, has compensated for the loss of federal jobs and a decline in manufacturing employment. In 1997, the state's unemployment rate was only 4.0 per-

cent, the household income median and the per capita personal income average exceeded the nation's, and the poverty rate was a little below the national average.

Growth has been most rapid in Northern Virginia, the state's portion of the Washington, DC metropolitan area, an area with a racially and ethnically diverse 1997 population of 2 million and the area that provided more than 30 percent of the state's jobs in 1997.

Prosperity has swelled the coffers of state government and some of the increased revenue is being used to reduce in-state tuition at state-supported colleges and universities, reduce sales taxes on food, and increase funding for a variety of state programs.

Average Annual Population Growth: 1990–97

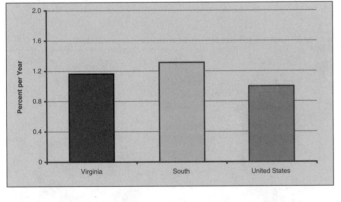

Median Household Income: 1989–97 (1997 dollars)

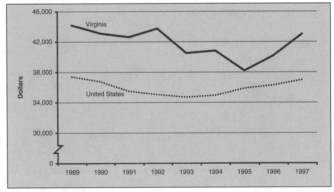

Unemployment Rate: 1989–97

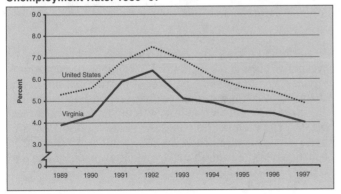

DURING THE 1990S, VIRGINIA'S UNEMPLOYMENT RATE HAS followed a pattern much like the nation's, pushed up by recession from 1990 to 1992 and falling each year thereafter. The Virginia rate remained well below the national rate at each stage of the cycle, however. The 1997 unemployment rate in Northern Virginia, the state's largest population center, was lower than the state-wide average of 4.0 percent, as was the rate in the Richmond-Petersburg area. However, the unemployment rate in the Norfolk-Virginia Beach-Newport News area was higher, 4.8 percent.

POPULATION AND LABOR FORCE

Virginia's 1.2 percent per year population growth from 1990 to 1997 exceeded the national average, but fell short of the state's 1.5 percent per year average growth during the 1980s. Immigration from abroad contributed 20 percent of the 1990 to 1997 population increase, in-migration from other states 25 percent, and natural increase (births minus deaths) the remainder.

With the continuing immigration, the state's population has become increasingly diverse. The Asian and Hispanic shares grew rapidly during the 1980s and the 1990s, each reaching 3.5 percent of the population by 1997. The share of the non-Hispanic Black population also has grown somewhat. Thus, the non-Hispanic White population, although it grew more rapidly than the national average from 1990 to 1997, declined as a share of the state's total population.

Population growth has been most rapid in metropolitan areas. Two-thirds of the population lives in the three largest metropolitan areas: Norfolk-Virginia Beach-Newport News, Richmond-Petersburg, and Northern Virginia (the state's portion of the Washington, DC metropolitan area). With a 1997 population of 2 million, Northern Virginia houses 20 percent of the state's population and more than one-half of its Asians and Hispanics.

Population and Labor Force

	1980	1990	1991	1992	1993	1994	1995	1996	1997	Change* State	Change* U.S.
Population											
Total number of persons (thousands)	5 347	6 214	6 284	6 384	6 467	6 539	6 602	6 667	6 737	1.2	1.0
Percent distribution:											
White, Non-Hispanic	78.3	76.1	75.6	75.1	74.7	74.4	74.0	73.6	73.2	0.6	0.4
Black, Non-Hispanic	18.7	18.4	18.9	19.1	19.2	19.4	19.5	19.6	19.7	2.1	1.4
Asian	1.3	2.7	2.7	2.9	3.0	3.1	3.2	3.3	3.5	5.0	4.1
Native American	0.2	0.3	0.3	0.3	0.3	0.3	0.3	0.3	0.3	1.0	1.6
Hispanic	1.5	2.7	2.7	2.8	2.9	3.0	3.2	3.4	3.5	4.9	3.8
In metropolitan areas	74.2	77.2	77.3	77.5	77.6	77.7	77.7	77.8	78.0	1.3	1.0
Total number of households (thousands)	1 863	2 292	2 332	2 383	2 414	2 439	2 476	2 511	NA	1.5	1.2
Labor Force (thousands)											
Population 16 and over	4 072	4 856	4 903	4 978	5 046	5 107	5 157	5 215	5 272	1.2	1.0
Civilian labor force	2 561	3 239	3 347	3 400	3 380	3 417	3 482	3 391	3 413	0.8	1.1
Employed	2 433	3 098	3 149	3 181	3 207	3 250	3 325	3 241	3 278	0.8	1.2
Percent of population	59.7	63.8	64.2	63.9	63.6	63.6	64.5	62.2	62.2		
Unemployment rate (percent)	5.0	4.3	5.9	6.4	5.1	4.9	4.5	4.4	4.0		

*Compound annual average percent change, 1990–1997; 1990–1996 for households.

Population Change and Components: 1990–97

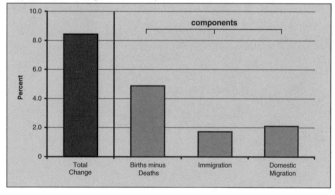

Average Annual Household and Population Growth

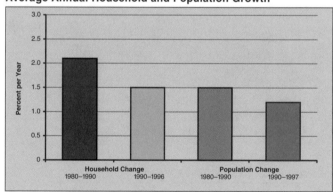

Population by Age; Births and Deaths

	1990 State	1990 U.S.	1997 State	1997 U.S.
Age distribution (percent)				
Under 5 years	7.3	7.6	6.7	7.2
5 to 17 years	17.1	18.2	17.7	18.8
18 to 64 years	64.8	61.8	64.4	61.3
65 years and over	10.7	12.5	11.2	12.7
Birth and death rates (per thousand population)				
Births	16.1	16.7	13.7	14.6
Deaths	7.8	8.6	8.0	8.6

In part because of its large military contingent, an unusually large proportion of Virginia's population is between age 18 and 64, and the proportions of the population in other age groups are correspondingly smaller. Virginia's birth rate fell in line with the nation's from 1990 to 1997. The high birth rate of the years around 1990 and the lower birth rate of the last few years are reflected in the shift in population shares from children under age five to those between ages five and seventeen.

HOUSEHOLD AND PERSONAL INCOME

HOUSEHOLD INCOME AND PERSONS IN POVERTY	1990	1995	1996	1997 State	1997 U.S.
Median household income (1997 dollars)	43 070	38 147	40 111	42 957	37 005
Persons in poverty (thousands)	705	648	795	858	35 574
Poverty rate (percent)	11.1	10.2	12.3	12.7	13.3

ADJUSTED FOR INFLATION, VIRGINIA'S MEDIAN HOUSEHOLD income has fluctuated from year to year during the 1990s, and the 1996-97 average was lower than in 1990. In both periods Virginia's median household income was more than 10 percent above the national average. The state's poverty rate in 1996-97 was a little higher than in 1990 and about equal to 1980; it was below the national average in each of these years. Real per capita personal income in Virginia has been above the national average since the early 1980s, reaching a relative peak of 106 percent from 1987 to 1989; since 1990 it has hovered around 104 percent.

Earnings provided 68 percent of Virginia personal income in 1997, compared to only 66 percent nationally. Almost 5 percent of these earnings came from earnings of Virginians working outside the state that exceeded the earnings in Virginia of residents of other states (shown in the "adjustment for residence" in the table). A large share of these out-of-state earnings came from Virginia residents commuting to jobs in other parts of the Washington, DC area.

Government transfer payments rose 65 percent from 1990 to 1997, compared to a U.S. average of 63 percent. Income maintenance payments rose more rapidly in the state than nationwide. "Other income maintenance," a category consisting largely of the earned income tax credit, was the most rapidly growing transfer program both in Virginia and in the nation. Supplemental Security Income and food stamp payments rose more rapidly in the state than nationally, and family assistance payments, which were about level for the nation as a whole, showed a small rise in Virginia.

Personal Income
(millions of dollars)

	1980	1989	1990	1991	1992	1993	1994	1995	1996	1997	Change*
Earnings by place of work	37 646	83 523	87 322	89 306	94 742	99 619	104 309	109 489	114 930	122 598	4.9
Wages and salaries	31 791	70 014	73 512	75 176	79 421	82 771	86 656	91 422	96 721	103 898	5.1
Other labor income	2 808	6 606	7 175	7 681	8 369	9 146	9 811	9 767	9 582	9 761	5.0
Proprietors' income	3 047	6 903	6 635	6 448	6 952	7 702	7 842	8 300	8 626	8 939	3.3
Farm	-50	477	471	416	447	321	386	314	288	186	-11.1
Nonfarm	3 098	6 426	6 164	6 032	6 505	7 381	7 456	7 987	8 338	8 753	3.9
(−) Personal contributions for social insurance	2 035	5 405	5 689	5 951	6 246	6 568	6 988	7 364	7 683	8 220	5.4
(+) Adjustment for residence	2 742	3 954	4 528	4 918	5 240	5 619	5 823	5 832	5 567	5 625	NA
(=) **Net earnings by state of residence**	38 352	82 072	86 161	88 273	93 735	98 670	103 144	107 957	112 814	120 003	4.9
(+) Dividends, interest, and rent	7 796	21 580	22 824	23 545	23 205	24 317	26 115	27 653	29 481	30 716	4.5
(+) Transfer payments	7 291	14 124	15 417	16 988	18 917	20 150	21 332	22 816	24 304	25 526	7.7
(=) **Total personal income**	53 439	117 776	124 401	128 807	135 857	143 137	150 591	158 426	166 599	176 245	5.2
Farm	88	621	639	581	605	496	555	487	468	364	-6.5
Nonfarm	53 351	117 155	123 762	128 226	135 252	142 641	150 036	157 939	166 131	175 882	5.2
Personal income per capita (dollars)											
Current dollars	9 954	19 244	20 021	20 503	21 283	22 139	23 034	24 000	24 992	26 172	3.9
1997 dollars	19 033	24 329	24 093	23 676	23 806	24 090	24 478	24 948	25 450	26 172	0.9

*Compound annual average percent change, 1989–1997

Government Transfer Payments

	Millions of dollars 1990	Millions of dollars 1997	Percent change* State	Percent change* U.S.
Total government payments to individuals	14 626	24 160	65.2	62.7
Retirement, disability, and insurance	9 771	15 072	54.3	48.2
Social Security	4 944	7 788	57.5	46.1
Government employee retirement	4 440	6 850	54.3	60.3
Medical payments	3 080	6 229	102.2	101.2
Income maintenance	884	1 647	86.4	58.0
Supplemental Security Income	273	528	93.5	75.4
Family assistance	188	195	3.8	-0.5
Food Stamps	261	358	37.4	27.1
Other income maintenance	162	566	249.6	189.8
Unemployment insurance benefits	190	182	-4.3	10.6
Veterans benefits and other	701	1 030	47.0	30.8

*Percent change, 1990–1997

Government Payments to Individuals: 1997

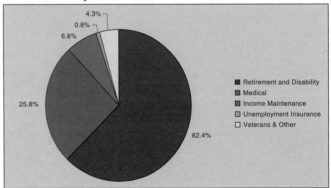

- Retirement and Disability — 62.4%
- Medical — 25.8%
- Income Maintenance — 6.8%
- Unemployment Insurance — 0.8%
- Veterans & Other — 4.3%

ECONOMIC STRUCTURE

LEADING PRIVATE INDUSTRIES, 1997 (Worker and proprietor earnings, millions of dollars)		FASTEST EARNINGS GROWTH, 1989–97 (percent increase)	
Business services	$10 079	Business services	121.5
Health services	8 266	Social services	116.4
Engineering and management services ..	7 234	Real estate	106.7
Construction specialties	4 802	Educational services	103.6
Banks and other credit institutions	3 109	Membership organizations	100.6

VIRGINIA HAS BECOME EVEN MORE OF A SERVICE ECONOMY during the 1990s, with employment in each goods producing-sector—manufacturing, mining, construction, and farming—declining from 1989 to 1997. The goods-producing industries provided only 18 percent of all jobs in 1997, and the service-producing industries provided 82 percent, compared to 80 percent nationwide. Each of the five industries that grew fastest from 1989 to 1997 is a service-producing industry as are four of the five largest industries, measured by worker and proprietor earnings.

The large federal presence in Northern Virginia and the large number of military personnel stationed in the Norfolk area bring the government share of employment well above the national average. Government employed 19 percent of all Virginia workers in 1997, compared to 14 percent nationwide. Government's share of the state's economy has been falling throughout the 1980s and 1990s, however, as both federal civilian and military employment have been reduced. The 19 percent

employment share in 1997 compares with 21 percent in 1989 and 24 percent in 1980. In absolute numbers, government employment rose by only 6,000 jobs from 1989 to 1997, as federal cutbacks very nearly offset growth of state and local employment.

The geographic pattern of employment has continued to shift toward Northern Virginia in the 1990s. Despite federal cutbacks, this region (a portion of the Washington DC metropolitan area) has had far more rapid employment growth than any other metropolitan area in the state from 1990 to 1997 and accounted for over 30 percent of the state's total employment in 1997. Employment growth in the state's two other large metropolitan areas, Norfolk-Virginia Beach-Newport News and Richmond-Petersburg, was a little slower than the statewide average, so that their shares of total employment diminished slightly. Even so, the Norfolk-Virginia Beach-Newport News area provided almost 21 percent of the state's jobs in 1997 and the Richmond-Petersburg area over 16 percent.

Employment and Earnings by Sector

	1980	1989	1990	1991	1992	1993	1994	1995	1996	1997 Number	1997 Percent of total	Change*
Employment *(thousands of persons)*												
Total	2 802	3 685	3 720	3 669	3 688	3 761	3 851	3 940	4 021	4 125	100.0	1.4
Farm	85	63	63	64	62	61	61	64	62	62	1.5	-0.1
Nonfarm	2 717	3 622	3 657	3 604	3 626	3 700	3 790	3 876	3 959	4 063	98.5	1.4
Private nonfarm	2 040	2 847	2 864	2 813	2 824	2 894	2 987	3 083	3 173	3 282	79.6	1.8
Agricultural service, forestry, and fishing ..	17	29	31	31	31	34	37	38	40	42	1.0	4.9
Mining	25	19	18	17	16	15	15	14	13	13	0.3	-4.3
Construction	161	259	245	213	208	214	226	233	243	255	6.2	-0.2
Manufacturing	422	440	437	424	420	418	419	417	415	420	10.2	-0.6
Transportation and public utilities	128	164	165	166	163	168	172	177	185	192	4.7	2.0
Wholesale trade	110	147	142	141	142	140	145	151	154	154	3.7	0.6
Retail trade	401	589	595	584	587	600	626	647	664	677	16.4	1.8
Finance, insurance, and real estate	204	258	260	252	243	251	264	268	275	285	6.9	1.3
Services	572	943	972	986	1 013	1 053	1 083	1 138	1 185	1 243	30.1	3.5
Government	677	775	793	791	802	806	803	793	786	781	18.9	0.1
Earnings *(millions of dollars)*												
Total	37 646	83 523	87 322	89 306	94 742	99 619	104 309	109 489	114 930	122 598	100.0	4.9
Farm	88	621	639	581	605	496	555	487	468	364	0.3	-6.5
Nonfarm	37 558	82 902	86 683	88 725	94 137	99 123	103 754	109 001	114 462	122 234	99.7	5.0
Private nonfarm	27 493	63 107	65 355	66 266	70 610	74 838	78 744	83 244	88 305	95 432	77.8	5.3
Agricultural service, forestry, and fishing ..	119	377	428	446	465	495	546	565	591	642	0.5	6.9
Mining	998	642	684	664	665	648	656	643	627	657	0.5	0.3
Construction	2 472	6 570	6 113	5 260	5 158	5 678	6 164	6 534	7 002	7 632	6.2	1.9
Manufacturing	7 121	12 704	13 073	13 252	13 900	14 163	14 742	15 024	15 326	16 117	13.1	3.0
Transportation and public utilities	2 640	5 655	5 647	5 906	6 203	6 559	6 791	7 020	7 573	8 240	6.7	4.8
Wholesale trade	2 061	4 589	4 718	4 861	5 063	5 177	5 510	5 907	6 259	6 628	5.4	4.7
Retail trade	3 633	7 813	8 022	8 057	8 411	8 726	9 293	9 669	10 094	10 669	8.7	4.0
Finance, insurance, and real estate	1 743	4 717	4 989	5 044	5 829	6 666	6 844	7 276	7 837	8 615	7.0	7.8
Services	6 706	20 041	21 681	22 775	24 915	26 727	28 198	30 606	32 997	36 231	29.6	7.7
Government	10 065	19 795	21 328	22 459	23 527	24 285	25 010	25 757	26 157	26 802	21.9	3.9

*Compound annual average percent change, 1989–1997

ECONOMIC STRUCTURE (Continued)

THE $29,330 ANNUAL WAGE OR SALARY EARNED BY THE AVERage Virginia worker in 1997 was within 2 percent of the U.S. average, and was the highest among the 12 states in the Southeast. Virginia workers' annual earnings in government, private services, agricultural services, transportation and public utilities, and wholesale trade were above national averages, but these were offset by below average wages in the other sectors. Retail trade paid the lowest wages and salaries of any nonfarm sector, both in the state and nationwide, and Virginia retail workers' earnings were 3 percent below the national average. The state's farm wages were the lowest of any sector and were the farthest below national norms, at only 70 percent of the U.S. average.

Manufacturing's share of Virginia's gross state product (GSP) has diminished during the 1990s. In 1996, it accounted for only 15.2 percent of Virginia GSP, compared to a 17.5 percent national average. Manufacturing value added per worker is above the national average, however, and has risen a bit more rapidly during the 1990s, indicating a modest shift toward higher-value industries. No one industry dominates the state's manufacturing scene. Industrial machinery and computers was the most rapidly growing from 1989 to 1997. Printing and publishing is the largest, with $1.7 billion in worker and proprietor earnings in 1997, and electronic and other electrical equipment is next with $1.6 billion. The state's third largest industry, transportation equipment other than motor vehicles, had almost no earnings growth from 1989 to 1997. This is the industry that includes shipbuilding—an industry segment that has been heavily impacted by cutbacks in defense spending. Virginia factories manufacture nearly 25 percent of the nation's output of tobacco products, but this small and declining industry provided less than 3 percent of all manufacturing jobs in the state in 1997.

Virginia's goods exports increased 16 percent from 1994 to 1997, a pace less than one-half the strong 34 percent national growth. Tobacco products dominate the state's export picture, accounting for 31 percent of all 1997 goods exports, and there was no growth of tobacco product exports from 1994 to 1997. Exports of industrial machinery and computers and electric and electronic equipment grew fairly strongly over these four years and together accounted for 18 percent of all goods exports in 1997, compared to 14 percent in 1994. Exports of bituminous coal and lignite doubled over the period, coming to rival transportation equipment as the state's fourth largest export category.

Average Annual Wages and Salaries by Sector
(dollars)

	1989	1996	1997 State	1997 U.S.
All wage and salary workers	21 892	28 010	29 330	29 809
Farm	10 083	12 494	11 495	16 442
Nonfarm	21 942	28 072	29 404	29 900
Private nonfarm	21 299	27 286	28 745	29 867
Agricultural service, forestry, and fishing	14 599	17 898	18 628	17 941
Mining	30 619	39 631	40 182	49 800
Construction	22 659	26 824	28 337	31 765
Manufacturing	25 149	32 272	33 716	38 351
Transportation and utilities	31 213	38 138	40 329	38 222
Wholesale trade	28 956	38 393	40 590	39 466
Retail trade	12 557	15 060	15 689	16 206
Finance, insurance, and real estate	26 012	35 976	39 104	44 993
Services	20 543	27 872	29 310	27 588
Government	23 941	30 724	31 719	30 062

Gross State Product and Manufacturing
(millions of dollars, except as noted)

	1989	1994	1995	1996
Gross state product, total	141 346	178 788	186 986	197 809
Manufacturing:				
Millions of dollars	22 825	27 805	29 079	29 986
Percent of total gross state product	16.1	15.6	15.6	15.2
Per worker (dollars)	51 877	66 410	69 766	72 320
New capital expenditures, manufacturing	NA	2 161	2 518	3 015

Exports of Goods
(millions of dollars)

	1994	1995	1996	1997
All goods	9 947	10 425	10 926	11 512
Manufactures	8 794	9 294	9 699	10 159
Agricultural and livestock products	631	486	409	391
Other commodities	523	645	818	963
Top goods exports, 1997:				
Tobacco products	3 506	3 185	3 647	3 530
Industrial machinery and computers	853	1 008	1 044	1 113
Electric and electronic equipment	566	652	727	1 014
Transportation equipment	980	989	869	821
Bituminous coal	404	500	674	821

HOUSING

IN 1989, VIRGINIA'S HOUSING DEMAND STILL REFLECTED THE rapid population growth of the 1980s, and the state's new home production rate per thousand population was quite high. Home-building activity then fell sharply during the 1990-91 recession, although the production rate remained above the national average even at the 1991 low. Home-building in the state picked up vigorously from 1991 through 1994, then leveled off at a rate somewhat above the national average from 1995 through 1997. Sales of existing homes slumped in 1990 and 1991, and, although they came back strongly in 1992, had not regained the 1989 pace by 1997.

The Virginia homeownership rate remained at 68 or 69 percent of all households from 1993 to 1997, compared to over 70 percent in 1989, but the rate still was above the U.S. average in 1997. Owning a home in the Washington, DC metropolitan area, where 20 percent of the state's population lives, is relatively expensive; the median sale price of existing homes there was $166,300 in 1997, compared to $124,100 nationwide. Prices in the Norfolk-Virginia Beach-Newport News area ($110,200) and the Richmond-Petersburg area ($114,200) were lower.

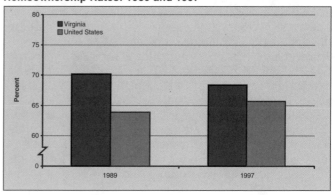

Homeownership Rates: 1989 and 1997

Housing Supply

	1989	1990	1991	1992	1993	1994	1995	1996	1997
Residential building permits (thousands)	56.9	42.1	33.7	40.2	45.0	46.8	43.1	45.9	45.5
New home production (including manufactured housing):									
Thousands of homes	63.1	48.2	39.4	45.7	51.1	52.8	49.8	51.4	50.5
Rate per 1,000 population									
Virginia	10.3	7.8	6.3	7.2	7.9	8.1	7.5	7.7	7.5
U.S.	6.2	5.2	4.5	5.1	5.6	6.4	6.3	6.6	6.5
Existing home sales:									
Thousands of homes	116.0	96.9	90.3	101.3	104.2	99.5	92.2	92.2	98.5
Change from previous year (percent)									
Virginia	-11.2	-16.5	-6.8	12.2	2.9	-4.5	-7.3	0.0	6.8
U.S.	-3.9	-4.0	0.0	9.2	8.2	4.8	-3.7	7.5	3.8
Home ownership rate (percent of households)	70.2	69.8	68.9	67.8	68.5	69.3	68.1	68.5	68.4
Rental vacancy rate (percent of rental housing units)	6.6	5.8	10.3	8.2	7.7	8.9	7.6	7.4	6.3

AGRICULTURE

VIRGINIA'S HORSE FARMS AND APPLE ORCHARDS CONTRIBUTE to its lovely countryside, but are not the economic heart of its agriculture. Poultry and its products accounted for 32 percent of all farm sales in 1997 and cattle and calves for another 17 percent. Only 4 percent of farms marketed poultry; for these farms, average poultry sales were $428,000. In contrast, 64 percent of farms marketed cattle, but received an average of only $15,000 per farm for cattle sales. Other leading agriculture activities are dairying (12 percent of 1997 sales), tobacco (8 percent), and nursery and greenhouse (7 percent). Receipts from farm sales grew from 1994 through 1997, but expenses grew more rapidly, so that net farm income declined each year.

VIRGINIA FARMS, 1997	
Number of farms	47 000
Total acres (thousands):	8 500
Average per farm	181
Value of land and buildings (millions of dollars)	17 255
Average per farm (dollars)	367 128

Farm Income
(millions of dollars)

	1980	1989	1990	1991	1992	1993	1994	1995	1996	1997
Gross income	1 770	2 561	2 636	2 546	2 582	2 580	2 612	2 650	2 802	2 845
Receipts from sales	1 563	2 208	2 285	2 269	2 291	2 282	2 332	2 368	2 493	2 545
Government payments	13	39	32	27	29	46	34	26	31	31
Imputed and miscellaneous income	194	315	319	251	262	252	246	256	279	270
(−) Production expenses	1 829	2 067	2 114	2 097	2 137	2 178	2 221	2 332	2 488	2 545
(=) Realized net income	-58	494	522	449	445	402	391	318	315	300
(+) Inventory change	-14	31	-1	1	54	-67	71	33	28	-82
(=) Net income	-72	526	521	450	499	335	462	351	343	218
Corporate income	-22	49	50	33	52	14	76	37	54	32
Farm proprietors income	-50	477	471	416	447	321	386	314	288	186

EDUCATION

EDUCATIONAL ATTAINMENT Percent of population age 25 and over, 1997	State	United States
High school graduate or higher	81.3	82.1
College graduate or higher	28.0	23.9

THE PERCENT OF VIRGINIANS AGE 25 AND OVER WHO HAVE completed four years of college has more than doubled in the past quarter-century, from 12.3 percent in 1970 to 28.0 percent in 1997. Virginia's 1996 percentage was well above the national average, ranking the state the eighth highest in the nation. Virginia's high school graduation rates also have increased, from 57.8 percent in 1970 to 81.3 percent in 1997, but national rates increased even more, so that Virginia's

rate now has dropped a little below the national average.

Like many states, Virginia has initiated comprehensive educational reforms in the 1990s, aimed at raising academic standards. Virginia's program, controversial within the state, emphasizes state-wide tests that students must pass in order to graduate, beginning with the class of 2004. Beginning in 2006-07, specified percentages of a school's students must pass the tests in order for the school to maintain its accreditation.

High School Completion: 1990–97

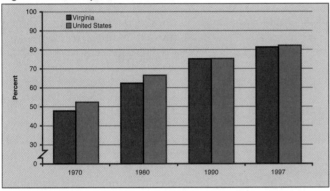

Education Indicators

	State	U.S.
Elementary and secondary schools		
Enrollment, 1995–96		
Total (thousands)	1 166	49 873
Percent in private schools	7.4	10.1
Expenditures per pupil (dollars), 1995–96	5 433	6 146
Average teacher salary (dollars), 1996–97	35 837	38 509
Higher education		
Enrollment, 1996–97		
Total (thousands)	354	14 218
Percent of population 18–34	20.1	21.8
Percent minority	24.8	26.1
Percent in private schools	17.3	22.6

HEALTH

VIRGINIA HAS SET A GOAL OF REDUCING THE STATE'S INFANT mortality rate to no more than 7 deaths per thousand live births. The reduction already achieved, from 10.2 in 1990 to 7.5 in 1997, has brought the state a considerable distance toward this goal. The state's Department of Health notes that much of the progress to date has been due to medical technology advances but that continued progress will require health promotion programs and improved

access to care for vulnerable members of society.

Adjusted for differences in the age distribution of the population, Virginia's overall death rate has fallen somewhat during the 1990s and remains just slightly above the national rate. Rates for most of the major causes of death are close to national averages. The percentage of the state's population lacking health insurance has fallen during the 1990s, while the national percentage has risen.

Health Indicators

	1990	1995	1996	1997
Infant mortality				
(rate per thousand live births)				
Virginia	10.2	7.8	7.4	7.5
U.S.	9.2	7.6	7.3	7.1
Total deaths, age-adjusted rate				
(rate per thousand population)				
Virginia	5.3	5.1	5.0	4.9
U.S.	5.2	5.0	4.9	4.8
Persons not covered by health insurance				
(percent of population)				
Virginia	15.7	13.5	12.5	12.6
U.S.	13.9	15.4	15.6	16.1

Leading Causes of Death, 1996
(deaths per 100,000 population)

	Age-adjusted		Not age-adjusted	
	State	U.S.	State	U.S.
Deaths from all causes	499.5	491.6	801.5	872.5
Heart disease	136.4	134.5	240.8	276.4
Cancer	132.0	127.9	190.4	203.4
Cerebrovascular diseases	29.0	26.4	57.8	60.3
Chronic obstructive pulmonary disease	20.0	21.0	33.9	40.0
Diabetes mellitus	12.6	13.6	18.9	23.3
Pneumonia and influenza	12.8	12.8	28.2	31.6
HIV	7.8	11.1	8.8	11.7
Liver disease	5.8	7.5	7.2	9.4
Alzheimer's disease	3.2	2.7	7.7	8.1
Accidents and adverse effects	27.7	30.4	33.5	35.8
Motor vehicle accidents	12.8	16.2	13.3	16.5
Suicide	11.4	10.8	12.4	11.6
Homicide	8.1	8.5	8.0	7.9
Injury by firearm	14.1	12.9	14.5	12.8

GOVERNMENT

STATE AND LOCAL TAXES, 1995–96	State	U.S.
Per capita (dollars)	2 287	2 477
Percent of personal income	9.6	10.8

IN THE 1995-96 FISCAL YEAR, VIRGINIA'S $2,287 PER CAPITA state and local taxes (excluding corporate income taxes) were 92 percent of the all-state average. With per capita personal income in Virginia about 3 percent higher than the national average, these taxes equaled only 9.6 percent of personal income, compared to 10.8 percent nationally. Local taxes were 44 percent of the state and local total, compared to a 41 percent national average.

State Government Finances, 1996–97

	Millions of dollars	Percent distribution	Dollars per capita	
			State	U.S.
General revenue	18 089	100.0	2 686	3 049
Intergovernmental revenue	3 545	19.6	526	863
Taxes	9 628	53.2	1 430	1 660
General sales	2 119	11.7	315	551
Selective sales	1 648	9.1	245	257
License taxes	431	2.4	64	106
Individual income	4 728	26.1	702	542
Corporation net income	425	2.4	63	115
Other taxes	277	1.5	41	90
Other general revenue	4 917	27.2	730	526
General expenditure	17 807	100.0	2 644	2 951
Intergovernmental expenditure	5 337	30.0	793	989
Direct expenditure	12 470	70.0	1 852	1 962
General expenditure, by function:				
Education	7 048	39.6	1 047	1 033
Public welfare	3 234	18.2	480	761
Hospitals and health	1 704	9.6	253	237
Highways	2 140	12.0	318	225
Police protection and corrections	1 150	6.5	171	137
Natural resources, parks and recreation	192	1.1	28	63
Governmental administration	776	4.4	115	107
Interest on general debt	599	3.4	89	99
Other and unallocable	965	5.4	143	290
Debt at end of fiscal year	9 941	NA	1 476	1 706
Cash and security holdings	42 855	NA	6 364	6 683

Federal Spending within State

	Federal funds, fiscal 1997		
	Millions of dollars	Percent distribution	Percent of U.S. total*
Total within state	53 178	100.0	3.7
Payments to individuals	20 259	38.1	2.6
Retirement and disability	14 012	26.3	3.1
Medicare	3 825	7.2	1.9
Food stamps	386	0.7	2.0
Supplemental Security Income	533	1.0	2.0
Grants	4 335	8.2	1.7
Medicaid and other health	1 532	2.9	1.3
Nutrition and family welfare	821	1.5	1.8
Education	356	0.7	2.1
Housing and community development	180	0.3	1.6
Salaries and wages	11 312	21.3	6.9
Defense procurement contracts	11 038	20.8	9.2
Non-defense procurement contracts	5 212	9.8	7.1

*State population is 2.5 percent of the U.S. total.

Virginia relies relatively heavily on its individual income tax, which provided 49 percent of total state-level tax revenue in fiscal year 1996-97, compared with an all-state average of 33 percent, and yielded $702 per capita compared with an all-state average of $542. General and selective sales taxes produced 39 percent, compared to the all-state average of 49 percent, while corporate income taxes yielded only 4 percent, compared to an all-state average of 7 percent.

Total state-level general expenditure per capita was 90 percent of the all-state average in 1996-97, but education spending was slightly above average. These figures are for state government spending only; local spending on education would appear to be somewhat below the national average, since total per-pupil expenditure in elementary and secondary schools was only 88 percent of the national average in 1995–96.

A prosperous economy recently has provided the state with a large budget surplus, part of which will be used to increase state spending on education and to reduce in-state tuition at state-supported colleges and universities. In addition, state sales taxes on food are to be reduced, and a variety of state programs will receive increased funding.

General debt and interest on that debt were somewhat below the national per capita averages in 1996-97, and cash and security holdings were more than 4 times the size of the debt.

Federal spending Virginia in fiscal 1997 substantially exceeded the state's share of the U.S. population. Payments to individuals living in Virginia were roughly in line with the state's population share, and grant payments were low relative to population. However, the shares for federal salaries and wages and for defense and non-defense procurement contracts were far above the state's population share. These large shares are explained primarily by the large numbers of federal workers and contractors located in Northern Virginia and by the large military presence and associated defense contracting in the Norfolk area.

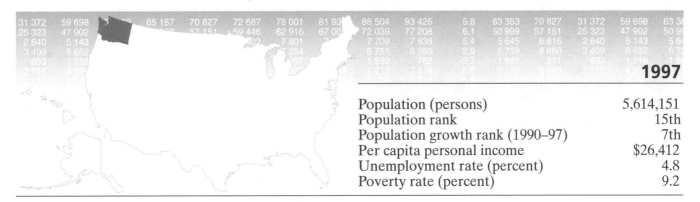

1997

Population (persons)	5,614,151
Population rank	15th
Population growth rank (1990–97)	7th
Per capita personal income	$26,412
Unemployment rate (percent)	4.8
Poverty rate (percent)	9.2

WASHINGTON'S ECONOMY WAS A FAST GROWING AND PROSPERous one, with computer related business an emerging dominant industry. The state's historical reliance on aircraft construction as a driving economic force, along with a major lumber industry, evolved into a diverse mix that mirrored the U.S. sectoral composition. Washington was in the vanguard of the computer software industry as host to Microsoft, part of the business services surge here. Earnings in business services surpassed those in transportation equipment in 1996 and in 1997 exceeded them by 34 percent. Earnings in agriculture, forestry and fishing were lower in 1997 than in 1990 and represent only 1 percent of earnings in the state. The strong showing in 1997 of both leading industries, aircraft manufacture and computer software production, led to income and employment increases well above the U.S. average for the year.

Population growth was among the fastest rates in the nation, with a 14.6 percent increase from 1990 to 1997. This was due to strong continuing in-migration from other states, particularly California, whose economic recession for much of the 1990s stimulated migration of workers to states with high job growth rates. Washington's population rank in the nation moved up from 18th to 15th within the 1990 to 1997 period. It continued to have an unusually small minority population and experienced less international immigration than average in 1990–97.

Average Annual Population Growth: 1990–97

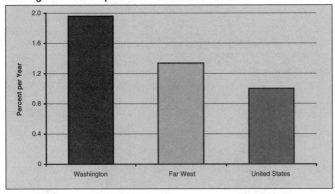

Median Household Income: 1989–97 (1997 dollars)

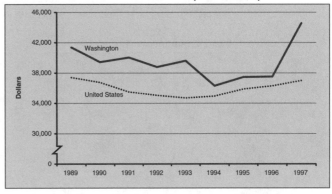

Unemployment Rate: 1989–97

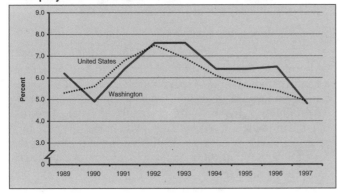

THE UNEMPLOYMENT RATE IN WASHINGTON DECLINED sharply in 1997 to 4.8 percent as employment gains accelerated. Job growth over the decade has been nearly double that in the United States, more than keeping up with rapid population growth in the state. Because the cyclically volatile aircraft industry still has an important presence, however, unemployment during the 1990s has averaged higher than nationwide.

POPULATION AND LABOR FORCE

TOTAL STATE POPULATION GREW AT DOUBLE THE RATE FOR THE United States from 1990 to 1997. The number of households increased even more strongly, further fueling high demand for housing. Half of the growth was the still-strong in-migration from other states, which contributed a 7.3 percent increase in population from 1990 to 1997. Adding foreign immigration, another 2 percent, total migration added more than 9 percent to the state's population in 1990–97, after 1980–90 migration rates that were about two-thirds that level. Though the growth of all minority populations exceeds that of White non-Hispanic, Washington retains an 84 percent White non-Hispanic population, with Hispanics and Asians as the two largest minority groups (each with around 6 percent of the population). Growth proceeded at the same high pace in both metropolitan and rural areas, and rapid growth occurred in Spokane and other smaller metro areas as well as Seattle.

The state's labor force grew even faster than the population, a torrid 2.4 percent annual average increase from 1990 to 1997. Job growth, equally high, led to an increasing proportion of the population at work. Washington had one of the highest percentages of adult population working, 65.8 percent in 1997.

Population and Labor Force

	1980	1990	1991	1992	1993	1994	1995	1996	1997	Change* State	Change* U.S.
Population											
Total number of persons (thousands)	4 132	4 901	5 015	5 143	5 249	5 336	5 433	5 519	5 614	2.0	1.0
Percent distribution:											
White, Non-Hispanic	90.4	86.5	86.4	85.9	85.6	85.1	84.7	84.2	83.8	1.5	0.4
Black, Non-Hispanic	2.5	3.3	3.0	3.1	3.1	3.1	3.2	3.2	3.3	1.8	1.4
Asian	2.7	4.4	4.6	4.8	4.9	5.1	5.3	5.4	5.5	5.2	4.1
Native American	1.5	1.8	1.8	1.8	1.8	1.8	1.8	1.8	1.8	2.1	1.6
Hispanic	2.9	4.5	4.6	4.8	5.1	5.3	5.6	5.8	6.1	6.4	3.8
In metropolitan areas	81.5	83.0	83.0	83.0	82.9	82.8	82.8	82.7	82.8	1.9	1.0
Total number of households (thousands)	1 541	1 872	1 922	1 978	2 019	2 049	2 097	2 139	NA	2.2	1.2
Labor Force (thousands)											
Population 16 and over	3 140	3 726	3 822	3 919	4 010	4 086	4 171	4 246	4 322	2.1	1.0
Civilian labor force	1 985	2 538	2 534	2 648	2 701	2 717	2 810	2 879	2 989	2.4	1.1
Employed	1 828	2 413	2 372	2 447	2 495	2 543	2 631	2 692	2 847	2.4	1.2
Percent of population	58.2	64.8	62.1	62.4	62.2	62.2	63.1	63.4	65.9		
Unemployment rate (percent)	7.9	4.9	6.4	7.6	7.6	6.4	6.4	6.5	4.8		

*Compound annual average percent change, 1990–1997; 1990–1996 for households.

Population Change and Components: 1990–97

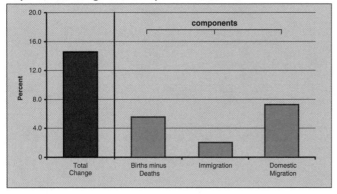

Average Annual Household and Population Growth

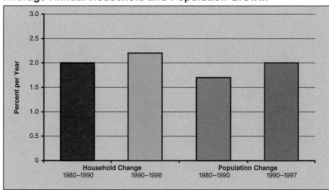

Population by Age; Births and Deaths

	1990 State	1990 U.S.	1997 State	1997 U.S.
Age distribution (percent)				
Under 5 years	7.8	7.6	6.9	7.2
5 to 17 years	18.7	18.2	19.0	18.8
18 to 64 years	61.7	61.8	62.5	61.3
65 years and over	11.8	12.5	11.5	12.7
Birth and death rates (per thousand population)				
Births	16.3	16.7	14.1	14.6
Deaths	7.6	8.6	7.6	8.6

WASHINGTON HAD A SMALLER THAN AVERAGE PROPORTION OF its population under 5 years old, but in-migration created a slightly higher than average number of school-age children. Similarly, in-migration led to a bulge in the working-age population, leaving a disproportionately small population 65 and older. Even with a slightly below-average birth rate, the lower death rates in this young state meant that the natural population increase was a bit above average.

HOUSEHOLD AND PERSONAL INCOME

HOUSEHOLD INCOME AND PERSONS IN POVERTY	1990	1995	1996	1997 State	1997 U.S.
Median household income (1997 dollars)	39 434	37 458	37 518	44 562	37 005
Persons in poverty (thousands)	434	677	666	529	35 574
Poverty rate (percent)	8.9	12.5	11.9	9.2	13.3

INCOMES WERE HIGHER THAN THE U.S. AVERAGE IN Washington and have been consistently so from 1990 to 1997. Median household income in the state spiked up by 19 percent in 1997, probably statistically overestimated but reflecting the very strong economy in that year. Personal income per capita was 4.4 percent higher than the U.S. average, led by employee and proprietor earnings, which were 6 percent above those of the United States on a per capita basis. With a higher than average share of the population working, earnings contributed a greater percentage to personal income than nationally. Dividend and interest income was also above average in the state, while transfer payments per capita were 3 percent lower than average. The adjustment for residence (which added 1.5 percent to resident earnings) indicates a net out commuting in Washington.

The state's poverty rate fell to 9.2 percent in 1997, in light of the rapid expansion of jobs, though the rate was still a bit higher than it had been in 1990.

Transfer payments grew faster than total personal income between 1990 and 1997, primarily because of a doubling of medical payments, which comprise 28 percent of all transfers. Social Security increased a more moderate 51 percent. Income maintenance spending increased 76 percent, more than the U.S. average (even after adjustment for population): increases in both Supplemental Security Income and family assistance outpaced the nation. The latter increased 11 percent, as reductions in welfare caseload were not as great as in many other states. Other income maintenance, primarily consisting of low income tax credits, tripled in size to become the second largest income maintenance program.

Personal Income
(millions of dollars)

	1980	1989	1990	1991	1992	1993	1994	1995	1996	1997	Change*
Earnings by place of work	33 129	61 048	68 111	72 844	79 301	82 799	86 060	90 763	97 190	105 885	7.1
Wages and salaries	27 017	48 863	54 167	57 971	62 906	64 638	67 733	71 911	77 297	85 205	7.2
Other labor income	2 340	4 620	5 309	5 945	6 612	7 181	7 588	7 598	7 600	7 976	7.1
Proprietors' income	3 773	7 565	8 635	8 928	9 783	10 980	10 739	11 254	12 293	12 704	6.7
Farm	601	626	560	625	905	1 117	567	445	824	363	-6.6
Nonfarm	3 172	6 938	8 074	8 303	8 878	9 863	10 173	10 809	11 469	12 341	7.5
(−) Personal contributions for social insurance	1 834	4 246	4 680	5 138	5 577	5 786	6 155	6 559	6 974	7 622	7.6
(+) Adjustment for residence	396	830	944	993	1 078	1 094	1 159	1 290	1 499	1 567	NA
(=) **Net earnings by state of residence**	31 691	57 632	64 375	68 699	74 802	78 106	81 064	85 493	91 716	99 830	7.1
(+) Dividends, interest, and rent	7 054	16 171	17 737	17 889	18 205	18 977	20 472	22 210	24 197	25 752	6.0
(+) Transfer payments	6 074	12 632	13 967	15 722	17 231	18 514	19 523	20 930	21 875	22 600	7.5
(=) **Total personal income**	44 818	86 435	96 079	102 310	110 238	115 597	121 058	128 633	137 788	148 182	7.0
Farm	890	1 057	1 085	1 152	1 418	1 683	1 162	1 114	1 580	1 127	0.8
Nonfarm	43 928	85 378	94 994	101 158	108 821	113 915	119 896	127 519	136 209	147 054	7.0
Personal income per capita (dollars)											
Current dollars	10 787	18 211	19 603	20 397	21 430	22 018	22 673	23 664	24 964	26 412	4.8
1997 dollars	20 625	23 023	23 590	23 553	23 971	23 959	24 095	24 599	25 422	26 412	1.7

*Compound annual average percent change, 1989–1997

Government Transfer Payments

	Millions of dollars 1990	Millions of dollars 1997	Percent change* State	Percent change* U.S.
Total government payments to individuals	13 354	21 590	61.7	62.7
Retirement, disability, and insurance	8 179	11 817	44.5	48.2
Social Security	4 590	6 928	50.9	46.1
Government employee retirement	2 423	3 695	52.5	60.3
Medical payments	3 091	6 327	104.7	101.2
Income maintenance	1 034	1 819	76.0	58.0
Supplemental Security Income	210	440	109.8	75.4
Family assistance	465	515	10.8	-0.5
Food Stamps	196	371	89.4	27.1
Other income maintenance	163	492	202.8	189.8
Unemployment insurance benefits	458	762	66.6	10.6
Veterans benefits and other	594	864	45.5	30.8

*Percent change, 1990–1997

Government Payments to Individuals: 1997

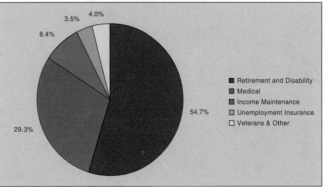

- Retirement and Disability — 54.7%
- Medical — 29.3%
- Income Maintenance — 8.4%
- Unemployment Insurance — 3.5%
- Veterans & Other — 4.0%

ECONOMIC STRUCTURE

LEADING PRIVATE INDUSTRIES, 1997 (Worker and proprietor earnings, millions of dollars)		FASTEST EARNINGS GROWTH, 1989–97 (percent increase)	
Business services	$9 504	Business services	343.9
Health services	7 788	Electric, gas, and sanitary services	219.4
Transportation equip., excl. motor veh.	7 069	Real estate	186.1
Construction specialties	4 030	Social services	151.9
Engineering and management services	3 635	Amusement and recreation services	149.9

WASHINGTON STATE IS UNUSUAL IN HAVING ITS FASTEST growing sector, business services, become its largest sector, with earnings growth from 1989 to 1997 nearly five times faster than total earnings for the state. The growth of the Microsoft computer company (with an estimated $14.5 billion in revenue), and the spin-off services, account for much of this. Business services as a category showed earnings growth of 344 percent (1989–97), compared to a healthy 73 percent increase for state earnings overall. Other service industries, especially real estate, social services, and tourism-related industries, also grew faster than the rest of the state economy. Employment in all levels of government grew much faster in Washington than in the United States from 1989 to 1997 (though not as fast as the private sector), with the highest earnings growth within the local government sector.

The dominant manufacturing industry—aircraft and other transportation equipment except motor vehicles—saw a very good year in 1997 and comprised 39 percent of all manufacturing earnings. Boeing Aircraft experienced a very strong level of orders for commercial jetliners in 1995–97 following four weak years, demonstrating the volatility of this industry. There is not necessarily any secular uptrend in this industry's future, so the strength of the business services sector provides a welcome cushion. Lumber manufacturing was a distant second place in size of earnings within the manufacturing sector.

Growth in the state economy was not geographically neutral within the state. Seattle and the adjacent metropolitan areas experienced higher growth in 1995–97, while the balance of the state was affected more by the slowdown in lumber and faces unemployment rates above the national average.

Employment and Earnings by Sector

	1980	1989	1990	1991	1992	1993	1994	1995	1996	1997 Number	1997 Percent of total	Change*
Employment *(thousands of persons)*												
Total	2 109	2 741	2 862	2 903	2 932	2 973	3 086	3 158	3 247	3 365	100.0	2.6
Farm	81	79	81	79	70	72	76	79	82	80	2.4	0.3
Nonfarm	2 028	2 662	2 780	2 824	2 862	2 902	3 010	3 079	3 165	3 284	97.6	2.7
Private nonfarm	1 636	2 204	2 304	2 338	2 366	2 402	2 504	2 565	2 645	2 756	81.9	2.8
Agricultural service, forestry, and fishing	32	46	49	51	49	53	56	57	59	61	1.8	3.8
Mining	4	6	6	6	5	5	6	5	5	5	0.2	-0.7
Construction	120	147	159	161	166	166	174	175	179	189	5.6	3.2
Manufacturing	318	381	388	370	366	361	361	356	368	396	11.8	0.5
Transportation and public utilities	100	123	128	128	128	129	134	139	145	155	4.6	3.0
Wholesale trade	107	135	140	144	148	147	153	158	158	163	4.9	2.4
Retail trade	337	450	467	475	490	499	527	544	558	572	17.0	3.0
Finance, insurance, and real estate	165	213	218	214	209	214	223	230	237	246	7.3	1.9
Services	452	705	748	790	804	827	870	902	935	967	28.7	4.0
Government	392	458	476	486	496	500	506	515	521	529	15.7	1.8
Earnings *(millions of dollars)*												
Total	33 129	61 048	68 111	72 844	79 301	82 799	86 060	90 763	97 190	105 885	100.0	7.1
Farm	890	1 057	1 085	1 152	1 418	1 683	1 162	1 114	1 580	1 127	1.1	0.8
Nonfarm	32 239	59 990	67 026	71 692	77 884	81 116	84 898	89 649	95 610	104 758	98.9	7.2
Private nonfarm	26 241	48 967	54 930	58 447	63 597	66 109	69 408	73 435	78 654	87 189	82.3	7.5
Agricultural service, forestry, and fishing	347	991	1 205	1 221	1 151	1 086	1 161	1 126	961	1 034	1.0	0.5
Mining	179	148	161	179	175	161	188	195	192	214	0.2	4.7
Construction	2 694	4 121	4 779	5 039	5 322	5 410	5 787	5 980	6 364	6 975	6.6	6.8
Manufacturing	7 566	12 882	13 851	13 852	14 696	14 539	14 955	15 253	16 228	18 117	17.1	4.4
Transportation and public utilities	2 322	4 090	4 486	4 748	5 094	5 269	5 642	5 791	6 356	6 805	7.3	8.2
Wholesale trade	2 219	3 813	4 295	4 575	4 918	5 078	5 419	5 785	6 102	6 607	6.2	7.1
Retail trade	3 455	6 140	6 802	7 222	7 708	8 063	8 570	8 944	9 378	9 949	9.4	6.2
Finance, insurance, and real estate	1 721	3 342	3 685	3 880	4 703	5 269	5 261	5 595	6 027	6 574	6.2	8.8
Services	5 738	13 440	15 665	17 732	19 830	20 862	22 275	24 200	26 597	30 031	28.4	10.6
Government	5 998	11 023	12 096	13 245	14 286	15 007	15 491	16 213	16 956	17 569	16.6	6.0

*Compound annual average percent change, 1989–1997

ECONOMIC STRUCTURE (Continued)

AVERAGE EARNINGS PER WORKER WERE 4.2 PERCENT ABOVE U.S. levels in 1997, as the strong job market in Washington boosted pay rates faster than average. Among major sectors, services workers had the highest earnings differential when compared with the same sector nationwide, 14 percent above those of the United States, reflecting the large computer industry presence in the sector. But even retail trade workers earned 9 percent higher on average than in the nation. Construction and manufacturing also paid wages 6 percent and 7 percent above the national rates, because of rapid growth in construction activity and the predominance of high-paid aircraft manufacturing jobs. Other large sectors were close to parity with the United States, except the finance sector, which lagged the national average by 16 percent.

Despite an outstanding year in 1997, the longer term picture for manufacturing, both in the aircraft and other industries, shows slow earnings growth measured against every other sector in the state. Only in industrial machinery and electronics, still small industries here, did earnings grow rapidly during the 1990s. The manufacturing sector actually grew faster than manufacturing nationwide, but it paled by comparison with the outstanding performance of other Washington state sectors. Manufacturing shrank in relative importance in the state: its employment comprised 11.8 percent of jobs in 1997, compared with 13.9 percent in 1989, and manufacturing output as a percentage of gross state product has declined 5 percentage points since 1989.

Exports were an important source of demand for the state's production, particularly of aircraft. Total exports of goods increased 26.7 percent in 1994–97, dominated by a 36 percent upsurge in aircraft exports. Though computer exports increased 55 percent in this period, they remained a small component of total exports. (Note that these data do not include exports of computer software and services, which are not counted as "goods.") The state ranked sixth in the nation in value of exports, and, considering exports as a percentage of economic output, Washington was one of the most dependent on export demand of any state in the country. However, aircraft exports showed volatile swings from year to year, and lumber exports failed to grow during the 1994–97 period, so foreign goods markets may not provide a consistent base for the state's continued economic expansion.

Average Annual Wages and Salaries by Sector
(dollars)

	1989	1996	1997	
			State	U.S.
All wage and salary workers	21 590	29 262	31 073	29 809
Farm	10 066	15 289	16 058	16 442
Nonfarm	21 802	29 517	31 327	29 900
Private nonfarm	21 643	29 387	31 487	29 867
Agricultural service, forestry, and fishing	17 308	19 780	20 478	17 941
Mining	33 773	41 291	43 936	49 800
Construction	24 403	31 769	33 513	31 765
Manufacturing	30 266	39 461	41 128	38 351
Transportation and utilities	29 088	36 721	39 499	38 222
Wholesale trade	26 601	36 180	37 970	39 466
Retail trade	12 991	16 946	17 588	16 206
Finance, insurance, and real estate	24 943	35 259	37 884	44 993
Services	18 091	28 710	31 623	27 588
Government	22 415	30 034	30 674	30 062

Gross State Product and Manufacturing
(millions of dollars, except as noted)

	1989	1994	1995	1996
Gross state product, total	103 408	144 721	150 001	159 602
Manufacturing:				
Millions of dollars	18 975	20 885	19 725	20 934
Percent of total gross state product	18.3	14.4	13.1	13.1
Per worker (dollars)	49 804	57 834	55 465	56 907
New capital expenditures, manufacturing	NA	1 976	2 104	2 211

Exports of Goods
(millions of dollars)

	1994	1995	1996	1997
All goods	25 062	22 032	25 498	31 746
Manufactures	22 356	18 946	22 741	29 185
Agricultural and livestock products	748	994	902	907
Other commodities	1 957	2 093	1 855	1 654
Top goods exports, 1997:				
Transportation equipment	14 450	9 582	13 403	19 711
Lumber and wood products	2 643	2 870	2 893	2 287
Fish and other marine products	1 691	1 755	1 512	1 298
Industrial machinery and computers	822	1 055	1 060	1 276
Paper products	1 019	1 600	1 285	1 241

HOUSING

HOUSING PRODUCTION HAS BEEN CONSISTENTLY STRONGER during the 1990s in Washington than in the United States because of the strong population increase from in-migration of households from other states. There was some cyclical downturn of production and sales in 1991, but the market recovered quickly and production per capita in 1997 was 28 percent above the U.S. average. Building permits issued in 1997 for the Seattle area placed it 13th in the nation, though local zoning and topography create limitations on how much building can occur in Seattle. Supply did not keep up with demand, so housing prices escalated in this area, with median existing home prices for the Seattle area reaching $171,300 in 1997.

Homeownership rates remained below national averages because of quickly escalating home prices and the flood of recent in-migrants who could not initially afford a home. The same factors make for a strong rental housing market, with active new construction of apartments and generally low vacancy rates.

Homeownership Rates: 1989 and 1997

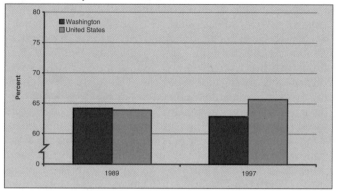

Housing Supply

	1989	1990	1991	1992	1993	1994	1995	1996	1997
Residential building permits (thousands)	48.2	48.4	33.0	39.7	41.3	44.0	38.2	39.6	41.1
New home production (including manufactured housing):									
Thousands of homes	53.4	54.2	39.4	45.6	48.1	51.0	44.8	45.0	46.7
Rate per 1,000 population									
Washington	11.3	11.1	7.9	8.9	9.2	9.6	8.2	8.2	8.3
U.S.	6.2	5.2	4.5	5.1	5.6	6.4	6.3	6.6	6.5
Existing home sales:									
Thousands of homes	90.8	87.7	86.9	91.3	97.0	101.2	95.5	101.5	116.5
Change from previous year (percent)									
Washington	23.7	-3.4	-0.9	5.1	6.2	4.3	-5.6	6.3	14.8
U.S.	-3.9	-4.0	0.0	9.2	8.2	4.8	-3.7	7.5	3.8
Home ownership rate (percent of households)	64.2	61.8	61.8	62.5	63.1	62.4	61.6	63.1	62.9
Rental vacancy rate (percent of rental housing units)	5.5	3.3	4.1	4.1	5.0	5.9	6.0	5.6	4.4

AGRICULTURE

WASHINGTON HAS A RELATIVELY DIVERSIFIED FARM SECTOR, with large meat, dairy, grain, and fruit sectors. On the whole it has performed better than in many other states during the 1990s, as flat sales of meat animals and modest growth in dairy product sales were offset by a 34 percent increase in grain sales and 23 percent rise in fruits and nuts, (looking at three-year averages). However, with steady increases in production costs, net income has not increased consistently during the 1990s; in three of the past six years performance was very profitable and in the other three it was poor. Agricultural exports were fairly strong in 1995–97.

WASHINGTON FARMS, 1997	
Number of farms	36 000
Total acres (thousands):	15 700
Average per farm	436
Value of land and buildings (millions of dollars)	19 311
Average per farm (dollars)	536 417

Farm Income
(millions of dollars)

	1980	1989	1990	1991	1992	1993	1994	1995	1996	1997
Gross income	2 981	4 457	4 687	5 147	5 289	5 695	5 813	6 186	6 473	6 428
Receipts from sales	2 733	3 894	4 021	4 500	4 564	4 883	5 010	5 433	5 670	5 665
Government payments	9	131	205	206	189	207	153	116	155	147
Imputed and miscellaneous income	238	432	460	441	536	604	650	637	648	616
(−) Production expenses	2 386	3 695	4 067	4 229	4 299	4 736	4 927	5 452	5 671	5 855
(=) Realized net income	595	761	620	918	990	959	886	734	802	574
(+) Inventory change	6	-6	58	-199	113	244	-94	-188	334	-88
(=) Net income	601	755	677	719	1 103	1 203	792	546	1 136	486
Corporate income	0	129	117	95	199	87	225	101	312	123
Farm proprietors income	601	626	560	625	905	1 117	567	445	824	363

EDUCATION

EDUCATIONAL ATTAINMENT Percent of population age 25 and over, 1997	State	United States
High school graduate or higher	88.8	82.1
College graduate or higher	26.1	23.9

WASHINGTON BOASTED HIGH RATES OF EDUCATIONAL ATTAIN-ment in its population, with the 15th highest percentage of college degree holders among all states, partly because its business expansion attracted a well-educated workforce from other states. Of young adults, 21.8 percent were enrolled in higher education in 1997, the same ratio as in the nation. The population holding high school diplomas also well exceeded the national average. However, public education budgets were stretched thin by the influx of new students migrating into the state, bringing per pupil spending down to 2 percent below the U.S. average. Average teacher salaries were also below average, possibly because of a large number of new hires of teachers. The proportion of children attending private schools was relatively low in the state.

High School Completion: 1990–97

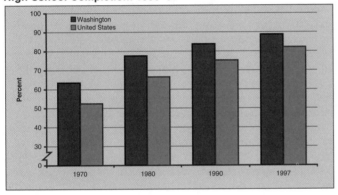

Education Indicators

	State	U.S.
Elementary and secondary schools		
Enrollment, 1995–96		
Total (thousands)	1 031	49 873
Percent in private schools	7.3	10.1
Expenditures per pupil (dollars), 1995–96	6 044	6 146
Average teacher salary (dollars), 1996–97	37 860	38 509
Higher education		
Enrollment, 1996–97		
Total (thousands)	292	14 218
Percent of population 18–34	21.8	21.8
Percent minority	18.1	26.1
Percent in private schools	13.8	22.6

HEALTH

INDICATORS SHOWED A HEALTHIER THAN AVERAGE STATE, DUE to its low poverty, young age distribution, and possibly the state's attraction of environment- and health-conscious in-migrants. The average 1996–97 infant mortality rate was the 4th lowest in the country, and the overall death rate was among the lowest quarter of states. Death rates from heart disease and cancer were substantially below average for the nation, even after adjustment for the state's age distribution. Death rates from accidents were about equal to the national average, while the suicide rate was high and the homicide rate was extremely low. The state also had a higher than average share of people covered by health insurance, not surprising in this prosperous, low-poverty state.

Health Indicators

	1990	1995	1996	1997
Infant mortality				
(rate per thousand live births)				
Washington	7.8	5.9	5.3	5.2
U.S.	9.2	7.6	7.3	7.1
Total deaths, age-adjusted rate				
(rate per thousand population)				
Washington	4.7	4.4	4.4	4.4
U.S.	5.2	5.0	4.9	4.8
Persons not covered by health insurance				
(percent of population)				
Washington	11.4	12.4	13.5	11.4
U.S.	13.9	15.4	15.6	16.1

Leading Causes of Death, 1996
(deaths per 100,000 population)

	Age-adjusted		Not age-adjusted	
	State	U.S.	State	U.S.
Deaths from all causes	442.2	491.6	763.7	872.5
Heart disease	107.7	134.5	212.1	276.4
Cancer	119.6	127.9	181.9	203.4
Cerebrovascular diseases	27.4	26.4	62.9	60.3
Chronic obstructive pulmonary disease	21.8	21.0	40.0	40.0
Diabetes mellitus	12.9	13.6	20.8	23.3
Pneumonia and influenza	11.9	12.8	29.3	31.6
HIV	6.4	11.1	7.2	11.7
Liver disease	6.8	7.5	8.3	9.4
Alzheimer's disease	3.4	2.7	9.7	8.1
Accidents and adverse effects	29.7	30.4	35.2	35.8
Motor vehicle accidents	14.2	16.2	14.3	16.5
Suicide	12.9	10.8	14.0	11.6
Homicide	4.9	8.5	4.7	7.9
Injury by firearm	10.6	12.9	11.1	12.8

GOVERNMENT

STATE AND LOCAL TAXES, 1995–96	State	U.S.
Per capita (dollars)	2 795	2 477
Percent of personal income	12.0	10.8

TOTAL STATE AND LOCAL TAXES PER CAPITA WERE ABOUT 13 percent higher in Washington than the national average in 1995–96 because of very high taxes at the state level (31 percent above average), even without having any income tax. Local taxes, in contrast, were substantially below average for the nation (13 percent less). The combination made this state one of the highest taxed in the country, even considering the high personal incomes in the state,

with 12 percent of income going to pay these taxes.

Washington's state government spent a lot on education, helping its local governments keep up with the demands of a 17 percent increase in the number of school-age children from 1990 to 1997. State-level spending on education in 1997 was 35 percent higher than the U.S. average per capita, with large intergovernmental transfers to the local level. Otherwise, its state spending levels generally followed national patterns. State spending on administration was only 75 percent of the national average, however. Washington's tax collections per capita exceeded the U.S. average, despite the absence of a state income tax (personal or corporate) because of an extremely high sales tax and a high rate of "other" taxes.

Federal spending in the state was proportional to the state's share of U.S. population in 1997, though the pattern of spending was unusual. Salaries paid to federal employees and military personnel on bases in the state comprised a larger than average share of spending, and there was substantial contract procurement in both defense and nondefense industries. The state's large computer sector probably accounted for much of this. With the younger than average population, there was substantially less Medicare spending than for a typical state, though payments for government retirement and Social Security reached average levels.

State Government Finances, 1996–97

	Millions of dollars	Percent distribution	Dollars per capita State	Dollars per capita U.S.
General revenue	18 213	100.0	3 247	3 049
Intergovernmental revenue	4 112	22.6	733	863
Taxes	11 202	61.5	1 997	1 660
General sales	6 572	36.1	1 172	551
Selective sales	1 717	9.4	306	257
License taxes	510	2.8	91	106
Individual income	0	0.0	0	542
Corporation net income	0	0.0	0	115
Other taxes	2 403	13.2	428	90
Other general revenue	2 898	15.9	517	526
General expenditure	18 803	100.0	3 352	2 951
Intergovernmental expenditure	5 682	30.2	1 013	989
Direct expenditure	13 121	69.8	2 339	1 962
General expenditure, by function:				
Education	7 803	41.5	1 391	1 033
Public welfare	4 059	21.6	724	761
Hospitals and health	1 574	8.4	281	237
Highways	1 558	8.3	278	225
Police protection and corrections	764	4.1	136	137
Natural resources, parks and recreation	537	2.9	96	63
Governmental administration	451	2.4	80	107
Interest on general debt	536	2.9	96	99
Other and unallocable	1 519	8.1	271	290
Debt at end of fiscal year	9 493	NA	1 692	1 706
Cash and security holdings	47 230	NA	8 419	6 683

Federal Spending within State

	Federal funds, fiscal 1997 Millions of dollars	Percent distribution	Percent of U.S. total*
Total within state	30 488	100.0	2.1
Payments to individuals	15 435	50.6	2.0
Retirement and disability	9 819	32.2	2.1
Medicare	3 130	10.3	1.5
Food stamps	395	1.3	2.0
Supplemental Security Income	422	1.4	1.6
Grants	5 386	17.7	2.2
Medicaid and other health	2 324	7.6	2.0
Nutrition and family welfare	1 103	3.6	2.4
Education	315	1.0	1.8
Housing and community development	196	0.6	1.7
Salaries and wages	4 574	15.0	2.8
Defense procurement contracts	2 586	8.5	2.2
Non-defense procurement contracts	2 015	6.6	2.8

*State population is 2.1 percent of the U.S. total.

1997

Population (persons)	1,815,231
Population rank	35th
Population growth rank (1990–97)	44th
Per capita personal income	$18,734
Unemployment rate (percent)	6.9
Poverty rate (percent)	16.4

WEST VIRGINIA'S ECONOMY HAS PERFORMED MUCH BETTER IN the 1990s than the 1980s, but the state still faces problems of an aging population, a high poverty rate, and limited job opportunities. During the 1980s West Virginia lost 8 percent of its population as unemployment soared and workers left the state in search of better job opportunities; from 1990 to 1997, the population increased, albeit very slightly. Employment grew and the unemployment rate fell, although at 6.9 percent in 1997 it still was one of the highest in the nation.

West Virginia's population of 1.8 million is predominantly rural. Only a small fraction of the work force is employed in farming, however, and farmers lost money from 1995 through 1997. Thus the state faces a problem of bringing other types of employment to rural areas, and many residents must travel long distances to work. Labor force participation is below national averages, contributing to low household incomes and a high poverty rate.

West Virginia has suffered large job losses in the coal mining industry. These losses began in the late 1970s and have continued into the 1990s. However, the state's economy has received a much needed boost from growth of employment in private services and the transfer of some federal jobs from the Washington, DC area. In addition, a growing logging and wood products industry has partially offset declines elsewhere in manufacturing.

Average Annual Population Growth: 1990–97

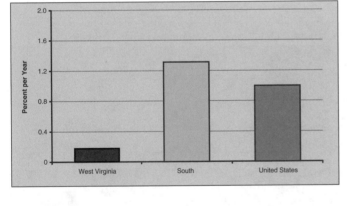

Median Household Income: 1989–97 (1997 dollars)

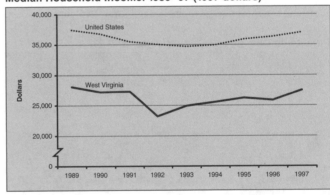

Unemployment Rate: 1989–97

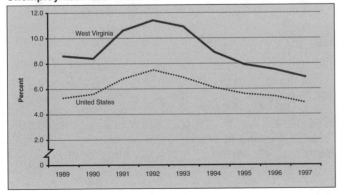

WEST VIRGINIA'S UNEMPLOYMENT RATE SOARED DURING THE early 1980s, reaching 18 percent in 1983. It subsequently declined, but still was at 8.4 percent in 1990, and it rose again in the early 1990s recession, reaching a 1992 peak of 11.4 percent. With employment growing after 1992, however, the unemployment rate then fell each year through 1997, and 1997's 6.9 percent, though still high by national standards, was the lowest since 1979. In part because of the state's limited job opportunities and the large share of older people in the population, the employment to population ratio, though it has risen since 1992, still is the nation's lowest.

415

POPULATION AND LABOR FORCE

WEST VIRGINIA'S MASSIVE POPULATION LOSS OF THE 1980S has been brought to a halt during the 1990s. From 1980 to 1990, the state lost 8 percent of its population as workers migrated to nearby states offering better job prospects. On average, those who migrated had higher levels of educational attainment than those who stayed behind, so that the state experienced a "brain drain." In contrast to the 1980s, West Virginia's population grew, although only slowly, from 1990 to 1995. The population then dipped slightly in 1996 and 1997, but the 1997 figure still was 1.3 percent above 1990.

The state's population growth in the 1990s was a result of net domestic in-migration and some natural increase. Because of the high average age of the population, natural increase (births minus deaths) has been growing smaller during the 1990s, and, by 1997, deaths actually exceeded births.

Over 95 percent of the state's population is White and non-Hispanic. Bucking the national trend, the Black and Hispanic populations have declined during the 1990s and the Asian population has grown only slowly, so that, on balance, the minority share of the population has not increased.

Population and Labor Force

	1980	1990	1991	1992	1993	1994	1995	1996	1997	Change* State	Change* U.S.
Population											
Total number of persons (thousands)	1 950	1 792	1 798	1 806	1 817	1 819	1 822	1 820	1 815	0.2	1.0
Percent distribution:											
White, Non-Hispanic	95.6	95.6	95.8	95.8	95.8	95.8	95.7	95.7	95.7	0.2	0.4
Black, Non-Hispanic	3.3	3.2	3.1	3.1	3.1	3.1	3.1	3.1	3.1	-0.2	1.4
Asian	0.3	0.5	0.4	0.5	0.5	0.5	0.5	0.5	0.5	0.7	4.1
Native American	0.1	0.1	0.1	0.1	0.1	0.1	0.1	0.1	0.1	-0.8	1.6
Hispanic	0.7	0.6	0.5	0.5	0.5	0.5	0.5	0.5	0.6	-1.7	3.8
In metropolitan areas	40.8	41.8	41.8	41.8	41.8	41.8	41.8	41.8	41.8	0.2	1.0
Total number of households (thousands)	686	689	695	702	705	705	709	714	NA	0.6	1.2
Labor Force (thousands)											
Population 16 and over	1 459	1 410	1 419	1 428	1 441	1 448	1 452	1 457	1 459	0.5	1.0
Civilian labor force	788	761	783	775	789	788	785	805	804	0.8	1.1
Employed	714	697	700	687	703	717	723	745	748	1.0	1.2
Percent of population	48.9	49.4	49.3	48.1	48.8	49.5	49.8	51.1	51.3		
Unemployment rate (percent)	9.4	8.4	10.6	11.4	10.9	8.9	7.9	7.5	6.9		

*Compound annual average percent change, 1990–1997; 1990–1996 for households.

Population Change and Components: 1990–97

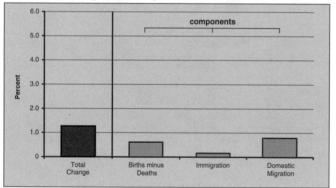

Average Annual Household and Population Growth

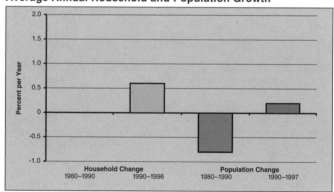

Population by Age; Births and Deaths

	1990 State	1990 U.S.	1997 State	1997 U.S.
Age distribution (percent)				
Under 5 years	5.9	7.6	5.7	7.2
5 to 17 years	18.4	18.2	17.0	18.8
18 to 64 years	60.7	61.8	62.2	61.3
65 years and over	15.0	12.5	15.1	12.7
Birth and death rates (per thousand population)				
Births	12.6	16.7	11.4	14.6
Deaths	10.8	8.6	11.6	8.6

WEST VIRGINIA'S LOSS OF WORKING-AGE POPULATION DURING the 1980s is reflected in the low percentage of the population in the 18 to 64 age group in 1990. By 1997, however, the population share of this group had risen above the national average. The share of the population age 65 and over in 1997 was the fourth highest of any state, and the large proportion of elderly helps explain the state's high death rate. The birth rate is low, as is the proportion of the population under age 18.

HOUSEHOLD AND PERSONAL INCOME

HOUSEHOLD INCOME AND PERSONS IN POVERTY	1990	1995	1996	1997	
				State	U.S.
Median household income (1997 dollars)	27 184	26 202	25 826	27 488	37 005
Persons in poverty (thousands)	328	300	323	286	35 574
Poverty rate (percent)	18.1	16.7	18.5	16.4	13.3

MEDIAN HOUSEHOLD INCOME IN WEST VIRGINIA TOOK A NOSE dive in 1992 and 1993, and the poverty rate rose above 22 percent. Since 1993, incomes have grown and poverty has declined. Even so, inflation-adjusted median household income in 1996–97 was 2 percent lower than in 1990 and was the lowest in the nation. The 1996–97 poverty rate of 17.5 percent was almost four percentage points higher than the national average of 13.5 percent.

In West Virginia, as in the nation, real per capita personal income has grown faster than median household income during the 1990s, rising almost 10 percent from 1990 to 1997. But, as of 1997, both income measures showed West Virginia at only 74 percent of the national average.

The state's low incomes and large share of elderly combine to make the state unusually reliant on transfer payments, which made up 26 percent of personal income in 1997, compared with only 16 percent nationally. Social Security and other government retirement and disability payments made up over one-half of all transfers and totaled 14 percent of personal income, compared with 8 percent nationally. These retirement and disability payments grew more slowly in the state than nationally from 1990 to 1997, however, rising only 32 percent, compared with 48 percent nationally. In part, this slower growth simply reflects the minimal growth of the state's population. Growth of medical payments exceeded the national average, and income maintenance payments rose at about the national rate. The most rapidly-growing transfer payments category—both nationally and in the state—was "other income maintenance," a category consisting largely of the earned income tax credit.

Personal Income
(millions of dollars)

	1980	1989	1990	1991	1992	1993	1994	1995	1996	1997	Change*
Earnings by place of work	11 713	15 435	16 501	16 975	17 974	18 664	19 712	20 242	20 794	21 402	4.2
Wages and salaries	9 528	12 468	13 311	13 713	14 467	14 889	15 716	16 285	16 865	17 461	4.3
Other labor income	1 138	1 342	1 485	1 584	1 728	1 875	2 015	1 979	1 915	1 874	4.3
Proprietors' income	1 046	1 625	1 705	1 678	1 779	1 899	1 980	1 978	2 015	2 066	3.0
Farm	-6	34	13	-1	25	33	28	-11	-35	-39	0.0
Nonfarm	1 053	1 591	1 692	1 679	1 755	1 866	1 952	1 989	2 050	2 105	3.6
(−) Personal contributions for social insurance	632	1 118	1 179	1 248	1 311	1 381	1 477	1 541	1 562	1 596	4.6
(+) Adjustment for residence	-315	27	72	71	90	91	126	166	187	257	NA
(=) **Net earnings by state of residence**	10 765	14 344	15 394	15 797	16 752	17 374	18 361	18 867	19 420	20 063	4.3
(+) Dividends, interest, and rent	1 937	3 964	4 174	4 273	4 223	4 200	4 384	4 563	4 909	5 005	3.0
(+) Transfer payments	3 055	5 447	5 841	6 570	7 334	8 045	8 077	8 354	8 657	8 949	6.4
(=) **Total personal income**	15 757	23 755	25 409	26 641	28 310	29 620	30 822	31 785	32 986	34 017	4.6
Farm	15	56	38	23	47	58	52	14	-10	-14	0.0
Nonfarm	15 742	23 699	25 371	26 618	28 262	29 561	30 770	31 771	32 995	34 030	4.6
Personal income per capita (dollars)											
Current dollars	8 075	13 149	14 176	14 816	15 679	16 307	16 946	17 446	18 120	18 734	4.5
1997 dollars	15 440	16 623	17 059	17 109	17 538	17 744	18 009	18 135	18 452	18 734	1.5

*Compound annual average percent change, 1989–1997

Government Transfer Payments

	Millions of dollars		Percent change*	
	1990	1997	State	U.S.
Total government payments to individuals	5 655	8 663	53.2	62.7
Retirement, disability, and insurance	3 518	4 651	32.2	48.2
Social Security	2 287	3 145	37.5	46.1
Government employee retirement	519	707	36.3	60.3
Medical payments	1 273	2 738	115.1	101.2
Income maintenance	507	816	60.9	58.0
Supplemental Security Income	146	297	103.8	75.4
Family assistance	117	109	-7.0	-0.5
Food Stamps	198	236	19.3	27.1
Other income maintenance	47	174	273.2	189.8
Unemployment insurance benefits	118	148	25.3	10.6
Veterans benefits and other	239	309	29.2	30.8

*Percent change, 1990–1997

Government Payments to Individuals: 1997

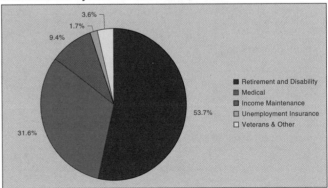

Retirement and Disability 53.7%
Medical 31.6%
Income Maintenance 9.4%
Unemployment Insurance 1.7%
Veterans & Other 3.6%

ECONOMIC STRUCTURE

LEADING PRIVATE INDUSTRIES, 1997 (Worker and proprietor earnings, millions of dollars)		FASTEST EARNINGS GROWTH, 1989–97 (percent increase)	
Health services	$2 467	Social services	208.6
Coal mining	1 284	Business services	108.1
Chemicals and allied products	991	General building contractors	93.9
Construction specialties	700	Legal services	82.6
Primary metal industries	637	Engineering and management services	81.0

WEST VIRGINIA IS A PREDOMINANTLY RURAL STATE. YET ONLY 3.1 percent of the West Virginia work force was employed in farming in 1990, and, by 1997, the farm share of employment had fallen to 2.6 percent. Rural dwellers, of course, undertake many kinds of work other than farming. Still, the high rural share of the population means that many of the state's residents must travel long distances to work and that others may be discouraged from participating in the work force at all.

Coal mining, long one of West Virginia's most important economic activities, remained the second largest industry in the state in 1997, measured by worker and proprietor earnings. But this industry provided only 20,000 jobs in 1997, less than one-third the 65,000 it provided in 1976 and only 2.3 percent of total employment. Earnings have been on a downtrend since 1982, with 1997 earnings only 60 percent of those in 1982. These earnings are in current dollars; were they to be adjusted for inflation, the drop would be much larger. Construction, on the other hand, provided a

greater share of employment and earnings than the national average in 1997 and grew faster from 1989 to 1997.

Service industries have been the major source of 1990s economic growth. Earnings in business services doubled from 1989 to 1997, and those in the smaller social services industry grew over 200 percent. The state's largest industry, health services, also grew fairly rapidly. Altogether, the service-producing sectors provided 78 percent of all West Virginia jobs in 1997, not far below the national average of 80 percent.

Government (federal, state, and local combined) employed 17.1 percent of the state's workers in 1997, compared with 13.9 percent nationwide. As elsewhere, federal employment was a fairly small share of this total. However, in contrast to the nation—which experienced a 16 percent drop in federal employment—the number of federal jobs in West Virginia grew by 16 percent from 1989 to 1997, a result, in part, of transfers of federal agency activities from the District of Columbia area.

Employment and Earnings by Sector

	1980	1989	1990	1991	1992	1993	1994	1995	1996	1997 Number	1997 Percent of total	Change*
Employment (thousands of persons)												
Total	784	762	782	784	795	807	829	843	854	864	100.0	1.6
Farm	26	25	24	23	23	23	22	22	22	22	2.6	-1.1
Nonfarm	758	737	758	761	772	784	807	821	832	842	97.4	1.7
Private nonfarm	621	604	621	623	630	642	662	676	684	694	80.3	1.8
Agricultural service, forestry, and fishing	3	4	5	5	5	5	6	6	6	6	0.7	4.8
Mining	68	40	42	40	36	32	34	33	30	29	3.3	-4.0
Construction	46	38	42	42	42	46	49	49	50	51	5.9	3.6
Manufacturing	123	92	91	87	86	86	86	86	86	86	9.9	-0.8
Transportation and public utilities	47	42	44	44	44	44	46	46	45	45	5.2	0.9
Wholesale trade	34	32	32	33	33	32	32	32	32	33	3.8	0.4
Retail trade	121	138	138	137	140	143	149	154	157	159	18.4	1.8
Finance, insurance, and real estate	37	37	38	38	37	38	39	40	40	41	4.8	1.5
Services	143	181	191	198	207	216	222	230	237	243	28.1	3.8
Government	136	134	137	138	142	142	145	145	148	148	17.1	1.3
Earnings (millions of dollars)												
Total	11 713	15 435	16 501	16 975	17 974	18 664	19 712	20 242	20 794	21 402	100.0	4.2
Farm	15	56	38	23	47	58	52	14	-10	-14	-0.1	NA
Nonfarm	11 697	15 379	16 463	16 952	17 927	18 606	19 659	20 228	20 804	21 415	100.1	4.2
Private nonfarm	10 051	12 724	13 599	13 887	14 658	15 157	16 023	16 452	16 870	17 355	81.1	4.0
Agricultural service, forestry, and fishing	20	46	54	57	63	67	72	73	70	75	0.4	6.3
Mining	2 014	1 590	1 768	1 726	1 690	1 442	1 588	1 587	1 527	1 492	7.0	-0.8
Construction	809	796	940	954	995	1 127	1 280	1 242	1 332	1 368	6.4	7.0
Manufacturing	2 636	2 945	3 000	2 906	3 043	3 136	3 219	3 297	3 345	3 337	15.6	1.6
Transportation and public utilities	1 023	1 306	1 377	1 444	1 521	1 583	1 664	1 684	1 676	1 682	7.9	3.2
Wholesale trade	573	788	824	856	902	903	939	961	1 000	1 064	5.0	3.8
Retail trade	1 062	1 540	1 566	1 611	1 691	1 781	1 880	1 954	2 013	2 102	9.8	4.0
Finance, insurance, and real estate	359	592	624	644	689	744	761	805	831	876	4.1	5.0
Services	1 555	3 121	3 446	3 689	4 064	4 373	4 618	4 849	5 077	5 359	25.0	7.0
Government	1 646	2 655	2 863	3 064	3 269	3 449	3 637	3 776	3 934	4 060	19.0	5.5

*Compound annual average percent change, 1989–1997

ECONOMIC STRUCTURE (Continued)

IN 1989, THE ANNUAL WAGE OR SALARY OF THE AVERAGE WEST Virginia worker was 88 percent of the national average, yet personal income per capita was only 72 percent of its U.S. average. The difference is explained by the state's high unemployment rate and low labor force participation. By 1997, the unemployment rate was lower. More people were at work, but wages had slipped relative to the national average; West Virginia workers' annual earnings were only 81 percent of the national average. Much of the drop can be attributed to changes in the industry mix. The number of relatively well-paid jobs in heavy industries such as coal mining and primary metals manufacturing fell while the number of jobs in lower wage service industries grew. Although high unemployment and low labor force participation still characterized the West Virginia economy in 1997, the picture had shifted somewhat toward more jobs, but relatively lower earnings per job.

Manufacturing contributed 19.4 percent of West Virginia's gross state product (GSP) at the 1989 business cycle peak. But recession then took its toll; in 1990 and 1991, the actual value of manufacturing output, as well as its share of GSP, declined, and employment in manufacturing declined 5 percent. In the subsequent recovery, manufacturing value added and employment rose through 1995, but then leveled off.

Manufacturing value added per worker in 1996 was about 12.5 percent above the U.S. average, reflecting the dominance in the state of the chemicals and primary metals industries, two relative high value-added industries. However, the chemicals industry grew only slowly from 1989 to 1997, and the primary metals industry actually declined 10 percent, measured by worker and proprietor earnings. The state's most rapidly growing manufacturing industry has been lumber and wood products, where earnings grew 74 percent from 1989 to 1997. Though still relatively small, this industry is expected to continued to grow.

Exports have been a bright spot in West Virginia's economy during the mid-1990s, showing a strong surge from 1993 to 1995 and continued growth through 1997. Coal is the top export product, and the value of coal exports doubled from 1993 to 1997, with most of the growth occurring from 1993 to 1995. Exports of primary metals doubled from 1994 to 1997, but chemicals exports, though fluctuating from year to year, have shown no clear trend. Two additional industries—industrial machinery and wood products—began to emerge as significant sources of export earnings from 1995 to 1997.

Average Annual Wages and Salaries by Sector
(dollars)

	1989	1996	1997 State	1997 U.S.
All wage and salary workers	19 614	23 620	24 195	29 809
Farm	6 968	11 802	9 426	16 442
Nonfarm	19 674	23 655	24 248	29 900
Private nonfarm	20 113	23 604	24 150	29 867
Agricultural service, forestry, and fishing	11 656	15 004	15 767	17 941
Mining	38 166	46 151	47 056	49 800
Construction	21 507	25 792	26 508	31 765
Manufacturing	28 006	33 947	34 203	38 351
Transportation and utilities	29 169	34 639	35 241	38 222
Wholesale trade	22 858	29 227	30 323	39 466
Retail trade	10 450	12 562	13 087	16 206
Finance, insurance, and real estate	19 710	24 795	25 639	44 993
Services	15 792	20 119	20 867	27 588
Government	18 035	23 848	24 624	30 062

Gross State Product and Manufacturing
(millions of dollars, except as noted)

	1989	1994	1995	1996
Gross state product, total	27 184	34 465	36 039	37 160
Manufacturing:				
Millions of dollars	5 266	5 928	6 716	6 716
Percent of total gross state product	19.4	17.2	18.6	18.1
Per worker (dollars)	57 528	69 164	77 845	78 029
New capital expenditures, manufacturing	NA	732	630	882

Exports of Goods
(millions of dollars)

	1994	1995	1996	1997
All goods	941	1 098	1 218	1 299
Manufactures	637	708	820	868
Agricultural and livestock products	6	12	6	8
Other commodities	297	377	392	423
Top goods exports, 1997:				
Bituminous coal	277	360	367	394
Primary metals	128	162	213	290
Chemical products	281	232	289	250
Industrial machinery and computers	50	57	75	80
Lumber and wood products	38	38	46	61

HOUSING

West Virginia's rapid population decline during the 1980s reduced the need for new home construction, and the new home production rate of 2.4 per thousand population in 1989 was far below the national average of 6.2. The state's new home production rate rose a little in the next two years, despite the recession, but remained well below even the nation's recession-impacted average. From 1991 to 1997, the state's rate rose a little faster than did the nation's but did not catch up to the national average. Throughout the 1990s, more than one-half of the state's new homes have been manufactured housing (mobile homes).

The state's high proportion of older people and limited migration of new residents into the state are reflected in a homeownership rate well above the national average. After some pick up from 1989 to 1990, sales of existing homes have shown only small year-to-year changes. In part because of the relatively inactive housing market and the state's low average incomes, the 1997 median sales price of existing homes in the Charleston area, the state's largest metropolitan area, was quite low, $87,800, or 70 percent of the U.S. average of $124,100.

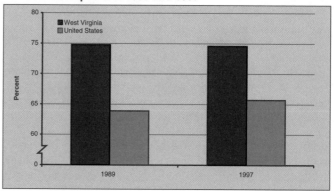

Homeownership Rates: 1989 and 1997

Housing Supply

	1989	1990	1991	1992	1993	1994	1995	1996	1997
Residential building permits (thousands)	1.7	1.8	2.0	2.3	2.6	3.9	3.7	3.6	4.1
New home production (including manufactured housing):									
Thousands of homes	4.4	5.5	5.2	6.1	7.2	9.7	9.2	8.9	9.4
Rate per 1,000 population									
West Virginia	2.4	3.1	2.9	3.4	4.0	5.3	5.0	4.9	5.2
U.S.	6.2	5.2	4.5	5.1	5.6	6.4	6.3	6.6	6.5
Existing home sales:									
Thousands of homes	36.8	42.0	43.3	46.8	45.7	45.8	44.2	43.8	45.2
Change from previous year (percent)									
West Virginia	1.1	14.1	3.1	8.1	-2.4	0.2	-3.5	-0.9	3.2
U.S.	-3.9	-4.0	0.0	9.2	8.2	4.8	-3.7	7.5	3.8
Home ownership rate (percent of households)	74.8	72.0	72.4	73.3	73.3	73.7	73.1	74.3	74.6
Rental vacancy rate (percent of rental housing units)	11.5	8.2	6.3	5.4	6.0	8.5	7.6	5.8	7.5

AGRICULTURE

Average agricultural sales per West Virginia farm are quite modest—only one-fourth the national average in 1997. Only 21 percent of farms had sales above $10,000, but these farms accounted for 91 percent of all sales.

Poultry and its products accounted for 50 percent of all farm sales in 1997 and cattle and calves for another 25 percent. Only 4 percent of farms marketed poultry, and average poultry sales were $308,000. In contrast, 65 percent of farms marketed cattle, receiving only $10,000 per farm for cattle sales.

WEST VIRGINIA FARMS, 1997	
Number of farms	20 000
Total acres (thousands):	3 700
Average per farm	185
Value of land and buildings (millions of dollars)	3 700
Average per farm (dollars)	185 000

Receipts from farm sales held fairly level from 1993 through 1997, but, due to inventory depletion and rising expenses, there were net losses from 1995 through 1997.

Farm Income
(millions of dollars)

	1980	1989	1990	1991	1992	1993	1994	1995	1996	1997
Gross income	299	430	422	420	437	518	518	496	486	502
Receipts from sales	238	327	354	353	362	439	439	415	403	415
Government payments	2	12	6	5	7	6	6	5	5	6
Imputed and miscellaneous income	59	91	62	61	67	73	74	75	79	81
(−) Production expenses	344	399	424	415	418	475	497	501	516	540
(=) Realized net income	-45	31	-3	5	19	43	21	-6	-30	-38
(+) Inventory change	37	5	17	-7	8	-8	12	-9	-16	-14
(=) Net income	-8	36	14	-2	27	34	32	-15	-46	-52
Corporate income	-2	3	1	-1	2	1	4	-4	-11	-13
Farm proprietors income	-6	34	13	-1	25	33	28	-11	-35	-39

EDUCATION

EDUCATIONAL ATTAINMENT Percent of population age 25 and over, 1997	State	United States
High school graduate or higher	77.3	82.1
College graduate or higher	14.7	23.9

THE PERCENT OF WEST VIRGINIA RESIDENTS AGE 25 AND OVER that had completed high school rose from 41.7 percent in 1970 to 66.0 percent in 1990 and 77.3 percent in 1997. The strong gains during the 1990s reduced the percentage-point gap with the national average by about one-half. The state's college completion rate doubled from 1970 to 1997, but even so, the state essentially was tied with Arkansas for lowest in the nation in 1997.

Elementary and secondary school expenditures per pupil have increased substantially during the 1990s and have exceeded the U.S. average since about 1994. The average teacher salary was 86 percent of the national average in 1997.

The percent of the population age 18 to 34 enrolled in higher education was a little below the national average in 1997, and the minority share of enrollment, though small, was greater than the minority share of West Virginia's total population.

High School Completion: 1990–97

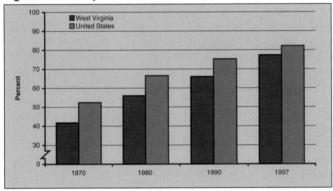

Education Indicators

	State	U.S.
Elementary and secondary schools		
Enrollment, 1995–96		
Total (thousands)	320	49 873
Percent in private schools	4.1	10.1
Expenditures per pupil (dollars), 1995–96	6 325	6 146
Average teacher salary (dollars), 1996–97	33 159	38 509
Higher education		
Enrollment, 1996–97		
Total (thousands)	86	14 218
Percent of population 18–34	20.4	21.8
Percent minority	6.2	26.1
Percent in private schools	12.8	22.6

HEALTH

WEST VIRGINIA HAS SET A GOAL OF REDUCING THE STATE'S infant mortality rate to no more than 7 deaths per thousand live births. The reduction already achieved, from 9.9 in 1990 to 8.2 in 1996 and 1997, has moved the state more than half-way toward this goal. Early prenatal care is key to reducing infant mortality, but access to this care may be hampered by lack of transportation, shortages of medical personnel, and failure to understand the importance of

early care. With start-up funds from the Robert Wood Johnson Foundation, the state is addressing these problems through its Right From the Start program.

Adjusted for differences in the age distribution of the population, West Virginia's death rate from heart disease was 25 percent above the national average in 1996, and reflecting the state's coal mining history, the rate from pulmonary (lung) diseases was 29 percent above.

Health Indicators

	1990	1995	1996	1997
Infant mortality				
(rate per thousand live births)				
West Virginia	9.9	7.9	8.2	8.2
U.S.	9.2	7.6	7.3	7.1
Total deaths, age-adjusted rate				
(rate per thousand population)				
West Virginia	5.7	5.5	5.5	5.5
U.S.	5.2	5.0	4.9	4.8
Persons not covered by health insurance				
(percent of population)				
West Virginia	13.8	15.3	14.9	17.2
U.S.	13.9	15.4	15.6	16.1

Leading Causes of Death, 1996
(deaths per 100,000 population)

	Age-adjusted		Not age-adjusted	
	State	U.S.	State	U.S.
Deaths from all causes	548.2	491.6	1118.4	872.5
Heart disease	167.8	134.5	386.4	276.4
Cancer	137.7	127.9	255.0	203.4
Cerebrovascular diseases	25.9	26.4	66.8	60.3
Chronic obstructive pulmonary disease	27.0	21.0	60.2	40.0
Diabetes mellitus	18.8	13.6	36.6	23.3
Pneumonia and influenza	11.8	12.8	33.8	31.6
HIV	3.3	11.1	3.1	11.7
Liver disease	7.4	7.5	10.6	9.4
Alzheimer's disease	2.9	2.7	10.4	8.1
Accidents and adverse effects	34.8	30.4	41.8	35.8
Motor vehicle accidents	18.6	16.2	18.5	16.5
Suicide	13.7	10.8	15.3	11.6
Homicide	5.1	8.5	4.8	7.9
Injury by firearm	13.7	12.9	15.1	12.8

GOVERNMENT

STATE AND LOCAL TAXES, 1995–96	State	U.S.
Per capita (dollars)	1 866	2 477
Percent of personal income	10.5	10.8

In the 1995-96 fiscal year, West Virginia's $1,866 per capita of state and local tax revenue (excluding corporate income taxes) was only 75 percent of the all-state average. Because of West Virginia's relatively low personal income per capita, this gap is substantially reduced when taxes are measured as a percent of personal income. State and local taxes were 10.5 percent of the state's personal income in 1995-96, compared to an all-state average of 10.8 percent.

State Government Finances, 1996–97

	Millions of dollars	Percent distribu- tion	Dollars per capita	
			State	U.S.
General revenue	6 038	100.0	3 325	3 049
Intergovernmental revenue	2 040	33.8	1 123	863
Taxes	2 906	48.1	1 600	1 660
General sales	831	13.8	458	551
Selective sales	683	11.3	376	257
License taxes	151	2.5	83	106
Individual income	786	13.0	433	542
Corporation net income	251	4.2	138	115
Other taxes	202	3.4	111	90
Other general revenue	1 092	18.1	601	526
General expenditure	6 099	100.0	3 358	2 951
Intergovernmental expenditure	1 626	26.7	895	989
Direct expenditure	4 473	73.3	2 463	1 962
General expenditure, by function:				
Education	2 386	39.1	1 314	1 033
Public welfare	1 603	26.3	883	761
Hospitals and health	217	3.6	120	237
Highways	783	12.8	431	225
Police protection and corrections	136	2.2	75	137
Natural resources, parks and recreation	192	3.2	106	63
Governmental administration	267	4.4	147	107
Interest on general debt	179	2.9	99	99
Other and unallocable	335	5.5	184	290
Debt at end of fiscal year	3 040	NA	1 674	1 706
Cash and security holdings	7 478	NA	4 118	6 683

Federal Spending within State

	Federal funds, fiscal 1997		
	Millions of dollars	Percent distribution	Percent of U.S. total*
Total within state	10 298	100.0	0.7
Payments to individuals	6 728	65.3	0.9
Retirement and disability	4 089	39.7	0.9
Medicare	1 581	15.4	0.8
Food stamps	240	2.3	1.2
Supplemental Security Income	302	2.9	1.1
Grants	2 119	20.6	0.9
Medicaid and other health	981	9.5	0.9
Nutrition and family welfare	350	3.4	0.7
Education	142	1.4	0.8
Housing and community development	60	0.6	0.5
Salaries and wages	863	8.4	0.5
Defense procurement contracts	150	1.5	0.1
Non-defense procurement contracts	352	3.4	0.5

*State population is 0.7 percent of the U.S. total.

Local taxes were only 26 percent of the state and local total, compared to a 41 percent national average, indicating considerably above average state-level responsibility for revenue collection.

General and selective sales taxes provided 52 percent of total state-level tax revenue in fiscal year 1996-97, a little above the all-state average of 49 percent. Revenue from the individual income tax made up 27 percent of the state's total, compared to an all-state average of 33 percent, while corporate income taxes yielded close to 9 percent, compared to an all-state average of 7 percent.

Total state-level general expenditure per capita was 14 percent higher than the all-state average in 1996-97, and education spending was 27 percent higher. The relatively high state contribution brought total per-pupil expenditure in elementary and secondary schools 3 percent above the national average in 1995–96. Also well above the national average in 1996-97 were per capita state spending on public welfare, highways, and natural resources, parks and recreation. Per capita health care spending was below average, however,

West Virginia's general debt of $1,674 per capita in 1996-97 was within 2 percent of the national average. The state's cash and security holdings, although about 2.5 times the general debt, did not reach the strong national average ratio of almost four times the size of the debt.

West Virginia's 0.7 percent share of federal funds distributed to states and their residents in fiscal 1997 was just equal to the state's 0.7 percent share of the U.S. population. The state has relatively low household incomes, a high poverty rate, and a relatively high share of elderly in its population. These factors were reflected in retirement, Medicare, food stamp and Supplementary Security Income payments that were high relative to the state's population share, as were Medicaid and other health related grants. In contrast, the state's share of federal salaries and wages and federal procurement contracts was low. Defense contracts totaled only $150 million, or only 1.5 percent of all federal payments within the state.

31 372	59 698		65 157	70 827	72 687	78 001	81 93		88 504	93 426	5.8	63 383	70 827	31 372	59 698	63 38
25 323	47 902		57 151	59 446	62 916	67 00		72 039	77 208	6.1	50 999	57 151	25 323	47 902	50 99
2 640	5 143			7 801				7 709	7 838	5.4	5 645	6 816	2 640	5 143	5 64
3 409	6 652			284				8 755	8 380	2.9	6 739	6 860	3 409	6 652	6 79
693	1 716							1 539	762	9.7	1 561	811	693	1 716	1 55
2 716								7 217	7 618	5.6	5 176	6 049	2 716		

1997

Population (persons)	5,201,226
Population rank	18th
Population growth rank (1990–97)	25th
Per capita personal income	$24,199
Unemployment rate (percent)	3.7
Poverty rate (percent)	8.2

IN THE 1990S WISCONSIN HAS REVERSED ITS FORTUNES, EXPE-riencing substantially better population and job growth than the sluggish increases it saw in the 1980s. Employment grew faster than the U.S. average in every major economic sector between 1989 and 1997. Because its population grew more slowly than the U.S. average, the strong employment growth led to a remarkable 70.8 per-cent of state population at work and fueled impressive gains in household income.

"America's Dairyland" suffered a significant downturn for its farm sector in the 1990s, but as a manufacturing powerhouse it saw gains. Manufacturing employment grew nearly 10 percent from 1989 to 1997, when the national trend was job losses in manufacturing. As of 1997, the state's diverse manufacturing sector boasted ten different industries with over $1 billion in earnings. Services and construction sectors grew strongly, complet-ing the picture of a diverse economy growing at healthy rates. Median household income has grown a bit faster in Wisconsin than nationwide in the 1990s.

Population trends have moved positively in the 1990s, though the total growth from 1990 to 1997 of 6.5 percent was below the national average (7.3 percent). Interstate migration added 1.7 percent to the state's population from 1990 to 1997; in the 1980s this factor had drained 2.7 per-cent of the state's population.

Average Annual Population Growth: 1990–97

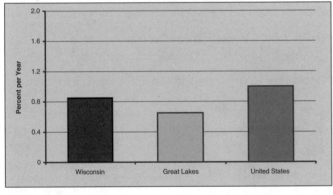

Median Household Income: 1989–97 (1997 dollars)

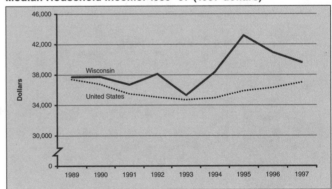

Unemployment Rate: 1989–97

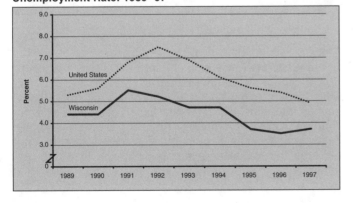

WITH STRONG STEADY JOB GROWTH THROUGH THE 1990S, unemployment has remained consistently below average in Wisconsin. The steadiness of unemployment was all the more remarkable because of the predominance of manu-facturing, which normally sees cyclical swings. The average unemployment rate of 3.6 percent over the 1996–97 peri-od was the seventh lowest in the nation. This remarkable performance came despite very large increases in the labor force, which grew at double the rate of growth of adult population (and substantially faster than the U.S. labor force).

POPULATION AND LABOR FORCE

WISCONSIN GRADUALLY SLIPPED LOWER IN THE POPULATION rankings among states, reaching 18th in 1997, as its moderate population growth of 1990–97 failed to keep pace with national averages (though it exceeded most Great Lakes states). It had grown even slower in the 1980s. While outmigration was the culprit during the 1980s, in the 1990s the migration pattern has been reversed by the strong prevailing job market in the state. The modest population growth can be traced instead to low birth rates: the 1997 birth rate was significantly below the U.S. rate.

While there was domestic in-migration equal to 1.7 percent of the 1990 population between 1990 and 1997, there was minimal foreign immigration, adding only 0.4 percent to the population over the seven years (much below the national average rate). Thus, Wisconsin maintained nearly the same high proportion of Whites non-Hispanic as previously: 89.9 percent of the population in 1997. Black non-Hispanic remained the largest minority group (5.4 percent); Hispanics and Asians combined represented only 4.0 percent of the population, despite rapid growth rates in percentage terms. The state's population became slightly less concentrated in metropolitan areas, and as of 1997 the share of the population in nonmetropolitan areas (about one-third) was above the national average.

Population and Labor Force

	1980	1990	1991	1992	1993	1994	1995	1996	1997	Change* State	Change* U.S.
Population											
Total number of persons (thousands)	4 706	4 902	4 953	5 005	5 056	5 095	5 137	5 174	5 201	0.8	1.0
Percent distribution:											
White, Non-Hispanic	93.7	90.9	91.1	90.9	90.7	90.5	90.3	90.1	89.9	0.6	0.4
Black, Non-Hispanic	3.9	5.1	5.0	5.1	5.2	5.2	5.3	5.4	5.4	1.5	1.4
Asian	0.5	1.2	1.2	1.2	1.3	1.3	1.4	1.4	1.5	4.4	4.1
Native American	0.7	0.8	0.8	0.8	0.9	0.9	0.9	0.9	0.9	1.7	1.6
Hispanic	1.3	2.1	2.0	2.0	2.1	2.2	2.3	2.4	2.5	3.0	3.8
In metropolitan areas	67.5	68.1	68.1	68.1	68.0	67.9	67.8	67.7	67.7	0.7	1.0
Total number of households (thousands)	1 652	1 822	1 842	1 868	1 883	1 891	1 917	1 943	NA	1.1	1.2
Labor Force (thousands)											
Population 16 and over	3 532	3 732	3 769	3 804	3 849	3 882	3 923	3 963	3 987	0.9	1.0
Civilian labor force	2 340	2 581	2 595	2 676	2 728	2 800	2 844	2 927	2 949	1.9	1.1
Employed	2 172	2 467	2 454	2 538	2 598	2 668	2 739	2 824	2 841	2.0	1.2
Percent of population	61.5	66.1	65.1	66.7	67.5	68.7	69.8	71.2	71.3		
Unemployment rate (percent)	7.2	4.4	5.5	5.2	4.7	4.7	3.7	3.5	3.7		

*Compound annual average percent change, 1990–1997; 1990–1996 for households.

Population Change and Components: 1990–97

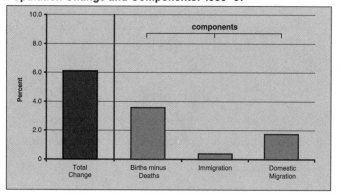

Average Annual Household and Population Growth

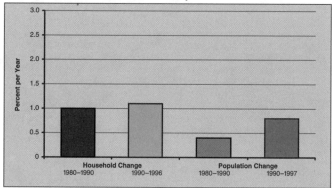

Population by Age; Births and Deaths

	1990 State	1990 U.S.	1997 State	1997 U.S.
Age distribution (percent)				
Under 5 years	7.5	7.6	6.5	7.2
5 to 17 years	19.1	18.2	19.6	18.8
18 to 64 years	60.1	61.8	60.7	61.3
65 years and over	13.3	12.5	13.2	12.7
Birth and death rates (per thousand population)				
Births	14.9	16.7	12.9	14.6
Deaths	8.7	8.6	8.7	8.6

THE AGE PATTERN OF THE STATE'S POPULATION WAS UNUSUAL. It had relatively few young children but a larger percentage of school-age children than average in the country. Since birth rates have been low for quite some time, it may be that the state's in-migrants have been families with children in the 5–17 year age bracket. The state also has had a somewhat high percentage of people age 65 and older, and a conversely smaller percentage of working-age adults.

HOUSEHOLD AND PERSONAL INCOME

HOUSEHOLD INCOME AND PERSONS IN POVERTY	1990	1995	1996	1997 State	1997 U.S.
Median household income (1997 dollars)	37 713	43 132	40 919	39 595	37 005
Persons in poverty (thousands)	448	449	460	422	35 574
Poverty rate (percent)	9.3	8.5	8.8	8.2	13.3

MEDIAN HOUSEHOLD INCOME IN WISCONSIN IN 1992–97 consistently stayed above the U.S. median. The median was 7 percent above that of the United States in 1997. This was an improvement from the approximate parity prevailing in 1989–90, not surprising considering the state's rapid growth of wage income. Poverty was a low 8.2 percent in 1997, continuing the state's favorable history that reflects high employment and a small population of minorities, who characteristically suffer from higher poverty rates.

Growth of personal income per capita outpaced U.S. growth rates, increasing 13.8 percent in real dollars from 1989 to 1997, though the level of per capita income still was about 4 percent lower than average in 1997. Earned income per capita was 2 percent below the U.S. level, dividend and interest income was 4 percent below average, and transfer payments were 13 percent less than average.

Because personal income includes the value of nonmoney transfers, Wisconsin's lower transfers weakened its total compared to that of other states. The adjustment for residence, which measures the effects of net commuting to a state, was positive, adding $2 billion (or about 2.3 percent) to resident income.

Transfer payments contributed a relatively small share of personal income in Wisconsin, and they grew slowly during the 1990–97 period. The fastest gains were in medical payments, but the growth was low in comparison to increases nationwide. Welfare rolls declined dramatically with the state's reform programs, which cut family assistance by 61 percent from 1990 to 1997. However, Supplemental Security Income grew rapidly as it did in the nation, and other income maintenance (mainly low-income tax credits) grew fastest of all.

Personal Income
(millions of dollars)

	1980	1989	1990	1991	1992	1993	1994	1995	1996	1997	Change*
Earnings by place of work	33 970	57 439	60 743	62 881	68 212	71 916	76 378	79 824	83 612	88 513	5.6
Wages and salaries	27 143	45 954	49 255	51 310	55 381	58 183	61 848	65 389	68 953	73 773	6.1
Other labor income	2 852	5 257	5 846	6 336	7 100	7 965	8 490	8 369	8 097	8 210	5.7
Proprietors' income	3 976	6 228	5 642	5 236	5 731	5 768	6 041	6 066	6 562	6 531	0.6
Farm	1 209	1 207	710	257	296	-44	3	-187	33	-290	0.0
Nonfarm	2 767	5 020	4 931	4 979	5 435	5 812	6 038	6 254	6 529	6 821	3.9
(−) Personal contributions for social insurance	1 761	3 587	3 807	4 039	4 334	4 581	4 953	5 246	5 437	5 794	6.2
(+) Adjustment for residence	534	1 245	1 325	1 361	1 458	1 462	1 590	1 722	1 866	1 990	NA
(=) **Net earnings by state of residence**	32 742	55 097	58 261	60 204	65 335	68 796	73 015	76 300	80 041	84 709	5.5
(+) Dividends, interest, and rent	7 230	14 840	15 750	16 102	16 223	16 476	17 520	19 099	20 925	21 656	4.8
(+) Transfer payments	6 672	11 782	12 715	14 014	15 188	15 887	16 528	17 517	18 075	18 734	6.0
(=) **Total personal income**	46 644	81 719	86 726	90 320	96 746	101 159	107 063	112 917	119 042	125 100	5.5
Farm	1 478	1 560	1 150	710	789	434	500	301	574	261	-20.0
Nonfarm	45 166	80 159	85 576	89 610	95 957	100 725	106 563	112 616	118 468	124 839	5.7
Personal income per capita (dollars)											
Current dollars	9 899	16 827	17 692	18 261	19 382	20 078	21 096	22 084	23 132	24 199	4.6
1997 dollars	18 927	21 273	21 290	21 087	21 680	21 848	22 419	22 956	23 556	24 199	1.6

*Compound annual average percent change, 1989–1997

Government Transfer Payments

	Millions of dollars 1990	Millions of dollars 1997	Percent change* State	Percent change* U.S.
Total government payments to individuals	12 024	17 815	48.2	62.7
Retirement, disability, and insurance	6 668	9 779	46.7	48.2
Social Security	5 383	7 535	40.0	46.1
Government employee retirement	1 132	2 063	82.2	60.3
Medical payments	3 455	5 815	68.3	101.2
Income maintenance	1 067	1 171	9.8	58.0
Supplemental Security Income	290	499	72.0	75.4
Family assistance	460	179	-61.1	-0.5
Food Stamps	186	151	-18.8	27.1
Other income maintenance	131	343	161.6	189.8
Unemployment insurance benefits	370	479	29.2	10.6
Veterans benefits and other	464	571	23.0	30.8

*Percent change, 1990–1997

Government Payments to Individuals: 1997

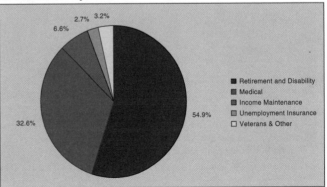

- Retirement and Disability — 54.9%
- Medical — 32.6%
- Income Maintenance — 6.6%
- Unemployment Insurance — 2.7%
- Veterans & Other — 3.2%

ECONOMIC STRUCTURE

LEADING PRIVATE INDUSTRIES, 1997 (Worker and proprietor earnings, millions of dollars)		FASTEST EARNINGS GROWTH, 1989–97 (percent increase)	
Health services	$8 014	Real estate	176.0
Industrial machinery manufacturing	5 184	Other transportation services	128.7
Construction specialties	3 716	Social services	121.5
Business services	3 505	Chemicals and allied products	78.5
Paper and allied products	2 750	Educational services	78.1

MANUFACTURING CONTINUED TO PLAY A LEADING ROLE IN the state economy, providing 19.2 percent of all jobs in 1997 (compared to only a 12.5 percent share for the whole country). However, the broad-based nature of the state economy meant that only two of the five largest-earning industries in 1997 were in manufacturing: industrial machinery and paper making. Construction was the fastest growing major sector in terms of employment, with a 35 percent increase from 1989 to 1997, a significant acceleration over the 1980s. Industries with the fastest growing earnings were mostly in the services sector, with the service-like real estate industry leading the list. Earnings at private social services agencies grew 121.5 percent from 1989 to 1997, possibly linked to the state's aggressive welfare-to-work programs. Overall, every major sector enjoyed stronger job growth than the averages for the nation.

Employment and Earnings by Sector

	1980	1989	1990	1991	1992	1993	1994	1995	1996	1997 Number	1997 Percent of total	Change*
Employment *(thousands of persons)*												
Total	2 449	2 760	2 829	2 862	2 917	2 974	3 070	3 148	3 203	3 268	100.0	2.1
Farm	151	114	115	113	110	108	109	110	105	105	3.2	-1.1
Nonfarm	2 298	2 646	2 714	2 749	2 808	2 867	2 962	3 038	3 098	3 163	96.8	2.3
Private nonfarm	1 968	2 289	2 349	2 382	2 428	2 484	2 579	2 654	2 712	2 775	84.9	2.4
Agricultural service, forestry, and fishing	15	21	23	25	25	26	28	29	30	31	1.0	4.7
Mining	4	3	4	4	4	3	4	4	3	4	0.1	0.2
Construction	97	117	125	125	134	136	143	147	153	158	4.8	3.8
Manufacturing	568	574	573	563	565	577	602	620	620	628	19.2	1.1
Transportation and public utilities	103	118	123	125	126	131	134	138	141	145	4.4	2.6
Wholesale trade	104	124	125	128	130	131	134	137	139	143	4.4	1.8
Retail trade	411	485	498	503	510	515	534	551	562	570	17.4	2.0
Finance, insurance, and real estate	173	178	185	189	189	195	206	213	217	222	6.8	2.8
Services	492	668	695	721	745	769	794	816	845	874	26.7	3.4
Government	330	357	365	367	379	383	383	384	386	388	11.9	1.1
Earnings *(millions of dollars)*												
Total	33 970	57 439	60 743	62 881	68 212	71 916	76 378	79 824	83 612	88 513	100.0	5.6
Farm	1 478	1 560	1 150	710	789	434	500	301	574	261	0.3	-20.0
Nonfarm	32 492	55 879	59 593	62 171	67 423	71 481	75 879	79 523	83 039	88 252	99.7	5.9
Private nonfarm	28 157	48 029	51 117	53 164	57 707	61 227	65 238	68 537	71 721	76 518	86.4	6.0
Agricultural service, forestry, and fishing	133	307	362	385	413	435	446	456	464	485	0.5	5.9
Mining	168	81	87	92	101	108	113	118	119	128	0.1	5.9
Construction	1 860	3 271	3 637	3 753	4 099	4 366	4 686	4 852	5 272	5 619	6.3	7.0
Manufacturing	11 528	17 107	17 766	18 019	19 413	20 443	22 093	23 116	23 574	25 157	28.4	4.9
Transportation and public utilities	2 109	3 374	3 648	3 825	4 043	4 317	4 597	4 774	4 902	5 174	5.8	5.5
Wholesale trade	2 024	3 466	3 705	3 844	4 116	4 299	4 540	4 772	5 055	5 459	6.2	5.8
Retail trade	3 336	5 377	5 708	5 937	6 312	6 596	7 023	7 300	7 613	7 991	9.0	5.1
Finance, insurance, and real estate	1 578	3 175	3 479	3 708	4 255	4 695	4 845	5 265	5 593	6 027	6.8	8.3
Services	5 420	11 870	12 726	13 601	14 956	15 968	16 897	17 884	19 128	20 477	23.1	7.1
Government	4 335	7 850	8 476	9 007	9 716	10 255	10 640	10 985	11 318	11 734	13.3	5.2

*Compound annual average percent change, 1989–1997

ECONOMIC STRUCTURE (Continued)

AVERAGE WAGES FOR WAGE AND SALARY WORKERS IN Wisconsin were 10 percent below the national averages in 1997, perhaps accounting for the state's attractiveness as a fast-expanding employment center. Employees in most sectors earned wages 8 percent to 9 percent below U.S. average levels, including the big manufacturing sector, even though the mix of industries there generally resembled the U.S. mix of high- and low-paying manufacturing industries. Pay in service jobs was particularly low, only 83 percent as high as the U.S. average in 1997. However, pay rates were higher than the U.S. norm within the construction sector, as well as for agricultural services and farm jobs. In contrast to the state's lower overall wage levels, rates of increase in wages were slightly above the national rate from 1989 to 1997.

Manufacturing occupied a central position supporting Wisconsin's economy, with value of output comprising 27.7 percent of gross state product (GSP) in 1996. This was the third highest ratio in the nation and above the average for the industrialized Great Lakes region (25.4 percent of its GSP was manufacturing). With the state's total gross state product growing an average of 5.7 percent annually from 1989 to 1996 (in current dollars), and manufacturing value increasing 4.8 percent per year, however, the relative size of the sector is decreasing slightly. The value of manufacturing output per worker was somewhat lower in Wisconsin than the national average. This is a bit surprising given the predominance of the industrial machinery and paper industries, which typically have high productivity, but the state also had significant production of food products and fabricated metals, which tend to have lower productivity.

Export demand has added a significant impetus to Wisconsin's growth in the 1990s, as exports of goods increased 41 percent from 1994 to 1997. The largest state export, industrial machinery and equipment, was also the fastest growing, with a 54 percent increase. Still, exports were a somewhat smaller element in the state economy than average because of its location and lower export rates for its large nondurable sectors. For example, the state's exports of paper products in 1997 were one-third as large as those from Washington state, and its agricultural exports were only a small fraction of such exports from Oregon.

Average Annual Wages and Salaries by Sector
(dollars)

	1989	1996	1997 State	1997 U.S.
All wage and salary workers	19 555	25 418	26 674	29 809
Farm	11 424	19 999	20 690	16 442
Nonfarm	19 655	25 469	26 727	29 900
Private nonfarm	19 572	25 284	26 610	29 867
Agricultural service, forestry, and fishing	15 441	19 316	19 649	17 941
Mining	27 277	35 806	37 139	49 800
Construction	25 458	31 898	33 570	31 765
Manufacturing	26 203	33 418	35 421	38 351
Transportation and utilities	25 087	30 550	31 833	38 222
Wholesale trade	25 105	32 754	34 591	39 466
Retail trade	10 262	13 154	13 732	16 206
Finance, insurance, and real estate	22 691	31 854	34 264	44 993
Services	16 208	21 964	22 880	27 588
Government	20 110	26 572	27 437	30 062

Gross State Product and Manufacturing
(millions of dollars, except as noted)

	1989	1994	1995	1996
Gross state product, total	94 522	125 831	132 704	139 160
Manufacturing:				
Millions of dollars	27 875	35 411	37 538	38 605
Percent of total gross state product	29.5	28.1	28.3	27.7
Per worker (dollars)	48 592	58 847	60 593	62 287
New capital expenditures, manufacturing	NA	3 321	3 507	3 986

Exports of Goods
(millions of dollars)

	1994	1995	1996	1997
All goods	6 928	8 004	8 410	9 792
Manufactures	6 637	7 643	8 095	9 455
Agricultural and livestock products	67	78	93	75
Other commodities	224	283	222	261
Top goods exports, 1997:				
Industrial machinery and computers	2 720	3 030	3 167	4 178
Scientific and measuring instruments	855	1 052	1 216	1 146
Electric and electronic equipment	591	726	770	860
Transportation equipment	450	503	480	603
Chemical products	301	347	368	442

HOUSING

HOUSING MARKETS IN WISCONSIN HAVE REFLECTED THE economy's robust growth of the 1990s, as new housing production per capita topped U.S. averages throughout the 1990s. The burst of construction reflects the rising household incomes in the state and the higher population growth compared to the 1980s. It may reflect pent-up demand from the slower growth and higher interest rate decade of the 1980s. Sales of existing homes grew steadily during the 1990s in parallel to the strong housing sales record in the United States overall, except for a weaker state performance in 1994–95. Home sales prices advanced but even in the largest metropolitan area, Milwaukee, median prices in 1997 of $125,300 were around the overall national median price level.

Rates of homeownership are above U.S. averages historically, and they remained that way in 1997 after some fluctuation during 1993–94. The state experienced less in-migration than average, had a relatively high proportion of residents over age 65, and moderate home prices, all of

Homeownership Rates: 1989 and 1997

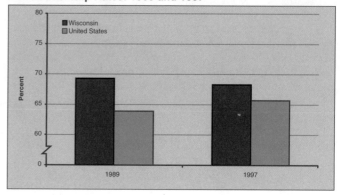

which contributed to the high rates of homeownership. Rental vacancy rates remained at very low levels in Wisconsin, as there has been little speculative overbuilding of apartments by developers in the past.

Housing Supply

	1989	1990	1991	1992	1993	1994	1995	1996	1997
Residential building permits (thousands)	26.9	27.3	25.1	31.0	32.1	34.6	32.4	33.3	31.9
New home production (including manufactured housing):									
Thousands of homes	29.8	30.2	27.4	34.1	35.9	38.7	36.0	37.1	35.2
Rate per 1,000 population									
Wisconsin	6.1	6.2	5.5	6.8	7.1	7.6	7.0	7.2	6.8
U.S.	6.2	5.2	4.5	5.1	5.6	6.4	6.3	6.6	6.5
Existing home sales:									
Thousands of homes	74.1	74.2	82.8	91.5	94.6	94.3	93.2	101.0	104.6
Change from previous year (percent)									
Wisconsin	-1.5	0.1	11.6	10.5	3.4	-0.3	-1.2	8.4	3.6
U.S.	-3.9	-4.0	0.0	9.2	8.2	4.8	-3.7	7.5	3.8
Home ownership rate (percent of households)	69.3	68.3	68.9	69.4	65.7	64.2	67.5	68.2	68.3
Rental vacancy rate (percent of rental housing units)	4.1	3.3	4.6	4.9	4.0	4.6	5.7	5.5	4.9

AGRICULTURE

THE FARM ECONOMY WEAKENED SIGNIFICANTLY OVER THE 1989–97 period, as sales revenues failed to keep up with inflation and government subsidies generally declined. Dairy products remained the leading category of output, but these sales have been flat in current dollars since 1990. Revenues from livestock sales have declined one-quarter since 1990, while grain sales have risen 50 percent. The result of flat revenues and escalating costs (including imputed cost of land) was a dismal net income perform-

ance for farming in the state. Net income has been negative during three of the latest five years, starting in 1993.

WISCONSIN FARMS, 1997	
Number of farms	79 000
Total acres (thousands):	16 800
Average per farm	213
Value of land and buildings (millions of dollars)	21 000
Average per farm (dollars)	265 823

Farm Income
(millions of dollars)

	1980	1989	1990	1991	1992	1993	1994	1995	1996	1997
Gross income	5 262	6 670	6 620	6 340	6 527	6 410	6 219	6 628	6 869	6 635
Receipts from sales	4 865	5 699	6 018	5 756	5 997	5 707	5 575	6 015	6 264	5 960
Government payments	12	522	181	150	166	310	236	184	158	177
Imputed and miscellaneous income	385	449	421	435	364	393	408	429	446	499
(−) Production expenses	4 433	5 674	5 936	5 987	5 991	6 253	6 660	6 571	6 774	7 125
(=) Realized net income	829	996	684	354	536	157	-440	57	94	-490
(+) Inventory change	379	302	82	-82	-214	-221	443	-312	-56	110
(=) Net income	1 208	1 298	766	272	322	-64	3	-255	38	-380
Corporate income	0	91	56	15	26	-20	0	-68	5	-90
Farm proprietors income	1 209	1 207	710	257	296	-44	3	-187	33	-290

EDUCATION

EDUCATIONAL ATTAINMENT Percent of population age 25 and over, 1997	State	United States
High school graduate or higher	87.1	82.1
College graduate or higher	22.4	23.9

WISCONSIN RANKED IN THE TOP TEN STATES IN THE PROPORtion of its population with a high school degree, consistent with the state's general prosperity, low poverty, and small immigrant population.   Public spending on elementary and secondary schools was substantially higher than the U.S. average, supported in part by strong state-level school aid programs.   Nonetheless, there was a large percentage of students attending private elementary and secondary schools, and the state experimented with pub-

licly funded vouchers to be used for private school tuition. The state ranked lower, 25th in the nation, in percent of population holding college degrees. The lower college attainment reflected the state's concentration of manufacturing jobs, low share of employment within computer and other business services, and the larger population within upper age brackets. A relatively high 24.4 percent of current young adults are enrolled in higher education, however.

High School Completion: 1990–97

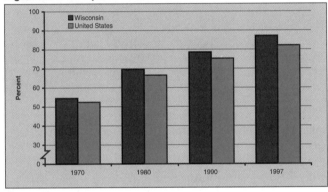

Education Indicators

	State	U.S.
Elementary and secondary schools Enrollment, 1995–96		
Total (thousands)	1 013	49 873
Percent in private schools	14.1	10.1
Expenditures per pupil (dollars), 1995–96	7 094	6 146
Average teacher salary (dollars), 1996–97	38 950	38 509
Higher education Enrollment, 1996–97		
Total (thousands)	299	14 218
Percent of population 18–34	24.4	21.8
Percent minority	9.6	26.1
Percent in private schools	18.2	22.6

HEALTH

MAJOR INDICATORS OF THE HEALTH OF THE STATE POPULATION were better than average for the nation. Infant mortality was below average, and the death rate was consistently less than average when adjusted for age distribution. Death rates from almost every major cause were below national rates, particularly from heart disease. Death from homicide and HIV were also especially low.

The health of the population was bolstered by its extremely high rate of coverage by health insurance. Only 8 percent of the population lacked health insurance, because of the state's low poverty rate and high rate of employment, and probably also because of its high number of jobs in the manufacturing sector, which typically offers superior employee benefits.

Health Indicators

	1990	1995	1996	1997
Infant mortality *(rate per thousand live births)*				
Wisconsin	8.2	7.3	7.5	6.3
U.S.	9.2	7.6	7.3	7.1
Total deaths, age-adjusted rate *(rate per thousand population)*				
Wisconsin	4.7	4.5	4.4	4.3
U.S.	5.2	5.0	4.9	4.8
Persons not covered by health insurance *(percent of population)*				
Wisconsin	6.7	7.3	8.4	8.0
U.S.	13.9	15.4	15.6	16.1

Leading Causes of Death, 1996
(deaths per 100,000 population)

	Age-adjusted		Not age-adjusted	
	State	U.S.	State	U.S.
Deaths from all causes	442.6	491.6	874.9	872.5
Heart disease	121.8	134.5	275.2	276.4
Cancer	121.4	127.9	203.2	203.4
Cerebrovascular diseases	26.5	26.4	71.4	60.3
Chronic obstructive pulmonary disease	18.4	21.0	38.8	40.0
Diabetes mellitus	12.0	13.6	22.7	23.3
Pneumonia and influenza	11.8	12.8	34.1	31.6
HIV	3.0	11.1	3.1	11.7
Liver disease	5.3	7.5	6.9	9.4
Alzheimer's disease	2.9	2.7	9.6	8.1
Accidents and adverse effects	27.8	30.4	35.8	35.8
Motor vehicle accidents	15.2	16.2	15.5	16.5
Suicide	10.9	10.8	11.6	11.6
Homicide	4.5	8.5	4.1	7.9
Injury by firearm	9.6	12.9	9.7	12.8

GOVERNMENT

STATE AND LOCAL TAXES, 1995–96	State	U.S.
Per capita (dollars)	2 826	2 477
Percent of personal income	12.8	10.8

THE TOTAL STATE AND LOCAL TAX BURDEN ON WISCONSIN CITIZENS was higher than the U.S. average, reflecting the state's tradition of activist government policies. In 1995–96, combined state and local taxes averaged $2,826 per capita in the state, about 14 percent higher than the U.S. national average. A slightly higher proportion of these taxes was at the state level, compared with national norms, while local taxes were closer to average. Calculated as a percent of total personal income, state and local taxes equaled 12.8 percent of total income (down slightly from its share in the previous year), while this percentage stood at 10.8 percent nationwide.

The state government in 1997 had higher than average rates of taxation and spending compared with the average among all states. Wisconsin was long known as a very high tax state, but the long tenure of its Republican governor in the 1990s has reversed this trend somewhat, and its policies have come closer to national norms. Taxes per capita in 1997 were 18.7 percent above the national average, while the state received less than average amounts of intergovernmental revenue from the federal government. The state made much larger than average transfers to local government, especially supporting education expenditures. Higher than average spending on education was partly balanced by lower than average spending on welfare and health, as the state embarked on ambitious welfare reform early in the 1990s.

The state received a below-average level of federal spending in 1997 compared to its share of population, mostly because of the low concentration of federal civilian and military employees. The state also received little in the way of procurement spending, especially in the defense area. In the larger spending categories of Social Security and retirement there was an average level of spending, though Medicare payments were disproportionately small (despite the somewhat higher than average elderly population.)

State Government Finances, 1996–97

	Millions of dollars	Percent distribution	Dollars per capita	
			State	U.S.
General revenue	16 916	100.0	3 272	3 049
Intergovernmental revenue	3 904	23.1	755	863
Taxes	10 187	60.2	1 970	1 660
General sales	2 865	16.9	554	551
Selective sales	1 366	8.1	264	257
License taxes	614	3.6	119	106
Individual income	4 538	26.8	878	542
Corporation net income	639	3.8	124	115
Other taxes	164	1.0	32	90
Other general revenue	2 826	16.7	547	526
General expenditure	16 229	100.0	3 139	2 951
Intergovernmental expenditure	6 993	43.1	1 353	989
Direct expenditure	9 236	56.9	1 786	1 962
General expenditure, by function:				
Education	6 286	38.7	1 216	1 033
Public welfare	3 223	19.9	623	761
Hospitals and health	943	5.8	182	237
Highways	1 277	7.9	247	225
Police protection and corrections	633	3.9	122	137
Natural resources, parks and recreation	355	2.2	69	63
Governmental administration	478	2.9	92	107
Interest on general debt	584	3.6	113	99
Other and unallocable	2 450	15.1	474	290
Debt at end of fiscal year	9 832	NA	1 902	1 706
Cash and security holdings	53 026	NA	10 256	6 683

Federal Spending within State

	Federal funds, fiscal 1997		
	Millions of dollars	Percent distribution	Percent of U.S. total*
Total within state	21 167	100.0	1.5
Payments to individuals	13 643	64.5	1.7
Retirement and disability	8 624	40.7	1.9
Medicare	3 198	15.1	1.6
Food stamps	156	0.7	0.8
Supplemental Security Income	399	1.9	1.5
Grants	4 350	20.6	1.7
Medicaid and other health	1 916	9.1	1.7
Nutrition and family welfare	936	4.4	2.0
Education	316	1.5	1.8
Housing and community development	154	0.7	1.4
Salaries and wages	1 363	6.4	0.8
Defense procurement contracts	565	2.7	0.5
Non-defense procurement contracts	740	3.5	1.0

*State population is 1.9 percent of the U.S. total.

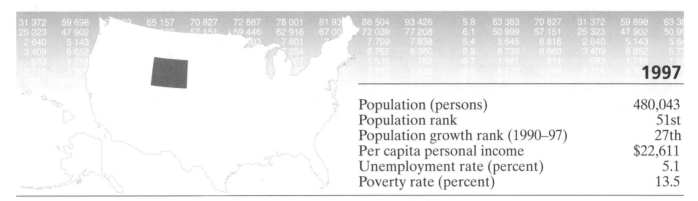

1997

Population (persons)	480,043
Population rank	51st
Population growth rank (1990–97)	27th
Per capita personal income	$22,611
Unemployment rate (percent)	5.1
Poverty rate (percent)	13.5

MEASURED BY POPULATION SIZE, WYOMING WAS THE NATION'S smallest state and, except for Alaska, the least densely populated. The state's population grew from 1990 to 1996, following a 3.4 percent decline during the 1980s, but again ceased to grow in 1997. From 1990 to 1997, Wyoming's population grew 5.9 percent, somewhat below the U.S. average. Natural increase (births minus deaths) accounted for 80 percent of the population growth from 1990 to 1997, but both immigration and domestic migration also were positive.

The 1990s have been a difficult period for the Wyoming economy. Every major sector grew more slowly than the U.S. average from 1990 to 1997. Since 1981, employment in the mining industry fell by over 20,000 jobs. With a minimal manufacturing base, the State has missed out on the recent U.S. export boom. Wyoming's disproportionate base of federal government employment, in this era of cutbacks, also hurt the state's economy. Reflecting the economic difficulties, inflation-adjusted median household incomes fell between 1990 and 1997 and the poverty rate rose.

Educational attainment of the state's residents was high, with over 91 percent of the adult population having completed high school. Health indicators were also good, with the fifth lowest infant mortality rate in 1996-97 and below average death rates for most causes.

Average Annual Population Growth: 1990–97

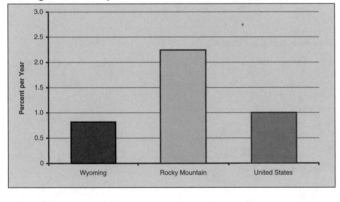

Median Household Income: 1989–97 (1997 dollars)

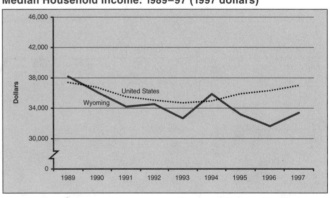

Unemployment Rate: 1989–97

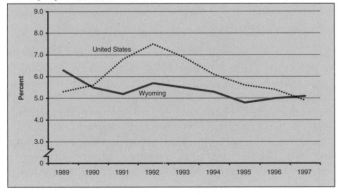

OVER THE PAST DECADE, WYOMING'S UNEMPLOYMENT RATE remained below the national average until 1997, when the unemployment rate increased to 5.1, just above the national average of 4.9. Despite relatively strong job growth and low population growth, the state's unemployment rate experienced little change over recent years. In 1997, Wyoming's unemployment rate was the 21st highest in the nation, which was a slight increase from its position at 25th highest in 1990. The state's labor force has grown less than the adult population since 1989, which has contributed to the fairly low unemployment rate.

POPULATION AND LABOR FORCE

WYOMING'S TOTAL POPULATION GREW 0.8 PERCENT ANNUALLY from 1990 to 1997, compared with the U.S. average of 1.0 percent per year. This rate amounted to an increase of just over 26,000 people. The decreased gap between birth and death rates contributed to the state's low population growth. In 1997, the state's birth rate remained lower than the national average, while, the death rate increased significantly from 7.1 deaths over 1,000 population in 1990 to 7.8 in 1997, drawing closer to the national average. Since 1990, the domestic migration levels have remained fairly equal, with a slightly greater number entering the state. International migration to Wyoming accounted for only 6 percent of the population increase from 1990 to 1997.

The breakdown of the state's population by race remained little changed from 1990 to 1997. The largest absolute growth was among the White, non-Hispanic population (+21,000), followed by Hispanics (+2,000), Native Americans (+1,000), and Asians (+1,000). The state's breakdown by metro and nonmetro population was the same in 1990 and 1997, with less than 30 percent of the state's residents living in metropolitan areas, making the state one of the most highly rural in the nation. Its largest metro area, Cheyenne, had a population of less than 80,000.

Population and Labor Force

	1980	1990	1991	1992	1993	1994	1995	1996	1997	Change* State	Change* U.S.
Population											
Total number of persons (thousands)	470	453	458	464	469	475	478	480	480	0.8	1.0
Percent distribution:											
White, Non-Hispanic	91.9	90.7	90.9	90.8	90.7	90.8	90.8	90.8	90.7	0.8	0.4
Black, Non-Hispanic	0.7	1.1	0.7	0.8	0.7	0.7	0.7	0.7	0.7	-5.8	1.4
Asian	0.4	0.7	0.7	0.7	0.7	0.7	0.7	0.8	0.8	3.7	4.1
Native American	1.8	2.1	2.2	2.2	2.3	2.2	2.2	2.2	2.2	1.4	1.6
Hispanic	5.2	5.7	5.8	5.8	5.8	5.8	5.8	5.8	5.9	1.3	3.8
In metropolitan areas	30.0	29.6	29.6	29.7	29.8	29.8	29.7	29.7	29.6	0.8	1.0
Total number of households (thousands)	166	169	170	174	176	178	181	184	NA	1.4	1.2
Labor Force (thousands)											
Population 16 and over	341	331	336	342	348	355	361	365	366	1.4	1.0
Civilian labor force	234	223	222	225	228	238	243	243	239	1.0	1.1
Employed	225	236	234	239	241	252	255	256	251	0.9	1.2
Percent of population	66.0	71.2	69.7	69.8	69.3	70.9	70.8	70.3	68.7		
Unemployment rate (percent)	4.0	5.5	5.2	5.7	5.5	5.3	4.8	5.0	5.1		

*Compound annual average percent change, 1990–1997; 1990–1996 for households.

Population Change and Components: 1990–97

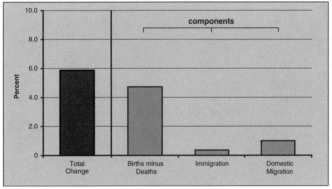

Average Annual Household and Population Growth

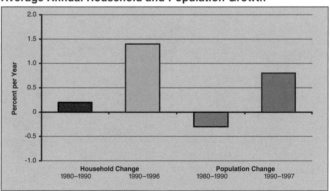

Population by Age; Births and Deaths

	1990 State	1990 U.S.	1997 State	1997 U.S.
Age distribution (percent)				
Under 5 years	7.8	7.6	6.5	7.2
5 to 17 years	22.2	18.2	21.0	18.8
18 to 64 years	59.6	61.8	61.2	61.3
65 years and over	10.4	12.5	11.3	12.7
Birth and death rates (per thousand population)				
Births	15.4	16.7	13.4	14.6
Deaths	7.1	8.6	7.8	8.6

THE AGE DISTRIBUTION OF WYOMING'S POPULATION SHIFTED significantly from 1990 to 1997. The state's population appears to be getting older. The percent of the population under the age of five fell from 7.8 percent in 1990 to 6.5 percent in 1997. There was also a decrease in the percentage of the population between the ages of 5 and 17, though it remained significantly higher than the national average. The percentage of Wyoming's population over 18 has gradually been growing closer to the national rates.

HOUSEHOLD AND PERSONAL INCOME

HOUSEHOLD INCOME AND PERSONS IN POVERTY	1990	1995	1996	1997	
				State	U.S.
Median household income (1997 dollars)	36 177	33 205	31 663	33 423	37 005
Persons in poverty (thousands)	51	59	58	66	35 574
Poverty rate (percent)	11.0	12.2	11.9	13.5	13.3

WYOMING'S REAL MEDIAN INCOME FELL CONSIDERABLY FROM 1990 to 1997. The 1997 median income was the 17th lowest in the nation, amounting to just over 90 percent of the national average. This level marked a substantial change from 1990, when median income in Wyoming was just over 98 percent of the national average. The state's poverty rate increased significantly in 1997; the 1997 rate of 13.5 percent was just above the national rate, and well above the 1996 rate of 11.9 percent. The 1997 rate was Wyoming's highest poverty rate in the past decade.

From 1989 to 1997, Wyoming's per capita income grew faster than the national average, though in 1997 Wyoming's per capita income remained below 90 percent of the national average. Wage earnings and proprietors' income grew by more than 45 percent during this time period, yet total earnings per capita in 1997 were only 84 percent as high as the U.S. average, the major reason for the state's low per capita income. Income from transfer payments and from dividends and interest both rose more rapidly than earnings during the 1989 to 1997 period.

Transfer payments grew by a faster rate than the national average. Medical payments grew faster than any other major program, paralleling the national escalation in health care spending. Family assistance fell by more than 40 percent from 1990 to 1997, while food stamps increased by only 6.2 percent, as compared to the national increase of 27.1 percent. This decrease occurred despite the substantial increase in Wyoming's poverty rate during the same period. Unemployment insurance benefits increased by nearly 30 percent from 1990 to 1997, while spending on other income maintenance, primarily consisting of earned income tax credits, mushroomed more than fourfold.

Personal Income
(millions of dollars)

	1980	1989	1990	1991	1992	1993	1994	1995	1996	1997	Change*
Earnings by place of work	4 453	5 026	5 445	5 846	6 072	6 477	6 575	6 797	6 939	7 325	4.8
Wages and salaries	3 533	3 933	4 221	4 443	4 629	4 849	5 096	5 256	5 405	5 702	4.8
Other labor income	331	363	414	460	494	540	571	558	544	549	5.3
Proprietors' income	589	731	810	943	950	1 088	907	983	990	1 074	4.9
Farm	28	37	94	165	157	224	22	10	-10	33	-1.4
Nonfarm	561	694	717	778	793	864	885	973	999	1 042	5.2
(–) Personal contributions for social insurance	233	334	359	387	409	428	454	472	484	509	5.4
(+) Adjustment for residence	-74	-13	-9	0	-9	-18	-24	-21	-19	-19	NA
(=) **Net earnings by state of residence**	4 146	4 680	5 077	5 459	5 654	6 031	6 097	6 304	6 436	6 798	4.8
(+) Dividends, interest, and rent	833	1 484	1 662	1 772	1 725	1 744	1 865	2 040	2 239	2 318	5.7
(+) Transfer payments	460	957	1 048	1 169	1 291	1 388	1 472	1 560	1 660	1 732	7.7
(=) **Total personal income**	5 439	7 121	7 787	8 399	8 670	9 163	9 434	9 903	10 336	10 848	5.4
Farm	86	82	144	213	204	276	89	83	63	110	3.8
Nonfarm	5 353	7 039	7 642	8 186	8 466	8 887	9 345	9 820	10 272	10 737	5.4
Personal income per capita (dollars)											
Current dollars	11 469	15 535	17 174	18 348	18 702	19 535	19 859	20 695	21 532	22 611	4.8
1997 dollars	21 929	19 640	20 667	21 187	20 919	21 257	21 104	21 512	21 927	22 611	1.8

*Compound annual average percent change, 1989–1997

Government Transfer Payments

	Millions of dollars		Percent change*	
	1990	1997	State	U.S.
Total government payments to individuals	988	1 648	66.7	62.7
Retirement, disability, and insurance	655	1 021	55.8	48.2
Social Security	387	606	56.6	46.1
Government employee retirement	172	288	67.7	60.3
Medical payments	198	426	115.3	101.2
Income maintenance	62	100	61.4	58.0
Supplemental Security Income	10	23	142.7	75.4
Family assistance	21	12	-43.3	-0.5
Food Stamps	21	22	6.2	27.1
Other income maintenance	10	42	331.6	189.8
Unemployment insurance benefits	23	30	29.1	10.6
Veterans benefits and other	51	71	40.8	30.8

*Percent change, 1990–1997

Government Payments to Individuals: 1997

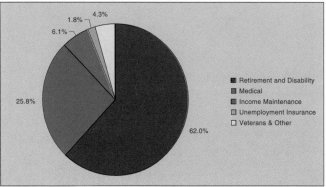

- Retirement and Disability — 62.0%
- Medical — 25.8%
- Income Maintenance — 6.1%
- Unemployment Insurance — 1.8%
- Veterans & Other — 4.3%

ECONOMIC STRUCTURE

LEADING PRIVATE INDUSTRIES, 1997 (Worker and proprietor earnings, millions of dollars)		FASTEST EARNINGS GROWTH, 1989–97 (percent increase)	
Oil and gas extraction	$614	Chemicals and allied products	292.8
Health services	395	General building contractors	132.9
Coal mining	312	Business services	104.1
Construction specialties	304	Engineering and management services	89.7
Railroad transportation	200	Hotels and lodging	75.9

SERVICES AND MINING HAVE DOMINATED AS WYOMING'S LEAD-ing private sectors since 1990. The state's leading mining industries were oil and gas extraction and coal mining, two of the top three largest industries (ranked by earnings). Until 1992, mining was the state's leading sector (as measured by earnings), then it was surpassed by the services industry. The largest service industry in the state was health care, the only service industry in the state's top five. The state's fastest growing industry was chemicals, which increased by nearly 300 percent from 1989 to 1997. Other fast-growing industries were general building contractors and business services. Construction has been one of Wyoming's leading growth industries since 1989, as construction employment grew 44 percent from 1989 to 1997. Mining showed a decrease of 7.5 percent in employment from 1989 to 1997. Farm employment decreased from 1990 to 1997, and farm earnings have been weak since 1994.

Government at all levels provided nearly 20 percent of the state's jobs, a significantly higher share than in the United States as a whole, yet growth in this sector has been minimal during the 1990s.

Employment and Earnings by Sector

	1980	1989	1990	1991	1992	1993	1994	1995	1996	1997 Number	1997 Percent of total	Change*
Employment *(thousands of persons)*												
Total	280	267	273	280	282	287	301	307	311	315	100.0	2.1
Farm	15	12	12	12	12	12	12	13	12	12	3.7	-0.8
Nonfarm	265	255	261	267	270	275	288	294	298	304	96.3	2.2
Private nonfarm	215	196	202	208	208	213	226	232	237	242	76.8	2.7
Agricultural service, forestry, and fishing	2	3	3	4	3	4	4	5	5	5	1.6	6.1
Mining	39	20	21	21	20	20	20	19	18	19	5.9	-1.0
Construction	26	15	16	17	17	18	20	21	21	22	6.9	4.7
Manufacturing	11	10	12	12	11	11	12	12	13	13	4.1	2.8
Transportation and public utilities	19	17	17	17	16	16	17	17	17	17	5.4	0.2
Wholesale trade	10	8	8	8	8	8	8	8	8	9	2.7	0.8
Retail trade	44	46	47	49	50	51	55	57	58	59	18.6	3.2
Finance, insurance, and real estate	16	18	17	17	17	17	17	19	20	21	6.6	2.1
Services	48	60	61	65	66	67	72	76	78	79	25.0	3.6
Government	50	58	59	60	61	61	62	62	62	62	19.5	0.6
Earnings *(millions of dollars)*												
Total	4 453	5 026	5 445	5 846	6 072	6 477	6 575	6 797	6 939	7 325	100.0	4.8
Farm	86	82	144	213	204	276	89	83	63	110	1.5	3.8
Nonfarm	4 367	4 945	5 301	5 633	5 868	6 201	6 486	6 713	6 876	7 215	98.5	4.8
Private nonfarm	3 663	3 706	3 987	4 248	4 423	4 711	4 953	5 130	5 274	5 581	76.2	5.2
Agricultural service, forestry, and fishing	15	35	39	47	52	51	52	51	50	53	0.7	5.5
Mining	1 136	861	920	1 012	998	1 035	1 026	1 066	1 050	1 152	15.7	3.7
Construction	540	351	373	413	411	436	512	533	548	583	8.0	6.5
Manufacturing	206	244	279	286	295	314	331	324	389	402	5.5	6.5
Transportation and public utilities	441	533	558	594	615	645	654	654	647	671	9.2	2.9
Wholesale trade	199	194	190	198	207	208	219	232	238	260	3.5	3.7
Retail trade	420	486	528	555	592	624	668	693	717	743	10.1	5.5
Finance, insurance, and real estate	141	180	184	191	220	278	304	297	315	334	4.6	8.0
Services	565	823	916	953	1 034	1 121	1 188	1 281	1 320	1 382	18.9	6.7
Government	704	1 239	1 314	1 384	1 445	1 490	1 533	1 583	1 602	1 635	22.3	3.5

*Compound annual average percent change, 1989–1997

ECONOMIC STRUCTURE (Continued)

IN 1997, WYOMING HAD THE EIGHTH LOWEST AVERAGE WAGE in the nation. The average wage of $23,840 amounted to only 80 percent of the national average. For most major sectors, Wyoming's wages were well below average. The two exceptions were farm wages and transportation and public utility wages. The largest gap between Wyoming's wages and the national averages was in finance, insurance, and real estate wages, which were less than 65 percent of the national average wage. Construction wages had the smallest increase from 1989 to 1997, growing only 19.0 percent, as compared to Wyoming's average wage, which increased by 26.0 percent.

Wyoming's gross state product (GSP) increased by more than 40 percent from 1989 to 1996, the same rate of growth as in the national economy in that period. Manufacturing played an increasing role in the state's economy. In 1989, manufacturing accounted for 4.0 percent of the state's GSP; by 1996 it had increased to 5.7 percent. The chemicals and allied products industry led Wyoming in manufacturing earnings. In 1996, manufacturing output value per worker jumped to $74,921, a substantial increase from the previous year, and nearly 8 percent higher than the national average. New capital expenditures decreased significantly from 1994 to 1996, however, falling by more than two-thirds.

Wyoming's exports to foreign markets increased by more than 84 percent from 1994 to 1997, without adjustment for inflation. This increase was significantly greater than the expansion of the overall state economy. It also was well above the 34 percent growth of U.S. exports, though export demand remained a tiny fraction of the state's overall economy. Wyoming's manufactures exports increased by only 52.3 percent, well below the increase for the state's total exports. The state's largest exports were chemical products and industrial machinery and computers. Chemical products exports increased by more than 128 percent from 1994 to 1997, while industrial machinery and computers exports grew by only 25.7 percent.

Average Annual Wages and Salaries by Sector
(dollars)

	1989	1996	1997 State	1997 U.S.
All wage and salary workers	18 927	22 825	23 840	29 809
Farm	11 843	19 221	25 695	16 442
Nonfarm	19 054	22 881	23 817	29 900
Private nonfarm	18 886	22 649	23 742	29 867
Agricultural service, forestry, and fishing	10 246	12 557	13 204	17 941
Mining	36 211	44 720	46 882	49 800
Construction	21 436	24 629	25 510	31 765
Manufacturing	21 653	29 277	30 644	38 351
Transportation and utilities	30 115	37 242	38 986	38 222
Wholesale trade	23 042	27 770	29 132	39 466
Retail trade	10 199	12 635	13 150	16 206
Finance, insurance, and real estate	19 622	27 256	28 882	44 993
Services	13 398	17 737	18 369	27 588
Government	19 472	23 527	24 031	30 062

Gross State Product and Manufacturing
(millions of dollars, except as noted)

	1989	1994	1995	1996
Gross state product, total	12 018	14 941	15 761	16 847
Manufacturing:				
Millions of dollars	482	685	699	967
Percent of total gross state product	4.0	4.6	4.4	5.7
Per worker (dollars)	46 262	56 198	59 082	74 921
New capital expenditures, manufacturing	NA	187	68	58

Exports of Goods
(millions of dollars)

	1994	1995	1996	1997
All goods	95	101	124	176
Manufactures	80	83	101	122
Agricultural and livestock products	2	2	3	5
Other commodities	13	17	20	48
Top goods exports, 1997:				
Chemical products	18	19	25	42
Industrial machinery and computers	27	20	24	34
Metallic ores and concentrates	0	0	0	17
Goods imported and returned unchanged	5	6	9	13
Fish and other marine products	0	0	1	10

HOUSING

HOUSING PRODUCTION IN WYOMING HAS UNDERGONE SLOW growth since the recession in 1990–91. The year 1994 marked the first time when the state's home production began to mirror the national rates. In 1996, the state's home production rate per capita exceeded the national rate for the first time during the past decade. Slower than average population growth contributed to the slow increase in home production. Sales of existing homes have been more volatile than the national trend, with strong sales in 1992–1994 and again in 1997, but weak sales in 1995–1996. The homeownership rate has been unsteady throughout the past several years. In 1997, homeownership reached 67.6 percent, which was lower than the rate in 1990, though the rate in 1997 was significantly higher than the decade low of 65.8 percent in 1994. Wyoming's rental vacancy rate has remained fairly low throughout the decade. In 1995, it fell to 5.0 percent, which was among the lowest in the nation, but by 1997 the rate had jumped to 8.2 percent.

Homeownership Rates: 1989 and 1997

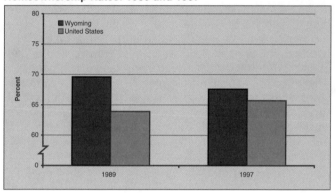

Housing Supply

	1989	1990	1991	1992	1993	1994	1995	1996	1997
Residential building permits (thousands)	0.6	0.7	0.6	1.0	1.2	2.0	1.7	2.2	1.7
New home production (including manufactured housing):									
Thousands of homes	0.9	0.7	0.9	1.2	1.6	3.0	2.7	3.3	2.8
Rate per 1,000 population									
Wyoming	2.0	1.5	2.0	2.6	3.4	6.3	5.6	6.9	5.8
U.S.	6.2	5.2	4.5	5.1	5.6	6.4	6.3	6.6	6.5
Existing home sales:									
Thousands of homes	7.3	7.4	8.2	9.9	10.9	11.0	9.4	8.6	9.5
Change from previous year (percent)									
Wyoming	-1.4	1.4	10.8	20.7	10.1	0.9	-14.5	-8.5	10.5
U.S.	-3.9	-4.0	0.0	9.2	8.2	4.8	-3.7	7.5	3.8
Home ownership rate (percent of households)	69.6	68.9	68.7	67.9	67.1	65.8	69.0	68.0	67.6
Rental vacancy rate (percent of rental housing units)	12.1	7.9	7.7	6.7	5.5	6.7	5.0	6.4	8.2

Note: Manufactured housing data for 1990 suppressed because estimate was based on too few responses.

AGRICULTURE

WYOMING HAS A LOW NUMBER OF FARMS, BUT THEY HAVE A very large average size of 3,802 acres per farm, well above the national average of 471 acres. The state's gross farm income increased by only 13.8 percent from 1989 to 1997. Production expenses increased by nearly 30 percent during the same period. In 1997, gross income exceeded production expenses by only $2 million. Wyoming derived 77.7 percent of its farm sales receipts from livestock, as there was a greater emphasis on ranching than crop production.

WYOMING FARMS, 1997	
Number of farms	9 100
Total acres (thousands):	34 600
Average per farm	3 802
Value of land and buildings (millions of dollars)	7 612
Average per farm (dollars)	836 484

Farm Income
(millions of dollars)

	1980	1989	1990	1991	1992	1993	1994	1995	1996	1997
Gross income	726	891	891	1 007	967	1 022	952	891	835	1 014
Receipts from sales	683	793	795	907	852	892	826	764	702	891
Government payments	7	34	31	33	37	43	38	31	25	22
Imputed and miscellaneous income	36	64	64	67	78	87	88	96	109	101
(–) Production expenses	704	781	783	905	797	847	884	907	908	1 012
(=) Realized net income	22	109	108	102	170	175	68	-16	-73	2
(+) Inventory change	7	-66	3	85	17	65	-38	28	56	40
(=) Net income	28	43	111	187	187	240	30	12	-18	42
Corporate income	0	7	17	22	30	16	8	2	-8	10
Farm proprietors income	28	37	94	165	157	224	22	10	-10	33

EDUCATION

EDUCATIONAL ATTAINMENT Percent of population age 25 and over, 1997	State	United States
High school graduate or higher	91.3	82.1
College graduate or higher	22.2	23.9

OVERALL, WYOMING APPEARS TO HAVE A GOOD RECORD WHEN it comes to education. The state had the second highest percentage of its population with high school degrees in the nation, behind only that of Alaska. In 1997, more than 91 percent of Wyoming's adults had earned high school diplomas. This level marked a substantial increase from 83 percent in 1990. The percentage of adults in Wyoming with college degrees was just below the national average, both of which have increased significantly from 1990. The

state's per pupil expenditure was above the national average, in part because of high overhead and transportation costs of school districts covering large geographic areas. The average teacher salary of $31,721 was much lower than the national average of $38,509, and ranked tenth lowest in the nation. Significantly fewer of Wyoming's students, at the elementary, secondary, and postsecondary levels, were enrolled in private schools than the national average.

High School Completion: 1990–97

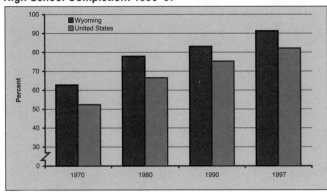

Education Indicators

	State	U.S.
Elementary and secondary schools		
Enrollment, 1995–96		
Total (thousands)	102	49 873
Percent in private schools	2.2	10.1
Expenditures per pupil (dollars), 1995–96	6 243	6 146
Average teacher salary (dollars), 1996–97	31 721	38 509
Higher education		
Enrollment, 1996–97		
Total (thousands)	31	14 218
Percent of population 18–34	28.6	21.8
Percent minority	8.0	26.1
Percent in private schools	2.6	22.6

HEALTH

DURING THE 1990S, THE GENERAL HEALTH OF WYOMING'S population has been above average, as shown by several leading health indicators. The state's infant mortality rate dropped substantially from 8.6 deaths per thousand live births in 1990 to 5.2 in 1997. The state's infant mortality rate was the fifth lowest in the nation based on the 1996-97 average. The overall death rates were lower in the state

than the national average. The death rates for leading causes were generally below the U.S. average, though the rates for suicide, motor vehicle deaths, and unintentional injuries appeared to be higher. The percentage of the population without health insurance increased from 13.5 percent in 1996 to 15.5 percent in 1997, though it remained below the U.S. average.

Health Indicators

	1990	1995	1996	1997
Infant mortality				
(rate per thousand live births)				
Wyoming	8.6	7.7	6.0	5.2
U.S.	9.2	7.6	7.3	7.1
Total deaths, age-adjusted rate				
(rate per thousand population)				
Wyoming	4.8	4.8	4.5	4.6
U.S.	5.2	5.0	4.9	4.8
Persons not covered by health insurance				
(percent of population)				
Wyoming	12.5	15.9	13.5	15.5
U.S.	13.9	15.4	15.6	16.1

Leading Causes of Death, 1996
(deaths per 100,000 population)

	Age-adjusted		Not age-adjusted	
	State	U.S.	State	U.S.
Deaths from all causes	454.7	491.6	748.2	872.5
Heart disease	109.0	134.5	197.1	276.4
Cancer	118.7	127.9	180.5	203.4
Cerebrovascular diseases	24.9	26.4	55.0	60.3
Chronic obstructive pulmonary disease	29.4	21.0	50.9	40.0
Diabetes mellitus	11.4	13.6	17.4	23.3
Pneumonia and influenza	10.3	12.8	25.1	31.6
HIV	NA	11.1	NA	11.7
Liver disease	5.7	7.5	7.7	9.4
Alzheimer's disease	3.8	2.7	10.4	8.1
Accidents and adverse effects	46.4	30.4	50.9	35.8
Motor vehicle accidents	25.2	16.2	24.5	16.5
Suicide	16.1	10.8	18.3	11.6
Homicide	NA	8.5	NA	7.9
Injury by firearm	16.4	12.9	17.7	12.8

GOVERNMENT

STATE AND LOCAL TAXES, 1995–96	State	U.S.
Per capita (dollars)	2 421	2 477
Percent of personal income	11.7	10.8

WYOMING'S PER CAPITA GENERAL REVENUE OF $4,365 IN FIS-cal 1997 was well above the national per capita revenue of $3,050. The state received a smaller per capita amount from taxes than the national average and a much higher then average transfer of intergovernmental revenue from the Federal government. Total state tax collections were 17 percent below the U.S. average on a per capita basis. Wyoming gained more of its revenue from "other" taxes and other general revenue, which helped to offset not having individual or corporate income taxes.

General expenditures in Wyoming were nearly $1,000 greater per capita than the national average. Education expenditures of $1,328 were well above the U.S. $1,033 per capita. The state also spent significantly more per capita on highway and national resources, parks, and recreation expenditures. Wyoming's per capita debt was just above the national average. Looking at local government combined with the state level, per capita state and local taxes amounted to $2421 in 1996, just below the national average of $2,477. In Wyoming, these taxes represented 11.7 percent of personal income, higher than the national average of 10.8 percent.

In 1997, Wyoming's population amounted to less than 0.2 percent of the U.S. total population. This made Wyoming the smallest in the nation. Generally, the state received a proportional share of U.S. total grants and payments to individuals. Procurements amounted to a smaller share of the U.S. total. In education grants and total grants, Wyoming received a greater than proportional share, both more than 0.3 percent of the U.S. total.

State Government Finances, 1996–97

	Millions of dollars	Percent distribu-tion	Dollars per capita State	Dollars per capita U.S.
General revenue	2 095	100.0	4 365	3 049
Intergovernmental revenue	851	40.6	1 774	863
Taxes	662	31.6	1 380	1 660
General sales	215	10.3	448	551
Selective sales	67	3.2	140	257
License taxes	78	3.7	163	106
Individual income	0	0.0	0	542
Corporation net income	0	0.0	0	115
Other taxes	302	14.4	630	90
Other general revenue	582	27.8	1 212	526
General expenditure	1 877	100.0	3 911	2 951
Intergovernmental expenditure	702	37.4	1 463	989
Direct expenditure	1 175	62.6	2 448	1 962
General expenditure, by function:				
Education	637	34.0	1 328	1 033
Public welfare	259	13.8	541	761
Hospitals and health	102	5.5	213	237
Highways	289	15.4	603	225
Police protection and corrections	51	2.7	107	137
Natural resources, parks and recreation	141	7.5	295	63
Governmental administration	88	4.7	184	107
Interest on general debt	57	3.0	119	99
Other and unallocable	251	13.4	523	290
Debt at end of fiscal year	872	NA	1 817	1 706
Cash and security holdings	6 955	NA	14 490	6 683

Federal Spending within State

	Federal funds, fiscal 1997		
	Millions of dollars	Percent distribution	Percent of U.S. total*
Total within state	2 612	100.0	0.2
Payments to individuals	1 264	48.4	0.2
Retirement and disability	840	32.2	0.2
Medicare	263	10.1	0.1
Food stamps	24	0.9	0.1
Supplemental Security Income	23	0.9	0.1
Grants	787	30.1	0.3
Medicaid and other health	153	5.9	0.1
Nutrition and family welfare	81	3.1	0.2
Education	54	2.1	0.3
Housing and community development	14	0.5	0.1
Salaries and wages	375	14.4	0.2
Defense procurement contracts	48	1.8	0.0
Non-defense procurement contracts	100	3.8	0.1

*State population is 0.2 percent of the U.S. total.

NOTES AND DEFINITIONS

The state chapters in this book follow a standard plan of organization, and the same data sources are used for the charts and tables in each chapter. For some states, supplementary sources of information were used in the text. These notes describe the standard data sources, presented by topic in the order in which the topics occur in the text. Definitions, brief descriptions of methodology, release dates, and sources of additional information are provided. Following the discussion of the standard data sources, the additional sources used for some text are listed.

GEOGRAPHIC CONCEPTS

REGIONAL DEFINITIONS. The Bureau of Economic Analysis (BEA), the source of much of the data used in this book, groups its state data into eight regions. These BEA regions are the ones most commonly used in this book, except that the editors have subdivided the large BEA Southeast Region into separate South Atlantic and South Central regions, and the term "Mid-Atlantic" had been substituted for the BEA term "Mideast." This set of regional definitions is used in the "Average Annual Population Growth: 1990–1997" chart shown for each state, as well as at various points in the text. The states included in each region are:

- New England: Connecticut, Maine, Massachusetts, New Hampshire, Rhode Island, Vermont.

- Mid-Atlantic: Delaware, District of Columbia, Maryland, New Jersey, New York, Pennsylvania.

- Great Lakes: Illinois, Indiana, Michigan, Ohio, Wisconsin.

- Plains: Iowa, Kansas, Minnesota, Missouri, Nebraska, North Dakota, South Dakota.

- South Atlantic: Florida, Georgia, North Carolina, South Carolina, Virginia.

- South Central: Alabama, Arkansas, Kentucky, Louisiana, Mississippi, Tennessee, West Virginia.

- Southwest: Arizona, New Mexico, Oklahoma, Texas.

- Rocky Mountain: Colorado, Idaho, Montana, Utah, Wyoming.

- Far West: Alaska, California, Hawaii, Nevada, Oregon, Washington.

The Bureau of the Census defines four broad regions: Northwest, Southeast, South, and West. These regions sometimes are used in the text in this book when more detailed geographic data are not available or when a conclusion applies generally to one or more of these broad regions. The Bureau of the Census further subdivides the four census regions into nine divisions. The states included in each census region and division are:

- Northeast Region:
  New England Division: Connecticut, Maine, Massachusetts, New Hampshire, Rhode Island, and Vermont.
  Middle Atlantic Division: New Jersey, New York, and Pennsylvania.

- Midwest Region:
  East North Central Division: Illinois, Indiana, Michigan, Ohio, and Wisconsin.
  West North Central Division: Iowa, Kansas, Minnesota, Missouri, Nebraska, North Dakota, and South Dakota.

- South Region
  South Atlantic Division: Delaware, District of Columbia, Florida, Georgia, Maryland, North Carolina, South Carolina, Virginia, West Virginia
  East South Central Division: Alabama, Kentucky, Mississippi, and Tennessee.
  West South Central Division: Arkansas, Louisiana, Oklahoma, and Texas.

- West Region
  Mountain Division: Arizona, Colorado, Idaho, Montana, Nevada, New Mexico, Utah, and Wyoming.
  Pacific Division: Alaska, California, Hawaii, Oregon, and Washington.

METROPOLITAN AREAS. In general, a metropolitan area is a geographic area consisting of a large population nucleus together with adjacent communities that have a high degree of economic and social integration with that nucleus. Except in New England, metropolitan areas, as officially defined by the federal government, consist of groups of counties. Although centered on a large concentration of urban population, these counties also may contain extensive rural areas. In New England, metropolitan areas are defined in terms of cities and towns, but 1997 data on that basis were not available for use in this book. An alternative concept, New England County Metropolitan Areas (NECMAs), was used. For all states, the percent living in metropolitan areas as shown in this book was obtained by totaling the populations of metropolitan counties within the state.

POPULATION; HOUSEHOLDS
Source: U.S. Department of Commerce, Bureau of the Census
Additional information: Statistical Information Staff, Population Division, U.S. Bureau of the Census (301-457-2422) or <http://www.census.gov/population/www>.

Population data for 1980 are from the 1980 Census of Population and are as of April 1, 1980. Data for 1990 through 1998 are from the Bureau of the Census Population Estimates Program and are as of July 1 of each year. All population data are for the resident population. The compound annual average percent changes were calculated by the editors.

POPULATION TOTALS. Data for the total resident population for 1990 through 1998 incorporate revisions and new estimates released by the Bureau of the Census in December 1998. The resident population of a state includes all residents (both civilian and armed forces) living in the state. The geographic universe for the resident population is the 50 states and the District of Columbia. It excludes Puerto Rico and the outlying areas under United States jurisdiction. The resident population excludes U.S. citizens living abroad.

Data for 1980 are from Summary Tape File (STF) 3 from the 1980 Census. The national total and the data for some states may differ from revised data subsequently issued by the Bureau of the Census.

AGE, RACE, AND ETHNICITY. Population estimates by age, race, and ethnicity incorporate revisions to the data for 1990 through 1997 released by the Bureau of the Census through September 1998. The percentage distributions were calculated by the editors based upon the Bureau of the Census estimates.

Estimates of the racial and ethnic distribution of the population necessarily are approximate, and comparisons over time should be interpreted with caution. Decennial census data on race and ethnicity are based on self-identification by the respondent. The same respondent may respond differently on different occasions. For example, someone of partly American Indian descent may have responded "Other race" in 1980 and "American Indian" in 1990. Estimates for intercensal years are developed by the Bureau of the Census using a method whereby each component of population change—births, deaths, domestic migration, and international migration—is estimated separately for each age group by sex, race, and Hispanic origin. The estimates incorporate information from birth and death records; sample data from tax returns and Social Security files (for estimates of domestic migration); Immigration and Naturalization Service records (for estimates of immigration); and other sources. A detailed description of the methodology is available from the Bureau of the Census.

In the decennial census data, the White population is defined as persons who indicated their race as White or who did not indicate a racial category but entered a nationality such as Canadian, German, Italian, Lebanese, or Polish. The Black population includes persons who indicated their race as Black or Negro or who reported entries such as Black Puerto Rican, Haitian, Jamaican, Nigerian, or West Indian. The Asian population includes persons who indicated their race as Chinese, Filipino, Japanese, Asian Indian, Korean, Vietnamese, Hawaiian, Samoan, or Guamanian. Also included are persons who provided write-in entries of other Asian or Pacific Island groups, such as Cambodian or Fiji Islander. The Native American population includes persons who indicated their race as Indian (American), Eskimo, or Aleut or who reported the name of an indian tribe.

Hispanic is an ethnic rather than a racial classification. The estimates shown in this book for the Hispanic population include Hispanics of all races. The estimates shown for the White and Black populations exclude Hispanics and are specifically identified as "non-Hispanic." The estimates shown for Native Americans and Asians include relatively small numbers of Hispanics, and these individuals thus may be included under two headings. Because of the small numbers involved and the margins of error inherent in population estimates by state, it is not appropriate to show separate figures for Hispanic and non-Hispanic Asians or Native Americans.

HOUSEHOLDS. A household consists of one or more persons occupying a single housing unit—a house, an apartment, or a room or rooms occupied as separate living quarters. A household may consist of a person living alone, a single family, two or more families living together, or any other group of related or unrelated individuals sharing a housing unit.

Census counts of the number of households equal the number of occupied housing units identified in the census. State estimates for intercensal years are developed by the Bureau of the Census using a model that applies the change in national household formation rates by age of householder to the 1990 decennial census state-specific household formation rates by age. This process produces estimates of state household formation rates by age. Next, the updated state household formation rates are applied to state population estimates by age to develop estimates of households by age of householder. The estimate of a state's total households is the sum of that state's households by age of householder. An estimate of the number of households in each state in 1997 was not available in time for inclusion in this book.

COMPONENTS OF POPULATION CHANGE. The components of demographic change consist of natural increase (births minus deaths), net domestic migration, net federal movement, and net international migration. In the data in this book, net federal movement, a small factor in most states, has been combined with net domestic migration.

Births are the total number of live births occurring to residents of an area during the period. Deaths are the total number of deaths occurring within the resident population of an area during the period. Births and deaths are as reported from the Census Bureau's Federal-State Cooperative Program for Population Estimates (FSCPE) and the National Center for Health Statistics.

Net domestic migration is the difference between domestic in-migration to an area and domestic out-migration from it during the period. Domestic in-migration and out-migration consist of moves where both the origins and destinations are within the United States (excluding Puerto Rico).

Net international migration is the difference between migration to an area from outside the United States (immigration) and migration from the area to outside the United States (emigration) during the period. For the purposes of these population estimates, the geographic extent of the United States is defined as excluding Puerto Rico. More specifically, net international migration consists of (1) legal immigration to the United States as reported by the Immigration and Naturalization Service, (2) an estimate of net undocumented immigration from abroad, (3) an estimate of emigration from the United States, and (4) net movement between Puerto Rico and the (balance of) the United States.

The state population estimates are constrained to sum to an independently derived estimate of the national population. The residual is the difference between an area's population as estimated by the state population estimation procedure before and after imposing this constraint. The residual is not a demographic component of population change; rather, it is a statistical artifact of the procedures employed in producing the estimates. Because of this residual, the percentage population changes due to each component (shown in the rankings on page ___) will not sum exactly to the total percentage population change.

LABOR FORCE, EMPLOYMENT, AND UNEMPLOYMENT

Source: U.S. Department of Labor, Bureau of Labor Statistics

Additional information: Local Area Unemployment Statistics, Bureau of Labor Statistics; lausinfo@bls.gov, or <http://stats.bls.gov/lauhome.htm>.

All data pertain to the civilian, noninstitutional population age 16 and over. Annual data are averages of the monthly estimates, updated by benchmarking and smoothing processes at the end of the year.

The employment to population ratio is the percentage of the civilian noninstitutional population (age 16 and over) that is employed. The civilian labor force is the sum of all civilians classified as employed or unemployed. The civilian unemployment rate is the number of unemployed as a percent of the civilian labor force. Unemployed persons are civilians who are not working but who are making specific efforts to find work or who are on layoff. Persons who are neither employed nor making specific efforts to find work are classified as "not in the labor force."

Over the years, a number of changes in the methods used to estimate state-level employment and unemployment have been introduced, and year-to-year changes in the data should be interpreted with caution. Since 1996, monthly estimates for all states and the District of Columbia have been produced using two models—one for the employment-to-population ratio and one for the unemployment rate. The employment-to-population ratio, rather than the employment level, and the unemployment rate, rather than the unemployment level, are estimated directly, primarily because these ratios are easier to estimate than levels.

The models draw on three sources of data—the Current Population Survey (CPS), which collects data each month from a sample of households in each state, the Current Employment Statistics (CES) program, which obtains data on payroll employment in all nonfarm industries from a large sample of employers, and information on unemployment insurance claims. The employment-to-population ratio model uses the relationship between the state's monthly employment estimates from the CES and the CPS. The model also includes trend components to account for long-run systematic differences between the two series. The unemployment rate model uses the rela-

tionship between the state's monthly unemployment insurance claims data and the CPS unemployment rate, along with a trend component to adjust for long-run systematic differences between the two series such as the inclusion in the CPS of unemployment not covered by insurance. Once the ratio and rate estimates are developed from the models, levels are calculated for employment, unemployment, and labor force.

BIRTHS AND DEATHS

Source: National Center for Health Statistics (NCHS), National Vital Statistics Report Series, Birth and Death Records.

BIRTHS AND DEATHS, 1990, 1997. The data are based on records of births and deaths that occurred during these years. Data for 1997 were received and processed by NCHS as of June 5, 1998, and are preliminary. State specific data were shown for both births and deaths if over 75 percent of all records had been processed. The number of death records processed for California was below the 75 percent criterion, and therefore mortality data were not shown for the state in 1997. Births and deaths are shown as rates per 1,000 population.

HOUSEHOLD INCOME; PERSONS IN POVERTY

Sources: U.S. Census Bureau, Current Population Survey (March Supplement) and 1990 Census of Population and Housing

MEDIAN HOUSEHOLD INCOME. Data for 1989 are from the 1990 "long form" census sample. Data for all other years are from the Current Population Survey (March Supplement). Household median income is defined as money income and is expressed as a median (the midpoint of all data) of income received by households. Money income, as defined by the Census Bureau, is the sum of: wage or salary income; nonfarm self-employment income; net farm self-employment income; Social Security and railroad retirement income; public assistance income; and all other regularly received income such as interest, dividends, veterans payments, pensions, unemployment compensation, and alimony. The total represents the amount of income received before deductions for personal income taxes, Social Security, bond purchases, union dues, Medicare deductions, etc.

PERSONS IN POVERTY. Poverty rates are based on data from the Current Population Survey (March Supplement). Poverty status is based on the definition prescribed by the U.S. Office of Management and Budget as the standard to be used by federal agencies for statistical purposes, which has been in use since the late 1960s. Families and persons are classified as below the poverty level if their total family income or unrelated individual income was less than the poverty threshold for the applicable family size, age of householder, and number of related children under age 18 present. The poverty threshold for a 4-person family was $16,400 in 1997. Several alternative measures of poverty, using other definitions of income and different survey methodologies, also are published by the Bureau of the Census.

PERSONAL INCOME; TRANSFER PAYMENTS; EMPLOYMENT AND EARNINGS; WAGES AND SALARIES

Source: U.S. Department of Commerce, Bureau of Economic Analysis (BEA)
Additional information: Regional Economic Measurement Division, BEA, (202-606-5360) or <http://www.bea.doc.gov>.

A comprehensive set of state-level data that include personal income and its components (earnings and employment by industry, taxes and transfers, and farm income) is prepared annually be BEA. These data provide a conceptually consistent set of measures of economic activity for each state, and these data have been used extensively in the sections of this book on Household and Personal Income, Economic Structure, and Agriculture.

Compound annual average rates of change from 1989 to 1997 have been calculated by the editors for personal income, employment, and earnings. The year 1989 was chosen as the base year for these calculations because it was the peak year of the most recent business cycle. Using 1990 (a recession year) as the base year would have tended to overstate the underlying trend in rate of growth. Except for constant dollar income per capita, the dollar figures for personal income, earnings, and average annual wages and salaries in the tables in this book are in current dollars, so the rates of change represent a combination of price increase and real growth.

PERSONAL INCOME. The personal income of a state is defined as the income received by, or on behalf of, all the residents of the state. Personal income consists of the income received by persons from all sources—that is, from participation in production, from both government and business transfer payments, and from government interest (which is treated like a transfer payment). In this context, "persons" consists of individuals, nonprofit institutions that primarily serve individuals, private noninsured welfare funds, and private trust funds. Personal income is calculated as the sum of wage and salary disbursements; other labor income (such as employer contributions to pension, profit-sharing, and health insurance plans); proprietors' income; and rental, dividend, and interest income received by persons; less personal contributions for social insurance. These definitions are essentially the same as those underlying the estimates of U.S. personal income in the national income and product accounts. However, the state estimates exclude the wages and salaries and other labor income of U.S. residents who are temporarily working and living abroad.

Information about earnings initially is collected based on the locations where people work. An "adjustment for residence" is then made to the data for each state to account for the earnings of those who work in one state and live in another (or in another country). A positive adjustment for residence indicates that, on balance, earnings are flowing into the state because residents cross state borders to work. A negative adjustment indicates that, on balance, workers are taking earnings out of the state to their residences elsewhere. The "adjustment for residence" in the U.S. totals is an estimate of the amount by which earnings within the United States by workers living in other countries exceed earnings of U.S. residents working abroad.

The definition of personal income differs from that of household income in a number of ways. One major difference is that personal income includes non-money income from sources such as Food Stamps and medical benefits, whereas the standard measure of household income is limited to money income. Per capita personal income is calculated as the total personal income of all the residents of a state divided by the midyear resident population of the state. It is an average, or mean. Household income is obtained from a survey of a sample of households, and median household income is the income of the household at the mid-point of a ranking of all households.

Income per capita in 1997 dollars was calculated by the editors using the personal consumption deflator from the national income and product accounts.

TRANSFER PAYMENTS. Transfer payments are payments to persons for which they do not render services in the current period. As a component of personal income, they are payments by government and business to individuals and nonprofit institutions. Although most transfer payments are made in cash, transfer payments also include some important in-kind payments, such as Medicare, Medicaid, and Food Stamps. Some government transfer payments are entitlements based on a combination of age and work history; examples are retirement payments to government employees and most Social Security benefits. Medicare is an entitlement based simply on age. Other transfer payments are "needs based," that is, eligibility for payment is based on low income, as is the case with Food Stamps, or on a combination of low income and age or disability, as is the case with Supplemental Security Income.

Social Security in the Government Transfer Payments table is Old age, Survivors and Disability Insurance (OASDI) payments. *Government employee retirement* includes payments to federal civilian and military and state and local government retirees. Categories of retirement, disability, and insurance included in the total but not shown separately include payments to retired railroad workers, workers' compensation payments, temporary disability payments, and payments to victims of black lung disease. *Medical payments* include Medicare and Medicaid and some smaller programs. Family assistance consists of Aid to Families with Dependent Children (AFDC) and, beginning with 1996, assistance programs operating under the Personal Responsibility and Work Opportunity Reconciliation Act of 1996 (often referred to as the "welfare reform" legislation). *Other income maintenance* largely consists of the earned income tax credit, a federal payment to qualifying low-income workers who file tax returns. These payments have grown rapidly during the 1990s due to program expansion, growth of employment, and increased awareness of the availability of this benefit. Other income maintenance also includes general assistance, emergency assistance, refugee assistance, foster home care payments, and energy assistance.

EMPLOYMENT AND EARNINGS BY SECTOR. The employment data are estimates of total employment in each sector and include the armed forces, civilian wage and salary employment, and self-employment. The estimates represent numbers of jobs, not of numbers of individuals. An individual holding two jobs will be counted twice, as will an individual who both holds a wage or salary job and also is self-employed. Estimates of self-employment rely in part on Schedule C filings on individual income tax returns. Thus a person engaged in two kinds of self-employment and filing two Schedule C forms also is counted twice.

This concept of employment differs from that in the Current Population Survey (CPS), which is the source of the employment data in the table on Population and Labor Force. The CPS is a household survey. It counts each individual only once, no matter how many jobs the person holds, and it includes only civilian employment. For these and other reasons, the BEA estimates of total employment differ from the estimates obtained from the CPS, and the BEA estimates typically are larger.

LEADING AND FASTEST GROWING PRIVATE INDUSTRIES. Identification of the leading and fastest growing industries was made by the editors, using data on worker and proprietor earnings. This is the same concept used for earnings in the Employment and Earning by Sector table, and the industry detail within each sector is the level of detail supplied by BEA in its comprehensive data set. In most cases, the industries are 2-digit industries as defined by the U.S. Standard Industrial Classification (or SIC—see "Industrial Classification" below). In a few cases, additional detail is used. For example, SIC 37, Transportation Equipment Manufacturing, is divided into Motor Vehicle Manufacturing and Other Transportation Equipment Manufacturing. Also in a few case, two or more 2-digit industries are combined. In a few cases, the title given the industry in this book differs from the official title used in the SIC and by BEA. These changes were made in order to provide titles that might be more meaningful to the general reader. For example, "Special Trade Contractors" (which includes construction specialties such as plumbing, electrical work, masonry, etc.) was changed to "Construction Specialties." Only private industries were ranked, and, in identifying the fastest growing industries, only those industries that accounted for at least one-half of one percent of 1996 Gross State Product were considered. A list of the industries available in the BEA data set is shown below.

Industries available in the BEA data set
(Editorial changes to the industry names are in parenthesis)
Agricultural services, forestry, fishing, and other
  Agricultural services
  Forestry
  Fisheries
  Other (Other agricultural services)
Mining
  Metal mining
  Coal mining
  Oil and gas extraction
  Nonmetallic minerals, excluding fuels
Construction
  General building contractors
  Heavy construction contractors
  Special trade contractors (Construction specialties)

Manufacturing
  Lumber and wood products
  Furniture and fixtures
  Stone, clay, and glass products
  Primary metal industries
  Fabricated metal products
  Industrial machinery and equipment (Industrial machinery manufacturing)
  Electronic and other electric equipment
  Motor vehicles and equipment
  Transportation equipment, excluding motor vehicles
  Instruments and related products
  Miscellaneous manufacturing industries (Miscellaneous manufacturing)
  Food and kindred products
  Tobacco products
  Textile mill products
  Apparel and other textile products
  Paper and allied products
  Printing and publishing
  Chemicals and allied products
  Petroleum and coal products
  Rubber and miscellaneous plastic products
  Leather and leather products
Transportation and public utilities
  Railroad transportation
  Trucking and warehousing
  Water transportation
  Other transportation
  Pipelines excluding natural gas
  Transportation services
  Communications
  Electric, gas, and sanitary services
Wholesale trade
Retail trade
  Building materials and garden equipment
  General merchandise stores
  Food stores
  Auto dealers and service stations
  Apparel and accessory stores
  Home furniture and furnishings stores
  Eating and drinking places
  Miscellaneous retail stores
Finance, insurance, and real estate
  Depository and nondepository credit institutions (Banks and other credit institutions)
  Security and commodity brokers and services (Security brokers)
  Insurance carriers
  Insurance agents, brokers, and services
  Real estate
  Holding and other investment companies
Services
  Hotels and other lodging places (Hotels)
  Personal services
  Private households
  Business services
  Auto repair, services, and parking
  Miscellaneous repair services
  Amusement and recreational services
  Motion pictures

Health services
Legal services
Educational services
Social services
Museums, botanical gardens, and zoos
Membership organizations
Engineering and management services
Miscellaneous services
Government and government enterprises
Federal civilian
Military
State and local
State
Local

INDUSTRIAL CLASSIFICATION. The Standard Industrial Classification (SIC) is the set of industry definitions that for many years has been used by the U.S. government—and by many private sources—to collect, tabulate, and publish statistical data by industry. The purpose of using a standard set of definitions is to provide analytically useful groupings of industrial activity and to promote comparability of data from different sources. Although there have been periodic revisions, the basic structure of the SIC has remained substantially the same for more than 50 years. In recent years the SIC has come to be criticized for having an overemphasis on manufacturing, inadequate service categories, and a lack of adequate classifications for new industries.

At present, the United States is in the process of moving to a new system of industrial classification, the North American Industry Classification System (NAICS). Canada and Mexico also are adopting this system. When fully implemented, NAICS will provide greatly improved delineation of service industries and better identification of new industries. It also will permit direct comparisons of industry data for Canada, Mexico, and the United States. The Bureau of the Census is collecting and publishing economic census data for 1997 on the new NAICS basis, but these data were not available in time for use in this book. The official government manual, North American Industry Classification System, United States 1997, defines each NAICS-based industry and provides a cross-walk to the SIC. The manual is available from Bernan Press (1-800-865-3457).

AVERAGE ANNUAL WAGES AND SALARIES. Average annual wages and salaries were calculated by the editors by dividing total wages and salaries paid during the year in each sector by annual average wage and salary employment in that sector. The data are not adjusted for inflation. They are appropriate for comparing annual average earnings across economic sectors and across states, but they do not directly measure changes over time in the purchasing power of these annual earnings.

Wages and salaries include not only the wages of production and nonsupervisory workers, but also the salaries of managerial and professional employees; the compensation of corporate officers; and commissions, tips, and bonuses. Thus, within any particular industry, the annual earnings of production or nonsupervisory workers typically are lower than the average for all types of workers as shown in this book.

Differences among economic sectors in annual average wage and salary earnings reflect differences in the length of the work week and of the work year as well as differences in hourly earnings. Work in construction and agriculture, for example, is highly seasonally; workers often are employed for less than a full year. Workers in retail trade and in many service industries work fewer hours per week, on average, than workers in manufacturing.

GROSS STATE PRODUCT AND MANUFACTURING
Source: U.S. Department of Commerce, Bureau of Economic Analysis (BEA)
Additional information: Regional Economic Measurement Division, BEA, (202-606-5360) or <http://www.bea.doc.gov>.

Gross state product (GSP) is a comprehensive measure of marketable goods and services produced within a state. It is the state counterpart of the nation's gross domestic product (GDP). GSP for a state is derived as the sum of the gross state product originating (GPO) in all industries in the state. In concept, an industry's GSP, or its "value added," is equivalent to its gross output (sales or receipts and other operating income, commodity taxes, and inventory change) minus its intermediate inputs (consumption of goods and services purchased from other U.S. industries or imported). In practice, GSP and GPO estimates are measured as the sum of the distributions by industry of the components of gross domestic income—that is, the sum of the costs incurred (such as compensation of employees, net interest, and indirect business taxes) and the profits earned in production.

The GSP estimates in this book are in current dollars and are appropriate for calculating the manufacturing share of GSP and for comparing one state with another. However, keep in mind that changes over time include price changes as well as changes in real output. The manufacturing value-added per worker was calculated by the editors by dividing manufacturing GPO by employment in manufacturing.

NEW CAPITAL EXPENDITURES, MANUFACTURING
Source: U.S. Department of Commerce, Bureau of the Census, 1996 Annual Survey of Manufactures.

The annual survey of manufactures (ASM) is conducted by the Bureau of the Census to provide measures of manufacturing activity by industry for intercensal years. More complete economic censuses are taken every five years. The most recent census collected data for 1997, but these 1997 data were not available in time to use in this book.

For establishments in operation and any known plants under construction, manufacturers are asked to report in the ASM their new expenditures for permanent additions and major alterations to manufacturing plants and for machinery and equipment used for replacement and additions to plant capacity. The totals for new expenditures include expenditures for plant and equipment leased from nonmanufacturing concerns through capital leases. New facilities owned by the federal government but operated under private contract by private companies, and plant and equipment furnished to the manufacturer by communities and nonprofit organizations are excluded.

EXPORTS OF GOODS

Source: U.S. Department of Commerce, Bureau of the Census, compiled by U.S. Department of Commerce, International Trade Administration, Office of Trade and Economic Analysis (OTEA).
Additional Information: Office of Trade and Economic Analysis <http://www.ita.doc.gov/tradestats>.

Exports of goods by state were compiled from the Bureau of the Census' Exporter Location (EL) series by OTEA. The EL series show the location of export sales by the exporter of record (the seller). About three-fourths of export sales of manufactured goods are made by manufacturers who do their own exporting. For these exports, production generally, but not always, occurs at the same location as sales. For the remaining one-fourth of manufactured exports and most nonmanufactured exports, the seller is not the producer. The production may or may not have occurred within the same state as the sale. Even when production occurs in the same state with the sale, the goods may well contain raw materials and components produced elsewhere. Thus, these export data provide an approximation, but not a complete and reliable record, of the production origin of U.S. exports.

The top ranking goods exports were identified by the editors using the commodity categories provided in the OTEA data. These categories are based on Standard Industrial Classification (SIC) product codes. These classifications may differ from the SIC industry classifications on which the employment and earnings data in this book are based. The industry classifications are based on the principal productive activity of each producing establishment (each plant, in the case of manufacturing). However, a single establishment sometimes may produce more than one category of goods. Export data are classified by product irrespective of whether the product was produced in an establishment primarily producing this product. Product classifications approximate industry classifications, but are not a precise match.

HOUSING SUPPLY

Sources: U.S. Bureau of the Census, Building Permits Survey, Survey of New Mobile Home Placements, and the Current Population Survey/Housing Vacancy Survey; National Association of Realtors, Homes Sales Median Home Prices.
Additional Information:
<http://www.cencus.gov/hhes/www/housing/hvs> and <http://nar.realtor.com/databank>.

Building permits data include permits issued for new construction of single family homes and multi-family apartments, and are from the Bureau of the Census' Building Permits Survey. Permit data exclude units renovated and building in areas that do not require permits.
New home production is the sum of building permits

and new manufactured housing (mobile homes) placements; mobile home data are from the Bureau of the Census Survey of New Mobile Home Placements.

Production per 1,000 population is calculated by the editors using resident population as of July 1 of each year.

Existing home sales are from the National Association of Realtors, and are available for nearly every state. The text of some chapters also contains data on median sales prices for existing homes in major metropolitan areas within the state.

Homeownership rate data are from the Bureau of the Census' Current Population Survey/Housing Vacancy Survey, and are based on the ratio of owner households to total occupied households. New survey weights were used starting in 1994, making comparability with previous years uncertain.

Rental vacancy rate data are from the Bureau of the Census' Current Population Survey/Housing Vacancy Survey, and equal the proportion of the rental inventory which is vacant and for rent.

AGRICULTURE; FARM INCOME

Sources: U.S. Department of Agriculture, National Agricultural Statistics Service (for general agricultural indicators) and U.S. Department of Commerce Bureau of Economic Analysis (for farm income).
Additional Information: National Agricultural Statistics Service Information Hotline 800-727-9540 or <http://www.usda.gov/nass/> and Regional Economic Measurement Division, Bureau of Economic Analysis (202-606-5360) or <http://www.bea.doc.gov>.

Estimates of the number of farms, acreage, and value of land and buildings in 1997 are those issued by the National Agricultural Statistics Services (NASS) prior to the availability of data from the 1997 Census of Agriculture and may differ somewhat from the census data. The census data became available as this book was being prepared and have been used as a source of supplementary information in the text of some chapters.

In federal statistics a farm is defined as any place with $1,000 of annual farm sales. Thus the total number of farms includes many for which farming generates only a minor fraction of total household income. In 1997, 50 percent of all farms had sales of less then $10,000, and 50 percent of all farm operators reported a principal occupation other than farming.

The *farm income data* are based on estimates prepared by the Department of Agriculture but have been modified by the Bureau of Economic Analysis to be consistent with the concepts and definitions used in their state-level personal income data set. Thus the Farm Income table in this book is on a basis fully consistent with the Personal Income, Employment and Earnings, and Average Annual Wages and Salaries tables.

EDUCATION

Sources: U.S. Bureau of the Census, Decennial Census and Current Population Survey; U.S. Department of Education, National Center for Education Statistics (NCES); National Education Association, Estimates of School Statistics.

EDUCATIONAL ATTAINMENT. Statistics for educational attainment are for persons age 25 and over. The 1970, 1980, and 1990 data were derived from the 1970, 1980, and 1990 censuses, respectively. The 1970 and 1980 census questionnaires asked for the highest number of years of education completed within each educational level; these results have been converted to be compatible with the 1990 questionnaire, which asked for the highest level of education completed. The 1997 data were derived from a similar question on the Current Population Survey. Persons who passed a high school equivalency examination were considered high school graduates. Schooling received in foreign schools was to be reported as the equivalent grade or year in the regular American school system.

ELEMENTARY AND SECONDARY SCHOOLS. Enrollment data on public school enrollment is from the NCES Common Core of Data for the 1995–96 school year, while those for private elementary and secondary enrollment are from the Private School Survey of 1995–96. The private school figure includes grades kindergarten through grade 12, including special education, vocational/technical education and alternative schools. Excluded from private enrollment is prekindergarten enrollment or enrollment in schools that do not offer first grade or above. Public school enrollment includes kindergarten through grade 12.

Per pupil spending data on per pupil spending are from the NCES Common Core of Data for 1995–96 and report the current expenditures for the regular school term divided by the average daily attendance of full-time pupils (or full time equivalency of pupils) during the term. Current expenditures include instruction, administration, operation and maintenance, and student transportation.

For *teacher salary data,* the National Education Association (NEA) reports instructional staff salary data in its annual publication, Estimates of School Statistics. Each year NEA prepares regression-based estimates of financial and other education statistics and submits them to the states for verification. Generally about 30 states adjust these estimates based on their own data. These preliminary data are published by NEA along with revised data from previous years. States are asked to revise previously submitted data as final figures become available. The most recent publication contains all changes reported to the NEA.

HIGHER EDUCATION. Total fall enrollment—public, private, and minority. The Integrated Postsecondary Education Data System (IPEDS) surveys approximately 11,000 post-secondary institutions, and is administered by the National Center for Education Statistics. The higher education portion of the survey is a census of all accredited 2- and 4-year colleges.

Population 18–34. These data are from the U.S. Bureau of the Census state population estimates for 1996. The estimated population is the computed number of persons living in an area as of July 1. See above notes on population for further information.

HEALTH
Sources: Center for Disease Control, National Center for Health Statistics, Mortality Statistics unpublished and as published in the National Vital Statistics Report, Vol.47,

No. 9; U.S. Bureau of the Census, Current Population Survey, Health Insurance report

TOTAL DEATHS, INFANT MORTALITY, AND LEADING CAUSES OF DEATH. The data for total deaths, infant mortality, and leading causes of death are released by the National Center for Health Statistics, in the National Vital Statistics Report series and on the Center for Disease Control's Wonder Website (http://wonder.cdc.gov), a set of databases with information on many health related issues, including mortality and infant mortality. Total deaths are expressed per 1,000 population, but deaths by cause are expressed as the number of deaths per 100,000 as deaths from some specific causes are relatively rare. Infant mortality is expressed as the number of infant deaths (under 1 year of age) per 1,000 births.

HEATH INSURANCE. The data for health insurance coverage are collected by the Bureau of the Census in the March Current Population Survey (CPS). The CPS is primarily a labor force survey, and interviewers have relatively little training in health insurance concepts. The data reflect the percentage of the population within an area without health insurance during the entire reported calendar year. Persons covered include those covered by private insurance (both employment-based and private plans) and government insurance (Medicare, Medicaid, military healthcare, and any other government plans).

GOVERNMENT FINANCE
Sources: U.S. Bureau of the Census, Governments Division, Annual Survey of Public Finance and Consolidated Federal Funds Report
Additional information: Governments Information: 1-800-242-2184 or
<http://www.census.gov/govs/www/index.html>.

STATE AND LOCAL TAXES PER CAPITA. These data are from the Bureau of the Census Governments Division, State and Local Finance series, fiscal 1996 (covering state and local fiscal years ending between July 1, 1995 and June 30, 1996). Total taxes reflect the sum of state plus local taxes, less corporate income taxes. Corporate income taxes were subtracted by the editors in order to better isolate taxes paid directly by individuals. Per capita amounts were calculated using resident population as of July 1, 1996. Taxes as a percentage of personal income were calculated by dividing taxes by total state personal income for 1995.

STATE GOVERNMENT FINANCE. These data are from the Bureau of the Census Governments Division, State Government Finance Data, fiscal 1997 (covering state and local fiscal years ending between July 1, 1996 and June 30, 1997), except for four states having later year-end dates. General revenue comprises all revenue except utility, liquor store, and insurance trust revenue. Intergovernmental revenue is funds from other governments, including general support, grants, shared taxes, and loans or advances.

FEDERAL SPENDING. Data are collected by the Bureau of the Census from a variety of sources within the federal government and compiled into the Consolidated Federal Funds Report.

ADDITIONAL SOURCES BY STATE

The great majority of the text in this book is based on the data in the accompanying tables or on related data from the federal statistical sources described above. For some states, supplementary sources specific to the individual state have been used. These are listed below. In most cases, this information was taken from World Wide Web sites, and the web addresses are included in the listings. Each state has its own web site, with an address of the form "http://www.state.al.us." In this example, the "al" is for Alabama. Other state sites are accessed by substituting the two-letter postal abbreviation for the state. These sites often have been valuable in preparing this book. Also valuable has been material found on web sites maintained by bureaus of business and economic research at state universities and by the regional Federal Reserve Banks.

ALABAMA

Industry growth in regions of the state: Federal Reserve Bank of Atlanta "Economic Outlook for Alabama Varies by Region," Regional Update VII N4. <http://www.frbatlanta.org>.

Education reform: Alabama State Department of Education, Alabama Education News, Vol. 22, No.3, October 1998. <http://www.alsde.edu>.

Infant mortality goal: Alabama Department of Public Health. < http://www.alapubhealth.org>.

ALASKA

Data on oil and oil field service employment: Alaska Department of Labor, Research and Analysis Section, "Alaska Economic Trends." <http://www.labor.state.ak.us/research/research.htm>. Alaska Permanent Fund information: Alaska Department of Revenue. Military personnel migration information: Alaska Department of Labor. Tourism's role in economy, air cargo landing information: Alaska Department of Labor.

DELAWARE

Leading employers: Delaware Economic Development Office, 1998 Statistical Overview of Delaware: Overview, "Delaware's Major Employers." <http://www.state.de.us/dedo/publications/databook/over view.htm>.

Data on incorporation: Delaware Division of Corporations, The Corporate Edge, "Delaware Incorporating Statistics," Spring 1998. <http://www.state.de.us/corp/graphs97.htm>.

DISTRICT OF COLUMBIA

Local government home purchase assistance: D.C. Department of Housing and Community Development.

FLORIDA

Forecast for service industry employment: Bureau of Business and Economic Research, Warrington College of Business Administration, University of Florida, "The Florida Long-term Economic Forecast 1998," July 1998. <http://www.cba.ufl.edu/bebr/>.

Citrus production, milk production, horse breeding: Florida Agricultural Statistics Service. <http://www.fl-ag.com/agFacts>.

GEORGIA

Environmental and infrastructure constraints on growth: Federal Reserve Bank of Atlanta, "What is Fueling Atlanta's Housing Growth?" Regional Update, VII N3. <http://www.frbatlanta.org>.

Georgia educational initiatives: <http://www.state.ga.us/index/educate.html> and <http://www.atlanta-info.com/atlanta-info/hope.html>.

Motor fuel tax: Terry College of Business Administration, University of Georgia, "The Georgia Outlook 1999." <http://www.selig.uga.edu>.

HAWAII

Hawaii Department of Business, Economic Development and Tourism. <http://www.hawaii.gov/dbedt>.

ILLINOIS

Leading employers and high-tech job information: Illinois Department of Commerce and Community Affairs. <http://www.commerce.state.il.us/>.

Corporate headquarters information from City of Chicago web site. <http://www.ci.chi.il.us/>.

INDIANA

Detailed industry production information: Indiana Department of Commerce: <http://www.state.in.us/doc>.

KANSAS

Information on aircraft industry: Kansas Department of Commerce and Housing.

KENTUCKY

Coal production: "Kentucky Facts," Cabinet for Economic Development, State of Kentucky. <http://www.state.ky.us>.

Per capita income: Mark C. Berger, "Kentucky's Per Capita Income: Catching up to the Rest of the Country," 1997Kentucky Annual Economic Report, University of Kentucky, Gatton College of Business and Economics, Center for Business and Economic Research. <http://gatton.gws.uky.edu.cber/cber.htm>.

Employment by industry: "Employment Growth in Kentucky, 1992-1997," Kentucky Business and Economic Outlook, Vol. 1, No.2, Spring 1998, University of Kentucky, Gatton College of Business and Economics, Center for Business and Economic Research. <http://gatton.gws.uky.edu.cber/cber.htm>.

Education reform: William H. Hoyt, "An Evaluation of the Kentucky Education Reform Act," 1999 Kentucky Annual Economic Report, University of Kentucky, Gatton College of Business and Economics, Center for Business and Economic Research. <http://gatton.gws.uky.edu.cber/cber.htm>; and Kentucky Department of Education, "The Kentucky Story." <http://www.kde.state.ky.us>.

LOUISIANA
Industry background, new oil industry technology: Federal Reserve Bank of Atlanta, Regional Updates, "Louisiana Economy Sends Mixed Signals," V10 N4; "Gulf of Mexico Oil Companies Gush Over New Drilling Technology," V11 N3, "Louisiana Expands, But Lower Gas Prices Temper Growth," V11 N4. <http://www.frbatlanta.org>.

Education reform: Louisiana Department of Education, "Louisiana Educational Assessment Program (LEAP)." <http://www.doe.state.la.us>.

Health status: Louisiana Office of Public Health, State Center for Health Statistics "1998 Louisiana Health Report Card," as revised July 23, 1998. <http://www.state.las.us>.

MICHIGAN
Housing construction background: U.S. Department of Housing and Urban Development regional market reports.

MISSISSIPPI
Industry background: Federal Reserve Bank of Atlanta, Regional Updates, "Some Bright Spots Emerge for Mississippi," V10 N4 and "Although Gambling Boom Ends, Mississippi's Economy is Stable," V11 N4. <http://www.frbatlanta.org>.

Education reform: Mississippi Department of Education "Mississippi Board of Education Proposed Assessment and Accreditation System." <http://www.mdek12.state.ms.us>.

Infant mortality goal: Mississippi State Department of Health "FY1998-2003 Strategic Plan," August 1997. <http://www.msdh.state.ms.us>.

NEBRASKA
Background on farm economy: Nebraska Bureau of Economic Research, Department of Economic Development.
Telecommunications growth: Nebraska Department of Economic Development press releases.

NEW HAMPSHIRE
Full-time employment: Economic and Labor Market Information Bureau, "Vital Signs: Economic and Social Indicators for New Hampshire, 1994-1997," January 1999.

NEW MEXICO
Information on high technology employment and

research: New Mexico Economic Development Department. <http://www.edd.state.nm.us/>.

NORTH CAROLINA
Geography: <http://www.state.nc.us>.

Agriculture compared to other states: "How North Carolina Agriculture Compares with Other States, 1998 Production." <http://www.agr.state.nc.us>.

Achievements in education: North Carolina Public Schools Infoweb, "How Are North Carolina Public Schools Really Doing?" <http://www.dpi.state.nc.us>.

Infant mortality goal: North Carolina Department of Health and Human Services "Building a Healthy North Carolina." <http://www.dhhs.state.nc.us>.

OHIO
Housing market information for areas within the state: U.S Department of Housing and Urban Development regional market reports.

OREGON
Information on employment in high technology industries and on composition of exports and markets in Asia: State of Oregon Department of Administrative Services, Office of Economic Analysis, <http://www.oea.das.state.or.us>.

Background on land use and growth policies and housing prices: "Growth Management in the Portland Region and the Housing Boom of the 1990s," G. Mildner, Portland State University, Urban Futures Program, Reason Public Policy Institute, Los Angeles CA.

SOUTH CAROLINA
Developing high tech industry: South Carolina Technology Advisory Council, "Strategies for Developing A Knowledge-Based Economy." <http://www.state.sc.us>.

SOUTH DAKOTA
Establishment of new businesses in business services and others: South Dakota Office of Economic Development press releases.

Business taxes: Office of Economic Development web site. <http://www.state.sd.us/oed>.

TENNESSEE
Industry background: Federal Reserve Bank of Atlanta, Regional Updates, "A Good but Not Great Year Ahead for Tennessee," V10 N4 and "National Slowing Will Affect Tennessee's Growth Prospects," V11 N4. <http://www.frbatlanta.org>.

Tenncare health plan: "TennCare Fact Sheet." http://www.state.tn.us; and "Tennessee Talks of Rolling Back Health Plan for 'Uninsurables' " New York Times May 1, 1999.

TEXAS

Sector information on high technology employment and output: Texas Department of Economic Development, Business and Industry Data Center. <http://www.bidc.state.tx.us>.

VIRGINIA

Employment by industry: Knapp, John L. "Virginia's Economy in the 1990s: Some Caution Is Warranted," The Virginia Newsletter, Vol.75, No.2, February 1999, Weldon Cooper Center for Public Service University of Virginia. <http://www.virginia.edu/~cpserv>/.

Education reform: "Virginia's K-12 Education Reform: Raising Student Achievement in Virginia," Virginia Department of Education. <http://www.pen.k12.va.us/>.

Infant mortality goal: "Healthy Virginia Communities," Virginia Department of Public Health December 1997. <http://www.vdh.state.va.us>.

WASHINGTON

Data on employment growth in Seattle compared to rest of the state and on Boeing Aircraft Company: State of Washington Employment Security Department: <http://www.wa.gov/esd/>.

Seattle housing market information: U.S. Department of Housing and Urban Development regional market reports.

WEST VIRGINIA

Industry background, population background: "Economic Growth Uneven Around State, Vol.3 No1, Winter 1997; "How High Are West Virginia Wages," Vol.3, Number 3, Fall 1997; "Wood Products Industry Creates More Jobs," Vol. 3, No.3, Summer 1997; and "Why in the World Has West Virginia's Population Growth Stopped?" Vol. 5, No. 1&2, Winter/Spring 1999; *West Virginia Economic Review* Bureau of Business and Economic Research, West Virgina University, <http://www.be.wvu.edu>.

INDEX

Because each eight-page chapter (except the chapter on the U.S.) in *State Profiles* is organized in the same way, and presents information for the same topics, this index lists, by state and for each state (and the District of Columbia), the topics and related page numbers. The topics are listed alphabetically and include: Overview, Agriculture, Economic Structure (two parts), Education, Government, Health, Housing, Income, Labor Force, and Population. Listed under each topic are more detailed entries that refer to the text, tables, and figures found on the page listing for the topic. The chapter on the U.S. lists page numbers for the more detailed entries, because this chapter expands on the standard layout of the state chapters.

United States—Overview, 1
  1998, Developments in, 18
    Population, Employment, Unemployment, and
      Exports, 19
  Agriculture, 13
    Farms (number, acreage, value), 13
    Farm Income, 13
  Economic Structure, 8
    Earnings Growth, Fastest, 8
    Employment and Earnings by Sector, 9
    Exports of Goods, 11
    Gross Domestic Product, 11
    Manufacturing, 10
    Private Industries, Leading, 8
    Wages and Salaries by Sector (Average Annual), 10
  Education, 14
    Education Indicators, 15
    Educational Attainment, 14
    High School Completion, 14
  Employment and Unemployment, 4
    Employment, Average Annual Increase in, 4
    Unemployment Rate, 4
  Government Finance, 16
    Federal Spending, 17
    Finances, State Government, 16
    Taxes, State and Local (Average), 16
  Health, 15
    Death, Leading Causes of, 16
    Health Indicators, 15
  Housing, 12
    Housing Supply, 12
    New Home Production, 12
  Income, 5
    Government Payments to Individuals, 7
    Income, Household, 5
    Income, Per Capita, 5
    Income, Personal, 6
    Poverty, Persons in, 5
    Transfer Payments, Government, 7
    Welfare Caseloads, Change in, 8
    Welfare Reform, the Impact of, 7
  Population, 1
    Births, 3
    Deaths, 3
    Growth, Household and Population (Average
      Annual), 3
    Population and Labor Force, 1
    Population by Age,
    Population Change and Components, 2
    Ten Fastest Growing States, Percent Population
      Change, 2

Alabama—Overview, 31
    Household Income, Median
    Population Growth (Average Annual)
    Unemployment Rate
  Agriculture, 36
    Farm Income
    Farms (number, acreage, value)
  Economic Structure, 34
    Earnings Growth, Fastest
    Employment and Earnings by Sector
    Private Industries, Leading
  Economic Structure (Continued), 35
    Exports of Goods
    Gross State Product
    Manufacturing
    Wages and Salaries by Sector (Average Annual)
  Education, 37
    Education Indicators
    Educational Attainment
    High School Completion
  Government, 38
    Federal Spending within State
    Finances, State Government
    Taxes, State and Local
  Health, 37
    Death, Leading Causes of
    Health Indicators
  Housing, 36
    Homeownership Rates
    Housing Supply
  Income, Household and Personal, 33
    Government Payments to Individuals
    Poverty, Persons in
    Transfer Payments, Government
  Labor Force, Employment and Unemployment, 32
    Employment to Population Ratio
    Unemployment Rate
  Population, 32
    Births
    Deaths
    Growth, Household and Population (Average Annual)
    Population by Age
    Population Change and Components

Alaska—Overview, 39
    Household Income, Median
    Population Growth (Average Annual)
    Unemployment Rate
  Agriculture, 44
    Farm Income
    Farms (number, acreage, value)

Economic Structure, 42
  Earnings Growth, Fastest
  Employment and Earnings by Sector
  Private Industries, Leading
Economic Structure (Continued), 43
  Exports of Goods
  Gross State Product
  Manufacturing
  Wages and Salaries by Sector (Average Annual)
Education, 45
  Education Indicators
  Educational Attainment
  High School Completion
Government, 46
  Federal Spending within State
  Finances, State Government
  Taxes, State and Local
Health, 45
  Death, Leading Causes of
  Health Indicators
Housing, 44
  Homeownership Rates
  Housing Supply
Income, Household and Personal, 41
  Government Payments to Individuals
  Poverty, Persons in
  Transfer Payments, Government
Labor Force, Employment and Unemployment, 40
  Employment to Population Ratio
  Unemployment Rate
Population, 40
  Births
  Deaths
  Growth, Household and Population (Average Annual)
  Population by Age
  Population Change and Components

Arizona—Overview, 47
  Household Income, Median
  Population Growth (Average Annual)
  Unemployment Rate
Agriculture, 52
  Farm Income
  Farms (number, acreage, value)
Economic Structure, 50
  Earnings Growth, Fastest
  Employment and Earnings by Sector
  Private Industries, Leading   ·
Economic Structure (Continued), 51
  Exports of Goods
  Gross State Product
  Manufacturing
  Wages and Salaries by Sector (Average Annual)
Education, 53
  Education Indicators
  Educational Attainment
  High School Completion
Government, 54
  Federal Spending within State
  Finances, State Government

  Taxes, State and Local
Health, 53
  Death, Leading Causes of
  Health Indicators
Housing, 52
  Homeownership Rates
  Housing Supply
Income, Household and Personal, 49
  Government Payments to Individuals
  Poverty, Persons in
  Transfer Payments, Government
Labor Force, Employment and Unemployment, 48
  Employment to Population Ratio
  Unemployment Rate
Population, 48
  Births
  Deaths
  Growth, Household and Population (Average Annual)
  Population by Age
  Population Change and Components

Arkansas—Overview, 55
  Household Income, Median
  Population Growth (Average Annual)
  Unemployment Rate
Agriculture, 60
  Farm Income
  Farms (number, acreage, value)
Economic Structure, 58
  Earnings Growth, Fastest
  Employment and Earnings by Sector
  Private Industries, Leading
Economic Structure (Continued), 59
  Exports of Goods
  Gross State Product
  Manufacturing
  Wages and Salaries by Sector (Average Annual)
Education, 61
  Education Indicators
  Educational Attainment
  High School Completion
Government, 62
  Federal Spending within State
  Finances, State Government
  Taxes, State and Local
Health, 61
  Death, Leading Causes of
  Health Indicators
Housing, 60
  Homeownership Rates
  Housing Supply
Income, Household and Personal, 57
  Government Payments to Individuals
  Poverty, Persons in
  Transfer Payments, Government
Labor Force, Employment and Unemployment, 56
  Employment to Population Ratio
  Unemployment Rate
Population, 56
  Births
  Deaths

Growth, Household and Population (Average Annual)
Population by Age
Population Change and Components

California—Overview, 63
Household Income, Median
Population Growth (Average Annual)
Unemployment Rate
Agriculture, 68
Farm Income
Farms (number, acreage, value)
Economic Structure, 66
Earnings Growth, Fastest
Employment and Earnings by Sector
Private Industries, Leading
Economic Structure (Continued), 67
Exports of Goods
Gross State Product
Manufacturing
Wages and Salaries by Sector (Average Annual)
Education, 69
Education Indicators
Educational Attainment
High School Completion
Government, 70
Federal Spending within State
Finances, State Government
Taxes, State and Local
Health, 69
Death, Leading Causes of
Health Indicators
Housing, 68
Homeownership Rates
Housing Supply
Income, Household and Personal, 65
Government Payments to Individuals
Poverty, Persons in
Transfer Payments, Government
Labor Force, Employment and Unemployment, 64
Employment to Population Ratio
Unemployment Rate
Population, 64
Births
Deaths
Growth, Household and Population (Average Annual)
Population by Age
Population Change and Components

Colorado—Overview, 71
Household Income, Median
Population Growth (Average Annual)
Unemployment Rate
Agriculture, 76
Farm Income
Farms (number, acreage, value)
Economic Structure, 74
Earnings Growth, Fastest
Employment and Earnings by Sector
Private Industries, Leading
Economic Structure (Continued), 75
Exports of Goods

Gross State Product
Manufacturing
Wages and Salaries by Sector (Average Annual)
Education, 77
Education Indicators
Educational Attainment
High School Completion
Government, 78
Federal Spending within State
Finances, State Government
Taxes, State and Local
Health, 77
Death, Leading Causes of
Health Indicators
Housing, 76
Homeownership Rates
Housing Supply
Income, Household and Personal, 73
Government Payments to Individuals
Poverty, Persons in
Transfer Payments, Government
Labor Force, Employment and Unemployment, 72
Employment to Population Ratio
Unemployment Rate
Population, 72
Births
Deaths
Growth, Household and Population (Average Annual)
Population by Age
Population Change and Components

Connecticut—Overview, 79
Household Income, Median
Population Growth (Average Annual)
Unemployment Rate
Agriculture, 84
Farm Income
Farms (number, acreage, value)
Economic Structure, 82
Earnings Growth, Fastest
Employment and Earnings by Sector
Private Industries, Leading
Economic Structure (Continued), 83
Exports of Goods
Gross State Product
Manufacturing
Wages and Salaries by Sector (Average Annual)
Education, 85
Education Indicators
Educational Attainment
High School Completion
Government, 86
Federal Spending within State
Finances, State Government
Taxes, State and Local
Health, 85
Death, Leading Causes of
Health Indicators
Housing, 84
Homeownership Rates
Housing Supply

Income, Household and Personal, 81
 Government Payments to Individuals
 Poverty, Persons in
 Transfer Payments, Government
Labor Force, Employment and Unemployment, 80
 Employment to Population Ratio
 Unemployment Rate
Population, 80
 Births
 Deaths
 Growth, Household and Population (Average Annual)
 Population by Age
 Population Change and Components

Delaware—Overview, 87
 Household Income, Median
 Population Growth (Average Annual)
 Unemployment Rate
Agriculture, 92
 Farm Income
 Farms (number, acreage, value)
Economic Structure, 90
 Earnings Growth, Fastest
 Employment and Earnings by Sector
 Private Industries, Leading
Economic Structure (Continued), 91
 Exports of Goods
 Gross State Product
 Manufacturing
 Wages and Salaries by Sector (Average Annual)
Education, 93
 Education Indicators
 Educational Attainment
 High School Completion
Government, 94
 Federal Spending within State
 Finances, State Government
 Taxes, State and Local
Health, 93
 Death, Leading Causes of
 Health Indicators
Housing, 92
 Homeownership Rates
 Housing Supply
Income, Household and Personal, 89
 Government Payments to Individuals
 Poverty, Persons in
 Transfer Payments, Government
Labor Force, Employment and Unemployment, 88
 Employment to Population Ratio
 Unemployment Rate
Population, 88
 Births
 Deaths
 Growth, Household and Population (Average Annual)
 Population by Age
 Population Change and Components

District of Columbia—Overview, 95
 Household Income, Median
 Population Growth (Average Annual)

 Unemployment Rate
Agriculture, 100
 Farm Income
 Farms (number, acreage, value)
Economic Structure, 98
 Earnings Growth, Fastest
 Employment and Earnings by Sector
 Private Industries, Leading
Economic Structure (Continued), 99
 Exports of Goods
 Gross State Product
 Manufacturing
 Wages and Salaries by Sector (Average Annual)
Education, 101
 Education Indicators
 Educational Attainment
 High School Completion
Government, 102
 Federal Spending within State
 Finances, State Government
 Taxes, State and Local
Health, 101
 Death, Leading Causes of
 Health Indicators
Housing, 100
 Homeownership Rates
 Housing Supply
Income, Household and Personal, 97
 Government Payments to Individuals
 Poverty, Persons in
 Transfer Payments, Government
Labor Force, Employment and Unemployment, 96
 Employment to Population Ratio
 Unemployment Rate
Population, 96
 Births
 Deaths
 Growth, Household and Population (Average Annual)
 Population by Age
 Population Change and Components

Florida—Overview, 103
 Household Income, Median
 Population Growth (Average Annual)
 Unemployment Rate
Agriculture, 108
 Farm Income
 Farms (number, acreage, value)
Economic Structure, 106
 Earnings Growth, Fastest
 Employment and Earnings by Sector
 Private Industries, Leading
Economic Structure (Continued), 107
 Exports of Goods
 Gross State Product
 Manufacturing
 Wages and Salaries by Sector (Average Annual)
Education, 109
 Education Indicators
 Educational Attainment
 High School Completion

Government, 110
  Federal Spending within State
  Finances, State Government
  Taxes, State and Local
Health, 109
  Death, Leading Causes of
  Health Indicators
Housing, 108
  Homeownership Rates
  Housing Supply
Income, Household and Personal, 105
  Government Payments to Individuals
  Poverty, Persons in
  Transfer Payments, Government
Labor Force, Employment and Unemployment, 104
  Employment to Population Ratio
  Unemployment Rate
Population, 104
  Births
  Deaths
  Growth, Household and Population (Average Annual)
  Population by Age
  Population Change and Components

Georgia—Overview, 111
  Household Income, Median
  Population Growth (Average Annual)
  Unemployment Rate
Agriculture, 116
  Farm Income
  Farms (number, acreage, value)
Economic Structure, 114
  Earnings Growth, Fastest
  Employment and Earnings by Sector
  Private Industries, Leading
Economic Structure (Continued), 115
  Exports of Goods
  Gross State Product
  Manufacturing
  Wages and Salaries by Sector (Average Annual)
Education, 117
  Education Indicators
  Educational Attainment
  High School Completion
Government, 118
  Federal Spending within State
  Finances, State Government
  Taxes, State and Local
Health, 117
  Death, Leading Causes of
  Health Indicators
Housing, 116
  Homeownership Rates
  Housing Supply
Income, Household and Personal, 113
  Government Payments to Individuals
  Poverty, Persons in
  Transfer Payments, Government
Labor Force, Employment and Unemployment, 112
  Employment to Population Ratio
  Unemployment Rate

Population, 112
  Births
  Deaths
  Growth, Household and Population (Average Annual)
  Population by Age
  Population Change and Components

Hawaii—Overview, 119
  Household Income, Median
  Population Growth (Average Annual)
  Unemployment Rate
Agriculture, 124
  Farm Income
  Farms (number, acreage, value)
Economic Structure, 122
  Earnings Growth, Fastest
  Employment and Earnings by Sector
  Private Industries, Leading
Economic Structure (Continued), 123
  Exports of Goods
  Gross State Product
  Manufacturing
  Wages and Salaries by Sector (Average Annual)
Education, 125
  Education Indicators
  Educational Attainment
  High School Completion
Government, 126
  Federal Spending within State
  Finances, State Government
  Taxes, State and Local
Health, 125
  Death, Leading Causes of
  Health Indicators
Housing, 124
  Homeownership Rates
  Housing Supply
Income, Household and Personal, 121
  Government Payments to Individuals
  Poverty, Persons in
  Transfer Payments, Government
Labor Force, Employment and Unemployment, 120
  Employment to Population Ratio
  Unemployment Rate
Population, 120
  Births
  Deaths
  Growth, Household and Population (Average Annual)
  Population by Age
  Population Change and Components

Idaho—Overview, 127
  Household Income, Median
  Population Growth (Average Annual)
  Unemployment Rate
Agriculture, 132
  Farm Income
  Farms (number, acreage, value)
Economic Structure, 130
  Earnings Growth, Fastest
  Employment and Earnings by Sector

Private Industries, Leading
Economic Structure (Continued), 131
Exports of Goods
Gross State Product
Manufacturing
Wages and Salaries by Sector (Average Annual)
Education, 133
Education Indicators
Educational Attainment
High School Completion
Government, 134
Federal Spending within State
Finances, State Government
Taxes, State and Local
Health, 133
Death, Leading Causes of
Health Indicators
Housing, 132
Homeownership Rates
Housing Supply
Income, Household and Personal, 129
Government Payments to Individuals
Poverty, Persons in
Transfer Payments, Government
Labor Force, Employment and Unemployment, 128
Employment to Population Ratio
Unemployment Rate
Population, 128
Births
Deaths
Growth, Household and Population (Average Annual)
Population by Age
Population Change and Components

Illinois—Overview, 135
Household Income, Median
Population Growth (Average Annual)
Unemployment Rate
Agriculture, 140
Farm Income
Farms (number, acreage, value)
Economic Structure, 138
Earnings Growth, Fastest
Employment and Earnings by Sector
Private Industries, Leading
Economic Structure (Continued), 139
Exports of Goods
Gross State Product
Manufacturing
Wages and Salaries by Sector (Average Annual)
Education, 141
Education Indicators
Educational Attainment
High School Completion
Government, 142
Federal Spending within State
Finances, State Government
Taxes, State and Local
Health, 141
Death, Leading Causes of
Health Indicators

Housing, 140
Homeownership Rates
Housing Supply
Income, Household and Personal, 137
Government Payments to Individuals
Poverty, Persons in
Transfer Payments, Government
Labor Force, Employment and Unemployment, 136
Employment to Population Ratio
Unemployment Rate
Population, 136
Births
Deaths
Growth, Household and Population (Average Annual)
Population by Age
Population Change and Components

Indiana—Overview, 143
Household Income, Median
Population Growth (Average Annual)
Unemployment Rate
Agriculture, 148
Farm Income
Farms (number, acreage, value)
Economic Structure, 146
Earnings Growth, Fastest
Employment and Earnings by Sector
Private Industries, Leading
Economic Structure (Continued), 147
Exports of Goods
Gross State Product
Manufacturing
Wages and Salaries by Sector (Average Annual)
Education, 149
Education Indicators
Educational Attainment
High School Completion
Government, 150
Federal Spending within State
Finances, State Government
Taxes, State and Local
Health, 149
Death, Leading Causes of
Health Indicators
Housing, 148
Homeownership Rates
Housing Supply
Income, Household and Personal, 145
Government Payments to Individuals
Poverty, Persons in
Transfer Payments, Government
Labor Force, Employment and Unemployment, 144
Employment to Population Ratio
Unemployment Rate
Population, 144
Births
Deaths
Growth, Household and Population (Average Annual)
Population by Age
Population Change and Components

Iowa—Overview, 151
  Household Income, Median
  Population Growth (Average Annual)
  Unemployment Rate
  Agriculture, 156
    Farm Income
    Farms (number, acreage, value)
  Economic Structure, 154
    Earnings Growth, Fastest
    Employment and Earnings by Sector
    Private Industries, Leading
  Economic Structure (Continued), 155
    Exports of Goods
    Gross State Product
    Manufacturing
    Wages and Salaries by Sector (Average Annual)
  Education, 157
    Education Indicators
    Educational Attainment
    High School Completion
  Government, 158
    Federal Spending within State
    Finances, State Government
    Taxes, State and Local
  Health, 157
    Death, Leading Causes of
    Health Indicators
  Housing, 156
    Homeownership Rates
    Housing Supply
  Income, Household and Personal, 153
    Government Payments to Individuals
    Poverty, Persons in
    Transfer Payments, Government
  Labor Force, Employment and Unemployment, 152
    Employment to Population Ratio
    Unemployment Rate
  Population, 152
    Births
    Deaths
    Growth, Household and Population (Average Annual)
    Population by Age
    Population Change and Components

Kansas—Overview, 159
  Household Income, Median
  Population Growth (Average Annual)
  Unemployment Rate
  Agriculture, 164
    Farm Income
    Farms (number, acreage, value)
  Economic Structure, 162
    Earnings Growth, Fastest
    Employment and Earnings by Sector
    Private Industries, Leading
  Economic Structure (Continued), 163
    Exports of Goods
    Gross State Product
    Manufacturing
    Wages and Salaries by Sector (Average Annual)
  Education, 165

    Education Indicators
    Educational Attainment
    High School Completion
  Government, 166
    Federal Spending within State
    Finances, State Government
    Taxes, State and Local
  Health, 165
    Death, Leading Causes of
    Health Indicators
  Housing, 164
    Homeownership Rates
    Housing Supply
  Income, Household and Personal, 161
    Government Payments to Individuals
    Poverty, Persons in
    Transfer Payments, Government
  Labor Force, Employment and Unemployment, 160
    Employment to Population Ratio
    Unemployment Rate
  Population, 160
    Births
    Deaths
    Growth, Household and Population (Average Annual)
    Population by Age
    Population Change and Components

Kentucky—Overview, 167
  Household Income, Median
  Population Growth (Average Annual)
  Unemployment Rate
  Agriculture, 172
    Farm Income
    Farms (number, acreage, value)
  Economic Structure, 170
    Earnings Growth, Fastest
    Employment and Earnings by Sector
    Private Industries, Leading
  Economic Structure (Continued), 171
    Exports of Goods
    Gross State Product
    Manufacturing
    Wages and Salaries by Sector (Average Annual)
  Education, 173
    Education Indicators
    Educational Attainment
    High School Completion
  Government, 174
    Federal Spending within State
    Finances, State Government
    Taxes, State and Local
  Health, 173
    Death, Leading Causes of
    Health Indicators
  Housing, 172
    Homeownership Rates
    Housing Supply
  Income, Household and Personal, 169
    Government Payments to Individuals
    Poverty, Persons in
    Transfer Payments, Government

Labor Force, Employment and Unemployment, 168
Employment to Population Ratio
Unemployment Rate
Population, 168
Births
Deaths
Growth, Household and Population (Average Annual)
Population by Age
Population Change and Components

Louisiana—Overview, 175
Household Income, Median
Population Growth (Average Annual)
Unemployment Rate
Agriculture, 180
Farm Income
Farms (number, acreage, value)
Economic Structure, 178
Earnings Growth, Fastest
Employment and Earnings by Sector
Private Industries, Leading
Economic Structure (Continued), 179
Exports of Goods
Gross State Product
Manufacturing
Wages and Salaries by Sector (Average Annual)
Education, 181
Education Indicators
Educational Attainment
High School Completion
Government, 182
Federal Spending within State
Finances, State Government
Taxes, State and Local
Health, 181
Death, Leading Causes of
Health Indicators
Housing, 180
Homeownership Rates
Housing Supply
Income, Household and Personal, 177
Government Payments to Individuals
Poverty, Persons in
Transfer Payments, Government
Labor Force, Employment and Unemployment, 176
Employment to Population Ratio
Unemployment Rate
Population, 176
Births
Deaths
Growth, Household and Population (Average Annual)
Population by Age
Population Change and Components

Maine—Overview, 183
Household Income, Median
Population Growth (Average Annual)
Unemployment Rate
Agriculture, 188
Farm Income
Farms (number, acreage, value)

Economic Structure, 186
Earnings Growth, Fastest
Employment and Earnings by Sector
Private Industries, Leading
Economic Structure (Continued), 187
Exports of Goods
Gross State Product
Manufacturing
Wages and Salaries by Sector (Average Annual)
Education, 189
Education Indicators
Educational Attainment
High School Completion
Government, 190
Federal Spending within State
Finances, State Government
Taxes, State and Local
Health, 189
Death, Leading Causes of
Health Indicators
Housing, 188
Homeownership Rates
Housing Supply
Income, Household and Personal, 185
Government Payments to Individuals
Poverty, Persons in
Transfer Payments, Government
Labor Force, Employment and Unemployment, 184
Employment to Population Ratio
Unemployment Rate
Population, 184
Births
Deaths
Growth, Household and Population (Average Annual)
Population by Age
Population Change and Components

Maryland—Overview, 191
Household Income, Median
Population Growth (Average Annual)
Unemployment Rate
Agriculture, 196
Farm Income
Farms (number, acreage, value)
Economic Structure, 194
Earnings Growth, Fastest
Employment and Earnings by Sector
Private Industries, Leading
Economic Structure (Continued), 195
Exports of Goods
Gross State Product
Manufacturing
Wages and Salaries by Sector (Average Annual)
Education, 197
Education Indicators
Educational Attainment
High School Completion
Government, 198
Federal Spending within State
Finances, State Government
Taxes, State and Local

Health, 197
  Death, Leading Causes of
  Health Indicators
Housing, 196
  Homeownership Rates
  Housing Supply
Income, Household and Personal, 193
  Government Payments to Individuals
  Poverty, Persons in
  Transfer Payments, Government
Labor Force, Employment and Unemployment, 192
  Employment to Population Ratio
  Unemployment Rate
Population, 192
  Births
  Deaths
  Growth, Household and Population (Average Annual)
  Population by Age
  Population Change and Components

Massachusetts—Overview, 199
  Household Income, Median
  Population Growth (Average Annual)
  Unemployment Rate
Agriculture, 204
  Farm Income
  Farms (number, acreage, value)
Economic Structure, 202
  Earnings Growth, Fastest
  Employment and Earnings by Sector
  Private Industries, Leading
Economic Structure (Continued), 203
  Exports of Goods
  Gross State Product
  Manufacturing
  Wages and Salaries by Sector (Average Annual)
Education, 205
  Education Indicators
  Educational Attainment
  High School Completion
Government, 206
  Federal Spending within State
  Finances, State Government
  Taxes, State and Local
Health, 205
  Death, Leading Causes of
  Health Indicators
Housing, 204
  Homeownership Rates
  Housing Supply
Income, Household and Personal, 201
  Government Payments to Individuals
  Poverty, Persons in
  Transfer Payments, Government
Labor Force, Employment and Unemployment, 200
  Employment to Population Ratio
  Unemployment Rate
Population, 200
  Births
  Deaths
  Growth, Household and Population (Average Annual)

Population by Age
Population Change and Components

Michigan—Overview, 207
  Household Income, Median
  Population Growth (Average Annual)
  Unemployment Rate
Agriculture, 212
  Farm Income
  Farms (number, acreage, value)
Economic Structure, 210
  Earnings Growth, Fastest
  Employment and Earnings by Sector
  Private Industries, Leading
Economic Structure (Continued), 211
  Exports of Goods
  Gross State Product
  Manufacturing
  Wages and Salaries by Sector (Average Annual)
Education, 213
  Education Indicators
  Educational Attainment
  High School Completion
Government, 214
  Federal Spending within State
  Finances, State Government
  Taxes, State and Local
Health, 213
  Death, Leading Causes of
  Health Indicators
Housing, 212
  Homeownership Rates
  Housing Supply
Income, Household and Personal, 209
  Government Payments to Individuals
  Poverty, Persons in
  Transfer Payments, Government
Labor Force, Employment and Unemployment, 208
  Employment to Population Ratio
  Unemployment Rate
Population, 208
  Births
  Deaths
  Growth, Household and Population (Average Annual)
  Population by Age
  Population Change and Components

Minnesota—Overview, 215
  Household Income, Median
  Population Growth (Average Annual)
  Unemployment Rate
Agriculture, 220
  Farm Income
  Farms (number, acreage, value)
Economic Structure, 218
  Earnings Growth, Fastest
  Employment and Earnings by Sector
  Private Industries, Leading
Economic Structure (Continued), 219
  Exports of Goods
  Gross State Product

Manufacturing
Wages and Salaries by Sector (Average Annual)
Education, 221
Education Indicators
Educational Attainment
High School Completion
Government, 222
Federal Spending within State
Finances, State Government
Taxes, State and Local
Health, 221
Death, Leading Causes of
Health Indicators
Housing, 220
Homeownership Rates
Housing Supply
Income, Household and Personal, 217
Government Payments to Individuals
Poverty, Persons in
Transfer Payments, Government
Labor Force, Employment and Unemployment, 216
Employment to Population Ratio
Unemployment Rate
Population, 216
Births
Deaths
Growth, Household and Population (Average Annual)
Population by Age
Population Change and Components

Mississippi—Overview, 223
Household Income, Median
Population Growth (Average Annual)
Unemployment Rate
Agriculture, 228
Farm Income
Farms (number, acreage, value)
Economic Structure, 226
Earnings Growth, Fastest
Employment and Earnings by Sector
Private Industries, Leading
Economic Structure (Continued), 227
Exports of Goods
Gross State Product
Manufacturing
Wages and Salaries by Sector (Average Annual)
Education, 229
Education Indicators
Educational Attainment
High School Completion
Government, 230
Federal Spending within State
Finances, State Government
Taxes, State and Local
Health, 229
Death, Leading Causes of
Health Indicators
Housing, 228
Homeownership Rates
Housing Supply
Income, Household and Personal, 225

Government Payments to Individuals
Poverty, Persons in
Transfer Payments, Government
Labor Force, Employment and Unemployment, 224
Employment to Population Ratio
Unemployment Rate
Population, 224
Births
Deaths
Growth, Household and Population (Average Annual)
Population by Age
Population Change and Components

Missouri—Overview, 231
Household Income, Median
Population Growth (Average Annual)
Unemployment Rate
Agriculture, 236
Farm Income
Farms (number, acreage, value)
Economic Structure, 234
Earnings Growth, Fastest
Employment and Earnings by Sector
Private Industries, Leading
Economic Structure (Continued), 235
Exports of Goods
Gross State Product
Manufacturing
Wages and Salaries by Sector (Average Annual)
Education, 237
Education Indicators
Educational Attainment
High School Completion
Government, 238
Federal Spending within State
Finances, State Government
Taxes, State and Local
Health, 237
Death, Leading Causes of
Health Indicators
Housing, 236
Homeownership Rates
Housing Supply
Income, Household and Personal, 233
Government Payments to Individuals
Poverty, Persons in
Transfer Payments, Government
Labor Force, Employment and Unemployment, 232
Employment to Population Ratio
Unemployment Rate
Population, 232
Births
Deaths
Growth, Household and Population (Average Annual)
Population by Age
Population Change and Components

Montana—Overview, 239
Household Income, Median
Population Growth (Average Annual)
Unemployment Rate

Agriculture, 244
  Farm Income
  Farms (number, acreage, value)
Economic Structure, 242
  Earnings Growth, Fastest
  Employment and Earnings by Sector
  Private Industries, Leading
Economic Structure (Continued), 243
  Exports of Goods
  Gross State Product
  Manufacturing
  Wages and Salaries by Sector (Average Annual)
Education, 245
  Education Indicators
  Educational Attainment
  High School Completion
Government, 246
  Federal Spending within State
  Finances, State Government
  Taxes, State and Local
Health, 245
  Death, Leading Causes of
  Health Indicators
Housing, 244
  Homeownership Rates
  Housing Supply
Income, Household and Personal, 241
  Government Payments to Individuals
  Poverty, Persons in
  Transfer Payments, Government
Labor Force, Employment and Unemployment, 240
  Employment to Population Ratio
  Unemployment Rate
Population, 240
  Births
  Deaths
  Growth, Household and Population (Average Annual)
  Population by Age
  Population Change and Components

Nebraska—Overview, 247
  Household Income, Median
  Population Growth (Average Annual)
  Unemployment Rate
Agriculture, 252
  Farm Income
  Farms (number, acreage, value)
Economic Structure, 250
  Earnings Growth, Fastest
  Employment and Earnings by Sector
  Private Industries, Leading
Economic Structure (Continued), 251
  Exports of Goods
  Gross State Product
  Manufacturing
  Wages and Salaries by Sector (Average Annual)
Education, 253
  Education Indicators
  Educational Attainment
  High School Completion
Government, 254

Federal Spending within State
  Finances, State Government
  Taxes, State and Local
Health, 253
  Death, Leading Causes of
  Health Indicators
Housing, 252
  Homeownership Rates
  Housing Supply
Income, Household and Personal, 249
  Government Payments to Individuals
  Poverty, Persons in
  Transfer Payments, Government
Labor Force, Employment and Unemployment, 248
  Employment to Population Ratio
  Unemployment Rate
Population, 248
  Births
  Deaths
  Growth, Household and Population (Average Annual)
  Population by Age
  Population Change and Components

Nevada—Overview, 255
  Household Income, Median
  Population Growth (Average Annual)
  Unemployment Rate
Agriculture, 260
  Farm Income
  Farms (number, acreage, value)
Economic Structure, 258
  Earnings Growth, Fastest
  Employment and Earnings by Sector
  Private Industries, Leading
Economic Structure (Continued), 259
  Exports of Goods
  Gross State Product
  Manufacturing
  Wages and Salaries by Sector (Average Annual)
Education, 261
  Education Indicators
  Educational Attainment
  High School Completion
Government, 262
  Federal Spending within State
  Finances, State Government
  Taxes, State and Local
Health, 261
  Death, Leading Causes of
  Health Indicators
Housing, 260
  Homeownership Rates
  Housing Supply
Income, Household and Personal, 257
  Government Payments to Individuals
  Poverty, Persons in
  Transfer Payments, Government
Labor Force, Employment and Unemployment, 256
  Employment to Population Ratio
  Unemployment Rate
Population, 256

Births
Deaths
Growth, Household and Population (Average Annual)
Population by Age
Population Change and Components

New Hampshire—Overview, 263
Household Income, Median
Population Growth (Average Annual)
Unemployment Rate
Agriculture, 268
Farm Income
Farms (number, acreage, value)
Economic Structure, 266
Earnings Growth, Fastest
Employment and Earnings by Sector
Private Industries, Leading
Economic Structure (Continued), 267
Exports of Goods
Gross State Product
Manufacturing
Wages and Salaries by Sector (Average Annual)
Education, 269
Education Indicators
Educational Attainment
High School Completion
Government, 270
Federal Spending within State
Finances, State Government
Taxes, State and Local
Health, 269
Death, Leading Causes of
Health Indicators
Housing, 268
Homeownership Rates
Housing Supply
Income, Household and Personal, 265
Government Payments to Individuals
Poverty, Persons in
Transfer Payments, Government
Labor Force, Employment and Unemployment, 264
Employment to Population Ratio
Unemployment Rate
Population, 264
Births
Deaths
Growth, Household and Population (Average Annual)
Population by Age
Population Change and Components

New Jersey—Overview, 271
Household Income, Median
Population Growth (Average Annual)
Unemployment Rate
Agriculture, 276
Farm Income
Farms (number, acreage, value)
Economic Structure, 274
Earnings Growth, Fastest
Employment and Earnings by Sector
Private Industries, Leading

Economic Structure (Continued), 275
Exports of Goods
Gross State Product
Manufacturing
Wages and Salaries by Sector (Average Annual)
Education, 277
Education Indicators
Educational Attainment
High School Completion
Government, 278
Federal Spending within State
Finances, State Government
Taxes, State and Local
Health, 277
Death, Leading Causes of
Health Indicators
Housing, 276
Homeownership Rates
Housing Supply
Income, Household and Personal, 273
Government Payments to Individuals
Poverty, Persons in
Transfer Payments, Government
Labor Force, Employment and Unemployment, 272
Employment to Population Ratio
Unemployment Rate
Population, 272
Births
Deaths
Growth, Household and Population (Average Annual)
Population by Age
Population Change and Components

New Mexico—Overview, 279
Household Income, Median
Population Growth (Average Annual)
Unemployment Rate
Agriculture, 284
Farm Income
Farms (number, acreage, value)
Economic Structure, 282
Earnings Growth, Fastest
Employment and Earnings by Sector
Private Industries, Leading
Economic Structure (Continued), 283
Exports of Goods
Gross State Product
Manufacturing
Wages and Salaries by Sector (Average Annual)
Education, 285
Education Indicators
Educational Attainment
High School Completion
Government, 286
Federal Spending within State
Finances, State Government
Taxes, State and Local
Health, 285
Death, Leading Causes of
Health Indicators
Housing, 284

Homeownership Rates
Housing Supply
Income, Household and Personal, 281
Government Payments to Individuals
Poverty, Persons in
Transfer Payments, Government
Labor Force, Employment and Unemployment, 280
Employment to Population Ratio
Unemployment Rate
Population, 280
Births
Deaths
Growth, Household and Population (Average Annual)
Population by Age
Population Change and Components

New York—Overview, 287
Household Income, Median
Population Growth (Average Annual)
Unemployment Rate
Agriculture, 292
Farm Income
Farms (number, acreage, value)
Economic Structure, 290
Earnings Growth, Fastest
Employment and Earnings by Sector
Private Industries, Leading
Economic Structure (Continued), 291
Exports of Goods
Gross State Product
Manufacturing
Wages and Salaries by Sector (Average Annual)
Education, 293
Education Indicators
Educational Attainment
High School Completion
Government, 294
Federal Spending within State
Finances, State Government
Taxes, State and Local
Health, 293
Death, Leading Causes of
Health Indicators
Housing, 292
Homeownership Rates
Housing Supply
Income, Household and Personal, 289
Government Payments to Individuals
Poverty, Persons in
Transfer Payments, Government
Labor Force, Employment and Unemployment, 288
Employment to Population Ratio
Unemployment Rate
Population, 288
Births
Deaths
Growth, Household and Population (Average Annual)
Population by Age
Population Change and Components

North Carolina—Overview, 295

Household Income, Median
Population Growth (Average Annual)
Unemployment Rate
Agriculture, 300
Farm Income
Farms (number, acreage, value)
Economic Structure, 298
Earnings Growth, Fastest
Employment and Earnings by Sector
Private Industries, Leading
Economic Structure (Continued), 299
Exports of Goods
Gross State Product
Manufacturing
Wages and Salaries by Sector (Average Annual)
Education, 301
Education Indicators
Educational Attainment
High School Completion
Government, 302
Federal Spending within State
Finances, State Government
Taxes, State and Local
Health, 301
Death, Leading Causes of
Health Indicators
Housing, 300
Homeownership Rates
Housing Supply
Income, Household and Personal, 297
Government Payments to Individuals
Poverty, Persons in
Transfer Payments, Government
Labor Force, Employment and Unemployment, 296
Employment to Population Ratio
Unemployment Rate
Population, 296
Births
Deaths
Growth, Household and Population (Average Annual)
Population by Age
Population Change and Components

North Dakota—Overview, 303
Household Income, Median
Population Growth (Average Annual)
Unemployment Rate
Agriculture, 308
Farm Income
Farms (number, acreage, value)
Economic Structure, 306
Earnings Growth, Fastest
Employment and Earnings by Sector
Private Industries, Leading
Economic Structure (Continued), 307
Exports of Goods
Gross State Product
Manufacturing
Wages and Salaries by Sector (Average Annual)
Education, 309
Education Indicators

Educational Attainment
High School Completion
Government, 310
Federal Spending within State
Finances, State Government
Taxes, State and Local
Health, 309
Death, Leading Causes of
Health Indicators
Housing, 308
Homeownership Rates
Housing Supply
Income, Household and Personal, 305
Government Payments to Individuals
Poverty, Persons in
Transfer Payments, Government
Labor Force, Employment and Unemployment, 304
Employment to Population Ratio
Unemployment Rate
Population, 304
Births
Deaths
Growth, Household and Population (Average Annual)
Population by Age
Population Change and Components

Ohio—Overview, 311
Household Income, Median
Population Growth (Average Annual)
Unemployment Rate
Agriculture, 316
Farm Income
Farms (number, acreage, value)
Economic Structure, 314
Earnings Growth, Fastest
Employment and Earnings by Sector
Private Industries, Leading
Economic Structure (Continued), 315
Exports of Goods
Gross State Product
Manufacturing
Wages and Salaries by Sector (Average Annual)
Education, 317
Education Indicators
Educational Attainment
High School Completion
Government, 318
Federal Spending within State
Finances, State Government
Taxes, State and Local
Health, 317
Death, Leading Causes of
Health Indicators
Housing, 316
Homeownership Rates
Housing Supply
Income, Household and Personal, 313
Government Payments to Individuals
Poverty, Persons in
Transfer Payments, Government
Labor Force, Employment and Unemployment, 312

Employment to Population Ratio
Unemployment Rate
Population, 312
Births
Deaths
Growth, Household and Population (Average Annual)
Population by Age
Population Change and Components

Oklahoma—Overview, 319
Household Income, Median
Population Growth (Average Annual)
Unemployment Rate
Agriculture, 324
Farm Income
Farms (number, acreage, value)
Economic Structure, 322
Earnings Growth, Fastest
Employment and Earnings by Sector
Private Industries, Leading
Economic Structure (Continued), 323
Exports of Goods
Gross State Product
Manufacturing
Wages and Salaries by Sector (Average Annual)
Education, 325
Education Indicators
Educational Attainment
High School Completion
Government, 326
Federal Spending within State
Finances, State Government
Taxes, State and Local
Health, 325
Death, Leading Causes of
Health Indicators
Housing, 324
Homeownership Rates
Housing Supply
Income, Household and Personal, 321
Government Payments to Individuals
Poverty, Persons in
Transfer Payments, Government
Labor Force, Employment and Unemployment, 320
Employment to Population Ratio
Unemployment Rate
Population, 320
Births
Deaths
Growth, Household and Population (Average Annual)
Population by Age
Population Change and Components

Oregon—Overview, 327
Household Income, Median
Population Growth (Average Annual)
Unemployment Rate
Agriculture, 332
Farm Income
Farms (number, acreage, value)
Economic Structure, 330

Earnings Growth, Fastest
Employment and Earnings by Sector
Private Industries, Leading
Economic Structure (Continued), 331
Exports of Goods
Gross State Product
Manufacturing
Wages and Salaries by Sector (Average Annual)
Education, 333
Education Indicators
Educational Attainment
High School Completion
Government, 334
Federal Spending within State
Finances, State Government
Taxes, State and Local
Health, 333
Death, Leading Causes of
Health Indicators
Housing, 332
Homeownership Rates
Housing Supply
Income, Household and Personal, 329
Government Payments to Individuals
Poverty, Persons in
Transfer Payments, Government
Labor Force, Employment and Unemployment, 328
Employment to Population Ratio
Unemployment Rate
Population, 328
Births
Deaths
Growth, Household and Population (Average Annual)
Population by Age
Population Change and Components

Pennsylvania—Overview, 335
Household Income, Median
Population Growth (Average Annual)
Unemployment Rate
Agriculture, 340
Farm Income
Farms (number, acreage, value)
Economic Structure, 338
Earnings Growth, Fastest
Employment and Earnings by Sector
Private Industries, Leading
Economic Structure (Continued), 339
Exports of Goods
Gross State Product
Manufacturing
Wages and Salaries by Sector (Average Annual)
Education, 341
Education Indicators
Educational Attainment
High School Completion
Government, 342
Federal Spending within State
Finances, State Government
Taxes, State and Local
Health, 341

Death, Leading Causes of
Health Indicators
Housing, 340
Homeownership Rates
Housing Supply
Income, Household and Personal, 337
Government Payments to Individuals
Poverty, Persons in
Transfer Payments, Government
Labor Force, Employment and Unemployment, 336
Employment to Population Ratio
Unemployment Rate
Population, 336
Births
Deaths
Growth, Household and Population (Average Annual)
Population by Age
Population Change and Components

Rhode Island—Overview, 343
Household Income, Median
Population Growth (Average Annual)
Unemployment Rate
Agriculture, 348
Farm Income
Farms (number, acreage, value)
Economic Structure, 346
Earnings Growth, Fastest
Employment and Earnings by Sector
Private Industries, Leading
Economic Structure (Continued), 347
Exports of Goods
Gross State Product
Manufacturing
Wages and Salaries by Sector (Average Annual)
Education, 349
Education Indicators
Educational Attainment
High School Completion
Government, 350
Federal Spending within State
Finances, State Government
Taxes, State and Local
Health, 349
Death, Leading Causes of
Health Indicators
Housing, 348
Homeownership Rates
Housing Supply
Income, Household and Personal, 345
Government Payments to Individuals
Poverty, Persons in
Transfer Payments, Government
Labor Force, Employment and Unemployment, 344
Employment to Population Ratio
Unemployment Rate
Population, 344
Births
Deaths
Growth, Household and Population (Average Annual)
Population by Age

Population Change and Components

South Carolina—Overview, 351
  Household Income, Median
  Population Growth (Average Annual)
  Unemployment Rate
 Agriculture, 356
  Farm Income
  Farms (number, acreage, value)
 Economic Structure, 354
  Earnings Growth, Fastest
  Employment and Earnings by Sector
  Private Industries, Leading
 Economic Structure (Continued), 355
  Exports of Goods
  Gross State Product
  Manufacturing
  Wages and Salaries by Sector (Average Annual)
 Education, 357
  Education Indicators
  Educational Attainment
  High School Completion
 Government, 358
  Federal Spending within State
  Finances, State Government
  Taxes, State and Local
 Health, 357
  Death, Leading Causes of
  Health Indicators
 Housing, 356
  Homeownership Rates
  Housing Supply
 Income, Household and Personal, 353
  Government Payments to Individuals
  Poverty, Persons in
  Transfer Payments, Government
 Labor Force, Employment and Unemployment, 352
  Employment to Population Ratio
  Unemployment Rate
 Population, 352
  Births
  Deaths
  Growth, Household and Population (Average Annual)
  Population by Age
  Population Change and Components

South Dakota—Overview, 359
  Household Income, Median
  Population Growth (Average Annual)
  Unemployment Rate
 Agriculture, 364
  Farm Income
  Farms (number, acreage, value)
 Economic Structure, 362
  Earnings Growth, Fastest
  Employment and Earnings by Sector
  Private Industries, Leading
 Economic Structure (Continued), 363
  Exports of Goods
  Gross State Product
  Manufacturing

  Wages and Salaries by Sector (Average Annual)
 Education, 365
  Education Indicators
  Educational Attainment
  High School Completion
 Government, 366
  Federal Spending within State
  Finances, State Government
  Taxes, State and Local
 Health, 365
  Death, Leading Causes of
  Health Indicators
 Housing, 364
  Homeownership Rates
  Housing Supply
 Income, Household and Personal, 361
  Government Payments to Individuals
  Poverty, Persons in
  Transfer Payments, Government
 Labor Force, Employment and Unemployment, 360
  Employment to Population Ratio
  Unemployment Rate
 Population, 360
  Births
  Deaths
  Growth, Household and Population (Average Annual)
  Population by Age
  Population Change and Components

Tennessee—Overview, 367
  Household Income, Median
  Population Growth (Average Annual)
  Unemployment Rate
 Agriculture, 372
  Farm Income
  Farms (number, acreage, value)
 Economic Structure, 370
  Earnings Growth, Fastest
  Employment and Earnings by Sector
  Private Industries, Leading
 Economic Structure (Continued), 371
  Exports of Goods
  Gross State Product
  Manufacturing
  Wages and Salaries by Sector (Average Annual)
 Education, 373
  Education Indicators
  Educational Attainment
  High School Completion
 Government, 374
  Federal Spending within State
  Finances, State Government
  Taxes, State and Local
 Health, 373
  Death, Leading Causes of
  Health Indicators
 Housing, 372
  Homeownership Rates
  Housing Supply
 Income, Household and Personal, 369
  Government Payments to Individuals

Poverty, Persons in
Transfer Payments, Government
Labor Force, Employment and Unemployment, 368
Employment to Population Ratio
Unemployment Rate
Population, 368
Births
Deaths
Growth, Household and Population (Average Annual)
Population by Age
Population Change and Components

Texas—Overview, 375
Household Income, Median
Population Growth (Average Annual)
Unemployment Rate
Agriculture, 380
Farm Income
Farms (number, acreage, value)
Economic Structure, 378
Earnings Growth, Fastest
Employment and Earnings by Sector
Private Industries, Leading
Economic Structure (Continued), 379
Exports of Goods
Gross State Product
Manufacturing
Wages and Salaries by Sector (Average Annual)
Education, 381
Education Indicators
Educational Attainment
High School Completion
Government, 382
Federal Spending within State
Finances, State Government
Taxes, State and Local
Health, 381
Death, Leading Causes of
Health Indicators
Housing, 380
Homeownership Rates
Housing Supply
Income, Household and Personal, 377
Government Payments to Individuals
Poverty, Persons in
Transfer Payments, Government
Labor Force, Employment and Unemployment, 376
Employment to Population Ratio
Unemployment Rate
Population, 376
Births
Deaths
Growth, Household and Population (Average Annual)
Population by Age
Population Change and Components

Utah—Overview, 383
Household Income, Median
Population Growth (Average Annual)
Unemployment Rate
Agriculture, 388

Farm Income
Farms (number, acreage, value)
Economic Structure, 386
Earnings Growth, Fastest
Employment and Earnings by Sector
Private Industries, Leading
Economic Structure (Continued), 387
Exports of Goods
Gross State Product
Manufacturing
Wages and Salaries by Sector (Average Annual)
Education, 389
Education Indicators
Educational Attainment
High School Completion
Government, 390
Federal Spending within State
Finances, State Government
Taxes, State and Local
Health, 389
Death, Leading Causes of
Health Indicators
Housing, 388
Homeownership Rates
Housing Supply
Income, Household and Personal, 385
Government Payments to Individuals
Poverty, Persons in
Transfer Payments, Government
Labor Force, Employment and Unemployment, 384
Employment to Population Ratio
Unemployment Rate
Population, 384
Births
Deaths
Growth, Household and Population (Average Annual)
Population by Age
Population Change and Components

Vermont—Overview, 391
Household Income, Median
Population Growth (Average Annual)
Unemployment Rate
Agriculture, 396
Farm Income
Farms (number, acreage, value)
Economic Structure, 394
Earnings Growth, Fastest
Employment and Earnings by Sector
Private Industries, Leading
Economic Structure (Continued), 395
Exports of Goods
Gross State Product
Manufacturing
Wages and Salaries by Sector (Average Annual)
Education, 397
Education Indicators
Educational Attainment
High School Completion
Government, 398
Federal Spending within State

Finances, State Government
Taxes, State and Local
Health, 397
Death, Leading Causes of
Health Indicators
Housing, 396
Homeownership Rates
Housing Supply
Income, Household and Personal, 393
Government Payments to Individuals
Poverty, Persons in
Transfer Payments, Government
Labor Force, Employment and Unemployment, 392
Employment to Population Ratio
Unemployment Rate
Population, 392
Births
Deaths
Growth, Household and Population (Average Annual)
Population by Age
Population Change and Components

Virginia—Overview, 399
Household Income, Median
Population Growth (Average Annual)
Unemployment Rate
Agriculture, 404
Farm Income
Farms (number, acreage, value)
Economic Structure, 402
Earnings Growth, Fastest
Employment and Earnings by Sector
Private Industries, Leading
Economic Structure (Continued), 403
Exports of Goods
Gross State Product
Manufacturing
Wages and Salaries by Sector (Average Annual)
Education, 405
Education Indicators
Educational Attainment
High School Completion
Government, 406
Federal Spending within State
Finances, State Government
Taxes, State and Local
Health, 405
Death, Leading Causes of
Health Indicators
Housing, 404
Homeownership Rates
Housing Supply
Income, Household and Personal, 401
Government Payments to Individuals
Poverty, Persons in
Transfer Payments, Government
Labor Force, Employment and Unemployment, 400
Employment to Population Ratio
Unemployment Rate
Population, 400
Births

Deaths
Growth, Household and Population (Average Annual)
Population by Age
Population Change and Components

Washington—Overview, 407
Household Income, Median
Population Growth (Average Annual)
Unemployment Rate
Agriculture, 412
Farm Income
Farms (number, acreage, value)
Economic Structure, 410
Earnings Growth, Fastest
Employment and Earnings by Sector
Private Industries, Leading
Economic Structure (Continued), 411
Exports of Goods
Gross State Product
Manufacturing
Wages and Salaries by Sector (Average Annual)
Education, 413
Education Indicators
Educational Attainment
High School Completion
Government, 414
Federal Spending within State
Finances, State Government
Taxes, State and Local
Health, 413
Death, Leading Causes of
Health Indicators
Housing, 412
Homeownership Rates
Housing Supply
Income, Household and Personal, 409
Government Payments to Individuals
Poverty, Persons in
Transfer Payments, Government
Labor Force, Employment and Unemployment, 408
Employment to Population Ratio
Unemployment Rate
Population, 408
Births
Deaths
Growth, Household and Population (Average Annual)
Population by Age
Population Change and Components

West Virginia—Overview, 415
Household Income, Median
Population Growth (Average Annual)
Unemployment Rate
Agriculture, 420
Farm Income
Farms (number, acreage, value)
Economic Structure, 418
Earnings Growth, Fastest
Employment and Earnings by Sector
Private Industries, Leading
Economic Structure (Continued), 419

Exports of Goods
Gross State Product
Manufacturing
Wages and Salaries by Sector (Average Annual)
Education, 421
Education Indicators
Educational Attainment
High School Completion
Government, 422
Federal Spending within State
Finances, State Government
Taxes, State and Local
Health, 421
Death, Leading Causes of
Health Indicators
Housing, 420
Homeownership Rates
Housing Supply
Income, Household and Personal, 417
Government Payments to Individuals
Poverty, Persons in
Transfer Payments, Government
Labor Force, Employment and Unemployment, 416
Employment to Population Ratio
Unemployment Rate
Population, 416
Births
Deaths
Growth, Household and Population (Average Annual)
Population by Age
Population Change and Components

Wisconsin—Overview, 423
Household Income, Median
Population Growth (Average Annual)
Unemployment Rate
Agriculture, 428
Farm Income
Farms (number, acreage, value)
Economic Structure, 426
Earnings Growth, Fastest
Employment and Earnings by Sector
Private Industries, Leading
Economic Structure (Continued), 427
Exports of Goods
Gross State Product
Manufacturing
Wages and Salaries by Sector (Average Annual)
Education, 429
Education Indicators
Educational Attainment
High School Completion
Government, 430
Federal Spending within State
Finances, State Government
Taxes, State and Local
Health, 429
Death, Leading Causes of
Health Indicators
Housing, 428
Homeownership Rates

Housing Supply
Income, Household and Personal, 425
Government Payments to Individuals
Poverty, Persons in
Transfer Payments, Government
Labor Force, Employment and Unemployment, 424
Employment to Population Ratio
Unemployment Rate
Population, 424
Births
Deaths
Growth, Household and Population (Average Annual)
Population by Age
Population Change and Components

Wyoming—Overview, 431
Household Income, Median
Population Growth (Average Annual)
Unemployment Rate
Agriculture, 436
Farm Income
Farms (number, acreage, value)
Economic Structure, 434
Earnings Growth, Fastest
Employment and Earnings by Sector
Private Industries, Leading
Economic Structure (Continued), 435
Exports of Goods
Gross State Product
Manufacturing
Wages and Salaries by Sector (Average Annual)
Education, 437
Education Indicators
Educational Attainment
High School Completion
Government, 438
Federal Spending within State
Finances, State Government
Taxes, State and Local
Health, 437
Death, Leading Causes of
Health Indicators
Housing, 436
Homeownership Rates
Housing Supply
Income, Household and Personal, 433
Government Payments to Individuals
Poverty, Persons in
Transfer Payments, Government
Labor Force, Employment and Unemployment, 432
Employment to Population Ratio
Unemployment Rate
Population, 432
Births
Deaths
Growth, Household and Population (Average Annual)
Population by Age
Population Change and Components